1999 Index
of Economic Freedom

Bryan T. Johnson,
Kim R. Holmes,
and Melanie Kirkpatrick

The Heritage Foundation

THE WALL STREET JOURNAL.

BRYAN T. JOHNSON is a Policy Analyst in International Economic Affairs in The Kathryn and Shelby Cullom Davis International Studies Center at The Heritage Foundation.

KIM R. HOLMES is Vice President, The Kathryn and Shelby Cullom Davis International Studies Center, at The Heritage Foundation.

MELANIE KIRKPATRICK is Assistant Editor of *The Wall Street Journal* Editorial Page.

Robert L. Bartley is Editor of *The Wall Street Journal*.

William W. Beach is John M. Olin Senior Fellow in Economics and Director of the Center for Data Analysis at The Heritage Foundation.

Gareth Davis is a Policy Analyst in the Center for Data Analysis at The Heritage Foundation.

Denise H. Froning is a Research Assistant in The Kathryn and Shelby Cullom Davis International Studies Center at The Heritage Foundation.

Claudia Rosett is a member of the Editorial Board of *The Wall Street Journal*. She is a former Editorial Page Editor of *The Asian Wall Street Journal* and former Chief of the *Journal*'s Moscow bureau.

Brett D. Schaefer is Jay Kingham Fellow in International Regulatory Affairs at The Heritage Foundation.

Copy editing, layout, and design by James V. Rutherford
Cover design and graphics by Thomas J. Timmons
Cover image copyright © 1996 by Cartesia Software

ISBN 0–89195–245–4
ISSN 1095–7308

The Heritage Foundation
214 Massachusetts Avenue, N.E.
Washington, D.C. 20002
(202) 546-4400
http://www.heritage.org

The Wall Street Journal
Dow Jones & Company, Inc.
200 Liberty Street
New York, N.Y. 10281
(212) 416-2000
http://wsj.com

Table of Contents

Chapter 6:
Methodology: Factors of the *Index of Economic Freedom* 51
by Bryan T. Johnson

Chapter 7:
The 1999 *Index of Economic Freedom*: The Countries 69
by Bryan T. Johnson

Acknowledgments

We would like to express our appreciation to several individuals at The Heritage Foundation who helped to complete the fifth edition of the *Index of Economic Freedom*. We are grateful to the staffs of The Kathryn and Shelby Cullom Davis International Studies Center, the Asian Studies Center, and the Center for Data Analysis that participated in Heritage's internal peer review process. The expertise of these analysts greatly enhanced the detailed analysis of the various countries included in this year's *Index*. The members of this group are James Anderson, Policy Analyst for Defense and National Security; Ariel Cohen, Senior Policy Analyst for Russian and Eurasian Affairs; John Dori, Research Associate, Asian Studies Center; Richard D. Fisher, Director, Asian Studies Center; Robert P. O'Quinn, formerly Policy Analyst for Asian Trade and Economics; James Phillips, Senior Policy Analyst for Middle East Affairs; James J. Przystup, former Director of the Asian Studies Center; Brett D. Schaefer, Jay Kingham Fellow in International Regulatory Affairs; John P. Sweeney, Policy Analyst for Trade and Latin American Affairs; and Stephen J. Yates, Policy Analyst for China.

Denise Froning of the Kathryn and Shelby Cullom Davis International Studies Center managed the data and the extensive research process. Denise was invaluable in providing the bulk of the research, crunching numbers, checking facts, and developing the charts and graphs as well as composing the Statistical Appendix. In addition, Yvette Campos and Amanda Deatherage provided vital production support. Without their help we would not have met our deadlines.

We also would like to thank Senior Editor Richard Odermatt, who was tasked with fine-tuning and editing the bulk of the book; Director of Publishing Services Ann Klucsarits; and the Heritage team that contributed so much to the final production of the book:

- Editing and Publishing Associate James V. Rutherford was responsible for copyediting the text, ensuring consistency from country to country, and designing the layout of the entire book.

• Manager of Graphic Design Services Thomas J. Timmons used a variety of source materials in developing both the regional and country maps: Cartesia Software's MapArt™, Mountain High Maps Frontiers™, and the CIA *World Factbook 1996*. He was responsible for formatting the charts and tables in this volume and also designed the *Index*'s cover.

The editorial and design skills of these two individuals were invaluable.

We also are grateful for the help of Copy Editor William T. Poole and Research Department Managing Editor Janice A. Smith.

Countless individuals serving with various accounting firms, businesses, research organizations, U.S. government agencies, embassies in Washington, D.C., and other organizations cooperated in providing us the data we use in the *Index*. Their assistance is much appreciated. So, too, is the help of Heritage interns. Jennifer Swanson, Iva Kovarikova, Bill Seiber, Ryan Storm, and Andrew

Coors were particularly helpful in producing this edition of the *Index*. Like their predecessors in 1997, they did the legwork, cheerfully running down data throughout the humid Washington summer. We wish them the best in their new ventures.

We are grateful to Heritage Trustee Ambassador J. William Middendorf for originally encouraging us to undertake such a study of global economic freedom. Many other people within Heritage generously have lent their expertise to our effort. We would like to express our appreciation to the many people who have praised the *Index of Economic Freedom* so enthusiastically. We have been pleased indeed at how well the *Index* has been received. The support and encouragement of people worldwide has been important in inspiring The Heritage Foundation to produce this edition in cooperation with *The Wall Street Journal* Editorial Page. We hope this effort matches the expectations of all our supporters.

B.T.J.
K.R.H.
M.K.

Foreword

Since the fall of the Berlin Wall in 1989, the cause of freedom has been sweeping the world, with increasing swaths of territory adopting at least the forms of political democracy and open and free markets. The *Index of Economic Freedom* was founded within those years and has had the pleasure of recording the spread of modern capitalism.

In 1998, however, the first real test emerged. Asia's "tiger economies" found themselves staggering if not imploding. Their storied growth formulas hit the rock of currency depreciation, and in several cases years of economic progress were wiped out almost in an instant, with such ugly reactions as anti-Chinese riots in Indonesia and political repression in Malaysia. Something clearly went wrong, and the issue became: Was it economic freedom itself?

The answer varied from country to country, and in a sense the rates of recovery in the next few years will be an empirical test. Malaysia imposed draconian currency controls, in effect isolating itself from the world economy; it will be instructive to watch this experiment over the next several years. Even Hong Kong, rating number one in economic freedom this year and last, conducted a massive market intervention, directly buying equities to bolster its sagging stock market. In the process it became the top shareholder in the huge Hong Kong & Shanghai Bank; these actions came after the June 30 closing date for these ratings, but no doubt will affect standings next year.

Yet a strong case can be made that many of the problems resulted from too little, not too much, openness in markets. This lesson is more than theoretical; in the midst of the currency crisis, Chile decided to relax rather than tighten its controls on foreign capital. "Crony capitalism," meaning bank loans to the politically powerful rather than economically efficient, has become a commonplace diagnosis. The Japanese model of industrial management, with banks at the service of cross-owned industrial corporations, seems discredited not only at home but in South Korea. Banking problems have been the common thread through the distressed economies, and most Asian countries are in the early stages of a slow and painful process of separating banks from their political and corporate alliances.

These experiences are still being digested not only by the countries involved but also by anyone trying to understand economic principles. We all are still learning. Yet when it comes to the structure of an index such as the present one, the imperative is year-to-year continuity. At times any consistent methodology will show occasional anomalies—in my own judgment the world has changed, for example, and in monetary policy I would certainly not award deflationary Japan a 1 and now-solid Argentina a 5. Yet the idea of this *Index* is to provide a constant yardstick against which events can be measured, not to construct measurements bending to each year's fashion. And the sweep of evidence, including the accumulated wealth of Japan, testifies that the *Index* measures something very real indeed.

As for lessons of the Asian test, my own view is that the capitalist world has underrated the importance of exchange-rate stability. The common question is, why shouldn't exchange rates be set in the free market? The answer is we do not live in some theoretical world of private currencies with the freedom of entry free-market theory specifies. In the real world, issuing currency is everywhere a government monopoly, and the only relevant question is: What guidepost should a monopolist central bank follow? For small economies like Hong Kong and Argentina, targeting the exchange rate has been a serviceable answer.

The Asian problem has been one of exchange rates. A series of competitive devaluations started with the Thai baht in 1997. Hong Kong's desperate stock-market intervention was intended to protect its peg to the U.S. dollar. We are learning again that devaluations only stir inflation. Internal prices have to adjust to world norms; the price of energy, for example, is everywhere set in dollars. As internal prices rise, any export advantage from a cheaper currency vanishes, leaving behind only the social upheaval inflation always causes. Most spectacularly, a banking system that earns local currency but has borrowed in dollars finds itself insolvent—as these ratings will no doubt reflect in the years after devaluation.

The great irony of 1998 is Hong Kong. Its economic freedom survived the reversion to Communist Chinese sovereignty but may be stumbling on a crisis of Asian capitalism. Precisely because its economic freedom was so successful, the Chinese government allowed it to maintain an important measure of political freedom—far from perfect by Western standards but amazing in a Chinese context. Meanwhile, the closing of economic freedom in Malaysia meant the closing of political freedom. And it is becoming increasingly evident that Russia's economic progress will depend on political progress toward the rule of law.

The big success story of 1998 was the birth of a European "tiger." The opening of Ireland's economy has produced growth rates unimagined in that part of the world; its per capita gross domestic product is poised to overtake that of Mother England. The dawning euro has protected small European economies from the currency crisis that ravaged Asia and threatens Latin America. The test of the euro bloc will be whether the continental welfare states will be forced to compete or whether their political influence will force the new Irish tiger to close its economy and curb its growth.

The *Index of Economic Freedom* provides a handy gauge for measuring these events. My own prediction is that it will continue to show that the answers lie not in less economic freedom but in more. The association between economic freedom and economic progress, and between economic freedom and political freedom, will survive the latest test as they have persisted over the years. I would venture, indeed, that these associations will emerge from the tests of 1998 not refuted but validated in the crucible of crisis.

Robert L. Bartley
Editor
The Wall Street Journal
October 1998

Preface

The main purpose of The Heritage Foundation's *Index of Economic Freedom* has been to document and substantiate the relationship between economic freedom and economic prosperity. To achieve this goal, this fifth edition, copublished with *The Wall Street Journal,* again measures the impact of tax laws, tariffs, business regulations, government intervention in the economy, corruption in the government, the judiciary, and the customs service along with a host of other economic factors in 161 different countries. Thus, the 1999 *Index of Economic Freedom* continues to offer policymakers and investors the most comprehensive, concise, and up-to-date measurement of the world's economies published.

Back in 1994, as the first-ever-published study of its kind, the *Index of Economic Freedom* established a benchmark by which global economic progress could be tracked. Previous editions of the *Index* show economic freedom improving around the world from 1994 through 1997. For the first time since our measurements began in 1994, however, this edition documents that global economic freedom has declined: Of the countries graded in both the 1998 and 1999 editions, 27 improved their overall scores this year, while 29 regressed. Why? Surely, one contributing factor has been the reaction of the governments in the region to the economic turmoil that began in Thailand and quickly spread throughout Asia in 1998, which, in fact, now threatens markets everywhere. Symptoms of that turmoil include the collapse of the Russian ruble, severe banking

problems in Japan, and serious concerns in the United States and elsewhere in the Group of Seven that the policies of the International Monetary Fund have contributed to the spread of this economic contagion.

Accompanying this worsening of economic conditions abroad is a host of accusations against the virtues of market capitalism. Much of this criticism centers on the notion that "too much" economic freedom (if indeed there is such a thing) caused this economic crisis not only to occur but also to worsen, and then to spread.

This argument is not borne out by the evidence in the *Index of Economic Freedom*. Our research shows that the current economic crisis is the result not of too much economic freedom but of the continued *lack* of economic freedom.

Past editions of the *Index* document the restrictions on economic freedom that are part of the root causes of the economic crisis in Asia. For example, previous editions of the *Index* note that countries like Thailand, Indonesia, and Malaysia were making significant progress toward economic freedom, but that such progress was uneven. Although these countries were opening their economies to increased trade and investment, establishing fewer distorting tax laws, and reducing some regulations on business, they also continued restrictions on the financial services industry and foreign bank entry, resorted to government allocation of credit, and tolerated high levels of corruption. These restrictions on economic freedom contributed to the rapid spread of the financial crisis, like a tsunami, across the Asia-Pacific region, until its breakers began to pound Wall Street.

Indeed, the scores for Indonesia and South Korea worsened this year, mainly because of their reactions to deteriorating conditions in the banking sector. In addition, countries like Malaysia have resorted to currency restrictions that inhibit the free flow of capital in and out of the country. (These restrictions were imposed too late for the authors to include in the official scoring for this edition.) In Russia (again, too late for official scoring this year), the government resorted to similar currency restrictions, manipulation of the banking system, and other restrictions on economic freedom. Thailand, whose score did not change, so far has resisted such interventions in the economy.

Critics of the free market believe that the troubled countries opened their economies to trade and investment too quickly and that, when investors decided to leave, this open investment policy contributed to the crisis. But what these observers ignore is the obvious question: What caused investors to flee? It was not low taxes, free trade, or other examples of economic freedom. Investors do not flee safe havens or investment environments based on sound market economics in which hefty returns can be made; instead, investors flee countries ravaged by government corruption, currency manipulation, unsound financial institutions, disdain for the rule of law, and other government policies. As Heritage analysts William W. Beach and Gareth G. Davis point out in Chapter 1, the historical overview of countries provided by the *Index* shows that those

Asian countries having the greatest currency fluctuation generally receive the poorest *Index* scores, a clear warning for investors. The more likely reason that investors left Asia is not because countries there had too much economic freedom, but because the harsh consequences of the level of corruption and crony capitalism were bad for business.

Consider the effects of the crisis on Hong Kong, the world's "most free" economy in previous editions of the *Index*. Unfortunately, in the wake of the economic turmoil, even Hong Kong began to clamp down on economic freedom. In August 1998 (again, too late for the authors to include in the official scoring for this publication), the government proceeded to use its funds to purchase private shares in its stock market. This interference in the market would mean that, if the scoring for the *Index* were done today, Hong Kong no longer could be ranked first. We hope that Hong Kong's government will reverse this action and return to the free-market practices that made its economy so strong in the past—or its ranking surely will fall in next year's edition of the *Index*.

Reactionary voices calling for a stronger, more restraining role for government should be ignored. As Heritage's Beach and Davis also point out in this edition, countries engulfed by the Asian financial crisis that have higher levels of economic freedom have weathered the storm better than those that have lower levels. Rather than increasing restrictions on the flow of capital, regulation, and state ownership of production or intervening in the stock market, governments of troubled economies should take immediate steps to establish or buttress the rule of law, create sound and open business environments, eliminate corruption, and implement policies that promote greater competition in the financial services.

Only when countries have an institutional framework based on the rule of law and free and competitive markets will their citizens have the freedom to work productively and enjoy the fruits of their labor. For with work comes the creation of wealth. And with freedom comes prosperity.

Edwin J. Feulner, Ph.D.
President
The Heritage Foundation
November 1998

Executive Summary

by Bryan T. Johnson, Kim R. Holmes, and Melanie Kirkpatrick

The concept of producing a user-friendly "index of economic freedom" as a tool for policymakers and investors was first discussed at The Heritage Foundation in the late 1980s. The goal then, as it is today, was to develop an index to measure empirically the level of economic freedom in countries around the world. To this end, a set of objective economic criteria was established; and since 1994, these criteria have been used to study and grade various countries for the annual publication of the *Index of Economic Freedom*. The *Index*, however, is more than just an empirical listing of scores; it is a careful analysis of the factors that contribute the most to the institutional setting for economic growth. And although many theories exist about the origins and causes of economic development, the findings of this study are conclusive: Countries that have the most economic freedom also tend to have higher rates of long-term economic growth and are more prosperous than those that have less economic freedom.

The Heritage Foundation/Wall Street Journal 1999 *Index of Economic Freedom* measures how well 161 countries score on a list of 50 independent criteria, divided into 10 broad economic factors. The higher the score on a factor, the greater the level of government interference in the economy and the less economic freedom. These 50 variables were grouped into the following 10 economic factors:

- Trade policy;
- Taxation;
- Government intervention in the economy;
- Monetary policy;
- Capital flows and foreign investment;
- Banking;
- Wage and price controls;
- Property rights;
- Regulation; and
- Black market.

The methodology chapter (Chapter 6) explains these factors in detail. Taken cumulatively, they offer an empirical snapshot of a country's level of economic freedom. An objective analysis of these factors continues to demonstrate unequivocally that countries with the highest levels of economic freedom also have the highest standards of living.

Similarly, countries with the lowest levels of economic freedom also have the lowest standards of living.

Five new countries are included in the study this year (60 have been added since the first edition). With these new countries, the *Index* offers its readers an even clearer vision of the world's most economically free and most repressed regions. And, as was true last year, most of the world's economies remain economically unfree. Of the 156 countries graded in both the 1998 and 1999 editions of the *Index,* 27 received better scores while 29 others regressed. This marks a departure from the trend established over the previous three years in which there were more improving scores than there were regressing scores. This is the first year since the *Index* began taking such measures that there has been a decrease in global economic freedom. Of the top 10 freest countries, 5 are in North America or Europe, 4 are in Asia, and 1 is in the Middle East. Most of the world's freest economies are in North America and Europe, while most of the world's most economically repressed countries are in Africa and the Middle East. Asia has a mixture of free and unfree economies.

By region, many interesting developments have occurred since last year's edition. For example:

North America and Europe. In 1997, North America and Europe made the second greatest overall progress toward economic freedom. Of the 42 countries graded for the 1998 and 1999 editions of the *Index,* 7 (17 percent) achieved better scores this year, and 4 worse. The region had the lowest percentage of declining scores (10 percent) for a net increase of 7 percent. The United States is the most economically free country in North America, while Switzerland is the most economically free country in Europe. The economies of Ireland, Luxembourg, the United Kingdom, the Czech Republic, Belgium, and Austria are the next most free. Former Marxist countries continue to make progress toward increasing economic freedom. The best examples are the Czech Republic and Estonia, both of which score well in the 1999 *Index.* These countries are following the models of Hong Kong and Singapore and promoting large economic growth rates by expanding economic freedom. The scores for Belarus and Albania have worsened for three years in a row. After improving last year, Russia's score has leveled off and remains the same as last year.[1]

Latin America and the Caribbean. In 1998, this region made the greatest overall progress toward economic freedom for the second year in a row. Of the 27 countries graded in this region, 10 (37 percent) improved their scores, and 3 regressed for this year's edition of the *Index.* Latin America and the Caribbean also had the second-lowest percentage of declining scores (11 percent) for a net increase of 26 percent. The Bahamas is the most economically free country in Latin America and the Caribbean. Chile is the most economically free country in Central and South America, and El Salvador is the second most free economy, followed by Panama, Argentina, Trinidad and Tobago, and Barbados. Mexico has improved this year, but remains mostly unfree. Despite a rush of media reports on purported economic reform in Cuba, the facts show that Havana continues to pursue economically repressive policies. Cuba remains the most economically unfree country in Latin America and one of the two most economically repressed countries in the world. In Central and South America, Argentina, Brazil, El Salvador, Guatemala, Guyana, Mexico, Peru, and Venezuela recorded improved scores this year. Colombia and Paraguay received lower scores. The rest remained the same.

Asia. Despite several years of progress, economic freedom decreased rapidly in Asia in 1998. Of the 32 countries graded, only 7 (22 percent) improved their scores while 9 (28 percent) regressed, for a net decrease of 6 percent. Three of the top five most free economies in the world are in Asia: Hong Kong, Singapore, and New Zealand; however, it is increasingly clear that some fallout from the Asian financial crisis is resulting in decreased economic freedom for many Asian countries. Despite the enthusiasm of the investment community, Vietnam remains economically unfree, ranking 10th in a listing of the world's most economically repressed countries. It continues to suffer from corrupt border officials, an inadequate foreign investment law, and a legal system that offers little protection for private property. It has a centrally planned economy with a marginal, albeit growing, free market. India's score remains the same; so does Japan's. China remains one of the most economically unfree countries in the world.

Hong Kong, which consistently has ranked first in the *Index,* appears in danger of surrendering that position. In August 1998 and the weeks that followed, Hong Kong's government spent some $15.2 billion to "ward off speculators" by buying private stock in the Hong Kong stock exchange. Not only has Hong Kong's government failed to allow its currency board to function properly, it has violated an important rule of free-market economics: Governments should avoid direct ownership of private companies. In so doing, Hong Kong has demonstrated that its commitment to the market may be weakening. Because these events occurred after the cutoff date for consideration in this edition of the *Index,* however, they did not affect this year's official score. Had this information been included, Hong Kong surely would have received a poorer score in the *Index,* ranking below Singapore. Thus, at the time of publication, in late 1998, Hong Kong no longer can be considered the freest economy in the world. If Hong Kong does not reverse this intervention in the stock market, its changed score will be reflected in the official listings and rankings of next year's *Index.*

North Africa and the Middle East. Economic freedom in North Africa and the Middle East suffered the greatest regional decline in 1998. Of the 18 countries graded, none improved their scores and 5 (28 percent) regressed. This region is the only one in which no countries improved over last year. Bahrain is the most economically free country in the Middle East and North Africa region, and it is the third-freest economy in the world. Bahrain's high ranking is chiefly the result of its lack of taxation on personal income or corporate profits. Thus, almost all income derived in Bahrain is tax-free. Bahrain also has one of the world's lowest levels of inflation, as well as a strong and efficient court system that upholds the rule of law. In the Middle East, the United Arab Emirates has the second most free economy, followed by Kuwait, Jordan, and Oman. Although Israel improved its "mostly unfree" designation to "mostly free" by the second edition of the *Index,* it has not made any additional progress since that time. In North Africa and the Middle East, Algeria, Egypt, Lebanon, Qatar, and Saudi Arabia have mostly unfree economies; Iran, Iraq, Libya, Syria, and Yemen have repressed economies.

Sub-Saharan Africa. As a whole, sub-Saharan Africa remains the most economically unfree—and by far the poorest—area in the world. Of the 42 sub-Saharan African countries graded, none received a rating of "free." Only 7 received a rating of "mostly free," 27 were rated "mostly unfree," and 8 were rated "repressed." Economic freedom in sub-Saharan Africa, in fact, declined in 1998; 3 countries (7 percent) received better scores this year, while 8 (19 percent) received worse scores, for a net decrease of 12 percent. The *Index* demonstrates quite clearly that sub-Saharan Africa's poverty is not the result of insufficient levels of foreign aid, weather patterns, or even internal strife; on a per capita basis, many sub-Saharan African countries rank among those receiving the highest levels of economic assistance in the world. Instead, the main cause of poverty in sub-Saharan Africa is the lack of economic freedom embodied in policies these countries have imposed on themselves.

The findings of the *Index* regarding sub-Saharan Africa cast doubt on the assertion that economic growth can be achieved by huge transfers of wealth from the industrialized economies to the less-developed world. The people of Angola, Mozambique, Haiti, and Ukraine are not poor because wealthy people in the West do not share their riches; they are poor because their governments pursue destructive economic policies that depress free enterprise. Only when they increase the economic freedom of their citizens and unleash the phenomenal power of the free market will the poor countries of the world begin to achieve true prosperity and economic growth. Anything short of this is not only economically unwise, it is inhumane.

The 1999 *Index of Economic Freedom* includes a chapter from *The Wall Street Journal* on the usefulness of the *Index* as an investment tool. For investors trying to judge how best to allocate scarce resources, the exciting shift toward free markets worldwide has brought along with it questions and uncertainties. These have been heightened, of course, by recent economic problems in Asia, Russia, and Latin America. In an increasingly competitive and lively world, in which old rules of thumb have become inadequate, the prudent investor needs the help of a good guide—which is what the *Index* aims to supply.

The *Index* again includes a chapter by Heritage economists on the statistical association between economic freedom and economic growth. The authors examine the economic benefits that flow from economic freedom and conclude there is strong evidence, both from the emerging field of New Growth Theory and from statistical tests that they themselves have conducted, linking the concepts measured in the *Index* to higher rates of growth and greater prosperity. This year, they also examined the assertion by critics of the market that government intervention is necessary to prevent the unequal distribution of income. Contrary to the critics, the analysis suggests that countries with a higher level of economic freedom tend to have more equal distributions of income. In addition, the authors looked at the Asian countries caught up in the region's economic crisis from the perspective of a basic indicator of economic health: the currency's exchange rate against the U.S. dollar. They found that currency devaluations have tended to be more drastic among countries in the region with lower levels of economic freedom.

Again this year, the *Index* includes a chapter of supplemental economic and social data that are important signposts for international investors. Most of these data are available only for a limited number of the world's economies. Thus, the authors provide this information solely to give additional information on issues relating to foreign investment. The chapter presents detailed information on member countries of the Organization for Economic Cooperation and Development (OECD), an organization that includes many of the world's most industrialized economies. OECD countries are the destination for the lion's share of global foreign investment. In addition, in recognition of the increasing importance of the developing world to investors, this chapter includes data on Brazil, India, Indonesia, the People's Republic of China, and Russia. The analysis of these data both underscores the importance of economic freedom to economic growth and provides international investors with supplemental information as a quick reference guide to the world's most important markets.

New this year is a chapter that explores the statistical relationship between economic freedom and political freedom. Comparing data from the respected survey of political freedom prepared by Freedom House with the *Index,* Heritage analysts find that countries that are more economically free also are more politically free and have higher levels of civil liberties than countries with less economic freedom.

Finally, the authors have added a new chapter this year that provides vital economic data on all the 161 countries graded in the *Index.* Presented as a statistical appendix to the 1999 edition, this chapter contains such essential economic data as gross domestic product (GDP) and per capita GDP presented in purchasing power parity as well as a list of major industries, agricultural production, and trading partners.

Note

[1] This edition of the *Index* includes an analysis of the second half of 1997 and the first half of 1998. It does not cover the late summer and early fall 1998 time frame in which Russia suffered its greatest economic setback in recent history. The author does quantify, however, the economic conditions that contributed to the recent economic downturn in the past several editions of the *Index.*

Global Distribution of Economic Freedom

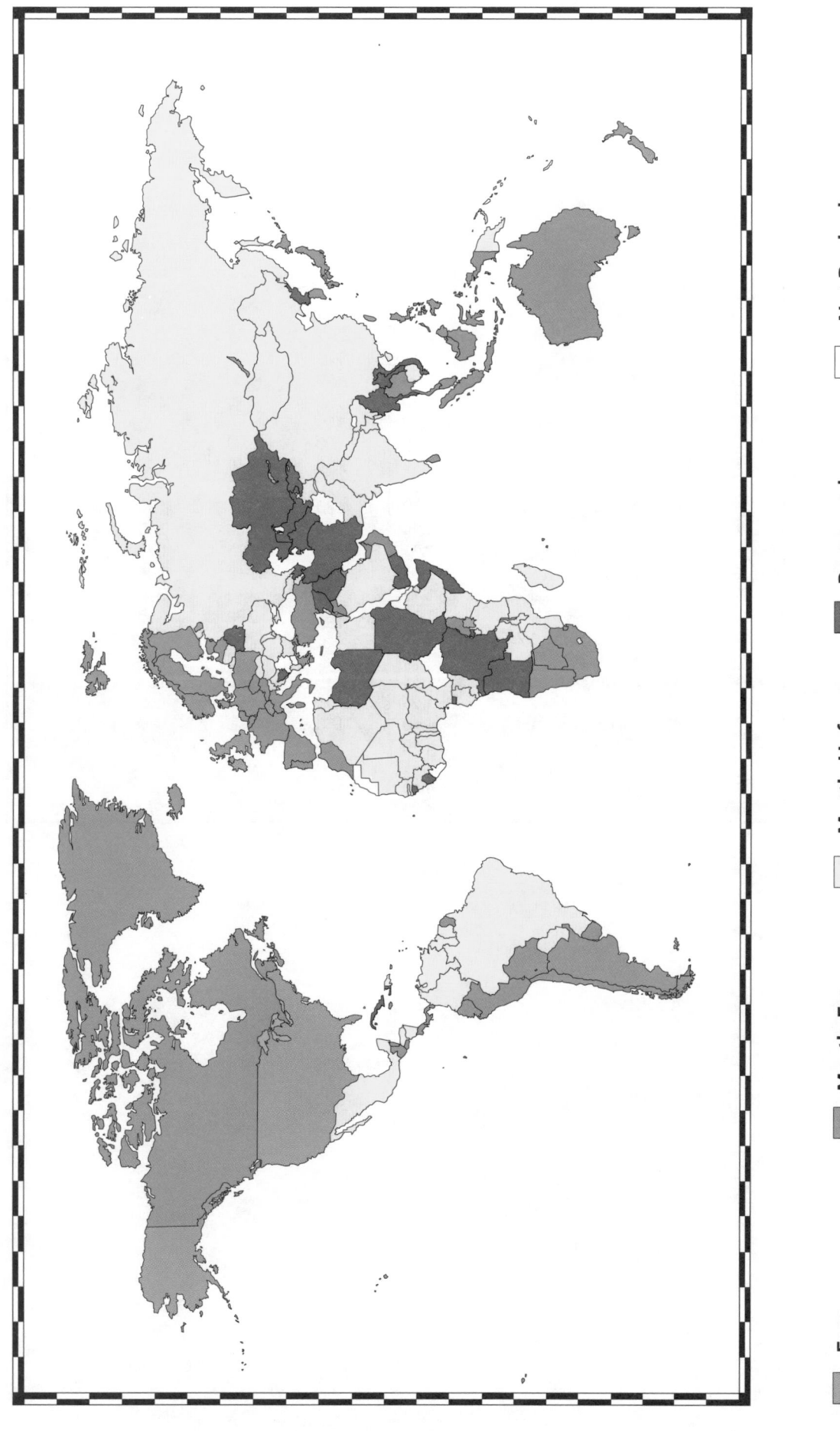

Free
Score: 1.00 to 1.99

Mostly Free
Score: 2.00 to 2.99

Mostly Unfree
Score: 3.00 to 3.99

Repressed
Score: 4.00 to 5.00

Not Ranked

Regional Rankings: Asia and the Pacific (32 Economies)

Regional Rank	World Rank		1999	1998	1997	1996	1995
6	14	Australia	2.10	2.05	2.15	2.10	2.20
25	143	Azerbaijan	4.30	4.40	4.60	4.70	-
22	129	Bangladesh	3.85	3.75	3.70	3.65	3.90
17	97	Cambodia	3.35	3.35	3.55	-	-
21	124	China	3.80	3.75	3.80	3.80	3.80
14	81	Fiji	3.10	3.20	3.20	3.10	3.30
1	1	Hong Kong	1.25	1.25	1.25	1.25	1.25
20	120	India	3.70	3.70	3.70	3.75	3.70
13	65	Indonesia	2.95	2.85	2.85	2.85	3.35
5	12	Japan	2.05	2.05	2.05	2.05	1.95
24	137	Kazakhstan	4.05	4.10	-	-	-
32	160	Korea, North	5.00	5.00	5.00	5.00	5.00
7	28	Korea, South	2.40	2.30	2.45	2.30	2.15
23	135	Kyrgyz Republic	4.00	4.00	-	-	-
31	157	Laos	4.90	5.00	5.00	5.00	-
7	28	Malaysia	2.40	2.40	2.60	2.40	2.15
16	88	Mongolia	3.20	3.10	3.30	3.50	3.33
25	143	Myanmar	4.30	4.30	4.30	4.30	-
19	104	Nepal	3.40	3.40	3.60	3.50	-
3	19	New Zealand	1.75	1.75	1.75	1.75	-
17	97	Pakistan	3.35	3.20	3.10	3.05	3.15
15	85	Papua New Guinea	3.15	3.15	3.10	3.10	-
11	48	Philippines	2.75	2.65	2.80	2.90	3.30
12	54	Samoa(former W. Samoa)	2.80	2.80	2.80	2.80	-
2	138	Singapore	1.30	1.30	1.30	1.30	1.25
10	38	Sri Lanka	2.55	2.45	2.45	2.65	2.80
4	7	Taiwan	1.95	1.95	1.95	1.95	1.95
27	147	Tajikistan	4.40	4.40	-	-	-
7	28	Thailand	2.40	2.40	2.30	2.30	2.30
29	149	Turkmenistan	4.45	4.50	-	-	-
27	147	Uzbekistan	4.40	4.55	-	-	-
30	152	Vietnam	4.60	4.70	4.70	4.70	4.70

Economic Freedom in Asia and the Pacific

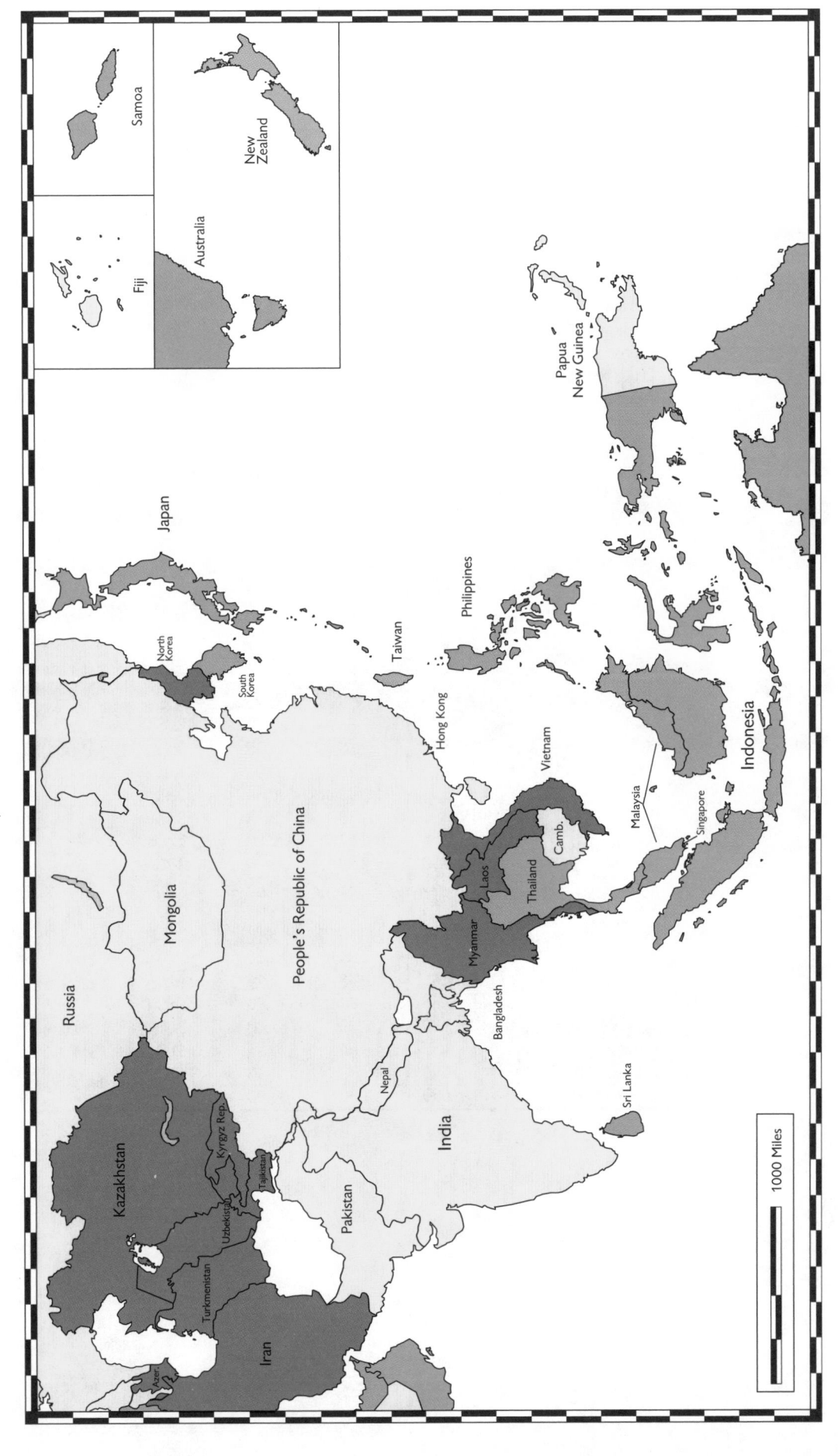

Free
Score: 1.00 to 1.99

Mostly Free
Score: 2.00 to 2.99

Mostly Unfree
Score: 3.00 to 3.99

Repressed
Score: 4.00 to 5.00

Not Ranked

Note: Fiji and Samoa are not to scale.

1000 Miles

Regional Rankings: North America and Europe (42 Economies)

Regional Rank	World Rank		1999	1998	1997	1996	1995
40	129	Albania	3.85	3.75	3.65	3.45	3.55
34	106	Armenia	3.45	3.45	3.45	3.75	-
9	18	Austria	2.15	2.15	2.15	2.05	2.05
41	140	Belarus	4.15	4.05	3.85	3.55	3.65
7	14	Belgium	2.10	2.10	2.10	2.10	-
42	155	Bosnia	4.80	4.80	-	-	-
34	106	Bulgaria	3.45	3.65	3.60	3.50	3.50
7	14	Canada	2.10	2.10	2.10	2.00	2.00
37	116	Croatia	3.65	3.75	3.70	3.70	-
22	45	Cyprus	2.70	2.60	2.60	2.60	-
6	12	Czech Republic	2.05	2.20	2.05	2.00	2.10
12	22	Denmark	2.25	2.25	2.05	1.95	-
9	18	Estonia	2.15	2.15	2.35	2.35	2.25
12	22	Finland	2.25	2.25	2.30	2.30	-
18	34	France	2.50	2.50	2.50	2.30	2.30
37	116	Georgia	3.65	3.65	3.85	3.85	-
14	25	Germany	2.30	2.30	2.20	2.10	2.00
25	62	Greece	2.90	2.90	2.85	2.80	2.80
25	62	Hungary	2.90	2.90	2.90	2.90	2.80
14	25	Iceland	2.30	2.30	2.50	-	-
3	7	Ireland	1.95	2.00	2.20	2.20	2.20
18	34	Italy	2.50	2.50	2.60	2.70	2.50
24	61	Latvia	2.85	2.85	2.95	3.05	-
29	72	Lithuania	3.00	3.00	3.10	3.50	-
3	7	Luxembourg	1.95	1.95	2.05	1.95	-
27	65	Malta	2.95	2.85	2.95	3.05	3.25
33	97	Moldova	3.35	3.35	3.35	3.45	4.10
9	18	Netherlands	2.15	2.20	2.00	1.85	-
16	27	Norway	2.35	2.35	2.45	2.45	-
27	65	Poland	2.95	2.95	3.15	3.05	3.25
21	38	Portugal	2.55	2.60	2.60	2.60	2.80
32	95	Romania	3.30	3.30	3.40	3.70	3.55
34	106	Russia	3.45	3.45	3.65	3.50	3.50
30	75	Slovak Republic	3.05	3.05	3.05	2.95	2.75
31	81	Slovenia	3.10	3.10	3.10	3.35	-
18	34	Spain	2.50	2.50	2.60	2.70	2.60
17	33	Sweden	2.45	2.45	2.45	2.55	2.65
1	34	Switzerland	1.85	1.90	1.90	1.80	-
23	54	Turkey	2.80	2.80	2.80	3.00	3.00
39	124	Ukraine	3.80	3.80	3.75	4.00	3.90
3	7	United Kingdom	1.95	1.95	1.95	1.95	1.95
2	6	United States	1.90	1.90	1.90	1.90	1.90

Economic Freedom in North America and Europe

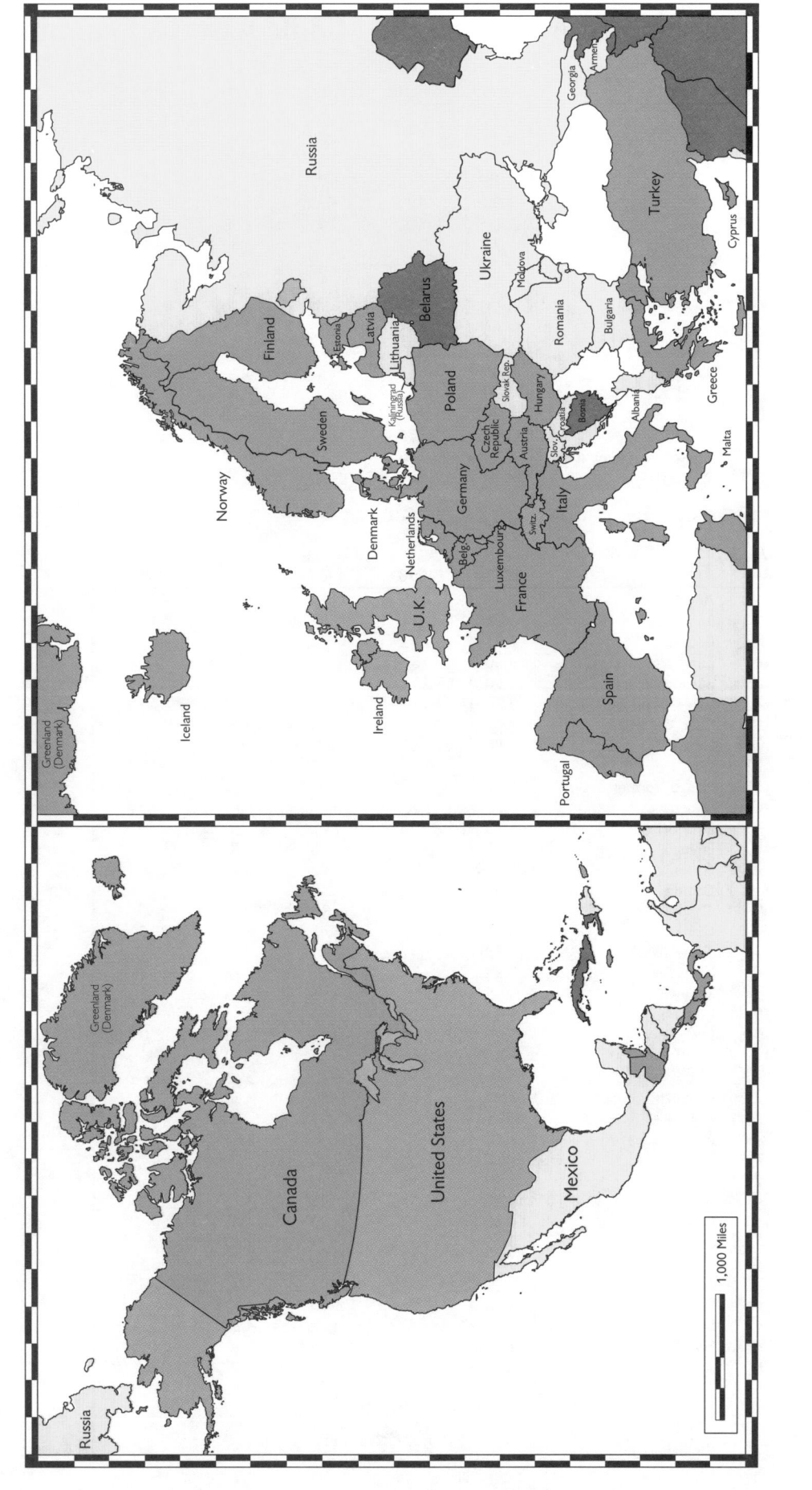

Free
Score: 1.00 to 1.99

Mostly Free
Score: 2.00 to 2.99

Mostly Unfree
Score: 3.00 to 3.99

Repressed
Score: 4.00 to 5.00

Not Ranked

Regional Rankings: North Africa and the Middle East (18 Economies)

Regional Rank	World Rank		1999	1998	1997	1996	1995
11	90	Algeria	3.25	3.25	3.25	3.25	3.15
1	12	Bahrain	1.70	1.70	1.60	1.70	1.60
13	97	Egypt	3.35	3.35	3.45	3.45	3.50
16	153	Iran	4.70	4.70	4.70	4.70	-
17	157	Iraq	4.90	4.90	4.90	4.90	-
6	54	Israel	2.80	2.80	2.80	2.90	3.10
4	48	Jordan	2.75	2.75	2.70	2.80	2.90
3	28	Kuwait	2.40	2.40	2.40	2.40	-
11	90	Lebanon	3.25	3.25	2.95	2.95	-
17	157	Libya	4.90	4.70	4.70	4.70	-
7	65	Morocco	2.95	2.95	2.75	2.70	2.90
4	48	Oman	2.75	2.65	2.75	2.85	2.65
10	75	Qatar	3.05	-	-	-	-
9	72	Saudi Arabia	3.00	2.80	2.80	2.90	-
15	141	Syria	4.20	4.00	4.20	4.20	-
7	65	Tunisia	2.95	2.75	2.75	2.65	2.85
2	14	United Arab Emirates	2.10	2.10	2.10	2.10	-
14	139	Yemen	4.10	4.10	3.90	3.75	3.75

Sub-Saharan Africa (37 Economies)

Regional Rank	World Rank		1999	1998	1997	1996	1995
39	149	Angola	4.45	4.35	4.35	4.35	4.35
9	75	Benin	3.05	2.95	2.95	2.95	-
2	48	Botswana	2.75	2.75	2.85	2.80	3.05
21	111	Burkina Faso	3.50	3.50	3.50	3.70	-
33	133	Burundi	3.90	3.90	3.80	-	-
21	111	Cameroon	3.50	3.50	3.60	3.60	3.60
25	119	Cape Verde	3.67	3.44	3.44	3.44	-
29	124	Chad	3.80	3.80	3.80	-	-
28	122	Congo	3.75	3.75	3.75	3.80	3.90
41	153	Congo (former Zaire)	4.70	4.70	4.20	4.20	-
13	88	Djibouti	3.20	3.20	3.00	-	-
37	143	Equatorial Guinea	4.30	-	-	-	-
26	120	Ethiopia	3.70	3.70	3.60	3.70	3.80
7	65	Gabon	2.95	2.95	2.95	3.06	3.06
23	115	Gambia	3.60	3.60	3.60	-	-
8	72	Ghana	3.00	3.00	3.10	3.20	3.30
17	97	Guinea	3.35	3.25	3.45	3.35	3.35
40	151	Guinea-Bissau	4.55	-	-	-	-
17	97	Ivory Coast	3.35	3.35	3.35	3.25	3.25
9	75	Kenya	3.05	3.05	3.05	3.05	3.05
19	106	Lesotho	3.45	3.50	3.65	3.65	-
19	106	Madagascar	3.45	3.35	3.25	3.35	3.50
24	116	Malawi	3.65	3.65	3.55	3.40	3.40
12	81	Mali	3.10	3.10	3.10	3.10	3.50
29	124	Mauritania	3.80	3.80	3.80	3.80	-
1	43	Mauritius	2.65	-	-	-	-
32	129	Mozambique	3.85	4.10	4.00	4.05	4.40
2	48	Namibia	2.75	2.75	2.95	-	-
26	120	Niger	3.70	3.70	3.70	3.70	-
16	95	Nigeria	3.30	3.30	3.20	3.25	3.15
37	143	Rwanda	4.30	4.30	4.20	-	-
14	90	Senegal	3.25	3.25	3.25	3.40	-
35	137	Sierra Leone	4.05	3.85	3.85	3.75	3.75
6	62	So. Africa	2.90	2.90	3.00	3.00	3.00
42	155	Somalia	4.80	4.70	4.70	4.70	-
36	141	Sudan	4.20	4.20	4.20	4.10	4.22
4	54	Swaziland	2.80	2.70	2.80	2.90	2.90
14	90	Tanzania	3.25	3.25	3.25	3.45	3.50
34	134	Togo	3.95	-	-	-	-
4	54	Uganda	2.80	2.80	2.90	2.83	2.94
9	75	Zambia	3.05	3.05	2.85	2.95	3.05
31	124	Zimbabwe	3.80	3.90	3.70	3.70	3.50

Economic Freedom in Africa and the Middle East

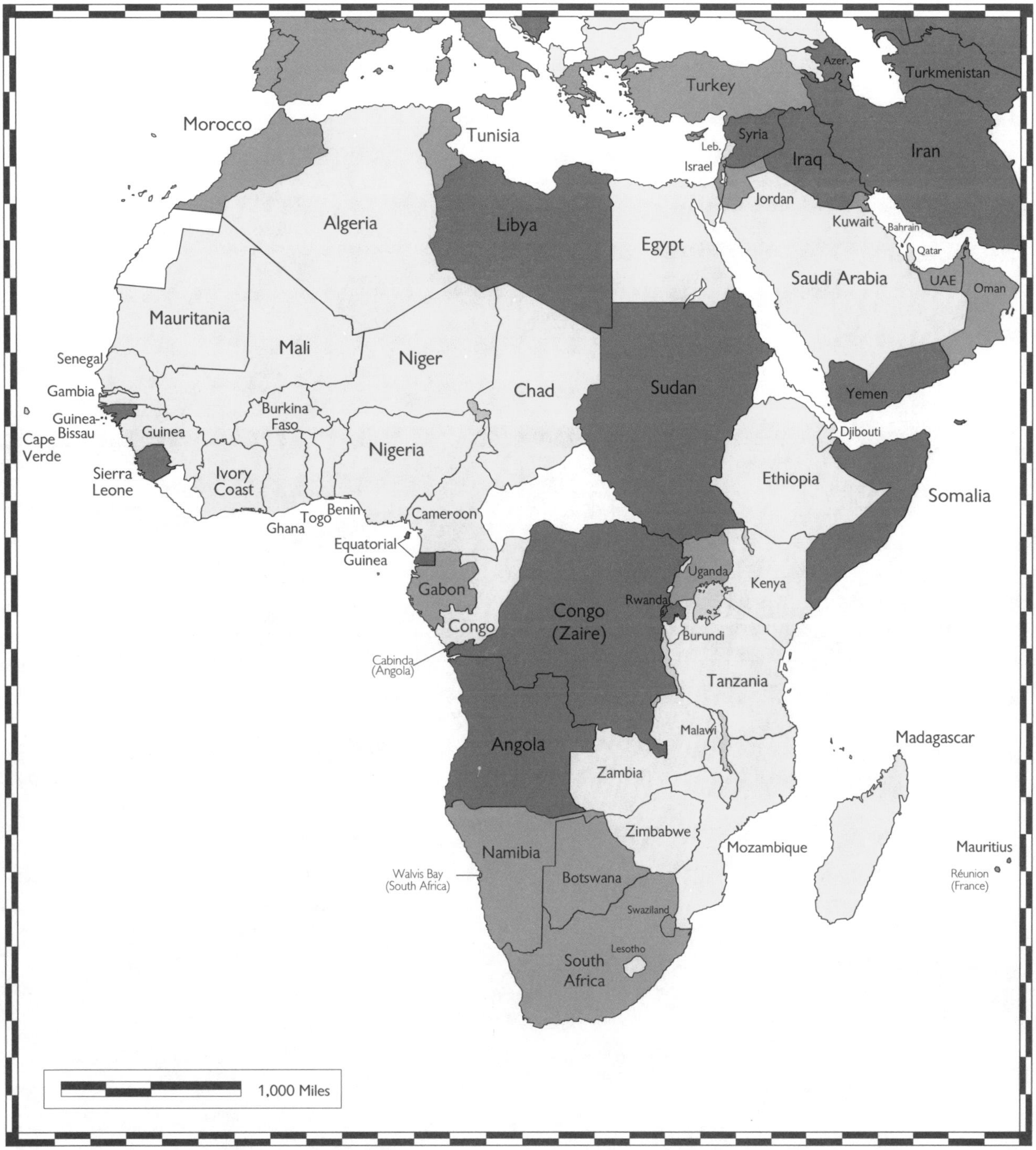

	Free		Mostly Free		Mostly Unfree		Repressed		Not Ranked
	Score: 1.00 to 1.99		Score: 2.00 to 2.99		Score: 3.00 to 3.99		Score: 4.00 to 5.00		

Regional Rankings: Latin America and the Caribbean (27 Economies)

Regional Rank	World Rank		1999	1998	1997	1996	1995
5	34	Argentina	2.50	2.60	2.65	2.65	2.85
1	11	Bahamas	2.00	2.00	2.00	2.00	2.10
7	41	Barbados	2.60	2.60	2.80	3.00	-
13	54	Belize	2.80	2.80	2.70	2.70	2.70
9	43	Bolivia	2.65	2.65	2.85	2.75	3.20
20	90	Brazil	3.25	3.35	3.35	3.45	3.30
2	18	Chile	2.15	2.15	2.25	2.45	2.50
17	81	Colombia	3.10	3.00	3.10	3.00	2.90
13	54	Costa Rica	2.80	2.80	2.80	2.80	2.90
27	160	Cuba	5.00	5.00	5.00	5.00	5.00
21	97	Dominican Republic	3.35	3.45	3.45	3.45	3.40
15	65	Ecuador	2.95	2.95	3.05	3.15	3.25
3	22	El Salvador	2.25	2.45	2.55	2.45	2.65
12	48	Guatemala	2.75	2.80	2.80	2.85	3.05
23	111	Guyana	3.50	3.60	3.50	3.40	3.70
26	135	Haiti	4.00	4.00	4.00	4.20	4.20
18	85	Honduras	3.15	3.15	3.15	3.15	3.15
10	45	Jamaica	2.70	2.60	2.60	2.70	2.80
18	85	Mexico	3.15	3.25	3.35	3.35	3.05
23	111	Nicaragua	3.50	3.50	3.60	3.60	3.90
4	28	Panama	2.40	2.40	2.50	2.40	2.70
16	75	Paraguay	3.05	2.85	2.75	2.65	2.75
7	41	Peru	2.60	2.80	2.90	3.00	3.40
25	129	Suriname	3.85	3.90	4.00	3.90	-
6	38	Trinidad and Tobago	2.55	2.55	2.55	2.50	-
10	45	Uruguay	2.70	2.70	2.70	2.80	2.90
22	104	Venezuela	3.40	3.50	3.60	3.50	3.00

Economic Freedom in South America

	Free		Mostly Free		Mostly Unfree		Repressed		Not
	Score: 1.00 to 1.99		Score: 2.00 to 2.99		Score: 3.00 to 3.99		Score: 4.00 to 5.00		Ranked

Economic Freedom in Central America and the Caribbean

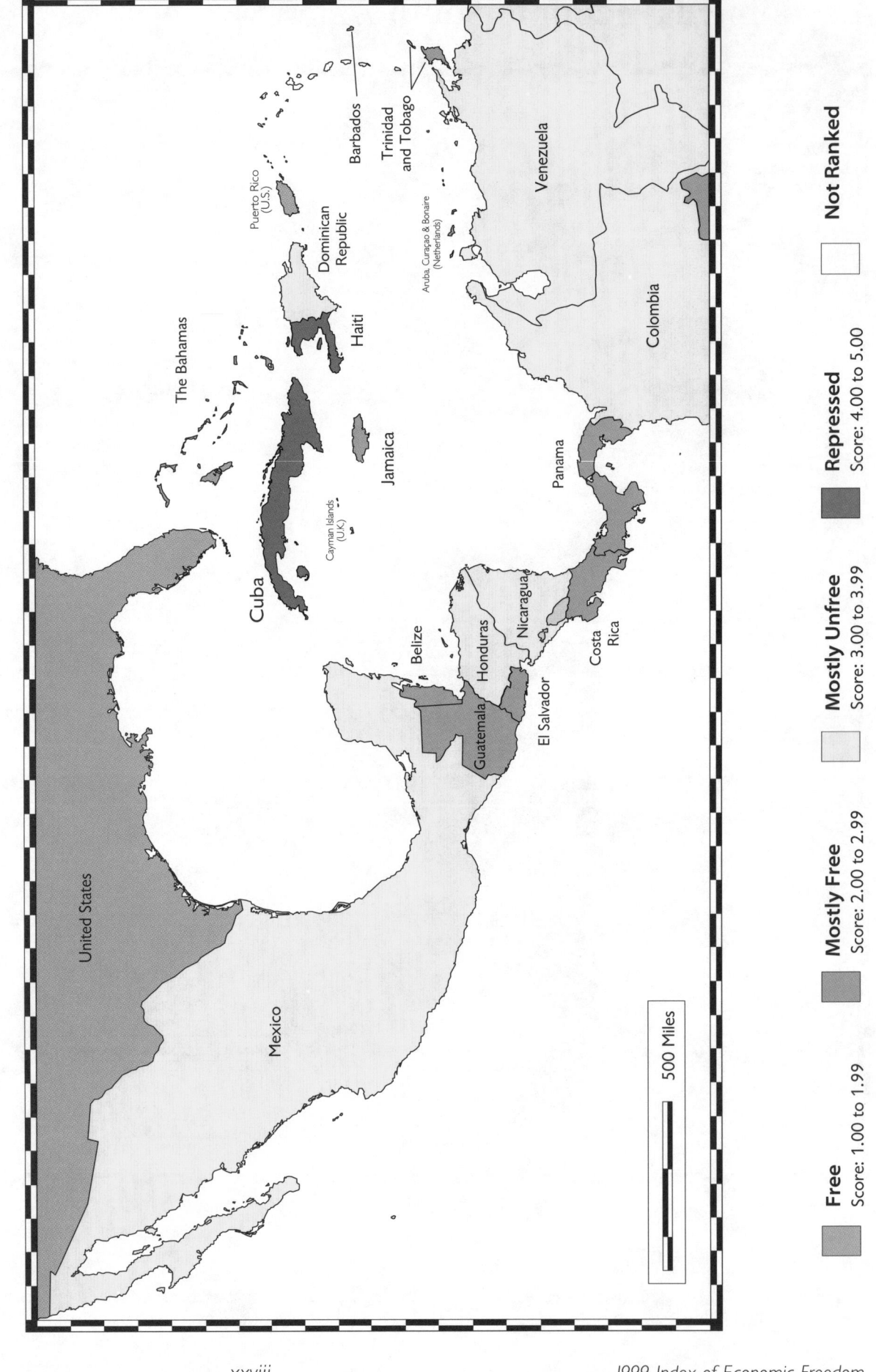

Free
Score: 1.00 to 1.99

Mostly Free
Score: 2.00 to 2.99

Mostly Unfree
Score: 3.00 to 3.99

Repressed
Score: 4.00 to 5.00

Not Ranked

500 Miles

Economic Freedom and Wealth

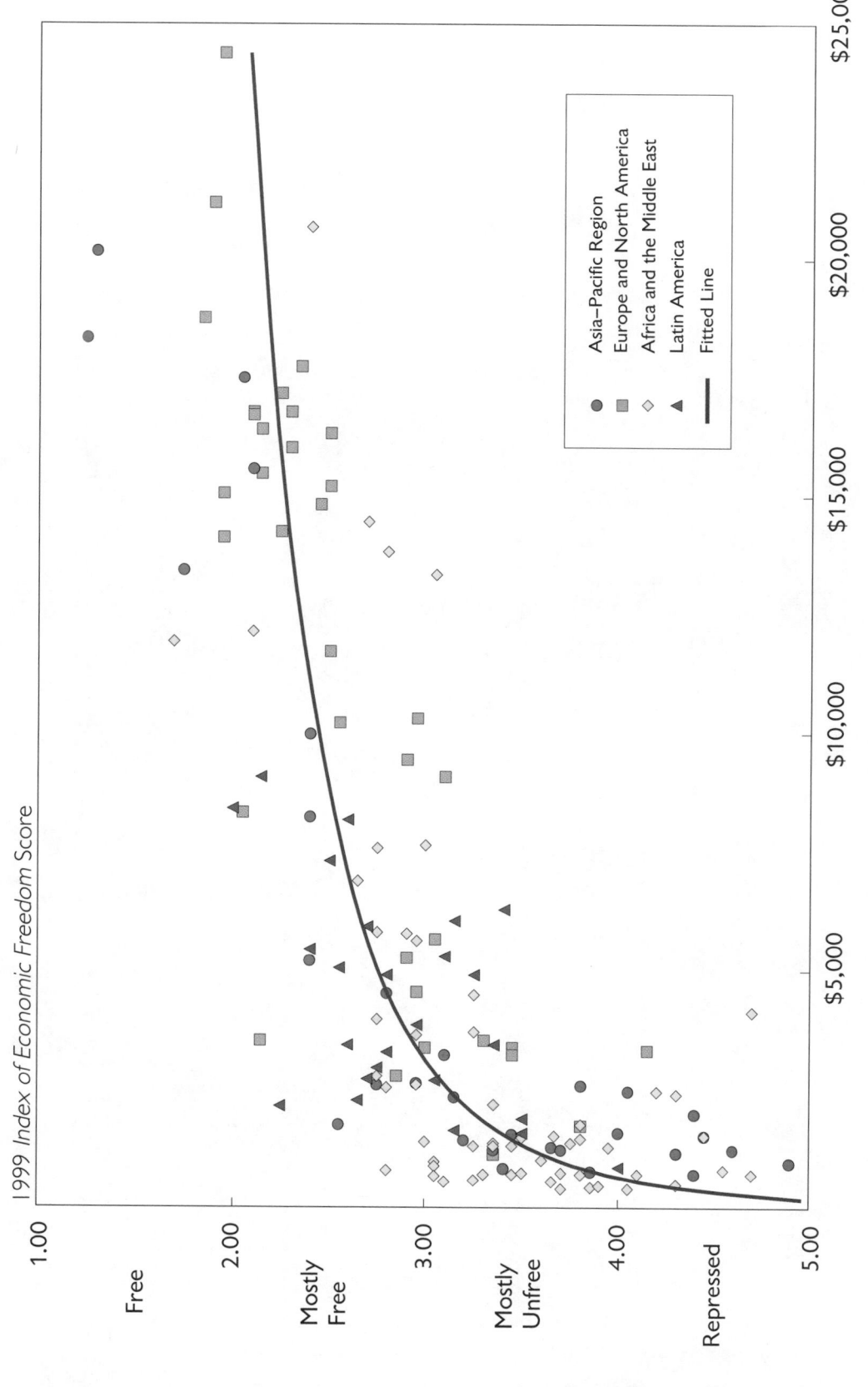

1999 *Index of Economic Freedom Score*

Per Capita GDP in Purchasing Power Parities

Legend:
- ● Asia–Pacific Region
- ■ Europe and North America
- ◇ Africa and the Middle East
- ▲ Latin America
- — Fitted Line

Y-axis: 1.00 (Free), 2.00 (Mostly Free), 3.00, 4.00 (Mostly Unfree), 5.00 (Repressed)

X-axis: $5,000 | $10,000 | $15,000 | $20,000 | $25,000

Note: Countries with unavailable per capita GDP figures have been left out of this chart. Per capita GDP figures are in 1987 international dollars and are from 1996, with the exception of the following: Armenia, Bahamas, Bahrain, Barbados, Bolivia, Gambia, Georgia, Iran, Israel, Kuwait, Malta, Saudi Arabia, Oman, Qatar, Syria, and U.A.E. figures are from 1995; Cyrpus figure is from 1994; Tanzania figure is from 1993.

Source: The World Bank, *1998 World Development Indicators on CD–ROM.*

Index of Economic Freedom Rankings

Rank	Country	1999 Score	1998 Score	1997 Score	1996 Score	1995 Score	Trade	Taxation	Government Intervention	Monetary Policy	Foreign Investment	Banking	Wage/Prices	Property Rights	Regulation	Black Market
1	Hong Kong*	1.25	1.25	1.25	1.25	1.25	1	1.5	1	2	1	1	2	1	1	1
2	Singapore	1.30	1.30	1.30	1.30	1.25	1	3	1	1	1	2	2	1	1	1
3	Bahrain	1.70	1.70	1.60	1.70	1.60	2	1	3	1	2	2	2	2	2	1
4	New Zealand	1.75	1.75	1.75	1.75		2	3.5	2	1	2	2	2	2	2	1
5	Switzerland	1.85 +	1.90	1.90	1.80	1.90	2	2.5+	3	1	2	1	2	3	3	1
6	United States	1.90	1.90	1.90	1.90	1.90	2	4	2	1	2	2	2	2	2	1
7	Ireland	1.95 +	2.00	2.20	2.20	2.20	2	4.5+	2	1	2	2	2	2	2	1
7	Luxembourg	1.95	1.95	2.05	1.95		2	3.5	3	1	2	2	2	2	2	1
7	Taiwan	1.95	1.95	1.95	1.95	1.95	2	2.5	2	1	3	3	2	2	2	1
7	United Kingdom	1.95	1.95	1.95	1.95	1.95	2	4.5	2	1	2	2	2	2	2	1
11	Bahamas	2.00	2.00	2.00	2.00	2.10	5	1	2	1	3	2	2	1	1	2
12	Czech Republic	2.05 +	2.20	2.05	2.00	2.10	1+	3.5+	2	2	2	3	2	2	2	3
12	Japan	2.05	2.05	2.05	2.05	1.95	2	4.5	1	1	3	3	2	2	2	1
14	Australia	2.10 -	2.05	2.15	2.10	2.20	2	5-	3	1	2	1	2	1	3	1
14	Belgium	2.10	2.10	2.10	2.10		2	5	2	1	2	2	2	1	3	1
14	Canada	2.10	2.10	2.10	2.00	2.00	2	5	2	1	3	2	2	1	2	1
14	United Arab Emirates	2.10	2.10	2.10	2.10		2	1	3	1	4	3	3	1	2	1
18	Austria	2.15	2.15	2.15	2.05	2.05	2	4.5	3	1	2	2	2	1	3	2
18	Chile	2.15	2.15	2.25	2.45	2.50	2	3.5	1	3	2	3	2	2	2	2
18	Estonia	2.15	2.15	2.35	2.35	2.25	1	3.5	2	4	1	2	2	2	2	2
18	Netherlands	2.15 +	2.20	2.00	1.85		2	4.5+	3	1	2	1	3	1	3	1
22	Denmark	2.25	2.25	2.05	1.95		2	4.5	4	1	2	2	1	1	2	3
22	El Salvador	2.25 +	2.45	2.55	2.45	2.65	3	2.5	1	3	1+	2	2	2+	3	3
22	Finland	2.25	2.25	2.30	2.30		2	4.5	3	1	2	3	2	1	3	1
25	Germany	2.30	2.30	2.20	2.10	2.00	2	5	2	1	2	3	2	1	4	1
25	Iceland	2.30	2.30	2.50			2	4	3	2	2	3	2	1	3	1
27	Norway	2.35	2.35	2.45	2.45		2	4.5	3	1	2	3	3	1	3	1
28	Korea, South	2.40 -	2.30	2.45	2.30	2.15	3	4	2	2	2	3-	2	1	3	2
28	Kuwait	2.40	2.40	2.40	2.40		2	1	4	2	4	3	3	1	2	2

Note: Countries whose scores have changed since last year are in **Bold**. Scores followed by a plus sign (+) have improved from last year. Those followed by a minus sign (-) have worsened.

*In August 1998 and the weeks that followed, the Hong Kong government spent some $15.2 billion to "ward off speculators" by buying private stock in the Hong Kong stock exchange. Not only has the Hong Kong government failed to allow its currency board to function properly by letting market forces take over, but it has violated a sacred rule of free-market economics: Governments should avoid direct ownership of private companies. In doing so, Hong Kong has demonstrated that its commitment to the market may be weakening. These events occurred after the cutoff date for consideration in this edition of the *Index of Economic Freedom*, however; had this information been included in this edition, Hong Kong would have ranked below Singapore in the *Index*. Thus, at the time of publication, in late 1998, Hong Kong no longer can be considered the freest economy in the world.

Index of Economic Freedom Rankings

Rank	Country	1999 Score	1998 Score	1997 Score	1996 Score	1995 Score	Trade	Taxation	Government Intervention	Monetary Policy	Foreign Investment	Banking	Wage/Prices	Property Rights	Regulation	Black Market
28	Malaysia	2.40	2.40	2.60	2.40	2.15	3	3	2	1	3	3	3	2	2	2
28	Panama	2.40	2.40	2.50	2.40	2.70	3	3	3	1	2	1	2	3	3	3
28	Thailand	2.40	2.40	2.30	2.30	2.30	3	3	2	1	2	3	3	3	3	2
33	Sweden	2.45	2.45	2.45	2.55	2.65	2	4.5	5	1	2	2	2	2	3	1
34	Argentina	2.50 +	2.60	2.65	2.65	2.85	3+	3	2	5	2	2	2	2	2	2
34	France	2.50	2.50	2.50	2.30	2.30	2	5	3	1	3	3	3	2	2	1
34	Italy	2.50	2.50	2.60	2.70	2.50	2	5	3	2	2	2	2	2	3	2
34	Spain	2.50	2.50	2.60	2.70	2.60	2	5	2	2	2	2	3	2	3	2
38	Portugal	2.55 +	2.60	2.60	2.60	2.80	2	4.5+	3	2	2	3	2	2	3	2
38	Sri Lanka	2.55 -	2.45	2.45	2.65	2.80	3	3.5	2	2	3	2	1	3	3-	3
38	Trinidad and Tobago	2.55	2.55	2.55	2.50		5	4.5	2	2	1	2	2	1	3	3
41	Barbados	2.60	2.60	2.80	3.00		3	5	3	1	2	2	2	2	3	3
41	Peru	2.60 +	2.80	2.90	3.00	3.40	2	3	1	5	2	2	2	2+	3+	4
43	Bolivia	2.65	2.65	2.85	2.75	3.20	2	2.5	3	3	2	2	3	3	4	4
43	Mauritius	2.65					4	4.5	2	2	3	2	3	2	2	2
45	Cyprus	2.70 -	2.60	2.60	2.60		3	4	3	1	3-	2	3	3	2	3
45	Jamaica	2.70 -	2.60	2.60	2.70	2.80	2	3	2	4	2	3-	3	2	3	3
45	Uruguay	2.70	2.70	2.70	2.80	2.90	2	3	3	5	2	2	2	3	3	3
48	Botswana	2.75	2.75	2.85	2.80	3.05	3	2.5	4	2	3	2	2	2	3	4
48	Guatemala	2.75 +	2.80	2.80	2.85	3.05	3	2.5+	1	3	3	2	3	3	4	3
48	Jordan	2.75	2.75	2.70	2.80	2.90	4	2.5	3	2	2	2	3	2	3	4
48	Namibia	2.75	2.75	2.95			4	3.5	4	2	2	2	2	2	3	3
48	Oman	2.75 -	2.65	2.75	2.85	2.65	2	2.5+	4	1	4-	4	3	2	3-	2
48	Philippines	2.75 -	2.65	2.80	2.90	3.30	3	3.5	1	2	3	3	2	2	4-	4
54	Belize	2.80	2.80	2.70	2.70	2.70	5	4	2	1	2	3	2	3	3	3
54	Costa Rica	2.80	2.80	2.80	2.80	2.90	4	3	2	3	2	3	2	2	3	3
54	Israel	2.80	2.80	2.80	2.90	3.10	2	5	4	3	1	3	2	2	2	4
54	Swaziland	2.80 -	2.70	2.80	2.90	2.90	3	3	2	3-	3	3	3	2	3	4
54	Turkey	2.80	2.80	2.80	3.00	3.00	2	4	2	5	2	2	3	2	3	3
54	Uganda	2.80	2.80	2.90	2.83	2.94	5	4	2	5	2	3	1	2	2	2
54	Samoa	2.80	2.80	2.80	2.80		3	4	2	2	3	3	3	3	3	2
61	Latvia	2.85	2.85	2.95	3.05		2	2.5	3	5	2	2	2	3	3	4
62	Greece	2.90	2.90	2.85	2.80	2.80	2	4	3	3	2	4	3	2	3	3

Note: Countries whose scores have changed since last year are in **Bold**. Scores followed by a plus sign (+) have improved from last year. Those followed by a minus sign (–) have worsened.

Index of Economic Freedom Rankings

Rank		1999 Score	1998 Score	1997 Score	1996 Score	1995 Score	Trade	Taxation	Government Intervention	Monetary Policy	Foreign Investment	Banking	Wage/ Prices	Property Rights	Regulation	Black Market
62	South Africa	2.90	2.90	3.00	3.00	3.00	4	4	2+	3	2	3	2	3	2	4-
65	Ecuador	2.95	2.95	3.05	3.15	3.25	3	2.5	1	5	2	3	2	3	4	4
65	Gabon	2.95	2.95	2.95	3.06	3.06	5	4.5	3	1	2	2	3	3	3	3
65	Indonesia	2.95 -	2.85	2.85	2.85	3.35	2	3.5	1	2	2	4-	3	3	4	5
65	Malta	2.95 -	2.85	2.95	3.05	3.25	4	3.5	3-	1	2	3	4	2	3	4
65	Morocco	2.95	2.95	2.75	2.70	2.90	5	3.5	3	1	2	3	3	3	3	3
65	Poland	2.95	2.95	3.15	3.05	3.25	2	3.5	3	5	2	3	3	2	3	3
65	Tunisia	2.95 -	2.75	2.75	2.65	2.85	5	3.5	3	2	2	3-	2	3	3-	3
72	Ghana	3.00	3.00	3.10	3.20	3.30	3	3	3	4	3	3	2	3	4	2
72	Lithuania	3.00	3.00	3.10	3.50		1	3	3	5	2	3	3	3	3	4
72	Saudi Arabia	3.00 -	2.80	2.80	2.90		4	4	4	1	4	3	3	2-	3-	2
75	Benin	3.05 -	2.95	2.95	2.95		4	3.5	3	1	3	3	3	3	3	4-
75	Kenya	3.05	3.05	3.05	3.05	3.05	4	3.5	3	2	3	2	3	3	4	3
75	Paraguay	3.05 -	2.85	2.75	2.65	2.75	2	2.5	3-	4	1	2	3	4	4-	5
75	Qatar	3.05					3	2.5	5	1	3	4	4	3	4	1
75	Slovak Republic	3.05	3.05	3.05	2.95	2.75	3	4.5	3	2	3	3	3	3	3	3
75	Zambia	3.05	3.05	2.85	2.95	3.05	3	3.5	3	5	2	2	2	3	4	3
81	Colombia	3.10 -	3.00	3.10	3.00	2.90	4-	4	2	4	2	2	2	3	3	5
81	Fiji	3.10 +	3.20	3.20	3.10	3.30	5	3	3	1	3	3	3	3	3+	4
81	Mali	3.10	3.10	3.10	3.10	3.50	3	5	3	1	2	3	3	3	3	5
81	Slovenia	3.10	3.10	3.10	3.35		4	4	3	5	2	2	3	2	3	3
85	Honduras	3.15	3.15	3.15	3.15	3.15	4	3.5	2-	2+	3	2	3	3	4	4-
85	Mexico	3.15 +	3.25	3.35	3.35	3.05	2+	3.5	2	5	2	4	3	3	4	3
85	Papua New Guinea	3.15	3.15	3.10	3.10		5	2.5	3	1	3	4	3	3	4	3
88	Djibouti	3.20	3.20	3.00			4	2	5	1	3	3	3	3	4	4-
88	Mongolia	3.20 -	3.10	3.30	3.50	3.33	1	4	3	5	3	3	3	3	4-	3
90	Algeria	3.25	3.25	3.25	3.25	3.15	5	3.5	3	3	3	3	3	3	3	3
90	Brazil	3.25 +	3.35	3.35	3.45	3.30	4	2.5	3	5	3	3	2+	3	3	4
90	Lebanon	3.25	3.25	2.95	2.95		5	2.5	2	5	3	2	2	3	3	5
90	Senegal	3.25	3.25	3.25	3.40		4	4.5	3	1	3	3	4	4	4	3
90	Tanzania	3.25	3.25	3.25	3.45	3.50	3	3.5	3	4	3	3	2	3	4	4
95	Nigeria	3.30	3.30	3.20	3.25	3.15	5	3	2	5	2	4	2	3	4	3
95	Romania	3.30	3.30	3.40	3.70	3.55	2	5	3	5	2	3	2	4	4	3

Note: Countries whose scores have changed since last year are in **Bold**. Scores followed by a plus sign (+) have improved from last year. Those followed by a minus sign (-) have worsened.

Index of Economic Freedom Rankings

Rank		1999 Score	1998 Score	1997 Score	1996 Score	1995 Score	Trade	Taxation	Government Intervention	Monetary Policy	Foreign Investment	Banking	Wage/ Prices	Property Rights	Regulation	Black Market
97	Cambodia	3.35	3.35	3.55			3	2.5	3	5	3	3	3	4	4	3
97	Dominican Republic	3.35 +	3.45	3.45	3.45	3.40	5	2.5	2	4+	3	3	2	4	4	4
97	Egypt	3.35	3.35	3.45	3.45	3.50	5	4.5	3	3	3	2	3	3	4	3
97	Guinea	3.35 -	3.25	3.45	3.35	3.35	3	4.5	3	3	3	3-	2	4	4	4
97	Ivory Coast	3.35	3.35	3.35	3.25	3.25	5	3.5	3	1	3	3	3	4	4	4
97	Moldova	3.35	3.35	3.35	3.45	4.10	3	3.5	3	5	3	3	3	3	3	4
97	Pakistan	3.35 -	3.20	3.10	3.05	3.15	5	3.5+	3	2	2	3	3	4-	4	4-
104	Nepal	3.40	3.40	3.60	3.50		3	3	2	2	4	4	4	3	4	5
104	Venezuela	3.40 +	3.50	3.60	3.50	3.00	3	3+	3	5	3	3	3	3	3	5
106	Armenia	3.45	3.45	3.45	3.75		2	3.5	3	5	4	3	3	3	4	4
106	Bulgaria	3.45 +	3.65	3.60	3.50	3.50	4	3.5+	3	5	2+	3	3	3	4	4
106	Lesotho	3.45 +	3.50	3.65	3.65		3	3.5+	3	3	3	4	4	3	4	4
106	Madagascar	3.45 -	3.35	3.25	3.35	3.50	5	3.5	2	4-	4	4	2	3	3	4
106	Russia	3.45	3.45	3.65	3.50	3.50	4	3.5	3	5	3	2	3	3	4	4
111	Burkina Faso	3.50	3.50	3.50	3.70		5	4	3	1	2	4	4	3	4	5
111	Cameroon	3.50	3.50	3.60	3.60	3.60	5	4	2	1	3	4	3	4	4	5
111	Guyana	3.50 +	3.60	3.50	3.40	3.70	5	4	2+	5	3	3	2	3	4	4
111	Nicaragua	3.50	3.50	3.60	3.60	3.90	4	3	2	5	2	3	3	4	4	5
115	Gambia	3.60	3.60	3.60			4	4	3	2	4	4	4	2	4	5
116	Croatia	3.65 +	3.75	3.70	3.70		3	3.5	4+	5	3	3	4	4	4	3
116	Georgia	3.65	3.65	3.85	3.85		3	2.5	2	5	3	4	4	3	4	5
116	Malawi	3.65	3.65	3.55	3.40	3.40	5	4.5	3	4	3	3	3	3	4	4
119	Cape Verde	3.67 -	3.44	3.44	3.44		5	N/A	5-	2	2	5	4	2	4	4
120	Ethiopia	3.70	3.70	3.60	3.70	3.80	5	4	3	2	4	4	3	4	4	4
120	India	3.70	3.70	3.70	3.75	3.70	5	3+	3	2	4-	4	4	3	4	5
120	Niger	3.70	3.70	3.70	3.70		5	4	3	1	4	4	4	3	4	5
123	Congo	3.75	3.75	3.75	3.80	3.90	5	4.5	3	1	4	4	3	4	4	5
124	Chad	3.80	3.80	3.80			5	4	3	1	4	4	4	4	4	5
124	China	3.80 -	3.75	3.80	3.80	3.80	5	4-	5	3	3	3	3	4	4	4
124	Mauritania	3.80	3.80	3.80	3.80		5	4	3	2	3	5	4	3	4	4
124	Ukraine	3.80	3.80	3.75	4.00	3.90	4	4	3	5	3	4	3	4	4	4
124	Zimbabwe	3.80 +	3.90	3.70	3.70	3.50	5	4	3+	4	4	3	3	4	4	4
129	Albania	3.85 -	3.75	3.65	3.45	3.55	4-	3.5	5	5	2	4	3	4	3	5

Note: Countries whose scores have changed since last year are in **Bold**. Scores followed by a plus sign (+) have improved from last year. Those followed by a minus sign (-) have worsened.

Index of Economic Freedom Rankings

Rank		1999 Score	1998 Score	1997 Score	1996 Score	1995 Score	Trade	Taxation	Government Intervention	Monetary Policy	Foreign Investment	Banking	Wage/ Prices	Property Rights	Regulation	Black Market
129	Bangladesh	3.85 -	3.75	3.70	3.65	3.90	5	3.5	3	2	3	4-	4	4	5	5
129	Mozambique	3.85 +	4.10	4.00	4.05	4.40	3+	3.5+	3	5	4	3	3	4	5	5
129	Suriname	3.85 +	3.90	4.00	3.90		5	3.5+	3	5	3	3	3	3	4	5
133	Burundi	3.90	3.90	3.80			5	4	3	2	4	4	4	4	4	5
134	Togo	3.95					4	4.5	3	2	3	4	4	4	5	5
135	Haiti	4.00	4.00	4.00	4.20	4.20	4	3	3	3	3	4	4	5	5	5
135	Kyrgyz Republic	4.00	4.00				4	3	3	5	3	4	4	4	4	5
137	Kazakhstan	4.05 +	4.10				4	3.5+	3	5	4	4	4	4	4	5
137	Sierra Leone	4.05 -	3.85	3.85	3.75	3.75	4	4.5	3	5	3	4	4-	4	4-	5
139	Yemen	4.10	4.10	3.90	3.75	3.75	5	3	4	5	4	4	3	4	4	5
140	Belarus	4.15 -	4.05	3.85	3.55	3.65	4	4.5	3	5	4	4-	4	5	4	5
141	Sudan	4.20	4.20	4.20	4.10	4.22	5	5	3	5	4	4	4	4	5	4
141	Syria	4.20 -	4.10	4.20	4.20		5	5	3	3	4	5	4	5	4-	5
143	Azerbaijan	4.30 +	4.40	4.60	4.70		5	4	4+	5	4	4	5	4	4	4
143	Equatorial Guinea	4.30					5	5	4	1	4	5	5	5	4	5
143	Myanmar	4.30	4.30	4.30	4.30		5	3	5	4	4	5	4	4	5	5
143	Rwanda	4.30	4.30	4.20			5	5	4	2	4	5	3	5	5	5
147	Tajikistan	4.40	4.40				5	5	4	5	4	4	5	4	4	5
147	Uzbekistan	4.40 +	4.55				5	4+	3+	5	4	5	4	4	5	5
149	Angola	4.45 -	4.35	4.35	4.35	4.35	5	3.5	5-	5	4	4	4	4	5	5
149	Turkmenistan	4.45 +	4.50				5	4.5+	4	5	5	5	4	4	4	5
151	Guinea-Bissau	4.55					5	3.5	4	5	4	4	4	5	5	5
152	Vietnam	4.60 +	4.70	4.70	4.70	4.70	5	5	5	4+	4	4	4	5	4	5
153	Congo (former Zaire)	4.70	4.70	4.20	4.20		5	5	4	5	5	5	4	5	4	5
153	Iran	4.70	4.70	4.70	4.70		5	5	5	4	5	5	4	5	4	5
155	Bosnia	4.80	4.80				5	5	5	5	4	5	4	5	5	5
155	Somalia	4.80 -	4.70	4.70	4.70		5	5	5	5	4	5	4-	5	5	5
157	Iraq	4.90	4.90	4.90	4.90		5	5	5	5	5	5	5	5	4	5
157	Laos	4.90 +	5.00	5.00	5.00		5	5	5	4+	5	5	5	5	5	5
157	Libya	4.90 -	4.70	4.70	4.70		5	5	5	4-	5	5	5	5	5	5
160	Cuba	5.00	5.00	5.00	5.00	5.00	5	5	5	5	5	5	5	5	5	5
160	North Korea	5.00	5.00	5.00	5.00	5.00	5	5	5	5	5	5	5	5	5	5

Note: Countries whose scores have changed since last year are in **Bold**. Scores followed by a plus sign (+) have improved from last year. Those followed by a minus sign (-) have worsened.

The Institutional Setting of Economic Growth

by William W. Beach and Gareth G. Davis

The haunting of economic policy circles has begun. A year after the abrupt emergence of the Asian financial crisis and year-long efforts to "solve" the crisis with loans and restructuring programs, some policymakers now are beginning to see the ghosts of depressions past. The "Asian flu" clearly spread to Latin and South American economies sometime in summer 1998. It appears also to have aided low oil prices in weakening Russia's economy. And stock markets around the world have spent much of the past year spooking one another in attempts to price correctly the extent of the global economic slowdown.

Official recessions exist at the end of 1998 in Japan, South Korea, the Philippines, Thailand, Indonesia (although it would be more correct to call that contraction a depression), and the flagship of Asia, Hong Kong. More significant, all these economies are in worse shape than many analysts believed as late as May 1998 when the International Monetary Fund (IMF) issued its annual economic outlook.[1] Economists widely expected Russia to spend much of 1998 in the black rather than deeply in the red. Few forecasters had any expectation of economic slowdowns in Latin and South America, but autumn 1998 brought with it economic crises in the region's largest economies: Brazil, Mexico, Argentina, Chile, and Venezuela. At his September 1998 briefing to Congress on the state of the U.S. economy, Alan Greenspan, the venerable chairman of the Federal Reserve's Board of Governors, hinted strongly that even the U.S.

economy would slow down as a result of the Asian crisis.

In the crisis atmosphere that grows denser around policy centers each day, a strong temptation will emerge to take dramatic actions. After all, the slowing of so many developed and developing economies more than just hints at the possibility of global economic recession; it appears to be a virtual recipe for it. Thus, policymakers will entertain such masterful moves as breaking the linkage between local currencies and the U.S. dollar, nationalizing banks and other key financial institutions, closing borders to the outward migration of capital, passing legislation to induce or force households to spend more and save less, and putting economies on a "wartime footing" of public works projects and military spending.

The casual reader of today's economic news justifiably might dismiss these dramatic moves as baseless possibilities, but the sad truth is that each has been advanced recently by key players in the current crisis. Malaysia has introduced currency controls that effectively make the government— not currency markets—the arbiter of the currency's international value. The Hong Kong Monetary Authority has abandoned its laissez-faire policy of permitting the Hong Kong dollar to find its value automatically through a currency board and now intervenes in the city's stock market when its currency appears to be slipping significantly.[2] Japan announced plans in late September to nationalize the most problematic of its major banks and unveiled massive tax cuts and spending programs to "grow" the economy out of its long recession.[3] Indonesia has attempted to reduce the outflow of capital through especially high rates of interest,[4] and Japan, again, talks of putting the second largest economy in the world on a "wartime footing"—whatever that means.[5]

Indeed, no less an economist than Paul Krugman of the Massachusetts Institute of Technology[6] writes in the September 1998 issue of *Fortune* magazine that free markets and IMF-guided financial restructuring might need to give way to currency controls and other "dramatic moves":

> [Exchange control] involves giving up for a time the business of trying to regain the confidence of international investors and forcibly breaking the link between domestic interest rates and the exchange rate. The policy freedom that Asia needs to rebuild its economies would clearly come at a price, but as the slump gets ever deeper, that price is starting to look more and more worth paying.[7]

It may well be, however, that this cry, and others, for regulatory action in fact indicate the degree to which open currency and capital markets have been successful in liquidating the speculative bubble in Asia. Open markets greatly facilitate the discovery of economic value in the many hidden places in which it exists. When an economy's productivity rises and wealth is being created, few people object to freewheeling investors' discovering new firms and products to support. When investors create opposite signals

through their flight from an economy, however, objections to their behavior are the only thing not in short supply.

Indeed, no moves by any government or international organization have been as "dramatic" as the efforts of savers and capitalists alike to rescue themselves from the consequences of crony capitalism and bad public policy. The hundreds of millions of financial transactions that, taken collectively, constitute the liquidation of speculative excesses throughout the region vastly overshadow any actions taken by regional governments or the IMF. Without the economic freedoms that allowed Asian businesses and households as well as the thousands of non-Asian investors to take these actions, the valuable elements of Asian economies would be sinking as fast as would the worthless. Indeed, without economic freedoms, Asian economies today would be facing the economic "dry rot" that plagued the People's Republic of China before Deng Xiaoping's economic reforms and was the real economic story of the old Soviet Union.

In fact, those countries with freer economic institutions and public policies appear to be weathering the current turmoil better than those countries with less economic freedom. Although any analysis of how freer economies are weathering the economic storms by necessity must be preliminary, insights about the relationship between economic performance and economic freedom can be found even in the midst of these great difficulties.

The ultimate measure of the impact of the recent crisis in economic terms will be its effect on the long-term rate of growth in gross domestic product (GDP). Unfortunately, data currently available on GDP in most of the afflicted countries predate the crisis. Even if such data were available, they would be subject to short-term fluctuations and possibly would not represent the ultimate measure of the long-term growth implications of the current crisis.

To measure the scale of the economic problems countries have faced in the past 12 months, our focus turns to a different variable: the percentage change in the value of a country's exchange rate against the U.S. dollar between January 1997 and September 1998. Data on both exchange rates and economic freedom are

2

Chart 1.1

Relationship of Exchange Rates to *Index* Values

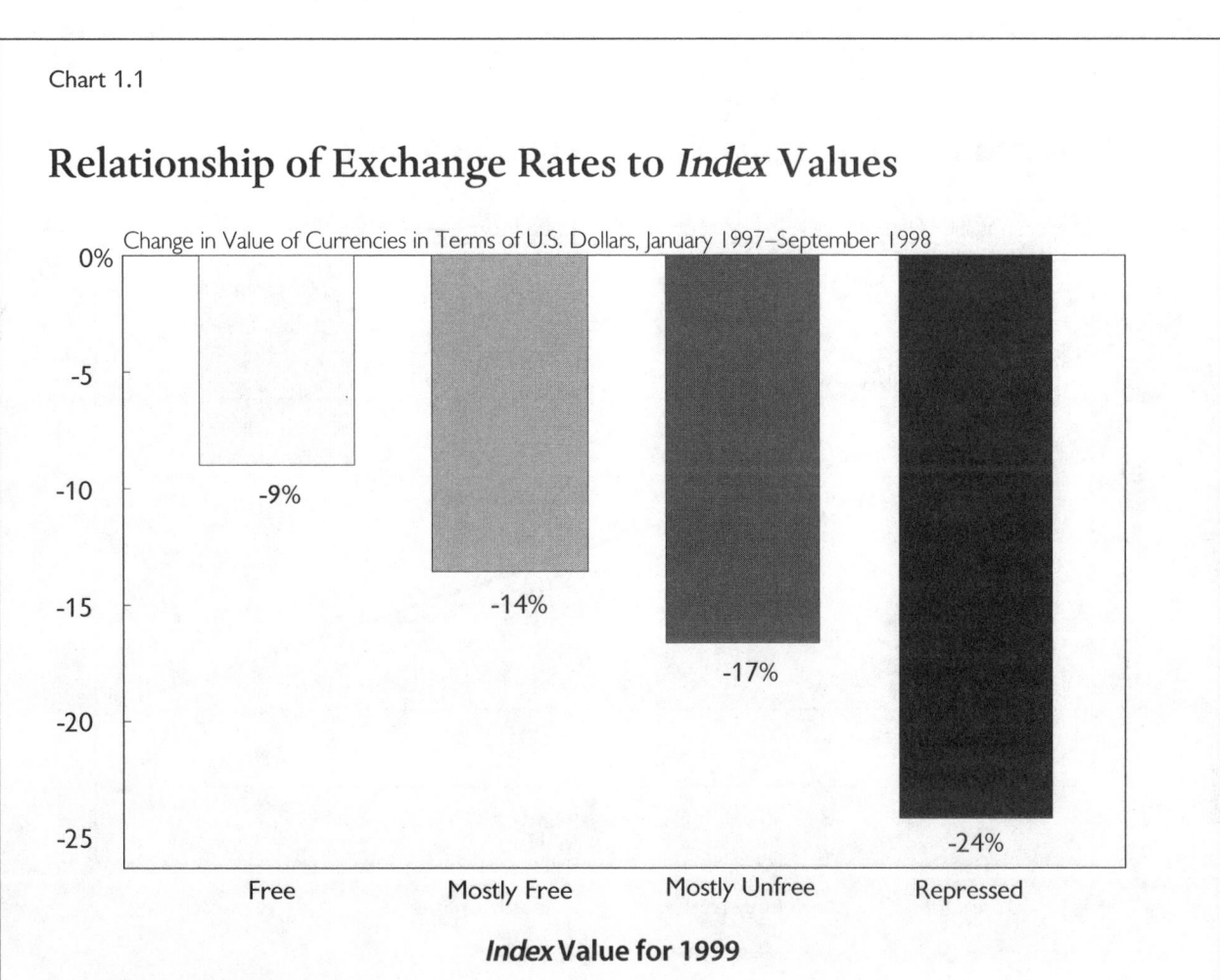

Change in Value of Currencies in Terms of U.S. Dollars, January 1997–September 1998

Index Value for 1999

Note: Exchange rate data were available for 137 of the 161 countries studied in this year's *Index*.
Source: Exchange rate data from WEFA International Financial Statistics.

available for 137 countries over this period. Economic freedom is measured by a country's score on the 1999 *Index of Economic Freedom,* while exchange rate data come from the WEFA Econometrics International Financial Statistics database.[8]

The use of exchange rate data has both advantages and disadvantages. The exchange rates are available for a wide range of developing and developed countries on a timely basis. Economists usually view exchange rates as prices that reflect information in financial markets about a country's economic health, the ability of its government to meet future obligations, and the sustainability of its monetary and fiscal policies; however, the exchange rate also is a price that can be affected by government controls and policies that prevent it from truly reflecting a country's economic fundamentals. For example, the intervention of its central bank on foreign exchange markets or even more directly through exchange and capital

controls may affect a country's exchange rate. With the exception of exchange controls, however, government policies seldom can offset market forces permanently in determining a currency's ultimate value (and even exchange controls will be circumvented by "black market" transactions). Although ultimately an imperfect measure of the severity of the recent economic crisis, the exchange rate does provide valuable information on a country's economic performance on a very timely and widespread basis.

We measure the degree of association between a country's commitment to free market policies and its exchange rate during the period between January 1997 and September 1998 using a linear regression. The results of this test of association show that a one-point increase in a country's *Index of Economic Freedom* score (higher scores reflect less economic freedom) implies a decline of 4.7 percent in the value of its currency against the U.S.

Chart 1.2

Relationship of Exchange Rates to *Index* Values in Asia

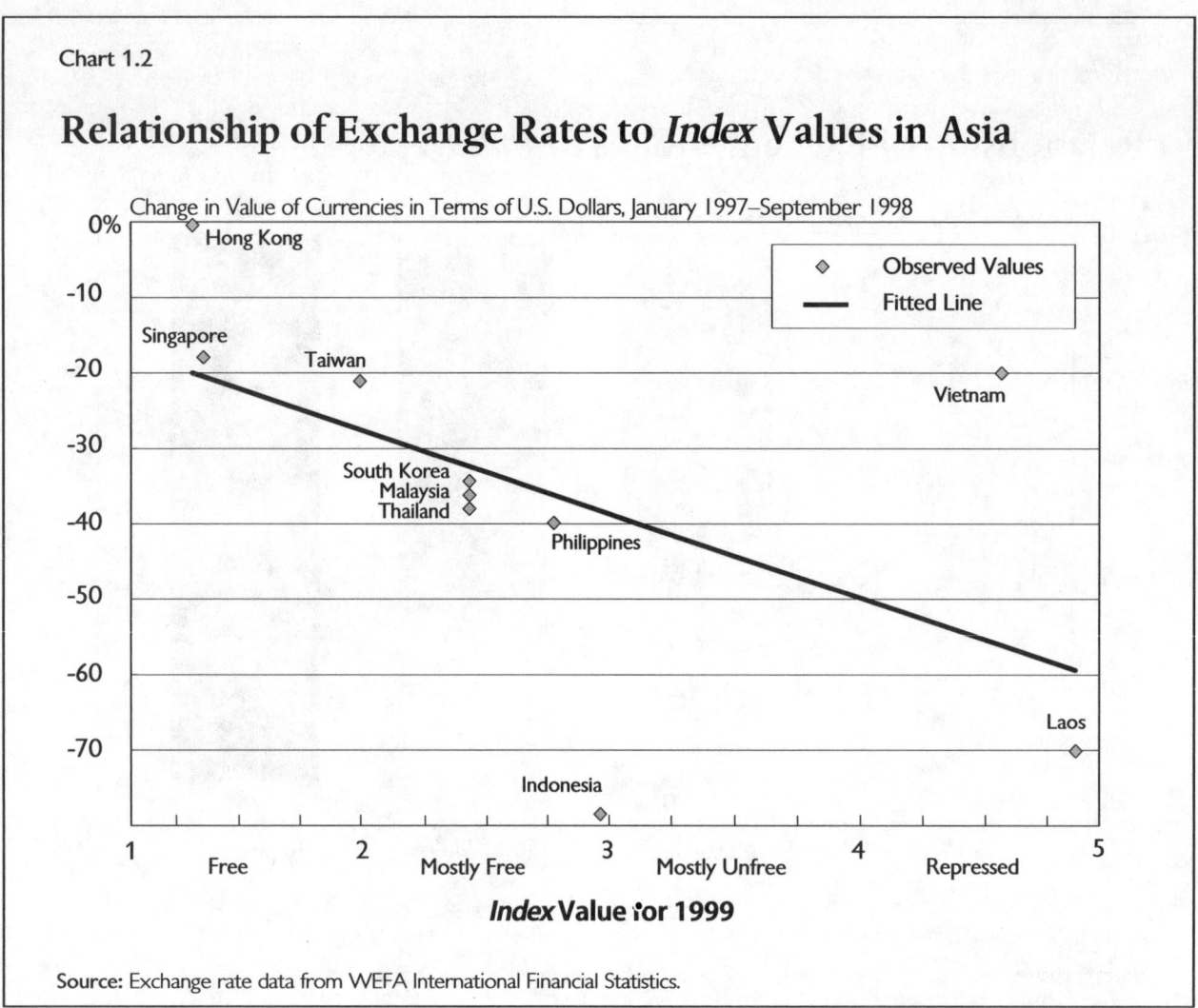

Change in Value of Currencies in Terms of U.S. Dollars, January 1997–September 1998

Source: Exchange rate data from WEFA International Financial Statistics.

dollar from January 1997 to September 1998.[9] This relationship also was found to be very robust. Evidence from the regression suggests there is less than a 2.0 percent chance that there is no positive relationship between economic freedom and the strength of a country's exchange rate during the 19 months up to September 1998.

Chart 1.1 illustrates in a dramatic manner the differences in economic performance between free and unfree economies during the previous 19 months. The dollar exchange rates of the countries ranked "free" in the 1999 *Index of Economic Freedom* (with *Index* scores between 1 and 2) fell at roughly half the rate of the currencies ranked "unfree" or "mostly unfree." The currencies of countries ranked "repressed" declined on average about three times more rapidly than the rate of decline among those rated "free." This relationship is even more impressive in the context of the fact that a disproportionately large number of

"repressed" and "mostly unfree" economies have had exchange and capital controls in place that hide the magnitude of the declines in their respective currencies since January 1997.

Critics might contend that it is the particular experiences of Northeast and Southeast Asian economies during the current economic crisis that are of most use to policymakers. This point is increasingly difficult to argue because the financial meltdown has spread to other regions of the world. Nevertheless, we applied our analysis to a smaller group of 10 countries that have been the most heavily publicized victims of recent economic turmoil.

Chart 1.2 shows the decline in exchange rate values and the 1999 *Index* scores for Hong Kong, Singapore, Taiwan, South Korea, Malaysia, Thailand, the Philippines, Indonesia, Vietnam, and Laos. As shown in Chart 1.2, currency devaluations have tended to be more drastic in countries with lower levels of economic freedom. Relative to other economies in the region, countries with higher levels of economic freedom, such as Hong Kong, have tended to have currencies that have weathered the economic typhoon of the previous 19 months better than those of countries with more restricted economies.

Extensive research already has shown a strong relationship between economic freedom, as measured by the components of the *Index of Economic Freedom,* and long-term rates of GDP growth. As the preliminary analysis above suggests, free-market policies may not work just over the long haul, but also are superior to government intervention even in the face of such economic crises as the one that currently is working its way around the globe.

Readers also should take some comfort in the great difference between today's economic crisis and the one that faced the world in 1930. Today, there is the wider understanding that long-term economic growth is much more dependent on the everyday institutional setting for economic activity than it is on the guiding hand of government. What ordinary businesspeople have understood for countless generations now is working its way back into mainstream economics and many policy circles. After a long and relatively barren period, economists and policymakers are paying full attention to the crucial role civil and political institutions play in shaping economic activity.

A remarkable feature of the current explosion of writing on the global economic crisis is the extent to which this discussion focuses on the institutional setting for economic growth—a focus that reminds historians of economic doctrine of problems that dominated the attention of the early classical economists like Adam Smith, David Ricardo, and John Stuart Mill. What set of rules and policies will best ensure a country's prosperity? What set of institutional arrangements most promotes economic growth? The modern economist's question about economic growth should be of concern to all citizens who care about their economic future: How can institutions and policies be changed so that higher levels of economic well-being and output are achieved?

Those who ask these types of questions can gain significant insight about how best to answer them by carefully studying the 1999 *Index of Economic Freedom.* Not only does the *Index* clearly identify successful countries that can serve as models for achieving higher levels of economic performance, it also identifies the institutional arrangements that appear conducive to achieving superior levels of well-being and growth. It may function in addition as an indicator of those countries that are most likely to weather today's rough economic water.

As this chapter will demonstrate, the *Index* draws on a rich body of scholarship on economic growth that encompasses insights as old as Adam Smith's and as recent as the New Growth Theory of the 1990s. In short, the *Index of Economic Freedom* is more than an interesting annual snapshot of international progress toward freer markets and freer people; it also can be a road map to help to reduce poverty and expand economic horizons around the world.

The Importance of the Institutional Context for Economic Growth

Adam Smith, the 18th century Scottish philosopher and founder of modern economics, devoted the whole of his *Inquiry into the Nature and Causes of the Wealth of Nations* to a seemingly simple question: Why do some countries prosper while others do not?[10] For Smith and his many followers, the answer is obvious: All economic growth flourishes from the single root of creatively dividing labor in the production of desirable goods, and blossoms in a political environment that protects private property, free exchange, and the justly deserved fruits of labor. Countries will experience opulence and peace, Smith argues, once they create the institutions that encourage entrepreneurship and savings (the stock of capital on which all production takes place). On the other hand, countries reap only poverty and despair when they discourage business and punish productive activities.

Subsequent generations of economists—in fact, nearly all major schools of economic thought since Smith—begin their work with the same question: What is economic growth? And all these perspectives on economic life—from Alfred Marshall and Karl Marx to John Maynard Keynes and Friedrich Hayek—emphasize the critical relationship between economic activity and its institutional setting when explaining the phenomenon of economic growth. Perhaps more important, much of the policymaking community and intellectually active public already recognizes that sustainable, long-term growth stems in some fashion from the synergy between freewheeling capitalism and the institutions that sustain civil society.

Even so, experts and laymen alike differ on what is meant by economic growth and the nature of its mediating institutions. Is economic growth merely the expansion of an economy's size, or is it the extension of improved well-being to all of a country's citizens? Do a country's imperial designs executed in the name of economic growth count at all in answering the basic question of what constitutes growth, or does growth in any meaningful sense occur only when peaceful domestic and international exchange leaves, as in David Ricardo's felicitous example, the English and the Portuguese both better off through trade in cloth and wine?[11]

Similarly, if government policy puts labor behind and capital ahead in the struggle for income shares, or strips capital owners of their property in the name of improved welfare for labor, is that really growth? Does public policy play any role at all in the long-term growth of an economy, or does economic expansion really stem only from changes in population and technology not related to public policy?

Considering these difficult questions, many of which are raised by experts on economic growth, is it any wonder that non-experts, from oil tycoons to short-order cooks, wonder what to believe? Nearly everyone lives in the massive currents of economic change, the swirl and rush of markets, the rise and tumble of great companies, and the ebb and flow of everyday working life. These are the economic rhythms that shape people's lives and punctuate their everyday work, and they leave precious little time for abstracting the big questions from the minutiae of living.

Although most people can sense that more income, more goods and services, and more economic opportunities promote economic growth, they, like many experts, puzzle over what ingredients are essential to facilitate that growth. They wonder about what public policies they should support, which politicians they should

believe, and what they can do to ensure a bigger economy for their children and grandchildren.

It is on these questions that The Heritage Foundation/Wall Street Journal *Index of Economic Freedom* sheds much-needed light. The *Index* measures a country's degree of economic freedom using a composite score consisting of 10 elements, each of which forms a major part of that country's institutional setting. These 10 elements are trade policy, taxes, government consumption of economic output, monetary policy, capital flows and foreign investment policy, banking regulation, wage and price controls, protection of property rights, business regulation, and the strength of the black market. Each element is scored separately, with the average of all elements for a country constituting a rating of that country's level of economic freedom.

What does this year's *Index of Economic Freedom* suggest about a country's prospects for superior economic growth? This chapter takes two approaches to answering this question. First, many economists of the New Growth Theory[12] school believe that the institutional setting strongly influences the rate of economic growth. A review of recent developments in this new field of research supports the position that low *Index* scores (greater economic freedom) imply superior rates of economic growth. Second, statistical work conducted independently by The Heritage Foundation also links *Index* scores to economic growth.

A Short Primer on the Economics of Growth

From the 1960s to the mid-1980s, the dominant academic theory of what causes economic growth was the Solow Growth Model, named after Nobel Laureate Robert Solow. From both a factual and a policy viewpoint, this theory performed poorly.

First, the theory offered meager advice to policymakers on how to generate economic growth. Solow argued that the only way a country could boost its level of growth was to save more and therefore accumulate physical capital. Even an increase in the rate of capital accumulation would bring about only a one-time boost in income, however, and only a short- or medium-term increase in economic growth rates. The long-run rate of economic growth (the "steady state" level) was determined by "technological innovation." This technological innovation was a mysterious force within Solow's model that could not be analyzed by economists or influenced by government policy. In the Solow model, to paraphrase the famous Cambridge economist Joan Robinson, technology (and hence growth) fell like manna from heaven.

Second, the major factual prediction of traditional growth theory (that poorer countries generally would grow faster and "converge" to the economic status of richer countries) has not been borne out in the real world.[13]

What Is the New Growth Theory?

In 1983, Professor Paul Romer, then at the University of Rochester, published a paper entitled "Increasing Returns and Long Run Growth."[14] Some 35 pages long and accessible only to those with a firm grasp of mathematics, this paper revolutionized the field of growth theory and led to the emergence of the New Growth Theory.

Romer argues that an initial increase in a society's productive capacity can feed on itself (because of what are known technically as *increasing returns*) to produce permanently higher rates of growth. This feedback effect stands in sharp contrast to the *decreasing returns* contained in the old theory, under which the growth effects of an increase in a society's productive capacity are only temporary. In other words, under the old theory of decreasing returns, policy changes can produce only a one-time boost to economic activity, after which the economy returns to its long-term growth rate. Under the new theory of increasing returns, however, it is possible to affect the long-term growth rate itself.

The old growth theory predicted that establishing sound policies would lead only to a one-time boost in income (and therefore only a transitory increase in economic growth rates). The theory of increasing returns, however, implies that instituting sensible policies can result in a GDP growth rate that is permanently higher. This means that the benefits of instituting wise economic policies (and the costs of pursuing misguided policies) are much greater than was thought to be the case under the old theories that assumed decreasing

returns. In this model, introducing a "good" policy can create a virtuous circle of economic expansion that will feed on itself to bring about a permanent acceleration in the growth of prosperity. Likewise, "bad" policies can mean permanently lower rates of growth and cost society more than earlier economists had thought possible.

Importance of Technology, Institutions, and Human Capital to Economic Growth. The New Growth Theory sometimes is referred to as *Endogenous Growth Theory* because key factors in economic growth (human capital, technology, innovation, and institutions) now are examined within and form an integral part of (that is, are "endogenous" to) this view of the world. No longer seen as mysterious and unfathomable, the New Growth Economics treats these factors as concrete entities over which policymakers can exercise some influence, whether for good or for ill. The focus of Romer's original paper is technology. Other theorists, such as 1995 Nobel Laureate Robert Lucas, examine the growth implications of human capital, institutions, and other factors. In the old growth theory, the only things for which its advocates could account were the accumulation of physical capital and population growth. Public policies could explain, predict, or influence none of the other factors that cause economic growth.

The Emphasis on Investigating the Causes of Economic Growth Using Statistical Tests. New Growth Economics extends beyond mere theory. These new theories have inspired economists to use statistical models. In the past eight years, a massive volume of econometric research has been carried out on explanations for the differences in growth rates across countries. This has been made possible by the recent emergence of internationally compatible and reliable long-run economic data for developing and developed countries. Even though this work is ongoing and in a state of relative infancy, several generalized findings have begun to emerge.

There is a striking correspondence between the elements of the *Index of Economic Freedom* and the key statistical findings of the New Growth Theory. New Growth economists show that high levels of growth are positively associated with (1) the level of private investment (especially in machinery); (2) "openness" to international trade and finance; (3) the educational attainment level of the

Sidebar:
Lessons from the New Growth Theory

- **Accumulate capital.** Increasing the stock of physical capital available for each worker in the economy is one of the best ways to increase per capita income.

- **Keep government small.** Government spending consumes scarce resources that could be used for productive investment and distorts the incentives faced by individuals and firms. State ownership of capital stock means that the output from those productive assets will be lower than if they were in private hands.

- **Open the economy to foreign trade and investment.** New Growth Theory has uncovered many previously unknown gains from foreign trade and investment, including the faster and deeper diffusion of technology from abroad, an increase in competition that improves efficiency, and more rapid capital accumulation.

- **Respect property rights and the rule of law.** Without adequate protection for property rights and a secure political environment, individuals and firms will face severe disincentives to invest and engage in productive activities.

- **Do not burden the productive sector with government regulations and controls.** Regulations, mandates, and wage and price controls are a drag on economic growth. They raise the cost of producing goods and services and make innovation and invention more expensive. Government controls also increase the opportunities for gains from corruption and thus divert entrepreneurship from productive activities to nonproductive "rent-seeking" activities.

- **Invest in "human capital."** Education, which increases worker productivity, is very important to growth, according to many leading New Growth economists. In this context, it is important that education systems operate primarily to educate students rather than to serve the ends of "social justice" or of powerful political groups.

population; and (4) the rule of law, political stability, and the protection of property rights. Economists in this field also associate slow or negative economic growth with hyperinflation, high levels of government consumption and taxation, and excessive regulation. The *Index* considers nearly all these factors to be crucial in evaluating economic freedom across countries.

Above all, the New Growth Theory strongly suggests that public policies *do* matter. In an essay on the reasons that some countries enjoy better economic performance than others, the late Mancur Olson, one of the world's leading economic theorists, observes that "Those countries with the best policies and institutions achieve most of their potential, while other countries achieve only a tiny faction of their potential income."[15] Olson further notes that

the large differences in per capita income across countries cannot be explained by differences in access to the world's stock of productive knowledge or to its capital markets, by differences in the ratio of population to land or natural resources, or by differences in the quality of marketable human capital or personal culture.... The only remaining plausible explanation is that the great differences in the wealth of nations are mainly due to differences in the quality of their institutions and economic policies.[16]

Chart 1.3

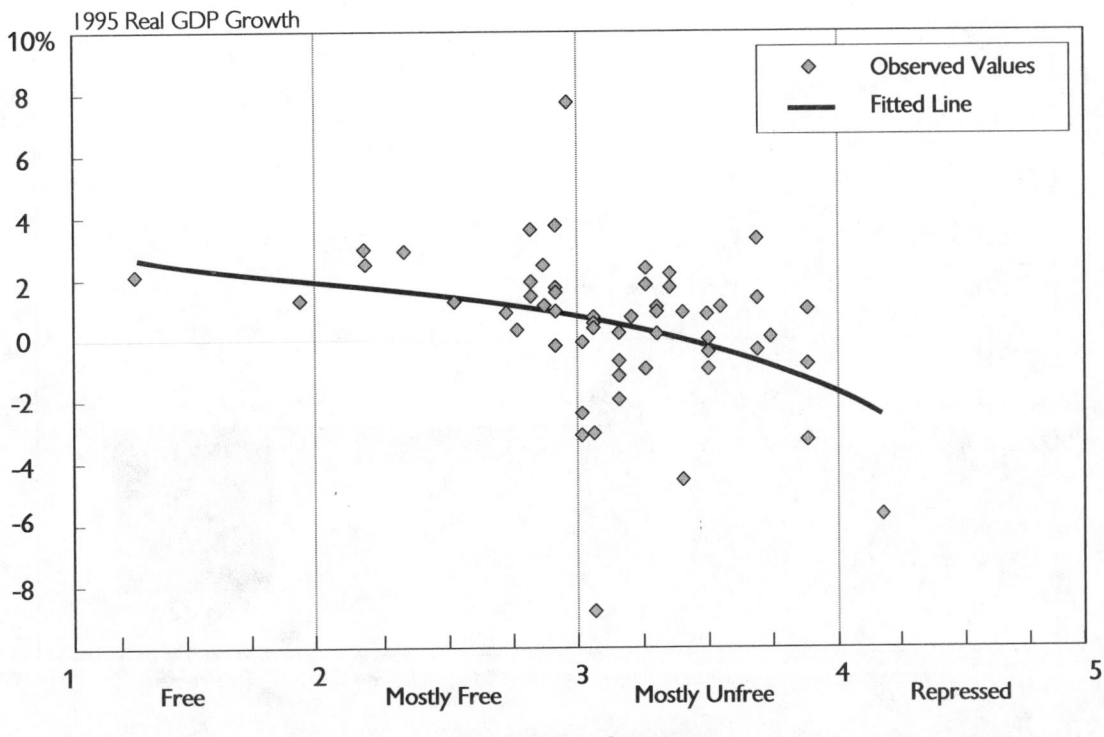

Relationship of Economic Growth to *Index* Values

1995 Real GDP Growth

Observed Values

Fitted Line

Index Value for 1995

Free · Mostly Free · Mostly Unfree · Repressed

Source: Michael Bruno, and William Easterly, "Inflation Crises and Long-Run Growth," *Journal of Monetary Economics*, 1997. These data are made available through the World Bank's Growth Project on the Internet at *http://www.worldbank.org/html/prdmg/grthweb/growth_t.htm.*

Statistical Relationship of the *Index* to Economic Growth

In addition to the strong support this scholarship affords the *Index* as an indicator of future economic performance, statistical tests performed by The Heritage Foundation further underscore the applicability of the *Index* to discussions of economic growth. Using one of the largest datasets designed for comparisons of inter-country growth,[17] Heritage analysts found statistically significant relationships both between the *Index* and country-by-country levels of economic development, and between the *Index* and economic growth rates.

Chart 1.3 shows the type of relationship observed between economic growth and *Index* values. In Chart 1.3, the vertical axis contains the percentage change in real GDP per capita for 1995.

The horizontal axis shows the *Index* values for 1995 based on data from the preceding year. This chart clearly shows a distinct association between lower *Index* numbers (freer economies) and higher levels of economic growth. In other words, this analysis strongly suggests that countries with free-market public policies grow faster than countries with repressed economies.[18]

Chart 1.4 demonstrates this correlation between economic freedom and economic growth as well by describing the average annual real per capita growth rate of countries in each *Index* category. Countries with repressed economies or mostly unfree economies in 1996 experienced negative per capita income growth on average over the period from 1980 to 1993. Free economies, and to a lesser extent mostly free economies, on average experienced positive real income growth.

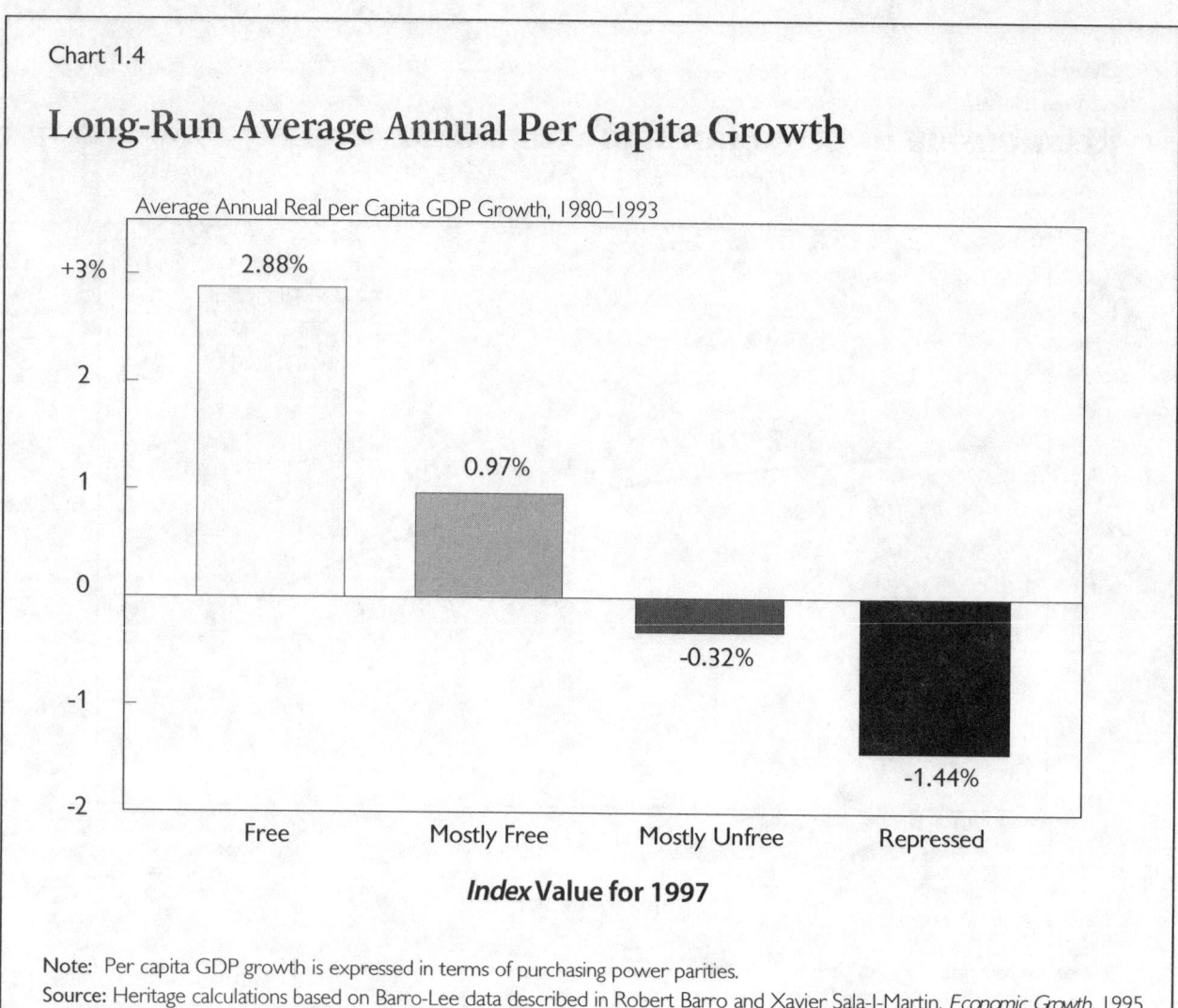

Chart 1.4

Long-Run Average Annual Per Capita Growth

Average Annual Real per Capita GDP Growth, 1980–1993

- Free: 2.88%
- Mostly Free: 0.97%
- Mostly Unfree: -0.32%
- Repressed: -1.44%

***Index* Value for 1997**

Note: Per capita GDP growth is expressed in terms of purchasing power parities.
Source: Heritage calculations based on Barro-Lee data described in Robert Barro and Xavier Sala-I-Martin, *Economic Growth,* 1995.

Despite the limitations of these and other data used to explore the implications of policy changes on cross-country growth rates, numerous other eminent scholars find similar and significant relationships between economic growth and government policies. For example, Robert Barro, a Harvard University professor and contributing editor of *The Wall Street Journal,* sees a strong positive relationship between growth rates and data that measure the degree to which a country rules itself by law as opposed to the whims and edicts of political strongmen. He also finds that growth rates are better in those countries in which government consumes a lower share of GDP than they are in those countries in which government consumes higher percentages of GDP. Barro determines that other policy and institutional or non-economic variables significantly related to growth include the rate of inflation, political

rights, the fertility rate, years of secondary and higher education, and the initial level of GDP.[19]

Responding to the Critics

As the *Index of Economic Freedom* gains stature as a measure of relative economic freedom, it naturally has attracted the attention of critics as well as the commendations of many readers worldwide. The authors, economists, and editors of the *Index* are delighted, of course, by the increasing scrutiny their work has received, and a number of criticisms made over the past year have resulted in additional explanation in this year's *Index.* The authors always review constructive criticisms seriously and use them, wherever possible, as the basis for improving future editions of the *Index.*

A recent review, however, merits special commentary. Bruce Scott of the Harvard Business

School raises questions about last year's *Index of Economic Freedom* that reveal misunderstandings about our work, and a few words here may clarify our objectives for readers of this year's edition.[20]

The world of growing economies is a complicated place, as Professor Scott reminds us, and he chides the authors of the *Index* for confusing cause and effect. If we understand him correctly, Professor Scott argues that economically emerging countries can afford to embrace economic freedoms only after building per capita income through public policies like "forced savings" and stiff tariffs. Professor Scott finds support for his view in recent economic data from China and, amazingly, in the economic history of the United States, Great Britain, the Netherlands, and postwar Germany.

Does Professor Scott seriously contend that China's recent explosion of economic prosperity is utterly unrelated to its rejection of Maoist socialism and the economic and social devastation of the Cultural Revolution? Could he possibly be ignorant of Deng Xiaoping's partial restoration of laws protecting private property and business contracts, as well as a judicial apparatus that advanced the rule of law rather than the edicts of the state? In identifying China's central government as the driving force behind that country's economic revival, Professor Scott, perhaps inadvertently, diminishes the deep and ancient cultural traditions of hard work, personal saving, and entrepreneurship that always resurface in China the moment the state relaxes its iron grip on the Chinese people. We suggest that China is a much more complicated economy and society than Professor Scott's theory would have it, and that the economic leadership of the special economic zones on the country's coastline explains in part the reason that "China had 30 individual provinces that would rank among the fastest growing major economies in the world."[21]

Professor Scott's spin on early American economic policy is interesting, if peculiar and at odds with conventional wisdom. As J. Willard Hurst and a host of more recent legal and economic historians argue, the principles of the American Revolution—individual liberty, private property, rule of law, limited government, low taxation, and free (internal) trade—explain this country's rapid economic growth better than Alexander Hamilton's flawed tariff policies. If Professor Scott would read closely Hamilton's *Report on Manufactures,* he would discern even there a vigorous exposition of the institutional setting for economic growth, made all the more interesting by Hamilton's tortuous effort to interpret Smithian economics in a fashion that justified the secretary of the Treasury's protectionist proposals. We happily admit that one major factor in the rapid economic growth of the United States after 1791 was the massive immigration from the Old World to America. We also invite Professor Scott to recognize that this migration of people and talents would have been much smaller without the guarantees of economic freedoms offered by the early Republic, and that the stock of talents and capital that these immigrants brought with them nullified the otherwise deleterious enterprise of protecting American manufacturers of nails and hooped barrels from foreign competition.

Professor Scott persists in misrepresenting our approach. We do not assert a "powerful causal linkage between economic growth and freedom." There is little doubt that governments can impose economic policies that cause their countries to lurch forward and perhaps even to catch up with developed countries. But growth in output and individual well-being seldom are achieved successfully and simultaneously and, as yet, never are sustained through those policies—as illustrated by the corpses of centrally managed economies that litter the historical landscape of the 20th century. Outside the show villages of the Soviet Union, life became increasingly grim during the 1960s and 1970s as the catch-up policies first introduced by Josef Stalin slowly undermined and ultimately destroyed much of that country's moral and economic capital. And today, in Asia, countries that tied their fortunes to industrial policies managed by central bureaucracies are collapsing rapidly while others more open to economic freedoms are weathering the financial storm.

The *Index of Economic Freedom* argues forcefully that the presence of economic freedoms is positively related to economic prosperity and economic growth. In fact, we go so far as to suggest that countries having more economic freedom enjoy higher levels of individual well-being and stronger, long-term economic growth than do countries having less economic freedom. Unfortunately, Professor Scott seems to have trouble grasping this straightforward message.

Does Government Intervention Enhance Economic Equality?

Even while acknowledging the beneficial effects of economic freedom in increasing GDP growth, opponents of economic liberalization often suggest that reducing government intervention leads to harmful "social" consequences. This has been especially the case in recent years, despite a growing body of professional literature that has shown a strong statistical link between economic liberty and long-term economic growth.[22] Critics of the market have responded by arguing that, even though the market may enhance efficiency, the state has a role in ensuring equity. An unfettered free market is held to undermine the "social protections" provided by the government, leading to growth in the gap between rich and poor. There are, however, severe problems both in principle and in practice with this view.

A strong case can be made that the equalization of income is not a proper policy goal for government. Differences in income often reflect differences in the choices made by individuals. For example, should the income of a person who chooses to work only 20 hours a week be made equal to that of a person who decides to work 40 hours? Pursuit of policies designed solely to reduce the difference between high- and low-income persons also can have effects that most people find objectionable. Taken to its logical conclusion, a policy of income-equalization would demand that a government not implement a growth-enhancing policy that would make everyone better off if the generated benefit were greater for the rich than for the poor.

There also are practical objections to the use of government intervention for the purposes of reducing inequalities of income. Many commentators—especially those on the Left—usually assume that governments are the modern equivalent of Plato's philosopher kings. Policy recommendations often are made on the basis that the state is a benign entity whose role is to implement such often abstract philosophical objectives as reducing inequality or pursuing some other definition of the public good. A large body of work by economists and political scientists, as well as the everyday common sense of ordinary people, however, now suggests that this generally is not the case.

Modern economics looks at the role of government in a much more realistic light. Research by such economists as Nobel Prize winner James Buchanan, Gordon Tullock, Mancur Olson, and Anne O. Krueger suggests that it is more valid to look at politicians as self-interested individuals who are more concerned with such objectives as maximizing their personal power, enhancing the security of their tenure, and increasing their personal wealth.[23]

In this context, the political process can be viewed as a forum for conflict over the allocation of resources. An expansion in the role of the government is most likely to benefit those who are politically powerful. In most societies and especially in lesser-developed countries, political power tends to be highly concentrated. In effect, an expansion in the role of the government is generally associated with policies that enrich powerful "insider" groups that are linked closely with the country's government elite.

For example, most agricultural policies pursued by third world governments have involved artificially driving down the prices received by producers of food. This benefits relatively affluent urban dwellers at the expense of farmers.[24] Tariffs and other trade restrictions often are introduced ostensibly for the purposes of "protecting" the jobs of ordinary workers. In practice, however, such policies usually are introduced at the behest of influential business owners whose firms, now freed from foreign competition, get to exercise monopoly control over a market.[25] The losers are ordinary consumers who now must pay higher prices for their goods.

To examine the question of whether government restrictions on economic liberty make the distribution of income more equal, we conducted a statistical examination of the relationship between economic freedom (as measured by the *Index of Economic Freedom*) and income inequality. The results, although by no means definitive, suggest that income inequality tends to be greater in countries with higher levels of government intervention. In fact, there is some evidence that countries with higher levels of economic freedom

Chart 1.5

Freer Economies Tend to Have
More Equal Distributions of Income

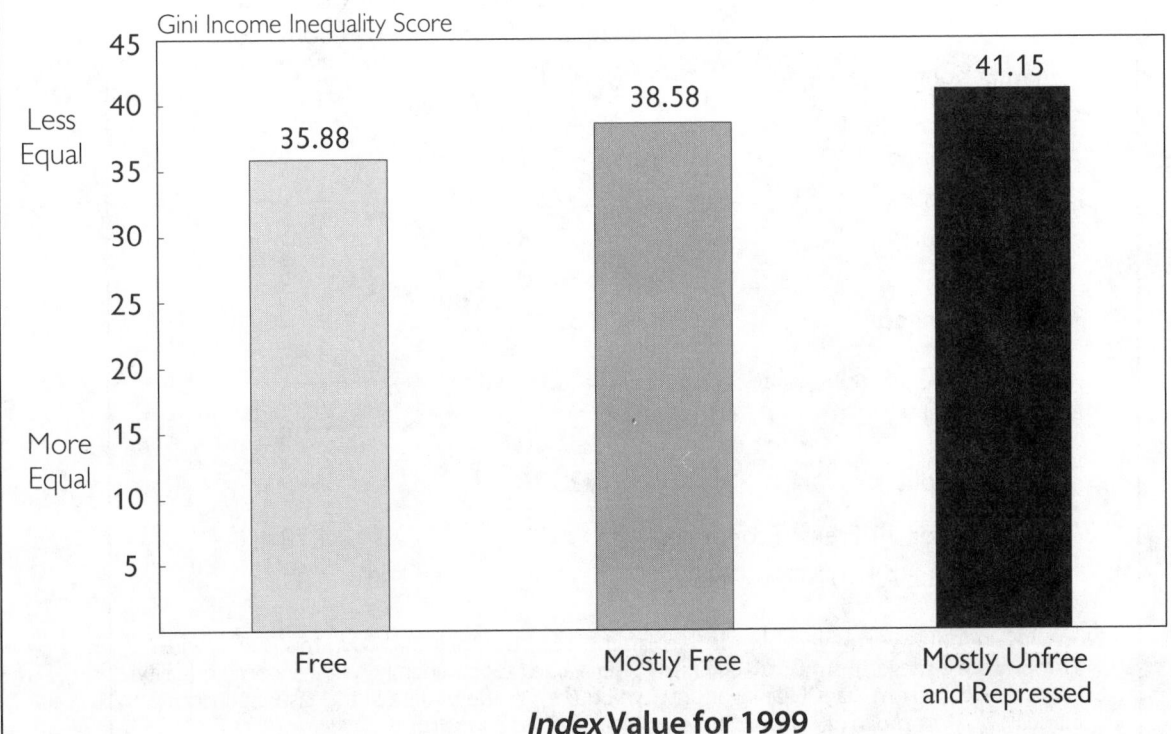

Gini Income Inequality Score

Less Equal

More Equal

35.88 — Free
38.58 — Mostly Free
41.15 — Mostly Unfree and Repressed

Index Value for 1999

Note: * Gini data were available for 102 of the 161 countries studied in this year's *Index.* The Gini scale ranges from 0 to 100, with lower values representing greater income equality.
Source: Gini data from Klaus Deininger and Lyn Squire, "A New Data Set Measuring Income Inequality," *World Bank Economic Review,* Vol. 10, No. 3 (1996).

tend to have more equal distributions of income.

A full description of the data and methods used to analyze the relationship between economic liberty and income equality is available in Appendix II to this chapter. The analysis in this section is based on scores from the 1999 *Index of Economic Freedom* and on inequality data for 102 countries that have been compiled by World Bank economists Klaus Deininger and Lyn Squire. Income inequality is measured by the Gini Inequality Score, with a higher Gini Inequality Score meaning that a society's level of inequality is greater. We examine the relationship between *Index of Economic Freedom* scores and income inequality using a Spearman rank-order correlation that compares a country's economic freedom ranking with its inequality ranking. We use an Ordinary Least Squares linear regression to examine the

magnitude of the link between economic freedom and income inequality.

From even a preliminary analysis of the data, it is obvious that there is little evidence that free-market policies are associated with increased levels of income inequality. Indeed, the data suggest the opposite: Those countries having high levels of economic freedom have a tendency toward more equal distributions of income. The Spearman rank correlation suggests there is a 76 percent probability that a better economic freedom ranking is related to a more equal distribution of income. The Ordinary Least Squares regression estimates that a 1 point increase in a country's *Index* score is associated with a 1.6 point increase in a country's inequality score. Therefore, if a country's *Index* score moves from 1 to 5, we can expect to see an increase in its Gini score of 6.4 points.

Table 1.1

Income Inequality in the 11 Economies with the Best *Index of Economic Freedom* Scores

	Gini Income Inequality Score	*Index of Economic Freedom* Score
Hong Kong	45.00	1.25
Singapore	39.00	1.30
New Zealand	40.21	1.75
United States	37.94	1.90
Luxembourg	27.13	1.95
Ireland	34.60	1.95
United Kingdom	32.40	1.95
Taiwan	30.78	1.95
Bahamas	45.29	2.00
Japan	35.00	2.05
Czech Republic	28.26	2.05
Average for 11 Freest Economies	35.96	1.78
Average for All 102 Economies*	39.58	2.92

Note: * Gini data were available for 102 of the 161 countries studied in this year's *Index*. The Gini scale ranges from 0 to 100, with lower values representing greater income equality.
Source: Gini data from Klaus Deininger and Lyn Squire, "A New Data Set Measuring Income Inequality," *World Bank Economic Review*, Vol. 10, No. 3 (1996).

This tendency also is apparent when we look at the individual countries themselves. We allocated the 102 countries into three groups, ranging from "free" countries (with *Index* scores less than 2) to countries that are classed as "mostly unfree" and "repressed" (with *Index* scores of 3 or greater). As the reader can see on Chart 1.5, the average level of inequality actually is lowest among those countries the *Index of Economic Freedom* rates "free."

Table 1.1 shows the freedom and inequality scores for the 11 countries having the highest economic freedom scores for which inequality data were available. These countries have an average level of income inequality (35.96) that falls well below the global average of 39.58. Indeed, only 3 of these 11 countries have levels of income inequality that lie below this global average; and, perhaps more striking, not a single country among these 11 ranks among the 25 percent most unequal countries.

This finding also holds when we examine the countries having the most unequal and the most equal income distributions.[26] The results are shown in Table 1.2. Among the 102 countries we analyze, those societies having the most uneven distributions of income tend to have below-average levels of economic liberty. Similarly, in countries having egalitarian distributions of income, the level of government intervention in the economy tends to be lower.

In addition to these analyses, professional studies also uncover a positive relationship between economic liberty and income inequality. In an extensive econometric study of 102 countries for the period 1975–1985, Swedish economist Nicholas Berggren discovers that increases in economic freedom lead to reductions in income inequality.[27] This relationship is especially strong over the long term and among the world's poorest countries. Berggren finds financial deregulation and trade liberalization to be particularly influential in reducing inequality.

In the face of a growing professional consensus that shows a strong relationship between long-term economic growth and the individual components used by the *Index of Economic Freedom* to measure economic freedom, advocates of intervention insist that the introduction of market-orientated policies will increase the gap between the haves and the have-nots. The argument that economic freedom sometimes must be restricted in order to ensure a more equal sharing of an economy's fruits cannot be supported from the evidence. Indeed, there is some evidence that a market economy tends to produce a more equal distribution of income than an economy featuring a high level of government intervention. In short, the alleged tradeoff between economic freedom and income inequality almost certainly is a false one.

There also is strong evidence that increased GDP causes improvements in "non-economic" indicators of welfare. One recent study by Harvard economist and Deputy Secretary of the U.S. Treasury Lawrence Summers and World Bank economist Lunt Pritchett uses advanced statistical analysis to demonstrate that higher economic growth causes decreases in infant mortality and increases in life expectancy.[28] One finding of this study is that reductions in economic growth during the 1980s alone (due in many cases to flawed economic policies) led to the deaths of 500,000 children worldwide during the 1990s. In the context of the evidence presented in this section, it is apparent that removing restrictions on private enterprise is very likely to represent more than just good economic policy; it may be good social policy, too.

Table 1.2

Index of Economic Freedom Scores by Level of Income Inequality

	Average *Index* Score
Ten Most Unequal Economies	3.15
Ten Most Equal Economies	2.53
All 102 Countries	2.92

Note: Inequality data were available for 102 of the 161 countries studied in this year's *Index*.
Source: Inequality data from Klaus Deininger and Lyn Squire, "A New Data Set Measuring Income Inequality," *World Bank Economic Review*, Vol. 10, No. 3 (1996).

Conclusion

Any country willing to embrace the policies of economic freedom could produce the powerful effects of pro-growth economic policies. Although cultural and political factors (including the frequency of wars) will make each country's response somewhat different, it appears to be a universal truth that free trade, free markets, and free men and women create stronger economies and better lives than is possible with any other "mix" of public policies.

The *Index of Economic Freedom* points clearly to those policies that reduce want and increase life spans. This makes the *Index* more than an intellectual exercise. This chapter begins with a discussion of the Asian economic crisis, ranges across discussions of 18th century social thought and long-term economic growth, and ends with a discussion of income inequality. This progression might strike some as odd, but Adam Smith—whose economics live squarely in the real world—certainly would understand.

Appendix I:
Evidence from New Growth Economics on Components of the *Index of Economic Freedom*

Evidence from New Growth literature, combined with the work of earlier economists, supports the argument that the concepts measured by the *Index of Economic Freedom* are related to economic growth. That is, conclusions from New Growth Economics link differences in the rate of economic growth across countries to a number of policy variables, many of which the *Index* attempts to measure.

Econometric studies by economists at Harvard, the World Bank, and the Federal Reserve Bank find that long-term growth rates rise as restraints on foreign trade and investment go down.[29] Calculations by Columbia University economist Richard Baldwin demonstrate that old models of growth tend to underestimate drastically the magnitude of gains from free trade.[30] A March 1996 cross-section/time series econometric analysis of over 120 countries by Columbia University economist Ann Harrison reveals a robust relationship between economic growth in developing countries and numerous measurements of the degree of openness to international trade and investment.[31] These results, which show a strong statistical link between free-trade policies and economic success, replicate the findings of a 1991 World Bank study of 95 developing countries over the period 1976–1986.[32]

The latest professional evidence also overwhelmingly supports the case that openness to international trade and foreign investment—not the reverse—causes economic growth. A recent National Bureau of Economic Research study by University of California at Berkeley economists Jeffrey Frankel, David Romer, and Teresa Cyrus clearly shows that, in a host of high-growth countries in East Asia, the direction of causation has been from free trade and open investment policies to economic growth.[33]

Likewise, numerous cross-country studies establish that high levels of government spending will slow the long-term rate of economic growth.[34] An econometric model calibrated by Professors Robert King and Sergio Rebelo of the University of Rochester finds that traditional growth models underestimate the negative growth effect of taxes by a magnitude of 40.[35]

Studies also have found links between inflation (particularly hyperinflation) and lower long-term GDP growth rates.[36] Recent statistical evidence also indicates the special importance of a strong, sophisticated, and unencumbered banking and financial system as a conduit for economic growth.[37]

Robert Barro of Harvard University and Xavier Sala-I-Martin of Yale University find a correlation between lower rates of growth and measures of the distortions caused by wage, price, and exchange controls and other forms of government regulation.[38] Economists also have succeeded recently in uncovering a robust empirical link between cross-country, long-term economic growth and the degree to which governments abide by the rule of law and respect and enforce property rights and contracts.[39]

After a decade of New Growth Economics, the scientific evidence is more persuasive than ever that the concepts measured in the *Index of Economic Freedom* indicate clearly the degree to which a country's current economic policies and institutions are friendly or unfriendly to economic growth.[40]

16

Appendix II:
Examining Economic Freedom
and Income Inequality

To examine the relationship between freedom and income inequality, we compare a country's score in the 1999 *Index of Economic Freedom* with its Gini Coefficient. (The Gini Coefficient is a statistic widely used by social scientists to measure the degree of inequality within an economy and is calculated on the basis of the shares of income accruing to various percentiles of a country's population.[41]) A Gini score of 100 would be the equivalent of complete inequality of income, with all of a country's income accruing to a single person. A Gini score of 0 means that a country has complete equality of income, with all residents receiving exactly the same income.

For many countries, especially those in the developing world, data on income inequality are available only on an irregular basis. The inequality data in this study come from hundreds of sources by World Bank economists Klaus Deininger and Lyn Squire.[42] In this study, only inequality data from the years between 1985 and 1996 are used. In every case, we use the most recent valid data available for a country to measure the level of inequality. Under these criteria, Gini Coefficients and *Index of Economic Freedom* scores are available for 102 countries.

It is easy to question the use of *Index of Economic Freedom* scores based on data from the last half of 1997 and the first half of 1998 alongside inequality statistics that date from between 1986 and 1996; however, we can make a number of points in defense of this technique. First, the great majority (84 observations) of the inequality data we use in this study date from the period after 1990. To test the time sensitivity of the results in this section, we complete two analyses. One uses only data from the period subsequent to 1990; the other relies only on data from the period subsequent to 1993. The major findings of these analyses do not differ in any material way from the main findings that we make using data from the 1986–1996 time period and report here. Second, although exceptions do exist, large variations in the level of economic freedom and in income inequality generally do not occur on a year-to-year basis.[43] It is likely that the relationships posited in this chapter have remained stable on a year-to-year basis, and we are confident that should more complete data become available in the future, the relationships that we uncover will be strengthened.

Notes

1. International Monetary Fund, *World Economic Outlook* (Washington, D.C.: International Monetary Fund, 1998).

2. Reuters News Service, August 18, 1998.

3. Kevin Sullivan and Mary Jordan, "Obuchi Defends Economic Policies: Japanese Leader Rules Out Boost in Defense Spending," *The Washington Post*, September 20, 1998, p. A1.

4. See Jeffrey Sachs, "Global Capitalism: Making It Work," *The Economist*, September 12, 1998, pp.23–25, for a critical review of efforts by Asian countries and the International Monetary Fund to stabilize declining economies.

5. Sullivan and Jordan, "Obuchi Defends Economic Policies," pp. A1, A29.

6. Paul Krugman is Ford International Professor of Economics at MIT. Among his writings are several well-known essays on economics and public policy: *Accidental Theorist & Other Dispatches from the Dismal Science* (1998); *The Age of Diminished Expectations* (Third Edition, 1997); *Development, Geography, and Economic Theory* (1997); and *Currencies and Crises* (1995).

7. Paul Krugman, "Saving Asia: It's Time to Get Radical," *Fortune*, September 7, 1998, p. 80.

8. The WEFA Group is a widely respected economic forecasting and data analysis firm founded by University of Pennsylvania professor and Nobel Laureate Lawrence Klein. WEFA clients include a number of U.S. federal government agencies and *Fortune* 500 corporations.

9. The regression was produced using the Ordinary Least Squares method and generated an F-value of 5.732. The coefficient value produced for the independent variable was negative with a t-value of 2.394. The authors use data from 137 countries in the regression.

10. Adam Smith, *An Inquiry into the Nature and Causes of the Wealth of Nations*, Glasgow Edition, R. H. Campbell and A. S. Skinner, eds. (Oxford, U.K.: Oxford University Press, 1976); published originally in 1776.

11. David Ricardo, *On the Principles of Political Economy and Taxation*, Third Edition, Piero Sraffa, ed. (Cambridge, U.K.: Cambridge University Press, 1951); published originally in 1821. See especially Chapter 7, "On Foreign Trade," for Ricardo's discussion on how two economies can grow by trading commodities in which each has a comparative advantage.

12. For a brief review of the New Growth literature, see Appendix I to this chapter.

13. Some economists have found evidence of convergence when they control for countries' differing savings rates, but this convergence has been very weak. In any case, the traditional model of growth has no explanation for what causes these international differences in savings rates and therefore no policy prescriptions in this regard.

14. Published in *Journal of Political Economy*, Vol. 94 (1986), pp. 1002–1037.

15. Mancur Olson, Jr., "Big Bills Left on the Sidewalk: Why Some Nations Are Rich, and Others Are Poor," *Journal of Economic Perspectives*, Vol. 10 (Spring 1996), p. 6.

16. *Ibid.*, p. 19.

17. Michael Bruno and William Easterly, "Inflation Crises and Long-Run Growth," *Journal of Monetary Economics*, 1997. These data are made available through the World Bank's Growth Project, available on the World Wide Web at *http://www.worldbank.org/html/prdmg/grthweb/datasets.htm*.

18. A number of qualifications must be made about the association contained in Chart 1.3. First, many factors outside the sphere of economic policy affect a country's growth rate: natural disasters, mineral discoveries, commodity price shifts, war, pestilence, the policies of other countries, to name just a few. A prudent use of the relationship illustrated above is valid, however; at the very least, it emphasizes a connection between economic performance and public policies. Second, only 56 countries out of 156 in the 1995 *Index* are present in this analysis. Even so, the array of countries contained in Chart 1.3 is

representative of the full set of countries scored in the 1995 *Index*.

19 Robert J. Barro, presentation to The Heritage Foundation Roundtable on Economic Growth, June 26, 1996; copies are available on request from The Heritage Foundation. See also Robert J. Barro, "Economic Growth in a Cross-Section of Countries," *Quarterly Journal of Economics*, Vol. 106 (1991), pp. 407–443.

20 Bruce R. Scott, Letter to the Editor, *Chief Executive Magazine*, April 1998.

21 *Ibid*.

22 See Appendix I on "Evidence from New Growth Economics on Components of the *Index of Economic Freedom*" at the end of this chapter for a review of the evidence on the link between economic freedom and long-term growth.

23 See James Buchanan and Gordon Tullock, *The Calculus of Consent* (Ann Arbor, Mich.: University of Michigan Press, 1965); Mancur Olson, *Logic of Collective Action* (Cambridge, Mass; Harvard University Press, 1971); and Anne O. Krueger, "The Political Economy of the Rent Seeking Society," *American Economic Review*, Vol. 64, No. 3 (June 1974), pp. 291–303.

24 P. T. Bauer, *Equality, the Third World and Economic Delusion* (Cambridge, Mass; Harvard University Press, 1981).

25 Krueger, "The Political Economy of the Rent Seeking Society."

26 The 10 countries having the most equal income distribution are, in order, Finland, Ukraine, Spain, Germany, Belgium, Latvia, Luxembourg, Canada, Hungary, and Slovenia. The 10 countries having the most unequal income distributions are, in order, South Africa, Malawi, Brazil, Guatemala, Zimbabwe, Chile, Panama, Guinea-Bissau, Lesotho, Kenya, and Botswana.

27 Nicholas Berggren, "Economic Freedom and Inequality: Friends or Foes," *Public Choice*, forthcoming.

28 Lunt Pritchett and Lawrence Summers, "Wealthier Is Healthier," *Journal of Human Resources*, Vol. 31 No. 4 (Fall 1996), pp. 841–868. Summers and Pritchett use advanced econometric methods to show that it is increased GDP that causes improvements in health, rather than improvements in health that cause increases in GDP.

29 Ross Levine and David Renelt, "A Sensitivity Analysis of Cross-Country Growth Regressions," *American Economic Review*, Vol. 82 (1990), pp. 943–963; David Gould and Roy Ruffin, "What Determines Economic Growth?" *Economic Review*, Federal Reserve Bank of Dallas, 1993, pp. 25–40.

30 Richard Baldwin, "The Growth Effects of 1992," *Economic Policy*, November 1989, pp. 248–283.

31 Ann Harrison, "Openness and Growth: A Time-Series, Cross-Country Analysis for Developing Countries," *Journal of Development Economics*, Vol. 48, No. 2 (March 1996), pp. 419–447.

32 D. Dollar, "Outward Oriented Developing Economies Really Do Grow More Rapidly: Evidence from 95 LDCs, 1976–85," *Economic Development and Cultural Change*, Vol. 40, No. 3 (1991), pp. 523–544.

33 Jeffrey Frankel, David Romer, and Teresa Cyrus, "Trade and Growth in East Asian Countries: Cause and Effect," National Bureau of Economic Research *Working Paper* No. 5732, August 1, 1996.

34 Barro, "Economic Growth in a Cross-Section of Countries"; Barro and Xavier Sala-I-Martin, *Economic Growth* (New York, N.Y.: McGraw-Hill, 1995), p. 434; Daniel Landau, "Government and Economic Growth in the Lesser Developed Countries: An Empirical Study for 1960–80," *Economic Development and Cultural Change*, Vol. 35 (October 1986), p. 68; Michael Marlow, "Links Between Taxes and Economic Growth: Some Empirical Evidence," *Journal of Economic Growth*, Vol. 1, No. 4 (1986); Eric Engen and Jonathan Skinner, "Fiscal Policy and Economic Growth," National Bureau of Economic Research *Working Paper* No. 4223, 1992; and Kevin Grier and Gordon Tullock, "An Empirical Analysis of Cross-National Economic Growth, 1951–80," *Journal of Monetary Economics*, Vol. 24 (1989), pp. 259–276.

[35] Robert King and Sergio Rebelo, "Public Policy and Economic Growth: Developing Neoclassical Implications," *Journal of Political Economy,* Vol. 98 (1990).

[36] For a full discussion of the evidence, see Kevin Dowd, "The Costs of Inflation and Disinflation," *Cato Journal,* Fall 1994. A 1993 panel and cross-sectional study by top Massachusetts Institute of Technology economist Stanley Fischer concludes that "high growth is not sustainable in the presence of high inflation." See Stanley Fischer, "The Role of Macroeconomic Factors in Growth," *Journal of Monetary Economics,* Vol. 32, No. 3 (1993), pp. 485–512.

[37] Robert King and Ross Levine, "Finance, Entrepreneurship and Growth: Theory and Evidence," *Journal of Monetary Economics,* Vol. 32, No. 3 (December 1993), pp. 513 542; see also Robert King and Ross Levine, "Finance and Growth: Schumpeter Might Be Right," *Quarterly Journal of Economics,* Vol. 108, No. 3 (August 1993), pp. 717–737.

[38] Barro and Sala-I-Martin, *Economic Growth,* pp. 434–435.

[39] Steven Knack and Philip Keefer, "Institutional and Economic Performance: Cross Country Tests Using Alternative Institutional Measures," *Economics and Politics,* Vol. 7 (1995), pp. 207–227, and Barro and Sala-I-Martin, *Economic Growth,* pp. 439–440.

[40] An introduction to the latest scientific research into the process of economic growth may be found at Oxford University's *Economic Growth Resources Home Page,* located on the World Wide Web at *http://www.nuff.ox.ac.uk/ Economics/Growth/.*

[41] For a description of how the Gini Coefficient is calculated and its characteristics, see Bruno Milanovic, "A Simple Way to Calculate the Gini Coefficient and Some Implications," *Economics Letters,* Vol. 56, No. 1 (September 1997), and Robert Dorfman, "A Formula for the Gini Coefficient," *Review of Economics and Statistics,* Vol. 61 No.1 (February 1979), pp. 146–149.

[42] Klaus Deininger and Lyn Squire, "A New Data Set Measuring Income Inequality," *World Bank Economic Review,* Vol. 10, No. 3 (1996), pp. 565–591.

[43] See, for example, Jeffrey Williamson, "American Prices and Urban Inequality Since 1820," *Journal of Economic History,* Vol. 36, No. 2 (June 1976), pp. 303–333.

2

Economic Freedom and Foreign Aid

by Bryan T. Johnson

Foreign aid bureaucrats have argued for years that assistance from the United States is vital to the economic well-being of less-developed countries. J. Brian Atwood, administrator of the U.S. Agency for International Development, which has responsibility for disbursing most of the $14 billion U.S. foreign aid budget, even has suggested that the overall economic prosperity of the post–World War II era can be attributed largely to the Marshall Plan and successive foreign aid efforts.[1] Such claims, however, grossly exaggerate the benefits of development aid and ignore its many harmful effects. Not only has the U.S. foreign aid program failed to promote economic growth in less-developed countries, many recipient countries are worse off today than they were before beginning to receive aid.

As the data presented in the *Index of Economic Freedom* demonstrate, economic freedom is the most important factor in creating the conditions for economic prosperity. Data presented in this chapter show that, instead of helping poor countries to lift themselves out of poverty, U.S. development aid frequently impedes economic growth and even damages fragile economies. Economic freedom matters far more than development aid in achieving economic development.

Data in the *Index of Economic Freedom* show as well that many long-term recipients of U.S. foreign aid have "unfree" or "repressed" economies. No matter how much money the United States and other donors give to such recipients as Tanzania, Sudan, and Ethiopia, economic development still is unlikely to result. Indeed, the countries the *Index*

scores as "mostly unfree" or "repressed" economies have yet to generate substantial levels of wealth. By comparison, countries ranked at the very top of the *Index* are among the wealthiest in the world.

The data compiled and compared for the *Index* demonstrate clearly that poverty is caused largely by ill-conceived and repressive economic policies. Such factors as history, culture, war, and climate may influence a country's development, but its level of economic freedom is far and away the most important determinant in the long run. The data show that no amount of foreign aid can offset the ill-effects of the conditions that exist in economically unfree economies. Some countries, in fact, have received U.S. foreign aid for over 50 years but are no better off today than they were before they began to receive aid.

A close look at the recipients of U.S. foreign aid and their economic performance over the past several decades supports these points:

- Of the 90 countries the *Index* ranks "mostly unfree" or "repressed," 38[2] have received U.S. foreign aid for at least 38 years—some for as long as 54 years[3] (see Table 2.1);
- Of these 38 countries, 27 are no better off economically today than they were in 1965; and
- Of these 27 recipients, 15 are poorer today than they were in 1965.

These facts raise several questions. If development aid is so important to economic growth, as Mr. Atwood claims, why are so many long-term recipients of foreign aid still so poor? If development aid is essential for economic growth and development, why are so many long-term recipients—over one-third, in fact—becoming poorer? And if development aid is essential to economic prosperity, why has there been so little progress by the countries that are the most dependent on foreign aid?

The answer to each of these questions is simple: Economic freedom—*not* aid—is the key to long-term economic development. Consider the following examples (see also Table 2.2):

1. **Haiti** has depended on U.S. foreign aid for 54 years, but it remains one of the world's poorest countries.[4] In 1965, Haiti's per capita gross domestic product (GDP) was $360; in 1996, it was even lower—$165.[5] During this time, Haiti received over $1 billion in foreign aid from the United States alone, not including the money the United States spent on a military operation to "restore" democracy in Haiti in 1994.
2. **Nicaragua** has received $1.4 billion in foreign aid from the United States over the past 51 years. In 1965, Nicaragua's GDP per capita was $1,752, but by 1996, it had shrunk to $845.
3. **Niger** has received over $500 million in U.S. foreign assistance over the past 39 years, but its per capita wealth fell by more than 59 percent from 1965 to 1996—from $617 to $261.

4. **Senegal** has received over $1 billion in U.S. foreign aid over the past 39 years. All the while, its per capita wealth shrank—from $752 in 1965 to only $309 in 1996, a reduction of 59 percent.
5. **Sudan** has been the recipient of U.S. foreign aid for 41 years. But how much has this aid helped it? In 1965, Sudan had a per capita wealth of only $806. Some three decades later, its per capita wealth has remained essentially stagnant ($800 in 1996).

Although there is little evidence that long-term receipt of foreign aid is associated closely with a country's economic prosperity, there is strong evidence that levels of economic freedom are associated closely with economic prosperity. This association becomes clear after analyzing the level of economic freedom for the 161 countries graded in the *Index* and comparing it with their level of per capita GDP expressed in purchasing power parity. The Economic Freedom and Wealth chart on p. xxix shows clearly that the higher the level of economic freedom in a country, in general, the higher the level of per capita wealth individuals enjoy. Thus, the evidence seems to indicate that economic freedom and per capita wealth are associated closely.

If the *Index of Economic Freedom* provides any insight into the economic development process, it is not to suggest which countries deserve economic development aid: no country does.[6] Instead, it is to show the general futility of providing economic development assistance in the first place. Although a well-intentioned foreign aid program may help a newly independent country to pay for the development of a commercial code, for example, it is far more likely to hinder the country's economic development process. Foreign aid delays economic growth by prolonging the implementation of such much-needed reforms as privatization of state-owned industries and the lowering of taxes, tariffs, and other factors measured by the *Index* that have a demonstrable impact on economic growth. Until the less-developed countries adopt these free-market reforms, they will continue to be impoverished no matter how much foreign aid money they receive.

Table 2.1

Economic Freedom and Economic Prosperity

	Index of Economic Freedom Score 1999	GDP per Capita 1965, Constant 1987 US$	GDP per Capita 1996, Constant 1987 US$	Increase in GDP per Capita 1965–1996	Years Receiving Aid
Free Countries					
Hong Kong	1.25	2422	12256	406%	-
Singapore	1.30	1685	14661	770%	-
Taiwan ++	1.95	833	9338	1021%	-
Unfree Countries					
Ghana	3.00	501	430	-14%	42
Benin	3.05	346	370	7%	41
Kenya	3.05	221	381	72%	46
Zambia	3.05	478	255	-47%	41
Colombia	3.10	690	1386	101%	54
Mali	3.10	227	261	15%	39
Honduras	3.15	746	910	22%	54
Mexico	3.15	1136	1903	68%	53
Senegal	3.25	752	658	-13%	39
Tanzania	3.25	134	**155**	16%	42
Nigeria	3.30	335	309	-8%	39
Dominican Republic	3.35	372	984	165%	47
Egypt	3.35	300	985	228%	47
Guinea *	3.35	386	436	13%	41
Nepal	3.40	151	213	41%	48
Lesotho	3.45	126	360	186%	39
Madagascar	3.45	320	208	-35%	41
Burkina Faso	3.50	180	265	47%	39
Cameroon	3.50	618	733	19%	40
Guyana	3.50	479	**539**	13%	46
Nicaragua	3.50	1752	845	-52%	51
Gambia	3.60	225	**241**	7%	42
Malawi	3.65	113	163	44%	44
Ethiopia **	3.70	187	166	-11%	51
India	3.70	217	464	114%	53
Niger	3.70	617	273	-56%	39
Chad	3.80	202	168	-17%	38
Mauritania	3.80	516	513	-1%	40
Burundi	3.90	124	157	27%	39
Togo	3.95	366	328	-10%	41
Repressed Countries					
Haiti	4.00	360	165	-54%	54
Sierra Leone	4.05	137	160	17%	45
Sudan#	4.20	806	800	-1%	42
Myanmar (Burma)#	4.30	210	267	27%	38
Rwanda	4.30	229	221	-3%	38
Congo (former Zaire)	4.70	282	108	-62%	44
Somalia +	4.80	111	115	4%	43

Note: While falling in the category of unfree countries that have received U.S. aid for 38 years or more, Lebanon is not included in this table due to a lack of GDP data. Shaded countries experienced growth of less than 1 percent per year. Figures in **Bold** are from 1995.

* First GDP/capita from 1986.　　　+ Second GDP/capita from 1990.　　　++ First GNP/capita from 1967,
** First GDP/capita from 1983.　　　# Second GDP/capita from 1994.　　　　　Second GNP/capita from 1996.

Sources: *World Data 1995* CD-ROM, The World Bank, 1996; *1997 World Development Indicators* CD-ROM, The World Bank, 1997; *1998 World Development Indicators* CD-ROM, The World Bank, 1998; *Foreign Aid Reduction Act of 1995*, Committee on Foreign Relations, U.S. Senate; *Congressional Presentation: Summary Tables, Fiscal Year 1999*, U.S. Agency for International Development; Taiwan figures from *The Republic of China Yearbook, 1997*, Government Information Office, Republic of China.

Table 2.2

Long-Term Recipients of U.S. Foreign Aid and Their Economic Performance: 1965–1995

Years Receiving Aid, FY1946–99	Country	GDP per Capita 1965, Constant 1987 US$	GDP per Capita 1996, Constant 1987 US$	Increase in GDP per Capita 1965–1996
54	Bolivia	$682	$790	16%
54	Chile	1236	2677	117%
54	Colombia	690	1386	101%
54	Costa Rica	1128	1860	65%
54	Ecuador	626	1242	98%
54	El Salvador	913	1006	10%
54	Guatemala	690	916	33%
54	Haiti	360	165	-54%
54	Honduras	746	910	22%
54	Panama	1371	2688	96%
54	Peru	1126	312	-72%
54	Philippines	464	634	37%
53	India	217	464	114%
53	Indonesia	189	761	302%
53	Mexico	1136	1903	68%
53	Turkey	834	1940	133%
53	Uruguay	434	2907	570%
52	Liberia +	627	495	-21%
51	Ethiopia ***	187	166	-11%
51	Nicaragua	1752	845	-52%
50	Lebanon	–	–	–
50	Thailand	366	1914	423%
49	Israel	4654	10505	126%
49	Jordan ***	2253	1966	-13%
48	Morocco	500	962	92%
48	Nepal	151	213	41%
47	Dominican Republic	372	984	165%
47	Egypt	300	985	228%
47	Tunisia	638	1512	137%
46	Guyana	479	**539**	12%
46	Kenya	221	381	73%
45	Sierra Leone	137	160	17%
45	Sri Lanka	213	526	147%
44	Afghanistan	–	–	–
44	Belize	$830	$2123	156%
44	Congo (former Zaire)	282	108	-62%
44	Jamaica	1272	1431	13%
44	Malawi	113	163	44%
43	Somalia ++	111	115	3%
43	Uganda ***	452	590	31%
42	Gambia	225	**241**	7%
42	Ghana	501	430	-14%
42	Portugal	1849	5389	191%
42	Tanzania	134	**155**	16%
41	Benin	346	370	7%
41	Guinea **	386	436	13%
41	Madagascar	320	208	-35%
41	Togo	366	328	-10%
41	Sudan#	806	800	-1%
41	Zambia	478	255	-47%
40	Cameroon	618	733	19%
40	Gabon	2798	4668	67%
40	Mauritania	516	513	-1%
40	Mauritius	968	2670	176%
39	Burkina Faso	180	265	47%
39	Central African Republic	408	157	-62%
39	Lesotho	126	372	195%
39	Mali	227	360	59%
39	Niger	617	261	-58%
39	Nigeria	335	273	-18%
39	Senegal	752	309	-59%
39	Seychelles	1918	658	-66%
39	Swaziland	478	4585	859%
38	Chad	202	924	357%
38	Rwanda	229	168	-27%
37	Burundi	124	265	114%
37	Myanmar (Burma)#	210	267	27%

Note: This table includes all countries that have received aid from the U.S. for at least 38 years. Shaded figures indicate countries whose per capita GDPs rose less than 1% per year. Figures in **Bold** are from 1995.

* First GDP/capita from 1986.　　** First GDP/capita from 1983.　　*** First GDP/capita from 1990.　　# Second GDP/capita from 1994.　　++ Second GDP/capita from 1995.　　+ Second GDP/capita from 1987.

Sources: *1997 World Development Indicators CD-ROM*, The World Bank, 1997; *1998 World Development Indicators CD-ROM*, The World Bank, 1998; *Foreign Aid Reduction Act of 1995*, Committee on Foreign Relations, U.S. Senate; *Congressional Presentation: Summary Tables, Fiscal Year 1999*, U.S. Agency for International Development, 1998.

Table 2.3

U.S. Economic and Military Bilateral Assistance: 1946–1999

Near East	Economic Assistance	Military Assistance	Total
Algeria	206.6	1.9	208.5
Bahrain	2.4	3.6	6.0
Egypt	31,371.4	29,017.3	60,388.8
Iran	767.7	1,404.9	2,172.6
Iraq	76.3	50.0	126.3
Israel	35,520.8	49,227.4	84,748.2
Jordan	2,444.7	2,160.8	4,605.5
Lebanon	518.4	280.9	799.4
Libya	212.5	17.6	230.1
Morocco	2,442.3	1,293.5	3,735.7
Oman	234.6	137.7	372.3
Saudi Arabia	31.8	292.3	324.1
Syria	353.0	0.1	353.1
Tunisia	1,308.9	797.5	2,106.3
West Bank	531.3	0.0	531.3
Yemen	526.8	30.7	557.5
Regional Total	**76,549.4**	**84,716.2**	**161,265.6**

Sub-Saharan Africa	Economic Assistance	Military Assistance	Total
Angola	334.3	0.6	334.9
Benin	282.5	2.6	285.1
Botswana	389.7	38.6	428.3
Burkina Faso	463.6	1.4	465.0
Burundi	219.1	2.5	221.6
Cameroon	410.2	34.9	445.1
Cape Verde	153.5	2.2	155.8
Central African Republic	92.7	3.3	96.1
Chad	330.7	40.0	370.7
Comoros	23.0	0.9	23.9
Democratic Republic of Congo (former Zaire)	1,306.5	438.8	1,745.3
Congo, Republic of	53.7	1.7	55.5
Djibouti	58.0	18.2	76.2
Entente States	8.5	0.0	8.5
Equatorial Guinea	20.1	2.0	22.2
Eritrea	119.2	1.8	120.9
Ethiopia	1,889.8	263.2	2,153.0
Gabon	64.3	23.5	87.8
Gambia	205.9	1.8	207.7
Ghana	1,071.1	8.0	1,079.1
Guinea	641.9	12.8	654.6
Guinea-Bissau	112.4	2.0	114.4
Ivory Coast	198.0	5.8	203.7
Kenya	1,180.7	287.4	1,468.1
Lesotho	375.2	1.2	376.4
Liberia	1,238.7	95.1	1,333.8
Madagascar	518.4	5.9	524.3
Malawi	746.8	11.6	758.5
Mali	840.5	7.0	847.5
Mauritania	211.4	0.9	212.2
Mauritius	85.3	0.5	85.8
Mozambique	1,273.9	1.6	1,275.5
Namibia	132.7	2.2	135.0

Sub-Saharan Africa	Economic Assistance	Military Assistance	Total
Niger	653.9	36.7	690.7
Nigeria	549.4	3.6	553.1
Rwanda	537.3	3.8	541.1
Sao Tome	19.8	1.5	21.3
Senegal	940.8	65.0	1,005.8
Seychelles	47.1	1.1	48.2
Sierra Leone	292.7	4.3	297.0
Somalia	905.8	240.8	1,146.6
South Africa	993.2	3.1	996.2
Sudan	1,706.8	375.7	2,082.5
Swaziland	218.2	1.5	219.7
Tanzania	750.8	1.8	752.7
Togo	238.0	1.0	239.1
Uganda	651.2	2.8	654.0
Zambia	737.7	1.7	739.4
Zimbabwe	701.3	5.4	706.7
Other	1,735.2	37.4	1,772.6
Regional Total	**26,731.9**	**2,107.2**	**28,839.1**

Europe	Economic Assistance	Military Assistance	Total
Albania	225.9	3.0	228.9
Armenia***	396.2	0.0	396.2
Austria	1,135.9	122.1	1,258.0
Azerbaijan	86.5	0.0	86.5
Balkan States**	10.4	0.0	10.4
Baltics***	13.6	2.9	16.5
Belarus**	34.8	1.1	35.8
Belgium-Luxembourg	589.1	1,275.3	1,864.4
Berlin, W.	131.9	0.0	131.9
Bosnia**	1,026.1	2.0	1,028.0
Bosnia-Herzegovina, Croatia and Kosovo**	144.1	0.0	144.1
Bulgaria	160.2	5.0	165.2
Croatia**	66.0	1.5	67.4
Cyprus	452.2	0.0	452.2
Czech Republic****	20.9	5.6	26.5
Czechoslovakia****	201.4	2.0	203.4
Denmark	276.5	640.1	916.6
Estonia+	1.8	2.7	4.4
Finland	51.2	0.8	52.1
France	3,917.0	4,548.6	8,465.6
Georgia***	246.2	1.4	247.6
Germany, East	0.8	0.0	0.8
Germany, West	3,843.4	939.4	4,782.8
Greece	2,602.9	9,524.6	12,127.4
Hungary	119.0	9.1	128.1
Iceland	76.9	0.3	77.2
Ireland	464.4	0.1	464.5
Italy	3,420.8	2,545.3	5,966.1
Kazakhstan***	201.5	2.2	203.8
Kyrgyz Republic***	116.9	1.2	118.1
Latvia***	16.2	2.7	18.9
Lithuania***	33.9	2.8	36.7

Note: Figures are in millions of current dollars.
*Aid to the former Yugoslavia broken down as follows: Yugoslavia in 1991; Balkan States – through 1991; NIS (former USSR), 1990; Armenia, 1992–1999; Croatia, 1993, 1994; Bosnia (and Bosnia-Herzegovina) 1995–1999; Croatia, 1995–1999; Macedonia, 1992–1999; Serbia and Montenegro.
**Aid to the former Yugoslavia broken down as follows: Bosnia-Herzegovina, Croatia & Kosovo, 1993, 1994; Bosnia-Herzegovina, Croatia & Kosovo, 1995–1999; Slovenia; 1993–1999.
***Aid to the former U.S.S.R. and Newly Independent States broken down as follows: USSR – through 1991; NIS (former USSR), 1990; Armenia, 1992–1999; Azerbaijan, 1995–1999; Baltics (and Baltic States), 1991 collectively, then for Peace Corps 1994–1999; Belarus, 1993–1999; Estonia, 1992–1999; Georgia, 1995–1999; Kazakhstan, 1993–1999; Kyrgyz Republic, 1993–1999; Latvia, 1992–1999; Lithuania, 1992–1999; Moldova, 1993–1999; Russia, 1992–1999; Tajikistan, 1995–1999; Turkmenistan, 1993–1999; Ukraine, 1992–1999; Uzbekistan, 1992–1999.
****Aid to the former Czechoslovakia is broken down as follows: Czechoslovakia, 1993; Czech Republic, 1994–1999; Slovak Republic, 1994–1999.
Sources: From Foreign Operations, Export Financing, and Related Programs Appropriations Bill, 1994, U.S. Senate Report No. 103-142, September 14, 1993; and U.S.A.I.D. Congressional Presentation Summary Tables, Fiscal Years 1991–1999, 1991–1998. Data for 1999 come from USAID's Request Funds for U.S. economic and military assistance; data for all other years are actual appropriations. Some "regional aid" — that is, U.S. aid given not to specific countries but to organizations like the World Bank for distribution to regions; and U.S aid designated directly for specific regions—is omitted from these figures.

Table 2.3

U.S. Economic and Military Bilateral Assistance: 1946–1999

Europe	Economic Assistance	Military Assistance	Total
Macedonia**	85.6	4.6	90.1
Malta	84.3	1.2	85.5
Moldova***	133.4	1.5	134.8
Netherlands	1,027.6	1,284.7	2,312.3
Norway	299.9	943.8	1,243.7
Poland	1,200.8	10.5	1,211.3
Portugal	1,651.4	2,004.4	3,655.9
Romania	303.4	4.6	308.0
Russia	964.0	5.4	969.3
Serbia & Montenegro**	27.0	0.0	27.0
Slovak Republic****	75.3	3.0	78.3
Slovenia**	10.5	2.3	12.8
Spain	1,084.5	3,447.4	4,531.9
Sweden	109.0	0.0	109.0
Tajikistan***	50.7	0.0	50.7
Turkey	6,459.5	14,868.4	21,327.9
Turkmenistan***	39.4	1.2	40.5
Ukraine***	1,075.1	6.0	1,081.1
U.K.	7,672.1	1,107.4	8,779.5
Uzbekistan***	109.7	1.4	111.1
U.S.S.R.***	191.4	0.0	191.4
Yugoslavia**	1,735.5	723.8	2,459.3
Other	1,523.5	0.2	1,523.7
Newly Independent States (former USSR)***	319.0	0.2	319.2
Regional Total	46,316.8	44,063.7	90,380.5

Latin America	Economic Assistance	Military Assistance	Total
Argentina	231.9	277.3	509.3
Bahamas	12.5	1.2	13.7
Barbados	4.1	0.5	4.6
Belize	166.3	7.2	173.5
Bolivia	2,432.5	293.2	2,725.7
Brazil	2,490.3	642.0	3,132.2
Chile	1,277.6	226.4	1,504.0
Colombia	1,961.8	622.8	2,584.6
Costa Rica	1,792.1	41.4	1,833.5
Cuba	4.0	16.1	20.1
Dominican Republic	1,577.1	101.5	1,678.6
Ecuador	952.2	201.0	1,153.2
El Salvador	4,654.2	1,266.6	5,920.8
Grenada	60.1	0.2	60.3
Guatemala	1,949.8	77.4	2,027.2
Guyana	142.9	6.7	149.6
Haiti	1,888.5	21.2	1,909.8
Honduras	2,011.8	589.0	2,600.8
Jamaica	1,950.7	54.0	2,004.6
Mexico	798.6	24.0	822.6
Nicaragua	1,347.9	31.4	1,379.3
Panama	1,127.3	77.5	1,204.8
Paraguay	275.7	33.6	309.3
Peru	3,115.4	374.0	3,489.3
Suriname	16.8	0.7	17.5
Trinidad and Tobago	44.3	3.8	48.1
Uruguay	182.4	94.8	277.2
Venezuela	214.3	157.4	371.7
Regional Total	32,683.1	5,242.7	37,925.7

Asia	Economic Assistance	Military Assistance	Total
Afghanistan	863.7	5.6	869.3
Bangladesh	3,558.2	6.9	3,565.1
Bhutan	9.3	0.0	9.3
Cambodia (former Kampuchea)	1,129.9	1,283.4	2,413.4
China, PRC	7.9	0.0	7.9
Cook Islands	0.4	0.0	0.4
Fiji	13.3	0.4	13.7
Hong Kong	43.8	0.0	43.8
India	13,130.6	151.6	13,282.2
Indochina Association States	825.6	731.5	1,557.1
Indonesia	4,266.9	724.1	4,991.0
Japan	2,685.9	1,239.6	3,925.5
Kiribati	5.3	0.3	5.6
Korea, South	6,085.3	8,797.8	14,883.1
Laos	938.7	1,606.8	2,545.5
Malaysia	92.0	199.7	291.7
Maldives	2.8	0.8	3.6
Marshall Islands	3.7	0.0	3.7
Micronesia & Palau	17.7	0.1	17.8
Mongolia	118.5	1.7	120.2
Myanmar (former Burma)	237.5	90.5	328.0
Nepal	717.6	5.3	722.9
Pakistan	7,972.3	2,952.0	10,924.3
Papua New Guinea	31.8	2.0	33.8
Philippines	6,281.6	2,582.5	8,864.1
Ryukyu Islands	413.8	0.0	413.8
Samoa & Niue	2.1	0.0	2.1
Samoa (former Western Samoa)	30.5	0.5	31.0
Singapore	2.8	19.7	22.5
Solomon Islands	11.1	0.7	11.8
Sri Lanka	1,586.2	9.5	1,595.7
Taiwan	2,219.1	4,360.4	6,579.5
Thailand	1,138.9	2,326.7	3,465.6
Tonga	8.8	0.0	8.8
Tuvalu	0.2	0.0	0.2
Vanuatu	5.2	0.5	5.7
Vietnam, South	6,950.5	16,416.1	23,366.6
Regional Total	61,409.2	43,517.4	104,926.6

Oceania and Others	Economic Assistance	Military Assistance	Total
Australia	8.0	115.6	123.6
New Zealand	4.3	4.3	8.6
Pacific Islands	824.2	0.0	824.2
Oceana Regional	234.8	1.8	236.6
Regional Total	1,071.3	121.7	1,193.0
Canada	17.5	13.0	30.5
Interregional Activities	65,806.0	4,764.2	70,570.2
Grand Total	310,585.1	184,546.1	495,131.2

Note: Figures are in millions of current dollars.
**Aid to the former Yugoslavia broken down as follows: Yugoslavia in 1991; Balkan States in 1992, 1993; Bosnia–Herzegovina, Croatia & Kosovo, 1993, 1994; Bosnia (and Bosnia–Herzegovina) 1995–1999; Croatia, 1995–1999; Macedonia, 1992–1999; Serbia and Montenegro, 1998–1999; Slovenia: 1993–1999.
***Aid to the former U.S.S.R. and Newly Independent States broken down as follows: USSR – through 1991; NIS (former USSR), 1990; Armenia, 1992–1999; Azerbaijan, 1995–1999; Baltics (and Baltic States) 1991 collectively, then for Peace Corps 1994–1999; Belarus, 1993–1999; Estonia, 1992–1999; Georgia, 1995–1999; Kazakhstan, 1993–1999; Kyrgyz Republic, 1993–1999; Latvia, 1992–1999; Lithuania, 1992–1999; Moldova, 1993–1999; Russia, 1992–1999; Tajikistan, 1995–1999; Turkmenistan, 1993–1999; Ukraine, 1993–1999; Uzbekistan, 1992–1999.
****Aid to the former Czechoslovakia is broken down as follows: Czechoslovakia, 1993; Czech Republic, 1994–1999; Slovak Republic, 1994–1999.
Sources: From Foreign Operations, Export Financing, and Related Programs Appropriations Bill, 1994; U.S. Senate Report No. 103-142, September 14, 1993; and U.S.A.I.D. Congressional Presentation Summary Tables, Fiscal Years 1991–1999, 1991–1998. Data for 1999 come from USAID's Request for Funds for U.S. economic and military assistance; data for all other years are actual appropriations. Some "regional aid" — that is, U.S. aid given not to specific countries but to organizations like the World Bank for distribution to regions, and U.S aid designated directly for specific regions—is omitted from these figures.

Notes

1   Remarks by AID Administrator J. Brian Atwood to Center for National Policy, Washington, D.C., December 14, 1994.

2   This listing does not include countries in which per capita GDP in constant 1987 U.S. dollar figures is not available.

3   Some aid recipients in sub-Saharan Africa and elsewhere have at least doubled their wealth in the past 30 years. In 1965, for example, Lesotho's per capita GDP (in constant 1987 dollars) was $126; by 1996, its per capita wealth had reached $360. Nevertheless, Lesotho obviously remains an extremely poor country. The growth rates for Lesotho and other aid-dependent countries pale in comparison to those of the "Asian Tigers," most of which increased their wealth over 500 percent during the same period. Thus, foreign aid recipients that have doubled or even tripled their economic wealth since 1965 are still worse off than the Asian Tigers, which had much higher growth rates without receiving much foreign aid. The most likely reason for the difference: economic freedom.

4   Figures include both military and economic assistance, although most assistance to less-developed countries has been in the form of economic aid. For example, of the $1.91 billion in U.S. foreign aid that Haiti received from 1946 to fiscal year 1999, $1.89 billion was in the form of economic assistance. For more information, see Chart 2.3.

5   All figures are GDP per capita, expressed in constant 1987 dollars; from World Bank, *World Data 1997, CD–ROM*, Washington, D.C., 1998.

6   Some U.S. military and security aid may help secure U.S. foreign policy interests abroad. For example, programs like the International Military Education Training Program, which allows the U.S. military to train with foreign militaries, when used prudently may improve the ability of the United States to defend its national security interests. In addition, some humanitarian and disaster relief provides much-needed help to victims of earthquakes, mass floods, and other natural disasters.

## 3

Comparing Economic Freedom and Political Freedom

by Bryan T. Johnson[1]

Just as economists long have assumed a relationship between economic freedom and economic growth, many economists also have assumed a relationship between economic freedom and political freedom. Indeed, even a cursory look at the *Index of Economic Freedom* and various existing political freedom reports shows that, in general, those countries that are most economically free generally are also the most politically free. Similarly, those countries that are most economically repressed also tend to be the most politically repressed.

An examination of the statistical relationship between economic freedom and political freedom provides evidence for those conclusions. Heritage analysts compare the economic freedom scores from the 1997 *Index of Economic Freedom*[2] with the findings of the *Comparative Survey of Freedom 1995–1996* published by Freedom House.[3] The Freedom House report examines such factors as free and fair elections, the right to organize in different political parties, free and independent media, equality under the law, access to an independent judiciary, and protection from unjustified imprisonment, exile, or torture.

Using one of the largest datasets designed for inter-country growth comparisons, Heritage analysts find statistically significant relationships between economic freedom and political freedom.

What Is Economic Freedom and How Is It Measured?

Economic freedom can be defined as the *absence of government coercion or constraint on the production, distribution, or consumption of goods and services.*

The *Index of Economic Freedom* analyzes 50 independent economic criteria organized into 10 broad economic factors. We then grade countries on a scale from 1 ("most free") to 5 ("least free").

Please see Chapter 6 for detailed information on the methodology of the *Index*.

What Is Political Freedom and How Is It Measured?

Since the 1970s, Freedom House, based in New York City, has published an annual survey that measures political freedom and civil liberties in over 190 countries. Freedom House defines

Sidebar:
Freedom House's Political Rights Checklist

1. Is the head of state and/or head of government or other chief authority elected through free and fair elections?

2. Are the legislative representatives elected through free and fair elections?

3. Are there fair electoral laws, equal campaigning opportunities, fair polling, and honest tabulation of ballots?

4. Are the voters able to endow their freely elected representatives with real power?

5. Do the people have the right to organize in different political parties or other competitive political groupings of their choice, and is the system open to rise and fall of these competing parties or groupings?

6. Is there a significant opposition vote, de facto opposition power, and a realistic possibility for the opposition to increase its support or gain power through elections?

7. Are people free from domination by the military, foreign powers, totalitarian parties, religious hierarchies, economic oligarchies or any other powerful group?

8. Do cultural, ethnic, religious and other minority groups have reasonable self-determination, self-government, autonomy or participation through informal consensus in the decision-making process?

Freedom House's Civil Liberties Checklist

1. Are there free and independent media, literature and other cultural expressions?

2. Is there open public discussion and free private discussion?

3. Is there freedom of assembly and demonstration?

4. Is there freedom of political or quasi-political organization?

5. Are citizens equal under the law, with access to an independent, nondiscriminatory judiciary, and are they respected by the security forces?

6. Is there protection from political terror, and from unjustified imprisonment, exile or torture, whether by groups that support or oppose the system, and freedom from war or insurgency situations?

7. Are there trade unions and peasant organizations or equivalents, and is there effective collective bargaining?

8. Are there free professional and other private organizations?

9. Are there free businesses or cooperatives?

10. Are there free religious institutions and free private and public religious expressions?

11. Are there personal social freedoms, which includes such aspects as gender equality, property rights, freedom of movement, choice of residence, and choice of marriage and size of family?

12. Is there equality of opportunity, which includes freedom from exploitation by or dependency on landlords, employers, union leaders, bureaucrats or any other type of denigrating obstacle to a share of legitimate economic gains?

13. Is there freedom from extreme government indifference and corruption?

Chart 3.1

Economic Freedom and Political Rights

1997 *Index of Economic Freedom* Score

1995–96 Freedom House Political Rights Score

More Free — Less Free

Sources: Heritage calculations, based on data from Freedom House, *Comparative Survey of Freedom, 1995–1996*, and The Heritage Foundation, 1997 *Index of Economic Freedom*.

political freedom as the ability of people "to chose their authoritative leaders freely from among competing groups and individuals who were not chosen by the government." It defines civil liberties as the "chance to act spontaneously in a variety of fields outside the control of government and other centers of potential domination."

Freedom House measures the level of political freedom based on an analysis of 8 factors, and of civil liberties based on an analysis of 13 factors (see Sidebar). The authors assign scores of 0 ("the worst") to 4 ("the best") for each factor. They then total these numbers and use them to categorize all countries into seven levels. Countries receive a final score between 1—the best for each category, political rights and civil liberties—and 7—the worst. Finally, the authors rank countries as "free," "partly free," or "not free" in both political rights and in civil liberties.

The Relationship Between Economic Freedom and Political Freedom

Armed with these data, it is possible to analyze the associations between economic freedoms and political freedoms. The findings of the *Index of Economic Freedom* and the *Comparative Survey of Freedom* can be graphed, and regression analyses run, to show any possible statistical relationships between these two annual surveys. This analysis is conducted both for economic freedom and political rights, and for economic freedom and civil liberties.

The standard statistical method for estimating the influence of one variable over another is called an *Ordinary Least-Squares Regression*. This method can be used to estimate a simple model of economic freedom and political rights, in which a country's political freedom is related to a country's level of economic freedom.

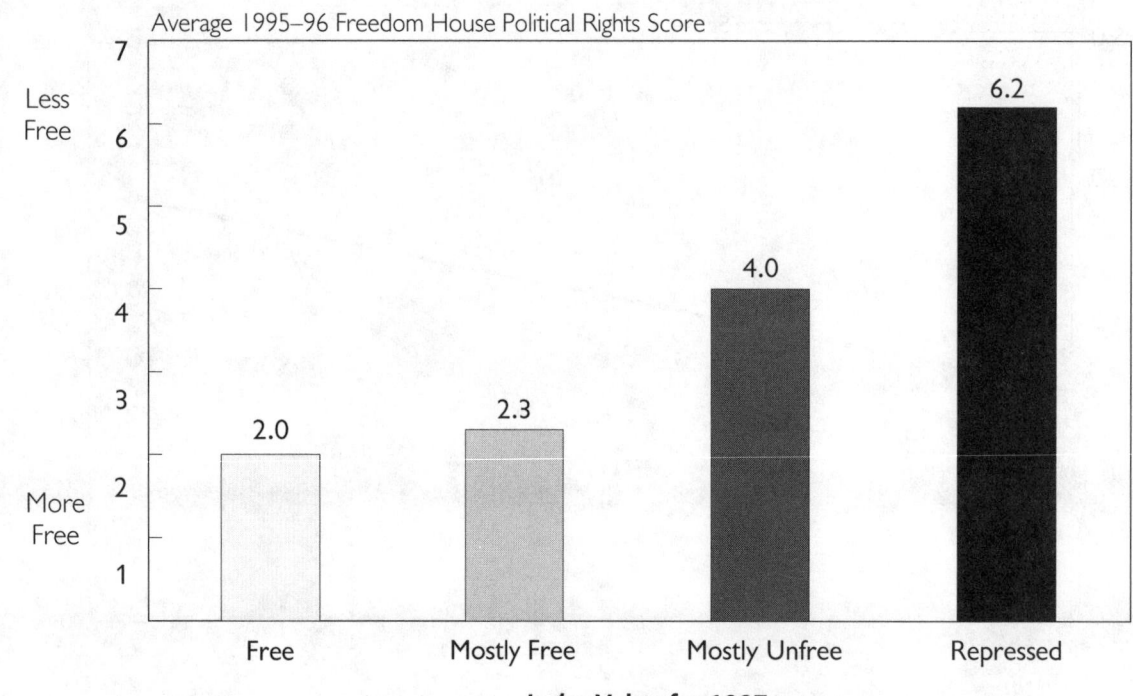

Chart 3.2

Economic Freedom and Political Rights

Average 1995–96 Freedom House Political Rights Score

Less Free

More Free

Free — 2.0

Mostly Free — 2.3

Mostly Unfree — 4.0

Repressed — 6.2

***Index* Value for 1997**

Sources: Heritage calculations, based on data from Freedom House, *Comparative Survey of Freedom, 1995–1996,* and The Heritage Foundation, 1997 *Index of Economic Freedom.*

Equation 1

$$P_n = a_1 + a_2(I_n)$$
Where:
- P_n = political rights score;
- I_n = a country's 1997 *Index of Economic Freedom* score;
- a_1 = the average ratio of P when I equals zero; and
- a_2 = the rate of change in political freedom as economic freedom varies.

Equation 1 explains a significant amount of the variation between Freedom House's index of political rights and the *Index of Economic Freedom.* The equation does not prove a causal link between economic and political freedom; however, it does indicate a strong statistical relationship between the two surveys. Equation 1 correctly predicts the level of political rights in 64 percent of the countries examined. In fact, the *t-statistic* (used to judge the statistical significance of the data) is over 10,

which means there is virtually no chance that the estimated relationship results from random associations. This analysis shows that the relationship between economic freedom and political rights is statistically significant at the 99 percent level (see Chart 3.1).

When broken into quartiles, the relationship between economic freedom and political freedom becomes even more apparent. In fact, those countries rated "free" in the *Index of Economic Freedom* also are the most politically free; likewise, those economies ranked as "repressed" in the *Index* are the most politically repressed (see Chart 3.2).

The relationship of economic freedom and civil liberties also can be expressed in an equation.

Equation 2

$$C_n = a_1 + a_2(I_n)$$
Where:
- C_n = civil liberties score;

Chart 3.3

Economic Freedom and Civil Liberties

1997 *Index of Economic Freedom* Score

1995–96 Freedom House Civil Liberties Score

More Free

Less Free

Sources: Heritage calculations, based on data from Freedom House, *Comparative Survey of Freedom, 1995–1996,* and The Heritage Foundation, 1997 *Index of Economic Freedom.*

- I_n = a country's 1997 *Index of Economic Freedom* score;
- a_1 = the average value of C when I equals zero; and
- a_2 = the rate of change in civil liberties as economic freedom varies.

This equation explains a significant amount of the variation between Freedom House's index of civil liberties and the *Index of Economic Freedom.* The equation correctly predicts civil liberties in 69 percent of countries examined, an even stronger correlation than the one between economic freedom and political rights. Indeed, the *t-statistic* is over 11, meaning that there is virtually no chance that the estimated relationship results from random associations. This analysis shows that the relationship between economic freedom and civil liberties is statistically significant at the 99 percent level.

When broken into quartiles, the relationship between economic freedom and civil liberties becomes more apparent. In fact, those countries

classified as "free" by the *Index of Economic Freedom* show the most freedom in civil liberties. Likewise, those economies ranked as "repressed" by the *Index* have the least freedom in civil liberties (see Chart 3.4).

Conclusion

Although it is nearly impossible to determine whether economic freedom or political freedom should come first, it is not impossible to see a statistically significant relationship between the two. Indeed, the findings of the *Index of Economic Freedom* show that those countries that are more economically free also are wealthier while those that are more economically repressed also are poorer. Likewise, the *Comparative Survey of Freedom 1995–1996* shows that those countries that have more political and civil freedom also have more wealth, while those with less political and civil freedom also have less wealth. But most important, this study shows that those countries

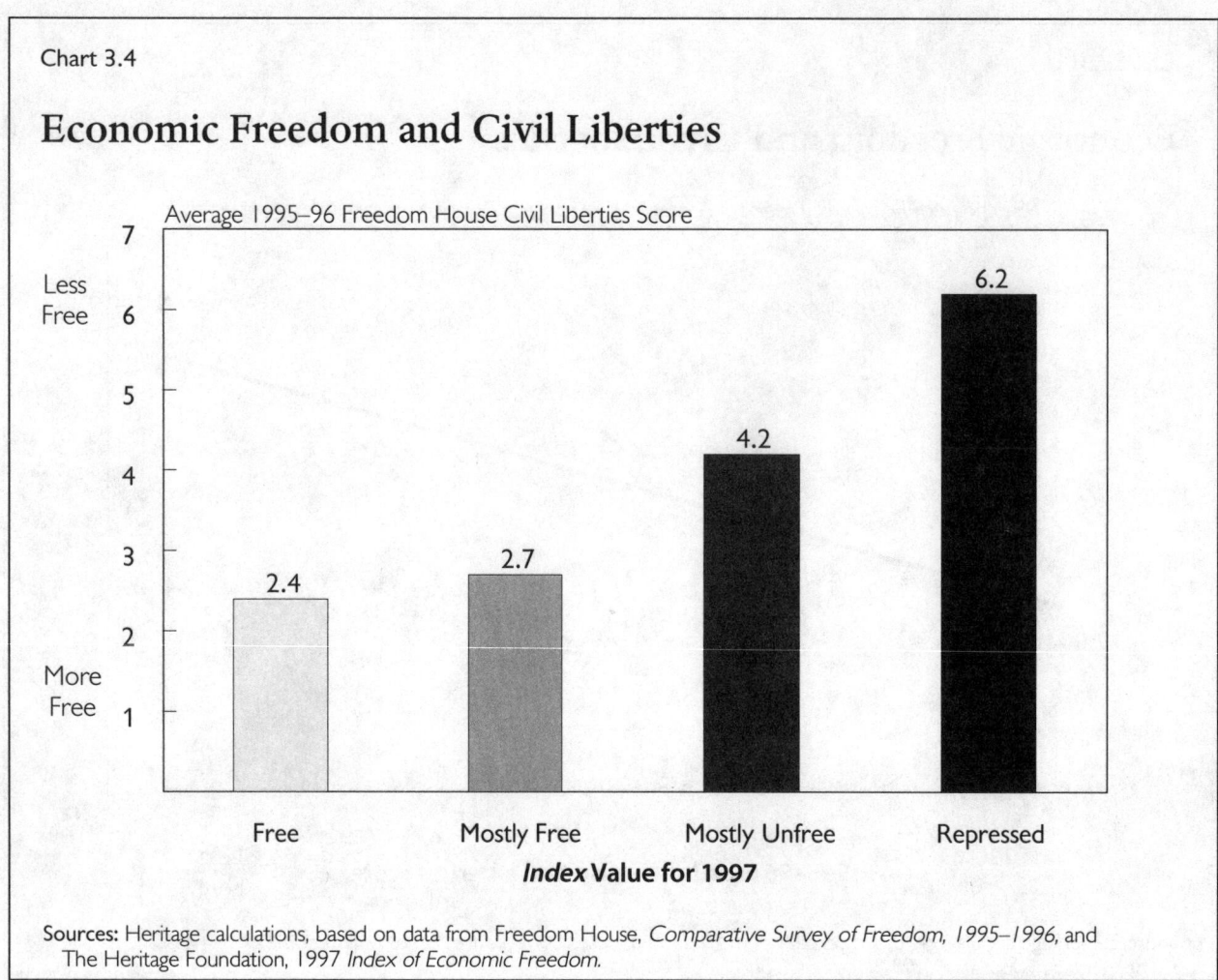

Chart 3.4

Economic Freedom and Civil Liberties

Average 1995–96 Freedom House Civil Liberties Score

Less Free

More Free

2.4 — Free
2.7 — Mostly Free
4.2 — Mostly Unfree
6.2 — Repressed

Index Value for 1997

Sources: Heritage calculations, based on data from Freedom House, *Comparative Survey of Freedom, 1995–1996,* and The Heritage Foundation, 1997 *Index of Economic Freedom.*

that are more economically free also are more politically free and have higher levels of civil liberties than those countries with less economic freedom. The message here is simple: Economic freedom and political freedom go hand in hand.

Notes

[1] The author thanks Heritage Foundation economists William W. Beach and Gareth G. Davis for their assistance with the research for this analysis.

[2] The 1997 *Index of Economic Freedom* includes scores that cover the last half of 1995 and the first half of 1996.

[3] "The Comparative Survey of Freedom 1995–1996: Survey Methodology" from the Freedom House Internet site: *http://www.freedomhouse.org/Political/method.htm.*

## 4

Mapping the New World Markets

by Claudia Rosett

One of the most poignant questions I have heard about economic development came from a North Korean refugee I interviewed in Moscow for *The Wall Street Journal* back in 1994. This man had come to Russia under official auspices from North Korea to work in a lumber camp in the Far East. From there, he had defected into post-communist Russia. When I met him, he was staying in a dingy Moscow apartment, hiding out from North Korean agents and hoping for asylum. To him, after the repression and hopeless poverty of North Korea, newly liberalizing Russia seemed a land of promise and opportunity—worth risking his life for a chance to stay. But he had a question: "Is it true," he asked, "that America is even better than this?"

This North Korean was no political agitator. He was simply seeking a better way of life. In crude form, he was setting up his own ranking of economic freedom, wondering where his personal resources of energy and skill might earn the best rewards. To compare North Korea, Russia, and the United States is, of course, to choose extreme cases. In the far more elaborate *Index of Economic Freedom* published here, North Korea ranks at the very bottom as the world's least economically free country—and, not coincidentally, one of its poorest. The United States stands among the most free—and the richest. Russia has begun a wild transition between the two. But this refugee, for all the apparent simplicity of his question, was pondering issues of economic freedom that in more subtle and detailed form concern investors

anywhere—whether they be individuals investing their own labor or titans of world finance moving billions through the markets.

Sometime during the past 15 years or so, after decades of scorning free markets, much of the world made the same conceptual leap as this North Korean lumberjack. In the more than 200-year-old tradition of Adam Smith's *Wealth of Nations,* it has again become accepted wisdom that when people are free, they get rich. Gone—for now—are the days in which state planning served as the popular prescription for development, when the Soviet Union played Big Brother and bizarre mentor to poor countries around the globe. At the more moderate end of the spectrum, we have also left behind the era in which Japanese industrial policy was debated as the true path and even the

United States—the Land of Liberty—was veering toward the kind of welfare state system already weighing down the economies of Europe.

Two main factors helped to work this change. One was raw evidence. By the 1980s, it had become stunningly clear that countries busy dictating the economic lives of their citizens were lagging far behind those in which people were free to choose. Communism provided some of the starkest comparisons: Taiwan versus Communist China; South versus North Korea; West versus East Germany. China, deciding it was more glorious to get rich than to suffer centrally planned famine, began easing its economic bindings and was rewarded with double-digit rates of growth. The Soviet Union, clinging to central planning, arrived at a stage of economic rot so pervasive that in 1991 the state collapsed. On the more moderate side, by 1991 Japan's bubble had burst, and industrial policy suddenly looked a lot less enticing. In the United States, thanks in part to President Ronald Reagan and in part to growing experience with an expanding state, the 1980s had already gone down as the decade of tax cuts and disenchantment with big government. By 1992, folks might vote for President Bill Clinton, who was fond of talking about "re-inventing" government, but they didn't much care for his more statist visions. Put to the test, Americans chose to spare themselves such horrors as Hillary Rodham Clinton's grand plan to socialize medicine.

Another large factor favoring the spread of freer markets has been rapidly advancing technology. In a world in which it is possible to process hundreds of millions of stock trades daily, or do computer programming in Bangalore, India, or fax a purchase order to rural China, it has become increasingly clear that the chief barriers to development are not mountains, oceans, and distance, but man-made rules of the game.

Binding together the thrust of evidence and technology has been the sheer force of competition. Once a country makes a serious bid to enter the world marketplace, it runs into a host of incentives to go on liberalizing. There is no other way to compete. The rewards are large enough so that even the most entrenched dictators and bureaucrats tend to take at least some notice. Cuba's Fidel Castro and Burma's junta, for example, have in recent years made motions toward plugging their countries back into the global economic grid, although clearly these tyrants are torn between a desire to dictate their countrymen's lives and greed to rule countries made richer—and more relevant to modern times—by even a small degree of economic reform. In the wake of Asia's economic rise of the 1980s, Latin America by the early 1990s was throwing off both its dictatorships and its economic stupor to rejoin the world. With the Soviet collapse, Eastern Europe and chunks of the former Soviet Union itself began a scramble to redevelop real markets. Even India and parts of Africa have been creaking toward freer economies. Deregulation, privatization, and freer trade have become policies that most countries want to advertise. One sign of this enthusiasm is that developing countries have in recent years celebrated in banner headlines any improvement in their own rankings in this *Index of Economic Freedom*.

All this augurs well. But if these are the best of times, they are also some of the most confusing. For investors trying to judge how best to allocate scarce resources, the shift toward the free market has brought its own dilemmas, questions, and discrepancies. To these, the emerging-market crises of the past year have added a touch of panic, grounded in fear of the unknown, or at least of the unfamiliar. Like explorers who set out long ago for the far reaches of the earth, we stand at the edge of uncharted economic terrain—facing for the first time the prospect of a truly global marketplace. To take a modest example, a visit to almost any discount store in the United States gives a sample of the vast turf these markets now span. T-shirt labels have become lessons in geography—made in places from Bangladesh to Botswana, Poland, Thailand, and Brazil. Thanks to computers, satellites, and fiber optic phone lines, buyers can shop the globe for the best goods and services at the lowest prices. Thanks to leaps in modern finance and communications, investors have available dramatically more efficient ways to put their capital to use. Out there lies a new world, fast-changing and tied together as never before by technology and trade, ready in theory to deliver a new Golden Age.

But whether, or where, all this promise might fully flower is no sure bet. To create a climate of economic freedom, many factors must combine—including in great measure those this *Index* attempts to quantify. As the past year's spreading crises in Asia and Russia have underscored, much depends on the evolution of policies and political institutions that will allow markets to thrive. Keeping track of where countries stand has become a huge job—due in part to the constant interplay of politics and economics. A glaring case this past year has been Malaysia, where, after years of growth and economic opening, Prime Minister Mohamad Mahathir responded to economic crisis by trying abruptly to sever ties to world markets—imposing capital controls that amount to state confiscation of private assets. An earlier example is Vietnam, which in the early 1990s briefly became the darling of Asia investors when Hanoi announced plans to open its markets. Unfortunately, Vietnam's Communist Party leaders could not bring themselves to reduce their own highly discretionary powers over property, profits, and trade. The result was a host of frustrated investors writing off a lot of time, effort, and cash poured into Vietnam. A glance at this *Index* suggests the basic problem: Of the 161 countries ranked, in descending order from best to worst in terms of economic freedom, Vietnam today comes in with one of the bottom scores, at 152.

In an increasingly competitive and lively world, many old rules of thumb have become inadequate guides. Anyone who figured a country's stock market offered a solid gauge of economic progress has by now had an eye-opener twice over in Russia. There, an early post-Soviet stock boom collapsed in 1994, when investors discovered they had no real property rights. Encouraged by further flailings at reform, enticed by Russia's vast store of natural resources, and shored up by the hope that the West would not let Russia collapse again, investors came back in far greater numbers. In 1997, Russia's stock market turned in a performance as the world's best, only to follow it up in 1998 with a crash that became one of the world's worst. Investors discovered for the second time that, in a country still lacking law, a rational tax system, and sound banking, they had no real property rights. Again, a look at this economic *Index* might have provided early warning to be at

least more cautious. Russia's score comes low on the list, at 106.

None of this is to suggest that investors should stay away from emerging markets. Rather, the increasingly clear message is that it helps to know what to look for, and to have a good map—which is what this *Index* aims to sketch out. Many standard labels can mislead because they do not take the larger picture into account. With privatization all the rage, for example, the world is full of finance ministers ready to promote their plans to sell off state assets. This is a good trend. But it is worth asking what institutions exist that will then allow buyers of privatized assets to turn reasonable profits. Western companies trying to invest directly in Russia's vast oil patch, for example, have repeatedly run into regulatory burdens too great to bear. At the other end of the scale, Ireland's market liberalizations of recent years have been thorough enough both to raise its score in the *Index* and to boost its economic growth rate to the highest in Europe.

This brings us to another vital factor in judging a country's prospects, which is the general direction of economic change. Snapshots are not enough. For example, China's ranking in this *Index* —124, which puts it below India and Ethiopia— would not by itself suggest the rapid growth of the past 15 years. What's telling is that, piece by piece, China has been liberalizing portions of an economy that has been recovering from the near-death of Maoist controls inflicted in the 1960s and 1970s. For years, that has given plenty of room for almost any market reform—such as the initial move of the early 1980s to decollectivize farms—to yield big returns. Investors would be wise, however, to keep in mind that China, for all its incremental improvements, is still far from a free-market economy. Unless Beijing's rulers have the courage to go ahead with further, major reforms—such as fostering a climate of law and the free flow of information that permits real banking—the day is coming in which the Middle Kingdom will hit the skids. It bears watching that China's score in the *Index* has dropped slightly this year, suggesting that Beijing is backing away from reform.

It is also telling that Hong Kong, long the world's leading example of economic freedom and accompanying growth, is set to topple from its position at the top of the *Index;* it would have dropped to number 2 this year had the cutoff date for inclusion of data not been June 30. In August, Hong Kong reacted to Asia's economic crisis by intervening to shore up the local stock market—a clear warning that the old wealth-engendering laissez-faire ways may be on the way out.

All of which brings us to the thunderclouds that by late 1998 were looming over the world economy—the Asia crisis, the Russia crisis, and the knock-on threats to Latin America. These show up only peripherally in this *Index* by way of reactions by individual economies, such as Hong Kong. It makes sense, as Robert L. Bartley, editor of *The Wall Street Journal,* suggests in his Foreword, to attribute these spreading problems less to specific national policies than to systemic troubles that hinder the smooth working of world markets. There is a case to be made that while individual countries have been liberalizing—and getting government out of business—global institutions such as the International Monetary Fund (IMF) have been putting government right back in charge. Starting with the 1994 bailout of Mexico, the U.S. Treasury and IMF have been broadcasting the message that big investors who make overly risky bets in emerging markets will be bailed out. Coupled with IMF urging of the devaluations that starting with Thailand plunged Asia into crisis in mid-1997, this policy has warped signals to world markets and set the stage for further crisis.

This growing problem, known as "moral hazard," is due in large part to the statist urges of the Clinton Presidency's Treasury and its confreres at the IMF. At both places, policy has been to pay lip service to free markets but to assume that the immense global economy wants hand-feeding and micro-managing by—guess who?—none other than the bureaucrats of the U.S. Treasury and IMF. This has placed the Treasury and the IMF in the intriguing position of prescribing free markets while dosing client countries with elaborate dictates tied to billions of dollars belonging to the taxpayers of the developed world—chiefly the United States. So, while many individual countries have been moving toward greater economic freedom at home, the world's most powerful multilateral agencies have been working overtime to impose their own version of central planning on any country that lands in their sights—and, by

extension, on the world economy. Although bailouts are advertised as help for the IMF's most troubled client countries, in practice they usually add up to compensation to big investors who got into dicey markets. That encourages lenders such as big U.S. and German banks to take on yet more risk than they otherwise might, expecting that the IMF will limit any losses.

The snowball effect, or "moral hazard," bred by these IMF rescues might even have its darkly comic side, were the damage to hundreds of millions of people less devastating. These folks at the IMF just don't want to learn. In 1997, the IMF stepped up with an $18 billion bailout for Thailand, and told the world all would be well. Then the IMF threw $43 billion into Indonesia, saying "Problem solved." It then ran through the same script to the tune of a $57 billion bailout for South Korea, followed by $23 billion for Russia. By late 1998, what the world had to show for this run of bailouts totaling $143 billion was a spiral of competitive currency debasement in emerging markets, blitzed economies in Thailand and South Korea, collapse and bloodshed in Indonesia, more economic collapse in Russia, fear and trembling in the markets of Latin America, and the prospect of world growth rates dropping in 1999 to 2 percent, or less than half what the IMF had been predicting a year before it began dictating policy to assorted emerging markets.

Threats on this scale can go beyond the powers of individual governments to easily fight off—especially in emerging markets still struggling to establish credibility. Probably there is room to incorporate in this *Index* some measure of how vulnerable countries are to systemic, global problems—such as the competitive devaluations that followed on IMF urgings to tinker with Asian exchange rates. Two of the hardest-hit countries, for example, Thailand and Malaysia, earned healthy rankings of 28 in this year's *Index.* That places them above, say, Spain or even Sweden, although both Thailand and Malaysia in the past year have clearly proved far worse places for investment.

It might be tempting to conclude that if a country can rank that high, but within the year be battling economic collapse, then there is small use to tracking individual rankings of economic freedom. I would argue the opposite. The jury is still out, for example, on how well and quickly Asia's stricken economies might recover. Meanwhile, we have what may well be passing blips, such as India's bragging up the benefits of its relative immunity to global contagion. What some of India's more forward-looking politicians will admit is that to achieve this insulation from crisis, India has had to suffer decades of disconnect from the world economy. This has probably cost India far more in terms of growth, and net wealth, than could have been lost even in a stretch of serious crisis. As it is, India's 950 million people have never been given the choice of having greater wealth—either to enjoy or to lose.

The causes and potential cures for the global economic crises of 1997 and 1998 are still matters of huge and complex debate. In navigating the reefs, investors and policymakers need the best guides they can find. Whether we look back across centuries of experience to the theories set forth in *The Wealth of Nations* or simply listen to the tale of a North Korean refugee, there is still every reason to believe that free markets provide the best climate for prosperity. The measures provided by this *Index* may be for the moment signposts in a storm, but they still tell us much about whether in the long run a country is headed for ruin or riches.

## 5

Signposts for the Foreign Investor: Economic Indicators for OECD and Select Developing Countries

by Brett D. Schaefer

As the economies of the world become more interdependent, businesses look increasingly to foreign countries as profitable destinations for investment. The Asian financial crisis shows, however, that international investment often is very risky. The prudent investor, therefore, undertakes careful research to identify countries that offer the most promise with the least risk. The 1999 *Index of Economic Freedom* is an invaluable resource of historical data that can illustrate economic trends.

The 1999 *Index of Economic Freedom* offers businesses an objective comparison of the economic environment in 161 countries. All are judged by the same criteria, allowing businesses to decide which countries might best suit their goals. The *Index* also indicates policies that are likely to lead to future economic growth. A study in Chapter 1 that examines the growth rates of real per capita gross domestic product (GDP) between 1980 and 1993 for 138 countries shows that policies supporting economic freedom correlate positively with increased economic growth. Countries ranked economically "free" experienced an average annual per capita GDP growth rate of 2.88

percent for that period, while countries ranked economically "repressed" experienced an annual per capita GDP growth rate of -1.44 percent. The bottom line: Increases in economic freedom correspond to increases in per capita wealth.

Analysis also indicates that increased economic freedom, as measured by the *Index,* improves the possibility of increased domestic consumption for exports and increased flows of foreign direct investment. Last year, Heritage economists conducted statistical analyses to determine whether a relationship exists between the amount of U.S. exports to and foreign direct investment in certain countries and the levels of economic freedom in

Table 5.1

Taxation Data for OECD Countries

	1999 *Index of Economic Freedom* Score	Tax Revenues as a Share of GDP 1991-96 *	Taxes on Income, Profit, and Capital Gains as a Share of Government Revenue 1991-96 **	Taxes on International Trade as a Share of Government Revenue 1991-96 **
Australia	2.10	22.17%	71.60%	3.15%
Austria	2.15	32.88	21.96	1.18
Belgium	2.10	42.58	34.87	0.00
Canada	2.10	18.64	55.69	2.63
Czech Republic	2.05	36.76	17.29	3.82
Denmark	2.25	34.41	44.90	0.06
Finland	2.25	28.58	32.73	0.73
France	2.50	37.87	19.05	0.00
Germany	2.30	29.26	16.53	0.00
Greece	2.90	18.99	33.01	0.11
Hungary	2.90	n/a	n/a	n/a
Iceland	2.30	25.58	24.34	5.18
Ireland	1.95	34.08	41.27	5.93
Italy	2.50	39.29	36.85	0.01
Japan	2.05	18.20	45.78	1.20
Korea	2.40	16.68	35.55	6.83
Luxembourg	1.95	40.59	33.93	0.00
Mexico	3.15	13.32	37.05	6.51
Netherlands	2.15	44.35	30.62	0.00
New Zealand	1.75	31.90	65.67	2.20
Norway	2.35	31.83	20.87	0.61
Poland	2.95	36.61	29.99	7.61
Portugal	2.55	31.25	27.90	0.18
Spain	2.50	29.09	33.47	0.42
Sweden	2.45	33.63	10.55	0.71
Switzerland	1.85	20.48	15.21	6.50
Turkey	2.80	13.86	44.84	3.85
United Kingdom	1.95	32.94	38.35	0.07
United States	1.90	18.31	55.92	1.46

Notes: * Poland data missing for 1991, 1992, and 1993; Czech Republic data missing for 1991 and 1992; Japan data missing for 1994, 1995, and 1996; Canada, Ireland and Spain data missing for 1995 and 1996; Austria, Belgium, Denmark, Finland, Greece, Iceland, Luxembourg, Mexico, Norway, Portugal, Switzerland, United Kingdom data missing for 1996.
** Poland data missing for 1991, 1992, and 1993; Czech Republic data missing for 1991 and 1992; Japan data missing for 1994, 1995, and 1996; Germany data missing for 1994 and 1996; Belgium, Canada, Ireland and Spain data missing for 1995 and 1996; Austria, Denmark, Finland, Greece, Iceland, Luxembourg, Mexico, Norway, Portugal, Switzerland, and the United Kingdom data missing for 1996.
Source: *1998 World Development Indicators*, World Bank.

those countries.[1] The analysis shows a statistically significant association between lower *Index* scores (indicating a higher level of economic freedom) and greater amounts of U.S. exports and higher levels of U.S. direct foreign investment.[2] This indicates, therefore, that investors can use the *Index* as a guide when seeking comparatively low-risk, profitable destinations for capital and strong, stable markets for goods and services.

This chapter presents historical data on member countries of the Organization for Economic Cooperation and Development (OECD) because they are the destinations for the majority of global investment.[3] Likewise, five developing countries (referred to collectively as the "Big 5"— Brazil, China, India, Indonesia, and Russia) were selected because they have been the largest recipients of foreign investment in the developing world over the past decade. Although the recent financial crises have affected foreign investment negatively, the Big 5 are likely to be the destination of the

lion's share of investment flowing to the developing world once again after the crises subside.

The following data present vital indicators or "signposts" that investors can use to determine where to invest in the future. The data are grouped into eight categories of economic indicators that are considered frequently by international investors. Four of the categories relate specifically to OECD countries, and four to the Big 5. Each category includes several distinct groups of data presented in tabular format with accompanying descriptions.[4] In many cases, the information is presented as a percentage of per capita GDP to aid in country comparisons.

Economic Indicators for OECD Countries

The leading economic indicators for OECD member countries fall within four general categories.

Table 5.2

Government Interference in the Economy for OECD Countries

	1999 Index of Economic Freedom Score	Government Consumption as a Share of GDP 1991-96*	Annual Growth in Government Consumption 1991–96*	Government Expenditure as a Share of GDP 1991–96**	Annual Growth in Government Expenditure 1991–96**	Subsidies and Other Current Transfers as a Share of Government Expenditure 1991–96***
Australia	2.10	18.23%	-1.03%	27.50%	0.81%	66.04%
Austria	2.15	19.79	1.66	40.39	2.32	57.94
Belgium	2.10	14.60	0.52	49.93	-0.01	57.66
Canada	2.10	20.99	-2.40	25.08	-0.41	60.85
Czech Republic	2.05	21.17	4.22	40.50	-3.76	67.22
Denmark	2.25	25.60	-0.26	42.93	1.56	63.04
Finland	2.25	23.11	-1.72	42.36	3.49	70.28
France	2.50	19.15	1.39	45.94	1.42	64.34
Germany	2.30	19.75	0.05	33.07	2.30	58.15
Greece	2.90	14.00	-0.42	32.96	-0.88	22.14
Hungary	2.90	11.52	-0.07	n/a	n/a	n/a
Iceland	2.30	20.46	1.09	33.06	-0.66	29.78
Ireland	1.95	15.45	-1.46	40.91	-0.50	58.09
Italy	2.50	17.28	-1.89	50.53	0.74	56.39
Japan	2.05	9.40	2.21	22.11	5.68	n/a
Korea	2.40	10.57	0.77	17.38	2.45	49.21
Luxembourg	1.95	12.99	-0.24	42.38	0.18	66.13
Mexico	3.15	4.88	1.67	14.97	1.64	33.09
Netherlands	2.15	14.51	-0.27	51.59	-1.47	71.81
New Zealand	1.75	15.71	-4.17	35.88	-4.94	39.31
Norway	2.35	21.55	-0.13	41.53	-1.80	69.38
Poland	2.95	20.86	-5.27	43.04	-2.30	60.45
Portugal	2.55	17.87	0.78	44.01	0.77	34.10
Spain	2.50	16.87	0.74	37.09	3.36	64.85
Sweden	2.45	27.02	-0.99	47.47	2.03	71.93
Switzerland	1.85	15.30	-0.34	25.61	3.36	62.36
Turkey	2.80	12.04	-1.08	23.11	5.68	31.06
United Kingdom	1.95	21.71	-0.35	41.87	1.33	56.40
United States	1.90	16.77	-2.90	23.40	-2.21	56.23

Notes: * Australia, Austria, Belgium, Canada, France, Germany, Greece, Ireland, Italy, Japan, Luxembourg, Mexico, Netherlands, New Zealand, Norway, Portugal, Spain, Switzerland, United Kingdom, and United States data missing for 1996.
** Poland data missing 1991, 1992, and 1993; Czech Republic data missing 1991 and 1992; Japan data missing 1994, 1995, and 1996; Canada, Ireland, and Spain data missing 1995 and 1996; Austria, Belgium, Denmark, Finland, Greece, Iceland, Luxembourg, Mexico, Norway, Portugal, Switzerland, and United Kingdom data missing 1996.
*** Poland data missing 1991, 1992, and 1993; Czech Republic data missing 1991 and 1992; Canada data from 1991 only; Ireland and Spain data missing 1995 and 1996; Austria, Belgium, Denmark, Finland, Greece, Iceland, Luxembourg, Mexico, Norway, Portugal, Switzerland, and United Kingdom data missing 1996.
Source: *1998 World Development Indicators*, World Bank.

Category 1: Taxation

Taxation is an impediment to investment, affecting nearly all facets of potential investment. It influences decisions over where and how much to invest and what form that investment should take. Investors need to examine the differences in taxation among countries.

Tax Revenue. Includes net taxes on citizens and business activity within the country or at the borders. Also includes interest and penalties collected on non- or late payment of taxes. In relation to GDP, taxation level is an impartial representation of the size of the state sector in the economy and its intrusion into the market.

Taxes on Income, Profit, and Capital Gains. Assessments on the reported or estimated net income of individuals, business profits, and capital gains (the difference between an asset's purchase and selling prices). Amount includes social security contributions after deductions and personal

exemptions; internal government payments are excluded. Presented as a percentage of total government revenue, demonstrating government's reliance on this source of income. Heavy government reliance on income, profit, and capital gains discourages investment by reducing returns on investments.

Taxes on International Trade. Includes import and export duties, profits of export or import monopolies, and profits and taxes earned in foreign exchange transactions. Presented as a percentage of total government revenue, demonstrating reliance on this source of income.

Category 2: Government Intervention in the Economy

Large-scale government intervention in the economy is detrimental to growth and long-term economic health. Through confiscation and redirection of resources through taxation,

Table 5.3

Economic Indicators for OECD Countries

	1999 Index of Economic Freedom Score	Trade as a Percentage of GDP 1995 *	Annual Growth in Exports of Goods and Services 1991–96 **	Annual Growth in Imports of Goods and Services 1991–96 **	Gross Domestic Savings as a Share of GDP 1991–96 ***	Average Interest Rate Spread 1991–96 ****	Annual Consumer Price Inflation 1991–96	Private Consumption as a Share of GDP 1991–96 ***
Australia	2.10	41.66%	7.91%	8.48%	20.58%	5.93	2.53%	61.19
Austria	2.15	78.22	4.26	4.85	24.40	n/a	3.01	55.82
Belgium	2.10	140.39	4.56	4.34	22.48	5.40	2.38	62.92
Canada	2.10	73.07	8.43	6.91	18.82	1.28	2.15	60.19
Czech Republic	2.05	116.91	n/a	n/a	25.81	6.17	n/a	53.02
Denmark	2.25	63.34	3.88	4.45	21.47	5.21	1.99	52.85
Finland	2.25	68.20	7.81	3.16	20.99	4.52	1.91	55.70
France	2.50	44.57	3.45	2.01	20.57	4.28	2.19	60.28
Germany	2.30	46.43	n/a	n/a	22.94	6.38	3.20	57.31
Greece	2.90	43.36	4.46	4.45	4.96	8.35	12.97	81.07
Hungary	2.90	79.36	0.50	2.53	18.52	7.34	25.05	69.96
Iceland	2.30	67.49	1.33	-0.59	18.42	7.38	3.39	61.19
Ireland	1.95	134.08	11.81	7.84	26.69	6.30	2.38	57.86
Italy	2.50	50.94	7.41	3.14	20.72	6.43	4.85	62.01
Japan	2.05	17.32	3.96	4.14	31.91	2.63	1.17	58.69
Korea	2.40	68.75	14.79	14.92	35.51	0.25	5.99	53.93
Luxembourg	1.95	172.32	4.59	2.94	25.05	2.06	2.56	61.66
Mexico	3.15	42.34	8.29	4.63	19.75	n/a	20.71	74.48
Netherlands	2.15	100.16	4.53	3.66	25.42	5.80	2.62	60.06
New Zealand	1.75	58.70	6.48	6.93	21.97	4.13	2.11	62.32
Norway	2.35	71.99	5.36	3.15	24.99	3.77	2.19	53.80
Poland	2.95	49.07	8.95	17.02	17.51	2.62	39.85	61.63
Portugal	2.55	73.86	5.76	6.76	16.25	6.49	6.54	66.01
Spain	2.50	46.94	9.81	6.81	20.45	2.97	4.90	62.68
Sweden	2.45	73.21	7.16	3.99	18.91	6.23	3.58	53.84
Switzerland	1.85	68.14	1.80	2.20	n/a	2.52	2.78	n/a
Turkey	2.80	48.99	11.21	11.36	20.68	n/a	79.48	67.28
United Kingdom	1.95	57.75	4.94	3.87	14.56	2.08	3.25	63.81
United States	1.90	24.12	6.99	7.26	15.44	n/a	3.09	67.79

Notes: * Czech Republic, Hungary, Korea, Mexico, Norway, Poland, Sweden, Switzerland and Turkey data from 1996.
** Australia, Belgium, Greece, Iceland, Ireland, Luxembourg, Netherlands, and Norway missing data from 1996.
*** Norway, Luxembourg, and the United Kingdom data from 1991 only; Portugal data from 1994, 1995, and 1996; Greece data missing 1995 and 1996; Australia, Austria, Belgium, Canada, Denmark, Finland, France, Germany, Iceland, Ireland, Italy, Japan, Netherlands, New Zealand, Spain, Sweden, and the United States missing data from 1996.
****Australia data from 1991 only; Czech Republic data missing 1991 and 1992; Belgium and Hungary data missing 1996.
Source: *1998 World Development Indicators*, World Bank..

governments exert tremendous influence over economic conditions in their respective economies. The size of government has a direct impact on all sectors of the economy and therefore should be considered carefully by investors before committing their resources.

Government Consumption. Includes all current expenditures on goods and services—as well as capital expenditures on national defense and security—by all levels of government, excluding most state-owned enterprises.

Government Expenditure. Includes current and capital expenditures that are not reimbursed, and excludes government lending, repayment to the government, or government acquisition of equity for public policy purposes.

Subsidies and Current Transfers. Includes all one-way current account transfers to private and public enterprises as well as costs incurred in departmental enterprise sales to the public.

Category 3: Key Economic Indicators

A number of factors affect the domestic economy and its relation to the global economy. Some influence economic stability and growth; others reflect the domestic economy's integration into, and its reliance on, the global trading system. Five characteristics of particular interest to investors are listed.

Trade. The sum of exports and imports of goods and services. The level of trade indirectly reflects domestic restrictions on international trade—typically in inverse proportion to the level of trade. It also reflects the domestic economy's competitiveness on the global stage.

Gross Domestic Savings. Gross domestic savings are the difference between GDP and total consumption. Domestic savings represent a potential pool of capital for financing all types of productive economic activity and, as such, bolster stable economic growth. The domestic savings

44

Table 5.4

Investment Data for OECD Countries

	1999 Index of Economic Freedom Score	Change in Direct Investment Inflows as a Percentage of GDP 1985–95	Change in Direct Investment Outflows as a Percentage of GDP 1985–95	Percentage Change in Inward Direct Investment Position 1984–94	Percentage Change in Outward Direct Investment Position 1984–94	Average Gross Domestic Investment as a Percentage of GDP 1991–96 *
Australia	2.10	-0.52	-1.65	n/a	n/a	20.98
Austria	2.15	1.44	0.13	300.00	729.64	24.09
Belgium	2.10	3.56	1.26	n/a	n/a	18.26
Canada	2.10	0.39	0.34	89.75	153.75	18.71
Czech Republic	2.05	n/a	n/a	n/a	n/a	26.34
Denmark	2.25	0.59	0.85	n/a	n/a	15.47
Finland	2.25	0.48	1.68	531.96	723.67	16.81
France	2.50	0.95	1.13	n/a	n/a	18.89
Germany	2.30	-0.25	0.17	754.54	594.08	22.56
Greece	2.90	n/a	n/a	n/a	n/a	15.16
Hungary	2.90	n/a	n/a	n/a	n/a	21.57
Iceland	2.30	-0.19	0.0	n/a	n/a	16.44
Ireland	1.95	2.6	n/a	n/a	n/a	15.28
Italy	2.50	0.28	0.01	247.56	516.36	18.45
Japan	2.05	0.0	-0.22	318.47	573.60	29.96
Korea	2.40	n/a	n/a	n/a	2069.42	36.98
Luxembourg	1.95	3.56	1.26	n/a	n/a	26.89
Mexico	3.15	-0.04	n/a	n/a	n/a	21.64
Netherlands	2.15	-0.89	0.26	390.54	272.11	19.82
New Zealand	1.75	2.85	2.02	n/a	n/a	19.46
Norway	2.35	0.84	1.27	n/a	n/a	16.91
Poland	2.95	n/a	n/a	n/a	n/a	17.48
Portugal	2.55	-0.12	0.75	n/a	n/a	24.59
Spain	2.50	-0.39	0.63	1252.26	652.86	21.63
Sweden	2.45	1.36	-1.19	n/a	n/a	15.45
Switzerland	1.85	-0.56	2.86	467.4	465.3	n/a
Turkey	2.80	0.14	n/a	n/a	n/a	24.15
United Kingdom	1.95	1.32	0.75	264.03	230.32	15.71
United States	1.90	0.3	0.74	203.38	209.01	16.54

Sources: World Bank, *1997 World Development Indicators on CD-ROM*; The Organization for Economic Cooperation and Development, *International Direct Investment Statistics Yearbook, 1997*.
* Norway, Luxembourg, and the United Kingdom data from 1991 only; Portugal data missing 1994, 1995, and 1996; Greece data missing 1995 and 1996; Australia, Austria, Belgium, Canada, Denmark, Finland, France, Germany, Iceland, Ireland, Italy, Japan, Netherlands, New Zealand, Spain, Sweden, and the United States missing data from 1996.

level also indicates whether a country's population possesses a positive impression of its country's economic prospects.

Interest Rate Spread. The interest rate charged by banks on loans minus the interest rate paid by commercial or similar banks for demand, time, or savings deposits. The interest rate spread indirectly represents confidence in the economy: Higher spreads indicate anticipation of inflation or similar government-induced costs of doing business. Investors also are interested in the interest rate spread if they are likely to seek financing in the domestic economy.

Inflation. Based on a consumer price index calculated by the World Bank. Consumer price indices reflect fluctuations in the cost of acquiring a set basket of goods and services. Inflation measured by consumer price fluctuations seldom is reliable for inter-country comparisons but offers insight into domestic economies. High rates of inflation are undesirable.

Private Consumption. Based on the market value of all goods and services, including durable products (such as cars, washing machines, and home computers) purchased or received as income in kind by households and nonprofit institutions. Includes imputed rent for owner-occupied dwellings but excludes purchases of dwellings. Also includes any statistical discrepancy in the use of resources.

Category 4: Investment Data

Investment strengthens an economy by providing resources for new ventures, overhauling inventories and assets, and supporting current businesses. A strong economy attracts investment because of the opportunities for return on investment and profit. Investment trends, therefore, can serve as an indicator of economic stability and strength. In addition, the presence of other investments lends an air of stability to an economy and indicates that

Table 5.5

Investment Data for the Big 5 Developing Countries

	1999 Index of Economic Freedom Score	Annual Increase in Net Private Capital Flows 1991–96	Annual Increase in Portfolio Investment (Bonds plus Equity) 1991–96	Official Development Assistance as a Percentage of GNP 1991–96	Net Inflows of Foreign Direct Investment as a Percentage of GDP 1991–96	Gross Domestic Investment as a Percentage of GDP 1991–96
Brazil	3.25	63.30%	51.10	0.04%	0.62	20.29
China	3.80	58.91	98.34	0.58	4.42	39.50
India	3.70	44.41	1286.47	0.76	0.34	24.19
Indonesia	2.95	137.81	181.26	1.11	1.76	29.92
Russia *	3.45	433.94	234.44	0.02	0.22	28.14

Note: * Portfolio Investment data 1994 to 1996
Sources: International Finance Corporation, *Emerging Markets Factbook 1998;* World Bank, *1997 World Development Indicators on CD-ROM.*

Table 5.6

Currency Stability for the Big 5 Developing Countries

	1999 Index of Economic Freedom Score	Consumer Price Inflation 1991–96	Annual Growth In Monetary Supply (M2) as a Share of GDP 1991–96	Monetary Supply (M2) as a Share of GDP 1996	Annual Change in Currency Exchange Rates to the US$ 1992–97
Brazil	3.25	905.32%	10.82%	26.38%	-54.99%
China	3.80	12.32	5.59	100.92	-10.75
India	3.70	10.24	1.11	45.44	-9.94
Indonesia	2.95	8.76	4.98	46.90	-11.28
Russia *	3.45	n/a	1.73	14.24	-11.90

Note: * Exchange rate data from 1996 and 1997, M2 data from 1994 to 1996.
Sources: International Finance Corporation, *Emerging Markets Factbook 1998;* World Bank, *1997 World Development Indicators on CD-ROM;* International Monetary Fund, *International Financial Statistics,* June 1997.

profitable opportunities exist.

Direct Investment Inflows. Indicates new real capital or financial assets invested, with a minimum of 10 percent equity ownership, in the domestic economy by foreign individuals or firms.

Direct Investment Outflows. Indicates new real capital or financial assets invested in foreign economies by individuals or firms.

Direct Investment Position. A measure of the net value of direct investment. Presented as a percentage change in value over time for both inflows and outflows. Significant changes in the flows reflect investor confidence in the domestic economy.

Gross Domestic Investment. Includes outlays to increase fixed assets (such as improvements in property, industrial capital, infrastructure, or buildings) and net changes in inventories.

Economic Indicators for the Big 5 Developing Countries[5]

The second four economic indicators apply to the Big 5 developing countries.

Category 1: Investment Data

Investment data for developing countries generally are not as accurate or readily available as they are for OECD countries. The manner and type of investment also are different. For example, OECD countries typically are donating development assistance, not receiving it. As a result, different groups of investment data are examined for the Big 5 countries. Table 5.5 presents data on six different aspects of investment:

Investment. Net total investment in the economy.

Net Private Capital Flows. Includes all private flows as well as debt flows from commercial bank

Table 5.7

Stock Market Performance for the Big 5 Developing Countries

	1999 *Index of Economic Freedom* Score	Annual Growth in Market Capitalization 1992–1997	Market Capitalization in US$ Millions 1997	Annual Growth in the Number of Domestic Companies Listed 1992–97	Number of Domestic Companies Listed 1997	Annual Growth in World Value Traded 1992–97	World Value Traded US$ Millions 1997
Brazil	3.25	50.55	255,478	-1.04	536	73.13	203,260
China	3.80	75.61	206,366	86.12	764	138.82	369,574
India	3.70	16.31	128,466	16.69	5,843	35.55	53,954
Indonesia	2.95	58.91	91,016	12.87	282	67.66	41,650
Russia	3.45	2286.30	128,207	80.26	208	354.26	16,362

Note: Russia world value traded from 1994–97.
Source: International Finance Corporation, *Emerging Markets Factbook 1998.*

Table 5.8

Demographic Trends for the Big 5 Developing Countries

	1999 *Index of Economic Freedom* Score	Population in Millions 1996	Urban Population 1996	Labor Force as a % of Population 1994	Labor Force in the Industrial Sector, 1994	Life Expectancy at Birth 1996	Literacy Rate 1995
Brazil	3.25	161	79%	44.72%	23%	67	83%
China	3.80	1,215	31	59.09	15	70	81
India	3.70	945	27	43.17	16	63	52
Indonesia	2.95	197	36	46.19	14	65	84
Russia	3.45	148	76	52.70	42	66	81

Note: Russian Literacy Rate is for 1994.
Sources: United Nations Development Program, *Human Development Report 1997*; World Bank, *1998 World Development Indicators* and *1998 World Bank Atlas.*

lending, bonds, and other private credit sources. Also includes foreign direct and portfolio equity investment.

Portfolio Investment. Includes the sum of country funds, depository receipts, direct foreign purchases of shares, and foreign-held bonds. Portfolio includes privately held bonds, both publicly guaranteed and non-guaranteed.

Official Development Assistance. Includes all disbursements of technical cooperation and assistance, loans, and grants (with a grant element of more than 25 percent) made bilaterally or through multilateral development agencies on concessional terms to promote economic development and welfare. High levels generally indicate a repressed economy and governmental resistance to market reform.

Foreign Direct Investment. A net figure of foreign acquisitions of 10 percent or more of voting stock in a business. Includes long- and short-term capital listed in the national balance of payments, equity investment, and reinvestment of earnings.

Gross Domestic Investment. Includes outlays to increase fixed assets, such as improvements in property, industrial capital, infrastructure, buildings, and net changes in inventories. High domestic investment indicates a commitment to maintain and improve domestic infrastructure (a key element for growth) as well as confidence in the economy by domestic businesses that increase inventories.

Category 2: Currency Stability

Investors often must use local currencies. If currencies lose value rapidly or fluctuate wildly, investors may suffer great losses. A strong currency indicates a healthy economy; a weak or declining currency raises import prices, deters foreign investment, lowers standards of living, and undermines business confidence. Investors place a high value on currency stability.[6] Table 5.6 presents three methods of measuring currency stability:

Inflation. Based on a consumer price index calculated by the World Bank. Consumer price indices reflect fluctuations in the cost of acquiring a set basket of goods and services. Inflation measured by consumer price fluctuations seldom is reliable for inter-country comparisons but can offer insight into domestic economies. High rates of inflation are undesirable.

Monetary Supply. Includes the amount of paper money outside banks, private demand deposits, current savings, and private foreign currency deposits. Presented both as an annual growth figure from 1991 to 1996 and as a percent of GDP in 1996. The amount of money in circulation has a direct impact on the value of a currency. Countries often instigate inflation by printing currency in excess of demand (growth in the economy or acquisition by foreign holders). Economists commonly refer to this grouping as "M2." Although growth in M2 is a necessary byproduct of economic growth and currency strength, it must correspond with economic growth. Rapid growth in M2 more often is a sign of poor economic management.

Exchange Rate versus the Dollar. Value fluctuations against the U.S. dollar are useful because most international transactions and contracts are valued in dollar terms. The stability of the dollar makes it a convenient benchmark against which to measure other currencies.

Category 3: Stock Market Performance

Many investments require the long-term commitment of resources. Investors may be unwilling to allocate capital to lengthy ventures, particularly in risky developing countries. Stock markets provide investors with the opportunity for short-term investments, allowing assets to be acquired quickly and abandoned just as quickly. They also provide vitally needed capital for long-term investments. Spurred by broad-based market liberalization, developing country stock markets in particular have grown in recent years. Three indicators are listed in this category, in performance between 1992 and 1997 and the 1997 value for perspective (see Table 5.7).

Market Capitalization. The price of the share multiplied by the number of shares outstanding. This represents the overall size and value of the stock market.

Number of Domestic Companies Listed. The number of companies that have offered and traded shares publicly on the market. The number of companies typically indicates the sophistication and breadth of the market in the local economy.

World Value Traded. The value traded refers to the total value of shares traded globally.

Category 4: Demographic Trends

It is impossible to overstate the importance of population as a source of labor and as a market for goods and services. Aspects of population that affect the labor force are presented. Level of education, for example, affects the efficiency of the work force, while increasing urbanization and distribution of employment define the size of the available labor force. Developed countries generally share such traits as low population growth, high literacy and educational achievement, better health with longer life spans, and predominantly urban populations. The populations of developing countries, however, have a broader range of characteristics that usually are quite different from those of developed countries. Therefore, six sets of demographic data that may be of particular interest to investors are presented on the Big 5 in Table 5.8.

Population. The 1996 estimated population. Population levels reveal the size of potential domestic markets and labor forces.

Urban Population. The percentage of the total population living in areas considered urban in that country. Advantages in investing in urban areas include access to shipping, resources, and labor.

Labor Force. The percentage of the population economically active, including both the employed and unemployed. This category includes people who have the potential to supply labor for production.

Labor Force in the Industrial Sector. The percentage of the labor force involved in the industrial sector. Provides insight into both the overall employment structure and the level of industrialization. Opportunities for investment in the industrial sector in developing countries include relatively cheaper labor, looser environmental regulations, and opportunities to purchase former state industries.

Life Expectancy. The number of years an infant can be expected to live under the health conditions of the year of his or her birth. Directly reflects the general population's level of health. Healthy populations are more productive, have fewer absences due to illness, are more efficient, and remain in the work force longer.

Literacy Rate. The percentage of the adult population (15 years of age and older) that is functionally literate. Literacy is an indirect indicator of education; greater levels of education generally make it easier for workers to learn new skills and be more productive.

Notes

[1]   U.S. exports and foreign direct investment position were chosen because the United States is the world's largest exporter and source of investment.

[2]   Kim R. Holmes and Brett D. Schaefer, "What Makes Economies Grow?" *Chief Executive Magazine*, April 1998, pp. 36–41. A description of the methodology used in this analysis is available on request.

[3]   The member countries of the OECD are Australia, Austria, Belgium, Canada, Czech Republic, Denmark, Finland, France, Germany, Greece, Hungary, Iceland, Ireland, Italy, Japan, Luxembourg, Mexico, the Netherlands, New Zealand, Norway, Poland, Portugal, South Korea, Spain, Sweden, Switzerland, Turkey, the United Kingdom, and the United States.

[4]   Descriptions based on definitions provided by source materials. Tables 5.1–5.7 contain columns of percentage-change data for five-year periods (1991 to 1996) where available. These data are average percentage changes for these time periods. Technical explanations of these calculations are available on request.

[5]   The recent financial crises in Asia and Russia have influenced the investment climate in the Big 5 dramatically—particularly in Russia and Indonesia. Although not affecting Brazil, China, and India to the same extent, the crises have had a detrimental impact on these economies. Unfortunately, the sources used for this chapter have not yet published data reflecting the crisis. Although other sources do contain more recent information, the data are not verified and could prove unreliable.

[6]   A weakening currency does benefit some foreign investors, however. Those producing goods for export may realize an advantage through relatively lower cost, thereby increasing their international competitiveness. Most exporters, however, rely on some imports whose cost will rise if the currency is weak, offsetting some benefits of lower domestic cost.

## 6

Methodology: Factors of the *Index* of *Economic Freedom*

by Bryan T. Johnson

Since 1995, the *Index of Economic Freedom* has offered the international community an in-depth examination of the factors that contribute most directly to a country's level of economic freedom and prosperity. As the first-ever-published comprehensive study of economic freedom, the *Index* in 1995 defined the method by which economic freedom and growth could be measured in such vastly different places as Hong Kong and Cuba, and in every country in between. Today, other studies are available that analyze such issues as trade or government intervention in the economy.[1] The *Index,* however, also analyzes such critical economic determinants as:

- **Corruption** in the judiciary, customs service, and government bureaucracy;
- **Non-tariff barriers** such as import bans and quotas, strict labeling and licensing requirements, and burdensome health, safety, and environmental regulations;
- **Taxation** such as capital gains, value-added, and payroll;
- **Rule of law,** efficiency within the judiciary, and the ability to enforce contracts;
- **Regulatory burdens** on business;
- **Restrictions on banks** regarding financial services, such as selling securities and insurance;
- **Labor market regulations,** such as established work weeks and mandatory separation pay; and
- **Black market activities,** including smuggling, piracy of intellectual property rights, and black market labor and provision of services.

Analyzing economic freedom on an annual basis is important. It permits the immediate inclusion of the most recent data available on a country-by-country basis. Not surprisingly, changes in government policy occur at an alarming rate in most less-developed countries. Some countries of the former Soviet Union, for example, make major economic policy reversals on an almost daily basis. Studies that are not published annually rely on information that may be grossly out of date by the time it is analyzed and published; consequently, such studies cannot track yearly trends for individual countries in important economic determinants like trade policy and regulation. The annual *Index of Economic Freedom* enables readers to see how recent changes may affect a country's overall level of economic freedom. For this fifth edition, five new countries have been added—Equatorial Guinea, Guinea-Bissau, Mauritius, Qatar, and Togo—to bring the total number of countries studied to 161.

Measuring Economic Freedom

The concept of economic freedom has been the subject of intense debate for centuries, but particularly since the 18th century and the emergence of the modern field of economics. The dictionary defines *freedom* as the "absence of necessity, coercion, or constraint on choice or action" and *economic* as "of, relating to, or based on the production, distribution, and consumption of goods and services."[2] Although leading economists and political theorists only now are reaching consensus on this important concept, economic freedom can be defined as the *absence of government coercion or constraint on the production, distribution, or consumption of goods and services.*

Governments have placed various constraints on economic activity throughout history; some of these constraints have been greater than others. Generally, these constraints can be measured. Because economic freedom is the degree to which individuals are free to produce, distribute, and consume goods and services, one way to measure it is to study the number of constraints a government has imposed. Government policies and conditions that either maximize or restrict personal economic choices can be examined objectively.

The purpose of the *Index of Economic Freedom* is to go one step further and explain the reason that some countries are rich today while others remain poor, even after years of development assistance from the international community. To do this, the *Index* has studied 50 independent economic variables to rate the level of economic freedom in each country. The variables fall into 10 broad

categories, or "factors," of economic freedom: trade policy, taxation, government intervention in the economy, monetary policy, foreign investment, banking, wage and price controls, property rights, regulation, and black market activity. (These factors and their respective variables will be discussed more fully later in this chapter.)

Inputs vs. Outputs. Most *Index* factors should be considered as inputs in the economic freedom equation; in other words, they are factors that measure the governmental policies that either maximize or restrict economic freedom. Such factors as trade policy and monetary policy do not represent outputs in the economic freedom equation;[3] that is, they do not measure the results or consequences of policies that are economically free or unfree as other studies do.[4] Instead, such factors as trade policy and monetary policy measure the specific restriction on economic activity. Studies that measure outputs often focus more on explaining the changes in economic growth rates than on understanding and describing the political, economic, and social environment necessary for economic activity. They measure economic freedom by looking at such outputs as the ability of a country's citizens to put their money in overseas bank accounts or the difference between a country's official currency exchange rate and its black market exchange rate. These elements are not inputs in determining economic freedom; they are not governmental policies. Instead, they are behavioral adaptations to a government's policies, or outputs by people and companies.

Attempting to measure economic freedom by analyzing outputs confuses context with content. The *Index of Economic Freedom* ranks the relative degree to which countries achieve economic freedom; in other words, it indicates the best context (or set of institutional inputs) for economic growth. Heritage analysts believe the activity from analyzing such inputs will lead more readily to superior levels of economic prosperity than economic activity that takes place in less free environments.

Weighting. The *Index of Economic Freedom* treats the 10 factors as equally important to the level of economic freedom in any country. Thus, to determine an overall score, the factors are weighted equally. This approach is the fairest and most consistent with the purpose of the *Index:* to produce a score of the institutional environment for economic activity in every country. Although other studies maintain that certain components are more important than others to the explanation of economic growth, they do not provide sufficient scientific support for their conclusions.[5] Other studies are designed primarily to explain changes in economic growth rates over time. By contrast, the *Index* is designed to analyze the institutional environment necessary for growth to occur in the first place.

The authors and editors of The Heritage Foundation/Wall Street Journal 1999 *Index of Economic Freedom* do not believe it is possible at this stage of academic research to know with a high degree of certainty which factors are more important than others. What *is* known is that, for a country to achieve long-term growth and economic well-being, it must perform well in all the factors evaluated in the *Index*'s methodology.

Heritage economists will continue to develop a statistical and scientifically supportable method for determining which factors play a larger role in economic freedom and how much weight each one deserves in relation to the others. Once leading economists have established and reviewed such statistical relationships, these relationships will be incorporated in the grading process for future editions of the *Index*. Until that time, however, the authors of the *Index* believe the most objective way to grade economic freedom is to weigh all factors of economic freedom equally.

The Grading Scale. Each country in the *Index* receives an overall economic freedom score based on the average of the 10 individual factor scores. Each factor is scored according to a grading scale unique for that factor. The scales run from 1 to 5: A score of 1 signifies a variable that is the most conducive to economic freedom, while a score of 5 signifies one that is the least conducive. In other words, factors rated with a 1 are variables of the most free economies, and factors rated with a 5 are variables of least free economies. In addition, each score is followed by a plus sign (+), a minus sign (–), or the word "Stable." This additional information indicates, respectively, whether the factor of economic freedom is improving, is getting worse, or has stayed the same compared with the country's score last year. Finally, the factors are added and averaged, and an overall

score is assigned and used to rank the countries.

The four broad rankings of economic freedom for the countries are:

- **Free:** Countries having an average overall score of 1.99 or less.
- **Mostly free:** Countries having an average overall score of 2.00 to 2.99.
- **Mostly not free:** Countries having an average overall score of 3.00 to 3.99.
- **Repressed:** Countries having an average overall score of 4.00 or higher.

Previous Scores. The *Index of Economic Freedom* includes a comprehensive listing of the 161 countries with their scores for each of the 10 factors. This year, the country listings include 1996, 1997, 1998, and 1999 overall scores. With this information, the reader can easily discern how rapidly a country has been increasing or reducing its level of economic freedom, or whether it has stayed the same over time.

Transparency. Because the *Index* is based on scientific methodology, it is both transparent and capable of analyzing a wide variety of data. The discussions that follow in this chapter explain the reason that the factor is an important element of economic freedom, how the five levels of economic freedom are broken down and scored for that factor, and what sources are used for its analysis. Thus, scoring is straightforward. If a country's banking system has a score of 3, it displays most of the characteristics spelled out on pp. 61–62 as level 3: There is heavy government influence on its banks, government owns or operates some of its banks, the government maintains strict control of credit, and there are significant barriers to the formation of domestic banks. Similarly, a country receiving a score of 5 in trade policy has an average tariff rate of at least 20 percent or very high non-tariff barriers that, for all practical purposes, close its markets to imports (see p. 55, Trade Policy).

A country must meet most, but not necessarily all, conditions specified for each grade level of a factor. In the banking factor, a country would rate a grade of 2 (which is better than a grade of 3) if its banking system has only some government limits on financial services and deposit insurance and minor barriers to new bank formation. It would receive a 4 (which is worse than a 3) if its banking system is in transition, the government keeps its banks under tight control, some corruption is present, or domestic bank formation is virtually nonexistent.

Period of Study. The 1999 *Index of Economic Freedom* generally examines the period from the last half of 1997 to the first half of 1998. Most of the information within the individual factors for most countries is current as of June 30, 1998. It is important to understand, however, that certain factors are based on historical information. For example, the Monetary Policy factor considers a ten-year average inflation rate. Other factors are current for the year in which the *Index* is published. For example, the Taxation factor considers tax rates that apply to the taxable year 1998 (the year in which the *1999 Index of Economic Freedom* is published).

Because the *Index* is published in December, or six months after the cutoff date for evaluation, there sometimes are major economic events occurring after the cutoff date that are not factored into the scores. In the past, these occurrences have been uncommon and isolated to one region of the world. The Asian financial crisis, for example, erupted after the *1998 Index of Economic Freedom* was ready to go to print. As a result, the impact of the crisis was not measured in last year's edition; instead, it is measured in this year's edition, which covers the time period of July 1, 1997, through June 30, 1998.

This year, a number of significant economic events occurred after the June 30, 1998, cutoff date, as the *Index* was being prepared for press. Although many of these economic events do not affect this year's scores, there are some egregious instances in which scores are likely to have changed had the events occurred during the time frame considered for grading the countries. These instances are discussed in notes to the introductory paragraphs of the specific country profiles. Changes that would have resulted in a changed score are noted. If those policies continue, they will register in the official *Index* ranking next year.

Not all potential score changes are noted in this way; only the most important ones are. The editors had to balance the desire to make reference to these economic changes against the need to meet a publication deadline.

Methodological and Scientific Continuity. Although the discussion of the likely impact of post–June 30 economic crises on *Index* scores is useful, it also highlights a serious methodological consideration. It would have been possible to delay the publication of the 1999 *Index of Economic Freedom* to incorporate new information into the 1999 scores. The result of such a decision, however, would have been neither methodologically sound nor scientifically credible.

One of the *Index*'s greatest contributions over the past five years has been in the establishment of a database of information that tracks the yearly economic conditions of over 100 countries. Indeed, this database serves as a significant research source not only for Heritage economists in their endeavor to establish statistical analysis of economic freedom and wealth creation but also for hundreds of other independent researchers who are engaged in the study of economic freedom.

The utility of the *Index* as a research source is based in part on the fact that its methodology has been consistently applied, using consistent sources and scoring methods. Thus, in order to protect the integrity of the data as well as the credibility of the methodological process employed in grading countries, it is crucial to maintain the same time frame for this year's *Index* as has been employed in previous editions: namely, the period covering the last half of a calendar year and the first half of the following year. Using identical time frames for each year yields a consistent and substantial database for economic research.

Sources. The author lists the primary sources used to determine how a country meets the criteria for each *Index* factor. The analysis relies heavily on these sources. Additional sources for data that are critical to a country's score also are documented. For example, a statement about the level of corruption in a country's customs service would be followed with a supporting quote from a reliable source. There are innumerable lesser sources of information, including conversations with government officials and visits to Internet sites. It would be cumbersome to cite all sources for every single variable of each factor, so specific endnotes are reserved for the most important information used for a score or score change.

A Summary of the Factor Variables

To grade each country for the *Index,* the author examines some 50 independent variables to determine the overall level of economic freedom. The author collected information pertaining to all 50 independent factors and analyzed it to determine which of the five grades established for each of the 10 factors most closely applies to the country. Even though all of the variables are studied, not all receive an individual score or specific mention in the text. For example, it is not necessary to mention the cases in which corruption is virtually nonexistent in a country's judiciary. This variable is mentioned only when corruption in the judiciary is a documented problem. Consequently, instead of grading each of the 50 variables for each of the 161 countries individually, the *Index* divides the 50 variables into the 10 broad factors of economic freedom. Although all of the 50 variables are analyzed, grades are provided only for the 10 broad factors of economic freedom. Such a system keeps the *Index* at a manageable length.

The independent variables are summarized in the callout box in the descriptions of each factor.

The Factors of Economic Freedom

Factor #1: Trade Policy

Trade policy is a key factor in measuring economic freedom. The degree to which government hinders the free flow of foreign commerce can have a direct bearing on a country's ability to maximize economic efficiency. Thus, trade policy is an important factor in the industrialization of developing economies. International trade enables a country's industries to maximize production by allowing them to import raw materials and foreign goods and services that are cheaper than those produced at home. It also offers access to the world market, which can lead to greater wealth.

Methodology. For trade policy, a score is given based on a country's average tariff rate—the higher the rate, the worse (or higher) the score. Whenever average tariff rates are not available, the average rate is determined by calculating the revenue raised from tariffs and duties as a percentage of total imports. In the event that this informa-

tion is not available, information on the overall tariff structure, its various rates, and the items to which these rates apply is analyzed and used to estimate an effective tariff rate.

Tariffs are not the only barriers to trade, however. Many countries increasingly impose import quotas, licensing requirements, and other mandates to restrict imports. These are referred to as non-tariff barriers (NTBs). Such NTBs are examined; if they exist in sufficient quantity, a country's score based solely on tariff rates receives an additional point on the scale (representing decreased economic freedom). The trade analysis also considers corruption within the customs service. This is an important consideration because, even though countries may have lower published tariff rates and no official NTBs, their customs officials may be corrupt and require bribes to allow products entry into their ports. Or there may be instances in which customs officials steal the goods for themselves, which also constitutes a barrier to trade. These circumstances are analyzed and documented whenever possible.

**Variables of Factor #1:
Trade Policy**

- Average tariff rate
- Non-tariff barriers
- Corruption in the customs service

Sources. Unless otherwise noted, the author utilizes the following sources to determine scores for trade policy: Arrowhead International, *World Trade and Customs Directory,* Winter 1998; Economist Intelligence Unit, *EIU Country Reports* and *Investing, Licensing and Trading Conditions Abroad* (*ILT Reports*); International Monetary Fund (IMF), *Government Finance Statistics Yearbook* and *International Financial Statistics Yearbook;* Office of the United States Trade Representative, *1998 National Trade Estimate Report on Foreign Trade Barriers;* U.S. Department of Commerce, *Country Commercial Guides,* 1998; U.S. Department of State, *Country Reports on Economic Policy and Trade Practices,* 1998; World Bank, *World Development Indicators 1998;* and various official government publications.

Trade Policy Grading Scale

Score	Levels of Protectionism	Criteria
1	Very low	Average tariff rate of less than 4 percent and/or very low non-tariff barriers.
2	Low	Average tariff rate of 5 percent to 9 percent and/or low non-tariff barriers.
3	Moderate	Average tariff rate of 10 percent to 14 percent and/or moderate non-tariff barriers.
4	High	Average tariff rate of 15 percent to 19 percent and/or high non-tariff barriers.
5	Very high	Average tariff rate of 20 percent and higher and/or very high non-tariff barriers that virtually close the market to imports.

Factor #2: Taxation

Taxes are a key factor in measuring economic freedom. All taxes are harmful to economic activity because a tax essentially is a government-imposed disincentive to perform the activity being taxed. For this reason, exorbitant taxes can slow economic growth. When analyzing taxation, the author measures taxes on corporate profits, income, and other significant activities.

Methodology. Many types of taxation are scored. First, each country is scored based on two major types of taxation: income and corporate. These scores then are averaged to achieve a single taxation score. Other taxes, such as value-added taxes, sales taxes, payroll taxes, and state and local taxes, also are examined; if they exist in sufficient quantity, the taxation score is moved 0.5 point higher on the scale, representing the relative impact of these other taxes on individual economic freedom. This 0.5 point increase signifies decreased economic freedom.

It should be noted that the author of the *Index* methodology also considered using the level of tax revenues as a percentage of the economy, based on the assumption that the higher the percentage, the lower the economic freedom. According to this assumption, taxes are higher when they equal a higher percentage of the overall economy. After the author examined this approach, however, he deemed it inaccurate and misleading.[6] Tax revenue data usually are several years old by the time they are published, whereas tax rate and tax bracket data are published yearly and therefore are current for the year in which the *Index* is published. By analyzing tax data based on rates and brackets, the author includes the most up-to-date information in each edition.

Variables of Factor #2: Taxation

- Top income tax rate
- Tax rate that applies to the average income level
- Top corporate tax rate
- Other taxes

Moreover, not only are the tax revenue data out of date by the time they are published, they also can be inaccurate. For example, the main source of tax revenue data available in a worldwide publication is the IMF's *Government Financial Statistics*. The data often are unreliable, however, because many of the less-developed countries listed in this publication are recipients of IMF loans. A conflict of interest exists for many IMF

Income Tax Grading Scale

This scale lists a score from 1 through 5. The higher the score, the higher the tax rate. In each case, the highest level that applies to a country becomes that country's score.

Score	Tax Rates	Criteria
1	Very low taxes	No taxes on income, or a flat tax rate on income of 10 percent or less.
2	Low taxes	A top tax rate of 25 percent or below, or a flat income tax between 10 percent and 20 percent, or a top rate of 40 percent or below and a tax on average income below 10 percent.
3	Moderate taxes	A top tax rate of 35 percent or below, or a tax on average income below 15 percent.
4	High taxes	A top income tax rate of 36 percent to 50 percent, or an average tax level between 15 percent and 20 percent, and a tax structure not fully developed by the government or in a state of disarray.
5	Very high taxes	A top rate above 50 percent and a tax on average income between 20 percent and 25 percent, or a tax rate on average income of 25 percent or above regardless of the top rate, or a tax system through which the government confiscates most economic output resulting from government ownership of most economic activity.

recipient countries between supplying reliable data for this survey and making their economies look better to attract additional aid. These figures therefore should be viewed with some skepticism.

The best way to measure a country's tax structure is to examine its tax rates, especially those that apply to the average taxpayer. This method, employed in the *Index,* allows Heritage economists to account for an increase, or a decrease, in economic freedom immediately as countries reduce or raise their rates of taxation.

Income Taxes. Some countries have relatively high top income tax rates, but these rates apply to very few people. For example, Japan has a top income tax rate of 50 percent, but the income levels on which it is levied are so large that very few people fall inside this bracket. The tax rate that applies to the average taxpayer in Japan is much lower. To measure taxation policy accu-

rately, it is necessary to examine not only the top income tax rate but also the rate that applies to the average income level. To discover the tax rate on the average income level, the author uses a country's per capita gross domestic product (GDP).[7] He then scores each country on (1) its top tax rate and (2) the tax rate that applies to the average income.

Sources. For each country, unless otherwise noted, the author utilizes the following sources for information on taxation: Economist Intelligence Unit, *ILT Reports;* Ernst & Young, *1998 Worldwide Executive Tax Guide and Directory* and *1998 Worldwide Corporate Tax Guide and Directory;* U.S. Department of Commerce, *Country Commercial Guides,* 1998, and reports available through its Internet site, *Stat–USA;* and various official government publications.

Corporate Tax Grading Scale

The second type of tax analyzed for each country is its corporate tax. Each country is scored according to a sliding scale based on corporate tax rates.

Score	Tax Rates	Criteria
1	Very low taxes	Limited or no taxes are imposed on corporate profits.
2	Low taxes	Flat corporate tax of less than 25 percent, or a progressive top tax of less than 25 percent.
3	Moderate taxes	A progressive corporate tax system with top rate of between 26 percent and 35 percent, or a flat tax system with tax levels above 25 percent.
4	High taxes	A progressive corporate tax system with a top rate of between 36 percent and 45 percent, and a tax structure not fully developed by the government or in a state of disarray.
5	Very high taxes	A cumbersome progressive tax system with top corporate tax rates of more than 46 percent, or a tax system in which the government confiscates most economic output resulting from government ownership of most economic activity.

Factor #3: Government Intervention in the Economy

The greater the degree to which the government intrudes in the economy, the less individuals are free to engage in their own economic activities. By taking government consumption as a percentage of GDP, one can begin to determine the level of government intervention in the economy. The higher the rate of government consumption as a percentage of GDP, the higher the *Index* score and, hence, the lower the level of economic freedom.

Methodology. Measuring government consumption as a percentage of GDP reveals only an approximation of the government's role in a country's economy.[8] In the United States, for example, the federal budget is about 24 percent of GDP. This figure includes servicing the federal budget deficit and transfer payments through entitlements like Medicaid. For most less-developed countries, government consumption figures do not include funds spent on servicing the budget deficit and some transfer payments. These figures

are included in government "expenditure" figures, but these figures are not available for all 161 countries graded in the *Index*. In addition, the figures that are available often are many years out of date. Government consumption figures, however, are available for nearly all countries and are up-to-date. Although government consumption figures probably understate total government intervention in the economy, they are useful as a starting point in gauging the degree of government intervention.

The next step in scoring government consumption is to determine the size of the state-owned sector of a country's economy. If a country has many state-owned enterprises, or if the state-owned sector produces a large portion of its GDP, the author scores it 1 point higher on the scale, signifying decreased economic freedom. This factor also examines the state of any privatization programs: If a country has a state-owned sector that is being privatized aggressively, he makes note of it. This puts into context any statements made about the size of the state-owned sector. If the

Government Intervention Grading Scale

Score	Level of Government Intervention in the Economy	Criteria
1	Very low	Less than 10 percent of GDP; virtually no government-owned enterprises.
2	Low	11 percent to 25 percent of GDP; a few government-owned enterprises, like the postal service; aggressive privatization program in place.
3	Moderate	26 percent to 35 percent of GDP; several government-owned enterprises like telecommunications, some banks, and energy production; stalled or limited privatization program.
4	High	36 percent to 45 percent of GDP; many government-owned enterprises like transportation, goods distributors, and manufacturing companies.
5	Very high	46 percent or more of GDP; mostly government-owned industries; few private companies.

privatization program has stalled, however, or one is not in place, the author makes mention of that, too.

Variables of Factor #3: Government Intervention in the Economy

- Government consumption as a percentage of the economy
- Government ownership of businesses and industries
- Economic output produced by the government

Sources. For each country, unless otherwise noted, the author utilizes the following sources for information on government intervention in the economy: U.S. Department of State and U.S. Department of Commerce, various reports; Economist Intelligence Unit, *EIU Country Reports;* and World Bank, *World Development Indicators 1998.*

Factor #4: Monetary Policy

The value of a country's currency is based largely on its monetary policy. When a government maintains a tight monetary policy—that is, the supply of currency does not exceed the demand—individuals have the economic freedom to engage in productive and profitable economic activities. If the government maintains a loose monetary policy—that is, it supplies more currency than the demand requires—the currency loses its value and individuals are less free to engage in productive and profitable economic activities. The best way to measure monetary policy is to analyze the inflation rate over a period of time because it is more difficult to maintain low stable inflation rates over a long period of time than over a short one. The inflation rate is linked directly with the government's ability to manage the money supply in the economy.

Methodology. The main criterion for this factor is a country's average annual rate of inflation from 1986 to 1996. Countries with high rates of inflation generally have a loose monetary policy and receive a poorer grade because they have less economic freedom than countries with

Monetary Policy Grading Scale

Score	Inflation Rate	Criteria
1	Very low	Below 6 percent.
2	Low	Between 7 percent and 13 percent.
3	Moderate	Between 14 percent and 20 percent.
4	High	Between 21 percent and 30 percent.
5	Very high	Over 30 percent.

lower inflation rates. Countries with low rates of inflation generally have a tight monetary policy and receive a better grade because they have more economic freedom.

Countries of the former Soviet Union pose a unique problem in determining average annual rates of inflation: Because these countries had command economies, average annual rates of inflation from 1986 to 1996 are misleading. Without a market-based system, the state can hold prices constant. Therefore, countries of the former Soviet Union are graded solely on an estimated average rate of inflation since 1992. Although these figures are high, especially because of the recent transformation of their economies to a market-based system, they are more accurate reflections of current conditions than are figures based on the Soviet era.

Variables of Factor #4: Monetary Policy

• Average inflation rate from 1986 to 1996

• Average inflation rate for 1997 (informational purposes only)

Moreover, measuring inflation on a historical basis may understate the current economic conditions within certain countries. If, for example, a country had high rates of inflation in the early 1980s but low rates today, the average rate of inflation still might be quite high. For this reason, it is important to include information that provides the most current rates of inflation available.

These figures appear at the end of the monetary policy section for each country. For purposes of grading monetary policy, however, the author uses them only to determine whether inflation is going down, increasing, or staying even with historical levels.

Sources. Unless otherwise noted, the main source for data on monetary policy is the World Bank, *World Development Indicators 1998*. For some countries, the average rate of inflation is not available. In other cases, the author uses consumer price inflation or only retail rates of inflation.

Factor #5: Capital Flows and Foreign Investment Policy

Foreign investment provides funds for economic expansion. Foreign investors often supply the capital domestic investors need to start or expand their businesses. Restrictions on foreign investment limit the inflow of capital and thus hamper economic freedom. By contrast, little or no restriction of foreign investment maximizes economic freedom and thus increases the flow of investments. For this category, the more restrictions a country imposes on foreign investment, the lower the level of economic freedom and the higher the score.

Methodology. This factor scrutinizes each country's policies toward foreign investment in order to determine its overall investment climate. It examines such variables as the extent to which foreign ownership limits domestic industries; the presence of a foreign investment code that defines the country's investment laws and procedures; whether the government encourages foreign investment through fair and equitable treatment

Capital Flows and Foreign Investment Grading Scale

Score	Barriers to Foreign Investment	Criteria
1	Very low	Open and impartial treatment of foreign investment; accessible foreign investment code.
2	Low	Restrictions on investments like utilities, companies vital to national security, and natural resources; limited, efficient approval process.
3	Moderate	Restrictions on many investments, but official policy that conforms to established foreign investment code; bureaucratic approval process.
4	High	Investment permitted on a case-by-case basis; possible presence of bureaucratic approval process and corruption.
5	Very high	Government that seeks actively to prevent foreign investment; rampant corruption.

of investors; whether foreign corporations are treated the same as domestic corporations under the law; and whether specific industries are closed to foreign investment. This analysis helps to develop an overall description of the investment climate in the country for this *Index*. The author then grades each country on its investment climate.

Sources. For each country, unless otherwise noted, the author utilizes the following sources for data on capital flows and foreign investment policy: Economist Intelligence Unit, *ILT Reports;* Office of the United States Trade Representative, *1998 National Trade Estimate Report on Foreign Trade Barriers;* U.S. Department of Commerce, *Country Commercial Guides,* 1998; U.S. Department of State, *Country Reports on Economic Policy and Trade Practices;* and official government publications of the respective countries.

Factor #6: Banking

In most countries, banks provide the economy with the financial means to operate. They lend money to start businesses; provide such services as real estate, insurance, and securities investments; and furnish a safe place for individuals to store their earnings. The more government controls banks, the less free they are to engage in these activities. The consequence of heavy regulation of banks is restricted economic freedom; therefore,

Variables of Factor #5: Capital Flows and Foreign Investment

- Foreign investment code
- Restrictions on foreign ownership of business
- Restrictions on the industries and companies open to foreign investors
- Restrictions and performance requirements on foreign companies
- Foreign ownership of land
- Equal treatment under the law for both foreign and domestic companies
- Restrictions on the repatriation of earnings
- Availability of local financing for foreign companies

Banking Grading Scale

Score	Restrictions on Banks	Criteria
1	Very low	Very few restrictions on foreign banks; banks can engage in all types of financial services; government controls few, if any, commercial banks; no government deposit insurance.
2	Low	Few limits on foreign banks; country may maintain some limits on financial services and have interstate banking restrictions and deposit insurance; domestic bank formation may face some barriers.
3	Moderate	Heavy influence on banks by government; government owns or operates some banks; strict government control of credit; domestic bank formation may face significant barriers.
4	High	Banking system in transition; banks tightly controlled by government; possible corruption; domestic bank formation virtually nonexistent.
5	Very High	Financial institutions in chaos; banks operate on primitive basis; most credit goes only to state-owned enterprises; corruption rampant.

Variables of Factor #6: Banking

- Government ownership of banks
- Restrictions on the ability of foreign banks to open branches and subsidiaries
- Government influence over the allocation of credit
- Government regulations, such as deposit insurance
- Freedom to offer all types of financial services, such as buying and selling real estate, securities, and insurance policies

the more a government restricts its banking sector, the higher its score and the lower the level of its economic freedom.

Methodology. The author scores this factor by determining the openness of a country's banking system: specifically, whether foreign banks are able to operate freely; how difficult it is to open domestic banks; how heavily regulated the banking system is; and whether banks are free to provide customers with insurance, sell real estate, and invest in securities. The author uses this analysis to develop a description of the country's banking climate. The *Index*'s banking factor measures the relative openness of a country's banking system.

Sources. For each country, unless otherwise noted, the author utilizes the following sources for data on banking: Economist Intelligence Unit, *EIU Country Reports* and *ILT Reports;* U.S. Department of Commerce, *Country Commercial Guides,* 1998, and National Trade Data Bank of the United States; U.S. Department of State, *1998 Country Reports on Economic Policy and Trade Practices;* official government publications of the respective countries; and the World Bank.

Wage and Price Controls Grading Scale

Score	Wage and Price Controls	Criteria
1	Very low	Wages and prices determined by the market; no minimum wage.
2	Low	Most prices determined by supply and demand, although some prices determined by the government or such monopolies as utilities; may or may not have minimum wage laws.
3	Moderate	Mixture of market forces and government-determined wages and prices, or heavy government control of either prices or wages.
4	High	Rationing, wage and price controls on most jobs and items.
5	Very high	Wages and prices almost completely controlled by the government.

Factor #7: Wage and Price Controls

A free economy is one that allows individual businesses to set not only the prices on the goods and services they sell but also the wages they pay to the workers they employ. Some governments mandate wage and price controls. In so doing, they restrict economic activity and curtail economic freedom. Therefore, the more a government intervenes and controls prices and wages, the higher its *Index* score and the lower its level of economic freedom.

Methodology. The author scores this factor by the extent to which a country allows the market or the government to set wages and prices. Specifically, this factor looks at which products have prices set by the government; whether the government controls such things as utilities; and whether the government has a minimum wage policy or sets other wages. The factor's scale measures the relative degree of government control over wages and prices. A "very low" score of 1 represents wages and prices that are set almost completely by the market, whereas a "very high" score of 5 means wages and prices are set almost completely by the government.

Sources. For each country, unless otherwise noted, the author utilizes the following sources for data on wage and price controls: Economist Intelligence Unit, *ILT Reports*; U.S. Department of Commerce, *Country Commercial Guides,* 1998; U.S. Department of State, *1998 Country Reports on Economic Policy and Trade Practices*; and the World Bank.

Variables of Factor #7: Wage and Price Controls

- Minimum wage laws
- Freedom to set prices privately without government influence
- Government price controls
- The extent to which government price controls are used
- Government subsidies to businesses that affect prices

Factor #8: Property Rights

The ability to accumulate private property is the main motivating force in a market economy, and the rule of law is vital to a fully functioning,

Property Rights Grading Scale

Score	Protection of Private Property	Criteria
1	Very high	Private property guaranteed by the government, and efficient court system enforces contracts; justice system punishes those who unlawfully confiscate private property; expropriation unlikely.
2	High	Private property guaranteed by the government, but enforcement lax; expropriation unlikely.
3	Moderate	Government recognizes some private property rights, such as land, but property can be nationalized; expropriation possible; judiciary may be influenced by other branches of government.
4	Low	Property ownership limited to personal items with little legal protection; communal property the rule; expropriation likely, and government does not protect private property adequately; judiciary subject to influence from other branches of government; possible corruption within judicial process; legal system has collapsed.
5	Very low	Private property outlawed; almost all property belongs to the state; expropriation certain, or country so corrupt and chaotic that property protection is nonexistent.

efficient market economy. This factor examines the extent to which the government protects private property and how safe private property is from expropriation. The less protection private property receives, the higher the score and the lower the level of economic freedom.

Methodology. This factor scores the degree to which private property is a guaranteed right, as it does the extent to which the government protects —and enforces laws that protect—private property. This factor also examines the expropriation of private property. In addition, it analyzes the independence of the judiciary, the existence of corruption within the judiciary, and the ability of individuals and businesses to enforce contracts. The less legal protection of property, the higher the score. Similarly, the greater the chances of government expropriation of property, the higher the score.

Variables of Factor #8: Property Rights

- Freedom from government influence over the judicial system
- Commercial code defining contracts
- Sanctioning of foreign arbitration of contract disputes
- Government expropriation of property
- Corruption within the judiciary
- Delays in receiving judicial decisions
- Legally granted and protected private property

Regulation Grading Scale

Score	Levels of Regulation	Criteria
1	Very low	Existing regulations straightforward and applied uniformly to all businesses; regulations not much of a burden for business; corruption nearly nonexistent.
2	Low	Simple licensing procedures; existing regulations relatively straightforward and applied uniformly most of the time, but still burdensome in some instances; corruption, although possible, rare and not a problem.
3	Moderate	Existing regulations may be applied haphazardly and in some instances are not even published by the government; complicated licensing procedure; regulations impose substantial burden on business; significant state-owned sector; corruption present and poses some minor strain on businesses.
4	High	Government-set production quotas and some state planning; major barriers to opening a business; complicated licensing process; very high fees; bribes sometimes necessary; corruption present and burdensome; regulations impose a great burden on business.
5	Very high	Government discourages the creation of new businesses; corruption rampant; regulations applied randomly.

Sources. For each country, unless otherwise noted, the author utilizes the following sources for information on property rights: Economist Intelligence Unit, *ILT Reports;* U.S. Department of Commerce, National Trade Data Bank of the United States and *Country Commercial Guides,* 1998; U.S. Department of State, *Country Reports on Human Rights Practices for 1997;* and the World Bank.

Factor #9: Regulation

In many less-developed economies, obtaining a business license to sell goods or services is nearly impossible. Regulations and restrictions make it difficult for entrepreneurs to create new businesses. In some cases, government officials frown on any private-sector initiative and even may make them illegal. Although many regulations hinder business, the most important are associated with licensing new companies and businesses. In some countries, such as the United States, obtaining a business license can be as simple as mailing in a registration form with a minimal fee. In others, especially in sub-Saharan Africa and parts of South America, obtaining a business license requires endless trips to a government building and countless bribes, and may take up to a year.

Once a business is open, government regulation does not always subside; in some cases, it increases. Some countries apply their regulations haphazardly. For example, an environmental regulation may be used to shut down one business but not another. Business owners are uncertain about which regulations they must obey. In addition, the existence of many regulations can support corruption as confused and harassed business owners try to work around the red tape.

Black Market Grading Scale

Score	Black Market Activity	Criteria
1	Very low	Very low level of black market activity; economies are free markets with black markets in such things as drugs and weapons.
2	Low	Low level of black market activity; economies may have some black market involvement in labor or pirating of intellectual property.
3	Moderate	Moderate level of black market activity; countries may have some black market activities in the labor, agriculture, and transportation sectors, and moderate levels of piracy in intellectual property.
4	High	High level of black market activity; countries may have substantial levels of black market activity in such areas as labor, pirated intellectual property, and smuggled consumer goods, and in such services as transportation, electricity, and telecommunications.
5	Very high	Very high level of black market activity; countries have black markets that are larger than their formal economies.

Variables of Factor #9: Regulation

- Licensing requirements to operate a business
- Ease of obtaining a business license
- Corruption within the bureaucracy
- Labor regulations, such as established work weeks, paid vacations, and maternity leave, as well as selected labor regulations
- Environmental, consumer safety, and worker health regulations
- Regulations that impose a burden on business

Methodology. This factor measures how easy or difficult it is to open and operate a business. The more regulations on business, the harder it is to open one. It also examines the degree of corruption and whether regulations are applied uniformly to all businesses. Another consideration is whether the country has state planning agencies that set production limits and quotas. The scale establishes a set of conditions for each of the five possible grades. These conditions include such items as the extent of government corruption, how uniformly regulations are applied, and the extent to which regulations impose a burden on business. At one end of the scale is the "very low" score of 1, at which corruption is nonexistent and regulations are minimal and applied uniformly. At the other end of the scale is the "very high" score of 5, at which corruption is rampant, regulations are applied randomly, and the general level of regulation is very high. A country need only meet a majority of the conditions in each score to receive that score.

Sources. For each country, unless otherwise noted, the author utilizes the following sources for data on regulation: U.S. Department of Commerce, National Trade Data Bank of the United

States and *Country Commercial Guides,* 1998; and official government publications of the respective countries.

Factor #10: Black Market

At first glance, one might think that the existence of a black market is positive: at least there is some ability to engage in entrepreneurship or to obtain scarce goods and services. Black markets, however, are the direct result of government intervention in the marketplace. A black market activity—the only kind of output measured in the *Index*—is one that the government has outlawed. Although it is common that many societies outlaw such activities as trafficking in illicit drugs and prostitution, others frequently limit individual liberty by outlawing such activities as private transportation and construction services. Furthermore, a government regulation or restriction in one area may create the need for a black market in another. For example, a country with high barriers to trade may have laws that protect its domestic market and prevent the import of foreign goods, but these barriers create incentives for smuggling, and a black market often is created for the barred products. In addition, governments that do not have strong property rights protection for items like intellectual property, or that do not enforce existing laws, encourage piracy and theft in these sectors.

For purposes of the *Index,* the larger the black market is in a particular country, the lower the country's level of economic freedom. The more prevalent these activities are, the worse the country's score. Conversely, the smaller the black market, the higher the country's level of economic freedom. The less prevalent these activities are, the better its score.

Methodology. This factor considers the extent to which black market activities occur. Although information on the size of black markets in less-developed countries is difficult to obtain, it has become more readily available. Information can be found on the extent of smuggling in a country, the level of piracy of intellectual property, and the level of black market labor. When information is available on these issues, the author uses it to determine the extent to which black market activities occur. He then uses the presence or absence of these types of activities to estimate the level of activity that occurs in the black market. The higher the level of black market activity, the higher a country's score and the lower its level of economic freedom. As newer data become available, it may become possible to document the percentage of black market activity in a country's overall economy.

Variables of Factor #10: Black Market

- Smuggling
- Piracy of intellectual property in the black market
- Agricultural production supplied on the black market
- Manufacturing supplied on the black market
- Services supplied on the black market
- Transportation supplied on the black market
- Labor supplied on the black market

Although this factor measures black market activity in the production, distribution, or consumption of goods and services, it does not measure such things as black market exchange rates, gambling, illegal narcotics, illegal arms, prostitution, or related activities. Such activities are very difficult to quantify with objectivity.

Sources. For this factor, unless otherwise noted, the author utilizes the following sources for information on black market activities: U.S. Department of Commerce, *Country Commercial Guide,* 1997; U.S. Department of State, *Country Reports on Economic Policy and Trade Practices;* official U.S. government cables supplied by the U.S. Department of Commerce and U.S. Department of State, available through the National Trade Data Bank of the United States; and official government publications of the respective countries.

Notes

1 See also James D. Gwartney and Robert A. Lawson, *Economic Freedom of the World 1997* (Vancouver, Canada: Fraser Institute, 1997), and Richard E. Messick, *World Survey of Economic Freedom: 1995–1996* (New Brunswick, NJ: Transaction Publishers, 1996).

2 *Webster's Ninth New Collegiate Dictionary* (Springfield, Mass.: Merriam Webster, Inc., 1997).

3 The black market factor is the only one in the *Index* that measures outputs. Black market activities are a direct result of government restrictions on economic freedom, so the black market factor serves to supplement the others, allowing the author to provide a more detailed analysis of the level of economic freedom in each country measured.

4 For example, see Gwartney and Lawson, *Economic Freedom of the World 1997*.

5 *Ibid.*

6 The author does rely on this approach, however, when information on tax rates is not available. These instances are noted.

7 Because these figures are readily available, this method allows the author to generate the average income level for nearly all countries.

8 GDP is used in most cases. When only gross national product (GNP) figures are available, this is so stated.

## 7

The 1999 *Index of Economic Freedom:* The Countries

by Bryan T. Johnson

This section is a compilation of countries, each graded in all 10 factors of the *Index of Economic Freedom*. Each country receives a 1 through 5 score for all 10 factors. Those scores then are averaged to get the final *Index of Economic Freedom* score. Countries with a score between 1 and 2 have the freest economies. Countries with a score around 3 are less free. Countries with a score near 4 are over-regulated and need significant economic reforms to achieve even the most basic increases in economic growth. Those with the score of 5 are the most economically oppressed countries. Please reference the Statistical Appendix for more information on each country.

Albania   3.85

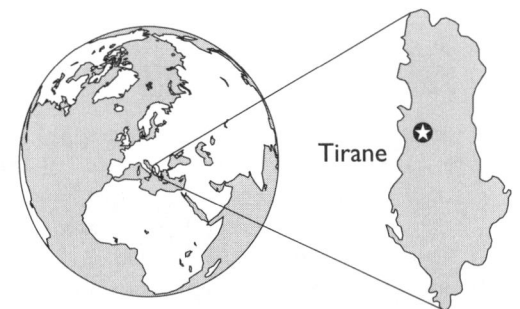

Tirane ✪

1998 Score: **3.75**	1997 Score: **3.65**	1996 Score: **3.45**

Trade	4	Banking	4
Taxation	3.5	Wages and Prices	3
Government Intervention	5	Property Rights	4
Monetary Policy	5	Regulation	3
Foreign Investment	2	Black Market	5

Albania gained its independence from the Ottoman Empire in 1912, but the struggle for independence resulted in the loss of about half its territory and 40 percent of its people to neighboring Greece and Serbia. During World War I, much of the country was destroyed. After the war, it was an independent state ruled by a monarch. But even though King Zog sought economic self-sufficiency, Albania became increasingly dependent on Benito Mussolini's Italy, which occupied parts of the country in 1939. The Albanian Communist Party was formed in 1941; after World War II, Albania became one of the world's most oppressive communist states. The communist regime was deposed in 1991, and Sali Berisha was elected to the presidency in 1992 and re-elected in 1996. A scandal surrounding a pyramid investment scheme, however, enabled the Socialist Party to regain control of the legislature amid widespread violence. (In July 1997, Berisha resigned from office and the Socialist Party won the ensuing elections to parliament.) Albania has been plagued by violence, rampant organized crime, and the collapse of its law enforcement system. Barriers to trade are rising. As a result, Albania's overall score is 0.1 point worse than last year.

TRADE POLICY
Score: 4– (high level of protectionism)

Albania's average tariff rate is 13.6 percent.[1] Recent evidence indicates, however, that corruption within the customs service is soaring.[2] Moreover, the U.S. State Department has issued a travel warning that indicates that attacks by "bands of thieves" are a regular occurrence in all parts of the country. In addition, getting goods into and out of the country is nearly impossible.[3] All of these factors demonstrate a significant increase in non-tariff barriers to trade. As a result, Albania's trade score is 1 point worse this year.

TAXATION
Score–Income taxation: 2–Stable (low tax rates)
Score–Corporate taxation: 3–Stable (moderate tax rates)
Final Taxation Score: 3.5–Stable (high tax rates)

Albania has a top income tax rate of 24 percent[4] and a top corporate tax rate of 30 percent. It also has a small business tax, a social contributions tax, and a turnover tax.

GOVERNMENT INTERVENTION IN THE ECONOMY
Score: 5–Stable (very high level)

The public sector generates about 50 percent of Albania's GDP.[5] The country has made significant progress toward privatizing some industries like agriculture, however, which could lead to less government intervention in the economy in the future.

1	Hong Kong	1.25	81	Fiji	3.10
2	Singapore	1.30	81	Mali	3.10
3	Bahrain	1.70	81	Slovenia	3.10
4	New Zealand	1.75	85	Honduras	3.15
5	Switzerland	1.85	85	Mexico	3.15
6	United States	1.90	85	Papua New Guinea	3.15
7	Ireland	1.95	88	Djibouti	3.20
7	Luxembourg	1.95	88	Mongolia	3.20
7	Taiwan	1.95	90	Algeria	3.25
7	United Kingdom	1.95	90	Brazil	3.25
11	Bahamas	2.00	90	Lebanon	3.25
12	Czech Republic	2.05	90	Senegal	3.25
12	Japan	2.05	90	Tanzania	3.25
14	Australia	2.10	95	Nigeria	3.30
14	Belgium	2.10	95	Romania	3.30
14	Canada	2.10	97	Cambodia	3.35
14	United Arab Emirates	2.10	97	Dominican Republic	3.35
18	Austria	2.15	97	Egypt	3.35
18	Chile	2.15	97	Guinea	3.35
18	Estonia	2.15	97	Ivory Coast	3.35
18	Netherlands	2.15	97	Moldova	3.35
22	Denmark	2.25	97	Pakistan	3.35
22	El Salvador	2.25	104	Nepal	3.40
22	Finland	2.25	104	Venezuela	3.40
25	Germany	2.30	106	Armenia	3.45
25	Iceland	2.30	106	Bulgaria	3.45
27	Norway	2.35	106	Lesotho	3.45
28	Korea, South	2.40	106	Madagascar	3.45
28	Kuwait	2.40	106	Russia	3.45
28	Malaysia	2.40	111	Burkina Faso	3.50
28	Panama	2.40	111	Cameroon	3.50
28	Thailand	2.40	111	Guyana	3.50
33	Sweden	2.45	111	Nicaragua	3.50
34	Argentina	2.50	115	Gambia	3.60
34	France	2.50	116	Croatia	3.65
34	Italy	2.50	116	Georgia	3.65
34	Spain	2.50	116	Malawi	3.65
38	Portugal	2.55	119	Cape Verde	3.67
38	Sri Lanka	2.55	120	Ethiopia	3.70
38	Trinidad and Tobago	2.55	120	India	3.70
41	Barbados	2.60	120	Niger	3.70
41	Peru	2.60	123	Congo	3.75
43	Bolivia	2.65	124	Chad	3.80
43	Mauritius	2.65	124	China	3.80
45	Cyprus	2.70	124	Mauritania	3.80
45	Jamaica	2.70	124	Ukraine	3.80
45	Uruguay	2.70	124	Zimbabwe	3.80
48	Botswana	2.75	129	Albania	3.85
48	Guatemala	2.75	129	Bangladesh	3.85
48	Jordan	2.75	129	Mozambique	3.85
48	Namibia	2.75	129	Suriname	3.85
48	Oman	2.75	133	Burundi	3.90
48	Philippines	2.75	134	Togo	3.95
54	Belize	2.80	135	Haiti	4.00
54	Costa Rica	2.80	135	Kyrgyz Rep.	4.00
54	Israel	2.80	137	Kazakhstan	4.05
54	Swaziland	2.80	137	Sierra Leone	4.05
54	Turkey	2.80	139	Yemen	4.10
54	Uganda	2.80	140	Belarus	4.15
54	Samoa	2.80	141	Sudan	4.20
61	Latvia	2.85	141	Syria	4.20
62	Greece	2.90	143	Azerbaijan	4.30
62	Hungary	2.90	143	Equatorial Guinea	4.30
62	So. Africa	2.90	143	Myanmar	4.30
65	Ecuador	2.95	143	Rwanda	4.30
65	Gabon	2.95	147	Tajikistan	4.40
65	Indonesia	2.95	147	Uzbekistan	4.40
65	Malta	2.95	149	Angola	4.45
65	Morocco	2.95	149	Turkmenistan	4.45
65	Poland	2.95	151	Guinea-Bissau	4.55
65	Tunisia	2.95	152	Vietnam	4.60
72	Ghana	3.00	153	Congo (Zaire)	4.70
72	Lithuania	3.00	153	Iran	4.70
72	Saudi Arabia	3.00	155	Bosnia	4.80
75	Benin	3.05	155	Somalia	4.80
75	Kenya	3.05	157	Iraq	4.90
75	Paraguay	3.05	157	Laos	4.90
75	Qatar	3.05	157	Libya	4.90
75	Slovak Republic	3.05	160	Cuba	5.00
75	Zambia	3.05	160	Korea, North	5.00
81	Colombia	3.10			

Mostly Unfree

MONETARY POLICY
Score: 5–Stable (very high level of inflation)

Inflation has been very high, but dropped from 226 percent in 1992 to 31 percent in 1993. The rate of inflation fell below 20 percent in 1994 but increased to 22 percent in 1995. In 1996, it fell to 12 percent. Inflation increased again in 1997, however, to about 22 percent. Although there are not enough data to develop an average inflation rate from 1986 to 1996, it is possible to estimate an average rate from 1992 to 1997: well over 30 percent.

CAPITAL FLOWS AND FOREIGN INVESTMENT
Score: 2–Stable (low barriers)

Albania has moved quickly to open its borders to desperately needed foreign capital and has passed laws forbidding state expropriation of foreign property. Foreign firms and domestic firms are treated equally under the law. No sectors are closed to foreign investment. Political instability, however, will work against foreign investment until order is reinstated.[6]

BANKING
Score: 4–Stable (high level of restrictions)

Although Albania has made significant strides toward replacing the communist central bank and providing avenues for implementing a competitive, market-driven system, the financial system still is not fully private. Albania's financial system consists of seven major banks: four state-owned banks, two joint ventures between state-owned banks and private banks, and only one bank that is fully private. The failure of several illegal pyramid investment schemes has curtailed many financial sector operations severely, hurling the industry into a financial crisis.

WAGE AND PRICE CONTROLS
Score: 3–Stable (moderate level)

Albania has a minimum wage. Although the government officially has ended price controls, most prices still are set by the huge state-owned sector of the economy, which continues to receive government subsidies. These state-owned enterprises often are able to control prices because they can undercut prices determined by the market.

PROPERTY RIGHTS
Score: 4–Stable (low level of protection)

Even though the government has made some strides toward privatization, the private sector remains small compared with the size of public holdings. In addition, the court system is not developed sufficiently to handle a growing caseload of property disputes. Recent reports on the court system point to a near collapse. According to the U.S. Department of State, for example, "The law on Major Constitutional Provisions provides for an independent judiciary, but with the breakdown of society, the judiciary was unable to function in many places as courts were burned and some judges fled their posts."[7]

REGULATION
Score: 3–Stable (moderate level)

Albania has made some progress toward streamlining its bureaucracy. Nevertheless, the bureaucracy has been unable to adapt to the emerging private sector; it remains large and inefficient.

BLACK MARKET
Score: 5–Stable (very high level of activity)

Albania's legal market may be growing, but many consumers and entrepreneurs still find it easier and more profitable to deal in the black market. Taxi and bus transportation are provided by black marketeers. Smugglers have discovered that the scarcities caused by high tariffs on auto parts present ample opportunity for profit on the black market. Moreover, black marketeers continue to provide many agricultural items. According to the U.S. Department of Commerce, "Customs tax evasion also results in Albanian import statistics that undercount the true quantity/value of imported poultry by almost half. Black market sales of perishable food items have also presented problems for the Albanian Food Inspection Service."[8]

NOTES

[1] World Bank, *World Development Indicators,* 1998.

[2] "Opposition Party Comments on Damning EU Report on Government Corruption," British Broadcasting Corporation, July 7, 1998.

[3] "Albania Travel Conditions," Market Research Reports, U.S. Department of State, August 16, 1997.

[4] Information with which to determine the tax on the average income level is not available.

[5] Budget figures are not available. Therefore, it is not possible to generate a government consumption figure. Albania's grade is based strictly on the fact that 50 percent of GDP is generated by the public sector.

[6] Most barriers to investment are the result of political instability; thus, they are not measurable. Such issues as rule of law, however, are taken into account in the other factors like property rights. Overall, Albania maintains low formal barriers to investment.

[7] U.S. Department of State, "Albania Country Report on Human Rights Practices for 1997," 1998.

[8] U.S. Department of Commerce, *Country Commercial Guide,* 1996.

Algeria   3.25

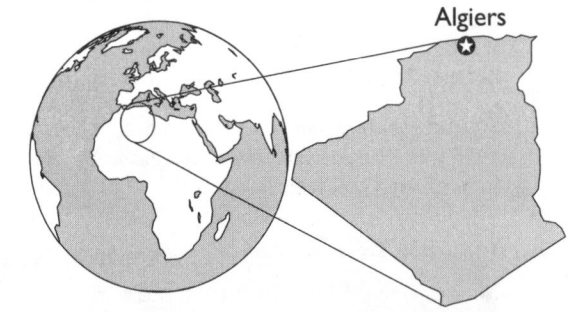

Algiers

1998 Score: **3.25**   1997 Score: **3.25**   1996 Score: **3.25**

Trade	5	Banking	3
Taxation	3.5	Wages and Prices	3
Government Intervention	3	Property Rights	3
Monetary Policy	3	Regulation	3
Foreign Investment	3	Black Market	3

Algeria has had a state-controlled socialist economy since gaining its independence from France in 1962. Years of government mismanagement coupled with low oil prices in the mid-1980s led to anti-government riots in 1988. In 1989, Algeria adopted a new constitution that ended one-party rule and called for multiparty elections, but the elections were canceled in January 1992 after the results of the first round of voting made it clear that the radical Islamic Salvation Front would take control. The cancellation precipitated a rebellion by Islamic radicals against the military-backed government. Since 1992, more than 60,000 Algerians have died in the ensuing, brutal civil war. Although Islamic terrorists have targeted foreigners in an effort to cut Algeria's economic links with the outside world and fuel discontent, the militants appear to have been stalemated by a harsh security crackdown. In this uncertain climate, economic growth has been negligible over the past several years. Under pressure from the international financial community, Algeria's government has made a commitment to economic liberalization, but the pursuit of economic reform has been erratic.

TRADE POLICY
Score: 5–Stable (very high level of protectionism)

The government reformed its tariff schedule in 1992, cutting the top rate from 120 percent to 60 percent and reducing the number of categories. Importers also must pay two other taxes, adding a combined 17 percent to 90 percent to the cost of imports. Algeria's average tariff rate is about 22.9 percent.[1] The importation of some 70 goods, including textiles and shoes, is banned. According to the U.S. Department of Commerce, "Customs operations are being modernized, but administrative procedures remain burdensome in some instances."[2]

TAXATION
Score–Income taxation: 3–Stable (moderate tax rates)
Score–Corporate taxation: 3–Stable (moderate tax rates)
Final Taxation Score: 3.5–Stable (high tax rates)

Algeria's top income tax rate is 50 percent. There is no tax on average income. Income earned by foreigners is taxed at a flat 20 percent; in the past, the rate has been as high as 70 percent. The corporate tax rate is 50 percent for business profits and 20 percent for earnings that are reinvested. Tax breaks are available for companies that choose to locate in poorer areas. Algeria also maintains a value-added tax of 21 percent.

GOVERNMENT INTERVENTION IN THE ECONOMY
Score: 3–Stable (moderate level)

State-controlled enterprises dominate most commerce and industry. Private-sector involvement is increasing slowly. Government consumes 15.7 percent of Algeria's GDP. Algeria's state sector is large, accounting for some 60 percent of national production. An announced privatization effort has made little progress, and opposition to it is mounting.

1	Hong Kong	1.25	81	Fiji	3.10
2	Singapore	1.30	81	Mali	3.10
3	Bahrain	1.70	81	Slovenia	3.10
4	New Zealand	1.75	85	Honduras	3.15
5	Switzerland	1.85	85	Mexico	3.15
6	United States	1.90	85	Papua New Guinea	3.15
7	Ireland	1.95	88	Djibouti	3.20
7	Luxembourg	1.95	88	Mongolia	3.20
7	Taiwan	1.95	90	Algeria	3.25
7	United Kingdom	1.95	90	Brazil	3.25
11	Bahamas	2.00	90	Lebanon	3.25
12	Czech Republic	2.05	90	Senegal	3.25
12	Japan	2.05	90	Tanzania	3.25
14	Australia	2.10	95	Nigeria	3.30
14	Belgium	2.10	95	Romania	3.30
14	Canada	2.10	97	Cambodia	3.35
14	United Arab Emirates	2.10	97	Dominican Republic	3.35
18	Austria	2.15	97	Egypt	3.35
18	Chile	2.15	97	Guinea	3.35
18	Estonia	2.15	97	Ivory Coast	3.35
18	Netherlands	2.15	97	Moldova	3.35
22	Denmark	2.25	97	Pakistan	3.35
22	El Salvador	2.25	104	Nepal	3.40
22	Finland	2.25	104	Venezuela	3.40
25	Germany	2.30	106	Armenia	3.45
25	Iceland	2.30	106	Bulgaria	3.45
27	Norway	2.35	106	Lesotho	3.45
28	Korea, South	2.40	106	Madagascar	3.45
28	Kuwait	2.40	106	Russia	3.45
28	Malaysia	2.40	111	Burkina Faso	3.50
28	Panama	2.40	111	Cameroon	3.50
28	Thailand	2.40	111	Guyana	3.50
33	Sweden	2.45	111	Nicaragua	3.50
34	Argentina	2.50	115	Gambia	3.60
34	France	2.50	116	Croatia	3.65
34	Italy	2.50	116	Georgia	3.65
34	Spain	2.50	116	Malawi	3.65
38	Portugal	2.55	119	Cape Verde	3.67
38	Sri Lanka	2.55	120	Ethiopia	3.70
38	Trinidad and Tobago	2.55	120	India	3.70
41	Barbados	2.60	120	Niger	3.70
41	Peru	2.60	123	Congo	3.75
43	Bolivia	2.65	124	Chad	3.80
43	Mauritius	2.65	124	China	3.80
45	Cyprus	2.70	124	Mauritania	3.80
45	Jamaica	2.70	124	Ukraine	3.80
45	Uruguay	2.70	124	Zimbabwe	3.80
48	Botswana	2.75	129	Albania	3.85
48	Guatemala	2.75	129	Bangladesh	3.85
48	Jordan	2.75	129	Mozambique	3.85
48	Namibia	2.75	129	Suriname	3.85
48	Oman	2.75	133	Burundi	3.90
48	Philippines	2.75	134	Togo	3.95
54	Belize	2.80	135	Haiti	4.00
54	Costa Rica	2.80	135	Kyrgyz Rep.	4.00
54	Israel	2.80	137	Kazakhstan	4.05
54	Swaziland	2.80	137	Sierra Leone	4.05
54	Turkey	2.80	139	Yemen	4.10
54	Uganda	2.80	140	Belarus	4.15
54	Samoa	2.80	141	Sudan	4.20
61	Latvia	2.85	141	Syria	4.20
62	Greece	2.90	143	Azerbaijan	4.30
62	Hungary	2.90	143	Equatorial Guinea	4.30
62	So. Africa	2.90	143	Myanmar	4.30
65	Ecuador	2.95	143	Rwanda	4.30
65	Gabon	2.95	147	Tajikistan	4.40
65	Indonesia	2.95	147	Uzbekistan	4.40
65	Malta	2.95	149	Angola	4.45
65	Morocco	2.95	149	Turkmenistan	4.45
65	Poland	2.95	151	Guinea-Bissau	4.55
65	Tunisia	2.95	152	Vietnam	4.60
72	Ghana	3.00	153	Congo (Zaire)	4.70
72	Lithuania	3.00	153	Iran	4.70
72	Saudi Arabia	3.00	155	Bosnia	4.80
75	Benin	3.05	155	Somalia	4.80
75	Kenya	3.05	157	Iraq	4.90
75	Paraguay	3.05	157	Laos	4.90
75	Qatar	3.05	157	Libya	4.90
75	Slovak Republic	3.05	160	Cuba	5.00
75	Zambia	3.05	160	Korea, North	5.00
81	Colombia	3.10			

Mostly Unfree

MONETARY POLICY
Score: 3–Stable (moderate level of inflation)

Algeria's average annual rate of inflation between 1986 and 1996 was 17.1 percent. Estimates place Algeria's rate of inflation at 5.0 percent for 1997.

CAPITAL FLOWS AND FOREIGN INVESTMENT
Score: 3–Stable (moderate barriers)

Algeria's 1993 investment code does not distinguish between foreign and domestic investment. It includes incentives for foreign investors, but the wording is vague. Laws governing oil and natural gas exploration have been liberalized, resulting in greater foreign investment. The large role played by state enterprises limits investment opportunities, and it is not uncommon for foreign investors to spend two years negotiating with the government officials charged with overseeing investments. Radical Islamic groups attacked and killed several foreign oil workers in 1995 and continue to pose a threat to all foreigners and to government officials.

BANKING
Score: 3–Stable (moderate level of restrictions)

Algeria has liberalized its heavily state-controlled banking sector. Foreign banks may establish operations in Algeria but must maintain the same level of capital as Algerian banks do. The central bank assumes nonperforming commercial loans made by five state banks, many of which are carried by state-controlled enterprises.

WAGE AND PRICE CONTROLS
Score: 3–Stable (moderate level)

The government controls the profit margins and sales of medicine, school supplies, tobacco, sugar, coffee, and vegetable oil. There has been, however, substantial progress toward eliminating price controls. In 1994, 89 percent of the prices of goods considered in the consumer price index were freely determined; in 1989, the figure was only 10 percent. The government's widespread participation in the economy, however, limits pricing competition. Subsidies on food items continue, although many were reduced in 1995. Algeria has a minimum wage.

PROPERTY RIGHTS
Score: 3–Stable (moderate level of protection)

Government expropriation is unlikely in Algeria. Collective farms recently have been parceled and made into lease properties, a modest advance for property rights. Overall, private property is reasonably well-protected. The constitution provides for an independent judiciary but, as the U.S. Department of State reports, "in practice, the Government does not always respect the independence of the judicial system."[3] The most significant threats to private property remain terrorist attacks and the confiscation of property by Islamic militants as they continue their struggle against the government.

REGULATION
Score: 3–Stable (moderate level)

Algeria's relatively few private-sector enterprises must contend with burdensome regulations. Workers cannot be dismissed easily; the norm is employment for life. This represents a considerable burden on foreign companies and the private sector. Setting up a business is fairly straightforward, and there has been some lessening of the difficulties encountered in hiring expatriate workers.

BLACK MARKET
Score: 3–Stable (moderate level of activity)

Subsidies on foodstuffs have led to the smuggling of goods into neighboring countries. There is considerable smuggling of high-tariff electronics and textiles. Algeria has advanced, efficient laws protecting such intellectual property rights. Enforcement is strict.

NOTES

1 World Bank, "Open Economies Work Better," *Policy Research Working Paper* No. 1636, 1996.
2 U.S. Department of Commerce, *Country Commercial Guide*, 1998.
3 U.S. Department of State, "Algeria Country Report on Human Rights Practices for 1997," 1998.

Angola   4.45

1998 Score: **4.35**	1997 Score: **4.35**	1996 Score: **4.35**

Trade	5	Banking	4
Taxation	3.5	Wages and Prices	4
Government Intervention	5	Property Rights	4
Monetary Policy	5	Regulation	5
Foreign Investment	4	Black Market	5

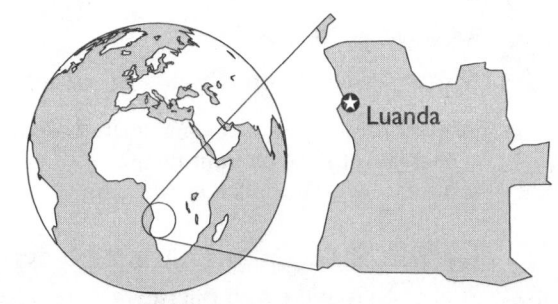

Angola went to war with colonial power Portugal in 1961 and finally won its independence in 1975. The government adopted a socialist economic system and established close ties with Cuba and the Soviet Union. Since 1975, Angola has been embroiled almost continually in civil war, including a 20-year conflict between the government and the National Union for the Total Independence of Angola (UNITA) that has left the country economically devastated and unable to take advantage of its considerable natural resources, which include oil, diamonds, and numerous minable ores. Despite apparent progress in late 1997 and early 1998 in implementing the 1994 peace agreement between the government of President Jose-Eduardo dos Santos and UNITA leader Jonas Savimbi, the peace process again is deteriorating and tensions between the two groups remain high; in fact, open conflict re-erupted in October 1998. GDP growth averaged 9.1 percent from 1994 to 1997. The economy remains vulnerable, however, to changes in the price of oil, which accounted for nearly 60 percent of GDP in 1996. Progress toward economic liberalization remains slow, and many key businesses remain in government hands. Government consumption has increased. As a result, Angola's overall score is 0.1 point worse than last year.

TRADE POLICY
Score: 5–Stable (very high level of protectionism)

Angola's market is virtually closed. The average tariff rate is about 30 percent, and the market is highly protected by a wall of trade quotas and import licenses that are required for all imports. Corruption in the customs service hampers foreign imports, and politically well-connected firms continue to dominate trade. "State owned firms in some service industries have in the recent past attempted to keep out foreign competition, sometimes with success," reports the U.S. Department of Commerce.[1] The United States has frozen UNITA's assets inside the United States and imposed a trade embargo against it.

TAXATION
Score–Income taxation: 2–Stable (low tax rates)
Score–Corporate taxation: 4–Stable (high tax rates)
Final Taxation Score: 3.5–Stable (high tax rates)

Angola's top marginal income tax rate is 40 percent. For the average income level, the rate is 4 percent. The government also imposes a top corporate tax rate of 40 percent, a 40 percent tax on capital gains, and a 7 percent social contributions tax.

GOVERNMENT INTERVENTION IN THE ECONOMY
Score: 5– (very high level)

Government consumes 46.1 percent of GDP, up from 33.9 percent in 1995. As a result, Angola's score in this factor is 1 point worse this year. Progress toward privatization has been minimal, and the government continues to control most economic sectors.

1	Hong Kong	1.25		81	Fiji	3.10
2	Singapore	1.30		81	Mali	3.10
3	Bahrain	1.70		81	Slovenia	3.10
4	New Zealand	1.75		85	Honduras	3.15
5	Switzerland	1.85		85	Mexico	3.15
6	United States	1.90		85	Papua New Guinea	3.15
7	Ireland	1.95		88	Djibouti	3.20
7	Luxembourg	1.95		88	Mongolia	3.20
7	Taiwan	1.95		90	Algeria	3.25
7	United Kingdom	1.95		90	Brazil	3.25
11	Bahamas	2.00		90	Lebanon	3.25
12	Czech Republic	2.05		90	Senegal	3.25
12	Japan	2.05		90	Tanzania	3.25
14	Australia	2.10		95	Nigeria	3.30
14	Belgium	2.10		95	Romania	3.30
14	Canada	2.10		97	Cambodia	3.35
14	United Arab Emirates	2.10		97	Dominican Republic	3.35
18	Austria	2.15		97	Egypt	3.35
18	Chile	2.15		97	Guinea	3.35
18	Estonia	2.15		97	Ivory Coast	3.35
18	Netherlands	2.15		97	Moldova	3.35
22	Denmark	2.25		97	Pakistan	3.35
22	El Salvador	2.25		104	Nepal	3.40
22	Finland	2.25		104	Venezuela	3.40
25	Germany	2.30		106	Armenia	3.45
25	Iceland	2.30		106	Bulgaria	3.45
27	Norway	2.35		106	Lesotho	3.45
28	Korea, South	2.40		106	Madagascar	3.45
28	Kuwait	2.40		106	Russia	3.45
28	Malaysia	2.40		111	Burkina Faso	3.50
28	Panama	2.40		111	Cameroon	3.50
28	Thailand	2.40		111	Guyana	3.50
33	Sweden	2.45		111	Nicaragua	3.50
34	Argentina	2.50		115	Gambia	3.60
34	France	2.50		116	Croatia	3.65
34	Italy	2.50		116	Georgia	3.65
34	Spain	2.50		116	Malawi	3.65
38	Portugal	2.55		119	Cape Verde	3.67
38	Sri Lanka	2.55		120	Ethiopia	3.70
38	Trinidad and Tobago	2.55		120	India	3.70
41	Barbados	2.60		120	Niger	3.70
41	Peru	2.60		123	Congo	3.75
43	Bolivia	2.65		124	Chad	3.80
43	Mauritius	2.65		124	China	3.80
45	Cyprus	2.70		124	Mauritania	3.80
45	Jamaica	2.70		124	Ukraine	3.80
45	Uruguay	2.70		124	Zimbabwe	3.80
48	Botswana	2.75		129	Albania	3.85
48	Guatemala	2.75		129	Bangladesh	3.85
48	Jordan	2.75		129	Mozambique	3.85
48	Namibia	2.75		129	Suriname	3.85
48	Oman	2.75		133	Burundi	3.90
48	Philippines	2.75		134	Togo	3.95
54	Belize	2.80		135	Haiti	4.00
54	Costa Rica	2.80		135	Kyrgyz Rep.	4.00
54	Israel	2.80		137	Kazakhstan	4.05
54	Swaziland	2.80		137	Sierra Leone	4.05
54	Turkey	2.80		139	Yemen	4.10
54	Uganda	2.80		140	Belarus	4.15
54	Samoa	2.80		141	Sudan	4.20
61	Latvia	2.85		141	Syria	4.20
62	Greece	2.90		143	Azerbaijan	4.30
62	Hungary	2.90		143	Equatorial Guinea	4.30
62	So. Africa	2.90		143	Myanmar	4.30
65	Ecuador	2.95		143	Rwanda	4.30
65	Gabon	2.95		147	Tajikistan	4.40
65	Indonesia	2.95		147	Uzbekistan	4.40
65	Malta	2.95		149	Angola	4.45
65	Morocco	2.95		149	Turkmenistan	4.45
65	Poland	2.95		151	Guinea-Bissau	4.55
65	Tunisia	2.95		152	Vietnam	4.60
72	Ghana	3.00		153	Congo (Zaire)	4.70
72	Lithuania	3.00		153	Iran	4.70
72	Saudi Arabia	3.00		155	Bosnia	4.80
75	Benin	3.05		155	Somalia	4.80
75	Kenya	3.05		157	Iraq	4.90
75	Paraguay	3.05		157	Laos	4.90
75	Qatar	3.05		157	Libya	4.90
75	Slovak Republic	3.05		160	Cuba	5.00
75	Zambia	3.05		160	Korea, North	5.00
81	Colombia	3.10				

Repressed

MONETARY POLICY
Score: 5–Stable (very high level of inflation)

Inflation has reached astronomical levels. The average annual rate of inflation from 1986 to 1996 was 458.4 percent; in 1997, the inflation rate was 160 percent.

CAPITAL FLOWS AND FOREIGN INVESTMENT
Score: 4–Stable (high barriers)

In effect, Angola is closed to most foreign investment. The economic and political crisis serves to deter foreign investment, which is prohibited in several sectors anyway. Red tape and corruption plague the investment-approval bureaucracy. All investments are approved on a case-by-case basis. Although there has been some easing of investment restrictions, several proposed projects languish because of government roadblocks. The U.S. Department of Commerce reports that "Foreign investment remains prohibited or limited in defense, law and order, banking, public telecommunications, energy, media, education, health and transport."[2]

BANKING
Score: 4–Stable (high level of restrictions)

For the most part, the government controls Angola's banks. Despite recent attempts to allow foreign investment in banks, little progress has been made. Three Portuguese banks have announced plans to expand operation to some of Angola's provincial capitals.

WAGE AND PRICE CONTROLS
Score: 4–Stable (high level)

The government has lifted price controls on some items but kept them in place for many other goods and services. The Ministry of Labor and Social Security sets wages and benefits. Petroleum price subsidies were eliminated recently, but large subsidies remain on a broad array of services, including transportation and telecommunications. According to the U.S. Department of State, "While the Government took some measures to increase the availability and control the prices of consumer staples, these unsustainable initiatives did not remedy the root causes of economic stability."[3]

PROPERTY RIGHTS
Score: 4–Stable (low level of protection)

The government has few means to protect private property, and expropriation is likely. Corruption and bureaucratic inefficiency still are pervasive. According to the U.S. Department of State, "The Constitution provides for an independent judiciary, but in practice the court system lacked the means, experience, and training to be truly independent from the influence of the President.... The judicial system was largely destroyed during the civil war and during 1996 did not function in large areas of the country."[4]

REGULATION
Score: 5–Stable (very high level)

Government regulations are a severe hindrance to business. Labor regulations are particularly onerous. Corruption and bureaucratic red tape have created an environment in which legal businesses find it nearly impossible to operate. According to the U.S. Department of Commerce, "Administrative chaos, corruption, hyperinflation, and war have vitiated normal economic activity and attempts at reform."[5] The U.S. Department of State reports that "Foreign nationals, especially independent entrepreneurs, are subject to arbitrary detention and/or deportation by immigration and police authorities."[6]

BLACK MARKET
Score: 5–Stable (very high level of activity)

A significant share of Angola's economic output goes through the black market. The government has been cracking down on "parallel economic activities," but both medicine and food are sold on the black market, and there is considerable smuggling of goods. An illegal diamond trade also exists. The civil war, too, has boosted black market activity. According to the U.S. Department of Commerce, "To date, Angola has not adhered to any of the principal international intellectual property rights conventions."[7]

NOTES

[1]   U.S. Department of Commerce, *Country Commercial Guide*, 1996.
[2]   *Ibid.*
[3]   U.S. Department of State, "Angola Country Report on Human Rights Practices for 1997," 1998.
[4]   *Ibid.*
[5]   U.S. Department of Commerce, *Country Commercial Guide*, 1996.
[6]   U.S. Department of State, "Angola—Travel Warning," April 18, 1997.
[7]   *Ibid.*

Argentina   2.50

Trade	3	Banking	2
Taxation	3	Wages and Prices	2
Government Intervention	2	Property Rights	2
Monetary Policy	5	Regulation	2
Foreign Investment	2	Black Market	2

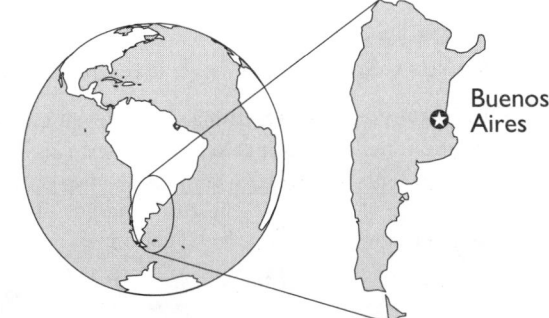

Buenos Aires

Argentina was the world's fourth richest country in the 1930s. Its standard of living was equal to those of the United States and much of Europe. Following World War II, however, the government introduced a series of social and economic policies that helped to send the economy into a spiraling decline. Argentina then retreated into a policy of isolationism that lasted until 1989. In 1990, under the leadership of President Carlos Menem, Argentina began a free-market revival that has increased economic freedom. As a result, inflation has stabilized and the economy is growing. From 1991 to 1994, the economy grew by an average of 8 percent annually. Economic growth slowed to 4.3 percent in 1996, but rebounded in 1997 with nearly 8 percent growth. Argentina's average tariff rate is shrinking. As a result, its overall score is 0.1 point better than last year.

TRADE POLICY
Score: 3+ (moderate level of protectionism)

Argentina's average tariff rate is about 9.4 percent, down from 10 percent last year.[1] As a result, Argentina's trade policy score is 1 point better than it was last year. Some non-tariff barriers remain in the country's rapidly opening market. For example, faced with the global proliferation of antidumping laws and duties, especially U.S. duties on Argentine exports to the United States, Argentina responded by enforcing its antidumping laws more aggressively. The result was higher duties on some items like textile products. There also are trade quotas for some imported automobiles. According to the U.S. Department of State, "Customs procedures are cumbersome and time consuming, thus raising the cost for importers."[2]

TAX POLICY
Score–Income taxation: 2-Stable (low tax rates)
Score–Corporate taxation: 3–Stable (moderate tax rates)
Final Taxation Score: 3-Stable (moderate tax rates)

Argentina has reduced its tax rates to stimulate the economy. The top income tax rate is 30 percent, and the rate for the average income level is 6 percent. The top marginal corporate tax rate is 33. Argentina also maintains a 33 percent capital gains tax and a value-added tax between 10.5 percent and 27 percent.

GOVERNMENT INTERVENTION IN THE ECONOMY
Score: 2–Stable (low level)

Government consumes about 15 percent of GDP. Argentina has undertaken a massive privatization program that is open to both foreign and domestic investors. Even some nuclear power plants are being privatized in part. If completed, this privatization program will reduce government involvement in the economy and expand opportunities for investors significantly. Argentina also is privatizing its pension fund, much as Chile has done.

1	Hong Kong	1.25		81	Fiji	3.10
2	Singapore	1.30		81	Mali	3.10
3	Bahrain	1.70		81	Slovenia	3.10
4	New Zealand	1.75		85	Honduras	3.15
5	Switzerland	1.85		85	Mexico	3.15
6	United States	1.90		85	Papua New Guinea	3.15
7	Ireland	1.95		88	Djibouti	3.20
7	Luxembourg	1.95		88	Mongolia	3.20
7	Taiwan	1.95		90	Algeria	3.25
7	United Kingdom	1.95		90	Brazil	3.25
11	Bahamas	2.00		90	Lebanon	3.25
12	Czech Republic	2.05		90	Senegal	3.25
12	Japan	2.05		90	Tanzania	3.25
14	Australia	2.10		95	Nigeria	3.30
14	Belgium	2.10		95	Romania	3.30
14	Canada	2.10		97	Cambodia	3.35
14	United Arab Emirates	2.10		97	Dominican Republic	3.35
18	Austria	2.15		97	Egypt	3.35
18	Chile	2.15		97	Guinea	3.35
18	Estonia	2.15		97	Ivory Coast	3.35
18	Netherlands	2.15		97	Moldova	3.35
22	Denmark	2.25		97	Pakistan	3.35
22	El Salvador	2.25		104	Nepal	3.40
22	Finland	2.25		104	Venezuela	3.40
25	Germany	2.30		106	Armenia	3.45
25	Iceland	2.30		106	Bulgaria	3.45
27	Norway	2.35		106	Lesotho	3.45
28	Korea, South	2.40		106	Madagascar	3.45
28	Kuwait	2.40		106	Russia	3.45
28	Malaysia	2.40		111	Burkina Faso	3.50
28	Panama	2.40		111	Cameroon	3.50
28	Thailand	2.40		111	Guyana	3.50
33	Sweden	2.45		111	Nicaragua	3.50
34	Argentina	2.50		115	Gambia	3.60
34	France	2.50		116	Croatia	3.65
34	Italy	2.50		116	Georgia	3.65
34	Spain	2.50		116	Malawi	3.65
38	Portugal	2.55		119	Cape Verde	3.67
38	Sri Lanka	2.55		120	Ethiopia	3.70
38	Trinidad and Tobago	2.55		120	India	3.70
41	Barbados	2.60		120	Niger	3.70
41	Peru	2.60		123	Congo	3.75
43	Bolivia	2.65		124	Chad	3.80
43	Mauritius	2.65		124	China	3.80
45	Cyprus	2.70		124	Mauritania	3.80
45	Jamaica	2.70		124	Ukraine	3.80
45	Uruguay	2.70		124	Zimbabwe	3.80
48	Botswana	2.75		129	Albania	3.85
48	Guatemala	2.75		129	Bangladesh	3.85
48	Jordan	2.75		129	Mozambique	3.85
48	Namibia	2.75		129	Suriname	3.85
48	Oman	2.75		133	Burundi	3.90
48	Philippines	2.75		134	Togo	3.95
54	Belize	2.80		135	Haiti	4.00
54	Costa Rica	2.80		135	Kyrgyz Rep.	4.00
54	Israel	2.80		137	Kazakhstan	4.05
54	Swaziland	2.80		137	Sierra Leone	4.05
54	Turkey	2.80		139	Yemen	4.10
54	Uganda	2.80		140	Belarus	4.15
54	Samoa	2.80		141	Sudan	4.20
61	Latvia	2.85		141	Syria	4.20
62	Greece	2.90		143	Azerbaijan	4.30
62	Hungary	2.90		143	Equatorial Guinea	4.30
62	So. Africa	2.90		143	Myanmar	4.30
65	Ecuador	2.95		143	Rwanda	4.30
65	Gabon	2.95		147	Tajikistan	4.40
65	Indonesia	2.95		147	Uzbekistan	4.40
65	Malta	2.95		149	Angola	4.45
65	Morocco	2.95		149	Turkmenistan	4.45
65	Poland	2.95		151	Guinea-Bissau	4.55
65	Tunisia	2.95		152	Vietnam	4.60
72	Ghana	3.00		153	Congo (Zaire)	4.70
72	Lithuania	3.00		153	Iran	4.70
72	Saudi Arabia	3.00		155	Bosnia	4.80
75	Benin	3.05		155	Somalia	4.80
75	Kenya	3.05		157	Iraq	4.90
75	Paraguay	3.05		157	Laos	4.90
75	Qatar	3.05		157	Libya	4.90
75	Slovak Republic	3.05		160	Cuba	5.00
75	Zambia	3.05		160	Korea, North	5.00
81	Colombia	3.10				

Mostly Free

MONETARY POLICY
Score: 5–Stable (very high level of inflation)

From 1986 to 1996, Argentina's average annual rate of inflation was over 300 percent. In 1997, it was less than 1 percent. This lower figure demonstrates Argentina's commitment to reducing inflation and pursuing sound monetary policies. If this trend continues, the average inflation rate can be expected to decrease over time.

CAPITAL FLOWS AND FOREIGN INVESTMENT
Score: 2–Stable (low barriers)

There are few barriers to investment in Argentina. Firms do not need to gain permission from the government to invest; most local companies may be wholly owned by foreign investors; and no permission is needed to own investment shares in the local stock exchange. These policies have resulted in a significant foreign corporate presence. Foreign investment is prohibited only in the shipbuilding, fishing, and nuclear power–generation industries.

BANKING
Score: 2–Stable (low level of restrictions)

Argentina's banking system is becoming more competitive because of privatization. As banks became profit-driven, they streamlined and modernized their business practices. The government recently reduced most barriers to foreign banking. There no longer are any distinctions between foreign and domestic banks; both are treated equally.

WAGE AND PRICE CONTROLS
Score: 2–Stable (low level)

Under the leadership of President Menem, the government has liberalized prices. Today, no major items are subject to price controls, and the market determines most wages. The government fixes wages for public-sector employees, however, and there is a minimum wage.

PROPERTY RIGHTS
Score: 2–Stable (high level of protection)

Private property is secure in Argentina, and the likelihood of expropriation is low. Court protection of private property, however, can be weak. According to the U.S. Department of State, "The Constitution provides for an independent judiciary. While the judiciary is nominally independent and impartial, its processes are inefficient, complicated, and at time, subject to political influence."[3]

REGULATION
Score: 2–Stable (low level)

Argentina has reduced cumbersome registration requirements. Thus, opening a business is generally easy. Existing regulations are relatively straightforward and, in general, are applied uniformly.

BLACK MARKET
Score: 2–Stable (low level of activity)

In the past, most of GDP was produced in the black market. As Argentina's market has become more integrated into the world economy, however, black market activity has shrunk to the point that it now is minimal. The government has passed new laws extending the protection of intellectual property rights to pharmaceuticals and computer software.

NOTES

[1]   Based on total taxes on international trade as a percentage of total imports. The Menem Administration has been successful in opening Argentina's market to imported goods. In joining the Southern Cone Common Market (Mercosur), however, Argentina raised some of its tariffs to meet the common external tariff of Mercosur members. Thus, the average tariff for non-Mercosur members is closer to 17 percent. Still, Argentina does much trade with Mercosur members Brazil, Paraguay, and Uruguay. Thus, its total trade-weighted average tariff is only 9.4 percent.

[2]   U.S. Department of State, *Country Reports on Economic Policy and Trade Practices,* 1998.

[3]   U.S. Department of State, "Argentina Country Report on Human Rights Practices for 1997," 1998.

Armenia   3.45

1998 Score: **3.45**	1997 Score: **3.45**	1996 Score: **3.75**

Trade	2	Banking	3
Taxation	3.5	Wages and Prices	3
Government Intervention	3	Property Rights	3
Monetary Policy	5	Regulation	4
Foreign Investment	4	Black Market	4

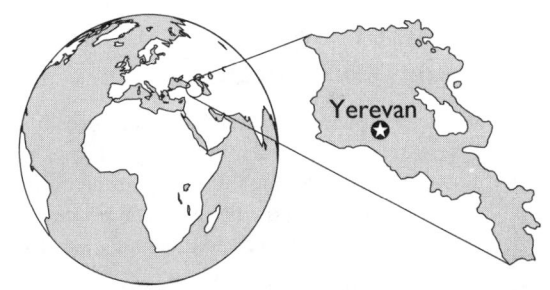

Yerevan

Armenia was an independent country from 1918 until 1922, when it was incorporated into the Soviet Union. Before 1918, it had been divided between the Russian and Ottoman Empires. Armenia became independent once again in September 1991. Since that time, it has attempted to shed its centrally planned, communist economy and adopt a system based on free markets. The move toward a free market, however, has been hindered by political instability, an entrenched bureaucracy, corruption, a war with neighboring Azerbaijan over the enclave of Nagorno-Karabakh, trade embargoes imposed by Azerbaijan and Turkey, and civil unrest in neighboring Georgia. Interruptions in supplies of fuel, natural gas, and electricity also have damaged the economy. Armenia held new elections in 1995, but many observers have questioned the validity of the outcome. Levon Ter-Petrosian, president from 1991 to 1998, strove to re-establish the government's credibility. In early 1998, he was forced out of office by his prime minister, Robert Kocharyan, who subsequently was elected president. Kocharyan's hard-line approach to Nagorno-Karabakh may complicate a solution to the conflict. Kocharyan and his prime minister, Armen Darpinyan (appointed in May 1998) intend to continue economic reform.

TRADE POLICY
Score: 2–Stable (low level of protectionism)

Armenia has an average tariff rate of less than 5 percent. It maintains non-tariff barriers in the form of licensing requirements for several products, including some pharmaceuticals.

TAXATION
Score–Income taxation: 3–Stable (moderate tax rates)
Score–Corporate taxation: 3–Stable (moderate tax rates)
Final Taxation Score: 3.5–Stable (high tax rates)

Armenia has a top income tax rate of 30 percent. The tax on the average income level is 12 percent to 15 percent. The top marginal corporate tax rate is 30 percent. The government also maintains a 20 percent value-added tax.

GOVERNMENT INTERVENTION IN THE ECONOMY
Score: 3–Stable (moderate level)

Government consumes about 13 percent of GDP.[1] Moreover, there is a substantial state-owned sector, and the conflict with Azerbaijan consumes considerable resources.

MONETARY POLICY
Score: 5–Stable (very high level of inflation)

Armenia has been plagued by high inflation rates: 729 percent in 1992, 1,920 percent in 1993, 4,964 percent in 1994, 175.5 percent in 1995, 18.7 percent in 1996, and 13.8 in 1997. Since gaining its independence, Armenia has had an average annual rate of inflation well above 500 percent.

1	Hong Kong	1.25	81	Fiji	3.10
2	Singapore	1.30	81	Mali	3.10
3	Bahrain	1.70	81	Slovenia	3.10
4	New Zealand	1.75	85	Honduras	3.15
5	Switzerland	1.85	85	Mexico	3.15
6	United States	1.90	85	Papua New Guinea	3.15
7	Ireland	1.95	88	Djibouti	3.20
7	Luxembourg	1.95	88	Mongolia	3.20
7	Taiwan	1.95	90	Algeria	3.25
7	United Kingdom	1.95	90	Brazil	3.25
11	Bahamas	2.00	90	Lebanon	3.25
12	Czech Republic	2.05	90	Senegal	3.25
12	Japan	2.05	90	Tanzania	3.25
14	Australia	2.10	95	Nigeria	3.30
14	Belgium	2.10	95	Romania	3.30
14	Canada	2.10	97	Cambodia	3.35
14	United Arab Emirates	2.10	97	Dominican Republic	3.35
18	Austria	2.15	97	Egypt	3.35
18	Chile	2.15	97	Guinea	3.35
18	Estonia	2.15	97	Ivory Coast	3.35
18	Netherlands	2.15	97	Moldova	3.35
22	Denmark	2.25	97	Pakistan	3.35
22	El Salvador	2.25	104	Nepal	3.40
22	Finland	2.25	104	Venezuela	3.40
25	Germany	2.30	106	Armenia	3.45
25	Iceland	2.30	106	Bulgaria	3.45
27	Norway	2.35	106	Lesotho	3.45
28	Korea, South	2.40	106	Madagascar	3.45
28	Kuwait	2.40	106	Russia	3.45
28	Malaysia	2.40	111	Burkina Faso	3.50
28	Panama	2.40	111	Cameroon	3.50
28	Thailand	2.40	111	Guyana	3.50
33	Sweden	2.45	111	Nicaragua	3.50
34	Argentina	2.50	115	Gambia	3.60
34	France	2.50	116	Croatia	3.65
34	Italy	2.50	116	Georgia	3.65
34	Spain	2.50	116	Malawi	3.65
38	Portugal	2.55	119	Cape Verde	3.67
38	Sri Lanka	2.55	120	Ethiopia	3.70
38	Trinidad and Tobago	2.55	120	India	3.70
41	Barbados	2.60	120	Niger	3.70
41	Peru	2.60	123	Congo	3.75
43	Bolivia	2.65	124	Chad	3.80
43	Mauritius	2.65	124	China	3.80
45	Cyprus	2.70	124	Mauritania	3.80
45	Jamaica	2.70	124	Ukraine	3.80
45	Uruguay	2.70	124	Zimbabwe	3.80
48	Botswana	2.75	129	Albania	3.85
48	Guatemala	2.75	129	Bangladesh	3.85
48	Jordan	2.75	129	Mozambique	3.85
48	Namibia	2.75	129	Suriname	3.85
48	Oman	2.75	133	Burundi	3.90
48	Philippines	2.75	134	Togo	3.95
54	Belize	2.80	135	Haiti	4.00
54	Costa Rica	2.80	135	Kyrgyz Rep.	4.00
54	Israel	2.80	137	Kazakhstan	4.05
54	Swaziland	2.80	137	Sierra Leone	4.05
54	Turkey	2.80	139	Yemen	4.10
54	Uganda	2.80	140	Belarus	4.15
54	Samoa	2.80	141	Sudan	4.20
61	Latvia	2.85	141	Syria	4.20
62	Greece	2.90	143	Azerbaijan	4.30
62	Hungary	2.90	143	Equatorial Guinea	4.30
62	So. Africa	2.90	143	Myanmar	4.30
65	Ecuador	2.95	143	Rwanda	4.30
65	Gabon	2.95	147	Tajikistan	4.40
65	Indonesia	2.95	147	Uzbekistan	4.40
65	Malta	2.95	149	Angola	4.45
65	Morocco	2.95	149	Turkmenistan	4.45
65	Poland	2.95	151	Guinea-Bissau	4.55
65	Tunisia	2.95	152	Vietnam	4.60
72	Ghana	3.00	153	Congo (Zaire)	4.70
72	Lithuania	3.00	153	Iran	4.70
72	Saudi Arabia	3.00	155	Bosnia	4.80
75	Benin	3.05	155	Somalia	4.80
75	Kenya	3.05	157	Iraq	4.90
75	Paraguay	3.05	157	Laos	4.90
75	Qatar	3.05	157	Libya	4.90
75	Slovak Republic	3.05	160	Cuba	5.00
75	Zambia	3.05	160	Korea, North	5.00
81	Colombia	3.10			

Mostly Unfree

CAPITAL FLOWS AND FOREIGN INVESTMENT
Score: 4–Stable (high barriers)

There are few official restrictions on investment, and investors are welcome in most industries. There are, however, many informal but substantial barriers to investment, including a slow privatization process, inadequate infrastructure, and inefficient banking and court systems.

BANKING
Score: 3–Stable (moderate level of restrictions)

The banking system is becoming more efficient, and there now are more than 40 private banks. These banks offer few services and inadequate lending potential to the private sector (see Capital Flows and Foreign Investment), however, and the government still owns and operates several banks.

WAGE AND PRICE CONTROLS
Score: 3–Stable (moderate level)

The market sets most prices. Price controls on rent, electricity, and public transportation remain in effect, however.

PROPERTY RIGHTS
Score: 3–Stable (moderate level of protection)

Private property is guaranteed by law, but neither legal enforcement nor the judicial system provides adequate protection. "According to the Foreign Investment Law," reports the U.S. Department of Commerce, "all disputes that may arise between a foreign investor and the Republic of Armenia must be settled in the Armenian courts."[2] This restricts the ability of property owners—especially foreign investors—to receive an impartial hearing. Moreover, the judiciary is not entirely independent. According to the U.S. Department of State, "The Constitution provides for an independent judiciary; however, in practice judges are subject to political pressure from the executive branch."[3] By global standards, however, Armenia provides a moderate level of protection of private property.

REGULATION
Score: 4–Stable (high level)

It is becoming easier to establish a business in Armenia. A corrupt bureaucracy, however, often applies the regulations haphazardly. According to the U.S. Department of Commerce, "Bureaucratic procedures may appear burdensome and time consuming when an investor is negotiating a contract with the Armenian government, as the contract may require approval by several ministries and usually goes back and forth many times."[4]

BLACK MARKET
Score: 4–Stable (high level of activity)

Some black market activity is found in the transportation and labor sectors. Because of trade embargoes, many goods (including foodstuffs) are smuggled, primarily from Iran. In addition, Armenia does not provide sufficient protection of intellectual property, and piracy is rampant. According to the U.S. Department of State, "Piracy of literary, video, audio materials and software is widespread and poorly controlled."[5]

NOTES

[1]   World Bank, *World Development Indicators,* 1998.
[2]   U.S. Department of Commerce, *Country Commercial Guide,* 1998.
[3]   U.S. Department of State, "Armenia Country Report on Human Rights Practices for 1997," 1998.
[4]   U.S. Department of Commerce, *Country Commercial Guide,* 1998.
[5]   U.S. Department of State, "Armenia Country Report on Human Rights Practices for 1997," 1998.

Australia   2.10

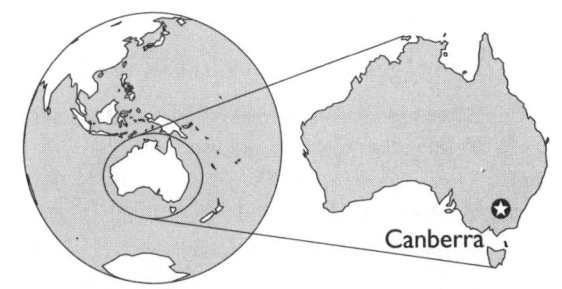

Canberra

| 1998 **2.05** | 1997 Score: **2.15** | 1996 Score: **2.10** |

Trade	2	Banking	1
Taxation	5	Wages and Prices	2
Government Intervention	3	Property Rights	1
Monetary Policy	1	Regulation	3
Foreign Investment	2	Black Market	1

Through most of its history, Australia maintained high trade barriers in order to promote industrialization, shunned trade with its Asian neighbors, and based wages and working conditions on principles of social justice rather than market conditions. With the election of a Labour Party government in 1983, Australia began to deregulate financial markets, remove substantial trade barriers, improve ties with Asia, and privatize many federally owned firms. Today, Australia is a leading force seeking trade liberalization in the World Trade Organization and the Asia Pacific Economic Cooperation forum. The Liberal–National Coalition government, headed by John Howard, was elected in March 1996 and has pledged to defederalize the labor market and reduce the swelling budget deficit—not by raising taxes, but by cutting spending. The first year's budget did curtail spending, and the government seems near its goal of reaching a budget surplus within three years. The tax on the average income level, however, is higher now than last year. Thus, Australia's overall score is 0.05 point worse this year.

TRADE POLICY
Score: 2–Stable (low level of protectionism)

Australia has an average tariff rate of 2.8 percent. It maintains non-tariff barriers in the form of strict health requirements on agricultural goods and strict import licenses for certain automobiles, textiles, clothing, and footwear.

TAXATION
Score–Income taxation: 5– (very high tax rates)
Score–Corporate taxation: 4–Stable (high tax rates)
Final Taxation Score: 5- (very high tax rates)

Australia's top income tax rate is 47 percent; the average income level is taxed at a rate of 34 percent, up from 20 percent. As a result, Australia's income taxation score is 1 point worse, making its final taxation score 0.5 point worse than last year. The top corporate tax rate is 36 percent, up from 33 percent in 1995. Australia has a 12 percent to 45 percent wholesale sales tax. Capital gains, after adjustment for inflation, are taxed at the same rate as other personal or corporate income.

GOVERNMENT INTERVENTION IN THE ECONOMY
Score: 3–Stable (moderate level)

The government consumes 16.5 percent of GDP. State-owned enterprises still exist in such industries as telecommunications, utilities, and railways. The Howard government, however, privatized some shares in a federally owned telecommunications firm in 1996, and one state, Victoria, privatized its electricity generation, distribution, and transmission system.

1	Hong Kong	1.25	81	Fiji	3.10
2	Singapore	1.30	81	Mali	3.10
3	Bahrain	1.70	81	Slovenia	3.10
4	New Zealand	1.75	85	Honduras	3.15
5	Switzerland	1.85	85	Mexico	3.15
6	United States	1.90	85	Papua New Guinea	3.15
7	Ireland	1.95	88	Djibouti	3.20
7	Luxembourg	1.95	88	Mongolia	3.20
7	Taiwan	1.95	90	Algeria	3.25
7	United Kingdom	1.95	90	Brazil	3.25
11	Bahamas	2.00	90	Lebanon	3.25
12	Czech Republic	2.05	90	Senegal	3.25
12	Japan	2.05	90	Tanzania	3.25
14	Australia	2.10	95	Nigeria	3.30
14	Belgium	2.10	95	Romania	3.30
14	Canada	2.10	97	Cambodia	3.35
14	United Arab Emirates	2.10	97	Dominican Republic	3.35
18	Austria	2.15	97	Egypt	3.35
18	Chile	2.15	97	Guinea	3.35
18	Estonia	2.15	97	Ivory Coast	3.35
18	Netherlands	2.15	97	Moldova	3.35
22	Denmark	2.25	97	Pakistan	3.35
22	El Salvador	2.25	104	Nepal	3.40
22	Finland	2.25	104	Venezuela	3.40
25	Germany	2.30	106	Armenia	3.45
25	Iceland	2.30	106	Bulgaria	3.45
27	Norway	2.35	106	Lesotho	3.45
28	Korea, South	2.40	106	Madagascar	3.45
28	Kuwait	2.40	106	Russia	3.45
28	Malaysia	2.40	111	Burkina Faso	3.50
28	Panama	2.40	111	Cameroon	3.50
28	Thailand	2.40	111	Guyana	3.50
33	Sweden	2.45	111	Nicaragua	3.50
34	Argentina	2.50	115	Gambia	3.60
34	France	2.50	116	Croatia	3.65
34	Italy	2.50	116	Georgia	3.65
34	Spain	2.50	116	Malawi	3.65
38	Portugal	2.55	119	Cape Verde	3.67
38	Sri Lanka	2.55	120	Ethiopia	3.70
38	Trinidad and Tobago	2.55	120	India	3.70
41	Barbados	2.60	120	Niger	3.70
41	Peru	2.60	123	Congo	3.75
43	Bolivia	2.65	124	Chad	3.80
43	Mauritius	2.65	124	China	3.80
45	Cyprus	2.70	124	Mauritania	3.80
45	Jamaica	2.70	124	Ukraine	3.80
45	Uruguay	2.70	124	Zimbabwe	3.80
48	Botswana	2.75	129	Albania	3.85
48	Guatemala	2.75	129	Bangladesh	3.85
48	Jordan	2.75	129	Mozambique	3.85
48	Namibia	2.75	129	Suriname	3.85
48	Oman	2.75	133	Burundi	3.90
48	Philippines	2.75	134	Togo	3.95
54	Belize	2.80	135	Haiti	4.00
54	Costa Rica	2.80	135	Kyrgyz Rep.	4.00
54	Israel	2.80	137	Kazakhstan	4.05
54	Swaziland	2.80	137	Sierra Leone	4.05
54	Turkey	2.80	139	Yemen	4.10
54	Uganda	2.80	140	Belarus	4.15
54	Samoa	2.80	141	Sudan	4.20
61	Latvia	2.85	141	Syria	4.20
62	Greece	2.90	143	Azerbaijan	4.30
62	Hungary	2.90	143	Equatorial Guinea	4.30
62	So. Africa	2.90	143	Myanmar	4.30
65	Ecuador	2.95	143	Rwanda	4.30
65	Gabon	2.95	147	Tajikistan	4.40
65	Indonesia	2.95	147	Uzbekistan	4.40
65	Malta	2.95	149	Angola	4.45
65	Morocco	2.95	149	Turkmenistan	4.45
65	Poland	2.95	151	Guinea-Bissau	4.55
65	Tunisia	2.95	152	Vietnam	4.60
72	Ghana	3.00	153	Congo (Zaire)	4.70
72	Lithuania	3.00	153	Iran	4.70
72	Saudi Arabia	3.00	155	Bosnia	4.80
75	Benin	3.05	155	Somalia	4.80
75	Kenya	3.05	157	Iraq	4.90
75	Paraguay	3.05	157	Laos	4.90
75	Qatar	3.05	157	Libya	4.90
75	Slovak Republic	3.05	160	Cuba	5.00
75	Zambia	3.05	160	Korea, North	5.00
81	Colombia	3.10			

Mostly Free

Monetary Policy
Score: 1–Stable (very low level of inflation)

From 1986 to 1996, inflation averaged 4.2 percent annually. In 1997, the inflation rate was 1 percent.

Capital Flows and Foreign Investment
Score: 2–Stable (low barriers)

Australia has opened its economy to foreign investment. It provides equal treatment for domestic and foreign firms and has opened particular service industries, such as insurance and accounting, to some foreign participation.

Banking
Score: 1–Stable (very low level of restrictions)

Banks are relatively free of intrusive government control. Foreigners are allowed to establish wholly owned institutions or branches. The banking system, once dominated by a few banks, has been deregulated substantially. In 1985, Australia began to allow foreign banks to enter the market, and over 30 foreign banks have obtained banking licenses thus far.

Wage and Price Controls
Score: 2–Stable (low level)

Minimum wages and working conditions are determined through a mandatory and centralized arbitration process involving labor, government, and business. The market determines most wages and almost all prices, however.

Property Rights
Score: 1–Stable (very high level of protection)

Property is very secure in Australia, which has an efficient legal and judicial system that enforces contracts and settles disputes. Government expropriation is highly unlikely.

Regulation
Score: 3–Stable (moderate level)

Some regulations are cumbersome, especially those affecting labor, occupational safety and health standards, and the environment. Australia maintains commodity boards in several agricultural products that regulate the distribution, and sometimes exports, of various agricultural goods.

Black Market
Score: 1–Stable (very low level of activity)

The size of Australia's black market activity is negligible. The government enforces intellectual property rights laws well, and it has reduced piracy in recorded music, film, and computer software significantly.

Austria

2.15

1998 **2.15**	1997 Score: **2.15**	1996 Score: **2.05**

Trade	2	Banking	2
Taxation	4.5	Wages and Prices	2
Government Intervention	3	Property Rights	1
Monetary Policy	1	Regulation	3
Foreign Investment	2	Black Market	1

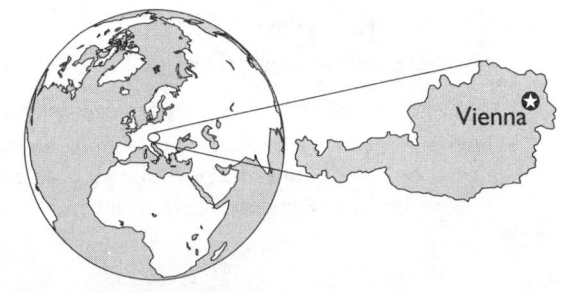
Vienna

The Republic of Austria emerged in 1918 from the ashes of the Austro-Hungarian Empire. After World War II, Austria was occupied by U.S. and Soviet troops; in 1955, it became an independent neutral country. Although ruled mainly by socialist parties since that time, Austria has pursued some free-market policies. It maintains a relatively high standard of living. Austria became a member of the European Union (EU) in 1995. Since then, most economic changes have been designed to bring the economy into conformity with EU standards.

TRADE POLICY
Score: 2–Stable (low level of protectionism)

When Austria entered the EU, 63 percent of its tariffs were lowered and 31 percent were increased. "Although Austria has reduced its customs duties in recent years," reports the Economist Intelligence Unit, "import tariffs at an average of 10.7 percent are higher than the EU average of 7.3 percent."[1] Sixty percent of all products from non-EU countries, however, enter without any tariff. Thus, weighted to take into account duty-free imports, Austria's average tariff rate is much lower: about 3.3 percent. Austria has non-tariff barriers common to other EU members, as well as additional certification requirements for some electronic goods that may restrict imports.

TAXATION
Score–Income taxation: 5–Stable (very high tax rates)
Score–Corporate taxation: 3–Stable (moderate tax rates)
Final Taxation Score: 4.5–Stable (very high tax rates)

Austria has a top income tax rate of 50 percent; the average income level is taxed at 32 percent. The top corporate tax rate is 34 percent. Austria also imposes several other taxes, including a 34 percent capital gains tax, a 20 percent value-added tax, and a 3.5 percent real estate tax.

GOVERNMENT INTERVENTION IN THE ECONOMY
Score: 3–Stable (moderate level)

Austria's government consumes 18.8 percent of GDP. There is a large state-owned industrial sector, however, and a recent privatization program is slowing. One-third of the work force is employed in the public sector. The government either owns outright or has controlling stakes in Austrian Radio and Television, Austrian Airlines, postal services, and long-distance busing. Nevertheless, government involvement in the economy is moderate by global standards.

MONETARY POLICY
Score: 1–Stable (very low level of inflation)

Austria had an average annual rate of inflation of 2.8 percent from 1986 to 1996. The rate was about 1.3 percent in 1997.

1	Hong Kong	1.25	81	Fiji	3.10
2	Singapore	1.30	81	Mali	3.10
3	Bahrain	1.70	81	Slovenia	3.10
4	New Zealand	1.75	85	Honduras	3.15
5	Switzerland	1.85	85	Mexico	3.15
6	United States	1.90	85	Papua New Guinea	3.15
7	Ireland	1.95	88	Djibouti	3.20
7	Luxembourg	1.95	88	Mongolia	3.20
7	Taiwan	1.95	90	Algeria	3.25
7	United Kingdom	1.95	90	Brazil	3.25
11	Bahamas	2.00	90	Lebanon	3.25
12	Czech Republic	2.05	90	Senegal	3.25
12	Japan	2.05	90	Tanzania	3.25
14	Australia	2.10	95	Nigeria	3.30
14	Belgium	2.10	95	Romania	3.30
14	Canada	2.10	97	Cambodia	3.35
14	United Arab Emirates	2.10	97	Dominican Republic	3.35
18	Austria	2.15	97	Egypt	3.35
18	Chile	2.15	97	Guinea	3.35
18	Estonia	2.15	97	Ivory Coast	3.35
18	Netherlands	2.15	97	Moldova	3.35
22	Denmark	2.25	97	Pakistan	3.35
22	El Salvador	2.25	104	Nepal	3.40
22	Finland	2.25	104	Venezuela	3.40
25	Germany	2.30	106	Armenia	3.45
25	Iceland	2.30	106	Bulgaria	3.45
27	Norway	2.35	106	Lesotho	3.45
28	Korea, South	2.40	106	Madagascar	3.45
28	Kuwait	2.40	106	Russia	3.45
28	Malaysia	2.40	111	Burkina Faso	3.50
28	Panama	2.40	111	Cameroon	3.50
28	Thailand	2.40	111	Guyana	3.50
33	Sweden	2.45	111	Nicaragua	3.50
34	Argentina	2.50	115	Gambia	3.60
34	France	2.50	116	Croatia	3.65
34	Italy	2.50	116	Georgia	3.65
34	Spain	2.50	116	Malawi	3.65
38	Portugal	2.55	119	Cape Verde	3.67
38	Sri Lanka	2.55	120	Ethiopia	3.70
38	Trinidad and Tobago	2.55	120	India	3.70
41	Barbados	2.60	120	Niger	3.70
41	Peru	2.60	123	Congo	3.75
43	Bolivia	2.65	124	Chad	3.80
43	Mauritius	2.65	124	China	3.80
45	Cyprus	2.70	124	Mauritania	3.80
45	Jamaica	2.70	124	Ukraine	3.80
45	Uruguay	2.70	124	Zimbabwe	3.80
48	Botswana	2.75	129	Albania	3.85
48	Guatemala	2.75	129	Bangladesh	3.85
48	Jordan	2.75	129	Mozambique	3.85
48	Namibia	2.75	129	Suriname	3.85
48	Oman	2.75	133	Burundi	3.90
48	Philippines	2.75	134	Togo	3.95
54	Belize	2.80	135	Haiti	4.00
54	Costa Rica	2.80	135	Kyrgyz Rep.	4.00
54	Israel	2.80	137	Kazakhstan	4.05
54	Swaziland	2.80	137	Sierra Leone	4.05
54	Turkey	2.80	139	Yemen	4.10
54	Uganda	2.80	140	Belarus	4.15
54	Samoa	2.80	141	Sudan	4.20
61	Latvia	2.85	141	Syria	4.20
62	Greece	2.90	143	Azerbaijan	4.30
62	Hungary	2.90	143	Equatorial Guinea	4.30
62	So. Africa	2.90	143	Myanmar	4.30
65	Ecuador	2.95	143	Rwanda	4.30
65	Gabon	2.95	147	Tajikistan	4.40
65	Indonesia	2.95	147	Uzbekistan	4.40
65	Malta	2.95	149	Angola	4.45
65	Morocco	2.95	149	Turkmenistan	4.45
65	Poland	2.95	151	Guinea-Bissau	4.55
65	Tunisia	2.95	152	Vietnam	4.60
72	Ghana	3.00	153	Congo (Zaire)	4.70
72	Lithuania	3.00	153	Iran	4.70
72	Saudi Arabia	3.00	155	Bosnia	4.80
75	Benin	3.05	155	Somalia	4.80
75	Kenya	3.05	157	Iraq	4.90
75	Paraguay	3.05	157	Laos	4.90
75	Qatar	3.05	157	Libya	4.90
75	Slovak Republic	3.05	160	Cuba	5.00
75	Zambia	3.05	160	Korea, North	5.00
81	Colombia	3.10			

Mostly Free

CAPITAL FLOWS AND FOREIGN INVESTMENT
Score: 2–Stable (low barriers)

Austria depends heavily on foreign investment and welcomes it openly. There are few restrictions, although foreign investors at times must deal with slow bureaucratic procedures to gain approval for new operations.

BANKING
Score: 2–Stable (low level of restrictions)

Foreign banks can operate in Austria so long as they have prior government approval. Austrian-owned banks are permitted to engage in all kinds of services, including the underwriting of loans and the brokering of securities and mutual funds. They may own subsidiaries that underwrite and sell insurance policies, and are allowed to invest in, develop, and manage real estate ventures. After six years, however, Austria failed to privatize one of its largest banks, Creditanstalt, and instead sold it to Bank Austria, which is controlled mainly by the government. This is a major setback for Austria's banking sector, which had been moving toward increased independence from the government.

WAGE AND PRICE CONTROLS
Score: 2–Stable (low level)

The market sets most wages and prices. Businesses voluntarily cooperate with the government, however, to set prices; thus, prices are not completely free. Some price controls still are in effect on rail travel, telecommunications, and parts of the energy sector. Austria maintains a minimum wage.

PROPERTY RIGHTS
Score: 1–Stable (very high level of protection)

Property is very secure in Austria, which has an efficient and well-established legal system that respects and protects private property and contractual agreements.

REGULATION
Score: 3–Stable (moderate level)

Although Austrians experienced long periods of economic growth after World War II, they also allowed the state to become involved in regulating the economy. A growing environmental movement threatens to shackle many businesses with burdensome regulations. Competitiveness is hindered further by extensive worker health and safety standards. According to the U.S. Department of Commerce, "The 'U.S. Investor Confidence Survey' recently conducted by the American Chamber of Commerce in Austria in cooperation with the U.S. Embassy in Vienna found that the current regulatory environment with its cumbersome enforcement procedures is unnecessarily complex, with overlapping authorities and a veritable jungle of permits and controls that stymie entrepreneurship."[2] Nevertheless, by global standards, Austria's economy is regulated only moderately.

BLACK MARKET
Score: 1–Stable (very low level of activity)

The size of Austria's black market is relatively small to nonexistent. Goods and services move fairly freely across the border, limiting the incentives for smuggling. The government passed legislation in 1995 to protect many types of intellectual property, including satellite broadcasting and cable television. There still is some piracy of video cassettes and computer software, although these activities are minuscule in comparison with the overall size of the economy.

NOTES

[1] Economist Intelligence Unit, *ILT Reports: Austria,* August 1996, updated February 1997.
[2] U.S. Department of Commerce, *Country Commercial Guide,* 1998.

Azerbaijan 4.30

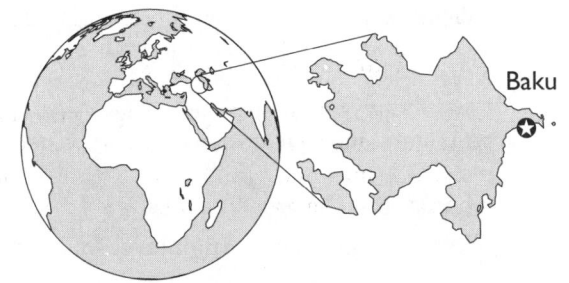
Baku

1998 Score: **4.40**   1997 Score: **4.60**   1996 Score: **4.70**

Trade	5	Banking	4
Taxation	4	Wages and Prices	5
Government Intervention	4	Property Rights	4
Monetary Policy	5	Regulation	4
Foreign Investment	4	Black Market	4

Azerbaijan is an oil-rich, post-Soviet state strategically located on the western coast of the Caspian Sea. Iran ceded territories of Turkic-speaking, predominantly Shiite Azerbaijan to Russia in 1813 and 1828. Azerbaijan gained its independence from Russia in 1918 and then was reconquered by the Soviet Union in 1920. In 1989, Azerbaijan claimed its sovereignty from the Soviet Union; by 1991, it had become fully independent. Since that time, the government (currently led by President Heydar Aliyev, who was re-elected amid controversy in October 1998) has embarked on a course of gradual reform, the success of which is threatened by a well-entrenched bureaucracy. The discovery of significant oil deposits on the shelf of the Caspian Sea (deposits larger than those of the North Sea) has attracted the attention of foreign investors, and several Western-led consortia are working on oil fields. Azerbaijan recently reduced its government consumption level; as a result, its overall score is 0.1 point better than last year.

TRADE POLICY
Score: 5–Stable (very high level of protectionism)

In January 1997, the government passed a new law to establish a uniform tariff rate of 15 percent, which is high by global standards. Azerbaijan imposes significant export tariffs as well, particularly on oil and oil products (70 percent), and significant non-tariff barriers exist, too. According to the U.S. Department of Commerce, "Companies often face problems in getting goods through customs due to officials who delay in hope of receiving bribes."[1]

TAXATION
Score—Income taxation: 4–Stable (high tax rates)
Score—Corporate taxation: 3–Stable (moderate tax rates)
Final Taxation Score: 4–Stable (high tax rates)

Azerbaijan's top income tax rate is 40 percent. The tax on the average income level is 15 percent. The top marginal corporate tax rate is 32 percent, down from 35 percent last year. There also is a 20 percent value-added tax.

GOVERNMENT INTERVENTION IN THE ECONOMY
Score: 4+ (high level)

Azerbaijan is privatizing its large state-owned sector. The economy remains dominated by large state enterprises, however, particularly in the agricultural sector. Reliable government consumption figures do not exist, but there is evidence that Azerbaijan's level of government consumption is shrinking.[2] Although some estimates indicate that the government consumption rate has fallen to only about 10 percent, it is probably closer to 15 percent or 20 percent. According to the U.S. Department of Commerce, "[D]espite the GOAZ's [government of Azerbaijan's] claims that it is moving toward a free market economy, government ownership remains pervasive throughout the industrial sector. Azerbaijan has yet to move decisively to break with the past and allow private ownership.... Large scale manufacturing enterprises, such as the oil

Rank	Country	Score	Rank	Country	Score
1	Hong Kong	1.25	81	Fiji	3.10
2	Singapore	1.30	81	Mali	3.10
3	Bahrain	1.70	81	Slovenia	3.10
4	New Zealand	1.75	85	Honduras	3.15
5	Switzerland	1.85	85	Mexico	3.15
6	United States	1.90	85	Papua New Guinea	3.15
7	Ireland	1.95	88	Djibouti	3.20
7	Luxembourg	1.95	88	Mongolia	3.20
7	Taiwan	1.95	90	Algeria	3.25
7	United Kingdom	1.95	90	Brazil	3.25
11	Bahamas	2.00	90	Lebanon	3.25
12	Czech Republic	2.05	90	Senegal	3.25
12	Japan	2.05	90	Tanzania	3.25
14	Australia	2.10	95	Nigeria	3.30
14	Belgium	2.10	95	Romania	3.30
14	Canada	2.10	97	Cambodia	3.35
14	United Arab Emirates	2.10	97	Dominican Republic	3.35
18	Austria	2.15	97	Egypt	3.35
18	Chile	2.15	97	Guinea	3.35
18	Estonia	2.15	97	Ivory Coast	3.35
18	Netherlands	2.15	97	Moldova	3.35
22	Denmark	2.25	97	Pakistan	3.35
22	El Salvador	2.25	104	Nepal	3.40
22	Finland	2.25	104	Venezuela	3.40
25	Germany	2.30	106	Armenia	3.45
25	Iceland	2.30	106	Bulgaria	3.45
27	Norway	2.35	106	Lesotho	3.45
28	Korea, South	2.40	106	Madagascar	3.45
28	Kuwait	2.40	106	Russia	3.45
28	Malaysia	2.40	111	Burkina Faso	3.50
28	Panama	2.40	111	Cameroon	3.50
28	Thailand	2.40	111	Guyana	3.50
33	Sweden	2.45	111	Nicaragua	3.50
34	Argentina	2.50	115	Gambia	3.60
34	France	2.50	116	Croatia	3.65
34	Italy	2.50	116	Georgia	3.65
34	Spain	2.50	116	Malawi	3.65
38	Portugal	2.55	119	Cape Verde	3.67
38	Sri Lanka	2.55	120	Ethiopia	3.70
38	Trinidad and Tobago	2.55	120	India	3.70
41	Barbados	2.60	120	Niger	3.70
41	Peru	2.60	123	Congo	3.75
43	Bolivia	2.65	124	Chad	3.80
43	Mauritius	2.65	124	China	3.80
45	Cyprus	2.70	124	Mauritania	3.80
45	Jamaica	2.70	124	Ukraine	3.80
45	Uruguay	2.70	124	Zimbabwe	3.80
48	Botswana	2.75	129	Albania	3.85
48	Guatemala	2.75	129	Bangladesh	3.85
48	Jordan	2.75	129	Mozambique	3.85
48	Namibia	2.75	129	Suriname	3.85
48	Oman	2.75	133	Burundi	3.90
48	Philippines	2.75	134	Togo	3.95
54	Belize	2.80	135	Haiti	4.00
54	Costa Rica	2.80	135	Kyrgyz Rep.	4.00
54	Israel	2.80	137	Kazakhstan	4.05
54	Swaziland	2.80	137	Sierra Leone	4.05
54	Turkey	2.80	139	Yemen	4.10
54	Uganda	2.80	140	Belarus	4.15
54	Samoa	2.80	141	Sudan	4.20
61	Latvia	2.85	141	Syria	4.20
62	Greece	2.90	143	Azerbaijan	4.30
62	Hungary	2.90	143	Equatorial Guinea	4.30
62	So. Africa	2.90	143	Myanmar	4.30
65	Ecuador	2.95	143	Rwanda	4.30
65	Gabon	2.95	147	Tajikistan	4.40
65	Indonesia	2.95	147	Uzbekistan	4.40
65	Malta	2.95	149	Angola	4.45
65	Morocco	2.95	149	Turkmenistan	4.45
65	Poland	2.95	151	Guinea-Bissau	4.55
65	Tunisia	2.95	152	Vietnam	4.60
72	Ghana	3.00	153	Congo (Zaire)	4.70
72	Lithuania	3.00	153	Iran	4.70
72	Saudi Arabia	3.00	155	Bosnia	4.80
75	Benin	3.05	155	Somalia	4.80
75	Kenya	3.05	157	Iraq	4.90
75	Paraguay	3.05	157	Laos	4.90
75	Qatar	3.05	157	Libya	4.90
75	Slovak Republic	3.05	160	Cuba	5.00
75	Zambia	3.05	160	Korea, North	5.00
81	Colombia	3.10			

Repressed

equipment industry and the petrochemical industry, remain in state hands and continue their steady deterioration."[3] Nevertheless, this rate is substantially lower than its 1995 level of 35 percent to 40 percent. Thus, Azerbaijan's government intervention score is 1 point better this year.

MONETARY POLICY
Score: 5–Stable (very high level of inflation)

Azerbaijan has made tremendous progress toward reducing inflation, which declined from rates as high as 616 percent in 1992, 1,130 percent in 1993, 1,664 percent in 1994, and 411 percent in 1995 to 19.9 percent in 1996. In 1997, the inflation rate was only 3.2 percent. Nevertheless, the rate of inflation remains very high by historical global standards.

CAPITAL FLOWS AND FOREIGN INVESTMENT
Score: 4–Stable (high barriers)

Although the government wants to increase foreign investment, relatively little non-petroleum investment has been forthcoming, chiefly because of an ineffective legal environment, an untrained and corrupt bureaucracy, and a weak infrastructure. Moreover, the government must approve nearly all foreign investment, and it forbade ownership of land until recently. As the U.S. Department of Commerce reports, "In theory, the GOAZ welcomes foreign investment. Inertia within government structures, corruption, lack of a predictable commercial legal framework combine to discourage established investors. Among major concerns are the considerable ambiguities exist concerning tax rates."[4]

BANKING
Score: 4–Stable (high level of restrictions)

The banking system is in disarray. The government owns most banks in whole or in part, and many are insolvent. Although some foreign banks are present, few have the ability or the capital to operate without government involvement.

WAGE AND PRICE CONTROLS
Score: 5–Stable (very high level)

Government ministries and the large state-owned sector control wages and prices. According to the U.S. Department of Commerce, "Several key commodities, including bread, natural gas and gasoline, remain under price controls. While the government raises these controlled prices periodically, they remain artificially low, and shortages of these goods occur along with corruption and black market activity."[5]

PROPERTY RIGHTS
Score: 4–Stable (low level of protection)

The legal system does not provide sufficient protection for private property. Until recently, foreigners could own land, and government expropriation was possible, but property rights still are not protected. The U.S. Department of Commerce reports that "There is no international arbitration mechanism in place to resolve disputes between the GOAZ and private companies. The existing state arbitration court and the supreme economic court reportedly do not work effectively.... Azerbaijan is not a member of the international center for the settlement of investment disputes."[6]

REGULATION
Score: 4–Stable (moderate level)

Establishing a business can be a tedious and time-consuming procedure that requires individuals to overcome numerous bureaucratic barriers. Some private businesses are opening in the retail sector, but racketeering and corruption are widespread. Azerbaijan is developing a formalized process, however, by which businesses will be able to register and obtain licenses. According to the U.S. Department of Commerce, "The lack of a western-style commercial legal framework remains a major problem. The impartiality of the Azeri legal system in disputes between foreign and Azeri firms has yet to be established."[7]

BLACK MARKET
Score: 4–Stable (high level of activity)

Smuggling is rampant. Because bartered trade is the norm, substantial underground economies exist in the trading of all kinds of goods. According to the U.S. Department of State, "More workers and unemployed persons turn to second jobs and makeshift employment in the informal sector, such as operating the family car as a taxi, selling produce from private gardens, or operating small roadside shops. Combinations of these and other strategies are the only way for broad sectors of the urban population to reach a subsistence income level."[8] Azerbaijan has passed a new intellectual property rights law to protect copyrights, trademarks, and patents, however, and it has curtailed some black market activity in this area.

NOTES

[1]   U.S. Department of Commerce, "Azerbaijan–Investment Climate," *Market Research Reports*, Washington, D.C., August 12, 1996.
[2]   World Bank, *World Development Indicators*, 1998.
[3]   U.S. Department of Commerce, *Country Commercial Guide*, 1998.
[4]   *Ibid.*
[5]   U.S. Department of Commerce, *Country Commercial Guide*, 1996.
[6]   U.S. Department of Commerce, *Country Commercial Guide*, 1998.
[7]   *Ibid.*
[8]   U.S. Department of State, "Azerbaijan Country Report on Human Rights Practices for 1997," 1998.

The Bahamas 2.00

1998 Score: **2.00**   1997 Score: **2.00**   1996 Score: **2.00**

Trade	5	Banking	2
Taxation	1	Wages and Prices	2
Government Intervention	2	Property Rights	1
Monetary Policy	1	Regulation	1
Foreign Investment	3	Black Market	2

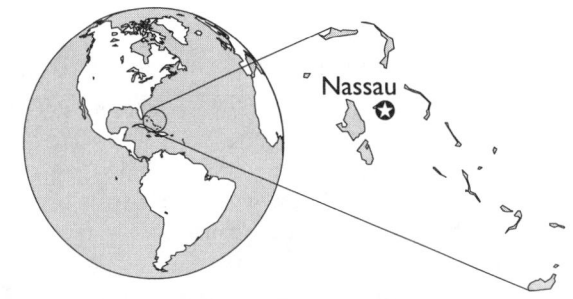

The Bahamas includes about 700 islands, of which only 30 are inhabited. The country is a member of the British Commonwealth and has a parliamentary democracy. Its biggest industry is tourism. With a few notable exceptions, the economy is essentially free of government control. According to the U.S. Department of State, "The Bahamas offers attractive features to the potential investor: a stable democratic environment; relief from personal and corporate income taxes; timely repatriation of corporate profits; proximity to the U.S. with extensive air and telecommunications links; and a good pool of skilled professional workers."[1]

TRADE POLICY
Score: 5–Stable (very high level of protectionism)

The absence of income, corporate, and inheritance taxes means that import duties are the main source of revenue for the government; as a result, tariff rates are very high. The general rate of duty charges on imports is 32.8 percent. There are no other significant barriers to trade.

TAXATION
Score–Income taxation: 1–Stable (very low tax rates)
Score–Corporate taxation: 1–Stable (very low tax rates)
Final Taxation Score: 1–Stable (very low tax rates)

The Bahamas has no income tax, no corporate income tax, no capital gains tax, no inheritance tax, and no value-added tax.

GOVERNMENT INTERVENTION IN THE ECONOMY
Score: 2–Stable (low level)

The government consumes 12.8 percent of GDP and plays only a limited role in the economy.

MONETARY POLICY
Score: 1–Stable (very low level of inflation)

From 1986 to 1996, the average annual rate of inflation was 3.5 percent. In 1997, the inflation rate was only 0.4 percent. The Bahamas pegs its currency on the U.S. dollar.

CAPITAL FLOWS AND FOREIGN INVESTMENT
Score: 3–Stable (moderate barriers)

The Bahamas has passed a new foreign investment law and seeks increased foreign investment. The government will restrict foreign investment, however, in areas that compete directly with Bahamian-owned businesses, such as construction and restaurants (except gourmet and ethnic restaurants). It does this by preventing foreign companies from obtaining business licenses and by imposing other requirements in areas in which Bahamian businesses already exist.

Rank	Country	Score	Rank	Country	Score
1	Hong Kong	1.25	81	Fiji	3.10
2	Singapore	1.30	81	Mali	3.10
3	Bahrain	1.70	81	Slovenia	3.10
4	New Zealand	1.75	85	Honduras	3.15
5	Switzerland	1.85	85	Mexico	3.15
6	United States	1.90	85	Papua New Guinea	3.15
7	Ireland	1.95	88	Djibouti	3.20
7	Luxembourg	1.95	88	Mongolia	3.20
7	Taiwan	1.95	90	Algeria	3.25
7	United Kingdom	1.95	90	Brazil	3.25
11	Bahamas	2.00	90	Lebanon	3.25
12	Czech Republic	2.05	90	Senegal	3.25
12	Japan	2.05	90	Tanzania	3.25
14	Australia	2.10	95	Nigeria	3.30
14	Belgium	2.10	95	Romania	3.30
14	Canada	2.10	97	Cambodia	3.35
14	United Arab Emirates	2.10	97	Dominican Republic	3.35
18	Austria	2.15	97	Egypt	3.35
18	Chile	2.15	97	Guinea	3.35
18	Estonia	2.15	97	Ivory Coast	3.35
18	Netherlands	2.15	97	Moldova	3.35
22	Denmark	2.25	97	Pakistan	3.35
22	El Salvador	2.25	104	Nepal	3.40
22	Finland	2.25	104	Venezuela	3.40
25	Germany	2.30	106	Armenia	3.45
25	Iceland	2.30	106	Bulgaria	3.45
27	Norway	2.35	106	Lesotho	3.45
28	Korea, South	2.40	106	Madagascar	3.45
28	Kuwait	2.40	106	Russia	3.45
28	Malaysia	2.40	111	Burkina Faso	3.50
28	Panama	2.40	111	Cameroon	3.50
28	Thailand	2.40	111	Guyana	3.50
33	Sweden	2.45	111	Nicaragua	3.50
34	Argentina	2.50	115	Gambia	3.60
34	France	2.50	116	Croatia	3.65
34	Italy	2.50	116	Georgia	3.65
34	Spain	2.50	116	Malawi	3.65
38	Portugal	2.55	119	Cape Verde	3.67
38	Sri Lanka	2.55	120	Ethiopia	3.70
38	Trinidad and Tobago	2.55	120	India	3.70
41	Barbados	2.60	120	Niger	3.70
41	Peru	2.60	123	Congo	3.75
43	Bolivia	2.65	124	Chad	3.80
43	Mauritius	2.65	124	China	3.80
45	Cyprus	2.70	124	Mauritania	3.80
45	Jamaica	2.70	124	Ukraine	3.80
45	Uruguay	2.70	124	Zimbabwe	3.80
48	Botswana	2.75	129	Albania	3.85
48	Guatemala	2.75	129	Bangladesh	3.85
48	Jordan	2.75	129	Mozambique	3.85
48	Namibia	2.75	129	Suriname	3.85
48	Oman	2.75	133	Burundi	3.90
48	Philippines	2.75	134	Togo	3.95
54	Belize	2.80	135	Haiti	4.00
54	Costa Rica	2.80	135	Kyrgyz Rep.	4.00
54	Israel	2.80	137	Kazakhstan	4.05
54	Swaziland	2.80	137	Sierra Leone	4.05
54	Turkey	2.80	139	Yemen	4.10
54	Uganda	2.80	140	Belarus	4.15
54	Samoa	2.80	141	Sudan	4.20
61	Latvia	2.85	141	Syria	4.20
62	Greece	2.90	143	Azerbaijan	4.30
62	Hungary	2.90	143	Equatorial Guinea	4.30
62	So. Africa	2.90	143	Myanmar	4.30
65	Ecuador	2.95	143	Rwanda	4.30
65	Gabon	2.95	147	Tajikistan	4.40
65	Indonesia	2.95	147	Uzbekistan	4.40
65	Malta	2.95	149	Angola	4.45
65	Morocco	2.95	149	Turkmenistan	4.45
65	Poland	2.95	151	Guinea-Bissau	4.55
65	Tunisia	2.95	152	Vietnam	4.60
72	Ghana	3.00	153	Congo (Zaire)	4.70
72	Lithuania	3.00	153	Iran	4.70
72	Saudi Arabia	3.00	155	Bosnia	4.80
75	Benin	3.05	155	Somalia	4.80
75	Kenya	3.05	157	Iraq	4.90
75	Paraguay	3.05	157	Laos	4.90
75	Qatar	3.05	157	Libya	4.90
75	Slovak Republic	3.05	160	Cuba	5.00
75	Zambia	3.05	160	Korea, North	5.00
81	Colombia	3.10			

Mostly Free

BANKING
Score: 2–Stable (low level of restrictions)

The Bahamas is one of the financial centers of the Caribbean. Financial services, for example, produces some 10 percent of GDP, making it the second-largest industry after tourism. The government seeks to attract foreign banks, and the financial sector is extremely open to foreigners.

WAGE AND PRICE CONTROLS
Score: 2–Stable (low level)

The Bahamas maintains some price controls on such items as automobiles, auto parts, gasoline, public transportation, and utilities, but the market mainly determines wages. A new minimum wage plan has gone into effect, but it applies only to government employees not on salary.

PROPERTY RIGHTS
Score: 1–Stable (very high level of protection)

Private property is easy to acquire and protect in the Bahamas, which has an advanced and efficient legal system based on English common law. The government never has expropriated private property and is very unlikely to do so in the future. According to the U.S. Department of State, "The judiciary, appointed by the Governor General on the advice, in most cases, of the Judicial and Legal Services Commission, has always been independent."[2]

REGULATION
Score: 1–Stable (very low level)

Regulation is virtually nonexistent in the Bahamas; the government follows a hands-off approach to business. There are no specific requirements for establishing a business, and English common law is used to enforce contracts. In addition, profits are not taxed, and businesses are free of burdensome regulation. A new labor law is being implemented, however, that requires paid vacations, sick leave, redundancy payments, and protection against unfair dismissal. It is yet unclear whether these new regulations pose a burden on business.

BLACK MARKET
Score: 2–Stable (low level of activity)

The black market in the Bahamas, like that in most developed countries, focuses on guns and drugs. Gambling is legalized. But because the government outlaws few things and businesses are free to operate as they see fit, the black market is very small—although high trade barriers encourage smuggling in such areas as auto parts and electronics. According to the U.S. Department of State, "Although local intellectual property laws exist, enforcement is generally weak."[3] Thus, there is a growing black market in such materials as pirated compact disks and videocassettes, although this increase is not substantial enough to warrant a change in score at this time. These activities remain minuscule in comparison with the overall size of the economy.

NOTES

[1]   U.S .Department of State, *The Bahamas: Background Notes,* No. 18, November 1997.
[2]   U.S. Department of State, "Bahamas Country Report on Human Rights Practices for 1997," 1998.
[3]   U.S. Department of State, *Country Reports on Economic Policy and Trade Practices,* 1998.

Bahrain   1.70

1998 Score: **1.70**   1997 Score: **1.60**   1996 Score: **1.70**

Trade	2	Banking	2
Taxation	1	Wages and Prices	2
Government Intervention	3	Property Rights	1
Monetary Policy	1	Regulation	2
Foreign Investment	2	Black Market	1

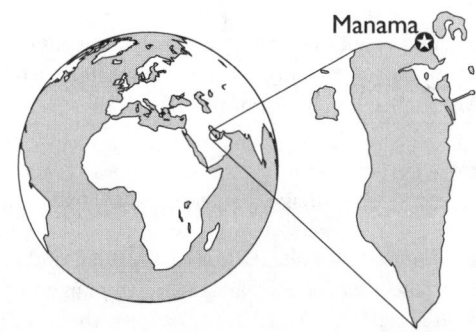

Manama

Bahrain declared its independence from the United Kingdom in 1971 and became a member of the United Nations and the Arab League. It has maintained a vibrant free-market economic system. Its principal export is oil; but because oil reserves are expected to last only 20 more years, the government is pursuing ways to diversify and modernize the economy. It also has reduced its level of spending. Since December 1994, Bahrain has been troubled by civil disturbances, arson attacks, and occasional bombings by disaffected members of the Shia community. The Shiites—about two-thirds of the population—suffer from a high rate of unemployment and claim religious discrimination by the Sunni-dominated government. Domestic disturbances have lessened since the June 1996 arrest of 44 people involved in an Iran-inspired plot to overthrow the government.

TRADE POLICY
Score: 2–Stable (low level of protectionism)

With an average tariff rate of 3.3 percent, Bahrain maintains few barriers to trade. The government maintains strict labeling requirements on imported products, however. This practice limits imports because exporters do not wish to spend the extra money to meet these requirements.

TAXATION
Score–Income taxation: 1–Stable (very low tax rates)
Score–Corporate taxation: 1–Stable (very low tax rates)
Final Taxation Score: 1–Stable (very low tax rates)

Bahrain imposes no taxes on income or corporate profits. It has no capital gains tax or value-added tax, either.

GOVERNMENT INTERVENTION IN THE ECONOMY
Score: 3–Stable (moderate level)

Government consumes 33.3 percent of GDP. The government also owns significant portions of some industries, including oil, which contributes most of the country's GDP. It privatized industrial and service companies in 1997.

MONETARY POLICY
Score: 1–Stable (very low level of inflation)

The average annual rate of inflation from 1986 to 1996 was less than 2 percent. In 1997, inflation fell to 1.5 percent. Bahrain's currency is pegged to the U.S. dollar.

CAPITAL FLOWS AND FOREIGN INVESTMENT
Score: 2–Stable (low barriers)

Bahrain has set up few barriers to foreign investment and has no foreign investment law, preferring to rely on various commercial codes. Bahrain permits 100

#	Country	Score		#	Country	Score
1	Hong Kong	1.25		81	Fiji	3.10
2	Singapore	1.30		81	Mali	3.10
3	Bahrain	1.70		81	Slovenia	3.10
4	New Zealand	1.75		85	Honduras	3.15
5	Switzerland	1.85		85	Mexico	3.15
6	United States	1.90		85	Papua New Guinea	3.15
7	Ireland	1.95		88	Djibouti	3.20
7	Luxembourg	1.95		88	Mongolia	3.20
7	Taiwan	1.95		90	Algeria	3.25
7	United Kingdom	1.95		90	Brazil	3.25
11	Bahamas	2.00		90	Lebanon	3.25
12	Czech Republic	2.05		90	Senegal	3.25
12	Japan	2.05		90	Tanzania	3.25
14	Australia	2.10		95	Nigeria	3.30
14	Belgium	2.10		95	Romania	3.30
14	Canada	2.10		97	Cambodia	3.35
14	United Arab Emirates	2.10		97	Dominican Republic	3.35
18	Austria	2.15		97	Egypt	3.35
18	Chile	2.15		97	Guinea	3.35
18	Estonia	2.15		97	Ivory Coast	3.35
18	Netherlands	2.15		97	Moldova	3.35
22	Denmark	2.25		97	Pakistan	3.35
22	El Salvador	2.25		104	Nepal	3.40
22	Finland	2.25		104	Venezuela	3.40
25	Germany	2.30		106	Armenia	3.45
25	Iceland	2.30		106	Bulgaria	3.45
27	Norway	2.35		106	Lesotho	3.45
28	Korea, South	2.40		106	Madagascar	3.45
28	Kuwait	2.40		106	Russia	3.45
28	Malaysia	2.40		111	Burkina Faso	3.50
28	Panama	2.40		111	Cameroon	3.50
28	Thailand	2.40		111	Guyana	3.50
33	Sweden	2.45		111	Nicaragua	3.50
34	Argentina	2.50		115	Gambia	3.60
34	France	2.50		116	Croatia	3.65
34	Italy	2.50		116	Georgia	3.65
34	Spain	2.50		116	Malawi	3.65
38	Portugal	2.55		119	Cape Verde	3.67
38	Sri Lanka	2.55		120	Ethiopia	3.70
38	Trinidad and Tobago	2.55		120	India	3.70
41	Barbados	2.60		120	Niger	3.70
41	Peru	2.60		123	Congo	3.75
43	Bolivia	2.65		124	Chad	3.80
43	Mauritius	2.65		124	China	3.80
45	Cyprus	2.70		124	Mauritania	3.80
45	Jamaica	2.70		124	Ukraine	3.80
45	Uruguay	2.70		124	Zimbabwe	3.80
48	Botswana	2.75		129	Albania	3.85
48	Guatemala	2.75		129	Bangladesh	3.85
48	Jordan	2.75		129	Mozambique	3.85
48	Namibia	2.75		129	Suriname	3.85
48	Oman	2.75		133	Burundi	3.90
48	Philippines	2.75		134	Togo	3.95
54	Belize	2.80		135	Haiti	4.00
54	Costa Rica	2.80		135	Kyrgyz Rep.	4.00
54	Israel	2.80		137	Kazakhstan	4.05
54	Swaziland	2.80		137	Sierra Leone	4.05
54	Turkey	2.80		139	Yemen	4.10
54	Uganda	2.80		140	Belarus	4.15
54	Samoa	2.80		141	Sudan	4.20
61	Latvia	2.85		141	Syria	4.20
62	Greece	2.90		143	Azerbaijan	4.30
62	Hungary	2.90		143	Equatorial Guinea	4.30
62	So. Africa	2.90		143	Myanmar	4.30
65	Ecuador	2.95		143	Rwanda	4.30
65	Gabon	2.95		147	Tajikistan	4.40
65	Indonesia	2.95		147	Uzbekistan	4.40
65	Malta	2.95		149	Angola	4.45
65	Morocco	2.95		149	Turkmenistan	4.45
65	Poland	2.95		151	Guinea-Bissau	4.55
65	Tunisia	2.95		152	Vietnam	4.60
72	Ghana	3.00		153	Congo (Zaire)	4.70
72	Lithuania	3.00		153	Iran	4.70
72	Saudi Arabia	3.00		155	Bosnia	4.80
75	Benin	3.05		155	Somalia	4.80
75	Kenya	3.05		157	Iraq	4.90
75	Paraguay	3.05		157	Laos	4.90
75	Qatar	3.05		157	Libya	4.90
75	Slovak Republic	3.05		160	Cuba	5.00
75	Zambia	3.05		160	Korea, North	5.00
81	Colombia	3.10				

Free

percent foreign ownership (although foreigners may not purchase or own land), requires no local sponsors for investments, and does not restrict the repatriation of funds.

BANKING
Score: 2–Stable (low level of restrictions)

Over the past 20 years, Bahrain has established itself as a financial center for the Persian Gulf region and the Arab world. "As of the end of 1996," reports the U.S. Department of Commerce, "there were 19 full commercial banks, two specialized banks, 41 representative offices, 28 investment banks, six foreign exchange and money brokers, and 27 money-changing companies registered in Bahrain."[1] The government has made it easy to establish a bank, both by streamlining the paperwork process and by placing few, if any, restrictions and requirements on new banks. Foreign banks are welcome.

WAGE AND PRICE CONTROLS
Score: 2–Stable (low level)

The market sets most wages and prices. According to the U.S. Department of State, "With the exception of a few basic foodstuffs and petroleum product prices, the Government of Bahrain does not attempt to control prices on the local market."[2] Importers of certain goods must pay a 5 percent fee to a local agent, which increases the cost of these goods. The government has removed several other price controls. Bahrain has a minimum wage, but only for public-sector employees.

PROPERTY RIGHTS
Score: 1–Stable (very high level of protection)

Property is secure, and expropriation is unlikely. According to the U.S. Department of Commerce, "The Bahraini legal system adequately protects and facilitates acquisition and disposition of property rights."[3]

REGULATION
Score: 2–Stable (low level)

Bahrain's bureaucracy is efficient and unobtrusive, and businesses are free to operate as they see fit. The government has established a fast-track business application process under which companies can be registered and licensed within seven days; most, in fact, are registered and licensed within only five days. Environmental and occupational health and safety regulations are not burdensome. Despite the existence of anticorruption laws, the U.S. Department of Commerce reports that "Corruption has occurred in Bahrain, and there are reports that this is increasingly the case."[4]

BLACK MARKET
Score: 1–Stable (very low level of activity)

Bahrain has virtually no black market. With few barriers to imports, smuggling is not a problem. There is almost no black market in pirated intellectual property, although the U.S. Department of State recently has documented instances of piracy of audio and visual recordings. The total cost of this piracy is not known, but it represents only a small fraction of Bahrain's overall economy.

NOTES
[1] U.S. Department of Commerce, *Country Commercial Guide,* 1998.
[2] U.S. Department of State, *Country Reports on Economic Policy and Trade Practices,* 1998.
[3] U.S. Department of Commerce, *Country Commercial Guide,* 1998.
[4] *Ibid.*

Bangladesh   3.85

1998 Score: **3.75**   1997 Score: **3.70**   1996 Score: **3.65**

Trade	5	Banking	4
Taxation	3.5	Wages and Prices	4
Government Intervention	3	Property Rights	4
Monetary Policy	2	Regulation	5
Foreign Investment	3	Black Market	5

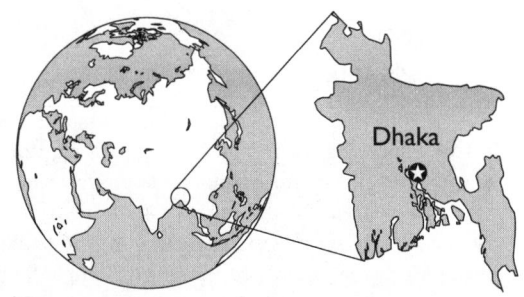

Dhaka

Bangladesh seceded from Pakistan in 1971, and since then has experienced several coups. One of the world's most densely populated countries, Bangladesh has struggled to produce and import enough food to feed its people. Some 60 percent of the labor force is engaged in agriculture. Bangladesh has received massive infusions of foreign aid, much of which has been squandered on unneeded buildings, roads, and bridges. In 1991, the government embarked on a path of economic reform. The banking system is near collapse. As a result, its overall score is 0.1 point worse than last year.

TRADE POLICY
Score: 5–Stable (very high level of protectionism)

Despite recent reductions in tariff rates, Bangladesh's average tariff rate is as high as 23 percent.[1] Moreover, according to the U.S. Department of State, "Customs procedures are lengthy and burdensome, and further complicated by corruption."[2]

TAXATION
Score–Income taxation: 2–Stable (low tax rates)
Score–Corporate taxation: 4–Stable (high tax rates)
Final Taxation Score: 3.5–Stable (high tax rates)

The top marginal income tax rate is 25 percent. The tax on the average income level is 0 percent. The top corporate tax rate is 40 percent.[3] Bangladesh also maintains a 15 percent value-added tax and a 4 percent turnover tax.

GOVERNMENT INTERVENTION IN THE ECONOMY
Score: 3–Stable (moderate level)

Government consumes 14 percent of GDP. Privatization has been slowed by opposition from many state-owned industries. According to the U.S. Department of State, "The state's presence in the economy continues to be large, and money-losing state enterprises have been a chronic drain on the treasury." [4] By global standards, however, government intervention in the economy is moderate.

MONETARY POLICY
Score: 2–Stable (low level of inflation)

Bangladesh's average annual rate of inflation from 1986 to 1996 was 6.97 percent. The inflation rate in 1997 was 3.9 percent.

CAPITAL FLOWS AND FOREIGN INVESTMENT
Score: 3–Stable (moderate barriers)

Some industries, like power generation, forestry, telecommunications, air transportation, railways, and mining, are closed to foreign investment. Nevertheless, Bangladesh has made modest efforts to attract foreign investment. Foreign and domestic investors now enjoy equal treatment.

1	Hong Kong	1.25		81	Fiji	3.10
2	Singapore	1.30		81	Mali	3.10
3	Bahrain	1.70		81	Slovenia	3.10
4	New Zealand	1.75		85	Honduras	3.15
5	Switzerland	1.85		85	Mexico	3.15
6	United States	1.90		85	Papua New Guinea	3.15
7	Ireland	1.95		88	Djibouti	3.20
7	Luxembourg	1.95		88	Mongolia	3.20
7	Taiwan	1.95		90	Algeria	3.25
7	United Kingdom	1.95		90	Brazil	3.25
11	Bahamas	2.00		90	Lebanon	3.25
12	Czech Republic	2.05		90	Senegal	3.25
12	Japan	2.05		90	Tanzania	3.25
14	Australia	2.10		95	Nigeria	3.30
14	Belgium	2.10		95	Romania	3.30
14	Canada	2.10		97	Cambodia	3.35
14	United Arab Emirates	2.10		97	Dominican Republic	3.35
18	Austria	2.15		97	Egypt	3.35
18	Chile	2.15		97	Guinea	3.35
18	Estonia	2.15		97	Ivory Coast	3.35
18	Netherlands	2.15		97	Moldova	3.35
22	Denmark	2.25		97	Pakistan	3.35
22	El Salvador	2.25		104	Nepal	3.40
22	Finland	2.25		104	Venezuela	3.40
25	Germany	2.30		106	Armenia	3.45
25	Iceland	2.30		106	Bulgaria	3.45
27	Norway	2.35		106	Lesotho	3.45
28	Korea, South	2.40		106	Madagascar	3.45
28	Kuwait	2.40		106	Russia	3.45
28	Malaysia	2.40		111	Burkina Faso	3.50
28	Panama	2.40		111	Cameroon	3.50
28	Thailand	2.40		111	Guyana	3.50
33	Sweden	2.45		111	Nicaragua	3.50
34	Argentina	2.50		115	Gambia	3.60
34	France	2.50		116	Croatia	3.65
34	Italy	2.50		116	Georgia	3.65
34	Spain	2.50		116	Malawi	3.65
38	Portugal	2.55		119	Cape Verde	3.67
38	Sri Lanka	2.55		120	Ethiopia	3.70
38	Trinidad and Tobago	2.55		120	India	3.70
41	Barbados	2.60		120	Niger	3.70
41	Peru	2.60		123	Congo	3.75
43	Bolivia	2.65		124	Chad	3.80
43	Mauritius	2.65		124	China	3.80
45	Cyprus	2.70		124	Mauritania	3.80
45	Jamaica	2.70		124	Ukraine	3.80
45	Uruguay	2.70		124	Zimbabwe	3.80
48	Botswana	2.75		129	Albania	3.85
48	Guatemala	2.75		129	Bangladesh	3.85
48	Jordan	2.75		129	Mozambique	3.85
48	Namibia	2.75		129	Suriname	3.85
48	Oman	2.75		133	Burundi	3.90
48	Philippines	2.75		134	Togo	3.95
54	Belize	2.80		135	Haiti	4.00
54	Costa Rica	2.80		135	Kyrgyz Rep.	4.00
54	Israel	2.80		137	Kazakhstan	4.05
54	Swaziland	2.80		137	Sierra Leone	4.05
54	Turkey	2.80		139	Yemen	4.10
54	Uganda	2.80		140	Belarus	4.15
54	Samoa	2.80		141	Sudan	4.20
61	Latvia	2.85		141	Syria	4.20
62	Greece	2.90		143	Azerbaijan	4.30
62	Hungary	2.90		143	Equatorial Guinea	4.30
62	So. Africa	2.90		143	Myanmar	4.30
65	Ecuador	2.95		143	Rwanda	4.30
65	Gabon	2.95		147	Tajikistan	4.40
65	Indonesia	2.95		147	Uzbekistan	4.40
65	Malta	2.95		149	Angola	4.45
65	Morocco	2.95		149	Turkmenistan	4.45
65	Poland	2.95		151	Guinea-Bissau	4.55
65	Tunisia	2.95		152	Vietnam	4.60
72	Ghana	3.00		153	Congo (Zaire)	4.70
72	Lithuania	3.00		153	Iran	4.70
72	Saudi Arabia	3.00		155	Bosnia	4.80
75	Benin	3.05		155	Somalia	4.80
75	Kenya	3.05		157	Iraq	4.90
75	Paraguay	3.05		157	Laos	4.90
75	Qatar	3.05		157	Libya	4.90
75	Slovak Republic	3.05		160	Cuba	5.00
75	Zambia	3.05		160	Korea, North	5.00
81	Colombia	3.10				

Mostly Unfree

BANKING
Score: 4– (high level of restrictions)

The government has initiated reforms that limit its control of the banking system, but the central bank still restricts some types of lending. Although some reforms are aimed at increasing access to banking services for poor people, parts of the system are chaotic and corrupt. The banking system is deteriorating, mainly resulting from unprofitable, money-losing, government-owned banks. As the U.S. Department of Commerce reports, "The Bangladesh banking sector is made up of nine government-owned banks, 18 domestic private banks, and 13 foreign banks. The government banks and many local private banks have a high percentage of non-performing loans—the government estimate is 40 percent. At the government banks, this resulted from directed lending, mostly to money-losing parastatals, diverting credit from the private sector. The banking system is impaired by a web of weak balance sheets, weak demand from credit-worthy borrowers, and heavy reliance on liquid asset-based lending." As a result, Bangladesh's banking score is 1 point worse this year.

WAGE AND PRICE CONTROLS
Score: 4–Stable (high)

Some price reform has been accomplished, but prices continue to be influenced by large state-owned and state-subsidized industrial sectors, such as textile production and jute and sugar processing. Heavy government subsidies affect prices negatively.

PROPERTY RIGHTS
Score: 4–Stable (low level of protection)

Even though private property is guaranteed by law, the U.S. Department of Commerce reports that "Underlying other impediments to investment in Bangladesh is a weak legal system in which the enforceability of contracts is in doubt.

Over ten years can pass between bringing a court case and executing a judgment. With no interest charged on judgments, there is no penalty for delaying proceedings. It is generally believed that in the lower courts where cases are first brought, private sector parties with the means to make 'good connections' with the judge have an advantage, even in cases where the government is the opposing party. Articles 115 and 116 of the Constitution allow the head of government to control and discipline judges, including Supreme Court justices."[5]

REGULATION
Score: 5–Stable (very high)

Bangladesh's largest regulatory problems are corruption and outdated business laws that do not protect private contracts. "Foreigners often find that the implementing ministries still require licenses and permissions which were supposedly done away with," says the U.S. Department of Commerce. "Added to these difficulties are such problems as slow government decisionmaking, corruption, labor militancy, an uncertain law and order situation, poor infrastructure, inadequate commercial laws and courts, and policy instability (i.e., policies being altered at the behest of special interests).... A large and recalcitrant bureaucracy often views its role more as controlling commercial activity than stimulating it. Corruption is endemic"[6]

BLACK MARKET
Score: 5–Stable (very high level of activity)

According to the U.S. Department of State, "Bangladesh has outdated intellectual property rights (IPR) laws, and an unwieldy system of registering and enforcing [IPR]. Intellectual property infringement is common, particularly of computer software, motion pictures, pharmaceuticals products and audio and video cassettes."[7] There remains much smuggling of textiles across Bangladesh's borders.

NOTES

[1]   U.S. Department of State, *Country Reports on Economic Policy and Trade Practices,* 1998.

[2]   *Ibid.*

[3]   For the taxable year 1998, all resident companies were subject to a corporate tax rate of 35 percent. All non-resident companies were taxed at 40 percent.

[4]   U.S. Department of State, *Country Reports on Economic Policy and Trade Practices,* 1998.

[5]   U.S. Department of Commerce, *Country Commercial Guide,* 1998.

[6]   *Ibid.*

[7]   U.S. Department of State, *Country Reports on Economic Policy and Trade Practices,* 1997, p. 378.

Barbados   2.60

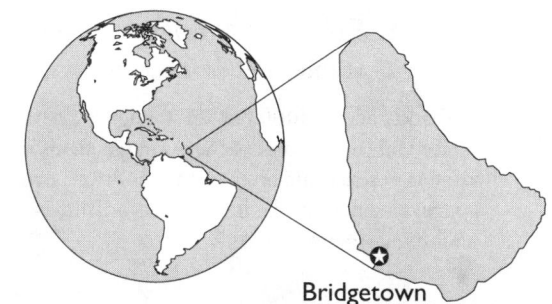

Bridgetown

| 1998 Score: **2.60** | 1997 Score: **2.80** | 1996 Score: **3.00** |

Trade	3	Banking	2
Taxation	5	Wages and Prices	2
Government Intervention	3	Property Rights	2
Monetary Policy	1	Regulation	3
Foreign Investment	2	Black Market	3

Barbados, a former British colony with a parliamentary democracy, has few natural resources and must import much of what it consumes, including energy, food, and most consumer goods. The country has a fairly large public sector. Recent reforms, however, have sought to open the economy to more foreign investment, trade, and competition. Since 1990, Barbados has achieved significant reform in specific areas of the economy. Barbados has lowered some barriers to trade, reformed its banking system, allowed more foreign investment, and slashed price controls.

TRADE POLICY
Score: 3–Stable (high level of protectionism)

Barbados is a member of the Caribbean Community and has tariffs common to the rest of the region. Tariffs range from 0 percent to 20 percent. The average tariff rate is about 11.5 percent,[1] and most non-tariff barriers have been removed.

TAXATION
Score–Income taxation: 5–Stable (very high tax rates)
Score–Corporate taxation: 4–Stable (high tax rates)
Final Taxation Score: 5–Stable (very high tax rates)

Barbados has a top income tax rate of 40 percent; the tax on the average income level is 25 percent. The top marginal corporate tax rate is 40 percent. There also is a value-added tax of 7.5 percent to 15 percent.

GOVERNMENT INTERVENTION IN THE ECONOMY
Score: 3–Stable (moderate level)

Government consumes about 21.5 percent of GDP. The government remains heavily involved in the economy, mainly through its generous spending and investment programs. According to the U.S. Department of Commerce, "The Government of Barbados focuses its resources on education and health care. Over the next five years, the government will be carrying out major investments in school computerization, the installation of a modern waste disposal system for the heavily populated south and west coasts, and upgrade of the sea and airports."[2]

MONETARY POLICY
Score: 1–Stable (very low level of inflation)

From 1986 to 1996, the average rate of inflation was 2.5 percent. In 1997, the inflation rate was 7.7 percent. For most of 1998, the inflation rate has been only 2 percent to 3 percent.

1	Hong Kong	1.25
2	Singapore	1.30
3	Bahrain	1.70
4	New Zealand	1.75
5	Switzerland	1.85
6	United States	1.90
7	Ireland	1.95
7	Luxembourg	1.95
7	Taiwan	1.95
7	United Kingdom	1.95
11	Bahamas	2.00
12	Czech Republic	2.05
12	Japan	2.05
14	Australia	2.10
14	Belgium	2.10
14	Canada	2.10
14	United Arab Emirates	2.10
18	Austria	2.15
18	Chile	2.15
18	Estonia	2.15
18	Netherlands	2.15
22	Denmark	2.25
22	El Salvador	2.25
22	Finland	2.25
25	Germany	2.30
25	Iceland	2.30
27	Norway	2.35
28	Korea, South	2.40
28	Kuwait	2.40
28	Malaysia	2.40
28	Panama	2.40
28	Thailand	2.40
33	Sweden	2.45
34	Argentina	2.50
34	France	2.50
34	Italy	2.50
34	Spain	2.50
38	Portugal	2.55
38	Sri Lanka	2.55
38	Trinidad and Tobago	2.55
41	Barbados	2.60
41	Peru	2.60
43	Bolivia	2.65
43	Mauritius	2.65
45	Cyprus	2.70
45	Jamaica	2.70
45	Uruguay	2.70
48	Botswana	2.75
48	Guatemala	2.75
48	Jordan	2.75
48	Namibia	2.75
48	Oman	2.75
48	Philippines	2.75
54	Belize	2.80
54	Costa Rica	2.80
54	Israel	2.80
54	Swaziland	2.80
54	Turkey	2.80
54	Uganda	2.80
54	Samoa	2.80
61	Latvia	2.85
62	Greece	2.90
62	Hungary	2.90
62	So. Africa	2.90
65	Ecuador	2.95
65	Gabon	2.95
65	Indonesia	2.95
65	Malta	2.95
65	Morocco	2.95
65	Poland	2.95
65	Tunisia	2.95
72	Ghana	3.00
72	Lithuania	3.00
72	Saudi Arabia	3.00
75	Benin	3.05
75	Kenya	3.05
75	Paraguay	3.05
75	Qatar	3.05
75	Slovak Republic	3.05
75	Zambia	3.05
81	Colombia	3.10

81	Fiji	3.10
81	Mali	3.10
81	Slovenia	3.10
85	Honduras	3.15
85	Mexico	3.15
85	Papua New Guinea	3.15
88	Djibouti	3.20
88	Mongolia	3.20
90	Algeria	3.25
90	Brazil	3.25
90	Lebanon	3.25
90	Senegal	3.25
90	Tanzania	3.25
95	Nigeria	3.30
95	Romania	3.30
97	Cambodia	3.35
97	Dominican Republic	3.35
97	Egypt	3.35
97	Guinea	3.35
97	Ivory Coast	3.35
97	Moldova	3.35
97	Pakistan	3.35
104	Nepal	3.40
104	Venezuela	3.40
106	Armenia	3.45
106	Bulgaria	3.45
106	Lesotho	3.45
106	Madagascar	3.45
106	Russia	3.45
111	Burkina Faso	3.50
111	Cameroon	3.50
111	Guyana	3.50
111	Nicaragua	3.50
115	Gambia	3.60
116	Croatia	3.65
116	Georgia	3.65
116	Malawi	3.65
119	Cape Verde	3.67
120	Ethiopia	3.70
120	India	3.70
120	Niger	3.70
123	Congo	3.75
124	Chad	3.80
124	China	3.80
124	Mauritania	3.80
124	Ukraine	3.80
124	Zimbabwe	3.80
129	Albania	3.85
129	Bangladesh	3.85
129	Mozambique	3.85
129	Suriname	3.85
133	Burundi	3.90
134	Togo	3.95
135	Haiti	4.00
135	Kyrgyz Rep.	4.00
137	Kazakhstan	4.05
137	Sierra Leone	4.05
139	Yemen	4.10
140	Belarus	4.15
141	Sudan	4.20
141	Syria	4.20
143	Azerbaijan	4.30
143	Equatorial Guinea	4.30
143	Myanmar	4.30
143	Rwanda	4.30
147	Tajikistan	4.40
147	Uzbekistan	4.40
149	Angola	4.45
149	Turkmenistan	4.45
151	Guinea-Bissau	4.55
152	Vietnam	4.60
153	Congo (Zaire)	4.70
153	Iran	4.70
155	Bosnia	4.80
155	Somalia	4.80
157	Iraq	4.90
157	Laos	4.90
157	Libya	4.90
160	Cuba	5.00
160	Korea, North	5.00

Mostly Free

Capital Flows and Foreign Investment
Score: 2–Stable (low barriers)

Barbados permits 100 percent foreign ownership of enterprises and treats domestic and foreign firms equally. There are few restrictions on investment. Prior government approval is needed for investment in utilities, broadcasting, banking, and insurance.

Banking
Score: 2–Stable (low level of restrictions)

The banking system is fairly open to competition. Some foreign banks already operate in Barbados, but government approval is needed for foreign investment in banks.

Wage and Price Controls
Score: 2–Stable (low level)

The market sets most wages and prices. The government, however, continues to set prices on some food items. Moreover, there are indications that prices are affected by a lack of competition. For example, the U.S. Department of Commerce reports, "Prices in Barbados are high, typically multiples of what a product would sell for in the United States. Import tariffs and taxes are high, competition at the wholesale and retail level is minimal. To escape high prices Barbadians frequently make shopping trips to San Juan, New York, and Miami."[3] This lack of competition, however, has only a small effect on all prices in Barbados. Thus, by global standards, wage and price controls in Barbados are low.

Property Rights
Score: 2–Stable (low level of protection)

Private property is a legal right. Barbados's legal tradition is based on British common law. Courts operate independently, although there are some delays.

Regulation
Score: 3–Stable (moderate level)

Establishing a business in Barbados is simple. Some newer regulations, however, like the environmental "green tax," hinder business formation and raise costs for consumers. According to the U.S. Department of Commerce, "The commercial environment is generally favorable, although tax rates and import tariffs remain high."[4]

Black Market
Score: 3–Stable (moderate level of activity)

According to the U.S. Department of Commerce, "Pirating of U.S. artistic products is the major problem now facing U.S. companies"[5] in intellectual property protection. Because this piracy represents only a small part of the economy, however, the overall level of black market activity is moderate by global standards.

Notes

[1]   Based on total taxes on international trade as a percentage of total imports. The author figures in tax revenues garnished from import duties as well as stamp duties applied by customs on imports. From "Economic and Financial Statistics," Central Bank of Barbados, Bridgetown, Barbados, April 1997.

[2]   U.S. Department of Commerce, *Country Commercial Guide*, 1998.

[3]   *Ibid.*

[4]   *Ibid.*

[5]   *Ibid.*

Belarus   4.15

Trade	4	Banking	4
Taxation	4.5	Wages and Prices	4
Government Intervention	3	Property Rights	4
Monetary Policy	5	Regulation	4
Foreign Investment	4	Black Market	5

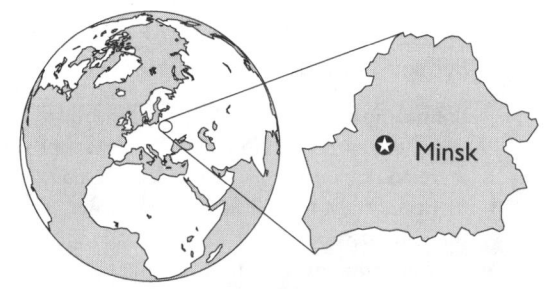

Minsk

Belarus had one of the highest income levels of all the republics of the former Soviet Union, but the collapse of the Soviet empire left its heavily industrialized economy in shambles. Market reforms have been halfhearted at best, and there are signs of a possible nationalist–socialist resurgence under President Oleksandr Lukashenka. The economy has shrunk in size and remains overburdened with regulations and an inefficient and corrupt bureaucracy. Lukashenka's anti-Western policies are scaring away foreign investors. Although the level of economic activity has been on the rise, much of this growth is the result of massive subsidies to the country's large, inefficient, and unprofitable state-owned industries. Some privatization is taking place, but it is confined mainly to small businesses; most medium- and large-sized government-owned businesses are not being privatized. Moreover, price controls continue to undermine market reforms. Finally, the banking system is in a state of collapse; as a result, the country's overall score is 0.1 point worse than last year.

TRADE POLICY
Score: 4–Stable (high level of protectionism)

The average tariff rate is 13.7 percent.[1] Non-tariff barriers include heavy user fees on imports and some currency requirements on those businesses trying to import raw materials.

TAXATION
Score–Income taxation: 5–Stable (very high tax rates)
Score–Corporate taxation: 3–Stable (moderate tax rates)
Final Taxation Score: 4.5–Stable (very high tax rates)

Income taxes in Belarus are among Europe's highest. The top income tax rate is 60 percent, and the average income level is taxed at 37 percent. The top corporate income tax rate is 30 percent.[2] Belarus also levies a value-added tax of 20 percent.

GOVERNMENT INTERVENTION IN THE ECONOMY
Score: 3–Stable (moderate level)

The government dominates Belarus's economy and consumes about 23 percent of GDP. Privatization has been halted and even reversed in some cases. Most enterprises still are state-owned. But, by global standards, the level of government intervention in the economy is moderate.

MONETARY POLICY
Score: 5–Stable (very high level of inflation)

Belarus has chronically high inflation rates: 2,096 percent in 1993, 2,059 percent in 1994, 709 percent in 1995, and 52 percent in 1996.[3] The rate for 1997 is unavailable.

1	Hong Kong	1.25	
2	Singapore	1.30	
3	Bahrain	1.70	
4	New Zealand	1.75	
5	Switzerland	1.85	
6	United States	1.90	
7	Ireland	1.95	
7	Luxembourg	1.95	
7	Taiwan	1.95	
7	United Kingdom	1.95	
11	Bahamas	2.00	
12	Czech Republic	2.05	
12	Japan	2.05	
14	Australia	2.10	
14	Belgium	2.10	
14	Canada	2.10	
14	United Arab Emirates	2.10	
18	Austria	2.15	
18	Chile	2.15	
18	Estonia	2.15	
18	Netherlands	2.15	
22	Denmark	2.25	
22	El Salvador	2.25	
22	Finland	2.25	
25	Germany	2.30	
25	Iceland	2.30	
27	Norway	2.35	
28	Korea, South	2.40	
28	Kuwait	2.40	
28	Malaysia	2.40	
28	Panama	2.40	
28	Thailand	2.40	
33	Sweden	2.45	
34	Argentina	2.50	
34	France	2.50	
34	Italy	2.50	
34	Spain	2.50	
38	Portugal	2.55	
38	Sri Lanka	2.55	
38	Trinidad and Tobago	2.55	
41	Barbados	2.60	
41	Peru	2.60	
43	Bolivia	2.65	
43	Mauritius	2.65	
45	Cyprus	2.70	
45	Jamaica	2.70	
45	Uruguay	2.70	
48	Botswana	2.75	
48	Guatemala	2.75	
48	Jordan	2.75	
48	Namibia	2.75	
48	Oman	2.75	
48	Philippines	2.75	
54	Belize	2.80	
54	Costa Rica	2.80	
54	Israel	2.80	
54	Swaziland	2.80	
54	Turkey	2.80	
54	Uganda	2.80	
54	Samoa	2.80	
61	Latvia	2.85	
62	Greece	2.90	
62	Hungary	2.90	
62	So. Africa	2.90	
65	Ecuador	2.95	
65	Gabon	2.95	
65	Indonesia	2.95	
65	Malta	2.95	
65	Morocco	2.95	
65	Poland	2.95	
65	Tunisia	2.95	
72	Ghana	3.00	
72	Lithuania	3.00	
72	Saudi Arabia	3.00	
75	Benin	3.05	
75	Kenya	3.05	
75	Paraguay	3.05	
75	Qatar	3.05	
75	Slovak Republic	3.05	
75	Zambia	3.05	
81	Colombia	3.10	
81	Fiji	3.10	
81	Mali	3.10	
81	Slovenia	3.10	
85	Honduras	3.15	
85	Mexico	3.15	
85	Papua New Guinea	3.15	
88	Djibouti	3.20	
88	Mongolia	3.20	
90	Algeria	3.25	
90	Brazil	3.25	
90	Lebanon	3.25	
90	Senegal	3.25	
90	Tanzania	3.25	
95	Nigeria	3.30	
95	Romania	3.30	
97	Cambodia	3.35	
97	Dominican Republic	3.35	
97	Egypt	3.35	
97	Guinea	3.35	
97	Ivory Coast	3.35	
97	Moldova	3.35	
97	Pakistan	3.35	
104	Nepal	3.40	
104	Venezuela	3.40	
106	Armenia	3.45	
106	Bulgaria	3.45	
106	Lesotho	3.45	
106	Madagascar	3.45	
106	Russia	3.45	
111	Burkina Faso	3.50	
111	Cameroon	3.50	
111	Guyana	3.50	
111	Nicaragua	3.50	
115	Gambia	3.60	
116	Croatia	3.65	
116	Georgia	3.65	
116	Malawi	3.65	
119	Cape Verde	3.67	
120	Ethiopia	3.70	
120	India	3.70	
120	Niger	3.70	
123	Congo	3.75	
124	Chad	3.80	
124	China	3.80	
124	Mauritania	3.80	
124	Ukraine	3.80	
124	Zimbabwe	3.80	
129	Albania	3.85	
129	Bangladesh	3.85	
129	Mozambique	3.85	
129	Suriname	3.85	
133	Burundi	3.90	
134	Togo	3.95	
135	Haiti	4.00	
135	Kyrgyz Rep.	4.00	
137	Kazakhstan	4.05	
137	Sierra Leone	4.05	
139	Yemen	4.10	
140	Belarus	4.15	
141	Sudan	4.20	
141	Syria	4.20	
143	Azerbaijan	4.30	
143	Equatorial Guinea	4.30	
143	Myanmar	4.30	
143	Rwanda	4.30	
147	Tajikistan	4.40	
147	Uzbekistan	4.40	
149	Angola	4.45	
149	Turkmenistan	4.45	
151	Guinea-Bissau	4.55	
152	Vietnam	4.60	
153	Congo (Zaire)	4.70	
153	Iran	4.70	
155	Bosnia	4.80	
155	Somalia	4.80	
157	Iraq	4.90	
157	Laos	4.90	
157	Libya	4.90	
160	Cuba	5.00	
160	Korea, North	5.00	

Repressed

CAPITAL FLOWS AND FOREIGN INVESTMENT
Score: 4–Stable (high barriers)

Political instability, anti-Western sentiment, an inefficient bureaucracy, corruption, and the lack of privatization all serve to hinder foreign investment. In addition, the government does not permit foreigners to own land. The Office of the United States Trade Representative reports that "Significant informal barriers to investment exist, notably an unstable, unpredictable business climate."[4]

BANKING
Score: 4– (high level of restrictions)

The government abolished most commercial banking regulations in 1994. The result was a boom in small banks. Belarus has over 44 commercial banks—one of which has as many as 20 branches—but the government still influences the country's largest banks. According to the U.S. Department of Commerce, "To date, most of the commercial banks in Belarus, including the four specialized banks, are largely owned by groups of state enterprises which exert powerful influence over their bank's operations and enjoy privileged treatment in their banking activities."[5] In addition, many government-owned banks are in serious arrears because of the government's direction of credit to preferred, money-losing state owned industries. Thus, many banks now are default and on the verge of collapse. As a result, Belarus's banking score is 1 point worse this year.

WAGE AND PRICE CONTROLS
Score: 4–Stable (high level)

Recent evidence indicates that price controls, shortages, and the rationing of certain items are on the rise. According to the U.S. Department of Commerce, "The state continues to be the largest operator in virtually every sphere of economic activity. Certain prices are set at illogical levels, leading to shortages (particularly of eggs and butter) or apparently unintentional bargains."[6]

PROPERTY RIGHTS
Score: 4–Stable (high level of protection)

The legal system does not protect private property in full, and the inefficient court system does not enforce contracts with consistency. The U.S. Department of State characterizes the judiciary as "not independent" and "largely unable to act as a check on the executive branch and its agents."[7]

REGULATION
Score: 4–Stable (high level)

Corruption is present, and regulations tend to be applied unevenly. Moreover, there are signs that the government is increasing the regulatory burden on business. According to the U.S. Department of Commerce, "There is very little understanding among GOB [government of Belarus] officials that businesses require a stable business environment to make plans.... Businesses also complain about tax officials who appear frequently and apply different laws each time they appear. These officials can enforce their decisions by unilaterally attaching funds to bank accounts. Resort to the courts is a theoretical possibility, but time-consuming, and tax authorities allegedly ignore court decisions if they disagree."[8]

BLACK MARKET
Score: 5–Stable (very high level of activity)

The black market, which was large even when Belarus was a Soviet Socialist Republic, has increased in size because of the slow pace of economic reform. Black market activity includes the smuggling of consumer goods, the provision of transportation and other services, and violations of intellectual property rights, such as the pirating of audio and video productions and software.

NOTES
[1] World Bank, *World Development Indicators,* 1998.
[2] The corporate income tax rate can be as high as 80 percent for income earned in auctions and through leases.
[3] Based on the consumer price index.
[4] Office of the United States Trade Representative, *1997 National Trade Estimate Report on Foreign Trade Barriers.*
[5] U.S. Department of Commerce, *Country Commercial Guide,* 1997.
[6] U.S. Department of Commerce, "Recent Commercial Developments in Belarus," May 26, 1997.
[7] U.S. Department of State, "Belarus Country Report on Human Rights Practices for 1997," 1998.
[8] "Recent Commercial Developments in Belarus."

Belgium   2.10

1998 Score: **2.10**	1997 Score: **2.10**	1996 **2.10**

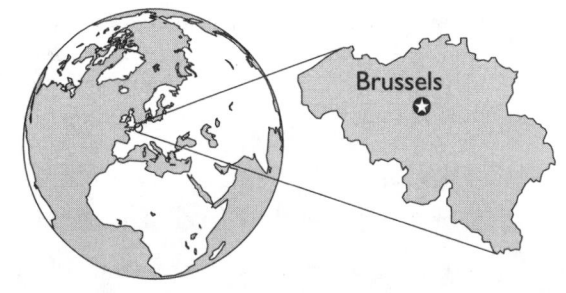

Brussels ⊛

Trade	2	Banking	2
Taxation	5	Wages and Prices	2
Government Intervention	2	Property Rights	1
Monetary Policy	1	Regulation	3
Foreign Investment	2	Black Market	1

Belgium was occupied by Germany during both World War I and World War II, and its monarchy fell victim to internal political strife immediately following World War II. Civil unrest between the French-speaking Walloons and the Flemings during the late 1960s led to the collapse of the government in 1968. In the 1970s, a socialist regime gained power and expanded the government's authority over the economy. In the 1990s, however, the government has implemented limited economic reforms. As a result of Belgium's integration into the European Union (EU), it has begun to consider a host of new reforms that eventually will open its economy further to trade and investment.

TRADE POLICY
Score: 2–Stable (low level of protectionism)

The average tariff rate is 3.6 percent. Belgium maintains non-tariff barriers (such as some government restrictions on trade in the telecommunications industry) that are common among EU members. The government has taken limited action to open portions of its telecommunication sector to foreign competition. For example, although the government maintains the majority share of the country's public telephone operator, Belgacom, a consortium of foreign companies now owns the other 49 percent.

TAXATION
Score–Income taxation: 5–Stable (very high tax rates)
Score–Corporate taxation: 4–Stable (high tax rates)
Final Taxation Score: 5–Stable (very high tax rates)

Belgium's top income tax rate is 55 percent; the average taxpayer is in the 45 percent tax bracket. The top marginal corporate tax rate is 40 percent. Belgium also maintains a 40 percent capital gains tax and a 21 percent value-added tax.

GOVERNMENT INTERVENTION IN THE ECONOMY
Score: 2–Stable (low level)

The government consumes 14.8 percent of GDP. Belgium has made significant progress in privatization; the government currently is selling portions of its telecommunications, mail, energy, and transportation services.

MONETARY POLICY
Score: 1–Stable (very low level of inflation)

From 1986 to 1996, Belgium's average rate of inflation was 3.1 percent. In 1997, the rate of inflation was about 2 percent.

CAPITAL FLOWS AND FOREIGN INVESTMENT
Score: 2–Stable (low barriers)

Belgium's foreign investment climate is one of the best in Europe. Foreign and domestic firms are treated equally, and there are few restrictions on foreign

1	Hong Kong	1.25	81	Fiji	3.10
2	Singapore	1.30	81	Mali	3.10
3	Bahrain	1.70	81	Slovenia	3.10
4	New Zealand	1.75	85	Honduras	3.15
5	Switzerland	1.85	85	Mexico	3.15
6	United States	1.90	85	Papua New Guinea	3.15
7	Ireland	1.95	88	Djibouti	3.20
7	Luxembourg	1.95	88	Mongolia	3.20
7	Taiwan	1.95	90	Algeria	3.25
7	United Kingdom	1.95	90	Brazil	3.25
11	Bahamas	2.00	90	Lebanon	3.25
12	Czech Republic	2.05	90	Senegal	3.25
12	Japan	2.05	90	Tanzania	3.25
14	Australia	2.10	95	Nigeria	3.30
14	Belgium	2.10	95	Romania	3.30
14	Canada	2.10	97	Cambodia	3.35
14	United Arab Emirates	2.10	97	Dominican Republic	3.35
18	Austria	2.15	97	Egypt	3.35
18	Chile	2.15	97	Guinea	3.35
18	Estonia	2.15	97	Ivory Coast	3.35
18	Netherlands	2.15	97	Moldova	3.35
22	Denmark	2.25	97	Pakistan	3.35
22	El Salvador	2.25	104	Nepal	3.40
22	Finland	2.25	104	Venezuela	3.40
25	Germany	2.30	106	Armenia	3.45
25	Iceland	2.30	106	Bulgaria	3.45
27	Norway	2.35	106	Lesotho	3.45
28	Korea, South	2.40	106	Madagascar	3.45
28	Kuwait	2.40	106	Russia	3.45
28	Malaysia	2.40	111	Burkina Faso	3.50
28	Panama	2.40	111	Cameroon	3.50
28	Thailand	2.40	111	Guyana	3.50
33	Sweden	2.45	111	Nicaragua	3.50
34	Argentina	2.50	115	Gambia	3.60
34	France	2.50	116	Croatia	3.65
34	Italy	2.50	116	Georgia	3.65
34	Spain	2.50	116	Malawi	3.65
38	Portugal	2.55	119	Cape Verde	3.67
38	Sri Lanka	2.55	120	Ethiopia	3.70
38	Trinidad and Tobago	2.55	120	India	3.70
41	Barbados	2.60	120	Niger	3.70
41	Peru	2.60	123	Congo	3.75
43	Bolivia	2.65	124	Chad	3.80
43	Mauritius	2.65	124	China	3.80
45	Cyprus	2.70	124	Mauritania	3.80
45	Jamaica	2.70	124	Ukraine	3.80
45	Uruguay	2.70	124	Zimbabwe	3.80
48	Botswana	2.75	129	Albania	3.85
48	Guatemala	2.75	129	Bangladesh	3.85
48	Jordan	2.75	129	Mozambique	3.85
48	Namibia	2.75	129	Suriname	3.85
48	Oman	2.75	133	Burundi	3.90
48	Philippines	2.75	134	Togo	3.95
54	Belize	2.80	135	Haiti	4.00
54	Costa Rica	2.80	135	Kyrgyz Rep.	4.00
54	Israel	2.80	137	Kazakhstan	4.05
54	Swaziland	2.80	137	Sierra Leone	4.05
54	Turkey	2.80	139	Yemen	4.10
54	Uganda	2.80	140	Belarus	4.15
54	Samoa	2.80	141	Sudan	4.20
61	Latvia	2.85	141	Syria	4.20
62	Greece	2.90	143	Azerbaijan	4.30
62	Hungary	2.90	143	Equatorial Guinea	4.30
62	So. Africa	2.90	143	Myanmar	4.30
65	Ecuador	2.95	143	Rwanda	4.30
65	Gabon	2.95	147	Tajikistan	4.40
65	Indonesia	2.95	147	Uzbekistan	4.40
65	Malta	2.95	149	Angola	4.45
65	Morocco	2.95	149	Turkmenistan	4.45
65	Poland	2.95	151	Guinea-Bissau	4.55
65	Tunisia	2.95	152	Vietnam	4.60
72	Ghana	3.00	153	Congo (Zaire)	4.70
72	Lithuania	3.00	153	Iran	4.70
72	Saudi Arabia	3.00	155	Bosnia	4.80
75	Benin	3.05	155	Somalia	4.80
75	Kenya	3.05	157	Iraq	4.90
75	Paraguay	3.05	157	Laos	4.90
75	Qatar	3.05	157	Libya	4.90
75	Slovak Republic	3.05	160	Cuba	5.00
75	Zambia	3.05	160	Korea, North	5.00
81	Colombia	3.10			

Mostly Free

investment that do not apply to domestic investment as well, except in industries vital to national defense. Restrictions remain on telecommunications, the retail sector, and broadcasting.

BANKING
Score: 2–Stable (low level of restrictions)

Foreign banks are allowed to operate in Belgium and are subject to relatively few restrictions. The domestic banking system often is tightly regulated by the government. According to the U.S. Department of Commerce, however, "Because of the lack of restrictions, easy tele-electronic communications, and fluent use of English, banking relationships with the U.S. and other countries are smooth."[1]

WAGE AND PRICE CONTROLS
Score: 2–Stable (low level)

Belgium's market determines most wages and prices. But both state ownership of some industries and a massive program of government subsidies affect pricing in many areas, such as electricity and agricultural products. Some price controls remain on household rent and certain pharmaceuticals. Belgium also maintains a minimum wage.

PROPERTY RIGHTS
Score: 1–Stable (very high level of protection)

Private property generally is safe from government expropriation in Belgium. According to the U.S. Department of State, "The Constitution provides for an independent judiciary, and the Government respects this provision in practice. The judiciary provides citizens with a fair and efficient judicial process."[2]

REGULATION
Score: 3–Stable (moderate level)

Establishing a business in Belgium can be easy if the business does not compete directly with government-owned industries (such as some utilities), and regulations are applied evenly in most cases. Belgium requires generous worker benefits, and regulations make it more difficult for some companies to survive. According to the U.S. Department of State, "Some U.S. retailers, including Toys 'R' Us, have experienced considerable difficulties in obtaining permits for outlets in Belgium. Current legislation is designed to protect small shopkeepers, and its application is not transparent."[3] But by global standards, the level of regulation is moderate.

BLACK MARKET
Score: 1–Stable (very low level of activity)

Belgium's black market is negligible. According to the U.S. Department of State, "[A]n estimated 20 percent of Belgium's video cassette and compact disc markets are composed of pirated products. For software, the share of pirated copies has dropped from 58 to 48 percent in one year, still representing a loss of $700 million to the industry."[4] This is small when compared with the overall size of the economy.

NOTES
[1] U.S. Department of Commerce, *Country Commercial Guide,*1998.
[2] U.S. Department of State, "Belgium Country Report on Human Rights Practices for 1997," 1998.
[3] U.S. Department of State, *Country Reports on Economic Policy and Trade Practices,* 1998.
[4] *Ibid.*

Belize   2.80

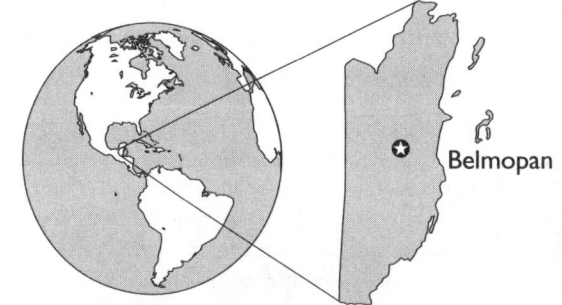

Belmopan

1998 Score: **2.80**	1997 Score: **2.70**	1996 Score: **2.70**

Trade	5	Banking	3
Taxation	4	Wages and Prices	2
Government Intervention	2	Property Rights	3
Monetary Policy	1	Regulation	3
Foreign Investment	2	Black Market	3

Belize, formerly British Honduras, received full independence from the United Kingdom in 1981. In the mid-1970s, Belize pegged its currency to the U.S. dollar, adopted a free-market philosophy and a liberal economic system. Belize has achieved significant economic gains since the early 1980s, when its main export (sugarcane) was hit by disease and the economy stagnated. Sound economic policies and favorable trade conditions in Latin and North America, the recipients of many of its exports, have led to extremely high rates of economic growth.

TRADE POLICY
Score: 5–Stable (very high level of protectionism)

Trade is a primary source of revenue for the government. Tariffs average almost 26 percent.[1] According to the U.S. Department of Commerce, "In order to protect certain domestic industries, the government maintains a list of 26 specific products which require import licenses. This list includes mostly consumer goods, such as sugar, citrus, flour, meats, jams/jellies, pepper sauce, pasta, matches, and peanut butter."[2]

TAXATION
Score–Income taxation: 4–Stable (high tax rates)
Score–Corporate taxation: 3–Stable (moderate tax rates)
Final Taxation Score: 4–Stable (high tax rates)

The top marginal income tax rate is 45 percent, and the average income level is taxed at 15 percent. The corporate income tax rate is a flat 35 percent. Belize has a social contributions tax, a value-added tax, a capital gains tax, and other taxes.

GOVERNMENT INTERVENTION IN THE ECONOMY
Score: 2–Stable (low level)

Government consumes 16 percent of GDP. There has been some progress toward privatization, but much remains to be done. As the U.S. Department of Commerce reports, "With the aim of divesting itself of inefficient public utilities, the GOB [government of Belize] privatized the local telecommunication company in 1992 and partially privatized the electric utility in 1993 through the sale of shares. However, Belize Electricity Limited (BEL) remains 51 percent government owned, and there are no immediate plans to continue the privatization program."[3]

MONETARY POLICY
Score: 1–Stable (very low level of inflation)

From 1986 to 1996 the average annual rate of inflation was 4.3 percent, In 1997, it was 4.2 percent.

1	Hong Kong	1.25
2	Singapore	1.30
3	Bahrain	1.70
4	New Zealand	1.75
5	Switzerland	1.85
6	United States	1.90
7	Ireland	1.95
7	Luxembourg	1.95
7	Taiwan	1.95
7	United Kingdom	1.95
11	Bahamas	2.00
12	Czech Republic	2.05
12	Japan	2.05
14	Australia	2.10
14	Belgium	2.10
14	Canada	2.10
14	United Arab Emirates	2.10
18	Austria	2.15
18	Chile	2.15
18	Estonia	2.15
18	Netherlands	2.15
22	Denmark	2.25
22	El Salvador	2.25
22	Finland	2.25
25	Germany	2.30
25	Iceland	2.30
27	Norway	2.35
28	Korea, South	2.40
28	Kuwait	2.40
28	Malaysia	2.40
28	Panama	2.40
28	Thailand	2.40
33	Sweden	2.45
34	Argentina	2.50
34	France	2.50
34	Italy	2.50
34	Spain	2.50
38	Portugal	2.55
38	Sri Lanka	2.55
38	Trinidad and Tobago	2.55
41	Barbados	2.60
41	Peru	2.60
43	Bolivia	2.65
43	Mauritius	2.65
45	Cyprus	2.70
45	Jamaica	2.70
45	Uruguay	2.70
48	Botswana	2.75
48	Guatemala	2.75
48	Jordan	2.75
48	Namibia	2.75
48	Oman	2.75
48	Philippines	2.75
54	Belize	2.80
54	Costa Rica	2.80
54	Israel	2.80
54	Swaziland	2.80
54	Turkey	2.80
54	Uganda	2.80
54	Samoa	2.80
61	Latvia	2.85
62	Greece	2.90
62	Hungary	2.90
62	So. Africa	2.90
65	Ecuador	2.95
65	Gabon	2.95
65	Indonesia	2.95
65	Malta	2.95
65	Morocco	2.95
65	Poland	2.95
65	Tunisia	2.95
72	Ghana	3.00
72	Lithuania	3.00
72	Saudi Arabia	3.00
75	Benin	3.05
75	Kenya	3.05
75	Paraguay	3.05
75	Qatar	3.05
75	Slovak Republic	3.05
75	Zambia	3.05
81	Colombia	3.10
81	Fiji	3.10
81	Mali	3.10
81	Slovenia	3.10
85	Honduras	3.15
85	Mexico	3.15
85	Papua New Guinea	3.15
88	Djibouti	3.20
88	Mongolia	3.20
90	Algeria	3.25
90	Brazil	3.25
90	Lebanon	3.25
90	Senegal	3.25
90	Tanzania	3.25
95	Nigeria	3.30
95	Romania	3.30
97	Cambodia	3.35
97	Dominican Republic	3.35
97	Egypt	3.35
97	Guinea	3.35
97	Ivory Coast	3.35
97	Moldova	3.35
97	Pakistan	3.35
104	Nepal	3.40
104	Venezuela	3.40
106	Armenia	3.45
106	Bulgaria	3.45
106	Lesotho	3.45
106	Madagascar	3.45
106	Russia	3.45
111	Burkina Faso	3.50
111	Cameroon	3.50
111	Guyana	3.50
111	Nicaragua	3.50
115	Gambia	3.60
116	Croatia	3.65
116	Georgia	3.65
116	Malawi	3.65
119	Cape Verde	3.67
120	Ethiopia	3.70
120	India	3.70
120	Niger	3.70
123	Congo	3.75
124	Chad	3.80
124	China	3.80
124	Mauritania	3.80
124	Ukraine	3.80
124	Zimbabwe	3.80
129	Albania	3.85
129	Bangladesh	3.85
129	Mozambique	3.85
129	Suriname	3.85
133	Burundi	3.90
134	Togo	3.95
135	Haiti	4.00
135	Kyrgyz Rep.	4.00
137	Kazakhstan	4.05
137	Sierra Leone	4.05
139	Yemen	4.10
140	Belarus	4.15
141	Sudan	4.20
141	Syria	4.20
143	Azerbaijan	4.30
143	Equatorial Guinea	4.30
143	Myanmar	4.30
143	Rwanda	4.30
147	Tajikistan	4.40
147	Uzbekistan	4.40
149	Angola	4.45
149	Turkmenistan	4.45
151	Guinea-Bissau	4.55
152	Vietnam	4.60
153	Congo (Zaire)	4.70
153	Iran	4.70
155	Bosnia	4.80
155	Somalia	4.80
157	Iraq	4.90
157	Laos	4.90
157	Libya	4.90
160	Cuba	5.00
160	Korea, North	5.00

Mostly Free

CAPITAL FLOWS AND FOREIGN INVESTMENT
Score: 2–Stable (low barriers)

Although Belize generally is open to foreign investment and has an established investment code, foreign investment is restricted in a variety of industries and economic activities. According to the U.S. Department of Commerce, "While non-Belizeans can invest in any sector of the economy, certain activities require special permits and licenses, which may not be granted to non-Belizeans."[4] These activities include merchandising, fishing (within the barrier reef), sugarcane cultivation, internal transportation, restaurants and bars, souvenir manufacturing for local market, bee-keeping, cruise ships, sightseeing tours, accounting, legal services, real estate, insurance, entertainment, and beauty salons.

BANKING
Score: 3–Stable (moderate level of restrictions)

Bank loans in Belize are closely regulated, and banks are under tight government control. Foreigners need official permission to operate, and government restrictions on the formation of new banks limit competition.

WAGE AND PRICE CONTROLS
Score: 2–Stable (low level)

The market sets most wages and prices, but there are price controls on some foodstuffs. Belize maintains a minimum wage.

PROPERTY RIGHTS
Score: 3–Stable (moderate level of protection)

The chances for expropriation remain remote, and the court system is adequate. According to the U.S. Department of State, however, there is political influence on the judiciary.[5]

REGULATION
Score: 3–Stable (moderate level)

Some regulations, like health and safety standards, can be onerous, especially for smaller companies. Regulations often are applied haphazardly, and obtaining a business license can be complicated. According to the U.S. Department of Commerce, "As with many countries in the region, corruption remains a problem in Belize."[6]

BLACK MARKET
Score: 3–Stable (moderate level of activity)

Black market activity takes many forms in Belize. Some construction, transportation, and other cash transactions are carried out primarily in the black market; and although the government is updating its copyright laws and other laws pertaining to intellectual property, there is a growing black market in pirated trademarks and prerecorded music and video tapes.

NOTES

[1] Based on total revenue from taxes on international transactions as a percentage of total imports.
[2] U.S. Department of Commerce, *Country Commercial Guide*, 1998.
[3] *Ibid.*
[4] *Ibid.*
[5] U.S. Department of State, "Belize Country Report on Human Rights Practices for 1997," 1998.
[6] U.S. Department of Commerce, *Country Commercial Guide*, 1998.

Benin   3.05

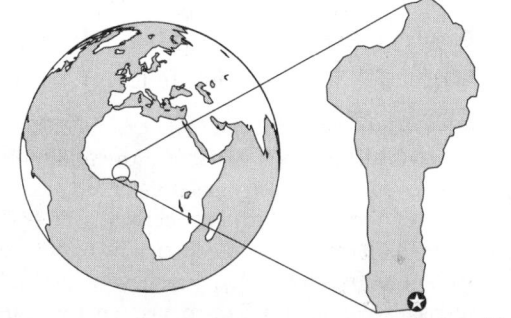

Porto-Novo

1998 Score: **2.95**	1997 Score: **2.95**	1996 Score: **2.95**

Trade	4	Banking	3
Taxation	3.5	Wages and Prices	3
Government Intervention	3	Property Rights	3
Monetary Policy	1	Regulation	3
Foreign Investment	3	Black Market	4

The Republic of Benin gained its independence from France in 1960 as Dahomey. In 1975, it was renamed by a Marxist government that had seized power in a 1972 coup. Free elections were held in 1991 following the adoption of a new constitution in 1990, which established a unitary republic. Its former dictator, Mathieu Kerekou, was elected president in 1996. Benin has not yet recovered from two decades of Marxism, and the World Bank ranked Benin as the world's ninth poorest country in 1997. Economic liberalization policies initiated in 1989, however, have led to consistent economic growth, averaging 4.8 percent between 1992 and 1996. Benin maintains close political and economic ties with France, including membership in the French Franc Zone. Recent indications that Benin has a sizable black market make its overall score 0.1 point worse than last year.

TRADE POLICY
Score: 4–Stable (high level of protectionism)

Benin has been liberalizing its trade policies. The tariff structure was simplified in 1993, but the average tariff rate remains at 13 percent, down from about 20 percent in 1996.[1] According to the World Trade Organization, "Import duties...are among the lowest in Africa, but administrative procedures at the border are complex, slow and prone to irregularities."[2] Thus, by global standards, Benin's overall level of protectionism is high.

TAXATION
Score–Income taxation: 3–Stable (moderate tax rates)
Score–Corporate taxation: 3–Stable (moderate tax rates)
Final Taxation Score: 3.5–Stable (high tax rates)

Benin's top income tax rate is 35 percent.[3] The corporate tax recently was reduced from 48 percent to 38 percent. An 18 percent value-added tax covering most goods was introduced in 1991.

GOVERNMENT INTERVENTION IN THE ECONOMY
Score: 3–Stable (moderate level)

Government consumes about 11.4 percent of GDP. There has been significant progress with privatization and the liquidation of state-owned enterprises over the past several years, but some 30 enterprises remain in state hands. The government plans further privatization.

MONETARY POLICY
Score: 1–Stable (very low level of inflation)

From 1986 to 1996, Benin's average annual rate of inflation was 5.27 percent. In 1997, it was 4.2 percent.

1	Hong Kong	1.25		81	Fiji	3.10
2	Singapore	1.30		81	Mali	3.10
3	Bahrain	1.70		81	Slovenia	3.10
4	New Zealand	1.75		85	Honduras	3.15
5	Switzerland	1.85		85	Mexico	3.15
6	United States	1.90		85	Papua New Guinea	3.15
7	Ireland	1.95		88	Djibouti	3.20
7	Luxembourg	1.95		88	Mongolia	3.20
7	Taiwan	1.95		90	Algeria	3.25
7	United Kingdom	1.95		90	Brazil	3.25
11	Bahamas	2.00		90	Lebanon	3.25
12	Czech Republic	2.05		90	Senegal	3.25
12	Japan	2.05		90	Tanzania	3.25
14	Australia	2.10		95	Nigeria	3.30
14	Belgium	2.10		95	Romania	3.30
14	Canada	2.10		97	Cambodia	3.35
14	United Arab Emirates	2.10		97	Dominican Republic	3.35
18	Austria	2.15		97	Egypt	3.35
18	Chile	2.15		97	Guinea	3.35
18	Estonia	2.15		97	Ivory Coast	3.35
18	Netherlands	2.15		97	Moldova	3.35
22	Denmark	2.25		97	Pakistan	3.35
22	El Salvador	2.25		104	Nepal	3.40
22	Finland	2.25		104	Venezuela	3.40
25	Germany	2.30		106	Armenia	3.45
25	Iceland	2.30		106	Bulgaria	3.45
27	Norway	2.35		106	Lesotho	3.45
28	Korea, South	2.40		106	Madagascar	3.45
28	Kuwait	2.40		106	Russia	3.45
28	Malaysia	2.40		111	Burkina Faso	3.50
28	Panama	2.40		111	Cameroon	3.50
28	Thailand	2.40		111	Guyana	3.50
33	Sweden	2.45		111	Nicaragua	3.50
34	Argentina	2.50		115	Gambia	3.60
34	France	2.50		116	Croatia	3.65
34	Italy	2.50		116	Georgia	3.65
34	Spain	2.50		116	Malawi	3.65
38	Portugal	2.55		119	Cape Verde	3.67
38	Sri Lanka	2.55		120	Ethiopia	3.70
38	Trinidad and Tobago	2.55		120	India	3.70
41	Barbados	2.60		120	Niger	3.70
41	Peru	2.60		123	Congo	3.75
43	Bolivia	2.65		124	Chad	3.80
43	Mauritius	2.65		124	China	3.80
45	Cyprus	2.70		124	Mauritania	3.80
45	Jamaica	2.70		124	Ukraine	3.80
45	Uruguay	2.70		124	Zimbabwe	3.80
48	Botswana	2.75		129	Albania	3.85
48	Guatemala	2.75		129	Bangladesh	3.85
48	Jordan	2.75		129	Mozambique	3.85
48	Namibia	2.75		129	Suriname	3.85
48	Oman	2.75		133	Burundi	3.90
48	Philippines	2.75		134	Togo	3.95
54	Belize	2.80		135	Haiti	4.00
54	Costa Rica	2.80		135	Kyrgyz Rep.	4.00
54	Israel	2.80		137	Kazakhstan	4.05
54	Swaziland	2.80		137	Sierra Leone	4.05
54	Turkey	2.80		139	Yemen	4.10
54	Uganda	2.80		140	Belarus	4.15
54	Samoa	2.80		141	Sudan	4.20
61	Latvia	2.85		141	Syria	4.20
62	Greece	2.90		143	Azerbaijan	4.30
62	Hungary	2.90		143	Equatorial Guinea	4.30
62	So. Africa	2.90		143	Myanmar	4.30
62	Ecuador	2.95		143	Rwanda	4.30
65	Gabon	2.95		147	Tajikistan	4.40
65	Indonesia	2.95		147	Uzbekistan	4.40
65	Malta	2.95		149	Angola	4.45
65	Morocco	2.95		149	Turkmenistan	4.45
65	Poland	2.95		151	Guinea-Bissau	4.55
65	Tunisia	2.95		152	Vietnam	4.60
72	Ghana	3.00		153	Congo (Zaire)	4.70
72	Lithuania	3.00		153	Iran	4.70
72	Saudi Arabia	3.00		155	Bosnia	4.80
75	Benin	3.05		155	Somalia	4.80
75	Kenya	3.05		157	Iraq	4.90
75	Paraguay	3.05		157	Laos	4.90
75	Qatar	3.05		157	Libya	4.90
75	Slovak Republic	3.05		160	Cuba	5.00
75	Zambia	3.05		160	Korea, North	5.00
81	Colombia	3.10				

Mostly Unfree

CAPITAL FLOWS AND FOREIGN INVESTMENT
Score: 3–Stable (moderate level)

Benin has improved its foreign investment climate considerably over the past few years. Investment incentives have been established, foreign investment has increased, and a one-stop foreign investment approval center is being planned. In the meantime, foreign investors must contend with numerous hurdles imposed by inefficient bureaucracies subject to corruption. The mining, energy, water, forestry, transport, and communication sectors remain under state control.

BANKING
Score: 3–Stable (moderate level of restrictions)

The banking sector collapsed in the late 1980s. Several state-controlled banks became bankrupt and subsequently were liquidated. Today, five private banks operate in Benin. The government remains involved in providing agricultural credit, and interest rates are dictated by the Central Bank of West Africa. New banks must meet minimum capital and other requirements.

WAGE AND PRICE CONTROLS
Score: 3–Stable (moderate level)

Although Benin's elaborate price control scheme has been dismantled, price controls on several foodstuffs have been re-imposed in an effort to combat inflation. There are price controls on cement, medicine, school equipment, electricity, and water, as well as a producer price for cotton, the country's largest export commodity. There is a minimum wage, and the government plays a significant role in guiding private-sector wage negotiations.

PROPERTY RIGHTS
Score: 3–Stable (moderate level of protection)

Private property is legal, but two decades of Marxist rule left Benin's court and legal system in disarray.

REGULATION
Score: 3–Stable (moderate level)

Benin's government has recognized the need to simplify business licensing procedures and revise the labor code to allow employers more flexibility in hiring and firing. The government recently reduced the licensing tax. According to the U.S. Department of Commerce, however, "Although the government has adopted a transparent policy to foster competition, bureaucratic red tape is a problem. The complicated steps are not streamlined to the extent that they need to be and often constitute a serious obstacle."[4]

BLACK MARKET
Score: 4– (high level of activity)

The re-imposition of price controls on several products has led to the establishment of surveillance teams to combat smuggling. There is, moreover, increasing evidence that the size of the black market in Benin is large. For example, according to the U.S. Department of Commerce, "Several factors should be considered when analyzing competition in Benin. The informal sector must be taken into account when determining competition within particular markets. Informal traders do not adhere to foreign investor guidelines, thereby avoiding both the time loss and expenses faced by formal sector traders. While no statistics accurately measure the full range and scale of informal activities, the informal sector clearly accounts for a large portion of household incomes.... The volume of informal trade at the Nigerian border is considerable.... The informal sector is linked as well to services, such as tailoring, catering, auto repair, hairdressing, and transportation."[5] As a result, Benin's score in this factor is 1 point worse than last year.

NOTES

[1] "Benin—Role As Trade Hub Would Be Strengthened by Greater Predictability of Import Duties and Liberalization of Services," World Trade Organization, Geneva, Switzerland, September 5, 1997.

[2] *Ibid.*

[3] The tax on the average income level is not available; therefore, Benin's income tax score is based solely on the top rate.

[4] U.S. Department of Commerce, *Country Commercial Guide,* 1998.

[5] *Ibid.*

Bolivia   2.65

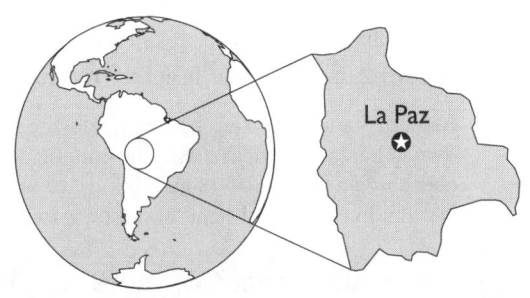

1998 Score: **2.65**	1997 Score: **2.85**	1996 Score: **2.75**

Trade	2		Banking	2
Taxation	2.5		Wages and Prices	1
Government Intervention	3		Property Rights	3
Monetary Policy	3		Regulation	4
Foreign Investment	2		Black Market	4

In June 1997, onetime president Hugo Banzer was elected president once again on the crest of a political coalition that is broad-based but ideologically inconsistent. Banzer took office as the government faced a severe financial crisis caused by the previous Sanchez de Lozada government's incomplete economic reforms. Banzer has pledged to continue Bolivia's economic liberalization, but his government's lack of political cohesion—as well as Banzer's populist inclinations—have stalled the reform process. Although the government has reformed the banking sector by selling state-owned banks, and has reduced inflation, too, Bolivia continues to lag behind many of its neighbors in overall economic freedom.

TRADE POLICY
Score: 2–Stable (low level of protectionism)

In 1990, the government reduced the average tariff rate from 16 percent to 10 percent on all but capital goods, which have a rate of 5 percent. The average tariff rate is 5.12 percent.[1] There are few, if any, non-tariff barriers.

TAXATION
Score–Income taxation: 2–Stable (low tax rates)
Score–Corporate taxation: 2–Stable (low tax rates)
Final Taxation Score: 2.5–Stable (moderate tax rates)

Bolivia has a flat income tax of 13 percent and a top corporate tax rate of 25 percent. It also has a 13 percent value-added tax and a variety of other transaction and property taxes.

GOVERNMENT INTERVENTION IN THE ECONOMY
Score: 3–Stable (moderate level)

The rate of government consumption is 13 percent, and total government spending accounts for some 27 percent of GDP, largely because of the country's state-owned industries. Privatization has helped to reduce spending, however, and overall government consumption and spending as a percentage of the economy have been decreasing steadily.

MONETARY POLICY
Score: 3–Stable (moderate level of inflation)

From 1986 to 1996, the average annual rate of inflation was 15 percent; in 1997, the rate was 7 percent.

CAPITAL FLOWS AND FOREIGN INVESTMENT
Score: 2–Stable (low barriers)

Bolivia encourages foreign investment. Few restrictions remain, and those that apply to the petroleum and mining industries are minimal.

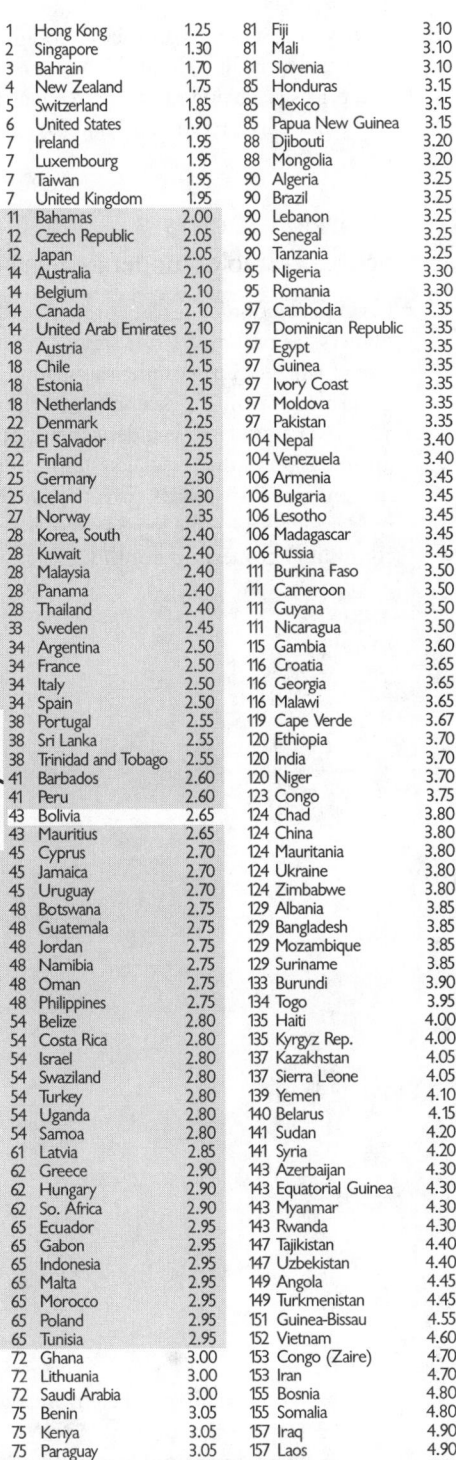

1	Hong Kong	1.25	81	Fiji	3.10
2	Singapore	1.30	81	Mali	3.10
3	Bahrain	1.70	81	Slovenia	3.10
4	New Zealand	1.75	85	Honduras	3.15
5	Switzerland	1.85	85	Mexico	3.15
6	United States	1.90	85	Papua New Guinea	3.15
7	Ireland	1.95	88	Djibouti	3.20
7	Luxembourg	1.95	88	Mongolia	3.20
7	Taiwan	1.95	90	Algeria	3.25
7	United Kingdom	1.95	90	Brazil	3.25
11	Bahamas	2.00	90	Lebanon	3.25
12	Czech Republic	2.05	90	Senegal	3.25
12	Japan	2.05	90	Tanzania	3.25
14	Australia	2.10	95	Nigeria	3.30
14	Belgium	2.10	95	Romania	3.30
14	Canada	2.10	97	Cambodia	3.35
14	United Arab Emirates	2.10	97	Dominican Republic	3.35
18	Austria	2.15	97	Egypt	3.35
18	Chile	2.15	97	Guinea	3.35
18	Estonia	2.15	97	Ivory Coast	3.35
18	Netherlands	2.15	97	Moldova	3.35
22	Denmark	2.25	97	Pakistan	3.35
22	El Salvador	2.25	104	Nepal	3.40
22	Finland	2.25	104	Venezuela	3.40
25	Germany	2.30	106	Armenia	3.45
25	Iceland	2.30	106	Bulgaria	3.45
27	Norway	2.35	106	Lesotho	3.45
28	Korea, South	2.40	106	Madagascar	3.45
28	Kuwait	2.40	106	Russia	3.45
28	Malaysia	2.40	111	Burkina Faso	3.50
28	Panama	2.40	111	Cameroon	3.50
28	Thailand	2.40	111	Guyana	3.50
33	Sweden	2.45	111	Nicaragua	3.50
34	Argentina	2.50	115	Gambia	3.60
34	France	2.50	116	Croatia	3.65
34	Italy	2.50	116	Georgia	3.65
34	Spain	2.50	116	Malawi	3.65
38	Portugal	2.55	119	Cape Verde	3.67
38	Sri Lanka	2.55	120	Ethiopia	3.70
38	Trinidad and Tobago	2.55	120	India	3.70
41	Barbados	2.60	120	Niger	3.70
41	Peru	2.60	123	Congo	3.75
43	Bolivia	2.65	124	Chad	3.80
43	Mauritius	2.65	124	China	3.80
45	Cyprus	2.70	124	Mauritania	3.80
45	Jamaica	2.70	124	Ukraine	3.80
45	Uruguay	2.70	124	Zimbabwe	3.80
48	Botswana	2.75	129	Albania	3.85
48	Guatemala	2.75	129	Bangladesh	3.85
48	Jordan	2.75	129	Mozambique	3.85
48	Namibia	2.75	129	Suriname	3.85
48	Oman	2.75	133	Burundi	3.90
48	Philippines	2.75	134	Togo	3.95
54	Belize	2.80	135	Haiti	4.00
54	Costa Rica	2.80	135	Kyrgyz Rep.	4.00
54	Israel	2.80	137	Kazakhstan	4.05
54	Swaziland	2.80	137	Sierra Leone	4.05
54	Turkey	2.80	139	Yemen	4.10
54	Uganda	2.80	140	Belarus	4.15
54	Samoa	2.80	141	Sudan	4.20
61	Latvia	2.85	141	Syria	4.20
62	Greece	2.90	143	Azerbaijan	4.30
62	Hungary	2.90	143	Equatorial Guinea	4.30
62	So. Africa	2.90	143	Myanmar	4.30
65	Ecuador	2.95	143	Rwanda	4.30
65	Gabon	2.95	147	Tajikistan	4.40
65	Indonesia	2.95	147	Uzbekistan	4.40
65	Malta	2.95	149	Angola	4.45
65	Morocco	2.95	149	Turkmenistan	4.45
65	Poland	2.95	151	Guinea-Bissau	4.55
65	Tunisia	2.95	152	Vietnam	4.60
72	Ghana	3.00	153	Congo (Zaire)	4.70
72	Lithuania	3.00	153	Iran	4.70
72	Saudi Arabia	3.00	155	Bosnia	4.80
75	Benin	3.05	155	Somalia	4.80
75	Kenya	3.05	157	Iraq	4.90
75	Paraguay	3.05	157	Laos	4.90
75	Qatar	3.05	157	Libya	4.90
75	Slovak Republic	3.05	160	Cuba	5.00
75	Zambia	3.05	160	Korea, North	5.00
81	Colombia	3.10			

Mostly Free

BANKING
Score: 2–Stable (low level of restrictions)

Bolivia's banking system has been reformed. Government-owned banks no longer exist. The banking industry is composed primarily of 18 institutions, of which 13 are private domestic banks and the rest are foreign-owned.

WAGE AND PRICE CONTROLS
Score: 1–Stable (very low level)

There are few price controls, although the government still reserves the right to limit the prices of foodstuffs. Wages and prices are being set more freely as more state-owned companies are privatized. There are no minimum wage laws.

PROPERTY RIGHTS
Score: 3–Stable (moderate level of protection)

Legal protection of private property is lax. Large property owners are particularly vulnerable because property can be seized without just compensation and "taxed" by corrupt government officials. According to the U.S. Department of State, "The judiciary is independent, but corruption and intimidation in the judicial system remain major problems."[2] But, by global standards, private property protection is moderate because the legal system is functional and communal property is not the rule.

REGULATION
Score: 4–Stable (high level)

Bolivia's economy often is regulated through haphazardly applied government requirements on business. According to the U.S. Department of Commerce, "Bureaucratic procedures have been reduced, but plenty of red tape and archaic policies still exist."[3] Moreover, even though the government maintains few occupational or environmental regulations, there are many complaints of corruption. The government has begun a crackdown on corruption, but the effects are not visible yet. According to the U.S. Department of Commerce, "potential investors should be aware that the country's judicial system is rife with corruption.... Corruption is an endemic problem."[4]

BLACK MARKET
Score: 4–Stable (high level of activity)

Some estimates place Bolivia's black market at about 30 percent of GDP. This share is being reduced, however. Piracy of intellectual property is widespread: Piracy in motion pictures, sound recordings, computer software, and books, for example, cost U.S. companies over $42 million in Bolivia during 1995.

NOTES

[1] Based on revenues gained from taxes on international trade as a percentage of total imports.
[2] U.S. Department of State, "Bolivia Country Report on Human Rights Practices for 1997," 1998.
[3] U.S. Department of Commerce, *Country Commercial Guide,* 1998.
[4] *Ibid.*

Bosnia and Herzegovina

4.80

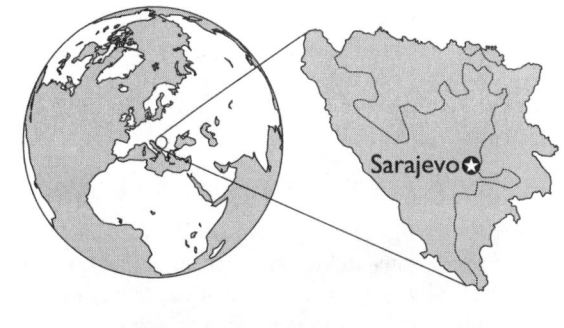

Sarajevo

1998 Score: **4.80**	1997 Score: **n/a**	1996 Score: **n/a**

Trade	5	Banking	5
Taxation	5	Wages and Prices	4
Government Intervention	5	Property Rights	5
Monetary Policy	5	Regulation	5
Foreign Investment	4	Black Market	5

The breakup of the former Yugoslavia in 1990 and 1991 created four independent countries, including Bosnia and Herzegovina. In 1992, the government of Bosnia and Herzegovina held a referendum on independence; the Bosnian Serbs, supported by nearby Serbia (another former Yugoslav republic), responded with armed resistance, seeking to divide Bosnia and Herzegovina largely along ethnic lines, with Serbian regions to join Serbia. Industrial production collapsed, and both inflation and unemployment skyrocketed. In 1994, Muslims and Croats in Bosnia and Herzegovina reached a ceasefire and signed an accord to create a Muslim–Croat confederation; the Serbs, however, controlled over 70 percent of the country, and fighting continued. A negotiated peace among the Serbs, Muslims, and Croats finally was achieved in Dayton, Ohio, in 1995, and an international peacekeeping force of 60,000 troops organized by the North Atlantic Treaty Organization entered the country later that year. The Dayton settlement calls for a multi-ethnic confederated state consisting of two administrative units: the Muslim–Croat Federation and the Serbian Republika Srpska. The results of elections held on September 12–13, 1998, were mixed: Hardliner Nikola Poplasen defeated moderate president Biljana Plavsic in the Republika Srpska, but moderate candidates made some gains in other races.

TRADE POLICY

Score: 5–Stable (very high level of protectionism)

The governments of Bosnia and Herzegovina have yet to establish fully functioning customs systems, and procedures that do exist are fraught with corruption. Official tariff rates generally average 13 percent for the Muslim–Croat Federation and 28 percent for the Republika Srpska.

TAXATION

Score–Income taxation: 5–Stable (very high tax rates)
Score–Corporate taxation: 5–Stable (very high tax rates)
Final Taxation Score: 5–Stable (very high tax rates)

The top income tax rate generally is 35 percent, and the top corporate tax rate is 30 percent. There are many other taxes, too, such as a 20 percent capital gains tax. Local and federal government entities are only beginning to establish tax administration offices, so tax collection is haphazard and applied arbitrarily. Much taxation still takes the form of government confiscation of goods produced by what little economic activity occurs; therefore, the true rates are very high.

GOVERNMENT INTERVENTION IN THE ECONOMY

Score: 5–Stable (very high level)

Government consumes almost all current GDP. With most economic output still going to the military, almost all revenue is spent before it is collected. The

1	Hong Kong	1.25	81	Fiji	3.10
2	Singapore	1.30	81	Mali	3.10
3	Bahrain	1.70	81	Slovenia	3.10
4	New Zealand	1.75	85	Honduras	3.15
5	Switzerland	1.85	85	Mexico	3.15
6	United States	1.90	85	Papua New Guinea	3.15
7	Ireland	1.95	88	Djibouti	3.20
7	Luxembourg	1.95	88	Mongolia	3.20
7	Taiwan	1.95	90	Algeria	3.25
7	United Kingdom	1.95	90	Brazil	3.25
11	Bahamas	2.00	90	Lebanon	3.25
12	Czech Republic	2.05	90	Senegal	3.25
12	Japan	2.05	90	Tanzania	3.25
14	Australia	2.10	95	Nigeria	3.30
14	Belgium	2.10	95	Romania	3.30
14	Canada	2.10	97	Cambodia	3.35
14	United Arab Emirates	2.10	97	Dominican Republic	3.35
18	Austria	2.15	97	Egypt	3.35
18	Chile	2.15	97	Guinea	3.35
18	Estonia	2.15	97	Ivory Coast	3.35
18	Netherlands	2.15	97	Moldova	3.35
22	Denmark	2.25	97	Pakistan	3.35
22	El Salvador	2.25	104	Nepal	3.40
22	Finland	2.25	104	Venezuela	3.40
25	Germany	2.30	106	Armenia	3.45
25	Iceland	2.30	106	Bulgaria	3.45
27	Norway	2.35	106	Lesotho	3.45
28	Korea, South	2.40	106	Madagascar	3.45
28	Kuwait	2.40	106	Russia	3.45
28	Malaysia	2.40	111	Burkina Faso	3.50
28	Panama	2.40	111	Cameroon	3.50
28	Thailand	2.40	111	Guyana	3.50
33	Sweden	2.45	111	Nicaragua	3.50
34	Argentina	2.50	115	Gambia	3.60
34	France	2.50	116	Croatia	3.65
34	Italy	2.50	116	Georgia	3.65
34	Spain	2.50	116	Malawi	3.65
38	Portugal	2.55	119	Cape Verde	3.67
38	Sri Lanka	2.55	120	Ethiopia	3.70
38	Trinidad and Tobago	2.55	120	India	3.70
41	Barbados	2.60	120	Niger	3.70
41	Peru	2.60	123	Congo	3.75
43	Bolivia	2.65	124	Chad	3.80
43	Mauritius	2.65	124	China	3.80
45	Cyprus	2.70	124	Mauritania	3.80
45	Jamaica	2.70	124	Ukraine	3.80
45	Uruguay	2.70	124	Zimbabwe	3.80
48	Botswana	2.75	129	Albania	3.85
48	Guatemala	2.75	129	Bangladesh	3.85
48	Jordan	2.75	129	Mozambique	3.85
48	Namibia	2.75	129	Suriname	3.85
48	Oman	2.75	133	Burundi	3.90
48	Philippines	2.75	134	Togo	3.95
54	Belize	2.80	135	Haiti	4.00
54	Costa Rica	2.80	135	Kyrgyz Rep.	4.00
54	Israel	2.80	137	Kazakhstan	4.05
54	Swaziland	2.80	137	Sierra Leone	4.05
54	Turkey	2.80	139	Yemen	4.10
54	Uganda	2.80	140	Belarus	4.15
54	Samoa	2.80	141	Sudan	4.20
61	Latvia	2.85	141	Syria	4.20
62	Greece	2.90	143	Azerbaijan	4.30
62	Hungary	2.90	143	Equatorial Guinea	4.30
62	So. Africa	2.90	143	Myanmar	4.30
65	Ecuador	2.95	143	Rwanda	4.30
65	Gabon	2.95	147	Tajikistan	4.40
65	Indonesia	2.95	147	Uzbekistan	4.40
65	Malta	2.95	149	Angola	4.45
65	Morocco	2.95	149	Turkmenistan	4.45
65	Poland	2.95	151	Guinea-Bissau	4.55
65	Tunisia	2.95	152	Vietnam	4.60
72	Ghana	3.00	153	Congo (Zaire)	4.70
72	Lithuania	3.00	153	Iran	4.70
72	Saudi Arabia	3.00	155	Bosnia	4.80
75	Benin	3.05	155	Somalia	4.80
75	Kenya	3.05	157	Iraq	4.90
75	Paraguay	3.05	157	Laos	4.90
75	Qatar	3.05	157	Libya	4.90
75	Slovak Republic	3.05	160	Cuba	5.00
75	Zambia	3.05	160	Korea, North	5.00
81	Colombia	3.10			

Repressed

governments continue to control most of the enterprises that were confiscated during the war and have yet to be given back to their rightful owners.

MONETARY POLICY
Score: 5–Stable (very high level of inflation)

Reliable figures on inflation in all of Bosnia and Herzegovina are not available, but inflation is known to be generally low in the Muslim–Croat Federation but rather high in the Serbian Republika Srpska. According to the U.S. Department of Commerce, "In the Federation, unemployment remains in the 40%–50% range and inflation is low. By contrast, growth in the Republika Srpska...was flat and inflation surpassed 30%."[1] Thus, the average annual rate of inflation for all of Bosnia and Herzegovina remains quite high.

CAPITAL FLOWS AND FOREIGN INVESTMENT
Score: 4–Stable (high barriers)

The current foreign investment code allows for investment in most areas of the economy. In practice, however, investments are allowed on a case-by-case basis. There are restrictions on investment in land, energy, transportation, telecommunications, forestry, public information, and utilities. According to the U.S. Department of Commerce, "Most international reconstruction projects in Bosnia are structured to employ as many Bosnians as possible and to utilize as many Bosnian building materials as possible. Although these regulations generally shut out foreign companies, there is a back-door approach to qualifying for these kinds of contracts. U.S. companies may establish a joint venture with a Bosnian company in order to be considered a legitimate Bosnian entity. At this time, the government of Bosnia & Herzegovina has not yet finalized and approved a new privatization law. Consequently, foreign companies may not yet acquire any stake of a state-owned commercial enterprise."[2]

BANKING
Score: 5–Stable (very high level of restrictions)

The banking system is in complete disarray. The governments own most banks and control most financial assets.

WAGE AND PRICE CONTROLS
Score: 4–Stable (high level)

The market alone does not set wages and prices. Price controls continue on public utilities, transportation, and items produced by the state-owned sector. There also are minimum wage laws.

PROPERTY RIGHTS
Score: 5–Stable (very low level of protection)

Private property is not safe in Bosnia and Herzegovina. According to the U.S. Department of State, "The Constitution provides for an independent judiciary, extends the judiciary's independence to the investigative division of the criminal justice system, and establishes a judicial police force that reports directly to the courts. However, Yugoslav and wartime practices in which the executive and the leading political parties exerted considerable influence over the judicial system persisted in all areas."[3]

REGULATION
Score: 5–Stable (very high level)

Corruption is widespread within many arms of the government, and existing regulations are applied haphazardly. Most regulatory functions and implementation are left to local governments, creating inconsistency and arbitrary enforcement.

BLACK MARKET
Score: 5–Stable (very high level of activity)

Almost all economic output is produced in the black market. According to the U.S. Department of Commerce, an "estimated two-thirds of the labor force is unemployed or working in the informal sector."[4]

NOTES

[1]   U.S. Department of Commerce, *Stat–USA* Internet site (*http://www.stat-usa.gov*).
[2]   *Ibid.*
[3]   U.S. Department of State, "Bosnia and Herzegovina Country Report on Human Rights Practices for 1997," 1998.
[4]   U.S. Department of Commerce, "Bosnia-Herzegovina: Annual Report on Prospects for Economic and Social Growth," 1997.

Botswana   2.75

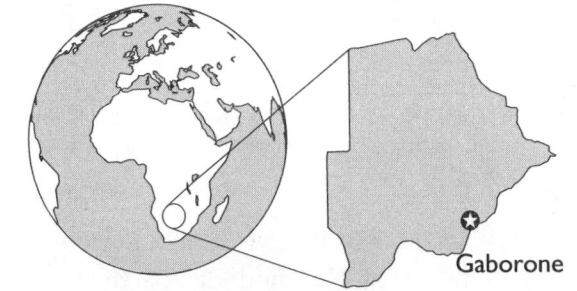
Gaborone

1998 Score: **2.75**	1997 Score: **2.85**	1996 Score: **2.80**

Trade	3	Banking	2
Taxation	2.5	Wages and Prices	2
Government Intervention	4	Property Rights	2
Monetary Policy	2	Regulation	3
Foreign Investment	3	Black Market	4

Botswana became a British protectorate in 1885 and gained its independence in 1966. One of the few African countries to experience continuous civilian rule since becoming independent, Botswana operates as a multiparty unitary republic. According to World Bank figures, Botswana enjoyed the world's fastest-growing economy between 1965 and 1996, averaging 13 percent growth in GNP over that period. This rate of growth has slowed over the past couple years, but the economy remains one of the most vibrant in Africa. As a landlocked country, Botswana largely depends on neighboring countries for access to international markets. It is a member of the Southern African Customs Union (SACU), whose member countries accounted for 78 percent of Botswana's imports and 21 percent of its exports in 1996.

TRADE POLICY
Score: 3-Stable (moderate level of protectionism)

Botswana is part of SACU with South Africa, Lesotho, Swaziland, and Namibia.[1] Its average tariff rate is less than 12 percent, down from around 30 percent in 1992. There are few, if any, non-tariff barriers.

TAXATION
Score–Income taxation: 2–Stable (low tax rates)
Score–Corporate taxation: 2–Stable (low tax rates)
Final Taxation Score: 2.5–Stable (moderate tax rates)

Botswana recently cut taxes and now has one of southern Africa's lower tax burdens. The top marginal income tax rate is 25 percent, down from 30 percent last year. The average income level is taxed at 0 percent. Botswana also has a 20 percent corporate tax rate, down from 25 percent last year.[2] It also has a 25 percent capital gains tax, a 10 percent sales tax, and a 12.5 percent tax on such transfers as inheritance.

GOVERNMENT INTERVENTION IN THE ECONOMY
Score: 4–Stable (high level)

Government consumes 28.9 percent of GDP, down from 34.9 percent in 1995. The state sector owns the majority of enterprises. According to the U.S. Department of Commerce, "The Government continued to be the primary employer, providing 100,000 public sector jobs. The private sector employed 135,000 workers in 1996, a 1.2 percent increase from 1995 but down from a peak of 145,000 in 1991. Nearly 1/4 of females actively seeking work remained unemployed, while 17 percent of male work-seekers could not find jobs. While Botswana can boast of high literacy rates and virtually universal access to primary education, employment growth is limited by a lack of technical and managerial skills among its workforce and relatively low worker productivity."[3]

1	Hong Kong	1.25	81	Fiji	3.10
2	Singapore	1.30	81	Mali	3.10
3	Bahrain	1.70	81	Slovenia	3.10
4	New Zealand	1.75	85	Honduras	3.15
5	Switzerland	1.85	85	Mexico	3.15
6	United States	1.90	85	Papua New Guinea	3.15
7	Ireland	1.95	88	Djibouti	3.20
7	Luxembourg	1.95	88	Mongolia	3.20
7	Taiwan	1.95	90	Algeria	3.25
7	United Kingdom	1.95	90	Brazil	3.25
11	Bahamas	2.00	90	Lebanon	3.25
12	Czech Republic	2.05	90	Senegal	3.25
12	Japan	2.05	90	Tanzania	3.25
14	Australia	2.10	95	Nigeria	3.30
14	Belgium	2.10	95	Romania	3.30
14	Canada	2.10	97	Cambodia	3.35
14	United Arab Emirates	2.10	97	Dominican Republic	3.35
18	Austria	2.15	97	Egypt	3.35
18	Chile	2.15	97	Guinea	3.35
18	Estonia	2.15	97	Ivory Coast	3.35
18	Netherlands	2.15	97	Moldova	3.35
22	Denmark	2.25	97	Pakistan	3.35
22	El Salvador	2.25	104	Nepal	3.40
22	Finland	2.25	104	Venezuela	3.40
25	Germany	2.30	106	Armenia	3.45
25	Iceland	2.30	106	Bulgaria	3.45
27	Norway	2.35	106	Lesotho	3.45
28	Korea, South	2.40	106	Madagascar	3.45
28	Kuwait	2.40	106	Russia	3.45
28	Malaysia	2.40	111	Burkina Faso	3.50
28	Panama	2.40	111	Cameroon	3.50
28	Thailand	2.40	111	Guyana	3.50
33	Sweden	2.45	111	Nicaragua	3.50
34	Argentina	2.50	115	Gambia	3.60
34	France	2.50	116	Croatia	3.65
34	Italy	2.50	116	Georgia	3.65
34	Spain	2.50	116	Malawi	3.65
38	Portugal	2.55	119	Cape Verde	3.67
38	Sri Lanka	2.55	120	Ethiopia	3.70
38	Trinidad and Tobago	2.55	120	India	3.70
41	Barbados	2.60	120	Niger	3.70
41	Peru	2.60	123	Congo	3.75
43	Bolivia	2.65	124	Chad	3.80
43	Mauritius	2.65	124	China	3.80
45	Cyprus	2.70	124	Mauritania	3.80
45	Jamaica	2.70	124	Ukraine	3.80
45	Uruguay	2.70	124	Zimbabwe	3.80
48	Botswana	2.75	129	Albania	3.85
48	Guatemala	2.75	129	Bangladesh	3.85
48	Jordan	2.75	129	Mozambique	3.85
48	Namibia	2.75	129	Suriname	3.85
48	Oman	2.75	133	Burundi	3.90
48	Philippines	2.75	134	Togo	3.95
54	Belize	2.80	135	Haiti	4.00
54	Costa Rica	2.80	135	Kyrgyz Rep.	4.00
54	Israel	2.80	137	Kazakhstan	4.05
54	Swaziland	2.80	137	Sierra Leone	4.05
54	Turkey	2.80	139	Yemen	4.10
54	Uganda	2.80	140	Belarus	4.15
54	Samoa	2.80	141	Sudan	4.20
61	Latvia	2.85	141	Syria	4.20
62	Greece	2.90	143	Azerbaijan	4.30
62	Hungary	2.90	143	Equatorial Guinea	4.30
62	So. Africa	2.90	143	Myanmar	4.30
65	Ecuador	2.95	143	Rwanda	4.30
65	Gabon	2.95	147	Tajikistan	4.40
65	Indonesia	2.95	147	Uzbekistan	4.40
65	Malta	2.95	149	Angola	4.45
65	Morocco	2.95	149	Turkmenistan	4.45
65	Poland	2.95	151	Guinea-Bissau	4.55
65	Tunisia	2.95	152	Vietnam	4.60
72	Ghana	3.00	153	Congo (Zaire)	4.70
72	Lithuania	3.00	153	Iran	4.70
72	Saudi Arabia	3.00	155	Bosnia	4.80
75	Benin	3.05	155	Somalia	4.80
75	Kenya	3.05	157	Iraq	4.90
75	Paraguay	3.05	157	Laos	4.90
75	Qatar	3.05	157	Libya	4.90
75	Slovak Republic	3.05	160	Cuba	5.00
75	Zambia	3.05	160	Korea, North	5.00
81	Colombia	3.10			

Mostly Free

MONETARY POLICY
Score: 2–Stable (low level of inflation)

From 1986 to 1996, Botswana's average annual rate of inflation was 14.2 percent The rate of inflation in 1997 was 6.5 percent.

CAPITAL FLOWS AND FOREIGN INVESTMENT
Score: 3–Stable (moderate barriers)

Some sectors, including most utilities, some smaller retail stores, and some restaurants and bars, are closed to private investment. The requirement that licenses be obtained for expatriate employees can be cumbersome. Botswana permits 100 percent foreign ownership.

BANKING
Score: 2–Stable (low level of restrictions)

Botswana's banking system is both competitive and advanced compared with those of most other African states, and three new foreign-controlled commercial banks have been established. The government, however, plays a significant regulatory role.

WAGE AND PRICE CONTROLS
Score: 2–Stable (low level)

Price controls have been eliminated, but some agriculture prices are established through negotiated agreements with the government.

PROPERTY RIGHTS
Score: 2–Stable (high level of protection)

Property is relatively safe in Botswana, and history illustrates few cases of expropriation. Because of financial constraints, however, the court system does not operate efficiently in all cases. According to the U.S. Department of State, "The civil courts remained unable to provide for timely, fair trials in many cases, however, due to severe staffing shortages and a back log of pending cases."[4]

REGULATION
Score: 3–Stable (moderate level)

Regulation is moderate by global standards, but government bureaucracy often is burdensome. A business license is relatively easy to obtain, for example, but the government regulates the length of the work week, maternity leave, and standards for hiring and firing. The government recently established an oversight agency to root out corrupt bureaucrats, and has stepped up its efforts to prosecute them. According to the U.S. Department of Commerce, "The Botswana constitution allows for a judiciary which is independent of both the executive and legislative powers. Civil law is based on Roman Dutch law while criminal law is built on familiar tenets of the English legal system. The legal system is sufficient to the conduct of secure commercial dealings."[5]

BLACK MARKET
Score: 4–Stable (high level of activity)

The elimination of price controls has diminished the level of black market activity, but, according to the U.S. Department of Commerce, "Copyright protection is virtually nonexistent in Botswana."[6] The government recognizes this problem and is working to establish copyright laws and their enforcement, but statistics show there is a growing informal economy. According to the U.S. Department of State, "Over 50 percent of the population is employed in the informal sector."[7]

NOTES

[1] SACU has a common external tariff of 12 percent.
[2] The basic corporate tax rate is 15 percent, although some companies are assessed an additional 10 percent.
[3] U.S. Department of Commerce, *Country Commercial Guide*, 1998.
[4] U.S. Department of State, "Botswana Country Report on Human Rights Practices for 1997," 1998.
[5] U.S. Department of Commerce, *Country Commercial Guide*, 1998.
[6] *Ibid.*
[7] U.S. Department of State, "Botswana Country Report on Human Rights Practices for 1997," 1998.

Brazil   3.25

1998 Score: **3.35**   1997 Score: **3.35**   1996 Score: **3.45**

Trade	4	Banking	3
Taxation	2.5	Wages and Prices	2
Government Intervention	3	Property Rights	3
Monetary Policy	5	Regulation	3
Foreign Investment	3	Black Market	4

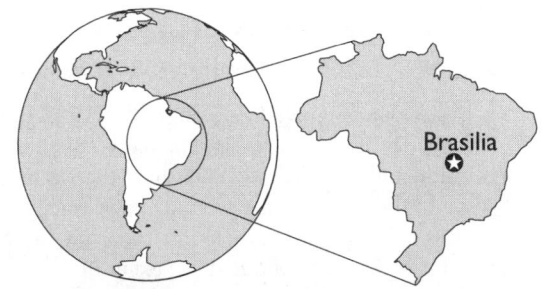

Brasilia

Brazil has the largest economy in Latin America. After decades of statist military governments, democracy was restored in the early 1990s. The former finance minister, Fernando Henrique Cardoso, was elected president in 1994 on the strength of his successful monetary plan to control Brazil's four-digit hyperinflation. Cardoso has focused on strengthening Brazil's economy, enacting constitutional reforms to enable important economic and structural reforms, and building strong diplomatic and commercial relations within the South American Common Market (Mercosur), to which Brazil belongs together with Argentina, Paraguay, and Uruguay. In July 1998, the Cardoso government privatized Telebras and Embratel, Brazil's state telecommunications monopoly and long-distance telephone carrier, respectively. Cardoso, who won re-election in October 1998, is determined to stay the course of market reform. The government's control over prices recently has been reduced; as a result, Brazil's overall score is 0.1 point better than last year. [1]

TRADE POLICY
Score: 4–Stable (high level of protectionism)

Brazil's average tariff rate is 13.8 percent.[2] It also has import licenses and other duties. "Import licenses are now used primarily for statistical purposes and generally are issued automatically within 5 days," reports the U.S. Department of State. "However, obtaining an import license can occasionally still be difficult."[3]

TAXATION
Score–Income taxation: 2–Stable (low tax rates)
Score–Corporate taxation: 2–Stable (low tax rates)
Final Taxation Score: 2.5–Stable (moderate tax rates)

Brazil's top income tax rate is 25 percent. The tax on the average income is 0 percent, and the maximum corporate tax rate is 15 percent. Brazil also has a capital gains tax of 15 percent, a federal value-added tax that ranges from 0 percent to 365.6 percent, a state value-added tax of 7 percent to 25 percent, and a maximum municipal service tax of 10 percent.

GOVERNMENT INTERVENTION IN THE ECONOMY
Score: 3–Stable (moderate level)

Government consumes 15.2 percent of GDP. The Cardoso administration's privatization program has not reduced the extent of government intervention significantly. The government still owns companies in the petroleum, electricity, and telecommunications industries, although it gradually is selling some of these assets to private investors.

MONETARY POLICY
Score: 5–Stable (very high level of inflation)

From 1986 to 1996, the average annual rate of inflation was 628.2 percent. The rate was 6.2 percent in 1997.[4]

1	Hong Kong	1.25	81	Fiji	3.10
2	Singapore	1.30	81	Mali	3.10
3	Bahrain	1.70	81	Slovenia	3.10
4	New Zealand	1.75	85	Honduras	3.15
5	Switzerland	1.85	85	Mexico	3.15
6	United States	1.90	85	Papua New Guinea	3.15
7	Ireland	1.95	88	Djibouti	3.20
7	Luxembourg	1.95	88	Mongolia	3.20
7	Taiwan	1.95	90	Algeria	3.25
7	United Kingdom	1.95	90	Brazil	3.25
11	Bahamas	2.00	90	Lebanon	3.25
12	Czech Republic	2.05	90	Senegal	3.25
12	Japan	2.05	90	Tanzania	3.25
14	Australia	2.10	95	Nigeria	3.30
14	Belgium	2.10	95	Romania	3.30
14	Canada	2.10	97	Cambodia	3.35
14	United Arab Emirates	2.10	97	Dominican Republic	3.35
18	Austria	2.15	97	Egypt	3.35
18	Chile	2.15	97	Guinea	3.35
18	Estonia	2.15	97	Ivory Coast	3.35
18	Netherlands	2.15	97	Moldova	3.35
22	Denmark	2.25	97	Pakistan	3.35
22	El Salvador	2.25	104	Nepal	3.40
22	Finland	2.25	104	Venezuela	3.40
25	Germany	2.30	106	Armenia	3.45
25	Iceland	2.30	106	Bulgaria	3.45
27	Norway	2.35	106	Lesotho	3.45
28	Korea, South	2.40	106	Madagascar	3.45
28	Kuwait	2.40	106	Russia	3.45
28	Malaysia	2.40	111	Burkina Faso	3.50
28	Panama	2.40	111	Cameroon	3.50
28	Thailand	2.40	111	Guyana	3.50
33	Sweden	2.45	111	Nicaragua	3.50
34	Argentina	2.50	115	Gambia	3.60
34	France	2.50	116	Croatia	3.65
34	Italy	2.50	116	Georgia	3.65
34	Spain	2.50	116	Malawi	3.65
38	Portugal	2.55	119	Cape Verde	3.67
38	Sri Lanka	2.55	120	Ethiopia	3.70
38	Trinidad and Tobago	2.55	120	India	3.70
41	Barbados	2.60	120	Niger	3.70
41	Peru	2.60	123	Congo	3.75
43	Bolivia	2.65	124	Chad	3.80
43	Mauritius	2.65	124	China	3.80
45	Cyprus	2.70	124	Mauritania	3.80
45	Jamaica	2.70	124	Ukraine	3.80
45	Uruguay	2.70	124	Zimbabwe	3.80
48	Botswana	2.75	129	Albania	3.85
48	Guatemala	2.75	129	Bangladesh	3.85
48	Jordan	2.75	129	Mozambique	3.85
48	Namibia	2.75	129	Suriname	3.85
48	Oman	2.75	133	Burundi	3.90
48	Philippines	2.75	134	Togo	3.95
54	Belize	2.80	135	Haiti	4.00
54	Costa Rica	2.80	135	Kyrgyz Rep.	4.00
54	Israel	2.80	137	Kazakhstan	4.05
54	Swaziland	2.80	137	Sierra Leone	4.05
54	Turkey	2.80	139	Yemen	4.10
54	Uganda	2.80	140	Belarus	4.15
54	Samoa	2.80	141	Sudan	4.20
61	Latvia	2.85	141	Syria	4.20
62	Greece	2.90	143	Azerbaijan	4.30
62	Hungary	2.90	143	Equatorial Guinea	4.30
62	So. Africa	2.90	143	Myanmar	4.30
65	Ecuador	2.95	143	Rwanda	4.30
65	Gabon	2.95	147	Tajikistan	4.40
65	Indonesia	2.95	147	Uzbekistan	4.40
65	Malta	2.95	149	Angola	4.45
65	Morocco	2.95	149	Turkmenistan	4.45
65	Poland	2.95	151	Guinea-Bissau	4.55
65	Tunisia	2.95	152	Vietnam	4.60
72	Ghana	3.00	153	Congo (Zaire)	4.70
72	Lithuania	3.00	153	Iran	4.70
72	Saudi Arabia	3.00	155	Bosnia	4.80
75	Benin	3.05	155	Somalia	4.80
75	Kenya	3.05	157	Yemen	4.90
75	Paraguay	3.05	157	Laos	4.90
75	Qatar	3.05	157	Libya	4.90
75	Slovak Republic	3.05	160	Cuba	5.00
75	Zambia	3.05	160	Korea, North	5.00
81	Colombia	3.10			

Mostly Unfree

CAPITAL FLOWS AND FOREIGN INVESTMENT
Score: 3–Stable (moderate barriers)

Restrictions on investment in the service industries can be high. The ability of foreigners to invest in internal transportation, public utilities, media, and others is limited. According to the Office of the United States Trade Representative, "Investment restrictions are an important limitation for U.S. firms seeking to conduct business in Brazil."[5] Brazil's Congress recently passed a new foreign investment law, however, that allows equal treatment for domestic and foreign firms and opens the overall economy to increased foreign investment.

BANKING
Score: 3–Stable (moderate level of restrictions)

Most banks are restricted in their ability to add branches or do business with state-owned companies. Private banks, both foreign and domestic, must compete with a substantial number of state-owned banks.

WAGE AND PRICE CONTROLS
Score: 2+ (low level)

Brazil has a long history of wage and price controls. It last froze prices in 1990 but has been easing controls gradually since that time. With the privatization of a variety of state-owned enterprises, the market gradually has taken over the responsibility for determining prices. According to the Economist Intelligence Unit, "[P]rivatization and public concessions in infrastructure services such as railways, telecommunications and electricity...have generally been accompanied by new regulations that try to raise competition and free prices."[6] As a result, Brazil's score in this category is 1 point better this year.

PROPERTY RIGHTS
Score: 3–Stable (moderate level of protection)

There is little chance that private property belonging to foreign investors will be expropriated in Brazil, where a number of major multinational corporations operate and the government is trying to attract additional foreign investment. The court system often is inefficient, however. The U.S. Department of State reports that "The judiciary has a large case backlog and is often unable to ensure the right to a fair trial. Justice is slow and often unreliable, especially in rural areas where powerful landowners use violence to settle land disputes and influence the local judiciary."[7] In addition, according to the U.S. Department of Commerce, "An overburdened court system is available for enforcing property rights; decisions take years. Decisions of the Supreme Federal Tribunal are not automatically binding on lower courts, leading to more appeals than would otherwise occur."[8]

REGULATION
Score: 3–Stable (moderate level)

Government regulation has begun to fall from its previously high level and now is moderate by global standards. But environmental, health, consumer, labor, financial, and other regulations still restrain business activity, and they frequently are not applied evenly or consistently. "Although some administrative improvements have been made," reports the U.S. Department of Commerce, "the Brazilian legal and regulatory system is far from transparent. The government has historically exercised considerable control over private business through extensive and frequently changing regulations.... Corruption is a persistent problem in Brazil."[9]

BLACK MARKET
Score: 4–Stable (high level of activity)

The level of black market activity is on the rise. According to the Office of the United States Trade Representative, the new intellectual property rights law "improves most aspects of Brazil's industrial property regime, but some problems remain."[10] There is significant pirating of patented and copyrighted materials. The U.S. Department of Commerce also reports a growing black market in labor: as much as 35 percent of the country's GDP is produced by such black market activities.[11]

NOTES

[1] Brazil's score improved in this edition of the *Index* on the basis of conditions that occurred during the last half of 1997 and the first half of 1998. In the second half of 1998, however, Brazil's economy began to feel the effects of the growing international financial crisis. As the *Index* went to press, the International Monetary Fund, the World Bank, and other international financial institutions, along with Brazil's government, were in the final stages of negotiating a new multibillion-dollar financial bailout. It is possible that such a bailout could be contingent on Brazil's restricting economic freedom through increased taxes, regulation, or other such policies. If so, any such restrictions will be included in next year's Brazil score.

[2] Office of the United States Trade Representative, *1998 National Trade Estimate Report on Foreign Trade Barriers*, 1998.

[3] U.S. Department of State, *Country Reports on Economic Policy and Trade Practices*, 1998.

[4] Based on the consumer price index.

[5] Office of the United States Trade Representative, *1998 National Trade Estimate Report on Foreign Trade Barriers*.

[6] Economist Intelligence Unit, *ILT Report*, January 1998.

[7] U.S. Department of State, "Brazil Country Report on Human Rights Practices for 1997," 1998.

[8] U.S. Department of Commerce, *Country Commercial Guide*, 1998.

[9] *Ibid.*

[10] U.S. Department of State, *Country Reports on Economic Policy and Trade Practices*, 1997, pp. 213–219.

[11] U.S. Department of Commerce, "Brazil–Sao Paulo Informal Market," *Market Research Reports*, November 1, 1996.

Bulgaria 3.45

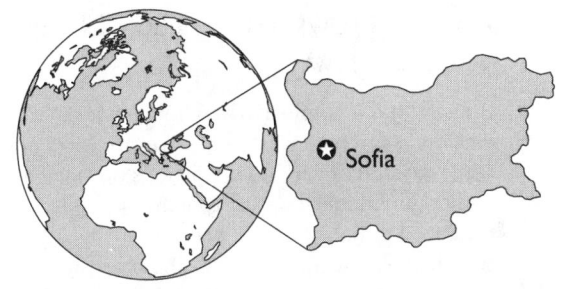

Sofia

1998 Score: **3.65**	1997 Score: **3.60**	1996 Score: **3.50**

Trade	4	Banking	3
Taxation	3.5	Wages and Prices	3
Government Intervention	3	Property Rights	3
Monetary Policy	5	Regulation	4
Foreign Investment	2	Black Market	4

Bulgaria began to move away from communism after the fall of the Berlin Wall in 1989 and finally succeeded in 1991. Pressure to slow the pace of economic reform is growing because of economic hardship, and a substantial slowdown followed the 1994 elections, which returned a neocommunist majority to parliament and brought in a cabinet controlled by former members of the Communist Party. But popular discontent swept the neocommunists out of power in the presidential and parliamentary elections in 1997. Although Bulgaria lags behind the Czech Republic, Hungary, and Poland in economic reform, it has made progress toward restoring land to its original owners and privatizing small businesses, primarily in the trade and services sectors. Bulgaria has cut taxes and implemented a new foreign investment law that removes barriers to investment. As a result, Bulgaria's overall score is 0.2 point better than last year.

TRADE POLICY
Score: 4–Stable (high level of protectionism)

Bulgaria's average tariff rate is 19.05 percent.[1] Neither the Office of the United States Trade Representative nor the U.S. Department of State reports any non-tariff barriers.

TAXATION
Score–Income taxation: 3+ (moderate tax rates)
Score–Corporate taxation: 3+ (moderate tax rates)
Final Taxation Score: 3.5+ (high tax rates)

Bulgaria's top income tax rate is 40 percent, down from 50 percent last year. The average income level is taxed at 0 percent, down from 20 percent last year; as a result, Bulgaria's income taxation score is 1 point better this year. Bulgaria has a top corporate tax rate of 30 percent, down from 36 percent last year; as a result, its corporate taxation score is 1 point better than last year. The improvement in both taxation scores gives Bulgaria a final taxation score that is 1 point better this year. Bulgaria also levies a 22 percent value-added tax.

GOVERNMENT INTERVENTION IN THE ECONOMY
Score: 3–Stable (moderate level)

Government consumption of GDP is 12.4 percent and falling. Some smaller businesses have been privatized, but most large state-owned industries have yet to be sold to the private sector.

MONETARY POLICY
Score: 5–Stable (very high level of inflation)

The rate of inflation was between 110 percent and 120 percent in 1994. It fell to 35 percent in 1995 but then jumped back up to 123 percent in 1996 and 594 percent in 1997. Bulgaria has adopted a currency board pegging its local currency to the German mark. This limits the government's ability to finance budget deficits by printing money, and may result in lower rates of inflation in the future.

#	Country	Score	#	Country	Score
1	Hong Kong	1.25	81	Fiji	3.10
2	Singapore	1.30	81	Mali	3.10
3	Bahrain	1.70	81	Slovenia	3.10
4	New Zealand	1.75	85	Honduras	3.15
5	Switzerland	1.85	85	Mexico	3.15
6	United States	1.90	85	Papua New Guinea	3.15
7	Ireland	1.95	88	Djibouti	3.20
7	Luxembourg	1.95	88	Mongolia	3.20
7	Taiwan	1.95	90	Algeria	3.25
7	United Kingdom	1.95	90	Brazil	3.25
11	Bahamas	2.00	90	Lebanon	3.25
12	Czech Republic	2.05	90	Senegal	3.25
12	Japan	2.05	90	Tanzania	3.25
14	Australia	2.10	95	Nigeria	3.30
14	Belgium	2.10	95	Romania	3.30
14	Canada	2.10	97	Cambodia	3.35
14	United Arab Emirates	2.10	97	Dominican Republic	3.35
18	Austria	2.15	97	Egypt	3.35
18	Chile	2.15	97	Guinea	3.35
18	Estonia	2.15	97	Ivory Coast	3.35
18	Netherlands	2.15	97	Moldova	3.35
22	Denmark	2.25	97	Pakistan	3.35
22	El Salvador	2.25	104	Nepal	3.40
22	Finland	2.25	104	Venezuela	3.40
25	Germany	2.30	106	Armenia	3.45
25	Iceland	2.30	106	Bulgaria	3.45
27	Norway	2.35	106	Lesotho	3.45
28	Korea, South	2.40	106	Madagascar	3.45
28	Kuwait	2.40	106	Russia	3.45
28	Malaysia	2.40	111	Burkina Faso	3.50
28	Panama	2.40	111	Cameroon	3.50
28	Thailand	2.40	111	Guyana	3.50
33	Sweden	2.45	111	Nicaragua	3.50
34	Argentina	2.50	115	Gambia	3.60
34	France	2.50	116	Croatia	3.65
34	Italy	2.50	116	Georgia	3.65
34	Spain	2.50	116	Malawi	3.65
38	Portugal	2.55	119	Cape Verde	3.67
38	Sri Lanka	2.55	120	Ethiopia	3.70
38	Trinidad and Tobago	2.55	120	India	3.70
41	Barbados	2.60	120	Niger	3.70
41	Peru	2.60	123	Congo	3.75
43	Bolivia	2.65	124	Chad	3.80
43	Mauritius	2.65	124	China	3.80
45	Cyprus	2.70	124	Mauritania	3.80
45	Jamaica	2.70	124	Ukraine	3.80
45	Uruguay	2.70	124	Zimbabwe	3.80
48	Botswana	2.75	129	Albania	3.85
48	Guatemala	2.75	129	Bangladesh	3.85
48	Jordan	2.75	129	Mozambique	3.85
48	Namibia	2.75	129	Suriname	3.85
48	Oman	2.75	133	Burundi	3.90
48	Philippines	2.75	134	Togo	3.95
54	Belize	2.80	135	Haiti	4.00
54	Costa Rica	2.80	135	Kyrgyz Rep.	4.00
54	Israel	2.80	137	Kazakhstan	4.05
54	Swaziland	2.80	137	Sierra Leone	4.05
54	Turkey	2.80	139	Yemen	4.10
54	Uganda	2.80	140	Belarus	4.15
54	Samoa	2.80	141	Sudan	4.20
61	Latvia	2.85	141	Syria	4.20
62	Greece	2.90	143	Azerbaijan	4.30
62	Hungary	2.90	143	Equatorial Guinea	4.30
62	So. Africa	2.90	143	Myanmar	4.30
65	Ecuador	2.95	143	Rwanda	4.30
65	Gabon	2.95	147	Tajikistan	4.40
65	Indonesia	2.95	147	Uzbekistan	4.40
65	Malta	2.95	149	Angola	4.45
65	Morocco	2.95	149	Turkmenistan	4.45
65	Poland	2.95	151	Guinea-Bissau	4.55
65	Tunisia	2.95	152	Vietnam	4.60
72	Ghana	3.00	153	Congo (Zaire)	4.70
72	Lithuania	3.00	153	Iran	4.70
72	Saudi Arabia	3.00	155	Bosnia	4.80
75	Benin	3.05	155	Somalia	4.80
75	Kenya	3.05	157	Iraq	4.90
75	Paraguay	3.05	157	Laos	4.90
75	Qatar	3.05	157	Libya	4.90
75	Slovak Republic	3.05	160	Cuba	5.00
75	Zambia	3.05	160	Korea, North	5.00
81	Colombia	3.10			

Mostly Unfree

CAPITAL FLOWS AND FOREIGN INVESTMENT
Score: 2+ (low)

Bulgaria has a nonrestrictive foreign investment code and welcomes foreign investment. Tax incentives are offered in some cases; there are no restrictions on foreign ownership; and requirements for local content of goods and services produced in Bulgaria have been eliminated. A well-entrenched bureaucracy remains the most significant obstacle to foreign investment, which until recently also was discouraged by the large state-owned sector and weak infrastructure. The government implemented a new foreign investment law in April 1998 that significantly reformed the investment environment. The new law, according to the Economist Intelligence Unit is, "clearer, less bureaucratic and more attractive for investors"; as a result, Bulgaria's score in this factor is 1 point better this year.

BANKING
Score: 3–Stable (moderate level of restrictions)

Foreign participation in Bulgarian banks requires permission from the government, which still owns several large banks that hold most of the country's industrial assets. Several of these banks went bankrupt in 1997, however, and have closed. A few banks from the Netherlands, Austria, and Greece have set up branches nevertheless.

WAGE AND PRICE CONTROLS
Score: 3–Stable (moderate level)

Despite attempts to adopt a free market, Bulgaria still has a mixed economy. Government-owned corporations supply subsidized raw materials to companies, thereby affecting the end prices of goods and services. Several items (mainly electricity, heating, domestic coal, postal services, and tobacco products) remain subject to price controls. Bulgaria has a minimum wage.

PROPERTY RIGHTS
Score: 3–Stable (moderate level of protection)

Private property has gained greater protection from a new legal code and an increasingly efficient legal system. According to the U.S. Department of State, "Under the Constitution, the judiciary is granted independent and coequal status with the legislative and executive branches. However, the judiciary continues to struggle with problems such as corruption, low salaries, understaffing, antiquated procedures, and a heavy backlog of cases."[2]

REGULATION
Score: 4–Stable (high level)

Bureaucrats held over from the communist era impose a significant burden on businesses. Previous U.S. Department of Commerce reports indicate that corruption was a problem in Bulgaria: "Racketeering and corruption are reportedly escalating."[3] The most recent U.S. Department of Commerce report states, however, that the "government procurement system is far from transparent (the Government Procurement Law of January 1997 has yet to show a track record), some business decisions seem to be made partly on political grounds, and some courts and law enforcement officers may be susceptible to influence (political or economic), but large-scale corruption in government circles does not appear to be as much of a problem as are bureaucratic impediments and regulations." Thus, even though a reduction in corruption is evident, bureaucratic impediments and regulations remain a problem.

BLACK MARKET
Score: 4–Stable (high level of activity)

Because economic reforms have yet to establish themselves fully, Bulgaria's black market still involves many activities like construction, transportation, and food production. The government estimates that as much as one-third of the active labor force is engaged in the black market. Even though Bulgaria maintains laws to protect intellectual property, enforcement is lax, and there is substantial black market activity in such pirated materials as computer software and prerecorded music and video.

NOTES

[1] This average tariff rate is based on official statistics from Bulgaria's government.
[2] U.S. Department of State, "Bulgaria Country Report on Human Rights Practices for 1997," 1998.
[3] U.S. Department of Commerce, *Country Commercial Guide*, 1997.

Burkina Faso 3.50

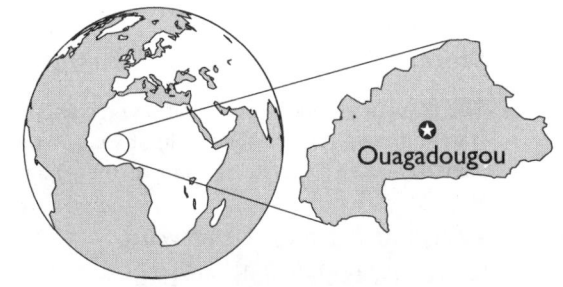

Ouagadougou

1998 Score: **3.50**	1997 Score: **3.50**	1996 Score: **3.70**

Trade	5	Banking	4
Taxation	4	Wages and Prices	4
Government Intervention	3	Property Rights	3
Monetary Policy	1	Regulation	4
Foreign Investment	2	Black Market	5

Burkina Faso, formerly Upper Volta, gained its independence from France in 1960. This landlocked country is one of the world's poorest: GNP per capita is $300. Over 80 percent of the population depends on subsistence agriculture. The government's commitment to its 1991 economic reform program appears to be bearing fruit: from 1995 to 1997, after years of poor growth, GDP growth averaged 5.2 percent. After years of poor progress, the privatization agenda appears to be gaining momentum, but many restrictions on economic freedom continue.

TRADE POLICY
Score: 5–Stable (very high level of protectionism)

Among other taxes, Burkina Faso imposes a 5 percent customs fee, a variable import duty, a variable value-added tax, a 4 percent statistical tax (an administrative fee), a 1 percent solidarity tax, and a 1 percent tax to support government enforcement of trade laws. All these taxes bring the average tariff rate to over 15 percent of an imported item's value. Burkina Faso also maintains some import bans and quotas.

TAXATION
Score–Income taxation: 3–Stable (moderate tax rates)
Score–Corporate taxation: 4–Stable (high tax rates)
Final Taxation Score: 4–Stable (high tax rates)

Burkina Faso has a top income tax rate of 35 percent and a top marginal corporate tax rate of 45 percent. It also maintains a 25 percent capital gains tax as well as real estate and other taxes.

GOVERNMENT INTERVENTION IN THE ECONOMY
Score: 3–Stable (moderate level)

Government consumes about 14.5 percent of GDP. There is a significant public sector.

MONETARY POLICY
Score: 1–Stable (very low level of inflation)

Burkina Faso had an average inflation rate of 3.8 percent from 1986 to 1996. The inflation rate for 1997 is unavailable.

CAPITAL FLOWS AND FOREIGN INVESTMENT
Score: 2–Stable (low barriers)

There are few restrictions on investment in Burkina Faso. In 1992, the government adopted a new investment code that treats foreign and domestic firms equally. Some tax incentives are granted. Corruption remains a problem, however.

1	Hong Kong	1.25		81	Fiji	3.10
2	Singapore	1.30		81	Mali	3.10
3	Bahrain	1.70		81	Slovenia	3.10
4	New Zealand	1.75		85	Honduras	3.15
5	Switzerland	1.85		85	Mexico	3.15
6	United States	1.90		85	Papua New Guinea	3.15
7	Ireland	1.95		88	Djibouti	3.20
7	Luxembourg	1.95		88	Mongolia	3.20
7	Taiwan	1.95		90	Algeria	3.25
7	United Kingdom	1.95		90	Brazil	3.25
11	Bahamas	2.00		90	Lebanon	3.25
12	Czech Republic	2.05		90	Senegal	3.25
12	Japan	2.05		90	Tanzania	3.25
14	Australia	2.10		95	Nigeria	3.30
14	Belgium	2.10		95	Romania	3.30
14	Canada	2.10		97	Cambodia	3.35
14	United Arab Emirates	2.10		97	Dominican Republic	3.35
18	Austria	2.15		97	Egypt	3.35
18	Chile	2.15		97	Guinea	3.35
18	Estonia	2.15		97	Ivory Coast	3.35
18	Netherlands	2.15		97	Moldova	3.35
22	Denmark	2.25		97	Pakistan	3.35
22	El Salvador	2.25		104	Nepal	3.40
22	Finland	2.25		104	Venezuela	3.40
25	Germany	2.30		106	Armenia	3.45
25	Iceland	2.30		106	Bulgaria	3.45
27	Norway	2.35		106	Lesotho	3.45
28	Korea, South	2.40		106	Madagascar	3.45
28	Kuwait	2.40		106	Russia	3.45
28	Malaysia	2.40		111	Burkina Faso	3.50
28	Panama	2.40		111	Cameroon	3.50
28	Thailand	2.40		111	Guyana	3.50
33	Sweden	2.45		111	Nicaragua	3.50
34	Argentina	2.50		115	Gambia	3.60
34	France	2.50		116	Croatia	3.65
34	Italy	2.50		116	Georgia	3.65
34	Spain	2.50		116	Malawi	3.65
38	Portugal	2.55		119	Cape Verde	3.67
38	Sri Lanka	2.55		120	Ethiopia	3.70
38	Trinidad and Tobago	2.55		120	India	3.70
41	Barbados	2.60		120	Niger	3.70
41	Peru	2.60		123	Congo	3.75
43	Bolivia	2.65		124	Chad	3.80
43	Mauritius	2.65		124	China	3.80
45	Cyprus	2.70		124	Mauritania	3.80
45	Jamaica	2.70		124	Ukraine	3.80
45	Uruguay	2.70		124	Zimbabwe	3.80
48	Botswana	2.75		129	Albania	3.85
48	Guatemala	2.75		129	Bangladesh	3.85
48	Jordan	2.75		129	Mozambique	3.85
48	Namibia	2.75		129	Suriname	3.85
48	Oman	2.75		133	Burundi	3.90
48	Philippines	2.75		134	Togo	3.95
54	Belize	2.80		135	Haiti	4.00
54	Costa Rica	2.80		135	Kyrgyz Rep.	4.00
54	Israel	2.80		137	Kazakhstan	4.05
54	Swaziland	2.80		137	Sierra Leone	4.05
54	Turkey	2.80		139	Yemen	4.10
54	Uganda	2.80		140	Belarus	4.15
54	Samoa	2.80		141	Sudan	4.20
61	Latvia	2.85		141	Syria	4.20
62	Greece	2.90		143	Azerbaijan	4.30
62	Hungary	2.90		143	Equatorial Guinea	4.30
62	So. Africa	2.90		143	Myanmar	4.30
65	Ecuador	2.95		143	Rwanda	4.30
65	Gabon	2.95		147	Tajikistan	4.40
65	Indonesia	2.95		147	Uzbekistan	4.40
65	Malta	2.95		149	Angola	4.45
65	Morocco	2.95		149	Turkmenistan	4.45
65	Poland	2.95		151	Guinea-Bissau	4.55
65	Tunisia	2.95		152	Vietnam	4.60
72	Ghana	3.00		153	Congo (Zaire)	4.70
72	Lithuania	3.00		153	Iran	4.70
72	Saudi Arabia	3.00		155	Bosnia	4.80
75	Benin	3.05		155	Somalia	4.80
75	Kenya	3.05		157	Iraq	4.90
75	Paraguay	3.05		157	Laos	4.90
75	Qatar	3.05		157	Libya	4.90
75	Slovak Republic	3.05		160	Cuba	5.00
75	Zambia	3.05		160	Korea, North	5.00
81	Colombia	3.10				

Mostly Unfree

BANKING
Score: 4–Stable (high level of restrictions)

The government heavily regulates and controls the banking system through direct ownership of many banks. There are plans, however, to privatize some of these banks.

WAGE AND PRICE CONTROLS
Score: 4–Stable (high level)

Wages and prices in Burkina Faso are affected mainly by significant government involvement in the economy. The government continues to subsidize many domestically produced products.

PROPERTY RIGHTS
Score: 3–Stable (moderate level of protection)

Private property in Burkina Faso is subject to government expropriation, and some cases can take years to resolve. The U.S. Department of Commerce reports that "Burkina Faso has a legal system which protects and facilitates acquisition and disposition of all property rights, including intellectual property."[1] According to the U.S. Department of State, "The Constitution provides for an independent judiciary; however, in practice it is subject to executive branch influence."[2]

REGULATION
Score: 4–Stable (high level)

Establishing a business in Burkina Faso can be difficult if the business intends to compete with a state-owned company. Regulations can be applied unevenly and inconsistently.

BLACK MARKET
Score: 5–Stable (very high level of activity)

By some estimates, the black market comprises almost half the formal economy. According to the U.S. Department of Commerce, "The tertiary sector, contributing about 41 percent in value added to the economy, is poised for growth. This sector is dominated by the so-called 'informal sector' (70 percent)."[3]

NOTES
[1]   U.S. Department of Commerce, *Country Commercial Guide,* 1998.
[2]   U.S. Department of State, "Burkina Faso Country Report on Human Rights Practices for 1997," 1998.
[3]   U.S. Department of Commerce, *Country Commercial Guide,* 1998.

Burundi   3.90

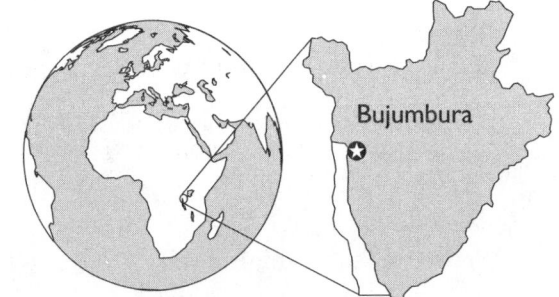

1998 Score: **3.90**	1997 Score: **3.80**	1996 Score: **n/a**

Trade	5	Banking	4
Taxation	4	Wages and Prices	4
Government Intervention	3	Property Rights	4
Monetary Policy	2	Regulation	4
Foreign Investment	4	Black Market	5

Burundi gained its independence from a Belgian-administered United Nations trusteeship in 1962. Its economy is primarily agricultural, with over 80 percent of the population engaged in subsistence farming. After gaining its independence, Burundi was one of the poorest countries in sub-Saharan Africa and quickly became embroiled in civil unrest and political instability. There was a coup d'état in 1996, and ethnic tension and violence continue. Open conflict erupts periodically between the government and rebel groups. Peace talks, begun in 1997, are progressing slowly. The economy shrank an average of 9.6 percent from 1994 to 1996; per capita GNP was $230 in 1996.

TRADE POLICY
Score: 5–Stable (very high level of protectionism)

Burundi's average tariff rate is 21.4 percent. Non-tariff barriers include difficult border crossing, inefficient customs service, and border thieves and bandits.

TAXATION
Score–Income taxation: 4–Stable (high tax rates)
Score–Corporate taxation: 4–Stable (high tax rates)
Final Taxation Score: 4–Stable (high tax rates)

Tax revenue as a percentage of GDP was over 25 percent in 1996.[1] Tax evasion is pervasive, indicating that the actual tax burden is quite high.

GOVERNMENT INTERVENTION IN THE ECONOMY
Score: 3–Stable (moderate level)

Government consumes about 11 percent of GDP, and the public sector generates most GDP overall. Burundi also has a large number of state-owned companies.

MONETARY POLICY
Score: 2–Stable (low level of inflation)

Burundi's average annual rate of inflation from 1986 to 1996 was 8.7 percent. The inflation rate for 1997 is not available.

CAPITAL FLOWS AND FOREIGN INVESTMENT
Score: 4–Stable (high barriers)

Burundi treats domestic and foreign firms equally and actively seeks investment, but it remains a country in turmoil. The most significant barriers to investment remain underdeveloped financial institutions, unsafe conditions, and insecure borders.

1	Hong Kong	1.25	81	Fiji	3.10
2	Singapore	1.30	81	Mali	3.10
3	Bahrain	1.70	81	Slovenia	3.10
4	New Zealand	1.75	85	Honduras	3.15
5	Switzerland	1.85	85	Mexico	3.15
6	United States	1.90	85	Papua New Guinea	3.15
7	Ireland	1.95	88	Djibouti	3.20
7	Luxembourg	1.95	88	Mongolia	3.20
7	Taiwan	1.95	90	Algeria	3.25
7	United Kingdom	1.95	90	Brazil	3.25
11	Bahamas	2.00	90	Lebanon	3.25
12	Czech Republic	2.05	90	Senegal	3.25
12	Japan	2.05	90	Tanzania	3.25
14	Australia	2.10	95	Nigeria	3.30
14	Belgium	2.10	95	Romania	3.30
14	Canada	2.10	97	Cambodia	3.35
14	United Arab Emirates	2.10	97	Dominican Republic	3.35
18	Austria	2.15	97	Egypt	3.35
18	Chile	2.15	97	Guinea	3.35
18	Estonia	2.15	97	Ivory Coast	3.35
18	Netherlands	2.15	97	Moldova	3.35
22	Denmark	2.25	97	Pakistan	3.35
22	El Salvador	2.25	104	Nepal	3.40
22	Finland	2.25	104	Venezuela	3.40
25	Germany	2.30	106	Armenia	3.45
25	Iceland	2.30	106	Bulgaria	3.45
27	Norway	2.35	106	Lesotho	3.45
28	Korea, South	2.40	106	Madagascar	3.45
28	Kuwait	2.40	106	Russia	3.45
28	Malaysia	2.40	111	Burkina Faso	3.50
28	Panama	2.40	111	Cameroon	3.50
28	Thailand	2.40	111	Guyana	3.50
33	Sweden	2.45	111	Nicaragua	3.50
34	Argentina	2.50	115	Gambia	3.60
34	France	2.50	116	Croatia	3.65
34	Italy	2.50	116	Georgia	3.65
34	Spain	2.50	116	Malawi	3.65
38	Portugal	2.55	119	Cape Verde	3.67
38	Sri Lanka	2.55	120	Ethiopia	3.70
38	Trinidad and Tobago	2.55	120	India	3.70
41	Barbados	2.60	120	Niger	3.70
41	Peru	2.60	123	Congo	3.75
43	Bolivia	2.65	124	Chad	3.80
43	Mauritius	2.65	124	China	3.80
45	Cyprus	2.70	124	Mauritania	3.80
45	Jamaica	2.70	124	Ukraine	3.80
45	Uruguay	2.70	124	Zimbabwe	3.80
48	Botswana	2.75	129	Albania	3.85
48	Guatemala	2.75	129	Bangladesh	3.85
48	Jordan	2.75	129	Mozambique	3.85
48	Namibia	2.75	129	Suriname	3.85
48	Oman	2.75	133	Burundi	3.90
48	Philippines	2.75	134	Togo	3.95
54	Belize	2.80	135	Haiti	4.00
54	Costa Rica	2.80	135	Kyrgyz Rep.	4.00
54	Israel	2.80	137	Kazakhstan	4.05
54	Swaziland	2.80	137	Sierra Leone	4.05
54	Turkey	2.80	139	Yemen	4.10
54	Uganda	2.80	140	Belarus	4.15
54	Samoa	2.80	141	Sudan	4.20
61	Latvia	2.85	141	Syria	4.20
62	Greece	2.90	143	Azerbaijan	4.30
62	Hungary	2.90	143	Equatorial Guinea	4.30
62	So. Africa	2.90	143	Myanmar	4.30
65	Ecuador	2.95	143	Rwanda	4.30
65	Gabon	2.95	147	Tajikistan	4.40
65	Indonesia	2.95	147	Uzbekistan	4.40
65	Malta	2.95	149	Angola	4.45
65	Morocco	2.95	149	Turkmenistan	4.45
65	Poland	2.95	151	Guinea-Bissau	4.55
65	Tunisia	2.95	152	Vietnam	4.60
72	Ghana	3.00	153	Congo (Zaire)	4.70
72	Lithuania	3.00	153	Iran	4.70
72	Saudi Arabia	3.00	155	Bosnia	4.80
75	Benin	3.05	155	Somalia	4.80
75	Kenya	3.05	157	Iraq	4.90
75	Paraguay	3.05	157	Laos	4.90
75	Qatar	3.05	157	Libya	4.90
75	Slovak Republic	3.05	160	Cuba	5.00
75	Zambia	3.05	160	Korea, North	5.00
81	Colombia	3.10			

Mostly Unfree

BANKING
Score: 4–Stable (high level of restrictions)

The banking system is heavily controlled by the government and is severely underdeveloped.

WAGE AND PRICE CONTROLS
Score: 4–Stable (high level)

Wages and prices in Burundi are affected by a large public sector, import substitution policies, and government subsidies.

PROPERTY RIGHTS
Score: 4–Stable (low level of protection)

Private property is subject to government expropriation and armed bandits. The government is attempting to privatize many state-owned enterprises, but crime and theft remain problems. According to the U.S. Department of State, "The decree of September 13 provides for an independent judiciary, but in practice the judiciary is dominated by Tutsis [a minority ethnic group that controls the army and is the primary support for the current government].... Besides the frequent lack of counsel...other major shortcomings in the legal system include a lack of adequate funding and an outmoded legal code."[2]

REGULATION
Score: 4–Stable (high level)

Establishing a business can be difficult because of a massive and corrupt bureaucracy. Bribery sometimes is present, as is embezzlement by government officials.

BLACK MARKET
Score: 5–Stable (very high level of activity)

Burundi's black market is larger than the formal market—and growing. Most of this activity occurs in smuggled consumer goods, labor, and pirated intellectual property.

NOTES
[1]   Tax rates for Burundi are not available; therefore, the author relies on total tax revenues as a percentage of the overall economy.
[2]   U.S. Department of State, "Burundi Country Report on Human Rights Practices for 1997," 1998.

Cambodia   3.35

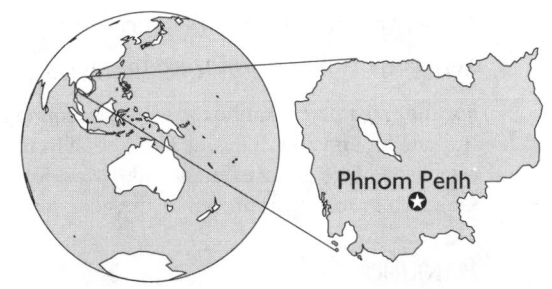

Phnom Penh

1998 Score: **3.35**	1997 Score: **3.55**	1996 Score: **n/a**

Trade	3	Banking	3
Taxation	2.5	Wages and Prices	3
Government Intervention	3	Property Rights	4
Monetary Policy	5	Regulation	4
Foreign Investment	3	Black Market	3

Since 1945, Cambodia has been ruled successively by France, a Cambodian monarch, and a military regime. After the United States ended its military and economic aid, the Khmer Rouge took power and killed over 1 million people. In 1979, Vietnam invaded Cambodia and installed its puppet Cambodia People's Party (CPP) in Phnom Penh. The CPP was opposed by remnants of the Khmer Rouge and Western-backed noncommunist factions in a war that continued until the 1991 Paris Peace Agreement, which called for a transitional government to be run by the United Nations until elections could be held in 1993. The 1993 elections saw the defeat of the CPP by the royalist party of Prince Ranariddh, but the CPP leader, Hun Sen, managed to force a coalition government on Ranariddh. Hun Sen came to dominate this government, and corruption and lawlessness flourished. Hun Sen ended the fiction of a coalition government in a 1997 coup that led Ranariddh and other opposition leaders to flee the country. International pressure forced Hun Sen to hold an election in July 1998, in which the CPP won a plurality. Although opposition parties may gain some political space, the continued dominance of the CPP does not bode well for economic reform.

TRADE POLICY
Score: 3–Stable (moderate level of protectionism)

Cambodia's average tariff is 8.5 percent. Import licenses have been abolished for most items but remain in effect for pharmaceuticals.

TAXATION
Score–Income taxation: 2–Stable (low tax rates)
Score–Corporate taxation: 2–Stable (low tax rates)
Final Taxation Score: 2.5–Stable (moderate tax rates)

Cambodia's top marginal income tax rate is 20 percent. The tax on the average income level is 5 percent. Cambodia's top corporate income tax rate also is 20 percent. In addition, Cambodia has a 4 percent sales tax as well as other taxes.

GOVERNMENT INTERVENTION IN THE ECONOMY
Score: 3–Stable (moderate level)

Government consumes 20 percent of GDP. The government sector also produces most of the country's GDP.

MONETARY POLICY
Score: 5–Stable (very high level of inflation)

Between 1986 and 1996, Cambodia's average annual rate of inflation was over 50 percent. In 1997, the inflation rate was 9.1 percent.

1	Hong Kong	1.25	81	Fiji	3.10
2	Singapore	1.30	81	Mali	3.10
3	Bahrain	1.70	81	Slovenia	3.10
4	New Zealand	1.75	85	Honduras	3.15
5	Switzerland	1.85	85	Mexico	3.15
6	United States	1.90	85	Papua New Guinea	3.15
7	Ireland	1.95	88	Djibouti	3.20
7	Luxembourg	1.95	88	Mongolia	3.20
7	Taiwan	1.95	90	Algeria	3.25
7	United Kingdom	1.95	90	Brazil	3.25
11	Bahamas	2.00	90	Lebanon	3.25
12	Czech Republic	2.05	90	Senegal	3.25
12	Japan	2.05	90	Tanzania	3.25
14	Australia	2.10	95	Nigeria	3.30
14	Belgium	2.10	95	Romania	3.30
14	Canada	2.10	97	Cambodia	3.35
14	United Arab Emirates	2.10	97	Dominican Republic	3.35
18	Austria	2.15	97	Egypt	3.35
18	Chile	2.15	97	Guinea	3.35
18	Estonia	2.15	97	Ivory Coast	3.35
18	Netherlands	2.15	97	Moldova	3.35
22	Denmark	2.25	97	Pakistan	3.35
22	El Salvador	2.25	104	Nepal	3.40
22	Finland	2.25	104	Venezuela	3.40
25	Germany	2.30	106	Armenia	3.45
25	Iceland	2.30	106	Bulgaria	3.45
27	Norway	2.35	106	Lesotho	3.45
28	Korea, South	2.40	106	Madagascar	3.45
28	Kuwait	2.40	106	Russia	3.45
28	Malaysia	2.40	111	Burkina Faso	3.50
28	Panama	2.40	111	Cameroon	3.50
28	Thailand	2.40	111	Guyana	3.50
33	Sweden	2.45	111	Nicaragua	3.50
34	Argentina	2.50	115	Gambia	3.60
34	France	2.50	116	Croatia	3.65
34	Italy	2.50	116	Georgia	3.65
34	Spain	2.50	116	Malawi	3.65
38	Portugal	2.55	119	Cape Verde	3.67
38	Sri Lanka	2.55	120	Ethiopia	3.70
38	Trinidad and Tobago	2.55	120	India	3.70
41	Barbados	2.60	120	Niger	3.70
41	Peru	2.60	123	Congo	3.75
43	Bolivia	2.65	124	Chad	3.80
43	Mauritius	2.65	124	China	3.80
45	Cyprus	2.70	124	Mauritania	3.80
45	Jamaica	2.70	124	Ukraine	3.80
45	Uruguay	2.70	124	Zimbabwe	3.80
48	Botswana	2.75	129	Albania	3.85
48	Guatemala	2.75	129	Bangladesh	3.85
48	Jordan	2.75	129	Mozambique	3.85
48	Namibia	2.75	129	Suriname	3.85
48	Oman	2.75	133	Burundi	3.90
48	Philippines	2.75	134	Togo	3.95
54	Belize	2.80	135	Haiti	4.00
54	Costa Rica	2.80	135	Kyrgyz Rep.	4.00
54	Israel	2.80	137	Kazakhstan	4.05
54	Swaziland	2.80	137	Sierra Leone	4.05
54	Turkey	2.80	139	Yemen	4.10
54	Uganda	2.80	140	Belarus	4.15
54	Samoa	2.80	141	Sudan	4.20
61	Latvia	2.85	141	Syria	4.20
62	Greece	2.90	143	Azerbaijan	4.30
62	Hungary	2.90	143	Equatorial Guinea	4.30
62	So. Africa	2.90	143	Myanmar	4.30
65	Ecuador	2.95	143	Rwanda	4.30
65	Gabon	2.95	147	Tajikistan	4.40
65	Indonesia	2.95	147	Uzbekistan	4.40
65	Malta	2.95	149	Angola	4.45
65	Morocco	2.95	149	Turkmenistan	4.45
65	Poland	2.95	151	Guinea-Bissau	4.55
65	Tunisia	2.95	152	Vietnam	4.60
72	Ghana	3.00	153	Congo (Zaire)	4.70
72	Lithuania	3.00	153	Iran	4.70
72	Saudi Arabia	3.00	155	Bosnia	4.80
75	Benin	3.05	155	Somalia	4.80
75	Kenya	3.05	157	Iraq	4.90
75	Paraguay	3.05	157	Laos	4.90
75	Qatar	3.05	157	Libya	4.90
75	Slovak Republic	3.05	160	Cuba	5.00
75	Zambia	3.05	160	Korea, North	5.00
81	Colombia	3.10			

Mostly Unfree

CAPITAL FLOWS AND FOREIGN INVESTMENT
Score: 3–Stable (moderate barriers)

For the most part, Cambodia welcomes foreign investment. It treats foreign and domestic firms equally and has an established foreign investment code. Most foreign investments still must be approved by the government, however.

BANKING
Score: 3–Stable (moderate level of restrictions)

Cambodia's banking system remains under government influence. There are 2 major state-owned banks and 17 private banks, but the government has plans to privatize its state-owned banks. By global standards, Cambodia's restrictions on banking are moderate.

WAGE AND PRICE CONTROLS
Score: 3–Stable (moderate level)

The market determines most wages and prices. There are some controls on such items as foodstuffs and some energy products. Companies in the large state-owned sector receive subsidies that allow them to offer goods and services at artificially low prices.

PROPERTY RIGHTS
Score: 4–Stable (low level of protection)

Cambodia's legal system does not protect private property effectively. "Cambodia's court system is weak," reports the U.S. Department of Commerce. "Judges have been trained either for a short period at home or under other systems of law, have little access to published Cambodian law and, because paid a minimal salary (USD20/month), are susceptible to corruption."[1]

REGULATION
Score: 4–Stable (high level)

Government corruption in Cambodia remains pervasive and often manifests itself in bribes, kickbacks, and payoffs. The bureaucracy is cumbersome and inefficient, making it difficult to open businesses and to keep them open.

BLACK MARKET
Score: 3–Stable (moderate level of activity)

Most of Cambodia's black market activity occurs in labor and pirated intellectual property.

NOTE
[1]   U.S. Department of Commerce, *Country Commercial Guide*, 1998.

Cameroon   3.50

1998 Score: **3.50**   1997 Score: **3.60**   1996 Score: **3.60**

Trade	5	Banking	4
Taxation	4	Wages and Prices	3
Government Intervention	2	Property Rights	4
Monetary Policy	1	Regulation	4
Foreign Investment	3	Black Market	5

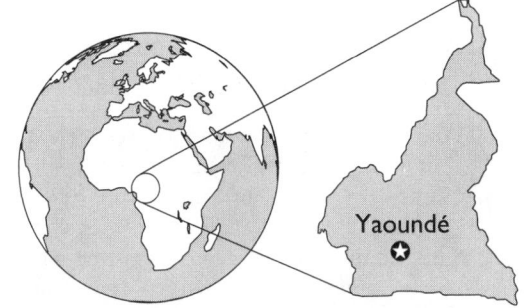

Yaoundé ✪

Cameroon gained its independence from a French-administered United Nations trusteeship in 1960. A one-party state was established, and political repression followed. Spurred by increasing domestic and international pressure for democratization, the government legalized opposition parties in 1990 and held elections—widely criticized by international observers as flawed—in 1992. President Paul Biya was re-elected in 1997 in a controversial election and amid allegations that he uses strong-arm tactics that stifle the democratic process. Despite its considerable resources, Cameroon's economy contracted from 1987 to 1994. The economy grew at 5 percent in 1995 and 1996, however, after the privatization of several state-owned industries and limited market reform.

TRADE POLICY
Score: 5–Stable (very high level of protectionism)

Cameroon's average tariff rate is around 20 percent.[1] Almost 40 percent of total government revenue is raised through tariffs, and countervailing and anti-dumping duties are used to protect inefficient domestic industries. According to the U.S. Department of Commerce, "Customs fraud is endemic in Cameroon and protracted negotiations with customs officers over the value of imported goods not subject to [official customs] valuation are common."[2]

TAXATION
Score–Income taxation: 3–Stable (moderate tax rates)
Score–Corporate taxation: 4–Stable (high tax rates)
Final Taxation Score: 4–Stable (high tax rates)

Cameroon's top income tax rate is 60 percent;[3] but the tax rate on the average income level is 0 percent. The top corporate tax rate is 38.5 percent. Cameroon also has a 38.5 percent capital gains tax and an 18.7 percent turnover tax.

GOVERNMENT INTERVENTION IN THE ECONOMY
Score: 2–Stable (low level)

Government consumes 8.3 percent of GDP. The public sector remains large, however, and privatization has been sluggish and plagued with scandal. The government continues to own enterprises in the airline industry, shipping, railroads, and investment funds.

MONETARY POLICY
Score: 1–Stable (very low level of inflation)

From 1986 to 1996, Cameroon's average annual rate of inflation was 2.95 percent. In 1997, inflation ran around 5 percent.

1	Hong Kong	1.25	81	Fiji	3.10
2	Singapore	1.30	81	Mali	3.10
3	Bahrain	1.70	81	Slovenia	3.10
4	New Zealand	1.75	85	Honduras	3.15
5	Switzerland	1.85	85	Mexico	3.15
6	United States	1.90	85	Papua New Guinea	3.15
7	Ireland	1.95	88	Djibouti	3.20
7	Luxembourg	1.95	88	Mongolia	3.20
7	Taiwan	1.95	90	Algeria	3.25
7	United Kingdom	1.95	90	Brazil	3.25
11	Bahamas	2.00	90	Lebanon	3.25
12	Czech Republic	2.05	90	Senegal	3.25
12	Japan	2.05	90	Tanzania	3.25
14	Australia	2.10	95	Nigeria	3.30
14	Belgium	2.10	95	Romania	3.30
14	Canada	2.10	97	Cambodia	3.35
14	United Arab Emirates	2.10	97	Dominican Republic	3.35
18	Austria	2.15	97	Egypt	3.35
18	Chile	2.15	97	Guinea	3.35
18	Estonia	2.15	97	Ivory Coast	3.35
18	Netherlands	2.15	97	Moldova	3.35
22	Denmark	2.25	97	Pakistan	3.35
22	El Salvador	2.25	104	Nepal	3.40
22	Finland	2.25	104	Venezuela	3.40
25	Germany	2.30	106	Armenia	3.45
25	Iceland	2.30	106	Bulgaria	3.45
27	Norway	2.35	106	Lesotho	3.45
28	Korea, South	2.40	106	Madagascar	3.45
28	Kuwait	2.40	106	Russia	3.45
28	Malaysia	2.40	111	Burkina Faso	3.50
28	Panama	2.40	111	Cameroon	3.50
28	Thailand	2.40	111	Guyana	3.50
33	Sweden	2.45	111	Nicaragua	3.50
34	Argentina	2.50	115	Gambia	3.60
34	France	2.50	116	Croatia	3.65
34	Italy	2.50	116	Georgia	3.65
34	Spain	2.50	116	Malawi	3.65
38	Portugal	2.55	119	Cape Verde	3.67
38	Sri Lanka	2.55	120	Ethiopia	3.70
38	Trinidad and Tobago	2.55	120	India	3.70
41	Barbados	2.60	120	Niger	3.70
41	Peru	2.60	123	Congo	3.75
43	Bolivia	2.65	124	Chad	3.80
43	Mauritius	2.65	124	China	3.80
45	Cyprus	2.70	124	Mauritania	3.80
45	Jamaica	2.70	124	Ukraine	3.80
45	Uruguay	2.70	124	Zimbabwe	3.80
48	Botswana	2.75	129	Albania	3.85
48	Guatemala	2.75	129	Bangladesh	3.85
48	Jordan	2.75	129	Mozambique	3.85
48	Namibia	2.75	129	Suriname	3.85
48	Oman	2.75	133	Burundi	3.90
48	Philippines	2.75	134	Togo	3.95
54	Belize	2.80	135	Haiti	4.00
54	Costa Rica	2.80	135	Kyrgyz Rep.	4.00
54	Israel	2.80	137	Kazakhstan	4.05
54	Swaziland	2.80	137	Sierra Leone	4.05
54	Turkey	2.80	139	Yemen	4.10
54	Uganda	2.80	140	Belarus	4.15
54	Samoa	2.80	141	Sudan	4.20
61	Latvia	2.85	141	Syria	4.20
62	Greece	2.90	143	Azerbaijan	4.30
62	Hungary	2.90	143	Equatorial Guinea	4.30
62	So. Africa	2.90	143	Myanmar	4.30
65	Ecuador	2.95	143	Rwanda	4.30
65	Gabon	2.95	147	Tajikistan	4.40
65	Indonesia	2.95	147	Uzbekistan	4.40
65	Malta	2.95	149	Angola	4.45
65	Morocco	2.95	149	Turkmenistan	4.45
65	Poland	2.95	151	Guinea-Bissau	4.55
65	Tunisia	2.95	152	Vietnam	4.60
72	Ghana	3.00	153	Congo (Zaire)	4.70
72	Lithuania	3.00	153	Iran	4.70
72	Saudi Arabia	3.00	155	Bosnia	4.80
75	Benin	3.05	155	Somalia	4.80
75	Kenya	3.05	157	Iraq	4.90
75	Paraguay	3.05	157	Laos	4.90
75	Qatar	3.05	157	Libya	4.90
75	Slovak Republic	3.05	160	Cuba	5.00
75	Zambia	3.05	160	Korea, North	5.00
81	Colombia	3.10			

Mostly Unfree

CAPITAL FLOWS AND FOREIGN INVESTMENT
Score: 3–Stable (moderate barriers)

Cameroon is open to foreign investment in most industries, but it remains partial to investments from France and, in some cases, blocks investment from other countries. Its corrupt bureaucracy and unstable legal institutions provide little comfort. Investment is approved on a case-by-case basis. Foreign direct investment is declining because of deteriorating economic conditions. "Cameroon's policies, as defined in law, contain all necessary elements of an open investment regime," reports the U.S. Department of Commerce. "However, current practice does not permit a fair, transparent and impartial implementation of the country's laws and policies."[4]

BANKING
Score: 4–Stable (high level of restrictions)

The banking sector is in crisis. Several state-owned banks are near collapse, and several French-owned banks are reducing their presence. Banks in Cameroon have been influenced heavily by the state and by France. Interest rates, for example, are controlled by the government and often do not reflect market conditions. There also is a domestic banking industry. According to the U.S. Department of Commerce, "Despite a system-wide restructuring exercise carried out in 1989–1992, Cameroon's banking system remains fragile with liabilities substantially in excess of any realistic valuation of its assets."[5]

WAGE AND PRICE CONTROLS
Score: 3–Stable (moderate level)

The government controls prices on some items, both by owning and operating enterprises and by officially dictating the prices of some goods that are produced by private firms and farms. There also is corruption in the price control bureaucracy. Price controls are imposed on pharmaceuticals, petroleum products, and goods and services provided by public monopolies. The market, however, still determines most prices. Thus, by global standards, Cameroon has a moderate level of wage and price controls.

PROPERTY RIGHTS
Score: 4–Stable (low level of protection)

Private property, although legal, is not entirely safe in Cameroon. A corrupt government and an uncertain legal environment can result in the confiscation of private property. According to the U.S. Department of Commerce, "The right to private ownership is recognized in Cameroon, but is limited in practice by a dysfunctional judiciary, inadequate definitions of property rights and widespread corruption in government decision-making."[6]

REGULATION
Score: 4–Stable (high level)

According to the U.S. Department of Commerce, "Corruption and a dysfunctional judicial system severely disrupt Cameroon's economy and society."[7] Existing regulations are applied unevenly and impose a huge burden on businesses. Establishing a business is a complicated procedure, and it is difficult to hire expatriate employees.

BLACK MARKET
Score: 5–Stable (very high level of activity)

Cameroon's black market is nearly as large as its legal market. Smugglers regularly bring in beef and other food products to circumvent the government's often high duties on agricultural products.

NOTES

[1] World Bank, *World Development Indicators*, 1998.
[2] U.S. Department of Commerce, *Country Commercial Guide*, 1998.
[3] Some estimates place the top income tax rate at 66 percent.
[4] U.S. Department of Commerce, *Country Commercial Guide*, 1998.
[5] *Ibid.*
[6] *Ibid.*
[7] *Ibid.*

Canada   2.10

1998 Score: **2.10**		1997 Score: **2.10**		1996 Score: **2.00**	
Trade	2	Banking	2
Taxation	5	Wages and Prices	2
Government Intervention	2	Property Rights	1
Monetary Policy	1	Regulation	2
Foreign Investment	3	Black Market	1

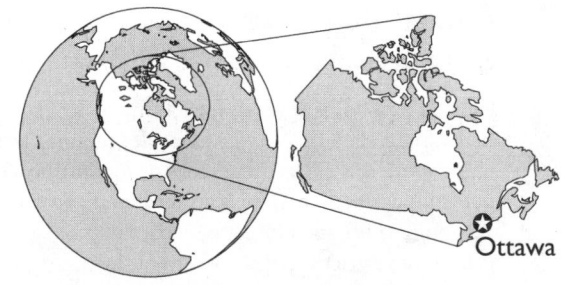
Ottawa

Canada has the world's seventh-largest market economy and is moving away from many of its formerly interventionist economic policies. In 1995, Ontario elected Mike Harris (Conservative Party) as prime minister on a platform of cutting provincial income taxes by 30 percent, balancing the budget, and reducing regulations; Harris already has accomplished most of these goals. By 1996, even Quebec had joined this trend: its prime minister, Lucien Bouchard (New Parti Quebeçois), proposed sharp spending reductions and a deregulation program and has implemented many of the cuts in spending. On the federal level, Prime Minister Jean Chrétien (Liberal Party) is curbing government spending to reduce the country's budget deficit. In June 1997, Canada held a national election in which the Liberal Party won a narrow majority in parliament. The Liberal Party has pledged to continue economic liberalization and work toward a balanced budget by 1999. This election, however, demonstrated the growing distance between Quebec and the rest of Canada, making another referendum on secession likely by the year 2000.

TRADE POLICY
Score: 2–Stable (low level of protectionism)

As a party to the North American Free Trade Agreement (NAFTA) with the United States and Mexico, Canada generally supports free trade. It has an average tariff rate of just over 4 percent.[1] Canada also maintains trade barriers, however, against such products as dairy, poultry, eggs, fresh fruit and vegetables, potatoes, processed horticultural products, and live swine.

TAXATION
Score–Income taxation: 4–Stable (high tax rates)
Score–Corporate taxation: 5–Stable (very high tax rates)
Final Taxation Score: 5–Stable (very high tax rates)

Canada's top income tax rate is 51.64 percent,[2] with the average income taxed at 17 percent. The top marginal corporate tax rate is 46.12 percent.[3] Canada also has a 21.84 percent capital gains tax and a 7 percent value-added tax (called the Goods and Services Tax).

GOVERNMENT INTERVENTION IN THE ECONOMY
Score: 2–Stable (low level)

Government consumes 20.6 percent of GDP. Since 1984, Canada has undertaken substantial privatization. Its provinces also are privatizing provincially owned firms, especially utilities.

MONETARY POLICY
Score: 1–Stable (very low level of inflation)

The Bank of Canada sets monetary policy. The average annual rate of inflation from 1986 to 1996 was 2.8 percent. Today, the rate is about 1.8 percent.

1	Hong Kong	1.25	81	Fiji	3.10
2	Singapore	1.30	81	Mali	3.10
3	Bahrain	1.70	81	Slovenia	3.10
4	New Zealand	1.75	85	Honduras	3.15
5	Switzerland	1.85	85	Mexico	3.15
6	United States	1.90	85	Papua New Guinea	3.15
7	Ireland	1.95	88	Djibouti	3.20
7	Luxembourg	1.95	88	Mongolia	3.20
7	Taiwan	1.95	90	Algeria	3.25
7	United Kingdom	1.95	90	Brazil	3.25
11	Bahamas	2.00	90	Lebanon	3.25
12	Czech Republic	2.05	90	Senegal	3.25
12	Japan	2.05	90	Tanzania	3.25
14	Australia	2.10	95	Nigeria	3.30
14	Belgium	2.10	95	Romania	3.30
14	Canada	2.10	97	Cambodia	3.35
14	United Arab Emirates	2.10	97	Dominican Republic	3.35
18	Austria	2.15	97	Egypt	3.35
18	Chile	2.15	97	Guinea	3.35
18	Estonia	2.15	97	Ivory Coast	3.35
18	Netherlands	2.15	97	Moldova	3.35
22	Denmark	2.25	97	Pakistan	3.35
22	El Salvador	2.25	104	Nepal	3.40
22	Finland	2.25	104	Venezuela	3.40
25	Germany	2.30	106	Armenia	3.45
25	Iceland	2.30	106	Bulgaria	3.45
27	Norway	2.35	106	Lesotho	3.45
28	Korea, South	2.40	106	Madagascar	3.45
28	Kuwait	2.40	106	Russia	3.45
28	Malaysia	2.40	111	Burkina Faso	3.50
28	Panama	2.40	111	Cameroon	3.50
28	Thailand	2.40	111	Guyana	3.50
33	Sweden	2.45	111	Nicaragua	3.50
34	Argentina	2.50	115	Gambia	3.60
34	France	2.50	116	Croatia	3.65
34	Italy	2.50	116	Georgia	3.65
34	Spain	2.50	116	Malawi	3.65
38	Portugal	2.55	119	Cape Verde	3.67
38	Sri Lanka	2.55	120	Ethiopia	3.70
38	Trinidad and Tobago	2.55	120	India	3.70
41	Barbados	2.60	120	Niger	3.70
41	Peru	2.60	123	Congo	3.75
43	Bolivia	2.65	124	Chad	3.80
43	Mauritius	2.65	124	China	3.80
45	Cyprus	2.70	124	Mauritania	3.80
45	Jamaica	2.70	124	Ukraine	3.80
45	Uruguay	2.70	124	Zimbabwe	3.80
48	Botswana	2.75	129	Albania	3.85
48	Guatemala	2.75	129	Bangladesh	3.85
48	Jordan	2.75	129	Mozambique	3.85
48	Namibia	2.75	129	Suriname	3.85
48	Oman	2.75	133	Burundi	3.90
48	Philippines	2.75	134	Togo	3.95
54	Belize	2.80	135	Haiti	4.00
54	Costa Rica	2.80	135	Kyrgyz Rep.	4.00
54	Israel	2.80	137	Kazakhstan	4.05
54	Swaziland	2.80	137	Sierra Leone	4.05
54	Turkey	2.80	139	Yemen	4.10
54	Uganda	2.80	140	Belarus	4.15
54	Samoa	2.80	141	Sudan	4.20
61	Latvia	2.85	141	Syria	4.20
62	Greece	2.90	143	Azerbaijan	4.30
62	Hungary	2.90	143	Equatorial Guinea	4.30
62	So. Africa	2.90	143	Myanmar	4.30
65	Ecuador	2.95	143	Rwanda	4.30
65	Gabon	2.95	147	Tajikistan	4.40
65	Indonesia	2.95	147	Uzbekistan	4.40
65	Malta	2.95	149	Angola	4.45
65	Morocco	2.95	149	Turkmenistan	4.45
65	Poland	2.95	151	Guinea-Bissau	4.55
65	Tunisia	2.95	152	Vietnam	4.60
72	Ghana	3.00	153	Congo (Zaire)	4.70
72	Lithuania	3.00	153	Iran	4.70
72	Saudi Arabia	3.00	155	Bosnia	4.80
75	Benin	3.05	155	Somalia	4.80
75	Kenya	3.05	157	Myanmar	4.90
75	Paraguay	3.05	157	Laos	4.90
75	Qatar	3.05	157	Libya	4.90
75	Slovak Republic	3.05	160	Cuba	5.00
75	Zambia	3.05	160	Korea, North	5.00
81	Colombia	3.10			

Mostly Free

CAPITAL FLOWS AND FOREIGN INVESTMENT
Score: 3–Stable (moderate barriers)

Canada maintains several restrictions on investment. The Investment Canada Act, for example, requires the government to review each foreign investment proposal to determine whether there is a "net benefit to Canada." Although most such investments are approved, the act often is used to restrict foreign investment in energy, publishing, telecommunications, broadcasting, and cable television.

BANKING
Score: 2–Stable (low level of restrictions)

Canada has a private financial system with some restrictions. In mid-1992, the government implemented a financial sector reform package that increased competition among banks, trust companies, and insurance companies. Canada's banking system, however, prohibits entry by foreign-owned branches. The country recently made some concessions to the World Trade Organization that would permit foreign bank branching. A new law is expected to be in place by June 30, 1999.

WAGE AND PRICE CONTROLS
Score: 2–Stable (low level)

The market sets most prices in Canada. Some notable exceptions include government-owned utilities, the health care system, and such agricultural goods as eggs, poultry, and dairy products.

PROPERTY RIGHTS
Score: 1–Stable (very high level of protection)

Private property is protected as a fundamental right in the Canada's political system. The legal and judicial system affords adequate protection. According to the U.S. Department of State, "The law provides for an independent judiciary, and the Government respects this provision in practice. The judiciary provides citizens with a fair and efficient judicial process and vigorously enforces the right to a fair trial."[4]

REGULATION
Score: 2–Stable (low level)

It is relatively easy to establish a business in Canada. Each business must be registered in its province (except in New Brunswick, which does not require registration). Canada does not have a single, uniform internal market, and regulations differ from province to province. The various provincial governments are seeking agreements that would establish common regulatory policies.

BLACK MARKET
Score: 1–Stable (very low level of activity)

Canada's black market is confined to the sale of goods and services considered harmful to public safety, principally weapons, drugs, and stolen merchandise. High taxes on alcohol and cigarettes encourage some smuggling of these products.

NOTES

[1] This rate does not take into account the large amount of trade that occurs between the United States and Canada, most of which takes place at reduced rates or duty-free under the U.S.–Canada Free Trade Agreement. When this reduction is taken into account, the average tariff rate is only 2.4 percent. For further explanation, see *World Trade and Customs Directory* (Washington, D.C.: Arrowhead International, 1998).

[2] This is a combined rate for 1997 in Ontario, which consists of a 31.32 percent federal tax and a 20.32 percent provincial tax. It is included here because both federal and provincial taxes are collected at the federal level. Thus, for all intents and purposes, the two tax rates are combined into one overall tax rate. Ontario is used because this is the rate reported in *Worldwide Executive Tax Guide and Directory,* 1998 edition (New York, N.Y.: Ernst & Young, 1998). Other provinces may have higher or lower taxes, but the average for Canada is about 53 percent.

[3] This rate includes both federal and provincial rates and was provided by *Worldwide Corporate Tax Guide and Directory,* 1998 edition (New York, N.Y.: Ernst & Young, 1998).

[4] U.S. Department of State, "Canada Country Report on Human Rights Practices for 1997," 1998.

Cape Verde   3.67

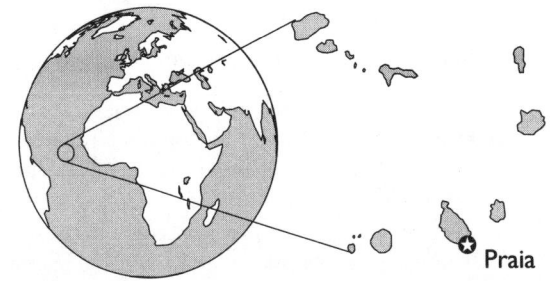
★ Praia

1998 Score: **3.44**	1997 Score: **3.44**	1996 Score: **3.44**

Trade	5	Banking	5
Taxation	n/a	Wages and Prices	4
Government Intervention	5	Property Rights	2
Monetary Policy	2	Regulation	4
Foreign Investment	2	Black Market	4

Cape Verde gained its independence from Portugal in 1975, but it maintains close ties with Portugal, its principal trading partner. In fact, there are negotiations under way aimed at associating Cape Verde's currency with or adopting Portugal's escudo. Cape Verde has few natural resources and is highly dependent on imports. The government maintains many restrictions on economic activity. Cape Verde typically is able to produce only a small percentage of its food requirements and relies heavily on international food aid. Higher levels of government consumption as a percentage of GDP have caused Cape Verde's overall score to drop by 0.23 point this year relative to last year.

TRADE POLICY
Score: 5–Stable (very high level of protectionism)

Cape Verde's tariff rates range from 5 percent to 50 percent; the average rate is about 20 percent. Imports are subject to a 7 percent tax on top of the tariff, in addition to a 5 percent to 20 percent consumption tax. Non-tariff barriers include strict import licenses and documentation requirements.

TAXATION
Score–Income taxation: Not scored
Score–Corporate taxation: Not scored
Final Taxation Score: Not scored

Tax information for Cape Verde is not available.

GOVERNMENT INTERVENTION IN THE ECONOMY
Score: 5– (very high level)

Government consumes about 30 percent of GDP.[1] Cape Verde has a significant state-owned sector.

MONETARY POLICY
Score: 2–Stable (low level of inflation)

Cape Verde had an average inflation rate of 6.55 percent from 1986 to 1996. The inflation rate for 1997 is not available.

CAPITAL FLOWS AND FOREIGN INVESTMENT
Score: 2–Stable (low barriers)

Nearly all sectors of the economy now are open to investment, but some restrictions remain. For example, delays often occur when revenue is converted to another currency and sent to the investor's home country; in addition, the approval process for some investments can be slow.

1	Hong Kong	1.25	81	Fiji	3.10
2	Singapore	1.30	81	Mali	3.10
3	Bahrain	1.70	81	Slovenia	3.10
4	New Zealand	1.75	85	Honduras	3.15
5	Switzerland	1.85	85	Mexico	3.15
6	United States	1.90	85	Papua New Guinea	3.15
7	Ireland	1.95	88	Djibouti	3.20
7	Luxembourg	1.95	88	Mongolia	3.20
7	Taiwan	1.95	90	Algeria	3.25
7	United Kingdom	1.95	90	Brazil	3.25
11	Bahamas	2.00	90	Lebanon	3.25
12	Czech Republic	2.05	90	Senegal	3.25
12	Japan	2.05	90	Tanzania	3.25
14	Australia	2.10	95	Nigeria	3.30
14	Belgium	2.10	95	Romania	3.30
14	Canada	2.10	97	Cambodia	3.35
14	United Arab Emirates	2.10	97	Dominican Republic	3.35
18	Austria	2.15	97	Egypt	3.35
18	Chile	2.15	97	Guinea	3.35
18	Estonia	2.15	97	Ivory Coast	3.35
18	Netherlands	2.15	97	Moldova	3.35
22	Denmark	2.25	97	Pakistan	3.35
22	El Salvador	2.25	104	Nepal	3.40
22	Finland	2.25	104	Venezuela	3.40
25	Germany	2.30	106	Armenia	3.45
25	Iceland	2.30	106	Bulgaria	3.45
27	Norway	2.35	106	Lesotho	3.45
28	Korea, South	2.40	106	Madagascar	3.45
28	Kuwait	2.40	106	Russia	3.45
28	Malaysia	2.40	111	Burkina Faso	3.50
28	Panama	2.40	111	Cameroon	3.50
28	Thailand	2.40	111	Guyana	3.50
33	Sweden	2.45	111	Nicaragua	3.50
34	Argentina	2.50	115	Gambia	3.60
34	France	2.50	116	Croatia	3.65
34	Italy	2.50	116	Georgia	3.65
34	Spain	2.50	116	Malawi	3.65
38	Portugal	2.55	119	Cape Verde	3.67
38	Sri Lanka	2.55	120	Ethiopia	3.70
38	Trinidad and Tobago	2.55	120	India	3.70
41	Barbados	2.60	120	Niger	3.70
41	Peru	2.60	123	Congo	3.75
43	Bolivia	2.65	124	Chad	3.80
43	Mauritius	2.65	124	China	3.80
45	Cyprus	2.70	124	Mauritania	3.80
45	Jamaica	2.70	124	Ukraine	3.80
45	Uruguay	2.70	124	Zimbabwe	3.80
48	Botswana	2.75	129	Albania	3.85
48	Guatemala	2.75	129	Bangladesh	3.85
48	Jordan	2.75	129	Mozambique	3.85
48	Namibia	2.75	129	Suriname	3.85
48	Oman	2.75	133	Burundi	3.90
48	Philippines	2.75	134	Togo	3.95
54	Belize	2.80	135	Haiti	4.00
54	Costa Rica	2.80	135	Kyrgyz Rep.	4.00
54	Israel	2.80	137	Kazakhstan	4.05
54	Swaziland	2.80	137	Sierra Leone	4.05
54	Turkey	2.80	139	Yemen	4.10
54	Uganda	2.80	140	Belarus	4.15
54	Samoa	2.80	141	Sudan	4.20
61	Latvia	2.85	141	Syria	4.20
62	Greece	2.90	143	Azerbaijan	4.30
62	Hungary	2.90	143	Equatorial Guinea	4.30
62	So. Africa	2.90	143	Myanmar	4.30
65	Ecuador	2.95	143	Rwanda	4.30
65	Gabon	2.95	147	Tajikistan	4.40
65	Indonesia	2.95	147	Uzbekistan	4.40
65	Malta	2.95	149	Angola	4.45
65	Morocco	2.95	149	Turkmenistan	4.45
65	Poland	2.95	152	Vietnam	4.60
65	Tunisia	2.95	151	Guinea-Bissau	4.55
72	Ghana	3.00	153	Congo (Zaire)	4.70
72	Lithuania	3.00	153	Iran	4.70
72	Saudi Arabia	3.00	155	Bosnia	4.80
75	Benin	3.05	155	Somalia	4.80
75	Kenya	3.05	157	Iraq	4.90
75	Paraguay	3.05	157	Laos	4.90
75	Qatar	3.05	157	Libya	4.90
75	Slovak Republic	3.05	160	Cuba	5.00
75	Zambia	3.05	160	Korea, North	5.00
81	Colombia	3.10			

Mostly Unfree

BANKING
Score: 5–Stable (very high level of restrictions)

Cape Verde's banking system is underdeveloped. According to the U.S. Department of Commerce, "Financial services to the private sector are limited, with the result that the existing system is considered inadequate to efficiently and effectively satisfy the private sector's needs for credit."[2] There is no stock market and no capital market, and banking accounting systems, although clear, are not always consistent with international norms. The government owns most banks.

WAGE AND PRICE CONTROLS
Score: 4–Stable (high level)

Wages and prices in Cape Verde are affected by the large public sector and the transfer of government subsidies to those institutions.

PROPERTY RIGHTS
Score: 2–Stable (high level of protection)

Private property is guaranteed in Cape Verde; the legal and judicial system is based on English law. Property can be expropriated, however, if such action is deemed to be in the national interest. According to the U.S. Department of State, "The Constitution provides for a judiciary independent of the executive branch, and the Government respects this provision in practice."[3]

REGULATION
Score: 4–Stable (high level)

Establishing a business can be cumbersome if the business is to compete with a state-owned enterprise. Regulations are applied evenly in most cases, but some corruption and a growing domestic monopoly in certain industries make it difficult to open a new business.

BLACK MARKET
Score: 4–Stable (high level of activity)

Cape Verde has a growing and pervasive black market, mainly in consumer goods, luxury items, and Western books, video and audio cassettes, and movies.

NOTES

[1] The score in this factor has changed from a "3" in 1998 to a "5" in 1999. Previously unavailable data provide a more accurate understanding of the country's performance. The government consumption rate is from World Bank, *World Development Indicators,* 1998. The methodology, however, remains unchanged.

[2] U.S. Department of Commerce, *Country Commercial Guide,* 1998.

[3] U.S. Department of State, "Cape Verde Country Report on Human Rights Practices for 1997," 1998.

Chad   3.80

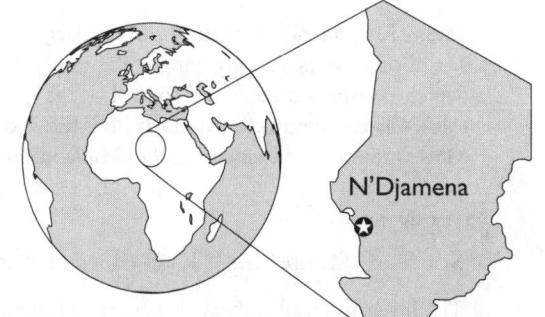

N'Djamena

1998 Score: **3.80**	1997 Score: **3.80**	1996 Score: **n/a**

Trade	5	Banking	4
Taxation	4	Wages and Prices	4
Government Intervention	3	Property Rights	4
Monetary Policy	1	Regulation	4
Foreign Investment	4	Black Market	5

Chad gained its independence from France in 1960. A majority of the population is engaged in subsistence farming and fishing, and agriculture accounted for over 40 percent of GNP in 1996. The oil sector is receiving considerable attention from international investors. After independence, Chad became one of the poorest and least politically cohesive of the former colonies in Africa; except for a brief respite following the 1996 presidential election, the country has experienced constant civil unrest and political instability. Chad remains extremely dependent on foreign aid, and the World Bank and the International Monetary Fund by and large dictate economic policy. Despite an economic liberalization agenda, little progress has been made. Economic growth averaged only 1.72 percent annually from 1992 to 1996, and per capita GNP was $160 in 1996.

TRADE POLICY
Score: 5–Stable (very high level of protectionism)

Chad's average tariff rate is 9.89 percent,[1] but the most significant deterrent to trade remains such non-tariff barriers as strict labeling, certification, documentation, and testing requirements.

TAXATION
Score–Income taxation: 4–Stable (high tax rates)
Score–Corporate taxation: 4–Stable (high tax rates)
Final Taxation Score: 4–Stable (high tax rates)

Chad's tax system changes constantly, and evasion is endemic. The main form of taxation is government expropriation of crops and goods produced by merchants. Such action—by government officials as well as by armed bandits—is common at the local level.[2]

GOVERNMENT INTERVENTION IN THE ECONOMY
Score: 3–Stable (moderate level)

Government consumes about 13 percent of GDP, most of which is generated by the public sector. Many companies are state-owned.

MONETARY POLICY
Score: 1–Stable (very low level of inflation)

Chad's average annual rate of inflation from 1986 to 1996 was 2.8 percent. No figure is available for 1997.

CAPITAL FLOWS AND FOREIGN INVESTMENT
Score: 4–Stable (high barriers)

Even though Chad provides equal treatment for domestic and foreign firms, most of its restrictions on foreign investment are informal. For example, according to the U.S. Department of Commerce, "The main obstacles to investments are the small scale of the economy, limited purchasing power, low

1	Hong Kong	1.25	81	Fiji	3.10
2	Singapore	1.30	81	Mali	3.10
3	Bahrain	1.70	81	Slovenia	3.10
4	New Zealand	1.75	85	Honduras	3.15
5	Switzerland	1.85	85	Mexico	3.15
6	United States	1.90	85	Papua New Guinea	3.15
7	Ireland	1.95	88	Djibouti	3.20
7	Luxembourg	1.95	88	Mongolia	3.20
7	Taiwan	1.95	90	Algeria	3.25
7	United Kingdom	1.95	90	Brazil	3.25
11	Bahamas	2.00	90	Lebanon	3.25
12	Czech Republic	2.05	90	Senegal	3.25
12	Japan	2.05	90	Tanzania	3.25
14	Australia	2.10	95	Nigeria	3.30
14	Belgium	2.10	95	Romania	3.30
14	Canada	2.10	97	Cambodia	3.35
14	United Arab Emirates	2.10	97	Dominican Republic	3.35
18	Austria	2.15	97	Egypt	3.35
18	Chile	2.15	97	Guinea	3.35
18	Estonia	2.15	97	Ivory Coast	3.35
18	Netherlands	2.15	97	Moldova	3.35
22	Denmark	2.25	97	Pakistan	3.35
22	El Salvador	2.25	104	Nepal	3.40
22	Finland	2.25	104	Venezuela	3.40
25	Germany	2.30	106	Armenia	3.45
25	Iceland	2.30	106	Bulgaria	3.45
27	Norway	2.35	106	Lesotho	3.45
28	Korea, South	2.40	106	Madagascar	3.45
28	Kuwait	2.40	106	Russia	3.45
28	Malaysia	2.40	111	Burkina Faso	3.50
28	Panama	2.40	111	Cameroon	3.50
28	Thailand	2.40	111	Guyana	3.50
33	Sweden	2.45	111	Nicaragua	3.50
34	Argentina	2.50	115	Gambia	3.60
34	France	2.50	116	Croatia	3.65
34	Italy	2.50	116	Georgia	3.65
34	Spain	2.50	116	Malawi	3.65
38	Portugal	2.55	119	Cape Verde	3.67
38	Sri Lanka	2.55	120	Ethiopia	3.70
38	Trinidad and Tobago	2.55	120	India	3.70
41	Barbados	2.60	120	Niger	3.70
41	Peru	2.60	123	Congo	3.75
43	Bolivia	2.65	124	Chad	3.80
43	Mauritius	2.65	124	China	3.80
45	Cyprus	2.70	124	Mauritania	3.80
45	Jamaica	2.70	124	Ukraine	3.80
45	Uruguay	2.70	124	Zimbabwe	3.80
48	Botswana	2.75	129	Albania	3.85
48	Guatemala	2.75	129	Bangladesh	3.85
48	Jordan	2.75	129	Mozambique	3.85
48	Namibia	2.75	129	Suriname	3.85
48	Oman	2.75	133	Burundi	3.90
48	Philippines	2.75	134	Togo	3.95
54	Belize	2.80	135	Haiti	4.00
54	Costa Rica	2.80	135	Kyrgyz Rep.	4.00
54	Israel	2.80	137	Kazakhstan	4.05
54	Swaziland	2.80	137	Sierra Leone	4.05
54	Turkey	2.80	139	Yemen	4.10
54	Uganda	2.80	140	Belarus	4.15
54	Samoa	2.80	141	Sudan	4.20
61	Latvia	2.85	141	Syria	4.20
62	Greece	2.90	143	Azerbaijan	4.30
62	Hungary	2.90	143	Equatorial Guinea	4.30
62	So. Africa	2.90	143	Myanmar	4.30
65	Ecuador	2.95	143	Rwanda	4.30
65	Gabon	2.95	147	Tajikistan	4.40
65	Indonesia	2.95	147	Uzbekistan	4.40
65	Malta	2.95	149	Angola	4.45
65	Morocco	2.95	149	Turkmenistan	4.45
65	Poland	2.95	151	Guinea-Bissau	4.55
65	Tunisia	2.95	152	Vietnam	4.60
72	Ghana	3.00	153	Congo (Zaire)	4.70
72	Lithuania	3.00	153	Iran	4.70
72	Saudi Arabia	3.00	155	Bosnia	4.80
75	Benin	3.05	155	Somalia	4.80
75	Kenya	3.05	157	Iraq	4.90
75	Paraguay	3.05	157	Laos	4.90
75	Qatar	3.05	157	Libya	4.90
75	Slovak Republic	3.05	160	Cuba	5.00
75	Zambia	3.05	160	Korea, North	5.00
81	Colombia	3.10			

Mostly Unfree

rates of capital accumulation and the fact that probably two thirds of GDP is actually generated in the informal sector, which is largely outside the control of the government. Also, Chad is landlocked and has high transportation costs. Government bureaucracy can be slow and inefficient."[3]

BANKING
Score: 4–Stable (high level of restrictions)

The little financial activity that occurs in the formal market is heavily controlled by the government. According to the U.S. Department of Commerce, "The cost of credit is very high and services are limited. Chad has no investment bank."[4]

WAGE AND PRICE CONTROLS
Score: 4–Stable (high level)

Wages and prices are affected by the large public sector, import substitution policies, and government subsidies.

PROPERTY RIGHTS
Score: 4–Stable (low level of protection)

Private property is subject to government expropriation, although there are few recent examples of nationalization. The government is attempting to privatize many state-owned enterprises, but crime and theft remain problems. According to the U.S. Department of Commerce, Chad has an "[u]ncertain legal protection and lack of an independent judiciary."[5]

REGULATION
Score: 4–Stable (high level)

Establishing a business is difficult because of Chad's massive and corrupt government bureaucracy. Bribery is sometimes present, as is embezzlement by those government officials who collect fees. Regulations often are applied haphazardly. According to the U.S. Department of Commerce, "It is widely assumed that corruption of some form exists at all levels of the Government."

BLACK MARKET
Score: 5–Stable (very high level of activity)

Chad's black market is larger than its formal market—and growing. The informal sector produces almost two-thirds of GDP.[6] Most activity occurs in smuggled consumer goods, labor, and pirated intellectual property.

NOTES
[1]   Based on taxation on international trade as a percentage of total imports.
[2]   Tax rate information is not available.
[3]   U.S. Department of Commerce, *Country Commercial Guide*, 1998.
[4]   *Ibid.*
[5]   *Ibid.*
[6]   *Ibid.*

Chile 2.15

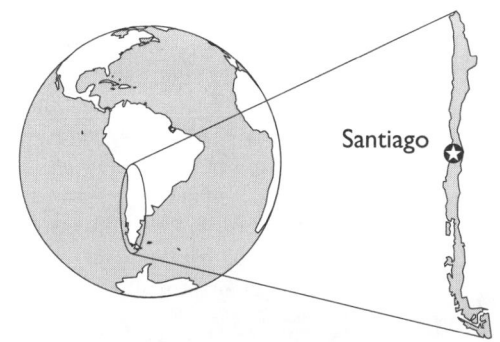
Santiago

1998 Score: **2.15**	1997 Score: **2.25**	1996 Score: **2.45**

Trade	2	Banking	3
Taxation	3.5	Wages and Prices	2
Government Intervention	1	Property Rights	1
Monetary Policy	3	Regulation	2
Foreign Investment	2	Black Market	2

Since 1960, most economic success stories have come from Asia, but Chile serves as an excellent example of a Latin American country enjoying economic success. A massive economic transformation during the 1980s created some of the fastest economic growth in the Western hemisphere and led Chile to adopt a series of political reforms that culminated in democratic elections in 1989. Chile's constitution defines and protects individual liberties, and President Eduardo Frei is continuing the country's free-market course.

TRADE POLICY
Score: 2–Stable (low level of protectionism)

International trade is the cornerstone of Chile's economy. The government maintains a flat tariff rate of 11 percent on most products; because the country has opened its borders to many of its neighbors and many items enter duty-free, the average tariff rate is less than 6 percent. Chile has removed most of its non-tariff barriers. Those that remain are minor and have little effect on trade flows.

TAXATION
Score–Income taxation: 4–Stable (high tax rates)
Score–Corporate taxation: 2–Stable (low tax rates)
Final Taxation Score: 3.5–Stable (high tax rates)

The top income tax rate is 45 percent; the average taxpayer is in the 10 percent bracket. The top corporate income tax rate is 15 percent. Chile maintains a 15 percent capital gains tax and an 18 percent value-added tax.

GOVERNMENT INTERVENTION IN THE ECONOMY
Score: 1–Stable (very low level)

Chile's example proves that reduced government intervention produces solid economic growth. Government consumes 8.1 percent of GDP; the country has achieved this low rate by permitting private enterprises to supply such "public" services as education, pension funds, social security, and some utilities.[1] Chile's social security system, for example, is privately owned and operated.

MONETARY POLICY
Score: 3–Stable (moderate level of inflation)

Chile's average annual rate of inflation from 1986 to 1996 was 17.3 percent. In 1997, the inflation rate was 5.9 percent.

CAPITAL FLOWS AND FOREIGN INVESTMENT
Score: 2–Stable (low barriers)

Chile aims to attract foreign investors by granting them quick government approval in some industries. But even though it has reformed its foreign investment code to attract investment, some barriers still exist. For example, according to the Office of the United States Trade Representative, "While Chile welcomes

1	Hong Kong	1.25
2	Singapore	1.30
3	Bahrain	1.70
4	New Zealand	1.75
5	Switzerland	1.85
6	United States	1.90
7	Ireland	1.95
7	Luxembourg	1.95
7	Taiwan	1.95
7	United Kingdom	1.95
11	Bahamas	2.00
12	Czech Republic	2.05
12	Japan	2.05
14	Australia	2.10
14	Belgium	2.10
14	Canada	2.10
14	United Arab Emirates	2.10
18	Austria	2.15
18	Chile	2.15
18	Estonia	2.15
18	Netherlands	2.15
22	Denmark	2.25
22	El Salvador	2.25
22	Finland	2.25
25	Germany	2.30
25	Iceland	2.30
27	Norway	2.35
28	Korea, South	2.40
28	Kuwait	2.40
28	Malaysia	2.40
28	Panama	2.40
28	Thailand	2.40
33	Sweden	2.45
34	Argentina	2.50
34	France	2.50
34	Italy	2.50
34	Spain	2.50
38	Portugal	2.55
38	Sri Lanka	2.55
38	Trinidad and Tobago	2.55
41	Barbados	2.60
41	Peru	2.60
43	Bolivia	2.65
43	Mauritius	2.65
45	Cyprus	2.70
45	Jamaica	2.70
45	Uruguay	2.70
48	Botswana	2.75
48	Guatemala	2.75
48	Jordan	2.75
48	Namibia	2.75
48	Oman	2.75
48	Philippines	2.75
54	Belize	2.80
54	Costa Rica	2.80
54	Israel	2.80
54	Swaziland	2.80
54	Turkey	2.80
54	Uganda	2.80
54	Samoa	2.80
61	Latvia	2.85
62	Greece	2.90
62	Hungary	2.90
62	So. Africa	2.90
65	Ecuador	2.95
65	Gabon	2.95
65	Indonesia	2.95
65	Malta	2.95
65	Morocco	2.95
65	Poland	2.95
65	Tunisia	2.95
72	Ghana	3.00
72	Lithuania	3.00
72	Saudi Arabia	3.00
75	Benin	3.05
75	Kenya	3.05
75	Paraguay	3.05
75	Qatar	3.05
75	Slovak Republic	3.05
75	Zambia	3.05
81	Colombia	3.10

81	Fiji	3.10
81	Mali	3.10
81	Slovenia	3.10
85	Honduras	3.15
85	Mexico	3.15
85	Papua New Guinea	3.15
88	Djibouti	3.20
88	Mongolia	3.20
90	Algeria	3.25
90	Brazil	3.25
90	Lebanon	3.25
90	Senegal	3.25
90	Tanzania	3.25
95	Nigeria	3.30
95	Romania	3.30
97	Cambodia	3.35
97	Dominican Republic	3.35
97	Egypt	3.35
97	Guinea	3.35
97	Ivory Coast	3.35
97	Moldova	3.35
97	Pakistan	3.35
104	Nepal	3.40
104	Venezuela	3.40
106	Armenia	3.45
106	Bulgaria	3.45
106	Lesotho	3.45
106	Madagascar	3.45
106	Russia	3.45
111	Burkina Faso	3.50
111	Cameroon	3.50
111	Guyana	3.50
111	Nicaragua	3.50
115	Gambia	3.60
116	Croatia	3.65
116	Georgia	3.65
116	Malawi	3.65
119	Cape Verde	3.67
120	Ethiopia	3.70
120	India	3.70
120	Niger	3.70
123	Congo	3.75
124	Chad	3.80
124	China	3.80
124	Mauritania	3.80
124	Ukraine	3.80
124	Zimbabwe	3.80
129	Albania	3.85
129	Bangladesh	3.85
129	Mozambique	3.85
129	Suriname	3.85
133	Burundi	3.90
134	Togo	3.95
135	Haiti	4.00
135	Kyrgyz Rep.	4.00
137	Kazakhstan	4.05
137	Sierra Leone	4.05
139	Yemen	4.10
140	Belarus	4.15
141	Sudan	4.20
141	Syria	4.20
143	Azerbaijan	4.30
143	Equatorial Guinea	4.30
143	Myanmar	4.30
143	Rwanda	4.30
147	Tajikistan	4.40
147	Uzbekistan	4.40
149	Angola	4.45
149	Turkmenistan	4.45
151	Guinea-Bissau	4.55
152	Vietnam	4.60
153	Congo (Zaire)	4.70
153	Iran	4.70
155	Bosnia	4.80
155	Somalia	4.80
157	Iraq	4.90
157	Laos	4.90
157	Libya	4.90
160	Cuba	5.00
160	Korea, North	5.00

Mostly Free

foreign investment, controls and restrictions do exist. Under the law that regulates nearly all foreign direct investment, profits may be repatriated immediately, but none of the original capital may be repatriated for one year. Foreign direct investment is also subject to pro forma screening by the Government of Chile."[2] The government restricts investment in the fishing, maritime transport, and oil and gas industries. By global standards, however, Chile has low barriers to foreign investment.

BANKING
Score: 3–Stable (moderate level of restrictions)

Although Chile's banking system is relatively free of government corruption, it is not fully competitive and market-oriented. According to the U.S. Department of Commerce, "Authorities have not allowed new banks to enter the market since the early 1980s financial crisis, except via purchasing existing banks. This restriction applies to domestic as well as foreign banks. Vigorous economic growth in recent years has strengthened bank profits, but restrictions remain on banks' ability to enter several rapidly growing area of business, including pension fund management, factoring and leasing."[3] Chile passed a new law in September 1997, however, that allows banks to move into insurance and other financial services. This law is being implemented currently.

WAGE AND PRICE CONTROLS
Score: 2–Stable (low level)

The market mainly determines pricing policy, although there are some exceptions, such as prices for urban and public transport and some utilities. The government determines minimum wages, hours worked, and safety regulations, but it has removed most price controls.

PROPERTY RIGHTS
Score: 1–Stable (very high level of protection)

Private property is gaining increasing protection from the government through greater efficiency in the court system and legal institutions. Chile has had a comprehensive program of privatization since the early 1980s, and it continues today.

REGULATION
Score: 2–Stable (low level)

Government regulation runs from nonexistent in some areas to overbearing in others, but opening a business is far easier in Chile than it is in many other Latin American countries. Regulations are moderate, although some can be burdensome for private businesses. The Ministry of Public Health, for example, regulates the production, storage, distribution, sale, and import of all food and drug products.

BLACK MARKET
Score: 2–Stable (low level of activity)

Like most other countries in Latin America, Chile has a black market. Piracy of intellectual property is decreasing, but the large black market business in this area continues. As much as 65 percent of computer software is pirated, and there still is a large black market in pirated pharmaceuticals from the United States. According to the U.S. Department of State, "Chilean authorities have taken aggressive enforcement measures against video, video game, audio, and computer software pirates in recent years, and piracy has declined in each of these areas."[4]

NOTES

[1]   Cristian V. Larroulet, ed., *The Chilean Experience: Private Solutions to Public Problems,* Instituto Libertad y Desarrollo and Center for International Private Enterprise, 1991.

[2]   Office of the United States Trade Representative, *National Trade Estimate on Foreign Trade Barriers,* 1998.

[3]   U.S. Department of Commerce, *Country Commercial Guide,* 1998.

[4]   U.S. Department of State, *Country Reports on Economic Policy and Trade Practices,* 1998.

China, People's Republic of   3.80

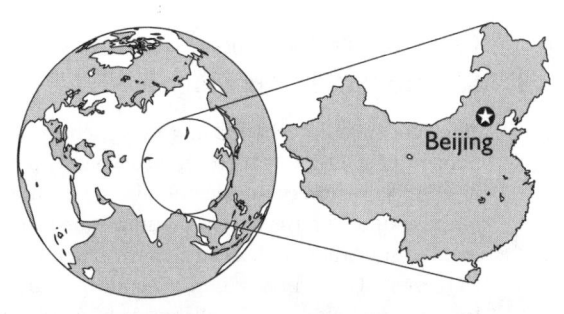

1998 Score: **3.75**   1997 Score: **3.80**   1996 Score: **3.80**

Trade	5	Banking	3
Taxation	4	Wages and Prices	3
Government Intervention	5	Property Rights	4
Monetary Policy	3	Regulation	4
Foreign Investment	3	Black Market	4

Although often criticized for its human rights abuses and communist political system, the People's Republic of China is more open and advanced economically today than it was two decades ago. Despite some twists and turns, economic reforms have remained on track, expanding since they began in the late 1970s. Several pockets within China's economy have performed well over the past several years and can be credited with causing most of the country's economic growth. The government continues to own over 118,000 companies, and a majority of these are losing money. State-owned enterprises employ almost two-thirds of the 170 million–strong urban workforce. Many foreign investors realize they severely underestimated the difficulties of doing business in a country striving to achieve the inherently contradictory goal of a "socialist market economy." Foreign investment fell in 1997 for the first time this decade, representing a 27 percent decrease from 1996. The government responded in January 1998 with new tax and tariff concessions for specific types of investment, which resulted in a slight increase in foreign investment through the first quarter 1998 over the same period in 1997. Still, China's economic growth is beginning to slow, falling from around 9 percent in 1997 to around 7 to 8 percent for 1998. The tax on the average income level is higher this year; as a result, China's overall score is 0.05 point worse than last year.

TRADE POLICY
Score: 5–Stable (very high level of protectionism)

China's average tariff rate is 20.9 percent.[1] In an effort to support its bid for accession to the World Trade Organization, China has announced that it will reduce its average tariff rate to 15 percent by 2000. According to the Office of the United States Trade Representative, "U.S. and other foreign businesses selling goods into China also complain about the lack of uniformity in customs valuation practices. Different ports of entry may charge significantly different duty rates on the same products."[2] Some tariffs are coming down, and over the next two years China will phase out tariff exemptions on capital equipment imported by foreign investors. Non-tariff barriers include "import licenses, import quotas, and other import controls."[3]

TAXATION
Score–Income taxation: 4– (High tax rates)
Score–Corporate taxation: 3–Stable (moderate tax rates)
Final Taxation Score: 4– (high tax rates)

China's top marginal income tax rate is 45 percent; the average income level is taxed at 15 percent, up from the previous 5 percent. Consequently, China's final taxation score is 0.5 point worse this year. The top corporate tax rate is 30 percent. China has a 33 percent capital gains tax, a 17 percent value-added tax, and a 3 percent to 20 percent business tax.

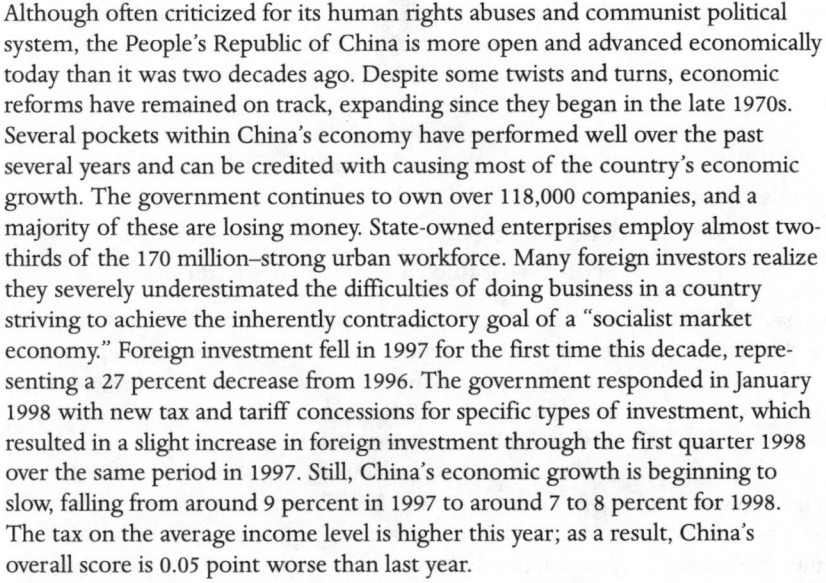

1	Hong Kong	1.25		81	Fiji	3.10
2	Singapore	1.30		81	Mali	3.10
3	Bahrain	1.70		81	Slovenia	3.10
4	New Zealand	1.75		85	Honduras	3.15
5	Switzerland	1.85		85	Mexico	3.15
6	United States	1.90		85	Papua New Guinea	3.15
7	Ireland	1.95		88	Djibouti	3.20
7	Luxembourg	1.95		88	Mongolia	3.20
7	Taiwan	1.95		90	Algeria	3.25
7	United Kingdom	1.95		90	Brazil	3.25
11	Bahamas	2.00		90	Lebanon	3.25
12	Czech Republic	2.05		90	Senegal	3.25
12	Japan	2.05		90	Tanzania	3.25
14	Australia	2.10		95	Nigeria	3.30
14	Belgium	2.10		95	Romania	3.30
14	Canada	2.10		97	Cambodia	3.35
14	United Arab Emirates	2.10		97	Dominican Republic	3.35
18	Austria	2.15		97	Egypt	3.35
18	Chile	2.15		97	Guinea	3.35
18	Estonia	2.15		97	Ivory Coast	3.35
18	Netherlands	2.15		97	Moldova	3.35
22	Denmark	2.25		97	Pakistan	3.35
22	El Salvador	2.25		104	Nepal	3.40
22	Finland	2.25		104	Venezuela	3.40
25	Germany	2.30		106	Armenia	3.45
25	Iceland	2.30		106	Bulgaria	3.45
27	Norway	2.35		106	Lesotho	3.45
28	Korea, South	2.40		106	Madagascar	3.45
28	Kuwait	2.40		106	Russia	3.45
28	Malaysia	2.40		111	Burkina Faso	3.50
28	Panama	2.40		111	Cameroon	3.50
28	Thailand	2.40		111	Guyana	3.50
33	Sweden	2.45		111	Nicaragua	3.50
34	Argentina	2.50		115	Gambia	3.60
34	France	2.50		116	Croatia	3.65
34	Italy	2.50		116	Georgia	3.65
34	Spain	2.50		116	Malawi	3.65
38	Portugal	2.55		119	Cape Verde	3.67
38	Sri Lanka	2.55		120	Ethiopia	3.70
38	Trinidad and Tobago	2.55		120	India	3.70
41	Barbados	2.60		120	Niger	3.70
41	Peru	2.60		123	Congo	3.75
43	Bolivia	2.65		124	Chad	3.80
43	Mauritius	2.65		124	China	3.80
45	Cyprus	2.70		124	Mauritania	3.80
45	Jamaica	2.70		124	Ukraine	3.80
45	Uruguay	2.70		124	Zimbabwe	3.80
48	Botswana	2.75		129	Albania	3.85
48	Guatemala	2.75		129	Bangladesh	3.85
48	Jordan	2.75		129	Mozambique	3.85
48	Namibia	2.75		129	Suriname	3.85
48	Oman	2.75		133	Burundi	3.90
48	Philippines	2.75		134	Togo	3.95
54	Belize	2.80		135	Haiti	4.00
54	Costa Rica	2.80		135	Kyrgyz Rep.	4.00
54	Israel	2.80		137	Kazakhstan	4.05
54	Swaziland	2.80		137	Sierra Leone	4.05
54	Turkey	2.80		139	Yemen	4.10
54	Uganda	2.80		140	Belarus	4.15
54	Samoa	2.80		141	Sudan	4.20
61	Latvia	2.85		141	Syria	4.20
62	Greece	2.90		143	Azerbaijan	4.30
62	Hungary	2.90		143	Equatorial Guinea	4.30
62	So. Africa	2.90		143	Myanmar	4.30
65	Ecuador	2.95		143	Rwanda	4.30
65	Gabon	2.95		147	Tajikistan	4.40
65	Indonesia	2.95		147	Uzbekistan	4.40
65	Malta	2.95		149	Angola	4.45
65	Morocco	2.95		149	Turkmenistan	4.45
65	Poland	2.95		151	Guinea-Bissau	4.55
65	Tunisia	2.95		152	Vietnam	4.60
72	Ghana	3.00		153	Congo (Zaire)	4.70
72	Lithuania	3.00		153	Iran	4.70
72	Saudi Arabia	3.00		155	Bosnia	4.80
75	Benin	3.05		155	Somalia	4.80
75	Kenya	3.05		157	Iraq	4.90
75	Paraguay	3.05		157	Laos	4.90
75	Qatar	3.05		157	Libya	4.90
75	Slovak Republic	3.05		160	Cuba	5.00
75	Zambia	3.05		160	Korea, North	5.00
81	Colombia	3.10				

Mostly Unfree

GOVERNMENT INTERVENTION IN THE ECONOMY
Score: 5–Stable (very high level)

The World Bank reports that government consumes only 11 percent of GDP,[4] but these figures severely understate the level of government intervention in the economy, primarily because official government consumption rates do not include education and social welfare expenditures made by state-owned enterprises. In most countries, these expenditures are included in official consumption figures. Although officially designated state-owned enterprises produce only 34 percent of industrial output, this figure rises to 75 percent if joint-venture companies with partial government ownership and local government cooperatives are included. Therefore, by global standards, government intervention in China's economy remains very high.

MONETARY POLICY
Score: 3–Stable (moderate level of inflation)

As a command economy, China's annual rate of inflation averaged only 9.75 percent from 1986 to 1996. Government subsidies and price controls, however, may serve to depress the rate artificially. If this is taken into account, the average annual rate of inflation during this period probably is higher than 13 percent, which is moderate by global standards.

CAPITAL FLOWS AND FOREIGN INVESTMENT
Score: 3–Stable (moderate barriers)

China always has maintained barriers to foreign investment. The government uses foreign investment policy to prevent foreign companies from competing with some state-owned industries while directing them toward other state-owned enterprises, such as power, telecommunications, aviation, and information technologies. According to the U.S. Department of State, "Multiple time consuming approval procedures adversely affect establishment of investments. Depending on the locality, investments above $30 million require national as well as local approval. Export requirements, local content requirements, and foreign exchange balancing requirements detract from China's investment climate.... China does not provide national treatment to foreign investors on establishment or operation of investments. In some key areas, such as input costs, foreign investors are often treated less favorably than Chinese firms. Foreign investors may not own land in China."[5] China does maintain special foreign investment zones in the south, however.

BANKING
Score: 3–Stable (moderate level of restrictions)

China controls its financial sector through four large state-owned commercial banks and one state-owned insurance company. Most of these firms are insolvent. Since 1988, however, the government has allowed some private domestic and foreign banks to engage in financial activity. Thus, by global standards, China's restrictions on banking are moderate.

WAGE AND PRICE CONTROLS
Score: 3–Stable (moderate level)

China has a history of price controls. After the 1993 recession, the government imposed controls on the prices of such items as foodstuffs and utilities. The government removed its controls on the prices of foodstuffs, but the government maintains its power to plan the production of items in some areas. China also has a minimum wage.

PROPERTY RIGHTS
Score: 4–Stable (low level of protection)

Because China remains a communist system, most property remains in government hands. The government is privatizing some major industries, however, and moving some state-owned assets into private hands; nevertheless, private property still is uncommon and the court system is both inefficient and far from impartial. According to the U.S. Department of State, "The Constitution states that the courts shall, in accordance with the law, exercise judicial power independently. However, in practice, the judiciary is subject to policy guidance from the Government and the Chinese Communist party, whose leaders use a variety of means to direct courts on verdicts and sentences in politically sensitive cases. Corruption and conflicts of interest also affect judicial decisionmaking"[6]

REGULATION
Score: 4–Stable (high level)

In an attempt to boost the private sector, China's bureaucracy sometimes does not enforce cumbersome regulations. The country still has a state planning agency that makes significant business and economic decisions, and this central planning results in high levels of regulation. Corruption also is a problem. According to the U.S. Department of Commerce, "From surveys reported in the western media and on the general views expressed by foreign business people and lawyers in China, it is clear that U.S. firms consider corruption in China a hindrance to foreign direct investment."[7]

BLACK MARKET
Score: 4–Stable (high level of activity)

Because of existing trade restrictions and central economic planning, the black market is rather large. There is extensive smuggling, both of automobiles from Hong Kong and of consumer electronic products like televisions and videocassette recorders. According to the U.S. Department of Commerce, "High duties on imported brands have given rise to smuggling. Restrictions on importation, distribution and foreign participation have also created a huge amount of illegal trade. Industry experts estimate that less than 5 percent of imported alcohol enters China legally. The remainder is brought in cheaply through corrupt customs officials in southern ports or by boat from Hong Kong."[8] The U.S. Department of Commerce further reports that "some companies and individuals have evaded the payment of customs duties or have otherwise smuggled foreign capital through local foreign trade firms by using fake clearance documents."[9]

NOTES

1   World Bank, *World Development Indicators,* 1998.
2   Office of the United States Trade Representative, *National Trade Estimate Report on Foreign Trade Barriers,* 1998.
3   *Ibid.*
4   World Bank, *World Development Indicators,* 1998.
5   U.S. Department of State, *Country Reports on Economic Policy and Trade Practices,* 1998.
6   U.S. Department of State, "China Country Report on Human Rights Practices for 1997," 1998.
7   U.S. Department of Commerce, *Country Commercial Guide,* 1998.
8   U.S. Department of Commerce, "China—Daily Briefing," *Market Research Reports,* March 11, 1997.
9   U.S. Department of Commerce, "China; Livestock; Frozen Pork Wholesale Market in Shanghai; Voluntary Report," *Agworld Attaché Reports,* 1996.

China, Republic of (Taiwan)

1.95

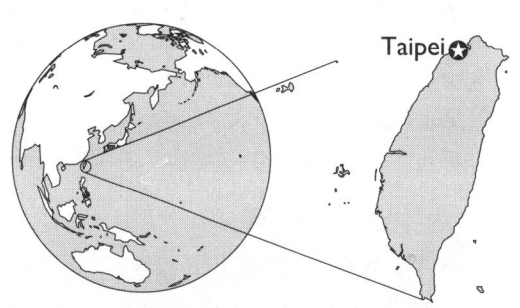

Taipei

1998 Score: **1.95**   1997 Score: **1.95**   1996 Score: **1.95**

Trade	2	Banking	3
Taxation	2.5	Wages and Prices	2
Government Intervention	2	Property Rights	1
Monetary Policy	1	Regulation	2
Foreign Investment	3	Black Market	1

The Republic of China on Taiwan has one of the world's fastest-growing economies. In the late 1950s, mired in conflict with the People's Republic of China, Taiwan had an inefficient and over-regulated economy. In the late 1960s, however, the government began to reform the economy. It guaranteed private property and set up a legal system to protect it, reformed the banking and financial sectors, stabilized taxes, gave public lands to private individuals, and allowed the free market to expand. These policies launched Taiwan, one of Asia's famous "tigers," into the industrialized world.[1] Today, annual economic growth is around 6 percent. Taiwan also has developed a functional democracy and conducted successful multiparty elections in both the legislative and executive branches of government. Elections will be held in December 1998 for the Legislative Yuan and the mayors of Taiwan's two largest cities, Taipei and Kaohsiung. These elections are expected to be a key measure of the relative strength of Taiwan's main opposition party, the Democratic Progressive Party (DPP), and may foreshadow the 2000 race for the presidency. Bipartisan proposals made at the December 1996 National Development Conference called for further deregulation and increasing the openness of the market to foreign competition. The recent economic chaos that has swept parts of Asia, including Indonesia and Thailand, by and large has been absent on Taiwan, principally due to the fact that its financial system remains more open to competition and experiences less government intervention.

TRADE POLICY
Score: 2–Stable (low level of protectionism)

Taiwan's average tariff rate is only about 3.5 percent. There are, however, several non-tariff barriers. For example, according to the Office of the United States Trade Representative, "Taiwan restricts the importation of 264 items, which may not be imported without special permission from the Taiwan authorities. Included in this category are agricultural items.... This amounts to a *de facto* ban on imports of many of these products since import approval is normally not granted."[2]

TAXATION
Score–Income taxation: 2–Stable (low tax rates)
Score–Corporate taxation: 2–Stable (low tax rates)
Final Taxation Score: 2.5–Stable (moderate tax rates)

Taiwan's top income tax rate is 40 percent, and the average income level is taxed at 6 percent. The maximum corporate tax rate is 25 percent. Taiwan also imposes a 25 percent capital gains tax and a 5 percent value-added tax.

1	Hong Kong	1.25		81	Fiji	3.10
2	Singapore	1.30		81	Mali	3.10
3	Bahrain	1.70		81	Slovenia	3.10
4	New Zealand	1.75		85	Honduras	3.15
5	Switzerland	1.85		85	Mexico	3.15
6	United States	1.90		85	Papua New Guinea	3.15
7	Ireland	1.95		88	Djibouti	3.20
7	Luxembourg	1.95		88	Mongolia	3.20
7	Taiwan	1.95		90	Algeria	3.25
7	United Kingdom	1.95		90	Brazil	3.25
11	Bahamas	2.00		90	Lebanon	3.25
12	Czech Republic	2.05		90	Senegal	3.25
12	Japan	2.05		90	Tanzania	3.25
14	Australia	2.10		95	Nigeria	3.30
14	Belgium	2.10		95	Romania	3.30
14	Canada	2.10		97	Cambodia	3.35
14	United Arab Emirates	2.10		97	Dominican Republic	3.35
18	Austria	2.15		97	Egypt	3.35
18	Chile	2.15		97	Guinea	3.35
18	Estonia	2.15		97	Ivory Coast	3.35
18	Netherlands	2.15		97	Moldova	3.35
22	Denmark	2.25		97	Pakistan	3.35
22	El Salvador	2.25		104	Nepal	3.40
22	Finland	2.25		104	Venezuela	3.40
25	Germany	2.30		106	Armenia	3.45
25	Iceland	2.30		106	Bulgaria	3.45
27	Norway	2.35		106	Lesotho	3.45
28	Korea, South	2.40		106	Madagascar	3.45
28	Kuwait	2.40		106	Russia	3.45
28	Malaysia	2.40		111	Burkina Faso	3.50
28	Panama	2.40		111	Cameroon	3.50
28	Thailand	2.40		111	Guyana	3.50
33	Sweden	2.45		111	Nicaragua	3.50
34	Argentina	2.50		115	Gambia	3.60
34	France	2.50		116	Croatia	3.65
34	Italy	2.50		116	Georgia	3.65
34	Spain	2.50		116	Malawi	3.65
38	Portugal	2.55		119	Cape Verde	3.67
38	Sri Lanka	2.55		120	Ethiopia	3.70
38	Trinidad and Tobago	2.55		120	India	3.70
41	Barbados	2.60		120	Niger	3.70
41	Peru	2.60		123	Congo	3.75
43	Bolivia	2.65		124	Chad	3.80
43	Mauritius	2.65		124	China	3.80
45	Cyprus	2.70		124	Mauritania	3.80
45	Jamaica	2.70		124	Ukraine	3.80
45	Uruguay	2.70		124	Zimbabwe	3.80
48	Botswana	2.75		129	Albania	3.85
48	Guatemala	2.75		129	Bangladesh	3.85
48	Jordan	2.75		129	Mozambique	3.85
48	Namibia	2.75		129	Suriname	3.85
48	Oman	2.75		133	Burundi	3.90
48	Philippines	2.75		134	Togo	3.95
54	Belize	2.80		135	Haiti	4.00
54	Costa Rica	2.80		135	Kyrgyz Rep.	4.00
54	Israel	2.80		137	Kazakhstan	4.05
54	Swaziland	2.80		137	Sierra Leone	4.05
54	Turkey	2.80		139	Yemen	4.10
54	Uganda	2.80		140	Belarus	4.15
54	Samoa	2.80		141	Sudan	4.20
61	Latvia	2.85		141	Syria	4.20
62	Greece	2.90		143	Azerbaijan	4.30
62	Hungary	2.90		143	Equatorial Guinea	4.30
62	So. Africa	2.90		143	Myanmar	4.30
65	Ecuador	2.95		143	Rwanda	4.30
65	Gabon	2.95		147	Tajikistan	4.40
65	Indonesia	2.95		147	Uzbekistan	4.40
65	Malta	2.95		149	Angola	4.45
65	Morocco	2.95		149	Turkmenistan	4.45
65	Poland	2.95		151	Guinea-Bissau	4.55
65	Tunisia	2.95		152	Vietnam	4.60
72	Ghana	3.00		153	Congo (Zaire)	4.70
72	Lithuania	3.00		153	Iran	4.70
72	Saudi Arabia	3.00		155	Bosnia	4.80
75	Benin	3.05		155	Somalia	4.80
75	Kenya	3.05		157	Iraq	4.90
75	Paraguay	3.05		157	Laos	4.90
75	Qatar	3.05		157	Libya	4.90
75	Slovak Republic	3.05		160	Cuba	5.00
75	Zambia	3.05		160	Korea, North	5.00
81	Colombia	3.10				

Free

GOVERNMENT INTERVENTION IN THE ECONOMY
Score: 2–Stable (low level)

Government consumes 14.2 percent of GDP. The state continues to privatize the remaining public companies.

MONETARY POLICY
Score: 1–Stable (very low level of inflation)

Taiwan's average annual rate of inflation during the 1980s was less than 2 percent.[3] From 1990 to 1994, the inflation rate was 3.8 percent; in 1995, 4.3 percent; in 1996, 3.1 percent; and in 1997, 2.6 percent.

CAPITAL FLOWS AND FOREIGN INVESTMENT
Score: 3–Stable (moderate barriers)

Foreign investment has been a major concern of government officials. Foreign investment in agriculture, cigarette manufacturing, housing construction, and liquor production still is banned, and foreign ownership of mining and shipping is limited. In 1997, however, the government passed new laws to open investment to previously closed industries, including mass media and telecommunications, radio broadcasting, wireless and cable television networks, cellular phone services, and pager and data mobile communications. Still, foreign participation in these areas is limited to just 20 percent.

BANKING
Score: 3–Stable (moderate level of restrictions)

Banks are competitive and serve as an important source of capital for Taiwan's expanding economy. In 1997, the government passed a host of new laws to remove many regulations on banks, including limits on a bank's foreign liabilities and restrictions on commercial paper guarantees. The number of foreign banks is increasing, as is competition in financial services. For example, as the U.S. Department of Commerce reports, "Foreign banking institutions are playing an increasingly important role on the financial scene. Foreign banks are essentially treated as domestic commercial banks—are permitted to engage in trade financing, foreign exchange dealings, lending to individuals and corporations, and various kinds of trust business."[4]

Some restrictions on foreign banks and individual investors remain, however. These include: ownership and investment fund limits, portfolio investment limits, and limits on foreign ownership of some companies listed on the Taiwan stock exchange. Moreover, according to the U.S. Department of Commerce, the "six largest banks are still owned by the public authorities."[5] Thus, by global standards, Taiwan has a moderate level of restrictions on banking.

WAGE AND PRICE CONTROLS
Score: 2–Stable (low level)

Taiwan maintains a minimum wage policy and requires equal pay for men and women. Prices are monitored regularly by the Commodity Price Supervisory Board, which is composed of members of the Ministry of Finance, the Ministry of Economic Affairs, the Agricultural Commission, and the Ministry of Communications. The board, however, does not have the power to set prices directly.

PROPERTY RIGHTS
Score: 1–Stable (very high level of protection)

Property rights are fully protected on Taiwan. The judiciary is efficient and independent of overt government influence.

REGULATION
Score: 2–Stable (low level)

Even though the government has established some moderately burdensome regulations, entrepreneurs can open a business with little difficulty. Most regulations are applied openly and evenly, and pose only a minor burden. By global standards, the level of regulation is low.

BLACK MARKET
Score: 1–Stable (very low level of activity)

Because Taiwan has a free economy, the size of its black market is very small. Taiwan has developed an advanced and efficient intellectual property rights protection law that is consistent with the World Trade Organization. Although there is some trade in pirated material, it is minuscule in comparison with the size of the economy overall, and the sources used in preparing the *Index* continue to indicate that black market activity is not significant.

NOTES

[1] Lawrence J. Lau and Lawrence R. Klein, *Models of Development: A Comparative Study of Economic Growth in South Korea and Taiwan* (San Francisco, Cal.: ICS Press, 1990).

[2] Office of the United States Trade Representative, *1998 National Trade Estimate on Foreign Trade Barriers*, 1998.

[3] Lau and Klein, p. 187.

[4] U.S. Department of Commerce, *Country Commercial Guide*, 1998.

[5] *Ibid.*

Colombia   3.10

Trade	4	Banking	2
Taxation	4	Wages and Prices	2
Government Intervention	2	Property Rights	3
Monetary Policy	4	Regulation	3
Foreign Investment	2	Black Market	5

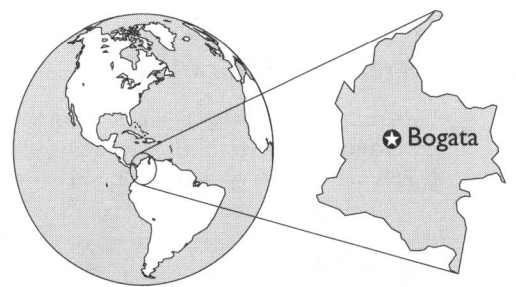

⭐ Bogata

Colombia's political system has come under growing pressure in recent years because drug traffickers have increased their influence within the government, thereby corrupting executive, legislative, and judicial institutions. After several years of economic stability and growth because of free-market reforms first applied in 1990 by President Cesar Gaviria, the economy has slowed since the end of 1994, due primarily to drug scandals involving former President Ernesto Samper and several current and former cabinet members. The level of government intervention in the economy increased under Samper, and the government has imposed more burdensome regulations. In June 1998, Andres Pastrana of the opposition Conservative Party was elected president, ending 12 years of Liberal Party rule. One of Pastrana's first actions as president-elect was to negotiate a cease-fire with Colombia's principal guerrilla organizations. He has pledged a peaceful settlement with the guerrillas, and has reaffirmed his commitment to trade liberalization and political reform. Pastrana also has called for greater economic and counter-drug assistance from the United States. Colombia recently increased its level of protectionism, making its overall score 0.1 point worse than last year.

TRADE POLICY
Score: 4– (high level of protectionism)

Colombia's average tariff rate is 10.9 percent, up from about 6 percent last year.[1] As a result, Colombia's trade policy score is 1 point worse this year than last year. Colombia still requires importers to obtain licenses for dairy, poultry, and other products. Moreover, the country's customs system remains plagued with corruption and bureaucracy. For example, according to the U.S. Department of Commerce, "Although significant progress has been achieved in this area, the Colombian government bureaucracy still constitutes a barrier to trade for both local and foreign companies. Pilferage in Customs warehouses and robberies of trucks on the roads is frequent. The absence of clear procedures to solve the problem of incorrect import documentation continues to be a barrier of sorts. Shipments have been detained indefinitely by Colombian Customs because of improper tariff schedule classification, use of an improper address, or any typing mistakes. When these mistakes are made by the exporter/importer, Customs presumes that it was done in bad faith and there is no clear procedure to correct the problem. The goods may be refused entry into Colombia and be returned at considerable expense to the exporter or importer."[2]

TAXATION
Score–Income taxation: 4–Stable (high tax rates)
Score–Corporate taxation: 3–Stable (moderate tax rates)
Final Taxation Score: 4–Stable (high tax rates)

Colombia's top income tax rate is 30 percent,[3] and the average income level is taxed at less than 5 percent. Many of these taxpayers are not required to fill out tax returns.[4] The government is cracking down on tax fraud, and more collections are being made than ever before. The top corporate tax rate is 35 percent, up from 30 percent in 1995. Colombia also has a 35 percent capital gains tax and a 16 percent value-added tax.

1	Hong Kong	1.25		81	Fiji	3.10
2	Singapore	1.30		81	Mali	3.10
3	Bahrain	1.70		81	Slovenia	3.10
4	New Zealand	1.75		85	Honduras	3.15
5	Switzerland	1.85		85	Mexico	3.15
6	United States	1.90		85	Papua New Guinea	3.15
7	Ireland	1.95		88	Djibouti	3.20
7	Luxembourg	1.95		88	Mongolia	3.20
7	Taiwan	1.95		90	Algeria	3.25
7	United Kingdom	1.95		90	Brazil	3.25
11	Bahamas	2.00		90	Lebanon	3.25
12	Czech Republic	2.05		90	Senegal	3.25
12	Japan	2.05		90	Tanzania	3.25
14	Australia	2.10		95	Nigeria	3.30
14	Belgium	2.10		95	Romania	3.30
14	Canada	2.10		97	Cambodia	3.35
14	United Arab Emirates	2.10		97	Dominican Republic	3.35
18	Austria	2.15		97	Egypt	3.35
18	Chile	2.15		97	Guinea	3.35
18	Estonia	2.15		97	Ivory Coast	3.35
18	Netherlands	2.15		97	Moldova	3.35
22	Denmark	2.25		97	Pakistan	3.35
22	El Salvador	2.25		104	Nepal	3.40
22	Finland	2.25		104	Venezuela	3.40
25	Germany	2.30		106	Armenia	3.45
25	Iceland	2.30		106	Bulgaria	3.45
27	Norway	2.35		106	Lesotho	3.45
28	Korea, South	2.40		106	Madagascar	3.45
28	Kuwait	2.40		106	Russia	3.45
28	Malaysia	2.40		111	Burkina Faso	3.50
28	Panama	2.40		111	Cameroon	3.50
28	Thailand	2.40		111	Guyana	3.50
33	Sweden	2.45		111	Nicaragua	3.50
34	Argentina	2.50		115	Gambia	3.60
34	France	2.50		116	Croatia	3.65
34	Italy	2.50		116	Georgia	3.65
34	Spain	2.50		116	Malawi	3.65
38	Portugal	2.55		119	Cape Verde	3.67
38	Sri Lanka	2.55		120	Ethiopia	3.70
38	Trinidad and Tobago	2.55		120	India	3.70
41	Barbados	2.60		120	Niger	3.70
41	Peru	2.60		123	Congo	3.75
43	Bolivia	2.65		124	Chad	3.80
43	Mauritius	2.65		124	China	3.80
45	Cyprus	2.70		124	Mauritania	3.80
45	Jamaica	2.70		124	Ukraine	3.80
45	Uruguay	2.70		124	Zimbabwe	3.80
48	Botswana	2.75		129	Albania	3.85
48	Guatemala	2.75		129	Bangladesh	3.85
48	Jordan	2.75		129	Mozambique	3.85
48	Namibia	2.75		129	Suriname	3.85
48	Oman	2.75		133	Burundi	3.90
48	Philippines	2.75		134	Togo	3.95
54	Belize	2.80		135	Haiti	4.00
54	Costa Rica	2.80		135	Kyrgyz Rep.	4.00
54	Israel	2.80		137	Kazakhstan	4.05
54	Swaziland	2.80		137	Sierra Leone	4.05
54	Turkey	2.80		139	Yemen	4.10
54	Uganda	2.80		140	Belarus	4.15
54	Samoa	2.80		141	Sudan	4.20
61	Latvia	2.85		141	Syria	4.20
62	Greece	2.90		143	Azerbaijan	4.30
62	Hungary	2.90		143	Equatorial Guinea	4.30
62	So. Africa	2.90		143	Myanmar	4.30
65	Ecuador	2.95		143	Rwanda	4.30
65	Gabon	2.95		147	Tajikistan	4.40
65	Indonesia	2.95		147	Uzbekistan	4.40
65	Malta	2.95		149	Angola	4.45
65	Morocco	2.95		149	Turkmenistan	4.45
65	Poland	2.95		151	Guinea-Bissau	4.55
65	Tunisia	2.95		152	Vietnam	4.60
72	Ghana	3.00		153	Congo (Zaire)	4.70
72	Lithuania	3.00		153	Iran	4.70
72	Saudi Arabia	3.00		155	Bosnia	4.80
75	Benin	3.05		155	Somalia	4.80
75	Kenya	3.05		157	Iraq	4.90
75	Paraguay	3.05		157	Laos	4.90
75	Qatar	3.05		157	Libya	4.90
75	Slovak Republic	3.05		160	Cuba	5.00
75	Zambia	3.05		160	Korea, North	5.00
81	Colombia	3.10				

Mostly Unfree

GOVERNMENT INTERVENTION IN THE ECONOMY
Score: 2–Stable (low level)

Government consumes 13.8 percent of GDP. Since 1991, the government has privatized ports, railroads, and cellular telephone services, as well as a number of chemical, agro-industrial, fishing, and gasoline companies and banks. It still owns some businesses that are engaged in oil exploration and development, financial services, energy, mining, telecommunications, and airports. The public sector, however, produces only a small portion of GDP.

MONETARY POLICY
Score: 4–Stable (high level of inflation)

From 1986 to 1996, Colombia's average annual rate of inflation was 24.6 percent. Since that time, the inflation rate has remained stable at around 20 percent.

CAPITAL FLOWS AND FOREIGN INVESTMENT
Score: 2–Stable (low barriers)

Colombia permits 100 percent foreign ownership in almost all sectors of its economy. The exceptions are in the national security and hazardous waste industries. Permission is needed for investments in the public service, water, waste, and transportation industries, or for large investments in mining and petroleum enterprises. A simple registration and licensing process is required for all investments.

BANKING
Score: 2–Stable (low level of restrictions)

Foreign banks have complete access to credit and the entire Colombian financial system, and the private sector directs almost all credit. "Foreign investors experience no discrimination in access to local credit," reports the U.S. Department of Commerce. "While the Colombian Government still directs credit to some areas (notably agriculture), credit is, for the most part, allocated by the private financial market."[5] Colombia has yet to achieve a completely free banking system, however. Domestic banks may sell securities, insurance policies, and investment services.

WAGE AND PRICE CONTROLS
Score: 2–Stable (low level)

Colombia's pricing policy is one of the most free-market in Latin America. According to the Economist Intelligence Unit, "Price controls apply only to a few pharmaceutical products, petroleum derivatives, gas, some petrochemicals, several basic consumer goods, school books, school tuition, residential rents and certain services—bus fares, utilities, and airline fares."[6] Thus, the market sets most prices. Colombia also maintains a minimum wage.

PROPERTY RIGHTS
Score: 3–Stable (moderate level of protection)

The most significant threats to private property are the violence created by the drug cartels and the government's attempt to distribute wealth more equally. Private property generally is protected, and the government is privatizing state-owned enterprises. The legal system is not always efficient: "The Colombian judicial system continues to be clogged and cumbersome," reports the U.S. Department of Commerce, "although its reform and streamlining are stated goals of the Samper administration."[7]

REGULATION
Score: 3–Stable (moderate level)

Obtaining a business license is not difficult; there is a limited registration process, and the government tends to allow businesses to operate as they see fit. A growing environmental movement is causing regulation of business to increase, however, and corruption within the bureaucracy is growing. According to the U.S. Department of Commerce, "It is generally acknowledged that corruption is pervasive in virtually all areas of Colombian public administration."[8]

BLACK MARKET
Score: 5–Stable (very high level of activity)

The drug trade makes the size of Colombia's black market very large. There also is a growing black market in pirated intellectual property, mainly because of lagging legal protection of rights in this area. According to the U.S. Department of Commerce, "The largest single IPR [intellectual property rights] problem is the government's failure to effectively combat trademark, patent, and copyright piracy. Enforcement problems arise not only at the police level, but also in the judicial system, where there have been complaints about lack of respect for preservation of evidence and frequent perjury."[9] The U.S. Department of Commerce also reports, "Labor regulations are unenforced and poorly observed in the large informal sector of the economy and child labor exists in several areas."[10] Moreover, according to the U.S. Department of State, "Colombia's extensive and expanding informal economy remains effectively outside government control. Some 800,000 children between the ages of 12 and 17 work, according to Labor Ministry studies. These children work—often under substandard conditions—in agriculture or in the informal sector, as street vendors, in leather tanning, and in small family-operated mines."[11]

NOTES

1   Arrowhead International, *World Trade and Customs Directory*, Winter 1998.
2   U.S. Department of Commerce, *Country Commercial Guide*, 1998.
3   Colombia's top marginal income tax rate is 55 percent: a top tax rate of 30 percent plus a 25 percent tax penalty for making more than a specific level of income. The 25 percent tax payment becomes a deduction on the following year's taxes, however. Thus, the author uses only the top rate of 30 percent in grading this factor.
4   For purposes of grading, the author uses the 5 percent figure.
5   U.S. Department of Commerce, *Country Commercial Guide*, 1998.
6   Economist Intelligence Unit, *ILT Reports, Colombia*, 1998, p. 20.
7   U.S. Department of Commerce, *Country Commercial Guide*, 1998.
8   *Ibid.*
9   *Ibid.*
10   *Ibid.*
11   U.S. Department of State, *Country Reports on Economic Policy and Trade Practices*, 1998.

Congo, Democratic Republic of (formerly Zaire)

4.70

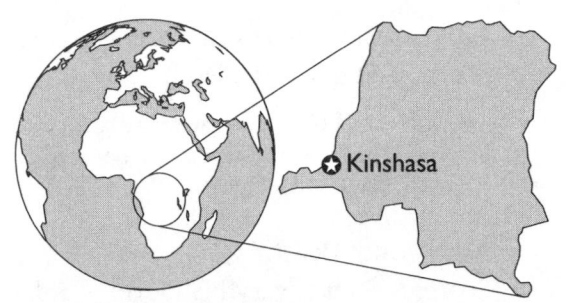

★ Kinshasa

1998 Score: 4.70   **1997 Score: 4.20**   **1996 Score: 4.20**

Trade	5	Banking	5
Taxation	5	Wages and Prices	4
Government Intervention	4	Property Rights	5
Monetary Policy	5	Regulation	4
Foreign Investment	5	Black Market	5

In May 1997, Zaire changed its name to the Democratic Republic of Congo.[1] The country had gained independence from Belgium in 1960 and quickly fell into turmoil as various regionally based and superpower-backed factions fought for control. A largely futile United Nations peacekeeping operation took place in what then was called the Congo. Then, in 1965, Mobutu Sese Seko seized control of the central government, changed the country's name to Zaire, and began decades of repression, forcing the people to live under a strict government-controlled economy. In May 1997, after years of relatively minor rebel activity, Zaire's government and Mobutu were overthrown by rebel leader Laurent Kabila. Three days after Mobutu had been ousted, Kabila proclaimed himself president of the renamed Democratic Republic of Congo. Kabila seems disinclined to embrace democracy. He has yet to solidify his grip on the country and currently is using aid from Angola, Namibia, and Zimbabwe to battle rebels backed by Uganda and Rwanda. According to the U.S. Department of Commerce, "The economy of Democratic Republic of the Congo has continued to disintegrate, although former Prime Minister Kengo had had some success in slowing the rate of economic decline. While meaningful economic figures are difficult to come by, the high rate of inflation, chronic large government deficits, and plunging mineral production have made it one of the world's poorest countries."[2]

TRADE POLICY
Score: 5–Stable (very high level of protectionism)

The change of government has decreased the movement of goods across the border severely. Corruption is rampant in what remains of the customs bureau as officials seek to confiscate imports arbitrarily or solicit bribes from importers to release goods.

TAXATION
Score–Income taxation: 5–Stable (very high tax rates)
Score–Corporate taxation: 5–Stable (very high tax rates)
Final Taxation Score: 5–Stable (very high tax rates)

Zaire had a top income tax rate of 45 percent and a top marginal corporate tax rate of 50 percent. The new government has yet to establish a system to collect and enforce taxes, and the result is arbitrary government raids on civilians and businesses to collect revenue. The breakdown of civil order has given rise to looting and banditry by citizens, government officials, and rebels.

1	Hong Kong	1.25	81	Fiji	3.10
2	Singapore	1.30	81	Mali	3.10
3	Bahrain	1.70	81	Slovenia	3.10
4	New Zealand	1.75	85	Honduras	3.15
5	Switzerland	1.85	85	Mexico	3.15
6	United States	1.90	85	Papua New Guinea	3.15
7	Ireland	1.95	88	Djibouti	3.20
7	Luxembourg	1.95	88	Mongolia	3.20
7	Taiwan	1.95	90	Algeria	3.25
7	United Kingdom	1.95	90	Brazil	3.25
11	Bahamas	2.00	90	Lebanon	3.25
12	Czech Republic	2.05	90	Senegal	3.25
12	Japan	2.05	90	Tanzania	3.25
14	Australia	2.10	95	Nigeria	3.30
14	Belgium	2.10	95	Romania	3.30
14	Canada	2.10	97	Cambodia	3.35
14	United Arab Emirates	2.10	97	Dominican Republic	3.35
18	Austria	2.15	97	Egypt	3.35
18	Chile	2.15	97	Guinea	3.35
18	Estonia	2.15	97	Ivory Coast	3.35
18	Netherlands	2.15	97	Moldova	3.35
22	Denmark	2.25	97	Pakistan	3.35
22	El Salvador	2.25	104	Nepal	3.40
22	Finland	2.25	104	Venezuela	3.40
25	Germany	2.30	106	Armenia	3.45
25	Iceland	2.30	106	Bulgaria	3.45
27	Norway	2.35	106	Lesotho	3.45
28	Korea, South	2.40	106	Madagascar	3.45
28	Kuwait	2.40	106	Russia	3.45
28	Malaysia	2.40	111	Burkina Faso	3.50
28	Panama	2.40	111	Cameroon	3.50
28	Thailand	2.40	111	Guyana	3.50
33	Sweden	2.45	111	Nicaragua	3.50
34	Argentina	2.50	115	Gambia	3.60
34	France	2.50	116	Croatia	3.65
34	Italy	2.50	116	Georgia	3.65
34	Spain	2.50	116	Malawi	3.65
38	Portugal	2.55	119	Cape Verde	3.67
38	Sri Lanka	2.55	120	Ethiopia	3.70
38	Trinidad and Tobago	2.55	120	India	3.70
41	Barbados	2.60	120	Niger	3.70
41	Peru	2.60	123	Congo	3.75
43	Bolivia	2.65	124	Chad	3.80
43	Mauritius	2.65	124	China	3.80
45	Cyprus	2.70	124	Mauritania	3.80
45	Jamaica	2.70	124	Ukraine	3.80
45	Uruguay	2.70	124	Zimbabwe	3.80
48	Botswana	2.75	129	Albania	3.85
48	Guatemala	2.75	129	Bangladesh	3.85
48	Jordan	2.75	129	Mozambique	3.85
48	Namibia	2.75	129	Suriname	3.85
48	Oman	2.75	133	Burundi	3.90
48	Philippines	2.75	134	Togo	3.95
54	Belize	2.80	135	Haiti	4.00
54	Costa Rica	2.80	135	Kyrgyz Rep.	4.00
54	Israel	2.80	137	Kazakhstan	4.05
54	Swaziland	2.80	137	Sierra Leone	4.05
54	Turkey	2.80	139	Yemen	4.10
54	Uganda	2.80	140	Belarus	4.15
54	Samoa	2.80	141	Sudan	4.20
61	Latvia	2.85	141	Syria	4.20
62	Greece	2.90	143	Azerbaijan	4.30
62	Hungary	2.90	143	Equatorial Guinea	4.30
62	So. Africa	2.90	143	Myanmar	4.30
65	Ecuador	2.95	143	Rwanda	4.30
65	Gabon	2.95	147	Tajikistan	4.40
65	Indonesia	2.95	147	Uzbekistan	4.40
65	Malta	2.95	149	Angola	4.45
65	Morocco	2.95	149	Turkmenistan	4.45
65	Poland	2.95	151	Guinea-Bissau	4.55
65	Tunisia	2.95	152	Vietnam	4.60
72	Ghana	3.00	153	Congo (Zaire)	4.70
72	Lithuania	3.00	153	Iran	4.70
72	Saudi Arabia	3.00	155	Bosnia	4.80
75	Benin	3.05	155	Somalia	4.80
75	Kenya	3.05	157	Iraq	4.90
75	Paraguay	3.05	157	Laos	4.90
75	Qatar	3.05	157	Libya	4.90
75	Slovak Republic	3.05	160	Cuba	5.00
75	Zambia	3.05	160	Korea, North	5.00
81	Colombia	3.10			

Repressed

GOVERNMENT INTERVENTION IN THE ECONOMY
Score: 4–Stable (high level)

The government is in disarray. Many civil servants have not been paid since the takeover, and major roads and bridges are being overtaken by jungle.

MONETARY POLICY
Score: 5–Stable (very high level of inflation)

Zaire historically had high average annual rates of inflation: over 2,000 percent from 1985 to 1993 and 5,000 percent in 1994. Today, control over the country's money supply is uncertain.

CAPITAL FLOWS AND FOREIGN INVESTMENT
Score: 5–Stable (very high barriers)

Although the Kabila government has stated publicly that it seeks to attract foreign investment and ensure the rights of current foreign investors, its actions prove otherwise. The breaking of a contract for the private operation of the country's main railway led to nationalization. Foreign investment has subsided to a trickle. It is not clear whether the former Zairian commercial code and foreign investment code still apply.

BANKING
Score: 5–Stable (very high level of restrictions)

The banking system has collapsed, and even though some small banks have tried to reopen for business, they remain hampered by an indeterminable and unreliable money supply. The Central Bank has been able to conduct some financial activity, restoring the Congolese franc some 23 years after it was supplanted by Zaire's currency. According to the U.S. Department of State, "Currency rules are in a state of flux in Democratic Republic of Congo's complex, mostly-cash economy.... Some travelers have complained about high fees, delays, and unavailability of cash at commercial banks for travelers checks and wire transfers."[3]

WAGE AND PRICE CONTROLS
Score: 4–Stable (high level)

Because of ongoing chaos, there is little official control over prices and wages. Most economic transactions are conducted as barter arrangements, and traditional market pricing mechanisms have ceased to exist, although market prices still apply for some goods in various rural parts of the country.

PROPERTY RIGHTS
Score: 5–Stable low level of protection)

Private property is not secure because of corruption and recent cases of government expropriation, including that of the country's largest railway. This expropriation broke a contract between a private firm and the former Mobutu government. According to the U.S. Department of State, "There continue to be reports of unofficial armed groups operating in parts of the country, as well as pillaging, vehicle thefts, carjackings, extrajudicial settling of differences, ethnic tensions, and continued military operations. Travelers run the risk of attack or detention."[4]

REGULATION
Score: 4–Stable (high level)

Kabila's troops have yet to establish the rule of law. Remaining businesses are harassed by corrupt bandits, former government officials, and renegade military personnel seeking bribes, kickbacks, and loot.

BLACK MARKET
Score: 5–Stable (very high level of activity)

Almost all economic activity is conducted in the black market.

NOTES

[1] For purposes of this study, the Democratic Republic of Congo is identified by its former name of Zaire whenever historical events before May 1997 are discussed.

[2] U.S. Department of Commerce, *Stat–USA* Internet site (*http://www.stat-usa.gov*).

[3] U.S. Department of State, "Travel Warning," December 1997.

[4] *Ibid.*

Congo, Republic of

3.75

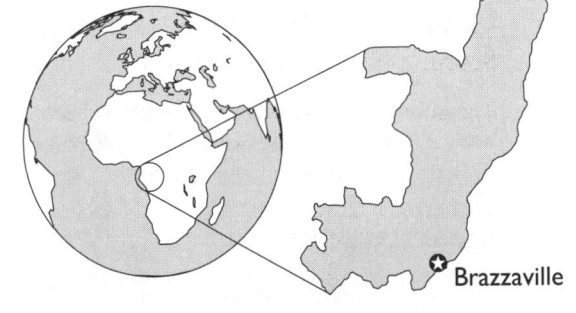

Brazzaville

1998 Score: **3.75**   1997 Score: **3.75**   1996 Score: **3.80**

Trade	5	Banking	4
Taxation	4.5	Wages and Prices	3
Government Intervention	3	Property Rights	4
Monetary Policy	1	Regulation	4
Foreign Investment	4	Black Market	5

Since receiving its independence from France in 1960, Congo has endured one-party rule, Marxist economic policies, political repression, and frequent military coups. In 1990, Congo abandoned Marxism and legalized other political parties. The country changed its name to the Republic of the Congo in 1991 and held multiparty elections in 1992. Congo's brief experiment with democracy ended in October 1997 when democratically elected President Pascal Lissouba was ousted by opposing militia leader and former President Denis Sassou Nguesso. The small progress toward fundamental democratic reform and market reforms that had been achieved by the Lissouba government has been undermined. The state plays a leading role in the stagnating economy, in which GDP growth averaged 1.1 percent annually from 1992 to 1996.

TRADE POLICY
Score: 5–Stable (very high level of protectionism)

Congo is a member of the Economic Union of Central Africa. This customs and economic union applies tariffs to non-members of 5 percent for essential goods; 15 percent for primary materials and capital equipment; 35 percent for intermediate and miscellaneous goods; and 50 percent for consumer goods—although this rate is expected to be reduced to 35 percent by 2000. In total, these various rates bring Congo's average tariff rate to over 30 percent. The most significant non-tariff barriers to trade remain import license requirements, red tape, an inefficient customs service, and the outright theft of imported goods by government officials.

TAXATION
Score–Income taxation: 4–Stable (high tax rates)
Score–Corporate taxation: 4–Stable (high tax rates)
Final Taxation Score: 4.5–Stable (very high tax rates)

Congo's top income tax rate is 50 percent, and the average income level is taxed at 15 percent. The top corporate tax is 45 percent. The government also imposes a 45 percent capital gains tax and a 18.09 percent goods and services tax.

GOVERNMENT INTERVENTION IN THE ECONOMY
Score: 3–Stable (moderate level)

Government consumes 20.6 percent of GDP, and the country's state-owned sector is extremely large. A privatization effort has yielded minimal results. According to the U.S. Department of Commerce, "Both under colonialism and Marxism, Congolese were oriented towards the public sector. As a result, the Congo currently spends an astronomical 54 percent of its budget on civil service salaries and roughly two-thirds of all persons employed in the formal sector work for the government."[1] But because the total government consumption is only 20.6 percent of GDP, Congo's government intervention in the economy is moderate by global standards.

1	Hong Kong	1.25	81	Fiji	3.10
2	Singapore	1.30	81	Mali	3.10
3	Bahrain	1.70	81	Slovenia	3.10
4	New Zealand	1.75	85	Honduras	3.15
5	Switzerland	1.85	85	Mexico	3.15
6	United States	1.90	85	Papua New Guinea	3.15
7	Ireland	1.95	88	Djibouti	3.20
7	Luxembourg	1.95	88	Mongolia	3.20
7	Taiwan	1.95	90	Algeria	3.25
7	United Kingdom	1.95	90	Brazil	3.25
11	Bahamas	2.00	90	Lebanon	3.25
12	Czech Republic	2.05	90	Senegal	3.25
12	Japan	2.05	90	Tanzania	3.25
14	Australia	2.10	95	Nigeria	3.30
14	Belgium	2.10	95	Romania	3.30
14	Canada	2.10	97	Cambodia	3.35
14	United Arab Emirates	2.10	97	Dominican Republic	3.35
18	Austria	2.15	97	Egypt	3.35
18	Chile	2.15	97	Guinea	3.35
18	Estonia	2.15	97	Ivory Coast	3.35
18	Netherlands	2.15	97	Moldova	3.35
22	Denmark	2.25	97	Pakistan	3.35
22	El Salvador	2.25	104	Nepal	3.40
22	Finland	2.25	104	Venezuela	3.40
25	Germany	2.30	106	Armenia	3.45
25	Iceland	2.30	106	Bulgaria	3.45
27	Norway	2.35	106	Lesotho	3.45
28	Korea, South	2.40	106	Madagascar	3.45
28	Kuwait	2.40	106	Russia	3.45
28	Malaysia	2.40	111	Burkina Faso	3.50
28	Panama	2.40	111	Cameroon	3.50
28	Thailand	2.40	111	Guyana	3.50
33	Sweden	2.45	111	Nicaragua	3.50
34	Argentina	2.50	115	Gambia	3.60
34	France	2.50	116	Croatia	3.65
34	Italy	2.50	116	Georgia	3.65
34	Spain	2.50	116	Malawi	3.65
38	Portugal	2.55	119	Cape Verde	3.67
38	Sri Lanka	2.55	120	Ethiopia	3.70
38	Trinidad and Tobago	2.55	120	India	3.70
41	Barbados	2.60	120	Niger	3.70
41	Peru	2.60	123	Congo	3.75
43	Bolivia	2.65	124	Chad	3.80
43	Mauritius	2.65	124	China	3.80
45	Cyprus	2.70	124	Mauritania	3.80
45	Jamaica	2.70	124	Ukraine	3.80
45	Uruguay	2.70	124	Zimbabwe	3.80
48	Botswana	2.75	129	Albania	3.85
48	Guatemala	2.75	129	Bangladesh	3.85
48	Jordan	2.75	129	Mozambique	3.85
48	Namibia	2.75	129	Suriname	3.85
48	Oman	2.75	133	Burundi	3.90
48	Philippines	2.75	134	Togo	3.95
54	Belize	2.80	135	Haiti	4.00
54	Costa Rica	2.80	135	Kyrgyz Rep.	4.00
54	Israel	2.80	137	Kazakhstan	4.05
54	Swaziland	2.80	137	Sierra Leone	4.05
54	Turkey	2.80	139	Yemen	4.10
54	Uganda	2.80	140	Belarus	4.15
54	Samoa	2.80	141	Sudan	4.20
61	Latvia	2.85	141	Syria	4.20
62	Greece	2.90	143	Azerbaijan	4.30
62	Hungary	2.90	143	Equatorial Guinea	4.30
62	So. Africa	2.90	143	Myanmar	4.30
65	Ecuador	2.95	143	Rwanda	4.30
65	Gabon	2.95	147	Tajikistan	4.40
65	Indonesia	2.95	147	Uzbekistan	4.40
65	Malta	2.95	149	Angola	4.45
65	Morocco	2.95	149	Turkmenistan	4.45
65	Poland	2.95	151	Guinea-Bissau	4.55
65	Tunisia	2.95	152	Vietnam	4.60
72	Ghana	3.00	153	Congo (Zaire)	4.70
72	Lithuania	3.00	153	Iran	4.70
72	Saudi Arabia	3.00	155	Bosnia	4.80
75	Benin	3.05	155	Somalia	4.80
75	Kenya	3.05	157	Iraq	4.90
75	Paraguay	3.05	157	Laos	4.90
75	Qatar	3.05	157	Libya	4.90
75	Slovak Republic	3.05	160	Cuba	5.00
75	Zambia	3.05	160	Korea, North	5.00
81	Colombia	3.10			

Mostly Unfree

MONETARY POLICY
Score: 1–Stable (very low level of inflation)

Congo's average annual rate of inflation from 1986 to 1996 was 2.3 percent. The inflation rate for 1997 is not available.

CAPITAL FLOWS AND FOREIGN INVESTMENT
Score: 4–Stable (high barriers)

Congo passed a new foreign investment code in 1992 and amended it again in 1996. Essentially, the code grants equal treatment for domestic and foreign investment. Congo is a member of the Economic Union of Central Africa, however, so the union's investment laws take precedence over the Congo investment code. This often creates confusion among investors. Moreover, according to the U.S. Department of Commerce, "There is host-government selection of foreign investment in specific circumstances such as the granting of oil and forestry concessions. These concessions are granted by a bidding process. However, there is often a marked lack of transparency in the process. Historical, cultural, and language ties combined with the absence of a French 'anti-corruption act' give the French a decided advantage in contracts which are granted by the Congolese government."[2]

BANKING
Score: 4–Stable (high level of restrictions)

Banks remain under the control or influence of corrupt government officials, and hostile labor conditions limit the ability of foreign banks to operate. The government claims that it may sell state banks to foreign investors. According to the U.S. Department of Commerce, "Congo's deteriorating financial sector has been a further obstacle to private sector development and investment. In the past 3 years, two major banks have gone bankrupt leaving the Congo with only one full-service bank, a network of credit unions, and a rural credit association. These institutions engage in very limited lending and none is a major injector of capital into the Congolese economy."[3]

WAGE AND PRICE CONTROLS
Score: 3–Stable (moderate level)

Prices are controlled through large state-owned companies, which also are subsidized by the government. There is a minimum wage.

PROPERTY RIGHTS
Score: 4–Stable (low level of protection)

Government expropriation of property remains possible. An insufficient judicial and legal framework means little government protection of private property. Although the courts are supposed to be independent, most are not. According to the U.S. Department of Commerce, "Judicial independence is a new concept and the courts are not yet able to effectively enforce property and contractual rights. There have been recent allegations of government interference in the courts.... The judicial system currently is not capable of securing land, building, and mortgage rights."[4]

REGULATION
Score: 4–Stable (high level)

Government regulators are corrupt and often require bribes. Regulations, in addition to being burdensome, are enforced haphazardly, and labor laws favor militant unions at the expense of employers. "Although the government has recently enacted measures to decrease bureaucratic red-tape," reports the U.S. Department of Commerce, "administrative procedures remain extremely time-consuming.... Corruption takes numerous forms and runs a gamut from a government official requesting a beer in return for a service to an apartment in France."[5]

BLACK MARKET
Score: 5–Stable (very high level of activity)

The size of Congo's black market is large. Corruption among customs officials creates a market for the smuggling of all types of goods, and high tariffs encourage the smuggling of many foodstuffs. There is considerable trade in illegal arms.

NOTES

[1] U.S. Department of Commerce, *Country Commercial Guide,* 1998.
[2] *Ibid.*
[3] *Ibid.*
[4] *Ibid.*
[5] *Ibid.*

Costa Rica   2.80

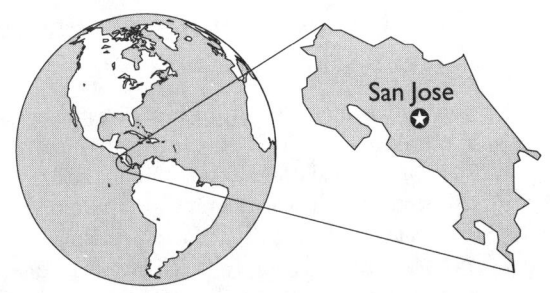
San Jose

Trade	4	Banking	3
Taxation	3	Wages and Prices	2
Government Intervention	2	Property Rights	3
Monetary Policy	3	Regulation	3
Foreign Investment	2	Black Market	3

Foreign aid to Costa Rica has decreased drastically since the end of the Cold War, while trade between the United States and Costa Rica has increased. The United States remains the country's largest trading partner. Costa Rica's economic growth has resulted primarily from increased trade and economic reforms. Inflation is rising again, however, and some economic reforms have slowed.[1]

TRADE POLICY
Score: 4–Stable (high level of protectionism)

Although Costa Rica has been moving toward greater openness, it remains a rather difficult market to penetrate. The average tariff rate is 11 percent,[2] and customs procedures are cumbersome and plagued with inefficiency. Many companies are forced to hire a customs specialist just to get their products across the border. As the U.S. Department of Commerce reports, "Customs procedures can be costly and complex. Most large enterprises must have customs specialists on the payroll, in addition to employing the services of customs brokers. Customs brokers must be bonded Costa Rican companies, which enjoy a monopoly on the handling of imports. All importers and exporters, including U.S. companies, suffer from defective customs procedures, poor administration and inadequate facilities. The government has implemented reforms to automate and streamline the system to improve efficiency."[3]

TAXATION
Score–Income taxation: 2–Stable (low tax rates)
Score–Corporate taxation: 3–Stable (moderate tax rates)
Final Taxation Score: 3–Stable (moderate tax rates)

Costa Rica's top marginal income tax rate is 25 percent, and the tax on the average income is 0 percent, down from 10 percent last year. The top corporate income tax rate is 30 percent. Costa Rica also has a 13 percent sales tax and a 42 percent payroll tax.

GOVERNMENT INTERVENTION IN THE ECONOMY
Score: 2–Stable (low level)

Government consumes about 17.5 percent of GDP. The government continues its privatization program.

MONETARY POLICY
Score: 3–Stable (high level of inflation)

Costa Rica's rate of inflation from 1986 to 1996 was 16.95 percent. The rate for 1997 was 13.3 percent.

1	Hong Kong	1.25		81	Fiji	3.10
2	Singapore	1.30		81	Mali	3.10
3	Bahrain	1.70		81	Slovenia	3.10
4	New Zealand	1.75		85	Honduras	3.15
5	Switzerland	1.85		85	Mexico	3.15
6	United States	1.90		85	Papua New Guinea	3.15
7	Ireland	1.95		88	Djibouti	3.20
7	Luxembourg	1.95		88	Mongolia	3.20
7	Taiwan	1.95		90	Algeria	3.25
7	United Kingdom	1.95		90	Brazil	3.25
11	Bahamas	2.00		90	Lebanon	3.25
12	Czech Republic	2.05		90	Senegal	3.25
12	Japan	2.05		90	Tanzania	3.25
14	Australia	2.10		95	Nigeria	3.30
14	Belgium	2.10		95	Romania	3.30
14	Canada	2.10		97	Cambodia	3.35
14	United Arab Emirates	2.10		97	Dominican Republic	3.35
18	Austria	2.15		97	Egypt	3.35
18	Chile	2.15		97	Guinea	3.35
18	Estonia	2.15		97	Ivory Coast	3.35
18	Netherlands	2.15		97	Moldova	3.35
22	Denmark	2.25		97	Pakistan	3.35
22	El Salvador	2.25		104	Nepal	3.40
22	Finland	2.25		104	Venezuela	3.40
25	Germany	2.30		106	Armenia	3.45
25	Iceland	2.30		106	Bulgaria	3.45
27	Norway	2.35		106	Lesotho	3.45
28	Korea, South	2.40		106	Madagascar	3.45
28	Kuwait	2.40		106	Russia	3.45
28	Malaysia	2.40		111	Burkina Faso	3.50
28	Panama	2.40		111	Cameroon	3.50
28	Thailand	2.40		111	Guyana	3.50
33	Sweden	2.45		111	Nicaragua	3.50
34	Argentina	2.50		115	Gambia	3.60
34	France	2.50		116	Croatia	3.65
34	Italy	2.50		116	Georgia	3.65
34	Spain	2.50		116	Malawi	3.65
38	Portugal	2.55		119	Cape Verde	3.67
38	Sri Lanka	2.55		120	Ethiopia	3.70
38	Trinidad and Tobago	2.55		120	India	3.70
41	Barbados	2.60		120	Niger	3.70
41	Peru	2.60		123	Congo	3.75
43	Bolivia	2.65		124	Chad	3.80
43	Mauritius	2.65		124	China	3.80
45	Cyprus	2.70		124	Mauritania	3.80
45	Jamaica	2.70		124	Ukraine	3.80
45	Uruguay	2.70		124	Zimbabwe	3.80
48	Botswana	2.75		129	Albania	3.85
48	Guatemala	2.75		129	Bangladesh	3.85
48	Jordan	2.75		129	Mozambique	3.85
48	Namibia	2.75		129	Suriname	3.85
48	Oman	2.75		133	Burundi	3.90
48	Philippines	2.75		134	Togo	3.95
54	Belize	2.80		135	Haiti	4.00
54	Costa Rica	2.80		135	Kyrgyz Rep.	4.00
54	Israel	2.80		137	Kazakhstan	4.05
54	Swaziland	2.80		137	Sierra Leone	4.05
54	Turkey	2.80		139	Yemen	4.10
54	Uganda	2.80		140	Belarus	4.15
54	Samoa	2.80		141	Sudan	4.20
61	Latvia	2.85		141	Syria	4.20
62	Greece	2.90		143	Azerbaijan	4.30
62	Hungary	2.90		143	Equatorial Guinea	4.30
62	So. Africa	2.90		143	Myanmar	4.30
65	Ecuador	2.95		143	Rwanda	4.30
65	Gabon	2.95		147	Tajikistan	4.40
65	Indonesia	2.95		147	Uzbekistan	4.40
65	Malta	2.95		149	Angola	4.45
65	Morocco	2.95		149	Turkmenistan	4.45
65	Poland	2.95		151	Guinea-Bissau	4.55
65	Tunisia	2.95		152	Vietnam	4.60
72	Ghana	3.00		153	Congo (Zaire)	4.70
72	Lithuania	3.00		153	Iran	4.70
72	Saudi Arabia	3.00		155	Bosnia	4.80
75	Benin	3.05		155	Somalia	4.80
75	Kenya	3.05		157	Iraq	4.90
75	Paraguay	3.05		157	Laos	4.90
75	Qatar	3.05		157	Libya	4.90
75	Slovak Republic	3.05		160	Cuba	5.00
75	Zambia	3.05		160	Korea, North	5.00
81	Colombia	3.10				

Mostly Free

CAPITAL FLOWS AND FOREIGN INVESTMENT
Score: 2–Stable (low barriers)

Costa Rica offers one of the best investment climates in Central America. There are no repatriation requirements; foreigners are allowed to take out all their profits; and the government offers a widening group of incentives, including tax holidays for some specific investments. Costa Rica does not discriminate against foreign investors; they are treated the same as local investors. Some restrictions remain on utilities and services, and investment in these areas is barred. According to the U.S. Department of Commerce, "Costa Rica has a relatively open international trade and investment regime. Since mid 1982, the Government has placed considerable emphasis on improving the investment climate, including the creation of the Ministry of Foreign Trade (COMEX), which coordinates government efforts in the trade and investment areas."[4]

BANKING
Score: 3–Stable (moderate level of restrictions)

Foreigners are prevented from engaging in some banking services, such as checking and savings. Banking competition is generally free and open in Costa Rica, although banks are not permitted to sell insurance policies and other services. The banking sector is mainly dominated by three state-owned banks; there are, however, new laws that allow increased competition from private banks.

WAGE AND PRICE CONTROLS
Score: 2–Stable (low level)

The market sets most wages and prices. Most price controls have been eliminated, except for those on a few basic foodstuffs. Costa Rica maintains a minimum wage.

PROPERTY RIGHTS
Score: 3–Stable (moderate level of protection)

Private property is not entirely safe in Costa Rica. "The Constitution and law provide for an independent judiciary, and the Government respects this provision in practice,"

reports the U.S. Department of State.[5] It also notes, however, that "Lengthy legal procedures...cause delays and case backlogs."[6] Moreover, the U.S. Department of Commerce reports that "Secured interests in both chattel and real property are recognized and enforced, and the concepts of a mortgage and title recording exist. However, recent property title disputes have suggested that abnormalities can exist in the National Registry, the Government entity recording property titles and boundaries.... On the other hand, much remains to be done to eliminate bottlenecks in public service providers, such as the Customs Service, and in the judicial system, which has little or no provision for punitive damage remedies for civil claims, and an average two year turnaround for cases involving criminal charges (intellectual property rights, squatter invasion of land, etc.). All judicial proceedings require highly specialized professional assistance."[7]

REGULATION
Score: 3–Stable (moderate level)

There are few major barriers to opening a business in Costa Rica. Regulations are easily understood and, for the most part, equally applied. There is scant evidence of corruption or bribery. Some regulations (for example, regulations requiring environmental impact studies) are moderately burdensome, and the government requires private companies to grant vacations, holidays, overtime, and social insurance. According to the U.S. Department of Commerce, "Bureaucratic procedures are frequently long and involved and tend to be discouraging to newcomers."[8]

BLACK MARKET
Score: 3–Stable (moderate level of activity)

Some construction, telephone installation, and transportation are performed in the black market. Intellectual property rights laws, although sufficient, are not enforced adequately. Thus, piracy in computer software, audio recordings, and videotapes remains a problem.

NOTES

[1]   Although inflation is on the rise, Costa Rica's annual average inflation rate has not reached the level that would warrant a score change.

[2]   Based on total taxes on international trade as a percentage of imports.

[3]   U.S. Department of Commerce, *Country Commercial Guide*, 1998.

[4]   *Ibid.*

[5]   U.S. Department of State, "Costa Rica Country Report on Human Rights Practices for 1997," 1998.

[6]   *Ibid.*

[7]   U.S. Department of Commerce, *Country Commercial Guide*, 1998.

[8]   *Ibid.*

Croatia   3.65

1998 Score: **3.75**   1997 Score: **3.70**   1996 Score: **3.70**

Trade	3	Banking	3
Taxation	3.5	Wages and Prices	4
Government Intervention	4	Property Rights	4
Monetary Policy	5	Regulation	4
Foreign Investment	3	Black Market	3

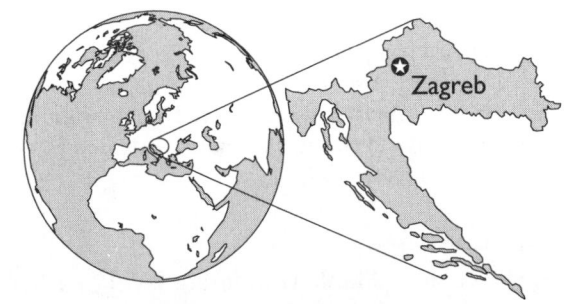

Zagreb

The collapse of the former Yugoslavia in 1990 and 1991 led to the creation of four independent countries, one of which is Croatia. Since 1991, Croatia has been involved in a civil war that has ravaged its economy—now only about half the size it was in 1990. The war, with its flow of dispossessed refugees, continues to strain the country. The government was forced to focus on military operations instead of instituting necessary economic reforms. Some 25 percent to 30 percent of the country's agricultural capacity has been decimated. Croatia has reduced government spending; as a result, its overall score is 0.1 point better than last year.

TRADE POLICY
Score: 3–Stable (moderate level of protectionism)

Croatia's average tariff rate is 10.64 percent.[1] Non-tariff barriers include strict testing and certification requirements for some foods, pharmaceuticals, and electronics.

TAXATION
Score–Income taxation: 3–Stable (moderate tax rates)
Score–Corporate taxation: 3–Stable (moderate tax rates)
Final Taxation Score: 3.5–Stable (high tax rates)

Croatia's top income tax rate is 35 percent; the average taxpayer is in the 25 percent bracket. The top marginal corporate tax rate is 35 percent. Croatia also imposes a host of other taxes, including a 22 percent value-added tax.

GOVERNMENT INTERVENTION IN THE ECONOMY
Score: 4+ (high level)

Government consumes about 30 percent of GDP, down from 45 percent in 1995. As a result, Croatia's score in this category is 1 point better this year. State-owned and -subsidized companies generate a substantial portion of GDP—as much as 45 percent.

MONETARY POLICY
Score: 5–Stable (very high level)

Chronic inflation has plagued Croatia until very recently. In 1992, retail inflation alone was 669 percent; in 1993, it was 1,517 percent. In 1994, Croatia's inflation rate was 98 percent. In 1995, it fell to 2 percent; and in 1996, it was 3.6 percent. In 1997, the inflation rate was 3.8 percent. Overall, however, Croatia has had very high rates of inflation since 1992.

CAPITAL FLOWS AND FOREIGN INVESTMENT
Score: 3–Stable (moderate barriers)

Croatia encourages foreign investment. It gives foreign companies national treatment, making them equal to domestic firms under the law. Foreign

1	Hong Kong	1.25	81	Fiji	3.10
2	Singapore	1.30	81	Mali	3.10
3	Bahrain	1.70	81	Slovenia	3.10
4	New Zealand	1.75	85	Honduras	3.15
5	Switzerland	1.85	85	Mexico	3.15
6	United States	1.90	85	Papua New Guinea	3.15
7	Ireland	1.95	88	Djibouti	3.20
7	Luxembourg	1.95	88	Mongolia	3.20
7	Taiwan	1.95	90	Algeria	3.25
7	United Kingdom	1.95	90	Brazil	3.25
11	Bahamas	2.00	90	Lebanon	3.25
12	Czech Republic	2.05	90	Senegal	3.25
12	Japan	2.05	90	Tanzania	3.25
14	Australia	2.10	95	Nigeria	3.30
14	Belgium	2.10	95	Romania	3.30
14	Canada	2.10	97	Cambodia	3.35
14	United Arab Emirates	2.10	97	Dominican Republic	3.35
18	Austria	2.15	97	Egypt	3.35
18	Chile	2.15	97	Guinea	3.35
18	Estonia	2.15	97	Ivory Coast	3.35
18	Netherlands	2.15	97	Moldova	3.35
22	Denmark	2.25	97	Pakistan	3.35
22	El Salvador	2.25	104	Nepal	3.40
22	Finland	2.25	104	Venezuela	3.40
25	Germany	2.30	106	Armenia	3.45
25	Iceland	2.30	106	Bulgaria	3.45
27	Norway	2.35	106	Lesotho	3.45
28	Korea, South	2.40	106	Madagascar	3.45
28	Kuwait	2.40	106	Russia	3.45
28	Malaysia	2.40	111	Burkina Faso	3.50
28	Panama	2.40	111	Cameroon	3.50
28	Thailand	2.40	111	Guyana	3.50
33	Sweden	2.45	111	Nicaragua	3.50
34	Argentina	2.50	115	Gambia	3.60
34	France	2.50	116	Croatia	3.65
34	Italy	2.50	116	Georgia	3.65
34	Spain	2.50	116	Malawi	3.65
38	Portugal	2.55	119	Cape Verde	3.67
38	Sri Lanka	2.55	120	Ethiopia	3.70
38	Trinidad and Tobago	2.55	120	India	3.70
41	Barbados	2.60	120	Niger	3.70
41	Peru	2.60	123	Congo	3.75
43	Bolivia	2.65	124	Chad	3.80
43	Mauritius	2.65	124	China	3.80
45	Cyprus	2.70	124	Mauritania	3.80
45	Jamaica	2.70	124	Ukraine	3.80
45	Uruguay	2.70	124	Zimbabwe	3.80
48	Botswana	2.75	129	Albania	3.85
48	Guatemala	2.75	129	Bangladesh	3.85
48	Jordan	2.75	129	Mozambique	3.85
48	Namibia	2.75	129	Suriname	3.85
48	Oman	2.75	133	Burundi	3.90
48	Philippines	2.75	134	Togo	3.95
54	Belize	2.80	135	Haiti	4.00
54	Costa Rica	2.80	135	Kyrgyz Rep.	4.00
54	Israel	2.80	137	Kazakhstan	4.05
54	Swaziland	2.80	137	Sierra Leone	4.05
54	Turkey	2.80	139	Yemen	4.10
54	Uganda	2.80	140	Belarus	4.15
54	Samoa	2.80	141	Sudan	4.20
61	Latvia	2.85	141	Syria	4.20
62	Greece	2.90	143	Azerbaijan	4.30
62	Hungary	2.90	143	Equatorial Guinea	4.30
62	So. Africa	2.90	143	Myanmar	4.30
65	Ecuador	2.95	143	Rwanda	4.30
65	Gabon	2.95	147	Tajikistan	4.40
65	Indonesia	2.95	147	Uzbekistan	4.40
65	Malta	2.95	149	Angola	4.45
65	Morocco	2.95	149	Turkmenistan	4.45
65	Poland	2.95	151	Guinea-Bissau	4.55
65	Tunisia	2.95	152	Vietnam	4.60
72	Ghana	3.00	153	Congo (Zaire)	4.70
72	Lithuania	3.00	153	Iran	4.70
72	Saudi Arabia	3.00	155	Bosnia	4.80
75	Benin	3.05	155	Somalia	4.80
75	Kenya	3.05	157	Iraq	4.90
75	Paraguay	3.05	157	Laos	4.90
75	Qatar	3.05	157	Libya	4.90
75	Slovak Republic	3.05	160	Cuba	5.00
75	Zambia	3.05	160	Korea, North	5.00
81	Colombia	3.10			

Mostly Unfree

investors are not allowed, however, to establish a fully owned company in the military-industrial, rail or air transport, insurance, publishing, or mass media sectors. The most formidable deterrents to foreign investment are political and civil unrest and an underdeveloped infrastructure.

BANKING
Score: 3–Stable (moderate level of restrictions)

The government regulates the banking system heavily. Foreign banks need permission in order to open branches, and banks may not engage in such nonbank services as selling insurance. The government continues to own many banks, either outright or through other state-owned companies that are major shareholders in many banks. Government-owned banks dominate the banking system, and the private banking industry remains underdeveloped. According to the U.S. Department of Commerce, "Privredna Banka and most of the medium-sized banks are indirectly owned by the government, through government-controlled companies that are major shareholders at these banks. Numerous privately owned banks have been established in the past few years are mostly very small.... Customer service in most of the banks is still relatively poor and transactions are complicated and time consuming."[2]

WAGE AND PRICE CONTROLS
Score: 4–Stable (high level)

The free market is not entirely responsible for setting wages and prices. Croatia continues to harbor a large public sector that controls prices and wages on many items. The government also extends large subsidies and price payments to farmers.

PROPERTY RIGHTS
Score: 4–Stable (low level of protection)

In general, property is free of expropriation, but it is unclear whether this will continue to be the case. A significant increase in political or civil unrest, for example, could increase the risk of expropriation. In addition, the court system is cumbersome and inefficient. According to the U.S. Department of Commerce, "The Croatian courts face a tremendous backlog, partly due to lack of judges, [and] settlement of commercial disputes is often a matter of years. In October 1995, there were more than a million cases pending in Croatian courts."[3]

REGULATION
Score: 4–Stable (high level)

Croatia's bureaucracy, like that of many other post-communist regimes, remains entrenched. Former party officials and bureaucrats frequently oppose the privatization of public firms, and corruption is present.

BLACK MARKET
Score: 3–Stable (moderate level of activity)

Croatia has a black market, primarily in labor services; the black market provides, for example, some transportation and construction services. The government has managed to stamp out other black market activity, however, particularly in the area of pirated intellectual property. A copyright law passed in 1993 provides stiff penalties for trafficking in pirated video and music recordings as well as in related materials. Over the past several years, Croatia has enforced these laws vigorously, in part to attract foreign investment.

NOTES

[1]   Based on official figures provided by the Embassy of Croatia.
[2]   U.S. Department of Commerce, *Country Commercial Guide*, 1998.
[3]   *Ibid.*

Cuba   5.00

| 1998 Score: **5.00** | 1997 Score: **5.00** | 1996 Score: **5.00** |

Trade	5	Banking	5
Taxation	5	Wages and Prices	5
Government Intervention	5	Property Rights	5
Monetary Policy	5	Regulation	5
Foreign Investment	5	Black Market	5

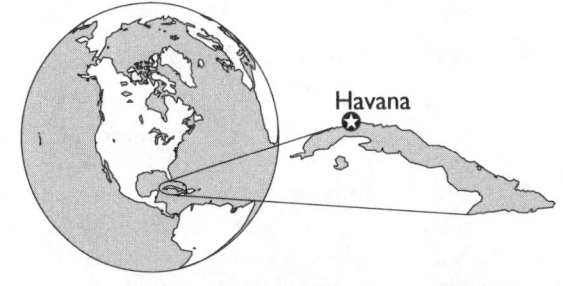

Havana

Cuba's economy—one of the world's most repressed, centralized, and government-planned—is rife with corruption and graft. Despite various news reports about the country's move toward the free market, there is a nearly complete lack of legal private economic activity. Individual economic freedom is virtually nonexistent. Although some forms of foreign investment are permitted, Cuba's constitution still outlaws foreign ownership of private property. Thus, even though foreign investment may be permitted if it is deemed beneficial to the communist, centrally planned economy, the constitution still makes it illegal. Moreover, there is no legal recourse to enforce property rights, contractual obligations, or the rule of law. In 1995, U.S. president Bill Clinton signed the Helms–Burton Act, passed by Congress to protect the property of Americans stolen by Fidel Castro's regime in 1959. President Clinton has postponed the implementation of much of this legislation since its signing, however, mainly because of complaints by members of the European Union. Despite the often rosy forecasts of European investors, and some in the U.S. business community, Cuba remains one of the world's most heavily regulated, corrupt, and poor countries.

TRADE POLICY

Score: 5–Stable (very high level of protectionism)

The Castro government inspects and approves all imports. In many cases, customs officials confiscate imports (especially scarce goods, like electronics) for their own use; such corruption enjoys official sanction. As a result, the government's trade barriers effectively bar most imports. Perhaps the biggest impediment to trade is Cuba's obsession with protecting its borders; this makes it nearly impossible for merchant ships to bring imports into the country. According to the U.S. Department of State, "Entering Cuban territory, territorial waters or airspace without prior authorization from the Cuban government may result in arrest or other enforcement action by Cuban authorities for violation of Cuban law. Any vessel or aircraft that enters the 12-mile limit off the coast of Cuba would be inside Cuban territorial waters or airspace and thus subject to the jurisdiction of the Cuban government. If persons enter Cuban territorial waters or airspace without prior permission, they may place themselves and others at serious personal risk."[1] Many businesses complain about their inability to import the goods and services needed to manufacture their products.

TAXATION

Score–Income taxation: 5–Stable (very high tax rates)
Score–Corporate taxation: 5–Stable (very high tax rates)
Final Taxation Score: 5–Stable (very high tax rates)

Because the government controls the entire economy, it essentially confiscates the proceeds of all economic activity. Because the government owns the fruits of almost all such activity, the rate of taxation effectively is 100 percent. Moreover, there are many reports of harassment of entrepreneurs by government officials and police, who confiscate earnings and steal their possessions. When outright theft does not occur, extortion often does.

1	Hong Kong	1.25	81	Fiji	3.10
2	Singapore	1.30	81	Mali	3.10
3	Bahrain	1.70	81	Slovenia	3.10
4	New Zealand	1.75	85	Honduras	3.15
5	Switzerland	1.85	85	Mexico	3.15
6	United States	1.90	85	Papua New Guinea	3.15
7	Ireland	1.95	88	Djibouti	3.20
7	Luxembourg	1.95	88	Mongolia	3.20
7	Taiwan	1.95	90	Algeria	3.25
7	United Kingdom	1.95	90	Brazil	3.25
11	Bahamas	2.00	90	Lebanon	3.25
12	Czech Republic	2.05	90	Senegal	3.25
12	Japan	2.05	90	Tanzania	3.25
14	Australia	2.10	95	Nigeria	3.30
14	Belgium	2.10	95	Romania	3.30
14	Canada	2.10	97	Cambodia	3.35
14	United Arab Emirates	2.10	97	Dominican Republic	3.35
18	Austria	2.15	97	Egypt	3.35
18	Chile	2.15	97	Guinea	3.35
18	Estonia	2.15	97	Ivory Coast	3.35
18	Netherlands	2.15	97	Moldova	3.35
22	Denmark	2.25	97	Pakistan	3.35
22	El Salvador	2.25	104	Nepal	3.40
22	Finland	2.25	104	Venezuela	3.40
25	Germany	2.30	106	Armenia	3.45
25	Iceland	2.30	106	Bulgaria	3.45
27	Norway	2.35	106	Lesotho	3.45
28	Korea, South	2.40	106	Madagascar	3.45
28	Kuwait	2.40	106	Russia	3.45
28	Malaysia	2.40	111	Burkina Faso	3.50
28	Panama	2.40	111	Cameroon	3.50
28	Thailand	2.40	111	Guyana	3.50
33	Sweden	2.45	111	Nicaragua	3.50
34	Argentina	2.50	115	Gambia	3.60
34	France	2.50	116	Croatia	3.65
34	Italy	2.50	116	Georgia	3.65
34	Spain	2.50	116	Malawi	3.65
38	Portugal	2.55	119	Cape Verde	3.67
38	Sri Lanka	2.55	120	Ethiopia	3.70
38	Trinidad and Tobago	2.55	120	India	3.70
41	Barbados	2.60	120	Niger	3.70
41	Peru	2.60	123	Congo	3.75
43	Bolivia	2.65	124	Chad	3.80
43	Mauritius	2.65	124	China	3.80
45	Cyprus	2.70	124	Mauritania	3.80
45	Jamaica	2.70	124	Ukraine	3.80
45	Uruguay	2.70	124	Zimbabwe	3.80
48	Botswana	2.75	129	Albania	3.85
48	Guatemala	2.75	129	Bangladesh	3.85
48	Jordan	2.75	129	Mozambique	3.85
48	Namibia	2.75	129	Suriname	3.85
48	Oman	2.75	133	Burundi	3.90
48	Philippines	2.75	134	Togo	3.95
54	Belize	2.80	135	Haiti	4.00
54	Costa Rica	2.80	135	Kyrgyz Rep.	4.00
54	Israel	2.80	137	Kazakhstan	4.05
54	Swaziland	2.80	137	Sierra Leone	4.05
54	Turkey	2.80	139	Yemen	4.10
54	Uganda	2.80	140	Belarus	4.15
54	Samoa	2.80	141	Sudan	4.20
61	Latvia	2.85	141	Syria	4.20
62	Greece	2.90	143	Azerbaijan	4.30
62	Hungary	2.90	143	Equatorial Guinea	4.30
62	So. Africa	2.90	143	Myanmar	4.30
65	Ecuador	2.95	143	Rwanda	4.30
65	Gabon	2.95	147	Tajikistan	4.40
65	Indonesia	2.95	147	Uzbekistan	4.40
65	Malta	2.95	149	Angola	4.45
65	Morocco	2.95	149	Turkmenistan	4.45
65	Poland	2.95	151	Guinea-Bissau	4.55
65	Tunisia	2.95	152	Vietnam	4.60
72	Ghana	3.00	153	Congo (Zaire)	4.70
72	Lithuania	3.00	153	Iran	4.70
72	Saudi Arabia	3.00	155	Bosnia	4.80
75	Benin	3.05	155	Somalia	4.80
75	Kenya	3.05	157	Iraq	4.90
75	Paraguay	3.05	157	Laos	4.90
75	Qatar	3.05	157	Libya	4.90
75	Slovak Republic	3.05	160	Cuba	5.00
75	Zambia	3.05	160	Korea, North	5.00
81	Colombia	3.10			

Repressed

GOVERNMENT INTERVENTION IN THE ECONOMY
Score: 5–Stable (very high level)

Although Castro permits some private (albeit highly restricted) economic activity, the means of production and most of the profits gained remain entirely in the hands of the state. The government owns and runs most of the country's economy. Castro and the highest echelons of his government directly control almost every economic and political apparatus in their country.

MONETARY POLICY
Score: 5–Stable (very high level of inflation)

The government claims that inflation does not exist on Cuba. This is fiction: If price controls were lifted and the true value of the currency were measured, inflation would be extremely high. The official prices of goods may be low because they are controlled and subsidized by the state, but the tremendous scarcity of goods and services attests to their real value. In short, Cuba's currency is worthless; it is not convertible on the international market.

CAPITAL FLOWS AND FOREIGN INVESTMENT
Score: 5–Stable (very high barriers)

Some foreign investment is permitted on Cuba. In September 1995, the government moved to allow foreigners—in exceptional cases—to control the majority share in some joint-venture operations. To say that Cuba has liberalized its foreign investment code, however, is misleading. Cuba's constitution still outlaws all foreign ownership of property and forbids any Cuban citizens from participating in joint ventures with foreigners. It still is illegal to hire Cubans directly: Foreign employers must pay the wages due their employees directly to the Cuban government, in hard currency. The government then pays the workers in Cuban pesos at a fraction of the value—sometimes less than 10 percent—of what the foreign business gives the government. Furthermore, although the new foreign investment law provides additional protection against expropriation, all arbitration must take place in corrupt, government-run ministries that afford the investor little protection. Thus, even though Cuba's government does not seek actively to prevent foreign investment, its constitution, economy, and corrupt legal and government institutions have the same effect. According to the U.S. Department of State, "Crimes against foreigners continue to increase. Foreigners are prime targets for purse snatchings, pickpocketing and thefts from hotel rooms, beaches, historic sites and other attractions."[2]

BANKING
Score: 5–Stable (very high level of restrictions)

Banks are owned and operated by the government and heavily influenced by the state-owned central bank. There is no free-market competition in this industry.

WAGE AND PRICE CONTROLS
Score: 5–Stable (very high level)

The government sets virtually all wages and prices.

PROPERTY RIGHTS
Score: 5–Stable (very low level of protection)

Cuba outlaws private property. Some individuals are allowed to operate self-employed businesses, but the government can confiscate all earnings from these activities if the individuals are deemed "unduly wealthy." Corrupt government and police officials often confiscate the money arbitrarily, especially if it is hard currency. There is no enforcement of contracts, and many European and Canadian investors have found that their investments can be renationalized and sold again to other uninformed investors. This has been particularly true in the hotel industry. Moreover, Cuba does not allow international arbitration of disputes, its court system is strongly influenced by the government, and corruption is rampant. According to the U.S. Department of State, "President Castro exercises control over all aspects of Cuban life through the Communist Party and its affiliated mass organizations, the government bureaucracy, and the state security apparatus.... The party controls all government positions, including judicial offices."[3]

REGULATION
Score: 5–Stable (very high level)

The government regulates the entire economy by owning and operating the means of production. Corrupt government officials and police routinely require those who are engaged in the few private-sector activities that are permitted to pay bribes or provide services free of charge.

BLACK MARKET
Score: 5–Stable (very high level of activity)

Cuba's black market is larger than its legal economy. As might be expected in a command economy, even basic economic activities—including the sale of milk and bread, transportation services, and housing—are performed in the black market. Smuggling is another big business; in addition to its importance as a major hub for illegal drugs entering the United States, Cuba has substantial smuggling of consumer goods.

NOTES

[1] U.S. Department of State Travel Advisory, 1997.
[2] *Ibid.*
[3] U.S. Department of State, "Cuba Country Report on Human Rights Practices for 1997," 1998.

Cyprus   2.70

1998 Score: **2.60**   1997 Score: **2.60**   1996 Score: **2.60**

Trade	3	Banking	2
Taxation	4	Wages and Prices	3
Government Intervention	3	Property Rights	3
Monetary Policy	1	Regulation	2
Foreign Investment	3	Black Market	3

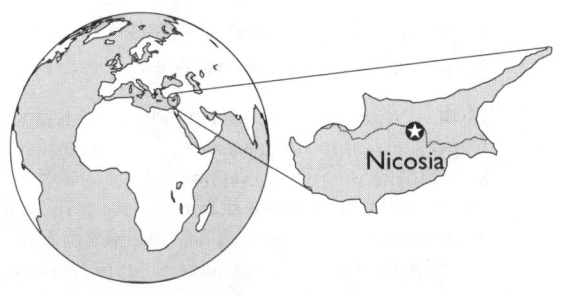
Nicosia

Cyprus gained its independence from Great Britain in 1960. Tensions between the ethnic Greek majority and the ethnic Turkish minority led to intercommunal strife in 1963 and 1967. In 1974, ethnic Greek military officers, supported by the military junta in Greece, staged a coup and sought unity with Greece. Turkey responded by dispatching troops to protect the ethnic Turkish minority. Today, the Cypriot government controls 59 percent of the island; the "Turkish Republic of Northern Cyprus," recognized only by Turkey, controls 37 percent, supported by 30,000 Turkish troops; and the United Nations, which is promoting negotiations to establish a federal, bicommunal republic, maintains peacekeeping forces in a buffer zone that comprises the remaining 4 percent. At the July 1997 summit of the North Atlantic Treaty Organization in Madrid, Greece and Turkey agreed not to use force or the threat of force over quarrels in the Aegean Sea. But tensions between Greece and Turkey are rising, in part due to the Cypriot government's purchase of Russian-made S–300 surface-to-air missiles, which were scheduled to be deployed in autumn 1998. There is increasing evidence that there are moderate barriers to foreign investment; as a result, Cyprus's overall score is 0.1 point worse than last year.

TRADE POLICY
Score: 3–Stable (moderate level of protectionism)

The average tariff rate on Cyprus is 6.1 percent.[1] Non-tariff barriers include licensing requirements and strict inspections.

TAXATION
Score–Income taxation: 5–Stable (very high tax rates)
Score–Corporate taxation: 2–Stable (low tax rates)
Final Taxation Score: 4–Stable (high tax rates)

Cyprus has a top income tax rate of 40 percent. The tax on the average income is 30 percent. The top corporate tax rate is 25 percent. Cyprus also has a 20 percent capital gains tax and an 8 percent value-added tax.

GOVERNMENT INTERVENTION IN THE ECONOMY
Score: 3–Stable (moderate level)

Government consumes 16.8 percent of GDP and continues to play a large role in many companies. For example, the government owns and operates the telecommunications industry.

MONETARY POLICY
Score: 1–Stable (very low level of inflation)

The average annual rate of inflation from 1986 to 1996 was 4.2 percent. In 1997, the rate was less than 4 percent.

1	Hong Kong	1.25		81	Fiji	3.10
2	Singapore	1.30		81	Mali	3.10
3	Bahrain	1.70		81	Slovenia	3.10
4	New Zealand	1.75		85	Honduras	3.15
5	Switzerland	1.85		85	Mexico	3.15
6	United States	1.90		85	Papua New Guinea	3.15
7	Ireland	1.95		88	Djibouti	3.20
7	Luxembourg	1.95		88	Mongolia	3.20
7	Taiwan	1.95		90	Algeria	3.25
7	United Kingdom	1.95		90	Brazil	3.25
11	Bahamas	2.00		90	Lebanon	3.25
12	Czech Republic	2.05		90	Senegal	3.25
12	Japan	2.05		90	Tanzania	3.25
14	Australia	2.10		95	Nigeria	3.30
14	Belgium	2.10		95	Romania	3.30
14	Canada	2.10		97	Cambodia	3.35
14	United Arab Emirates	2.10		97	Dominican Republic	3.35
18	Austria	2.15		97	Egypt	3.35
18	Chile	2.15		97	Guinea	3.35
18	Estonia	2.15		97	Ivory Coast	3.35
18	Netherlands	2.15		97	Moldova	3.35
22	Denmark	2.25		97	Pakistan	3.35
22	El Salvador	2.25		104	Nepal	3.40
22	Finland	2.25		104	Venezuela	3.40
25	Germany	2.30		106	Armenia	3.45
25	Iceland	2.30		106	Bulgaria	3.45
27	Norway	2.35		106	Lesotho	3.45
28	Korea, South	2.40		106	Madagascar	3.45
28	Kuwait	2.40		106	Russia	3.45
28	Malaysia	2.40		111	Burkina Faso	3.50
28	Panama	2.40		111	Cameroon	3.50
28	Thailand	2.40		111	Guyana	3.50
33	Sweden	2.45		111	Nicaragua	3.50
34	Argentina	2.50		115	Gambia	3.60
34	France	2.50		116	Croatia	3.65
34	Italy	2.50		116	Georgia	3.65
34	Spain	2.50		116	Malawi	3.65
38	Portugal	2.55		119	Cape Verde	3.67
38	Sri Lanka	2.55		120	Ethiopia	3.70
38	Trinidad and Tobago	2.55		120	India	3.70
41	Barbados	2.60		120	Niger	3.70
41	Peru	2.60		123	Congo	3.75
43	Bolivia	2.65		124	Chad	3.80
43	Mauritius	2.65		124	China	3.80
45	Cyprus	2.70		124	Mauritania	3.80
45	Jamaica	2.70		124	Ukraine	3.80
45	Uruguay	2.70		124	Zimbabwe	3.80
48	Botswana	2.75		129	Albania	3.85
48	Guatemala	2.75		129	Bangladesh	3.85
48	Jordan	2.75		129	Mozambique	3.85
48	Namibia	2.75		129	Suriname	3.85
48	Oman	2.75		133	Burundi	3.90
48	Philippines	2.75		134	Togo	3.95
54	Belize	2.80		135	Haiti	4.00
54	Costa Rica	2.80		135	Kyrgyz Rep.	4.00
54	Israel	2.80		137	Kazakhstan	4.05
54	Swaziland	2.80		137	Sierra Leone	4.05
54	Turkey	2.80		139	Yemen	4.10
54	Uganda	2.80		140	Belarus	4.15
54	Samoa	2.80		141	Sudan	4.20
61	Latvia	2.85		141	Syria	4.20
62	Greece	2.90		143	Azerbaijan	4.30
62	Hungary	2.90		143	Equatorial Guinea	4.30
62	So. Africa	2.90		143	Myanmar	4.30
65	Ecuador	2.95		143	Rwanda	4.30
65	Gabon	2.95		147	Tajikistan	4.40
65	Indonesia	2.95		147	Uzbekistan	4.40
65	Malta	2.95		149	Angola	4.45
65	Morocco	2.95		149	Turkmenistan	4.45
65	Poland	2.95		151	Guinea-Bissau	4.55
65	Tunisia	2.95		152	Vietnam	4.60
72	Ghana	3.00		153	Congo (Zaire)	4.70
72	Lithuania	3.00		153	Iran	4.70
72	Saudi Arabia	3.00		155	Bosnia	4.80
75	Benin	3.05		155	Somalia	4.80
75	Kenya	3.05		157	Iraq	4.90
75	Paraguay	3.05		157	Laos	4.90
75	Qatar	3.05		157	Libya	4.90
75	Slovak Republic	3.05		160	Cuba	5.00
75	Zambia	3.05		160	Korea, North	5.00
81	Colombia	3.10				

Mostly Free

CAPITAL FLOWS AND FOREIGN INVESTMENT
Score: 3– (moderate barriers)

Most of the few restrictions on foreign investment on Cyprus are imposed in areas vital to national security. The government requires an approval process for some investments; even though this may cause some delays, until recently there was no evidence it served to hinder investment. A 1997 U.S. Department of State report concludes, however, "The government offers tax incentives to encourage foreign direct investment. Majority ownership by foreigners is rarely approved, although exceptions occur."[2] Thus, based on this recent evidence that majority foreign ownership is the exception instead of the rule, Cyprus's score in this factor is 1 point worse than last year.

BANKING
Score: 2–Stable (low level of restrictions)

The banking system is open and competitive. There are more than 28 foreign banks on Cyprus.

WAGE AND PRICE CONTROLS
Score: 3–Stable (moderate level)

The market principally sets wages and prices. The government plays a large role in setting wages for Cyprus's state-owned companies, however, and controls some prices, particularly in the state-owned telecommunications industry and through large subsidies to the agricultural sector.

PROPERTY RIGHTS
Score: 3–Stable (moderate level of protection)

Private property on Cyprus is protected from government expropriation. Although legal enforcement sometimes is lax, expropriation is unlikely.

REGULATION
Score: 2–Stable (low level)

Establishing a business is relatively easy on Cyprus. Regulations are applied evenly in most cases, although some (such as worker health and safety laws) are burdensome. Corruption is nearly nonexistent, but the bureaucracy often is inefficient and laden with red tape.

BLACK MARKET
Score: 3–Stable (moderate level of activity)

There is some smuggling of pirated video and audio cassettes, as well as of copied books and other materials.

NOTES
[1] Based on total tax revenues on international trade as a percentage of total imports.
[2] U.S. Department of State, "Background Notes: Cyprus," September 1997.

Czech Republic   2.05

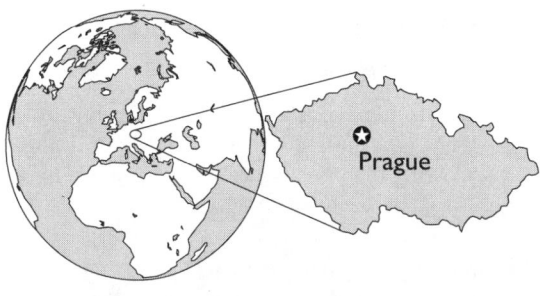
Prague

1998 Score: **2.20**	1997 Score: **2.05**	1996 Score: **2.00**

Trade	1	Banking	1
Taxation	3.5	Wages and Prices	2
Government Intervention	2	Property Rights	2
Monetary Policy	2	Regulation	2
Foreign Investment	2	Black Market	3

The Czech Republic became independent in January 1993 after separating from the Slovak Republic. Since the breakup of the Warsaw Pact in 1989, it has pursued economic liberalization, trading mainly with the European Union (EU) and countries of the former Soviet Union; more than half its foreign trade now is with EU countries, especially Germany. Vaclav Klaus, prime minister from 1992 to 1997, was one of the most progressive free-market reformers among leaders of Europe's former communist states. In June 1998 elections for the lower house of parliament, the Czech Social Democratic Party edged out Klaus's Civil Democratic Party to win the first leftist party victory since 1989. The new government, led by Milos Zeman, may slow down the pace of reform in a populist attempt to address social problems before repairing the economy. In May 1997, the Czech currency plummeted in value against the German mark and the U.S. dollar. Despite attempts by the Central Bank to maintain the currency by raising interest rates, its value has continued to decline, and annual economic growth has dropped to about 2 percent from 5 percent in 1995. The Czech Republic recently reduced some non-tariff barriers and cut corporate tax rates. As a result, the country's overall score is 0.15 point better this year than last year.

TRADE POLICY

Score: 1+ (very low level of protectionism)

The Czech Republic has one of Europe's most open markets. The average tariff rate is about 2.6 percent. In April 1997, the government instituted a policy requiring importers of selected consumer products and foodstuffs to place a six-month interest-free deposit of 20 percent of the value of the goods into a Czech bank. The main reason for this policy was to create barriers to imported goods; the government was concerned with a rapidly increasing trade deficit. This policy was noted in last year's edition of the *Index of Economic Freedom,* and the Czech Republic's score was reduced accordingly. Under increased criticism of the policy, however, the government moved to abolish the requirement in August 1997.[1] Thus, the Czech Republic's trade policy score is 1 point better this year.

TAXATION

Score–Income taxation: 4–Stable (high tax rates)
Score–Corporate taxation: 3+ (Moderate tax rates)
Final Taxation Score: 3.5+ (high tax rates)

The Czech Republic's top marginal income tax rate is 39 percent, and the tax on the average income level is 16.4 percent.[2] The top marginal corporate income tax rate is 35 percent, down from 39 percent in 1997. As a result, the Czech Republic's corporate tax score is 1 point better this year than last year, making the overall tax score 0.5 point better than last year's. The Czech Republic also has a 35 percent capital gains tax, a 22 percent value-added tax, and a real estate transfer tax.

1	Hong Kong	1.25		81	Fiji	3.10
2	Singapore	1.30		81	Mali	3.10
3	Bahrain	1.70		81	Slovenia	3.10
4	New Zealand	1.75		85	Honduras	3.15
5	Switzerland	1.85		85	Mexico	3.15
6	United States	1.90		85	Papua New Guinea	3.15
7	Ireland	1.95		88	Djibouti	3.20
7	Luxembourg	1.95		88	Mongolia	3.20
7	Taiwan	1.95		90	Algeria	3.25
7	United Kingdom	1.95		90	Brazil	3.25
11	Bahamas	2.00		90	Lebanon	3.25
12	Czech Republic	2.05		90	Senegal	3.25
12	Japan	2.05		90	Tanzania	3.25
14	Australia	2.10		95	Nigeria	3.30
14	Belgium	2.10		95	Romania	3.30
14	Canada	2.10		97	Cambodia	3.35
14	United Arab Emirates	2.10		97	Dominican Republic	3.35
18	Austria	2.15		97	Egypt	3.35
18	Chile	2.15		97	Guinea	3.35
18	Estonia	2.15		97	Ivory Coast	3.35
18	Netherlands	2.15		97	Moldova	3.35
22	Denmark	2.25		97	Pakistan	3.35
22	El Salvador	2.25		104	Nepal	3.40
22	Finland	2.25		104	Venezuela	3.40
25	Germany	2.30		106	Armenia	3.45
25	Iceland	2.30		106	Bulgaria	3.45
27	Norway	2.35		106	Lesotho	3.45
28	Korea, South	2.40		106	Madagascar	3.45
28	Kuwait	2.40		106	Russia	3.45
28	Malaysia	2.40		111	Burkina Faso	3.50
28	Panama	2.40		111	Cameroon	3.50
28	Thailand	2.40		111	Guyana	3.50
33	Sweden	2.45		111	Nicaragua	3.50
34	Argentina	2.50		115	Gambia	3.60
34	France	2.50		116	Croatia	3.65
34	Italy	2.50		116	Georgia	3.65
34	Spain	2.50		116	Malawi	3.65
38	Portugal	2.55		119	Cape Verde	3.67
38	Sri Lanka	2.55		120	Ethiopia	3.70
38	Trinidad and Tobago	2.55		120	India	3.70
41	Barbados	2.60		120	Niger	3.70
41	Peru	2.60		123	Congo	3.75
43	Bolivia	2.65		124	Chad	3.80
43	Mauritius	2.65		124	China	3.80
45	Cyprus	2.70		124	Mauritania	3.80
45	Jamaica	2.70		124	Ukraine	3.80
45	Uruguay	2.70		124	Zimbabwe	3.80
48	Botswana	2.75		129	Albania	3.85
48	Guatemala	2.75		129	Bangladesh	3.85
48	Jordan	2.75		129	Mozambique	3.85
48	Namibia	2.75		129	Suriname	3.85
48	Oman	2.75		133	Burundi	3.90
48	Philippines	2.75		134	Togo	3.95
54	Belize	2.80		135	Haiti	4.00
54	Costa Rica	2.80		135	Kyrgyz Rep.	4.00
54	Israel	2.80		137	Kazakhstan	4.05
54	Swaziland	2.80		137	Sierra Leone	4.05
54	Turkey	2.80		139	Yemen	4.10
54	Uganda	2.80		140	Belarus	4.15
54	Samoa	2.80		141	Sudan	4.20
61	Latvia	2.85		141	Syria	4.20
62	Greece	2.90		143	Azerbaijan	4.30
62	Hungary	2.90		143	Equatorial Guinea	4.30
62	So. Africa	2.90		143	Myanmar	4.30
65	Ecuador	2.95		143	Rwanda	4.30
65	Gabon	2.95		147	Tajikistan	4.40
65	Indonesia	2.95		147	Uzbekistan	4.40
65	Malta	2.95		149	Angola	4.45
65	Morocco	2.95		149	Turkmenistan	4.45
65	Poland	2.95		151	Guinea-Bissau	4.55
65	Tunisia	2.95		152	Vietnam	4.60
72	Ghana	3.00		153	Congo (Zaire)	4.70
72	Lithuania	3.00		153	Iran	4.70
72	Saudi Arabia	3.00		155	Bosnia	4.80
75	Benin	3.05		155	Somalia	4.80
75	Kenya	3.05		157	Iraq	4.90
75	Paraguay	3.05		157	Laos	4.90
75	Qatar	3.05		157	Libya	4.90
75	Slovak Republic	3.05		160	Cuba	5.00
75	Zambia	3.05		160	Korea, North	5.00
81	Colombia	3.10				

Mostly Free

GOVERNMENT INTERVENTION IN THE ECONOMY
Score: 2–Stable (low level)

Government consumes about 19.2 percent of GDP. The Klaus government initiated a massive privatization program, allowing the private sector to generate between 70 percent and 80 percent of GDP.

MONETARY POLICY
Score: 2–Stable (low level of inflation)

The Czech Republic has pursued an anti-inflationary monetary policy since 1992 and, according to the U.S. Department of State, has one of the world's most stable currencies.[3] When the government decided to float the koruna, international currency traders lost confidence in the currency, and it lost value. The inflation rate now is moving up again. The rate of inflation was 11 percent in 1992, 20.8 percent in 1993, 8.6 percent in 1994, 7.7 percent in 1995, and 8.8 percent in 1996—an average of about 11.3 percent. In 1997, the inflation rate was about 10 percent.

CAPITAL FLOWS AND FOREIGN INVESTMENT
Score: 2–Stable (low barriers)

With the exception of defense-related industries, all sectors of the economy are open to foreign investment. The Czech Republic attracts more foreign investment per capita than any other country in Central and Eastern Europe, although that level has been declining in recent years. According to the U.S. Department of Commerce, "An open investment climate has been a key element of the Czech Republic's economic transition. The country's investment grade ratings from the international credit rating agencies and its membership in the prestigious OECD [Organization for Economic Cooperation and Development] testify to its positive economic fundamentals."[4]

BANKING
Score: 1–Stable (very low level of restrictions)

Competition in the Czech Republic's banking system is increasing, and there are few, if any, barriers to opening either a foreign or domestic bank. Banks also are open to foreign participation; a foreign bank may establish a wholly owned bank, buy into an existing bank, or open a branch. Private Czech banks are allowed to sell securities and make some investments.

WAGE AND PRICE CONTROLS
Score: 2–Stable (low level)

The market sets most wages and prices. The prices of many utilities, the price of rail and bus transport, and rent paid on government-owned housing remain controlled, however. The Czech Republic maintains a minimum wage.

PROPERTY RIGHTS
Score: 2–Stable (high level of protection)

Private property receives a high level of protection in the Czech Republic. According to the U.S. Department of State, "The Constitution provides for an independent judiciary, and is impartial and independent in practice. Judges are not fired or transferred for political reasons."[5] Delays sometimes are a problem, however.

REGULATION
Score: 2–Stable (low level)

The Czech Republic imposes few regulations on businesses, and most companies do not need a license to begin operation. The government is planning additional reductions in its regulation of business activity. But increased economic activity has brought growth in bureaucratic procedures and some minor signs of corruption. According to the U.S. Department of State, "American business people often cite a convoluted—or in some cases corrupt—bureaucratic system at both national and local levels which can act as an impediment to market access."[6]

BLACK MARKET
Score: 3–Stable (moderate level of activity)

Some goods and services still are supplied on the black market, but recent legislation to combat the piracy of intellectual property, combined with increased enforcement, has reduced significantly the piracy of prerecorded videocassettes and computer software. Any remaining activity represents only a moderate portion of the total economy.

NOTES

[1] U.S. Department of State, *Country Reports on Economic Policy and Trade Practices,* 1998
[2] Based on an average income in local currency of 118,830 koruna. The tax on the first 84,000 koruna is 15 percent; the remainder is taxed at 20 percent, for a total tax of 19,566 koruna, or about 16.4 percent of the average income level.
[3] U.S. Department of Commerce, *Country Commercial Guide,* 1998
[4] *Ibid.*
[5] U.S. Department of State, "Czech Republic Country Report on Human Rights Practices for 1997," 1998
[6] U.S. Department of State, *Country Reports on Economic Policy and Trade Practices,* 1998.

Denmark   2.25

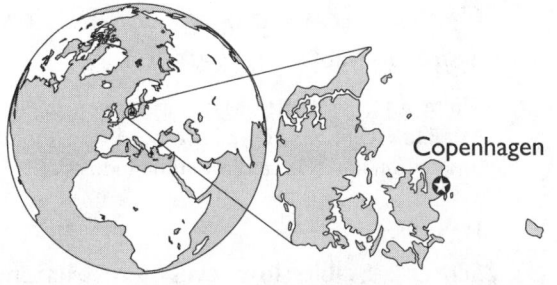

Copenhagen

1998 Score: **2.25**	1997 Score: **2.05**	1996 Score: **1.95**

Trade	2	Banking	2
Taxation	4.5	Wages and Prices	1
Government Intervention	4	Property Rights	1
Monetary Policy	1	Regulation	2
Foreign Investment	2	Black Market	3

Denmark, a constitutional monarchy since 1849, remained neutral during World War I but was invaded and occupied by Nazi Germany during World War II. Following the war, Denmark developed from an economy based to a large extent on agriculture into a modern industrial and post-industrial country. Denmark joined the European Community, now the European Union (EU) in 1973, but has chosen not to participate in the EU's common currency, the euro. However, Denmark's currency will be fixed to the euro within a narrow band of plus or minus 2.35 percent. The Danish economy remains open to trade and investment, provides substantial property rights protection, and allows the market to set most prices and wages. Tax rates, however, remain among the highest in the world.

TRADE POLICY
Score: 2–Stable (low level of protectionism)

Although its average tariff rate is 3.6 percent, Denmark maintains trade restrictions common to other EU members (for example, in financial services, credit cards, insurance, and legal services). Because standards apply to all members, however, Denmark has led the fight within the EU to reduce non-tariff barriers to imports.

TAXATION
Score–Income taxation: 5–Stable (very high tax rates)
Score–Corporate taxation: 3–Stable (moderate tax rates)
Final Taxation Score: 4.5–Stable (very high tax rates)

Denmark's top income tax rate is 60 percent; the tax on the average income level is 47 percent, up from 42 percent last year. The top marginal corporate tax rate is 34 percent. Denmark also has a 34 percent capital gains tax and a 25 percent value-added tax.

GOVERNMENT INTERVENTION IN THE ECONOMY
Score: 4–Stable (high level)

Government consumes about 26 percent of GDP, but this probably understates the extent to which it consumes economic output. According to the Economist Intelligence Unit, the state "holds stakes of 50% or more in 30 companies and a range of holdings from less than 1% to 49% in 18 more. The combined share capital is around Dkr38bn [$5.7 billion], and the combined workforce is about 53,000."[1]

MONETARY POLICY
Score: 1–Stable (very low level of inflation)

Denmark's average rate of inflation from 1986 to 1996 was 2.9 percent. In 1997, the inflation rate was 2.2 percent, where it remains today.

1	Hong Kong	1.25
2	Singapore	1.30
3	Bahrain	1.70
4	New Zealand	1.75
5	Switzerland	1.85
6	United States	1.90
7	Ireland	1.95
7	Luxembourg	1.95
7	Taiwan	1.95
7	United Kingdom	1.95
11	Bahamas	2.00
12	Czech Republic	2.05
12	Japan	2.05
14	Australia	2.10
14	Belgium	2.10
14	Canada	2.10
14	United Arab Emirates	2.10
18	Austria	2.15
18	Chile	2.15
18	Estonia	2.15
18	Netherlands	2.15
22	Denmark	2.25
22	El Salvador	2.25
22	Finland	2.25
25	Germany	2.30
25	Iceland	2.30
27	Norway	2.35
28	Korea, South	2.40
28	Kuwait	2.40
28	Malaysia	2.40
28	Panama	2.40
28	Thailand	2.40
33	Sweden	2.45
34	Argentina	2.50
34	France	2.50
34	Italy	2.50
34	Spain	2.50
38	Portugal	2.55
38	Sri Lanka	2.55
38	Trinidad and Tobago	2.55
41	Barbados	2.60
41	Peru	2.60
43	Bolivia	2.65
43	Mauritius	2.65
45	Cyprus	2.70
45	Jamaica	2.70
45	Uruguay	2.70
48	Botswana	2.75
48	Guatemala	2.75
48	Jordan	2.75
48	Namibia	2.75
48	Oman	2.75
48	Philippines	2.75
54	Belize	2.80
54	Costa Rica	2.80
54	Israel	2.80
54	Swaziland	2.80
54	Turkey	2.80
54	Uganda	2.80
54	Samoa	2.80
61	Latvia	2.85
62	Greece	2.90
62	Hungary	2.90
62	So. Africa	2.90
65	Ecuador	2.95
65	Gabon	2.95
65	Indonesia	2.95
65	Malta	2.95
65	Morocco	2.95
65	Poland	2.95
65	Tunisia	2.95
72	Ghana	3.00
72	Lithuania	3.00
72	Saudi Arabia	3.00
75	Benin	3.05
75	Kenya	3.05
75	Paraguay	3.05
75	Qatar	3.05
75	Slovak Republic	3.05
75	Zambia	3.05
81	Colombia	3.10

81	Fiji	3.10
81	Mali	3.10
81	Slovenia	3.10
85	Honduras	3.15
85	Mexico	3.15
85	Papua New Guinea	3.15
88	Djibouti	3.20
88	Mongolia	3.20
90	Algeria	3.25
90	Brazil	3.25
90	Lebanon	3.25
90	Senegal	3.25
90	Tanzania	3.25
95	Nigeria	3.30
95	Romania	3.30
97	Cambodia	3.35
97	Dominican Republic	3.35
97	Egypt	3.35
97	Guinea	3.35
97	Ivory Coast	3.35
97	Moldova	3.35
97	Pakistan	3.35
104	Nepal	3.40
104	Venezuela	3.40
106	Armenia	3.45
106	Bulgaria	3.45
106	Lesotho	3.45
106	Madagascar	3.45
106	Russia	3.45
111	Burkina Faso	3.50
111	Cameroon	3.50
111	Guyana	3.50
111	Nicaragua	3.50
115	Gambia	3.60
116	Croatia	3.65
116	Georgia	3.65
116	Malawi	3.65
119	Cape Verde	3.67
120	Ethiopia	3.70
120	India	3.70
120	Niger	3.70
123	Congo	3.75
124	Chad	3.80
124	China	3.80
124	Mauritania	3.80
124	Ukraine	3.80
124	Zimbabwe	3.80
129	Albania	3.85
129	Bangladesh	3.85
129	Mozambique	3.85
129	Suriname	3.85
133	Burundi	3.90
134	Togo	3.95
135	Haiti	4.00
135	Kyrgyz Rep.	4.00
137	Kazakhstan	4.05
137	Sierra Leone	4.05
139	Yemen	4.10
140	Belarus	4.15
141	Sudan	4.20
141	Syria	4.20
143	Azerbaijan	4.30
143	Equatorial Guinea	4.30
143	Myanmar	4.30
143	Rwanda	4.30
147	Tajikistan	4.40
147	Uzbekistan	4.40
149	Angola	4.45
149	Turkmenistan	4.45
151	Guinea-Bissau	4.55
152	Vietnam	4.60
153	Congo (Zaire)	4.70
153	Iran	4.70
155	Bosnia	4.80
155	Somalia	4.80
157	Iraq	4.90
157	Laos	4.90
157	Libya	4.90
160	Cuba	5.00
160	Korea, North	5.00

Mostly Free

CAPITAL FLOWS AND FOREIGN INVESTMENT
Score: 2–Stable (low barriers)

There are few restrictions on investments in Denmark. Notable exceptions are the hydrocarbon exploration, arms production, aircraft, and maritime industries.

BANKING
Score: 2–Stable (low level of restrictions)

Denmark's banking system is open to foreign investment and largely independent of government. The law allows banks to engage in securities and insurance services, but there are restrictions on real estate activities.

WAGE AND PRICE CONTROLS
Score: 1–Stable (very low level)

The market sets wages and prices. There is no minimum wage.

PROPERTY RIGHTS
Score: 1–Stable (very high level of protection)

Private property in Denmark is safe from government expropriation. The legal and judicial system is efficient. According to the U.S. Department of State, "The law provides for an independent judiciary, and the Government respects this provision in practice. The judiciary provides citizens with a fair and efficient judicial process."[2]

REGULATION
Score: 2–Stable (low level)

Establishing a business in Denmark is a simple process. Regulations are applied evenly in most cases, although such regulations as safety and health standards make it more difficult for some businesses to keep their doors open. According to the U.S. Department of Commerce, "Bureaucratic procedures appear streamlined and transparent."[3]

BLACK MARKET
Score: 3–Stable (moderate level of activity)

An underground economy has developed in Denmark, primarily in labor. The tax system, the rates of which currently are among the highest in the world, may encourage workers to accept payments "under the table." According to the U.S. Department of State, "[M]any Danes believe the tax system needs further overhaul to improve incentives for work and investment and to reduce the underground economy, which may account for as much as 10 percent of GDP."[4] Moreover, even though Denmark has very strong intellectual property rights (IPR) laws and a long history of strictly enforcing these laws, there are signs of increased black market activity in pirated copyrighted materials, primarily computer software. In May 1997, the United States complained to the World Trade Organization that Denmark has failed to meet the stipulations of international agreements on IPR protection.

NOTES
[1] Economist Intelligence Unit, *ILT Report*, February 1998, p. 8.
[2] U.S. Department of State, "Denmark Country Report on Human Rights Practices for 1997," 1998.
[3] U.S. Department of Commerce, *Country Commercial Guide*, 1998.
[4] U.S. Department of State, *Country Reports on Economic Policy and Trade Practices*, 1997, p. 108.

Djibouti, Republic of

3.20

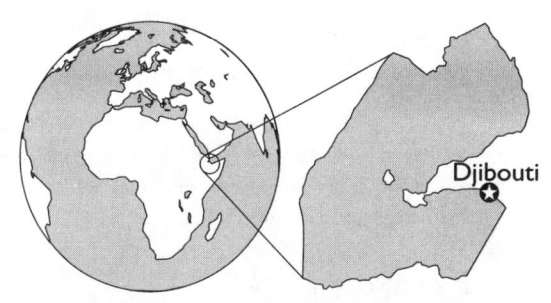

Djibouti

1998 Score: **3.20**	1997 Score: **3.00**	1996 Score: **n/a**

Trade	4	Banking	3
Taxation	2	Wages and Prices	3
Government Intervention	5	Property Rights	3
Monetary Policy	1	Regulation	4
Foreign Investment	3	Black Market	4

The Republic of Djibouti won its independence from France in 1977. It remains a major overseas military base for France, although the latter's troop presence recently has been reduced. During the 1980s, Djibouti focused on maintaining political order and avoiding civil unrest. In 1991, crisis finally erupted and led to increased civil unrest and calls for multiparty democratic elections. Long-term economic planning was supplanted by short-term crisis management and was undermined by political fragmentation; as a result, the country has made little progress toward developing sustainable levels of economic growth. From 1992 to 1996, economic growth actually contracted an average of 1.38 percent annually.

TRADE POLICY
Score: 4–Stable (high level of protectionism)

The most significant barriers to imports are corruption in the customs service, inadequate infrastructure to bring products into the country, and poor banking and financial services. Djibouti lies in the crucial maritime shipping lanes between the Mediterranean Sea and the Indian Ocean. With its ports so strategically located, the regime feels some pressure to liberalize its trade laws.

TAXATION
Score–Income taxation: 2–Stable (low tax rates)
Score–Corporate taxation: 2–Stable (low tax rates)
Final Taxation Score: 2–Stable (low tax rates)

Djibouti has a top income tax rate of 20 percent. The average income level is taxed at 6 percent. The top corporate tax rate is 20 percent. The capital gains tax also is 20 percent. Djibouti also imposes other taxes.

GOVERNMENT INTERVENTION IN THE ECONOMY
Score: 5–Stable (very high level)

Government consumes 36 percent of GDP. Moreover, much of the country's GDP is produced by the state, which continues to own large sections of the transportation industry, including some ports, airports, and maritime shipping.

MONETARY POLICY
Score: 1–Stable (very low level of inflation)

Djibouti has maintained the value of its currency over a considerable period of time. The average annual rate of inflation from 1985 to 1994 was 4.4 percent. No data are available for 1995, 1996, or 1997.

1	Hong Kong	1.25	81	Fiji	3.10
2	Singapore	1.30	81	Mali	3.10
3	Bahrain	1.70	81	Slovenia	3.10
4	New Zealand	1.75	85	Honduras	3.15
5	Switzerland	1.85	85	Mexico	3.15
6	United States	1.90	85	Papua New Guinea	3.15
7	Ireland	1.95	88	Djibouti	3.20
7	Luxembourg	1.95	88	Mongolia	3.20
7	Taiwan	1.95	90	Algeria	3.25
7	United Kingdom	1.95	90	Brazil	3.25
11	Bahamas	2.00	90	Lebanon	3.25
12	Czech Republic	2.05	90	Senegal	3.25
12	Japan	2.05	90	Tanzania	3.25
14	Australia	2.10	95	Nigeria	3.30
14	Belgium	2.10	95	Romania	3.30
14	Canada	2.10	97	Cambodia	3.35
14	United Arab Emirates	2.10	97	Dominican Republic	3.35
18	Austria	2.15	97	Egypt	3.35
18	Chile	2.15	97	Guinea	3.35
18	Estonia	2.15	97	Ivory Coast	3.35
18	Netherlands	2.15	97	Moldova	3.35
22	Denmark	2.25	97	Pakistan	3.35
22	El Salvador	2.25	104	Nepal	3.40
22	Finland	2.25	104	Venezuela	3.40
25	Germany	2.30	106	Armenia	3.45
25	Iceland	2.30	106	Bulgaria	3.45
27	Norway	2.35	106	Lesotho	3.45
28	Korea, South	2.40	106	Madagascar	3.45
28	Kuwait	2.40	106	Russia	3.45
28	Malaysia	2.40	111	Burkina Faso	3.50
28	Panama	2.40	111	Cameroon	3.50
28	Thailand	2.40	111	Guyana	3.50
33	Sweden	2.45	111	Nicaragua	3.50
34	Argentina	2.50	115	Gambia	3.60
34	France	2.50	116	Croatia	3.65
34	Italy	2.50	116	Georgia	3.65
34	Spain	2.50	116	Malawi	3.65
38	Portugal	2.55	119	Cape Verde	3.67
38	Sri Lanka	2.55	120	Ethiopia	3.70
38	Trinidad and Tobago	2.55	120	India	3.70
41	Barbados	2.60	120	Niger	3.70
41	Peru	2.60	123	Congo	3.75
43	Bolivia	2.65	124	Chad	3.80
43	Mauritius	2.65	124	China	3.80
45	Cyprus	2.70	124	Mauritania	3.80
45	Jamaica	2.70	124	Ukraine	3.80
45	Uruguay	2.70	124	Zimbabwe	3.80
48	Botswana	2.75	129	Albania	3.85
48	Guatemala	2.75	129	Bangladesh	3.85
48	Jordan	2.75	129	Mozambique	3.85
48	Namibia	2.75	129	Suriname	3.85
48	Oman	2.75	133	Burundi	3.90
48	Philippines	2.75	134	Togo	3.95
54	Belize	2.80	135	Haiti	4.00
54	Costa Rica	2.80	135	Kyrgyz Rep.	4.00
54	Israel	2.80	137	Kazakhstan	4.05
54	Swaziland	2.80	137	Sierra Leone	4.05
54	Turkey	2.80	139	Yemen	4.10
54	Uganda	2.80	140	Belarus	4.15
54	Samoa	2.80	141	Sudan	4.20
61	Latvia	2.85	141	Syria	4.20
62	Greece	2.90	143	Azerbaijan	4.30
62	Hungary	2.90	143	Equatorial Guinea	4.30
62	So. Africa	2.90	143	Myanmar	4.30
65	Ecuador	2.95	143	Rwanda	4.30
65	Gabon	2.95	147	Tajikistan	4.40
65	Indonesia	2.95	147	Uzbekistan	4.40
65	Malta	2.95	149	Angola	4.45
65	Morocco	2.95	149	Turkmenistan	4.45
65	Poland	2.95	151	Guinea-Bissau	4.55
65	Tunisia	2.95	152	Vietnam	4.60
72	Ghana	3.00	153	Congo (Zaire)	4.70
72	Lithuania	3.00	153	Iran	4.70
72	Saudi Arabia	3.00	155	Bosnia	4.80
75	Benin	3.05	155	Somalia	4.80
75	Kenya	3.05	157	Iraq	4.90
75	Paraguay	3.05	157	Laos	4.90
75	Qatar	3.05	157	Libya	4.90
75	Slovak Republic	3.05	160	Cuba	5.00
75	Zambia	3.05	160	Korea, North	5.00
81	Colombia	3.10			

Mostly Unfree

CAPITAL FLOWS AND FOREIGN INVESTMENT
Score: 3–Stable (moderate barriers)

Djibouti is open to foreign investment. Investments must be reviewed by the government, however, and some sectors—mainly in areas the government has determined are vital to national security—are closed.

BANKING
Score: 3–Stable (moderate level of restrictions)

The banking system is very open and competitive. According to the U.S. Department of Commerce, "Djibouti has one of the most liberal economic regimes in Africa, with almost unrestricted banking and commerce sectors."[1] The most significant problem, however, is the lack of sufficient capital to finance economic expansion. The government controls capital.

WAGE AND PRICE CONTROLS
Score: 3–Stable (moderate level)

The market principally sets wages and prices for most products. The government, however, controls prices on electricity and transportation services.

PROPERTY RIGHTS
Score: 3–Stable (moderate level of protection)

Private property rights are respected in Djibouti, although the courts often are overburdened and the enforcement of contracts can be both time-consuming and cumbersome. According to the U.S. Department of State, there is evidence that Djibouti's judiciary is not entirely free of government influence.[2]

REGULATION
Score: 4–Stable (high level)

Government corruption is a burden on business, and bribes often are necessary. Health and safety regulations also add to the cost of doing business.

BLACK MARKET
Score: 4–Stable (high level of activity)

Much of Djibouti's economic activity, especially trade in pirated trademarks and computer software, occurs in the black market. Laws protecting intellectual property are not enforced in full.

NOTES
[1]   U.S. Department of Commerce, National Trade Data Bank and Economic Bulletin Board, products of *Stat–USA* Internet site (*www.stat-usa.gov*).
[2]   U.S. Department of State, "Djibouti Country Report on Human Rights Practices for 1996," 1997.

Dominican Republic   3.35

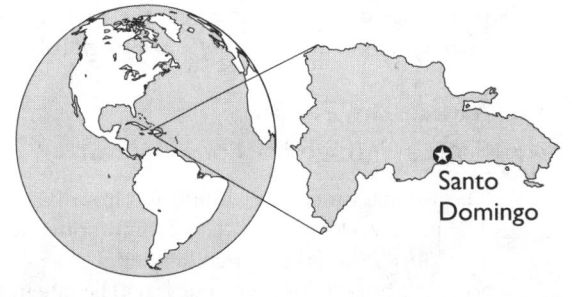
Santo Domingo

1998 Score: **3.45**   1997 Score: **3.45**   1996 Score: **3.45**

Trade	5	Banking	3
Taxation	2.5	Wages and Prices	2
Government Intervention	2	Property Rights	4
Monetary Policy	4	Regulation	4
Foreign Investment	3	Black Market	4

The Dominican Republic has a large agriculture industry. The government has intervened often in this and other industries. In the 1980s, the country suffered a major economic crisis when bad weather, coupled with socialist economic policies, ruined its agricultural production. Since 1990, the government has been trying to reform the economy. Even though it has made significant progress in reducing inflation, reforming its investment laws, and reducing its barriers to trade, substantial restrictions on economic freedom remain in effect, particularly in the areas of trade policy and monetary policy. The inflation rate has been decreasing; as a result, the Dominican Republic's overall score is 0.1 point better than last year.

TRADE POLICY
Score: 5–Stable (very high level of protectionism)

The Dominican Republic's average tariff rate is 15.4 percent. Non-tariff barriers include arbitrary customs clearance procedures and a burdensome licensing requirement for selected imports. According to the U.S. Department of State, "Arbitrary customs clearance procedures sometimes cause problems for business. The use of 'negotiated fee' practices to gain faster customs clearance continues to put some U.S. firms at a competitive disadvantage in the Dominican market. Customs officials routinely reject invoice prices for computing duties and customs fees and use their own assumed value database."[1]

TAXATION
Score–Income taxation: 2–Stable (low tax rates)
Score–Corporate taxation: 2–Stable (low tax rates)
Final Taxation Score: 2.5–Stable (moderate tax rates)

The Dominican Republic's marginal top income tax rate is 25 percent; the tax on the average income level is 0 percent. The top corporate tax rate is 25 percent. The Dominican Republic also has a 25 percent capital gains tax and an 8 percent value-added tax.

GOVERNMENT INTERVENTION IN THE ECONOMY
Score: 2–Stable (low level)

Government consumes about 5 percent of GDP. The state-owned sector, however, is large. According to the U.S. Department of Commerce, "The Dominican government has traditionally played a large role in the country's economic life. The government is the owner of all public utilities (except telecommunications), an insurance company, the country's largest bank (Banco de Reservas), and factories producing a variety of items....The large government presence in the economy and a web of complicated regulations means that many economic decisions are politicized and businesspersons spend time 'lobbying' the government."[2] Nevertheless, because of its low level of consumption as a

#	Country	Score
1	Hong Kong	1.25
2	Singapore	1.30
3	Bahrain	1.70
4	New Zealand	1.75
5	Switzerland	1.85
6	United States	1.90
7	Ireland	1.95
7	Luxembourg	1.95
7	Taiwan	1.95
7	United Kingdom	1.95
11	Bahamas	2.00
12	Czech Republic	2.05
12	Japan	2.05
14	Australia	2.10
14	Belgium	2.10
14	Canada	2.10
14	United Arab Emirates	2.10
18	Austria	2.15
18	Chile	2.15
18	Estonia	2.15
18	Netherlands	2.15
22	Denmark	2.25
22	El Salvador	2.25
22	Finland	2.25
25	Germany	2.30
25	Iceland	2.30
27	Norway	2.35
28	Korea, South	2.40
28	Kuwait	2.40
28	Malaysia	2.40
28	Panama	2.40
28	Thailand	2.40
33	Sweden	2.45
34	Argentina	2.50
34	France	2.50
34	Italy	2.50
34	Spain	2.50
38	Portugal	2.55
38	Sri Lanka	2.55
38	Trinidad and Tobago	2.55
41	Barbados	2.60
41	Peru	2.60
43	Bolivia	2.65
43	Mauritius	2.65
45	Cyprus	2.70
45	Jamaica	2.70
45	Uruguay	2.70
48	Botswana	2.75
48	Guatemala	2.75
48	Jordan	2.75
48	Namibia	2.75
48	Oman	2.75
48	Philippines	2.75
54	Belize	2.80
54	Costa Rica	2.80
54	Israel	2.80
54	Swaziland	2.80
54	Turkey	2.80
54	Uganda	2.80
54	Samoa	2.80
61	Latvia	2.85
62	Greece	2.90
62	Hungary	2.90
62	So. Africa	2.90
65	Ecuador	2.95
65	Gabon	2.95
65	Indonesia	2.95
65	Malta	2.95
65	Morocco	2.95
65	Poland	2.95
65	Tunisia	2.95
72	Ghana	3.00
72	Lithuania	3.00
72	Saudi Arabia	3.00
75	Benin	3.05
75	Kenya	3.05
75	Paraguay	3.05
75	Qatar	3.05
75	Slovak Republic	3.05
75	Zambia	3.05
81	Colombia	3.10
81	Fiji	3.10
81	Mali	3.10
81	Slovenia	3.10
85	Honduras	3.15
85	Mexico	3.15
85	Papua New Guinea	3.15
88	Djibouti	3.20
88	Mongolia	3.20
90	Algeria	3.25
90	Brazil	3.25
90	Lebanon	3.25
90	Senegal	3.25
90	Tanzania	3.25
95	Nigeria	3.30
95	Romania	3.30
97	Cambodia	3.35
97	Dominican Republic	3.35
97	Egypt	3.35
97	Guinea	3.35
97	Ivory Coast	3.35
97	Moldova	3.35
97	Pakistan	3.35
104	Nepal	3.40
104	Venezuela	3.40
106	Armenia	3.45
106	Bulgaria	3.45
106	Lesotho	3.45
106	Madagascar	3.45
106	Russia	3.45
111	Burkina Faso	3.50
111	Cameroon	3.50
111	Guyana	3.50
111	Nicaragua	3.50
115	Gambia	3.60
116	Croatia	3.65
116	Georgia	3.65
116	Malawi	3.65
119	Cape Verde	3.67
120	Ethiopia	3.70
120	India	3.70
120	Niger	3.70
123	Congo	3.75
124	Chad	3.80
124	China	3.80
124	Mauritania	3.80
124	Ukraine	3.80
124	Zimbabwe	3.80
129	Albania	3.85
129	Bangladesh	3.85
129	Mozambique	3.85
129	Suriname	3.85
133	Burundi	3.90
134	Togo	3.95
135	Haiti	4.00
135	Kyrgyz Rep.	4.00
137	Kazakhstan	4.05
137	Sierra Leone	4.05
139	Yemen	4.10
140	Belarus	4.15
141	Sudan	4.20
141	Syria	4.20
143	Azerbaijan	4.30
143	Equatorial Guinea	4.30
143	Myanmar	4.30
143	Rwanda	4.30
147	Tajikistan	4.40
147	Uzbekistan	4.40
149	Angola	4.45
149	Turkmenistan	4.45
151	Guinea-Bissau	4.55
152	Vietnam	4.60
153	Congo (Zaire)	4.70
153	Iran	4.70
155	Bosnia	4.80
155	Somalia	4.80
157	Iraq	4.90
157	Laos	4.90
157	Libya	4.90
160	Cuba	5.00
160	Korea, North	5.00

Mostly Unfree

percentage of the total economy, the level of government intervention in the economy is low by global standards.

MONETARY POLICY
Score: 4+ (high level of inflation)

The average annual rate of inflation from 1986 to 1996 was 22.6 percent, down from 26.3 percent for the period 1985 to 1995. As a result, the Dominican Republic's monetary policy score is 1 point better than last year. The rate in 1997 was 8.37 percent.

CAPITAL FLOWS AND FOREIGN INVESTMENT
Score: 3–Stable (moderate barriers)

The government has made significant progress toward removing most barriers to foreign investment. According to the Office of the United States Trade Representative, "The December 1995 investment law is designed to remove barriers to investment and to provide equal access for foreign investors to all sectors of the economy except toxic waste disposal, public health and environment, and defense, for which express presidential authorization is required."[3] The U.S. Department of State, however, notes the existence of continuing barriers to foreign investment: Investors "must receive approval from the Foreign Investment Directorate of the Central Bank to qualify for repatriation of profits.... Foreign employees may not exceed 20 percent of a firm's work force. This is not applicable when foreign employees only perform managerial or administrative functions.... [E]xpropriation standards (e.g., in the 'public interest') do not appear to be consistent with international law standards.... The Dominican Republic does not recognize the general right of investors to binding international arbitration."[4] Nevertheless, by global standards, restrictions on foreign investment remain moderate.

BANKING
Score: 3–Stable (moderate level of restrictions)

According to the Office of the United States Trade Representative, "Until recently, foreign participation in the financial services sector was restricted by law. The 1995 foreign investment law, and financial-monetary code now before the Dominican Congress, permit foreign participation in the financial services sector. However, the practical impact of these provisions is not clear. There is no secondary securities market in the Dominican Republic so questions of brokerage services and securities underwriting, trading, etc., do not arise."[5] State-owned banks continue to play a vital role in the financial system, controlling almost one-third of all assets. Because of the lack of financial services, like securities underwriting and trading, the continued government control of financial resources, and the lack of an assessment of financial-sector liberalization policies now being enacted, the Dominican Republic's banking score remains the same as last year.

WAGE AND PRICE CONTROLS
Score: 2–Stable (low level)

The market sets most wages and prices. According to the U.S. Department of State, "Most domestic prices are determined by market forces, although distortionary government policies sometimes limit the operation of these forces."[6]

PROPERTY RIGHTS
Score: 4–Stable (low level of protection)

The court system is inefficient; corruption and bureaucratic red tape run high; and the government can expropriate property. The U.S. Department of State explains, "Although the Constitution stipulates an independent judiciary, interference from other public and private entities, including the executive branch, has substantially undermined judicial independence.... The judicial system is plagued by chronic delays."[7]

REGULATION
Score: 4–Stable (high level)

Regulations are not applied evenly or honestly. According to the U.S. Department of Commerce, "As in many developing countries...red tape and differences between law and actual practice remain significant problems."[8] Moreover, corruption also presents a significant barrier. "Corruption with the Government and among judges, prosecutors, and law enforcement officers," reports the U.S. Department of Commerce, "is endemic."[9]

BLACK MARKET
Score: 4–Stable (high level of activity)

The Dominican Republic has a high level of black market activity, particularly in labor services. Competition for workers is so intense that many legal labor regulations are ignored. There also is no regard for the protection of intellectual property. According to the U.S. Department of State, "Although the Dominican Republic is a signatory to the Paris Convention and the Universal Copyright Convention, and in 1991 became a member of the World Intellectual Property Organization, the lack of a strong regulatory environment results in inadequate protection of intellectual property rights.... In general, copyright laws are adequate, but...enforcement is weak, resulting in widespread piracy."[10]

NOTES

[1]   U.S. Department of State, *Country Reports on Economic Policy and Trade Practices,* 1998.
[2]   U.S. Department of Commerce, *Country Commercial Guide,* 1998.
[3]   Office of the United States Trade Representative, *1998 National Trade Estimate Report on Foreign Trade Barriers.*
[4]   U.S. Department of State, *Country Reports on Economic Policy and Trade Practices,* 1998.
[5]   Office of the United States Trade Representative, *1998 National Trade Estimate Report on Foreign Trade Barriers.*
[6]   U.S. Department of State, *Country Reports on Economic Policy and Trade Practices,* 1998.
[7]   U.S. Department of State, "Dominican Republic Country Report on Human Rights Practices for 1997," 1998.
[8]   U.S. Department of Commerce, *Country Commercial Guide,* 1998.
[9]   *Ibid.*
[10]   U.S. Department of State, *Country Reports on Economic Policy and Trade Practices,* 1998.

Ecuador   2.95

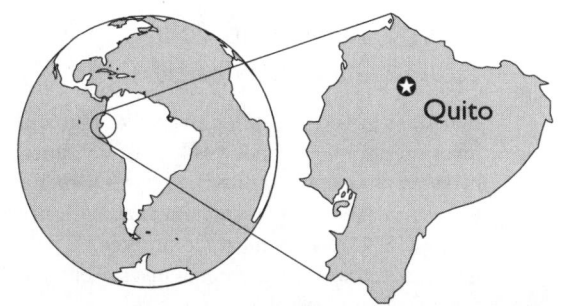

1998 Score: **2.95**	1997 Score: **3.05**	1996 Score: **3.15**

Trade	3	Banking	3
Taxation	2.5	Wages and Prices	2
Government Intervention	1	Property Rights	3
Monetary Policy	5	Regulation	4
Foreign Investment	2	Black Market	4

Ecuador has been plagued since the 1980s by a succession of economic and political crises, including steep drops in the prices of oil and bananas, the mainstays of its economy. Throughout the 1990s, efforts to advance free-market reforms have been thwarted repeatedly by political forces that are broadly opposed to economic liberalization. In 1996, the country also underwent a constitutional crisis when President Abdala Bucaram was impeached and forced out of office. His elected successor, Jamil Mahuad, was inaugurated in August 1998. Despite a long history of political instability, Ecuador overcame the constitutional crisis precipitated by Bucaram's removal without intervention by the military. The new political leadership has yet to carry out any meaningful economic and democratic reforms. President Mahuad has pledged to pursue these long-overdue reforms, but political resistance to change remains very strong.

TRADE POLICY
Score: 3–Stable (moderate level of protectionism)

Ecuador's average tariff rate is 8 percent.[1] Importers must obtain import licenses, which can serve to delay the movement of goods into the country. The government has made some progress toward reforming cumbersome customs procedures. According to the U.S. Department of State, "Customs procedures can be difficult, but they are not normally used to discriminate against U.S. products."[2]

TAXATION
Score–Income taxation: 2–Stable (low tax rates)
Score–Corporate taxation: 2–Stable (low tax rates)
Final Taxation Score: 2.5–Stable (moderate tax rates)

Ecuador's top marginal income tax rate is 25 percent, and the average income level is taxed at 0 percent. The top tax rate on corporate profits is 25 percent. Ecuador also has a 10 percent value-added tax.

GOVERNMENT INTERVENTION IN THE ECONOMY
Score: 1–Stable (very low level)

Government consumes only 9.1 percent of GDP. This share may seem very low, considering that the government employs 25 percent of the workforce and state-owned firms dominate many industries, but the vast majority of firms are privately owned. The state-owned sector contributes less than 8 percent of GDP.

MONETARY POLICY
Score: 5–Stable (very high level of inflation)

Ecuador's main monetary goal has been to stabilize inflation by controlling the money supply. From 1986 to 1996, the average annual rate of inflation was 40.3 percent. In 1997, the inflation rate was 32 percent.

1	Hong Kong	1.25	81	Fiji	3.10
2	Singapore	1.30	81	Mali	3.10
3	Bahrain	1.70	81	Slovenia	3.10
4	New Zealand	1.75	85	Honduras	3.15
5	Switzerland	1.85	85	Mexico	3.15
6	United States	1.90	85	Papua New Guinea	3.15
7	Ireland	1.95	88	Djibouti	3.20
7	Luxembourg	1.95	88	Mongolia	3.20
7	Taiwan	1.95	90	Algeria	3.25
7	United Kingdom	1.95	90	Brazil	3.25
11	Bahamas	2.00	90	Lebanon	3.25
12	Czech Republic	2.05	90	Senegal	3.25
12	Japan	2.05	90	Tanzania	3.25
14	Australia	2.10	95	Nigeria	3.30
14	Belgium	2.10	95	Romania	3.30
14	Canada	2.10	97	Cambodia	3.35
14	United Arab Emirates	2.10	97	Dominican Republic	3.35
18	Austria	2.15	97	Egypt	3.35
18	Chile	2.15	97	Guinea	3.35
18	Estonia	2.15	97	Ivory Coast	3.35
18	Netherlands	2.15	97	Moldova	3.35
22	Denmark	2.25	97	Pakistan	3.35
22	El Salvador	2.25	104	Nepal	3.40
22	Finland	2.25	104	Venezuela	3.40
25	Germany	2.30	106	Armenia	3.45
25	Iceland	2.30	106	Bulgaria	3.45
27	Norway	2.35	106	Lesotho	3.45
28	Korea, South	2.40	106	Madagascar	3.45
28	Kuwait	2.40	106	Russia	3.45
28	Malaysia	2.40	111	Burkina Faso	3.50
28	Panama	2.40	111	Cameroon	3.50
28	Thailand	2.40	111	Guyana	3.50
33	Sweden	2.45	111	Nicaragua	3.50
34	Argentina	2.50	115	Gambia	3.60
34	France	2.50	116	Croatia	3.65
34	Italy	2.50	116	Georgia	3.65
34	Spain	2.50	116	Malawi	3.65
38	Portugal	2.55	119	Cape Verde	3.67
38	Sri Lanka	2.55	120	Ethiopia	3.70
38	Trinidad and Tobago	2.55	120	India	3.70
41	Barbados	2.60	120	Niger	3.70
41	Peru	2.60	123	Congo	3.75
43	Bolivia	2.65	124	Chad	3.80
43	Mauritius	2.65	124	China	3.80
45	Cyprus	2.70	124	Mauritania	3.80
45	Jamaica	2.70	124	Ukraine	3.80
45	Uruguay	2.70	124	Zimbabwe	3.80
48	Botswana	2.75	129	Albania	3.85
48	Guatemala	2.75	129	Bangladesh	3.85
48	Jordan	2.75	129	Mozambique	3.85
48	Namibia	2.75	129	Suriname	3.85
48	Oman	2.75	133	Burundi	3.90
48	Philippines	2.75	134	Togo	3.95
54	Belize	2.80	135	Haiti	4.00
54	Costa Rica	2.80	135	Kyrgyz Rep.	4.00
54	Israel	2.80	137	Kazakhstan	4.05
54	Swaziland	2.80	137	Sierra Leone	4.05
54	Turkey	2.80	139	Yemen	4.10
54	Uganda	2.80	140	Belarus	4.15
54	Samoa	2.80	141	Sudan	4.20
61	Latvia	2.85	141	Syria	4.20
62	Greece	2.90	143	Azerbaijan	4.30
62	Hungary	2.90	143	Equatorial Guinea	4.30
62	So. Africa	2.90	143	Myanmar	4.30
65	Ecuador	2.95	143	Rwanda	4.30
65	Gabon	2.95	147	Tajikistan	4.40
65	Indonesia	2.95	147	Uzbekistan	4.40
65	Malta	2.95	149	Angola	4.45
65	Morocco	2.95	149	Turkmenistan	4.45
65	Poland	2.95	151	Guinea-Bissau	4.55
65	Tunisia	2.95	152	Vietnam	4.60
72	Ghana	3.00	153	Congo (Zaire)	4.70
72	Lithuania	3.00	153	Iran	4.70
72	Saudi Arabia	3.00	155	Bosnia	4.80
75	Benin	3.05	155	Somalia	4.80
75	Kenya	3.05	157	Iraq	4.90
75	Paraguay	3.05	157	Laos	4.90
75	Qatar	3.05	157	Libya	4.90
75	Slovak Republic	3.05	160	Cuba	5.00
75	Zambia	3.05	160	Korea, North	5.00
81	Colombia	3.10			

Mostly Free

CAPITAL FLOWS AND FOREIGN INVESTMENT
Score: 2–Stable (low barriers)

Ecuador's government has worked to liberalize its foreign investment policies since 1990. Most investors are free to invest in almost any industry, except for such strategic industries as mining and state-owned enterprises. According to the U.S. Department of Commerce, "The Ecuadorian government welcomes foreign investment and offers an open foreign investment regime."[3]

BANKING
Score: 3–Stable (moderate level of restrictions)

Ecuador has more private banks than most of its neighbors. Domestically owned banks are relatively competitive with foreign banks; however, these privately owned banks must compete with state-owned development banks that provide a variety of subsidized loans to farmers, ranchers, and small businessmen.

WAGE AND PRICE CONTROLS
Score: 2–Stable (low level)

Although there are fewer price controls today than there were several years ago, the government still sets prices on such items as natural gas and electricity and some agricultural goods for export. Ecuador maintains a minimum wage policy.

PROPERTY RIGHTS
Score: 3–Stable (moderate level of protection)

According to the U.S. Department of Commerce, "For the most part, Ecuadorian law provides adequate protection for property rights, but it can be difficult to gain effective protection via the legal system due in part to problems of transparency."[4] In 1994, the government passed a law to uphold the rights of rural landowners, but corruption still plagues the legal framework, making it unnecessarily difficult to enforce property rights.

REGULATION
Score: 4–Stable (high level)

The Superintendency of Companies, the Superintendency of Banks and Insurance Companies, and the Ecuadorian Standards Institute are Ecuador's primary regulatory bodies. Corruption causes these and other agencies to enforce regulations haphazardly. According to the U.S. Department of Commerce, "The regulatory system in Ecuador's economy has not been specifically geared toward fostering competition and is insufficiently transparent."[5]

BLACK MARKET
Score: 4–Stable (high level of activity)

Because of bureaucratic inefficiency and corruption, many entrepreneurs resort to the black market. The government has reduced many trade tariffs on items that were being sold as contraband. According to the U.S. Department of State, however, "Copyright infringement occurs and there is widespread local trade in pirated audio and video recordings, as well as computer software."[6]

NOTES

[1] Based on total taxation on international trade as a percentage of total imports.
[2] U.S. Department of State, *Country Reports on Economic Policy and Trade Practices,* 1998.
[3] U.S. Department of Commerce, *Country Commercial Guide,* 1998.
[4] *Ibid.*
[5] *Ibid.*
[6] U.S. Department of State, *Country Reports on Economic Policy and Trade Practices,* 1998.

Egypt

3.35

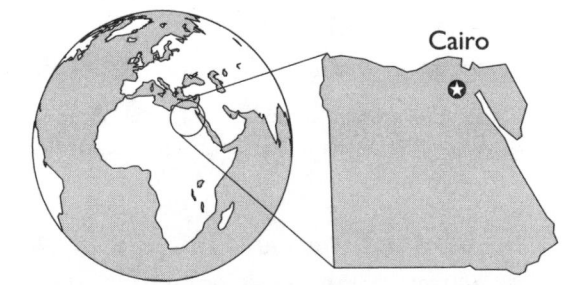

Cairo

1998 Score: 3.35   **1997 Score: 3.45**   **1996 Score: 3.45**

Trade	5	Banking	2
Taxation	4.5	Wages and Prices	3
Government Intervention	3	Property Rights	3
Monetary Policy	3	Regulation	4
Foreign Investment	3	Black Market	3

Egypt today is a social democracy ruled by President Hosni Mubarak. It also is the second largest annual recipient of U.S. foreign aid. In 1991, the government launched a desperately needed market liberalization program; but, despite attempts to remove the state from the market, little progress has been made toward privatizing Egypt's massive and inefficient public sector. Little has been done to reform and reduce the size of the bureaucracy, either. Egypt has made some progress toward lowering extremely high tariffs and establishing greater fiscal discipline.

TRADE POLICY
Score: 5–Stable (very high level of protectionism)

Despite progress over the past several years in liberalizing its trade policy, Egypt remains one of the world's most heavily protected markets, with an exceptionally high average tariff rate of 14.6 percent, although this rate has steadily come down since 1990. According to the Office of the United States Trade Representative, however, Egypt "discriminates against some imports by imposing offsetting sales taxes."[1] Moreover, according to the U.S. Department of Commerce, "Egyptian customs procedures are complicated and rigid in areas such as duty rates. They are designed to eliminate trading loopholes. Authorities do not have to explain or justify their decisions and there is no formal appeal process for customs officers' decisions. Customs procedures are subjective when it comes to identifying whether a commodity fits in one tariff category or another."[2] Even so, Egypt is attempting to offset its cumbersome customs service by implementing "offshore customs services" that allow exporters to finalize necessary paperwork prior to arriving in an Egyptian port, thus reducing the time it takes to clear customs. Import bans now apply only to textiles and apparels, and the government must eliminate them eventually as part of the World Trade Organization agreement. Import licenses no longer are required.

TAXATION
Score–Income taxation: 4–Stable (high tax rates)
Score–Corporate taxation: 4–Stable (high tax rates)
Final Taxation Score: 4.5–Stable (very high tax rates)

Egypt has a top income tax rate of 40 percent. The tax on the average income level is 20 percent, and corporate income is taxed at a rate of 40 percent. Egypt also has a 40 percent capital gains tax, a sales tax, and a social insurance tax.

GOVERNMENT INTERVENTION IN THE ECONOMY
Score: 3–Stable (moderate level)

Government consumes 11.2 percent of GDP. With plans for wide-scale privatization proceeding at a slow pace, the large and inefficient state sector still accounts for the majority of industrial production.

1	Hong Kong	1.25		81	Fiji	3.10
2	Singapore	1.30		81	Mali	3.10
3	Bahrain	1.70		81	Slovenia	3.10
4	New Zealand	1.75		85	Honduras	3.15
5	Switzerland	1.85		85	Mexico	3.15
6	United States	1.90		85	Papua New Guinea	3.15
7	Ireland	1.95		88	Djibouti	3.20
7	Luxembourg	1.95		88	Mongolia	3.20
7	Taiwan	1.95		90	Algeria	3.25
7	United Kingdom	1.95		90	Brazil	3.25
11	Bahamas	2.00		90	Lebanon	3.25
12	Czech Republic	2.05		90	Senegal	3.25
12	Japan	2.05		90	Tanzania	3.25
14	Australia	2.10		95	Nigeria	3.30
14	Belgium	2.10		95	Romania	3.30
14	Canada	2.10		97	Cambodia	3.35
14	United Arab Emirates	2.10		97	Dominican Republic	3.35
18	Austria	2.15		97	Egypt	3.35
18	Chile	2.15		97	Guinea	3.35
18	Estonia	2.15		97	Ivory Coast	3.35
18	Netherlands	2.15		97	Moldova	3.35
22	Denmark	2.25		97	Pakistan	3.35
22	El Salvador	2.25		104	Nepal	3.40
22	Finland	2.25		104	Venezuela	3.40
25	Germany	2.30		106	Armenia	3.45
25	Iceland	2.30		106	Bulgaria	3.45
27	Norway	2.35		106	Lesotho	3.45
27	Korea, South	2.40		106	Madagascar	3.45
28	Kuwait	2.40		106	Russia	3.45
28	Malaysia	2.40		111	Burkina Faso	3.50
28	Panama	2.40		111	Cameroon	3.50
28	Thailand	2.40		111	Guyana	3.50
33	Sweden	2.45		111	Nicaragua	3.50
34	Argentina	2.50		115	Gambia	3.60
34	France	2.50		116	Croatia	3.65
34	Italy	2.50		116	Georgia	3.65
34	Spain	2.50		116	Malawi	3.65
38	Portugal	2.55		119	Cape Verde	3.67
38	Sri Lanka	2.55		120	Ethiopia	3.70
38	Trinidad and Tobago	2.55		120	India	3.70
41	Barbados	2.60		120	Niger	3.70
41	Peru	2.60		123	Congo	3.75
43	Bolivia	2.65		124	Chad	3.80
43	Mauritius	2.65		124	China	3.80
45	Cyprus	2.70		124	Mauritania	3.80
45	Jamaica	2.70		124	Ukraine	3.80
45	Uruguay	2.70		124	Zimbabwe	3.80
48	Botswana	2.75		129	Albania	3.85
48	Guatemala	2.75		129	Bangladesh	3.85
48	Jordan	2.75		129	Mozambique	3.85
48	Namibia	2.75		129	Suriname	3.85
48	Oman	2.75		133	Burundi	3.90
48	Philippines	2.75		134	Togo	3.95
54	Belize	2.80		135	Haiti	4.00
54	Costa Rica	2.80		135	Kyrgyz Rep.	4.00
54	Israel	2.80		137	Kazakhstan	4.05
54	Swaziland	2.80		137	Sierra Leone	4.05
54	Turkey	2.80		139	Yemen	4.10
54	Uganda	2.80		140	Belarus	4.15
54	Samoa	2.80		141	Sudan	4.20
61	Latvia	2.85		141	Syria	4.20
62	Greece	2.90		143	Azerbaijan	4.30
62	Hungary	2.90		143	Equatorial Guinea	4.30
62	So. Africa	2.90		143	Myanmar	4.30
65	Ecuador	2.95		143	Rwanda	4.30
65	Gabon	2.95		147	Tajikistan	4.40
65	Indonesia	2.95		147	Uzbekistan	4.40
65	Malta	2.95		149	Angola	4.45
65	Morocco	2.95		149	Turkmenistan	4.45
65	Poland	2.95		151	Guinea-Bissau	4.55
65	Tunisia	2.95		152	Vietnam	4.60
72	Ghana	3.00		153	Congo (Zaire)	4.70
72	Lithuania	3.00		153	Iran	4.70
72	Saudi Arabia	3.00		155	Bosnia	4.80
75	Benin	3.05		155	Somalia	4.80
75	Kenya	3.05		157	Iraq	4.90
75	Paraguay	3.05		157	Laos	4.90
75	Qatar	3.05		157	Libya	4.90
75	Slovak Republic	3.05		160	Cuba	5.00
75	Zambia	3.05		160	Korea, North	5.00
81	Colombia	3.10				

Mostly Unfree

MONETARY POLICY
Score: 3–Stable (moderate level of inflation)

Egypt's average annual rate of inflation from 1986 to 1996 was 13.27 percent. The estimated rate for 1997 was 4.6 percent.

CAPITAL FLOWS AND FOREIGN INVESTMENT
Score: 3–Stable (moderate barriers)

Egypt's government has established business zones free of customs duties, sales taxes, and other taxes. Despite these improvements, however, a cumbersome bureaucracy continues to frustrate foreign investment. Foreign investors occasionally face official discrimination, particularly when their proposals threaten public-sector interests. In practice, 100 percent foreign ownership, although legally permitted in most sectors, is approved only in rare cases. Most foreigners, particularly non-Arabs, are likely to find themselves excluded from Egypt's still embryonic privatization process. Foreigners are prohibited from owning agricultural land.

BANKING
Score: 2–Stable (low level of restrictions)

Egypt's banking industry is dominated by four large commercial banks, some of which are undergoing privatization. Over 20 foreign banks operate branches in Egypt, and there are plans for further privatization of the banking sector. In June 1996, Egypt passed a new banking law that allows up to 100 percent foreign ownership of Egyptian banks.

WAGE AND PRICE CONTROLS
Score: 3–Stable (moderate level)

Price controls have been removed on most products, with the notable exceptions of pharmaceutical products, sugar, edible oils, and cigarettes. Basic foods and transportation are subsidized, although not as much as in recent years. The existence of a massive public sector limits the private sector's ability to set wages and prices. The government limits the amount of profit earned on some imported goods and also is involved in setting wages. There is a minimum wage.

PROPERTY RIGHTS
Score: 3–Stable (moderate level of protection)

Egypt's privatization effort has bogged down. Although private property is protected by the constitution, the judiciary is inefficient. "In some instances," according to the U.S. Department of Commerce, "Government entities refuse for years to accept contractual requirements to arbitrate even if arbitration is explicitly written into the contract. Local lawyers insist, however, that the recalcitrant party cannot prevent indefinitely the initiation of arbitration. It requires time, sometimes numerous court proceedings which in many cases average five years to reach primary court decision, and sometimes numerous appeals to senior Government officials. Legal appeal procedures can extend court cases to 15 years or longer."[3]

REGULATION
Score: 4–Stable (high level)

Corruption is endemic and bribery is the norm in Egypt's bureaucracy, which is massive and inefficient. The business environment is over-regulated, with managers spending an estimated 30 percent of their time handling bureaucratic paperwork. The labor market is heavily regulated as well. According to the U.S. Department of Commerce, "Egypt's accounting system is not consistent with international norms. The often arbitrary imposition of bureaucratic impediments and the length of time which must be spent resolving them remain significant obstacles to increased private sector investment in Egypt."[4]

BLACK MARKET
Score: 3–Stable (moderate level of activity)

With its long commitment to a command economy, and with economic reform proceeding at a slow pace, Egypt retains a large black market. According to the U.S. Department of Commerce, "No reliable data exist on Egypt's large informal sector, which may account for 30% of economic activity and serves as the employer of last resort for many Egyptians."[5] Even though most goods are available in shops, substantial trade restrictions encourage smuggling.

NOTES

[1]   Office of the United States Trade Representative, *1998 National Trade Estimate Report on Foreign Trade Barriers*, 1998.
[2]   U.S. Department of Commerce, *Country Commercial Guide*, 1998.
[3]   *Ibid.*
[4]   *Ibid.*
[5]   *Ibid.*

El Salvador   2.25

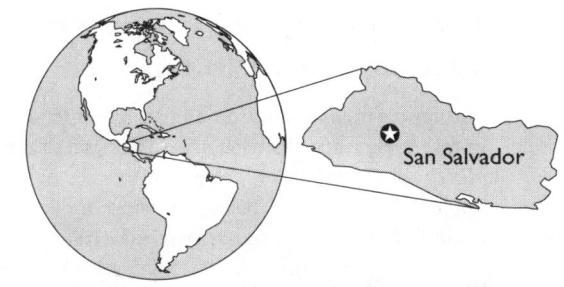

San Salvador

1998 Score: **2.45**	1997 Score: **2.55**	1996 Score: **2.45**

Trade	3	Banking	2
Taxation	2.5	Wages and Prices	2
Government Intervention	1	Property Rights	2
Monetary Policy	3	Regulation	3
Foreign Investment	1	Black Market	3

El Salvador suffered a terrible civil war in the 1980s. Despite massive infusions of foreign aid, its economy grew by an average of only 2 percent annually from 1982 to 1989. After peace was established in 1991, however, the government began to implement market reforms; the economy slowly began to recover, growing by about 6 percent annually between 1990 and 1997. Under President Alfredo Cristiani, the government abolished price controls, slashed import tariffs, privatized most of the financial system, and followed a relatively tight monetary policy. Although some problems remain, the economy continues to grow and shows signs of increasing prosperity. President Armando Calderon Sol has maintained Cristiani's reforms. El Salvador recently further liberalized its foreign investment laws and reformed its judiciary; as a result, its overall score is 0.2 point better than last year.

TRADE POLICY
Score: 3–Stable (moderate level of protectionism)

El Salvador recently slashed tariff rates and probably will continue to cut them through 1999. It now has an average tariff rate of 6 percent. Many non-tariff barriers also have been removed, but arbitrary sanitation requirements on poultry imports, as well as some non-tariff restrictions on selected agricultural imports, continue.

TAXATION
Score–Income taxation: 2–Stable (low tax rates)
Score–Corporate taxation: 2–Stable (low tax rates)
Final Taxation Score: 2.5–Stable (moderate tax rates)

El Salvador's top marginal income tax rate is 30 percent;[1] the rate for the average income level is 0 percent. The top corporate income tax rate is 25 percent. El Salvador also has a 13 percent value-added tax.

GOVERNMENT INTERVENTION IN THE ECONOMY
Score: 1–Stable (very low level)

Government consumes 7.7 percent of GDP, down from 14 percent in 1980. Recent legislation makes the country's telecommunications industry one of the most competitive in the world. Other privatization programs are nearly complete, and the government's role in the economy has been reduced significantly. El Salvador currently is privatizing its state-owned telephone company, four electricity companies, sugar mills, and the administration of its pension funds.

MONETARY POLICY
Score: 3–Stable (moderate level of inflation)

El Salvador's average annual rate of inflation from 1986 to 1996 was 15 percent. In 1997, the rate was 3.5 percent.

1	Hong Kong	1.25
2	Singapore	1.30
3	Bahrain	1.70
4	New Zealand	1.75
5	Switzerland	1.85
6	United States	1.90
7	Ireland	1.95
7	Luxembourg	1.95
7	Taiwan	1.95
7	United Kingdom	1.95
11	Bahamas	2.00
12	Czech Republic	2.05
12	Japan	2.05
14	Australia	2.10
14	Belgium	2.10
14	Canada	2.10
14	United Arab Emirates	2.10
18	Austria	2.15
18	Chile	2.15
18	Estonia	2.15
18	Netherlands	2.15
22	Denmark	2.25
22	El Salvador	2.25
22	Finland	2.25
25	Germany	2.30
25	Iceland	2.30
27	Norway	2.35
28	Korea, South	2.40
28	Kuwait	2.40
28	Malaysia	2.40
28	Panama	2.40
28	Thailand	2.40
33	Sweden	2.45
34	Argentina	2.50
34	France	2.50
34	Italy	2.50
34	Spain	2.50
38	Portugal	2.55
38	Sri Lanka	2.55
38	Trinidad and Tobago	2.55
41	Barbados	2.60
41	Peru	2.60
43	Bolivia	2.65
43	Mauritius	2.65
45	Cyprus	2.70
45	Jamaica	2.70
45	Uruguay	2.70
48	Botswana	2.75
48	Guatemala	2.75
48	Jordan	2.75
48	Namibia	2.75
48	Oman	2.75
48	Philippines	2.75
54	Belize	2.80
54	Costa Rica	2.80
54	Israel	2.80
54	Swaziland	2.80
54	Turkey	2.80
54	Uganda	2.80
54	Samoa	2.80
61	Latvia	2.85
62	Greece	2.90
62	Hungary	2.90
62	So. Africa	2.90
65	Ecuador	2.95
65	Gabon	2.95
65	Indonesia	2.95
65	Malta	2.95
65	Morocco	2.95
65	Poland	2.95
65	Tunisia	2.95
72	Ghana	3.00
72	Lithuania	3.00
72	Saudi Arabia	3.00
75	Benin	3.05
75	Kenya	3.05
75	Paraguay	3.05
75	Qatar	3.05
75	Slovak Republic	3.05
75	Zambia	3.05
81	Colombia	3.10
81	Fiji	3.10
81	Mali	3.10
81	Slovenia	3.10
85	Honduras	3.15
85	Mexico	3.15
85	Papua New Guinea	3.15
88	Djibouti	3.20
88	Mongolia	3.20
90	Algeria	3.25
90	Brazil	3.25
90	Lebanon	3.25
90	Senegal	3.25
90	Tanzania	3.25
95	Nigeria	3.30
95	Romania	3.30
97	Cambodia	3.35
97	Dominican Republic	3.35
97	Egypt	3.35
97	Guinea	3.35
97	Ivory Coast	3.35
97	Moldova	3.35
97	Pakistan	3.35
104	Nepal	3.40
104	Venezuela	3.40
106	Armenia	3.45
106	Bulgaria	3.45
106	Lesotho	3.45
106	Madagascar	3.45
106	Russia	3.45
111	Burkina Faso	3.50
111	Cameroon	3.50
111	Guyana	3.50
111	Nicaragua	3.50
115	Gambia	3.60
116	Croatia	3.65
116	Georgia	3.65
116	Malawi	3.65
119	Cape Verde	3.67
120	Ethiopia	3.70
120	India	3.70
120	Niger	3.70
123	Congo	3.75
124	Chad	3.80
124	China	3.80
124	Mauritania	3.80
124	Ukraine	3.80
124	Zimbabwe	3.80
129	Albania	3.85
129	Bangladesh	3.85
129	Mozambique	3.85
129	Suriname	3.85
133	Burundi	3.90
134	Togo	3.95
135	Haiti	4.00
135	Kyrgyz Rep.	4.00
137	Kazakhstan	4.05
137	Sierra Leone	4.05
139	Yemen	4.10
140	Belarus	4.15
141	Sudan	4.20
141	Syria	4.20
143	Azerbaijan	4.30
143	Equatorial Guinea	4.30
143	Myanmar	4.30
143	Rwanda	4.30
147	Tajikistan	4.40
147	Uzbekistan	4.40
149	Angola	4.45
149	Turkmenistan	4.45
151	Guinea-Bissau	4.55
152	Vietnam	4.60
153	Congo (Zaire)	4.70
153	Iran	4.70
155	Bosnia	4.80
155	Somalia	4.80
157	Iraq	4.90
157	Laos	4.90
157	Libya	4.90
160	Cuba	5.00
160	Korea, North	5.00

Mostly Free

CAPITAL FLOWS AND FOREIGN INVESTMENT
Score: 1+ (very low barriers)

Foreigners previously were able to invest in almost any enterprise except electricity. With the privatization of four electricity firms in 1997, however, this restriction no longer applies. As a result, El Salvador's score under this factor is 1 point better than it was last year. According to the U.S. Department of Commerce, "El Salvador has significantly reduced bureaucratic impediments to trade and investment in the last few years. It offers virtually unrestricted remittance of net profits for investors in industrial activities, a fixed tax rate for resident corporations, income tax exemption, and duty free importation of raw materials, intermediate products and machinery for free trade zone investors."[2]

BANKING
Score: 2–Stable (low level of restrictions)

Foreign banks are permitted to operate in El Salvador as though they were domestically owned. All restrictions on foreign banks have been removed, and most local and foreign banks are allowed to compete in offering a wide range of financial services. According to the U.S. Department of Commerce, "The Salvadoran banking system, which was state-owned from 1980 to 1990, is now controlled by private investors. In 1990 and 1991, the government implemented market-oriented reforms that encouraged competitiveness in the financial system."[3]

WAGE AND PRICE CONTROLS
Score: 2–Stable (low level)

The government has eliminated price controls on some 240 goods, although controls remain in effect for bus fares and utilities. El Salvador has a minimum wage.

PROPERTY RIGHTS
Score: 2+ (high level of protection)

The government has undertaken a massive privatization program and is returning banks, hotels, and other enterprises to the private sector. According to the U.S. Department of State, "The Constitution provides for an independent judiciary, and the Government respects this provision in practice."[4] This official report has replaced previous language claiming there was corruption in the judiciary. A report by the U.S. Department of Commerce adds, "Although the laws of El Salvador protect property rights, in practice, these laws are not always enforced even-handedly. The judicial system is being reformed, and corrupt judges and administrators generally have been removed from their posts. However, investors must be aware that the legal and regulatory system can act arbitrarily, and should take all due precautions to protect their property and investments."[5] In light of these recent improvements in property rights protection, El Salvador's property rights score this year is 1 point better than last year.

REGULATION
Score: 3–Stable (moderate level)

Because price controls have been abolished, the government maintains little regulatory control over most businesses. Even though the regulatory system is relative streamlined, however, there remain some instances in which red tape and bureaucracy can be burdensome. According to the U.S. Department of Commerce, "The laws and policies of El Salvador are relatively transparent and generally foster competition. Bureaucratic procedures, although cumbersome, have improved in recent years and are relatively streamlined for foreign investors."[6]

BLACK MARKET
Score: 3–Stable (moderate level of activity)

Some labor, such as construction, is provided by the black market. El Salvador's intellectual property laws suffer from a lack of enforcement, as well as from an inefficient bureaucracy.

NOTES
[1] The effective tax rate may not exceed 25 percent of taxable income.
[2] U.S. Department of Commerce, *Country Commercial Guide*, 1998.
[3] *Ibid.*
[4] U.S. Department of State, "El Salvador Country Report on Human Rights Practices for 1997," 1998
[5] U.S. Department of Commerce, *Country Commercial Guide*, 1998.
[6] *Ibid.*

Equatorial Guinea 4.30

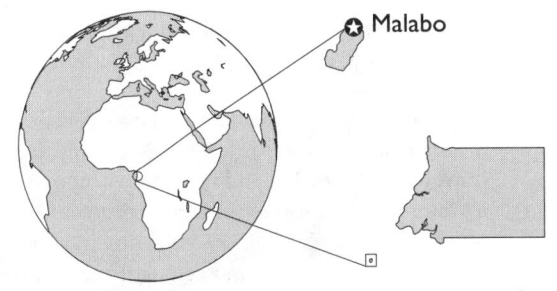
Malabo

| 1998 Score: **n/a** | 1997 Score: **n/a** | 1996 Score: **n/a** |

Trade	5	Banking	5
Taxation	5	Wages and Prices	5
Government Intervention	4	Property Rights	5
Monetary Policy	1	Regulation	4
Foreign Investment	4	Black Market	5

Equatorial Guinea was formed in 1963 with the joining of the provinces of Fernando Po and Rio Muni. It gained full independence from Spain in 1968. Opposition parties were banned in 1970, and the country has undergone several violent power struggles ever since. In 1992, a new law was passed to permit new opposition parties. The first multi-party elections were held in 1993, but some international observers question the democratic process in the country and criticize frequent human rights abuses.[1] Former dictator Teodoro Obiang Nguema M'basogo was re-elected to the presidency in a 1996 election that most opposition parties boycotted. Equatorial Guinea's economy is primarily agricultural: over 30 percent of GDP is derived from agriculture, forestry, and fishing. Petroleum is playing an increasing role, however, and GDP growth averaged a huge 17.2 percent from 1992 to 1996 largely because of the oil industry. Much of the economy remains in government hands and little economic liberalization has occurred.

TRADE POLICY
Score: 5–Stable (very high level of protectionism)

The average tariff rate is unavailable. Most imports, however, must be cleared through an inefficient and corrupt customs service that significantly adds to the cost of business activities. In addition, there is little infrastructure with which to conduct trade: Roads are in poor shape and often require four-wheel-drive vehicles to navigate them, and there are no commercial airports.

TAXATION
Score–Income taxation: 5–Stable (very high tax rates)
Score–Corporate taxation: 5–Stable (very high tax rates)
Final Taxation Score: 5–Stable (very high tax rates)

Equatorial Guinea has no known official tax rates. Most economic activity takes place in the form of barter. Government taxation often takes the form of confiscated property, bribes, extortion, and corruption.

GOVERNMENT INTERVENTION IN THE ECONOMY
Score: 4–Stable (high level)

Government consumes about 31 percent of GDP. Most economic activity is controlled by the government and government-owned companies, which produce most of the country's economic output. There is, however, a small and growing private sector. Of the 12 major enterprises the government owned in the early 1990s, 3 have been privatized in full.

MONETARY POLICY
Score: 1–Stable (very low level of inflation)

From 1986 to 1996, Equatorial Guinea's average annual rate of inflation was less than 4 percent. The rate for 1997 is not available.

1	Hong Kong	1.25		81	Fiji	3.10
2	Singapore	1.30		81	Mali	3.10
3	Bahrain	1.70		81	Slovenia	3.10
4	New Zealand	1.75		85	Honduras	3.15
5	Switzerland	1.85		85	Mexico	3.15
6	United States	1.90		85	Papua New Guinea	3.15
7	Ireland	1.95		88	Djibouti	3.20
7	Luxembourg	1.95		88	Mongolia	3.20
7	Taiwan	1.95		90	Algeria	3.25
7	United Kingdom	1.95		90	Brazil	3.25
11	Bahamas	2.00		90	Lebanon	3.25
12	Czech Republic	2.05		90	Senegal	3.25
12	Japan	2.05		90	Tanzania	3.25
14	Australia	2.10		95	Nigeria	3.30
14	Belgium	2.10		95	Romania	3.30
14	Canada	2.10		97	Cambodia	3.35
14	United Arab Emirates	2.10		97	Dominican Republic	3.35
18	Austria	2.15		97	Egypt	3.35
18	Chile	2.15		97	Guinea	3.35
18	Estonia	2.15		97	Ivory Coast	3.35
18	Netherlands	2.15		97	Moldova	3.35
22	Denmark	2.25		97	Pakistan	3.35
22	El Salvador	2.25		104	Nepal	3.40
22	Finland	2.25		104	Venezuela	3.40
25	Germany	2.30		106	Armenia	3.45
25	Iceland	2.30		106	Bulgaria	3.45
27	Norway	2.35		106	Lesotho	3.45
28	Korea, South	2.40		106	Madagascar	3.45
28	Kuwait	2.40		106	Russia	3.45
28	Malaysia	2.40		111	Burkina Faso	3.50
28	Panama	2.40		111	Cameroon	3.50
28	Thailand	2.40		111	Guyana	3.50
33	Sweden	2.45		111	Nicaragua	3.50
34	Argentina	2.50		115	Gambia	3.60
34	France	2.50		116	Croatia	3.65
34	Italy	2.50		116	Georgia	3.65
34	Spain	2.50		116	Malawi	3.65
38	Portugal	2.55		119	Cape Verde	3.67
38	Sri Lanka	2.55		120	Ethiopia	3.70
38	Trinidad and Tobago	2.55		120	India	3.70
41	Barbados	2.60		120	Niger	3.70
41	Peru	2.60		123	Congo	3.75
43	Bolivia	2.65		124	Chad	3.80
43	Mauritius	2.65		124	China	3.80
45	Cyprus	2.70		124	Mauritania	3.80
45	Jamaica	2.70		124	Ukraine	3.80
45	Uruguay	2.70		124	Zimbabwe	3.80
48	Botswana	2.75		129	Albania	3.85
48	Guatemala	2.75		129	Bangladesh	3.85
48	Jordan	2.75		129	Mozambique	3.85
48	Namibia	2.75		129	Suriname	3.85
48	Oman	2.75		133	Burundi	3.90
48	Philippines	2.75		134	Togo	3.95
54	Belize	2.80		135	Haiti	4.00
54	Costa Rica	2.80		135	Kyrgyz Rep.	4.00
54	Israel	2.80		137	Kazakhstan	4.05
54	Swaziland	2.80		137	Sierra Leone	4.05
54	Turkey	2.80		139	Yemen	4.10
54	Uganda	2.80		140	Belarus	4.15
54	Samoa	2.80		141	Sudan	4.20
61	Latvia	2.85		141	Syria	4.20
62	Greece	2.90		143	Azerbaijan	4.30
62	Hungary	2.90		143	Equatorial Guinea	4.30
62	So. Africa	2.90		143	Myanmar	4.30
65	Ecuador	2.95		143	Rwanda	4.30
65	Gabon	2.95		147	Tajikistan	4.40
65	Indonesia	2.95		147	Uzbekistan	4.40
65	Malta	2.95		149	Angola	4.45
65	Morocco	2.95		149	Turkmenistan	4.45
65	Poland	2.95		151	Guinea-Bissau	4.55
65	Tunisia	2.95		152	Vietnam	4.60
72	Ghana	3.00		153	Congo (Zaire)	4.70
72	Lithuania	3.00		153	Iran	4.70
72	Saudi Arabia	3.00		155	Bosnia	4.80
75	Benin	3.05		155	Somalia	4.80
75	Kenya	3.05		157	Iraq	4.90
75	Paraguay	3.05		157	Laos	4.90
75	Qatar	3.05		157	Libya	4.90
75	Slovak Republic	3.05		160	Cuba	5.00
75	Zambia	3.05		160	Korea, North	5.00
81	Colombia	3.10				

Repressed

CAPITAL FLOWS AND FOREIGN INVESTMENT
Score: 4–Stable (high barriers)

Equatorial Guinea has been opening its economy to foreign investment since the early 1990s. Many restrictions remain, however, both formal and informal. Although there is some investment, the process remains obscure and nontransparent. In addition, government approval for investment is required; and getting it can involve a tedious and corrupt process.

BANKING
Score: 5–Stable (very high level of restrictions)

The government owns most banks. The majority is either bankrupt or on the verge of bankruptcy, and few financial services are available. The government exercises significant control over the financial status of the country and rarely publishes public finance data. As the U.S. Department of State sums up, "The country's economic potential continues to be undermined by poor fiscal management and a lack of transparency in public finance."[2]

WAGE AND PRICE CONTROLS
Score: 5–Stable (very high level)

Little economic activity takes place using market-based pricing. In fact, most economic activity occurs in the form of barter. Barter is a "major aspect of the economy," according to the U.S. Department of State.[3]

PROPERTY RIGHTS
Score: 5–Stable (very low level of protection)

Although private property is not specifically outlawed, neither is it legally protected. Government corruption, an inefficient judiciary, and poor law enforcement all prevent legal protection. According to the U.S. Department of State, "The judiciary is not independent; judges serve at the pleasure of the President and are appointed, transferred, and dismissed for political reasons. Corruption is rampant."[4]

REGULATION
Score: 4–Stable (high level)

Regulations are neither transparent nor applied consistently. Rampant corruption places increased burdens on entrepreneurship.

BLACK MARKET
Score: 5–Stable (very high level of activity)

Equatorial Guinea has a huge black market, the size of which eclipses that of the formal market.

NOTES

[1]   U.S. Department of State, "Equatorial Guinea, Country Report on Human Rights Practices for 1997," 1998.
[2]   *Ibid.*
[3]   *Ibid.*
[4]   *Ibid.*

Estonia   2.15

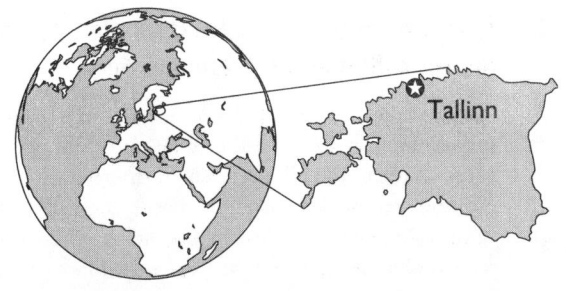

1998 Score: **2.15**	1997 Score: **2.35**	1996 Score: **2.35**

Trade	1	Banking	2
Taxation	3.5	Wages and Prices	2
Government Intervention	2	Property Rights	2
Monetary Policy	4	Regulation	2
Foreign Investment	1	Black Market	2

Estonia gained its independence in 1918, but the Soviet Union forcibly annexed it in 1940. The most Western-oriented country of the former Soviet Union, with a clear Scandinavian and North European orientation, Estonia has associate membership in the European Union and is applying for full membership. The government has undertaken a massive program of privatization, including the selling of many state-owned enterprises, and has established its own national currency, the kroon, which is both stable and convertible. The rate of inflation has fallen dramatically, and trade with the West has grown 500 percent since 1991. Mart Siimann, prime minister since 1997, and the government formed by the 1995 electoral victories of the Coalition Party and Rural People's Union plan further privatization.

TRADE POLICY
Score: 1–Stable (very low level of protectionism)

Estonia is essentially a duty-free country. There are few, if any, non-tariff barriers.

TAXATION
Score–Income taxation: 3–Stable (moderate tax rates)
Score–Corporate taxation: 3–Stable (moderate tax rates)
Final Taxation Score: 3.5–Stable (high tax rates)

Estonia has a flat income tax rate of 26 percent and a top corporate tax rate of 26 percent. It also has a 26 percent capital gains tax, an 18 percent value-added tax, a 20 percent social security tax, a 13 percent social insurance tax, and a 1 percent land tax.

GOVERNMENT INTERVENTION IN THE ECONOMY
Score: 2–Stable (low level)

Government consumes 24.7 percent of GDP, up from 16 percent in 1995. Estonia has been successful in privatizing many state-owned companies and continues to privatize remaining firms. For example, the largest privatization in Estonia to date is the sale of 70 percent of the government's stake in the Estonian Shipping Company.

MONETARY POLICY
Score: 4–Stable (high level of inflation)

Although inflation is historically high in Estonia because of the 1992 monetary crisis in the former Soviet Union, it has dropped dramatically over the past two years. In 1992, the annual rate of inflation was 1,069 percent. In 1993, it fell to about 89 percent; in 1994, it was 47 percent; in 1995, it fell to about 29 percent; in 1996, it fell again to about 23 percent; and in 1997, it fell to just 11.3 percent. Over all, however, the average rate of inflation since 1992 has remained high.

1	Hong Kong	1.25		81	Fiji	3.10
2	Singapore	1.30		81	Mali	3.10
3	Bahrain	1.70		81	Slovenia	3.10
4	New Zealand	1.75		85	Honduras	3.15
5	Switzerland	1.85		85	Mexico	3.15
6	United States	1.90		85	Papua New Guinea	3.15
7	Ireland	1.95		88	Djibouti	3.20
7	Luxembourg	1.95		88	Mongolia	3.20
7	Taiwan	1.95		90	Algeria	3.25
7	United Kingdom	1.95		90	Brazil	3.25
11	Bahamas	2.00		90	Lebanon	3.25
12	Czech Republic	2.05		90	Senegal	3.25
12	Japan	2.05		90	Tanzania	3.25
14	Australia	2.10		95	Nigeria	3.30
14	Belgium	2.10		95	Romania	3.30
14	Canada	2.10		97	Cambodia	3.35
14	United Arab Emirates	2.10		97	Dominican Republic	3.35
18	Austria	2.15		97	Egypt	3.35
18	Chile	2.15		97	Guinea	3.35
18	Estonia	2.15		97	Ivory Coast	3.35
18	Netherlands	2.15		97	Moldova	3.35
22	Denmark	2.25		97	Pakistan	3.35
22	El Salvador	2.25		104	Nepal	3.40
22	Finland	2.25		104	Venezuela	3.40
25	Germany	2.30		106	Armenia	3.45
25	Iceland	2.30		106	Bulgaria	3.45
27	Norway	2.35		106	Lesotho	3.45
28	Korea, South	2.40		106	Madagascar	3.45
28	Kuwait	2.40		106	Russia	3.45
28	Malaysia	2.40		111	Burkina Faso	3.50
28	Panama	2.40		111	Cameroon	3.50
28	Thailand	2.40		111	Guyana	3.50
33	Sweden	2.45		111	Nicaragua	3.50
34	Argentina	2.50		115	Gambia	3.60
34	France	2.50		116	Croatia	3.65
34	Italy	2.50		116	Georgia	3.65
34	Spain	2.50		116	Malawi	3.65
38	Portugal	2.55		119	Cape Verde	3.67
38	Sri Lanka	2.55		120	Ethiopia	3.70
38	Trinidad and Tobago	2.55		120	India	3.70
41	Barbados	2.60		120	Niger	3.70
41	Peru	2.60		123	Congo	3.75
43	Bolivia	2.65		124	Chad	3.80
43	Mauritius	2.65		124	China	3.80
45	Cyprus	2.70		124	Mauritania	3.80
45	Jamaica	2.70		124	Ukraine	3.80
45	Uruguay	2.70		124	Zimbabwe	3.80
48	Botswana	2.75		129	Albania	3.85
48	Guatemala	2.75		129	Bangladesh	3.85
48	Jordan	2.75		129	Mozambique	3.85
48	Namibia	2.75		129	Suriname	3.85
48	Oman	2.75		133	Burundi	3.90
48	Philippines	2.75		134	Togo	3.95
54	Belize	2.80		135	Haiti	4.00
54	Costa Rica	2.80		135	Kyrgyz Rep.	4.00
54	Israel	2.80		137	Kazakhstan	4.05
54	Swaziland	2.80		137	Sierra Leone	4.05
54	Turkey	2.80		139	Yemen	4.10
54	Uganda	2.80		140	Belarus	4.15
54	Samoa	2.80		141	Sudan	4.20
61	Latvia	2.85		141	Syria	4.20
62	Greece	2.90		143	Azerbaijan	4.30
62	Hungary	2.90		143	Equatorial Guinea	4.30
62	So. Africa	2.90		143	Myanmar	4.30
65	Ecuador	2.95		143	Rwanda	4.30
65	Gabon	2.95		147	Tajikistan	4.40
65	Indonesia	2.95		147	Uzbekistan	4.40
65	Malta	2.95		149	Angola	4.45
65	Morocco	2.95		149	Turkmenistan	4.45
65	Poland	2.95		151	Guinea-Bissau	4.55
65	Tunisia	2.95		152	Vietnam	4.60
72	Ghana	3.00		153	Congo (Zaire)	4.70
72	Lithuania	3.00		153	Iran	4.70
72	Saudi Arabia	3.00		155	Bosnia	4.80
75	Benin	3.05		155	Somalia	4.80
75	Kenya	3.05		157	Iraq	4.90
75	Paraguay	3.05		157	Laos	4.90
75	Qatar	3.05		157	Libya	4.90
75	Slovak Republic	3.05		160	Cuba	5.00
75	Zambia	3.05		160	Korea, North	5.00
81	Colombia	3.10				

Mostly Free

Capital Flows and Foreign Investment
Score: 1–Stable (very low barriers)

There are relatively few restrictions on foreign investors. Investments are permitted in all areas of industry, including some utilities, and all foreign investment ventures are granted "national treatment"; that is, they are treated the same as businesses owned by Estonians. There are no repatriation limitations that force investors to keep their capital in the country.

Banking
Score: 2–Stable (low level of restrictions)

Banks in Estonia have been made more accessible to foreign operation, and private banks are growing. There still are some restrictions, however, on banks' selling investments and securities.

Wage and Price Controls
Score: 2–Stable (low level)

The government has removed price controls on 95 percent of goods and services; the only remaining controls are on the prices of items like electricity and energy-producing agents like shale. There is a minimum wage.

Property Rights
Score: 2–Stable (high level of protection)

Estonia has made significant progress toward establishing an independent judiciary. According to the U.S. Department of State, "The Constitution establishes an independent judicial branch and the judiciary is independent in practice."[1] The court system and enforcement of court awards may be slightly inefficient, however.

Regulation
Score: 2–Stable (low level)

Some regulations are burdensome. Increased attention to health, safety, and the environment, as well as product testing and environmental standards, for example, inhibit business creation. Obtaining a business license, however, is relatively easy and corruption-free.

Black Market
Score: 2–Stable (low level of activity)

Because of reduced barriers to trade and a limited regulatory environment, the black market is shrinking. There had been widespread piracy in video and audio tapes and compact disks, but a recent government crackdown has reduced some of this activity. In addition, port authorities have focused their efforts on fighting corruption, which have resulted in a reduction in smuggling.

Note

[1] U.S. Department of State, "Estonia Country Report on Human Rights Practices for 1997," 1998

Ethiopia   3.70

1998 Score: **3.70**	1997 Score: **3.60**	1996 Score: **3.70**

Trade	5	Banking	4
Taxation	4	Wages and Prices	3
Government Intervention	3	Property Rights	4
Monetary Policy	2	Regulation	4
Foreign Investment	4	Black Market	4

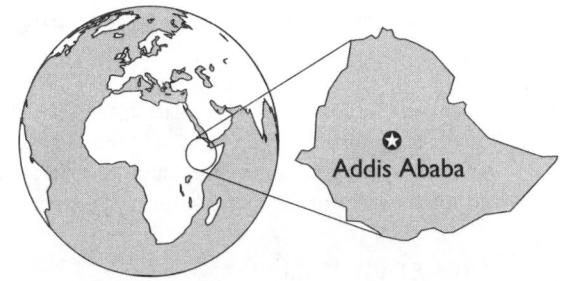

Addis Ababa

Years of civil war and Marxist economic policies have devastated Ethiopia, the second most populous country in sub-Saharan Africa—and one of the poorest, with an estimated per capita GNP of $100 in 1996. The Ethiopian People's Revolutionary Democratic Party seized power in 1991 after ousting the Marxist regime of Mengistu Haile Mariam. The transitional government of Prime Minister Meles Zenawi adopted a new constitution in December 1995. Democratic elections were held in 1995 but were boycotted by the major opposition parties. The province of Eritrea successfully declared its independence in 1993. Peace talks between the two countries are moving slowly: They have yet to resolve a border dispute, and conflict erupts sporadically. Ethiopia's government has made some strides on privatization, but has yet to take firm action on corruption or to reduce government expenditures. The economy is based primarily on agriculture; 85 percent of the population is employed in the agricultural sector. Annual GDP growth averaged 6.5. percent between 1992 and 1996.

TRADE POLICY

Score: 5–Stable (very high level of protectionism)

Although Ethiopia has liberalized trade somewhat, partly by eliminating the negative list of imports and lowering its maximum tariff to 50 percent, the average tariff rate is 25 percent.[1] The customs bureaucracy is cumbersome and inefficient, and delays in bringing goods into the country are not uncommon. As the U.S. Department of Commerce describes the problems: "Ethiopia levies fairly high customs duties on a wide range of imports, despite three reductions in the past two years.... There are no quantitative restrictions on imports, and import licensing requirements do not present a notable barrier to trade, although customs clearance remains a hindrance to the business of importing. Not only is the process of clearance slow, but imported goods are sometimes charged at an attributed value instead of at invoice values, even when the invoice has been certified by trade officials of the exporting country.... The Ministry of Trade and Industry has the power to restrict and/or limit imports and exports. There are restrictions on the importation of products which compete with locally produced goods, particularly in agricultural sectors. Automobile or motor vehicle imports require approval from the Ministry of Transport and Communications."[2]

TAXATION

Score–Income taxation: 5–Stable (very high tax rates)
Score–Corporate taxation: 3–Stable (moderate tax rates)
Total Taxation Score: 4–Stable (high tax rates)

Ethiopia recently reduced taxes, but its top income tax rate remains over 50 percent, and the average income level is taxed at rates higher than 25 percent. The corporate tax rate is 50 percent.[3]

#	Country	Score	#	Country	Score
1	Hong Kong	1.25	81	Fiji	3.10
2	Singapore	1.30	81	Mali	3.10
3	Bahrain	1.70	81	Slovenia	3.10
4	New Zealand	1.75	85	Honduras	3.15
5	Switzerland	1.85	85	Mexico	3.15
6	United States	1.90	85	Papua New Guinea	3.15
7	Ireland	1.95	88	Djibouti	3.20
7	Luxembourg	1.95	88	Mongolia	3.20
7	Taiwan	1.95	90	Algeria	3.25
7	United Kingdom	1.95	90	Brazil	3.25
11	Bahamas	2.00	90	Lebanon	3.25
12	Czech Republic	2.05	90	Senegal	3.25
12	Japan	2.05	90	Tanzania	3.25
14	Australia	2.10	95	Nigeria	3.30
14	Belgium	2.10	95	Romania	3.30
14	Canada	2.10	97	Cambodia	3.35
14	United Arab Emirates	2.10	97	Dominican Republic	3.35
18	Austria	2.15	97	Egypt	3.35
18	Chile	2.15	97	Guinea	3.35
18	Estonia	2.15	97	Ivory Coast	3.35
18	Netherlands	2.15	97	Moldova	3.35
22	Denmark	2.25	97	Pakistan	3.35
22	El Salvador	2.25	104	Nepal	3.40
22	Finland	2.25	104	Venezuela	3.40
25	Germany	2.30	106	Armenia	3.45
25	Iceland	2.30	106	Bulgaria	3.45
27	Norway	2.35	106	Lesotho	3.45
28	Korea, South	2.40	106	Madagascar	3.45
28	Kuwait	2.40	106	Russia	3.45
28	Malaysia	2.40	111	Burkina Faso	3.50
28	Panama	2.40	111	Cameroon	3.50
28	Thailand	2.40	111	Guyana	3.50
33	Sweden	2.45	111	Nicaragua	3.50
34	Argentina	2.50	115	Gambia	3.60
34	France	2.50	116	Croatia	3.65
34	Italy	2.50	116	Georgia	3.65
34	Spain	2.50	116	Malawi	3.65
38	Portugal	2.55	119	Cape Verde	3.67
38	Sri Lanka	2.55	120	Ethiopia	3.70
38	Trinidad and Tobago	2.55	120	India	3.70
41	Barbados	2.60	120	Niger	3.70
41	Peru	2.60	123	Congo	3.75
43	Bolivia	2.65	124	Chad	3.80
43	Mauritius	2.65	124	China	3.80
45	Cyprus	2.70	124	Mauritania	3.80
45	Jamaica	2.70	124	Ukraine	3.80
45	Uruguay	2.70	124	Zimbabwe	3.80
48	Botswana	2.75	129	Albania	3.85
48	Guatemala	2.75	129	Bangladesh	3.85
48	Jordan	2.75	129	Mozambique	3.85
48	Namibia	2.75	129	Suriname	3.85
48	Oman	2.75	133	Burundi	3.90
48	Philippines	2.75	134	Togo	3.95
54	Belize	2.80	135	Haiti	4.00
54	Costa Rica	2.80	135	Kyrgyz Rep.	4.00
54	Israel	2.80	137	Kazakhstan	4.05
54	Swaziland	2.80	137	Sierra Leone	4.05
54	Turkey	2.80	139	Yemen	4.10
54	Uganda	2.80	140	Belarus	4.15
54	Samoa	2.80	141	Sudan	4.20
61	Latvia	2.85	141	Syria	4.20
62	Greece	2.90	143	Azerbaijan	4.30
62	Hungary	2.90	143	Equatorial Guinea	4.30
62	So. Africa	2.90	143	Myanmar	4.30
65	Ecuador	2.95	143	Rwanda	4.30
65	Gabon	2.95	147	Tajikistan	4.40
65	Indonesia	2.95	147	Uzbekistan	4.40
65	Malta	2.95	149	Angola	4.45
65	Morocco	2.95	149	Turkmenistan	4.45
65	Poland	2.95	151	Guinea-Bissau	4.55
65	Tunisia	2.95	152	Vietnam	4.60
72	Ghana	3.00	153	Congo (Zaire)	4.70
72	Lithuania	3.00	153	Iran	4.70
72	Saudi Arabia	3.00	155	Bosnia	4.80
75	Benin	3.05	155	Somalia	4.80
75	Kenya	3.05	157	Iraq	4.90
75	Paraguay	3.05	157	Laos	4.90
75	Qatar	3.05	157	Libya	4.90
75	Slovak Republic	3.05	160	Cuba	5.00
75	Zambia	3.05	160	Korea, North	5.00
81	Colombia	3.10			

Mostly Unfree

GOVERNMENT INTERVENTION IN THE ECONOMY
Score: 3–Stable (moderate level)

Government consumes 12.3 percent of GDP. The industrial sector is dominated by 15 public enterprises, and progress with planned privatization has been slow. State enterprises account for almost all manufacturing production.

MONETARY POLICY
Score: 2–Stable (low level of inflation)

Historically, Ethiopia's inflation rate has been low. The average annual rate of inflation from 1986 through 1996 was only 4.6 percent, although this was artificially low because Ethiopia was a communist country until 1991.

CAPITAL FLOWS AND FOREIGN INVESTMENT
Score: 4–Stable (high barriers)

The government of Prime Minister Zenawi has made modest progress in dismantling the hostile foreign investment climate created by the previous Marxist regime. Sectors remaining off-limits to private investment include the defense industry, large-scale electric power generation, and postal, telecommunications, financial, some export/import, and major transportation services. Ethiopians are granted priority for investment opportunities, and bureaucratic decision-making is slow. According to the U.S. Department of Commerce, "Despite the new investment proclamation, some fields remain off limits for foreign investors: financial services (banking and insurance), large-scale power production (over 20 megawatts), telecommunications, other public utilities, and small-scale personal services. Some other areas are limited to foreign investors acting in partnership with domestic investors, such as engineering, metallurgical, pharmaceutical, basic chemical, petrochemical, and fertilizer industries."[4]

BANKING
Score: 4–Stable (high level of restrictions)

The financial sector, nationalized in 1975, has been liberalized, and private investment in banking and insurance was permitted in 1994. The dominant Commercial Bank of Ethiopia and the Ethiopian Insurance Corporation remain under full state ownership. Private investment is limited to newly established bank and insurance operations, of which a few were established last year; the latter remain of marginal importance. Limits on banking and insurance ownership apply to individuals and families, and the government allows no foreign ownership of banks. Foreign banks may not operate in the country, either. According to the U.S. Department of Commerce, "All transactions in foreign exchange must be carried out through authorized dealers under the control of the National Bank. All payments abroad require licenses issued by the Controller of Exchange."[5]

WAGE AND PRICE CONTROLS
Score: 3–Stable (moderate level)

Government-imposed price controls have been removed on all but a few products, although a slow and sometimes ineffective privatization program leaves large sections of the economy in government hands, often hindering price competition. State-owned retail and distribution companies, for example, reduce price and wage competition in these sectors because the government directly subsidizes their activities. Because the government owns many distribution companies, the prices on the goods they handle are affected negatively.

PROPERTY RIGHTS
Score: 4–Stable (low level of protection)

The Mengistu regime nationalized most industries and vast tracts of agricultural land, and the current government's failure to address adequately the status of rural land frustrates proposals for commercial agricultural development. Privatization of state farms is a long-term objective, but urban land will remain the property of the state, available to the private sector only through revocable long-term leases. Bureaucratic red tape and corruption further weaken property rights in Ethiopia. The judicial system remains subject to political influence. According to the U.S. Department of Commerce, "Secured interests in property are protected and enforced, although land ownership remains in the hands of the State.... Ethiopia's judicial system remains underdeveloped, although efforts are underway to strengthen its capacity. While property and contractual rights are recognized, and there are written commercial and bankruptcy laws, there is thus far no experience by which to judge the level of acceptance of foreign court rulings."[6] Property may be expropriated legally with compensation.

REGULATION
Score: 4–Stable (high level)

Impromptu police clearings of street stalls and other persecutions of merchants who threaten politically favored businesses are common. The business permit system is used to favor certain ethnic groups and is subject to corruption. Businesses targeted for government crackdowns include schools teaching computer skills, foreign languages, and typing. Ethiopia's regulatory regime greatly impedes legitimate business activity. The U.S. Department of Commerce reports that "Ethiopia presents many bureaucratic barriers to investors, which are frequently cited by U.S. business representatives as major problems. These include difficulties with customs clearance, obtaining telephone/fax service and public utility hookups, locating appropriate office space, leasing land, and obtaining work permits and various government offices and unsatisfactory coordination between federal and regional governments."[7]

BLACK MARKET
Score: 4–Stable (high level of activity)

Many legitimate economic activities, especially retailing, are driven underground by repressive authorities. There is considerable smuggling of coffee, fruits and vegetables, cigarettes, alcohol, textiles, and electronics. Because Ethiopia has no legal protection of many intellectual property products—for example, there are no trademark or patent laws—piracy is rampant.

NOTES

[1] Office of the United States Trade Representative, *National Trade Estimate Report of Foreign Trade Barriers,* 1998.

[2] U.S. Department of Commerce, *Country Commercial Guide,* 1998.

[3] Tax information from *Foreign Tax and Trade Briefs,* Matthew Bender and Co., Inc., June 1994.

[4] U.S. Department of Commerce, *Country Commercial Guide,* 1998.

[5] *Ibid.*

[6] *Ibid.*

[7] *Ibid.*

Fiji   3.10

1998 Score: **3.20**	1997 Score: **3.20**	1996 Score: **3.10**

Trade	5	Banking	3
Taxation	3	Wages and Prices	3
Government Intervention	3	Property Rights	3
Monetary Policy	1	Regulation	3
Foreign Investment	3	Black Market	4

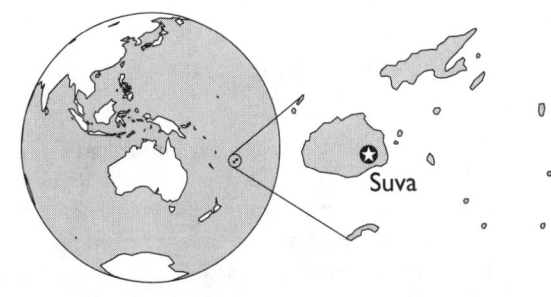

Suva

Fiji gained its independence from Great Britain in 1970 and shortly thereafter developed a democratic constitution. During the 1980s, however, several military coups occurred. This political instability has prevented Fiji from adopting significant, long-lasting economic reform and achieving sustained economic growth, although the government has reduced taxes and cut its consumption of GDP. According to the U.S. Department of Commerce, "Since the late 1980s, the Fiji Government has been pursuing policies aimed at deregulating the economy and reducing the role of the public sector. An important part of the reform package is reform of the public enterprise sector."[1] Fiji recently reduced its level of regulation. As a result, its overall score is 0.1 point better than last year.

TRADE POLICY
Score: 5–Stable (very high level of protectionism)

Fiji's average tariff rate is 16 percent.[2] Its many non-tariff barriers include special licenses. According to the U.S. Department of Commerce, "Most goods may be imported without an import license. Products subject to specific import licensing are powdered milk, bulk butter, seed potatoes, rice, coffee, canned fish, lubricants, transformer and circuit breaker oils, cleansing oils and hydraulic brake oils."[3]

TAXATION
Score–Income taxation: 2–Stable (low tax rates)
Score–Corporate taxation: 3–Stable (moderate tax rates)
Final Taxation Score: 3–Stable (moderate tax rates)

Fiji's top income tax rate is 35 percent; the tax rate for the average income is 0 percent. The top corporate income tax rate is 35 percent. Fiji also has a 10 percent value-added tax and a social contributions tax ranging between 7 percent and 23 percent.

GOVERNMENT INTERVENTION IN THE ECONOMY
Score: 3–Stable (moderate level)

Government consumes 20 percent of GDP. The government continues to own many companies in various industries, including banking.

MONETARY POLICY
Score: 1–Stable (very low level of inflation)

Fiji's average annual rate of inflation from 1986 to 1996 was 5.5 percent. The inflation rate for 1997 is unavailable. Fiji devalued its currency by 20 percent in January 1998 in response to the currency devaluations in East Asia. This may have a long-term impact on inflation.

1	Hong Kong	1.25	81	Fiji	3.10
2	Singapore	1.30	81	Mali	3.10
3	Bahrain	1.70	81	Slovenia	3.10
4	New Zealand	1.75	85	Honduras	3.15
5	Switzerland	1.85	85	Mexico	3.15
6	United States	1.90	85	Papua New Guinea	3.15
7	Ireland	1.95	88	Djibouti	3.20
7	Luxembourg	1.95	88	Mongolia	3.20
7	Taiwan	1.95	90	Algeria	3.25
7	United Kingdom	1.95	90	Brazil	3.25
11	Bahamas	2.00	90	Lebanon	3.25
12	Czech Republic	2.05	90	Senegal	3.25
12	Japan	2.05	90	Tanzania	3.25
14	Australia	2.10	95	Nigeria	3.30
14	Belgium	2.10	95	Romania	3.30
14	Canada	2.10	97	Cambodia	3.35
14	United Arab Emirates	2.10	97	Dominican Republic	3.35
18	Austria	2.15	97	Egypt	3.35
18	Chile	2.15	97	Guinea	3.35
18	Estonia	2.15	97	Ivory Coast	3.35
18	Netherlands	2.15	97	Moldova	3.35
22	Denmark	2.25	97	Pakistan	3.35
22	El Salvador	2.25	104	Nepal	3.40
22	Finland	2.25	104	Venezuela	3.40
25	Germany	2.30	106	Armenia	3.45
25	Iceland	2.30	106	Bulgaria	3.45
27	Norway	2.35	106	Lesotho	3.45
28	Korea, South	2.40	106	Madagascar	3.45
28	Kuwait	2.40	106	Russia	3.45
28	Malaysia	2.40	111	Burkina Faso	3.50
28	Panama	2.40	111	Cameroon	3.50
28	Thailand	2.40	111	Guyana	3.50
33	Sweden	2.45	111	Nicaragua	3.50
34	Argentina	2.50	115	Gambia	3.60
34	France	2.50	116	Croatia	3.65
34	Italy	2.50	116	Georgia	3.65
34	Spain	2.50	116	Malawi	3.65
38	Portugal	2.55	119	Cape Verde	3.67
38	Sri Lanka	2.55	120	Ethiopia	3.70
38	Trinidad and Tobago	2.55	120	India	3.70
41	Barbados	2.60	120	Niger	3.70
41	Peru	2.60	123	Congo	3.75
43	Bolivia	2.65	124	Chad	3.80
43	Mauritius	2.65	124	China	3.80
45	Cyprus	2.70	124	Mauritania	3.80
45	Jamaica	2.70	124	Ukraine	3.80
45	Uruguay	2.70	124	Zimbabwe	3.80
48	Botswana	2.75	129	Albania	3.85
48	Guatemala	2.75	129	Bangladesh	3.85
48	Jordan	2.75	129	Mozambique	3.85
48	Namibia	2.75	129	Suriname	3.85
48	Oman	2.75	133	Burundi	3.90
48	Philippines	2.75	134	Togo	3.95
54	Belize	2.80	135	Haiti	4.00
54	Costa Rica	2.80	135	Kyrgyz Rep.	4.00
54	Israel	2.80	137	Kazakhstan	4.05
54	Swaziland	2.80	137	Sierra Leone	4.05
54	Turkey	2.80	139	Yemen	4.10
54	Uganda	2.80	140	Belarus	4.15
54	Samoa	2.80	141	Sudan	4.20
61	Latvia	2.85	141	Syria	4.20
62	Greece	2.90	143	Azerbaijan	4.30
62	Hungary	2.90	143	Equatorial Guinea	4.30
62	So. Africa	2.90	143	Myanmar	4.30
65	Ecuador	2.95	143	Rwanda	4.30
65	Gabon	2.95	147	Tajikistan	4.40
65	Indonesia	2.95	147	Uzbekistan	4.40
65	Malta	2.95	149	Angola	4.45
65	Morocco	2.95	149	Turkmenistan	4.45
65	Poland	2.95	151	Guinea-Bissau	4.55
65	Tunisia	2.95	152	Vietnam	4.60
72	Ghana	3.00	153	Congo (Zaire)	4.70
72	Lithuania	3.00	153	Iran	4.70
72	Saudi Arabia	3.00	155	Bosnia	4.80
75	Benin	3.05	155	Somalia	4.80
75	Kenya	3.05	157	Iraq	4.90
75	Paraguay	3.05	157	Laos	4.90
75	Qatar	3.05	157	Libya	4.90
75	Slovak Republic	3.05	160	Cuba	5.00
75	Zambia	3.05	160	Korea, North	5.00
81	Colombia	3.10			

Mostly Unfree

CAPITAL FLOWS AND FOREIGN INVESTMENT
Score: 3–Stable (moderate barriers)

There are many restrictions on foreign investment in Fiji. The government does not permit foreign investors to buy into and gain a controlling share in any domestically owned business, and it must approve all investments. Most foreign-owned enterprises are discouraged from seeking local financing. According to the U.S. Department of Commerce, "Government approval (through the Ministry of Finance) is required for all foreign investment in Fiji. Investment proposals are assessed in light of their contribution to the following national objectives: assist in developing Fiji on a sound economic basis; create employment and income-earning opportunities; promote an equitable distribution of the benefits of development and improve standards of living; contribute to skill development and training of locals; and, involve maximum processing of products in Fiji."[4] Fiji does conform to an established foreign investment code, however; and, by global standards, Fiji's barriers to foreign investment are moderate.

BANKING
Score: 3–Stable (moderate level of restrictions)

Fiji has few direct restrictions on banking. Although the government's ownership of banks inhibits competition, there is a growing private banking industry. Some local banks are encouraged not to lend to foreign-owned enterprises.

WAGE AND PRICE CONTROLS
Score: 3–Stable (moderate level)

Fiji maintains price controls on a select group of commodities and consumer goods. It also has a minimum wage.

PROPERTY RIGHTS
Score: 3–Stable (moderate level of protection)

Property expropriation in Fiji remains possible. According to the U.S. Department of State, "The judiciary is independent under the Constitution and in practice."[5] But the Economist Intelligence Unit reports that "Fijian lawyers have expressed concern about the administration of the higher court and magisterial court systems. Some judges have also criticized the long delays, procedural irregularities and the incompetence of court staff and even magistrates."[6]

REGULATION
Score: 3+ (moderate level)

Fiji's economy slowly is becoming deregulated. For example, according to the U.S. Department of Commerce, "Generally the government has removed excessive controls and regulations to encourage risk-taking and improve efficiency and productivity. The size of the government in relation to the private sector has shrunk since 1990, giving a wider range of choices for consumers and eliminating some bureaucratic red tape."[7] As a result, Fiji's regulation score is 1 point better than it was last year. Some regulatory burdens continue, however, including the government's strict monitoring of prices and inefficiency in the bureaucracy.

BLACK MARKET
Score: 4–Stable (high level of activity)

Fiji's relatively closed market for imports creates a substantial black market in smuggled items. There is rampant piracy of such intellectual property as video and sound recordings and motion pictures.

NOTES
[1] U.S. Department of Commerce, *Country Commercial Guide*, 1998.
[2] The World Bank, *World Development Indicators 1998*, 1998.
[3] U.S. Department of Commerce, *Country Commercial Guide*, 1998.
[4] *Ibid.*
[5] U.S. Department of State, "Fiji Report on Human Rights Practices for 1996," 1997.
[6] Economist Intelligence Unit, *Country Report, Fiji*, 1997.
[7] U.S. Department of Commerce, *Country Commercial Guide*, 1998.

Finland   2.25

1998 Score: **2.25**   1997 Score: **2.30**   1996 Score: **2.30**

Trade	2	Banking	3
Taxation	4.5	Wages and Prices	2
Government Intervention	3	Property Rights	1
Monetary Policy	1	Regulation	3
Foreign Investment	2	Black Market	1

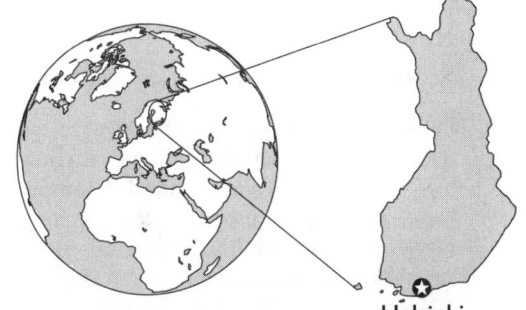

Helsinki

Once part of Sweden, Finland fought both the Soviet Union and Germany during World War II. During the Cold War, it adopted a policy of neutrality between East and West. Finland has been ruled by coalition governments for most of the post–World War II period. The economic depression in Russia (Finland's major trading partner) after the dissolution of the Soviet Union contributed to the shrinkage of 13 percent in Finland's economy from 1990 to 1993. In 1995, Finland joined the European Union (EU). Its economy now is recovering and may reach annual growth rates of 4 percent over the next several years.

TRADE POLICY
Score: 2–Stable (low level of protectionism)

Finland's average tariff rate is 5.9 percent, which is slightly higher than the average for members of the EU; its trade restrictions are the same as those of other EU members. Most non-tariff barriers, including import licensing, have been eliminated.

TAXATION
Score–Income taxation: 5–Stable (very high tax rates)
Score–Corporate taxation: 3–Stable (moderate tax rates)
Final Taxation Score: 4.5–Stable (very high tax rates)

Finland's top income tax rate is 56 percent; the average taxpayer is in the 26 percent bracket. The top marginal corporate tax rate is 28 percent. The government also imposes many other taxes, including a 28 percent capital gains tax and a 22 percent value-added tax.

GOVERNMENT INTERVENTION IN THE ECONOMY
Score: 3–Stable (moderate level)

Government consumes 20.8 percent of GDP. Its presence in the economy is considerable, however: State-owned companies comprise almost 19 percent of GDP, and the government owns shares in many Finnish companies. According to the U.S. Department of State, "[F]our of Finland's ten largest companies are majority state-owned."[1]

MONETARY POLICY
Score: 1–Stable (very low level of inflation)

Finland's rate of inflation averaged 3.8 percent from 1986 to 1996. In 1997, the inflation rate was 1.2 percent.

CAPITAL FLOWS AND FOREIGN INVESTMENT
Score: 2–Stable (low barriers)

Finland welcomes foreign investment, although there are some restrictions on investments in areas related to national security, transportation, and mining.

1	Hong Kong	1.25	
2	Singapore	1.30	
3	Bahrain	1.70	
4	New Zealand	1.75	
5	Switzerland	1.85	
6	United States	1.90	
7	Ireland	1.95	
7	Luxembourg	1.95	
7	Taiwan	1.95	
7	United Kingdom	1.95	
11	Bahamas	2.00	
12	Czech Republic	2.05	
12	Japan	2.05	
14	Australia	2.10	
14	Belgium	2.10	
14	Canada	2.10	
14	United Arab Emirates	2.10	
18	Austria	2.15	
18	Chile	2.15	
18	Estonia	2.15	
18	Netherlands	2.15	
22	Denmark	2.25	
22	El Salvador	2.25	
22	Finland	2.25	
25	Germany	2.30	
25	Iceland	2.30	
27	Norway	2.35	
28	Korea, South	2.40	
28	Kuwait	2.40	
28	Malaysia	2.40	
28	Panama	2.40	
28	Thailand	2.40	
33	Sweden	2.45	
34	Argentina	2.50	
34	France	2.50	
34	Italy	2.50	
34	Spain	2.50	
38	Portugal	2.55	
38	Sri Lanka	2.55	
38	Trinidad and Tobago	2.55	
41	Barbados	2.60	
41	Peru	2.60	
43	Bolivia	2.65	
43	Mauritius	2.65	
45	Cyprus	2.70	
45	Jamaica	2.70	
45	Uruguay	2.70	
48	Botswana	2.75	
48	Guatemala	2.75	
48	Jordan	2.75	
48	Namibia	2.75	
48	Oman	2.75	
48	Philippines	2.75	
54	Belize	2.80	
54	Costa Rica	2.80	
54	Israel	2.80	
54	Swaziland	2.80	
54	Turkey	2.80	
54	Uganda	2.80	
54	Samoa	2.80	
61	Latvia	2.85	
62	Greece	2.90	
62	Hungary	2.90	
62	So. Africa	2.90	
65	Ecuador	2.95	
65	Gabon	2.95	
65	Indonesia	2.95	
65	Malta	2.95	
65	Morocco	2.95	
65	Poland	2.95	
65	Tunisia	2.95	
72	Ghana	3.00	
72	Lithuania	3.00	
72	Saudi Arabia	3.00	
75	Benin	3.05	
75	Kenya	3.05	
75	Paraguay	3.05	
75	Qatar	3.05	
75	Slovak Republic	3.05	
75	Zambia	3.05	
81	Colombia	3.10	
81	Fiji	3.10	
81	Mali	3.10	
81	Slovenia	3.10	
85	Honduras	3.15	
85	Mexico	3.15	
85	Papua New Guinea	3.15	
88	Djibouti	3.20	
88	Mongolia	3.20	
90	Algeria	3.25	
90	Brazil	3.25	
90	Lebanon	3.25	
90	Senegal	3.25	
90	Tanzania	3.25	
95	Nigeria	3.30	
95	Romania	3.30	
97	Cambodia	3.35	
97	Dominican Republic	3.35	
97	Egypt	3.35	
97	Guinea	3.35	
97	Ivory Coast	3.35	
97	Moldova	3.35	
97	Pakistan	3.35	
104	Nepal	3.40	
104	Venezuela	3.40	
106	Armenia	3.45	
106	Bulgaria	3.45	
106	Lesotho	3.45	
106	Madagascar	3.45	
106	Russia	3.45	
111	Burkina Faso	3.50	
111	Cameroon	3.50	
111	Guyana	3.50	
111	Nicaragua	3.50	
115	Gambia	3.60	
116	Croatia	3.65	
116	Georgia	3.65	
116	Malawi	3.65	
119	Cape Verde	3.67	
120	Ethiopia	3.70	
120	India	3.70	
120	Niger	3.70	
123	Congo	3.75	
124	Chad	3.80	
124	China	3.80	
124	Mauritania	3.80	
124	Ukraine	3.80	
124	Zimbabwe	3.80	
129	Albania	3.85	
129	Bangladesh	3.85	
129	Mozambique	3.85	
129	Suriname	3.85	
133	Burundi	3.90	
134	Togo	3.95	
135	Haiti	4.00	
135	Kyrgyz Rep.	4.00	
137	Kazakhstan	4.05	
137	Sierra Leone	4.05	
139	Yemen	4.10	
140	Belarus	4.15	
141	Sudan	4.20	
141	Syria	4.20	
143	Azerbaijan	4.30	
143	Equatorial Guinea	4.30	
143	Myanmar	4.30	
143	Rwanda	4.30	
147	Tajikistan	4.40	
147	Uzbekistan	4.40	
149	Angola	4.45	
149	Turkmenistan	4.45	
151	Guinea-Bissau	4.55	
152	Vietnam	4.60	
153	Congo (Zaire)	4.70	
153	Iran	4.70	
155	Bosnia	4.80	
155	Somalia	4.80	
157	Iraq	4.90	
157	Laos	4.90	
157	Libya	4.90	
160	Cuba	5.00	
160	Korea, North	5.00	

Mostly Free

BANKING
Score: 3–Stable (moderate level of restrictions)

Finland's banking system generally is in line with the rest of the EU. Even though the government continues to own (or has ownership stakes in) banks that compete with private banks, the industry is open to foreign competition. Banks may engage in some financial services, such as the buying and selling of securities.

WAGE AND PRICE CONTROLS
Score: 2–Stable (low level)

Finland's market sets wages and prices, but the government can control prices through massive transfers of subsidies to such sectors as agriculture and manufacturing. It also can control the prices of some pharmaceuticals through its medical reimbursement programs; drugs subject to government reimbursement must abide by government-established pricing standards.

PROPERTY RIGHTS
Score: 1–Stable (very high level of protection)

Private property is safe in Finland. The legal and judicial system is efficient, and there is no history of government expropriation. According to the U.S. Department of State, "The Constitution provides an independent judiciary, and the Government respects this provision in practice."[2]

REGULATION
Score: 3–Stable (moderate level)

Establishing a business is a simple process. Regulations are applied evenly in most cases, although increased regulation, primarily in financial services, is making it more difficult to acquire the capital needed to expand or open new businesses. Finland still maintains onerous health, safety, and employment requirements. The U.S. Department of State characterizes the country's health and safety laws as "among the strictest in the world."[3]

BLACK MARKET
Score: 1–Stable (very low level of activity)

The size of Finland's black market is negligible. The laws that protect intellectual property are very strong, and the levels of computer software and prerecorded music and video piracy are among the world's lowest.

NOTES

[1] U.S. Department of State, *Country Reports on Economic Policy and Trade Practices,* 1998
[2] U.S. Department of State, "Finland Country Report on Human Rights Practices for 1997," 1998.
[3] U.S. Department of State, *Country Reports on Economic Policy and Trade Practices,* 1998.

France   2.50

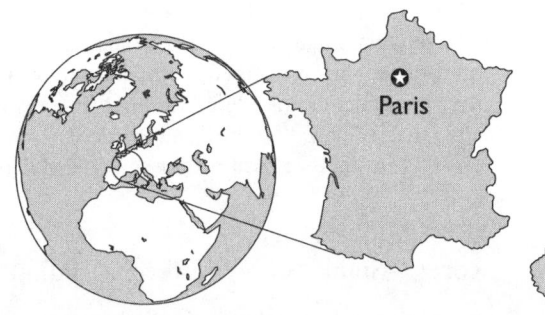

Paris

1998 Score: **2.50**	1997 Score: **2.50**	1996 Score: **2.30**

Trade	2	Banking	3
Taxation	5	Wages and Prices	3
Government Intervention	3	Property Rights	2
Monetary Policy	1	Regulation	2
Foreign Investment	3	Black Market	1

France is a founding member of the European Union (EU) and has the world's fourth largest industrialized economy. Although essentially a free market, France has a history of centralized administrative control over many parts of its economy. After getting elected to the presidency in May 1995, Jacques Chirac appointed Alain Juppe to the prime minister's post to lead a center-right coalition of the Rally for the Republic and the Union for a Democratic France in the National Assembly. Juppe's government took some cautious steps toward economic liberalization, but its major focus was on reducing France's budget deficit through spending cuts and tax increases to meet Maastricht Treaty criteria for budget deficits and government debt and to qualify for the monetary union. In June 1997, voters rejected the center-right coalition and returned a leftist majority composed of the Socialist, Communist, and Green Parties. At this point, Chirac was forced to appoint the Socialist Party's Lionel Jospin to the prime minister's post.

TRADE POLICY
Score: 2–Stable (low level of protectionism)

Because France is a member of the EU, its trade policy is the same as those of other EU members. Imports are subject to the common EU external tariff of 3.6 percent. Even though economic integration has reduced some trade barriers, it has raised others. Particularly affected are electronics, audio-visual products, telecommunications equipment, medical and veterinary equipment, and agricultural products.

TAXATION
Score–Income taxation: 5–Stable (very high tax rates)
Score–Corporate taxation: 4–Stable (high tax rates)
Final Taxation Score: 5–Stable (very high tax rates)

France's top income tax rate is 52 percent; the rate for the average income is 32 percent. The corporate tax is 33.33 percent. The government also imposes a capital gains tax of 19 percent to 33.33 percent, a value-added tax of 20.6 percent, a business activity tax of up to 22 percent, and a social contributions tax of 12 percent to 45 percent.

GOVERNMENT INTERVENTION IN THE ECONOMY
Score: 3–Stable (moderate level)

Government consumes 19.6 percent of GDP. The government has monopoly control over several parts of the economy, such as energy generation and supply, rail transportation, postal services, telecommunications, and tobacco production and distribution. Attempts to privatize some of these and other industries have failed. State-owned companies dominate various industrial sectors, skewing pricing and adding inefficiency to the entire economy. In 1996, reports the U.S. Department of Commerce, "total general government outlays amounted to over 54% of GDP. According to a study, 70 state-owned enterprises accounted for approximately 30% of GDP at the beginning of 1993. Privatizations since 1993

1	Hong Kong	1.25	81	Fiji	3.10
2	Singapore	1.30	81	Mali	3.10
3	Bahrain	1.70	81	Slovenia	3.10
4	New Zealand	1.75	85	Honduras	3.15
5	Switzerland	1.85	85	Mexico	3.15
6	United States	1.90	85	Papua New Guinea	3.15
7	Ireland	1.95	88	Djibouti	3.20
7	Luxembourg	1.95	88	Mongolia	3.20
7	Taiwan	1.95	90	Algeria	3.25
7	United Kingdom	1.95	90	Brazil	3.25
11	Bahamas	2.00	90	Lebanon	3.25
12	Czech Republic	2.05	90	Senegal	3.25
12	Japan	2.05	90	Tanzania	3.25
14	Australia	2.10	95	Nigeria	3.30
14	Belgium	2.10	95	Romania	3.30
14	Canada	2.10	97	Cambodia	3.35
14	United Arab Emirates	2.10	97	Dominican Republic	3.35
18	Austria	2.15	97	Egypt	3.35
18	Chile	2.15	97	Guinea	3.35
18	Estonia	2.15	97	Ivory Coast	3.35
18	Netherlands	2.15	97	Moldova	3.35
22	Denmark	2.25	97	Pakistan	3.35
22	El Salvador	2.25	104	Nepal	3.40
22	Finland	2.25	104	Venezuela	3.40
25	Germany	2.30	106	Armenia	3.45
25	Iceland	2.30	106	Bulgaria	3.45
27	Norway	2.35	106	Lesotho	3.45
28	Korea, South	2.40	106	Madagascar	3.45
28	Kuwait	2.40	106	Russia	3.45
28	Malaysia	2.40	111	Burkina Faso	3.50
28	Panama	2.40	111	Cameroon	3.50
28	Thailand	2.40	111	Guyana	3.50
33	Sweden	2.45	111	Nicaragua	3.50
34	Argentina	2.50	115	Gambia	3.60
34	France	2.50	116	Croatia	3.65
34	Italy	2.50	116	Georgia	3.65
34	Spain	2.50	116	Malawi	3.65
38	Portugal	2.55	119	Cape Verde	3.67
38	Sri Lanka	2.55	120	Ethiopia	3.70
38	Trinidad and Tobago	2.55	120	India	3.70
41	Barbados	2.60	120	Niger	3.70
41	Peru	2.60	123	Congo	3.75
43	Bolivia	2.65	124	Chad	3.80
43	Mauritius	2.65	124	China	3.80
45	Cyprus	2.70	124	Mauritania	3.80
45	Jamaica	2.70	124	Ukraine	3.80
45	Uruguay	2.70	124	Zimbabwe	3.80
48	Botswana	2.75	129	Albania	3.85
48	Guatemala	2.75	129	Bangladesh	3.85
48	Jordan	2.75	129	Mozambique	3.85
48	Namibia	2.75	129	Suriname	3.85
48	Oman	2.75	133	Burundi	3.90
48	Philippines	2.75	134	Togo	3.95
54	Belize	2.80	135	Haiti	4.00
54	Costa Rica	2.80	135	Kyrgyz Rep.	4.00
54	Israel	2.80	137	Kazakhstan	4.05
54	Swaziland	2.80	137	Sierra Leone	4.05
54	Turkey	2.80	139	Yemen	4.10
54	Uganda	2.80	140	Belarus	4.15
54	Samoa	2.80	141	Sudan	4.20
61	Latvia	2.85	141	Syria	4.20
62	Greece	2.90	143	Azerbaijan	4.30
62	Hungary	2.90	143	Equatorial Guinea	4.30
62	So. Africa	2.90	143	Myanmar	4.30
65	Ecuador	2.95	143	Rwanda	4.30
65	Gabon	2.95	147	Tajikistan	4.40
65	Indonesia	2.95	147	Uzbekistan	4.40
65	Malta	2.95	149	Angola	4.45
65	Morocco	2.95	149	Turkmenistan	4.45
65	Poland	2.95	151	Guinea-Bissau	4.55
65	Tunisia	2.95	152	Vietnam	4.60
72	Ghana	3.00	153	Congo (Zaire)	4.70
72	Lithuania	3.00	153	Iran	4.70
72	Saudi Arabia	3.00	155	Bosnia	4.80
75	Benin	3.05	155	Somalia	4.80
75	Kenya	3.05	157	Iraq	4.90
75	Paraguay	3.05	157	Laos	4.90
75	Qatar	3.05	157	Libya	4.90
75	Slovak Republic	3.05	160	Cuba	5.00
75	Zambia	3.05	160	Korea, North	5.00
81	Colombia	3.10			

Mostly Free

have somewhat reduced the economic role of state-owned enterprises, which nonetheless remains strong. The government maintains a large presence in industries such as aeronautics, defense, banking, insurance and manufacturing, and can still exert control over privatized firms."[1]

MONETARY POLICY
Score: 1–Stable (very low level of inflation)

France's average annual rate of inflation from 1986 to 1996 was 2.8 percent. In 1997, the rate was 1.3 percent.

CAPITAL FLOWS AND FOREIGN INVESTMENT
Score: 3–Stable (moderate barriers)

EU directives determine much of France's investment policy, but the government places additional restrictions on investments. According to the U.S. Department of Commerce, "[W]hile today's foreign investors face much less interference from government officials than was once the case, over a decade of rapid deregulation has not entirely overcome the French state's very old tradition of extensive control of business and the economy."[2]

BANKING
Score: 3–Stable (moderate level of restrictions)

Although France has made significant progress toward reforming its banking industry, increasing competition, and opening many financial services to foreign banks, the government remains a major player in this industry. According to the U.S. Department of Commerce, "The French government has sold its equity stake in major banks and insurance companies. However, it retains ownership in several major financial institutions, such as Credit Agricole, Credit Lyonnais and the Caisse des Depots et Consignations (CDC)."[3]

WAGE AND PRICE CONTROLS
Score: 3–Stable (moderate level)

France has a long history of legalized monopolies in such areas as telecommunications, public infrastructure, electricity, and rail transportation. In 1987, the government removed price controls, and the market began to set most prices. Products still subject to price controls are pharmaceuticals, books, agricultural products, and electricity. France has a minimum wage, and the government still controls some wages.

PROPERTY RIGHTS
Score: 2–Stable (high level of protection)

Property rights are uniform throughout France, and enforcement is adequate. There are some impediments, however, to acquiring property. The constitution states that any company defined as a national public service or natural monopoly must pass into state ownership. It also allows the state to nationalize companies that fall into this category. Both in practice and by global standards, however, the level of property protection is high.

REGULATION
Score: 2–Stable (low level)

EU reforms have made it easier to open a business. Obtaining a business license is relatively easy, although some hurdles still must be overcome. A company must obtain a registration number from the district commercial court, and a copy of its lease and other documentation must accompany the application. The government has helped to streamline this cumbersome process by incorporating all the registration requirements into one office.

BLACK MARKET
Score: 1–Stable (very low level of activity)

The principal areas of black market activity are gambling and the buying and selling of illegal weapons, drugs, and stolen merchandise.

NOTES

[1] U.S. Department of Commerce, *Country Commercial Guide,* 1998.
[2] *Ibid.*
[3] *Ibid.*

Gabon   2.95

1998 Score: **2.95**   1997 Score: **2.95**   1996 Score: **3.06**

Trade	5	Banking	2
Taxation	4.5	Wages and Prices	3
Government Intervention	3	Property Rights	3
Monetary Policy	1	Regulation	3
Foreign Investment	2	Black Market	3

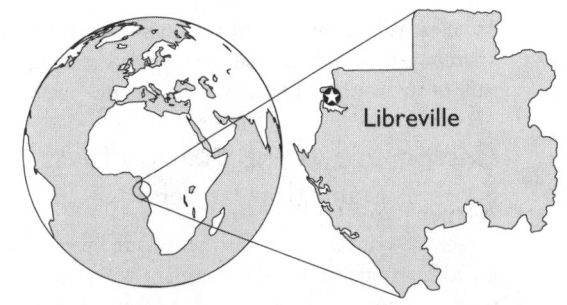

Libreville

Gabon gained its independence from France in 1960. Due to generous deposits of oil and such valuable minerals as uranium and manganese, and to its small population of about 1.4 million, Gabon is one of the most prosperous countries in sub-Saharan Africa. Per capita GNP was $6,300 in 1996. Gabon maintains close economic and political ties with France, including membership in the French Franc Zone, but non-French companies are becoming an increasing presence. Although a number of political parties exist, the Parti Democratique Gabonais (PDG) unquestionably is in control, occupying 89 of parliament's 120 seats, and President Omar Bongo, a PDG member, is expected to win re-election in December 1998. Economic liberalization has been moving very slowly, and the government remains the dominant force in the economy.

TRADE POLICY
Score: 5–Stable (very high level of protectionism)

Gabon's average tariff rate is a high 32.54 percent, and the tariff on electronics and vehicles is even higher. There are quantitative import restrictions on sugar, vegetable oil, soap, mineral water, and cement; rice and wheat are subject to import licenses. The customs process is slow and cumbersome, and fraud is a problem.[1] Import bans on mineral water, cement, soap, and other items have been lifted.

TAXATION
Score–Income taxation: 5–Stable (very high tax rates)
Score–Corporate taxation: 3–Stable (moderate tax rates)
Final Taxation Score: 4.5–Stable (very high tax rates)

The highest tax bracket is 60.5 percent;[2] the tax on the average income is 15 percent. The corporate tax rate is 35 percent, down from 40 percent in 1997, but companies must pay 5 percent of their pretax profits into the Gabonese Investment Fund. Gabon also has a 35 percent capital gains tax and an 18 percent value-added tax. The latter was introduced in 1995 to replace other taxes, including the business turnover tax.

GOVERNMENT INTERVENTION IN THE ECONOMY
Score: 3–Stable (moderate level)

Government consumes 12.6 percent of GDP, and the public sector remains bloated despite retrenchment efforts. Although some state-owned enterprises have been liquidated, there has been little privatization of larger state-owned companies.

MONETARY POLICY
Score: 1–Stable (very low level of inflation)

Gabon's average annual rate of inflation between 1986 and 1996 was 3.2 percent. Under the Franc Zone Mechanism, Gabon's currency is pegged to the French franc, and the government thus exercises only limited control over its monetary

1	Hong Kong	1.25		81	Fiji	3.10
2	Singapore	1.30		81	Mali	3.10
3	Bahrain	1.70		81	Slovenia	3.10
4	New Zealand	1.75		85	Honduras	3.15
5	Switzerland	1.85		85	Mexico	3.15
6	United States	1.90		85	Papua New Guinea	3.15
7	Ireland	1.95		88	Djibouti	3.20
7	Luxembourg	1.95		88	Mongolia	3.20
7	Taiwan	1.95		90	Algeria	3.25
7	United Kingdom	1.95		90	Brazil	3.25
11	Bahamas	2.00		90	Lebanon	3.25
12	Czech Republic	2.05		90	Senegal	3.25
12	Japan	2.05		90	Tanzania	3.25
14	Australia	2.10		95	Nigeria	3.30
14	Belgium	2.10		95	Romania	3.30
14	Canada	2.10		97	Cambodia	3.35
14	United Arab Emirates	2.10		97	Dominican Republic	3.35
18	Austria	2.15		97	Egypt	3.35
18	Chile	2.15		97	Guinea	3.35
18	Estonia	2.15		97	Ivory Coast	3.35
18	Netherlands	2.15		97	Moldova	3.35
22	Denmark	2.25		97	Pakistan	3.35
22	El Salvador	2.25		104	Nepal	3.40
22	Finland	2.25		104	Venezuela	3.40
25	Germany	2.30		106	Armenia	3.45
25	Iceland	2.30		106	Bulgaria	3.45
27	Norway	2.35		106	Lesotho	3.45
28	Korea, South	2.40		106	Madagascar	3.45
28	Kuwait	2.40		106	Russia	3.45
28	Malaysia	2.40		111	Burkina Faso	3.50
28	Panama	2.40		111	Cameroon	3.50
28	Thailand	2.40		111	Guyana	3.50
33	Sweden	2.45		111	Nicaragua	3.50
34	Argentina	2.50		115	Gambia	3.60
34	France	2.50		116	Croatia	3.65
34	Italy	2.50		116	Georgia	3.65
34	Spain	2.50		116	Malawi	3.65
38	Portugal	2.55		119	Cape Verde	3.67
38	Sri Lanka	2.55		120	Ethiopia	3.70
38	Trinidad and Tobago	2.55		120	India	3.70
41	Barbados	2.60		120	Niger	3.70
41	Peru	2.60		123	Congo	3.75
43	Bolivia	2.65		124	Chad	3.80
43	Mauritius	2.65		124	China	3.80
45	Cyprus	2.70		124	Mauritania	3.80
45	Jamaica	2.70		124	Ukraine	3.80
45	Uruguay	2.70		124	Zimbabwe	3.80
48	Botswana	2.75		129	Albania	3.85
48	Guatemala	2.75		129	Bangladesh	3.85
48	Jordan	2.75		129	Mozambique	3.85
48	Namibia	2.75		129	Suriname	3.85
48	Oman	2.75		133	Burundi	3.90
48	Philippines	2.75		134	Togo	3.95
54	Belize	2.80		135	Haiti	4.00
54	Costa Rica	2.80		135	Kyrgyz Rep.	4.00
54	Israel	2.80		137	Kazakhstan	4.05
54	Swaziland	2.80		137	Sierra Leone	4.05
54	Turkey	2.80		139	Yemen	4.10
54	Uganda	2.80		140	Belarus	4.15
54	Samoa	2.80		141	Sudan	4.20
61	Latvia	2.85		141	Syria	4.20
62	Greece	2.90		143	Azerbaijan	4.30
62	Hungary	2.90		143	Equatorial Guinea	4.30
62	So. Africa	2.90		143	Myanmar	4.30
65	Ecuador	2.95		143	Rwanda	4.30
65	Gabon	2.95		147	Tajikistan	4.40
65	Indonesia	2.95		147	Uzbekistan	4.40
65	Malta	2.95		149	Angola	4.45
65	Morocco	2.95		149	Turkmenistan	4.45
65	Poland	2.95		151	Guinea-Bissau	4.55
65	Tunisia	2.95		152	Vietnam	4.60
72	Ghana	3.00		153	Congo (Zaire)	4.70
72	Lithuania	3.00		153	Iran	4.70
72	Saudi Arabia	3.00		155	Bosnia	4.80
75	Benin	3.05		155	Somalia	4.80
75	Kenya	3.05		157	Iraq	4.90
75	Paraguay	3.05		157	Laos	4.90
75	Qatar	3.05		157	Libya	4.90
75	Slovak Republic	3.05		160	Cuba	5.00
75	Zambia	3.05		160	Korea, North	5.00
81	Colombia	3.10				

Mostly Free

policies. When the European Union establishes its common currency, the euro, Gabon will peg its currency to it. The rate of inflation in 1997 was 4.1 percent.

CAPITAL FLOWS AND FOREIGN INVESTMENT
Score: 2–Stable (low barriers)

A 1989 rewrite of the investment code liberalized conditions for foreign businesses. Government participation in investment no longer is required. A requirement that all private companies established in Gabon contribute 10 percent of their shares to the government was repealed in 1994. Foreign investors face only minimal restrictions in most areas, and the government has allowed foreign-owned operations to compete with local businesses. Very few areas are off-limits to foreign investors, but the government dominates the most lucrative sectors of the marketplace. Foreign investors encounter protracted delays in the investment approval process. There are no free trade zones in Gabon, but tax holidays for certain investors are available.

BANKING
Score: 2–Stable (low level of restrictions)

The government exercises little control over the banking system, which is composed primarily of competitive foreign banks. According to the U.S. Department of Commerce, "The banking system, dominated by French banks, is relatively sophisticated and offers most corporate banking services or can procure them through affiliates abroad."[3]

WAGE AND PRICE CONTROLS
Score: 3–Stable (moderate level)

Price controls are imposed on 17 goods and most services, including insurance and construction. A relatively high minimum wage has attracted many unskilled immigrants from neighboring African countries. The minimum wage for non-Gabonese is 80 percent of what Gabonese workers must be paid.

PROPERTY RIGHTS
Score: 3–Stable (moderate level of protection)

Expropriation of foreign property is not likely. There have been charges, however, that government officials use coercion to obtain control of successful businesses. Property also is threatened by ethnic clashes, the lack of progress toward greater democracy, and the growing resentment of foreign business. According to the U.S. Department of State, "The judiciary is independent but remains vulnerable to government manipulation."[4]

REGULATION
Score: 3–Stable (moderate level)

Although the bureaucracy is generally effective, lengthy delays in the processing of some business investments and expansions are common; corruption is present; and regulations make the business environment increasingly complicated. According to the U.S. Department of Commerce, "Public sector finances have been poorly managed in the past, creating possibilities for officials to exploit their positions for illicit enrichment."[5] The success of Gabonese enterprises depends largely on their political connections. A "Gabonization" program instituted in 1992 forces employers to decrease the number of foreigners in their workforce. This has led to inefficiency.

BLACK MARKET
Score: 3–Stable (moderate level of activity)

The level of government control of and influence over economic activity encourages black market activity, and high tariffs on luxury goods and automobiles encourage smuggling.

NOTES
[1] U.S. Department of State, *Country Reports on Economic Policy and Trade Practices*, 1997, p. 8.
[2] Includes a 5.5 percent supplementary tax.
[3] U.S. Department of Commerce, *Country Commercial Guide*, 1998.
[4] U.S. Department of State, "Gabon Country Report on Human Rights Practices for 1997," 1998.
[5] U.S. Department of Commerce, *Country Commercial Guide*, 1998.

The Gambia　　　3.60

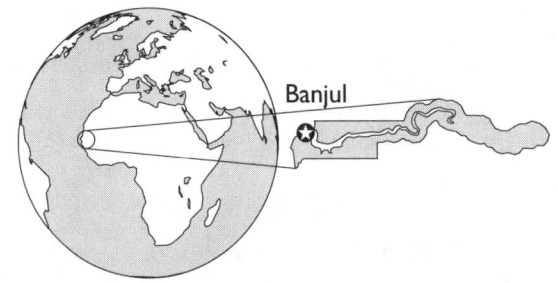
Banjul

1998 Score: **3.60**	1997 Score: **3.60**	1996 Score: **n/a**

Trade	4	Banking	4
Taxation	4	Wages and Prices	4
Government Intervention	3	Property Rights	2
Monetary Policy	2	Regulation	4
Foreign Investment	4	Black Market	5

The Gambia gained its independence from Great Britain in 1965 and established a multiparty system that held elections every five years. Until the government was overthrown in 1994 in a military coup led by Colonel Yahyah Jammeh, the country had been ruled continuously by President Dawda Kairaba Jawara, who had been re-elected five times. In September 1996, the Gambia held elections in which Colonel Jammeh became president; the U.S. Department of State referred to these elections as neither free nor fair.[1] Jammeh has solidified his position, however, and generally is recognized by foreign leaders. He has not yet fulfilled his promise to strengthen legal institutions and deregulate the economy. Economic growth has been poor, averaging 0.86 percent annually from 1993 to 1997, and GDP per capita was estimated to be $360 in 1997.

TRADE POLICY
Score: 4–Stable (high level of protectionism)

The Gambia's average tariff rate is 14.3 percent.[2] Import bans apply mainly to over-the-counter medicines.

TAXATION
Score–Income taxation: 4–Stable (high tax rates)
Score–Corporate taxation: 4–Stable (high tax rates)
Final Taxation Score: 4–Stable (high tax rates)

Total government revenues represent about 23 percent of GDP. This is higher than comparable figures for most other countries in sub-Saharan Africa.[3]

GOVERNMENT INTERVENTION IN THE ECONOMY
Score: 3–Stable (moderate level)

Government consumes about 17 percent of GDP, most of which is generated by the public sector. Many companies are government-owned.

MONETARY POLICY
Score: 2–Stable (low level of inflation)

The Gambia's average annual rate of inflation from 1986 to 1996 was 11.45 percent. In 1997, the inflation rate was 2.9 percent.

CAPITAL FLOWS AND FOREIGN INVESTMENT
Score: 4–Stable (high barriers)

The Gambia grants equal treatment to domestic and foreign firms and actively seeks foreign investment. The government must approve all investments, however, which it does on a case-by-case basis.

1	Hong Kong	1.25		81	Fiji	3.10
2	Singapore	1.30		81	Mali	3.10
3	Bahrain	1.70		81	Slovenia	3.10
4	New Zealand	1.75		85	Honduras	3.15
5	Switzerland	1.85		85	Mexico	3.15
6	United States	1.90		85	Papua New Guinea	3.15
7	Ireland	1.95		88	Djibouti	3.20
7	Luxembourg	1.95		88	Mongolia	3.20
7	Taiwan	1.95		90	Algeria	3.25
7	United Kingdom	1.95		90	Brazil	3.25
11	Bahamas	2.00		90	Lebanon	3.25
12	Czech Republic	2.05		90	Senegal	3.25
12	Japan	2.05		90	Tanzania	3.25
14	Australia	2.10		95	Nigeria	3.30
14	Belgium	2.10		95	Romania	3.30
14	Canada	2.10		97	Cambodia	3.35
14	United Arab Emirates	2.10		97	Dominican Republic	3.35
18	Austria	2.15		97	Egypt	3.35
18	Chile	2.15		97	Guinea	3.35
18	Estonia	2.15		97	Ivory Coast	3.35
18	Netherlands	2.15		97	Moldova	3.35
22	Denmark	2.25		97	Pakistan	3.35
22	El Salvador	2.25		104	Nepal	3.40
22	Finland	2.25		104	Venezuela	3.40
25	Germany	2.30		106	Armenia	3.45
25	Iceland	2.30		106	Bulgaria	3.45
27	Norway	2.35		106	Lesotho	3.45
28	Korea, South	2.40		106	Madagascar	3.45
28	Kuwait	2.40		106	Russia	3.45
28	Malaysia	2.40		111	Burkina Faso	3.50
28	Panama	2.40		111	Cameroon	3.50
28	Thailand	2.40		111	Guyana	3.50
33	Sweden	2.45		111	Nicaragua	3.50
34	Argentina	2.50		115	Gambia	3.60
34	France	2.50		116	Croatia	3.65
34	Italy	2.50		116	Georgia	3.65
34	Spain	2.50		116	Malawi	3.65
38	Portugal	2.55		119	Cape Verde	3.67
38	Sri Lanka	2.55		120	Ethiopia	3.70
38	Trinidad and Tobago	2.55		120	India	3.70
41	Barbados	2.60		120	Niger	3.70
41	Peru	2.60		123	Congo	3.75
43	Bolivia	2.65		124	Chad	3.80
43	Mauritius	2.65		124	China	3.80
45	Cyprus	2.70		124	Mauritania	3.80
45	Jamaica	2.70		124	Ukraine	3.80
45	Uruguay	2.70		124	Zimbabwe	3.80
48	Botswana	2.75		129	Albania	3.85
48	Guatemala	2.75		129	Bangladesh	3.85
48	Jordan	2.75		129	Mozambique	3.85
48	Namibia	2.75		129	Suriname	3.85
48	Oman	2.75		133	Burundi	3.90
48	Philippines	2.75		134	Togo	3.95
54	Belize	2.80		135	Haiti	4.00
54	Costa Rica	2.80		135	Kyrgyz Rep.	4.00
54	Israel	2.80		137	Kazakhstan	4.05
54	Swaziland	2.80		137	Sierra Leone	4.05
54	Turkey	2.80		139	Yemen	4.10
54	Uganda	2.80		140	Belarus	4.15
54	Samoa	2.80		141	Sudan	4.20
61	Latvia	2.85		141	Syria	4.20
62	Greece	2.90		143	Azerbaijan	4.30
62	Hungary	2.90		143	Equatorial Guinea	4.30
62	So. Africa	2.90		143	Myanmar	4.30
65	Ecuador	2.95		143	Rwanda	4.30
65	Gabon	2.95		147	Tajikistan	4.40
65	Indonesia	2.95		147	Uzbekistan	4.40
65	Malta	2.95		149	Angola	4.45
65	Morocco	2.95		149	Turkmenistan	4.45
65	Poland	2.95		152	Guinea-Bissau	4.55
65	Tunisia	2.95		152	Vietnam	4.60
72	Ghana	3.00		153	Congo (Zaire)	4.70
72	Lithuania	3.00		153	Iran	4.70
72	Saudi Arabia	3.00		155	Bosnia	4.80
75	Benin	3.05		155	Somalia	4.80
75	Kenya	3.05		157	Iraq	4.90
75	Paraguay	3.05		157	Laos	4.90
75	Qatar	3.05		157	Libya	4.90
75	Slovak Republic	3.05		160	Cuba	5.00
75	Zambia	3.05		160	Korea, North	5.00
81	Colombia	3.10				

Mostly Unfree

BANKING
Score: 4–Stable (high level of restrictions)

The banking system is heavily controlled by the government and is severely underdeveloped.

WAGE AND PRICE CONTROLS
Score: 4–Stable (high level)

The Gambia's large public sector sometimes has a significant effect on wages and prices. Heavy government subsidies influence prices, too, as do the country's import substitution policies.

PROPERTY RIGHTS
Score: 2–Stable (high level of protection)

The legal system in the Gambia is efficient, fair, and independent. It also is overburdened at times, however, with a backlog of unresolved cases, and judgments can take several years. According to the U.S. Department of State, "The Constitution provides for an independent judiciary; however, the judiciary reportedly has been at times subject to executive branch pressure, but courts demonstrated their independence in 1997 in a number of cases."[4]

REGULATION
Score: 4–Stable (high level)

Establishing a business in the Gambia can be difficult because of corruption in the government bureaucracy. Bribery and embezzlement are prevalent among the government officials who are responsible for collecting fees.

BLACK MARKET
Score: 5–Stable (very high level of activity)

The size of the Gambia's black market is large. Most of this activity occurs in smuggled consumer goods, labor, and pirated intellectual property.

NOTES
[1] U.S. Department of State, "The Gambia Country Report on Human Rights Practices for 1997," 1998.
[2] Based on total taxation on international trade as a percentage of total imports.
[3] Tax information is not available for the Gambia
[4] U.S. Department of State, "The Gambia Country Report on Human Rights Practices for 1997," 1998.

Georgia   3.65

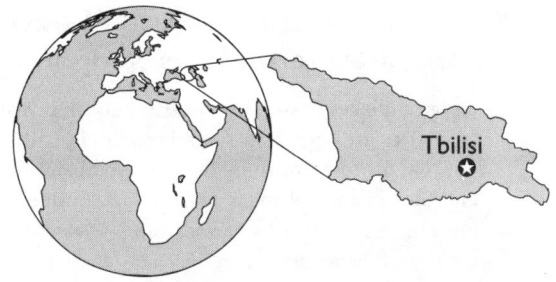

Tbilisi

1998 Score: **3.65**	1997 Score: **3.85**	1996 Score: **3.85**

Trade	3	Banking	4
Taxation	2.5	Wages and Prices	4
Government Intervention	2	Property Rights	4
Monetary Policy	5	Regulation	4
Foreign Investment	3	Black Market	5

Georgia was independent from 1918 to 1921, at which time it was conquered by the consolidating Soviet Union. It has a developed agricultural sector that includes citrus production as well as resorts, light industry, and some high-tech enterprises. Ethnic unrest and two civil wars since becoming independent again in 1991 have hampered the development of a free market. Georgia has been plagued by hyperinflation and declines in industrial output. The administration of President Eduard Shevardnadze has achieved an economic turnaround by applying responsible economic policies. For example, Georgia has privatized many state-owned industries, opened its market to imports and foreign investment, and established a commercial code.

TRADE POLICY
Score: 3–Stable (moderate level of protectionism)

According to the U.S. Department of Commerce, "Import duties on most goods are set at 12 percent. Under the terms of the new customs law which came into effect January 1, 1997, capital goods, spare parts and goods intended for manufacturing are subject to a 5 percent tariff."[1] When these lower rates are taken into account, Georgia has an average tariff rate of about 8 percent. There are no import bans, but some government licenses are required for particular goods like medical equipment. Georgia also maintains import quotas.

TAXATION
Score–Income taxation: 2–Stable (low tax rates)
Score–Corporate taxation: 2–Stable (low tax rates)
Final Taxation Score: 2.5–Stable (moderate tax rates)

Georgia's top income tax rate is 20 percent; the average taxpayer lands in the 15 percent bracket. The top marginal corporate tax rate is 20 percent. The government levies several other taxes, too, including a 20 percent value-added tax. Tax collection is hampered by an inefficient bureaucracy and by separatist local administrations in parts of the country.

GOVERNMENT INTERVENTION IN THE ECONOMY
Score: 2–Stable (low level)

Government consumes over 7 percent of GDP, but the state-owned sector accounts for most GDP. Because the government's consumption figure has fallen significantly, however, its level of intervention in the economy is low by global standards. The government is moving to privatize some of the enterprises it owns.

MONETARY POLICY
Score: 5–Stable (very high level of inflation)

Georgia suffers from chronic inflation; for example, from 1993 to 1994, prices increased roughly 60 percent per month. In 1996, inflation fell to 48 percent for the year and, in 1997, to just 7.1 percent. But, by global standards, Georgia's average annual rate of inflation remains very high.

1	Hong Kong	1.25	81	Fiji	3.10
2	Singapore	1.30	81	Mali	3.10
3	Bahrain	1.70	81	Slovenia	3.10
4	New Zealand	1.75	85	Honduras	3.15
5	Switzerland	1.85	85	Mexico	3.15
6	United States	1.90	85	Papua New Guinea	3.15
7	Ireland	1.95	88	Djibouti	3.20
7	Luxembourg	1.95	88	Mongolia	3.20
7	Taiwan	1.95	90	Algeria	3.25
7	United Kingdom	1.95	90	Brazil	3.25
11	Bahamas	2.00	90	Lebanon	3.25
12	Czech Republic	2.05	90	Senegal	3.25
12	Japan	2.05	90	Tanzania	3.25
14	Australia	2.10	95	Nigeria	3.30
14	Belgium	2.10	95	Romania	3.30
14	Canada	2.10	97	Cambodia	3.35
14	United Arab Emirates	2.10	97	Dominican Republic	3.35
18	Austria	2.15	97	Egypt	3.35
18	Chile	2.15	97	Guinea	3.35
18	Estonia	2.15	97	Ivory Coast	3.35
18	Netherlands	2.15	97	Moldova	3.35
22	Denmark	2.25	97	Pakistan	3.35
22	El Salvador	2.25	104	Nepal	3.40
22	Finland	2.25	104	Venezuela	3.40
25	Germany	2.30	106	Armenia	3.45
25	Iceland	2.30	106	Bulgaria	3.45
27	Norway	2.35	106	Lesotho	3.45
28	Korea, South	2.40	106	Madagascar	3.45
28	Kuwait	2.40	106	Russia	3.45
28	Malaysia	2.40	111	Burkina Faso	3.50
28	Panama	2.40	111	Cameroon	3.50
28	Thailand	2.40	111	Guyana	3.50
33	Sweden	2.45	111	Nicaragua	3.50
34	Argentina	2.50	115	Gambia	3.60
34	France	2.50	116	Croatia	3.65
34	Italy	2.50	116	Georgia	3.65
34	Spain	2.50	116	Malawi	3.65
38	Portugal	2.55	119	Cape Verde	3.67
38	Sri Lanka	2.55	120	Ethiopia	3.70
38	Trinidad and Tobago	2.55	120	India	3.70
41	Barbados	2.60	120	Niger	3.70
41	Peru	2.60	123	Congo	3.75
43	Bolivia	2.65	124	Chad	3.80
43	Mauritius	2.65	124	China	3.80
45	Cyprus	2.70	124	Mauritania	3.80
45	Jamaica	2.70	124	Ukraine	3.80
45	Uruguay	2.70	124	Zimbabwe	3.80
48	Botswana	2.75	129	Albania	3.85
48	Guatemala	2.75	129	Bangladesh	3.85
48	Jordan	2.75	129	Mozambique	3.85
48	Namibia	2.75	129	Suriname	3.85
48	Oman	2.75	133	Burundi	3.90
48	Philippines	2.75	134	Togo	3.95
54	Belize	2.80	135	Haiti	4.00
54	Costa Rica	2.80	135	Kyrgyz Rep.	4.00
54	Israel	2.80	137	Kazakhstan	4.05
54	Swaziland	2.80	137	Sierra Leone	4.05
54	Turkey	2.80	139	Yemen	4.10
54	Uganda	2.80	140	Belarus	4.15
54	Samoa	2.80	141	Sudan	4.20
61	Latvia	2.85	141	Syria	4.20
62	Greece	2.90	143	Azerbaijan	4.30
62	Hungary	2.90	143	Equatorial Guinea	4.30
62	So. Africa	2.90	143	Myanmar	4.30
65	Ecuador	2.95	143	Rwanda	4.30
65	Gabon	2.95	147	Tajikistan	4.40
65	Indonesia	2.95	147	Uzbekistan	4.40
65	Malta	2.95	149	Angola	4.45
65	Morocco	2.95	149	Turkmenistan	4.45
65	Poland	2.95	151	Guinea-Bissau	4.55
65	Tunisia	2.95	152	Vietnam	4.60
72	Ghana	3.00	153	Congo (Zaire)	4.70
72	Lithuania	3.00	153	Iran	4.70
72	Saudi Arabia	3.00	155	Bosnia	4.80
75	Benin	3.05	155	Somalia	4.80
75	Kenya	3.05	157	Iraq	4.90
75	Paraguay	3.05	157	Laos	4.90
75	Qatar	3.05	157	Libya	4.90
75	Slovak Republic	3.05	160	Cuba	5.00
75	Zambia	3.05	160	Korea, North	5.00
81	Colombia	3.10			

Mostly Unfree

CAPITAL FLOWS AND FOREIGN INVESTMENT
Score: 3–Stable (moderate barriers)

Georgia places few official restrictions on investment. Most industries are open to foreign investment, although the lack of legal protection, an inefficient and bloated bureaucracy, and the collapse of many state-owned businesses can present problems. Laws concerning private ownership of land can be confusing and unclear.

BANKING
Score: 4–Stable (high level of restrictions)

The banking system is in shambles. The government has a heavy hand in controlling the domestic banking system, and many state-owned banks are inefficient and led by officials who lack common business knowledge. According to the U.S. Department of Commerce, "Georgian law does permit the free flow of financial resources. But in practice, the flow is restrained because of poor and unreliable interbank communication (regular banking transactions within Georgia can take several days)."[2]

WAGE AND PRICE CONTROLS
Score: 4–Stable (high level)

The government still sets some wages and prices. Government subsidies to state-owned industries cause goods to be sold at artificially low prices, and the government establishes prices for electricity, bread, and some municipal services.

PROPERTY RIGHTS
Score: 4–Stable (low level of protection)

The lack of effective government control over parts of Georgia's territory hampers the protection of private property. As yet, there is neither a fully functioning court system nor a legal environment conducive to the protection of private property. "The Constitution provides for an independent judiciary," says the U.S. Department of State, "but in practice the judiciary often does not exercise independence."[3]

REGULATION
Score: 4–Stable (high level)

Establishing a business can be difficult, especially if the business intends to compete directly with a state-owned company. Regulations generally are applied unevenly, and corruption frequently is present. The U.S. Department of Commerce identifies the "high level of crime and corruption" and "remnants of central planning and bureaucracy" as additional deterrents.[4]

BLACK MARKET
Score: 5–Stable (very high level of activity)

Some estimates indicate that Georgia's black market is equal in size to its formal market. It includes such activities as the sale of pirated computer software, compact discs, and videos as well as labor. Smuggling from neighboring Turkey, Russia, Armenia, and Azerbaijan also is prevalent.

NOTES
[1]   U.S. Department of Commerce, "Georgia: Economic and Trade Overview," May 26, 1997.
[2]   *Ibid.*
[3]   U.S. Department of State, "Georgia Country Report on Human Rights Practices for 1997," 1998.
[4]   U.S. Department of Commerce, *Country Commercial Guide,* 1998.

Germany 2.30

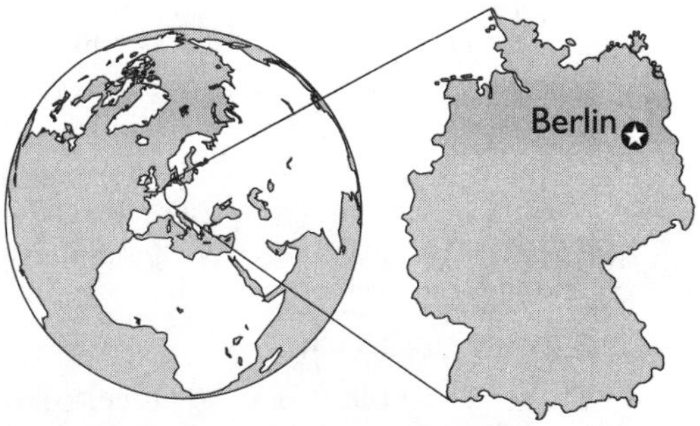

1998 Score: **2.30**	1997 Score: **2.20**	1996 Score: **2.10**

Trade	2	Banking	3
Taxation	5	Wages and Prices	2
Government Intervention	2	Property Rights	1
Monetary Policy	1	Regulation	4
Foreign Investment	2	Black Market	1

Germany is the largest economic power in the European Union (EU). Since the reunification of West and East Germany, however, the country has experienced unemployment of around 10 percent per year. To ease the pain of reunification, the government increased social spending, which has placed a burden on the economy. According to the U.S. Department of Commerce, "The state of the German economy has been a major topic of debate in 1997. The pressure to meet the Maastricht Treaty's fiscal deficit criterion, high and growing unemployment, fiscal revenue shortfalls, the economic burden of supporting eastern German development and the need to restructure the economy have added to the general level of uncertainty.... German business efforts to remain competitive by restructuring (with job-shedding) and investing in new techniques and machinery have fueled rising unemployment (currently 4.3 million people are officially unemployed)"[1] In national elections to parliament in September 1998, the Social Democratic Party won a narrow majority of seats, thus ending Helmut Kohl's 16-year rule as chancellor and leader of the Christian Democratic Party. As leader of the Social Democratic Party, Chancellor Gerhard Schröder formed a coalition government with the Green Party while pledging to reduce the country's unemployment, push for tax reform, and maintain continuity in Germany's foreign policy.

Trade Policy

Score: 2–Stable (low level of protectionism)

Germany's average tariff rate is about 2.8 percent.[2] Non-tariff barriers include overbearing consumer regulations on the labeling and testing of products. According to the U.S. Department of Commerce, "Germany's regulations and bureaucratic procedures can be a difficult hurdle for companies wishing to enter the market, requiring close attention by U.S. exporters."[3] By global standards, however, Germany's level of protectionism is low.

Taxation

Score–Income taxation: 5–Stable (very high tax rates)

Score–Corporate taxation: 4–Stable (high tax rates)

Final Taxation Score: 5–Stable (very high tax rates)

Germany's taxes remain among the highest in both the industrialized world and the EU. The top income tax bracket is 53 percent, and the tax on the average income level is over 35 percent. The top corporate tax rate is 45 percent, but corporations also pay a 7.5 percent "surcharge" tax, and municipality taxes on profits can increase the total corporate tax rate to over 70 percent. Germany also has a 45 percent capital gains tax, a 15 percent value-added tax, and land, property, and real estate taxes.

Government Intervention in the Economy

Score: 2–Stable (low level)

Government consumes 19.7 percent of GDP. After reunification, the government extended its generous social welfare system to the former East Germany and expanded subsidies for private investment. These expenditures have

Mostly Free

1	Hong Kong	1.25	81	Fiji	3.10
2	Singapore	1.30	81	Mali	3.10
3	Bahrain	1.70	81	Slovenia	3.10
4	New Zealand	1.75	85	Honduras	3.15
5	Switzerland	1.85	85	Mexico	3.15
6	United States	1.90	85	Papua New Guinea	3.15
7	Ireland	1.95	88	Djibouti	3.20
7	Luxembourg	1.95	88	Mongolia	3.20
7	Taiwan	1.95	90	Algeria	3.25
7	United Kingdom	1.95	90	Brazil	3.25
11	Bahamas	2.00	90	Lebanon	3.25
12	Czech Republic	2.05	90	Senegal	3.25
12	Japan	2.05	90	Tanzania	3.25
14	Australia	2.10	95	Nigeria	3.30
14	Belgium	2.10	95	Romania	3.30
14	Canada	2.10	97	Cambodia	3.35
14	United Arab Emirates	2.10	97	Dominican Republic	3.35
18	Austria	2.15	97	Egypt	3.35
18	Chile	2.15	97	Guinea	3.35
18	Estonia	2.15	97	Ivory Coast	3.35
18	Netherlands	2.15	97	Moldova	3.35
22	Denmark	2.25	97	Pakistan	3.35
22	El Salvador	2.25	104	Nepal	3.40
22	Finland	2.25	104	Venezuela	3.40
25	Germany	2.30	106	Armenia	3.45
25	Iceland	2.30	106	Bulgaria	3.45
27	Norway	2.35	106	Lesotho	3.45
28	Korea, South	2.40	106	Madagascar	3.45
28	Kuwait	2.40	106	Russia	3.45
28	Malaysia	2.40	111	Burkina Faso	3.50
28	Panama	2.40	111	Cameroon	3.50
28	Thailand	2.40	111	Guyana	3.50
33	Sweden	2.45	111	Nicaragua	3.50
34	Argentina	2.50	115	Gambia	3.60
34	France	2.50	116	Croatia	3.65
34	Italy	2.50	116	Georgia	3.65
34	Spain	2.50	116	Malawi	3.65
38	Portugal	2.55	119	Cape Verde	3.67
38	Sri Lanka	2.55	120	Ethiopia	3.70
38	Trinidad and Tobago	2.55	120	India	3.70
41	Barbados	2.60	120	Niger	3.70
41	Peru	2.60	123	Congo	3.75
43	Bolivia	2.65	124	Chad	3.80
43	Mauritius	2.65	124	China	3.80
45	Cyprus	2.70	124	Mauritania	3.80
45	Jamaica	2.70	124	Ukraine	3.80
45	Uruguay	2.70	124	Zimbabwe	3.80
48	Botswana	2.75	129	Albania	3.85
48	Guatemala	2.75	129	Bangladesh	3.85
48	Jordan	2.75	129	Mozambique	3.85
48	Namibia	2.75	129	Suriname	3.85
48	Oman	2.75	133	Burundi	3.90
48	Philippines	2.75	134	Togo	3.95
54	Belize	2.80	135	Haiti	4.00
54	Costa Rica	2.80	135	Kyrgyz Rep.	4.00
54	Israel	2.80	137	Kazakhstan	4.05
54	Swaziland	2.80	137	Sierra Leone	4.05
54	Turkey	2.80	139	Yemen	4.10
54	Uganda	2.80	140	Belarus	4.15
54	Samoa	2.80	141	Sudan	4.20
61	Latvia	2.85	141	Syria	4.20
62	Greece	2.90	143	Azerbaijan	4.30
62	Hungary	2.90	143	Equatorial Guinea	4.30
62	So. Africa	2.90	143	Myanmar	4.30
65	Ecuador	2.95	143	Rwanda	4.30
65	Gabon	2.95	147	Tajikistan	4.40
65	Indonesia	2.95	147	Uzbekistan	4.40
65	Malta	2.95	149	Angola	4.45
65	Morocco	2.95	149	Turkmenistan	4.45
65	Poland	2.95	151	Guinea-Bissau	4.55
65	Tunisia	2.95	152	Vietnam	4.60
72	Ghana	3.00	153	Congo (Zaire)	4.70
72	Lithuania	3.00	153	Iran	4.70
72	Saudi Arabia	3.00	155	Bosnia	4.80
75	Benin	3.05	155	Somalia	4.80
75	Kenya	3.05	157	Iraq	4.90
75	Paraguay	3.05	157	Laos	4.90
75	Qatar	3.05	157	Libya	4.90
75	Slovak Republic	3.05	160	Cuba	5.00
75	Zambia	3.05	160	Korea, North	5.00
81	Colombia	3.10			

increased the government's role in the economy. The government also continues to be involved through local and state regulations. Attempts to privatize sections of the economy stalled in 1995, but progress resumed in 1996. Most of the telecommunications network has been privatized or is being privatized, as are some postal services.

MONETARY POLICY
Score: 1–Stable (very low level of inflation)

The inflation rate is among the world's lowest: 2.4 percent annually from 1986 to 1996 and less than 1.8 percent in 1997.

CAPITAL FLOWS AND FOREIGN INVESTMENT
Score: 2–Stable (low barriers)

Germany welcomes foreign investment and is one of the few countries to impose no permanent currency or administrative controls on foreign investments. Some government regulations, such as those regulating monopolies and competition, can present barriers to investment. According to the U.S. Department of Commerce, "Foreign companies with complaints about investment problems in Germany generally list the same investment problems that domestic companies suffer, such as high tax rates and burdensome regulatory requirements and indicate they are not being less well treated than domestic companies."[4]

BANKING
Score: 3–Stable (moderate level of restrictions)

Germany is a world financial center. According to the U.S. Department of Commerce, "Germany has a basically non-discriminatory, well developed financial services infrastructure. Germany's universal banking system allows the country's more than 45,000 bank offices not only to take deposits and make loans to customers, but also to trade in securities."[5] The state-owned banking sector, however, controls a significant portion of the market. For example, as the U.S. Department of Commerce also reports, "Private banks control roughly 30 percent of the market, while publicly-owned savings banks controlled by state and local governments account for 50 percent of banking turnover, and cooperative banks make up the balance."[6]

WAGE AND PRICE CONTROLS
Score: 2–Stable (low level)

Germany's free-enterprise system is based on market-set prices and wages. Even though the market by and large determines wages, the government still maintains a Federal Cartel Office to monitor the prices of specific goods and services. With the exception of rents and some agricultural goods, there are virtually no price controls in Germany.

PROPERTY RIGHTS
Score: 1–Stable (very high level of protection)

Germany's economy, based on the private ownership of property, is undergoing extensive privatization, especially in the former East Germany. The government is pursuing the privatization of state-owned property, and the chances of expropriation are virtually nonexistent. The court system provides a very high level of property protection; it is efficient and available for all types of dispute resolution. According to the U.S. Department of State, "The court system is highly developed and provides full legal protection and numerous possibilities for judicial review."[7]

REGULATION
Score: 4–Stable (high level)

Establishing a business can be relatively easy. Few barriers exist; for example, new businesses must notify the local economic supervisory office, which supplies them with a certificate. Laws on employment, product safety, and the environment, however, impose some burdens. For example, according to the U.S. Department of Commerce, "Certain aspects of German tax, labor, health, environmental and safety regulations are excessively burdensome and serve as an effective impediment to new investment."[8] In addition, the U.S. Department of State reports, "Despite the progress in recent years, lack of competition remains a problem in many protected sectors, which drives up business costs in Germany. Services which continue to be subject to excessive regulation and market access restrictions include communications, energy, banking and insurance."[9]

BLACK MARKET
Score: 1–Stable (very low level of activity)

The black market involves such illegal activities as trafficking in drugs and guns. Prostitution is legal, as are some forms of gambling. Germany's protection of intellectual property is among the best in the world, leaving only a negligible black market in pirated materials.

NOTES

1. U.S. Department of Commerce, *Country Commercial Guide,* 1998.
2. Based on the applied tariff rate. See Arrowhead International, *World Trade and Customs Directory,* Washington, D.C., 1998.
3. U.S. Department of Commerce, *Country Commercial Guide,* 1998.
4. *Ibid.*
5. *Ibid.*
6. *Ibid.*
7. U.S. Department of State, "Germany Country Report on Human Rights Practices for 1997," 1998.
8. U.S. Department of Commerce, *Market Research Reports,* June 24, 1997.
9. U.S. Department of State, "Germany Country Report on Human Rights Practices for 1997," 1998.

Ghana   3.00

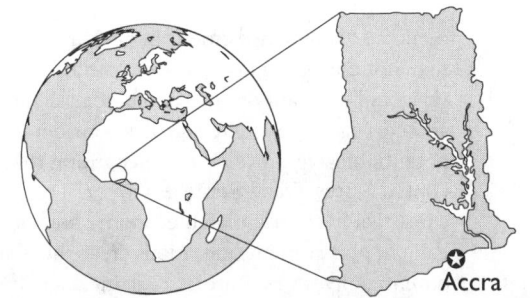

1998 Score: **3.00**	1997 Score: **3.20**	1996 Score: **3.20**

Trade	3	Banking	3
Taxation	3	Wages and Prices	2
Government Intervention	3	Property Rights	3
Monetary Policy	4	Regulation	4
Foreign Investment	3	Black Market	2

Ghana became the first independent state in sub-Saharan Africa when it gained its independence from Great Britain in 1957. Prime Minister Kwame Nkrumah quickly transformed Ghana into a one-party socialist state. Flight Lieutenant J. J. Rawlings seized power though a military coup in 1981. He legalized political parties, won Ghana's presidential election in 1992, and was re-elected in December 1996. The opposition party protested the elections, but international observers found them free and transparent. An economic liberalization program begun by Rawlings has improved what was a collapsing socialist economy. GDP growth has averaged over 5 percent annually between 1995 and 1997.

TRADE POLICY
Score: 3–Stable (moderate level of protectionism)

Ghana's average tariff rate is 11.66 percent.[1] The government has eliminated import licenses and quotas, and significant non-tariff barriers no longer exist.

TAXATION
Score–Income taxation: 2–Stable (low tax rates)
Score–Corporate taxation: 3–Stable (moderate tax rates)
Final Taxation Score: 3–Stable (moderate tax rates)

Ghana has a progressive income tax system with a top bracket of 35 percent; the average taxpayer falls within the 0 percent bracket. The government taxes corporate profits at a top rate of 35 percent. Ghana also has a 5 percent capital gains tax and a gift tax that ranges from 0 percent to 15 percent.

GOVERNMENT INTERVENTION IN THE ECONOMY
Score: 3–Stable (moderate level)

Government consumes 11.7 percent of GDP; state-owned enterprises dominate many sectors, including the petroleum, steel, diamond, timber marketing, retail, and construction industries. Ghana's public sector continues to be one of the largest in sub-Saharan Africa. Organized labor generally opposes the government's privatization program, which has stalled.

MONETARY POLICY
Score: 4–Stable (high level of inflation)

Ghana's average annual rate of inflation from 1986 to 1996 was 31.4 percent. In 1997, inflation was 28 percent.

CAPITAL FLOWS AND FOREIGN INVESTMENT
Score: 3–Stable (moderate barriers)

In 1992, the government developed a new investment code that eased restrictions on private-sector investment in Ghana, but restrictions on foreign investment remain in place. Some economic activities are closed to foreign investors or subject to a high minimum investment, and wholly owned foreign firms must

1	Hong Kong	1.25		81	Fiji	3.10
2	Singapore	1.30		81	Mali	3.10
3	Bahrain	1.70		81	Slovenia	3.10
4	New Zealand	1.75		85	Honduras	3.15
5	Switzerland	1.85		85	Mexico	3.15
6	United States	1.90		85	Papua New Guinea	3.15
7	Ireland	1.95		88	Djibouti	3.20
7	Luxembourg	1.95		88	Mongolia	3.20
7	Taiwan	1.95		90	Algeria	3.25
7	United Kingdom	1.95		90	Brazil	3.25
11	Bahamas	2.00		90	Lebanon	3.25
12	Czech Republic	2.05		90	Senegal	3.25
12	Japan	2.05		90	Tanzania	3.25
14	Australia	2.10		95	Nigeria	3.30
14	Belgium	2.10		95	Romania	3.30
14	Canada	2.10		97	Cambodia	3.35
14	United Arab Emirates	2.10		97	Dominican Republic	3.35
18	Austria	2.15		97	Egypt	3.35
18	Chile	2.15		97	Guinea	3.35
18	Estonia	2.15		97	Ivory Coast	3.35
18	Netherlands	2.15		97	Moldova	3.35
22	Denmark	2.25		97	Pakistan	3.35
22	El Salvador	2.25		104	Nepal	3.40
22	Finland	2.25		104	Venezuela	3.40
25	Germany	2.30		106	Armenia	3.45
25	Iceland	2.30		106	Bulgaria	3.45
27	Norway	2.35		106	Lesotho	3.45
28	Korea, South	2.40		106	Madagascar	3.45
28	Kuwait	2.40		106	Russia	3.45
28	Malaysia	2.40		111	Burkina Faso	3.50
28	Panama	2.40		111	Cameroon	3.50
28	Thailand	2.40		111	Guyana	3.50
33	Sweden	2.45		111	Nicaragua	3.50
34	Argentina	2.50		115	Gambia	3.60
34	France	2.50		116	Croatia	3.65
34	Italy	2.50		116	Georgia	3.65
34	Spain	2.50		116	Malawi	3.65
38	Portugal	2.55		119	Cape Verde	3.67
38	Sri Lanka	2.55		120	Ethiopia	3.70
38	Trinidad and Tobago	2.55		120	India	3.70
41	Barbados	2.60		120	Niger	3.70
41	Peru	2.60		123	Congo	3.75
43	Bolivia	2.65		124	Chad	3.80
43	Mauritius	2.65		124	China	3.80
45	Cyprus	2.70		124	Mauritania	3.80
45	Jamaica	2.70		124	Ukraine	3.80
45	Uruguay	2.70		124	Zimbabwe	3.80
48	Botswana	2.75		129	Albania	3.85
48	Guatemala	2.75		129	Bangladesh	3.85
48	Jordan	2.75		129	Mozambique	3.85
48	Namibia	2.75		129	Suriname	3.85
48	Oman	2.75		133	Burundi	3.90
48	Philippines	2.75		134	Togo	3.95
54	Belize	2.80		135	Haiti	4.00
54	Costa Rica	2.80		135	Kyrgyz Rep.	4.00
54	Israel	2.80		137	Kazakhstan	4.05
54	Swaziland	2.80		137	Sierra Leone	4.05
54	Turkey	2.80		139	Yemen	4.10
54	Uganda	2.80		140	Belarus	4.15
54	Samoa	2.80		141	Sudan	4.20
61	Latvia	2.85		141	Syria	4.20
62	Greece	2.90		143	Azerbaijan	4.30
62	Hungary	2.90		143	Equatorial Guinea	4.30
62	So. Africa	2.90		143	Myanmar	4.30
65	Ecuador	2.95		143	Rwanda	4.30
65	Gabon	2.95		147	Tajikistan	4.40
65	Indonesia	2.95		147	Uzbekistan	4.40
65	Malta	2.95		149	Angola	4.45
65	Morocco	2.95		149	Turkmenistan	4.45
65	Poland	2.95		151	Guinea-Bissau	4.55
65	Tunisia	2.95		152	Vietnam	4.60
72	Ghana	3.00		153	Congo (Zaire)	4.70
72	Lithuania	3.00		153	Iran	4.70
72	Saudi Arabia	3.00		155	Bosnia	4.80
75	Benin	3.05		155	Somalia	4.80
75	Kenya	3.05		157	Iraq	4.90
75	Paraguay	3.05		157	Laos	4.90
75	Qatar	3.05		157	Libya	4.90
75	Slovak Republic	3.05		160	Cuba	5.00
75	Zambia	3.05		160	Korea, North	5.00
81	Colombia	3.10				

Mostly Unfree

meet a $200,000 investment minimum. Foreign investors may not engage in taxi services, lotteries, and certain services like beauty salons and barber shops. An inefficient and corrupt bureaucracy creates considerable barriers to potential foreign investment. According to the Office of the United States Trade Representative, "The residual effects of a drastically overregulated economy and lack of transparency in government operations create an element of risk for potential investors. Bureaucratic inertia is sometimes a problem in government ministries, and administrative approvals often take longer than they should. Entrenched local interests sometimes have the ability to derail or delay new entrants, and securing government approvals may depend on an applicant's contacts."[2]

BANKING
Score: 3–Stable (moderate level of restrictions)

Five private commercial and investment banks are chartered in Ghana, and there is considerable competition among them. The Central Bank has abolished interest rate controls, but the bank otherwise maintains tight control over financial activities. There is a government monopoly on personal insurance. Several state-owned banks are being divested from government control. The government has a strong influence on the Central Bank, however, and public-sector borrowing crowds out that by the private sector. According to the U.S. Department of Commerce, "Until recently the sector was dominated by state-owned institutions and showed few signs of competition. Within the last two years, however, two state-owned banks have been privatized under the government's Divestiture Implementation Program, and others are to follow suit in the near future."[3]

WAGE AND PRICE CONTROLS
Score: 2–Stable (low level)

Although employers and workers generally are encouraged to negotiate wages and working conditions, Ghana has a minimum wage. The government maintains some food subsidies.

PROPERTY RIGHTS
Score: 3–Stable (moderate level of protection)

Ghana's investment code guarantees private property against expropriation, so seizure remains unlikely. Domestically owned property is less secure than foreign-owned property; during the past several years, there have been cases of arbitrary seizure of domestic commercial property. There is no central land registry. According to the U.S. Department of State, "Inadequate resources and a system vulnerable to political influence compromised the integrity of the overburdened judicial system."[4] By global standards, however, Ghana's protection of private property is moderate.

REGULATION
Score: 4–Stable (high level)

Private-sector investors face a burdensome licensing process, and regulations require foreign firms to hire local employees. Additional problems include the need to gain bureaucratic approval for acquiring and selling land. Bureaucratic inertia and politically inspired administrative judgments reduce competition among domestic firms.

BLACK MARKET
Score: 2–Stable (low level of activity)

The dismantling of price controls has reduced the number of Ghana's once-legion "economic criminals" and removed a large incentive to engage in black market activity. There is little piracy of intellectual property.[5]

NOTES

[1] Based on total taxes on international trade as a percentage of total imports.
[2] Office of the United State Trade Representative, *1998 National Trade Estimate Report on Foreign Trade Barriers.*
[3] U.S. Department of Commerce, *Country Commercial Guide,* 1998.
[4] U.S. Department of State, "Ghana Country Report on Human Rights Practices for 1997," 1998.
[5] U.S. Department of State, *Country Reports on Economic Policy and Trade Practices,* 1998.

Greece   2.90

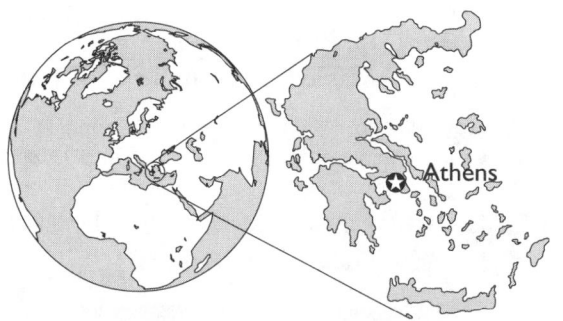

1998 Score: **2.90**	1997 Score: **2.85**	1996 Score: **2.80**

Trade	2	Banking	4
Taxation	4	Wages and Prices	3
Government Intervention	3	Property Rights	2
Monetary Policy	3	Regulation	3
Foreign Investment	2	Black Market	3

From 1941 until 1944, Greece was occupied by Nazi Germany. In 1946, a Soviet-backed attempt by communists to take over the country led to a bloody civil war. Greece emerged from this ordeal as a pro-Western democracy and joined the North Atlantic Treaty Organization in 1952. It also has been involved in a bitter standoff with Turkey over Cyprus. Since joining the European Union (EU) in 1981, Greece has worked to bring its economy in line with those of other European democracies. In September 1996, the voters re-elected a parliament with a Panhellenic Socialist Party majority, led by Prime Minister Constantinos Simitis. The prime minister's privatization and austerity measures have met with strong opposition. Plans to bolster the defense budget may undermine Simitis's goal of curbing government spending.

TRADE POLICY
Score: 2–Stable (low level of protectionism)

Greece has an average tariff rate of 3.6 percent. As a member of the EU, it must conform to that organization's trade standards and practices. In addition to common EU trade restrictions, Greece maintains nationality requirements on a variety of services, such as those provided by lawyers, architects, and accountants. These restrictions have a severe effect on imported services.

TAXATION
Score–Income taxation: 3–Stable (moderate tax rates)
Score–Corporate taxation: 4–Stable (high tax rates)
Final Taxation Score: 4–Stable (high tax rates)

Greece's top income tax rate is 45 percent, and the rate for the average income level has increased to 15 percent. The top corporate income tax is 40 percent. Greece also has a 35 percent capital gains tax and an 18 percent value-added tax.

GOVERNMENT INTERVENTION IN THE ECONOMY
Score: 3–Stable (moderate level)

Government consumes 14.3 percent of GDP. State-owned industries still make up a significant portion of the economy, however—about 40 percent of GDP. According to the U.S. Department of Commerce, "General government expenditures, which according to Maastricht Treaty definitions, include those of the central government, social insurance funds, and local authorities, amounted to 43.6 percent of GDP (including interest payments) in 1996. The government controls 7 social insurance funds, 48 public enterprises and directly or indirectly some 75 percent of the banking system. The government owns or controls all public utilities and the national airline Olympic Airways."[1] Still, because government consumption is only 14.3 percent, by global standards the level of government intervention in the economy is moderate.

1	Hong Kong	1.25	81	Fiji	3.10
2	Singapore	1.30	81	Mali	3.10
3	Bahrain	1.70	81	Slovenia	3.10
4	New Zealand	1.75	85	Honduras	3.15
5	Switzerland	1.85	85	Mexico	3.15
6	United States	1.90	85	Papua New Guinea	3.15
7	Ireland	1.95	88	Djibouti	3.20
7	Luxembourg	1.95	88	Mongolia	3.20
7	Taiwan	1.95	90	Algeria	3.25
7	United Kingdom	1.95	90	Brazil	3.25
11	Bahamas	2.00	90	Lebanon	3.25
12	Czech Republic	2.05	90	Senegal	3.25
12	Japan	2.05	90	Tanzania	3.25
14	Australia	2.10	95	Nigeria	3.30
14	Belgium	2.10	95	Romania	3.30
14	Canada	2.10	97	Cambodia	3.35
14	United Arab Emirates	2.10	97	Dominican Republic	3.35
18	Austria	2.15	97	Egypt	3.35
18	Chile	2.15	97	Guinea	3.35
18	Estonia	2.15	97	Ivory Coast	3.35
18	Netherlands	2.15	97	Moldova	3.35
22	Denmark	2.25	97	Pakistan	3.35
22	El Salvador	2.25	104	Nepal	3.40
22	Finland	2.25	104	Venezuela	3.40
25	Germany	2.30	106	Armenia	3.45
25	Iceland	2.30	106	Bulgaria	3.45
27	Norway	2.35	106	Lesotho	3.45
28	Korea, South	2.40	106	Madagascar	3.45
28	Kuwait	2.40	106	Russia	3.45
28	Malaysia	2.40	111	Burkina Faso	3.50
28	Panama	2.40	111	Cameroon	3.50
28	Thailand	2.40	111	Guyana	3.50
33	Sweden	2.45	111	Nicaragua	3.50
34	Argentina	2.50	115	Gambia	3.60
34	France	2.50	116	Croatia	3.65
34	Italy	2.50	116	Georgia	3.65
34	Spain	2.50	116	Malawi	3.65
38	Portugal	2.55	119	Cape Verde	3.67
38	Sri Lanka	2.55	120	Ethiopia	3.70
38	Trinidad and Tobago	2.55	120	India	3.70
41	Barbados	2.60	120	Niger	3.70
41	Peru	2.60	123	Congo	3.75
43	Bolivia	2.65	124	Chad	3.80
43	Mauritius	2.65	124	China	3.80
45	Cyprus	2.70	124	Mauritania	3.80
45	Jamaica	2.70	124	Ukraine	3.80
45	Uruguay	2.70	124	Zimbabwe	3.80
48	Botswana	2.75	129	Albania	3.85
48	Guatemala	2.75	129	Bangladesh	3.85
48	Jordan	2.75	129	Mozambique	3.85
48	Namibia	2.75	129	Suriname	3.85
48	Oman	2.75	133	Burundi	3.90
48	Philippines	2.75	134	Togo	3.95
54	Belize	2.80	135	Haiti	4.00
54	Costa Rica	2.80	135	Kyrgyz Rep.	4.00
54	Israel	2.80	137	Kazakhstan	4.05
54	Swaziland	2.80	137	Sierra Leone	4.05
54	Turkey	2.80	139	Yemen	4.10
54	Uganda	2.80	140	Belarus	4.15
54	Samoa	2.80	141	Sudan	4.20
61	Latvia	2.85	141	Syria	4.20
62	Greece	2.90	143	Azerbaijan	4.30
62	Hungary	2.90	143	Equatorial Guinea	4.30
62	So. Africa	2.90	143	Myanmar	4.30
65	Ecuador	2.95	143	Rwanda	4.30
65	Gabon	2.95	147	Tajikistan	4.40
65	Indonesia	2.95	147	Uzbekistan	4.40
65	Malta	2.95	149	Angola	4.45
65	Morocco	2.95	149	Turkmenistan	4.45
65	Poland	2.95	151	Guinea-Bissau	4.55
65	Tunisia	2.95	152	Vietnam	4.60
72	Ghana	3.00	153	Congo (Zaire)	4.70
72	Lithuania	3.00	153	Iran	4.70
72	Saudi Arabia	3.00	155	Bosnia	4.80
75	Benin	3.05	155	Somalia	4.80
75	Kenya	3.05	157	Iraq	4.90
75	Paraguay	3.05	157	Laos	4.90
75	Qatar	3.05	157	Libya	4.90
75	Slovak Republic	3.05	160	Cuba	5.00
75	Zambia	3.05	160	Korea, North	5.00
81	Colombia	3.10			

Mostly Free

MONETARY POLICY
Score: 3–Stable (moderate level of inflation)

From 1986 to 1996, Greece's average annual rate of inflation was 13.6 percent. In 1997, the rate fell to 5.7 percent.

CAPITAL FLOWS AND FOREIGN INVESTMENT
Score: 2–Stable (low barriers)

Greece has an open foreign investment code that invites many investments. There are some restrictions, however, especially with regard to banks, that require prior government approval and rarely result in 100 percent foreign ownership. According to the U.S. Department of Commerce, "The Greek government encourages private foreign investment as a matter of policy. Investments are screened only when the investor wants to take advantage of government provided tax and investment incentives. In such cases, foreign and domestic investors face the same screening criteria. Greece restricts foreign and domestic private investment in public utilities (with the exception of cellular telephony and energy from renewable sources). There are also restrictions for land purchases in border regions and on certain islands (on national security grounds). U.S. and other non-EU investors receive less advantageous treatment than domestic or EU investors in the banking, mining, broadcasting, maritime, and air transport sectors."[2] Still, investment in all other areas is unrestricted and foreign investors receive national treatment. Thus, by global standards, Greece's restrictions on foreign investment are few.

BANKING
Score: 4–Stable (high level of restrictions)

Although the government has liberalized the banking system considerably as a condition of membership in the EU, it still owns a significant number of banks, and foreign competition is minimal. According to the U.S. Department of Commerce, "State-controlled banks and specialized financial institutions together control about 76 percent of deposits and 73 percent of loans. Foreign-owned banks (including other EU-based banks) control about 7 percent of deposits and 10 percent of loans. Greek-owned private banks retain control of the remaining 17 percent of deposits and 17 percent of loans."[3]

WAGE AND PRICE CONTROLS
Score: 3–Stable (moderate level)

The government sets some prices, including those for bread, freight charges, motor vehicle insurance, pharmaceuticals, and telephone service. The government also controls the price of fuel.

PROPERTY RIGHTS
Score: 2–Stable (high level of protection)

Property expropriation is unlikely in Greece. There are signs, however, of inefficiency in the judicial system. As the U.S. Department of Commerce reports, "Greece has an independent judiciary and effective, albeit time-consuming, means for enforcing property and contractual rights. However, foreign companies often feel that Greek courts do not always provide unbiased and effective recourse. Although an investment agreement could be drafted subject to foreign legal jurisdiction, this is highly unlikely particularly if one of the contracting parties is the Greek state."[4]

REGULATION
Factor Score: 3–Stable (moderate level)

Greece's government is highly bureaucratic, and many regulations are burdensome. According to the U.S. Department of Commerce, "As an EU member, Greece is required to have transparent policies and effective laws for fostering competition. In practice, however, the process is not transparent due to overlapping laws and confusion in their application. Foreign companies consider the complexity of government regulations and procedures—and their implementation by the Greek civil administration—to be the greatest impediment to operating in Greece."[5] When compared with other countries, however, Greece's regulatory burden is moderate.

BLACK MARKET
Score: 3–Stable (moderate level of activity)

Greece is a popular place for smuggling, particularly of recorded music and videos. According to the U.S. Department of Commerce, "Despite Greece's legal framework for and voiced commitment to copyright protection, piracy of copyrighted material, especially audio-visual works for television, remains widespread."[6]

NOTES

1   U.S. Department of Commerce, *Country Commercial Guide,* 1998.
2   *Ibid.*
3   *Ibid.*
4   *Ibid.*
5   *Ibid.*
6   *Ibid.*

Guatemala 2.75

1998 Score: **2.80**	1997 Score: **2.80**	1996 Score: **2.85**

Trade	3	Banking	2
Taxation	2.5	Wages and Prices	3
Government Intervention	1	Property Rights	3
Monetary Policy	3	Regulation	4
Foreign Investment	3	Black Market	3

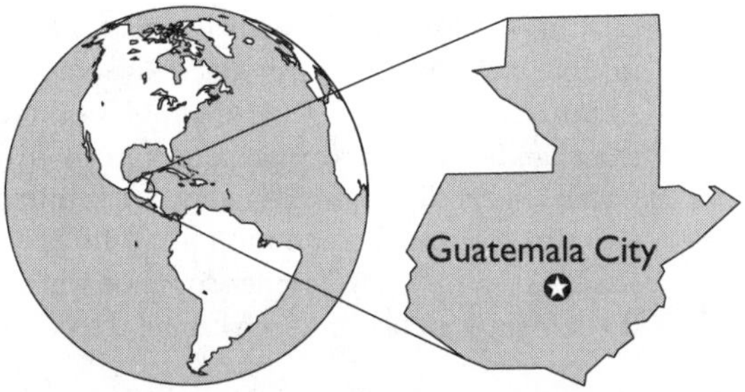

In 1997, the government of President Alvaro Arzu signed a peace agreement with Guatemalan guerrillas, ending a civil war that had raged for decades. Following his election in January 1996, President Arzu nominated several business leaders to cabinet-level and other government positions and launched a new economic liberalization program. Arzu faces a legislature that largely opposes market reforms, however. Nevertheless, Guatemala recently reduced some taxes. As a result, its overall score is 0.05 point better than last year.

Trade Policy

Score: 3–Stable (moderate level of protectionism)

Guatemala's average tariff rate is 8 percent.[1] Non-tariff barriers include the arbitrary application of customs procedures and red tape in the customs agency. There are some restrictions on poultry imports. According to the U.S. Department of Commerce, "Exporters to Guatemala enjoy an increasingly open trade regime. Imports are generally not subject to non-tariff trade barriers, though there are occasional cases of arbitrary customs valuation and excessive bureaucratic obstacles that can create delays."[2]

Taxation

Score–Income taxation: 2+ (low tax rates)
Score–Corporate taxation: 2–Stable (low tax rates)
Final Taxation Score: 2.5+ (moderate tax rates)

Guatemala's top tax rate is 25 percent, down from 30 percent in 1997. As a result, Guatemala's income tax score is 1 point lower this year than last year, making the overall tax score 0.5 point lower this year. The average income level is taxed at 15 percent. The top corporate income tax is 30 percent. Guatemala also has a 10 percent capital gains tax, a 10 percent value-added tax, and a land tax.

Government Intervention in the Economy

Score: 1–Stable (very low level)

Government consumes 8.4 percent of GDP. The government has completed privatizing some state-owned sectors in telecommunications, electricity, and railways. According to the U.S. Department of Commerce, "Government has traditionally played a minor role in the economy."[3]

Monetary Policy

Score: 3–Stable (moderate level of inflation)

From 1986 to 1996, Guatemala's average annual rate of inflation was 15.5 percent. In 1997, the rate was 9 percent.

Capital Flows and Foreign Investment

Score: 3–Stable (moderate barriers)

Foreign investment usually is welcome, although the government imposes restrictions on investment in utilities and such domestic industries as fishing,

Mostly Free

1	Hong Kong	1.25	81	Fiji	3.10
2	Singapore	1.30	81	Mali	3.10
3	Bahrain	1.70	81	Slovenia	3.10
4	New Zealand	1.75	85	Honduras	3.15
5	Switzerland	1.85	85	Mexico	3.15
6	United States	1.90	85	Papua New Guinea	3.15
7	Ireland	1.95	88	Djibouti	3.20
7	Luxembourg	1.95	88	Mongolia	3.20
7	Taiwan	1.95	90	Algeria	3.25
7	United Kingdom	1.95	90	Brazil	3.25
11	Bahamas	2.00	90	Lebanon	3.25
12	Czech Republic	2.05	90	Senegal	3.25
12	Japan	2.05	90	Tanzania	3.25
14	Australia	2.10	95	Nigeria	3.30
14	Belgium	2.10	95	Romania	3.30
14	Canada	2.10	97	Cambodia	3.35
14	United Arab Emirates	2.10	97	Dominican Republic	3.35
18	Austria	2.15	97	Egypt	3.35
18	Chile	2.15	97	Guinea	3.35
18	Estonia	2.15	97	Ivory Coast	3.35
18	Netherlands	2.15	97	Moldova	3.35
22	Denmark	2.25	97	Pakistan	3.35
22	El Salvador	2.25	104	Nepal	3.40
22	Finland	2.25	104	Venezuela	3.40
25	Germany	2.30	106	Armenia	3.45
25	Iceland	2.30	106	Bulgaria	3.45
27	Norway	2.35	106	Lesotho	3.45
28	Korea, South	2.40	106	Madagascar	3.45
28	Kuwait	2.40	106	Russia	3.45
28	Malaysia	2.40	111	Burkina Faso	3.50
28	Panama	2.40	111	Cameroon	3.50
28	Thailand	2.40	111	Guyana	3.50
33	Sweden	2.45	111	Nicaragua	3.50
34	Argentina	2.50	115	Gambia	3.60
34	France	2.50	116	Croatia	3.65
34	Italy	2.50	116	Georgia	3.65
34	Spain	2.50	116	Malawi	3.65
38	Portugal	2.55	119	Cape Verde	3.67
38	Sri Lanka	2.55	120	Ethiopia	3.70
38	Trinidad and Tobago	2.55	120	India	3.70
41	Barbados	2.60	120	Niger	3.70
41	Peru	2.60	123	Congo	3.75
43	Bolivia	2.65	124	Chad	3.80
43	Mauritius	2.65	124	China	3.80
45	Cyprus	2.70	124	Mauritania	3.80
45	Jamaica	2.70	124	Ukraine	3.80
45	Uruguay	2.70	124	Zimbabwe	3.80
48	Botswana	2.75	129	Albania	3.85
48	Guatemala	2.75	129	Bangladesh	3.85
48	Jordan	2.75	129	Mozambique	3.85
48	Namibia	2.75	129	Suriname	3.85
48	Oman	2.75	133	Burundi	3.90
48	Philippines	2.75	134	Togo	3.95
54	Belize	2.80	135	Haiti	4.00
54	Costa Rica	2.80	135	Kyrgyz Rep.	4.00
54	Israel	2.80	137	Kazakhstan	4.05
54	Swaziland	2.80	137	Sierra Leone	4.05
54	Turkey	2.80	139	Yemen	4.10
54	Uganda	2.80	140	Belarus	4.15
54	Samoa	2.80	141	Sudan	4.20
61	Latvia	2.85	141	Syria	4.20
62	Greece	2.90	143	Azerbaijan	4.30
62	Hungary	2.90	143	Equatorial Guinea	4.30
62	So. Africa	2.90	143	Myanmar	4.30
65	Ecuador	2.95	143	Rwanda	4.30
65	Gabon	2.95	147	Tajikistan	4.40
65	Indonesia	2.95	147	Uzbekistan	4.40
65	Malta	2.95	149	Angola	4.45
65	Morocco	2.95	149	Turkmenistan	4.45
65	Poland	2.95	151	Guinea-Bissau	4.55
65	Tunisia	2.95	152	Vietnam	4.60
72	Ghana	3.00	153	Congo (Zaire)	4.70
72	Lithuania	3.00	153	Iran	4.70
72	Saudi Arabia	3.00	155	Bosnia	4.80
75	Benin	3.05	155	Somalia	4.80
75	Kenya	3.05	157	Iraq	4.90
75	Paraguay	3.05	157	Laos	4.90
75	Qatar	3.05	157	Libya	4.90
75	Slovak Republic	3.05	160	Cuba	5.00
75	Zambia	3.05	160	Korea, North	5.00
81	Colombia	3.10			

mining, and forestry. Investments in banks, auditing, and insurance services also are subject to some restrictions. According to the U.S. Department of Commerce, "Guatemala can be an attractive place for foreign investment, which is generally afforded national treatment. Investors face time-consuming administrative obstacles and occasional arbitrary impediments, some of which occur after the investment is in place, which can be discouraging."[4]

BANKING
Score: 2–Stable (low level of restrictions)

The government recently liberalized the banking sector to allow for more foreign participation and domestic competition. According to the U.S. Department of Commerce, "Capital markets in Guatemala have been developing rapidly in recent years but remain fairly shallow. There are now 34 private commercial banks, up from 21 just three years ago.... Also a number of informal, extralegal financial institutions operate independent of any government supervision. These include moneychangers, informal investment firms, and traditional rural moneylenders. Government intervention in the financial sector is limited to implementation of monetary policy and to prudential regulation of the banks, investment firms, bonded warehouses and exchange houses. Credit is not rationed or otherwise directed by the government with the minor exception of a small amount of lending subsidized by the government—principally for small businesses, small farms or low-income housing."[5]

WAGE AND PRICE CONTROLS
Score: 3–Stable (moderate level)

Guatemala has a minimum wage law. The government imposes no official price controls but does use "price bands" for some agricultural goods. A price band defines the price level of a given product; if the price rises above this level, the government may step in to impose a lower price. The effect, therefore, quite often is to control prices.

PROPERTY RIGHTS
Score: 3–Stable (moderate level of protection)

Property is not subject to expropriation; in fact, none has been expropriated since the 1950s. The dispute settlement system often is cumbersome, however. According to the U.S. Department of Commerce, "On paper, Guatemalan procedures for enforcing agreements do not differ significantly from those of the United States. In practice, however, the process is less transparent, cumbersome and poorly implemented. The time required to complete these procedures can be significant and Guatemala does not allow the parties to proceed to arbitration or obtain a default award until those procedures are completed. The procedures for enforcing foreign awards are even more cumbersome. The party against whom enforcement is sought can raise a number of procedural objections through the judicial process, in a manner that is inconsistent with the New York Convention."[6]

REGULATION
Score: 4–Stable (high level)

Guatemala's regulations are ambiguous, interpreted by bureaucrats who apply them arbitrarily. "Bureaucratic hurdles are common for both domestic and foreign companies wishing to operate in Guatemala," reports the U.S. Department of Commerce. "Not infrequently, companies are subject to ambiguous requirements, applied inconsistently by different government agencies. Regulations—where they exist—often contain few explicit criteria for the government decision maker, creating uncertainty. Public participation in the promulgation of regulations is rare and there is no consistent judicial review of administrative rule making."[7] Corruption also is present, according to the U.S. Department of Commerce: "Corruption is a serious problem which companies may encounter at any level. Bribery is illegal under the penal code, however, enforcement has not been effective. Although there are basic laws that are aimed at combating corruption, there is a lack of enforcement and compliance."[8]

BLACK MARKET
Score: 3–Stable (moderate level of activity)

Guatemala provides no effective protection for intellectual property, so there is black market activity in this area. "Protection of intellectual property is inadequate and an impediment to investment," reports the U.S. Department of Commerce. "Enforcement mechanisms are virtually nonexistent, penalties are weak, and an overburdened, poorly trained judiciary does not understand the issues."[9]

NOTES
[1] Based on total taxes on international trade as a percentage of total imports.
[2] U.S. Department of Commerce, *Country Commercial Guide*, 1998.
[3] *Ibid.*
[4] *Ibid.*
[5] *Ibid.*
[6] *Ibid.*
[7] *Ibid.*
[8] *Ibid.*
[9] *Ibid.*

Guinea   3.35

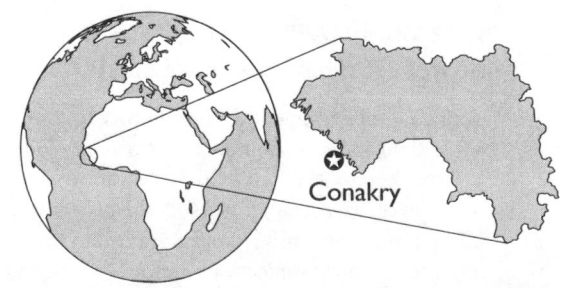
Conakry

1998 Score: **3.25**   1997 Score: **3.45**   1996 Score: **3.35**

Trade	3	Banking	3
Taxation	4.5	Wages and Prices	2
Government Intervention	3	Property Rights	4
Monetary Policy	3	Regulation	4
Foreign Investment	3	Black Market	4

Guinea was colonized by France in 1891 and gained its independence in 1958, after which the new government established a socialist state. Despite abundant natural resources, including bauxite, diamonds, and gold, Guinea's state-controlled economy stagnated. In 1984, General Lansana Conté seized power and initiated an economic liberalization program. GDP growth averaged 4.1 percent from 1992 to 1996. A new constitution adopted in 1990 allowed for limited political and economic reforms, and opposition parties were legalized in 1992. Conté, the former dictator and current president, is strongly favored to win re-election in December 1998. Although foreign aid donors, including the International Monetary Fund, have been disappointed with the slow progress of economic reform, they continue to provide the country with considerable aid. Restrictions on banking recently have increased. As a result, Guinea's overall score is 0.1 point worse than last year.

TRADE POLICY
Score: 3–Stable (moderate level of protectionism)

Guinea's average tariff rate is about 7 percent.[1] Licenses are required for "restricted goods" like cement, rice, wheat flour, and other agricultural products. Some imports require special authorization from the Central Bank.

TAXATION
Score–Income taxation: 5–Stable (very high tax rates)
Score–Corporate taxation: 3–Stable (moderate tax rates)
Final Taxation Score: 4.5–Stable (very high tax rates)

Guinea's top income tax rate is 40 percent; the average income level is taxed at 25 percent. The top corporate tax rate is 35 percent. The government also imposes a 35 percent capital gains tax and an 18 percent value-added tax.

GOVERNMENT INTERVENTION IN THE ECONOMY
Score: 3–Stable (moderate level)

Government consumes 11.1 percent of GDP. In an attempt to downsize a swollen government, Guinea plans to privatize schools and return doctors to the private sector by ending the state-supplied health care system. The pace of privatization has been slow, and Guinea still has a large state-owned sector.

MONETARY POLICY
Score: 3–Stable (moderate level of inflation)

From 1986 to 1996, Guinea's average annual rate of inflation was 16.4 percent. In 1997, the rate was about 3 percent.

1	Hong Kong	1.25		81	Fiji	3.10
2	Singapore	1.30		81	Mali	3.10
3	Bahrain	1.70		81	Slovenia	3.10
4	New Zealand	1.75		85	Honduras	3.15
5	Switzerland	1.85		85	Mexico	3.15
6	United States	1.90		85	Papua New Guinea	3.15
7	Ireland	1.95		88	Djibouti	3.20
7	Luxembourg	1.95		88	Mongolia	3.20
7	Taiwan	1.95		90	Algeria	3.25
7	United Kingdom	1.95		90	Brazil	3.25
11	Bahamas	2.00		90	Lebanon	3.25
12	Czech Republic	2.05		90	Senegal	3.25
12	Japan	2.05		90	Tanzania	3.25
14	Australia	2.10		95	Nigeria	3.30
14	Belgium	2.10		95	Romania	3.30
14	Canada	2.10		97	Cambodia	3.35
14	United Arab Emirates	2.10		97	Dominican Republic	3.35
18	Austria	2.15		97	Egypt	3.35
18	Chile	2.15		97	Guinea	3.35
18	Estonia	2.15		97	Ivory Coast	3.35
18	Netherlands	2.15		97	Moldova	3.35
22	Denmark	2.25		97	Pakistan	3.35
22	El Salvador	2.25		104	Nepal	3.40
22	Finland	2.25		104	Venezuela	3.40
25	Germany	2.30		106	Armenia	3.45
25	Iceland	2.30		106	Bulgaria	3.45
27	Norway	2.35		106	Lesotho	3.45
28	Korea, South	2.40		106	Madagascar	3.45
28	Kuwait	2.40		106	Russia	3.45
28	Malaysia	2.40		111	Burkina Faso	3.50
28	Panama	2.40		111	Cameroon	3.50
28	Thailand	2.40		111	Guyana	3.50
33	Sweden	2.45		111	Nicaragua	3.50
34	Argentina	2.50		115	Gambia	3.60
34	France	2.50		116	Croatia	3.65
34	Italy	2.50		116	Georgia	3.65
34	Spain	2.50		116	Malawi	3.65
38	Portugal	2.55		119	Cape Verde	3.67
38	Sri Lanka	2.55		120	Ethiopia	3.70
38	Trinidad and Tobago	2.55		120	India	3.70
41	Barbados	2.60		120	Niger	3.70
41	Peru	2.60		123	Congo	3.75
43	Bolivia	2.65		124	Chad	3.80
43	Mauritius	2.65		124	China	3.80
45	Cyprus	2.70		124	Mauritania	3.80
45	Jamaica	2.70		124	Ukraine	3.80
45	Uruguay	2.70		124	Zimbabwe	3.80
48	Botswana	2.75		129	Albania	3.85
48	Guatemala	2.75		129	Bangladesh	3.85
48	Jordan	2.75		129	Mozambique	3.85
48	Namibia	2.75		129	Suriname	3.85
48	Oman	2.75		133	Burundi	3.90
48	Philippines	2.75		134	Togo	3.95
54	Belize	2.80		135	Haiti	4.00
54	Costa Rica	2.80		135	Kyrgyz Rep.	4.00
54	Israel	2.80		137	Kazakhstan	4.05
54	Swaziland	2.80		137	Sierra Leone	4.05
54	Turkey	2.80		139	Yemen	4.10
54	Uganda	2.80		140	Belarus	4.15
54	Samoa	2.80		141	Sudan	4.20
61	Latvia	2.85		141	Syria	4.20
62	Greece	2.90		143	Azerbaijan	4.30
62	Hungary	2.90		143	Equatorial Guinea	4.30
62	So. Africa	2.90		143	Myanmar	4.30
65	Ecuador	2.95		143	Rwanda	4.30
65	Gabon	2.95		147	Tajikistan	4.40
65	Indonesia	2.95		147	Uzbekistan	4.40
65	Malta	2.95		149	Angola	4.45
65	Morocco	2.95		149	Turkmenistan	4.45
65	Poland	2.95		151	Guinea-Bissau	4.55
65	Tunisia	2.95		152	Vietnam	4.60
72	Ghana	3.00		153	Congo (Zaire)	4.70
72	Lithuania	3.00		153	Iran	4.70
72	Saudi Arabia	3.00		155	Bosnia	4.80
75	Benin	3.05		155	Somalia	4.80
75	Kenya	3.05		157	Iraq	4.90
75	Paraguay	3.05		157	Laos	4.90
75	Qatar	3.05		157	Libya	4.90
75	Slovak Republic	3.05		160	Cuba	5.00
75	Zambia	3.05		160	Korea, North	5.00
81	Colombia	3.10				

Mostly Unfree

CAPITAL FLOWS AND FOREIGN INVESTMENT
Score: 3–Stable (moderate barriers)

Guinea has been opening its economy to foreign investment since 1990 and has adopted an investment code based on a system used by the Ivory Coast that allows investment in many industrial sectors. In 1992, the government began to allow 100 percent private participation in the mining sector, and the telecommunications sector was opened partially to private participation. The government carefully screens new investment, and it restricts some repatriation of capital.

BANKING
Score: 3– (moderate level of restrictions)

There are few restrictions on banks. Most are in private hands as a result of a massive privatization of the banking industry in the late 1980s and early 1990s. Foreign banks are welcome, and six commercial banks currently operate in the country. The government has tightened lending regulations, however, raised reserve requirements, and made borrower qualifications more strict. Moreover, a recent assessment of the banking system by the U.S. Department of Commerce has uncovered several lingering problems: "Because of the lack of competition, the uncertain financial health of some banks, and the uncertainty of profitability and law enforcement, the banking system has a narrow base, is very fragile and is unable to meet the development needs of the private sector."[2] As a result of this new assessment, Guinea's banking score is 1 point worse this year.

WAGE AND PRICE CONTROLS
Score: 2–Stable (low level)

Price controls have been removed on most items but remain on fuel, taxis, and bus fares. The Ministry of Trade reserves the right to introduce emergency price control measures. There is no minimum wage.

PROPERTY RIGHTS
Score: 4–Stable (low level of protection)

Property is not completely secure. According to the U.S. Department of Commerce, "As with ownership of business enterprises, both foreign and national individuals have the right to own property. However, enforcement of these rights depends on a corrupt and inefficient Guinean legal and administrative system. As of yet, few cases exist which demonstrate that the legal system provides much effective protection in property rights dispute cases."[3]

REGULATION
Score: 4–Stable (high level)

Although the government has taken steps to end its interference in private business, a huge bureaucracy remains an impediment to free enterprise. The U.S. Department of Commerce reports, "According to local and expatriate businesspersons the GOG [Government of Guinea] lacks transparency in the application of the law. However, businesspersons assert that application procedures are sufficiently opaque to allow for significant corruption, and regulatory activity is often applied based on personal interest."[4]

BLACK MARKET
Score: 4–Stable (high level of activity)

Guinea has a large black market, especially in luxury goods (which otherwise would face a 40 percent tariff rate). Moreover, a large segment of the population works in the informal sector. For example, some 50 percent of the working population officially is "unemployed," but 90 percent of those individuals actually work in the informal sector.[5]

NOTES

1   World Bank, *World Development Indicators*, 1998.
2   U.S. Department of Commerce, *Country Commercial Guide*, 1998.
3   *Ibid.*
4   *Ibid.*
5   *Ibid.*

Guinea-Bissau   4.55

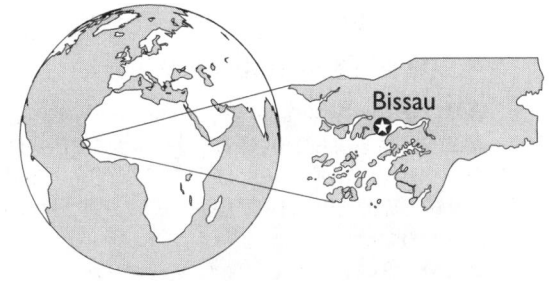

1997 Score: **n/a**	1996 Score: **n/a**	1995 Score: **n/a**

Trade	5	Banking	5
Taxation	3.5	Wages and Prices	4
Government Intervention	4	Property Rights	5
Monetary Policy	5	Regulation	5
Foreign Investment	4	Black Market	5

Guinea-Bissau gained independence from Portugal in September 1974. After a coup in 1980 overthrew the existing government, a provisional government existed until 1984, when a new legislature and president were elected. Army chief Ansomane Mane attempted a coup d'état in June 1998, citing government corruption under President Joao Bernado Vieira. The country today is in the midst of a civil war. The socialist economic programs of the late 1970s resulted in extensive foreign debt and failed enterprises. Today, Guinea-Bissau remains one of the least developed countries in the world and one of the ten poorest, with a GNP per capita of $250 in 1996. At that time, Guinea-Bissau had little infrastructure and its total industry consisted of only one factory. Agriculture dominates the economy; it accounts for 45 percent of GDP, nearly 100 percent of exports, and about 90 percent of employment.

TRADE POLICY
Score: 5–Stable (very high level of protectionism)

Guinea-Bissau's average tariff rate is unknown. The current level of political unrest, however, has caused movement of goods across the border nearly to cease. What little trade does occur is funneled through a corrupt and inefficient customs service that regularly confiscates imports or charges arbitrary rates.

TAXATION
Score–Income taxation: 3–Stable (moderate tax rates)
Score–Corporate taxation: 3–Stable (moderate tax rates)
Final Taxation Score: 3.5–Stable (high tax rates)

Guinea-Bissau's tax revenue as a percentage of GDP is about 10 percent.[1] Moreover, the country has a capital gains tax, a value-added tax, and some sales taxes.[2]

GOVERNMENT INTERVENTION IN THE ECONOMY
Score: 4–Stable (high level)

Government consumes only 7 percent of GDP. This figure significantly understates the level of government intervention in the economy, however: The government partly or completely owns companies involved in almost all facets of the economy. Thus, if actual government expenditures are taken into account, government's consumption rate probably is closer to 30 percent. In addition, government continues to produce most of the country's GDP.

MONETARY POLICY
Score: 5–Stable (very high level of inflation)

From 1986 to 1996, Guinea-Bissau's average annual rate of inflation was 67.2 percent. In 1997, the rate fell to about 30 percent.

1	Hong Kong	1.25	81	Fiji	3.10
2	Singapore	1.30	81	Mali	3.10
3	Bahrain	1.70	81	Slovenia	3.10
4	New Zealand	1.75	85	Honduras	3.15
5	Switzerland	1.85	85	Mexico	3.15
6	United States	1.90	85	Papua New Guinea	3.15
7	Ireland	1.95	88	Djibouti	3.20
7	Luxembourg	1.95	88	Mongolia	3.20
7	Taiwan	1.95	90	Algeria	3.25
7	United Kingdom	1.95	90	Brazil	3.25
11	Bahamas	2.00	90	Lebanon	3.25
12	Czech Republic	2.05	90	Senegal	3.25
12	Japan	2.05	90	Tanzania	3.25
14	Australia	2.10	95	Nigeria	3.30
14	Belgium	2.10	95	Romania	3.30
14	Canada	2.10	97	Cambodia	3.35
14	United Arab Emirates	2.10	97	Dominican Republic	3.35
18	Austria	2.15	97	Egypt	3.35
18	Chile	2.15	97	Guinea	3.35
18	Estonia	2.15	97	Ivory Coast	3.35
18	Netherlands	2.15	97	Moldova	3.35
22	Denmark	2.25	97	Pakistan	3.35
22	El Salvador	2.25	104	Nepal	3.40
22	Finland	2.25	104	Venezuela	3.40
25	Germany	2.30	106	Armenia	3.45
25	Iceland	2.30	106	Bulgaria	3.45
27	Norway	2.35	106	Lesotho	3.45
28	Korea, South	2.40	106	Madagascar	3.45
28	Kuwait	2.40	106	Russia	3.45
28	Malaysia	2.40	111	Burkina Faso	3.50
28	Panama	2.40	111	Cameroon	3.50
28	Thailand	2.40	111	Guyana	3.50
33	Sweden	2.45	111	Nicaragua	3.50
34	Argentina	2.50	115	Gambia	3.60
34	France	2.50	116	Croatia	3.65
34	Italy	2.50	116	Georgia	3.65
34	Spain	2.50	116	Malawi	3.65
38	Portugal	2.55	119	Cape Verde	3.67
38	Sri Lanka	2.55	120	Ethiopia	3.70
38	Trinidad and Tobago	2.55	120	India	3.70
41	Barbados	2.60	120	Niger	3.70
41	Peru	2.60	123	Congo	3.75
43	Bolivia	2.65	124	Chad	3.80
43	Mauritius	2.65	124	China	3.80
45	Cyprus	2.70	124	Mauritania	3.80
45	Jamaica	2.70	124	Ukraine	3.80
45	Uruguay	2.70	124	Zimbabwe	3.80
48	Botswana	2.75	129	Albania	3.85
48	Guatemala	2.75	129	Bangladesh	3.85
48	Jordan	2.75	129	Mozambique	3.85
48	Namibia	2.75	129	Suriname	3.85
48	Oman	2.75	133	Burundi	3.90
48	Philippines	2.75	134	Togo	3.95
54	Belize	2.80	135	Haiti	4.00
54	Costa Rica	2.80	135	Kyrgyz Rep.	4.00
54	Israel	2.80	137	Kazakhstan	4.05
54	Swaziland	2.80	137	Sierra Leone	4.05
54	Turkey	2.80	139	Yemen	4.10
54	Uganda	2.80	140	Belarus	4.15
54	Samoa	2.80	141	Sudan	4.20
61	Latvia	2.85	141	Syria	4.20
62	Greece	2.90	143	Azerbaijan	4.30
62	Hungary	2.90	143	Equatorial Guinea	4.30
62	So. Africa	2.90	143	Myanmar	4.30
65	Ecuador	2.95	143	Rwanda	4.30
65	Gabon	2.95	147	Tajikistan	4.40
65	Indonesia	2.95	147	Uzbekistan	4.40
65	Malta	2.95	149	Angola	4.45
65	Morocco	2.95	149	Turkmenistan	4.45
65	Poland	2.95	151	Guinea-Bissau	4.55
65	Tunisia	2.95	152	Vietnam	4.60
72	Ghana	3.00	153	Congo (Zaire)	4.70
72	Lithuania	3.00	153	Iran	4.70
72	Saudi Arabia	3.00	155	Bosnia	4.80
75	Benin	3.05	155	Somalia	4.80
75	Kenya	3.05	157	Iraq	4.90
75	Paraguay	3.05	157	Laos	4.90
75	Qatar	3.05	157	Libya	4.90
75	Slovak Republic	3.05	160	Cuba	5.00
75	Zambia	3.05	160	Korea, North	5.00
81	Colombia	3.10			

Repressed

CAPITAL FLOWS AND FOREIGN INVESTMENT
Score: 4–Stable (high barriers)

Although some foreign investment is occurring in Guinea-Bissau, the country has yet to establish an official and transparent investment code. Moreover, the government allows foreign investment only on a case-by-case basis.

BANKING
Score: 5–Stable (very high level of restrictions)

The banking system is nearly all government-owned and -operated. In addition, what financial system the country does have is in disarray.

WAGE AND PRICE CONTROLS
Score: 4–Stable (low level)

Guinea-Bissau's large government sector exerts a great influence over prices. The government continues to subsidize some industries, including agriculture and fishing, thus influencing the prices of related products. In addition, the large number of government jobs has a de facto control over wages.

PROPERTY RIGHTS
Score: 5–Stable (very low level of protection)

There is no judicial system in Guinea-Bissau. Although the government does not outlaw private property directly, neither is there any official apparatus for its protection.

REGULATION
Score: 5–Stable (very high level)

Government regulations are neither transparent nor applied consistently. Corruption is pervasive and adds significantly to the cost of doing business in Guinea-Bissau.

BLACK MARKET
Score: 5–Stable (very high level of activity)

Guinea-Bissau has a black market so large that it eclipses the legal market.

NOTES

[1]   The top income tax and corporate tax rate is not known. Thus, total tax revenue as a percentage of GDP is used to first categorize the level of taxation in Guinea-Bissau. The government also imposes random taxation on the population, however, so official taxation figures are misleading.

[2]   Tax evasion is widespread, a phenomenon that explains the relatively low tax revenues as a percentage of GDP.

Guyana   3.50

1998 Score: **3.60**   1997 Score: **3.50**   1996 Score: **3.40**

Trade	5	Banking	3
Taxation	4	Wages and Prices	2
Government Intervention	2	Property Rights	3
Monetary Policy	5	Regulation	4
Foreign Investment	3	Black Market	4

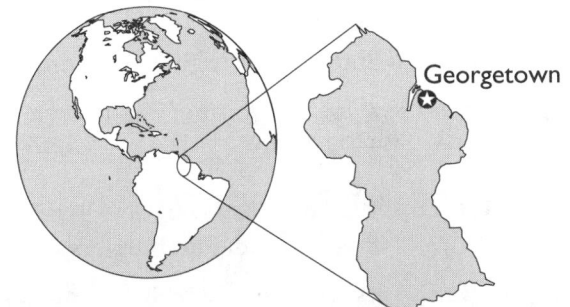

Georgetown

Since winning its independence from the United Kingdom in 1966, Guyana has followed a mainly socialist economic course and today is among the world's poorest countries. The government is controlled by the People's Progressive Party; since 1992, it has made sweeping reforms aimed at attracting foreign investment by relying on the free market. Recently, Guyana reduced its government consumption of GDP by limiting the size of its public sector, reforming its banking industry, and cutting back on some black market activities. The government recently privatized the National Bank of Industry, thus reducing its level of intervention in the economy. As a result, Guyana's overall score this year is 0.1 point better than last year.

TRADE POLICY
Score: 5–Stable (very high level of protectionism)

Despite an easing of formal barriers to trade, Guyana's tariffs still range from 0 percent to 20 percent. The average tariff rate is about 17 percent. Government paperwork, corruption, and informal obstacles remain substantial barriers to trade. According to the U.S. Department of Commerce, "All shipments are inspected, both imports and exports. Since the Customs Department (like many government agencies) is extremely understaffed, the mandatory inspection often results in extended waits on the wharf. There are special provisions for perishable goods. Some businesses allege that obstacles are created by individuals who frustrate processing in hopes of attaining inducements to expedite clearances. There is a proposal under consideration to create an independent agency for customs and tax collection. If implemented, this may help to alleviate some of the difficulties currently endemic to the system."[1]

TAXATION
Score–Income taxation: 3–Stable (moderate tax rates)
Score–Corporate taxation: 4–Stable (high tax rates)
Final Taxation Score: 4–Stable (high tax rates)

Guyana's tax on income is a flat 33.3 percent, and its top corporate tax rate is 45 percent.[2] Guyana also has a 20 percent capital gains tax and a property tax.

GOVERNMENT INTERVENTION IN THE ECONOMY
Score: 2+ (low level)

The central government consumes about 12.8 percent of GDP. According to the Economist Intelligence Unit, the government's privatization drive has been "slow and erratic."[3] The government recently privatized its National Bank of Industry, however; as a result, the government's influence over the market has diminished significantly. As a result, Guyana's government intervention score is 1 point better than last year.

1	Hong Kong	1.25
2	Singapore	1.30
3	Bahrain	1.70
4	New Zealand	1.75
5	Switzerland	1.85
6	United States	1.90
7	Ireland	1.95
7	Luxembourg	1.95
7	Taiwan	1.95
7	United Kingdom	1.95
11	Bahamas	2.00
12	Czech Republic	2.05
12	Japan	2.05
14	Australia	2.10
14	Belgium	2.10
14	Canada	2.10
14	United Arab Emirates	2.10
18	Austria	2.15
18	Chile	2.15
18	Estonia	2.15
18	Netherlands	2.15
22	Denmark	2.25
22	El Salvador	2.25
22	Finland	2.25
25	Germany	2.30
25	Iceland	2.30
27	Norway	2.35
28	Korea, South	2.40
28	Kuwait	2.40
28	Malaysia	2.40
28	Panama	2.40
28	Thailand	2.40
33	Sweden	2.45
34	Argentina	2.50
34	France	2.50
34	Italy	2.50
34	Spain	2.50
38	Portugal	2.55
38	Sri Lanka	2.55
38	Trinidad and Tobago	2.55
41	Barbados	2.60
41	Peru	2.60
43	Bolivia	2.65
43	Mauritius	2.65
45	Cyprus	2.70
45	Jamaica	2.70
45	Uruguay	2.70
48	Botswana	2.75
48	Guatemala	2.75
48	Jordan	2.75
48	Namibia	2.75
48	Oman	2.75
48	Philippines	2.75
54	Belize	2.80
54	Costa Rica	2.80
54	Israel	2.80
54	Swaziland	2.80
54	Turkey	2.80
54	Uganda	2.80
54	Samoa	2.80
61	Latvia	2.85
62	Greece	2.90
62	Hungary	2.90
62	So. Africa	2.90
65	Ecuador	2.95
65	Gabon	2.95
65	Indonesia	2.95
65	Malta	2.95
65	Morocco	2.95
65	Poland	2.95
65	Tunisia	2.95
72	Ghana	3.00
72	Lithuania	3.00
72	Saudi Arabia	3.00
75	Benin	3.05
75	Kenya	3.05
75	Paraguay	3.05
75	Qatar	3.05
75	Slovak Republic	3.05
75	Zambia	3.05
81	Colombia	3.10

81	Fiji	3.10
81	Mali	3.10
81	Slovenia	3.10
85	Honduras	3.15
85	Mexico	3.15
85	Papua New Guinea	3.15
88	Djibouti	3.20
88	Mongolia	3.20
90	Algeria	3.25
90	Brazil	3.25
90	Lebanon	3.25
90	Senegal	3.25
90	Tanzania	3.25
95	Nigeria	3.30
95	Romania	3.30
97	Cambodia	3.35
97	Dominican Republic	3.35
97	Egypt	3.35
97	Guinea	3.35
97	Ivory Coast	3.35
97	Moldova	3.35
97	Pakistan	3.35
104	Nepal	3.40
104	Venezuela	3.40
106	Armenia	3.45
106	Bulgaria	3.45
106	Lesotho	3.45
106	Madagascar	3.45
106	Russia	3.45
111	Burkina Faso	3.50
111	Cameroon	3.50
111	Guyana	3.50
111	Nicaragua	3.50
115	Gambia	3.60
116	Croatia	3.65
116	Georgia	3.65
116	Malawi	3.65
119	Cape Verde	3.67
120	Ethiopia	3.70
120	India	3.70
120	Niger	3.70
123	Congo	3.75
124	Chad	3.80
124	China	3.80
124	Mauritania	3.80
124	Ukraine	3.80
124	Zimbabwe	3.80
129	Albania	3.85
129	Bangladesh	3.85
129	Mozambique	3.85
129	Suriname	3.85
133	Burundi	3.90
134	Togo	3.95
135	Haiti	4.00
135	Kyrgyz Rep.	4.00
137	Kazakhstan	4.05
137	Sierra Leone	4.05
139	Yemen	4.10
140	Belarus	4.15
141	Sudan	4.20
141	Syria	4.20
143	Azerbaijan	4.30
143	Equatorial Guinea	4.30
143	Myanmar	4.30
143	Rwanda	4.30
147	Tajikistan	4.40
147	Uzbekistan	4.40
149	Angola	4.45
149	Turkmenistan	4.45
151	Guinea-Bissau	4.55
152	Vietnam	4.60
153	Congo (Zaire)	4.70
153	Iran	4.70
155	Bosnia	4.80
155	Somalia	4.80
157	Iraq	4.90
157	Laos	4.90
157	Libya	4.90
160	Cuba	5.00
160	Korea, North	5.00

Mostly Unfree

MONETARY POLICY
Score: 5–Stable (very high level of inflation)

Guyana's average annual rate of inflation from 1986 to 1996 was 45.3 percent. In 1997, the rate was 4.1 percent.

CAPITAL FLOWS AND FOREIGN INVESTMENT
Score: 3–Stable (moderate barriers)

There are few restrictions on foreign investment, although investors are concerned about civil unrest, crime, and corruption. According to the U.S. Department of Commerce, "After years of a state-dominated economy, the mechanisms for private investment, domestic or foreign, are still evolving.... While there is no 'screening' of investment, the centralized process of decision-making and its lack of transparency can result in delays and frustration for foreign investors."[4]

BANKING
Score: 3–Stable (moderate level of restrictions)

Guyana's banking system is becoming more competitive. The government still owns portions of some banks, but there are plans to privatize these holdings. According to the U.S. Department of Commerce, "Any foreign borrower applying to borrow [over 2 million in local currency] must be given permission by the Minister of Finance."[5]

WAGE AND PRICE CONTROLS
Score: 2–Stable (low level)

Guyana maintains a minimum wage as well as price controls on electricity rates.

PROPERTY RIGHTS
Score: 3–Stable (moderate level of protection)

Private property is guaranteed and receives legal protection, but several Western firms are engaged in legal battles with the government over contracts. The judicial system often is slow and inefficient. According to the U.S. Department of State, "There is a constitutionally independent, albeit somewhat inefficient, judiciary."[6]

REGULATION
Score: 4–Stable (high level)

Some sectors of the economy, such as utilities and other state-owned industries, are highly regulated, and corruption often hinders the ability of companies in these sectors to do business. The U.S. Department of Commerce reports that "Attempts to reform bureaucratic procedures have not succeeded in limiting red tape: for example, businesses find that clearing shipments through customs is a long, tedious, and contentious process."[7]

BLACK MARKET
Score: 4–Stable (very high level of activity)

Guyana has a rather large black market, mainly because of trademark and copyright infringement and the massive pirating of video and audio recordings, and computer software. According to the U.S. Department of Commerce, "At present, there is no enforcement mechanism to protect intellectual property rights. Patent and trademark infringement are also common. Pirating of TV satellite signals is widespread and takes place with impunity."[8]

NOTES

[1] U.S. Department of Commerce, *Country Commercial Guide*, 1998.
[2] This rate applies to profits of commercial companies.
[3] Economist Intelligence Unit, "Guyana Investment: Slow and Erratic Privatisation Drive," *EIU ViewsWire*, April 6, 1998.
[4] U.S. Department of Commerce, *Country Commercial Guide*, 1998.
[5] *Ibid.*
[6] U.S. Department of State, "Guyana Country Report on Human Rights Practices for 1997," 1998.
[7] U.S. Department of Commerce, *Country Commercial Guide*, 1998.
[8] *Ibid.*

Haiti   4.00

1998 Score: **4.00**	1997 Score: **4.00**	1996 Score: **4.20**

Trade	4	Banking	4
Taxation	3	Wages and Prices	4
Government Intervention	3	Property Rights	5
Monetary Policy	3	Regulation	5
Foreign Investment	4	Black Market	5

Port-au-Prince

Haiti has little economic freedom, and its current president, René Préval, is no advocate of free markets. Former leader Jean-Bertrand Aristide remains the country's most powerful and influential political figure. Following his ouster by military coup in September 1991, Haiti became isolated economically and subject to a United Nations embargo. In October 1994, Aristide returned to power after armed intervention by the United States; Préval was elected in 1995, but Haiti's economy has not improved. An inefficient, well-entrenched, and corrupt bureaucracy continues to hinder the development of free and open markets, and political violence could destroy the economy. Haiti remains plagued by outdated regulations, corruption, and an almost total absence of property rights. Aristide, moreover, has emerged as the single greatest obstacle to democracy and free-market reforms.

TRADE POLICY
Score: 4–Stable (high level of protectionism)

Haiti has slashed tariffs to an average rate of 11.6 percent, but crime, corruption, and poor infrastructure make its market inaccessible to most imports. According to the U.S. Department of Commerce, "[C]orruption among customs officers does pose a problem in that petty bribes are sometimes necessary to clear shipments expeditiously. Some importers also reportedly negotiate customs duties with inspectors."[1]

TAXATION
Score–Income taxation: 3–Stable (moderate tax rates)
Score–Corporate taxation: 3–Stable (moderate tax rates)
Final Taxation Score: 3–Stable (high tax rates)

Haiti's top income tax rate is 30 percent, but the tax collection system is so poor that it is impossible to determine the rate that applies to the average income. Tax evasion is massive, and direct taxes represent only 25 percent of total receipts.[2] The top corporate income tax rate is 35 percent.

GOVERNMENT INTERVENTION IN THE ECONOMY
Score: 3–Stable (moderate level)

Government consumes about 20 percent of GDP, a significant portion of which is produced by the state-owned sector. Préval wants to privatize many large state-owned enterprises, but this initiative is being resisted by Aristide and the bureaucracy.

MONETARY POLICY
Score: 3–Stable (moderate level of inflation)

Haiti's average annual rate of inflation from 1986 to 1996 was 15.25 percent. In 1997, the rate was 16.2 percent.

1	Hong Kong	1.25	81	Fiji	3.10
2	Singapore	1.30	81	Mali	3.10
3	Bahrain	1.70	81	Slovenia	3.10
4	New Zealand	1.75	85	Honduras	3.15
5	Switzerland	1.85	85	Mexico	3.15
6	United States	1.90	85	Papua New Guinea	3.15
7	Ireland	1.95	88	Djibouti	3.20
7	Luxembourg	1.95	88	Mongolia	3.20
7	Taiwan	1.95	90	Algeria	3.25
7	United Kingdom	1.95	90	Brazil	3.25
11	Bahamas	2.00	90	Lebanon	3.25
12	Czech Republic	2.05	90	Senegal	3.25
12	Japan	2.05	90	Tanzania	3.25
14	Australia	2.10	95	Nigeria	3.30
14	Belgium	2.10	95	Romania	3.30
14	Canada	2.10	97	Cambodia	3.35
14	United Arab Emirates	2.10	97	Dominican Republic	3.35
18	Austria	2.15	97	Egypt	3.35
18	Chile	2.15	97	Guinea	3.35
18	Estonia	2.15	97	Ivory Coast	3.35
18	Netherlands	2.15	97	Moldova	3.35
22	Denmark	2.25	97	Pakistan	3.35
22	El Salvador	2.25	104	Nepal	3.40
22	Finland	2.25	104	Venezuela	3.40
25	Germany	2.30	106	Armenia	3.45
25	Iceland	2.30	106	Bulgaria	3.45
27	Norway	2.35	106	Lesotho	3.45
28	Korea, South	2.40	106	Madagascar	3.45
28	Kuwait	2.40	106	Russia	3.45
28	Malaysia	2.40	111	Burkina Faso	3.50
28	Panama	2.40	111	Cameroon	3.50
28	Thailand	2.40	111	Guyana	3.50
33	Sweden	2.45	111	Nicaragua	3.50
34	Argentina	2.50	115	Gambia	3.60
34	France	2.50	116	Croatia	3.65
34	Italy	2.50	116	Georgia	3.65
34	Spain	2.50	116	Malawi	3.65
38	Portugal	2.55	119	Cape Verde	3.67
38	Sri Lanka	2.55	120	Ethiopia	3.70
38	Trinidad and Tobago	2.55	120	India	3.70
41	Barbados	2.60	120	Niger	3.70
41	Peru	2.60	123	Congo	3.75
43	Bolivia	2.65	124	Chad	3.80
43	Mauritius	2.65	124	China	3.80
45	Cyprus	2.70	124	Mauritania	3.80
45	Jamaica	2.70	124	Ukraine	3.80
45	Uruguay	2.70	124	Zimbabwe	3.80
48	Botswana	2.75	129	Albania	3.85
48	Guatemala	2.75	129	Bangladesh	3.85
48	Jordan	2.75	129	Mozambique	3.85
48	Namibia	2.75	129	Suriname	3.85
48	Oman	2.75	133	Burundi	3.90
48	Philippines	2.75	134	Togo	3.95
54	Belize	2.80	135	Haiti	4.00
54	Costa Rica	2.80	135	Kyrgyz Rep.	4.00
54	Israel	2.80	137	Kazakhstan	4.05
54	Swaziland	2.80	137	Sierra Leone	4.05
54	Turkey	2.80	139	Yemen	4.10
54	Uganda	2.80	140	Belarus	4.15
54	Samoa	2.80	141	Sudan	4.20
61	Latvia	2.85	141	Syria	4.20
62	Greece	2.90	143	Azerbaijan	4.30
62	Hungary	2.90	143	Equatorial Guinea	4.30
62	So. Africa	2.90	143	Myanmar	4.30
65	Ecuador	2.95	143	Rwanda	4.30
65	Gabon	2.95	147	Tajikistan	4.40
65	Indonesia	2.95	147	Uzbekistan	4.40
65	Malta	2.95	149	Angola	4.45
65	Morocco	2.95	149	Turkmenistan	4.45
65	Poland	2.95	151	Guinea-Bissau	4.55
65	Tunisia	2.95	152	Vietnam	4.60
72	Ghana	3.00	153	Congo (Zaire)	4.70
72	Lithuania	3.00	153	Iran	4.70
72	Saudi Arabia	3.00	155	Bosnia	4.80
75	Benin	3.05	155	Somalia	4.80
75	Kenya	3.05	157	Iraq	4.90
75	Paraguay	3.05	157	Laos	4.90
75	Qatar	3.05	157	Libya	4.90
75	Slovak Republic	3.05	160	Cuba	5.00
75	Zambia	3.05	160	Korea, North	5.00
81	Colombia	3.10			

Repressed

CAPITAL FLOWS AND FOREIGN INVESTMENT
Score: 4–Stable (high barriers)

Haiti has opened its market to foreign investment, providing equal treatment to domestic and foreign firms. Its investment laws remain outdated, however, and are not always enforced by the corrupt bureaucracy. According to the U.S. Department of Commerce, "The protection and guarantees which Haitian law extends to investors are severely compromised by weak enforcement mechanisms, a poor judicial system and an antiquated legal system."[3] Moreover, although some foreign arbitration is allowed, foreign court decisions are not enforceable in Haitian courts.

BANKING
Score: 4–Stable (high level of restrictions)

Although Haiti now welcomes foreign banks, and recent changes allow foreign banks to engage in a variety of financial services, the banking system remains underdeveloped and in disarray. "Under Haitian law," reports the U.S. Department of Commerce, "banks are neither required to comply with internationally recognized accounting standards, nor to be audited by internationally recognized accounting firms.... Access to credit is restricted by the difficulty in assessing client risk and the lack of legal remedies for the lender in the event of default. Lack of a civil register, the absence of proper titles and problems with creating security interests pose additional institutional problems. As a result, banks lend only to their most trusted and credit-worthy clients."[4]

WAGE AND PRICE CONTROLS
Score: 4–Stable (high level)

With most of the economy a shambles, Haiti's government has attempted to eliminate its direct control of prices. It still directly controls prices on some items, however, including cement, gasoline, and a variety of staples like food; it also indirectly controls prices on other items. Under Aristide, the government established "communitarian" shops to provide basic goods. These shops, because they are subsidized by the government, depress prices for legitimate store operators and limit competition. Haiti has a minimum wage.

PROPERTY RIGHTS
Score: 5–Stable (very low level of protection)

Private property enjoys little or no protection in Haiti. The judiciary is notoriously corrupt, and even though expropriation is unlikely, property remains subject to crime and thievery. Haiti's police force also is corrupt, and oppression of the country's people is routine. According to the U.S. Department of State, "The judicial system—while theoretically independent—remained weak, disorganized, and corrupt after decades of government interference, financial neglect, and corruption.... The protection and guarantees which Haitian law extends to investors are severely compromised by weak enforcement mechanisms, a poor judicial system and an antiquated legal system"[5]

REGULATION
Score: 5–Stable (very high level)

It is virtually impossible to open a business legally under Haitian law. "Haiti's commercial code," reports the U.S. Department of Commerce, "dates from 1826 and underwent its last significant revision in 1944.... Bureaucratic procedures are not uniform and frequently involve excess red tape.... Tax, labor, and health and safety laws and policies are theoretically universally applicable, but are not universally applied or observed.... Haitian law is different in a number of areas, including operation of the judicial system; organization and operation of the executive branch; publication of laws; regulations and official notices; establishment of companies; land tenure and real property law and procedures; bank and credit operations; insurance and pension regulation; accounting standards; civil status documentation; customs law and administration; international trade and investment promotion; foreign investment regime; regulation of market concentration and competition; and privatization."[6] Haiti is among the world's most government-regulated countries.

BLACK MARKET
Score: 5–Stable (very high level of activity)

Even before the embargo, price controls and other inefficient government policies had created a large black market. At that time, the black market comprised around 40 percent of GDP; today, it surpasses GDP. According to the U.S. Department of Commerce, "Smuggling remains a major problem, with contraband accounting for a large percentage of the market for manufactured consumables."[7]

NOTES

[1] U.S. Department of Commerce, *Country Commercial Guide,* 1998.
[2] For this factor, Haiti is graded only on its top income tax rate.
[3] U.S. Department of Commerce, *Country Commercial Guide,* 1998.
[4] *Ibid.*
[5] U.S. Department of State, "Haiti Country Report on Human Rights Practices for 1997," 1998.
[6] U.S. Department of Commerce, *Country Commercial Guide,* 1998.
[7] *Ibid.*

Honduras   3.15

1998 Score: **3.15**	1997 Score: **3.15**		1996 Score: **3.15**	
Trade	4	Banking	3	
Taxation	3.5	Wages and Prices	3	
Government Intervention	2	Property Rights	3	
Monetary Policy	2	Regulation	4	
Foreign Investment	3	Black Market	4	

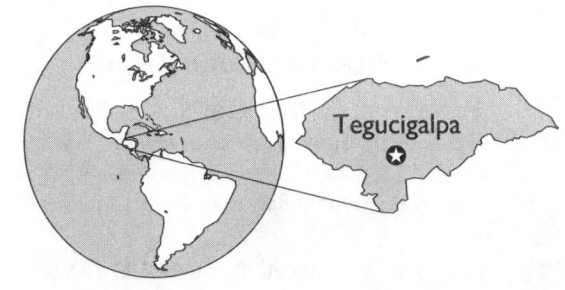

Tegucigalpa

Honduras is one of the poorest countries in the Western Hemisphere, despite its abundant natural resources and substantial U.S. and multilateral economic assistance.[1] From 1990 until 1993, the government implemented an ambitious economic reform program that included dismantling price controls, lowering import tariff duties, and removing many non-tariff barriers to trade. In 1992 and 1993, however, a sharp increase in public-sector investment spending reversed the fiscal progress that had been achieved, and domestic inflation increased. President Carlos Roberto Reina, inaugurated in 1994, took over a stagnant economy suffering from an energy crisis, falling output of key agricultural commodities, and extravagant public investment policies. He responded by cutting spending, improving tax collections, curtailing public-sector employment, and reducing the deficit. The Reina government also enacted modern financial reform legislation and authorized the privatization of the national telecommunications company and international airports. Anti-inflationary Central Bank policies have been tightened further, and strict limits imposed on public-sector borrowing. Government spending is rising again, however, although inflation is decreasing. The resulting two score changes cancel each other out, leaving Honduras's overall score unchanged.

TRADE POLICY
Score: 4–Stable (high level of protectionism)

Tariffs range from 5 percent to 20 percent; the average tariff rate is about 11 percent. Non-tariff barriers include strict labeling and sanitary requirements. According to the U.S. Department of State, "Honduras' customs administrative procedures are burdensome. There are extensive documentary requirements and red tape involving the payment of numerous import duties, customs surcharges, selective consumption taxes, consular fees and warehouse levies."[2]

TAXATION
Score–Income taxation: 2–Stable (low tax rates)
Score–Corporate taxation: 4–Stable (high tax rates)
Final Taxation Score: 3.5–Stable (high tax rates)

The top income tax rate is 40 percent; no taxes are imposed on the average level of income. The top corporate tax rate is 40.25 percent. There also is a 40.25 percent capital gains tax, a 7 percent sales tax, and various local taxes.

GOVERNMENT INTERVENTION IN THE ECONOMY
Score: 2– (low level)

Honduras's government consumes 10.5 percent of GDP, up from 8.8 percent last year; as a result, its score in this category is 1 point worse this year.

1	Hong Kong	1.25		81	Fiji	3.10
2	Singapore	1.30		81	Mali	3.10
3	Bahrain	1.70		81	Slovenia	3.10
4	New Zealand	1.75		85	Honduras	3.15
5	Switzerland	1.85		85	Mexico	3.15
6	United States	1.90		85	Papua New Guinea	3.15
7	Ireland	1.95		88	Djibouti	3.20
7	Luxembourg	1.95		88	Mongolia	3.20
7	Taiwan	1.95		90	Algeria	3.25
7	United Kingdom	1.95		90	Brazil	3.25
11	Bahamas	2.00		90	Lebanon	3.25
12	Czech Republic	2.05		90	Senegal	3.25
12	Japan	2.05		90	Tanzania	3.25
14	Australia	2.10		95	Nigeria	3.30
14	Belgium	2.10		95	Romania	3.30
14	Canada	2.10		97	Cambodia	3.35
14	United Arab Emirates	2.10		97	Dominican Republic	3.35
18	Austria	2.15		97	Egypt	3.35
18	Chile	2.15		97	Guinea	3.35
18	Estonia	2.15		97	Ivory Coast	3.35
18	Netherlands	2.15		97	Moldova	3.35
22	Denmark	2.25		97	Pakistan	3.35
22	El Salvador	2.25		104	Nepal	3.40
22	Finland	2.25		104	Venezuela	3.40
25	Germany	2.30		106	Armenia	3.45
25	Iceland	2.30		106	Bulgaria	3.45
27	Norway	2.35		106	Lesotho	3.45
28	Korea, South	2.40		106	Madagascar	3.45
28	Kuwait	2.40		106	Russia	3.45
28	Malaysia	2.40		111	Burkina Faso	3.50
28	Panama	2.40		111	Cameroon	3.50
28	Thailand	2.40		111	Guyana	3.50
33	Sweden	2.45		111	Nicaragua	3.50
34	Argentina	2.50		115	Gambia	3.60
34	France	2.50		116	Croatia	3.65
34	Italy	2.50		116	Georgia	3.65
34	Spain	2.50		116	Malawi	3.65
38	Portugal	2.55		119	Cape Verde	3.67
38	Sri Lanka	2.55		120	Ethiopia	3.70
38	Trinidad and Tobago	2.55		120	India	3.70
41	Barbados	2.60		120	Niger	3.70
41	Peru	2.60		123	Congo	3.75
43	Bolivia	2.65		124	Chad	3.80
43	Mauritius	2.65		124	China	3.80
45	Cyprus	2.70		124	Mauritania	3.80
45	Jamaica	2.70		124	Ukraine	3.80
45	Uruguay	2.70		124	Zimbabwe	3.80
48	Botswana	2.75		129	Albania	3.85
48	Guatemala	2.75		129	Bangladesh	3.85
48	Jordan	2.75		129	Mozambique	3.85
48	Namibia	2.75		129	Suriname	3.85
48	Oman	2.75		133	Burundi	3.90
48	Philippines	2.75		134	Togo	3.95
54	Belize	2.80		135	Haiti	4.00
54	Costa Rica	2.80		135	Kyrgyz Rep.	4.00
54	Israel	2.80		137	Kazakhstan	4.05
54	Swaziland	2.80		137	Sierra Leone	4.05
54	Turkey	2.80		139	Yemen	4.10
54	Uganda	2.80		140	Belarus	4.15
54	Samoa	2.80		141	Sudan	4.20
61	Latvia	2.85		141	Syria	4.20
62	Greece	2.90		143	Azerbaijan	4.30
62	Hungary	2.90		143	Equatorial Guinea	4.30
62	So. Africa	2.90		143	Myanmar	4.30
65	Ecuador	2.95		143	Rwanda	4.30
65	Gabon	2.95		147	Tajikistan	4.40
65	Indonesia	2.95		147	Uzbekistan	4.40
65	Malta	2.95		149	Angola	4.45
65	Morocco	2.95		149	Turkmenistan	4.45
65	Poland	2.95		151	Guinea-Bissau	4.55
65	Tunisia	2.95		152	Vietnam	4.60
72	Ghana	3.00		153	Congo (Zaire)	4.70
72	Lithuania	3.00		153	Iran	4.70
72	Saudi Arabia	3.00		155	Bosnia	4.80
75	Benin	3.05		155	Somalia	4.80
75	Kenya	3.05		157	Iraq	4.90
75	Paraguay	3.05		157	Laos	4.90
75	Qatar	3.05		157	Libya	4.90
75	Slovak Republic	3.05		160	Cuba	5.00
75	Zambia	3.05		160	Korea, North	5.00
81	Colombia	3.10				

Mostly Unfree

MONETARY POLICY
Score: 2+ (low level of inflation)

From 1986 to 1996, the average annual rate of inflation was 12.6 percent, down from 14.2 percent from 1985 to 1995. As a result, Honduras's score in this area is 1 point better this year. In 1997, the inflation rate was 15 percent.

CAPITAL FLOWS AND FOREIGN INVESTMENT
Score: 3–Stable (moderate barriers)

Honduras maintains some restrictions on foreign investment. Special state authorization must be obtained for investments in air transport, forestry, telecommunications, basic health services, fishing and aquaculture, exploration of "subsurface" resources, insurance and financial services, private education services, and agriculture and agro-industrial activities. The government requires that a majority of certain types of businesses be owned by Hondurans.

BANKING
Score: 3–Stable (moderate level of restrictions)

Foreigners must obtain government permission to engage in some types of banking services. Domestic banks are under the control of the government and the Central Bank, and are unduly influenced by Honduran business interests. According to the U.S. Department of Commerce, "Most [Honduran] banks are associated with powerful economic groups, and lend primarily to businesses owned by the group of which they are a part. The system has been criticized for permitting excessive amounts of unsecured lending to major stockholders or bank principals."[3]

WAGE AND PRICE CONTROLS
Score: 3–Stable (moderate level)

After years of eliminating price controls, Honduras imposed new controls on the prices of 44 goods in 1993, including certain foodstuffs. The government still controls the prices of coffee, medicines, some housing rents, and petroleum products. Honduras has a minimum wage.

PROPERTY RIGHTS
Score: 3–Stable (moderate level of protection)

Expropriation remains possible. The government does not protect property in full; corruption is a continuing problem; and those seeking legal recourse to protect their property frequently face an inefficient and ill-functioning court system. The U.S. Department of Commerce describes the Honduran legal system as "slow and generally unsatisfactory."[4]

REGULATION
Score: 4–Stable (high level)

Honduras's bureaucracy suffers from corruption and cronyism. According to the U.S. Department of Commerce, "Most of the Honduran laws dealing with business, trade, labor, and finance are outdated.... The Government of Honduras often lacks resources to implement or enforce those laws on the books.... [R]ed tape is still very common on procedures and activities that require government approval."[5]

BLACK MARKET
Score: 4–Stable (high level of activity)

Because Honduras maintains significant barriers to trade, the size of its black market is rather large; in fact, the black market supplies nearly 50 percent of the labor force. Although Honduras has passed laws to protect intellectual property rights, piracy continues. According to the U.S. Department of State, "The piracy of books, sound and video recordings, compact discs, computer software, and television programs is widespread in Honduras."[6]

NOTES

[1]   U.S. Department of State, *Country Reports on Economic Policy and Trade Practices,* 1998.
[2]   *Ibid.*
[3]   U.S. Department of Commerce, *Country Commercial Guide,* 1998.
[4]   *Ibid.*
[5]   *Ibid.*
[6]   U.S. Department of State, *Country Reports on Economic Policy and Trade Practices,* 1998.

Hong Kong   1.25

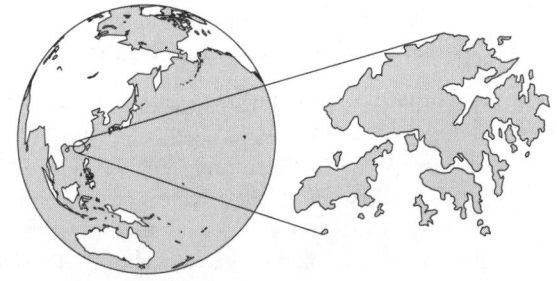

Trade	1	Banking	1
Taxation	1.5	Wages and Prices	2
Government Intervention	1	Property Rights	1
Monetary Policy	2	Regulation	1
Foreign Investment	1	Black Market	1

Hong Kong became a "special administrative region" (SAR) of the People's Republic of China on July 1, 1997. There continues to be little government interference in the marketplace; taxes remain low and predictable; increases in government spending are linked closely with economic growth; foreign trade still is free; and regulations, in addition to being transparent, continue to be applied both uniformly and consistently. As the U.S. Department of Commerce forecast, "The keys to Hong Kong's economic success—its free-market philosophy, entrepreneurial drive, absence of trade barriers, well established rule of law, low and predictable taxes, transparent regulations, and complete freedom of capital movement—are all expected to remain intact through the transition to Chinese sovereignty."[1] In May 1998, Hong Kong held its first democratic elections under China's sovereignty; 53 percent of eligible voters cast ballots for a new Legislative Council. This year's score in the *Index of Economic Freedom* reflects the first full-year review of Hong Kong's economy under China's sovereignty. In August 1998 and the weeks that followed, Hong Kong's government spent some $15.2 billion to "ward off speculators" by buying private stock in the country's stock exchange.[2] Not only has the government failed to allow its currency board to function properly by allowing market forces to take over; it has violated a sacred rule of free-market economics: Governments should avoid direct ownership of private companies. This action demonstrates that the new government's commitment to the market may be weakening. But these events occurred after the cutoff date for consideration in this edition of the *Index of Economic Freedom;* had this information been included in this edition, Hong Kong surely would have received a worse score, ranking below Singapore in the *Index.* If Hong Kong does not reverse its intervention in the stock market, its changed score will be reflected in the official listings and rankings of next year's *Index of Economic Freedom.*

TRADE POLICY
Score: 1–Stable (very low level of protectionism)

Hong Kong levies virtually no import tariffs or duties and is considered a duty-free port.[3] There are, in fact, very few barriers to imports in Hong Kong, which has one of the world's most accessible markets. It is a vital market for U.S. exports, and consumes U.S. manufactured and agricultural goods at a higher rate per capita than most of the world's other economies.

TAXATION
Score–Income taxation: 2–Stable (low tax rates)
Score–Corporate taxation: 1–Stable (very low tax rates)
Final Taxation Score: 1.5–Stable (low tax rates)

The top marginal personal income tax rate is 20 percent;[4] the tax on the average income level is 2 percent. The corporate tax is a flat 16.5 percent.

1	Hong Kong	1.25		81	Fiji	3.10
2	Singapore	1.30		81	Mali	3.10
3	Bahrain	1.70		81	Slovenia	3.10
4	New Zealand	1.75		85	Honduras	3.15
5	Switzerland	1.85		85	Mexico	3.15
6	United States	1.90		85	Papua New Guinea	3.15
7	Ireland	1.95		88	Djibouti	3.20
7	Luxembourg	1.95		88	Mongolia	3.20
7	Taiwan	1.95		90	Algeria	3.25
7	United Kingdom	1.95		90	Brazil	3.25
11	Bahamas	2.00		90	Lebanon	3.25
12	Czech Republic	2.05		90	Senegal	3.25
12	Japan	2.05		90	Tanzania	3.25
14	Australia	2.10		95	Nigeria	3.30
14	Belgium	2.10		95	Romania	3.30
14	Canada	2.10		97	Cambodia	3.35
14	United Arab Emirates	2.10		97	Dominican Republic	3.35
18	Austria	2.15		97	Egypt	3.35
18	Chile	2.15		97	Guinea	3.35
18	Estonia	2.15		97	Ivory Coast	3.35
18	Netherlands	2.15		97	Moldova	3.35
22	Denmark	2.25		97	Pakistan	3.35
22	El Salvador	2.25		104	Nepal	3.40
22	Finland	2.25		104	Venezuela	3.40
25	Germany	2.30		106	Armenia	3.45
25	Iceland	2.30		106	Bulgaria	3.45
27	Norway	2.35		106	Lesotho	3.45
28	Korea, South	2.40		106	Madagascar	3.45
28	Kuwait	2.40		106	Russia	3.45
28	Malaysia	2.40		111	Burkina Faso	3.50
28	Panama	2.40		111	Cameroon	3.50
28	Thailand	2.40		111	Guyana	3.50
33	Sweden	2.45		111	Nicaragua	3.50
34	Argentina	2.50		115	Gambia	3.60
34	France	2.50		116	Croatia	3.65
34	Italy	2.50		116	Georgia	3.65
34	Spain	2.50		116	Malawi	3.65
38	Portugal	2.55		119	Cape Verde	3.67
38	Sri Lanka	2.55		120	Ethiopia	3.70
38	Trinidad and Tobago	2.55		120	India	3.70
41	Barbados	2.60		120	Niger	3.70
41	Peru	2.60		123	Congo	3.75
43	Bolivia	2.65		124	Chad	3.80
43	Mauritius	2.65		124	China	3.80
45	Cyprus	2.70		124	Mauritania	3.80
45	Jamaica	2.70		124	Ukraine	3.80
45	Uruguay	2.70		124	Zimbabwe	3.80
48	Botswana	2.75		129	Albania	3.85
48	Guatemala	2.75		129	Bangladesh	3.85
48	Jordan	2.75		129	Mozambique	3.85
48	Namibia	2.75		129	Suriname	3.85
48	Oman	2.75		133	Burundi	3.90
48	Philippines	2.75		134	Togo	3.95
54	Belize	2.80		135	Haiti	4.00
54	Costa Rica	2.80		135	Kyrgyz Rep.	4.00
54	Israel	2.80		137	Kazakhstan	4.05
54	Swaziland	2.80		137	Sierra Leone	4.05
54	Turkey	2.80		139	Yemen	4.10
54	Uganda	2.80		140	Belarus	4.15
54	Samoa	2.80		141	Sudan	4.20
61	Latvia	2.85		141	Syria	4.20
62	Greece	2.90		143	Azerbaijan	4.30
62	Hungary	2.90		143	Equatorial Guinea	4.30
62	So. Africa	2.90		143	Myanmar	4.30
65	Ecuador	2.95		143	Rwanda	4.30
65	Gabon	2.95		147	Tajikistan	4.40
65	Indonesia	2.95		147	Uzbekistan	4.40
65	Malta	2.95		149	Angola	4.45
65	Morocco	2.95		149	Turkmenistan	4.45
65	Poland	2.95		151	Guinea-Bissau	4.55
65	Tunisia	2.95		152	Vietnam	4.60
72	Ghana	3.00		153	Congo (Zaire)	4.70
72	Lithuania	3.00		153	Iran	4.70
72	Saudi Arabia	3.00		155	Bosnia	4.80
75	Benin	3.05		155	Somalia	4.80
75	Kenya	3.05		157	Iraq	4.90
75	Paraguay	3.05		157	Laos	4.90
75	Qatar	3.05		157	Libya	4.90
75	Slovak Republic	3.05		160	Cuba	5.00
75	Zambia	3.05		160	Korea, North	5.00
81	Colombia	3.10				

Free

GOVERNMENT INTERVENTION IN THE ECONOMY
Score: 1–Stable (very low level)

According to the U.S. Department of Commerce, "The Hong Kong Government pursues a generally non-interventionist approach to economic policy that stresses the predominant role of the private sector. Economic policy is based primarily on minimal interference with market forces."[5] Government consumes about 8.9 percent of GDP.

MONETARY POLICY
Score: 2–Stable (low level of inflation)

The Hong Kong dollar has been linked to the U.S. dollar since 1983. During late 1997 and early 1998, Hong Kong's government came under pressure to de-link the Hong Kong dollar from the U.S. dollar because of the Asian financial crisis. Hong Kong's government defended the link, however, and has overcome any initial inflationary pressures. The annual rate of inflation has averaged 7.8 percent since 1986.

CAPITAL FLOWS AND FOREIGN INVESTMENT
Score: 1–Stable (very low barriers)

The government encourages foreign investment and is one of the most receptive to investment in the world. There are virtually no restrictions on foreign capital or investment, except in the media sector.

BANKING
Score: 1–Stable (very low level of restrictions)

Hong Kong is a world banking center and one of the world's most stable banking environments. Banks are independent of the government. Foreign banks are free to operate with only limited restrictions on the number of automated teller machines and branches.

WAGE AND PRICE CONTROLS
Score: 2–Stable (low level)

Hong Kong's market largely sets wages and prices (the only exception pertains to certain telecommunications services). There are, however, price controls on rent, public transport, and electricity. The government has the power to enforce minimum wages, but rarely does so.

PROPERTY RIGHTS
Score: 1–Stable (very high level of protection)

The government fully protects private property rights. The legal system to protect these rights is both highly efficient and effective. According to the U.S. Department of State, "Until June 30 [1997], the judicial and legal systems were organized by principles of British constitutional law and legal precedent for an independent judiciary, which the Government respected in practice. An independent judiciary endured after Hong Kong's reversion, underpinned by the Basic Law's provision that Hong Kong's common law tradition be maintained."[6]

REGULATION
Score: 1–Stable (very low level)

Hong Kong has a simple system to license businesses. The regulations imposed on business are few, not burdensome, and applied uniformly. According to the U.S. Department of Commerce, "Hong Kong's body of law and regulation implicitly and explicitly promotes competition in all forms of economic endeavor.... Tax, labor, health and safety and other laws and policies avoid distortions or impediments to the efficient mobilization and allocation of investment. Bureaucratic procedures and 'red tape' are held to the minimum and are equally transparent to local and foreign investors."[7]

BLACK MARKET
Score: 1–Stable (very low level of activity)

The black market is virtually nonexistent. There is no significant smuggling, and black market activity in pirated intellectual property is minuscule compared with the size of the economy.[8] According to the U.S. Department of State, "With respect to the legislative arena and international conventions, Hong Kong's [intellectual property] framework is world class."[9] To the extent that piracy does exist in Hong Kong's market, it is being met with increasingly vigorous law enforcement, as evidenced by major crackdowns in late April and early May 1998 in which the government confiscated millions of pirated videos and software programs.

NOTES

1   U.S. Department of Commerce, *Country Commercial Guide, Fiscal Year 1998*, August 1997.
2   Christina Mungan and Jon E. Hilsenrath, "Hong Kong Spent $15.2 Billion to Buy Up Stocks," *Wall Street Journal*, October 27, 1998, p. A15.
3   Minor import duties exist on alcoholic beverages, tobacco, and cosmetics.
4   The income tax on individuals is a progressive rate from 2 percent to 20 percent after deductions and allowances, or at a flat rate of 15 percent on gross salary—whichever produces the lower tax liability. For the purposes of grading Hong Kong's income tax rate, the author uses the flat 15 percent rate.
5   U.S. Department of Commerce, *Country Commercial Guide, Fiscal Year 1998*.
6   U.S. Department of State, "Hong Kong Country Report on Human Rights Practices for 1997," 1998.
7   U.S. Department of Commerce, *Country Commercial Guide, Fiscal Year 1998*.
8   Although some pirated intellectual property from other parts of China finds its way into the Hong Kong SAR, the customs bureau is among the best in the world; as a result, most pirated material from the mainland is confiscated at the border. Although some pirated products remain for sale in Hong Kong, few are exported to other countries.
9   U.S. Department of State, *Country Reports on Economic Policy and Trade Practices*, 1997, p. 34.

Hungary   2.90

1998 Score: **2.90**   1997 Score: **2.90**   1996 Score: **2.90**

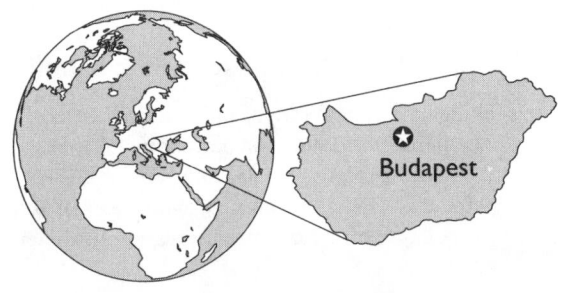

Budapest

Trade	4	Banking	2
Taxation	4	Wages and Prices	2
Government Intervention	3	Property Rights	2
Monetary Policy	4	Regulation	3
Foreign Investment	2	Black Market	3

Once part of the Austro–Hungarian Empire, Hungary was incorporated into the Soviet bloc after World War II. The government, which had practiced a type of reform communism, collapsed in 1989 and a democratically elected government introduced market reforms soon thereafter. Despite the victory of a Socialist–Free Democrat coalition in 1994 elections to parliament, Hungary's economic policy of market reform has continued and its political climate remains relatively stable. A coalition of center-right and populist parties won elections to parliament in May 1998, allowing Viktor Orbán to become prime minister. His government may pursue further liberalization. Hungary has an efficient system to protect intellectual property rights, weak labor unions, and a liberal foreign trade policy. It also has pursued an extensive program of privatization.

TRADE POLICY
Score: 4–Stable (high level of protectionism)

Hungary's average tariff rate is 10.9 percent.[1] The government also maintains import quotas that mainly affect such consumer products as automobiles, clothing, leather footwear, and some foodstuffs. The government has replaced other quotas, such as the one on agricultural products, with tariffs. According to the U.S. Department of Commerce, "Non-tariff barriers include lack of transparency with respect to the creation and application of laws and regulations. Furthermore, the absence of a prior notice or review period often leaves companies with little opportunity to influence the outcome or plan ahead."[2]

TAXATION
Score–Income taxation: 5–Stable (very high tax rates)
Score–Corporate taxation: 2–Stable (low tax rates)
Final Taxation Score: 4–Stable (high tax rates)

Hungary's top income tax rate is 42 percent, down from 48 percent last year. The average income level is taxed at 35 percent, down from 44 percent last year. The top corporate income tax rate is 18 percent (the government cut corporate taxes by half in 1995). Hungary also levies an 18 percent capital gains tax, a 12 percent to 25 percent value-added tax, and various local taxes.

GOVERNMENT INTERVENTION IN THE ECONOMY
Score: 3–Stable (moderate level)

Government consumes 11.9 percent of GDP; the public sector generates more than 30 percent of this. The government remains heavily involved in energy, telecommunications, transportation, pharmaceuticals, and other areas. Privatization continues. According to the U.S. Department of Commerce, "Since 1989, the private sector in Hungary has grown from approximately 20% to over 70% of GDP. The socialist-led [until May 1998] government has accelerated the privatization process, with significant progress in 1995 and 1996, notably in energy, banking and telecommunication. Since 1989, the state has liquidated or privatized 75% percent of its holdings and aims to increase this figure to 80% by the end of the century. Government expenditures are expected to be under 50% of GDP in 1997."[3]

1	Hong Kong	1.25	81	Fiji	3.10
2	Singapore	1.30	81	Mali	3.10
3	Bahrain	1.70	81	Slovenia	3.10
4	New Zealand	1.75	85	Honduras	3.15
5	Switzerland	1.85	85	Mexico	3.15
6	United States	1.90	85	Papua New Guinea	3.15
7	Ireland	1.95	88	Djibouti	3.20
7	Luxembourg	1.95	88	Mongolia	3.20
7	Taiwan	1.95	90	Algeria	3.25
7	United Kingdom	1.95	90	Brazil	3.25
11	Bahamas	2.00	90	Lebanon	3.25
12	Czech Republic	2.05	90	Senegal	3.25
12	Japan	2.05	90	Tanzania	3.25
14	Australia	2.10	95	Nigeria	3.30
14	Belgium	2.10	95	Romania	3.30
14	Canada	2.10	97	Cambodia	3.35
14	United Arab Emirates	2.10	97	Dominican Republic	3.35
18	Austria	2.15	97	Egypt	3.35
18	Chile	2.15	97	Guinea	3.35
18	Estonia	2.15	97	Ivory Coast	3.35
18	Netherlands	2.15	97	Moldova	3.35
22	Denmark	2.25	97	Pakistan	3.35
22	El Salvador	2.25	104	Nepal	3.40
22	Finland	2.25	104	Venezuela	3.40
25	Germany	2.30	106	Armenia	3.45
25	Iceland	2.30	106	Bulgaria	3.45
27	Norway	2.35	106	Lesotho	3.45
28	Korea, South	2.40	106	Madagascar	3.45
28	Kuwait	2.40	106	Russia	3.45
28	Malaysia	2.40	111	Burkina Faso	3.50
28	Panama	2.40	111	Cameroon	3.50
28	Thailand	2.40	111	Guyana	3.50
33	Sweden	2.45	111	Nicaragua	3.50
34	Argentina	2.50	115	Gambia	3.60
34	France	2.50	116	Croatia	3.65
34	Italy	2.50	116	Georgia	3.65
34	Spain	2.50	116	Malawi	3.65
38	Portugal	2.55	119	Cape Verde	3.67
38	Sri Lanka	2.55	120	Ethiopia	3.70
38	Trinidad and Tobago	2.55	120	India	3.70
41	Barbados	2.60	120	Niger	3.70
41	Peru	2.60	123	Congo	3.75
43	Bolivia	2.65	124	Chad	3.80
43	Mauritius	2.65	124	China	3.80
45	Cyprus	2.70	124	Mauritania	3.80
45	Jamaica	2.70	124	Ukraine	3.80
45	Uruguay	2.70	124	Zimbabwe	3.80
48	Botswana	2.75	129	Albania	3.85
48	Guatemala	2.75	129	Bangladesh	3.85
48	Jordan	2.75	129	Mozambique	3.85
48	Namibia	2.75	129	Suriname	3.85
48	Oman	2.75	133	Burundi	3.90
48	Philippines	2.75	134	Togo	3.95
54	Belize	2.80	135	Haiti	4.00
54	Costa Rica	2.80	135	Kyrgyz Rep.	4.00
54	Israel	2.80	137	Kazakhstan	4.05
54	Swaziland	2.80	137	Sierra Leone	4.05
54	Turkey	2.80	139	Yemen	4.10
54	Uganda	2.80	140	Belarus	4.15
54	Samoa	2.80	141	Sudan	4.20
61	Latvia	2.85	141	Syria	4.20
62	Greece	2.90	143	Azerbaijan	4.30
62	Hungary	2.90	143	Equatorial Guinea	4.30
62	So. Africa	2.90	143	Myanmar	4.30
65	Ecuador	2.95	143	Rwanda	4.30
65	Gabon	2.95	147	Tajikistan	4.40
65	Indonesia	2.95	147	Uzbekistan	4.40
65	Malta	2.95	149	Angola	4.45
65	Morocco	2.95	149	Turkmenistan	4.45
65	Poland	2.95	151	Guinea-Bissau	4.55
65	Tunisia	2.95	152	Vietnam	4.60
72	Ghana	3.00	153	Congo (Zaire)	4.70
72	Lithuania	3.00	153	Iran	4.70
72	Saudi Arabia	3.00	155	Bosnia	4.80
75	Benin	3.05	155	Somalia	4.80
75	Kenya	3.05	157	Iraq	4.90
75	Paraguay	3.05	157	Laos	4.90
75	Qatar	3.05	157	Libya	4.90
75	Slovak Republic	3.05	160	Cuba	5.00
75	Zambia	3.05	160	Korea, North	5.00
81	Colombia	3.10			

Mostly Free

MONETARY POLICY
Score: 4–Stable (high level of inflation)

Hungary's annual rate of inflation was 18 percent in 1997, 23.6 percent in 1996, 28.2 percent in 1995, 18.8 percent in 1994, 22.5 percent in 1993, 23.0 percent in 1992, and 35 percent in 1991.[4] The average annual rate of inflation since the collapse of the communist regime has been about 24 percent.

CAPITAL FLOWS AND FOREIGN INVESTMENT
Score: 2–Stable (low barriers)

Hungary is very open to foreign investment and is leading the way on foreign investment reform, attracting more investment from the United States than any other country in the region. Even though 100 percent ownership is guaranteed to foreign investors, the government sometimes opposes such ownership for newly privatized businesses. Once a foreign investor's business is located in Hungary, the law is applied evenly to both foreign and domestic firms. According to the U.S. Department of Commerce, "Hungary attracted $16.5 billion in all forms of foreign investment, including foreign direct investment (FDI) and in-kind contributions, from 1989–1996. This amounts to over one-third of all FDI invested in Central and Eastern Europe during the period. According to a World Bank report, Hungary ranks among the top 12 investment target countries, which received 73 percent of all private investment in 1996."[5]

BANKING
Score: 2–Stable (low level of restrictions)

The privatization of Hungary's banking industry is progressing. The government may not own more than 25 percent of a bank. The banking industry is becoming increasingly competitive, and banks are relatively free from burdensome government oversight. According to the U.S. Department of Commerce, "The Hungarian banking system has gone through a remarkable transformation in recent years from money-losing state-owned monoliths to private enterprises, and the strong presence of foreign financial institutions. More than two-thirds of Hungary's banks are fully or partially foreign owned."[6]

WAGE AND PRICE CONTROLS
Score: 2–Stable (low level)

Hungary has eliminated most price controls. According to the U.S. Department of State, however, "[P]rices for public transport, utilities such as gas, electricity and water, pharmaceuticals, and vehicle fuel continue to be partially set by the state."[7] Hungary has a minimum wage.

PROPERTY RIGHTS
Score: 2–Stable (high level of protection)

There is little chance of property expropriation in Hungary. There have been no cases of government expropriation of foreign-owned assets since the 1950s, and private property is guaranteed by law. The legal system is at times corrupt, ineffective, and inefficient, but the U.S. Department of State reports that the Constitution "provides for an independent judiciary, and the Government respects this in practice."[8]

REGULATION
Score: 3–Stable (moderate level)

A business license is required only for a few activities. New laws on consumer protection and the environment, however, are becoming burdensome. The environmental law, for example, imposes a "green tax" on certain businesses engaged in manufacturing such products as tires and refrigerators. In addition, there sometimes is a lack of transparency in regulations. For example, according to the U.S. Department of Commerce, "A lack of transparency is a common complaint of U.S. companies doing business in Hungary."[9] The U.S. Department of Commerce also reports that "Corruption is not pervasive or institutional on the government level, although some U.S. companies have complained about corruption incidents occurring."[10]

BLACK MARKET
Score: 3–Stable (moderate level of activity)

As Hungary moves closer to the free market, the level of black market activity decreases. According to the U.S. Department of Commerce, black market activity equals about one-third of the economy.[11] There is some infringement of intellectual property, and a significant black market exists in pirated materials, especially pharmaceuticals. By global standards, however, Hungary's black market is moderate in size.

NOTES

[1]   Based on the trade-weighted mean average tariff rate. See World Bank, *World Development Indicators 1997*, 1998.
[2]   U.S. Department of Commerce, *Country Commercial Guide*, 1998.
[3]   *Ibid.*
[4]   Based on consumer price inflation; see U.S. Department of State, *1997 Country Reports on Economic Policy and Trade Practices*, 1998, 1997, 1996, and 1995.
[5]   U.S. Department of Commerce, *Country Commercial Guide*, 1998.
[6]   *Ibid.*
[7]   *Ibid.*
[8]   U.S. Department of State, "Hungary Report on Human Rights Practices for 1997," 1998.
[9]   U.S. Department of Commerce, *Country Commercial Guide*, 1998.
[10] U.S. Department of Commerce, *Country Commercial Guide*, 1998.
[11] *Ibid.*

Iceland 2.30

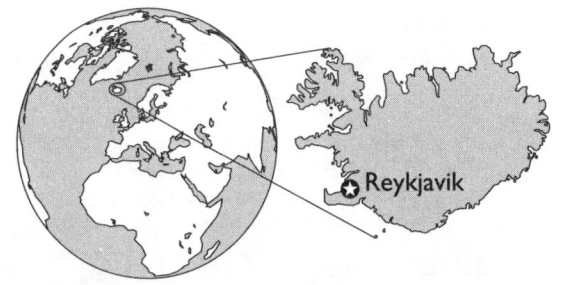

1998 Score: **2.30**	1997 Score: **2.50**	1996 Score: **n/a**

Trade	2	Banking	3
Taxation	4	Wages and Prices	2
Government Intervention	3	Property Rights	1
Monetary Policy	2	Regulation	3
Foreign Investment	2	Black Market	1

Iceland is the westernmost outpost of Europe. During the 1800s, it was primarily an agricultural and fishing country, and these industries produced substantial economic growth. But by the 1900s, Iceland had an established industrial base. The country won its independence from Denmark in 1944. It has an advanced market economy and is a major export base for manufactured goods.

TRADE POLICY
Score: 2–Stable (low level of protectionism)

Iceland's average tariff rate is about 1.58 percent.[1] Non-tariff barriers continue in the form of quotas and some licensing requirements. According to the U.S. Department of State, "Iceland's relatively liberal trading policy has been strengthened by accession to the European Economic Area in 1993 and by the Uruguay Round agreement, which also brought significantly improved market access for Iceland's exports, particularly seafood products. However, the agricultural sector remains heavily subsidized and protected, with some tariffs ranging as high as 700%."[2]

TAXATION
Score–Income taxation: 4–Stable (high tax rates)
Score–Corporate taxation: 3–Stable (moderate tax rates)
Final Taxation Score: 4–Stable (high tax rates)

Iceland has a flat income tax rate of 41.94 percent and a top marginal corporate tax rate of 33 percent. It also has a 33 percent capital gains tax and a 24.5 percent value-added tax.

GOVERNMENT INTERVENTION IN THE ECONOMY
Score: 3–Stable (moderate level)

Government consumes about 20.7 percent of GDP, a substantial portion of which is produced by publicly owned companies.

MONETARY POLICY
Score: 2–Stable (low level of inflation)

Iceland's average annual rate of inflation from 1986 to 1996 was 12.5 percent. Inflation was lower than 3 percent in 1997.

CAPITAL FLOWS AND FOREIGN INVESTMENT
Score: 2–Stable (low barriers)

Iceland generally welcomes foreign investment, although the government still maintains some restrictions on foreign investment in fishing and primary fish processing, commercial banks, airlines, and industries considered vital to national security.

#	Country	Score	#	Country	Score
1	Hong Kong	1.25	81	Fiji	3.10
2	Singapore	1.30	81	Mali	3.10
3	Bahrain	1.70	81	Slovenia	3.10
4	New Zealand	1.75	85	Honduras	3.15
5	Switzerland	1.85	85	Mexico	3.15
6	United States	1.90	85	Papua New Guinea	3.15
7	Ireland	1.95	88	Djibouti	3.20
7	Luxembourg	1.95	88	Mongolia	3.20
7	Taiwan	1.95	90	Algeria	3.25
7	United Kingdom	1.95	90	Brazil	3.25
11	Bahamas	2.00	90	Lebanon	3.25
12	Czech Republic	2.05	90	Senegal	3.25
12	Japan	2.05	90	Tanzania	3.25
14	Australia	2.10	95	Nigeria	3.30
14	Belgium	2.10	95	Romania	3.30
14	Canada	2.10	97	Cambodia	3.35
14	United Arab Emirates	2.10	97	Dominican Republic	3.35
18	Austria	2.15	97	Egypt	3.35
18	Chile	2.15	97	Guinea	3.35
18	Estonia	2.15	97	Ivory Coast	3.35
18	Netherlands	2.15	97	Moldova	3.35
22	Denmark	2.25	97	Pakistan	3.35
22	El Salvador	2.25	104	Nepal	3.40
22	Finland	2.25	104	Venezuela	3.40
25	Germany	2.30	106	Armenia	3.45
25	Iceland	2.30	106	Bulgaria	3.45
27	Norway	2.35	106	Lesotho	3.45
28	Korea, South	2.40	106	Madagascar	3.45
28	Kuwait	2.40	106	Russia	3.45
28	Malaysia	2.40	111	Burkina Faso	3.50
28	Panama	2.40	111	Cameroon	3.50
28	Thailand	2.40	111	Guyana	3.50
33	Sweden	2.45	111	Nicaragua	3.50
34	Argentina	2.50	115	Gambia	3.60
34	France	2.50	116	Croatia	3.65
34	Italy	2.50	116	Georgia	3.65
34	Spain	2.50	116	Malawi	3.65
38	Portugal	2.55	119	Cape Verde	3.67
38	Sri Lanka	2.55	120	Ethiopia	3.70
38	Trinidad and Tobago	2.55	120	India	3.70
41	Barbados	2.60	120	Niger	3.70
41	Peru	2.60	123	Congo	3.75
43	Bolivia	2.65	124	Chad	3.80
43	Mauritius	2.65	124	China	3.80
45	Cyprus	2.70	124	Mauritania	3.80
45	Jamaica	2.70	124	Ukraine	3.80
45	Uruguay	2.70	124	Zimbabwe	3.80
48	Botswana	2.75	129	Albania	3.85
48	Guatemala	2.75	129	Bangladesh	3.85
48	Jordan	2.75	129	Mozambique	3.85
48	Namibia	2.75	129	Suriname	3.85
48	Oman	2.75	133	Burundi	3.90
48	Philippines	2.75	134	Togo	3.95
54	Belize	2.80	135	Haiti	4.00
54	Costa Rica	2.80	135	Kyrgyz Rep.	4.00
54	Israel	2.80	137	Kazakhstan	4.05
54	Swaziland	2.80	137	Sierra Leone	4.05
54	Turkey	2.80	139	Yemen	4.10
54	Uganda	2.80	140	Belarus	4.15
54	Samoa	2.80	141	Sudan	4.20
61	Latvia	2.85	141	Syria	4.20
62	Greece	2.90	143	Azerbaijan	4.30
62	Hungary	2.90	143	Equatorial Guinea	4.30
62	So. Africa	2.90	143	Myanmar	4.30
65	Ecuador	2.95	143	Rwanda	4.30
65	Gabon	2.95	147	Tajikistan	4.40
65	Indonesia	2.95	147	Uzbekistan	4.40
65	Malta	2.95	149	Angola	4.45
65	Morocco	2.95	149	Turkmenistan	4.45
65	Poland	2.95	152	Guinea-Bissau	4.55
65	Tunisia	2.95	152	Vietnam	4.60
72	Ghana	3.00	153	Congo (Zaire)	4.70
72	Lithuania	3.00	153	Iran	4.70
72	Saudi Arabia	3.00	155	Bosnia	4.80
75	Benin	3.05	155	Somalia	4.80
75	Kenya	3.05	157	Iraq	4.90
75	Paraguay	3.05	157	Laos	4.90
75	Qatar	3.05	157	Libya	4.90
75	Slovak Republic	3.05	160	Cuba	5.00
75	Zambia	3.05	160	Korea, North	5.00
81	Colombia	3.10			

Mostly Free

BANKING
Score: 3–Stable (moderate level of restrictions)

Iceland's banking system is becoming more liberalized, but some banks remain under state ownership. Although the government plans to privatize a few of these banks, little progress has been made toward that goal.

WAGE AND PRICE CONTROLS
Score: 2–Stable (low level)

The market sets most wages and prices in Iceland. The government has implemented policies to limit its own impact on some prices. The government can affect prices, however, through its use of various trade restrictions and production quotas in agriculture.

PROPERTY RIGHTS
Score: 1–Stable (very high level of protection)

Private property is safe from government confiscation. Iceland has an efficient and independent legal system. According to the U.S. Department of State, "The Constitution and law provide for an independent judiciary, and the Government respects this provision in practice."[3]

REGULATION
Score: 3–Stable (moderate level)

Some of Iceland's economy—especially fishing, agriculture, and such service industries as telecommunications and the airlines—remains heavily regulated. Strict environmental laws also can add to the cost of doing business.

BLACK MARKET
Score: 1–Stable (very low level of activity)

Iceland has a very small black market and strong and efficient laws regarding intellectual property rights. Piracy in these products is virtually nonexistent.

NOTES

[1] Based on total government taxation of international transactions as a percentage of imports.
[2] U.S. Department of State, "Iceland: Background Notes," June 1997
[3] U.S. Department of State, "1997 Human Rights Report: Iceland," March 1998.

India   3.70

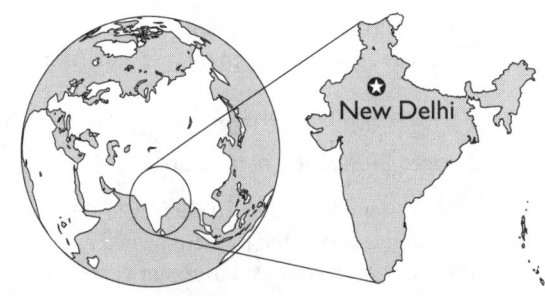

New Delhi

1998 Score: 3.70   **1997 Score: 3.70**   **1996 Score: 3.75**

Trade	5	Banking	4
Taxation	3	Wages and Prices	4
Government Intervention	3	Property Rights	3
Monetary Policy	2	Regulation	4
Foreign Investment	4	Black Market	5

India gained its independence from the United Kingdom in 1947 and became a republic in 1950. Over the next four decades, the socialist-democratic government restricted economic growth by imposing exhaustive controls on production, prices, and employment; nationalizing industries; limiting competition through licensing; discouraging foreign investment; and raising tariffs and taxes. Following a foreign exchange crisis in 1991, the government under Prime Minister P. V. Narashima Rao began to liberalize the economy by accepting foreign investment and reducing barriers to trade. From 1990 to 1995, India's economy grew by an average of 4.6 percent annually. The government also has undergone frequent change during the past several years. Prime Minister H. D. Deve Gowda, who took office in June 1996 and headed a center-left coalition government, resigned in March 1997 after his government lost a parliamentary vote of confidence. Minister of External Affairs I. K. Gujral became prime minister in April 1997. In March 1998, a Bharatiya Janata Party–led government took power that is inclined toward increasing protection for domestic industries. India recently reduced taxes, which caused the country's final taxation score to improve by 1 point this year. The country has raised its barriers to foreign investment, however, thereby making its foreign investment score 1 point worse. Because these score changes cancel one another out, India's overall score remains unchanged.

TRADE POLICY
Score: 5–Stable (very high level of protectionism)

India recently agreed to abolish all tariff and other trade restrictions on computers, telecommunications equipment, software, semiconductors, and printed circuit boards by 2000. The average tariff rate is 28 percent. India also maintains a number of non-tariff barriers. According to the Office of the United States Trade Representative, "Despite recent tariff reductions and the relaxation of many quantitative restrictions, India's near total ban on consumer goods imports, quantitative restrictions under its negative import list, and relatively high tariffs remain a serious impediment to U.S. trade, especially in agricultural and consumer items."[1] Moreover, the U.S. Department of State reports, "Documentation requirements, including ex-factory bills of sale, are extensive and delays frequent. There have also been private sector reports of misclassification and incorrect valuation of goods for the purposes of duty assessment, in addition to corruption."[2]

TAXATION
Score–Income taxation: 2+ (low tax rates)
Score–Corporate taxation: 3+ (moderate tax rates)
Final Taxation Score: 3+ (moderate tax rates)

India's top income tax level is 30 percent, down from 40 percent last year. As a result, India's income tax score is 1 point better this year. The tax on the average income level is 0 percent. The top corporate tax rate is 35 percent, down from 40 percent last year. As a result, India's corporate taxation score is 1 point better than last year. When the two tax scores are averaged, India's final taxation score

1	Hong Kong	1.25		81	Fiji	3.10
2	Singapore	1.30		81	Mali	3.10
3	Bahrain	1.70		81	Slovenia	3.10
4	New Zealand	1.75		85	Honduras	3.15
5	Switzerland	1.85		85	Mexico	3.15
6	United States	1.90		85	Papua New Guinea	3.15
7	Ireland	1.95		88	Djibouti	3.20
7	Luxembourg	1.95		88	Mongolia	3.20
7	Taiwan	1.95		90	Algeria	3.25
7	United Kingdom	1.95		90	Brazil	3.25
11	Bahamas	2.00		90	Lebanon	3.25
12	Czech Republic	2.05		90	Senegal	3.25
12	Japan	2.05		90	Tanzania	3.25
14	Australia	2.10		95	Nigeria	3.30
14	Belgium	2.10		95	Romania	3.30
14	Canada	2.10		97	Cambodia	3.35
14	United Arab Emirates	2.10		97	Dominican Republic	3.35
18	Austria	2.15		97	Egypt	3.35
18	Chile	2.15		97	Guinea	3.35
18	Estonia	2.15		97	Ivory Coast	3.35
18	Netherlands	2.15		97	Moldova	3.35
22	Denmark	2.25		97	Pakistan	3.35
22	El Salvador	2.25		104	Nepal	3.40
22	Finland	2.25		104	Venezuela	3.40
25	Germany	2.30		106	Armenia	3.45
25	Iceland	2.30		106	Bulgaria	3.45
27	Norway	2.35		106	Lesotho	3.45
28	Korea, South	2.40		106	Madagascar	3.45
28	Kuwait	2.40		106	Russia	3.45
28	Malaysia	2.40		111	Burkina Faso	3.50
28	Panama	2.40		111	Cameroon	3.50
28	Thailand	2.40		111	Guyana	3.50
33	Sweden	2.45		111	Nicaragua	3.50
34	Argentina	2.50		115	Gambia	3.60
34	France	2.50		116	Croatia	3.65
34	Italy	2.50		116	Georgia	3.65
34	Spain	2.50		116	Malawi	3.65
38	Portugal	2.55		119	Cape Verde	3.67
38	Sri Lanka	2.55		120	Ethiopia	3.70
38	Trinidad and Tobago	2.55		120	India	3.70
41	Barbados	2.60		120	Niger	3.70
41	Peru	2.60		123	Congo	3.75
43	Bolivia	2.65		124	Chad	3.80
43	Mauritius	2.65		124	China	3.80
45	Cyprus	2.70		124	Mauritania	3.80
45	Jamaica	2.70		124	Ukraine	3.80
45	Uruguay	2.70		124	Zimbabwe	3.80
48	Botswana	2.75		129	Albania	3.85
48	Guatemala	2.75		129	Bangladesh	3.85
48	Jordan	2.75		129	Mozambique	3.85
48	Namibia	2.75		129	Suriname	3.85
48	Oman	2.75		133	Burundi	3.90
48	Philippines	2.75		134	Togo	3.95
54	Belize	2.80		135	Haiti	4.00
54	Costa Rica	2.80		135	Kyrgyz Rep.	4.00
54	Israel	2.80		137	Kazakhstan	4.05
54	Swaziland	2.80		137	Sierra Leone	4.05
54	Turkey	2.80		139	Yemen	4.10
54	Uganda	2.80		140	Belarus	4.15
54	Samoa	2.80		141	Sudan	4.20
61	Latvia	2.85		141	Syria	4.20
62	Greece	2.90		143	Azerbaijan	4.30
62	Hungary	2.90		143	Equatorial Guinea	4.30
62	So. Africa	2.90		143	Myanmar	4.30
65	Ecuador	2.95		143	Rwanda	4.30
65	Gabon	2.95		147	Tajikistan	4.40
65	Indonesia	2.95		147	Uzbekistan	4.40
65	Malta	2.95		149	Angola	4.45
65	Morocco	2.95		149	Turkmenistan	4.45
65	Poland	2.95		151	Guinea-Bissau	4.55
65	Tunisia	2.95		152	Vietnam	4.60
72	Ghana	3.00		153	Congo (Zaire)	4.70
72	Lithuania	3.00		153	Iran	4.70
72	Saudi Arabia	3.00		155	Bosnia	4.80
75	Benin	3.05		155	Somalia	4.80
75	Kenya	3.05		157	Iraq	4.90
75	Paraguay	3.05		157	Laos	4.90
75	Qatar	3.05		157	Libya	4.90
75	Slovak Republic	3.05		160	Cuba	5.00
75	Zambia	3.05		160	Korea, North	5.00
81	Colombia	3.10				

Mostly Unfree

this year improves by 1 point. India also levies a 20 percent capital gains tax and both interest and sales taxes.

GOVERNMENT INTERVENTION IN THE ECONOMY
Score: 3–Stable (moderate level)

Government consumes 10 percent of GDP, a large portion of which is generated by state-owned enterprises. Privatization has slowed in recent years. Although shares of such formerly state-owned firms as Bharat Electronics and the Steel Authority of India now are traded on the Bombay stock exchange, the government retains managerial control. In addition, the government continues to provide large subsidies to many businesses. According to the Department of Commerce, India provides almost $30 billion a year in subsidies, or almost 10 percent of GDP.[3]

MONETARY POLICY
Score: 2–Stable (low level of inflation)

From 1986 to 1996, India's average annual rate of inflation was 8.6 percent. In 1997, the rate was 9 percent.

CAPITAL FLOWS AND FOREIGN INVESTMENT
Score: 4– (high barriers)

India has reduced some barriers to foreign investment. Foreign investors, however, may not own 100 percent of an Indian concern without prior government approval. According to the Office of the United States Trade Representative, "Industries have expressed concern with the Indian Government's stringent and non-transparent regulations and procedures governing local share-holding. Current price control regulations have undermined incentives to increase equity holdings in India. Some companies report forced renegotiations of contracts in the power sector to accommodate government changes at the state and central levels. They report that this practice makes India an expensive, complicated and frustrating environment in which to do business."[4] In addition, new evidence of corruption within the government procurement approval process has emerged, further frustrating foreign investment. For example, according to the U.S. Department of Commerce, "The government procurement area has been particularly subject to allegations of corruption."[5] Thus, as a result of the bureaucratic investment regime and evidence of corruption, India's foreign investment score is 1 point worse this year.

BANKING
Score: 4–Stable (high level of restrictions)

The government exercises a heavy hand in controlling India's banking sector. According to the U.S. Department of Commerce, "All large Indian banks are nationalized, and all Indian financial institutions are in the public sector."[6] The government plans to permit only 5 licenses per year for foreign bank branches or extensions of current operations. Only 12 such licenses have been granted over the years, only 8 of which have begun operations.

WAGE AND PRICE CONTROLS
Score: 4–Stable (high level)

Central and state governments still regulate the pricing of most essential products, including cereals, sugar, basic medicines, some energy, coal, and many industrial inputs. India has a minimum wage.

PROPERTY RIGHTS
Score: 3–Stable (moderate level of protection)

Even though India has an efficient court system, property remains at risk in rural areas because of long delays. According to the U.S. Department of Commerce, "Indian courts provide adequate safeguards for the enforcement of property and contractual rights. However, case backlogs frequently lead to long procedural delays."[7]

REGULATION
Score: 4–Stable (high level)

India's economy is heavily regulated. The large public sector must meet all kinds of burdensome requirements, including restrictive licensing requirements, to operate. In addition, the U.S. Department of Commerce reports that "Investors, foreign and domestic, still complain that the regulatory system allows far too much leeway for bureaucratic discretion.... Indian industry remains highly regulated by a powerful bureaucracy armed with excessive rules and broad discretion."[8]

BLACK MARKET
Score: 5–Stable (very high level of activity)

India's huge tariffs make it very profitable to smuggle foreign goods into the country. Many goods are smuggled in from Myanmar (Burma). Although some progress has been made, there continues to be evidence of a massive black market. According to the U.S. Department of Commerce,

"India has both organized and unorganized channels for selling goods. Before import liberalization, smuggling such luxury consumer items as color TV's, videotape machines, air conditioners, jewelry and gold developed into a thriving 'unorganized' sector or black market of the economy. By avoiding taxes and customs duties and using cash transactions, the unorganized merchants could offer better prices than those in the organized sector."[9]

NOTES

[1] U.S. Department of Commerce, *Country Commercial Guide*, 1998.
[2] Office of the United States Trade Representative, *National Trade Estimate Report on Foreign Trade Barriers*, 1998.
[3] U.S. Department of Commerce, *Country Commercial Guide*, 1998.
[4] Office of the United States Trade Representative, *National Trade Estimate Report on Foreign Trade Barriers*, 1998.
[5] U.S. Department of Commerce, *Country Commercial Guide*, 1998.
[6] *Ibid.*
[7] *Ibid.*
[8] *Ibid.*
[9] *Ibid.*

Indonesia   2.95

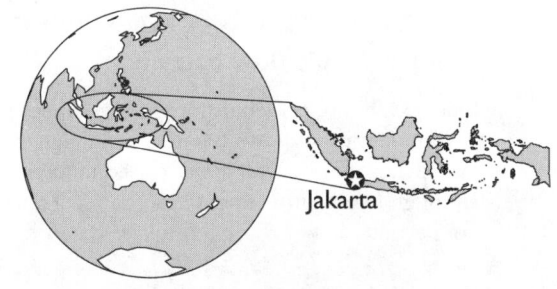

Jakarta

| Score 1998: **2.85** | 1997 Score: **2.85** | 1996 Score: **2.85** |

Trade	2	Banking	4
Taxation	3.5	Wages and Prices	3
Government Intervention	1	Property Rights	3
Monetary Policy	2	Regulation	4
Foreign Investment	2	Black Market	5

Indonesia gained its independence from the Netherlands in 1945. It has received large sums of foreign aid from the international community. It also has pursued such policy reforms as cutting taxes, lowering barriers to trade, and opening the economy to foreign investment. Indonesia has been adversely affected by the Asian financial crisis, however: since the crisis began, the International Monetary Fund was slated to send Indonesia $43 billion in stabilization assistance. Under increasing protest, President Suharto stepped down from office in May 1998, ending his 32-year rule of the country. Suharto's hand-picked replacement, B. J. Habibie, has called for democratic elections in 1999. In the meantime, Indonesia is working to stabilize its economy, which continues to suffer from the after-shocks of the Asian financial crisis. Many Indonesian banks have become insolvent as a result of the financial crisis, and the country's banking system is becoming increasingly unstable; as a result, Indonesia's overall score is 0.1 point worse than last year.

TRADE POLICY
Score: 2–Stable (low level of protectionism)

Indonesia's average tariff rate is 6 percent. There are strict licensing requirements on a number of products, including flour, sugar, and rice.

TAXATION
Score–Income taxation: 3–Stable (moderate tax rates)
Score–Corporate taxation: 3–Stable (moderate tax rates)
Final Taxation Score: 3.5–Stable (high tax rates)

Indonesia's top income tax rate is 30 percent, and the average income level is taxed at 10 percent. The top corporate income tax rate is 30 percent. Indonesia also imposes a 10 percent value-added tax and a sales tax.

GOVERNMENT INTERVENTION IN THE ECONOMY
Score: 1–Stable (very low level)

Government consumes 7.7 percent of GDP. According to the Economist Intelligence Unit, "The State continues to play a major role in Indonesian industry, though the government increasingly requires state firms to meet private-sector accounting and competitive standards. At the same time it is phasing out subsidies and a multitude of preferences, and making privatization a serious goal."[1]

MONETARY POLICY
Score: 2–Stable (low level of inflation)

Indonesia's average annual rate of inflation from 1986 to 1996 was 8.8 percent. In 1997, the rate was 10 percent.

1	Hong Kong	1.25		81	Fiji	3.10
2	Singapore	1.30		81	Mali	3.10
3	Bahrain	1.70		81	Slovenia	3.10
4	New Zealand	1.75		85	Honduras	3.15
5	Switzerland	1.85		85	Mexico	3.15
6	United States	1.90		85	Papua New Guinea	3.15
7	Ireland	1.95		88	Djibouti	3.20
7	Luxembourg	1.95		88	Mongolia	3.20
7	Taiwan	1.95		90	Algeria	3.25
7	United Kingdom	1.95		90	Brazil	3.25
11	Bahamas	2.00		90	Lebanon	3.25
12	Czech Republic	2.05		90	Senegal	3.25
12	Japan	2.05		90	Tanzania	3.25
14	Australia	2.10		95	Nigeria	3.30
14	Belgium	2.10		95	Romania	3.30
14	Canada	2.10		97	Cambodia	3.35
14	United Arab Emirates	2.10		97	Dominican Republic	3.35
18	Austria	2.15		97	Egypt	3.35
18	Chile	2.15		97	Guinea	3.35
18	Estonia	2.15		97	Ivory Coast	3.35
18	Netherlands	2.15		97	Moldova	3.35
22	Denmark	2.25		97	Pakistan	3.35
22	El Salvador	2.25		104	Nepal	3.40
22	Finland	2.25		104	Venezuela	3.40
25	Germany	2.30		106	Armenia	3.45
25	Iceland	2.30		106	Bulgaria	3.45
27	Norway	2.35		106	Lesotho	3.45
28	Korea, South	2.40		106	Madagascar	3.45
28	Kuwait	2.40		106	Russia	3.45
28	Malaysia	2.40		111	Burkina Faso	3.50
28	Panama	2.40		111	Cameroon	3.50
28	Thailand	2.40		111	Guyana	3.50
33	Sweden	2.45		111	Nicaragua	3.50
34	Argentina	2.50		115	Gambia	3.60
34	France	2.50		116	Croatia	3.65
34	Italy	2.50		116	Georgia	3.65
34	Spain	2.50		116	Malawi	3.65
38	Portugal	2.55		119	Cape Verde	3.67
38	Sri Lanka	2.55		120	Ethiopia	3.70
38	Trinidad and Tobago	2.55		120	India	3.70
41	Barbados	2.60		120	Niger	3.70
41	Peru	2.60		123	Congo	3.75
43	Bolivia	2.65		124	Chad	3.80
43	Mauritius	2.65		124	China	3.80
45	Cyprus	2.70		124	Mauritania	3.80
45	Jamaica	2.70		124	Ukraine	3.80
45	Uruguay	2.70		124	Zimbabwe	3.80
48	Botswana	2.75		129	Albania	3.85
48	Guatemala	2.75		129	Bangladesh	3.85
48	Jordan	2.75		129	Mozambique	3.85
48	Namibia	2.75		129	Suriname	3.85
48	Oman	2.75		133	Burundi	3.90
48	Philippines	2.75		134	Togo	3.95
54	Belize	2.80		135	Haiti	4.00
54	Costa Rica	2.80		135	Kyrgyz Rep.	4.00
54	Israel	2.80		137	Kazakhstan	4.05
54	Swaziland	2.80		137	Sierra Leone	4.05
54	Turkey	2.80		139	Yemen	4.10
54	Uganda	2.80		140	Belarus	4.15
54	Samoa	2.80		141	Sudan	4.20
61	Latvia	2.85		141	Syria	4.20
62	Greece	2.90		143	Azerbaijan	4.30
62	Hungary	2.90		143	Equatorial Guinea	4.30
62	So. Africa	2.90		143	Myanmar	4.30
65	Ecuador	2.95		143	Rwanda	4.30
65	Gabon	2.95		147	Tajikistan	4.40
65	Indonesia	2.95		147	Uzbekistan	4.40
65	Malta	2.95		149	Angola	4.45
65	Morocco	2.95		149	Turkmenistan	4.45
65	Poland	2.95		151	Guinea-Bissau	4.55
65	Tunisia	2.95		152	Vietnam	4.60
72	Ghana	3.00		153	Congo (Zaire)	4.70
72	Lithuania	3.00		153	Iran	4.70
72	Saudi Arabia	3.00		155	Bosnia	4.80
75	Benin	3.05		155	Somalia	4.80
75	Kenya	3.05		157	Iraq	4.90
75	Paraguay	3.05		157	Laos	4.90
75	Qatar	3.05		157	Libya	4.90
75	Slovak Republic	3.05		160	Cuba	5.00
75	Zambia	3.05		160	Korea, North	5.00
81	Colombia	3.10				

Mostly Free

CAPITAL FLOWS AND FOREIGN INVESTMENT
Score: 2–Stable (low barriers)

Indonesia has reformed its foreign investment code. The government now allows 100 percent foreign ownership and has opened many sectors once closed to foreign investors, although foreign investment in some retail operations still is not permitted.

BANKING
Score: 4– (high level of restrictions)

From 1969 until the late 1980s, foreign banks were prohibited from receiving a license. There have been some changes to allow greater participation, but foreign banks remain highly regulated. In many cases, they can operate only through joint ventures with Indonesian banks. Moreover, 100 percent foreign-owned banks are not permitted. The banking system is in a state of transition. Many of Indonesia's banks are insolvent as a result of the Asian financial crisis. Some of these banks are being closed; others are being restructured. Thus, because the banking system has moved from a relatively stable operating environment to one of insolvency and closure, Indonesia's banking score is 1 point worse this year.

WAGE AND PRICE CONTROLS
Score: 3–Stable (moderate level)

The market sets most prices, although the government maintains control over the prices of many products, including sugar, soybeans, and rice. According to the Economist Intelligence Unit, "Where [price] controls exist, they are normally set at the retail level. In pharmaceuticals, companies seeking to raise prices must justify the increase to the Ministry of Health."[2] Indonesia has a minimum wage.

PROPERTY RIGHTS
Score: 3–Stable (moderate level of protection)

Indonesia's legal framework is based on Dutch commercial codes that have not been updated since colonial times. Court rulings can be arbitrary and inconsistent. As the U.S. Department of Commerce notes, "In general, the court system does not provide effective recourse for solving commercial disputes. Enforcement of secured interests is problematic."[3]

REGULATION
Score: 4–Stable (high level)

Indonesia's regulatory environment is characterized by bribery, kickbacks, and other corruption. Many regulations are applied arbitrarily, and payoffs may become necessary to receive an "exemption" from a government regulation. The U.S. Department of Commerce reports that corruption continues at some port facilities in which bribes often are required to get some goods through customs. In addition, "Despite major improvements in its economic environment, Indonesia continues to have a reputation as a difficult place to do business. The regulatory and legal environment can be tangled, confusing and time-consuming.... In recent years, considerable attention has focused on the costs of corruption and influence-peddling to local and foreign businesses, and the economy as a whole. Local and foreign companies report that corruption is commonplace, and surveys of business executives working in Asia have ranked Indonesia among countries where corrupt practices are most pervasive and act as a disincentive to direct foreign investment. Complaints arise from irregular fees and/or commissions that companies are asked to pay to operate businesses in a timely, efficient manner. Foreign companies frequently report difficulties in obtaining and renewing necessary immigration permits for expatriate staff based in Indonesia. Government efforts to combat corruption have not been effective. Foreign companies have little success in filing formal complaints, either through legal or administrative channels."[4]

BLACK MARKET
Score: 5–Stable (very high level of activity)

Indonesia has a very large black market, mainly in labor and manufacturing. According to the U.S. Department of Commerce, "The informal sector in Indonesia is significant, with some estimates placing two thirds of the labor force in the sector."[5] Another cause of black market activity is the lack of protection for intellectual property. The U.S. government has targeted Indonesia for intellectual property rights violations; and even though Indonesia's government has undertaken a swift crackdown on pirated copyrighted materials like video and audio tapes, pirated computer software remains rampant. Biotechnology products do not enjoy protection yet under Indonesian law, although they may in the future.

NOTES
[1]   Economist Intelligence Unit, *ILT Reports, Indonesia,* 1998.
[2]   *Ibid.*
[3]   U.S. Department of Commerce, *Country Commercial Guide,* 1998.
[4]   *Ibid.*
[5]   U.S. Department of Commerce, "Indonesia Labor Trends, 1992–94, Foreign Labor Trends," 1996; see also Ministry of Manpower, Republic of Indonesia, "Manpower and Employment Situation in Indonesia, 1992," p. 77.

Iran   4.70

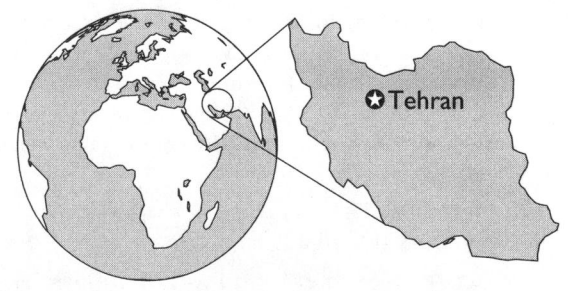

1998 Score: **4.70**	1997 Score: **4.70**	1996 Score: **4.70**

Trade	5	Banking	5
Taxation	5	Wages and Prices	4
Government Intervention	5	Property Rights	5
Monetary Policy	4	Regulation	4
Foreign Investment	5	Black Market	5

Iran had one of the most advanced economies in the Middle East before the 1979 revolution, the 1980–1988 Iran–Iraq War, and widespread economic mismanagement crippled it. The country's radical Islamic leaders established an economic system that discourages private enterprise and favors state-run enterprises. President Ali Akbar Rafsanjani enjoyed only limited success in pushing for economic liberalization during his two terms in office (1989–1997); a corrupt and intransigent bureaucracy allied with hard-line Islamic militants in parliament fought his proposed reforms. Iran's new president, Mohammed Khatami, campaigned in the May 1997 election in favor of limited economic and political reforms. Much of Iran's political power structure, however, including supreme leader Ayatollah Ali Khamenei and many members of parliament, remains opposed to extensive economic reform.

TRADE POLICY
Score: 5–Stable (very high level of protectionism)

Iran controls imports through its exorbitant tariff rates, import bans, licensing, and a customs service that confiscates many goods that cross the border. The average tariff rate is about 14.53 percent, but once other taxes on imports are taken into account, it can increase to over 100 percent.[1] Many Western goods, especially those representing Western culture, are banned. Iran imports little except for goods that the government deems vital—mainly raw materials, food, and medicine. According to the *Economist*, "Iranian industries are seldom self-sufficient, most of them depending on imported capital equipment. When imports are stopped or delayed by the need for permits and licenses, or shoot up in price because they have been smuggled in from Dubai, a business is reduced to a crawl."[2]

TAXATION
Score–Income taxation: 5–Stable (very high tax rates)
Score–Corporate taxation: 5–Stable (very high tax rates)
Final Taxation Score: 5–Stable (very high tax rates)

Iran's top income tax rate is 54 percent, and the average taxpayer is in the 35 percent bracket. The top marginal corporate tax rate is 54 percent. Iran maintains many other taxes, too, including a 10 percent capital gains tax, a 3 percent municipality tax, and a social contributions tax.

GOVERNMENT INTERVENTION IN THE ECONOMY
Score: 5–Stable (very high level)

Government produces most GDP. The private sector is discouraged, and the state owns the banking, petroleum, transportation, utilities, and mining sectors, although it plans to privatize portions of the banking sector. The public sector generates 86 percent of GDP; the remaining 14 percent is generated mainly by religious foundations called *bonyads,* which exist outside the government but get direct government capital support through subsidies. According to the U.S. Department of State, "Iran has a mixed economy. The Government owns the

1	Hong Kong	1.25	81	Fiji	3.10
2	Singapore	1.30	81	Mali	3.10
3	Bahrain	1.70	81	Slovenia	3.10
4	New Zealand	1.75	85	Honduras	3.15
5	Switzerland	1.85	85	Mexico	3.15
6	United States	1.90	85	Papua New Guinea	3.15
7	Ireland	1.95	88	Djibouti	3.20
7	Luxembourg	1.95	88	Mongolia	3.20
7	Taiwan	1.95	90	Algeria	3.25
7	United Kingdom	1.95	90	Brazil	3.25
11	Bahamas	2.00	90	Lebanon	3.25
12	Czech Republic	2.05	90	Senegal	3.25
12	Japan	2.05	90	Tanzania	3.25
14	Australia	2.10	95	Nigeria	3.30
14	Belgium	2.10	95	Romania	3.30
14	Canada	2.10	97	Cambodia	3.35
14	United Arab Emirates	2.10	97	Dominican Republic	3.35
18	Austria	2.15	97	Egypt	3.35
18	Chile	2.15	97	Guinea	3.35
18	Estonia	2.15	97	Ivory Coast	3.35
18	Netherlands	2.15	97	Moldova	3.35
22	Denmark	2.25	97	Pakistan	3.35
22	El Salvador	2.25	104	Nepal	3.40
22	Finland	2.25	104	Venezuela	3.40
25	Germany	2.30	106	Armenia	3.45
25	Iceland	2.30	106	Bulgaria	3.45
27	Norway	2.35	106	Lesotho	3.45
28	Korea, South	2.40	106	Madagascar	3.45
28	Kuwait	2.40	106	Russia	3.45
28	Malaysia	2.40	111	Burkina Faso	3.50
28	Panama	2.40	111	Cameroon	3.50
28	Thailand	2.40	111	Guyana	3.50
33	Sweden	2.45	111	Nicaragua	3.50
34	Argentina	2.50	115	Gambia	3.60
34	France	2.50	116	Croatia	3.65
34	Italy	2.50	116	Georgia	3.65
34	Spain	2.50	116	Malawi	3.65
38	Portugal	2.55	119	Cape Verde	3.67
38	Sri Lanka	2.55	120	Ethiopia	3.70
38	Trinidad and Tobago	2.55	120	India	3.70
41	Barbados	2.60	120	Niger	3.70
41	Peru	2.60	123	Congo	3.75
43	Bolivia	2.65	124	Chad	3.80
43	Mauritius	2.65	124	China	3.80
45	Cyprus	2.70	124	Mauritania	3.80
45	Jamaica	2.70	124	Ukraine	3.80
45	Uruguay	2.70	124	Zimbabwe	3.80
48	Botswana	2.75	129	Albania	3.85
48	Guatemala	2.75	129	Bangladesh	3.85
48	Jordan	2.75	129	Mozambique	3.85
48	Namibia	2.75	129	Suriname	3.85
48	Oman	2.75	133	Burundi	3.90
48	Philippines	2.75	134	Togo	3.95
54	Belize	2.80	135	Haiti	4.00
54	Costa Rica	2.80	135	Kyrgyz Rep.	4.00
54	Israel	2.80	137	Kazakhstan	4.05
54	Swaziland	2.80	137	Sierra Leone	4.05
54	Turkey	2.80	139	Yemen	4.10
54	Uganda	2.80	140	Belarus	4.15
54	Samoa	2.80	141	Sudan	4.20
61	Latvia	2.85	141	Syria	4.20
62	Greece	2.90	143	Azerbaijan	4.30
62	Hungary	2.90	143	Equatorial Guinea	4.30
62	So. Africa	2.90	143	Myanmar	4.30
65	Ecuador	2.95	143	Rwanda	4.30
65	Gabon	2.95	147	Tajikistan	4.40
65	Indonesia	2.95	147	Uzbekistan	4.40
65	Malta	2.95	149	Angola	4.45
65	Morocco	2.95	149	Turkmenistan	4.45
65	Poland	2.95	151	Guinea-Bissau	4.55
65	Tunisia	2.95	152	Vietnam	4.60
72	Ghana	3.00	153	Congo (Zaire)	4.70
72	Lithuania	3.00	153	Iran	4.70
72	Saudi Arabia	3.00	155	Bosnia	4.80
75	Benin	3.05	155	Somalia	4.80
75	Kenya	3.05	157	Iraq	4.90
75	Paraguay	3.05	157	Laos	4.90
75	Qatar	3.05	157	Libya	4.90
75	Slovak Republic	3.05	160	Cuba	5.00
75	Zambia	3.05	160	Korea, North	5.00
81	Colombia	3.10			

Repressed

petroleum and utilities industries and the banks. Large charitable foundations called bonyads, most with strong connection to the Government, control properties expropriated from the former Shah and figures associated with his regime. The bonyads exercise considerable influence in the economy."[3]

MONETARY POLICY
Score: 4–Stable (high level of inflation)

Iran's average rate of inflation from 1986 to 1996 was 25.8 percent. In 1997, the rate was 17.7 percent.

CAPITAL FLOWS AND FOREIGN INVESTMENT
Score: 5–Stable (very high barriers)

Iran has removed some restrictions on foreign investment, but it generally is hostile to foreigners, especially non-Muslims. Foreign ownership is prohibited in banking, domestic trade, construction, and most defense-related industries. According to the *Economist*, "[T]he combination of a laborious bureaucracy and the need to hand out baksheesh [bribes] at every turn makes doing business in Iran...like coping with the combined bad habits of the old Soviet Union and the new Nigeria."[4]

BANKING
Score: 5–Stable (very high level of restrictions)

The banking system is completely government-owned.

WAGE AND PRICE CONTROLS
Score: 4–Stable (high level)

The government controls wages and prices through the large public sector. Price controls apply to essential goods and services like gasoline, bread, and electricity.

PROPERTY RIGHTS
Score: 5–Stable (very low level of protection)

Iran's legal and judicial system is corrupt and inefficient. The government has confiscated huge amounts of private property—particularly property owned by supporters of the former shah, political dissidents, or Westerners—and has outlawed private ownership of satellite dishes because people were using them to watch Western movies and television programs. According to the U.S. Department of State, "The traditional court system is not independent and is subject to government and religious influence."[5]

REGULATION
Score: 4–Stable (high level)

The government discourages the establishment of a business. Regulations are applied unevenly in most cases, and corruption is rampant. According to the *Economist*, "[The] government...last year alone issued more than 250 regulations on imports and exports. Would-be investors say the problem is not so much that there are too many rules, but that the rules keep changing at the whim of ministers."[6]

BLACK MARKET
Score: 5–Stable (very high level of activity)

Because the government manages the level of imports, and because it maintains import bans on many consumer goods, smuggling is rampant. According to the *Economist*, "[I]mports [are] sharply restricted (although they can be smuggled in)."[7]

NOTES

[1]   The 15 percent average tariff rate is based on total revenues from tariffs as a percentage of total imports. According to the World Bank, however, if total import charges for all products are taken into account, the rate increases to 100.9 percent. See World Bank, "Open Economies Work Better," *Policy Research Working Paper* No. 1636, August 1996.

[2]   "Hard Times," *Economist*, January 18, 1997, pp. 12–15.

[3]   U.S. Department of State, "Iran Country Report on Human Rights Practices for 1997," 1998

[4]   "Hard Times."

[5]   U.S. Department of State, "Iran Country Report on Human Rights Practices for 1997," 1998.

[6]   "Hard Times."

[7]   *Ibid.*

Iraq   4.90

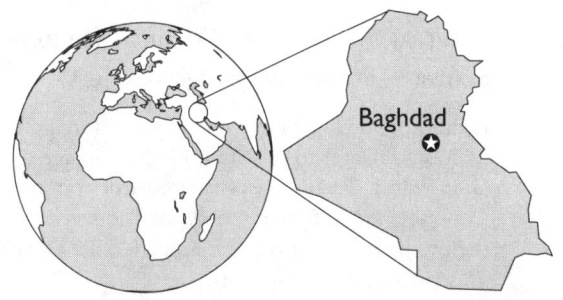

Trade	5	Banking	5
Taxation	5	Wages and Prices	5
Government Intervention	5	Property Rights	5
Monetary Policy	5	Regulation	4
Foreign Investment	5	Black Market	5

Iraq gained its independence from Great Britain in 1932. A military coup in 1958 replaced the monarchy, however, and ushered in a period of political instability. The Ba'ath Socialist Party, which came to power in a 1968 coup, nationalized large portions of the economy. Although Iraq's oil reserves are second only to Saudi Arabia's, its economy has been devastated by government mismanagement, the 1980–1988 war with Iran, the disastrous 1991 Persian Gulf War, and continuing United Nations economic sanctions. The government is dedicated to a socialist economic ideology and public ownership. Although some private-sector initiatives are permitted, the government regularly executes businessmen who charge excessive prices for scarce imported goods.

TRADE POLICY
Score: 5–Stable (very high level of protectionism)

Customs officials apply tariff rates arbitrarily. The government inspects and controls all imports, although there is considerable smuggling across most of Iraq's borders.

TAXATION
Score–Income taxation: 5–Stable (very high tax rates)
Score–Corporate taxation: 5–Stable (very high tax rates)
Final Taxation Score: 5–Stable (very high tax rates)

Taxes generally take the form of confiscated property, much as they do in North Korea and Cuba. Farmers are permitted to grow their own crops, but much of the harvest is confiscated and rationed. Thus, Iraq has the equivalent of very high tax rates.

GOVERNMENT INTERVENTION IN THE ECONOMY
Score: 5–Stable (very high level)

Most economic output is produced by the government or performed in the black market, which the government is trying to restrict. There is little entrepreneurship; where it does occur, it often is subject to government extortion. According to the U.S. Department of Commerce, "The Ba'athist regime engages in extensive central planning and management of industrial production and foreign trade while leaving some small-scale industry and services and most agriculture to private enterprise."[1]

MONETARY POLICY
Score: 5–Stable (very high level of inflation)

Iraq's average annual rate of inflation from 1989 to 1996 was 207 percent. In 1997, the inflation rate was 200 percent.

1	Hong Kong	1.25	81	Fiji	3.10
2	Singapore	1.30	81	Mali	3.10
3	Bahrain	1.70	81	Slovenia	3.10
4	New Zealand	1.75	85	Honduras	3.15
5	Switzerland	1.85	85	Mexico	3.15
6	United States	1.90	85	Papua New Guinea	3.15
7	Ireland	1.95	88	Djibouti	3.20
7	Luxembourg	1.95	88	Mongolia	3.20
7	Taiwan	1.95	90	Algeria	3.25
7	United Kingdom	1.95	90	Brazil	3.25
11	Bahamas	2.00	90	Lebanon	3.25
12	Czech Republic	2.05	90	Senegal	3.25
12	Japan	2.05	90	Tanzania	3.25
14	Australia	2.10	95	Nigeria	3.30
14	Belgium	2.10	95	Romania	3.30
14	Canada	2.10	97	Cambodia	3.35
14	United Arab Emirates	2.10	97	Dominican Republic	3.35
18	Austria	2.15	97	Egypt	3.35
18	Chile	2.15	97	Guinea	3.35
18	Estonia	2.15	97	Ivory Coast	3.35
18	Netherlands	2.15	97	Moldova	3.35
22	Denmark	2.25	97	Pakistan	3.35
22	El Salvador	2.25	104	Nepal	3.40
22	Finland	2.25	104	Venezuela	3.40
25	Germany	2.30	106	Armenia	3.45
25	Iceland	2.30	106	Bulgaria	3.45
27	Norway	2.35	106	Lesotho	3.45
28	Korea, South	2.40	106	Madagascar	3.45
28	Kuwait	2.40	106	Russia	3.45
28	Malaysia	2.40	111	Burkina Faso	3.50
28	Panama	2.40	111	Cameroon	3.50
28	Thailand	2.40	111	Guyana	3.50
33	Sweden	2.45	111	Nicaragua	3.50
34	Argentina	2.50	115	Gambia	3.60
34	France	2.50	116	Croatia	3.65
34	Italy	2.50	116	Georgia	3.65
34	Spain	2.50	116	Malawi	3.65
38	Portugal	2.55	119	Cape Verde	3.67
38	Sri Lanka	2.55	120	Ethiopia	3.70
38	Trinidad and Tobago	2.55	120	India	3.70
41	Barbados	2.60	120	Niger	3.70
41	Peru	2.60	123	Congo	3.75
43	Bolivia	2.65	124	Chad	3.80
43	Mauritius	2.65	124	China	3.80
45	Cyprus	2.70	124	Mauritania	3.80
45	Jamaica	2.70	124	Ukraine	3.80
45	Uruguay	2.70	124	Zimbabwe	3.80
48	Botswana	2.75	129	Albania	3.85
48	Guatemala	2.75	129	Bangladesh	3.85
48	Jordan	2.75	129	Mozambique	3.85
48	Namibia	2.75	129	Suriname	3.85
48	Oman	2.75	133	Burundi	3.90
48	Philippines	2.75	134	Togo	3.95
54	Belize	2.80	135	Haiti	4.00
54	Costa Rica	2.80	135	Kyrgyz Rep.	4.00
54	Israel	2.80	137	Kazakhstan	4.05
54	Swaziland	2.80	137	Sierra Leone	4.05
54	Turkey	2.80	139	Yemen	4.10
54	Uganda	2.80	140	Belarus	4.15
54	Samoa	2.80	141	Sudan	4.20
61	Latvia	2.85	141	Syria	4.20
62	Greece	2.90	143	Azerbaijan	4.30
62	Hungary	2.90	143	Equatorial Guinea	4.30
62	So. Africa	2.90	143	Myanmar	4.30
65	Ecuador	2.95	143	Rwanda	4.30
65	Gabon	2.95	147	Tajikistan	4.40
65	Indonesia	2.95	147	Uzbekistan	4.40
65	Malta	2.95	149	Angola	4.45
65	Morocco	2.95	149	Turkmenistan	4.45
65	Poland	2.95	151	Guinea-Bissau	4.55
65	Tunisia	2.95	152	Vietnam	4.60
72	Ghana	3.00	153	Congo (Zaire)	4.70
72	Lithuania	3.00	153	Iran	4.70
72	Saudi Arabia	3.00	155	Bosnia	4.80
75	Benin	3.05	155	Somalia	4.80
75	Kenya	3.05	157	Iraq	4.90
75	Paraguay	3.05	157	Laos	4.90
75	Qatar	3.05	157	Libya	4.90
75	Slovak Republic	3.05	160	Cuba	5.00
75	Zambia	3.05	160	Korea, North	5.00
81	Colombia	3.10			

Repressed

CAPITAL FLOWS AND FOREIGN INVESTMENT
Score: 5–Stable (very high barriers)

Even though Iraq has permitted some foreign investment, mainly to help it to rebuild from the damage of the Persian Gulf War, it discourages such investment in most areas. Contracts are not guaranteed, and there is little recourse in the event their enforcement is needed. Investment is allowed only on a case-by-case basis.

BANKING
Score: 5–Stable (very high level of restrictions)

Although some private banks exist, most are under the indirect and sometimes even direct control of the government. The banking system is in complete disarray.

WAGE AND PRICE CONTROLS
Score: 5–Stable (very high level)

Rationing is the norm in Iraq. The government confiscates most durable goods from producers in order to ration them. The regime does not allow private merchants to establish their own prices. It also regularly executes businessman who profit from the high prices charged for scarce and smuggled goods.

PROPERTY RIGHTS
Score: 5–Stable (very low level of protection)

Saddam Hussein's dictatorship does not respect private property. The legal and judicial system is corrupt and inefficient, and the state regularly confiscates private property. According to the U.S. Department of State, "The judiciary is not independent and there is no check on the President's power to override any court decision."[2]

REGULATION
Score: 4–Stable (high level)

Iraq executes government officials convicted of corruption. The bureaucracy is large and inefficient, however, and, despite the capital punishment for such activity, corruption remains rampant, particularly among Saddam Hussein's inner circle. Officially sanctioned extortion is increasing as the government seeks to force merchants to turn a larger portion of their products over to the state.

BLACK MARKET
Score: 5–Stable (very high level of activity)

Smuggling of all kinds of products is rampant. According to the U.S. Department of Commerce, "Many consumer goods and basic necessities, including medicine, are available on the black market at highly inflated prices."[3] In an attempt to crack down on black market activity, the government has resorted to execution. The Department of Commerce also reports that "Capital punishment has been decreed for those smuggling cars and trucks from the country and harsh penalties have been levied on currency traders and 'profiteers.'"[4]

NOTES

[1] U.S. Department of Commerce, *Stat–USA* Internet site (*http://www.stat-usa.gov*).
[2] U.S. Department of State, "Iraq Country Report on Human Rights Practices for 1997," 1998.
[3] U.S. Department of Commerce, *Country Commercial Guide,* 1996.
[4] *Ibid.*

Ireland   1.95

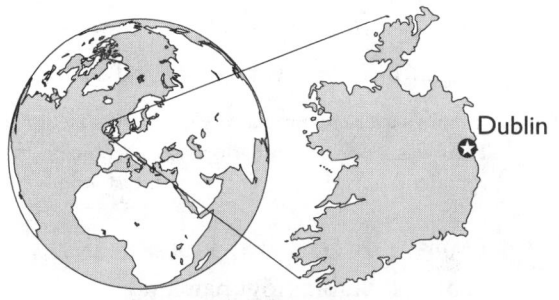

Dublin

1998 Score: **2.00**	1997 Score: **2.20**	1996 Score: **2.20**

Trade	2	Banking	2
Taxation	4.5	Wages and Prices	2
Government Intervention	2	Property Rights	1
Monetary Policy	1	Regulation	2
Foreign Investment	2	Black Market	1

Throughout much of its history, Ireland has been an agricultural country. Since the mid-1950s, however, it has become increasingly industrialized. Today, mining, manufacturing, construction, and public utilities account for about 37 percent of GDP; agriculture accounts for only 12 percent. Because of the creation of a largely open trade and investment environment during the late 1980s and early 1990s, Ireland became a base for the production of advanced consumer electronics. Many high-tech companies, both foreign and domestic, now operate in Ireland. Due to an agreement with the European Union Commission in July 1998, the Irish government announced plans to instate a uniform corporate tax rate of 12.5 percent by 2003. Parliamentary elections held in June 1997 brought to power a coalition government of the Fianna Fail and the Progressive Democrats led by Prime Minister Bertie Ahern. Ireland recently reduced its corporate taxes. As a result, its overall score is .05 point better this year.

TRADE POLICY
Score: 2–Stable (low level of protectionism)

As part of the European Union (EU), Ireland has an average tariff rate of 3.6 percent. It also maintains some of the EU's strictest plant and animal health standards, although there have been some attempts to remove some of these restrictions, which often present barriers to the importation of such items as meat and vegetables.

TAXATION
Score–Income taxation: 5–Stable (very high tax rates)
Score–Corporate taxation: 3+ (moderate tax rates)
Final Taxation Score: 4.5+ (very high tax rates)

Ireland's top income tax rate is 48 percent, and the average income level is taxed at 26 percent. The top corporate income tax rate is 32 percent, down from 38 percent in 1997. As a result, Ireland's corporate tax score has improved by 1 point since last year, making its overall taxation score 0.5 point better this year than last year. Ireland also has a 40 percent capital gains tax and a 21 percent value-added tax. To attract high-tech companies, the government has instituted a top corporate tax of 10 percent on some companies involved in manufacturing, international finance, data processing, and research and development.

GOVERNMENT INTERVENTION IN THE ECONOMY
Score: 2–Stable (low level)

Government consumes 14.8 percent of GDP. The government has sold most state-owned industries, including some transportation, energy, and communications companies. There are no prohibitions on private-sector involvement in any sector of the economy. State-owned industries are confined to such areas as energy production and telecommunications.

1	Hong Kong	1.25	81	Fiji	3.10
2	Singapore	1.30	81	Mali	3.10
3	Bahrain	1.70	81	Slovenia	3.10
4	New Zealand	1.75	85	Honduras	3.15
5	Switzerland	1.85	85	Mexico	3.15
6	United States	1.90	85	Papua New Guinea	3.15
7	Ireland	1.95	88	Djibouti	3.20
7	Luxembourg	1.95	88	Mongolia	3.20
7	Taiwan	1.95	90	Algeria	3.25
7	United Kingdom	1.95	90	Brazil	3.25
11	Bahamas	2.00	90	Lebanon	3.25
12	Czech Republic	2.05	90	Senegal	3.25
12	Japan	2.05	90	Tanzania	3.25
14	Australia	2.10	95	Nigeria	3.30
14	Belgium	2.10	95	Romania	3.30
14	Canada	2.10	97	Cambodia	3.35
14	United Arab Emirates	2.10	97	Dominican Republic	3.35
18	Austria	2.15	97	Egypt	3.35
18	Chile	2.15	97	Guinea	3.35
18	Estonia	2.15	97	Ivory Coast	3.35
18	Netherlands	2.15	97	Moldova	3.35
22	Denmark	2.25	97	Pakistan	3.35
22	El Salvador	2.25	104	Nepal	3.40
22	Finland	2.25	104	Venezuela	3.40
25	Germany	2.30	106	Armenia	3.45
25	Iceland	2.30	106	Bulgaria	3.45
27	Norway	2.35	106	Lesotho	3.45
28	Korea, South	2.40	106	Madagascar	3.45
28	Kuwait	2.40	106	Russia	3.45
28	Malaysia	2.40	111	Burkina Faso	3.50
28	Panama	2.40	111	Cameroon	3.50
28	Thailand	2.40	111	Guyana	3.50
33	Sweden	2.45	111	Nicaragua	3.50
34	Argentina	2.50	115	Gambia	3.60
34	France	2.50	116	Croatia	3.65
34	Italy	2.50	116	Georgia	3.65
34	Spain	2.50	116	Malawi	3.65
38	Portugal	2.55	119	Cape Verde	3.67
38	Sri Lanka	2.55	120	Ethiopia	3.70
38	Trinidad and Tobago	2.55	120	India	3.70
41	Barbados	2.60	120	Niger	3.70
41	Peru	2.60	123	Congo	3.75
43	Bolivia	2.65	124	Chad	3.80
43	Mauritius	2.65	124	China	3.80
45	Cyprus	2.70	124	Mauritania	3.80
45	Jamaica	2.70	124	Ukraine	3.80
45	Uruguay	2.70	124	Zimbabwe	3.80
48	Botswana	2.75	129	Albania	3.85
48	Guatemala	2.75	129	Bangladesh	3.85
48	Jordan	2.75	129	Mozambique	3.85
48	Namibia	2.75	129	Suriname	3.85
48	Oman	2.75	133	Burundi	3.90
48	Philippines	2.75	134	Togo	3.95
54	Belize	2.80	135	Haiti	4.00
54	Costa Rica	2.80	135	Kyrgyz Rep.	4.00
54	Israel	2.80	137	Kazakhstan	4.05
54	Swaziland	2.80	137	Sierra Leone	4.05
54	Turkey	2.80	139	Yemen	4.10
54	Uganda	2.80	140	Belarus	4.15
54	Samoa	2.80	141	Sudan	4.20
61	Latvia	2.85	141	Syria	4.20
62	Greece	2.90	143	Azerbaijan	4.30
62	Hungary	2.90	143	Equatorial Guinea	4.30
62	So. Africa	2.90	143	Myanmar	4.30
65	Ecuador	2.95	143	Rwanda	4.30
65	Gabon	2.95	147	Tajikistan	4.40
65	Indonesia	2.95	147	Uzbekistan	4.40
65	Malta	2.95	149	Angola	4.45
65	Morocco	2.95	149	Turkmenistan	4.45
65	Poland	2.95	151	Guinea-Bissau	4.55
65	Tunisia	2.95	152	Vietnam	4.60
72	Ghana	3.00	153	Congo (Zaire)	4.70
72	Lithuania	3.00	153	Iran	4.70
72	Saudi Arabia	3.00	155	Bosnia	4.80
75	Benin	3.05	155	Somalia	4.80
75	Kenya	3.05	157	Iraq	4.90
75	Paraguay	3.05	157	Laos	4.90
75	Qatar	3.05	157	Libya	4.90
75	Slovak Republic	3.05	160	Cuba	5.00
75	Zambia	3.05	160	Korea, North	5.00
81	Colombia	3.10			

MONETARY POLICY
Score: 1–Stable (very low level of inflation)

Ireland's average annual rate of inflation from 1986 to 1996 was 3 percent. Inflation was 1.6 percent in 1997 and remained below 2 percent for most of 1998.

CAPITAL FLOWS AND FOREIGN INVESTMENT
Score: 2–Stable (low barriers)

Ireland welcomes foreign investment and offers such incentives as a guaranteed 10 percent maximum tax on investment profits for manufacturing companies. Foreign investment, however, is restricted in natural gas, transportation, and some telecommunications.

BANKING
Score: 2–Stable (low level of restrictions)

Ireland has a highly competitive and advanced banking and financial system. Foreign banks are welcome and are treated the same as domestic banks.

WAGE AND PRICE CONTROLS
Score: 2–Stable (low level)

Ireland has no price controls but maintains a minimum wage for certain low-wage jobs.

PROPERTY RIGHTS
Score: 1–Stable (very high level of protection)

Property expropriation is highly unlikely. Property receives sufficient protection from the court system. According to the U.S. Department of State, "The Constitution provides for an independent judiciary, and the Government respects this provision in practice. The judiciary provides citizens with a fair and efficient judicial process."[1]

REGULATION
Score: 2–Stable (low level)

Regulations are applied uniformly and are not substantially onerous. The level of regulation has been increasing, however. The environmental movement is putting a great strain on business, especially on manufacturing companies, which must comply with stringent air quality laws. Some occupational health and safety laws also are burdensome. According to the U.S. Department of Commerce, "Most tax, labor, health and safety, and other laws are compatible with European Union regulations, and they do not adversely affect investment. Bureaucratic procedures generally are transparent and reasonably efficient."[2]

BLACK MARKET
Score: 1–Stable (very low level of activity)

The level of black market activity is minimal, although some pirating of computer software does take place.

NOTES

[1] U.S. Department of State, "1997 Human Rights Report: Ireland," March 1998.
[2] U.S. Department of Commerce, *Country Commercial Guide*, 1998.

Israel   2.80

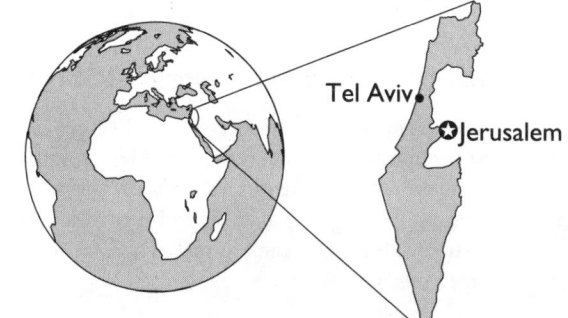

Tel Aviv ·
⊕ Jerusalem

1998 Score: **2.80**	1997 Score: **2.80**	1996 Score: **2.90**

Trade	2	Banking	3
Taxation	5	Wages and Prices	2
Government Intervention	4	Property Rights	2
Monetary Policy	3	Regulation	2
Foreign Investment	1	Black Market	4

Since gaining independence in 1948, Israel technically has been at war with most of its Arab neighbors. This has imposed a heavy defense burden that has been alleviated only slightly by peace treaties with Egypt in 1979 and Jordan in 1994. Because of limited natural resources, Israel depends on imports of oil, grain, and raw materials. It usually posts current account deficits, which are exacerbated by large transfer payments from abroad, as well as by foreign loans and foreign aid. A free trade area formed with the United States in 1985 has increased trade between the two countries. Prime Minister Benjamin Netanyahu, elected in May 1996, has called for economic liberalization and a gradual reduction of U.S. foreign aid. Netanyahu's economic reform program has proceeded at a slow pace, however.

TRADE POLICY
Score: 2–Stable (low level of protectionism)

Israel's average tariff rate is less than 1 percent. Non-tariff barriers include import bans, strict product standards, and import quotas.

TAXATION
Score–Income taxation: 5–Stable (very high tax rates)
Score–Corporate taxation: 4–Stable (high tax rates)
Final Taxation Score: 5–Stable (very high tax rates)

Israel's top income tax level is 50 percent; the average income level is taxed at 30 percent. The top corporate tax rate is over 36 percent. Israel also has a 36 percent capital gains tax and a 17 percent value-added tax.

GOVERNMENT INTERVENTION IN THE ECONOMY
Score: 4–Stable (high level)

Government consumes 29.2 percent of GDP, primarily because of military expenditures and social welfare programs. The Economist Intelligence Unit describes the government as "a major player in the business world."[1] The government continues to own large portions of the utility, chemical, airline, and shipyard industries.

MONETARY POLICY
Score: 3–Stable (moderate level of inflation)

Israel's average annual rate of inflation from 1986 to 1996 was 19.6 percent. In 1997, consumer price inflation was 9 percent.

CAPITAL FLOWS AND FOREIGN INVESTMENT
Score: 1–Stable (very low barriers)

There are no significant barriers to foreign investment. The government permits 100 percent foreign ownership of businesses and offers such investment incentives as tax holidays.

1	Hong Kong	1.25
2	Singapore	1.30
3	Bahrain	1.70
4	New Zealand	1.75
5	Switzerland	1.85
6	United States	1.90
7	Ireland	1.95
7	Luxembourg	1.95
7	Taiwan	1.95
7	United Kingdom	1.95
11	Bahamas	2.00
12	Czech Republic	2.05
12	Japan	2.05
14	Australia	2.10
14	Belgium	2.10
14	Canada	2.10
14	United Arab Emirates	2.10
18	Austria	2.15
18	Chile	2.15
18	Estonia	2.15
18	Netherlands	2.15
22	Denmark	2.25
22	El Salvador	2.25
22	Finland	2.25
25	Germany	2.30
25	Iceland	2.30
27	Norway	2.35
28	Korea, South	2.40
28	Kuwait	2.40
28	Malaysia	2.40
28	Panama	2.40
28	Thailand	2.40
33	Sweden	2.45
34	Argentina	2.50
34	France	2.50
34	Italy	2.50
34	Spain	2.50
38	Portugal	2.55
38	Sri Lanka	2.55
38	Trinidad and Tobago	2.55
41	Barbados	2.60
41	Peru	2.60
43	Bolivia	2.65
43	Mauritius	2.65
45	Cyprus	2.70
45	Jamaica	2.70
45	Uruguay	2.70
48	Botswana	2.75
48	Guatemala	2.75
48	Jordan	2.75
48	Namibia	2.75
48	Oman	2.75
48	Philippines	2.75
54	Belize	2.80
54	Costa Rica	2.80
54	Israel	2.80
54	Swaziland	2.80
54	Turkey	2.80
54	Uganda	2.80
54	Samoa	2.80
61	Latvia	2.85
62	Greece	2.90
62	Hungary	2.90
62	So. Africa	2.90
65	Ecuador	2.95
65	Gabon	2.95
65	Indonesia	2.95
65	Malta	2.95
65	Morocco	2.95
65	Poland	2.95
65	Tunisia	2.95
72	Ghana	3.00
72	Lithuania	3.00
72	Saudi Arabia	3.00
75	Benin	3.05
75	Kenya	3.05
75	Paraguay	3.05
75	Qatar	3.05
75	Slovak Republic	3.05
75	Zambia	3.05
81	Colombia	3.10

81	Fiji	3.10
81	Mali	3.10
81	Slovenia	3.10
85	Honduras	3.15
85	Mexico	3.15
85	Papua New Guinea	3.15
88	Djibouti	3.20
88	Mongolia	3.20
90	Algeria	3.25
90	Brazil	3.25
90	Lebanon	3.25
90	Senegal	3.25
90	Tanzania	3.25
95	Nigeria	3.30
95	Romania	3.30
97	Cambodia	3.35
97	Dominican Republic	3.35
97	Egypt	3.35
97	Guinea	3.35
97	Ivory Coast	3.35
97	Moldova	3.35
97	Pakistan	3.35
104	Nepal	3.40
104	Venezuela	3.40
106	Armenia	3.45
106	Bulgaria	3.45
106	Lesotho	3.45
106	Madagascar	3.45
106	Russia	3.45
111	Burkina Faso	3.50
111	Cameroon	3.50
111	Guyana	3.50
111	Nicaragua	3.50
115	Gambia	3.60
116	Croatia	3.65
116	Georgia	3.65
116	Malawi	3.65
119	Cape Verde	3.67
120	Ethiopia	3.70
120	India	3.70
120	Niger	3.70
123	Congo	3.75
124	Chad	3.80
124	China	3.80
124	Mauritania	3.80
124	Ukraine	3.80
124	Zimbabwe	3.80
129	Albania	3.85
129	Bangladesh	3.85
129	Mozambique	3.85
129	Suriname	3.85
133	Burundi	3.90
134	Togo	3.95
135	Haiti	4.00
135	Kyrgyz Rep.	4.00
137	Kazakhstan	4.05
137	Sierra Leone	4.05
139	Yemen	4.10
140	Belarus	4.15
141	Sudan	4.20
141	Syria	4.20
143	Azerbaijan	4.30
143	Equatorial Guinea	4.30
143	Myanmar	4.30
143	Rwanda	4.30
147	Tajikistan	4.40
147	Uzbekistan	4.40
149	Angola	4.45
149	Turkmenistan	4.45
151	Guinea-Bissau	4.55
152	Vietnam	4.60
153	Congo (Zaire)	4.70
153	Iran	4.70
155	Bosnia	4.80
155	Somalia	4.80
157	Iraq	4.90
157	Laos	4.90
157	Libya	4.90
160	Cuba	5.00
160	Korea, North	5.00

Mostly Free

BANKING
Score: 3–Stable (moderate level of restrictions)

Israel's government continues to sell shares of state-owned banks, but these banks remain highly centralized. The government manipulates a significant portion of the industry through regulations and controls. Banks are restricted from investing in real estate, insurance, and some other business activities.

WAGE AND PRICE CONTROLS
Score: 2–Stable (low level)

Although most price controls have been lifted, they remain in effect in a few areas, such as transportation. Israel has a minimum wage.

PROPERTY RIGHTS
Score: 2–Stable (high level of protection)

Expropriation of property is unlikely. "Israel has a modern legal system based on mandate and British case law," reports the U.S. Department of Commerce. "Effective means exist for enforcing property and contractual rights. Courts are independent; there is no government interference in the court system."[2]

REGULATION
Score: 2–Stable (low level)

Although Israel is reducing its regulatory burden, some impediments to business remain. For example, according to the U.S. Department of Commerce, "Tax, labor, health, and safety laws are frequently an impediment to the foreign investor in Israel.... Although there is a current trend towards deregulation, Israel's bureaucracy can still be difficult to navigate, especially for the foreign investor unfamiliar with the system."[3]

BLACK MARKET
Score: 4–Stable (high level of activity)

Although the size of Israel's black market is shrinking, the level of non-tariff barriers still encourages fairly extensive smuggling of some consumer goods. Smuggling of consumer electronics equipment is diminishing, but the black market in pirated videos and other forms of entertainment is substantial. According to the U.S. Department of State, "Cable, television, video, and software piracy is common in Israel. Israel currently has an antiquated copyright law which together with the low priority given to IPR [intellectual property rights] enforcement by the authorities, has allowed an upsurge in piracy."[4] Illegal showings of pirated U.S. movies and television programs and black market versions of U.S. music continue to flourish.

NOTES

[1] Economist Intelligence Unit, *ILT Country Reports, Israel,* 1997.
[2] U.S. Department of Commerce, *Country Commercial Guide,* 1998.
[3] *Ibid.*
[4] U.S. Department of State, *Country Reports on Economic Policy and Trade Practices,* 1998.

Italy   2.50

1998 Score: **2.50**	1997 Score: **2.60**	1996 Score: **2.70**

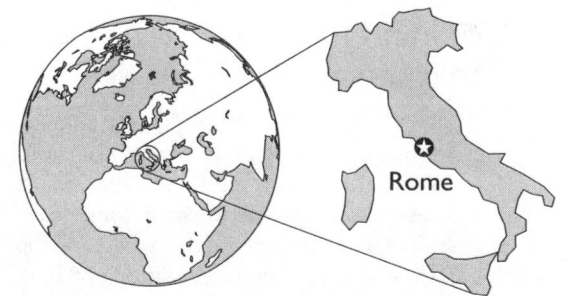

Rome

Trade	2	Banking	2
Taxation	5	Wages and Prices	2
Government Intervention	3	Property Rights	2
Monetary Policy	2	Regulation	3
Foreign Investment	2	Black Market	2

Italy was unified under a constitutional monarchy in 1861. After World War I, it became a fascist dictatorship, but became a republic after World War II. A founding member of the European Union (EU), Italy is the world's fifth-largest economy and is one of the Group of Seven advanced industrialized countries. Parliamentary elections in April 1996 failed to establish a majority in both chambers for any one party or coalition. As a result, Prime Minister Romano Prodi of the Olive Tree coalition had difficulty in achieving economic liberalization, although there has been some progress. In October 1998, Prodi resigned after his center-left government lost a vote of confidence in parliament. His successor, Prime Minister Massimo D'Alema—a former communist and leader of the Democratic Party of the Left—has pledged to reduce Italy's level of unemployment and budget deficit.

TRADE POLICY
Score: 2–Stable (low level of protectionism)

As a member of the EU, Italy has an average tariff rate of 3.6 percent. But customs procedures can be both strict and arbitrary, particularly with respect to agricultural goods; this affects imports from non-EU countries. "In Italy," reports the U.S. Department of State, "fragmented, often non-transparent government procurement practices and previous problems with corruption have created obstacles to U.S. firms' participation in Italian government procurement."[1]

TAXATION
Score–Income taxation: 5–Stable (very high tax rates)
Score–Corporate taxation: 4–Stable (high tax rates)
Final Taxation Score: 5–Stable (very high tax rates)

Italy's top income tax rate is 46 percent, down from 51 percent; the average income level is taxed at 34 percent. The top corporate income tax rate is 37 percent. Italy also maintains a 37 percent capital gains tax and a 20 percent value-added tax.[2]

GOVERNMENT INTERVENTION IN THE ECONOMY
Score: 3–Stable (moderate level)

Government consumes about 16.6 percent of GDP and is responsible for about 40 percent of all economic output. The government owns portions of the telephone utility, Telecom Italia, as well as energy utilities and transportation companies.

MONETARY POLICY
Score: 2–Stable (low level)

Italy's average annual rate of inflation from 1986 to 1996 was 5.7 percent. Inflation was 1.9 percent in 1997.

1	Hong Kong	1.25	81	Fiji	3.10
2	Singapore	1.30	81	Mali	3.10
3	Bahrain	1.70	81	Slovenia	3.10
4	New Zealand	1.75	85	Honduras	3.15
5	Switzerland	1.85	85	Mexico	3.15
6	United States	1.90	85	Papua New Guinea	3.15
7	Ireland	1.95	88	Djibouti	3.20
7	Luxembourg	1.95	88	Mongolia	3.20
7	Taiwan	1.95	90	Algeria	3.25
7	United Kingdom	1.95	90	Brazil	3.25
11	Bahamas	2.00	90	Lebanon	3.25
12	Czech Republic	2.05	90	Senegal	3.25
12	Japan	2.05	90	Tanzania	3.25
14	Australia	2.10	95	Nigeria	3.30
14	Belgium	2.10	95	Romania	3.30
14	Canada	2.10	97	Cambodia	3.35
14	United Arab Emirates	2.10	97	Dominican Republic	3.35
18	Austria	2.15	97	Egypt	3.35
18	Chile	2.15	97	Guinea	3.35
18	Estonia	2.15	97	Ivory Coast	3.35
18	Netherlands	2.15	97	Moldova	3.35
22	Denmark	2.25	97	Pakistan	3.35
22	El Salvador	2.25	104	Nepal	3.40
22	Finland	2.25	104	Venezuela	3.40
25	Germany	2.30	106	Armenia	3.45
25	Iceland	2.30	106	Bulgaria	3.45
27	Norway	2.35	106	Lesotho	3.45
28	Korea, South	2.40	106	Madagascar	3.45
28	Kuwait	2.40	106	Russia	3.45
28	Malaysia	2.40	111	Burkina Faso	3.50
28	Panama	2.40	111	Cameroon	3.50
28	Thailand	2.40	111	Guyana	3.50
33	Sweden	2.45	111	Nicaragua	3.50
34	Argentina	2.50	115	Gambia	3.60
34	France	2.50	116	Croatia	3.65
34	Italy	2.50	116	Georgia	3.65
34	Spain	2.50	116	Malawi	3.65
38	Portugal	2.55	119	Cape Verde	3.67
38	Sri Lanka	2.55	120	Ethiopia	3.70
38	Trinidad and Tobago	2.55	120	India	3.70
41	Barbados	2.60	120	Niger	3.70
41	Peru	2.60	123	Congo	3.75
43	Bolivia	2.65	124	Chad	3.80
43	Mauritius	2.65	124	China	3.80
45	Cyprus	2.70	124	Mauritania	3.80
45	Jamaica	2.70	124	Ukraine	3.80
45	Uruguay	2.70	124	Zimbabwe	3.80
48	Botswana	2.75	129	Albania	3.85
48	Guatemala	2.75	129	Bangladesh	3.85
48	Jordan	2.75	129	Mozambique	3.85
48	Namibia	2.75	129	Suriname	3.85
48	Oman	2.75	133	Burundi	3.90
48	Philippines	2.75	134	Togo	3.95
54	Belize	2.80	135	Haiti	4.00
54	Costa Rica	2.80	135	Kyrgyz Rep.	4.00
54	Israel	2.80	137	Kazakhstan	4.05
54	Swaziland	2.80	137	Sierra Leone	4.05
54	Turkey	2.80	139	Yemen	4.10
54	Uganda	2.80	140	Belarus	4.15
54	Samoa	2.80	141	Sudan	4.20
61	Latvia	2.85	141	Syria	4.20
62	Greece	2.90	143	Azerbaijan	4.30
62	Hungary	2.90	143	Equatorial Guinea	4.30
62	So. Africa	2.90	143	Myanmar	4.30
65	Ecuador	2.95	143	Rwanda	4.30
65	Gabon	2.95	147	Tajikistan	4.40
65	Indonesia	2.95	147	Uzbekistan	4.40
65	Malta	2.95	149	Angola	4.45
65	Morocco	2.95	149	Turkmenistan	4.45
65	Poland	2.95	151	Guinea-Bissau	4.55
65	Tunisia	2.95	152	Vietnam	4.60
72	Ghana	3.00	153	Congo (Zaire)	4.70
72	Lithuania	3.00	153	Iran	4.70
72	Saudi Arabia	3.00	155	Bosnia	4.80
75	Benin	3.05	155	Somalia	4.80
75	Kenya	3.05	157	Iraq	4.90
75	Paraguay	3.05	157	Laos	4.90
75	Qatar	3.05	157	Libya	4.90
75	Slovak Republic	3.05	160	Cuba	5.00
75	Zambia	3.05	160	Korea, North	5.00
81	Colombia	3.10			

Mostly Free

CAPITAL FLOWS AND FOREIGN INVESTMENT
Score: 2–Stable (low barriers)

As part of the EU, Italy generally welcomes foreign investment, mainly because of its importance in bringing new technologies to ailing industries. There are a few restrictions and bans on foreign investment in domestic air transport, aircraft manufacturing, and some state monopolies. Industrial projects require a multitude of approvals and permits. Nevertheless, overall barriers to foreign investment are low by global standards.

BANKING
Score: 2–Stable (low level of restrictions)

Banks face some government restrictions and regulations, although Italy has undertaken some financial reform, including the privatization of several large banks.

WAGE AND PRICE CONTROLS
Score: 2–Stable (low level)

Although few direct price controls exist, the government affects prices through state-owned and -subsidized industries for which pricing policies are not determined by market forces. The government has abolished many of its price controls on pharmaceuticals and other products; and, because the government has privatized many businesses, it has much less control over prices now than it had a few years ago. Thus, Italy's wage and price controls today are low by global standards.

PROPERTY RIGHTS
Score: 2–Stable (high level of protection)

Property is safe from arbitrary government expropriation. Italy has an advanced legal system to protect property. According to the U.S. Department of State, "The Constitution provides for an independent judiciary, and the Government respects this provision in practice. The judiciary provides citizens with a fair and efficient judicial process."[3] There often are delays, however, in Italy's court system. For example, according to the U.S. Department of Commerce, "Given the slowness of the Italian judicial system (normally 3–5 years for trial in a civil matter and two automatic appeals), companies are well advised to choose arbitration, which can be Italian or international."[4]

REGULATION
Score: 3–Stable (moderate level)

Despite recent government initiatives to eliminate burdensome regulations that could lead to corruption, Italy's political crisis has led to the return of corruption. Although it is easy to open businesses, and bribes no longer are necessary, cumbersome laws regarding workers rights undermine the competitiveness of many Italian companies. According to the U.S. Department of Commerce, "Difficult bureaucratic procedures impede new investment in Italy for both Italian and foreign firms.... Business has identified corruption as a significant disincentive to investment, particularly in the south."[5] By global standards, however, Italy's level of regulation is moderate.

BLACK MARKET
Score: 2–Stable (low level of activity)

Italy's organized criminals are involved heavily in drugs and guns, but black market activity in smuggling, transportation services, and the construction industries is limited; in addition, the government is making some progress in stamping out organized crime.[6] It has enacted severe penalties for engaging in the piracy of protected intellectual property. Pirated computer software represented some 86 percent of the market in 1992; today, it accounts for less than half. Pirated video sales represent some 40 percent of the market. Compared with the size of Italy's economy, however, these activities are negligible.

NOTES

[1] U.S. Department of State, *Country Reports on Economic Policy and Trade Practices*, 1998.
[2] It is important to point out that many Italians probably avoid paying taxes altogether.
[3] U.S. Department of State, "Italy Country Report on Human Rights Practices for 1997," 1998.
[4] U.S. Department of Commerce, *Country Commercial Guide*, 1998
[5] U.S. Department of Commerce, *Country Commercial Guide*, 1998.
[6] The methodology for this factor considers only black market activity that results from government restrictions on free enterprise. For a detailed explanation, see Chapter 4.

Ivory Coast   3.35

1998 Score: **3.35**	1997 Score: **3.35**	1996 Score: **3.25**

Trade	5	Banking	3
Taxation	3.5	Wages and Prices	3
Government Intervention	3	Property Rights	4
Monetary Policy	1	Regulation	4
Foreign Investment	3	Black Market	4

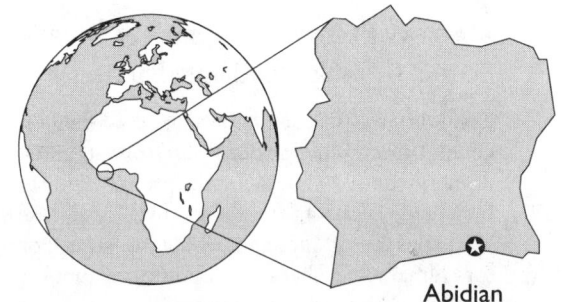

Abidjan

The Ivory Coast gained its independence from France in 1960, although its cultural, economic, and military ties with its former colonial power remain very close. The Ivory Coast embraced socialism on gaining independence and remained committed to socialist economic policies into the 1990s. Until his death in 1993, President Felix Houphouet-Boigny ruled the country with little regard for democracy. His successor, Henri Konan Bédié, has made modest strides toward promoting political and economic reforms, which also are being pushed by foreign aid donors. The government recently accelerated economic liberalization policies, including the privatization of 44 state industries and agreement with an International Monetary Fund agenda to liberalize the cocoa and coffee industries, which account for 20 percent of GDP and 44 percent of exports. Growth in GDP averaged only 0.8 percent annually from 1990 to 1994, although it was strong from 1995 to 1997, averaging 6.7 percent per annum.

TRADE POLICY
Score: 5–Stable (very high level of protectionism)

The Ivory Coast has been reducing tariffs to some extent, but they remain high. The average tariff rate is 25.5 percent,[1] and there is a quota system for some goods. The government has a monopoly on rice imports and bans other imports, such as poultry products. Import quotas also exist to restrict some imports such as fuels and lubricants, coffee, cocoa, sugar, certain textiles, used clothing, and specific types of vehicles.

TAXATION
Score–Income taxation: 3–Stable (moderate tax rates)
Score–Corporate taxation: 3–Stable (moderate tax rates)
Final Taxation Score: 3.5–Stable (high tax rates)

Taxes in the Ivory Coast are moderately high. The top income tax rate is 60 percent, and the average income is taxed at 10 percent. The top corporate income tax level is 35 percent. The Ivory Coast also has a 35 percent capital gains tax, a 20 percent value-added tax, and a turnover tax of 10 percent to 25 percent on services and interest provided by banks and financial companies.

GOVERNMENT INTERVENTION IN THE ECONOMY
Score: 3–Stable (moderate level)

Government consumes 11.6 percent of GDP, which is generated primarily by a significant state-owned sector. There has been some progress in privatization, including the sale of the country's largest rubber producer to a Belgian company.

MONETARY POLICY
Score: 1–Stable (very low level of inflation)

The Ivory Coast's average annual rate of inflation from 1986 to 1996 was 5.3 percent. In 1997, the rate of inflation was about 5 percent.

1	Hong Kong	1.25		81	Fiji	3.10
2	Singapore	1.30		81	Mali	3.10
3	Bahrain	1.70		81	Slovenia	3.10
4	New Zealand	1.75		85	Honduras	3.15
5	Switzerland	1.85		85	Mexico	3.15
6	United States	1.90		85	Papua New Guinea	3.15
7	Ireland	1.95		88	Djibouti	3.20
7	Luxembourg	1.95		88	Mongolia	3.20
7	Taiwan	1.95		90	Algeria	3.25
7	United Kingdom	1.95		90	Brazil	3.25
11	Bahamas	2.00		90	Lebanon	3.25
12	Czech Republic	2.05		90	Senegal	3.25
12	Japan	2.05		90	Tanzania	3.25
14	Australia	2.10		95	Nigeria	3.30
14	Belgium	2.10		95	Romania	3.30
14	Canada	2.10		97	Cambodia	3.35
14	United Arab Emirates	2.10		97	Dominican Republic	3.35
18	Austria	2.15		97	Egypt	3.35
18	Chile	2.15		97	Guinea	3.35
18	Estonia	2.15		97	Ivory Coast	3.35
18	Netherlands	2.15		97	Moldova	3.35
22	Denmark	2.25		97	Pakistan	3.35
22	El Salvador	2.25		104	Nepal	3.40
22	Finland	2.25		104	Venezuela	3.40
25	Germany	2.30		106	Armenia	3.45
25	Iceland	2.30		106	Bulgaria	3.45
27	Norway	2.35		106	Lesotho	3.45
28	Korea, South	2.40		106	Madagascar	3.45
28	Kuwait	2.40		106	Russia	3.45
28	Malaysia	2.40		111	Burkina Faso	3.50
28	Panama	2.40		111	Cameroon	3.50
28	Thailand	2.40		111	Guyana	3.50
33	Sweden	2.45		111	Nicaragua	3.50
34	Argentina	2.50		115	Gambia	3.60
34	France	2.50		116	Croatia	3.65
34	Italy	2.50		116	Georgia	3.65
34	Spain	2.50		116	Malawi	3.65
38	Portugal	2.55		119	Cape Verde	3.67
38	Sri Lanka	2.55		120	Ethiopia	3.70
38	Trinidad and Tobago	2.55		120	India	3.70
41	Barbados	2.60		120	Niger	3.70
41	Peru	2.60		123	Congo	3.75
43	Bolivia	2.65		124	Chad	3.80
43	Mauritius	2.65		124	China	3.80
45	Cyprus	2.70		124	Mauritania	3.80
45	Jamaica	2.70		124	Ukraine	3.80
45	Uruguay	2.70		124	Zimbabwe	3.80
48	Botswana	2.75		129	Albania	3.85
48	Guatemala	2.75		129	Bangladesh	3.85
48	Jordan	2.75		129	Mozambique	3.85
48	Namibia	2.75		129	Suriname	3.85
48	Oman	2.75		133	Burundi	3.90
48	Philippines	2.75		134	Togo	3.95
54	Belize	2.80		135	Haiti	4.00
54	Costa Rica	2.80		135	Kyrgyz Rep.	4.00
54	Israel	2.80		137	Kazakhstan	4.05
54	Swaziland	2.80		137	Sierra Leone	4.05
54	Turkey	2.80		139	Yemen	4.10
54	Uganda	2.80		140	Belarus	4.15
54	Samoa	2.80		141	Sudan	4.20
61	Latvia	2.85		141	Syria	4.20
62	Greece	2.90		143	Azerbaijan	4.30
62	Hungary	2.90		143	Equatorial Guinea	4.30
62	So. Africa	2.90		143	Myanmar	4.30
65	Ecuador	2.95		143	Rwanda	4.30
65	Gabon	2.95		147	Tajikistan	4.40
65	Indonesia	2.95		147	Uzbekistan	4.40
65	Malta	2.95		149	Angola	4.45
65	Morocco	2.95		149	Turkmenistan	4.45
65	Poland	2.95		151	Guinea-Bissau	4.55
65	Tunisia	2.95		152	Vietnam	4.60
72	Ghana	3.00		153	Congo (Zaire)	4.70
72	Lithuania	3.00		153	Iran	4.70
72	Saudi Arabia	3.00		155	Bosnia	4.80
75	Benin	3.05		155	Somalia	4.80
75	Kenya	3.05		157	Iraq	4.90
75	Paraguay	3.05		157	Laos	4.90
75	Qatar	3.05		157	Libya	4.90
75	Slovak Republic	3.05		160	Cuba	5.00
75	Zambia	3.05		160	Korea, North	5.00
81	Colombia	3.10				

Mostly Unfree

CAPITAL FLOWS AND FOREIGN INVESTMENT
Score: 3–Stable (moderate barriers)

The Ivory Coast recently developed a foreign investment code. Although there is little discrimination between domestic and foreign investors, proposals for total foreign ownership of assets are not approved in all cases, and some industries are off-limits to private investors. Foreign investors remain wary because of crime, corruption, an inefficient and abusive bureaucracy, and unstable legal protections. For example, according to the U.S. Department of Commerce, "Most US-based companies in Côte d'Ivoire [i.e., the Ivory Coast] have experienced harassment by tax, customs, and judicial officials, as well as unfair competition from well-connected competitors in contract awards and regulatory matters."[2]

BANKING
Score: 3–Stable (moderate level of restrictions)

The Ivory Coast is a member of the Communaute Financiere Africaine (CFA), a financial grouping of several African countries that base the value of their currency on the French franc, and its government exercises only moderate control of banking institutions, although it still owns shares in some banks. Ten commercial banks operate inside the country.

WAGE AND PRICE CONTROLS
Score: 3–Stable (moderate level)

The government has made some progress toward liberalizing prices. In 1994, price controls were imposed on 30 goods and services for three months in the wake of the CFA's devaluation of the franc.[3] State dominance of several sectors of the economy reduces price competition; the state both sets the producer price and engages in the marketing of coffee and cocoa exports. There also are price controls on wheat and rice. The Ivory Coast has a minimum wage law.

PROPERTY RIGHTS
Score: 4–Stable (low level of protection)

The Ivory Coast's court system, although much more efficient than in the past, is unable to protect private property adequately. According to the U.S. Department of Commerce, "Enforcement of contract rights can be a time consuming and expensive process. Not all cases are decided quickly, and some do not appear to be judged on their legal or contractual merits. This has led to a widely-held view within the business community that there are elements within the judiciary which can be corrupted."[4] Even when corruption is not present, the courts frequently disregard employment contracts and rule against businesses, regardless of the legal merits of the case. Thus, businesses often are at a legal disadvantage when being sued by their employees. According to the U.S. Department of Commerce, "The Ivorian courts have historically been viewed as favoring the employee in labor disputes."[5]

REGULATION
Score: 4–Stable (high level)

The Ivory Coast's bureaucracy is cumbersome, corrupt, and subject to political manipulation. Individuals sometimes find it difficult to complete the paperwork required to open a business. The government has tried—with very modest success—to reduce bureaucratic barriers by making it easier for businesses to conform to government regulations, but the private sector remains highly regulated. Labor legislation is more onerous than in many developed countries, and foreign companies are under increasing informal pressure to use local labor. Corruption also remains a problem. "Corruption is widely assumed to exist at all branches of the government," reports the U.S. Department of Commerce.[6]

BLACK MARKET
Score: 4–Stable (high level of activity)

The Ivory Coast's high trade barriers make the smuggling of many items, primarily consumer goods, a lucrative business. There is a growing black market in food aid, in addition to substantial activity in such pirated intellectual property as videos and computer software. According to the U.S. Department of Commerce, "Though in theory prohibited, counterfeit clothing, textiles, footwear, watches, and audio and video tapes can be found, particularly among street vendors and in local markets."[7]

NOTES

1. Based on total taxes on international trade as a percentage of total imports.
2. U.S. Department of Commerce, *Country Commercial Guide*, 1998.
3. The CFA franc, a form of common currency, is used by African member countries that have agreed to peg their national currencies to a set value of the French franc.
4. U.S. Department of Commerce, *Country Commercial Guide*, 1998.
5. *Ibid.*
6. *Ibid.*
7. *Ibid.*

Jamaica   2.70

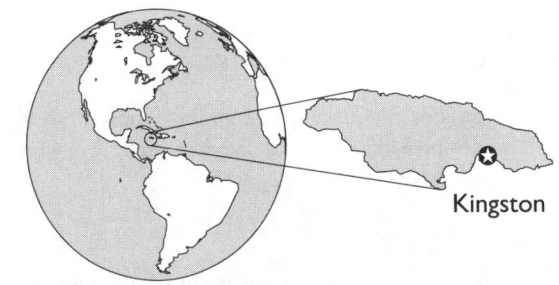

Kingston

1998 Score: **2.60**	1997 Score: **2.60**	1996 Score: **2.70**

Trade	2	Banking	3
Taxation	3	Wages and Prices	3
Government Intervention	2	Property Rights	2
Monetary Policy	4	Regulation	3
Foreign Investment	2	Black Market	3

Jamaica seldom uses free-market approaches to economic policy. During the 1970s and part of the 1980s, the government was the primary player in the economy, and it did not encourage entrepreneurship; in fact, the country was well on its way toward developing a socialist economy. Until recently, Jamaica's economy was characterized by a high level of protectionism and government intervention. The government has opened the economy to foreign investment in the past several years, however, and has reduced both taxes and tariffs. Jamaica's economy went into a severe recession beginning in 1996 and continuing into 1997. According to the U.S. Department of State, this recession was caused by "losses and failures of major financial companies necessitating sector wide government support; slow growth in the agricultural sector due to prolonged drought, low prices and high production costs of export crops such as sugar; the lack of export competitiveness in the manufacturing sector; high interest rates and internal debt burden; and low levels of investment."[1] A recent banking crisis forced the government to increase regulations and control of the banking system. As a result, Jamaica's overall score is 0.1 point worse than last year.

TRADE POLICY
Score: 2–Stable (low level of protectionism)

Jamaica's tariff rates range from 0 percent to 30 percent. The average tariff rate is 9 percent. There are no significant non-tariff barriers. According to the U.S. Department of Commerce, "There have been some improvements as a result of the government of Jamaica's efforts to streamline customs procedures. In order to facilitate the movement of goods, the government simplified the documentation and clearance requirements for exporters. Computerization of the entire system is in progress."[2]

TAXATION
Score–Income taxation: 2–Stable (low tax rates)
Score–Corporate taxation: 3–Stable (moderate tax rates)
Final Taxation Score: 3–Stable (moderate tax rates)

Jamaica's top marginal income tax rate is 25 percent; the average income level is not taxed at all. The top marginal corporate tax rate is 33.33 percent. Jamaica also has a consumption tax of up to 15 percent.

GOVERNMENT INTERVENTION IN THE ECONOMY
Score: 2–Stable (low level)

Government consumes 12.5 percent of GDP, down from around 20 percent in 1980. In an effort to limit budget deficits and stimulate the private sector, the government has undertaken an aggressive program of privatization.

MONETARY POLICY
Score: 4–Stable (high level of inflation)

Jamaica's average annual rate of inflation between 1985 and 1995 was 28.3 percent. The rate fell to 15.7 percent in 1996.

1	Hong Kong	1.25	81	Fiji	3.10
2	Singapore	1.30	81	Mali	3.10
3	Bahrain	1.70	81	Slovenia	3.10
4	New Zealand	1.75	85	Honduras	3.15
5	Switzerland	1.85	85	Mexico	3.15
6	United States	1.90	85	Papua New Guinea	3.15
7	Ireland	1.95	88	Djibouti	3.20
7	Luxembourg	1.95	88	Mongolia	3.20
7	Taiwan	1.95	90	Algeria	3.25
7	United Kingdom	1.95	90	Brazil	3.25
11	Bahamas	2.00	90	Lebanon	3.25
12	Czech Republic	2.05	90	Senegal	3.25
12	Japan	2.05	90	Tanzania	3.25
14	Australia	2.10	95	Nigeria	3.30
14	Belgium	2.10	95	Romania	3.30
14	Canada	2.10	97	Cambodia	3.35
14	United Arab Emirates	2.10	97	Dominican Republic	3.35
18	Austria	2.15	97	Egypt	3.35
18	Chile	2.15	97	Guinea	3.35
18	Estonia	2.15	97	Ivory Coast	3.35
18	Netherlands	2.15	97	Moldova	3.35
22	Denmark	2.25	97	Pakistan	3.35
22	El Salvador	2.25	104	Nepal	3.40
22	Finland	2.25	104	Venezuela	3.40
25	Germany	2.30	106	Armenia	3.45
25	Iceland	2.30	106	Bulgaria	3.45
27	Norway	2.35	106	Lesotho	3.45
28	Korea, South	2.40	106	Madagascar	3.45
28	Kuwait	2.40	106	Russia	3.45
28	Malaysia	2.40	111	Burkina Faso	3.50
28	Panama	2.40	111	Cameroon	3.50
28	Thailand	2.40	111	Guyana	3.50
33	Sweden	2.45	111	Nicaragua	3.50
34	Argentina	2.50	115	Gambia	3.60
34	France	2.50	116	Croatia	3.65
34	Italy	2.50	116	Georgia	3.65
34	Spain	2.50	116	Malawi	3.65
38	Portugal	2.55	119	Cape Verde	3.67
38	Sri Lanka	2.55	120	Ethiopia	3.70
38	Trinidad and Tobago	2.55	120	India	3.70
41	Barbados	2.60	120	Niger	3.70
41	Peru	2.60	123	Congo	3.75
43	Bolivia	2.65	124	Chad	3.80
43	Mauritius	2.65	124	China	3.80
45	Cyprus	2.70	124	Mauritania	3.80
45	Jamaica	2.70	124	Ukraine	3.80
45	Uruguay	2.70	124	Zimbabwe	3.80
48	Botswana	2.75	129	Albania	3.85
48	Guatemala	2.75	129	Bangladesh	3.85
48	Jordan	2.75	129	Mozambique	3.85
48	Namibia	2.75	129	Suriname	3.85
48	Oman	2.75	133	Burundi	3.90
48	Philippines	2.75	134	Togo	3.95
54	Belize	2.80	135	Haiti	4.00
54	Costa Rica	2.80	135	Kyrgyz Rep.	4.00
54	Israel	2.80	137	Kazakhstan	4.05
54	Swaziland	2.80	137	Sierra Leone	4.05
54	Turkey	2.80	139	Yemen	4.10
54	Uganda	2.80	140	Belarus	4.15
54	Samoa	2.80	141	Sudan	4.20
61	Latvia	2.85	141	Syria	4.20
62	Greece	2.90	143	Azerbaijan	4.30
62	Hungary	2.90	143	Equatorial Guinea	4.30
62	So. Africa	2.90	143	Myanmar	4.30
65	Ecuador	2.95	143	Rwanda	4.30
65	Gabon	2.95	147	Tajikistan	4.40
65	Indonesia	2.95	147	Uzbekistan	4.40
65	Malta	2.95	149	Angola	4.45
65	Morocco	2.95	149	Turkmenistan	4.45
65	Poland	2.95	151	Guinea-Bissau	4.55
65	Tunisia	2.95	152	Vietnam	4.60
72	Ghana	3.00	153	Congo (Zaire)	4.70
72	Lithuania	3.00	153	Iran	4.70
72	Saudi Arabia	3.00	155	Bosnia	4.80
75	Benin	3.05	155	Somalia	4.80
75	Kenya	3.05	157	Iraq	4.90
75	Paraguay	3.05	157	Laos	4.90
75	Qatar	3.05	157	Libya	4.90
75	Slovak Republic	3.05	160	Cuba	5.00
75	Zambia	3.05	160	Korea, North	5.00
81	Colombia	3.10			

Mostly Free

CAPITAL FLOWS AND FOREIGN INVESTMENT
Score: 2–Stable (low barriers)

Jamaica encourages foreign investment in nearly all areas. It also provides some incentives to investors who use Jamaican raw materials and supplies.

BANKING
Score: 3– (moderate level of restrictions)

Jamaica has a mixture of domestic and foreign banks. There are few direct restrictions on the formation of banks, and the government had reduced its control of the financial system. A recent financial crisis brought on by bad loans, overvalued investments, and collusion with the insurance industry, however, led the government to re-establish a high level of control over the financial services industry. As the U.S. Department of Commerce explains, "Due to what is widely termed a 'mismatch of assets and liabilities' (such as holding long term securities and costly real estate which did not appreciate or cover costs as expected) coupled with large portfolios of bad debts, the [financial services] sector recorded an overall decline of 5.2 percent. The Century Financial Institutions (now in litigation) were the worst affected. They were taken over by the Government of Jamaica in July 1996. In March 1997, the Government, through its new agent, FINSAC, again intervened to take over institutions of the troubled Eagle Financial Network (including inter alia, Eagle Commercial Bank, Eagle Merchant Bank and Crowne Eagle Insurance Company) due to liquidity problems and to prevent further erosion of the situation."[3] As a result of greater government influence in the banking sector, Jamaica's banking score is 1 point worse than last year.

WAGE AND PRICE CONTROLS
Score: 3–Stable (moderate level)

Price controls remain on many items, including bus fares, water, electricity, telecommunications, and kerosene. Jamaica has a minimum wage law.

PROPERTY RIGHTS
Score: 2–Stable (high level of protection)

The likelihood of expropriation is remote. Private property receives adequate protection. According to the U.S. Department of State, "The Constitution provides for an independent judiciary, which exists in practice. However, the judicial system is overburdened and operates with inadequate resources."[4]

REGULATION
Score: 3–Stable (moderate level)

Most regulations are only moderately burdensome. Bribery and corruption exist in government, but they are minimal.

BLACK MARKET
Score: 3–Stable (moderate level of activity)

Smuggling is big business in Jamaica because prices remain high in many areas, such as consumer electronics. Pirated broadcasts, video tapes, and recorded music are found frequently on the black market. The U.S. Department of State reports that "Video and broadcast piracy is illegal but widespread."[5]

NOTES

[1] U.S. Department of State, *Country Reports on Economic Policy and Trade Practices*, 1998.
[2] U.S. Department of Commerce, *Country Commercial Guide*, 1998.
[3] *Ibid.*
[4] U.S. Department of State, "Jamaica Country Report on Human Rights Practices for 1997," 1998.
[5] U.S. Department of State, *Country Reports on Economic Policy and Trade Practices*, 1998.

Japan   2.05

1998 **2.05**	1997 Score: **2.05**	1996 Score: **2.05**

Trade	2	Banking	3
Taxation	4.5	Wages and Prices	2
Government Intervention	1	Property Rights	1
Monetary Policy	1	Regulation	2
Foreign Investment	3	Black Market	1

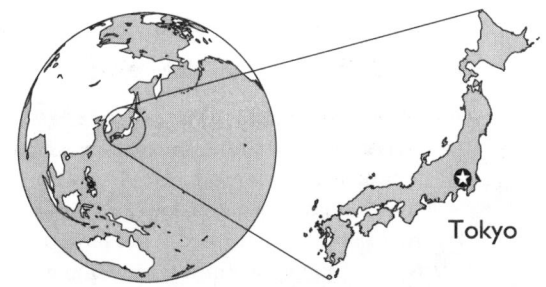

Tokyo

Since the end of World War II, Japan has had one of the world's fastest-growing economies. With its economy in ruins but democracy in place by 1946, it began to adopt the basics of a free-market system. These moves helped to propel Japan's economy to its current level. The government, however, continues to impose controls on the economy, sometimes formally but often informally. Government mismanagement of the economy sent Japan into a dismal economic recession with three straight years of less than 1 percent growth from 1993 to 1995. The economy rebounded slightly, posting a gain of almost 4 percent in 1996. This rebound was short-lived, however, because the economy grew by less than 2 percent in 1997 and it entered a recession in 1998. This is partially the result of the financial crisis in East Asia, in which Japan remains a large creditor. It also is the result of the crisis in Japan's own banking system, weighed down by bad loans. Despite efforts by Prime Minister Ryutaro Hashimoto to address the banking crisis and to stimulate the economy through public works spending and the promise of permanent tax cuts, his party was defeated in July 1998 elections. His successor, Keizo Obuchi, has committed his government to economic reform, including the reduction of the top marginal income tax rate from 65 percent to 50 percent.

TRADE POLICY
Score: 2–Stable (low level of protectionism)

Many economists argue that Japan is very protectionist; but the country's average tariff rate is among the world's lowest: less than 3 percent, which is lower even than that of the United States. Tariffs have never been the problem with Japan, however; it continues to be plagued with non-tariff barriers, including government red tape, exclusionary private business practices, a fragmented distribution system, and a relatively unapproachable government bureaucracy. Although these may prove impediments to some imports, Japan's market remains more accessible than those of most other countries. Therefore, by global standards—and especially when compared with countries like Bangladesh, India, and Yemen—Japan's trade barriers are relatively low. Since 1994, Japan has achieved several agreements with other countries—within the General Agreement on Tariffs and Trade and bilaterally with the United States—to reduce many non-tariff barriers, including an import ban on rice.

TAXATION
Score–Income taxation: 4–Stable (high tax rates)
Score–Corporate taxation: 4–Stable (high tax rates)
Final Taxation Score: 4.5–Stable (very high tax rates)

Japan's top income tax rate is 50 percent;[1] the tax on the average income level is 20 percent. The top marginal corporate tax rate is 37.5 percent. Japan also has prefectural and municipal taxes, an inhabitant's tax paid to the prefecture or municipality in which the company is located, a capital gains tax of 37.5 percent, and an enterprise tax of 6 percent to 12.6 percent. It raised its consumption tax to 5 percent in 1997. Japan also has a social insurance tax of 17.6 percent paid by both the employee and the employer.

1	Hong Kong	1.25	81	Fiji	3.10
2	Singapore	1.30	81	Mali	3.10
3	Bahrain	1.70	81	Slovenia	3.10
4	New Zealand	1.75	85	Honduras	3.15
5	Switzerland	1.85	85	Mexico	3.15
6	United States	1.90	85	Papua New Guinea	3.15
7	Ireland	1.95	88	Djibouti	3.20
7	Luxembourg	1.95	88	Mongolia	3.20
7	Taiwan	1.95	90	Algeria	3.25
7	United Kingdom	1.95	90	Brazil	3.25
11	Bahamas	2.00	90	Lebanon	3.25
12	Czech Republic	2.05	90	Senegal	3.25
12	Japan	2.05	90	Tanzania	3.25
14	Australia	2.10	95	Nigeria	3.30
14	Belgium	2.10	95	Romania	3.30
14	Canada	2.10	97	Cambodia	3.35
14	United Arab Emirates	2.10	97	Dominican Republic	3.35
18	Austria	2.15	97	Egypt	3.35
18	Chile	2.15	97	Guinea	3.35
18	Estonia	2.15	97	Ivory Coast	3.35
18	Netherlands	2.15	97	Moldova	3.35
22	Denmark	2.25	97	Pakistan	3.35
22	El Salvador	2.25	104	Nepal	3.40
22	Finland	2.25	104	Venezuela	3.40
25	Germany	2.30	106	Armenia	3.45
25	Iceland	2.30	106	Bulgaria	3.45
27	Norway	2.35	106	Lesotho	3.45
28	Korea, South	2.40	106	Madagascar	3.45
28	Kuwait	2.40	106	Russia	3.45
28	Malaysia	2.40	111	Burkina Faso	3.50
28	Panama	2.40	111	Cameroon	3.50
28	Thailand	2.40	111	Guyana	3.50
33	Sweden	2.45	111	Nicaragua	3.50
34	Argentina	2.50	115	Gambia	3.60
34	France	2.50	116	Croatia	3.65
34	Italy	2.50	116	Georgia	3.65
34	Spain	2.50	116	Malawi	3.65
38	Portugal	2.55	119	Cape Verde	3.67
38	Sri Lanka	2.55	120	Ethiopia	3.70
38	Trinidad and Tobago	2.55	120	India	3.70
41	Barbados	2.60	120	Niger	3.70
41	Peru	2.60	123	Congo	3.75
43	Bolivia	2.65	124	Chad	3.80
43	Mauritius	2.65	124	China	3.80
45	Cyprus	2.70	124	Mauritania	3.80
45	Jamaica	2.70	124	Ukraine	3.80
45	Uruguay	2.70	124	Zimbabwe	3.80
48	Botswana	2.75	129	Albania	3.85
48	Guatemala	2.75	129	Bangladesh	3.85
48	Jordan	2.75	129	Mozambique	3.85
48	Namibia	2.75	129	Suriname	3.85
48	Oman	2.75	133	Burundi	3.90
48	Philippines	2.75	134	Togo	3.95
54	Belize	2.80	135	Haiti	4.00
54	Costa Rica	2.80	135	Kyrgyz Rep.	4.00
54	Israel	2.80	137	Kazakhstan	4.05
54	Swaziland	2.80	137	Sierra Leone	4.05
54	Turkey	2.80	139	Yemen	4.10
54	Uganda	2.80	140	Belarus	4.15
54	Samoa	2.80	141	Sudan	4.20
61	Latvia	2.85	141	Syria	4.20
62	Greece	2.90	143	Azerbaijan	4.30
62	Hungary	2.90	143	Equatorial Guinea	4.30
62	So. Africa	2.90	143	Myanmar	4.30
65	Ecuador	2.95	143	Rwanda	4.30
65	Gabon	2.95	147	Tajikistan	4.40
65	Indonesia	2.95	147	Uzbekistan	4.40
65	Malta	2.95	149	Angola	4.45
65	Morocco	2.95	149	Turkmenistan	4.45
65	Poland	2.95	151	Guinea-Bissau	4.55
65	Tunisia	2.95	152	Vietnam	4.60
72	Ghana	3.00	153	Congo (Zaire)	4.70
72	Lithuania	3.00	153	Iran	4.70
72	Saudi Arabia	3.00	155	Bosnia	4.80
75	Benin	3.05	155	Somalia	4.80
75	Kenya	3.05	157	Iraq	4.90
75	Paraguay	3.05	157	Laos	4.90
75	Qatar	3.05	157	Libya	4.90
75	Slovak Republic	3.05	160	Cuba	5.00
75	Zambia	3.05	160	Korea, North	5.00
81	Colombia	3.10			

Mostly Free

GOVERNMENT INTERVENTION IN THE ECONOMY
Score: 1–Stable (very low level)

Government consumes 9.8 percent of GDP. The government has gone from granting extensive subsidies to opening up its market for such products as rice. Government expenditures have been kept lower than those of other countries because the United States has provided for Japan's defense. Although government spending will be a large part of any Japanese economic program, that spending is declining as a percentage of GDP.

MONETARY POLICY
Score: 1–Stable (very low level of inflation)

Japan's average annual rate of inflation was less than 1 percent from 1986 to 1996. It has remained at less than 1 percent since.

CAPITAL FLOWS AND FOREIGN INVESTMENT
Score: 3–Stable (moderate barriers)

Japan's foreign investment procedures received an overhaul in the early 1990s, which included the elimination of the need to notify the government in advance of investment in all areas except agriculture, aircraft, atomic energy, fisheries, forestry, leather goods, oil and gas production, and space development. The close relationship between government and private businesses, however, continues to impede foreign investment because some businesses and government agencies collude to make it too costly.

BANKING
Score: 3–Stable (moderate level of restrictions)

The banking industry is very competitive. The government places few restrictions on Japanese banks and their ability to engage in a variety of services. Banks may underwrite, deal, and broker all kinds of securities through subsidiaries. This allows them to be more competitive. The government, however, maintains significant regulations on banks. Such regulations make is difficult, for example, for banks to liquidate bad loans by selling them off to buyers at a discount, and banks may not list a loan as "in default" until it has been in arrears for at least six months (compared with only three months in the United States). These and other regulations make it difficult to diversify risk and recoup

losses on bad loans. The government also has imposed a host of new regulations to deal with the financial crisis and has agreed to bail out many failing financial institutions. Although the government plans to relax some of its recent regulations on the financial sector, it has made little progress. [2]

WAGE AND PRICE CONTROLS
Score: 2–Stable (low level)

With the exception of rice, there are no price controls. For the most part, the market sets wages, although Japan has a minimum wage.

PROPERTY RIGHTS
Score: 1–Stable (very high level of protection)

Japan has an efficient legal and court system that is able to protect property rights. Government expropriation is unlikely.

REGULATION
Score: 2–Stable (low level)

Although Japan's economy often is characterized as heavily regulated, most businesses enjoy a large amount of freedom. The government has made the process for opening a business easier in the past several years. Even though some regulations may impose a burden on individuals, regulations on businesses are aimed at allowing them enough room to maximize profits; many either are not enforced or are not significantly burdensome. Japan rarely enforces its antitrust laws, which allows businesses to join forces without the threat of antimonopoly litigation from competitors. By global standards, the level of regulation is low.

BLACK MARKET
Score: 1–Stable (very low level of activity)

The government has undertaken a large crackdown on such illegal activities as the buying and selling of guns and narcotics. Even though Japan has very strong protection for intellectual property rights, black market activity in pirated sound recording and computer software continues to some degree and the government has increased its prosecution of those who violate such laws. These activities represent a minuscule portion of Japan's $4 trillion economy.

NOTES

1. Japanese income tax rates do not include a local inhabitant tax that could raise the top rate to as high as 65 percent.
2. Some economists have charged that Japan's government has intervened in the stock market in an attempt to manipulate it. (See Mark Magnier, "Asian Governments Risk Ruin to Prop Up Economies: Hong Kong, Malaysia, Japan Use Public Funds to Buy Stocks in Strategy That Is Widely Criticized," *Los Angeles Times*, August 25, 1998, p. 1.) Such an intervention could affect Japan's score in banking or regulation. The government reportedly has denied engaging in this practice. (*Ibid.*) The Heritage Foundation has requested formally from Japan's Ministry of Finance an official confirmation, denial, or explanation of the charges of stock-market interference. When a response is received, the information will be analyzed for inclusion in next year's edition of the *Index*.

Jordan   2.75

| 1998 Score: **2.75** | 1997 Score: **2.70** | 1996 Score: **2.80** |

Trade	4	Banking	2
Taxation	2.5	Wages and Prices	3
Government Intervention	3	Property Rights	2
Monetary Policy	2	Regulation	3
Foreign Investment	2	Black Market	4

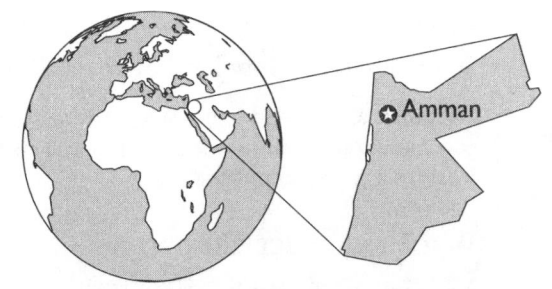

Jordan gained its independence from the United Kingdom in 1946, and King Hussein, the longest-ruling leader in the Middle East, has provided able political leadership since 1953. In 1988, he began a series of economic reforms to correct lagging growth rates. The king is attempting to reduce Jordan's budget deficit through controlled spending, reduced subsidies and tariffs, and lower taxes.

TRADE POLICY
Score: 4–Stable (high level of protectionism)

Jordan's average tariff rate is 14.4 percent.[1] Taxes on items like automobiles are particularly high, ranging from 44 percent to 200 percent, and customs procedures are plagued by bureaucratic red tape. For example, according to the U.S. Department of State, "Cumbersome customs procedures continue to undermine Jordan's business and investment climate. Overlapping areas of authority and difficult clearance procedures remain in place. Actual appraisal and tariff assessment practices are frequently arbitrary and may even differ from written regulations. Customs officers often make discretionary decisions about tariff applications when regulations and instructions conflict or lack specificity. Delays in clearing customs are routine."[2]

TAXATION
Score–Income taxation: 2-Stable (low tax rates)
Score–Corporate taxation: 3–Stable (moderate tax rates)
Final Taxation Score: 2.5-Stable (moderate tax rates)

The top marginal income tax rate in Jordan is 30 percent. The average income level is taxed at 5 percent. The top corporate tax rate is 35 percent.

GOVERNMENT INTERVENTION IN THE ECONOMY
Score: 3–Stable (moderate level)

Government consumes 23.2 percent of GDP. Recent statistics demonstrate that nearly 50 percent of GDP is produced by government-owned companies and industries.

MONETARY POLICY
Score: 2–Stable (low level of inflation)

Jordan's annual rate of inflation from 1986 to 1996 averaged 7.25 percent. In 1997, the inflation rate was 4 percent.

CAPITAL FLOWS AND FOREIGN INVESTMENT
Score: 2–Stable (low barriers)

Jordan maintains few restrictions on foreign investment. But industries deemed vital to national security, such as utilities, are not open to outside investors, and there are some ownership restrictions in trade and transportation industries.

1	Hong Kong	1.25	
2	Singapore	1.30	
3	Bahrain	1.70	
4	New Zealand	1.75	
5	Switzerland	1.85	
6	United States	1.90	
7	Ireland	1.95	
7	Luxembourg	1.95	
7	Taiwan	1.95	
7	United Kingdom	1.95	
11	Bahamas	2.00	
12	Czech Republic	2.05	
12	Japan	2.05	
14	Australia	2.10	
14	Belgium	2.10	
14	Canada	2.10	
14	United Arab Emirates	2.10	
18	Austria	2.15	
18	Chile	2.15	
18	Estonia	2.15	
18	Netherlands	2.15	
22	Denmark	2.25	
22	El Salvador	2.25	
22	Finland	2.25	
25	Germany	2.30	
25	Iceland	2.30	
27	Norway	2.35	
28	Korea, South	2.40	
28	Kuwait	2.40	
28	Malaysia	2.40	
28	Panama	2.40	
28	Thailand	2.40	
33	Sweden	2.45	
34	Argentina	2.50	
34	France	2.50	
34	Italy	2.50	
34	Spain	2.50	
38	Portugal	2.55	
38	Sri Lanka	2.55	
38	Trinidad and Tobago	2.55	
41	Barbados	2.60	
41	Peru	2.60	
43	Bolivia	2.65	
43	Mauritius	2.65	
45	Cyprus	2.70	
45	Jamaica	2.70	
45	Uruguay	2.70	
48	Botswana	2.75	
48	Guatemala	2.75	
48	Jordan	2.75	
48	Namibia	2.75	
48	Oman	2.75	
48	Philippines	2.75	
54	Belize	2.80	
54	Costa Rica	2.80	
54	Israel	2.80	
54	Swaziland	2.80	
54	Turkey	2.80	
54	Uganda	2.80	
54	Samoa	2.80	
61	Latvia	2.85	
62	Greece	2.90	
62	Hungary	2.90	
62	So. Africa	2.90	
65	Ecuador	2.95	
65	Gabon	2.95	
65	Indonesia	2.95	
65	Malta	2.95	
65	Morocco	2.95	
65	Poland	2.95	
65	Tunisia	2.95	
72	Ghana	3.00	
72	Lithuania	3.00	
72	Saudi Arabia	3.00	
75	Benin	3.05	
75	Kenya	3.05	
75	Paraguay	3.05	
75	Qatar	3.05	
75	Slovak Republic	3.05	
75	Zambia	3.05	
81	Colombia	3.10	
81	Fiji	3.10	
81	Mali	3.10	
81	Slovenia	3.10	
85	Honduras	3.15	
85	Mexico	3.15	
85	Papua New Guinea	3.15	
88	Djibouti	3.20	
88	Mongolia	3.20	
90	Algeria	3.25	
90	Brazil	3.25	
90	Lebanon	3.25	
90	Senegal	3.25	
90	Tanzania	3.25	
95	Nigeria	3.30	
95	Romania	3.30	
97	Cambodia	3.35	
97	Dominican Republic	3.35	
97	Egypt	3.35	
97	Guinea	3.35	
97	Ivory Coast	3.35	
97	Moldova	3.35	
97	Pakistan	3.35	
104	Nepal	3.40	
104	Venezuela	3.40	
106	Armenia	3.45	
106	Bulgaria	3.45	
106	Lesotho	3.45	
106	Madagascar	3.45	
106	Russia	3.45	
111	Burkina Faso	3.50	
111	Cameroon	3.50	
111	Guyana	3.50	
111	Nicaragua	3.50	
115	Gambia	3.60	
116	Croatia	3.65	
116	Georgia	3.65	
116	Malawi	3.65	
119	Cape Verde	3.67	
120	Ethiopia	3.70	
120	India	3.70	
120	Niger	3.70	
123	Congo	3.75	
124	Chad	3.80	
124	China	3.80	
124	Mauritania	3.80	
124	Ukraine	3.80	
124	Zimbabwe	3.80	
129	Albania	3.85	
129	Bangladesh	3.85	
129	Mozambique	3.85	
129	Suriname	3.85	
133	Burundi	3.90	
134	Togo	3.95	
135	Haiti	4.00	
135	Kyrgyz Rep.	4.00	
137	Kazakhstan	4.05	
137	Sierra Leone	4.05	
139	Yemen	4.10	
140	Belarus	4.15	
141	Sudan	4.20	
141	Syria	4.20	
143	Azerbaijan	4.30	
143	Equatorial Guinea	4.30	
143	Myanmar	4.30	
143	Rwanda	4.30	
147	Tajikistan	4.40	
147	Uzbekistan	4.40	
149	Angola	4.45	
149	Turkmenistan	4.45	
151	Guinea-Bissau	4.55	
152	Vietnam	4.60	
153	Congo (Zaire)	4.70	
153	Iran	4.70	
155	Bosnia	4.80	
155	Somalia	4.80	
157	Iraq	4.90	
157	Laos	4.90	
157	Libya	4.90	
160	Cuba	5.00	
160	Korea, North	5.00	

Mostly Free

BANKING
Score: 2–Stable (low level of restrictions)

Foreigners are allowed to invest in Jordanian banks. The government maintains some control over banks through strict reserve requirements.

WAGE AND PRICE CONTROLS
Score: 3–Stable (moderate level)

The government sets prices for "non-strategic commodities," including bread, automobile spare parts, construction materials, household cleaning materials, soft drinks, and some food and beverages served in restaurants. There is a minimum wage for specific trades.

PROPERTY RIGHTS
Score: 2–Stable (high level of protection)

Expropriation is unlikely in Jordan. Property receives adequate protection from legal institutions and the police force.

REGULATION
Score: 3–Stable (moderate level)

Jordan's regulatory environment is moderately bureaucratic and burdensome. Under a 1993 disabilities law, for example, many businesses had to retrofit their buildings to accommodate the hearing-, sight-, and physically disabled. This expense proved to be a substantial burden on many businesses.

BLACK MARKET
Score: 4–Stable (high level of activity)

Because levels of trade protectionism are so high, smuggling is big business in Jordan. Computer software and related items provide significant business for black marketeers. According to the U.S. Department of State, "The practice of pirating audio and video tapes for commercial purposes is widespread, and the government makes no effort to intervene. Pirated books are sold in Jordan, though few, if any, are published within the country."[3]

NOTES

[1] Based on International Monetary Fund statistics for taxes on international transactions as a percentage of total imports; from International Monetary Fund, *Government Financial Statistics,* 1996.
[2] U.S. Department of State, *Country Reports on Economic Policy and Trade Practices,* 1998.
[3] *Ibid.*

Kazakhstan 4.05

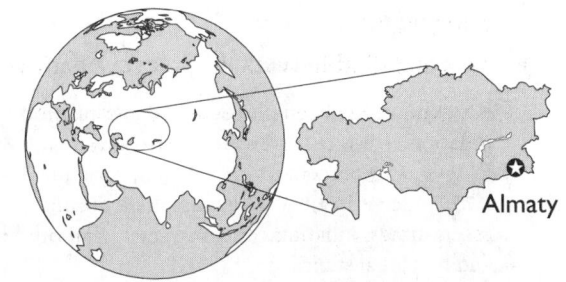

Almaty

1998 Score: **4.10**   1997 Score: **n/a**   1996 Score: **n/a**

Trade	4	Banking	4
Taxation	3.5	Wages and Prices	4
Government Intervention	3	Property Rights	4
Monetary Policy	5	Regulation	4
Foreign Investment	4	Black Market	5

Kazakhstan became an autonomous republic of the Russian Federation in 1920 but was incorporated into the Soviet Union in 1936. During some 70 years of Soviet rule, Moscow used part of Kazakhstan as a penal colony. (In fact, its railways and mining quarries were built largely by prison labor.) In the early stages of the Cold War, Josef Stalin used some areas of Kazakhstan as a nuclear test center, turning parts of the country into lethal, radioactive deserts. Under Nikita Khrushchev, the Soviet Union built Baikonur, its major space center, in Kazakhstan. Since gaining its independence in 1991, Kazakhstan has moved to adopt the fundamentals of a market-based economy. Economic development, however, remains hindered by a quasi-authoritarian regime and an intransigent bureaucracy plagued with corruption. Kazakhstan has reduced some taxes, however; as a result, its overall score is 0.05 point better than last year.

TRADE POLICY
Score: 4–Stable (high level of protectionism)

The average tariff rate is about 12 percent. Non-tariff barriers take the form of unevenly applied testing and standards requirements as well as strict labeling requirements. According to the U.S. Department of Commerce, "The existence of significant delays in customs clearances has impeded foreign investment."[1]

TAXATION
Score–Income taxation: 3+ (moderate tax rates)
Score–Corporate taxation: 3–Stable (moderate tax rates)
Final Taxation Score: 3.5+ (high tax rates)

Kazakhstan's top income tax rate is 40 percent. The tax on the average income is 10 percent. As a result, Kazakhstan's income taxation score is 1 point better this year.[2] The top marginal corporate tax rate is 30 percent. Kazakhstan also has a 30 percent capital gains tax, a 20 percent value-added tax, and a payroll tax between 2 percent and 25 percent. The corporate taxation score, when averaged with the income taxation score, results in 0.05 point improvement in the final taxation score this year.

GOVERNMENT INTERVENTION IN THE ECONOMY
Score: 3–Stable (moderate level)

Kazakhstan is privatizing its large state-owned sector, although the economy remains dominated by large state-owned enterprises, particularly in the agricultural sector. According to the U.S. Department of Commerce, the government "remains an equity partner in a wide variety of parastatals—from banks to agriculture joint stock companies."[3] Government consumption as a percentage of GDP, however, is 15 percent, which means government intervention in the economy is moderate by global standards.

1	Hong Kong	1.25		81	Fiji	3.10
2	Singapore	1.30		81	Mali	3.10
3	Bahrain	1.70		81	Slovenia	3.10
4	New Zealand	1.75		85	Honduras	3.15
5	Switzerland	1.85		85	Mexico	3.15
6	United States	1.90		85	Papua New Guinea	3.15
7	Ireland	1.95		88	Djibouti	3.20
7	Luxembourg	1.95		88	Mongolia	3.20
7	Taiwan	1.95		90	Algeria	3.25
7	United Kingdom	1.95		90	Brazil	3.25
11	Bahamas	2.00		90	Lebanon	3.25
12	Czech Republic	2.05		90	Senegal	3.25
12	Japan	2.05		90	Tanzania	3.25
14	Australia	2.10		95	Nigeria	3.30
14	Belgium	2.10		95	Romania	3.30
14	Canada	2.10		97	Cambodia	3.35
14	United Arab Emirates	2.10		97	Dominican Republic	3.35
18	Austria	2.15		97	Egypt	3.35
18	Chile	2.15		97	Guinea	3.35
18	Estonia	2.15		97	Ivory Coast	3.35
18	Netherlands	2.15		97	Moldova	3.35
22	Denmark	2.25		97	Pakistan	3.35
22	El Salvador	2.25		104	Nepal	3.40
22	Finland	2.25		104	Venezuela	3.40
25	Germany	2.30		106	Armenia	3.45
25	Iceland	2.30		106	Bulgaria	3.45
27	Norway	2.35		106	Lesotho	3.45
28	Korea, South	2.40		106	Madagascar	3.45
28	Kuwait	2.40		106	Russia	3.45
28	Malaysia	2.40		111	Burkina Faso	3.50
28	Panama	2.40		111	Cameroon	3.50
28	Thailand	2.40		111	Guyana	3.50
33	Sweden	2.45		111	Nicaragua	3.50
34	Argentina	2.50		115	Gambia	3.60
34	France	2.50		116	Croatia	3.65
34	Italy	2.50		116	Georgia	3.65
34	Spain	2.50		116	Malawi	3.65
38	Portugal	2.55		119	Cape Verde	3.67
38	Sri Lanka	2.55		120	Ethiopia	3.70
38	Trinidad and Tobago	2.55		120	India	3.70
41	Barbados	2.60		120	Niger	3.70
41	Peru	2.60		123	Congo	3.75
43	Bolivia	2.65		124	Chad	3.80
43	Mauritius	2.65		124	China	3.80
45	Cyprus	2.70		124	Mauritania	3.80
45	Jamaica	2.70		124	Ukraine	3.80
45	Uruguay	2.70		124	Zimbabwe	3.80
48	Botswana	2.75		129	Albania	3.85
48	Guatemala	2.75		129	Bangladesh	3.85
48	Jordan	2.75		129	Mozambique	3.85
48	Namibia	2.75		129	Suriname	3.85
48	Oman	2.75		133	Burundi	3.90
48	Philippines	2.75		134	Togo	3.95
54	Belize	2.80		135	Haiti	4.00
54	Costa Rica	2.80		135	Kyrgyz Rep.	4.00
54	Israel	2.80		137	Kazakhstan	4.05
54	Swaziland	2.80		137	Sierra Leone	4.05
54	Turkey	2.80		139	Yemen	4.10
54	Uganda	2.80		140	Belarus	4.15
54	Samoa	2.80		141	Sudan	4.20
61	Latvia	2.85		141	Syria	4.20
62	Greece	2.90		143	Azerbaijan	4.30
62	Hungary	2.90		143	Equatorial Guinea	4.30
62	So. Africa	2.90		143	Myanmar	4.30
65	Ecuador	2.95		143	Rwanda	4.30
65	Gabon	2.95		147	Tajikistan	4.40
65	Indonesia	2.95		147	Uzbekistan	4.40
65	Malta	2.95		149	Angola	4.45
65	Morocco	2.95		149	Turkmenistan	4.45
65	Poland	2.95		151	Guinea-Bissau	4.55
65	Tunisia	2.95		152	Vietnam	4.60
72	Ghana	3.00		153	Congo (Zaire)	4.70
72	Lithuania	3.00		153	Iran	4.70
72	Saudi Arabia	3.00		155	Bosnia	4.80
75	Benin	3.05		155	Somalia	4.80
75	Kenya	3.05		157	Iraq	4.90
75	Paraguay	3.05		157	Laos	4.90
75	Qatar	3.05		157	Libya	4.90
75	Slovak Republic	3.05		160	Cuba	5.00
75	Zambia	3.05		160	Korea, North	5.00
81	Colombia	3.10				

Repressed

MONETARY POLICY
Score: 5–Stable (very high level of inflation)

Kazakhstan has been plagued by hyperinflation. The inflation rate was 17 percent in 1997 but it was 39.1 percent in 1996, 60.3 percent in 1995, 1,171 percent in 1994, and 1,758 percent in 1993. Thus, despite a drastic reduction in recent times, inflation remains very high, both historically and by global standards.

CAPITAL FLOWS AND FOREIGN INVESTMENT
Score: 4–Stable (high barriers)

Even though the government wants to promote and increase foreign investment, it still maintains some barriers. Despite improvement in investment laws, the government still screens much of the foreign capital entering the country. According to the U.S. Department of Commerce, "Foreign investment proposals are screened by host government officials, sometimes at the highest level. Although the government has promised that tendering will be done in an open and fair manner, there continue to be complaints that the tendering process is not always transparent and fair."[4] Corruption within the foreign investment approval process also remains a problem. Even though Kazakhstan's criminal code "contains special articles on penalties for accepting and giving bribes," reports the U.S. Department of Commerce, "corruption in all economic sectors is a problem.... U.S. firms and other foreign companies consider corruption an obstacle to investment."[5]

BANKING
Score: 4–Stable (high level of restrictions)

As the U.S. Department of Commerce reports, Kazakhstan's banking system is a "system in transition, in the midst of a difficult phase of consolidation, increased competition and adaptation to international standards."[6] The government continues to own many banks and controls most assets of the financial system.

WAGE AND PRICE CONTROLS
Score: 4–Stable (high level)

Powerful state-owned industries control wages and prices. Price controls continue on such items as agricultural products, transportation, and utilities.

PROPERTY RIGHTS
Score: 4–Stable (low level of protection)

Kazakhstan's legal system does not provide sufficient protection for private property. Legal reform is a major priority of the government, but the judiciary remains weak and corrupt. According to the U.S. Department of State, "The judiciary remained under the control of the President and the executive branch. The lack of an independent judiciary made it difficult to root out corruption, which is pervasive throughout the Government."[7]

REGULATION
Score: 4–Stable (high level)

Establishing a business can be a tedious and time-consuming procedure that requires individuals to overcome numerous bureaucratic barriers. Although a 1995 business licensing decree established the legal framework for providing business licenses, its implementation has been extremely inadequate. According to the U.S. Department of Commerce, "An April 1995 Licensing Law established the legal framework for licensing activities.... It requires the relevant agency to issue a license within one month of submitting all required documents. Unfortunately, the full implementation of this Law has been grossly inadequate. For example, most of the qualification and procedural requirements for issuing licenses have not yet been approved by the government. As a consequence, licensing authorities are either using old requirements to license those activities licensed prior to the adoption of the 1995 Law or they are unable to issue licenses for those activities that did not previously require licensing. This situation has left some businesses vulnerable to inspection bodies, who have threatened them with fines and shut-downs for not having licenses that are, in many instances, legally impossible to obtain."[8]

BLACK MARKET
Score: 5–Stable (very high level of activity)

Smuggling is rampant; in fact, most imports are smuggled into the country. According to the U.S. Department of Commerce, "As reported by the Chairman of the Custom Committee, approximately 80 percent of imported goods...are smuggled."[9] Despite the existence of laws protecting intellectual property rights, significant piracy in computer software continues.

NOTES

[1]   U.S. Department of Commerce, *Country Commercial Guide,* 1998.
[2]   The score in this factor has changed from a "4" in 1998 to a "3" in 1999 because previously unavailable information provides a more accurate picture of the conditions. Last year, the tax on the average income was not available; this information now is available; as a result, Kazakhstan's income taxation score has changed.
[3]   U.S. Department of Commerce, *Country Commercial Guide,* 1998.
[4]   *Ibid.*
[5]   *Ibid.*
[6]   *Ibid.*
[7]   U.S. Department of State, "Kazakstan Country Report on Human Rights Practices for 1996," 1997.
[8]   U.S. Department of Commerce, *Country Commercial Guide,* 1998.
[9]   U.S. Department of Commerce, "Kazakhstan; Tobacco Annual 1997," *Annual Report, Agworld Attaché Reports,* 1997.

Kenya   3.05

1998 Score: **3.05**   1997 Score: **3.05**   1996 Score: **3.05**

Trade	4	Banking	2
Taxation	3.5	Wages and Prices	3
Government Intervention	3	Property Rights	3
Monetary Policy	2	Regulation	4
Foreign Investment	3	Black Market	3

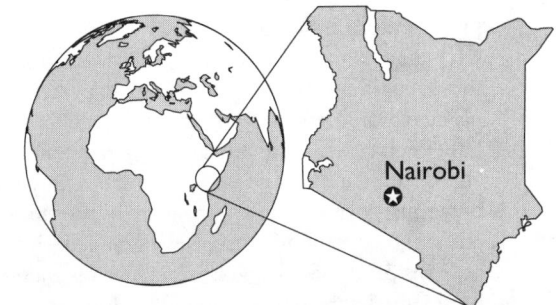

Nairobi

Kenya gained its independence from Great Britain in 1963. A long period of one-party rule ended in 1991 with the legalization of opposition political parties through a constitutional amendment. Political freedoms, however, remain fairly constricted, and the economy—once one of Africa's freest and most prosperous—has fallen victim to government corruption and mismanagement. Economic growth averaged 2.6 percent annually from 1992 to 1996, and per capita GNP had reached only $320 by 1996. Over the past several years, the government of President Daniel arap Moi has been in frequent conflict with Western donors and international financial institutions over Kenya's level of corruption and lack of economic reform, leading them to withhold credit and aid in July 1997. Kenya also is plagued with serious ethnic conflict.

TRADE POLICY
Score: 4–Stable (high level of protectionism)

Kenya's average tariff rate is 14 percent.[1] In 1993, import licenses were abolished for most goods. According to the U.S. Department of Commerce, "The stumbling block is high operational costs and export and import delays at customs. The clearing process at Mombassa harbor, the main seaport, is slow, and charges at the ports of entry high."[2] Some imports, including dairy products, are banned.

TAXATION
Score—Income taxation: 3–Stable (moderate tax rates)
Score–Corporate taxation: 3–Stable (moderate tax rates)
Total Taxation Score: 3.5–Stable (high tax rates)

Kenya's top income tax rate is 32.5 percent; the average income is taxed at approximately 10 percent. The top corporate income tax is 32.5 percent. Kenya also has a value-added tax that ranges from 10 percent to 16 percent.

GOVERNMENT INTERVENTION IN THE ECONOMY
Score: 3–Stable (moderate level)

Government consumes 16.5 percent of GDP. It also plans to privatize over 100 state-owned companies, although at least 31 will be kept under state control. To date, little progress has been made toward privatization.

MONETARY POLICY
Score: 2–Stable (low level of inflation)

Kenya's average annual rate of inflation between 1986 and 1996 was 12.2 percent.

CAPITAL FLOWS AND FOREIGN INVESTMENT
Score: 3–Stable (moderate barriers)

Kenya permits complete foreign ownership of some enterprises, and most sectors are open to foreign participation. The government also has suggested that foreigners would be acceptable buyers of state-owned enterprises slated for

1	Hong Kong	1.25	81	Fiji	3.10
2	Singapore	1.30	81	Mali	3.10
3	Bahrain	1.70	81	Slovenia	3.10
4	New Zealand	1.75	85	Honduras	3.15
5	Switzerland	1.85	85	Mexico	3.15
6	United States	1.90	85	Papua New Guinea	3.15
7	Ireland	1.95	88	Djibouti	3.20
7	Luxembourg	1.95	88	Mongolia	3.20
7	Taiwan	1.95	90	Algeria	3.25
7	United Kingdom	1.95	90	Brazil	3.25
11	Bahamas	2.00	90	Lebanon	3.25
12	Czech Republic	2.05	90	Senegal	3.25
12	Japan	2.05	90	Tanzania	3.25
14	Australia	2.10	95	Nigeria	3.30
14	Belgium	2.10	95	Romania	3.30
14	Canada	2.10	97	Cambodia	3.35
14	United Arab Emirates	2.10	97	Dominican Republic	3.35
18	Austria	2.15	97	Egypt	3.35
18	Chile	2.15	97	Guinea	3.35
18	Estonia	2.15	97	Ivory Coast	3.35
18	Netherlands	2.15	97	Moldova	3.35
22	Denmark	2.25	97	Pakistan	3.35
22	El Salvador	2.25	104	Nepal	3.40
22	Finland	2.25	104	Venezuela	3.40
25	Germany	2.30	106	Armenia	3.45
25	Iceland	2.30	106	Bulgaria	3.45
27	Norway	2.35	106	Lesotho	3.45
28	Korea, South	2.40	106	Madagascar	3.45
28	Kuwait	2.40	106	Russia	3.45
28	Malaysia	2.40	111	Burkina Faso	3.50
28	Panama	2.40	111	Cameroon	3.50
28	Thailand	2.40	111	Guyana	3.50
33	Sweden	2.45	111	Nicaragua	3.50
34	Argentina	2.50	115	Gambia	3.60
34	France	2.50	116	Croatia	3.65
34	Italy	2.50	116	Georgia	3.65
34	Spain	2.50	116	Malawi	3.65
38	Portugal	2.55	119	Cape Verde	3.67
38	Sri Lanka	2.55	120	Ethiopia	3.70
38	Trinidad and Tobago	2.55	120	India	3.70
41	Barbados	2.60	120	Niger	3.70
41	Peru	2.60	123	Congo	3.75
43	Bolivia	2.65	124	Chad	3.80
43	Mauritius	2.65	124	China	3.80
45	Cyprus	2.70	124	Mauritania	3.80
45	Jamaica	2.70	124	Ukraine	3.80
45	Uruguay	2.70	124	Zimbabwe	3.80
48	Botswana	2.75	129	Albania	3.85
48	Guatemala	2.75	129	Bangladesh	3.85
48	Jordan	2.75	129	Mozambique	3.85
48	Namibia	2.75	129	Suriname	3.85
48	Oman	2.75	133	Burundi	3.90
48	Philippines	2.75	134	Togo	3.95
54	Belize	2.80	135	Haiti	4.00
54	Costa Rica	2.80	135	Kyrgyz Rep.	4.00
54	Israel	2.80	137	Kazakhstan	4.05
54	Swaziland	2.80	137	Sierra Leone	4.05
54	Turkey	2.80	139	Yemen	4.10
54	Uganda	2.80	140	Belarus	4.15
54	Samoa	2.80	141	Sudan	4.20
61	Latvia	2.85	141	Syria	4.20
62	Greece	2.90	143	Azerbaijan	4.30
62	Hungary	2.90	143	Equatorial Guinea	4.30
62	So. Africa	2.90	143	Myanmar	4.30
65	Ecuador	2.95	143	Rwanda	4.30
65	Gabon	2.95	147	Tajikistan	4.40
65	Indonesia	2.95	147	Uzbekistan	4.40
65	Malta	2.95	149	Angola	4.45
65	Morocco	2.95	149	Turkmenistan	4.45
65	Poland	2.95	151	Guinea-Bissau	4.55
65	Tunisia	2.95	152	Vietnam	4.60
72	Ghana	3.00	153	Congo (Zaire)	4.70
72	Lithuania	3.00	153	Iran	4.70
72	Saudi Arabia	3.00	155	Bosnia	4.80
75	Benin	3.05	155	Somalia	4.80
75	Kenya	3.05	157	Iraq	4.90
75	Paraguay	3.05	157	Laos	4.90
75	Qatar	3.05	157	Libya	4.90
75	Slovak Republic	3.05	160	Cuba	5.00
75	Zambia	3.05	160	Korea, North	5.00
81	Colombia	3.10			

Mostly Unfree

privatization, although enterprises on the Kenyan Stock Exchange, which previously were limited to 20 percent foreign participation, are limited to 40 percent foreign participation. Export Promotion Zones offering tax breaks have been established; but because investment proposals are approved on a case-by-case basis and the procedures for obtaining government approval are burdensome, arbitrary, and often corrupt, foreign investment is declining. President Moi has been railing against foreign investment, and presidential approval is required for foreign acquisition of agricultural land. The government does not permit foreign investment in insurance or in government-sanctioned monopolies.

BANKING
Score: 2–Stable (low level of restrictions)

Two state-controlled banks make loans to state-owned industries. The National Bank of Kenya has been privatized in part. Lending levels for agriculture are mandated, and commercial banks are required to store a percentage of their deposits with the Central Bank. But Kenya also has deregulated its banking industry. The U.S. Department of Commerce reports that "The financial sector, particularly banking, has been liberalized.... [M]ost banks are privately owned and operated."[3]

WAGE AND PRICE CONTROLS
Score: 3–Stable (moderate level)

The government has lifted price controls in almost every sector of the economy. The pricing of petroleum products has been freed, too. Some agricultural products, however, including coffee, must be sold through monopolistic government marketing boards. Monopolies, many of them government-sanctioned, control approximately half the market, reducing price competition. Most wages are negotiated, although Kenya has a minimum wage.

PROPERTY RIGHTS
Score: 3–Stable (moderate level of protection)

Property is constitutionally protected from compulsory state takeover. In the exceptional case of expropriation, owners receive compensation, albeit in local currency. In some cases, foreign investors have been deported and business licenses arbitrarily revoked. According to the U.S. Department of State, "Although the Constitution provides for an independent judiciary, it is subject to executive branch influence in practice."[4]

REGULATION
Score: 4–Stable (high level)

Companies are registered with relative ease, although some have found their operating licenses arbitrarily suspended. Businesses are required to file monthly reports on their activities, and it is difficult to terminate employees. To reduce unemployment, the government pressures firms to use labor-intensive methods of production instead of technology, and companies often find themselves over-staffed and facing excessively high payroll demands. Some progress has been made in cracking down on government corruption, but the U.S. Department of Commerce reports that "Public institutions are poorly managed and corruption remains widespread."[5]

BLACK MARKET
Score: 3–Stable (moderate level of activity)

The government's monopoly on the distribution of some agricultural products encourages illegal trading, and the heavy regulation of business likewise encourages "illegal" commerce in many items. There is significant piracy of stolen intellectual property. According to the Office of the United States Trade Representative, "Pirated sound record-ings are common, and virtually all videos available in shops are unlicensed."[6] These activities, however, affect Kenya's $6.6 billion economy only moderately.

NOTES

[1] Based on taxation revenue on international trade as a percentage of total imports.
[2] U.S. Department of Commerce, *Country Commercial Guide,* 1998.
[3] U.S. Department of Commerce, "Kenya Economic Trends," *Market Research Reports,* March 14, 1997.
[4] U.S. Department of State, "Kenya Country Report on Human Rights Practices for 1997," 1998.
[5] U.S. Department of Commerce, "Kenya Economic Trends," March 14, 1997.
[6] Office of the United States Trade Representative, *1998 National Trade Estimate Report on Foreign Trade Barriers.*

Korea, Democratic People's Republic of (North Korea)

5.00

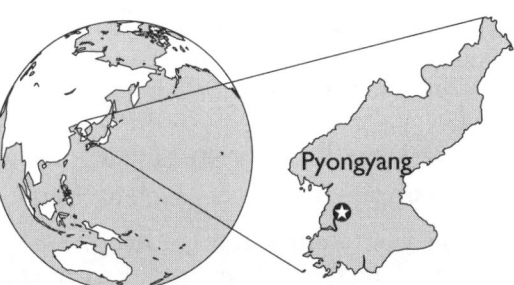

Pyongyang

1998 Score: **5.00**   1997 Score: **5.00**   1996 Score: **5.00**

Trade	5	Banking	5
Taxation	5	Wages and Prices	5
Government Intervention	5	Property Rights	5
Monetary Policy	5	Regulation	5
Foreign Investment	5	Black Market	5

North Korea is one of the world's most economically repressed countries. Its economy is controlled by the central government, few entrepreneurial activities are legal, and little economic growth has occurred over the past decade. Although some signs point toward eventual economic liberalization, there is scant evidence that North Korea is headed down the economic path taken by the People's Republic of China. The country currently is facing a severe food shortage that will place increasing strain on its already weak economy. North Korea's economic problems are structural and long-term in nature, and overcoming them will require fundamental market-oriented reform.

TRADE POLICY
Score: 5–Stable (very high level of protectionism)

The government controls and inspects all imports into and exports from North Korea. There is an effective ban on many imports from Western countries. Essentially, North Korea is closed to trade, except for some imports manufactured in South Korea.

TAXATION
Score–Income taxation: 5–Stable (very high tax rates)
Score–Corporate taxation: 5–Stable (very high tax rates)
Final Taxation Score: 5–Stable (very high tax rates)
Because North Korea is a communist state, the government owns all property. The government confiscates all economic output, resulting in real tax rates of 100 percent.

GOVERNMENT INTERVENTION IN THE ECONOMY
Score: 5–Stable (very high level)

North Korea has a command economy in which the government owns all property and sets production levels on most products. State-owned industries account for nearly all GDP. According to the U.S. Department of State, "The State directs all significant economic activity, and only government-controlled labor unions are permitted."[1]

MONETARY POLICY
Score: 5–Stable (very high level of inflation)

As a communist state, North Korea does not admit officially to having inflation. But even though the official prices of goods may be low because they are controlled and subsidized by the state, the tremendous scarcity of goods and services attests to their real value. The government covers its huge domestic

1	Hong Kong	1.25	81	Fiji	3.10
2	Singapore	1.30	81	Mali	3.10
3	Bahrain	1.70	81	Slovenia	3.10
4	New Zealand	1.75	85	Honduras	3.15
5	Switzerland	1.85	85	Mexico	3.15
6	United States	1.90	85	Papua New Guinea	3.15
7	Ireland	1.95	88	Djibouti	3.20
7	Luxembourg	1.95	88	Mongolia	3.20
7	Taiwan	1.95	90	Algeria	3.25
7	United Kingdom	1.95	90	Brazil	3.25
11	Bahamas	2.00	90	Lebanon	3.25
12	Czech Republic	2.05	90	Senegal	3.25
12	Japan	2.05	90	Tanzania	3.25
14	Australia	2.10	95	Nigeria	3.30
14	Belgium	2.10	95	Romania	3.30
14	Canada	2.10	97	Cambodia	3.35
14	United Arab Emirates	2.10	97	Dominican Republic	3.35
18	Austria	2.15	97	Egypt	3.35
18	Chile	2.15	97	Guinea	3.35
18	Estonia	2.15	97	Ivory Coast	3.35
18	Netherlands	2.15	97	Moldova	3.35
22	Denmark	2.25	97	Pakistan	3.35
22	El Salvador	2.25	104	Nepal	3.40
22	Finland	2.25	104	Venezuela	3.40
25	Germany	2.30	106	Armenia	3.45
25	Iceland	2.30	106	Bulgaria	3.45
27	Norway	2.35	106	Lesotho	3.45
28	Korea, South	2.40	106	Madagascar	3.45
28	Kuwait	2.40	106	Russia	3.45
28	Malaysia	2.40	111	Burkina Faso	3.50
28	Panama	2.40	111	Cameroon	3.50
28	Thailand	2.40	111	Guyana	3.50
33	Sweden	2.45	111	Nicaragua	3.50
34	Argentina	2.50	115	Gambia	3.60
34	France	2.50	116	Croatia	3.65
34	Italy	2.50	116	Georgia	3.65
34	Spain	2.50	116	Malawi	3.65
38	Portugal	2.55	119	Cape Verde	3.67
38	Sri Lanka	2.55	120	Ethiopia	3.70
38	Trinidad and Tobago	2.55	120	India	3.70
41	Barbados	2.60	120	Niger	3.70
41	Peru	2.60	123	Congo	3.75
43	Bolivia	2.65	124	Chad	3.80
43	Mauritius	2.65	124	China	3.80
45	Cyprus	2.70	124	Mauritania	3.80
45	Jamaica	2.70	124	Ukraine	3.80
45	Uruguay	2.70	124	Zimbabwe	3.80
48	Botswana	2.75	129	Albania	3.85
48	Guatemala	2.75	129	Bangladesh	3.85
48	Jordan	2.75	129	Mozambique	3.85
48	Namibia	2.75	129	Suriname	3.85
48	Oman	2.75	133	Burundi	3.90
48	Philippines	2.75	134	Togo	3.95
54	Belize	2.80	135	Haiti	4.00
54	Costa Rica	2.80	135	Kyrgyz Rep.	4.00
54	Israel	2.80	137	Kazakhstan	4.05
54	Swaziland	2.80	137	Sierra Leone	4.05
54	Turkey	2.80	139	Yemen	4.10
54	Uganda	2.80	140	Belarus	4.15
54	Samoa	2.80	141	Sudan	4.20
61	Latvia	2.85	141	Syria	4.20
62	Greece	2.90	143	Azerbaijan	4.30
62	Hungary	2.90	143	Equatorial Guinea	4.30
62	So. Africa	2.90	143	Myanmar	4.30
65	Ecuador	2.95	143	Rwanda	4.30
65	Gabon	2.95	147	Tajikistan	4.40
65	Indonesia	2.95	147	Uzbekistan	4.40
65	Malta	2.95	149	Angola	4.45
65	Morocco	2.95	149	Turkmenistan	4.45
65	Poland	2.95	151	Guinea-Bissau	4.55
65	Tunisia	2.95	152	Vietnam	4.60
72	Ghana	3.00	153	Congo (Zaire)	4.70
72	Lithuania	3.00	153	Iran	4.70
72	Saudi Arabia	3.00	155	Bosnia	4.80
75	Benin	3.05	155	Somalia	4.80
75	Kenya	3.05	157	Iraq	4.90
75	Paraguay	3.05	157	Laos	4.90
75	Qatar	3.05	157	Libya	4.90
75	Slovak Republic	3.05	160	Cuba	5.00
75	Zambia	3.05	160	Korea, North	5.00
81	Colombia	3.10			

Repressed

debts simply by printing more money. As a result, the currency is worth little and is not convertible on the international market.

CAPITAL FLOWS AND FOREIGN INVESTMENT
Score: 5–Stable (very high barriers)

Although North Korea's government recently claimed to recognize the importance of foreign investment, foreign investors still do not receive equal treatment under the law. The government must remain a majority owner in a business, and investments are effectively banned in most industries.

BANKING
Score: 5–Stable (very high level of restrictions)

The government controls the financial system. Foreigners are barred from using banking services.

WAGE AND PRICE CONTROLS
Score: 5–Stable (very high level)

The government determines wages and prices.

PROPERTY RIGHTS
Score: 5–Stable (very low level of protection)

North Korea bans the ownership of private property. According to the U.S. Department of State, "The Constitution states that courts are independent and that judicial proceedings are to be carried out in strict accordance with the law; however, an independent judiciary and individual rights do not exist in [North Korea]."[2] According to the U.S. Department of Commerce, "More than 90% of this command economy is socialized; agricultural land is collectivized; and state-owned industry produces 95% of manufactured goods. State control of economic affairs is unusually tight even for a communist country because of the small size and homogeneity of the society and the strict rule of KIM Il-song in the past and now his son, KIM Chong-il."[3]

REGULATION
Score: 5–Stable (very high level)

As North Korea's principal economic player, the government regulates the economy heavily.

BLACK MARKET
Score: 5–Stable (very high level of activity)

The size of North Korea's black market is immense, despite the fact that the government imprisons many who engage in such activity.

NOTES

[1] U.S. Department of State, "Democratic People's Republic of Korea Report on Human Rights Practices for 1997," 1998.

[2] *Ibid.*

[3] U.S. Department of Commerce, *Stat–USA* Internet site (*http://www.stat-usa.gov*).

Korea, Republic of (South Korea)

2.40

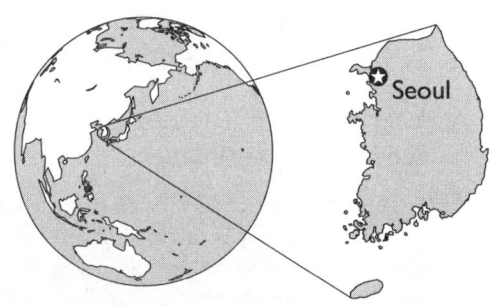

Seoul

1998 Score: **2.30**   1997 Score: **2.45**   1996 Score: **2.30**

Trade	3	Banking	3
Taxation	4	Wages and Prices	2
Government Intervention	2	Property Rights	1
Monetary Policy	2	Regulation	3
Foreign Investment	2	Black Market	2

Following the cessation of overt hostilities in Korean War, economic liberalization became the standard in the Republic of Korea, while nationalization and collectivization were the norm in communist North Korea. In the 1960s, faced with a potential reduction in U.S. foreign aid, South Korea reformed its economy to attract foreign investment and develop export industries. As a result, it became one of the world's fastest-growing economies, averaging roughly 9 percent GDP growth for most of the past 30 years. South Korea has been hit hard by the Asian economic crisis that began in 1997, and its economy could contract by as much as 2 percent to 3 percent in 1998. Several structural economic problems have caused South Korea's economy some recent pains. For example, according to the U.S. Department of State, "Much of this downturn has been ascribed to a cyclic worsening in Korea's terms of trade, especially lower prices for some key exports (i.e., semiconductors, chemicals and steel) and the weakening of the Japanese yen. A string of bankruptcies of large business conglomerates in 1997 and the strains this has placed on the banking system have contributed to the slower economic growth rate."[1] Thus, South Korea's banking system is coming under increased control of the government. As a result, the country's overall score is 0.1 point worse than last year. After taking office in February 1998, new President Kim Dae Jung proposed sweeping economic liberalization measures to address the economic crisis. Among other things, the government is opening some markets to foreign investment, including real estate and telecommunications. It also has ended majority foreign ownership restrictions in many sectors. It remains to be seen, however, whether the reforms will succeed in the face of likely opposition by powerful entrenched bureaucrats.

TRADE POLICY
Score: 3–Stable (moderate level of protectionism)

South Korea's average tariff rate is 7.7 percent, down from the 7.9 reported in last year's edition of the *Index*.[2] Non-tariff barriers remain stringent. According to the U.S. Department of State, "The typical trade barriers U.S. exporters experience today are mostly nontariff-related...and are rooted in non-transparent regulations which give too much discretion to officials, but offer little recourse or compensation. These affect licensing, inspections, type approval, marking/labeling requirements and other standards."[3]

TAXATION
Score–Income taxation: 3-Stable (moderate tax rates)
Score–Corporate taxation: 4–Stable (high tax rates)
Total Taxation Score: 4-Stable (high tax rates)

South Korea's top income tax rate is 40 percent; the average income level is taxed at 10 percent. The top corporate income tax rate is 28 percent, although a

1	Hong Kong	1.25	81	Fiji	3.10
2	Singapore	1.30	81	Mali	3.10
3	Bahrain	1.70	81	Slovenia	3.10
4	New Zealand	1.75	85	Honduras	3.15
5	Switzerland	1.85	85	Mexico	3.15
6	United States	1.90	85	Papua New Guinea	3.15
7	Ireland	1.95	88	Djibouti	3.20
7	Luxembourg	1.95	88	Mongolia	3.20
7	Taiwan	1.95	90	Algeria	3.25
7	United Kingdom	1.95	90	Brazil	3.25
11	Bahamas	2.00	90	Lebanon	3.25
12	Czech Republic	2.05	90	Senegal	3.25
12	Japan	2.05	90	Tanzania	3.25
14	Australia	2.10	95	Nigeria	3.30
14	Belgium	2.10	95	Romania	3.30
14	Canada	2.10	97	Cambodia	3.35
14	United Arab Emirates	2.10	97	Dominican Republic	3.35
18	Austria	2.15	97	Egypt	3.35
18	Chile	2.15	97	Guinea	3.35
18	Estonia	2.15	97	Ivory Coast	3.35
18	Netherlands	2.15	97	Moldova	3.35
22	Denmark	2.25	97	Pakistan	3.35
22	El Salvador	2.25	104	Nepal	3.40
22	Finland	2.25	104	Venezuela	3.40
25	Germany	2.30	106	Armenia	3.45
25	Iceland	2.30	106	Bulgaria	3.45
27	Norway	2.35	106	Lesotho	3.45
28	Korea, South	2.40	106	Madagascar	3.45
28	Kuwait	2.40	106	Russia	3.45
28	Malaysia	2.40	111	Burkina Faso	3.50
28	Panama	2.40	111	Cameroon	3.50
28	Thailand	2.40	111	Guyana	3.50
33	Sweden	2.45	111	Nicaragua	3.50
34	Argentina	2.50	115	Gambia	3.60
34	France	2.50	116	Croatia	3.65
34	Italy	2.50	116	Georgia	3.65
34	Spain	2.50	116	Malawi	3.65
38	Portugal	2.55	119	Cape Verde	3.67
38	Sri Lanka	2.55	120	Ethiopia	3.70
38	Trinidad and Tobago	2.55	120	India	3.70
41	Barbados	2.60	120	Niger	3.70
41	Peru	2.60	123	Congo	3.75
43	Bolivia	2.65	124	Chad	3.80
43	Mauritius	2.65	124	China	3.80
45	Cyprus	2.70	124	Mauritania	3.80
45	Jamaica	2.70	124	Ukraine	3.80
45	Uruguay	2.70	124	Zimbabwe	3.80
48	Botswana	2.75	129	Albania	3.85
48	Guatemala	2.75	129	Bangladesh	3.85
48	Jordan	2.75	129	Mozambique	3.85
48	Namibia	2.75	129	Suriname	3.85
48	Oman	2.75	133	Burundi	3.90
48	Philippines	2.75	134	Togo	3.95
54	Belize	2.80	135	Haiti	4.00
54	Costa Rica	2.80	135	Kyrgyz Rep.	4.00
54	Israel	2.80	137	Kazakhstan	4.05
54	Swaziland	2.80	137	Sierra Leone	4.05
54	Turkey	2.80	139	Yemen	4.10
54	Uganda	2.80	140	Belarus	4.15
54	Samoa	2.80	141	Sudan	4.20
61	Latvia	2.85	141	Syria	4.20
62	Greece	2.90	143	Azerbaijan	4.30
62	Hungary	2.90	143	Equatorial Guinea	4.30
62	So. Africa	2.90	143	Myanmar	4.30
65	Ecuador	2.95	143	Rwanda	4.30
65	Gabon	2.95	147	Tajikistan	4.40
65	Indonesia	2.95	147	Uzbekistan	4.40
65	Malta	2.95	149	Angola	4.45
65	Morocco	2.95	149	Turkmenistan	4.45
65	Poland	2.95	151	Guinea-Bissau	4.55
65	Tunisia	2.95	152	Vietnam	4.60
72	Ghana	3.00	153	Congo (Zaire)	4.70
72	Lithuania	3.00	153	Iran	4.70
72	Saudi Arabia	3.00	155	Bosnia	4.80
75	Benin	3.05	155	Somalia	4.80
75	Kenya	3.05	157	Iraq	4.90
75	Paraguay	3.05	157	Laos	4.90
75	Qatar	3.05	157	Libya	4.90
75	Slovak Republic	3.05	160	Cuba	5.00
75	Zambia	3.05	160	Korea, North	5.00
81	Colombia	3.10			

Mostly Free

10 percent "resident surtax" increases it to over 35 percent. South Korea also has a 28 percent capital gains tax.

GOVERNMENT INTERVENTION IN THE ECONOMY
Score: 2–Stable (low level)

Government consumes 8.9 percent of GDP. The government remains heavily involved in such industries as banking, utilities, and services as well as in some heavy manufacturing, but has been reducing its level of involvement in these and other areas in an effort to reduce government spending. Although previously a low priority, an aggressive program of privatization was announced in July 1998.

MONETARY POLICY
Score: 2–Stable (low level of inflation)

South Korea's average annual rate of inflation from 1986 to 1996 was 5.5 percent. Inflation fell to 4.5 percent in 1997. South Korea currently is under an agreement with the International Monetary Fund as a result of the ongoing Asian financial crisis.

CAPITAL FLOWS AND FOREIGN INVESTMENT
Score: 2–Stable (low barriers)

The government has relied on foreign investment to build its export economy. Foreign investments have been useful particularly in developing high-tech industries, which are heavily involved in exports. In December 1996, the government passed legislation to eliminate the possibility of variable interpretation of the foreign direct investment code, which had not been applied systematically.

BANKING
Score: 3– (moderate level of restrictions)

Foreign banks were welcome in South Korea as early as 1967. The government occasionally tries to steer capital to small businesses, but it has been removed from direct ownership of banks since the early 1990s. Local banks are permitted to underwrite, deal, and broker all kinds of securities and to invest in some real estate ventures. The Asian financial crisis has resulted in South Korea's banking sector's coming increasingly under the control of the government. Although some of South Korea's new banking laws may help to increase long-term competition in financial services, today there is less competition than there was one year ago. As a result, South Korea's banking score is 1 point worse this year.

WAGE AND PRICE CONTROLS
Score: 2–Stable (low level)

The market sets most prices, although the government imposes controls on some utilities. The government also maintains stockpiles of foodstuffs that it releases into the market to raise or lower prices. South Korea has a minimum wage law, but some companies are exempt.

PROPERTY RIGHTS
Score: 1–Stable (very high level of protection)

Private property is secure, and expropriation is highly unlikely. South Korea has a stable and efficient legal system to protect private property.

REGULATION
Score: 3–Stable (moderate level)

Obtaining a business license can be simple. All businesses must be registered, but the process is efficient and not significantly burdensome. According to the U.S. Department of Commerce, however, "The Korean regulatory environment is difficult for domestic firms to work through and poses an even greater challenge to foreign firms. Laws and regulations are framed in general terms and are subject to differing bureaucratic interpretations. Basic concepts of administrative procedure are not well-developed, despite the enactment of an administrative procedures law in 1996. The regulatory process is not transparent and frequent informal discussions with the bureaucracy are necessary. Mid-level bureaucrats rely on unpublished ministerial guidelines and unwritten administrative advice for direction. No formal rule-making procedure exists. Proposed rules are often not published prior to promulgation, or are published with insufficient time to permit either full public comment or an adequate period for industry adjustment. After promulgation, rules can be applied retroactively and arbitrarily."[4] Still, by global standards, regulation in South Korea is moderate.

BLACK MARKET
Score: 2–Stable (low level of activity)

South Korea has a fairly small black market. A sizable number of employers tries to avoid the minimum wage laws, however. The government has set up stringent laws regarding intellectual property rights, and its recent crackdowns on pirated material are beginning to have an effect. The piracy of computer software, although still widespread, represents just a small portion of the economy.

NOTES
[1] U.S. Department of State, *Country Reports on Economic Policy and Trade Practices,* 1998.
[2] Based on the applied rate. See Arrowhead International, *World Trade and Customs Directory,* 1998.
[3] U.S. Department of State, *Country Reports on Economic Policy and Trade Practices,* 1998.
[4] U.S. Department of Commerce, *Country Commercial Guide,* 1998.

Kuwait

2.40

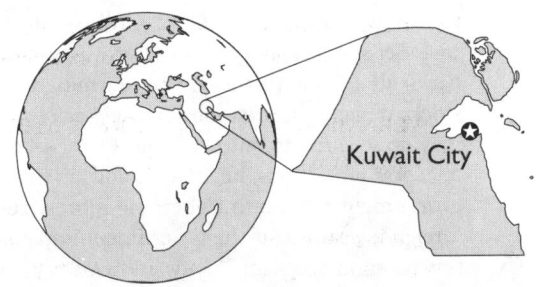

Kuwait City

| 1998 Score: **2.40** | 1997 Score: **2.40** | 1996 Score: **2.40** |

Trade	2	Banking	3
Taxation	1	Wages and Prices	3
Government Intervention	4	Property Rights	1
Monetary Policy	2	Regulation	2
Foreign Investment	4	Black Market	2

Kuwait is a Persian Gulf emirate with a small and relatively open oil-rich economy. Its reserves of 94 billion barrels of crude oil make up about 10 percent of the world's total. This assures that Kuwait will remain affluent well into the next century, absent external interference. The economy has undergone several major shocks over the past two decades, including massive government intervention in the late 1970s, the collapse of the securities market in 1982, the collapse of world oil prices in the mid-1980s, and invasion by Iraq in 1990. The government continues to control oil production. Oil revenues should enable the government to keep import tariffs and taxation to a minimum.

TRADE POLICY
Score: 2–Stable (low level of protectionism)

Kuwait's average tariff rate is 3.5 percent.[1] Government procurement policies cater generally to Kuwaiti firms, and non-tariff barriers include strict standards on imports, especially food. For example, according to the U.S. Department of State, "Kuwait, like other GCC [Gulf Cooperation Council] member states, maintains restrictive standards which impede the marketing of U.S. exports."[2]

TAXATION
Score–Income taxation: 1–Stable (very low tax rates)
Score–Corporate taxation: 1–Stable (very low tax rates)
Final Taxation Score: 1–Stable (very low tax rates)

Kuwait has no income tax, corporate tax (except on some foreign firms), or other significant tax.

GOVERNMENT INTERVENTION IN THE ECONOMY
Score: 4–Stable (high level)

Government consumes about 30 percent of GDP. Most GDP comes from oil production, nearly all of which is owned by the government.

MONETARY POLICY
Score: 2–Stable (low level of inflation)

Kuwait's average rate of inflation from 1989 to 1995 was about 10.5 percent. In 1996, the rate of inflation fell to about 4.7 percent.

CAPITAL FLOWS AND FOREIGN INVESTMENT
Score: 4–Stable (high barriers)

In general, Kuwait is open to some types of foreign investment, but significant restrictions still exist. For example, according to the U.S. Department of Commerce, "[F]oreign ownership in joint ventures with Kuwaiti firms is now limited to 49 percent. Foreign firms may not invest in the upstream petroleum sector, but are allowed to invest in joint venture petrochemical projects. Foreign firms may own up to 40 percent of banks. Foreign investment in real estate is limited

1	Hong Kong	1.25		81	Fiji	3.10
2	Singapore	1.30		81	Mali	3.10
3	Bahrain	1.70		81	Slovenia	3.10
4	New Zealand	1.75		85	Honduras	3.15
5	Switzerland	1.85		85	Mexico	3.15
6	United States	1.90		85	Papua New Guinea	3.15
7	Ireland	1.95		88	Djibouti	3.20
7	Luxembourg	1.95		88	Mongolia	3.20
7	Taiwan	1.95		90	Algeria	3.25
7	United Kingdom	1.95		90	Brazil	3.25
11	Bahamas	2.00		90	Lebanon	3.25
12	Czech Republic	2.05		90	Senegal	3.25
12	Japan	2.05		90	Tanzania	3.25
14	Australia	2.10		95	Nigeria	3.30
14	Belgium	2.10		95	Romania	3.30
14	Canada	2.10		97	Cambodia	3.35
14	United Arab Emirates	2.10		97	Dominican Republic	3.35
18	Austria	2.15		97	Egypt	3.35
18	Chile	2.15		97	Guinea	3.35
18	Estonia	2.15		97	Ivory Coast	3.35
18	Netherlands	2.15		97	Moldova	3.35
22	Denmark	2.25		97	Pakistan	3.35
22	El Salvador	2.25		104	Nepal	3.40
22	Finland	2.25		104	Venezuela	3.40
25	Germany	2.30		106	Armenia	3.45
25	Iceland	2.30		106	Bulgaria	3.45
27	Norway	2.35		106	Lesotho	3.45
28	Korea, South	2.40		106	Madagascar	3.45
28	Kuwait	2.40		106	Russia	3.45
28	Malaysia	2.40		111	Burkina Faso	3.50
28	Panama	2.40		111	Cameroon	3.50
28	Thailand	2.40		111	Guyana	3.50
33	Sweden	2.45		111	Nicaragua	3.50
34	Argentina	2.50		115	Gambia	3.60
34	France	2.50		116	Croatia	3.65
34	Italy	2.50		116	Georgia	3.65
34	Spain	2.50		116	Malawi	3.65
38	Portugal	2.55		119	Cape Verde	3.67
38	Sri Lanka	2.55		120	Ethiopia	3.70
38	Trinidad and Tobago	2.55		120	India	3.70
41	Barbados	2.60		120	Niger	3.70
41	Peru	2.60		123	Congo	3.75
43	Bolivia	2.65		124	Chad	3.80
43	Mauritius	2.65		124	China	3.80
45	Cyprus	2.70		124	Mauritania	3.80
45	Jamaica	2.70		124	Ukraine	3.80
45	Uruguay	2.70		124	Zimbabwe	3.80
48	Botswana	2.75		129	Albania	3.85
48	Guatemala	2.75		129	Bangladesh	3.85
48	Jordan	2.75		129	Mozambique	3.85
48	Namibia	2.75		129	Suriname	3.85
48	Oman	2.75		133	Burundi	3.90
48	Philippines	2.75		134	Togo	3.95
54	Belize	2.80		135	Haiti	4.00
54	Costa Rica	2.80		135	Kyrgyz Rep.	4.00
54	Israel	2.80		137	Kazakhstan	4.05
54	Swaziland	2.80		137	Sierra Leone	4.05
54	Turkey	2.80		139	Yemen	4.10
54	Uganda	2.80		140	Belarus	4.15
54	Samoa	2.80		141	Sudan	4.20
61	Latvia	2.85		141	Syria	4.20
62	Greece	2.90		143	Azerbaijan	4.30
62	Hungary	2.90		143	Equatorial Guinea	4.30
62	So. Africa	2.90		143	Myanmar	4.30
65	Ecuador	2.95		143	Rwanda	4.30
65	Gabon	2.95		147	Tajikistan	4.40
65	Indonesia	2.95		147	Uzbekistan	4.40
65	Malta	2.95		149	Angola	4.45
65	Morocco	2.95		149	Turkmenistan	4.45
65	Poland	2.95		151	Guinea-Bissau	4.55
65	Tunisia	2.95		152	Vietnam	4.60
72	Ghana	3.00		153	Congo (Zaire)	4.70
72	Lithuania	3.00		153	Iran	4.70
72	Saudi Arabia	3.00		155	Bosnia	4.80
75	Benin	3.05		155	Somalia	4.80
75	Kenya	3.05		157	Iraq	4.90
75	Paraguay	3.05		157	Laos	4.90
75	Qatar	3.05		157	Libya	4.90
75	Slovak Republic	3.05		160	Cuba	5.00
75	Zambia	3.05		160	Korea, North	5.00
81	Colombia	3.10				

Mostly Free

to nationals of the other GCC-[Gulf Cooperation Council] member states. Foreigners (with the exception of GCC nationals and Egyptians) are not permitted to invest in stocks directly through the Kuwait Stock Exchange, but they may do so through mutual funds. Other sectors such as telecommunications, health care and airlines are still government-run, but may become more accessible to foreign investment if the government implements a privatization program."[3] Kuwaiti firms pay no corporate tax, but foreign firms must pay a corporate tax as high as 55 percent.

BANKING
Score: 3–Stable (moderate level of restrictions)

Banking in Kuwait is competitive, and banks are relatively free of government control. With the exception of investment banking, the financial services industry is virtually closed to foreigners. For example, according to the U.S. Department of Commerce, "[F]oreign investment is discriminated against in several ways: through the bar on majority ownership [and] the bar on investment in prohibited sectors such as oil and financial services."[4] Still, some foreign ownership is allowed. Thus, by global standards, Kuwait's restrictions on banking are moderate.

WAGE AND PRICE CONTROLS
Score: 3–Stable (moderate level)

The market sets most wages and prices. The government continues to offer subsidies to many businesses, however, thereby distorting prices on some goods and services, like food.

PROPERTY RIGHTS
Score: 1–Stable (very high level of protection)

Private property is protected in Kuwait. The country has an efficient legal and judicial system.

REGULATION
Score: 2–Stable (low level)

Establishing a business in Kuwait is easy if the business will not compete directly with state-owned concerns. Regulations are applied evenly in most cases.

BLACK MARKET
Score: 2–Stable (low level of activity)

The black market is confined mainly to pirated software, video and cassette recordings, and similar products. The government continues to combat violations.

NOTES

[1]   Based on total taxes on international trade as a percentage of total imports.
[2]   U.S. Department of State, *Country Reports on Economic Policy and Trade Practices,* 1998.
[3]   U.S. Department of Commerce, *Country Commercial Guide,* 1998.
[4]   *Ibid.*

Kyrgyz Republic 4.00

1998 Score: **4.00**	1997 Score: **n/a**	1996 Score: **n/a**

Trade	4	Banking	4
Taxation	4	Wages and Prices	4
Government Intervention	3	Property Rights	4
Monetary Policy	5	Regulation	4
Foreign Investment	3	Black Market	5

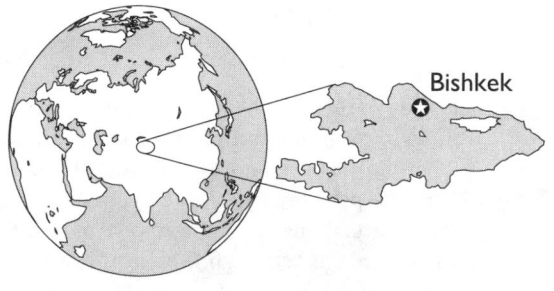

Bishkek

The Kyrgyz Republic became an autonomous republic of the Russian Federation in 1921 and was incorporated into the Soviet Union in 1936. During some 70 years of Soviet rule, the Kyrgyz Republic underwent political, economic, and cultural repression, although some modernization and industrialization occurred in some urban areas of the country. Since becoming independent in 1991, the Kyrgyz Republic has tried to transform its centrally planned economy into a more market-based economy. Success has been sporadic, however, and the country remains hindered by an intransigent bureaucracy.

TRADE POLICY
Score: 4–Stable (high level of protectionism)

The Kyrgyz Republic's average tariff rate is about 10 percent. Among its non-tariff barriers are corrupt customs officials, who often charge arbitrary duty rates. According to the U.S. Department of Commerce, "Corruption is evident in tax and customs collection and in the enforcement of many laws and regulations and is especially noticeable in trade and in construction."[1]

TAXATION
Score–Income taxation: 4–Stable (high tax rates)
Score–Corporate taxation: 3–Stable (moderate tax rates)
Final Taxation Score: 4–Stable (high tax rates)

The Kyrgyz Republic has a top income tax rate of 40 percent[2] and a top marginal corporate tax rate of 30 percent. It also has a 30 percent capital gains tax and a 20 percent value-added tax.

GOVERNMENT INTERVENTION IN THE ECONOMY
Score: 3–Stable (moderate level)

The Kyrgyz Republic is privatizing its large state-owned sector. Government consumes 17 percent of GDP.[3] The economy remains dominated by large state-owned enterprises, particularly in utilities and transportation. In 1997, however, the government passed a new law that paves the way for eventual privatization of state-owned enterprises in mining, aviation, energy, telecommunications, agriculture, and publishing. The government has yet to complete such privatizations; but it has made some progress toward the privatization of Kyrgyztelecom, the national telecommunications company, which now is a joint-stock company under the control of the largest shareholder, the State Property Fund, and is seeking private investors. The State Property Fund is the principal privatization agency of the government. It already has privatized 56.3 percent of the government's holdings in construction, 47.1 percent in transportation, and 79.2 percent in other industrial sectors.

1	Hong Kong	1.25		81	Fiji	3.10
2	Singapore	1.30		81	Mali	3.10
3	Bahrain	1.70		81	Slovenia	3.10
4	New Zealand	1.75		85	Honduras	3.15
5	Switzerland	1.85		85	Mexico	3.15
6	United States	1.90		85	Papua New Guinea	3.15
7	Ireland	1.95		88	Djibouti	3.20
7	Luxembourg	1.95		88	Mongolia	3.20
7	Taiwan	1.95		90	Algeria	3.25
7	United Kingdom	1.95		90	Brazil	3.25
11	Bahamas	2.00		90	Lebanon	3.25
12	Czech Republic	2.05		90	Senegal	3.25
12	Japan	2.05		90	Tanzania	3.25
14	Australia	2.10		95	Nigeria	3.30
14	Belgium	2.10		95	Romania	3.30
14	Canada	2.10		97	Cambodia	3.35
14	United Arab Emirates	2.10		97	Dominican Republic	3.35
18	Austria	2.15		97	Egypt	3.35
18	Chile	2.15		97	Guinea	3.35
18	Estonia	2.15		97	Ivory Coast	3.35
18	Netherlands	2.15		97	Moldova	3.35
22	Denmark	2.25		97	Pakistan	3.35
22	El Salvador	2.25		104	Nepal	3.40
22	Finland	2.25		104	Venezuela	3.40
25	Germany	2.30		106	Armenia	3.45
25	Iceland	2.30		106	Bulgaria	3.45
27	Norway	2.35		106	Lesotho	3.45
28	Korea, South	2.40		106	Madagascar	3.45
28	Kuwait	2.40		106	Russia	3.45
28	Malaysia	2.40		111	Burkina Faso	3.50
28	Panama	2.40		111	Cameroon	3.50
28	Thailand	2.40		111	Guyana	3.50
33	Sweden	2.45		111	Nicaragua	3.50
34	Argentina	2.50		115	Gambia	3.60
34	France	2.50		116	Croatia	3.65
34	Italy	2.50		116	Georgia	3.65
34	Spain	2.50		116	Malawi	3.65
38	Portugal	2.55		119	Cape Verde	3.67
38	Sri Lanka	2.55		120	Ethiopia	3.70
38	Trinidad and Tobago	2.55		120	India	3.70
41	Barbados	2.60		120	Niger	3.70
41	Peru	2.60		123	Congo	3.75
43	Bolivia	2.65		124	Chad	3.80
43	Mauritius	2.65		124	China	3.80
45	Cyprus	2.70		124	Mauritania	3.80
45	Jamaica	2.70		124	Ukraine	3.80
45	Uruguay	2.70		124	Zimbabwe	3.80
48	Botswana	2.75		129	Albania	3.85
48	Guatemala	2.75		129	Bangladesh	3.85
48	Jordan	2.75		129	Mozambique	3.85
48	Namibia	2.75		129	Suriname	3.85
48	Oman	2.75		133	Burundi	3.90
48	Philippines	2.75		134	Togo	3.95
54	Belize	2.80		135	Haiti	4.00
54	Costa Rica	2.80		135	Kyrgyz Rep.	4.00
54	Israel	2.80		137	Kazakhstan	4.05
54	Swaziland	2.80		137	Sierra Leone	4.05
54	Turkey	2.80		139	Yemen	4.10
54	Uganda	2.80		140	Belarus	4.15
54	Samoa	2.80		141	Sudan	4.20
61	Latvia	2.85		141	Syria	4.20
62	Greece	2.90		143	Azerbaijan	4.30
62	Hungary	2.90		143	Equatorial Guinea	4.30
62	So. Africa	2.90		143	Myanmar	4.30
65	Ecuador	2.95		143	Rwanda	4.30
65	Gabon	2.95		147	Tajikistan	4.40
65	Indonesia	2.95		147	Uzbekistan	4.40
65	Malta	2.95		149	Angola	4.45
65	Morocco	2.95		149	Turkmenistan	4.45
65	Poland	2.95		151	Guinea-Bissau	4.55
65	Tunisia	2.95		152	Vietnam	4.60
72	Ghana	3.00		153	Congo (Zaire)	4.70
72	Lithuania	3.00		153	Iran	4.70
72	Saudi Arabia	3.00		155	Bosnia	4.80
75	Benin	3.05		155	Somalia	4.80
75	Kenya	3.05		157	Iraq	4.90
75	Paraguay	3.05		157	Laos	4.90
75	Qatar	3.05		157	Libya	4.90
75	Slovak Republic	3.05		160	Cuba	5.00
75	Zambia	3.05		160	Korea, North	5.00
81	Colombia	3.10				

Repressed

MONETARY POLICY
Score: 5–Stable (very high level of inflation)

The Kyrgyz Republic has been plagued with hyperinflation. Although inflation was projected to be less than 35 percent in 1997 and 1996, it was 42.6 percent in 1995, 278 percent in 1994, 1,209 percent in 1993, and 855 percent in 1992. Thus, although greatly reduced, the average annual rate of inflation remains very high, both historically and by global standards.

CAPITAL FLOWS AND FOREIGN INVESTMENT
Score: 3–Stable (moderate barriers)

Although the government wants to raise the level of foreign investment, it still maintains some barriers. The Kyrgyz Republic has opened most of its economy to foreign investment but forbids complete foreign ownership of mining companies and forestry. Foreigners may not own land, but they may lease it. The government announced the creation of a new State Agency on Foreign Investments to assist foreign investment in the country.

BANKING
Score: 4–Stable (high level of restrictions)

The banking system is not fully functional. According to the U.S. Department of Commerce, "The banking system is a private banking system supervised by a strong and independent central bank. The banking system is very weak and undercapitalized."[4] Although there are few official restrictions, the very fact that the system has yet to develop fully is a primary hindrance. Capital is scarce; lending policies usually are tightly controlled; and financial transactions are difficult. Domestic bank formation is virtually nonexistent, and the government is revoking the licenses of many existing banks. The U.S. Department of Commerce reports that "Four banks recently had their licenses revoked, two of them being completely insolvent former state banks."[5]

WAGE AND PRICE CONTROLS
Score: 4–Stable (high level)

The large number of state-owned industries controls wages and prices. Price controls continue in such areas as agricultural products, transportation, and utilities.

PROPERTY RIGHTS
Score: 4–Stable (low level of protection)

The Kyrgyz Republic's legal system does not afford private property sufficient protection. Although legal reform is a major government priority, the judiciary remains weak and corrupt. According to the U.S. Department of State, "The Constitution provides for an independent judiciary; however, the court system remains largely unreformed, and the executive branch dominates the judiciary."[6]

REGULATION
Score: 4–Stable (high level)

Establishing a business can be a tedious and time-consuming procedure that requires individuals to overcome numerous bureaucratic barriers. According to the U.S. Department of Commerce, "Because of the state of flux, bureaucratic procedures are unclear and those in charge of implementing laws may not know what the law in fact is. This can cause a general state of confusion and lack of transparency in some issues."[7]

BLACK MARKET
Score: 5–Stable (very high level of activity)

Smuggling is rampant and includes many imports. According to the U.S. Department of Commerce, "Most foreign manufactured brands reportedly are smuggled."[8] Despite the existence of laws to protect intellectual property rights, piracy in computer software remains a significant problem.

NOTES

[1] U.S. Department of Commerce, *Country Commercial Guide*, 1997.
[2] The tax on the average level of income is not available. Therefore, the Kyrgyz Republic is graded strictly on its top income tax rates.
[3] World Bank, *World Development Indicators*, 1998.
[4] U.S. Department of Commerce, *Country Commercial Guide*, 1997.
[5] *Ibid.*
[6] U.S. Department of State, "Kyrgyzstan Country Report on Human Rights Practices for 1997," 1998.
[7] U.S. Department of Commerce, *Country Commercial Guide*, 1997.
[8] U.S. Department of Commerce, "Kyrgyzstan: Tobacco Situation," *Voluntary Report, Agworld Attaché Reports*, 1997.

Laos   4.90

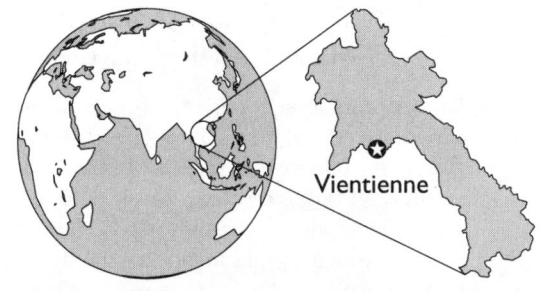

Vientienne

1998 Score: **5.00**	1997 Score: **5.00**	1996 Score: **5.00**

Trade	5	Banking	5
Taxation	5	Wages and Prices	5
Government Intervention	5	Property Rights	5
Monetary Policy	4	Regulation	5
Foreign Investment	5	Black Market	5

Laos, a constitutional monarchy before 1975, has one of the world's most repressed economies. It is a one-party communist state with a highly centralized, government-planned economy that is riddled with corruption and graft. The Clinton Administration recently removed a restriction on U.S. foreign aid to Laos, paving the way for the sending of U.S. development assistance to the regime. With such a highly corrupt and restricted system, however, Laos's government is most likely to use this foreign aid to maintain the country's centrally planned economy. Inflation recently dropped, however; as a result, Laos's overall score is 0.1 point better than last year.

TRADE POLICY
Score: 5–Stable (very high level of protectionism)

Import tariffs range from 0 percent to 200 percent, with most imports subject to a tariff of 45 percent. All imports are inspected by a corrupt customs service that arbitrarily applies customs duties and taxes imports. Officials sometimes simply confiscate imports at the border. In addition to this rampant corruption—sanctioned and supported by customs officials—trade barriers effectively bar most imports.

TAXATION
Score–Income taxation: 5–Stable (very high tax rates)
Score–Corporate taxation: 5–Stable (very high tax rates)
Final Taxation Score: 5–Stable (very high tax rates)

Because of its total control of the economy, the government is able to confiscate the proceeds of all economic activity. By "owning" the fruits of economic activity, it imposes an effective rate of taxation that approaches 100 percent.

GOVERNMENT INTERVENTION IN THE ECONOMY
Score: 5–Stable (very high level)

Laos permits some restricted private economic activity, but the means of production and most of the profits gained from that production remain entirely in the hands of the state. The government owns and runs most of the country's primarily agricultural economy.

MONETARY POLICY
Score: 4+ (high level of inflation)

The official average annual rate of inflation from 1986 to 1996 is 24.4 percent, down from 29.6 percent from 1985 to 1995; as a result, Laos's monetary policy score is 1 point better this year. The inflation rate in 1997 was 17 percent.

1	Hong Kong	1.25
2	Singapore	1.30
3	Bahrain	1.70
4	New Zealand	1.75
5	Switzerland	1.85
6	United States	1.90
7	Ireland	1.95
7	Luxembourg	1.95
7	Taiwan	1.95
7	United Kingdom	1.95
11	Bahamas	2.00
12	Czech Republic	2.05
12	Japan	2.05
14	Australia	2.10
14	Belgium	2.10
14	Canada	2.10
14	United Arab Emirates	2.10
18	Austria	2.15
18	Chile	2.15
18	Estonia	2.15
18	Netherlands	2.15
22	Denmark	2.25
22	El Salvador	2.25
22	Finland	2.25
25	Germany	2.30
25	Iceland	2.30
27	Norway	2.35
28	Korea, South	2.40
28	Kuwait	2.40
28	Malaysia	2.40
28	Panama	2.40
28	Thailand	2.40
33	Sweden	2.45
34	Argentina	2.50
34	France	2.50
34	Italy	2.50
34	Spain	2.50
38	Portugal	2.55
38	Sri Lanka	2.55
38	Trinidad and Tobago	2.55
41	Barbados	2.60
41	Peru	2.60
43	Bolivia	2.65
43	Mauritius	2.65
45	Cyprus	2.70
45	Jamaica	2.70
45	Uruguay	2.70
48	Botswana	2.75
48	Guatemala	2.75
48	Jordan	2.75
48	Namibia	2.75
48	Oman	2.75
48	Philippines	2.75
54	Belize	2.80
54	Costa Rica	2.80
54	Israel	2.80
54	Swaziland	2.80
54	Turkey	2.80
54	Uganda	2.80
54	Samoa	2.80
61	Latvia	2.85
62	Greece	2.90
62	Hungary	2.90
62	So. Africa	2.90
65	Ecuador	2.95
65	Gabon	2.95
65	Indonesia	2.95
65	Malta	2.95
65	Morocco	2.95
65	Poland	2.95
65	Tunisia	2.95
72	Ghana	3.00
72	Lithuania	3.00
72	Saudi Arabia	3.00
75	Benin	3.05
75	Kenya	3.05
75	Paraguay	3.05
75	Qatar	3.05
75	Slovak Republic	3.05
75	Zambia	3.05
81	Colombia	3.10
81	Fiji	3.10
81	Mali	3.10
81	Slovenia	3.10
85	Honduras	3.15
85	Mexico	3.15
85	Papua New Guinea	3.15
88	Djibouti	3.20
88	Mongolia	3.20
90	Algeria	3.25
90	Brazil	3.25
90	Lebanon	3.25
90	Senegal	3.25
90	Tanzania	3.25
95	Nigeria	3.30
95	Romania	3.30
97	Cambodia	3.35
97	Dominican Republic	3.35
97	Egypt	3.35
97	Guinea	3.35
97	Ivory Coast	3.35
97	Moldova	3.35
97	Pakistan	3.35
104	Nepal	3.40
104	Venezuela	3.40
106	Armenia	3.45
106	Bulgaria	3.45
106	Lesotho	3.45
106	Madagascar	3.45
106	Russia	3.45
111	Burkina Faso	3.50
111	Cameroon	3.50
111	Guyana	3.50
111	Nicaragua	3.50
115	Gambia	3.60
116	Croatia	3.65
116	Georgia	3.65
116	Malawi	3.65
119	Cape Verde	3.67
120	Ethiopia	3.70
120	India	3.70
120	Niger	3.70
123	Congo	3.75
124	Chad	3.80
124	China	3.80
124	Mauritania	3.80
124	Ukraine	3.80
124	Zimbabwe	3.80
129	Albania	3.85
129	Bangladesh	3.85
129	Mozambique	3.85
129	Suriname	3.85
133	Burundi	3.90
134	Togo	3.95
135	Haiti	4.00
135	Kyrgyz Rep.	4.00
137	Kazakhstan	4.05
137	Sierra Leone	4.05
139	Yemen	4.10
140	Belarus	4.15
141	Sudan	4.20
141	Syria	4.20
143	Azerbaijan	4.30
143	Equatorial Guinea	4.30
143	Myanmar	4.30
143	Rwanda	4.30
147	Tajikistan	4.40
147	Uzbekistan	4.40
149	Angola	4.45
149	Turkmenistan	4.45
151	Guinea-Bissau	4.55
152	Vietnam	4.60
153	Congo (Zaire)	4.70
153	Iran	4.70
155	Bosnia	4.80
155	Somalia	4.80
157	Iraq	4.90
157	Laos	4.90
157	Libya	4.90
160	Cuba	5.00
160	Korea, North	5.00

Repressed

CAPITAL FLOWS AND FOREIGN INVESTMENT
Score: 5–Stable (very high barriers)

Laos permits some foreign investment, and the government allows 100 percent foreign ownership of investments in almost all areas of the economy. But it would be a mistake to interpret this as meaning Laos is open to foreign investment: Corruption and arbitrary government confiscation of profits through a multitude of constantly changing fees, taxes, stipends, and other charges make it nearly impossible to conduct business. Bribes to government officials are implicitly mandatory when establishing a business, and foreigners often are subject to government surveillance. Property is confiscated and foreigners are expelled on a regular basis. Although Laos does not seek actively to prevent foreign investment, its centralized, corrupt, and bureaucratic economy and one-party communist rule have had the same effect. Finally, foreign investors are not permitted to own land.

BANKING
Score: 5–Stable (very high level of restrictions)

Banks are owned and operated by the government, as well as influenced heavily by the state-owned central bank. There is no free-market competition in the banking industry.

WAGE AND PRICE CONTROLS
Score: 5–Stable (very high level)

The government sets virtually all wages and prices in Laos—particularly on such products as rice, sugar, cloth, and gasoline.

PROPERTY RIGHTS
Score: 5–Stable (very low level of protection)

Individuals are free to accumulate some private property, such as a home or a piece of land, but all such property is subject to expropriation, pillaging by the Vietnamese "security" forces that routinely enter Laos, extortion by corrupt local government officials, and destruction by criminal elements sanctioned by the government. The corrupt, state-controlled legal system rarely rules in favor of private citizens in complaints against the government. According to the U.S. Department of Commerce, "Laos' legal system is evolving. The administrative and judicial systems have not changed very much from the Soviet mode."[1]

REGULATION
Score: 5–Stable (very high level)

The government regulates the entire economy by owning and operating all means of production. According to the U.S. Department of Commerce, "The Lao bureaucracy may be described as arcane and deliberate."[2]

BLACK MARKET
Score: 5–Stable (very high level of activity)

The black market is larger than the official or legal economy. As in other command economies, even basic economic activity in Laos is performed in the black market.

NOTES

[1]   U.S. Department of Commerce, "Laos—Investment Climate," *Market Research Reports,* August 1997.
[2]   U.S. Department of Commerce, "Laos—Investment Climate," *Market Research Reports,* August 1996.

Latvia   2.85

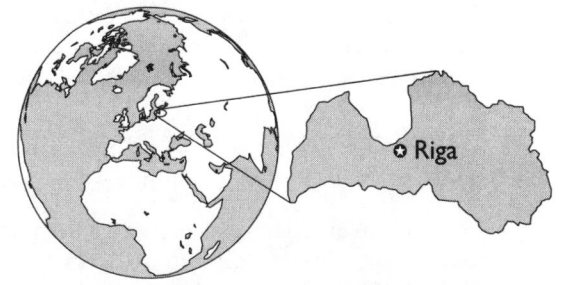

1998 Score: **2.85**	1997 Score: **2.95**	1996 Score: **3.05**

Trade	2	Banking	2
Taxation	2.5	Wages and Prices	2
Government Intervention	3	Property Rights	3
Monetary Policy	5	Regulation	3
Foreign Investment	2	Black Market	4

Latvia was an independent republic from 1918 to 1940, at which time it was annexed by the Soviet Union. Since declaring its independence in August 1991, it has liberalized its economy and made substantial progress in opening its borders to trade and investment despite some remaining roadblocks. Latvia enjoys a highly trained labor force and is home to several high-tech enterprises, as well as major ports on the Baltic Sea. After a 50 percent drop in GDP from 1991 to 1993, the economy began to recover in 1994 and has stabilized. The government has applied for membership in the European Union. President Guntis Ulmanis was elected for a three-year term in 1996. The pro-business People's Party won a slim majority of seats in elections to parliament in October 1998. As of this writing, a coalition government has not been formed or a prime minister named.

TRADE POLICY
Score: 2–Stable (low level of protectionism)

Latvia's average tariff rate is less than 2 percent.[1] According to the U.S. Department of Commerce, "Latvia currently licenses imports of sugar, grains, alcohol and arms. There are no other quantitative constraints on imports."[2]

TAXATION
Score–Income taxation: 2–Stable (low tax rates)
Score–Corporate taxation: 2–Stable (low tax rates)
Final Taxation Score: 2.5–Stable (moderate tax rates)

Latvia has a flat income tax rate of 25 percent and a flat corporate tax rate of 25 percent. It also has an 18 percent value-added tax and a 37 percent social payments tax.

GOVERNMENT INTERVENTION IN THE ECONOMY
Score: 3–Stable (moderate level)

Government consumes about 22.2 percent of GDP, almost 40 percent of which still is produced by the public sector.[3] But this level is low by global standards.

MONETARY POLICY
Score: 5–Stable (very high level of inflation)

Latvia's rate of inflation was 124.5 percent in 1991, 951.2 percent in 1992, 109.2 percent in 1993, 35.9 percent in 1994, 25 percent in 1995, and 17.7 percent in 1996. Thus, even though Latvia has made tremendous progress toward reducing inflation, the average annual rate since independence is still over 200 percent.

CAPITAL FLOWS AND FOREIGN INVESTMENT
Score: 2–Stable (low barriers)

There are few restrictions on investing in Latvia. Foreigners are permitted to invest in most industries but are restricted from acquiring majority shares in companies related to national defense. Investors now may own land if there is an

Rank	Country	Score	Rank	Country	Score
1	Hong Kong	1.25	81	Fiji	3.10
2	Singapore	1.30	81	Mali	3.10
3	Bahrain	1.70	81	Slovenia	3.10
4	New Zealand	1.75	85	Honduras	3.15
5	Switzerland	1.85	85	Mexico	3.15
6	United States	1.90	85	Papua New Guinea	3.15
7	Ireland	1.95	88	Djibouti	3.20
7	Luxembourg	1.95	88	Mongolia	3.20
7	Taiwan	1.95	90	Algeria	3.25
7	United Kingdom	1.95	90	Brazil	3.25
11	Bahamas	2.00	90	Lebanon	3.25
12	Czech Republic	2.05	90	Senegal	3.25
12	Japan	2.05	90	Tanzania	3.25
14	Australia	2.10	95	Nigeria	3.30
14	Belgium	2.10	95	Romania	3.30
14	Canada	2.10	97	Cambodia	3.35
14	United Arab Emirates	2.10	97	Dominican Republic	3.35
18	Austria	2.15	97	Egypt	3.35
18	Chile	2.15	97	Guinea	3.35
18	Estonia	2.15	97	Ivory Coast	3.35
18	Netherlands	2.15	97	Moldova	3.35
22	Denmark	2.25	97	Pakistan	3.35
22	El Salvador	2.25	104	Nepal	3.40
22	Finland	2.25	104	Venezuela	3.40
25	Germany	2.30	106	Armenia	3.45
25	Iceland	2.30	106	Bulgaria	3.45
27	Norway	2.35	106	Lesotho	3.45
28	Korea, South	2.40	106	Madagascar	3.45
28	Kuwait	2.40	106	Russia	3.45
28	Malaysia	2.40	111	Burkina Faso	3.50
28	Panama	2.40	111	Cameroon	3.50
28	Thailand	2.40	111	Guyana	3.50
33	Sweden	2.45	111	Nicaragua	3.50
34	Argentina	2.50	115	Gambia	3.60
34	France	2.50	116	Croatia	3.65
34	Italy	2.50	116	Georgia	3.65
34	Spain	2.50	116	Malawi	3.65
38	Portugal	2.55	119	Cape Verde	3.67
38	Sri Lanka	2.55	120	Ethiopia	3.70
38	Trinidad and Tobago	2.55	120	India	3.70
41	Barbados	2.60	120	Niger	3.70
41	Peru	2.60	123	Congo	3.75
43	Bolivia	2.65	124	Chad	3.80
43	Mauritius	2.65	124	China	3.80
45	Cyprus	2.70	124	Mauritania	3.80
45	Jamaica	2.70	124	Ukraine	3.80
45	Uruguay	2.70	124	Zimbabwe	3.80
48	Botswana	2.75	129	Albania	3.85
48	Guatemala	2.75	129	Bangladesh	3.85
48	Jordan	2.75	129	Mozambique	3.85
48	Namibia	2.75	129	Suriname	3.85
48	Oman	2.75	133	Burundi	3.90
48	Philippines	2.75	134	Togo	3.95
54	Belize	2.80	135	Haiti	4.00
54	Costa Rica	2.80	135	Kyrgyz Rep.	4.00
54	Israel	2.80	137	Kazakhstan	4.05
54	Swaziland	2.80	137	Sierra Leone	4.05
54	Turkey	2.80	139	Yemen	4.10
54	Uganda	2.80	140	Belarus	4.15
54	Samoa	2.80	141	Sudan	4.20
61	Latvia	2.85	141	Syria	4.20
62	Greece	2.90	143	Azerbaijan	4.30
62	Hungary	2.90	143	Equatorial Guinea	4.30
62	So. Africa	2.90	143	Myanmar	4.30
65	Ecuador	2.95	143	Rwanda	4.30
65	Gabon	2.95	147	Tajikistan	4.40
65	Indonesia	2.95	147	Uzbekistan	4.40
65	Malta	2.95	149	Angola	4.45
65	Morocco	2.95	149	Turkmenistan	4.45
65	Poland	2.95	151	Guinea-Bissau	4.55
65	Tunisia	2.95	152	Vietnam	4.60
72	Ghana	3.00	153	Congo (Zaire)	4.70
72	Lithuania	3.00	153	Iran	4.70
72	Saudi Arabia	3.00	155	Bosnia	4.80
75	Benin	3.05	155	Somalia	4.80
75	Kenya	3.05	157	Iraq	4.90
75	Paraguay	3.05	157	Laos	4.90
75	Qatar	3.05	157	Libya	4.90
75	Slovak Republic	3.05	160	Cuba	5.00
75	Zambia	3.05	160	Korea, North	5.00
81	Colombia	3.10			

Mostly Free

existing investment protection agreement between Latvia and the country in which the investor is based. The foreign investment code has been streamlined and updated.

BANKING
Score: 2–Stable (low level of restrictions)

Latvia's banking sector underwent significant transformation in 1995, when less competitive banks went out of business. Financial crisis in the banking industry in neighboring Russia also has caused some Latvian banks to collapse. Today, the banking system is beginning to stabilize; it is competitive and mostly free of onerous government regulation. The government has partially privatized the State Savings Bank (Krajbanka) and Unibank; however, the Bank of Latvia must approve all foreign investments in domestic banks and all foreign bank branches.

WAGE AND PRICE CONTROLS
Score: 2–Stable (low level)

The private sector sets most wages and prices, although the government continues to set prices on some goods and services, such as electricity, rents for government-controlled housing, and telecommunications.

PROPERTY RIGHTS
Score: 3–Stable (moderate level of protection)

Since independence, the government has not expropriated any property. The court system is becoming more efficient, and laws are being drafted to reflect Western standards more closely. There is no indication that the government influences the legal process unduly. According to the U.S. Department of State, there is evidence that the "judiciary is independent but not well-trained, efficient, or free from corruption."[4]

REGULATION
Score: 3–Stable (moderate level)

Establishing a business is relatively easy, and many private businesses are opening. There is some corruption, and some regulations are applied unevenly. "As in other countries to emerge from the old Soviet Bloc," reports the U.S. Department of Commerce, "government bureaucracy, corruption and organized crime are the most significant hurdles to U.S. trade and investment in Latvia."[5]

BLACK MARKET
Score: 4–Stable (high level of activity)

The black market involves mainly agricultural goods, transportation, and labor. The government estimates that black market activity is equivalent to one-third of the official economy. There is significant trafficking in pirated videotapes and motion pictures, as well as increasing black market activity in the smuggling of commodities from Russia. Some banking operations also are performed in the black market.

NOTES
[1]   This is a trade-weighted average tariff for all imports. It is based on total taxation on international trade as a percentage of imports.
[2]   U.S. Department of Commerce, *Country Commercial Guide*, 1998.
[3]   Government of Latvia, *Latvia, Country Profile*, from Embassy of Latvia, Washington, D.C.
[4]   U.S. Department of State, "Latvia Country Report on Human Rights Practices for 1997," 1998.
[5]   U.S. Department of Commerce, *Country Commercial Guide*, 1998.

Lebanon   3.25

1998 Score: **3.25**   1997 Score: **2.95**   1996 Score: **2.95**

Trade	5	Banking	2
Taxation	2.5	Wages and Prices	2
Government Intervention	2	Property Rights	3
Monetary Policy	5	Regulation	3
Foreign Investment	3	Black Market	5

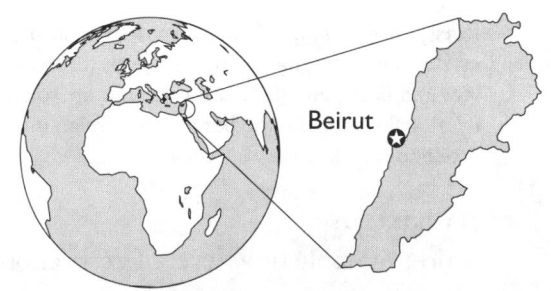

Beirut

After 17 years of bloody civil war, Lebanon elected Rafiq Hariri as prime minister in 1992. Hariri embarked on an ambitious reform plan aimed at stimulating the economy. The war-torn country suffers from a shattered infrastructure, outdated utilities, and the destruction of much of Beirut, formerly one of the Arab world's foremost financial and trade centers. Hariri's reconstruction plans have opened significant opportunities to businesses, which are rushing to rebuild the country as Lebanon tries to implement a more open foreign investment regime. Parts of the economy are among the freest in the world; most restrictions on economic freedom are the result of civil war, the lack of the rule of law, and the intimidating presence of more than 30,000 Syrian troops, who engage extensively in car theft and smuggling.

TRADE POLICY
Score: 5–Stable (very high level of protectionism)

Lebanon's average tariff rate is 24.2 percent.[1] There are few non-tariff barriers, although the government does require import licenses for firearms and ammunition. The operations of the customs service are marred by some corruption and inefficiency.

TAXATION
Score–Income taxation: 2–Stable (low tax rates)
Score–Corporate taxation: 2–Stable (low tax rates)
Final Taxation Score: 2.5–Stable (moderate tax rates)

Lebanon's top income tax rate is 10 percent, with the average taxpayer in the 2 percent bracket. The top marginal corporate tax rate is 10 percent. Lebanon also has a 6 percent capital gains tax and a 12 percent social contributions tax.

GOVERNMENT INTERVENTION IN THE ECONOMY
Score: 2–Stable (low level)

Government consumes about 11.6 percent of GDP, but the government has established a significant privatization program to reduce its role in the economy. "Lebanon has traditionally enjoyed a free-market economy and a strong laissez-faire commercial tradition," reports the U.S. Department of Commerce.[2]

MONETARY POLICY
Score: 5–Stable (very high level of inflation)

Lebanon's average annual rate of inflation from 1986 to 1996 was about 43 percent.

CAPITAL FLOWS AND FOREIGN INVESTMENT
Score: 3–Stable (moderate barriers)

According to the U.S. Department of Commerce, "Lebanon offers the most liberal investment climate in the Middle East, with no significant restrictions on

1	Hong Kong	1.25	81	Fiji	3.10
2	Singapore	1.30	81	Mali	3.10
3	Bahrain	1.70	81	Slovenia	3.10
4	New Zealand	1.75	85	Honduras	3.15
5	Switzerland	1.85	85	Mexico	3.15
6	United States	1.90	85	Papua New Guinea	3.15
7	Ireland	1.95	88	Djibouti	3.20
7	Luxembourg	1.95	88	Mongolia	3.20
7	Taiwan	1.95	90	Algeria	3.25
7	United Kingdom	1.95	90	Brazil	3.25
11	Bahamas	2.00	90	Lebanon	3.25
12	Czech Republic	2.05	90	Senegal	3.25
12	Japan	2.05	90	Tanzania	3.25
14	Australia	2.10	95	Nigeria	3.30
14	Belgium	2.10	95	Romania	3.30
14	Canada	2.10	97	Cambodia	3.35
14	United Arab Emirates	2.10	97	Dominican Republic	3.35
18	Austria	2.15	97	Egypt	3.35
18	Chile	2.15	97	Guinea	3.35
18	Estonia	2.15	97	Ivory Coast	3.35
18	Netherlands	2.15	97	Moldova	3.35
22	Denmark	2.25	97	Pakistan	3.35
22	El Salvador	2.25	104	Nepal	3.40
22	Finland	2.25	104	Venezuela	3.40
25	Germany	2.30	106	Armenia	3.45
25	Iceland	2.30	106	Bulgaria	3.45
27	Norway	2.35	106	Lesotho	3.45
28	Korea, South	2.40	106	Madagascar	3.45
28	Kuwait	2.40	106	Russia	3.45
28	Malaysia	2.40	111	Burkina Faso	3.50
28	Panama	2.40	111	Cameroon	3.50
28	Thailand	2.40	111	Guyana	3.50
33	Sweden	2.45	111	Nicaragua	3.50
34	Argentina	2.50	115	Gambia	3.60
34	France	2.50	116	Croatia	3.65
34	Italy	2.50	116	Georgia	3.65
34	Spain	2.50	116	Malawi	3.65
38	Portugal	2.55	119	Cape Verde	3.67
38	Sri Lanka	2.55	120	Ethiopia	3.70
38	Trinidad and Tobago	2.55	120	India	3.70
41	Barbados	2.60	120	Niger	3.70
41	Peru	2.60	123	Congo	3.75
43	Bolivia	2.65	124	Chad	3.80
43	Mauritius	2.65	124	China	3.80
45	Cyprus	2.70	124	Mauritania	3.80
45	Jamaica	2.70	124	Ukraine	3.80
45	Uruguay	2.70	124	Zimbabwe	3.80
48	Botswana	2.75	129	Albania	3.85
48	Guatemala	2.75	129	Bangladesh	3.85
48	Jordan	2.75	129	Mozambique	3.85
48	Namibia	2.75	129	Suriname	3.85
48	Oman	2.75	133	Burundi	3.90
48	Philippines	2.75	134	Togo	3.95
54	Belize	2.80	135	Haiti	4.00
54	Costa Rica	2.80	135	Kyrgyz Rep.	4.00
54	Israel	2.80	137	Kazakhstan	4.05
54	Swaziland	2.80	137	Sierra Leone	4.05
54	Turkey	2.80	139	Yemen	4.10
54	Uganda	2.80	140	Belarus	4.15
54	Samoa	2.80	141	Sudan	4.20
61	Latvia	2.85	141	Syria	4.20
62	Greece	2.90	143	Azerbaijan	4.30
62	Hungary	2.90	143	Equatorial Guinea	4.30
62	So. Africa	2.90	143	Myanmar	4.30
65	Ecuador	2.95	143	Rwanda	4.30
65	Gabon	2.95	147	Tajikistan	4.40
65	Indonesia	2.95	147	Uzbekistan	4.40
65	Malta	2.95	149	Angola	4.45
65	Morocco	2.95	149	Turkmenistan	4.45
65	Poland	2.95	151	Guinea-Bissau	4.55
65	Tunisia	2.95	152	Vietnam	4.60
72	Ghana	3.00	153	Congo (Zaire)	4.70
72	Lithuania	3.00	153	Iran	4.70
72	Saudi Arabia	3.00	155	Bosnia	4.80
75	Benin	3.05	155	Somalia	4.80
75	Kenya	3.05	157	Iraq	4.90
75	Paraguay	3.05	157	Laos	4.90
75	Qatar	3.05	157	Libya	4.90
75	Slovak Republic	3.05	160	Cuba	5.00
75	Zambia	3.05	160	Korea, North	5.00
81	Colombia	3.10			

Mostly Unfree

foreign investment."[3] It does restrict the amount of real estate foreigners may own, however, still lacks in the rule of law, and needs an efficient investment approval regime. But by global standards, the barriers to foreign investment are moderate.

BANKING
Score: 2–Stable (low level of restrictions)

Lebanon's banking system is highly competitive and saturated with private banks. There are over 70 commercial banks. Foreign banks, however, may not open wholly owned branches.

WAGE AND PRICE CONTROLS
Score: 2–Stable (low level)

The market sets most wages and prices with very little government involvement, although the government's consumer protection agency can establish price controls.

PROPERTY RIGHTS
Score: 3–Stable (moderate level of protection)

The most significant threats to private property are the illegal activity and seizure of property by Syrian soldiers, the lack of an efficient legal system, and the inconsistent application of the rule of law. According to the U.S. Department of Commerce, "The legal system, modeled after the French, is being studied, and plans exist for modernization. New laws tend to follow international patterns. Court cases are not settled rapidly because of a shortage of judges and inadequate support structure. There is occasional government interference in the court system."[4]

REGULATION
Score: 3–Stable (moderate level)

Establishing a business in Lebanon is easy, but corruption and crime can hinder normal business operations. According to the U.S. Department of Commerce, "Unnecessary red tape is a problem in Lebanon.... It is widely believed that investors in many cases need to pay bribes to win contracts."[5]

BLACK MARKET
Score: 5–Stable (very high level of activity)

Lebanon's black market includes extensive trade in pirated intellectual property like trademarks, patents, and copyrights. Many services, such as transportation and construction, also are performed in the black market.

NOTES

[1] See International Monetary Fund, *Adjusting to New Realities: MENA, The Uruguay Round, and the EU-Mediterranean Initiative,* January 1997.

[2] U.S. Department of Commerce, *Country Commercial Guide,* 1998.

[3] *Ibid.*

[4] *Ibid.*

[5] *Ibid.*

Lesotho   3.45

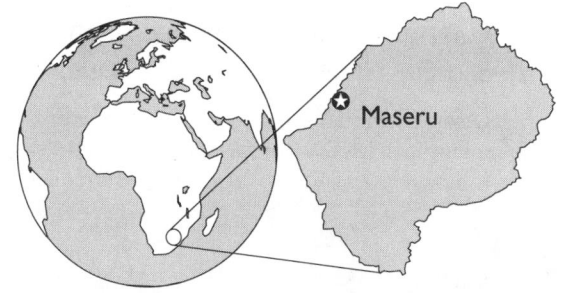

Maseru

| 1998 Score: **3.50** | 1997 Score: **3.65** | 1996 Score: **3.65** |

Trade	3	Banking	4
Taxation	3.5	Wages and Prices	4
Government Intervention	3	Property Rights	3
Monetary Policy	3	Regulation	4
Foreign Investment	3	Black Market	4

Lesotho gained its independence from the United Kingdom in 1966. It is a constitutional monarchy, but executive power has resided with the prime minister since the 1993 constitution stripped the king of such authority. The Lesotho Congress for Democracy won 78 of 80 seats in parliament in May 1998. Despite protests from opposition parties, international monitors declared the elections free and fair. Lesotho is encircled completely by South Africa and depends on it for access to trade and employment opportunities. Employment in the South African mines accounts for over 40 percent of Lesotho's GNP. The economy has grown at over 10 percent annually from 1994 to 1996. Lesotho recently reduced income taxes; as a result, its overall score has improved by 0.05 point over last year. Lesotho recently experienced considerable civil unrest stemming from allegations that the ruling party had rigged elections in May 1998.

TRADE POLICY
Score: 3–Stable (moderate level of protectionism)

The Southern African Customs Union, of which Lesotho is a member with South Africa, Botswana, Namibia, and Swaziland, has a common external tariff rate of 12 percent.

TAXATION
Score–Income taxation: 3+ (moderate tax rates)
Score–Corporate taxation: 3–Stable (moderate tax rates)
Final Taxation Score: 3.5+ (high tax rates)

Lesotho's top income tax rate is 35 percent, down from 40 percent last year. As a result, Lesotho's income tax score is 1 point better this year. The tax on the average income is 15 percent. The top marginal corporate tax rate is 35 percent. Because the income taxation score and the corporate taxation score are averaged, Lesotho's final taxation score is 0.5 point better this year. Lesotho also has a 35 percent capital gains tax and a 10 percent general services tax.

GOVERNMENT INTERVENTION IN THE ECONOMY
Score: 3–Stable (moderate level)

Government consumes about 20 percent of GDP, a significant portion of which is generated by the state-owned sector.

MONETARY POLICY
Score: 3–Stable (moderate level of inflation)

Lesotho's average annual rate of inflation from 1986 to 1996 was 11.9 percent. In 1997, inflation was 10 percent.

1	Hong Kong	1.25		81	Fiji	3.10
2	Singapore	1.30		81	Mali	3.10
3	Bahrain	1.70		81	Slovenia	3.10
4	New Zealand	1.75		85	Honduras	3.15
5	Switzerland	1.85		85	Mexico	3.15
6	United States	1.90		85	Papua New Guinea	3.15
7	Ireland	1.95		88	Djibouti	3.20
7	Luxembourg	1.95		88	Mongolia	3.20
7	Taiwan	1.95		90	Algeria	3.25
7	United Kingdom	1.95		90	Brazil	3.25
11	Bahamas	2.00		90	Lebanon	3.25
12	Czech Republic	2.05		90	Senegal	3.25
12	Japan	2.05		90	Tanzania	3.25
14	Australia	2.10		95	Nigeria	3.30
14	Belgium	2.10		95	Romania	3.30
14	Canada	2.10		97	Cambodia	3.35
14	United Arab Emirates	2.10		97	Dominican Republic	3.35
18	Austria	2.15		97	Egypt	3.35
18	Chile	2.15		97	Guinea	3.35
18	Estonia	2.15		97	Ivory Coast	3.35
18	Netherlands	2.15		97	Moldova	3.35
22	Denmark	2.25		97	Pakistan	3.35
22	El Salvador	2.25		104	Nepal	3.40
22	Finland	2.25		104	Venezuela	3.40
25	Germany	2.30		106	Armenia	3.45
25	Iceland	2.30		106	Bulgaria	3.45
27	Norway	2.35		106	Lesotho	3.45
28	Korea, South	2.40		106	Madagascar	3.45
28	Kuwait	2.40		106	Russia	3.45
28	Malaysia	2.40		111	Burkina Faso	3.50
28	Panama	2.40		111	Cameroon	3.50
28	Thailand	2.40		111	Guyana	3.50
33	Sweden	2.45		111	Nicaragua	3.50
34	Argentina	2.50		115	Gambia	3.60
34	France	2.50		116	Croatia	3.65
34	Italy	2.50		116	Georgia	3.65
34	Spain	2.50		116	Malawi	3.65
38	Portugal	2.55		119	Cape Verde	3.67
38	Sri Lanka	2.55		120	Ethiopia	3.70
38	Trinidad and Tobago	2.55		120	India	3.70
41	Barbados	2.60		120	Niger	3.70
41	Peru	2.60		123	Congo	3.75
43	Bolivia	2.65		124	Chad	3.80
43	Mauritius	2.65		124	China	3.80
45	Cyprus	2.70		124	Mauritania	3.80
45	Jamaica	2.70		124	Ukraine	3.80
45	Uruguay	2.70		124	Zimbabwe	3.80
48	Botswana	2.75		129	Albania	3.85
48	Guatemala	2.75		129	Bangladesh	3.85
48	Jordan	2.75		129	Mozambique	3.85
48	Namibia	2.75		129	Suriname	3.85
48	Oman	2.75		133	Burundi	3.90
48	Philippines	2.75		134	Togo	3.95
54	Belize	2.80		135	Haiti	4.00
54	Costa Rica	2.80		135	Kyrgyz Rep.	4.00
54	Israel	2.80		137	Kazakhstan	4.05
54	Swaziland	2.80		137	Sierra Leone	4.05
54	Turkey	2.80		139	Yemen	4.10
54	Uganda	2.80		140	Belarus	4.15
54	Samoa	2.80		141	Sudan	4.20
61	Latvia	2.85		141	Syria	4.20
62	Greece	2.90		143	Azerbaijan	4.30
62	Hungary	2.90		143	Equatorial Guinea	4.30
62	So. Africa	2.90		143	Myanmar	4.30
65	Ecuador	2.95		143	Rwanda	4.30
65	Gabon	2.95		147	Tajikistan	4.40
65	Indonesia	2.95		147	Uzbekistan	4.40
65	Malta	2.95		149	Angola	4.45
65	Morocco	2.95		149	Turkmenistan	4.45
65	Poland	2.95		151	Guinea-Bissau	4.55
65	Tunisia	2.95		152	Vietnam	4.60
72	Ghana	3.00		153	Congo (Zaire)	4.70
72	Lithuania	3.00		153	Iran	4.70
72	Saudi Arabia	3.00		155	Bosnia	4.80
75	Benin	3.05		155	Somalia	4.80
75	Kenya	3.05		157	Iraq	4.90
75	Paraguay	3.05		157	Laos	4.90
75	Qatar	3.05		157	Libya	4.90
75	Slovak Republic	3.05		160	Cuba	5.00
75	Zambia	3.05		160	Korea, North	5.00
81	Colombia	3.10				

Mostly Unfree

CAPITAL FLOWS AND FOREIGN INVESTMENT
Score: 3–Stable (moderate barriers)

Lesotho maintains some informal restrictions on investments in areas that compete with domestic local investment. It has an established investment code but offers few incentives.

BANKING
Score: 4–Stable (high level of restrictions)

The banking system is heavily regulated by the government, which also owns one of the country's largest banks. According to the U.S. Department of Commerce, "There are three commercial banks in Lesotho, each targeting a distinct niche market. One of the three is wholly owned, but not operated, by the government."[1] These banks enable the government to control a large portion of the banking industry's assets.

WAGE AND PRICE CONTROLS
Score: 4–Stable (high level)

Wages and prices are affected by the large state sector, which receives government subsidies. The government continues to set some prices on utilities, as well as on some agricultural goods.

PROPERTY RIGHTS
Score: 3–Stable (moderate level of protection)

Private property is guaranteed, and expropriation is unlikely. Foreigners, however, are not permitted to own land. As the U.S. Department of State reports, "The Constitution provides for an independent judiciary. However, magistrates appear to be subject at times to government and chieftainship influence."[2]

REGULATION
Score: 4–Stable (high level)

Establishing a business can be difficult if the business plans to compete directly with a state-owned company or government-sanctioned monopoly. Some corruption exists.

BLACK MARKET
Score: 4–Stable (high level of activity)

Lesotho has a substantial black market, primarily in consumer goods.

NOTES

1. U.S. Department of Commerce, *Country Commercial Guide,* 1998.
2. U.S. Department of State, "Lesotho Report on Human Rights Practices for 1997," 1998.

Libya   4.90

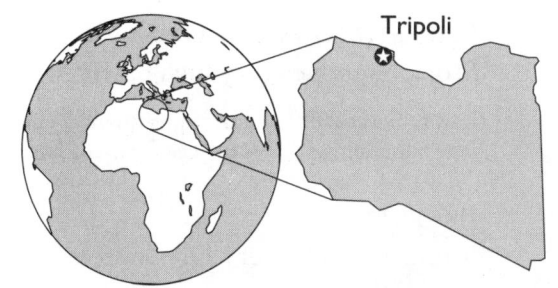
Tripoli

1998 Score: **4.70**   1997 Score: **4.70**   1996 Score: **4.70**

Trade	5	Banking	5
Taxation	5	Wages and Prices	5
Government Intervention	5	Property Rights	5
Monetary Policy	4	Regulation	5
Foreign Investment	5	Black Market	5

Libya's state-dominated socialist economy depends primarily on oil revenues, which contribute almost all export earnings and about one-third of GDP. In 1992, the United Nations imposed sanctions on Libya for its support of terrorist activities. Libya's dictator, Muammar Qadhafi, has hinted at mild economic reforms, but he remains hostile to capitalism and dedicated to quasi-Marxist economic theories. Libya remains one of the world's most economically repressed countries. Government mismanagement of the economy has caused inflation to soar; as a result, Libya's overall score is 0.2 point worse than last year.

TRADE POLICY
Score: 5–Stable (very high level of protectionism)

Libya's average tariff rate is over 18 percent, but tariffs represent only a small portion of the fees that importers generally must pay. If all these fees are taken into account, Libya's average tariff rate is over 34 percent.[1] The government controls almost all imports and exports, and it remains difficult to move goods and services across the border. The government also bans many imports, especially imports of goods like audio and video recordings that reflect Western culture. According to the U.S. Department of Commerce, "Import restrictions and inefficient resource allocations have led to periodic shortages of basic goods and foodstuffs."[2]

TAXATION
Score–Income taxation: 5–Stable (very high tax rates)
Score–Corporate taxation: 5–Stable (very high tax rates)
Final Taxation Score: 5–Stable (very high tax rates)

Libya's government maintains its dedication to the redistribution of wealth as well as its hostility to individual wealth. Its top income tax rate is 90 percent, with the average taxpayer in the 35 percent bracket. The top marginal corporate tax rate is 60 percent. Libya also has a 60 percent capital gains tax and a *jihad* (holy war) tax of up to 4 percent of income.

GOVERNMENT INTERVENTION IN THE ECONOMY
Score: 5–Stable (very high level)

Government produces nearly all GDP. The government controls some 70 percent of economic output.[3]

MONETARY POLICY
Score: 4– (high level of inflation)

Libya's average annual rate of inflation from 1990 to 1996 was 23.3 percent, up from 10 percent for the period 1990–1994. As a result, Libya's monetary policy score is 2 points worse than last year.[4]

1	Hong Kong	1.25	81	Fiji	3.10
2	Singapore	1.30	81	Mali	3.10
3	Bahrain	1.70	81	Slovenia	3.10
4	New Zealand	1.75	85	Honduras	3.15
5	Switzerland	1.85	85	Mexico	3.15
6	United States	1.90	85	Papua New Guinea	3.15
7	Ireland	1.95	88	Djibouti	3.20
7	Luxembourg	1.95	88	Mongolia	3.20
7	Taiwan	1.95	90	Algeria	3.25
7	United Kingdom	1.95	90	Brazil	3.25
11	Bahamas	2.00	90	Lebanon	3.25
12	Czech Republic	2.05	90	Senegal	3.25
12	Japan	2.05	90	Tanzania	3.25
14	Australia	2.10	95	Nigeria	3.30
14	Belgium	2.10	95	Romania	3.30
14	Canada	2.10	97	Cambodia	3.35
14	United Arab Emirates	2.10	97	Dominican Republic	3.35
18	Austria	2.15	97	Egypt	3.35
18	Chile	2.15	97	Guinea	3.35
18	Estonia	2.15	97	Ivory Coast	3.35
18	Netherlands	2.15	97	Moldova	3.35
22	Denmark	2.25	97	Pakistan	3.35
22	El Salvador	2.25	104	Nepal	3.40
22	Finland	2.25	104	Venezuela	3.40
25	Germany	2.30	106	Armenia	3.45
25	Iceland	2.30	106	Bulgaria	3.45
27	Norway	2.35	106	Lesotho	3.45
28	Korea, South	2.40	106	Madagascar	3.45
28	Kuwait	2.40	106	Russia	3.45
28	Malaysia	2.40	111	Burkina Faso	3.50
28	Panama	2.40	111	Cameroon	3.50
28	Thailand	2.40	111	Guyana	3.50
33	Sweden	2.45	111	Nicaragua	3.50
34	Argentina	2.50	115	Gambia	3.60
34	France	2.50	116	Croatia	3.65
34	Italy	2.50	116	Georgia	3.65
34	Spain	2.50	116	Malawi	3.65
38	Portugal	2.55	119	Cape Verde	3.67
38	Sri Lanka	2.55	120	Ethiopia	3.70
38	Trinidad and Tobago	2.55	120	India	3.70
41	Barbados	2.60	120	Niger	3.70
41	Peru	2.60	123	Congo	3.75
43	Bolivia	2.65	124	Chad	3.80
43	Mauritius	2.65	124	China	3.80
45	Cyprus	2.70	124	Mauritania	3.80
45	Jamaica	2.70	124	Ukraine	3.80
45	Uruguay	2.70	124	Zimbabwe	3.80
48	Botswana	2.75	129	Albania	3.85
48	Guatemala	2.75	129	Bangladesh	3.85
48	Jordan	2.75	129	Mozambique	3.85
48	Namibia	2.75	129	Suriname	3.85
48	Oman	2.75	133	Burundi	3.90
48	Philippines	2.75	134	Togo	3.95
54	Belize	2.80	135	Haiti	4.00
54	Costa Rica	2.80	135	Kyrgyz Rep.	4.00
54	Israel	2.80	137	Kazakhstan	4.05
54	Swaziland	2.80	137	Sierra Leone	4.05
54	Turkey	2.80	139	Yemen	4.10
54	Uganda	2.80	140	Belarus	4.15
54	Samoa	2.80	141	Sudan	4.20
61	Latvia	2.85	141	Syria	4.20
62	Greece	2.90	143	Azerbaijan	4.30
62	Hungary	2.90	143	Equatorial Guinea	4.30
62	So. Africa	2.90	143	Myanmar	4.30
65	Ecuador	2.95	143	Rwanda	4.30
65	Gabon	2.95	147	Tajikistan	4.40
65	Indonesia	2.95	147	Uzbekistan	4.40
65	Malta	2.95	149	Angola	4.45
65	Morocco	2.95	149	Turkmenistan	4.45
65	Poland	2.95	151	Guinea-Bissau	4.55
65	Tunisia	2.95	152	Vietnam	4.60
72	Ghana	3.00	153	Congo (Zaire)	4.70
72	Lithuania	3.00	153	Iran	4.70
72	Saudi Arabia	3.00	155	Bosnia	4.80
75	Benin	3.05	155	Somalia	4.80
75	Kenya	3.05	157	Iraq	4.90
75	Paraguay	3.05	157	Laos	4.90
75	Qatar	3.05	157	Libya	4.90
75	Slovak Republic	3.05	160	Cuba	5.00
75	Zambia	3.05	160	Korea, North	5.00
81	Colombia	3.10			

Repressed

CAPITAL FLOWS AND FOREIGN INVESTMENT
Score: 5–Stable (very high barriers)

Libya tolerates little foreign investment. In instances in which it is allowed, it is on a case-by-case basis.

BANKING
Score: 5–Stable (very high level of restrictions)

The government owns the entire banking system.

WAGE AND PRICE CONTROLS
Score: 5–Stable (very high level)

The government sets most wages and prices. According to the U.S. Department of State, "Despite efforts to diversify the economy and encourage private sector participation, the economy continues to be constrained by a system of extensive controls and regulations covering prices, credit, trade, and foreign exchange."[5]

PROPERTY RIGHTS
Score: 5–Stable (very low level of protection)

Private property is not legal in Libya, although there is growing tolerance of it as government officials often look the other way when individuals acquire property. The U.S. Department of State reports that the judiciary "is not independent from the government."[6]

REGULATION
Score: 5–Stable (very high level)

Establishing a business is nearly impossible. Although there is growing tolerance for some small private stores and shops, the government often makes it very difficult for private businesses to operate. According to the U.S. Department of Commerce, "The Government's mismanagement of the economy has caused high levels of inflation, increased import prices, and hampered economic expansion.... [M]uch of the country's income has been lost to waste [and] corruption."[7]

BLACK MARKET
Score: 5–Stable (very high level of activity)

Libya's black market is almost as large as its formal economy. Most consumer items must be smuggled into the country.

NOTES

[1] The 18 percent average tariff rate is based on total revenues from tariffs as a percentage of total imports. According to the World Bank, however, if total import charges for all products are taken into account, the rate increases to 34.7 percent. See World Bank, "Open Economies Work Better," *Policy Research Working Paper* No. 1636, August 1996.

[2] U.S. Department of Commerce, *Stat–USA* Internet site (*http://www.stat-usa.gov*).

[3] Quest Economics Database, "Libya: Africa Review 1998," Janet Matthews Information Services, March 1998.

[4] Figures for the average annual rate of inflation from 1986 to 1996 are not available.

[5] U.S. Department of State, "Libya Country Report on Human Rights Practices for 1997," 1998.

[6] *Ibid.*

[7] *Ibid.*

Lithuania   3.00

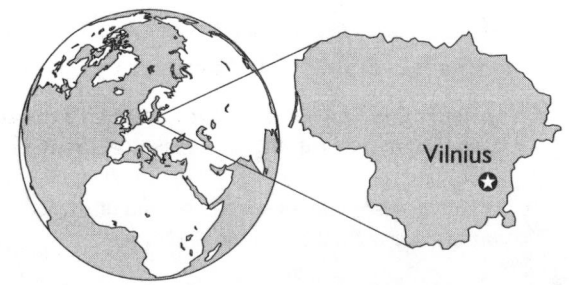

Vilnius

1998 Score: **3.00**	1997 Score: **3.10**	1996 Score: **3.50**

Trade	1	Banking	3
Taxation	3	Wages and Prices	3
Government Intervention	3	Property Rights	3
Monetary Policy	5	Regulation	3
Foreign Investment	2	Black Market	4

Independent from 1918 to 1940, at which time the Soviet Union forcibly annexed it, Lithuania regained its sovereignty in 1990. Since that time, it has undergone intensive economic reform. For example, the government has instituted a privatization program and is selling off some state-owned enterprises. Entrenched bureaucrats, former Communist Party officials, and large state-owned monopolies, however, have slowed the process of reform. In the 1997 elections, a conservative–nationalist party established a majority in parliament. Both President Valdas Adamkus, in office since January 1998, and Prime Minister Gediminas Vagnorius, in office since 1996, have indicated they will continue reforms and the integration of Lithuania into the European Union. Like many of its European neighbors, Lithuania relies heavily on aid from the World Bank, International Monetary Fund, European Bank for Reconstruction and Development, and U.S. Agency for International Development.

TRADE POLICY
Score: 1–Stable (very low level of protectionism)

Lithuania has reduced its average tariff to less than 2 percent.[1] It also raises no significant non-tariff barriers.

TAXATION
Score–Income taxation: 2–Stable (low tax rates)
Score–Corporate taxation: 3–Stable (moderate tax rates)
Final Taxation Score: 3–Stable (moderate tax rates)

Lithuania's top income tax rate is 33 percent; the average taxpayer is in the 10 percent bracket. The top marginal corporate tax rate is 29 percent. The government also imposes an 18 percent value-added tax and a 30 percent social security tax.

GOVERNMENT INTERVENTION IN THE ECONOMY
Score: 3–Stable (moderate level)

Government consumes 18.4 percent of GDP. The country's large state-owned sector accounts for about 30 percent of GDP.

MONETARY POLICY
Score: 5–Stable (very high level of inflation)

Lithuania's rate of inflation was 1,163 percent in 1992, 189 percent in 1993, 45 percent in 1994, 39.6 percent in 1995, 24.6 percent in 1996 and 8.4 percent in 1997. Even though the country has made great progress toward reducing inflation since 1992, the rate remains very high.

1	Hong Kong	1.25	81	Fiji	3.10
2	Singapore	1.30	81	Mali	3.10
3	Bahrain	1.70	81	Slovenia	3.10
4	New Zealand	1.75	85	Honduras	3.15
5	Switzerland	1.85	85	Mexico	3.15
6	United States	1.90	85	Papua New Guinea	3.15
7	Ireland	1.95	88	Djibouti	3.20
7	Luxembourg	1.95	88	Mongolia	3.20
7	Taiwan	1.95	90	Algeria	3.25
7	United Kingdom	1.95	90	Brazil	3.25
11	Bahamas	2.00	90	Lebanon	3.25
12	Czech Republic	2.05	90	Senegal	3.25
12	Japan	2.05	90	Tanzania	3.25
14	Australia	2.10	95	Nigeria	3.30
14	Belgium	2.10	95	Romania	3.30
14	Canada	2.10	97	Cambodia	3.35
14	United Arab Emirates	2.10	97	Dominican Republic	3.35
18	Austria	2.15	97	Egypt	3.35
18	Chile	2.15	97	Guinea	3.35
18	Estonia	2.15	97	Ivory Coast	3.35
18	Netherlands	2.15	97	Moldova	3.35
22	Denmark	2.25	97	Pakistan	3.35
22	El Salvador	2.25	104	Nepal	3.40
22	Finland	2.25	104	Venezuela	3.40
25	Germany	2.30	106	Armenia	3.45
25	Iceland	2.30	106	Bulgaria	3.45
27	Norway	2.35	106	Lesotho	3.45
28	Korea, South	2.40	106	Madagascar	3.45
28	Kuwait	2.40	106	Russia	3.45
28	Malaysia	2.40	111	Burkina Faso	3.50
28	Panama	2.40	111	Cameroon	3.50
28	Thailand	2.40	111	Guyana	3.50
33	Sweden	2.45	111	Nicaragua	3.50
34	Argentina	2.50	115	Gambia	3.60
34	France	2.50	116	Croatia	3.65
34	Italy	2.50	116	Georgia	3.65
34	Spain	2.50	116	Malawi	3.65
38	Portugal	2.55	119	Cape Verde	3.67
38	Sri Lanka	2.55	120	Ethiopia	3.70
38	Trinidad and Tobago	2.55	120	India	3.70
41	Barbados	2.60	120	Niger	3.70
41	Peru	2.60	123	Congo	3.75
43	Bolivia	2.65	124	Chad	3.80
43	Mauritius	2.65	124	China	3.80
45	Cyprus	2.70	124	Mauritania	3.80
45	Jamaica	2.70	124	Ukraine	3.80
45	Uruguay	2.70	124	Zimbabwe	3.80
48	Botswana	2.75	129	Albania	3.85
48	Guatemala	2.75	129	Bangladesh	3.85
48	Jordan	2.75	129	Mozambique	3.85
48	Namibia	2.75	129	Suriname	3.85
48	Oman	2.75	133	Burundi	3.90
48	Philippines	2.75	134	Togo	3.95
54	Belize	2.80	135	Haiti	4.00
54	Costa Rica	2.80	135	Kyrgyz Rep.	4.00
54	Israel	2.80	137	Kazakhstan	4.05
54	Swaziland	2.80	137	Sierra Leone	4.05
54	Turkey	2.80	139	Yemen	4.10
54	Uganda	2.80	140	Belarus	4.15
54	Samoa	2.80	141	Sudan	4.20
61	Latvia	2.85	141	Syria	4.20
62	Greece	2.90	143	Azerbaijan	4.30
62	Hungary	2.90	143	Equatorial Guinea	4.30
62	So. Africa	2.90	143	Myanmar	4.30
65	Ecuador	2.95	143	Rwanda	4.30
65	Gabon	2.95	147	Tajikistan	4.40
65	Indonesia	2.95	147	Uzbekistan	4.40
65	Malta	2.95	149	Angola	4.45
65	Morocco	2.95	149	Turkmenistan	4.45
65	Poland	2.95	151	Guinea-Bissau	4.55
65	Tunisia	2.95	152	Vietnam	4.60
72	Ghana	3.00	153	Congo (Zaire)	4.70
72	Lithuania	3.00	153	Iran	4.70
72	Saudi Arabia	3.00	155	Bosnia	4.80
75	Benin	3.05	155	Somalia	4.80
75	Kenya	3.05	157	Iraq	4.90
75	Paraguay	3.05	157	Laos	4.90
75	Qatar	3.05	157	Libya	4.90
75	Slovak Republic	3.05	160	Cuba	5.00
75	Zambia	3.05	160	Korea, North	5.00
81	Colombia	3.10			

Mostly Unfree

CAPITAL FLOWS AND FOREIGN INVESTMENT
Score: 2–Stable (low barriers)

Lithuania has moved quickly to open its market to foreign investment, and this presents many opportunities. Foreign companies are accorded the same treatment as domestic firms. Investments in such government-owned monopolies as utilities are not permitted, however.

BANKING
Score: 3–Stable (moderate level of restrictions)

Lithuania's banking system collapsed in 1995. In the assessment of the U.S. Department of Commerce, "The underlying weakness of [the] banking system became apparent in late December 1995 when followed by the collapse of a number of smaller banks, the Government imposed moratorium on [the] two largest commercial banks 'Litimpex' and 'Akcinis Inovacinis Bankas'. Unsustainable deposit interest payments, inadequate banking laws and regulations as well as risky lending practices and insider trading were the main factors causing the crisis."[2] The government passed legislation in June 1996, however, that aims to create more favorable conditions for banking. These new laws have helped to rebuild the country's banking system and bring about more stability. The government recently implemented new reserve requirements on foreign currency liabilities of commercial banks in order to make foreign borrowing more expensive. This new regulation hinders competition. Moreover, three large state-owned banks continue to compete directly with private banks.

WAGE AND PRICE CONTROLS
Score: 3–Stable (moderate level)

The government continues to set some wages and prices. For example, price controls remain on some agricultural products. Lithuania has a minimum wage.

PROPERTY RIGHTS
Score: 3–Stable (moderate level of protection)

A more efficient legal structure is providing better protection for private property. The court system, although sometimes slow, operates independently. The judiciary has yet to transform itself into a market-oriented system, however, and enforcement of contracts remains very weak.

REGULATION
Score: 3–Stable (moderate level)

Establishing a business can be easy if the business does not intend to compete directly with state-owned industries, and regulations are applied evenly in most cases. Lithuania has passed many new health and safety regulations that, if enforced, will prove burdensome, but these requirements are in line with those of other European countries. By general European standards, Lithuania's level of regulation is moderate.

BLACK MARKET
Score: 4–Stable (high level of activity)

The black market mainly involves the sale of goods and services that compete with state-owned industries. Consumer goods are sold on the black market as well. Lithuania maintains some protection of intellectual property and, according to the U.S. Department of Commerce, is considering the adoption of several new laws to protect copyrights and patents. Nevertheless, the level of black market activity in pirated computer software, compact discs, and prerecorded music and video tapes is substantial.

NOTES

[1]   Based on total taxes on international trade as a percentage of total imports.

[2]   U.S. Department of Commerce, *Country Commercial Guide,* 1998.

Luxembourg   1.95

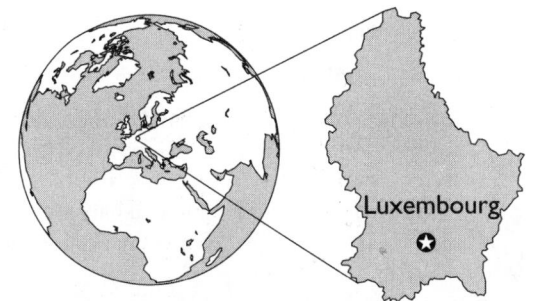

1998 Score: 1.95   **1997 Score: 2.05**   **1996 Score: 1.95**

Trade	2	Banking	2
Taxation	3.5	Wages and Prices	2
Government Intervention	3	Property Rights	1
Monetary Policy	1	Regulation	2
Foreign Investment	2	Black Market	1

Luxembourg, a constitutional monarchy, was recognized as a sovereign, independent state in 1839. Traditionally, Luxembourg had an agrarian society. Throughout most of the 20th century, however, it has developed into a manufacturing and services society and one of the world's richest and most highly industrialized countries. It is a member of the European Union (EU) and has a free and thriving economic system.

TRADE POLICY
Score: 2–Stable (low level of protectionism)

Luxembourg has an average tariff rate of less than 3 percent and maintains non-tariff barriers common to all EU countries, including restrictions on telecommunications, television, and broadcasting as well as quotas on agricultural products like bananas.

TAXATION
Score–Income taxation: 3-Stable (moderate tax rates)
Score–Corporate taxation: 3–Stable (moderate tax rates)
Final Taxation Score: 3.5-Stable (high tax rates)

Luxembourg's top income tax rate is 51.25 percent; the average taxpayer falls in the 14.54 percent bracket. The top marginal corporate tax rate is 30 percent, down from 32 percent in 1997 and from 33 percent in 1996. Luxembourg also has a 51.25 percent capital gains tax and a 15 percent value-added tax.

GOVERNMENT INTERVENTION IN THE ECONOMY
Score: 3–Stable (moderate level)

Government consumes 13.4 percent of GDP and, despite recent attempts to privatize portions of the economy, it remains entrenched in many sectors. The government continues to own and operate the railways, as well as the mail and telephone service (known as the P&T), and either owns or is a major shareholder in companies that provide banking, electricity, air transport, and financial services.

MONETARY POLICY
Score: 1–Stable (very low level of inflation)

Luxembourg's average rate of inflation from 1986 to 1996 was 3.6 percent. In 1997, the rate was 1.4 percent and remained below 2 percent for most of 1998.

CAPITAL FLOWS AND FOREIGN INVESTMENT
Score: 2–Stable (low barriers)

Luxembourg has a very open foreign investment regime. Foreign and domestic businesses receive equal treatment, and there are no local content requirements. The government restricts investments that directly affect national security, however, as well as those in some utilities.

1	Hong Kong	1.25	81	Fiji	3.10
2	Singapore	1.30	81	Mali	3.10
3	Bahrain	1.70	81	Slovenia	3.10
4	New Zealand	1.75	85	Honduras	3.15
5	Switzerland	1.85	85	Mexico	3.15
6	United States	1.90	85	Papua New Guinea	3.15
7	Ireland	1.95	88	Djibouti	3.20
7	Luxembourg	1.95	88	Mongolia	3.20
7	Taiwan	1.95	90	Algeria	3.25
7	United Kingdom	1.95	90	Brazil	3.25
11	Bahamas	2.00	90	Lebanon	3.25
12	Czech Republic	2.05	90	Senegal	3.25
12	Japan	2.05	90	Tanzania	3.25
14	Australia	2.10	95	Nigeria	3.30
14	Belgium	2.10	95	Romania	3.30
14	Canada	2.10	97	Cambodia	3.35
14	United Arab Emirates	2.10	97	Dominican Republic	3.35
18	Austria	2.15	97	Egypt	3.35
18	Chile	2.15	97	Guinea	3.35
18	Estonia	2.15	97	Ivory Coast	3.35
18	Netherlands	2.15	97	Moldova	3.35
22	Denmark	2.25	97	Pakistan	3.35
22	El Salvador	2.25	104	Nepal	3.40
22	Finland	2.25	104	Venezuela	3.40
25	Germany	2.30	106	Armenia	3.45
25	Iceland	2.30	106	Bulgaria	3.45
27	Norway	2.35	106	Lesotho	3.45
28	Korea, South	2.40	106	Madagascar	3.45
28	Kuwait	2.40	106	Russia	3.45
28	Malaysia	2.40	111	Burkina Faso	3.50
28	Panama	2.40	111	Cameroon	3.50
28	Thailand	2.40	111	Guyana	3.50
33	Sweden	2.45	111	Nicaragua	3.50
34	Argentina	2.50	115	Gambia	3.60
34	France	2.50	116	Croatia	3.65
34	Italy	2.50	116	Georgia	3.65
34	Spain	2.50	116	Malawi	3.65
38	Portugal	2.55	119	Cape Verde	3.67
38	Sri Lanka	2.55	120	Ethiopia	3.70
38	Trinidad and Tobago	2.55	120	India	3.70
41	Barbados	2.60	120	Niger	3.70
41	Peru	2.60	123	Congo	3.75
43	Bolivia	2.65	124	Chad	3.80
43	Mauritius	2.65	124	China	3.80
45	Cyprus	2.70	124	Mauritania	3.80
45	Jamaica	2.70	124	Ukraine	3.80
45	Uruguay	2.70	124	Zimbabwe	3.80
48	Botswana	2.75	129	Albania	3.85
48	Guatemala	2.75	129	Bangladesh	3.85
48	Jordan	2.75	129	Mozambique	3.85
48	Namibia	2.75	129	Suriname	3.85
48	Oman	2.75	133	Burundi	3.90
48	Philippines	2.75	134	Togo	3.95
54	Belize	2.80	135	Haiti	4.00
54	Costa Rica	2.80	135	Kyrgyz Rep.	4.00
54	Israel	2.80	137	Kazakhstan	4.05
54	Swaziland	2.80	137	Sierra Leone	4.05
54	Turkey	2.80	139	Yemen	4.10
54	Uganda	2.80	140	Belarus	4.15
54	Samoa	2.80	141	Sudan	4.20
61	Latvia	2.85	141	Syria	4.20
62	Greece	2.90	143	Azerbaijan	4.30
62	Hungary	2.90	143	Equatorial Guinea	4.30
62	So. Africa	2.90	143	Myanmar	4.30
65	Ecuador	2.95	143	Rwanda	4.30
65	Gabon	2.95	147	Tajikistan	4.40
65	Indonesia	2.95	147	Uzbekistan	4.40
65	Malta	2.95	149	Angola	4.45
65	Morocco	2.95	149	Turkmenistan	4.45
65	Poland	2.95	151	Guinea-Bissau	4.55
65	Tunisia	2.95	152	Vietnam	4.60
72	Ghana	3.00	153	Congo (Zaire)	4.70
72	Lithuania	3.00	153	Iran	4.70
72	Saudi Arabia	3.00	155	Bosnia	4.80
75	Benin	3.05	155	Somalia	4.80
75	Kenya	3.05	157	Iraq	4.90
75	Paraguay	3.05	157	Laos	4.90
75	Qatar	3.05	157	Libya	4.90
75	Slovak Republic	3.05	160	Cuba	5.00
75	Zambia	3.05	160	Korea, North	5.00
81	Colombia	3.10			

BANKING
Score: 2–Stable (low level of restrictions)

Banking is one of Luxembourg's largest industries: There are over 150 foreign banks in Luxembourg. The banking system is both highly competitive and subject to little government regulation, although banks are restricted in their ability to engage in some financial services like real estate.

WAGE AND PRICE CONTROLS
Score: 2–Stable (low level)

The market sets most wages and prices. Prices also are affected by such government policies as subsidies to the state-owned sector and direct price controls on energy.

PROPERTY RIGHTS
Score: 1–Stable (very high level of protection)

Private property is safe from government expropriation in Luxembourg. The legal and judicial system is advanced and efficient. According to the U.S. Department of State, "The judiciary provides citizens with a fair and efficient judicial process."[1]

REGULATION
Score: 2–Stable (low level)

Establishing a business in Luxembourg is simple. Regulations are applied evenly in most cases, and businesses generally are free to operate with minimal intrusion from the government.

BLACK MARKET
Score: 1–Stable (very low level of activity)

The black market in Luxembourg is almost nonexistent. Protection of intellectual property is strong, and there is little piracy.

Note
[1] U.S. Department of State, "Luxembourg Country Report on Human Rights Practices for 1997," 1998.

Madagascar   3.45

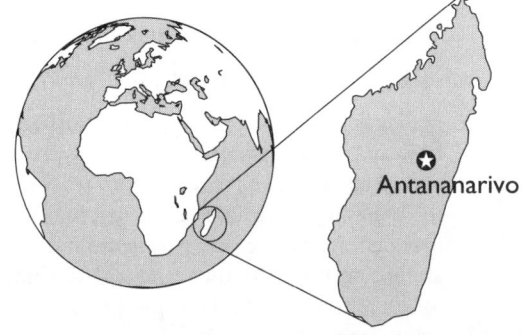

Antananarivo

1998 Score: **3.35**	1997 Score: **3.25**	1996 Score: **3.35**

Trade	5	Banking	4
Taxation	3.5	Wages and Prices	2
Government Intervention	2	Property Rights	3
Monetary Policy	4	Regulation	3
Foreign Investment	4	Black Market	4

Madagascar, the world's fourth-largest island, gained its independence from France in 1960. It has a mostly agrarian economy, with rice as its primary crop. Much of its agricultural industry is state-owned, although some large plots of land are privately owned. Former dictator Didier Ratsiraka was elected president in a widely criticized election in 1996. An advocate of socialism during his previous 16-year rule, President Ratsiraka claims to support economic liberalization, although substantial change has yet to materialize. Populist political opposition has been an impediment to liberalization, but some barriers to trade have been reduced. Three decades of slow economic growth have left Madagascar impoverished; the World Bank ranks it among the world's 10 poorest countries, with a GNP per capita of $250 in 1996. Economic growth has been poor, averaging 1.4 percent annually between 1992 and 1996 and not exceeding 2.01 percent during that time. Inflation is on the rise; as a result, Madagascar's overall score is 0.1 point worse than last year.

TRADE POLICY
Score: 5–Stable (very high level of protectionism)

Madagascar's average tariff rate is 29 percent.[1] There are no significant formal non-tariff barriers, except for a ban on the importation of pornographic materials.[2] Most non-tariff barriers exist in the form of an inefficient customs service and extensive bureaucracy.

TAXATION
Score–Income taxation: 3–Stable (moderate tax rates)
Score–Corporate taxation: 3–Stable (moderate tax rates)
Total Taxation Score: 3.5–Stable (high tax rates)

Madagascar's top income tax rate is 35 percent.[3] The top corporate income tax rate also is 35 percent. In addition, the island has a 25 percent value-added tax and a 45 percent excess profits tax.

GOVERNMENT INTERVENTION IN THE ECONOMY
Score: 2–Stable (low level)

Government consumes 6 percent of GDP. Despite some progress toward privatization, the state-owned sector remains large.

MONETARY POLICY
Score: 4– (high level of inflation)

Madagascar's average annual rate of inflation from 1986 to 1996 was 21.7 percent, up from 17 percent for the previous period. As a result, Madagascar's score in this factor is 1 point worse this year.

1	Hong Kong	1.25	81	Fiji	3.10
2	Singapore	1.30	81	Mali	3.10
3	Bahrain	1.70	81	Slovenia	3.10
4	New Zealand	1.75	85	Honduras	3.15
5	Switzerland	1.85	85	Mexico	3.15
6	United States	1.90	85	Papua New Guinea	3.15
7	Ireland	1.95	88	Djibouti	3.20
7	Luxembourg	1.95	88	Mongolia	3.20
7	Taiwan	1.95	90	Algeria	3.25
7	United Kingdom	1.95	90	Brazil	3.25
11	Bahamas	2.00	90	Lebanon	3.25
12	Czech Republic	2.05	90	Senegal	3.25
12	Japan	2.05	90	Tanzania	3.25
14	Australia	2.10	95	Nigeria	3.30
14	Belgium	2.10	95	Romania	3.30
14	Canada	2.10	97	Cambodia	3.35
14	United Arab Emirates	2.10	97	Dominican Republic	3.35
18	Austria	2.15	97	Egypt	3.35
18	Chile	2.15	97	Guinea	3.35
18	Estonia	2.15	97	Ivory Coast	3.35
18	Netherlands	2.15	97	Moldova	3.35
22	Denmark	2.25	97	Pakistan	3.35
22	El Salvador	2.25	104	Nepal	3.40
22	Finland	2.25	104	Venezuela	3.40
25	Germany	2.30	106	Armenia	3.45
25	Iceland	2.30	106	Bulgaria	3.45
27	Norway	2.35	106	Lesotho	3.45
28	Korea, South	2.40	106	Madagascar	3.45
28	Kuwait	2.40	106	Russia	3.45
28	Malaysia	2.40	111	Burkina Faso	3.50
28	Panama	2.40	111	Cameroon	3.50
28	Thailand	2.40	111	Guyana	3.50
33	Sweden	2.45	111	Nicaragua	3.50
34	Argentina	2.50	115	Gambia	3.60
34	France	2.50	116	Croatia	3.65
34	Italy	2.50	116	Georgia	3.65
34	Spain	2.50	116	Malawi	3.65
38	Portugal	2.55	119	Cape Verde	3.67
38	Sri Lanka	2.55	120	Ethiopia	3.70
38	Trinidad and Tobago	2.55	120	India	3.70
41	Barbados	2.60	120	Niger	3.70
41	Peru	2.60	123	Congo	3.75
43	Bolivia	2.65	124	Chad	3.80
43	Mauritius	2.65	124	China	3.80
45	Cyprus	2.70	124	Mauritania	3.80
45	Jamaica	2.70	124	Ukraine	3.80
45	Uruguay	2.70	124	Zimbabwe	3.80
48	Botswana	2.75	129	Albania	3.85
48	Guatemala	2.75	129	Bangladesh	3.85
48	Jordan	2.75	129	Mozambique	3.85
48	Namibia	2.75	129	Suriname	3.85
48	Oman	2.75	133	Burundi	3.90
48	Philippines	2.75	134	Togo	3.95
54	Belize	2.80	135	Haiti	4.00
54	Costa Rica	2.80	135	Kyrgyz Rep.	4.00
54	Israel	2.80	137	Kazakhstan	4.05
54	Swaziland	2.80	137	Sierra Leone	4.05
54	Turkey	2.80	139	Yemen	4.10
54	Uganda	2.80	140	Belarus	4.15
54	Samoa	2.80	141	Sudan	4.20
61	Latvia	2.85	141	Syria	4.20
62	Greece	2.90	143	Azerbaijan	4.30
62	Hungary	2.90	143	Equatorial Guinea	4.30
62	So. Africa	2.90	143	Myanmar	4.30
65	Ecuador	2.95	143	Rwanda	4.30
65	Gabon	2.95	147	Tajikistan	4.40
65	Indonesia	2.95	147	Uzbekistan	4.40
65	Malta	2.95	149	Angola	4.45
65	Morocco	2.95	149	Turkmenistan	4.45
65	Poland	2.95	151	Guinea-Bissau	4.55
65	Tunisia	2.95	152	Vietnam	4.60
72	Ghana	3.00	153	Congo (Zaire)	4.70
72	Lithuania	3.00	153	Iran	4.70
72	Saudi Arabia	3.00	155	Bosnia	4.80
75	Benin	3.05	155	Somalia	4.80
75	Kenya	3.05	157	Iraq	4.90
75	Paraguay	3.05	157	Laos	4.90
75	Qatar	3.05	157	Libya	4.90
75	Slovak Republic	3.05	160	Cuba	5.00
75	Zambia	3.05	160	Korea, North	5.00
81	Colombia	3.10			

Mostly Unfree

CAPITAL FLOWS AND FOREIGN INVESTMENT
Score: 4–Stable (high barriers)

Madagascar has a free trade zone. Outside this zone, however, foreign investors are not treated as well as domestic investors. There are restrictions on foreign investments in the banking and insurance, energy, water, hydrocarbon production, mining, and petroleum industries; foreigners are not permitted to own land; and the bureaucratic process for establishing a new enterprise is time-consuming and not transparent. There are political considerations to be weighed, and foreign investors must demonstrate the social value of their investments.

BANKING
Score: 4–Stable (high level of restrictions)

Only five banks operate on Madagascar. Both private banking and foreign investment are limited, and the banking system remains under strict government control, particularly in such areas as credit extension. The government still owns significant shares in some major banks, although two banks are undergoing privatization.

WAGE AND PRICE CONTROLS
Score: 2–Stable (low level)

The government has freed most prices and lifted administered prices for all agricultural goods except vanilla, but there is a consumer subsidy for wheat and flour. Madagascar has a minimum wage.

PROPERTY RIGHTS
Score: 3–Stable (moderate level of protection)

Property expropriation is unlikely. The current government slowly has been settling expropriations claims dating back to the 1970s. Private property, however, does not receive full legal protection in all cases because the legal system is sometimes inefficient. According to the U.S. Department of Commerce, "Investors in Madagascar face a legal environment in which the security of private property and the enforcement of contracts is inadequately protected by the judicial system."[4] Thus, by global standards, the level of property rights protection is moderate.

REGULATION
Score: 3–Stable (moderate level)

The government maintains moderate regulations on Madagascar's economy. Obtaining business licenses and permits often involves bribery, and the bureaucracy tends to operate in a capricious manner. According to the U.S. Department of Commerce, "Madagascar has laws to combat corruption but they are not efficiently enforced. Corruption is most pervasive in the administrative sector (project approval, government procurements, judicial matters, etc.)."[5]

BLACK MARKET
Score: 4–Stable (high level of activity)

Madagascar has a large black market because of high tariffs and government controls, although the removal of most price controls has reduced the size of the informal economy in recent years. Intellectual property rights are not fully protected; according to the U.S. Department of Commerce, "Major brand names and franchise rights are respected, but pirated copies of videotaped movies and music cassettes sell openly."[6]

NOTES

[1] World Bank, *World Development Indicators,* 1998.

[2] U.S. Department of Commerce, *Country Commercial Guide,* 1998.

[3] It is not possible to determine the tax on the average income level. Therefore, Madagascar's score is based on its top income tax rate.

[4] U.S. Department of Commerce, *Country Commercial Guide,* 1998.

[5] *Ibid.*

[6] *Ibid.*

Malawi   3.65

1998 Score: **3.65**	1997 Score: **3.55**	1996 Score: **3.40**

Trade	5	Banking	3
Taxation	4.5	Wages and Prices	3
Government Intervention	3	Property Rights	3
Monetary Policy	4	Regulation	4
Foreign Investment	3	Black Market	4

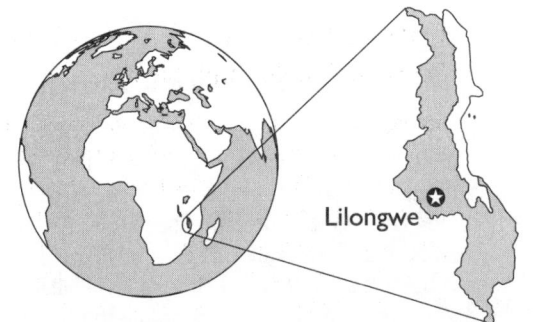

Lilongwe

Malawi gained its independence from the United Kingdom in 1964. During the rest of that decade and into the 1970s, it used increased agricultural production as an engine for economic growth. GDP more than doubled, with annual growth rates of 3 percent. The economy sank into a deep recession in the 1980s, however, as drought brought widespread agricultural depression and refugees from the civil war in nearby Mozambique flowed into the country. GDP growth was poor during the 1980s, averaging just 1.4 percent annually. Malawi's heavily agricultural economy has been characterized by dramatic performance swings in the 1990s; the economy contracted 7.9 percent in 1992 and 12.4 percent in 1994 before growing about 10 percent in 1993, 1995, and 1996. Tentative plans to privatize state-owned enterprises have been announced.

TRADE POLICY
Score: 5–Stable (very high level of protectionism)

Malawi's average tariff rate is 23.5 percent. Non-tariff barriers include strict import licenses on imports of fresh meat, gold, sugar, and military and hunting items.

TAXATION
Score–Income taxation: 4–Stable (high tax rates)
Score–Corporate taxation: 4–Stable (high tax rates)
Final Taxation Score: 4.5–Stable (very high tax rates)

The top income tax rate is 38 percent.[1] The top corporate tax rate is 38 percent. Malawi also levies municipal taxes, a border tax, and a capital gains tax.

GOVERNMENT INTERVENTION IN THE ECONOMY
Score: 3–Stable (moderate level)

Government consumes 22.7 percent of GDP. Malawi has a large public sector that operates marketing boards for some agricultural products. These boards allow the government to confiscate crops, pay lower-than-market-value prices for them, and then export them at higher prices, keeping the profits. According to the U.S. Department of Commerce, "The Government emphasizes a facilitative rather than a regulatory role in economic activities. However, government ownership/control of much of the modern economy deters private investment."[2]

MONETARY POLICY
Score: 4–Stable (high level of inflation)

Malawi's average annual rate of inflation from 1986 to 1996 was 26.6 percent. In 1997, the rate was 22 percent.

1	Hong Kong	1.25	81	Fiji	3.10
2	Singapore	1.30	81	Mali	3.10
3	Bahrain	1.70	81	Slovenia	3.10
4	New Zealand	1.75	85	Honduras	3.15
5	Switzerland	1.85	85	Mexico	3.15
6	United States	1.90	85	Papua New Guinea	3.15
7	Ireland	1.95	88	Djibouti	3.20
7	Luxembourg	1.95	88	Mongolia	3.20
7	Taiwan	1.95	90	Algeria	3.25
7	United Kingdom	1.95	90	Brazil	3.25
11	Bahamas	2.00	90	Lebanon	3.25
12	Czech Republic	2.05	90	Senegal	3.25
12	Japan	2.05	90	Tanzania	3.25
14	Australia	2.10	95	Nigeria	3.30
14	Belgium	2.10	95	Romania	3.30
14	Canada	2.10	97	Cambodia	3.35
14	United Arab Emirates	2.10	97	Dominican Republic	3.35
18	Austria	2.15	97	Egypt	3.35
18	Chile	2.15	97	Guinea	3.35
18	Estonia	2.15	97	Ivory Coast	3.35
18	Netherlands	2.15	97	Moldova	3.35
22	Denmark	2.25	97	Pakistan	3.35
22	El Salvador	2.25	104	Nepal	3.40
22	Finland	2.25	104	Venezuela	3.40
25	Germany	2.30	106	Armenia	3.45
25	Iceland	2.30	106	Bulgaria	3.45
27	Norway	2.35	106	Lesotho	3.45
28	Korea, South	2.40	106	Madagascar	3.45
28	Kuwait	2.40	106	Russia	3.45
28	Malaysia	2.40	111	Burkina Faso	3.50
28	Panama	2.40	111	Cameroon	3.50
28	Thailand	2.40	111	Guyana	3.50
33	Sweden	2.45	111	Nicaragua	3.50
34	Argentina	2.50	115	Gambia	3.60
34	France	2.50	116	Croatia	3.65
34	Italy	2.50	116	Georgia	3.65
34	Spain	2.50	116	Malawi	3.65
38	Portugal	2.55	119	Cape Verde	3.67
38	Sri Lanka	2.55	120	Ethiopia	3.70
38	Trinidad and Tobago	2.55	120	India	3.70
41	Barbados	2.60	120	Niger	3.70
41	Peru	2.60	123	Congo	3.75
43	Bolivia	2.65	124	Chad	3.80
43	Mauritius	2.65	124	China	3.80
45	Cyprus	2.70	124	Mauritania	3.80
45	Jamaica	2.70	124	Ukraine	3.80
45	Uruguay	2.70	124	Zimbabwe	3.80
48	Botswana	2.75	129	Albania	3.85
48	Guatemala	2.75	129	Bangladesh	3.85
48	Jordan	2.75	129	Mozambique	3.85
48	Namibia	2.75	129	Suriname	3.85
48	Oman	2.75	133	Burundi	3.90
48	Philippines	2.75	134	Togo	3.95
54	Belize	2.80	135	Haiti	4.00
54	Costa Rica	2.80	135	Kyrgyz Rep.	4.00
54	Israel	2.80	137	Kazakhstan	4.05
54	Swaziland	2.80	137	Sierra Leone	4.05
54	Turkey	2.80	139	Yemen	4.10
54	Uganda	2.80	140	Belarus	4.15
54	Samoa	2.80	141	Sudan	4.20
61	Latvia	2.85	141	Syria	4.20
62	Greece	2.90	143	Azerbaijan	4.30
62	Hungary	2.90	143	Equatorial Guinea	4.30
62	So. Africa	2.90	143	Myanmar	4.30
65	Ecuador	2.95	143	Rwanda	4.30
65	Gabon	2.95	147	Tajikistan	4.40
65	Indonesia	2.95	147	Uzbekistan	4.40
65	Malta	2.95	149	Angola	4.45
65	Morocco	2.95	149	Turkmenistan	4.45
65	Poland	2.95	151	Guinea-Bissau	4.55
65	Tunisia	2.95	152	Vietnam	4.60
72	Ghana	3.00	153	Congo (Zaire)	4.70
72	Lithuania	3.00	153	Iran	4.70
72	Saudi Arabia	3.00	155	Bosnia	4.80
75	Benin	3.05	155	Somalia	4.80
75	Kenya	3.05	157	Iraq	4.90
75	Paraguay	3.05	157	Laos	4.90
75	Qatar	3.05	157	Libya	4.90
75	Slovak Republic	3.05	160	Cuba	5.00
75	Zambia	3.05	160	Korea, North	5.00
81	Colombia	3.10			

Mostly Unfree

CAPITAL FLOWS AND FOREIGN INVESTMENT
Score: 3–Stable (moderate barriers)

The government encourages foreign investment in industries that produce goods for export. Thus, it does not restrict foreign investment in the coffee, sugar, or tea industries. Non-citizens must obtain labor licenses to work in Malawi, and these licenses are not granted if the government determines that Malawi citizens are available and able to do the work. For example, according to the U.S. Department of Commerce, "Under the Immigration Act, foreign nationals who work or invest in Malawi must have either a visitors' permit; business visitors' permit; temporary residence permit; temporary employment permit (TEP); or a business residence permit. TEPs have become a major impediment to foreign investment. The processing of applications is slow and inconsistent, and the government's longstanding commitment to streamline the process has yet to produce noticeable results."[3]

BANKING
Score: 3–Stable (moderate level of restrictions)

Only a few banks are free of government ownership. Although the government released interest rates in 1992, it still exercises a great deal of control over the financial system. Malawi plans to allow two foreign banks to open in the near future.

WAGE AND PRICE CONTROLS
Score: 3–Stable (moderate level)

The government has lifted price controls on almost all products, although those on some food items and energy remain in effect. Malawi has a minimum wage.

PROPERTY RIGHTS
Score: 3–Stable (moderate level of protection)

Malawi has begun a huge privatization program aimed at selling its largest state-owned enterprises. Despite plans to eliminate them, however, marketing boards still control the sale of such agricultural products as corn and fertilizer. The court system, while independent, is inefficient. The U.S. Department of Commerce reports that "Malawi has a fairly independent but overburdened judiciary system which derives its procedures from English Common Law.... It is commonly accepted that administration of the courts is weak, and due process can be very slow."

REGULATION
Score: 4–Stable (high level)

The government heavily regulates the sale of such agricultural products as corn and fertilizer. It also enforces health and safety regulations erratically, causing confusion among businesses. Corruption is becoming more prevalent. According to the U.S. Department of Commerce, "[P]rocedural delays, red tape, and corrupt practices continue to impede the business and investment approval process. These include decision making which is often neither transparent nor based purely on merit; land access approvals, and slow and arbitrary processing of expatriate work permits."[4]

BLACK MARKET
Score: 4–Stable (high level of activity)

Because the government strictly controls the importation of food, there is a huge black market in such items as eggs and poultry, which often are imported illegally. Because the government provides insufficient legal protection for intellectual property rights, there is a rather large black market in pirated computer software and recorded music and video.

NOTES
[1] The tax on the average income level is unavailable. Therefore, the income tax score is based solely on the top rate.
[2] U.S. Department of Commerce, *Country Commercial Guide*, 1998.
[3] *Ibid.*
[4] U.S. Department of Commerce, "Malawi, Investment Climate," *Market Research Reports*, June 12, 1997.

Malaysia   2.40

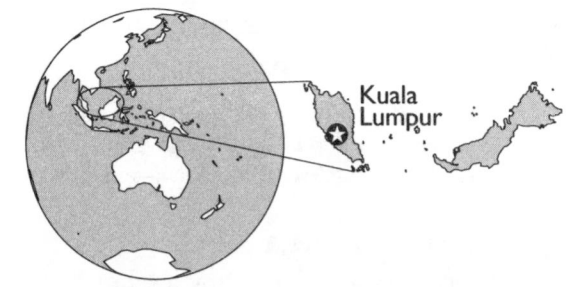

Kuala Lumpur

1998 Score: **2.40**	1997 Score: **2.60**	1996 Score: **2.40**

Trade	3	Banking	3
Taxation	3	Wages and Prices	3
Government Intervention	2	Property Rights	2
Monetary Policy	1	Regulation	2
Foreign Investment	3	Black Market	2

Malaysia gained its independence from the United Kingdom in 1957. In 1963, Singapore, Sarawak, and Sabah (North Borneo) joined the Federation of Malaya to form Malaysia. (Singapore withdrew in 1964 to become an independent country.) Although Malaysia experienced civil unrest in its early years, recent governments have moved to address the sources of ethnic and social tension and thus have enhanced political stability. Economic reforms begun in the 1970s have helped Malaysia to develop a more open market economy. Malaysia's economy has been embroiled in the Asian financial crisis, however, suffering from a devalued currency and growing debt. Unlike other countries affected by the crisis, Malaysia has refused aid from the International Monetary Fund. In September 1998, Prime Minister Mahathir Mohamed fired his deputy, Anwar Ibrahim, who had been closely associated with the market reforms opposed by Mahathir. The subsequent arrest and brutal mistreatment of Anwar have prompted widespread protest. Also in September 1998, the government announced it would impose a series of foreign-exchange control regulations, including an immediate end to the trading of Malaysia's currency, the ringgit, outside the country. Thus, individuals holding ringgits no longer have the ability to exchange them for U.S. dollars, German marks, or other hard currencies. This represents a significant foreign investment barrier. These events occurred after the cutoff date for consideration in this edition of the *Index of Economic Freedom*, however; had this information been included in this edition, Malaysia surely would have received a worse score. If these events remain unchanged—or worsen—they will be reflected in next year's score.

TRADE POLICY

Score: 3–Stable (moderate level of protectionism)

Malaysia's average trade-weighted tariff rate has decreased to less than 6.4 percent, according to the U.S. Department of State.[1] Non-tariff barriers include import bans, licensing requirements, and strict labeling requirements. For example, according to the Office of the United States Trade Representative, "Tariffs are the main instrument used to regulate the importation of goods in Malaysia. However, 17 percent of Malaysia's tariff lines (principally in the construction equipment, forestry, logging, agricultural, mineral, and motor vehicle sectors) are also subject to non-automatic import licensing designed to protect import-sensitive or strategic industries."[2]

TAXATION

Score–Income taxation: 2–Stable (low tax rates)
Score–Corporate taxation: 3–Stable (moderate tax rates)
Total Taxation Score: 3–Stable (moderate tax rates)

Malaysia's top income tax rate is 30 percent, down from 32 percent last year; the average income level is taxed at 6 percent. The top corporate tax is 28 percent, down from 30 percent in 1997. Malaysia also levies a sales tax between 10 percent and 15 percent. Neither of these tax reductions is significant enough to result in a score change.

1	Hong Kong	1.25	81	Fiji	3.10
2	Singapore	1.30	81	Mali	3.10
3	Bahrain	1.70	81	Slovenia	3.10
4	New Zealand	1.75	85	Honduras	3.15
5	Switzerland	1.85	85	Mexico	3.15
6	United States	1.90	85	Papua New Guinea	3.15
7	Ireland	1.95	88	Djibouti	3.20
7	Luxembourg	1.95	88	Mongolia	3.20
7	Taiwan	1.95	90	Algeria	3.25
7	United Kingdom	1.95	90	Brazil	3.25
11	Bahamas	2.00	90	Lebanon	3.25
12	Czech Republic	2.05	90	Senegal	3.25
12	Japan	2.05	90	Tanzania	3.25
14	Australia	2.10	95	Nigeria	3.30
14	Belgium	2.10	95	Romania	3.30
14	Canada	2.10	97	Cambodia	3.35
14	United Arab Emirates	2.10	97	Dominican Republic	3.35
18	Austria	2.15	97	Egypt	3.35
18	Chile	2.15	97	Guinea	3.35
18	Estonia	2.15	97	Ivory Coast	3.35
18	Netherlands	2.15	97	Moldova	3.35
22	Denmark	2.25	97	Pakistan	3.35
22	El Salvador	2.25	104	Nepal	3.40
22	Finland	2.25	104	Venezuela	3.40
25	Germany	2.30	106	Armenia	3.45
25	Iceland	2.30	106	Bulgaria	3.45
27	Norway	2.35	106	Lesotho	3.45
28	Korea, South	2.40	106	Madagascar	3.45
28	Kuwait	2.40	106	Russia	3.45
28	Malaysia	2.40	111	Burkina Faso	3.50
28	Panama	2.40	111	Cameroon	3.50
28	Thailand	2.40	111	Guyana	3.50
33	Sweden	2.45	111	Nicaragua	3.50
34	Argentina	2.50	115	Gambia	3.60
34	France	2.50	116	Croatia	3.65
34	Italy	2.50	116	Georgia	3.65
34	Spain	2.50	116	Malawi	3.65
38	Portugal	2.55	119	Cape Verde	3.67
38	Sri Lanka	2.55	120	Ethiopia	3.70
38	Trinidad and Tobago	2.55	120	India	3.70
41	Barbados	2.60	120	Niger	3.70
41	Peru	2.60	123	Congo	3.75
43	Bolivia	2.65	124	Chad	3.80
43	Mauritius	2.65	124	China	3.80
45	Cyprus	2.70	124	Mauritania	3.80
45	Jamaica	2.70	124	Ukraine	3.80
45	Uruguay	2.70	124	Zimbabwe	3.80
48	Botswana	2.75	129	Albania	3.85
48	Guatemala	2.75	129	Bangladesh	3.85
48	Jordan	2.75	129	Mozambique	3.85
48	Namibia	2.75	129	Suriname	3.85
48	Oman	2.75	133	Burundi	3.90
48	Philippines	2.75	134	Togo	3.95
54	Belize	2.80	135	Haiti	4.00
54	Costa Rica	2.80	135	Kyrgyz Rep.	4.00
54	Israel	2.80	137	Kazakhstan	4.05
54	Swaziland	2.80	137	Sierra Leone	4.05
54	Turkey	2.80	139	Yemen	4.10
54	Uganda	2.80	140	Belarus	4.15
54	Samoa	2.80	141	Sudan	4.20
61	Latvia	2.85	141	Syria	4.20
62	Greece	2.90	143	Azerbaijan	4.30
62	Hungary	2.90	143	Equatorial Guinea	4.30
62	So. Africa	2.90	143	Myanmar	4.30
65	Ecuador	2.95	143	Rwanda	4.30
65	Gabon	2.95	147	Tajikistan	4.40
65	Indonesia	2.95	147	Uzbekistan	4.40
65	Malta	2.95	149	Angola	4.45
65	Morocco	2.95	149	Turkmenistan	4.45
65	Poland	2.95	151	Guinea-Bissau	4.55
65	Tunisia	2.95	152	Vietnam	4.60
72	Ghana	3.00	153	Congo (Zaire)	4.70
72	Lithuania	3.00	153	Iran	4.70
72	Saudi Arabia	3.00	155	Bosnia	4.80
75	Benin	3.05	155	Somalia	4.80
75	Kenya	3.05	157	Iraq	4.90
75	Paraguay	3.05	157	Laos	4.90
75	Qatar	3.05	157	Libya	4.90
75	Slovak Republic	3.05	160	Cuba	5.00
75	Zambia	3.05	160	Korea, North	5.00
81	Colombia	3.10			

Mostly Free

GOVERNMENT INTERVENTION IN THE ECONOMY
Score: 2–Stable (low level)

Government consumes 12.7 percent of GDP, down from 13.5 percent one year ago. The government still has many holdings among several companies and industries.

MONETARY POLICY
Score: 1–Stable (very low level of inflation)

The average annual rate of inflation from 1986 to 1996 was 2.95 percent. In 1997, the rate was 2.6 percent.

CAPITAL FLOWS AND FOREIGN INVESTMENT
Score: 3–Stable (moderate barriers)

Malaysia is relatively open to foreign investment. Most restrictions apply to investments in utilities and industries considered essential to national security, although the government also restricts foreign participation in such services as law, architecture, and banking.

BANKING
Score: 3–Stable (moderate level of restrictions)

Competition in the banking industry is limited by government restrictions that prevent banks from providing a full range of financial services. The government also limits foreign participation in banking.

WAGE AND PRICE CONTROLS
Score: 3–Stable (moderate level)

The market determines most wages and prices, although the government has added price controls on key goods and maintains controls on the prices of fuel, public utilities, motor vehicles, rice, flour, sugar, and tobacco. Malaysia has a minimum wage.

PROPERTY RIGHTS
Score: 2–Stable (high level of protection)

Protection of private property by the courts sometimes is lax. According to some private-sector complaints, there is a "widening web of patronage and privilege between some influential politicians and private business groups."[3] This has created an incentive for the government to expropriate private property, give compensation for it at levels below the market, and then use government-owned development firms to develop it for a profit. In one recent case, the government expropriated 6,520 acres from a private company and offered compensation equal to only 25 percent of the property's market value. Such occurrences, however, represent the exception to an otherwise high level of protection of private property.

REGULATION
Score: 2–Stable (low level)

Malaysia has eliminated the majority of its most burdensome regulations. Its regulatory regime is efficient and relatively free of corruption. According to the U.S. Department of Commerce, "Malaysia has an open system of Government economic and business regulation."[4]

BLACK MARKET
Score: 2–Stable (low level of activity)

The level of black market activity is minimal. Most services are supplied legally, and there is little incentive to engage in the black market. There is a small but growing black market in such pirated intellectual property as computer software and music and video tapes.

NOTES

1   U.S. Department of State, *Country Reports on Economic Policy and Trade Practices,* 1997, p. 54.
2   Office of the United States Trade Representative, *National Trade Estimate Report on Foreign Trade Barriers,* 1998.
3   See Raphael Pura, "Property Firms' Suit Against Malaysian State Spotlights Controversial Land Acquisition Law," *Asian Wall Street Journal,* June 19, 1995, p. 1.
4   U.S. Department of Commerce, *Country Commercial Guide,* 1998.

Mali 3.10

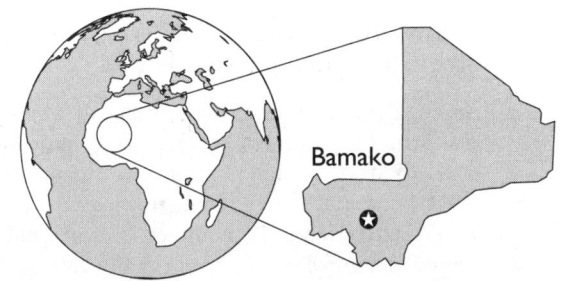

Bamako

1998 Score: **3.10**	1997 Score: **3.10**	1996 Score: **3.10**

Trade	3	Banking	3
Taxation	5	Wages and Prices	3
Government Intervention	3	Property Rights	3
Monetary Policy	1	Regulation	3
Foreign Investment	2	Black Market	5

Mali, a vast and sparsely populated country, is also one of the world's poorest, with a per capita GDP of only $240 in 1996. Mali gained independence from France in 1960 and immediately adopted socialist economic policies under the leadership of President Modibo Keita. After years of state-dominated economic policy, however, the country is beginning to rely more on the market for everyday economic decisions. Its predominantly agrarian economy has improved recently, with GDP growth averaging 4.95 percent from 1994 to 1997 after contracting 4.5 percent in 1993. Mali held its second presidential election in June 1997; Apha Oumar Konare emerged as the winner. Although judged to be free and fair by international observers, the election was contested by a number of political parties, and partisan quibbling has stalled the political process.

TRADE POLICY
Score: 3–Stable (moderate level of protectionism)

Mali's average tariff rate is about 10 percent. The government also uses a complex system of "fiscal duties" ranging from 5 percent to 30 percent.[1] Most import barriers have been lifted, although import licenses still are required. Import taxes on many goods were lowered or eliminated in 1994.

TAXATION
Score–Income taxation: 4–Stable (high tax rates)
Score–Corporate taxation: 5–Stable (very high tax rates)
Final Taxation Score: 5–Stable (very high tax rates)

Mali's top income and corporate tax rates are over 50 percent.[2] The government also levies a capital gains tax and a turnover tax.

GOVERNMENT INTERVENTION IN THE ECONOMY
Score: 3–Stable (moderate level)

Government consumes 10.6 percent of GDP. The state sector is dominant, but several state enterprises have been liquidated or privatized over the past few years.

MONETARY POLICY
Score: 1–Stable (very low level of inflation)

Mali's average annual rate of inflation from 1986 to 1996 was 5.8 percent. Inflation currently is running at 3 percent.

CAPITAL FLOWS AND FOREIGN INVESTMENT
Score: 2–Stable (low barriers)

The government has an established investment code and permits investment in almost all areas. Foreign investors are offered some incentives and face few restrictions. Because of its poor economic state, Mali has received very little foreign investment to date, although there has been an upturn in recent years.

1	Hong Kong	1.25	81	Fiji	3.10
2	Singapore	1.30	81	Mali	3.10
3	Bahrain	1.70	81	Slovenia	3.10
4	New Zealand	1.75	85	Honduras	3.15
5	Switzerland	1.85	85	Mexico	3.15
6	United States	1.90	85	Papua New Guinea	3.15
7	Ireland	1.95	88	Djibouti	3.20
7	Luxembourg	1.95	88	Mongolia	3.20
7	Taiwan	1.95	90	Algeria	3.25
7	United Kingdom	1.95	90	Brazil	3.25
11	Bahamas	2.00	90	Lebanon	3.25
12	Czech Republic	2.05	90	Senegal	3.25
12	Japan	2.05	90	Tanzania	3.25
14	Australia	2.10	95	Nigeria	3.30
14	Belgium	2.10	95	Romania	3.30
14	Canada	2.10	97	Cambodia	3.35
14	United Arab Emirates	2.10	97	Dominican Republic	3.35
18	Austria	2.15	97	Egypt	3.35
18	Chile	2.15	97	Guinea	3.35
18	Estonia	2.15	97	Ivory Coast	3.35
18	Netherlands	2.15	97	Moldova	3.35
22	Denmark	2.25	97	Pakistan	3.35
22	El Salvador	2.25	104	Nepal	3.40
22	Finland	2.25	104	Venezuela	3.40
25	Germany	2.30	106	Armenia	3.45
25	Iceland	2.30	106	Bulgaria	3.45
27	Norway	2.35	106	Lesotho	3.45
28	Korea, South	2.40	106	Madagascar	3.45
28	Kuwait	2.40	106	Russia	3.45
28	Malaysia	2.40	111	Burkina Faso	3.50
28	Panama	2.40	111	Cameroon	3.50
28	Thailand	2.40	111	Guyana	3.50
33	Sweden	2.45	111	Nicaragua	3.50
34	Argentina	2.50	115	Gambia	3.60
34	France	2.50	116	Croatia	3.65
34	Italy	2.50	116	Georgia	3.65
34	Spain	2.50	116	Malawi	3.65
38	Portugal	2.55	119	Cape Verde	3.67
38	Sri Lanka	2.55	120	Ethiopia	3.70
38	Trinidad and Tobago	2.55	120	India	3.70
41	Barbados	2.60	120	Niger	3.70
41	Peru	2.60	123	Congo	3.75
43	Bolivia	2.65	124	Chad	3.80
43	Mauritius	2.65	124	China	3.80
45	Cyprus	2.70	124	Mauritania	3.80
45	Jamaica	2.70	124	Ukraine	3.80
45	Uruguay	2.70	124	Zimbabwe	3.80
48	Botswana	2.75	129	Albania	3.85
48	Guatemala	2.75	129	Bangladesh	3.85
48	Jordan	2.75	129	Mozambique	3.85
48	Namibia	2.75	129	Suriname	3.85
48	Oman	2.75	133	Burundi	3.90
48	Philippines	2.75	134	Togo	3.95
54	Belize	2.80	135	Haiti	4.00
54	Costa Rica	2.80	135	Kyrgyz Rep.	4.00
54	Israel	2.80	137	Kazakhstan	4.05
54	Swaziland	2.80	137	Sierra Leone	4.05
54	Turkey	2.80	139	Yemen	4.10
54	Uganda	2.80	140	Belarus	4.15
54	Samoa	2.80	141	Sudan	4.20
61	Latvia	2.85	141	Syria	4.20
62	Greece	2.90	143	Azerbaijan	4.30
62	Hungary	2.90	143	Equatorial Guinea	4.30
62	So. Africa	2.90	143	Myanmar	4.30
65	Ecuador	2.95	143	Rwanda	4.30
65	Gabon	2.95	147	Tajikistan	4.40
65	Indonesia	2.95	147	Uzbekistan	4.40
65	Malta	2.95	149	Angola	4.45
65	Morocco	2.95	149	Turkmenistan	4.45
65	Poland	2.95	151	Guinea-Bissau	4.55
65	Tunisia	2.95	152	Vietnam	4.60
72	Ghana	3.00	153	Congo (Zaire)	4.70
72	Lithuania	3.00	153	Iran	4.70
72	Saudi Arabia	3.00	155	Bosnia	4.80
75	Benin	3.05	155	Somalia	4.80
75	Kenya	3.05	157	Iraq	4.90
75	Paraguay	3.05	157	Laos	4.90
75	Qatar	3.05	157	Libya	4.90
75	Slovak Republic	3.05	160	Cuba	5.00
75	Zambia	3.05	160	Korea, North	5.00
81	Colombia	3.10			

Mostly Unfree

BANKING
Score: 3–Stable (moderate level of restrictions)

Among the most serious impediments to efficient banking are corrupt government bureaucrats, collusion by some banks to maintain high rates of interest, and a generally chaotic financial system. Some restrictions have been liberalized, however. Six commercial banks, either privately owned or controlled by a majority of private-sector owners, now are permitted to invest in foreign capital markets.

WAGE AND PRICE CONTROLS
Score: 3–Stable (moderate level)

The government has lifted most price controls, but prices continue to be influenced by the large public sector. Mali has a minimum wage.

PROPERTY RIGHTS
Score: 3–Stable (moderate level of protection)

Property is at risk because of high crime rates and an inefficient (although generally fair) court system. Some property has been destroyed because of separatist strife in the north. Government expropriation is not likely under the current regime. The U.S. Department of State reports that "The Constitution provides for an independent judiciary, but the executive branch continues to exert influence over the judicial system."[3]

REGULATION
Score: 3–Stable (moderate level)

Regulations are applied sporadically, and government corruption increases the risk of doing business. According to the U.S. Department of Commerce, corruption remains a problem for many businesses: "The rule of law is generally respected, although petty corruption is endemic at the lower and middle levels of the government."[4] Mali has simplified its business registration procedures and liberalized its commerce and labor codes over the past few years.

BLACK MARKET
Score: 5–Stable (very high level of activity)

Mali has a large black market in smuggled consumer electronics equipment like videocassette recorders. In addition, auto parts are stolen from operating cars to be resold by black marketeers, and cattle rustling is growing.

NOTES

[1] Mali's average tariff rate does not include fiscal duties, which increase the rate to between 10 percent and 15 percent.

[2] According to the U.S. Department of State, total taxation on income and corporate profits is over 50 percent. It was not possible to obtain the tax rate on the average income level. Therefore, Mali's score is based only on the top rate.

[3] U.S. Department of State, "Mali Country Report on Human Rights Practices for 1997," 1998.

[4] U.S. Department of Commerce, *Country Commercial Guide*, 1998.

Malta   2.95

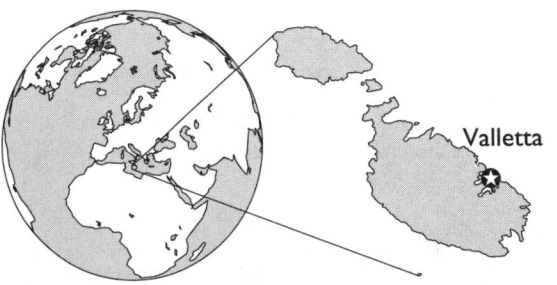
Valletta

1998 Score: **2.85**	1997 Score: **2.95**	1996 Score: **3.05**

Trade	4	Banking	3
Taxation	3.5	Wages and Prices	4
Government Intervention	3	Property Rights	2
Monetary Policy	1	Regulation	3
Foreign Investment	2	Black Market	4

Malta gained its independence from the United Kingdom in 1964. During the 1970s, the government owned and controlled many businesses. Instead of allowing these businesses to fail, the government intervened and nationalized them, causing the budget to become bloated. In recent times, Malta has made progress toward free-market reform by reducing some taxes, maintaining a tight money supply, and welcoming most foreign investment. It also has managed to reduce black market activity by cracking down on smuggling. Legal protection of private property has been strengthened recently. There is increasing evidence that the level of government intervention in the economy has risen, however; as a result, Malta's overall score is 0.1 point worse than last year.

TRADE POLICY
Score: 4–Stable (high level of protectionism)

Malta's average tariff rate is 12 percent, up from about 8 percent last year.[1] Some import licenses are required, especially for health and environmental products.

TAXATION
Score–Income taxation: 3–Stable (moderate tax rates)
Score–Corporate taxation: 3–Stable (moderate tax rates)
Total Taxation Score: 3.5–Stable (high tax rates)

Malta's top marginal income tax rate is 35 percent, and citizens making the average income pay 15 percent, down from 20 percent last year. The top corporate tax rate is 35 percent. Malta also has a 35 percent capital gains tax and a 2 percent to 7 percent stamp duty (a tax on the transfer of property).

GOVERNMENT INTERVENTION IN THE ECONOMY
Score: 3– (moderate level)

Government consumes 21.1 percent of GDP. The government has failed to privatize many inefficient industries, and it remains the largest source of economic activity. As the U.S. Department of Commerce explains, "The Government of Malta (GOM) is a major contributor to the economy, with government spending accounting for almost half of GDP. A major presence on the capital markets, the GOM borrowed USD 280 million in 1996 to finance revenue shortfalls. Public enterprises are not considered efficient nor are they profitable, as the GOM must finance recurrent operational deficits. This is especially the case for the Malta Drydocks, a major drain on the GOM's budget. However, the GOM is not considering privatization of any of these enterprises at this time."[2] As a result, Malta's score in this factor is 1 point worse this year.

MONETARY POLICY
Score: 1–Stable (very low level of inflation)

The average annual rate of inflation from 1986 to 1996 was 2.9 percent. In 1997, the rate rose to 4 percent.

1	Hong Kong	1.25
2	Singapore	1.30
3	Bahrain	1.70
4	New Zealand	1.75
5	Switzerland	1.85
6	United States	1.90
7	Ireland	1.95
7	Luxembourg	1.95
7	Taiwan	1.95
7	United Kingdom	1.95
11	Bahamas	2.00
12	Czech Republic	2.05
12	Japan	2.05
14	Australia	2.10
14	Belgium	2.10
14	Canada	2.10
14	United Arab Emirates	2.10
18	Austria	2.15
18	Chile	2.15
18	Estonia	2.15
18	Netherlands	2.15
22	Denmark	2.25
22	El Salvador	2.25
22	Finland	2.25
25	Germany	2.30
25	Iceland	2.30
27	Norway	2.35
28	Korea, South	2.40
28	Kuwait	2.40
28	Malaysia	2.40
28	Panama	2.40
28	Thailand	2.40
33	Sweden	2.45
34	Argentina	2.50
34	France	2.50
34	Italy	2.50
34	Spain	2.50
38	Portugal	2.55
38	Sri Lanka	2.55
38	Trinidad and Tobago	2.55
41	Barbados	2.60
41	Peru	2.60
43	Bolivia	2.65
43	Mauritius	2.65
45	Cyprus	2.70
45	Jamaica	2.70
45	Uruguay	2.70
48	Botswana	2.75
48	Guatemala	2.75
48	Jordan	2.75
48	Namibia	2.75
48	Oman	2.75
48	Philippines	2.75
54	Belize	2.80
54	Costa Rica	2.80
54	Israel	2.80
54	Swaziland	2.80
54	Turkey	2.80
54	Uganda	2.80
54	Samoa	2.80
61	Latvia	2.85
62	Greece	2.90
62	Hungary	2.90
62	So. Africa	2.90
65	Ecuador	2.95
65	Gabon	2.95
65	Indonesia	2.95
65	Malta	2.95
65	Morocco	2.95
65	Poland	2.95
65	Tunisia	2.95
72	Ghana	3.00
72	Lithuania	3.00
72	Saudi Arabia	3.00
75	Benin	3.05
75	Kenya	3.05
75	Paraguay	3.05
75	Qatar	3.05
75	Slovak Republic	3.05
75	Zambia	3.05
81	Colombia	3.10

81	Fiji	3.10
81	Mali	3.10
81	Slovenia	3.10
85	Honduras	3.15
85	Mexico	3.15
85	Papua New Guinea	3.15
88	Djibouti	3.20
88	Mongolia	3.20
90	Algeria	3.25
90	Brazil	3.25
90	Lebanon	3.25
90	Senegal	3.25
90	Tanzania	3.25
95	Nigeria	3.30
95	Romania	3.30
97	Cambodia	3.35
97	Dominican Republic	3.35
97	Egypt	3.35
97	Guinea	3.35
97	Ivory Coast	3.35
97	Moldova	3.35
97	Pakistan	3.35
104	Nepal	3.40
104	Venezuela	3.40
106	Armenia	3.45
106	Bulgaria	3.45
106	Lesotho	3.45
106	Madagascar	3.45
106	Russia	3.45
111	Burkina Faso	3.50
111	Cameroon	3.50
111	Guyana	3.50
111	Nicaragua	3.50
115	Gambia	3.60
116	Croatia	3.65
116	Georgia	3.65
116	Malawi	3.65
119	Cape Verde	3.67
120	Ethiopia	3.70
120	India	3.70
120	Niger	3.70
123	Congo	3.75
124	Chad	3.80
124	China	3.80
124	Mauritania	3.80
124	Ukraine	3.80
124	Zimbabwe	3.80
129	Albania	3.85
129	Bangladesh	3.85
129	Mozambique	3.85
129	Suriname	3.85
133	Burundi	3.90
134	Togo	3.95
135	Haiti	4.00
135	Kyrgyz Rep.	4.00
137	Kazakhstan	4.05
137	Sierra Leone	4.05
139	Yemen	4.10
140	Belarus	4.15
141	Sudan	4.20
141	Syria	4.20
143	Azerbaijan	4.30
143	Equatorial Guinea	4.30
143	Myanmar	4.30
143	Rwanda	4.30
147	Tajikistan	4.40
147	Uzbekistan	4.40
149	Angola	4.45
149	Turkmenistan	4.45
151	Guinea-Bissau	4.55
152	Vietnam	4.60
153	Congo (Zaire)	4.70
153	Iran	4.70
155	Bosnia	4.80
155	Somalia	4.80
157	Iraq	4.90
157	Laos	4.90
157	Libya	4.90
160	Cuba	5.00
160	Korea, North	5.00

Mostly Free

CAPITAL FLOWS AND FOREIGN INVESTMENT
Score: 2–Stable (low barriers)

With the exception of utilities, almost all companies on Malta are open to foreign investment. There are few restrictions. According to the U.S. Department of Commerce, "in the last several years, the private sector has been playing an increasingly important role. The Malta Development Corporation (MDC) actively promotes investment in local industry, provides information to prospective investors, processes applications for industrial projects and serves as liaison between investors and other government entities. MDC is also responsible for the construction and management of Malta's 12 industrial parks."[3]

BANKING
Score: 3–Stable (moderate level of restrictions)

Most domestic banks are privately owned, with only a few still owned by the government, and there is competition to attract customers. Foreign banks are increasing their presence.

WAGE AND PRICE CONTROLS
Score: 4–Stable (high level)

The Department of Trade is responsible for pricing most items sold on Malta. There also is a minimum wage. According to the U.S. Department of Commerce, "Despite these pressures, consumer price inflation has remained low, reflecting the impact of a fixed exchange rate policy and lingering price controls."[4]

PROPERTY RIGHTS
Score: 2–Stable (high level of protection)

There have been cases of government expropriation in the past, but such action is much less likely today. The judicial system has been strengthened. According to the U.S. Department of State, Malta's judiciary "upholds the Constitution's protections for individual rights and freedoms.... The judiciary is independent of the executive and legislative branches."[5] There may be delays in some court cases, however.

REGULATION
Score: 3–Stable (moderate level)

Malta has new consumer safety regulations that conform to European Union standards. Environmental regulations are enforced stringently and carry large fines for violations. Opening a business can be difficult, and licenses must be granted by many bureaucracies, including the police.

BLACK MARKET
Score: 4–Stable (high level of activity)

Malta is a major center for smuggling, and its location makes it a preferred base for black market activity. The government has cracked down on smuggling and other black market activities, however, thereby reducing them to some extent.

NOTES

[1] Malta removed its 15 percent value-added tax in July 1997. In its place, it created a 15 percent excise tax on most imports. This raises its average tariff rate to around 12 percent.

[2] U.S. Department of Commerce, *Country Commercial Guide,* 1998.

[3] *Ibid.*

[4] *Ibid.*

[5] U.S. Department of State, "Malta Country Report on Human Rights Practices for 1997," 1998.

Mauritania 3.80

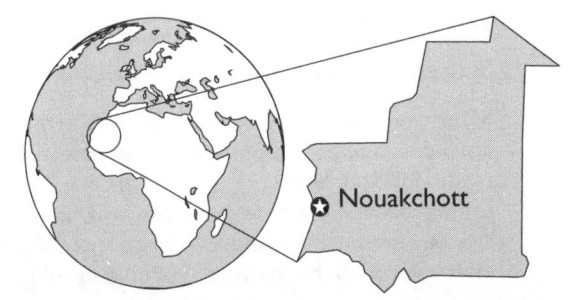

Nouakchott

1998 Score: **3.80**	1997 Score: **3.80**	1996 Score: **3.80**

Trade	5	Banking	5
Taxation	4	Wages and Prices	4
Government Intervention	3	Property Rights	4
Monetary Policy	2	Regulation	4
Foreign Investment	3	Black Market	4

Mauritania gained its independence from France in 1960. Its territory consists primarily of flat, dry plains and desert. In 1991, opposition parties were legalized and a new constitution was adopted. Maaouya Ould Sidi Ahmed Taya, who has ruled since 1984, won the 1992 presidential election and was elected to another six-year term in 1997. Despite irregularities, international observers accepted the 1997 election result as reasonable (the U.S. Department of State had characterized the 1992 election as "fraudulent").[1] During most of the 1980s, the government pursued a highly interventionist policy toward the economy, which consists predominantly of fishing, agriculture, and mining. In the 1990s, Mauritania has struggled to adopt a series of economic reforms. The government has run a budget surplus since 1995 and pledged to continue this policy despite plans to increase spending in the coming year. GDP growth averaged 4.9 percent annually from 1993 to 1997. Although the government has plans to reduce barriers to trade, liberalize the economy, and draft new legal codes, it has made only limited progress.

TRADE POLICY
Score: 5–Stable (very high level of protectionism)

Mauritania's average tariff rate is 35 percent.[2] Trade restrictions include strict labeling and inspection requirements as well as a sometimes corrupt and inefficient customs agency.

TAXATION
Score–Income taxation: 4–Stable (high tax rates)
Score–Corporate taxation: 4–Stable (high tax rates)
Final Taxation Score: 4–Stable (high tax rates)

Because top income and corporate tax rates are not available, the author uses total government revenue as a percentage of GDP (over 25 percent[3]) to grade Mauritania's levels of taxation.

GOVERNMENT INTERVENTION IN THE ECONOMY
Score: 3–Stable (moderate level)

Government consumes about 14 percent of GDP. Even though much of the economy has been privatized, the government still owns some companies, including those that produce electricity and water.

MONETARY POLICY
Score: 2–Stable (low level of inflation)

Mauritania's average annual rate of inflation from 1986 to 1996 was 7 percent. In 1997, the rate was about 5 percent.

1	Hong Kong	1.25	81	Fiji	3.10
2	Singapore	1.30	81	Mali	3.10
3	Bahrain	1.70	81	Slovenia	3.10
4	New Zealand	1.75	85	Honduras	3.15
5	Switzerland	1.85	85	Mexico	3.15
6	United States	1.90	85	Papua New Guinea	3.15
7	Ireland	1.95	88	Djibouti	3.20
7	Luxembourg	1.95	88	Mongolia	3.20
7	Taiwan	1.95	90	Algeria	3.25
7	United Kingdom	1.95	90	Brazil	3.25
11	Bahamas	2.00	90	Lebanon	3.25
12	Czech Republic	2.05	90	Senegal	3.25
12	Japan	2.05	90	Tanzania	3.25
14	Australia	2.10	95	Nigeria	3.30
14	Belgium	2.10	95	Romania	3.30
14	Canada	2.10	97	Cambodia	3.35
14	United Arab Emirates	2.10	97	Dominican Republic	3.35
18	Austria	2.15	97	Egypt	3.35
18	Chile	2.15	97	Guinea	3.35
18	Estonia	2.15	97	Ivory Coast	3.35
18	Netherlands	2.15	97	Moldova	3.35
22	Denmark	2.25	97	Pakistan	3.35
22	El Salvador	2.25	104	Nepal	3.40
22	Finland	2.25	104	Venezuela	3.40
25	Germany	2.30	106	Armenia	3.45
25	Iceland	2.30	106	Bulgaria	3.45
27	Norway	2.35	106	Lesotho	3.45
28	Korea, South	2.40	106	Madagascar	3.45
28	Kuwait	2.40	106	Russia	3.45
28	Malaysia	2.40	111	Burkina Faso	3.50
28	Panama	2.40	111	Cameroon	3.50
28	Thailand	2.40	111	Guyana	3.50
33	Sweden	2.45	111	Nicaragua	3.50
34	Argentina	2.50	115	Gambia	3.60
34	France	2.50	116	Croatia	3.65
34	Italy	2.50	116	Georgia	3.65
34	Spain	2.50	116	Malawi	3.65
38	Portugal	2.55	119	Cape Verde	3.67
38	Sri Lanka	2.55	120	Ethiopia	3.70
38	Trinidad and Tobago	2.55	120	India	3.70
41	Barbados	2.60	120	Niger	3.70
41	Peru	2.60	123	Congo	3.75
43	Bolivia	2.65	124	Chad	3.80
43	Mauritius	2.65	124	China	3.80
45	Cyprus	2.70	124	Mauritania	3.80
45	Jamaica	2.70	124	Ukraine	3.80
45	Uruguay	2.70	124	Zimbabwe	3.80
48	Botswana	2.75	129	Albania	3.85
48	Guatemala	2.75	129	Bangladesh	3.85
48	Jordan	2.75	129	Mozambique	3.85
48	Namibia	2.75	129	Suriname	3.85
48	Oman	2.75	133	Burundi	3.90
48	Philippines	2.75	134	Togo	3.95
54	Belize	2.80	135	Haiti	4.00
54	Costa Rica	2.80	135	Kyrgyz Rep.	4.00
54	Israel	2.80	137	Kazakhstan	4.05
54	Swaziland	2.80	137	Sierra Leone	4.05
54	Turkey	2.80	139	Yemen	4.10
54	Uganda	2.80	140	Belarus	4.15
54	Samoa	2.80	141	Sudan	4.20
61	Latvia	2.85	141	Syria	4.20
62	Greece	2.90	143	Azerbaijan	4.30
62	Hungary	2.90	143	Equatorial Guinea	4.30
62	So. Africa	2.90	143	Myanmar	4.30
65	Ecuador	2.95	143	Rwanda	4.30
65	Gabon	2.95	147	Tajikistan	4.40
65	Indonesia	2.95	147	Uzbekistan	4.40
65	Malta	2.95	149	Angola	4.45
65	Morocco	2.95	149	Turkmenistan	4.45
65	Poland	2.95	151	Guinea-Bissau	4.55
65	Tunisia	2.95	152	Vietnam	4.60
72	Ghana	3.00	153	Congo (Zaire)	4.70
72	Lithuania	3.00	153	Iran	4.70
72	Saudi Arabia	3.00	155	Bosnia	4.80
75	Benin	3.05	155	Somalia	4.80
75	Kenya	3.05	157	Iraq	4.90
75	Paraguay	3.05	157	Laos	4.90
75	Qatar	3.05	157	Libya	4.90
75	Slovak Republic	3.05	160	Cuba	5.00
75	Zambia	3.05	160	Korea, North	5.00
81	Colombia	3.10			

Mostly Unfree

CAPITAL FLOWS AND FOREIGN INVESTMENT
Score: 3–Stable (moderate barriers)

Mauritania has passed laws with the idea to attract foreign investors. Foreign and domestic firms generally enjoy equal treatment, and there are few legal barriers. Overall, despite some problems—such as corruption among officials, the lack of infrastructure, and a very poor population—the new investment code has been successful in opening the economy to foreign investment.

BANKING
Score: 5–Stable (very high level of restrictions)

Despite the introduction of some reforms, the banking system remains chaotic. The government strictly controls most banks, and the entire industry remains undeveloped and small. According to the U.S. Department of Commerce, "With only five commercial banks and two small credit agencies, Mauritania's banking system remains underdeveloped."[4]

WAGE AND PRICE CONTROLS
Score: 4–Stable (high level)

Wages and prices are controlled through subsidies to businesses, as well as to state-owned utilities like electricity.

PROPERTY RIGHTS
Score: 4–Stable (low level of protection)

Private property is not safe in Mauritania. The legal and judicial system is chaotic and sometimes corrupt. According to the U.S. Department of Commerce, the country's banks "have had difficulty getting local courts to enforce a bank's right under loan agreements to seize pledged assets from local merchants."[5]

REGULATION
Score: 4–Stable (high level)

Establishing a business is becoming easier. Regulations, although cumbersome, are applied fairly evenly in most cases. Corrupt government bureaucrats, however, sometimes impose arbitrary requirements on businesses. According to the U.S. Department of Commerce, "[I]mportant problems remain to be resolved: improvement and development of management practices, improving transparency of government procedures, abolition of corruption within the administration, and improvement of the labor and banking laws."[6]

BLACK MARKET
Score: 4–Stable (high level of activity)

Mauritania's large informal market is confined principally to consumer goods and entertainment products, especially computer software.

NOTES

[1] U.S. Department of State, "Mauritania Country Report on Human Rights Practices for 1996," 1997, p. 1.
[2] U.S. Department of Commerce, *Country Commercial Guide,* 1998.
[3] This compares with about 13 percent in Japan, which has a top income tax rate of 50 percent.
[4] *Ibid.*
[5] *Ibid.*
[6] *Ibid.*

Mauritius 2.65

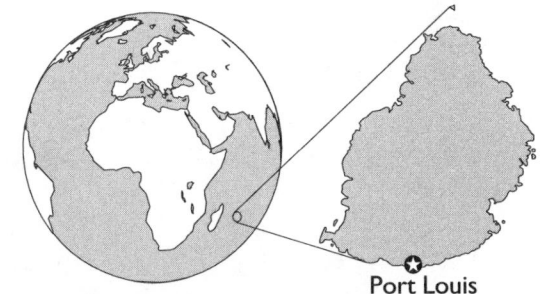

Port Louis

1998 Score: **n/a**	1997 Score: **n/a**	1996 Score: **n/a**

Trade	4	Banking	2
Taxation	4.5	Wages and Prices	3
Government Intervention	2	Property Rights	2
Monetary Policy	2	Regulation	2
Foreign Investment	3	Black Market	2

Mauritius at different times was a colony of both France and the United Kingdom. It took its first steps toward democracy in 1947, when it held elections for a national legislature. The United Kingdom agreed in 1961 to allow more self-rule, and the country elected its first prime minister in 1968. Mauritius has maintained a stable democracy since becoming a republic in 1992. That year, voters elected Cassam Uteem as their first president. The economy grew at an average rate of 5.7 percent annually from 1992 to 1996.

TRADE POLICY
Score: 4–Stable (high level of protectionism)

Mauritius has as average tariff rate of 14 percent.[1] Non-tariff barriers exist. As the U.S. Department of Commerce summarizes, "Mauritius operates a relatively streamlined trade regime, although peculiarities remain. The most significant is a two-tiered system whereby imports from certain countries are given preferential duties.... Import permits are required for foodstuffs (milk, potatoes, corn, rice, beans, wheat, fruits, infant formulas, food additives, spices, fats and oils), pharmaceuticals, cigarettes, insecticides, petroleum products, cement, PVC pipes, plastic feeding bottles, corrugated iron sheets, gold, weighing machinery, baking equipment, syringes, electric water heaters, motor vehicles (including used vehicles, parts and accessories), crash helmets and fireworks.... [S]tate enterprises control the import of several commodities: State Trading Corporation (rice, wheat flour, petroleum, cement), Agricultural Marketing Board (products that compete with domestic goods), Tea Board, Tobacco Board and the Mauritius Sugar Syndicate."[2]

TAXATION
Score–Income taxation: 5–Stable (very high tax rates)
Score–Corporate taxation: 3–Stable (moderate tax rates)
Total Taxation Score: 4.5–Stable (very high tax rates)

The top income tax rate is 30 percent. The tax on the average income level also is 30 percent. The top corporate income tax rate is 35 percent. Mauritius also has an 8 percent to 10 percent sales tax and a 9 percent pension tax.

GOVERNMENT INTERVENTION IN THE ECONOMY
Score: 2–Stable (low level)

Government consumes 9.8 percent of GDP. According to the U.S. Department of Commerce, "Government's share of GDP is modest but it controls several key sectors directly or through parastatals, including electricity, water, postal services, telecommunications (except cellular), and broadcasting. The State Trading Corporation controls imports of rice, flour, petroleum products, and cement, and the Agricultural Marketing Board controls imports of potatoes, onions and some spices that compete with locally grown produce."[3]

1	Hong Kong	1.25	81	Fiji	3.10
2	Singapore	1.30	81	Mali	3.10
3	Bahrain	1.70	81	Slovenia	3.10
4	New Zealand	1.75	85	Honduras	3.15
5	Switzerland	1.85	85	Mexico	3.15
6	United States	1.90	85	Papua New Guinea	3.15
7	Ireland	1.95	88	Djibouti	3.20
7	Luxembourg	1.95	88	Mongolia	3.20
7	Taiwan	1.95	90	Algeria	3.25
7	United Kingdom	1.95	90	Brazil	3.25
11	Bahamas	2.00	90	Lebanon	3.25
12	Czech Republic	2.05	90	Senegal	3.25
12	Japan	2.05	90	Tanzania	3.25
14	Australia	2.10	95	Nigeria	3.30
14	Belgium	2.10	95	Romania	3.30
14	Canada	2.10	97	Cambodia	3.35
14	United Arab Emirates	2.10	97	Dominican Republic	3.35
18	Austria	2.15	97	Egypt	3.35
18	Chile	2.15	97	Guinea	3.35
18	Estonia	2.15	97	Ivory Coast	3.35
18	Netherlands	2.15	97	Moldova	3.35
22	Denmark	2.25	97	Pakistan	3.35
22	El Salvador	2.25	104	Nepal	3.40
22	Finland	2.25	104	Venezuela	3.40
25	Germany	2.30	106	Armenia	3.45
25	Iceland	2.30	106	Bulgaria	3.45
27	Norway	2.35	106	Lesotho	3.45
28	Korea, South	2.40	106	Madagascar	3.45
28	Kuwait	2.40	106	Russia	3.45
28	Malaysia	2.40	111	Burkina Faso	3.50
28	Panama	2.40	111	Cameroon	3.50
28	Thailand	2.40	111	Guyana	3.50
33	Sweden	2.45	111	Nicaragua	3.50
34	Argentina	2.50	115	Gambia	3.60
34	France	2.50	116	Croatia	3.65
34	Italy	2.50	116	Georgia	3.65
34	Spain	2.50	116	Malawi	3.65
38	Portugal	2.55	119	Cape Verde	3.67
38	Sri Lanka	2.55	120	Ethiopia	3.70
38	Trinidad and Tobago	2.55	120	India	3.70
41	Barbados	2.60	120	Niger	3.70
41	Peru	2.60	123	Congo	3.75
43	Bolivia	2.65	124	Chad	3.80
43	**Mauritius**	**2.65**	124	China	3.80
45	Cyprus	2.70	124	Mauritania	3.80
45	Jamaica	2.70	124	Ukraine	3.80
45	Uruguay	2.70	124	Zimbabwe	3.80
48	Botswana	2.75	129	Albania	3.85
48	Guatemala	2.75	129	Bangladesh	3.85
48	Jordan	2.75	129	Mozambique	3.85
48	Namibia	2.75	129	Suriname	3.85
48	Oman	2.75	133	Burundi	3.90
48	Philippines	2.75	134	Togo	3.95
54	Belize	2.80	135	Haiti	4.00
54	Costa Rica	2.80	135	Kyrgyz Rep.	4.00
54	Israel	2.80	137	Kazakhstan	4.05
54	Swaziland	2.80	137	Sierra Leone	4.05
54	Turkey	2.80	139	Yemen	4.10
54	Uganda	2.80	140	Belarus	4.15
54	Samoa	2.80	141	Sudan	4.20
61	Latvia	2.85	141	Syria	4.20
62	Greece	2.90	143	Azerbaijan	4.30
62	Hungary	2.90	143	Equatorial Guinea	4.30
62	So. Africa	2.90	143	Myanmar	4.30
65	Ecuador	2.95	143	Rwanda	4.30
65	Gabon	2.95	147	Tajikistan	4.40
65	Indonesia	2.95	147	Uzbekistan	4.40
65	Malta	2.95	149	Angola	4.45
65	Morocco	2.95	149	Turkmenistan	4.45
65	Poland	2.95	151	Guinea-Bissau	4.55
65	Tunisia	2.95	152	Vietnam	4.60
72	Ghana	3.00	153	Congo (Zaire)	4.70
72	Lithuania	3.00	153	Iran	4.70
72	Saudi Arabia	3.00	155	Bosnia	4.80
75	Benin	3.05	155	Somalia	4.80
75	Kenya	3.05	157	Iraq	4.90
75	Paraguay	3.05	157	Laos	4.90
75	Qatar	3.05	157	Libya	4.90
75	Slovak Republic	3.05	160	Cuba	5.00
75	Zambia	3.05	160	Korea, North	5.00
81	Colombia	3.10			

Mostly Free / *Mostly Free*

MONETARY POLICY
Score: 2–Stable (low level of inflation)

The average annual rate of inflation from 1986 to 1996 was 8.6 percent. In 1997, the rate of inflation was around 6.6 percent.

CAPITAL FLOWS AND FOREIGN INVESTMENT
Score: 3–Stable (moderate barriers)

Mauritius generally welcomes foreign investment. It has a transparent and well-defined foreign investment code and an efficient investment approval process. There are, however, significant limitations on foreign investors. Foreigners are prohibited from owning land, for example, which is a significant impediment because it restricts investors from using land as collateral. In addition, according to the U.S. Department of Commerce, "Foreign participation may be limited to 49% for investments serving the domestic market, and is generally not encouraged in areas where Mauritius has already mastered the technology.... Foreign ownership of services such as accountancy, law, medicine, computer services, international marketing, and management consultancy, is limited to 30%."[4]

BANKING
Score: 2–Stable (low level of restrictions)

Mauritius has an open, efficient, and competitive banking system. There are, however, some restrictions on banks' engaging in such financial services as selling real estate, insurance policies, and some forms of investments.

WAGE AND PRICE CONTROLS
Score: 3–Stable (moderate level)

Mauritius maintains a modest level of price controls on a variety of goods and services. According to the U.S. Department of Commerce, "The government controls prices and/or markups on a range of goods. Imports subject to price control include rice, flour, cement, cooking gas, infant milk powder, cheese, fertilizer, frozen fish, iron and steel bars, petroleum products, coconut oil, and salted fish. Maximum markups apply to refrigerators and certain appliances, tires, pharmaceuticals, sporting goods, tiles, crash helmets, glass panes, plywood, sanitary wares, textbooks and timber. Markup limits vary between 20–50%."[5]

PROPERTY RIGHTS
Score: 2–Stable (high level of protection)

Property expropriation is unlikely. Mauritius has an efficient and transparent legal system. According to the U.S. Department of Commerce, "Mauritius maintains a sophisticated and impartial legal system based on both Napoleonic code and British common law. The system protects the acquisition and disposition of all property, including land, buildings, and mortgages. Long-standing legislation, inherited from the United Kingdom, protects patents and trademarks."[6] Foreigners, as noted above, are not permitted to purchase land.

REGULATION
Score: 2–Stable (moderate level)

Regulations generally are transparent and applied consistently. The U.S. Department of Commerce reports, "Business regulations are generally transparent."[7] Special permits are required, however, for foreign workers, and the process to acquire them sometimes is lengthy. "Some corruption exists at all levels of government but does not present an obstacle for most investors," the U.S. Department of Commerce adds.[8]

BLACK MARKET
Score: 2–Stable (low level of activity)

Mauritius has a strong intellectual property rights law, and piracy in this area is minimal. According to the U.S. Department of Commerce, "Legislation protecting artistic, literary, and scientific works, was enacted in 1986 and amended in 1988 to bring the period of copyright protection into conformity with the Berne Convention."[9] There is little other activity in the informal sector.

NOTES

1. The World Bank, *World Development Indicators*, 1998.
2. U.S. Department of Commerce, *Country Commercial Guide*, 1998.
3. *Ibid.*
4. *Ibid.*
5. *Ibid.*
6. *Ibid.*
7. *Ibid.*
8. *Ibid.*
9. *Ibid.*

Mexico   3.15

1998 Score: **3.25**	1997 Score: **3.35**		1996 Score: **3.35**

Trade	2	Banking	4
Taxation	3.5	Wages and Prices	3
Government Intervention	2	Property Rights	3
Monetary Policy	5	Regulation	4
Foreign Investment	2	Black Market	3

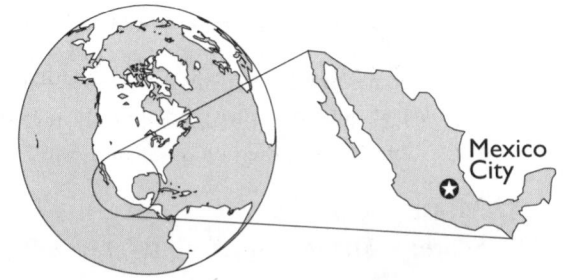
Mexico City

After decades of socialist economic policies and limited economic freedom, Mexico is trying to liberalize its market. As in other countries trying to reform their economies, many of the benefits of the free market are only beginning to take effect. Efforts to integrate the economy with those of the United States and Canada through the North American Free Trade Agreement (NAFTA) are promoting economic liberalization, but Mexico still limits economic freedom, especially with respect to trade with non-NAFTA countries, and has not reformed its political system as rapidly as it has reformed its economy. Restricted economic freedom and a lack of political openness were behind the December 1994 collapse of the peso, which caused an economic recession from which Mexico only now is on the road to recovery. In 1997, Mexico became the second largest market for U.S. merchandise goods exports, surpassing Japan. This mainly is the result of a continual downward trend in Mexico's barriers to trade. For example, Mexico's average tariff rate is shrinking; as a result, its overall score is 0.1 point better than last year.

TRADE POLICY
Score: 2+ (low level of protectionism)

Mexico's average tariff rate is 4 percent, down from 5.1 percent last year.[1] As a result, Mexico's score in this factor has improved by 1 point over last year. Non-tariff barriers, however, continue to discourage imports into Mexico. As the Office of the United States Trade Representative reports, "U.S. exporters continue to register complaints about certain aspects of Mexican customs administration, including the lack of prior notification of procedural changes, inconsistent interpretation of regulatory requirements for imports at different border posts, new requirements that particular goods may enter only through certain ports, and discriminatory and capricious enforcement of Mexican standards and labeling rules."[2] These non-tariff barriers, however, are exceptions in a market increasingly open to trade. Moreover, Mexico's average tariff rate puts it on par with most industrialized countries. Thus, by global standards, Mexico's level of protectionism is low.

TAXATION
Score–Income taxation: 3–Stable (moderate tax rates)
Score–Corporate taxation: 3–Stable (moderate tax rates)
Total Taxation Score: 3.5–Stable (high tax rates)

Mexico's top marginal tax rate is 35 percent, and the average income level is taxed at 17 percent. The top corporate tax rate is 34 percent. Mexico also has a 15 percent value-added tax, a 34 percent capital gains tax, a state tax on salaries, and a resident tax.

GOVERNMENT INTERVENTION IN THE ECONOMY
Score: 2–Stable (low level)

Government consumes 10.9 percent of GDP. The recent economic crisis caused Mexico's privatization program to slow in some sectors, but that trend is

1	Hong Kong	1.25	
2	Singapore	1.30	
3	Bahrain	1.70	
4	New Zealand	1.75	
5	Switzerland	1.85	
6	United States	1.90	
7	Ireland	1.95	
7	Luxembourg	1.95	
7	Taiwan	1.95	
7	United Kingdom	1.95	
11	Bahamas	2.00	
12	Czech Republic	2.05	
12	Japan	2.05	
14	Australia	2.10	
14	Belgium	2.10	
14	Canada	2.10	
14	United Arab Emirates	2.10	
18	Austria	2.15	
18	Chile	2.15	
18	Estonia	2.15	
18	Netherlands	2.15	
22	Denmark	2.25	
22	El Salvador	2.25	
22	Finland	2.25	
25	Germany	2.30	
25	Iceland	2.30	
27	Norway	2.35	
28	Korea, South	2.40	
28	Kuwait	2.40	
28	Malaysia	2.40	
28	Panama	2.40	
28	Thailand	2.40	
33	Sweden	2.45	
34	Argentina	2.50	
34	France	2.50	
34	Italy	2.50	
34	Spain	2.50	
38	Portugal	2.55	
38	Sri Lanka	2.55	
38	Trinidad and Tobago	2.55	
41	Barbados	2.60	
41	Peru	2.60	
43	Bolivia	2.65	
43	Mauritius	2.65	
45	Cyprus	2.70	
45	Jamaica	2.70	
45	Uruguay	2.70	
48	Botswana	2.75	
48	Guatemala	2.75	
48	Jordan	2.75	
48	Namibia	2.75	
48	Oman	2.75	
48	Philippines	2.75	
54	Belize	2.80	
54	Costa Rica	2.80	
54	Israel	2.80	
54	Swaziland	2.80	
54	Turkey	2.80	
54	Uganda	2.80	
54	Samoa	2.80	
61	Latvia	2.85	
62	Greece	2.90	
62	Hungary	2.90	
62	So. Africa	2.90	
65	Ecuador	2.95	
65	Gabon	2.95	
65	Indonesia	2.95	
65	Malta	2.95	
65	Morocco	2.95	
65	Poland	2.95	
65	Tunisia	2.95	
72	Ghana	3.00	
72	Lithuania	3.00	
72	Saudi Arabia	3.00	
75	Benin	3.05	
75	Kenya	3.05	
75	Paraguay	3.05	
75	Qatar	3.05	
75	Slovak Republic	3.05	
75	Zambia	3.05	
81	Colombia	3.10	
81	Fiji	3.10	
81	Mali	3.10	
81	Slovenia	3.10	
85	Honduras	3.15	
85	Mexico	3.15	
85	Papua New Guinea	3.15	
88	Djibouti	3.20	
88	Mongolia	3.20	
90	Algeria	3.25	
90	Brazil	3.25	
90	Lebanon	3.25	
90	Senegal	3.25	
90	Tanzania	3.25	
95	Nigeria	3.30	
95	Romania	3.30	
97	Cambodia	3.35	
97	Dominican Republic	3.35	
97	Egypt	3.35	
97	Guinea	3.35	
97	Ivory Coast	3.35	
97	Moldova	3.35	
97	Pakistan	3.35	
104	Nepal	3.40	
104	Venezuela	3.40	
106	Armenia	3.45	
106	Bulgaria	3.45	
106	Lesotho	3.45	
106	Madagascar	3.45	
106	Russia	3.45	
111	Burkina Faso	3.50	
111	Cameroon	3.50	
111	Guyana	3.50	
111	Nicaragua	3.50	
115	Gambia	3.60	
116	Croatia	3.65	
116	Georgia	3.65	
116	Malawi	3.65	
119	Cape Verde	3.67	
120	Ethiopia	3.70	
120	India	3.70	
120	Niger	3.70	
123	Congo	3.75	
124	Chad	3.80	
124	China	3.80	
124	Mauritania	3.80	
124	Ukraine	3.80	
124	Zimbabwe	3.80	
129	Albania	3.85	
129	Bangladesh	3.85	
129	Mozambique	3.85	
129	Suriname	3.85	
133	Burundi	3.90	
134	Togo	3.95	
135	Haiti	4.00	
135	Kyrgyz Rep.	4.00	
137	Kazakhstan	4.05	
137	Sierra Leone	4.05	
139	Yemen	4.10	
140	Belarus	4.15	
141	Sudan	4.20	
141	Syria	4.20	
143	Azerbaijan	4.30	
143	Equatorial Guinea	4.30	
143	Myanmar	4.30	
143	Rwanda	4.30	
147	Tajikistan	4.40	
147	Uzbekistan	4.40	
149	Angola	4.45	
149	Turkmenistan	4.45	
151	Guinea-Bissau	4.55	
152	Vietnam	4.60	
153	Congo (Zaire)	4.70	
153	Iran	4.70	
155	Bosnia	4.80	
155	Somalia	4.80	
157	Iraq	4.90	
157	Laos	4.90	
157	Libya	4.90	
160	Cuba	5.00	
160	Korea, North	5.00	

Mostly Unfree

reversing and privatization has resumed. Mexico has privatized over 1,000 enterprises since 1986. The government also has developed plans to privatize some port facilities, airports, electricity generating plants, and railroads.

MONETARY POLICY
Score: 5–Stable (very high level of inflation)

Even though Mexico has made great strides toward containing inflation since 1988, its overall record in this area has been poor. From 1986 to 1996, the average annual rate of inflation was 52 percent; in 1997, the rate of inflation was 16 percent.[3]

CAPITAL FLOWS AND FOREIGN INVESTMENT
Score: 2–Stable (low barriers)

Mexico has reformed its foreign investment code to attract more investors, allowing for more equal treatment of foreign and domestic firms. Investors from non-NAFTA countries, however, may not own majority shares in many service industries, including banking.

BANKING
Score: 4–Stable (high level of restrictions)

Since the collapse of the peso in December 1994, the government has allowed 100 percent U.S. and Canadian ownership of banks, although government authorization is required for some investments. The economic situation has led the government to bail out many private banks, effectively acquiring control of many institutions, and domestic banks are prohibited from investing in real estate and industrial firms. Thus, the government remains fully entrenched in the country's troubled financial sector.[4] There is some corruption in the dispensing of loans to state-owned companies.

WAGE AND PRICE CONTROLS
Score: 3–Stable (moderate level)

In 1994, 60 product areas were subject to price controls; in 1995, the number decreased to 28. Some controls, such as those on corn flour, bread, and certain quantities of milk, remain in effect. Mexico has a minimum wage with incremental cost-of-living increases.

PROPERTY RIGHTS
Score: 3–Stable (moderate level of protection)

Mexico's constitution guarantees private property, and legal protection of private property will increase as more state-owned property is privatized. Considering current levels of corruption and government-sanctioned cronyism, however, as well as the growing trade in illegal drugs, private property also faces increased risk. According to the U.S. Department of State, "The judiciary is nominally independent; however, on occasion it has been influenced by the executive branch. Corruption and inefficiency are problems and are more widespread in some states than others. Judicial reforms have begun to address these problems."[5] By global standards, protection of private property is moderate.

REGULATION
Score: 4–Stable (high level)

Opening a business remains a complicated task. Each business must obtain a license or some other form of certification from numerous government agencies, including the Public Registry of Commerce, the Bureau of Statistics, federal and local tax authorities, the Mexican Social Security Institute, and the National Housing Fund. Some localities require each business to belong to a local chamber of commerce and trade association, and additional licenses may be required from the Ministry of Health and other agencies. Although Mexico is attempting to end corruption, its current regulatory environment remains an obstacle to business creation.

BLACK MARKET
Score: 3–Stable (moderate level of activity)

A black market in such transportation services as taxis and busing is prevalent in many cities, and black market labor often is available to businesses that want to skirt minimum wage laws. Some estimates put black market labor in Mexico City at over 40 percent. The country also is plagued with black market activity in the construction industry, and there continues to be some piracy of such intellectual property as computer software.

NOTES
[1] World Bank, *World Development Indicators*, 1998.
[2] Office of the United States Trade Representative, *1998 National Trade Estimate Report on Foreign Trade Barriers*, 1998.
[3] Based on consumer price inflation.
[4] Economist Intelligence Unit, *EIU Country Reports*, 1997.
[5] U.S. Department of State, "1997 Human Rights Report: Mexico," 1998.

Moldova   3.35

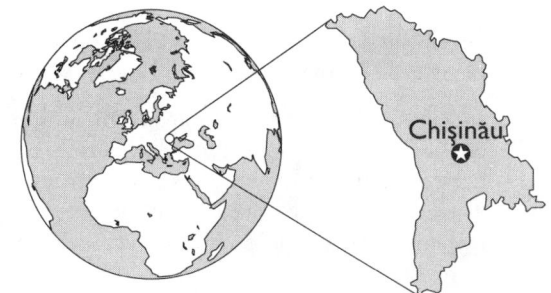

1998 Score: **3.35**	1997 Score: **3.35**	1996 Score: **3.45**

Trade	3	Banking	3
Taxation	3.5	Wages and Prices	3
Government Intervention	3	Property Rights	3
Monetary Policy	5	Regulation	3
Foreign Investment	3	Black Market	4

Moldova gained its independence from the Soviet Union in 1991. Pro-Russian communist separatists in the Transdniestr region mounted an armed conflict in 1992. Moldova remains divided; the Organization for Security and Cooperation in Europe, Russia, and Ukraine act as mediators. (Although the international community has not recognized the independence of the Transdniestr "republic," it has its own executive and parliament.) As a Soviet Socialist Republic, Moldova was a large food producer. Since independence, its economy has shrunk, unemployment has grown, and inflation has skyrocketed. The government has made some progress, however, toward stabilizing the economy and laying the groundwork for the creation of a market infrastructure. The current president, Petru Lucinschi, a former member of the Central Committee of the Communist Party of the Soviet Union, began his five-year term in 1997. Ion Ciubuc is prime minister. Although the Communists are the strongest party in the parliament elected in March 1998, the government consists of three democratic parties.

TRADE POLICY
Score: 3–Stable (moderate level of protectionism)

Moldova has an average tariff rate of around 5 percent. It also maintains non-tariff barriers to trade in several areas. For example, the government imposes quotas on imports of unprocessed leather, energy products, and cereals.

TAXATION
Score–Income taxation: 3–Stable (moderate tax rates)
Score–Corporate taxation: 3–Stable (moderate tax rates)
Total Taxation Score: 3.5–Stable (high tax rates)

Moldova's top income tax rate is 50 percent; the average income level is taxed at 10 percent.[1] Moldova also has a 30 percent corporate tax and a 20 percent value-added tax.[2]

GOVERNMENT INTERVENTION IN THE ECONOMY
Score: 3–Stable (moderate level)

Government consumes 20 percent of GDP, of which the public sector produces almost half.

MONETARY POLICY
Score: 5–Stable (very high level of inflation)

The government has made substantial progress toward reducing the hyperinfla-tion of 1992, caused by the collapse of the Russian ruble. The rate of inflation was 1,276 percent in 1992, 837 percent in 1993, 108 percent in 1994, 23.8 percent in 1995, and 25.5 percent in 1996. Nevertheless, the average annual rate of inflation from 1991 to 1996 was very high. In 1997, the rate was 11.2 percent, the lowest level since the collapse of the Soviet Union.

1	Hong Kong	1.25	81	Fiji	3.10
2	Singapore	1.30	81	Mali	3.10
3	Bahrain	1.70	81	Slovenia	3.10
4	New Zealand	1.75	85	Honduras	3.15
5	Switzerland	1.85	85	Mexico	3.15
6	United States	1.90	85	Papua New Guinea	3.15
7	Ireland	1.95	88	Djibouti	3.20
7	Luxembourg	1.95	88	Mongolia	3.20
7	Taiwan	1.95	90	Algeria	3.25
7	United Kingdom	1.95	90	Brazil	3.25
11	Bahamas	2.00	90	Lebanon	3.25
12	Czech Republic	2.05	90	Senegal	3.25
12	Japan	2.05	90	Tanzania	3.25
14	Australia	2.10	95	Nigeria	3.30
14	Belgium	2.10	95	Romania	3.30
14	Canada	2.10	97	Cambodia	3.35
14	United Arab Emirates	2.10	97	Dominican Republic	3.35
18	Austria	2.15	97	Egypt	3.35
18	Chile	2.15	97	Guinea	3.35
18	Estonia	2.15	97	Ivory Coast	3.35
18	Netherlands	2.15	97	Moldova	3.35
22	Denmark	2.25	97	Pakistan	3.35
22	El Salvador	2.25	104	Nepal	3.40
22	Finland	2.25	104	Venezuela	3.40
25	Germany	2.30	106	Armenia	3.45
25	Iceland	2.30	106	Bulgaria	3.45
27	Norway	2.35	106	Lesotho	3.45
28	Korea, South	2.40	106	Madagascar	3.45
28	Kuwait	2.40	106	Russia	3.45
28	Malaysia	2.40	111	Burkina Faso	3.50
28	Panama	2.40	111	Cameroon	3.50
28	Thailand	2.40	111	Guyana	3.50
33	Sweden	2.45	111	Nicaragua	3.50
34	Argentina	2.50	115	Gambia	3.60
34	France	2.50	116	Croatia	3.65
34	Italy	2.50	116	Georgia	3.65
34	Spain	2.50	116	Malawi	3.65
38	Portugal	2.55	119	Cape Verde	3.67
38	Sri Lanka	2.55	120	Ethiopia	3.70
38	Trinidad and Tobago	2.55	120	India	3.70
41	Barbados	2.60	120	Niger	3.70
41	Peru	2.60	123	Congo	3.75
43	Bolivia	2.65	124	Chad	3.80
43	Mauritius	2.65	124	China	3.80
45	Cyprus	2.70	124	Mauritania	3.80
45	Jamaica	2.70	124	Ukraine	3.80
45	Uruguay	2.70	124	Zimbabwe	3.80
48	Botswana	2.75	129	Albania	3.85
48	Guatemala	2.75	129	Bangladesh	3.85
48	Jordan	2.75	129	Mozambique	3.85
48	Namibia	2.75	129	Suriname	3.85
48	Oman	2.75	133	Burundi	3.90
48	Philippines	2.75	134	Togo	3.95
54	Belize	2.80	135	Haiti	4.00
54	Costa Rica	2.80	135	Kyrgyz Rep.	4.00
54	Israel	2.80	137	Kazakhstan	4.05
54	Swaziland	2.80	137	Sierra Leone	4.05
54	Turkey	2.80	139	Yemen	4.10
54	Uganda	2.80	140	Belarus	4.15
54	Samoa	2.80	141	Sudan	4.20
61	Latvia	2.85	141	Syria	4.20
62	Greece	2.90	143	Azerbaijan	4.30
62	Hungary	2.90	143	Equatorial Guinea	4.30
62	So. Africa	2.90	143	Myanmar	4.30
65	Ecuador	2.95	143	Rwanda	4.30
65	Gabon	2.95	147	Tajikistan	4.40
65	Indonesia	2.95	147	Uzbekistan	4.40
65	Malta	2.95	149	Angola	4.45
65	Morocco	2.95	149	Turkmenistan	4.45
65	Poland	2.95	151	Guinea-Bissau	4.55
65	Tunisia	2.95	152	Vietnam	4.60
72	Ghana	3.00	153	Congo (Zaire)	4.70
72	Lithuania	3.00	153	Iran	4.70
72	Saudi Arabia	3.00	155	Bosnia	4.80
75	Benin	3.05	155	Somalia	4.80
75	Kenya	3.05	157	Iraq	4.90
75	Paraguay	3.05	157	Laos	4.90
75	Qatar	3.05	157	Libya	4.90
75	Slovak Republic	3.05	160	Cuba	5.00
75	Zambia	3.05	160	Korea, North	5.00
81	Colombia	3.10			

Mostly Unfree

CAPITAL FLOWS AND FOREIGN INVESTMENT
Score: 3–Stable (moderate barriers)

Moldova has moved to develop foreign investment and commercial codes. Some foreign ownership of land is legal now, but 100 percent foreign ownership is not permitted. The government also prevents 100 percent foreign ownership in banking, securities and bonds, and natural resources.

BANKING
Score: 3–Stable (moderate level of restrictions)

Although Moldova's banking system is becoming more competitive and less subject to government control, it remains underdeveloped. There are 26 private foreign banks operating in the country, but foreigners are not permitted to own 100 percent of banks and other financial institutions.

WAGE AND PRICE CONTROLS
Score: 3–Stable (moderate level)

The market sets most prices, but the government still controls those of goods produced by some state-run monopolies. Moldova has a minimum wage.

PROPERTY RIGHTS
Score: 3–Stable (moderate level of protection)

Moldova has passed laws guaranteeing private property and strengthening the judiciary. According to the U.S. Department of Commerce, "The independence of Moldova's judiciary has increased since the 1991 dissolution of the Soviet Union, partly due to provisions for tenure designed to increase judicial independence. A series of reforms approved in 1995 have begun to be implemented, including creation of a court to deal with constitutional issues and a system of appeals courts."[3] The enforcement of property rights can be cumbersome, and 100 percent ownership of land by foreign investors is not permitted.

REGULATION
Score: 3–Stable (moderate level)

Moldova is establishing a regulatory regime that will stress environmental protection and consumer safety. Existing regulations, in addition to being burdensome, are applied haphazardly. State planning has been reduced considerably.

BLACK MARKET
Score: 4–Stable (high level of activity)

"In 1995," reports the U.S. Department of Commerce, "Moldova adopted a [law] on protection of intellectual and industrial [property]. The law and its enforcement are inadequate to curb infringements, which take place in all sectors: software, cable television, audio and video cassettes, books and other [items]."[4] This law has allowed a substantial black market to develop in these pirated items.

NOTES

[1]   U.S. Department of Commerce, "Moldova—Economic and Trade Overview," 1997.
[2]   *Ibid.*
[3]   U.S. Department of Commerce, National Trade Data Bank and Economic Bulletin Board, products of *Stat–USA* Internet site (*http://www.stat-usa.gov*).
[4]   U.S. Department of Commerce, "Moldova—Economic and Trade Overview," 1997.

Mongolia 3.20

1998 Score: **3.10**   1997 Score: **3.30**   1996 Score: **3.50**

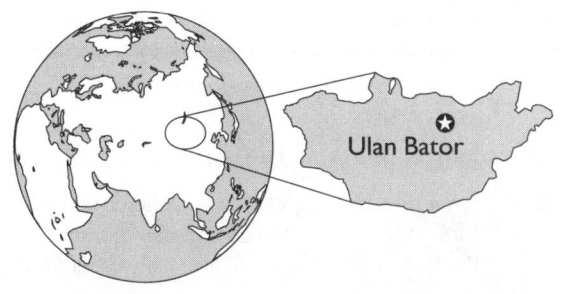

Ulan Bator

Trade	1	Banking	3
Taxation	4	Wages and Prices	3
Government Intervention	3	Property Rights	3
Monetary Policy	5	Regulation	4
Foreign Investment	3	Black Market	3

Mongolia regained its independence from the Soviet Union in 1921. Its economy remained closely linked with that of the Soviet Union, however, and it copied the Soviet model of central economic planning. After the collapse of the Soviet Union in 1991, Mongolia embarked on a program of economic liberalization; and although much remains to be done, there has been significant progress. Democratic elections were held in June 1996, and the new government agreed to accelerate the process of economic reform. Mongolia eliminated tariffs and taxes on all imports in 1997. The regulatory burden is rising, however; as a result, its overall score is 0.1 point worse than last year.

TRADE POLICY
Score: 1–Stable (very low level of protectionism)

Mongolia abolished all forms of tariffs and taxes on imports in April 1997. It is the only country with no taxes of any kind on imports. Mongolia also has streamlined its customs bureau, making it much more efficient, and there no longer are any significant non-tariff barriers.

TAXATION
Score–Income taxation: 4–Stable (high tax rates)
Score–Corporate taxation: 4–Stable (high tax rates)
Total Taxation Score: 4–Stable (high tax rates)

Mongolia has a top income tax rate of 40 percent and a top corporate tax rate of 40 percent. It also has a 10 percent sales tax.

GOVERNMENT INTERVENTION IN THE ECONOMY
Score: 3–Stable (high level)

Government consumes 25 percent of GDP. Although the government has undertaken a substantial privatization program, the state-owned sector remains significant and still generates almost 50 percent of GNP.

MONETARY POLICY
Score: 5–Stable (very high level of inflation)

Mongolia's rate of inflation averaged 52.2 percent during the 1986–1996 period. The inflation rate was 58 percent in 1997.

CAPITAL FLOWS AND FOREIGN INVESTMENT
Score: 3–Stable (moderate barriers)

Mongolia recently passed legislation to protect private property and foreign investments from government expropriation. New laws also provide equal treatment for Mongolian- and foreign-owned companies, and restrictions on currencies and profits have been removed. Although no industry is formally restricted, the government maintains a list of industries in which foreign investment is discouraged; examples include state-owned enterprises, liquor,

1	Hong Kong	1.25	81	Fiji	3.10
2	Singapore	1.30	81	Mali	3.10
3	Bahrain	1.70	81	Slovenia	3.10
4	New Zealand	1.75	85	Honduras	3.15
5	Switzerland	1.85	85	Mexico	3.15
6	United States	1.90	85	Papua New Guinea	3.15
7	Ireland	1.95	88	Djibouti	3.20
7	Luxembourg	1.95	88	Mongolia	3.20
7	Taiwan	1.95	90	Algeria	3.25
7	United Kingdom	1.95	90	Brazil	3.25
11	Bahamas	2.00	90	Lebanon	3.25
12	Czech Republic	2.05	90	Senegal	3.25
12	Japan	2.05	90	Tanzania	3.25
14	Australia	2.10	95	Nigeria	3.30
14	Belgium	2.10	95	Romania	3.30
14	Canada	2.10	97	Cambodia	3.35
14	United Arab Emirates	2.10	97	Dominican Republic	3.35
18	Austria	2.15	97	Egypt	3.35
18	Chile	2.15	97	Guinea	3.35
18	Estonia	2.15	97	Ivory Coast	3.35
18	Netherlands	2.15	97	Moldova	3.35
22	Denmark	2.25	97	Pakistan	3.35
22	El Salvador	2.25	104	Nepal	3.40
22	Finland	2.25	104	Venezuela	3.40
25	Germany	2.30	106	Armenia	3.45
25	Iceland	2.30	106	Bulgaria	3.45
27	Norway	2.35	106	Lesotho	3.45
28	Korea, South	2.40	106	Madagascar	3.45
28	Kuwait	2.40	106	Russia	3.45
28	Malaysia	2.40	111	Burkina Faso	3.50
28	Panama	2.40	111	Cameroon	3.50
28	Thailand	2.40	111	Guyana	3.50
33	Sweden	2.45	111	Nicaragua	3.50
34	Argentina	2.50	115	Gambia	3.60
34	France	2.50	116	Croatia	3.65
34	Italy	2.50	116	Georgia	3.65
34	Spain	2.50	116	Malawi	3.65
38	Portugal	2.55	119	Cape Verde	3.67
38	Sri Lanka	2.55	120	Ethiopia	3.70
38	Trinidad and Tobago	2.55	120	India	3.70
41	Barbados	2.60	120	Niger	3.70
41	Peru	2.60	123	Congo	3.75
43	Bolivia	2.65	124	Chad	3.80
43	Mauritius	2.65	124	China	3.80
45	Cyprus	2.70	124	Mauritania	3.80
45	Jamaica	2.70	124	Ukraine	3.80
45	Uruguay	2.70	124	Zimbabwe	3.80
48	Botswana	2.75	129	Albania	3.85
48	Guatemala	2.75	129	Bangladesh	3.85
48	Jordan	2.75	129	Mozambique	3.85
48	Namibia	2.75	129	Suriname	3.85
48	Oman	2.75	133	Burundi	3.90
48	Philippines	2.75	134	Togo	3.95
54	Belize	2.80	135	Haiti	4.00
54	Costa Rica	2.80	135	Kyrgyz Rep.	4.00
54	Israel	2.80	137	Kazakhstan	4.05
54	Swaziland	2.80	137	Sierra Leone	4.05
54	Turkey	2.80	139	Yemen	4.10
54	Uganda	2.80	140	Belarus	4.15
54	Samoa	2.80	141	Sudan	4.20
61	Latvia	2.85	141	Syria	4.20
62	Greece	2.90	143	Azerbaijan	4.30
62	Hungary	2.90	143	Equatorial Guinea	4.30
62	So. Africa	2.90	143	Myanmar	4.30
65	Ecuador	2.95	143	Rwanda	4.30
65	Gabon	2.95	147	Tajikistan	4.40
65	Indonesia	2.95	147	Uzbekistan	4.40
65	Malta	2.95	149	Angola	4.45
65	Morocco	2.95	149	Turkmenistan	4.45
65	Poland	2.95	151	Guinea-Bissau	4.55
65	Tunisia	2.95	152	Vietnam	4.60
72	Ghana	3.00	153	Congo (Zaire)	4.70
72	Lithuania	3.00	153	Iran	4.70
72	Saudi Arabia	3.00	155	Bosnia	4.80
75	Benin	3.05	155	Somalia	4.80
75	Kenya	3.05	157	Iraq	4.90
75	Paraguay	3.05	157	Laos	4.90
75	Qatar	3.05	157	Libya	4.90
75	Slovak Republic	3.05	160	Cuba	5.00
75	Zambia	3.05	160	Korea, North	5.00
81	Colombia	3.10			

Mostly Unfree

securities, mining, animal skins, pharmaceuticals, and chemicals. Foreigners still may not own land.

BANKING
Score: 3–Stable (moderate level of restrictions)

Even though progress has been made toward deregulating Mongolia's banks, the government continues to control them. The banking system remains underdeveloped.

WAGE AND PRICE CONTROLS
Score: 3–Stable (moderate level)

Mongolia controls prices through a complex system of government procurement. For example, the government may buy a significant amount of a product in order to control its supply, thereby affecting the price. Noteworthy progress has been made toward liberalizing prices, however, as the government has begun to allow the market to play a more prominent role. Mongolia has a minimum wage.

PROPERTY RIGHTS
Score: 3–Stable (moderate level of protection)

Expropriation of existing private property is unlikely. The government has instituted new laws to protect property owners. Enforcement of laws protecting private property, however, is inefficient, and the state still holds a significant amount of land that stands little chance of being privatized in the near future. According to the U.S. Department of Commerce, "While there is no reason to believe that the judiciary is unduly influenced either by the government or by any individual or entity in Mongolia, it is important to note that there is a countrywide lack of expertise in Western business practices that certainly extends to judges. In addition, many of the recent laws in Mongolia have not been thoroughly tested."[1]

REGULATION
Score: 4– (high level)

The growing private sector—especially newly privatized companies—remains subject to significant government control. Moreover, the government has implemented a host of new regulations in the past several years that increase the burden on business, but there continue to be problems with enforcement. For example, according to the U.S. Department of Commerce, "Mongolia does not suffer from a shortage of laws and regulations; what it lacks are experience and enforcement capability. The system is transparent in the sense that copies of the laws are readily available, oftentimes in English and officials do try to live up to the spirit and letter of the legislation as written. The problem is the sheer volume of new laws that have gone on the books in the last few years. Since 1993, new laws or amendments to previous ones that have been drafted and passed and impact directly on foreign investment include legislation on accounting, anti-corruption, banking law amendments, bankruptcy of economic entities, the chamber of commerce and industry, communications, consumer protection, copyright, currency regulation, customs, deposits, settlements & credits, economic entities, energy, environmental protection, excise tax, foreign investment, foreign trade arbitration, general taxation, income tax of economic entities & organizations, labor, minerals, partnership & company, patent, petroleum, railway transportation safety, rights of trade unions, securities, and transport facilities & vehicle tax."[2] As a result of this increase in the regulatory burden, Mongolia's regulation score is 1 point worse this year.

BLACK MARKET
Score: 3–Stable (moderate level of activity)

Mongolia's government buys many goods through its complex procurement program. This distorts prices for food commodities. The result is a black market for these and other government-regulated goods. There also is a moderate level of smuggling.

NOTES

1   U.S. Department of Commerce, *Country Commercial Guide,* 1998.
2   *Ibid.*

Morocco   2.95

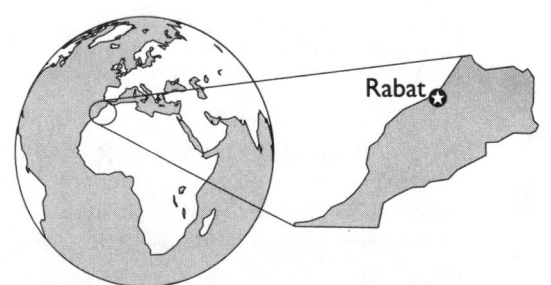
Rabat

1998 Score: **2.95**	1997 Score: **2.75**	1996 Score: **2.70**

Trade	5	Banking	3
Taxation	3.5	Wages and Prices	3
Government Intervention	3	Property Rights	3
Monetary Policy	1	Regulation	3
Foreign Investment	2	Black Market	3

Morocco, which gained its independence from France in 1956, is a constitutional monarchy. The government of King Hassan II has imposed free-market reforms on the country's mixed economy, which has experienced slow but steady rate of growth in recent years despite a 1995 drought. Morocco aspires to become a major manufacturing base, serving markets in both Europe and Africa, and is undergoing modest political liberalization along with economic modernization. Its military effort to retain control of the disputed Western Sahara, however, has caused both a large expensive and a diplomatic headache.

TRADE POLICY
Score: 5–Stable (very high level of protectionism)

Morocco has an average tariff of about 20 percent. Bananas still are protected by non-tariff barriers. According to the U.S. Department of Commerce, "In principle, customs procedures are simple and straightforward, but in practice they are sometimes marked by delays."[1]

TAXATION
Score–Income taxation: 3–Stable (moderate tax rates)
Score–Corporate taxation: 3–Stable (moderate tax rates)
Total Taxation Score: 3.5–Stable (high tax rates)

Morocco's highest income tax rate is 44 percent; the average income is taxed at a rate of 0 percent. The corporate tax rate is fixed at 35 percent of profits. A value-added tax is payable at rates of 7 percent or 20 percent on sales and 7 percent on banking activities. Morocco also has a capital gains tax of 35 percent.

GOVERNMENT INTERVENTION IN THE ECONOMY
Score: 3–Stable (moderate level)

Government consumes 18.4 percent of GDP. Under an ambitious privatization program begun in 1992, over 100 state-owned enterprises, worth over $2 billion, were targeted to be sold by 1995. This goal has yet to be met, although there has been steady progress. The government sold some 27 operations, including 8 hotels, in 1994. Privatization slowed in 1995 but rebounded in 1996. The government still owns substantial portions of the economy, mainly some financial institutions and steel and fertilizer companies.

MONETARY POLICY
Score: 1–Stable (very low level of inflation)

Morocco's average annual rate of inflation between 1986 and 1996 was 5 percent. In 1997, the rate was 2.5 percent.

1	Hong Kong	1.25	
2	Singapore	1.30	
3	Bahrain	1.70	
4	New Zealand	1.75	
5	Switzerland	1.85	
6	United States	1.90	
7	Ireland	1.95	
7	Luxembourg	1.95	
7	Taiwan	1.95	
7	United Kingdom	1.95	
11	Bahamas	2.00	
12	Czech Republic	2.05	
12	Japan	2.05	
14	Australia	2.10	
14	Belgium	2.10	
14	Canada	2.10	
14	United Arab Emirates	2.10	
18	Austria	2.15	
18	Chile	2.15	
18	Estonia	2.15	
18	Netherlands	2.15	
22	Denmark	2.25	
22	El Salvador	2.25	
22	Finland	2.25	
25	Germany	2.30	
25	Iceland	2.30	
27	Norway	2.35	
28	Korea, South	2.40	
28	Kuwait	2.40	
28	Malaysia	2.40	
28	Panama	2.40	
28	Thailand	2.40	
33	Sweden	2.45	
34	Argentina	2.50	
34	France	2.50	
34	Italy	2.50	
34	Spain	2.50	
38	Portugal	2.55	
38	Sri Lanka	2.55	
38	Trinidad and Tobago	2.55	
41	Barbados	2.60	
41	Peru	2.60	
43	Bolivia	2.65	
43	Mauritius	2.65	
45	Cyprus	2.70	
45	Jamaica	2.70	
45	Uruguay	2.70	
48	Botswana	2.75	
48	Guatemala	2.75	
48	Jordan	2.75	
48	Namibia	2.75	
48	Oman	2.75	
48	Philippines	2.75	
54	Belize	2.80	
54	Costa Rica	2.80	
54	Israel	2.80	
54	Swaziland	2.80	
54	Turkey	2.80	
54	Uganda	2.80	
54	Samoa	2.80	
61	Latvia	2.85	
62	Greece	2.90	
62	Hungary	2.90	
62	So. Africa	2.90	
65	Ecuador	2.95	
65	Gabon	2.95	
65	Indonesia	2.95	
65	Malta	2.95	
65	Morocco	2.95	
65	Poland	2.95	
65	Tunisia	2.95	
72	Ghana	3.00	
72	Lithuania	3.00	
72	Saudi Arabia	3.00	
75	Benin	3.05	
75	Kenya	3.05	
75	Paraguay	3.05	
75	Qatar	3.05	
75	Slovak Republic	3.05	
75	Zambia	3.05	
81	Colombia	3.10	

81	Fiji	3.10	
81	Mali	3.10	
81	Slovenia	3.10	
85	Honduras	3.15	
85	Mexico	3.15	
85	Papua New Guinea	3.15	
88	Djibouti	3.20	
88	Mongolia	3.20	
90	Algeria	3.25	
90	Brazil	3.25	
90	Lebanon	3.25	
90	Senegal	3.25	
90	Tanzania	3.25	
95	Nigeria	3.30	
95	Romania	3.30	
97	Cambodia	3.35	
97	Dominican Republic	3.35	
97	Egypt	3.35	
97	Guinea	3.35	
97	Ivory Coast	3.35	
97	Moldova	3.35	
97	Pakistan	3.35	
104	Nepal	3.40	
104	Venezuela	3.40	
106	Armenia	3.45	
106	Bulgaria	3.45	
106	Lesotho	3.45	
106	Madagascar	3.45	
106	Russia	3.45	
111	Burkina Faso	3.50	
111	Cameroon	3.50	
111	Guyana	3.50	
111	Nicaragua	3.50	
115	Gambia	3.60	
116	Croatia	3.65	
116	Georgia	3.65	
116	Malawi	3.65	
119	Cape Verde	3.67	
120	Ethiopia	3.70	
120	India	3.70	
120	Niger	3.70	
123	Congo	3.75	
124	Chad	3.80	
124	China	3.80	
124	Mauritania	3.80	
124	Ukraine	3.80	
124	Zimbabwe	3.80	
129	Albania	3.85	
129	Bangladesh	3.85	
129	Mozambique	3.85	
129	Suriname	3.85	
133	Burundi	3.90	
134	Togo	3.95	
135	Haiti	4.00	
135	Kyrgyz Rep.	4.00	
137	Kazakhstan	4.05	
137	Sierra Leone	4.05	
139	Yemen	4.10	
140	Belarus	4.15	
141	Sudan	4.20	
141	Syria	4.20	
143	Azerbaijan	4.30	
143	Equatorial Guinea	4.30	
143	Myanmar	4.30	
143	Rwanda	4.30	
147	Tajikistan	4.40	
147	Uzbekistan	4.40	
149	Angola	4.45	
149	Turkmenistan	4.45	
151	Guinea-Bissau	4.55	
152	Vietnam	4.60	
153	Congo (Zaire)	4.70	
153	Iran	4.70	
155	Bosnia	4.80	
155	Somalia	4.80	
157	Iraq	4.90	
157	Laos	4.90	
157	Libya	4.90	
160	Cuba	5.00	
160	Korea, North	5.00	

Mostly Free

CAPITAL FLOWS AND FOREIGN INVESTMENT
Score: 2–Stable (low barriers)

Morocco's government treats foreign-owned and locally owned investments equally; the government also permits 100 percent foreign ownership. Neither foreigners nor Moroccans may invest, however, in industries that compete with the state's water monopoly, rail and transportation services, or the mining and processing of phosphates.

BANKING
Score: 3–Stable (moderate level of restrictions)

Foreign banks may possess controlling interests in Moroccan banks. Local banks are expanding their activities to include capital market activity. Even though the government has privatized one major bank and plans to privatize another, it still owns several other financial and credit institutions. According to the U.S. Department of Commerce, "The banking system is still used by the government...as a way to channel domestic savings to finance government debt, and the banks are required to hold a part of their assets in bonds paying below market interest rates."[2]

WAGE AND PRICE CONTROLS
Score: 3–Stable (moderate level)

Most price controls have been eliminated, although they remain on bread, cereals, milk, sugar, and other basics. The state subsidizes these products, too. Even though wage and salary increases are negotiated freely between the government and businesses, there is a minimum wage. When the Central Commission for Prices and Wages records an increase of at least 5 percent in the cost of living, the government can raise all wages and prices by decree.

PROPERTY RIGHTS
Score: 3–Stable (moderate level of protection)

Morocco's constitution prohibits the expropriation of private property except in special cases prescribed by law. There has been no expropriation since the early 1970s, and there are no outstanding cases of expropriation or nationalization of investments. The U.S. Department of State reports that the constitution "provides for an independent judiciary, but all courts are subject to extrajudicial pressures, including bribery and government influence."[3]

REGULATION
Score: 3–Stable (moderate level)

Although establishing a business is fairly straightforward in Morocco, foreign businesses face complicated procedures and corruption. Government procedures are not always transparent, and routine business permits can be difficult to obtain, particularly from local authorities. Labor legislation makes it difficult to terminate workers. According to the U.S. Department of Commerce, "Morocco's economic reform program has included improvements in the regulatory environment. In particular, the liberalization of the foreign exchange allocation system, the import regime, and the financial sector have reduced the government's role in the economy. Deficiencies remain in other areas, however, such as the labor law which limits firms' ability to hire and fire workers. Even in areas where the regulations are favorable on paper, there are often problems in practice. Government procedures are not always transparent, efficient or quick. Routine permits, especially those required by local governments, can be difficult to obtain. The Moroccan legal system is often inadequate for resolving disputes, particularly those involving foreign investors."[4]

BLACK MARKET
Score: 3–Stable (moderate level of activity)

The black market accounts for an estimated 20 percent of GDP. There is considerable smuggling of consumer goods, as well as a lively trade in contraband. Because Morocco's laws governing intellectual property do not cover computer software, black market activity in this area is on the rise. Trademark violations, mainly in the clothing industry, also constitute a growing problem.

NOTES

[1]   U.S. Department of State, *Country Reports on Economic Policy and Trade Practices,* 1998.
[2]   U.S. Department of Commerce, *Country Commercial Guide,* 1998.
[3]   U.S. Department of State, "Morocco Country Report on Human Rights Practices for 1997," 1998.
[4]   U.S. Department of Commerce, *Country Commercial Guide,* 1998.

Mozambique   3.85

1998 Score: **4.10**   1997 Score: **4.00**   1996 Score: **4.05**

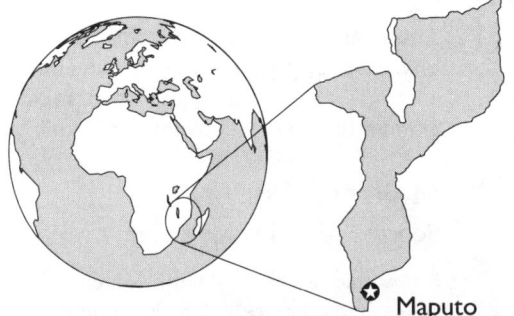

Maputo

Trade	3	Banking	3
Taxation	3.5	Wages and Prices	3
Government Intervention	3	Property Rights	4
Monetary Policy	5	Regulation	5
Foreign Investment	4	Black Market	5

Mozambique won a decade-long conflict for independence from Portugal in 1975. Two years later, it became engulfed in a bloody civil war that lasted until 1992. Since then, it has been reasonably successful in constructing a democratic government and rebuilding the economy. Mozambique held its first multiparty democratic elections in 1994. The government has abandoned the Marxist policies that dominated the economy for decades; these policies had caused Mozambique's economy to become one of the most heavily dependent on aid. Growth in GDP averaged 6.6 percent from 1992 to 1996; per capita GNP, however, was estimated at just $80 in 1996. The government has slashed tariffs and eliminated non-tariff barriers—even allowing a private company to take over customs as a means for eliminating corruption—and privatized over 900 companies. Moreover, it has reduced taxes on the average income level; as a result, Mozambique's overall score is 0.25 point better than last year.

TRADE POLICY
Score: 3+ (moderate level of protectionism)

Mozambique's tariff rates range from 0 percent to 40 percent. The U.S. Department of Commerce previously had estimated that the average tariff was about 27 percent; this rate has fallen to 11 percent. As a result, Mozambique's trade policy score is 2 points better this year. The government has worked to liberalize trade by eliminating nearly all non-tariff barriers and simplifying licensing procedures. Although the customs bureau had been riddled with corruption, the government recently allowed private managers to take it over. This has had a tremendous impact on eliminating corruption within customs. According to the U.S. Department of Commerce, "[Customs] procedures are becoming more routinized. Company profiling data is being gathered. Corrupt employees are being identified and summarily released. New employees are being hired and trained. And more efficient procedures are being developed."[1]

TAXATION
Score–Income taxation: 2+ (low tax rates)
Score–Corporate taxation: 4–Stable (high tax rates)
Total Taxation Score: 3.5+ (high tax rates)

Mozambique adjusted personal income taxes in 1995. The highest bracket now is 30 percent, up from 15 percent in 1995, and the tax on the average income is 8 percent, down from 15 percent last year. As a result, Mozambique's income taxation score is 1 point better than last year. The top corporate income tax rate is 45 percent. Mozambique also has a 45 percent capital gains tax and a 75 percent consumption tax. When the tax scores are averaged, Mozambique's total taxation score is 0.5 point better than last year.

GOVERNMENT INTERVENTION IN THE ECONOMY
Score: 3–Stable (moderate level)

Government consumes 12 percent of GDP. Many small enterprises have been privatized (including a brewery and cement factory that were sold to South

1	Hong Kong	1.25	81	Fiji	3.10
2	Singapore	1.30	81	Mali	3.10
3	Bahrain	1.70	81	Slovenia	3.10
4	New Zealand	1.75	85	Honduras	3.15
5	Switzerland	1.85	85	Mexico	3.15
6	United States	1.90	85	Papua New Guinea	3.15
7	Ireland	1.95	88	Djibouti	3.20
7	Luxembourg	1.95	88	Mongolia	3.20
7	Taiwan	1.95	90	Algeria	3.25
7	United Kingdom	1.95	90	Brazil	3.25
11	Bahamas	2.00	90	Lebanon	3.25
12	Czech Republic	2.05	90	Senegal	3.25
12	Japan	2.05	90	Tanzania	3.25
14	Australia	2.10	95	Nigeria	3.30
14	Belgium	2.10	95	Romania	3.30
14	Canada	2.10	97	Cambodia	3.35
14	United Arab Emirates	2.10	97	Dominican Republic	3.35
18	Austria	2.15	97	Egypt	3.35
18	Chile	2.15	97	Guinea	3.35
18	Estonia	2.15	97	Ivory Coast	3.35
18	Netherlands	2.15	97	Moldova	3.35
22	Denmark	2.25	97	Pakistan	3.35
22	El Salvador	2.25	104	Nepal	3.40
22	Finland	2.25	104	Venezuela	3.40
25	Germany	2.30	106	Armenia	3.45
25	Iceland	2.30	106	Bulgaria	3.45
27	Norway	2.35	106	Lesotho	3.45
28	Korea, South	2.40	106	Madagascar	3.45
28	Kuwait	2.40	106	Russia	3.45
28	Malaysia	2.40	111	Burkina Faso	3.50
28	Panama	2.40	111	Cameroon	3.50
28	Thailand	2.40	111	Guyana	3.50
33	Sweden	2.45	111	Nicaragua	3.50
34	Argentina	2.50	115	Gambia	3.60
34	France	2.50	116	Croatia	3.65
34	Italy	2.50	116	Georgia	3.65
34	Spain	2.50	116	Malawi	3.65
38	Portugal	2.55	119	Cape Verde	3.67
38	Sri Lanka	2.55	120	Ethiopia	3.70
38	Trinidad and Tobago	2.55	120	India	3.70
41	Barbados	2.60	120	Niger	3.70
41	Peru	2.60	123	Congo	3.75
43	Bolivia	2.65	124	Chad	3.80
43	Mauritius	2.65	124	China	3.80
45	Cyprus	2.70	124	Mauritania	3.80
45	Jamaica	2.70	124	Ukraine	3.80
45	Uruguay	2.70	124	Zimbabwe	3.80
48	Botswana	2.75	129	Albania	3.85
48	Guatemala	2.75	129	Bangladesh	3.85
48	Jordan	2.75	129	Mozambique	3.85
48	Namibia	2.75	129	Suriname	3.85
48	Oman	2.75	133	Burundi	3.90
48	Philippines	2.75	134	Togo	3.95
54	Belize	2.80	135	Haiti	4.00
54	Costa Rica	2.80	135	Kyrgyz Rep.	4.00
54	Israel	2.80	137	Kazakhstan	4.05
54	Swaziland	2.80	137	Sierra Leone	4.05
54	Turkey	2.80	139	Yemen	4.10
54	Uganda	2.80	140	Belarus	4.15
54	Samoa	2.80	141	Sudan	4.20
61	Latvia	2.85	141	Syria	4.20
62	Greece	2.90	143	Azerbaijan	4.30
62	Hungary	2.90	143	Equatorial Guinea	4.30
62	So. Africa	2.90	143	Myanmar	4.30
65	Ecuador	2.95	143	Rwanda	4.30
65	Gabon	2.95	147	Tajikistan	4.40
65	Indonesia	2.95	147	Uzbekistan	4.40
65	Malta	2.95	149	Angola	4.45
65	Morocco	2.95	149	Turkmenistan	4.45
65	Poland	2.95	151	Guinea-Bissau	4.55
65	Tunisia	2.95	152	Vietnam	4.60
72	Ghana	3.00	153	Congo (Zaire)	4.70
72	Lithuania	3.00	153	Iran	4.70
72	Saudi Arabia	3.00	155	Bosnia	4.80
75	Benin	3.05	155	Somalia	4.80
75	Kenya	3.05	157	Iraq	4.90
75	Paraguay	3.05	157	Laos	4.90
75	Qatar	3.05	157	Libya	4.90
75	Slovak Republic	3.05	160	Cuba	5.00
75	Zambia	3.05	160	Korea, North	5.00
81	Colombia	3.10			

Mostly Unfree

African and Portuguese concerns), and plans for additional privatizations are on the table. In the meantime, public enterprises will continue to account for a considerable amount of the formal sector's economic output.

MONETARY POLICY
Score: 5–Stable (very high level of inflation)

Mozambique's average annual rate of inflation from 1986 to 1996 was 59.7 percent. The inflation data for 1997 are not available.

CAPITAL FLOWS AND FOREIGN INVESTMENT
Score: 4–Stable (high barriers)

A recent change in the investment law has improved the climate for foreign investors. Mozambique has established a one-stop shop for approval of foreign investment, and the government is granting land concessions to South African farmers in remote, underutilized areas. At the same time, however, feasibility study requirements and a corrupt government bureaucracy frustrate foreign investment, especially by small-scale investors. Infrastructure and a few other areas are off-limits to private investment. Free-trade zones were established in 1993, but their terms are not comparatively attractive. Restrictions remain on the ownership of land, as do local content requirements.

BANKING
Score: 3–Stable (moderate level of restrictions)

State banks dominate banking, although the government is liberalizing the system. The government also has freed interest rates and privatized the Commercial Bank of Mozambique, which accounts for some 70 percent of banking assets. There still are only a few private banks, which remain at a disadvantage when trying to compete with the state-owned banks, in which corruption is a problem.

WAGE AND PRICE CONTROLS
Score: 3–Stable (moderate level)

The government lifted price controls on several products in 1994. Remaining price controls apply to wheat, flour, bread, rents, fuels, utilities, newspapers, transportation, and a few other services. Mozambique has a minimum wage.

PROPERTY RIGHTS
Score: 4–Stable (low level of protection)

Despite some progress in bolstering property rights, Mozambique's land tenure and property rights regime remains fairly chaotic. Technically, all land still belongs to the state, and the vast majority of housing is state-owned, although the government has made some progress toward residential privatization. The government recently announced that it would not make restitution for pre-independence property claims. Mozambique's underdeveloped court system is unable to protect private property adequately. "The judicial system in Mozambique is not effective in resolving commercial disputes," according to the U.S. Department of Commerce.[2]

REGULATION
Score: 5–Stable (very high level)

Bureaucratic corruption characterizes Mozambique's regulatory environment. Registering a company is a cumbersome and secretive process, with considerable red tape. According to the U.S. Department of Commerce, "Until recently, the battle against corruption was waged through privatization: banks, parastatals, and even customs operations. Currently, the battle revolves around strengthening the country's judicial system, streamlining and simplifying regulations, reducing government bureaucracy, improving the salary of and training of government workers, and improving enforcement."[3]

BLACK MARKET
Score: 5–Stable (very high level of activity)

Mozambique is a center for drug trafficking and money laundering, and international crime organizations use it as a clearinghouse for black market trade between Asia and Europe. According to the U.S. Department of Commerce, "At nearly $1 billion, unofficial imports are five times official exports. These figures exclude a vibrant and growing informal sector that conducts much of the trade along the porous borders with six neighboring countries and outside of the formal economy."[4]

NOTES
[1]   U.S. Department of Commerce, *Country Commercial Guide,* 1998.
[2]   *Ibid.*
[3]   *Ibid.*
[4]   *Ibid.*

Myanmar (formerly Burma)

4.30

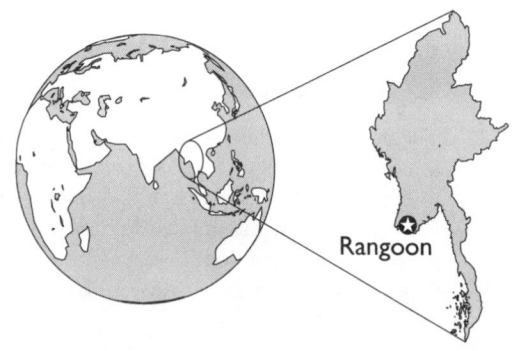
Rangoon

1998 Score: **4.30**   1997 Score: **4.30**   1996 Score: **4.30**

Trade	5	Banking	4
Taxation	3	Wages and Prices	4
Government Intervention	5	Property Rights	4
Monetary Policy	4	Regulation	5
Foreign Investment	4	Black Market	5

Burma, now known as Myanmar, gained its independence from the United Kingdom in 1948. A fragile parliamentary democracy arose, but the military overthrew it in 1962. The country then embarked on a self-imposed state of isolation. In 1974, it declared itself a "socialist republic." In 1988, an economic crisis led to some opening to foreign investment, particularly in energy and tourism, although tight controls over other sectors have kept the level of foreign investment far below that of neighboring countries. A new military government began to introduce some free-market and democratic reforms, but they were put on hold in 1990 after opposition parties won national elections and the regime refused to relinquish power. Today, the military government continues to suppress democratic opposition. Myanmar gained membership in the Association of Southeast Asian Nations in 1997. President Bill Clinton imposed U.S. trade sanctions on Myanmar in May 1997 because of human rights abuses.

TRADE POLICY
Score: 5–Stable (very high level of protectionism)

Myanmar's average tariff rate is more than 61 percent.[1] Non-tariff barriers include licenses and import bans.

TAXATION
Score–Income taxation: 2–Stable (low tax rates)
Score–Corporate taxation: 3–Stable (moderate tax rates)
Final Taxation Score: 3–Stable (moderate tax rates)

Myanmar's top income tax rate is 30 percent; the average taxpayer is in the 3 percent bracket. The top marginal corporate tax rate is 30 percent. A commercial tax ranges from 0 percent to 200 percent.

GOVERNMENT INTERVENTION IN THE ECONOMY
Score: 5–Stable (very high level)

The government is privatizing several companies, but the economy remains largely state-controlled, with most GDP generated by government sources. According to the U.S. Department of Commerce, "No large SEE [State Economic Enterprise] has been privatized, and no major privatization initiative appears imminent."[2]

MONETARY POLICY
Score: 4–Stable (high level of inflation)

Myanmar's average annual rate of inflation from 1986 to 1996 was 24.7 percent. In 1997, the rate was 29.4 percent.

1	Hong Kong	1.25	81	Fiji	3.10
2	Singapore	1.30	81	Mali	3.10
3	Bahrain	1.70	81	Slovenia	3.10
4	New Zealand	1.75	85	Honduras	3.15
5	Switzerland	1.85	85	Mexico	3.15
6	United States	1.90	85	Papua New Guinea	3.15
7	Ireland	1.95	88	Djibouti	3.20
7	Luxembourg	1.95	88	Mongolia	3.20
7	Taiwan	1.95	90	Algeria	3.25
7	United Kingdom	1.95	90	Brazil	3.25
11	Bahamas	2.00	90	Lebanon	3.25
12	Czech Republic	2.05	90	Senegal	3.25
12	Japan	2.05	90	Tanzania	3.25
14	Australia	2.10	95	Nigeria	3.30
14	Belgium	2.10	95	Romania	3.30
14	Canada	2.10	97	Cambodia	3.35
14	United Arab Emirates	2.10	97	Dominican Republic	3.35
18	Austria	2.15	97	Egypt	3.35
18	Chile	2.15	97	Guinea	3.35
18	Estonia	2.15	97	Ivory Coast	3.35
18	Netherlands	2.15	97	Moldova	3.35
22	Denmark	2.25	97	Pakistan	3.35
22	El Salvador	2.25	104	Nepal	3.40
22	Finland	2.25	104	Venezuela	3.40
25	Germany	2.30	106	Armenia	3.45
25	Iceland	2.30	106	Bulgaria	3.45
27	Norway	2.35	106	Lesotho	3.45
28	Korea, South	2.40	106	Madagascar	3.45
28	Kuwait	2.40	106	Russia	3.45
28	Malaysia	2.40	111	Burkina Faso	3.50
28	Panama	2.40	111	Cameroon	3.50
28	Thailand	2.40	111	Guyana	3.50
33	Sweden	2.45	111	Nicaragua	3.50
34	Argentina	2.50	115	Gambia	3.60
34	France	2.50	116	Croatia	3.65
34	Italy	2.50	116	Georgia	3.65
34	Spain	2.50	116	Malawi	3.65
38	Portugal	2.55	119	Cape Verde	3.67
38	Sri Lanka	2.55	120	Ethiopia	3.70
38	Trinidad and Tobago	2.55	120	India	3.70
41	Barbados	2.60	120	Niger	3.70
41	Peru	2.60	123	Congo	3.75
43	Bolivia	2.65	124	Chad	3.80
43	Mauritius	2.65	124	China	3.80
45	Cyprus	2.70	124	Mauritania	3.80
45	Jamaica	2.70	124	Ukraine	3.80
45	Uruguay	2.70	124	Zimbabwe	3.80
48	Botswana	2.75	129	Albania	3.85
48	Guatemala	2.75	129	Bangladesh	3.85
48	Jordan	2.75	129	Mozambique	3.85
48	Namibia	2.75	129	Suriname	3.85
48	Oman	2.75	133	Burundi	3.90
48	Philippines	2.75	134	Togo	3.95
54	Belize	2.80	135	Haiti	4.00
54	Costa Rica	2.80	135	Kyrgyz Rep.	4.00
54	Israel	2.80	137	Kazakhstan	4.05
54	Swaziland	2.80	137	Sierra Leone	4.05
54	Turkey	2.80	139	Yemen	4.10
54	Uganda	2.80	140	Belarus	4.15
54	Samoa	2.80	141	Sudan	4.20
61	Latvia	2.85	141	Syria	4.20
62	Greece	2.90	143	Azerbaijan	4.30
62	Hungary	2.90	143	Equatorial Guinea	4.30
62	So. Africa	2.90	143	Myanmar	4.30
65	Ecuador	2.95	143	Rwanda	4.30
65	Gabon	2.95	147	Tajikistan	4.40
65	Indonesia	2.95	147	Uzbekistan	4.40
65	Malta	2.95	149	Angola	4.45
65	Morocco	2.95	149	Turkmenistan	4.45
65	Poland	2.95	151	Guinea-Bissau	4.55
65	Tunisia	2.95	152	Vietnam	4.60
72	Ghana	3.00	153	Congo (Zaire)	4.70
72	Lithuania	3.00	153	Iran	4.70
72	Saudi Arabia	3.00	155	Bosnia	4.80
75	Benin	3.05	155	Somalia	4.80
75	Kenya	3.05	157	Iraq	4.90
75	Paraguay	3.05	157	Laos	4.90
75	Qatar	3.05	157	Libya	4.90
75	Slovak Republic	3.05	160	Cuba	5.00
75	Zambia	3.05	160	Korea, North	5.00
81	Colombia	3.10			

Repressed

CAPITAL FLOWS AND FOREIGN INVESTMENT
Score: 4–Stable (high barriers)

The government heavily restricts investment. Even though it has moved to open some sectors of the economy to foreign investment, most of the economy remains closed. Foreign investors face a massive bureaucracy and extensive government corruption. Investments are approved only if they are deemed to benefit Myanmar, and only on a case-by-case basis.

BANKING
Score: 4–Stable (high level of restrictions)

The government controls the banking system almost completely. There is little competition, although the private banking industry is growing. According to the U.S. Department of Commerce, "At the end of FY 94/95, 82 percent of the outstanding loans of the legal banking system were to the central government, up from 79 percent two years before."[3]

WAGE AND PRICE CONTROLS
Score: 4–Stable (high level)

In many industries (such as public utilities and some agricultural goods), the government has primary responsibility for setting wages and prices. The government controls prices, too, through direct ownership of such industries as postal services, telecommunications, utilities, and rice. Prices are becoming more liberalized, however.

PROPERTY RIGHTS
Score: 4–Stable (low level of protection)

Private property owned by foreigners as a result of foreign investment is exempt from expropriation, but the property of Myanmar's citizens still is subject to confiscation. Government corruption makes it difficult to seek legal protection for property. The judiciary is both inefficient and subject to extensive government influence. According to the U.S. Department of Commerce, "The government continues sporadically to seize land and other property from its citizens and forcibly to relocate people. Such seizures are done without due process or transparency of purpose, and are not in accordance with international law.... Seeking protection for property rights from Burmese courts can be difficult. Although Burma has a well-developed legal system based on British law, in practice the system is undermined by corruption, unprofessional behavior on the part of some legal officials, and blatant interference in some cases by the military government."[4] As the U.S. Department of State reports, "The judiciary is not independent of the executive."[5]

REGULATION
Score: 5–Stable (very high level)

Establishing a business can be time-consuming and costly. Bureaucrats are corrupt and often seek bribes, and regulations can be applied unevenly and inconsistently. According to the U.S. Department of Commerce, "Enforcement of tax, labor, health and other regulations is haphazard and can be arbitrary."[6] According to the U.S. Department of State, "Some economic improvement has ensued, but major obstacles to economic reform persist. These include extensive overt and covert state involvement in economic activity, state monopolization of leading exports, a bloated bureaucracy prone to arbitrary and opaque governance, corruption, poor human and physical infrastructure, and disproportionately large military spending."[7]

BLACK MARKET
Score: 5–Stable (very high level of activity)

Myanmar's black market, mainly in consumer goods and pirated intellectual property from Western counties, continues to grow in size. "There is no effective protection of patents, copyrights, trademarks or any other intellectual property in Burma," reports the U.S. Department of Commerce. "A Patents and Design Act was introduced in 1945, but never brought into force.... Pirating of books, software, designs, etc., is rampant.... Civil action can be taken against misuse of a trademark, but is cumbersome and costly. Burma does not belong to any international conventions on patents, trademarks or copyrights."[8]

NOTES
[1]   Based on total taxes on international trade as a percentage of total imports.
[2]   U.S. Department of Commerce, *Country Commercial Guide*, 1998.
[3]   U.S. Department of Commerce, *Country Commercial Guide*, 1997.
[4]   *Ibid.*
[5]   U.S. Department of State, "Burma Country Report on Human Rights Practices for 1997," 1998.
[6]   U.S. Department of Commerce, *Country Commercial Guide*, 1997.
[7]   U.S. Department of State, "Burma Country Report on Human Rights Practices for 1997."
[8]   U.S. Department of Commerce, *Country Commercial Guide*, 1997.

Namibia   2.75

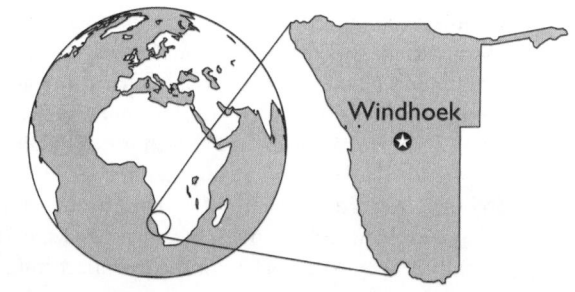

1998 Score: **2.75**	1997 Score: **2.95**	1996 Score: **n/a**

Trade	4	Banking	2
Taxation	3.5	Wages and Prices	2
Government Intervention	4	Property Rights	2
Monetary Policy	2	Regulation	3
Foreign Investment	2	Black Market	3

Namibia was a colony of Germany prior to World War I and later became a colony of South Africa, gaining its independence in 1990. The government is committed to opening the market to trade and investment, but is resisting the privatization of state industries. Namibia has achieved moderately high, but stable, levels of economic growth relative to most other countries in sub-Saharan Africa: an average of over 4 percent annually from 1992 to 1996. Namibia retains close ties with South Africa, its primary trading partner and the source of 87 percent of its imports in 1996, through membership in the Common (Rand) Monetary Area and the Southern African Customs Union (SACU).

TRADE POLICY
Score: 4–Stable (high level of protectionism)

Namibia's average tariff rate is 12 percent. Namibia belongs to the SACU, a regional trade arrangement that also includes Botswana, Lesotho, South Africa, and Swaziland. Non-tariff barriers include letters of credit that discriminate against some imports.

TAXATION
Score–Income taxation: 3–Stable (moderate tax rates)
Score–Corporate taxation: 3–Stable (moderate tax rates)
Final Taxation Score: 3.5–Stable (high tax rates)

Namibia's top income tax rate is 35 percent; the rate for the average income level is 0 percent. The top corporate tax rate is 35 percent. The government also imposes a sales tax of 8 percent to 11 percent and a special sales levy on certain manufactured goods of 0 percent to 15 percent.

GOVERNMENT INTERVENTION IN THE ECONOMY
Score: 4–Stable (high level)

Government consumes about 29.9 percent of GDP, and the public sector of the economy is substantial.

MONETARY POLICY
Score: 2–Stable (low level of inflation)

Namibia's average annual rate of inflation from 1986 to 1996 was 11.3 percent. In 1997, the rate was 8 percent.

CAPITAL FLOWS AND FOREIGN INVESTMENT
Score: 2–Stable (low barriers)

Namibia provides equal treatment for domestic and foreign firms and actively seeks foreign investment. Its modern investment code provides significant protection and incentives. According to the U.S. Department of Commerce, "The government is actively seeking foreign investment as a way to develop the economy, generate employment and boost foreign exchange earnings. In this

#	Country	Score	#	Country	Score
1	Hong Kong	1.25	81	Fiji	3.10
2	Singapore	1.30	81	Mali	3.10
3	Bahrain	1.70	81	Slovenia	3.10
4	New Zealand	1.75	85	Honduras	3.15
5	Switzerland	1.85	85	Mexico	3.15
6	United States	1.90	85	Papua New Guinea	3.15
7	Ireland	1.95	88	Djibouti	3.20
7	Luxembourg	1.95	88	Mongolia	3.20
7	Taiwan	1.95	90	Algeria	3.25
7	United Kingdom	1.95	90	Brazil	3.25
11	Bahamas	2.00	90	Lebanon	3.25
12	Czech Republic	2.05	90	Senegal	3.25
12	Japan	2.05	90	Tanzania	3.25
14	Australia	2.10	95	Nigeria	3.30
14	Belgium	2.10	95	Romania	3.30
14	Canada	2.10	97	Cambodia	3.35
14	United Arab Emirates	2.10	97	Dominican Republic	3.35
18	Austria	2.15	97	Egypt	3.35
18	Chile	2.15	97	Guinea	3.35
18	Estonia	2.15	97	Ivory Coast	3.35
18	Netherlands	2.15	97	Moldova	3.35
22	Denmark	2.25	97	Pakistan	3.35
22	El Salvador	2.25	104	Nepal	3.40
22	Finland	2.25	104	Venezuela	3.40
25	Germany	2.30	106	Armenia	3.45
25	Iceland	2.30	106	Bulgaria	3.45
27	Norway	2.35	106	Lesotho	3.45
28	Korea, South	2.40	106	Madagascar	3.45
28	Kuwait	2.40	106	Russia	3.45
28	Malaysia	2.40	111	Burkina Faso	3.50
28	Panama	2.40	111	Cameroon	3.50
28	Thailand	2.40	111	Guyana	3.50
33	Sweden	2.45	111	Nicaragua	3.50
34	Argentina	2.50	115	Gambia	3.60
34	France	2.50	116	Croatia	3.65
34	Italy	2.50	116	Georgia	3.65
34	Spain	2.50	116	Malawi	3.65
38	Portugal	2.55	119	Cape Verde	3.67
38	Sri Lanka	2.55	120	Ethiopia	3.70
38	Trinidad and Tobago	2.55	120	India	3.70
41	Barbados	2.60	120	Niger	3.70
41	Peru	2.60	123	Congo	3.75
43	Bolivia	2.65	124	Chad	3.80
43	Mauritius	2.65	124	China	3.80
45	Cyprus	2.70	124	Mauritania	3.80
45	Jamaica	2.70	124	Ukraine	3.80
45	Uruguay	2.70	124	Zimbabwe	3.80
48	Botswana	2.75	129	Albania	3.85
48	Guatemala	2.75	129	Bangladesh	3.85
48	Jordan	2.75	129	Mozambique	3.85
48	Namibia	2.75	129	Suriname	3.85
48	Oman	2.75	133	Burundi	3.90
48	Philippines	2.75	134	Togo	3.95
54	Belize	2.80	135	Haiti	4.00
54	Costa Rica	2.80	135	Kyrgyz Rep.	4.00
54	Israel	2.80	137	Kazakhstan	4.05
54	Swaziland	2.80	137	Sierra Leone	4.05
54	Turkey	2.80	139	Yemen	4.10
54	Uganda	2.80	140	Belarus	4.15
54	Samoa	2.80	141	Sudan	4.20
61	Latvia	2.85	141	Syria	4.20
62	Greece	2.90	143	Azerbaijan	4.30
62	Hungary	2.90	143	Equatorial Guinea	4.30
62	So. Africa	2.90	143	Myanmar	4.30
65	Ecuador	2.95	143	Rwanda	4.30
65	Gabon	2.95	147	Tajikistan	4.40
65	Indonesia	2.95	147	Uzbekistan	4.40
65	Malta	2.95	149	Angola	4.45
65	Morocco	2.95	149	Turkmenistan	4.45
65	Poland	2.95	151	Guinea-Bissau	4.55
65	Tunisia	2.95	152	Vietnam	4.60
72	Ghana	3.00	153	Congo (Zaire)	4.70
72	Lithuania	3.00	153	Iran	4.70
72	Saudi Arabia	3.00	155	Bosnia	4.80
75	Benin	3.05	155	Somalia	4.80
75	Kenya	3.05	157	Iraq	4.90
75	Paraguay	3.05	157	Laos	4.90
75	Qatar	3.05	157	Libya	4.90
75	Slovak Republic	3.05	160	Cuba	5.00
75	Zambia	3.05	160	Korea, North	5.00
81	Colombia	3.10			

Mostly Free

regard, the government has taken a number of positive steps to establish a system and environment conducive to foreign investment. Namibia's Foreign Investment Act guarantees foreign investors treatment equal to that given to Namibian firms, fair compensation in the event of expropriation, international arbitration of disputes between the investors and the government, the right to remit profits and access to foreign exchange. Investment incentives and special tax incentives are also available for the manufacturing sector."[1]

BANKING
Score: 2–Stable (low level of restrictions)

Namibia's banking system is entirely private, with minimal government intrusion or regulation. There is no deposit insurance, but commercial banks are regulated by a central bank. As the U.S. Department of Commerce reports, "The banking system is modern and efficient. Namibian banks are capable of handling international financial transactions and trade finances."[2]

WAGE AND PRICE CONTROLS
Score: 2–Stable (low level)

The government abolished most price controls, and the market now sets most wages and prices. Petroleum prices still are controlled, however, and a growing "buy Namibian" movement impedes competition and raises prices on some domestically produced goods and services.

PROPERTY RIGHTS
Score: 2–Stable (high level of protection)

Namibia's legal system is efficient, fair, and independent. According to the U.S. Department of Commerce, "The local court system provides an effective means to enforce property and contractual rights."[3] There is a shortage of lawyers, however, and the courts often become backlogged. According to the U.S. Department of State, "The constitutional right to a fair trail...is generally afforded by the judiciary. However, long delays in hearing cases in regular courts and problems associated with the traditional system limit this right in practice."[4]

REGULATION
Score: 3–Stable (moderate level)

Namibia has begun to enforce its recent anticorruption legislation rigorously. According to the U.S. Department of Commerce, "Allegations of alleged favoritism and nepotism in the awarding of some significant contracts to SWAPO-affiliated concerns are raised from time to time."[5] The government also has introduced new and potentially burdensome regulations on business, however, including both health and safety standards and a requirement that businesses submit an environmental impact statement for proposed new investments and construction.

BLACK MARKET
Score: 3–Stable (moderate level of activity)

Black market activity is moderate and confined mainly to goods smuggled from South Africa. The smuggling of gold and diamonds is a particular problem.

NOTES
[1]   U.S. Department of Commerce, *Country Commercial Guide,* 1998.
[2]   *Ibid.*
[3]   *Ibid.*
[4]   U.S. Department of State, "Namibia Country Report on Human Rights Practices for 1997," 1998.
[5]   U.S. Department of Commerce, *Country Commercial Guide,* 1998. SWAPO, the South West Africa People's Organization, is the current ruling party in Namibia.

Nepal

3.40

1998 Score: **3.40**   1997 Score: **3.60**   1996 Score: **3.50**

Trade	3
Taxation	3
Government Intervention	2
Monetary Policy	2
Foreign Investment	4

Banking	4
Wages and Prices	4
Property Rights	3
Regulation	4
Black Market	5

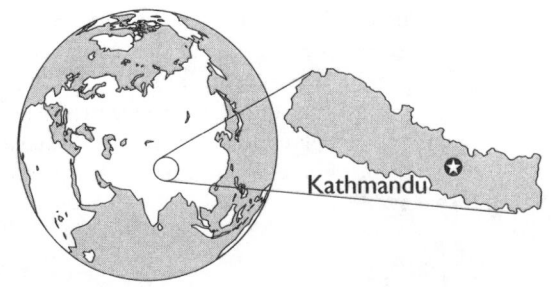

Kathmandu

In 1992, Nepal established a constitutional monarchy with a multiparty parliament; in late 1994, however, communists gained the majority of seats. Nepal's economy is mainly agricultural, and tight government controls have helped to make it one of the poorest in the world. Nevertheless, there are indications that the government supports aggressive economic reform. For example, a substantial program of privatization is in place. This process has only begun, however, and much remains to be done.

TRADE POLICY
Score: 3–Stable (moderate level of protectionism)

Nepal's average tariff rate is about 10 percent.[1] According to the U.S. Department of Commerce, "U.S. firms and other foreign investors have identified pervasive corruption as an obstacle to maintaining and expanding direct investment."[2] Nepal bans imports of beef.

TAXATION
Score–Income taxation: 3–Stable (moderate tax rates)
Score–Corporate taxation: 3–Stable (moderate tax rates)
Final Taxation Score: 3–Stable (moderate tax rates)

Nepal's top income tax rate is 35 percent, and government revenues equal 15.3 percent of GDP.[3]

GOVERNMENT INTERVENTION IN THE ECONOMY
Score: 2–Stable (low level)

Government consumes about 10 percent of GDP. The public sector, however, is large; the government still owns significant portions of the national airlines, telecommunications companies, and energy companies.

MONETARY POLICY
Score: 2–Stable (low level of inflation)

Nepal's average annual rate of inflation from 1986 to 1996 was 11.3 percent.

CAPITAL FLOWS AND FOREIGN INVESTMENT
Score: 4–Stable (high barriers)

Nepal has opened some of its market to foreign investment, but many investments are permitted only in the form of joint ventures, either with government-owned firms or with other private companies. Bureaucratic red tape and government corruption often postpone, prolong, or terminate foreign investment initiatives. According to the U.S. Department of Commerce, "The Government officially welcomes foreign direct investment, but policy implementation is hampered by bureaucratic delay and inefficiency.... Implementation of official policy is slow and often haphazard once the investment has been made. Foreign investors constantly complain about complex and opaque Government

1	Hong Kong	1.25	81	Fiji	3.10
2	Singapore	1.30	81	Mali	3.10
3	Bahrain	1.70	81	Slovenia	3.10
4	New Zealand	1.75	85	Honduras	3.15
5	Switzerland	1.85	85	Mexico	3.15
6	United States	1.90	85	Papua New Guinea	3.15
7	Ireland	1.95	88	Djibouti	3.20
7	Luxembourg	1.95	88	Mongolia	3.20
7	Taiwan	1.95	90	Algeria	3.25
7	United Kingdom	1.95	90	Brazil	3.25
11	Bahamas	2.00	90	Lebanon	3.25
12	Czech Republic	2.05	90	Senegal	3.25
12	Japan	2.05	90	Tanzania	3.25
14	Australia	2.10	95	Nigeria	3.30
14	Belgium	2.10	95	Romania	3.30
14	Canada	2.10	97	Cambodia	3.35
14	United Arab Emirates	2.10	97	Dominican Republic	3.35
18	Austria	2.15	97	Egypt	3.35
18	Chile	2.15	97	Guinea	3.35
18	Estonia	2.15	97	Ivory Coast	3.35
18	Netherlands	2.15	97	Moldova	3.35
22	Denmark	2.25	97	Pakistan	3.35
22	El Salvador	2.25	104	Nepal	3.40
22	Finland	2.25	104	Venezuela	3.40
25	Germany	2.30	106	Armenia	3.45
25	Iceland	2.30	106	Bulgaria	3.45
27	Norway	2.35	106	Lesotho	3.45
28	Korea, South	2.40	106	Madagascar	3.45
28	Kuwait	2.40	106	Russia	3.45
28	Malaysia	2.40	111	Burkina Faso	3.50
28	Panama	2.40	111	Cameroon	3.50
28	Thailand	2.40	111	Guyana	3.50
33	Sweden	2.45	111	Nicaragua	3.50
34	Argentina	2.50	115	Gambia	3.60
34	France	2.50	116	Croatia	3.65
34	Italy	2.50	116	Georgia	3.65
34	Spain	2.50	116	Malawi	3.65
38	Portugal	2.55	119	Cape Verde	3.67
38	Sri Lanka	2.55	120	Ethiopia	3.70
38	Trinidad and Tobago	2.55	120	India	3.70
41	Barbados	2.60	120	Niger	3.70
41	Peru	2.60	123	Congo	3.75
43	Bolivia	2.65	124	Chad	3.80
43	Mauritius	2.65	124	China	3.80
45	Cyprus	2.70	124	Mauritania	3.80
45	Jamaica	2.70	124	Ukraine	3.80
45	Uruguay	2.70	124	Zimbabwe	3.80
48	Botswana	2.75	129	Albania	3.85
48	Guatemala	2.75	129	Bangladesh	3.85
48	Jordan	2.75	129	Mozambique	3.85
48	Namibia	2.75	129	Suriname	3.85
48	Oman	2.75	133	Burundi	3.90
48	Philippines	2.75	134	Togo	3.95
54	Belize	2.80	135	Haiti	4.00
54	Costa Rica	2.80	135	Kyrgyz Rep.	4.00
54	Israel	2.80	137	Kazakhstan	4.05
54	Swaziland	2.80	137	Sierra Leone	4.05
54	Turkey	2.80	139	Yemen	4.10
54	Uganda	2.80	140	Belarus	4.15
54	Samoa	2.80	141	Sudan	4.20
61	Latvia	2.85	141	Syria	4.20
62	Greece	2.90	143	Azerbaijan	4.30
62	Hungary	2.90	143	Equatorial Guinea	4.30
62	So. Africa	2.90	143	Myanmar	4.30
65	Ecuador	2.95	143	Rwanda	4.30
65	Gabon	2.95	147	Tajikistan	4.40
65	Indonesia	2.95	147	Uzbekistan	4.40
65	Malta	2.95	149	Angola	4.45
65	Morocco	2.95	149	Turkmenistan	4.45
65	Poland	2.95	151	Guinea-Bissau	4.55
65	Tunisia	2.95	152	Vietnam	4.60
72	Ghana	3.00	153	Congo (Zaire)	4.70
72	Lithuania	3.00	153	Iran	4.70
72	Saudi Arabia	3.00	155	Bosnia	4.80
75	Benin	3.05	155	Somalia	4.80
75	Kenya	3.05	157	Iraq	4.90
75	Paraguay	3.05	157	Laos	4.90
75	Qatar	3.05	157	Libya	4.90
75	Slovak Republic	3.05	160	Cuba	5.00
75	Zambia	3.05	160	Korea, North	5.00
81	Colombia	3.10			

Mostly Unfree

procedures and a working-level attitude that is more hostile than accommodating. Indeed, the Government continues to refuse to even recognize the existence of the Foreign Investors in Nepal (FIIN), an organization representing the majority of the non-Indian investors in the country, since it insists that its Board of Directors must contain at least seven Nepalese."[4]

BANKING
Score: 4–Stable (high level of restrictions)

Since 1984, Nepal has opened its banking system to foreign competition. Yet only a few banks have opened, primarily because the government prefers foreign banks to open branches through joint ventures with domestic banks. Foreign competition therefore is limited. The government owns significant shares of most banks, although it does plan to privatize the 100 percent state-owned Rastriya Banija Bank over the next several years.

WAGE AND PRICE CONTROLS
Score: 4–Stable (high level)

Nepal controls most wages and prices through its large government-owned sector and the substantial subsidies it provides to these companies.

PROPERTY RIGHTS
Score: 3–Stable (moderate level of protection)

The main threats to private property are crime and government corruption. Despite recent judicial reform, protection of private property by the legal and judicial system is insufficient. According to the U.S. Department of Commerce, "There is an effective means of enforcing property rights as all such transactions must be registered and property holdings cannot be transferred without following procedures. Even so, property disputes account for half of the current backlog in Nepal's court system and such cases can take years to be settled."[5] By global standards, however, the judiciary provides a moderate level of protection for private property.

REGULATION
Score: 4–Stable (high level)

Establishing a business in Nepal can be difficult if the business is to compete with a state-owned company. Instead of creating new competition for existing state-owned companies, the government attempts to redirect private investment toward companies that are being privatized. In some cases, regulations are applied haphazardly by corrupt government bureaucracies. A practical problem, according to the U.S. Department of Commerce, "is the reluctance of the bureaucracy to accept legal precedents established in similar cases that have been decided in the courts. As a consequence, businesses are often forced to relitigate issues that have already been settled by the courts."[6]

BLACK MARKET
Score: 5–Stable (very high level of activity)

The size of Nepal's black market is substantial, especially in consumer goods, labor, construction, and pirated intellectual property from Western countries. Computer software and semiconductor designs are not protected adequately, and piracy is prevalent in these areas.

NOTES
[1] World Bank, *World Development Indicators*, 1998.
[2] U.S. Department of Commerce, *Country Commercial Guide*, 1998.
[3] Nepal's tax rates are unavailable. Therefore, the country was graded solely on total government revenues as a percentage of GDP.
[4] U.S. Department of Commerce, *Country Commercial Guide*, 1998.
[5] *Ibid.*
[6] *Ibid.*

The Netherlands   2.15

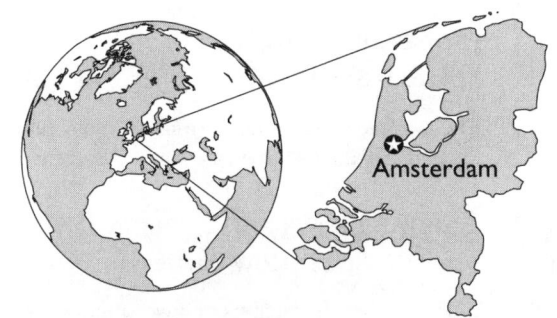
Amsterdam

1998 Score: **2.20**   1997 Score: **2.00**   1996 Score: **1.85**

Trade	2	Banking	1
Taxation	4.5	Wages and Prices	3
Government Intervention	3	Property Rights	1
Monetary Policy	1	Regulation	3
Foreign Investment	2	Black Market	1

The Netherlands declared its independence from Spain in 1579, although it did not become truly independent for several more years. During the 17th and 18th centuries, the Netherlands was a driving force in global trade and the establishment of colonies overseas. In the 19th century, Napoleon transformed it into the Kingdom of Holland, which lasted until independence was restored in 1815. The remainder of the 19th century saw the development of parliamentary democracy. After World War II, the Netherlands re-established a stable government and built a market-oriented economic system. The country maintains a large social welfare program funded by taxes that are among the world's highest, but economic freedom in other areas, such as banking and monetary policy, is far greater than in most other countries. The Netherlands recently reduced its corporate income tax rate; as a result, its overall score is .05 point better than last year.

TRADE POLICY
Score: 2–Stable (low level of protectionism)

According to the U.S. Department of State, "Dutch trade and investment policy is among the most open in the world."[1] But even though the average tariff rate is 3.6 percent, the government also maintains trade restrictions common to all members of the European Union (EU), such as restrictions on foreign participation in telecommunication systems like broadcasting.

TAXATION
Score–Income taxation: 5–Stable (very high tax rates)
Score–Corporate taxation: 3+ (moderate tax rates)
Final Taxation Score: 4.5+ (very high tax rates)

The Netherlands has a top income tax rate of 60 percent, although there is a proposal to reduce it to 50 percent. The average taxpayer is in the 6.15 percent bracket.[2] The top marginal corporate tax rate is 35 percent, down from 36 percent in 1997. Therefore, the Netherlands' corporate taxation score is 1 point better this year, making the final taxation score 0.5 point better than last year. The government also levies several other taxes, including a 35 percent capital gains tax and a 17.5 percent value-added tax.

GOVERNMENT INTERVENTION IN THE ECONOMY
Score: 3–Stable (moderate level)

In 1994, the government undertook a massive reduction in spending and made substantial progress in slashing its budget deficit, now about 3 percent of GDP. Government consumes about 14 percent of GDP and plays a relatively moderate role in the economy. It subsidizes private-sector research and development programs, provides funds to help some companies restructure, dominates the energy sector, and plays a large role in aviation, chemicals, steel, telecommunications, and transportation.

1	Hong Kong	1.25	81	Fiji	3.10
2	Singapore	1.30	81	Mali	3.10
3	Bahrain	1.70	81	Slovenia	3.10
4	New Zealand	1.75	85	Honduras	3.15
5	Switzerland	1.85	85	Mexico	3.15
6	United States	1.90	85	Papua New Guinea	3.15
7	Ireland	1.95	88	Djibouti	3.20
7	Luxembourg	1.95	88	Mongolia	3.20
7	Taiwan	1.95	90	Algeria	3.25
7	United Kingdom	1.95	90	Brazil	3.25
11	Bahamas	2.00	90	Lebanon	3.25
12	Czech Republic	2.05	90	Senegal	3.25
12	Japan	2.05	90	Tanzania	3.25
14	Australia	2.10	95	Nigeria	3.30
14	Belgium	2.10	95	Romania	3.30
14	Canada	2.10	97	Cambodia	3.35
14	United Arab Emirates	2.10	97	Dominican Republic	3.35
18	Austria	2.15	97	Egypt	3.35
18	Chile	2.15	97	Guinea	3.35
18	Estonia	2.15	97	Ivory Coast	3.35
18	Netherlands	2.15	97	Moldova	3.35
22	Denmark	2.25	97	Pakistan	3.35
22	El Salvador	2.25	104	Nepal	3.40
22	Finland	2.25	104	Venezuela	3.40
25	Germany	2.30	106	Armenia	3.45
25	Iceland	2.30	106	Bulgaria	3.45
27	Norway	2.35	106	Lesotho	3.45
28	Korea, South	2.40	106	Madagascar	3.45
28	Kuwait	2.40	106	Russia	3.45
28	Malaysia	2.40	111	Burkina Faso	3.50
28	Panama	2.40	111	Cameroon	3.50
28	Thailand	2.40	111	Guyana	3.50
33	Sweden	2.45	111	Nicaragua	3.50
34	Argentina	2.50	115	Gambia	3.60
34	France	2.50	116	Croatia	3.65
34	Italy	2.50	116	Georgia	3.65
34	Spain	2.50	116	Malawi	3.65
38	Portugal	2.55	119	Cape Verde	3.67
38	Sri Lanka	2.55	120	Ethiopia	3.70
38	Trinidad and Tobago	2.55	120	India	3.70
41	Barbados	2.60	120	Niger	3.70
41	Peru	2.60	123	Congo	3.75
43	Bolivia	2.65	124	Chad	3.80
43	Mauritius	2.65	124	China	3.80
45	Cyprus	2.70	124	Mauritania	3.80
45	Jamaica	2.70	124	Ukraine	3.80
45	Uruguay	2.70	124	Zimbabwe	3.80
48	Botswana	2.75	129	Albania	3.85
48	Guatemala	2.75	129	Bangladesh	3.85
48	Jordan	2.75	129	Mozambique	3.85
48	Namibia	2.75	129	Suriname	3.85
48	Oman	2.75	133	Burundi	3.90
48	Philippines	2.75	134	Togo	3.95
54	Belize	2.80	135	Haiti	4.00
54	Costa Rica	2.80	135	Kyrgyz Rep.	4.00
54	Israel	2.80	137	Kazakhstan	4.05
54	Swaziland	2.80	137	Sierra Leone	4.05
54	Turkey	2.80	139	Yemen	4.10
54	Uganda	2.80	140	Belarus	4.15
54	Samoa	2.80	141	Sudan	4.20
61	Latvia	2.85	141	Syria	4.20
62	Greece	2.90	143	Azerbaijan	4.30
62	Hungary	2.90	143	Equatorial Guinea	4.30
62	So. Africa	2.90	143	Myanmar	4.30
65	Ecuador	2.95	143	Rwanda	4.30
65	Gabon	2.95	147	Tajikistan	4.40
65	Indonesia	2.95	147	Uzbekistan	4.40
65	Malta	2.95	149	Angola	4.45
65	Morocco	2.95	149	Turkmenistan	4.45
65	Poland	2.95	151	Guinea-Bissau	4.55
65	Tunisia	2.95	152	Vietnam	4.60
72	Ghana	3.00	153	Congo (Zaire)	4.70
72	Lithuania	3.00	153	Iran	4.70
72	Saudi Arabia	3.00	155	Bosnia	4.80
75	Benin	3.05	155	Somalia	4.80
75	Kenya	3.05	157	Iraq	4.90
75	Paraguay	3.05	157	Laos	4.90
75	Qatar	3.05	157	Libya	4.90
75	Slovak Republic	3.05	160	Cuba	5.00
75	Zambia	3.05	160	Korea, North	5.00
81	Colombia	3.10			

Mostly Free

MONETARY POLICY
Score: 1–Stable (very low level of inflation)

The average annual rate of inflation from 1986 to 1996 was 1.1 percent. In 1997, the rate was 2.1 percent.

CAPITAL FLOWS AND FOREIGN INVESTMENT
Score: 2–Stable (low barriers)

There are few restrictions on investment in the Netherlands. Most restrictions apply to investment in defense-related industries, such as the manufacturing of weapons.

BANKING
Score: 1–Stable (very low level of restrictions)

The Netherlands has been one of Europe's financial and banking centers for centuries, and its banking system operates freely with almost no government regulation. Banks established in the Netherlands may engage in a variety of financial services, such as buying, selling, and holding securities, insurance policies, and real estate. There are few investment restrictions imposed on banks, and most financial institutions are not subject to supervision by the central bank. Over 80 foreign banks operate in the Netherlands today.

WAGE AND PRICE CONTROLS
Score: 3–Stable (moderate level)

The market in the Netherlands primarily sets wages and prices, although price controls on many pharmaceutical products under a law passed in June 1996 now affect some 3,000 medicines and are expected eventually to cover some 7,000 items. There is a minimum wage. Traditionally, the government has sanctioned cartels, especially in the utilities area; but the country's entrance into the EU has forced the government to crack down on cartels, and most are being eliminated.

PROPERTY RIGHTS
Score: 1–Stable (very high level of protection)

Private property in the Netherlands is safe from expropriation. The legal and judicial system is advanced, efficient, and independent. According to the U.S. Department of State, "The Constitution provides for an independent judiciary, and the Government respects this provision in practice. The judiciary provides citizens with a fair and efficient judicial process."[3]

REGULATION
Score: 3–Stable (moderate level)

Establishing a business in the Netherlands is a simple procedure, and regulations are applied evenly in most cases. While reducing some regulations in some sectors, the Netherlands recently passed laws requiring businesses to provide disability insurance. Moreover, regulations establishing minimum work weeks, mandatory leave, and separation pay for terminated workers are burdensome. The government has expanded laws allowing for increased part-time work, however. With businesses free to access a larger pool of the work force, the Netherlands has one of the lowest unemployment rates in continental Europe.

BLACK MARKET
Score: 1–Stable (very low level of activity)

Because so few things are illegal in the Netherlands (even prostitution and drugs are legal), there is little incentive to engage in black market activity. Sales of pirated intellectual property are minuscule in comparison with the overall size of the economy.

NOTES
[1]   U.S. Department of State, *Country Reports on Economic Policy and Trade Practices*, 1998.
[2]   This rate may increase to 37.65 percent because of a national insurance tax that can be levied on top of the lowest tax bracket. Therefore, the income tax score for the Netherlands is based on this higher rate.
[3]   U.S. Department of State, "The Netherlands Country Reports on Human Rights Practices for 1997," 1998.

New Zealand 1.75

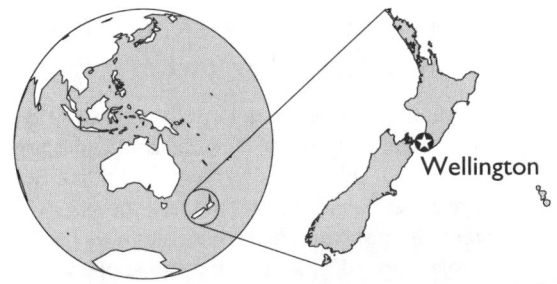
Wellington

1998 Score: **1.75**   1997 Score: **1.75**   1996 Score: **1.75**

Trade	2	Banking	1
Taxation	3.5	Wages and Prices	2
Government Intervention	2	Property Rights	1
Monetary Policy	1	Regulation	2
Foreign Investment	2	Black Market	1

New Zealand achieved independence from the United Kingdom in 1932. For the next five decades, both Labour and National Party governments pursued an economic policy of "insulationism" that included high tariffs, import licensing, foreign exchange controls, high tax rates, strict regulations, and government provision of many commercial activities. After Labour's victory in 1984, the government of Prime Minister David Lange reversed course and launched what the Organization for Economic Cooperation and Development considers the most comprehensive economic liberalization program ever undertaken in a developed country. Following the National Party's triumph in the 1990 election, the government of Prime Minister Jim Bolger expanded the economic liberalization program by deregulating the labor market, balancing the budget, and cutting income tax rates. In 1993, New Zealand voted to replace its British-style "first-past-the-post" parliament with a German-style "mixed membership" parliament based on proportional representation. The first election under the new system was held in October 1996, but no clear winner emerged. After intensive negotiations between the parties, a coalition of the National Party and New Zealand First Party was formed. The coalition government has agreed to maintain the existing course of economic liberalization.

TRADE POLICY
Score: 2–Stable (low level of protectionism)

New Zealand's average tariff rate is about 3.8 percent.[1] The government has accelerated its earlier plan to eliminate all tariffs by 2004 to be completed by 2000. Indeed, tariffs on motor vehicles, the last major protected sector, were abolished in 1998. All import licensing and other quantitative restrictions were abolished in 1992. New Zealand has a comprehensive free-trade and -investment agreement with Australia and is seeking one with the United States. The government has abolished most non-tariff barriers to imports, although business-run marketing boards and private associations still can impede imports, mainly in the agricultural sector.

TAXATION
Score–Income taxation: 3–Stable (moderate tax rates)
Score–Corporate taxation: 3–Stable (moderate tax rates)
Final Taxation Score: 3.5–Stable (high tax rates)

The top income tax rate is 33 percent, and the average income level is taxed at 21.5 percent. New Zealand has a flat 33 percent corporate tax. In addition, it also has a 12.5 percent goods and services tax, a 49 percent fringe benefits tax, and a risk-based 1 percent to 8 percent levy on gross salaries and wages to pay for accident compensation insurance. New Zealand has no capital gains or estate taxes.

1	Hong Kong	1.25	81	Fiji	3.10
2	Singapore	1.30	81	Mali	3.10
3	Bahrain	1.70	81	Slovenia	3.10
4	New Zealand	1.75	85	Honduras	3.15
5	Switzerland	1.85	85	Mexico	3.15
6	United States	1.90	85	Papua New Guinea	3.15
7	Ireland	1.95	88	Djibouti	3.20
7	Luxembourg	1.95	88	Mongolia	3.20
7	Taiwan	1.95	90	Algeria	3.25
7	United Kingdom	1.95	90	Brazil	3.25
11	Bahamas	2.00	90	Lebanon	3.25
12	Czech Republic	2.05	90	Senegal	3.25
12	Japan	2.05	90	Tanzania	3.25
14	Australia	2.10	95	Nigeria	3.30
14	Belgium	2.10	95	Romania	3.30
14	Canada	2.10	97	Cambodia	3.35
14	United Arab Emirates	2.10	97	Dominican Republic	3.35
18	Austria	2.15	97	Egypt	3.35
18	Chile	2.15	97	Guinea	3.35
18	Estonia	2.15	97	Ivory Coast	3.35
18	Netherlands	2.15	97	Moldova	3.35
22	Denmark	2.25	97	Pakistan	3.35
22	El Salvador	2.25	104	Nepal	3.40
22	Finland	2.25	104	Venezuela	3.40
25	Germany	2.30	106	Armenia	3.45
25	Iceland	2.30	106	Bulgaria	3.45
27	Norway	2.35	106	Lesotho	3.45
28	Korea, South	2.40	106	Madagascar	3.45
28	Kuwait	2.40	106	Russia	3.45
28	Malaysia	2.40	111	Burkina Faso	3.50
28	Panama	2.40	111	Cameroon	3.50
28	Thailand	2.40	111	Guyana	3.50
33	Sweden	2.45	111	Nicaragua	3.50
34	Argentina	2.50	115	Gambia	3.60
34	France	2.50	116	Croatia	3.65
34	Italy	2.50	116	Georgia	3.65
34	Spain	2.50	116	Malawi	3.65
38	Portugal	2.55	119	Cape Verde	3.67
38	Sri Lanka	2.55	120	Ethiopia	3.70
38	Trinidad and Tobago	2.55	120	India	3.70
41	Barbados	2.60	120	Niger	3.70
41	Peru	2.60	123	Congo	3.75
43	Bolivia	2.65	124	Chad	3.80
43	Mauritius	2.65	124	China	3.80
45	Cyprus	2.70	124	Mauritania	3.80
45	Jamaica	2.70	124	Ukraine	3.80
45	Uruguay	2.70	124	Zimbabwe	3.80
48	Botswana	2.75	129	Albania	3.85
48	Guatemala	2.75	129	Bangladesh	3.85
48	Jordan	2.75	129	Mozambique	3.85
48	Namibia	2.75	129	Suriname	3.85
48	Oman	2.75	133	Burundi	3.90
48	Philippines	2.75	134	Togo	3.95
54	Belize	2.80	135	Haiti	4.00
54	Costa Rica	2.80	135	Kyrgyz Rep.	4.00
54	Israel	2.80	137	Kazakhstan	4.05
54	Swaziland	2.80	137	Sierra Leone	4.05
54	Turkey	2.80	139	Yemen	4.10
54	Uganda	2.80	140	Belarus	4.15
54	Samoa	2.80	141	Sudan	4.20
61	Latvia	2.85	141	Syria	4.20
62	Greece	2.90	143	Azerbaijan	4.30
62	Hungary	2.90	143	Equatorial Guinea	4.30
62	So. Africa	2.90	143	Myanmar	4.30
65	Ecuador	2.95	143	Rwanda	4.30
65	Gabon	2.95	147	Tajikistan	4.40
65	Indonesia	2.95	147	Uzbekistan	4.40
65	Malta	2.95	149	Angola	4.45
65	Morocco	2.95	149	Turkmenistan	4.45
65	Poland	2.95	151	Guinea-Bissau	4.55
65	Tunisia	2.95	152	Vietnam	4.60
72	Ghana	3.00	153	Congo (Zaire)	4.70
72	Lithuania	3.00	153	Iran	4.70
72	Saudi Arabia	3.00	155	Bosnia	4.80
75	Benin	3.05	155	Somalia	4.80
75	Kenya	3.05	157	Iraq	4.90
75	Paraguay	3.05	157	Laos	4.90
75	Qatar	3.05	157	Libya	4.90
75	Slovak Republic	3.05	160	Cuba	5.00
75	Zambia	3.05	160	Korea, North	5.00
81	Colombia	3.10			

GOVERNMENT INTERVENTION IN THE ECONOMY
Score: 2–Stable (low level)

Government consumes 15 percent of GDP. During the 1970s and early 1980s, New Zealand had a large state-owned sector that received government subsidies. Recent privatization efforts have reduced the size of this sector, and remaining state-owned companies have been "corporatized," meaning they must operate the same way commercial companies do. The government has eliminated all subsidies to these businesses.

MONETARY POLICY
Score: 1–Stable (very low level of inflation)

New Zealand's average annual rate of inflation from 1986 to 1996 was 6.1 percent. In 1997, the rate was 1.2 percent.

CAPITAL FLOWS AND FOREIGN INVESTMENT
Score: 2–Stable (low barriers)

Government approval is required for certain large direct investments and for the purchase of commercial fishing assets and rural land. New Zealand actively encourages direct foreign investment, however, and approval is routine.

BANKING
Score: 1–Stable (very low level of restrictions)

New Zealand's banking system is deregulated, and foreign banks are welcome. The Reserve Bank of New Zealand is limited to prudential supervision. The government does not impose deposit insurance on financial institutions; instead, banks provide full disclosure of their financial condition to the public.

WAGE AND PRICE CONTROLS
Score: 2–Stable (low level)

The market largely determines wages and prices. New Zealand enforces a relatively low minimum wage for most adult workers.

PROPERTY RIGHTS
Score: 1–Stable (very high level of protection)

Private property is a fundamental right. The legal and judicial system is efficient and provides adequate protection. Government expropriation is highly unlikely.

REGULATION
Score: 2–Stable (low level)

Establishing a business in New Zealand is easy. Regulations are applied evenly and consistently, although environmental and safety regulations can be burdensome.

BLACK MARKET
Score: 1–Stable (very low level of activity)

New Zealand's negligible black market is confined to the sale of goods and services considered harmful to society, such as guns and drugs. There is virtually no black market in smuggling or pirated intellectual property.

NOTE
[1] Based on total revenues from taxation on international trade as a percentage of total imports.

Nicaragua   3.50

1998 Score: **3.50**   1997 Score: **3.60**   1996 Score: **3.60**

Trade	4	Banking	3
Taxation	3	Wages and Prices	3
Government Intervention	2	Property Rights	4
Monetary Policy	5	Regulation	4
Foreign Investment	2	Black Market	5

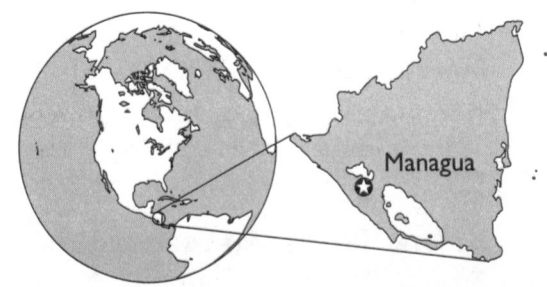

Managua

Nicaragua became a socialist state in 1979 under the Sandinista regime. Despite infusions of foreign aid, the economy stalled. The election of Violeta Chamorro to the presidency in 1990 marked the beginning of the country's transition from a centralized economy to one more market-oriented. The Chamorro administration succeeded in controlling inflation, liberalizing the trade regime, and jump-starting economic growth: From 1994 to 1996, Nicaragua's economy grew between 3 percent and 4.5 percent annually. The pace of economic reform accelerated in 1997 with the inauguration of President Arnoldo Aleman of the center-right Liberal Alliance. Nicaragua remains an agricultural economy with a small manufacturing base. It imports most of its manufactured, processed, and consumer goods. A member of the World Trade Organization, Nicaragua has reduced tariffs and eliminated some non-tariff barriers and foreign exchange controls. The United States is Nicaragua's largest trading partner. The Sandinistas, who still hold key posts in the military and police, have blocked some reforms, especially the privatization of state-owned enterprises and other nationalized sectors of the economy.

TRADE POLICY
Score: 4–Stable (high level of protectionism)

Nicaragua's average tariff rate is 10.43 percent.[1] There remain significant non-tariff barriers. The U.S. Department of State reports that "Importers complain of steep secondary customs costs, including customs declaration form charges and consular fees. In addition, importers are required to utilize the services of licensed customs agents, adding further costs."[2]

TAXATION
Score–Income taxation: 2–Stable (low tax rates)
Score–Corporate taxation: 3–Stable (moderate tax rates)
Total Taxation Score: 3–Stable (moderate tax rates)

Nicaragua's top marginal income tax rate is 30 percent, with the average income taxed at 0 percent. The top corporate tax rate also is 30 percent. Nicaragua also maintains a 10 percent capital gains tax, a 15 percent general sales tax, a consumption tax, and a municipality tax.

GOVERNMENT INTERVENTION IN THE ECONOMY
Score: 2–Stable (low level)

Government consumes 13 percent of GDP. The government has privatized much of the economy, so that the private sector now produces most of the country's GDP. According to the U.S. Department of Commerce, "Since 1990, all state monopolies except for public utilities have been eliminated, virtually all price controls have been phased out, and more than 300 state enterprises have been privatized."[3]

1	Hong Kong	1.25	81	Fiji	3.10
2	Singapore	1.30	81	Mali	3.10
3	Bahrain	1.70	81	Slovenia	3.10
4	New Zealand	1.75	85	Honduras	3.15
5	Switzerland	1.85	85	Mexico	3.15
6	United States	1.90	85	Papua New Guinea	3.15
7	Ireland	1.95	88	Djibouti	3.20
7	Luxembourg	1.95	88	Mongolia	3.20
7	Taiwan	1.95	90	Algeria	3.25
7	United Kingdom	1.95	90	Brazil	3.25
11	Bahamas	2.00	90	Lebanon	3.25
12	Czech Republic	2.05	90	Senegal	3.25
12	Japan	2.05	90	Tanzania	3.25
14	Australia	2.10	95	Nigeria	3.30
14	Belgium	2.10	95	Romania	3.30
14	Canada	2.10	97	Cambodia	3.35
14	United Arab Emirates	2.10	97	Dominican Republic	3.35
18	Austria	2.15	97	Egypt	3.35
18	Chile	2.15	97	Guinea	3.35
18	Estonia	2.15	97	Ivory Coast	3.35
18	Netherlands	2.15	97	Moldova	3.35
22	Denmark	2.25	97	Pakistan	3.35
22	El Salvador	2.25	104	Nepal	3.40
22	Finland	2.25	104	Venezuela	3.40
25	Germany	2.30	106	Armenia	3.45
25	Iceland	2.30	106	Bulgaria	3.45
27	Norway	2.35	106	Lesotho	3.45
28	Korea, South	2.40	106	Madagascar	3.45
28	Kuwait	2.40	106	Russia	3.45
28	Malaysia	2.40	111	Burkina Faso	3.50
28	Panama	2.40	111	Cameroon	3.50
28	Thailand	2.40	111	Guyana	3.50
33	Sweden	2.45	111	**Nicaragua**	**3.50**
34	Argentina	2.50	115	Gambia	3.60
34	France	2.50	116	Croatia	3.65
34	Italy	2.50	116	Georgia	3.65
34	Spain	2.50	116	Malawi	3.65
38	Portugal	2.55	119	Cape Verde	3.67
38	Sri Lanka	2.55	120	Ethiopia	3.70
38	Trinidad and Tobago	2.55	120	India	3.70
41	Barbados	2.60	120	Niger	3.70
41	Peru	2.60	123	Congo	3.75
43	Bolivia	2.65	124	Chad	3.80
43	Mauritius	2.65	124	China	3.80
45	Cyprus	2.70	124	Mauritania	3.80
45	Jamaica	2.70	124	Ukraine	3.80
45	Uruguay	2.70	124	Zimbabwe	3.80
48	Botswana	2.75	129	Albania	3.85
48	Guatemala	2.75	129	Bangladesh	3.85
48	Jordan	2.75	129	Mozambique	3.85
48	Namibia	2.75	129	Suriname	3.85
48	Oman	2.75	133	Burundi	3.90
48	Philippines	2.75	134	Togo	3.95
54	Belize	2.80	135	Haiti	4.00
54	Costa Rica	2.80	135	Kyrgyz Rep.	4.00
54	Israel	2.80	137	Kazakhstan	4.05
54	Swaziland	2.80	137	Sierra Leone	4.05
54	Turkey	2.80	139	Yemen	4.10
54	Uganda	2.80	140	Belarus	4.15
54	Samoa	2.80	141	Sudan	4.20
61	Latvia	2.85	141	Syria	4.20
62	Greece	2.90	143	Azerbaijan	4.30
62	Hungary	2.90	143	Equatorial Guinea	4.30
62	So. Africa	2.90	143	Myanmar	4.30
65	Ecuador	2.95	143	Rwanda	4.30
65	Gabon	2.95	147	Tajikistan	4.40
65	Indonesia	2.95	147	Uzbekistan	4.40
65	Malta	2.95	149	Angola	4.45
65	Morocco	2.95	149	Turkmenistan	4.45
65	Poland	2.95	151	Guinea-Bissau	4.55
65	Tunisia	2.95	152	Vietnam	4.60
72	Ghana	3.00	153	Congo (Zaire)	4.70
72	Lithuania	3.00	153	Iran	4.70
72	Saudi Arabia	3.00	155	Bosnia	4.80
75	Benin	3.05	155	Somalia	4.80
75	Kenya	3.05	157	Iraq	4.90
75	Paraguay	3.05	157	Laos	4.90
75	Qatar	3.05	157	Libya	4.90
75	Slovak Republic	3.05	160	Cuba	5.00
75	Zambia	3.05	160	Korea, North	5.00
81	Colombia	3.10			

Mostly Unfree

MONETARY POLICY
Score: 5–Stable (very high level of inflation)

Nicaragua's average annual rate of inflation from 1986 to 1996 was 2,408 percent. In 1997, the rate was around 8 percent.

CAPITAL FLOWS AND FOREIGN INVESTMENT
Score: 2–Stable (low barriers)

Nicaragua has liberalized its foreign investment code to allow for 100 percent foreign ownership. Most industries are open to investment.

BANKING
Score: 3–Stable (moderate level of restrictions)

Despite some progress toward ending state control, some of Nicaragua's banks remain in government hands. The government owns 3 of the 14 commercial banks now operating inside the country.

WAGE AND PRICE CONTROLS
Score: 3–Stable (moderate level)

The government has lifted nearly all price controls, but it still maintains a significant degree of control over some prices: petroleum products, public utilities, sugar, and locally produced soft drinks and beer. It also affects free-market pricing by purchasing "emergency stores" of such important basic foods as sugar, beans, and grain.

PROPERTY RIGHTS
Score: 4–Stable (low level of protection)

Private property is not safe: It can be confiscated by armed criminals and corrupt local governments; the court system is ill-equipped to deal with claims of confiscation; and local law enforcement remains inadequate. According to the U.S. Department of Commerce, "On the whole, the legal system is cumbersome, and enforcement of judicial determinations is uncertain and sometimes subject to non-judicial considerations."[4]

REGULATION
Score: 4–Stable (high level)

Government regulation remains a serious problem. The environmental impact studies required of businesses, for example, can prevent the expansion of existing businesses and the formation of new ones. In addition, regulations are applied haphazardly, and corruption persists. For example, according to the U.S. Department of Commerce, "Despite significant streamlining during the past five years, Nicaragua's legal and regulatory framework remains cumbersome and an impediment to investment. The rules are not transparent, and much business is still conducted on a 'who you know' basis. Lack of reliable dispute resolution mechanisms—whether judicial or administrative—complicates even relatively minor disputes with the authorities or Nicaraguan business contacts. The Labor Code contains many provisions concerning hiring/firing of the workforce and benefits."[5]

BLACK MARKET
Score: 5–Stable (very high level of activity)

Nicaragua has a large black market in several goods, including pharmaceuticals and agricultural products, and there is rampant piracy of goods from Canada, the United States, and Latin America. With unemployment rates of 40 percent, large numbers of people engage in black market activity. "Pirated videos are readily available in video rental stores nationwide, as are pirated audio cassettes," reports the U.S. Department of State. "In addition, cable television operators are known to intercept and retransmit U.S. satellite signals, a practice that continues despite a trend of negotiating contracts with U.S. sports and news satellite programmers."[6]

NOTES

[1]   Based on taxation of international transactions as a percentage of total imports.
[2]   U.S. Department of State, *Country Reports on Economic Policy and Trade Practices,* 1998.
[3]   U.S. Department of Commerce, *Country Commercial Guide,* 1998.
[4]   *Ibid.*
[5]   *Ibid.*
[6]   U.S. Department of State, *Country Reports on Economic Policy and Trade Practices,* 1998.

Niger   3.70

1998 Score: **3.70**   1997 Score: **3.70**   1996 Score: **3.70**

Trade	5	Banking	4
Taxation	4	Wages and Prices	4
Government Intervention	3	Property Rights	3
Monetary Policy	1	Regulation	4
Foreign Investment	4	Black Market	5

Niamey

Niger gained its independence from France in 1960 and has a long history of political instability and dictatorial governments, punctuated by brief periods of civilian rule. Most recently, Brigadier General Ibrahim Baré Maïnassara led a successful coup and became president in 1996 through an election that opposition parties boycotted and the U.S. Department of State characterized as "seriously flawed."[1] Some 85 percent of Niger's economy is based on subsistence agriculture, herding, and informal markets. According to the United Nations, Niger is one of the five poorest countries in the world. GDP growth averaged only 0.3 percent annually from 1991 to 1995, and per capita GDP was only $200 in 1996. The economy remains plagued by a large public sector, a bloated bureaucracy, corruption, and an immense black market. The government has announced an economic liberalization agenda that includes significant privatization, but substantial public resistance and strikes may hinder implementation.

TRADE POLICY
Score: 5–Stable (very high level of protectionism)

Niger's average tariff rate is 18.3 percent. There are some non-tariff barriers, primarily import bans and import substitution policies. Many items, such as bottled carbonated drinks, sheet metal, and soap, require special authorization from the Ministry of Commerce. According to the U.S. Department of Commerce, "This list most likely reflects measures to protect the position of well-entrenched local importers and producers."[2]

TAXATION
Score–Income taxation: 3–Stable (moderate tax rates)
Score–Corporate taxation: 4–Stable (high tax rates)
Final Taxation Score: 4–Stable (high tax rates)

Niger's top income tax rate is 60 percent; the average taxpayer finds himself in the 2 percent bracket. The top marginal corporate tax rate is 45 percent. Niger also has a value-added tax and a capital gains tax.

GOVERNMENT INTERVENTION IN THE ECONOMY
Score: 3–Stable (moderate level)

Government consumes 14.5 percent of GDP, most of which is generated by the public sector. The government employs about half the workers in the formal sector.[3]

MONETARY POLICY
Score: 1–Stable (very low level of inflation)

Niger's average annual rate of inflation from 1986 to 1996 was 3.95 percent. Inflation data for 1997 are unavailable.

1	Hong Kong	1.25	81	Fiji	3.10
2	Singapore	1.30	81	Mali	3.10
3	Bahrain	1.70	81	Slovenia	3.10
4	New Zealand	1.75	85	Honduras	3.15
5	Switzerland	1.85	85	Mexico	3.15
6	United States	1.90	85	Papua New Guinea	3.15
7	Ireland	1.95	88	Djibouti	3.20
7	Luxembourg	1.95	88	Mongolia	3.20
7	Taiwan	1.95	90	Algeria	3.25
7	United Kingdom	1.95	90	Brazil	3.25
11	Bahamas	2.00	90	Lebanon	3.25
12	Czech Republic	2.05	90	Senegal	3.25
12	Japan	2.05	90	Tanzania	3.25
14	Australia	2.10	95	Nigeria	3.30
14	Belgium	2.10	95	Romania	3.30
14	Canada	2.10	97	Cambodia	3.35
14	United Arab Emirates	2.10	97	Dominican Republic	3.35
18	Austria	2.15	97	Egypt	3.35
18	Chile	2.15	97	Guinea	3.35
18	Estonia	2.15	97	Ivory Coast	3.35
18	Netherlands	2.15	97	Moldova	3.35
22	Denmark	2.25	97	Pakistan	3.35
22	El Salvador	2.25	104	Nepal	3.40
22	Finland	2.25	104	Venezuela	3.40
25	Germany	2.30	106	Armenia	3.45
25	Iceland	2.30	106	Bulgaria	3.45
27	Norway	2.35	106	Lesotho	3.45
28	Korea, South	2.40	106	Madagascar	3.45
28	Kuwait	2.40	106	Russia	3.45
28	Malaysia	2.40	111	Burkina Faso	3.50
28	Panama	2.40	111	Cameroon	3.50
28	Thailand	2.40	111	Guyana	3.50
33	Sweden	2.45	111	Nicaragua	3.50
34	Argentina	2.50	115	Gambia	3.60
34	France	2.50	116	Croatia	3.65
34	Italy	2.50	116	Georgia	3.65
34	Spain	2.50	116	Malawi	3.65
38	Portugal	2.55	119	Cape Verde	3.67
38	Sri Lanka	2.55	120	Ethiopia	3.70
38	Trinidad and Tobago	2.55	120	India	3.70
41	Barbados	2.60	120	Niger	3.70
41	Peru	2.60	123	Congo	3.75
43	Bolivia	2.65	124	Chad	3.80
43	Mauritius	2.65	124	China	3.80
45	Cyprus	2.70	124	Mauritania	3.80
45	Jamaica	2.70	124	Ukraine	3.80
45	Uruguay	2.70	124	Zimbabwe	3.80
48	Botswana	2.75	129	Albania	3.85
48	Guatemala	2.75	129	Bangladesh	3.85
48	Jordan	2.75	129	Mozambique	3.85
48	Namibia	2.75	129	Suriname	3.85
48	Oman	2.75	133	Burundi	3.90
48	Philippines	2.75	134	Togo	3.95
54	Belize	2.80	135	Haiti	4.00
54	Costa Rica	2.80	135	Kyrgyz Rep.	4.00
54	Israel	2.80	137	Kazakhstan	4.05
54	Swaziland	2.80	137	Sierra Leone	4.05
54	Turkey	2.80	139	Yemen	4.10
54	Uganda	2.80	140	Belarus	4.15
54	Samoa	2.80	141	Sudan	4.20
61	Latvia	2.85	141	Syria	4.20
62	Greece	2.90	143	Azerbaijan	4.30
62	Hungary	2.90	143	Equatorial Guinea	4.30
62	So. Africa	2.90	143	Myanmar	4.30
65	Ecuador	2.95	143	Rwanda	4.30
65	Gabon	2.95	147	Tajikistan	4.40
65	Indonesia	2.95	147	Uzbekistan	4.40
65	Malta	2.95	149	Angola	4.45
65	Morocco	2.95	149	Turkmenistan	4.45
65	Poland	2.95	151	Guinea-Bissau	4.55
65	Tunisia	2.95	152	Vietnam	4.60
72	Ghana	3.00	153	Congo (Zaire)	4.70
72	Lithuania	3.00	153	Iran	4.70
72	Saudi Arabia	3.00	155	Bosnia	4.80
75	Benin	3.05	155	Somalia	4.80
75	Kenya	3.05	157	Iraq	4.90
75	Paraguay	3.05	157	Laos	4.90
75	Qatar	3.05	157	Libya	4.90
75	Slovak Republic	3.05	160	Cuba	5.00
75	Zambia	3.05	160	Korea, North	5.00
81	Colombia	3.10			

Mostly Unfree

CAPITAL FLOWS AND FOREIGN INVESTMENT
Score: 4–Stable (high barriers)

Niger provides equal treatment for domestic and foreign firms, although it also has a strict investment-review process, a hostile state-owned sector, and corruption. The bureaucracy is cumbersome and often delays investments. According to the U.S. Department of Commerce, "The government now promises final authorization for an investment three months from the date of applications. Nevertheless, investors should be prepared for delays caused by the process of acquiring various approvals."[4]

BANKING
Score: 4–Stable (high level of restrictions)

The banking system remains small, and banks generally are restricted as to the kinds of financial services they can offer. According to the U.S. Department of Commerce, "While the government's financial policies do not limit the free flow of capital, the private banking sector is small and conservative. Since 1988 four banks have ceased operations. The remaining ones have tightened lending criteria. Generally only well-established businesses obtain bank credit and the cost of credit is high. Banks offer only a limited array of financial instruments: letters of credit and short- and long-term loans."[5]

WAGE AND PRICE CONTROLS
Score: 4–Stable (high level)

Niger's large public sector affects wages and prices, as do import substitution policies and government subsidies.

PROPERTY RIGHTS
Score: 3–Stable (moderate level of protection)

Private property is subject to expropriation, although there are few recent examples of nationalization. Niger's court system, however, is not independent. According to the U.S. Department of State, "The Constitution provides for an independent judiciary, but it is subject to executive interference."[6]

REGULATION
Score: 4–Stable (high level)

Establishing a business can be difficult. The government bureaucracy is both massive and corrupt, bribery sometimes is present, and there is embezzlement by those government officials responsible for collecting fees. According to the U.S. Department of Commerce, "Complaints have focused on occasional petty hassling by low-level officials who hope for a gift."[7] In addition, regulations often are applied haphazardly.

BLACK MARKET
Score: 5–Stable (very high level of activity)

The black market is larger than the formal market—and growing. The U.S. Department of Commerce reports that the economy "mainly comprises subsistence agriculture and informal market activity."[8]

NOTES

1   U.S. Department of State, "Niger Country Report on Human Rights Practices for 1996," 1997.
2   U.S. Department of Commerce, *Country Commercial Guide*, 1997.
3   *Ibid.*
4   *Ibid.*
5   *Ibid.*
6   U.S. Department of State, "Niger Country Report on Human Rights Practices for 1997," 1998.
7   U.S. Department of Commerce, *Country Commercial Guide*, 1998.
8   *Ibid.*

Nigeria

3.30

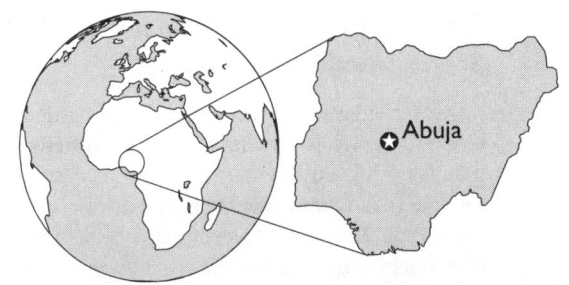

Abuja

1998 Score: **3.30**	1997 Score: **3.20**	1996 Score: **3.25**

Trade	5	Banking	4
Taxation	3	Wages and Prices	2
Government Intervention	2	Property Rights	3
Monetary Policy	5	Regulation	4
Foreign Investment	2	Black Market	3

Nigeria gained its independence from the United Kingdom in 1960. It is rich in natural resources, including oil, coal, natural gas, and fertile soil; it also has the largest population in Africa, estimated at 115 million in 1996. Despite Nigeria's resources, mismanagement and endemic corruption have crippled economic performance. The economy has been in decline; annual per capita GNP fell by more than 75 percent—to just $240—between 1985 and 1996. Nigeria is a center for both the narcotics trade and international crime. The recent deaths of General Sani Abacha, who seized power in a 1993 coup, and leading civilian candidate Chief Moshood Abiola have thrown the political scene into chaos. The military maintains control under General Abdulsalam Abubakar, but plans call for a transfer to civilian rule in May 1999.

TRADE POLICY
Score: 5–Stable (very high level of protectionism)

Despite 1995 reductions in import duties on many goods, Nigeria's average import duty is 18.3 percent. All goods are subject to additional administrative surcharges totaling 6 percent. The list of banned imports, including maize, eggs, processed wood, textiles, and used vehicles, is substantial even though the ban on wheat imports has been lifted. The customs process is burdensome.

TAXATION
Score–Income taxation: 2–Stable (low tax rates)
Score–Corporate taxation: 3–Stable (moderate tax rates)
Total Taxation Score: 3–Stable (moderate tax rates)

Nigeria's top income tax rate is 25 percent. The rate for the average taxpayer is 0 percent. The corporate tax rate is 30 percent. In 1994, the government introduced a 5 percent value-added tax that applies to 17 categories of goods and 24 services. The government also levies a capital gains tax.

GOVERNMENT INTERVENTION IN THE ECONOMY
Score: 2–Stable (low level)

Government consumes 11 percent of GDP.[1] Privatization has stalled, and government-controlled companies—many of which are unprofitable—dominate many basic manufacturing industries.

MONETARY POLICY
Score: 5–Stable (very high level of inflation)

Nigeria's average annual rate of inflation from 1986 to 1996 was 33.3 percent. The rate for 1997 was 12.5 percent.

1	Hong Kong	1.25		81	Fiji	3.10
2	Singapore	1.30		81	Mali	3.10
3	Bahrain	1.70		81	Slovenia	3.10
4	New Zealand	1.75		85	Honduras	3.15
5	Switzerland	1.85		85	Mexico	3.15
6	United States	1.90		85	Papua New Guinea	3.15
7	Ireland	1.95		88	Djibouti	3.20
7	Luxembourg	1.95		88	Mongolia	3.20
7	Taiwan	1.95		90	Algeria	3.25
7	United Kingdom	1.95		90	Brazil	3.25
11	Bahamas	2.00		90	Lebanon	3.25
12	Czech Republic	2.05		90	Senegal	3.25
12	Japan	2.05		90	Tanzania	3.25
14	Australia	2.10		95	Nigeria	3.30
14	Belgium	2.10		95	Romania	3.30
14	Canada	2.10		97	Cambodia	3.35
14	United Arab Emirates	2.10		97	Dominican Republic	3.35
18	Austria	2.15		97	Egypt	3.35
18	Chile	2.15		97	Guinea	3.35
18	Estonia	2.15		97	Ivory Coast	3.35
18	Netherlands	2.15		97	Moldova	3.35
22	Denmark	2.25		97	Pakistan	3.35
22	El Salvador	2.25		104	Nepal	3.40
22	Finland	2.25		104	Venezuela	3.40
25	Germany	2.30		106	Armenia	3.45
25	Iceland	2.30		106	Bulgaria	3.45
27	Norway	2.35		106	Lesotho	3.45
28	Korea, South	2.40		106	Madagascar	3.45
28	Kuwait	2.40		106	Russia	3.45
28	Malaysia	2.40		111	Burkina Faso	3.50
28	Panama	2.40		111	Cameroon	3.50
28	Thailand	2.40		111	Guyana	3.50
33	Sweden	2.45		111	Nicaragua	3.50
34	Argentina	2.50		115	Gambia	3.60
34	France	2.50		116	Croatia	3.65
34	Italy	2.50		116	Georgia	3.65
34	Spain	2.50		116	Malawi	3.65
38	Portugal	2.55		119	Cape Verde	3.67
38	Sri Lanka	2.55		120	Ethiopia	3.70
38	Trinidad and Tobago	2.55		120	India	3.70
41	Barbados	2.60		120	Niger	3.70
41	Peru	2.60		123	Congo	3.75
43	Bolivia	2.65		124	Chad	3.80
43	Mauritius	2.65		124	China	3.80
45	Cyprus	2.70		124	Mauritania	3.80
45	Jamaica	2.70		124	Ukraine	3.80
45	Uruguay	2.70		124	Zimbabwe	3.80
48	Botswana	2.75		129	Albania	3.85
48	Guatemala	2.75		129	Bangladesh	3.85
48	Jordan	2.75		129	Mozambique	3.85
48	Namibia	2.75		129	Suriname	3.85
48	Oman	2.75		133	Burundi	3.90
48	Philippines	2.75		134	Togo	3.95
54	Belize	2.80		135	Haiti	4.00
54	Costa Rica	2.80		135	Kyrgyz Rep.	4.00
54	Israel	2.80		137	Kazakhstan	4.05
54	Swaziland	2.80		137	Sierra Leone	4.05
54	Turkey	2.80		139	Yemen	4.10
54	Uganda	2.80		140	Belarus	4.15
54	Samoa	2.80		141	Sudan	4.20
61	Latvia	2.85		141	Syria	4.20
62	Greece	2.90		143	Azerbaijan	4.30
62	Hungary	2.90		143	Equatorial Guinea	4.30
62	So. Africa	2.90		143	Myanmar	4.30
65	Ecuador	2.95		143	Rwanda	4.30
65	Gabon	2.95		147	Tajikistan	4.40
65	Indonesia	2.95		147	Uzbekistan	4.40
65	Malta	2.95		149	Angola	4.45
65	Morocco	2.95		149	Turkmenistan	4.45
65	Poland	2.95		151	Guinea-Bissau	4.55
65	Tunisia	2.95		152	Vietnam	4.60
72	Ghana	3.00		153	Congo (Zaire)	4.70
72	Lithuania	3.00		153	Iran	4.70
72	Saudi Arabia	3.00		155	Bosnia	4.80
75	Benin	3.05		155	Somalia	4.80
75	Kenya	3.05		157	Iraq	4.90
75	Paraguay	3.05		157	Laos	4.90
75	Qatar	3.05		157	Libya	4.90
75	Slovak Republic	3.05		160	Cuba	5.00
75	Zambia	3.05		160	Korea, North	5.00
81	Colombia	3.10				

Mostly Unfree

CAPITAL FLOWS AND FOREIGN INVESTMENT
Score: 2–Stable (low barriers)

In 1995, the government implemented various foreign investment reforms, including the scrapping of laws that mandated the employment of Nigerians. As a result, foreigners now may own 100 percent of any Nigerian enterprise. The ministry charged with approving foreign investment often acts arbitrarily, however, and there can be long delays in the project-approval process. In recent years, Nigeria has proved unable to attract significant foreign investment outside the oil and gas sectors.

BANKING
Score: 4–Stable (high level of restrictions)

More than 100 domestic and foreign banks now operate branch offices in Nigeria; nevertheless, the banking sector is doing poorly. Although 60 percent Nigerian ownership no longer is required for foreign ventures, licensing refusals are common and the government has taken control of four large, recently privatized commercial banks. The Central Bank (which the president controls directly) fixes the discount rate, mandates lending to the agricultural and manufacturing sectors, and heavily regulates and controls the country's other banks. Private banks recently have been forced to purchase government securities.

WAGE AND PRICE CONTROLS
Score: 2–Stable (low level)

Price controls were abolished in 1987, although some products, including petroleum, are subsidized. Wages are determined by negotiations between employers and unions, and the government has the final word on wage increases. Nigeria has a minimum wage.

PROPERTY RIGHTS
Score: 3–Stable (moderate level of protection)

There is strong resistance to privatization among Nigeria's labor unions, and the enforcement of laws protecting property remains lax. According to the U.S. Department of Commerce, "The Government has taken several steps to undercut the independence and integrity of the judiciary.... [T]he Government's frequent refusal to respect court rulings also undermines the integrity of the judicial process."[2]

REGULATION
Score: 4–Stable (high level)

The government has streamlined the process for establishing a business, but problems remain: Foreign investors must deal with bureaucratic delays, rampant corruption, and a complex web of restrictions and regulations. The U.S. Department of Commerce reports that "Nigeria offers potential investors a low-cost labor pool, abundant natural resources, and the largest domestic market in sub-Saharan Africa. However, these advantages must be weighed against Nigeria's autocratic military government, inadequate and poorly maintained infrastructure, increasing labor problems, complicated, confusing and inconsistent regulatory environment, the importance of personal ties in doing business and endemic corruption."[3] It may take several years just to acquire building permits.

BLACK MARKET
Score: 3–Stable (moderate level of activity)

High tariffs and bans on textile and agricultural imports provide incentives for smuggling. Government monopolies on sugar and fertilizer distribution also encourage illegal trade, and a high duty on cigarettes and luxury goods makes smuggling in these areas very lucrative. According to the Office of the United States Trade Representative, "[Import] bans are compromised by widespread smuggling."[4] The black market in pirated computer software is substantial.

NOTES

[1] World Bank, *World Development Indicators,* 1998.
[2] U.S. Department of Commerce, *Country Commercial Guide,* 1997.
[3] U.S. Department of Commerce, *Country Commercial Guide,* 1998.
[4] Office of the United States Trade Representative, *1998 National Trade Estimate Report on Foreign Trade Barriers.*

Norway — 2.35

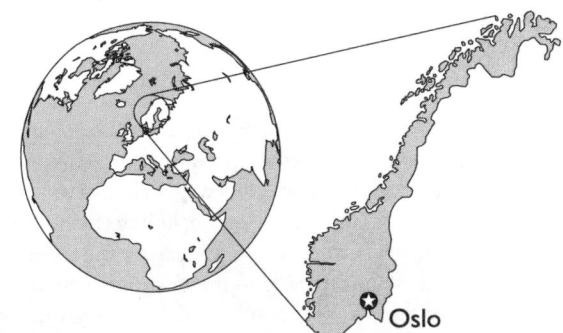

1998 Score: **2.35**	1997 Score: **2.45**	1996 Score: **2.45**

Trade	2	Banking	3
Taxation	4.5	Wages and Prices	3
Government Intervention	3	Property Rights	1
Monetary Policy	1	Regulation	3
Foreign Investment	2	Black Market	1

Norway won its independence from Sweden in 1905. It remained neutral during World War I and was occupied by Nazi Germany during World War II, before which time it had an established socialized economy with generous social welfare programs. When the legitimate government was restored in 1945, new elections resulted in a powerful victory for the Labor Party, which remained in power for the next 20 years and oversaw the consolidation of the social welfare state. During the late 1950s, Norway began to pursue free trade with its neighbors, becoming a member of the European Free Trade Association in 1959. It twice has rejected full membership in the European Union (EU) but remains closely linked with the EU through the European Economic Area, which affords favorable access to the EU market for most Norwegian products.

TRADE POLICY
Score: 2–Stable (low level of protectionism)

Norway has decreased its average tariff to about 1.32 percent.[1] Non-tariff barriers include quotas and other restrictions on agricultural imports.

TAXATION
Score–Income taxation: 5–Stable (very high tax rates)
Score–Corporate taxation: 3–Stable (moderate tax rates)
Final Taxation Score: 4.5–Stable (very high tax rates)

Norway's top income tax rate is 41.7 percent, and the average citizen is taxed at more than 28 percent. The top marginal corporate tax rate is 28 percent. Norway also has a 28 percent capital gains tax and a 23 percent value-added tax.

GOVERNMENT INTERVENTION IN THE ECONOMY
Score: 3–Stable (moderate level)

Government consumes 20.5 percent of GDP, almost half of which is produced by state-owned industries.

MONETARY POLICY
Score: 1–Stable (very low level of inflation)

From 1986 to 1996, Norway had an average inflation rate of 2.9 percent. In 1997, the rate was 2.5 percent.

CAPITAL FLOWS AND FOREIGN INVESTMENT
Score: 2–Stable (low barriers)

Although Norway generally welcomes foreign investment, the government still maintains restrictions on investments in telecommunications, public utilities, and industries considered vital to national security. According to the U.S. Department of Commerce, "While the Norwegian government officially endorses a 'level playing field' for foreign investors, existing regulations, standards and practices often marginally favor Norwegian, Scandinavian and European Economic Area investors, in that order."[2]

1	Hong Kong	1.25		81	Fiji	3.10
2	Singapore	1.30		81	Mali	3.10
3	Bahrain	1.70		81	Slovenia	3.10
4	New Zealand	1.75		85	Honduras	3.15
5	Switzerland	1.85		85	Mexico	3.15
6	United States	1.90		85	Papua New Guinea	3.15
7	Ireland	1.95		88	Djibouti	3.20
7	Luxembourg	1.95		88	Mongolia	3.20
7	Taiwan	1.95		90	Algeria	3.25
7	United Kingdom	1.95		90	Brazil	3.25
11	Bahamas	2.00		90	Lebanon	3.25
12	Czech Republic	2.05		90	Senegal	3.25
12	Japan	2.05		90	Tanzania	3.25
14	Australia	2.10		95	Nigeria	3.30
14	Belgium	2.10		95	Romania	3.30
14	Canada	2.10		97	Cambodia	3.35
14	United Arab Emirates	2.10		97	Dominican Republic	3.35
18	Austria	2.15		97	Egypt	3.35
18	Chile	2.15		97	Guinea	3.35
18	Estonia	2.15		97	Ivory Coast	3.35
18	Netherlands	2.15		97	Moldova	3.35
22	Denmark	2.25		97	Pakistan	3.35
22	El Salvador	2.25		104	Nepal	3.40
22	Finland	2.25		104	Venezuela	3.40
25	Germany	2.30		106	Armenia	3.45
25	Iceland	2.30		106	Bulgaria	3.45
27	Norway	2.35		106	Lesotho	3.45
28	Korea, South	2.40		106	Madagascar	3.45
28	Kuwait	2.40		106	Russia	3.45
28	Malaysia	2.40		111	Burkina Faso	3.50
28	Panama	2.40		111	Cameroon	3.50
28	Thailand	2.40		111	Guyana	3.50
33	Sweden	2.45		111	Nicaragua	3.50
34	Argentina	2.50		115	Gambia	3.60
34	France	2.50		116	Croatia	3.65
34	Italy	2.50		116	Georgia	3.65
34	Spain	2.50		116	Malawi	3.65
38	Portugal	2.55		119	Cape Verde	3.67
38	Sri Lanka	2.55		120	Ethiopia	3.70
38	Trinidad and Tobago	2.55		120	India	3.70
41	Barbados	2.60		120	Niger	3.70
41	Peru	2.60		123	Congo	3.75
43	Bolivia	2.65		124	Chad	3.80
43	Mauritius	2.65		124	China	3.80
45	Cyprus	2.70		124	Mauritania	3.80
45	Jamaica	2.70		124	Ukraine	3.80
45	Uruguay	2.70		124	Zimbabwe	3.80
48	Botswana	2.75		129	Albania	3.85
48	Guatemala	2.75		129	Bangladesh	3.85
48	Jordan	2.75		129	Mozambique	3.85
48	Namibia	2.75		129	Suriname	3.85
48	Oman	2.75		133	Burundi	3.90
48	Philippines	2.75		134	Togo	3.95
54	Belize	2.80		135	Haiti	4.00
54	Costa Rica	2.80		135	Kyrgyz Rep.	4.00
54	Israel	2.80		137	Kazakhstan	4.05
54	Swaziland	2.80		137	Sierra Leone	4.05
54	Turkey	2.80		139	Yemen	4.10
54	Uganda	2.80		140	Belarus	4.15
54	Samoa	2.80		141	Sudan	4.20
61	Latvia	2.85		141	Syria	4.20
62	Greece	2.90		143	Azerbaijan	4.30
62	Hungary	2.90		143	Equatorial Guinea	4.30
62	So. Africa	2.90		143	Myanmar	4.30
65	Ecuador	2.95		143	Rwanda	4.30
65	Gabon	2.95		147	Tajikistan	4.40
65	Indonesia	2.95		147	Uzbekistan	4.40
65	Malta	2.95		149	Angola	4.45
65	Morocco	2.95		149	Turkmenistan	4.45
65	Poland	2.95		151	Guinea-Bissau	4.55
65	Tunisia	2.95		152	Vietnam	4.60
72	Ghana	3.00		153	Congo (Zaire)	4.70
72	Lithuania	3.00		153	Iran	4.70
72	Saudi Arabia	3.00		155	Bosnia	4.80
75	Benin	3.05		155	Somalia	4.80
75	Kenya	3.05		157	Iraq	4.90
75	Paraguay	3.05		157	Laos	4.90
75	Qatar	3.05		157	Libya	4.90
75	Slovak Republic	3.05		160	Cuba	5.00
75	Zambia	3.05		160	Korea, North	5.00
81	Colombia	3.10				

Mostly Free

BANKING
Score: 3–Stable (moderate level of restrictions)

Norway's banking system is becoming more liberalized. Non-European banks are permitted to establish subsidiaries (but not branches), and Norwegian banks may engage in a variety of financial services, including the buying and selling of securities, insurance policies, real estate, and other investments. According to the U.S. Department of State, "While there has been substantial banking reform, competition in this sector still remains distorted due to government ownership of the two largest commercial banks, and the existence of specialized state banks which offer subsidized loans in certain sectors and geographic locations."[3]

WAGE AND PRICE CONTROLS
Score: 3–Stable (moderate level)

The market sets wages and prices, although the government exercises indirect control over many wages and prices through the large public sector. Large agricultural subsidies also continue to affect prices. According to the Economist Intelligence Unit, "Indirect price controls and price fixing exist in several industrial sectors," such as oil and electricity.[4]

PROPERTY RIGHTS
Score: 1–Stable (very high level of protection)

Private property is safe from expropriation. Norway has an efficient legal system. The U.S. Department of State reports that "The Constitution provides for an independent judiciary, and the Government respects this provision in practice."[5]

REGULATION
Score: 3–Stable (moderate level)

Some of Norway's economy (especially agriculture and such service industries as telecommunications and transportation) remains heavily regulated. The government, however, also continues to reduce expenditures and privatize some businesses.

BLACK MARKET
Score: 1–Stable (very low level of activity)

Norway has a minuscule black market. Because it also has strong and efficient laws concerning intellectual property rights, piracy in such products is virtually nonexistent.

NOTES

[1] Based on total government taxation of international transactions as a percentage of imports.
[2] U.S. Department of Commerce, *Country Commercial Guide,* 1998.
[3] U.S. Department of State, *Country Reports on Economic Policy and Trade Practices,* 1998.
[4] The Economist Intelligence Unit, *ILT Report,* April 1997.
[5] U.S. Department of State, "Norway Country Report on Human Rights Practices for 1997," 1998.

Oman   2.75

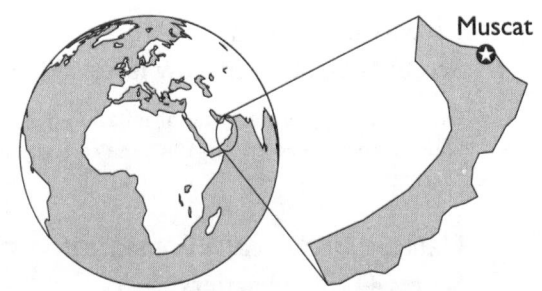
Muscat

1998 Score: **2.65**	1997 Score: **2.75**	1996 Score: **2.85**

Trade	2	Banking	4
Taxation	2.5	Wages and Prices	3
Government Intervention	4	Property Rights	2
Monetary Policy	1	Regulation	3
Foreign Investment	4	Black Market	2

Oman is an absolute monarchy. Sultan Qaboos bin Said al-Said has a 60-member consultative council with limited advisory powers, however. The economy depends heavily on oil revenues, which account for 85 percent of export earnings and about 40 percent of GDP. According to the U.S. Department of State, "A significant proportion of its rural population lives in poverty. An annual population growth of no less than 3.7 percent for Omani nationals surpasses growth in non-petroleum domestic production and presents ever greater demand on infrastructure. The Sultanate seeks to lessen its dependence on oil export revenues by diversifying, primarily to natural gas-based industry."[1] Oman recently reduced some taxes on corporations. There is an increase, however, in foreign investment restrictions and in the regulatory burden; as a result, Oman's overall score is 0.1 point worse than last year.

TRADE POLICY
Score: 2–Stable (low level of protectionism)

Oman's average tariff rate has decreased to lower than 3 percent. Non-tariff barriers take the form of import licenses, which are required for all imports. The U.S. Department of State reports that "Oman's customs procedures are complex. There are complaints of sudden changes in the enforcement of regulations. Until superior officers can be contacted, an occasional customs officer can cause temporary delays and confusion by insisting that documentation or shipments comply with suspended boycott regulations."[2]

TAXATION
Score–Income taxation: 1–Stable (low tax rates)
Score–Corporate taxation: 3+ (moderate high tax rates)
Total Taxation Score: 2.5+ (moderate tax rates)

Income taxes are not imposed on individuals. The top corporate tax rate is 30 percent, down from 50 percent last year.[3] As a result, Oman's corporate taxation score is 2 points better this year; thus, its final taxation score is 1 point better than last year. Oman also has a 30 percent capital gains tax, a training levy taken from non-Omani employees, and a social contributions tax.

GOVERNMENT INTERVENTION IN THE ECONOMY
Score: 4–Stable (high level)

Government consumes 26 percent of GDP. It also owns nearly all of the country's oil production. According to the U.S. Department of State, "Oman operates a free market economy, but the government is at present the most important economic actor, both in terms of employment and as a purchaser of goods and services."[4]

#	Country	Score		#	Country	Score
1	Hong Kong	1.25		81	Fiji	3.10
2	Singapore	1.30		81	Mali	3.10
3	Bahrain	1.70		81	Slovenia	3.10
4	New Zealand	1.75		85	Honduras	3.15
5	Switzerland	1.85		85	Mexico	3.15
6	United States	1.90		85	Papua New Guinea	3.15
7	Ireland	1.95		88	Djibouti	3.20
7	Luxembourg	1.95		88	Mongolia	3.20
7	Taiwan	1.95		90	Algeria	3.25
7	United Kingdom	1.95		90	Brazil	3.25
11	Bahamas	2.00		90	Lebanon	3.25
12	Czech Republic	2.05		90	Senegal	3.25
12	Japan	2.05		90	Tanzania	3.25
14	Australia	2.10		95	Nigeria	3.30
14	Belgium	2.10		95	Romania	3.30
14	Canada	2.10		97	Cambodia	3.35
14	United Arab Emirates	2.10		97	Dominican Republic	3.35
18	Austria	2.15		97	Egypt	3.35
18	Chile	2.15		97	Guinea	3.35
18	Estonia	2.15		97	Ivory Coast	3.35
18	Netherlands	2.15		97	Moldova	3.35
22	Denmark	2.25		97	Pakistan	3.35
22	El Salvador	2.25		104	Nepal	3.40
22	Finland	2.25		104	Venezuela	3.40
25	Germany	2.30		106	Armenia	3.45
25	Iceland	2.30		106	Bulgaria	3.45
27	Norway	2.35		106	Lesotho	3.45
28	Korea, South	2.40		106	Madagascar	3.45
28	Kuwait	2.40		106	Russia	3.45
28	Malaysia	2.40		111	Burkina Faso	3.50
28	Panama	2.40		111	Cameroon	3.50
28	Thailand	2.40		111	Guyana	3.50
33	Sweden	2.45		111	Nicaragua	3.50
34	Argentina	2.50		115	Gambia	3.60
34	France	2.50		116	Croatia	3.65
34	Italy	2.50		116	Georgia	3.65
34	Spain	2.50		116	Malawi	3.65
38	Portugal	2.55		119	Cape Verde	3.67
38	Sri Lanka	2.55		120	Ethiopia	3.70
38	Trinidad and Tobago	2.55		120	India	3.70
41	Barbados	2.60		120	Niger	3.70
41	Peru	2.60		123	Congo	3.75
43	Bolivia	2.65		124	Chad	3.80
43	Mauritius	2.65		124	China	3.80
45	Cyprus	2.70		124	Mauritania	3.80
45	Jamaica	2.70		124	Ukraine	3.80
45	Uruguay	2.70		124	Zimbabwe	3.80
48	Botswana	2.75		129	Albania	3.85
48	Guatemala	2.75		129	Bangladesh	3.85
48	Jordan	2.75		129	Mozambique	3.85
48	Namibia	2.75		129	Suriname	3.85
48	**Oman**	**2.75**		133	Burundi	3.90
48	Philippines	2.75		134	Togo	3.95
54	Belize	2.80		135	Haiti	4.00
54	Costa Rica	2.80		135	Kyrgyz Rep.	4.00
54	Israel	2.80		137	Kazakhstan	4.05
54	Swaziland	2.80		137	Sierra Leone	4.05
54	Turkey	2.80		139	Yemen	4.10
54	Uganda	2.80		140	Belarus	4.15
54	Samoa	2.80		141	Sudan	4.20
61	Latvia	2.85		141	Syria	4.20
62	Greece	2.90		143	Azerbaijan	4.30
62	Hungary	2.90		143	Equatorial Guinea	4.30
62	So. Africa	2.90		143	Myanmar	4.30
65	Ecuador	2.95		143	Rwanda	4.30
65	Gabon	2.95		147	Tajikistan	4.40
65	Indonesia	2.95		147	Uzbekistan	4.40
65	Malta	2.95		149	Angola	4.45
65	Morocco	2.95		149	Turkmenistan	4.45
65	Poland	2.95		151	Guinea-Bissau	4.55
65	Tunisia	2.95		152	Vietnam	4.60
72	Ghana	3.00		153	Congo (Zaire)	4.70
72	Lithuania	3.00		153	Iran	4.70
72	Saudi Arabia	3.00		155	Bosnia	4.80
75	Benin	3.05		155	Somalia	4.80
75	Kenya	3.05		157	Iraq	4.90
75	Paraguay	3.05		157	Laos	4.90
75	Qatar	3.05		157	Libya	4.90
75	Slovak Republic	3.05		160	Cuba	5.00
75	Zambia	3.05		160	Korea, North	5.00
81	Colombia	3.10				

Mostly Free

MONETARY POLICY
Score: 1–Stable (very low level of inflation)

Oman's average annual rate of inflation from 1986 to 1996 was less than 1 percent. In 1997, the rate was less than 1 percent.

CAPITAL FLOWS AND FOREIGN INVESTMENT
Score: 4– (high barriers)

With few exceptions, companies must be owned fully by Omanis. Foreign investment is allowed only through joint ventures and joint-stock companies. There are some tax incentives for investment. There are increasing indications, however, that Oman is undertaking a program aimed at encouraging businesses to hire only, or primarily, Omani citizens. This further discourages foreign investment. As a result, Oman's foreign investment score is 1 point worse than it was last year.

BANKING
Score: 4–Stable (high level of restrictions)

Oman has a thriving banking sector, but competition is limited because foreigners are not permitted to open new banks.

WAGE AND PRICE CONTROLS
Score: 3–Stable (moderate level)

There are few official price controls, but government is the main consumer of goods and services, and its purchases therefore affect prices. Oman has a minimum wage law.

PROPERTY RIGHTS
Score: 2–Stable (high level of protection)

Property expropriation is not likely. Oman's court system is efficient, and private property is well protected, although the judicial system is not completely free of government influence.

REGULATION
Score: 3– (moderate level)

Oman's relatively straightforward regulations have been applied consistently in most cases. There is growing evidence, however, that regulations are increasing and are becoming a greater burden on the economy. For example, according to the U.S. Department of Commerce, "Although the government officially supports the free market, the regulatory environment it fosters hampers investment and commercial activity. In addition to the ownership, visa and agency requirements,...general licensing of business activities can be time-consuming and complicated. The absence of a particular clearance will stall the entire process. For example, processing shipments in and out of the Mina Qaboos port can add significantly to the amount of time it takes to get goods to the market or inputs to a project. Oman is also moving forward with a variety of environmental regulations but enforcement of the rules is inconsistent."[5] As a result, Oman's score is 1 point worse this year.

BLACK MARKET
Score: 2–Stable (low level of activity)

Oman has a negligible black market. There is some traffic in pirated intellectual property (primarily sound and video recordings); but laws are strictly enforced, and black market activity in this area is minimal.

NOTES

[1] U.S. Department of State, *Country Reports on Economic Policy and Trade Practices*, 1998.

[2] *Ibid.*

[3] Oman had a top corporate tax rate of 50 percent for joint venture firms with less than 10 percent Omani ownership. That tax rate was removed and now is capped at 30 percent.

[4] U.S. Department of State, *Country Reports on Economic Policy and Trade Practices*, 1998.

[5] U.S. Department of Commerce, *Country Commercial Guide*, 1998.

Pakistan 3.35

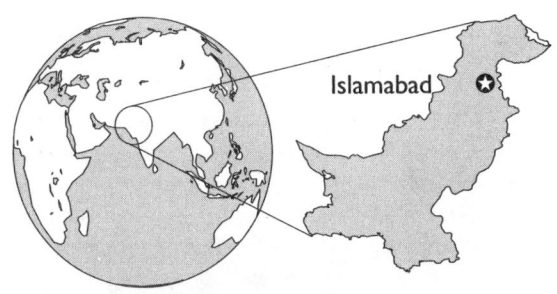

Islamabad

1998 Score: 3.20   **1997 Score: 3.10**   **1996 Score: 3.05**

Trade	5	Banking	3
Taxation	3.5	Wages and Prices	3
Government Intervention	3	Property Rights	4
Monetary Policy	2	Regulation	4
Foreign Investment	2	Black Market	4

Since gaining its independence following the partition of the Indian subcontinent and the end of British rule in 1947, Pakistan has received huge amounts of foreign aid—much of which has been squandered—and has remained poor. In 1990, the government of Prime Minister Nawaz Sharif undertook a program of economic liberalization to increase foreign and domestic private investment, but the pace of reform slowed after Benazir Bhutto became prime minister in 1993. Terrorist attacks and political violence among warring religious and ethnic factions have destabilized Karachi, Pakistan's business center. Prime Minister Bhutto was removed from office in November 1996 under accusations of corruption, and a new government headed once again by Sharif was elected in February 1997. Inheriting an economy in deep recession, Sharif has responded by cutting some taxes, which has improved Pakistan's taxation score. There has been a decrease in the level of property rights protection, however, as well as an increase in black market activity; as a result, Pakistan's overall score is 0.15 point worse this year.

TRADE POLICY
Score: 5–Stable (very high level of protectionism)

Pakistan's average tariff rate is 28 percent.[1] Non-tariff barriers include import licenses and fees. According to the U.S. Department of State, "Charges that customs officers demand bribes are also common."[2]

TAXATION
Score–Income taxation: 2+ (low tax rates)
Score–Corporate taxation: 4–Stable (high tax rates)
Total Taxation Score: 3.5+ (moderate tax rates)

Pakistan's top income tax rate is 20 percent, down from 35 percent last year. The average income is taxed at 5 percent, down from 10 percent last year; as a result, Pakistan's income taxation score is 1 point better than last year, improving its final taxation score by 0.5 point. The top corporate income tax rate is 40 percent. Pakistan also has a 40 percent capital gains tax, a sales tax, state and local taxes, and a capital value tax that is added to certain properties like factories and automobiles.

GOVERNMENT INTERVENTION IN THE ECONOMY
Score: 3–Stable (moderate level)

Government consumes 11.5 percent of GDP. Although proceeding with significant privatization, the government continues to own many financial institutions as well as companies in the energy and utilities, transportation, and marketing sectors.

MONETARY POLICY
Score: 2–Stable (low level of inflation)

Pakistan's average annual rate of inflation from 1986 to 1996 was 8.9 percent. The rate for 1997 was 11.4 percent.

1	Hong Kong	1.25		81	Fiji	3.10
2	Singapore	1.30		81	Mali	3.10
3	Bahrain	1.70		81	Slovenia	3.10
4	New Zealand	1.75		85	Honduras	3.15
5	Switzerland	1.85		85	Mexico	3.15
6	United States	1.90		85	Papua New Guinea	3.15
7	Ireland	1.95		88	Djibouti	3.20
7	Luxembourg	1.95		88	Mongolia	3.20
7	Taiwan	1.95		90	Algeria	3.25
7	United Kingdom	1.95		90	Brazil	3.25
11	Bahamas	2.00		90	Lebanon	3.25
12	Czech Republic	2.05		90	Senegal	3.25
12	Japan	2.05		90	Tanzania	3.25
14	Australia	2.10		95	Nigeria	3.30
14	Belgium	2.10		95	Romania	3.30
14	Canada	2.10		97	Cambodia	3.35
14	United Arab Emirates	2.10		97	Dominican Republic	3.35
18	Austria	2.15		97	Egypt	3.35
18	Chile	2.15		97	Guinea	3.35
18	Estonia	2.15		97	Ivory Coast	3.35
18	Netherlands	2.15		97	Moldova	3.35
22	Denmark	2.25		97	Pakistan	3.35
22	El Salvador	2.25		104	Nepal	3.40
22	Finland	2.25		104	Venezuela	3.40
25	Germany	2.30		106	Armenia	3.45
25	Iceland	2.30		106	Bulgaria	3.45
27	Norway	2.35		106	Lesotho	3.45
28	Korea, South	2.40		106	Madagascar	3.45
28	Kuwait	2.40		106	Russia	3.45
28	Malaysia	2.40		111	Burkina Faso	3.50
28	Panama	2.40		111	Cameroon	3.50
28	Thailand	2.40		111	Guyana	3.50
33	Sweden	2.45		111	Nicaragua	3.50
34	Argentina	2.50		115	Gambia	3.60
34	France	2.50		116	Croatia	3.65
34	Italy	2.50		116	Georgia	3.65
34	Spain	2.50		116	Malawi	3.65
38	Portugal	2.55		119	Cape Verde	3.67
38	Sri Lanka	2.55		120	Ethiopia	3.70
38	Trinidad and Tobago	2.55		120	India	3.70
41	Barbados	2.60		120	Niger	3.70
41	Peru	2.60		123	Congo	3.75
43	Bolivia	2.65		124	Chad	3.80
43	Mauritius	2.65		124	China	3.80
45	Cyprus	2.70		124	Mauritania	3.80
45	Jamaica	2.70		124	Ukraine	3.80
45	Uruguay	2.70		124	Zimbabwe	3.80
48	Botswana	2.75		129	Albania	3.85
48	Guatemala	2.75		129	Bangladesh	3.85
48	Jordan	2.75		129	Mozambique	3.85
48	Namibia	2.75		129	Suriname	3.85
48	Oman	2.75		133	Burundi	3.90
48	Philippines	2.75		134	Togo	3.95
54	Belize	2.80		135	Haiti	4.00
54	Costa Rica	2.80		135	Kyrgyz Rep.	4.00
54	Israel	2.80		137	Kazakhstan	4.05
54	Swaziland	2.80		137	Sierra Leone	4.05
54	Turkey	2.80		139	Yemen	4.10
54	Uganda	2.80		140	Belarus	4.15
54	Samoa	2.80		141	Sudan	4.20
61	Latvia	2.85		141	Syria	4.20
62	Greece	2.90		143	Azerbaijan	4.30
62	Hungary	2.90		143	Equatorial Guinea	4.30
62	So. Africa	2.90		143	Myanmar	4.30
65	Ecuador	2.95		143	Rwanda	4.30
65	Gabon	2.95		147	Tajikistan	4.40
65	Indonesia	2.95		147	Uzbekistan	4.40
65	Malta	2.95		149	Angola	4.45
65	Morocco	2.95		149	Turkmenistan	4.45
65	Poland	2.95		151	Guinea-Bissau	4.55
65	Tunisia	2.95		152	Vietnam	4.60
72	Ghana	3.00		153	Congo (Zaire)	4.70
72	Lithuania	3.00		153	Iran	4.70
72	Saudi Arabia	3.00		155	Bosnia	4.80
75	Benin	3.05		155	Somalia	4.80
75	Kenya	3.05		157	Iraq	4.90
75	Paraguay	3.05		157	Laos	4.90
75	Qatar	3.05		157	Libya	4.90
75	Slovak Republic	3.05		160	Cuba	5.00
75	Zambia	3.05		160	Korea, North	5.00
81	Colombia	3.10				

Mostly Unfree

CAPITAL FLOWS AND FOREIGN INVESTMENT
Score: 2–Stable (low barriers)

There are no restrictions on the amount of foreign investment in Pakistani industries. Domestic and foreign firms are treated equally. According to the U.S. Department of Commerce, "The Government of Pakistan is open to foreign investment and offers a package of incentives to attract foreign investors. Considering the openness of the investment regime, foreign investment activity to date has been relatively modest and in 1996–97 registered a substantial drop in new FDI [foreign direct investment]. Possible reasons for this include inadequate infrastructure, perceptions of political instability, law and order difficulties, policy inconsistencies, and resistance to the new policies by some elements of the bureaucracy who have not yet fully adjusted to the new, open economic environment."[3]

BANKING
Score: 3–Stable (moderate level of restrictions)

Foreigners are gaining greater access to banks in Pakistan, although foreign banks are subject to higher taxes than domestic banks are. Local banks are permitted to engage in securities and investments, but not in insurance and real estate ventures. Despite recent attempts to privatize more banks, the government continues to own several banking institutions; new data show that state-owned banks control over 70 percent of total commercial bank assets. By global standards, however, the level of restrictions on banking is only moderate.

WAGE AND PRICE CONTROLS
Score: 3–Stable (moderate level)

Pakistan maintains price controls on many products. Prices are set generally on products (such as automobiles) manufactured by state-operated firms, on petroleum, and on electricity. Pakistan has a minimum wage.

PROPERTY RIGHTS
Score: 4– (low level of protection)

Property is protected in most cases, and expropriation is unlikely. The courts do not enforce property rights in all cases, however, and recent political strife has highlighted the government's control over the judiciary. According to the U.S. Department of State, "The Constitution provides for an independent judiciary; however, in practice, the judiciary is subject to political influence."[4] Moreover, recent political turmoil has revealed the existence of corruption within the judiciary. For example, according to the Economist Intelligence Unit, "The judiciary and the civil service have become heavily politicized, and they are accused of widespread corruption."[5] As a result, Pakistan's property rights score is 1 point worse than last year.

REGULATION
Score: 4–Stable (high level)

Pakistan's economy is heavily regulated, and laws like the Environmental Protection Ordinance of 1983, the Industrial Relations Ordinance of 1974, and the Factories Act often are burdensome. Corruption also remains a problem. According to the U.S. Department of Commerce, "Corruption is prevalent in both public and private sectors in Pakistan."[6]

BLACK MARKET
Score: 4– (high level of activity)

Smuggling is encouraged by extremely high tariffs on many consumer goods. Illicit trade in consumer electronics and recorded music is substantial. According to the U.S. Department of State, "Pakistani enforcement of intellectual property rights is weak, resulting in widespread piracy, especially of copyrighted materials."[7] Moreover, smuggling is increasing, causing the size of the black market to grow. The Xinhua News Agency reports, "Increasingly rampant smuggling has caused serious concern in Pakistan as this South Asian nation is suffering losses estimated at hundreds of millions of U.S. dollars annually."[8] Additionally, the U.S. Department of Commerce notes, Pakistan "has had to rely on import and excise taxes for a very high share of revenues, thus protecting inefficient industries and encouraging smuggling."[9] As a result, Pakistan's score in this factor is 1 point worse this year.

NOTES
[1] World Bank, *World Development Indicators 1998*, 1998.
[2] U.S. Department of State, *Country Reports on Economic Policy and Trade Practices*, 1998.
[3] U.S. Department of Commerce, *Country Commercial Guide*, 1998.
[4] U.S. Department of State, "Pakistan Country Report on Human Rights Practices for 1997," 1998.
[5] Economist Intelligence Unit, *ILT Reports*, September 1997; and March 1998 update.
[6] U.S. Department of Commerce, *Country Commercial Guide*, 1998.
[7] U.S. Department of State, *Country Reports on Economic Policy and Trade Practices*, 1998.
[8] "Pakistan Faces Daunting Task of Anti-Smuggling," Xinhua News Agency, Islamabad, April 11, 1998.
[9] U.S. Department of Commerce, *Country Commercial Guide*, 1998.

Panama   2.40

1998 Score: **2.40**   1997 Score: **2.50**   1996 Score: **2.40**

Trade	3
Taxation	3
Government Intervention	3
Monetary Policy	1
Foreign Investment	2

Banking	1
Wages and Prices	2
Property Rights	3
Regulation	3
Black Market	3

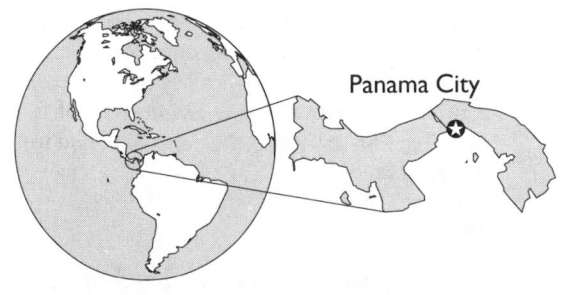

Panama City

Panama, site of the U.S.-built Panama Canal, held democratic elections in May 1994. President Ernesto Perez Balladares advocates a strong policy of economic liberalization. Privatization efforts have stalled, however, leaving many businesses and utilities in government hands. Panama adopted the U.S. dollar as its official currency in 1904. This significant economic reform removed the government's ability to inflate the currency to cover government spending and is a major reason that the inflation rate is less than 3 percent, and that Panama has enjoyed a degree of price stability that has eluded the rest of Latin America.

TRADE POLICY
Score: 3–Stable (moderate level of protectionism)

Panama's average tariff rate is 8.73 percent.[1] Non-tariff barriers, however, have increased to include strict labeling, testing, and certification requirements, especially on poultry, pork, and beef products.

TAXATION
Score–Income taxation: 2–Stable (low tax rates)
Score–Corporate taxation: 3–Stable (moderate tax rates)
Total Taxation Score: 3–Stable (moderate tax rates)

Panama's top marginal tax rate is 30 percent, but the average income level is taxed at 0 percent. The top corporate tax rate is 30 percent. Panama also has a 30 percent capital gains tax.

GOVERNMENT INTERVENTION IN THE ECONOMY
Score: 3–Stable (moderate level)

Government consumes 15.7 percent of GDP. The government also owns some telephone, electricity, and water systems, as well as some manufacturing companies.

MONETARY POLICY
Score: 1–Stable (very low level of inflation)

Panama has made its most significant progress in monetary policy, removing the government almost completely from supplying the currency. The average annual rate of inflation between 1986 and 1996 was 1.9 percent, primarily because Panama has used the U.S. dollar as its currency since 1904. This prevents the government from printing money to cover deficit spending. The inflation rate was 1.5 percent in 1997.

CAPITAL FLOWS AND FOREIGN INVESTMENT
Score: 2–Stable (low barriers)

Most sectors of Panama's economy are open to foreign investment, although there are a few restrictions on "national interest" industries and retail activities. According to the U.S. Department of Commerce, "Taking its cue from Panama's

#	Country	Score	#	Country	Score
1	Hong Kong	1.25	81	Fiji	3.10
2	Singapore	1.30	81	Mali	3.10
3	Bahrain	1.70	81	Slovenia	3.10
4	New Zealand	1.75	85	Honduras	3.15
5	Switzerland	1.85	85	Mexico	3.15
6	United States	1.90	85	Papua New Guinea	3.15
7	Ireland	1.95	88	Djibouti	3.20
7	Luxembourg	1.95	88	Mongolia	3.20
7	Taiwan	1.95	90	Algeria	3.25
7	United Kingdom	1.95	90	Brazil	3.25
11	Bahamas	2.00	90	Lebanon	3.25
12	Czech Republic	2.05	90	Senegal	3.25
12	Japan	2.05	90	Tanzania	3.25
14	Australia	2.10	95	Nigeria	3.30
14	Belgium	2.10	95	Romania	3.30
14	Canada	2.10	97	Cambodia	3.35
14	United Arab Emirates	2.10	97	Dominican Republic	3.35
18	Austria	2.15	97	Egypt	3.35
18	Chile	2.15	97	Guinea	3.35
18	Estonia	2.15	97	Ivory Coast	3.35
18	Netherlands	2.15	97	Moldova	3.35
22	Denmark	2.25	97	Pakistan	3.35
22	El Salvador	2.25	104	Nepal	3.40
22	Finland	2.25	104	Venezuela	3.40
25	Germany	2.30	106	Armenia	3.45
25	Iceland	2.30	106	Bulgaria	3.45
27	Norway	2.35	106	Lesotho	3.45
28	Korea, South	2.40	106	Madagascar	3.45
28	Kuwait	2.40	106	Russia	3.45
28	Malaysia	2.40	111	Burkina Faso	3.50
28	Panama	2.40	111	Cameroon	3.50
28	Thailand	2.40	111	Guyana	3.50
33	Sweden	2.45	111	Nicaragua	3.50
34	Argentina	2.50	115	Gambia	3.60
34	France	2.50	116	Croatia	3.65
34	Italy	2.50	116	Georgia	3.65
34	Spain	2.50	116	Malawi	3.65
38	Portugal	2.55	119	Cape Verde	3.67
38	Sri Lanka	2.55	120	Ethiopia	3.70
38	Trinidad and Tobago	2.55	120	India	3.70
41	Barbados	2.60	120	Niger	3.70
41	Peru	2.60	123	Congo	3.75
43	Bolivia	2.65	124	Chad	3.80
43	Mauritius	2.65	124	China	3.80
45	Cyprus	2.70	124	Mauritania	3.80
45	Jamaica	2.70	124	Ukraine	3.80
45	Uruguay	2.70	124	Zimbabwe	3.80
48	Botswana	2.75	129	Albania	3.85
48	Guatemala	2.75	129	Bangladesh	3.85
48	Jordan	2.75	129	Mozambique	3.85
48	Namibia	2.75	129	Suriname	3.85
48	Oman	2.75	133	Burundi	3.90
48	Philippines	2.75	134	Togo	3.95
54	Belize	2.80	135	Haiti	4.00
54	Costa Rica	2.80	135	Kyrgyz Rep.	4.00
54	Israel	2.80	137	Kazakhstan	4.05
54	Swaziland	2.80	137	Sierra Leone	4.05
54	Turkey	2.80	139	Yemen	4.10
54	Uganda	2.80	140	Belarus	4.15
54	Samoa	2.80	141	Sudan	4.20
61	Latvia	2.85	141	Syria	4.20
62	Greece	2.90	143	Azerbaijan	4.30
62	Hungary	2.90	143	Equatorial Guinea	4.30
62	So. Africa	2.90	143	Myanmar	4.30
65	Ecuador	2.95	143	Rwanda	4.30
65	Gabon	2.95	147	Tajikistan	4.40
65	Indonesia	2.95	147	Uzbekistan	4.40
65	Malta	2.95	149	Angola	4.45
65	Morocco	2.95	149	Turkmenistan	4.45
65	Poland	2.95	151	Guinea-Bissau	4.55
65	Tunisia	2.95	152	Vietnam	4.60
72	Ghana	3.00	153	Congo (Zaire)	4.70
72	Lithuania	3.00	153	Iran	4.70
72	Saudi Arabia	3.00	155	Bosnia	4.80
75	Benin	3.05	155	Somalia	4.80
75	Kenya	3.05	157	Iraq	4.90
75	Paraguay	3.05	157	Laos	4.90
75	Qatar	3.05	157	Libya	4.90
75	Slovak Republic	3.05	160	Cuba	5.00
75	Zambia	3.05	160	Korea, North	5.00
81	Colombia	3.10			

Mostly Free

central geographic location and its limited manufacturing and agricultural sectors, the Government of Panama and the business community actively promote this country's long-standing reputation as an international trading, banking, and services center, and as a site for foreign direct investment."[2]

BANKING
Score: 1–Stable (very low level of restrictions)

Domestic competition in banking is relatively high, and major banks from all over the world operate in Panama. Domestic banks may sell securities and real estate and make some investments, but they are not permitted to sell insurance. There are few restrictions on opening banks. The U.S. Department of Commerce describes Panama's banking sector as one of the most dynamic areas of the economy.[3]

WAGE AND PRICE CONTROLS
Score: 2–Stable (low level)

The market sets most wages and prices, although the government controls the prices of a few basic foodstuffs, industrial products, medicines, public transportation, and rent. Panama also imposes minimum wages.

PROPERTY RIGHTS
Score: 3–Stable (moderate level of protection)

Property rights are constitutionally protected in Panama, but the legal system is not always independent. According to the U.S. Department of State, "The Constitution provides for an independent judiciary; however, the judiciary is susceptible to corruption and outside influence, including from other branches of government."[4]

REGULATION
Score: 3–Stable (moderate level)

Opening a business is a relatively easy process that requires obtaining a license from the Ministry of Commerce and Industry. Bureaucratic red tape remains burdensome, however, as does some corruption.

BLACK MARKET
Score: 3–Stable (moderate level of activity)

Panama has a large black market in pirated computer software and prerecorded sound and video tapes. According to the U.S. Department of Commerce, "In general, protection for intellectual property rights in Panama has in the past been less than adequate in several areas. The U.S.–Panama Bilateral Investment Treaty, negotiated in 1983 but not put into effect until 1992, does not contain an intellectual property annex. Representatives of some U.S. firms allege that Panama provides inadequate copyright and trademark protection. In 1995, Nintendo of America and associated video game manufacturers petitioned the U.S. Trade Representative to remove Panama's benefits under the Generalized System of Preferences (GSP) program for this reason; that case is pending. In 1997, USTR placed Panama on the Special 301 'Watch List' for failure to protect American intellectual property rights. The notice cited transshipment of counterfeited goods through Panama and lack of enforcement in the Colon Free Zone."[5] By global standards, however, the level of Panama's black market activity is moderate.

NOTES
[1]   Based on taxes on international trade as a percentage of total imports.
[2]   U.S. Department of Commerce, *Country Commercial Guide*, 1998.
[3]   *Ibid.*
[4]   U.S. Department of State, *1997 Human Rights Report: Panama*, 1998.
[5]   U.S. Department of Commerce, *Country Commercial Guide*, 1998.

Papua New Guinea 3.15

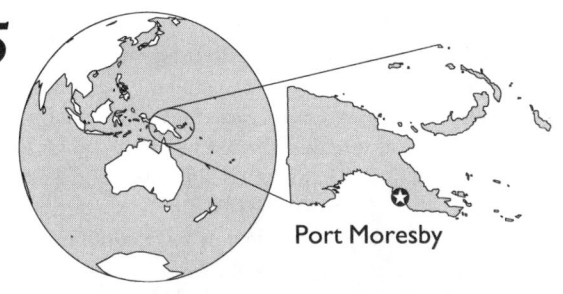

Port Moresby

1998 Score: **3.15**	1997 Score: **3.10**	1996 Score: **3.10**

Trade	5	Banking	4
Taxation	2.5	Wages and Prices	3
Government Intervention	3	Property Rights	3
Monetary Policy	1	Regulation	4
Foreign Investment	3	Black Market	3

Papua New Guinea gained its independence from Australia in 1975. Its parliamentary democracy is raucous but weak, beset by corruption, costly and overlapping local governments, and the expense of fighting a secessionist movement on the island of Bougainville. The country's high economic growth is due largely to mining, logging, and oil projects; but it also relies heavily on foreign aid. In 1994, faced with a chronic budget deficit that threatened the government with bankruptcy, it began to cut some trade restrictions while raising taxes and fees. In June 1996, Papua New Guinea joined the World Trade Organization, thereby obligating the government to reduce its barriers to international trade and investment and to establish laws to protect intellectual property rights.

TRADE POLICY
Score: 5–Stable (very high level of protectionism)

The average tariff rate is 21.3 percent.[1] Non-tariff barriers include an inefficient bureaucracy and local government requirements that tend to hamper imports of products that compete directly with domestic firms.

TAXATION
Score–Income taxation: 2-Stable (low tax rates)
Score–Corporate taxation: 2–Stable (low tax rates)
Final Taxation Score: 2.5-Stable (moderate tax rates)

Papua New Guinea's top income tax rate is 35 percent; the average taxpayer is in the 0 percent bracket. The top marginal corporate tax rate is 25 percent. The government also levies a sales tax of varying rates.

GOVERNMENT INTERVENTION IN THE ECONOMY
Score: 3–Stable (moderate level)

Government consumes about 22.4 percent of GDP. The government also owns substantial portions of the economy, especially in the mining sector. About one-third of those employed in the formal sector work for the government.

MONETARY POLICY
Score: 1–Stable (very low level of inflation)

Papua New Guinea's average annual rate of inflation from 1986 to 1996 was 5.2 percent.

CAPITAL FLOWS AND FOREIGN INVESTMENT
Score: 3–Stable (moderate barriers)

The government is opening more sectors to foreign investment, but some barriers still exist. Not all foreign companies are treated the same as their domestic counterparts; several industrial sectors, such as mining, are closed to foreign investment; and hostility to foreign investment in the lower levels of the

1	Hong Kong	1.25
2	Singapore	1.30
3	Bahrain	1.70
4	New Zealand	1.75
5	Switzerland	1.85
6	United States	1.90
7	Ireland	1.95
7	Luxembourg	1.95
7	Taiwan	1.95
7	United Kingdom	1.95
11	Bahamas	2.00
12	Czech Republic	2.05
12	Japan	2.05
14	Australia	2.10
14	Belgium	2.10
14	Canada	2.10
14	United Arab Emirates	2.10
18	Austria	2.15
18	Chile	2.15
18	Estonia	2.15
18	Netherlands	2.15
22	Denmark	2.25
22	El Salvador	2.25
22	Finland	2.25
25	Germany	2.30
25	Iceland	2.30
27	Norway	2.35
28	Korea, South	2.40
28	Kuwait	2.40
28	Malaysia	2.40
28	Panama	2.40
28	Thailand	2.40
33	Sweden	2.45
34	Argentina	2.50
34	France	2.50
34	Italy	2.50
34	Spain	2.50
38	Portugal	2.55
38	Sri Lanka	2.55
38	Trinidad and Tobago	2.55
41	Barbados	2.60
41	Peru	2.60
43	Bolivia	2.65
43	Mauritius	2.65
45	Cyprus	2.70
45	Jamaica	2.70
45	Uruguay	2.70
48	Botswana	2.75
48	Guatemala	2.75
48	Jordan	2.75
48	Namibia	2.75
48	Oman	2.75
48	Philippines	2.75
54	Belize	2.80
54	Costa Rica	2.80
54	Israel	2.80
54	Swaziland	2.80
54	Turkey	2.80
54	Uganda	2.80
54	Samoa	2.80
61	Latvia	2.85
62	Greece	2.90
62	Hungary	2.90
62	So. Africa	2.90
65	Ecuador	2.95
65	Gabon	2.95
65	Indonesia	2.95
65	Malta	2.95
65	Morocco	2.95
65	Poland	2.95
65	Tunisia	2.95
72	Ghana	3.00
72	Lithuania	3.00
72	Saudi Arabia	3.00
75	Benin	3.05
75	Kenya	3.05
75	Paraguay	3.05
75	Qatar	3.05
75	Slovak Republic	3.05
75	Zambia	3.05
81	Colombia	3.10
81	Fiji	3.10
81	Mali	3.10
81	Slovenia	3.10
85	Honduras	3.15
85	Mexico	3.15
85	Papua New Guinea	3.15
88	Djibouti	3.20
88	Mongolia	3.20
90	Algeria	3.25
90	Brazil	3.25
90	Lebanon	3.25
90	Senegal	3.25
90	Tanzania	3.25
95	Nigeria	3.30
95	Romania	3.30
97	Cambodia	3.35
97	Dominican Republic	3.35
97	Egypt	3.35
97	Guinea	3.35
97	Ivory Coast	3.35
97	Moldova	3.35
97	Pakistan	3.35
104	Nepal	3.40
104	Venezuela	3.40
106	Armenia	3.45
106	Bulgaria	3.45
106	Lesotho	3.45
106	Madagascar	3.45
106	Russia	3.45
111	Burkina Faso	3.50
111	Cameroon	3.50
111	Guyana	3.50
111	Nicaragua	3.50
115	Gambia	3.60
116	Croatia	3.65
116	Georgia	3.65
116	Malawi	3.65
119	Cape Verde	3.67
120	Ethiopia	3.70
120	India	3.70
120	Niger	3.70
123	Congo	3.75
124	Chad	3.80
124	China	3.80
124	Mauritania	3.80
124	Ukraine	3.80
124	Zimbabwe	3.80
129	Albania	3.85
129	Bangladesh	3.85
129	Mozambique	3.85
129	Suriname	3.85
133	Burundi	3.90
134	Togo	3.95
135	Haiti	4.00
135	Kyrgyz Rep.	4.00
137	Kazakhstan	4.05
137	Sierra Leone	4.05
139	Yemen	4.10
140	Belarus	4.15
141	Sudan	4.20
141	Syria	4.20
143	Azerbaijan	4.30
143	Equatorial Guinea	4.30
143	Myanmar	4.30
143	Rwanda	4.30
147	Tajikistan	4.40
147	Uzbekistan	4.40
149	Angola	4.45
149	Turkmenistan	4.45
151	Guinea-Bissau	4.55
152	Vietnam	4.60
153	Congo (Zaire)	4.70
153	Iran	4.70
155	Bosnia	4.80
155	Somalia	4.80
157	Iraq	4.90
157	Laos	4.90
157	Libya	4.90
160	Cuba	5.00
160	Korea, North	5.00

Mostly Unfree

bureaucracy can create delays in obtaining necessary documents and meeting licensing requirements. "Though the government favors investment," reports the U.S. Department of Commerce, "many investors trying to enter the market remain frustrated with the process. Potential investors often experience difficulties and delay in obtaining necessary clearances from a cumbersome bureaucracy. Large developments are inevitably contentious and quickly become political issues, necessitating cabinet decisions. Without consensus at this level, the investor faces additional delay. Several reports in the Australian and local media have charged corruption on the part of decision-makers. Some companies have reported delays in receiving investment approvals which they believe were attributable to their refusal to pay bribes."[2]

BANKING
Score: 4–Stable (high level of restrictions)

The government exercises a great deal of influence over the banking system. Banks are not free to engage in all types of financial services.

WAGE AND PRICE CONTROLS
Score: 3–Stable (moderate level)

Both the private and public sectors set wages and prices. The government sets prices on some goods and services, such as certain foodstuffs and agricultural goods.

PROPERTY RIGHTS
Score: 3–Stable (moderate level of protection)

Private property is safe from government expropriation, and the legal and judicial system is efficient. According to the U.S. Department of Commerce, Papua New Guinea "has a

Western legal system inherited primarily from Australia. The courts, which are insulated from Government interference, provide a meaningful forum in which to enforce property and contractual rights, though the country does not have a written commercial code. The insolvency act is the source of bankruptcy law and controls the dissolution of failed corporations."[3] The lack of a commercial code, however, sometimes makes enforcement of property claims costly and ineffective.

REGULATION
Score: 4–Stable (high level)

Establishing a business can be difficult, especially if it requires extensive contact with lower levels of the bureaucracy and with local government. The government recently increased its regulation of the economy. According to the U.S. Department of Commerce, "The government has intervened heavily in economic activity through an extensive system of licensing and approval requirements and through trade restrictions, tariffs, and price controls." Some recent laws, including health and safety regulations and strict environmental policies, are making compliance increasingly burdensome, and corruption within the bureaucracy remains a problem. According to the U.S. Department of Commerce, "The bureaucratic procedure for resolving interagency differences is cumbersome; differences often cannot be solved except at the highest political levels. This involves delay and frustration for many investors."[4]

BLACK MARKET
Score: 3–Stable (moderate level of activity)

The black market is limited primarily to illegal and smuggled goods, as well as to pirated video and audio cassettes.

NOTES
[1] World Bank, *World Development Indicators 1998,* 1998
[2] U.S. Department of Commerce, *Country Commercial Guide,* 1998.
[3] *Ibid.*
[4] *Ibid.*

Paraguay

3.05

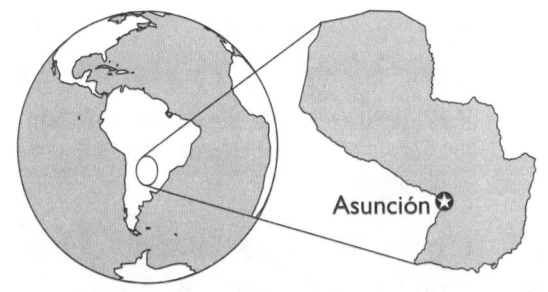

Asunción ✪

1998 Score: **2.85**	1997 Score: **2.75**	1996 Score: **2.65**

Trade	2	Banking	2
Taxation	2.5	Wages and Prices	3
Government Intervention	3	Property Rights	4
Monetary Policy	4	Regulation	4
Foreign Investment	1	Black Market	5

Paraguay held its first free democratic election May 1993. The government of President Juan Carlos Wasmosy attempted to control government spending, reduce customs duties and inflation, and attract foreign investment, but had little success. President Raul Cubas Grau, elected in May 1998, has pledged to reform the country's weakened financial system. Although its economic liberalization policies have pushed Paraguay ahead of many of its neighbors in Latin America, the country remains plagued with corruption and a repressive police force. Recently, Paraguay increased its level of government intervention in the economy and its regulatory burden on business; as a result, its overall score is 0.2 point worse than last year.

TRADE POLICY
Score: 2–Stable (low level of protectionism)

According to the U.S. Department of Commerce, "Since 1995 Paraguay has applied the Mercosur Common External Tariff of 0–20% to all but 399 items on its list of exceptions. The duties on these items are to converge to the Mercosur level by 2006."[1] Paraguay's average tariff rate is 9.3 percent.[2] The country maintains no major non-tariff barriers to trade, although it has erected barriers to some agricultural imports like poultry.

TAXATION
Score–Income taxation: 1–Stable (very low tax rates)
Score–Corporate taxation: 3–Stable (moderate tax rates)
Total Taxation Score: 2.5–Stable (moderate tax rates)

Paraguay imposes no taxes on income derived from personal work, services provided, or professional services rendered.[3] The top corporate tax rate is 30 percent. The government also levies a 30 percent capital gains tax, a 10 percent value-added tax, and a 26 percent payroll tax.

GOVERNMENT INTERVENTION IN THE ECONOMY
Score: 3– (moderate level)

Government consumes 7.8 percent of GDP. Paraguay had a successful privatization program that involved selling off its airlines and other companies. Recent moves by the legislature have slowed this process, however, and many large firms remain government-owned. According to the U.S. Department of Commerce, "The Paraguayan government continues to be the primary actor in the economy. It is the largest employer and the budget represents almost 40% of GDP (although only about half the budget was actually spent). Of the budget spent, 80% went to salaries and other current expenditures, 15% for servicing foreign debt, and 5% for investment. The government has followed a stringent monetary policy aimed at controlling inflation (8.2% in 1996, with a 9% target for 1997) and maintaining the value of the local currency, the Guarani (devaluation has averaged 4–5% during the last four years). Reform efforts, including privatization, are effectively on hold until after the 1998 elections."[4] As a result of the stalled privatization program, Paraguay's score for government intervention is 1 point worse this year.

1	Hong Kong	1.25	81	Fiji	3.10
2	Singapore	1.30	81	Mali	3.10
3	Bahrain	1.70	81	Slovenia	3.10
4	New Zealand	1.75	85	Honduras	3.15
5	Switzerland	1.85	85	Mexico	3.15
6	United States	1.90	85	Papua New Guinea	3.15
7	Ireland	1.95	88	Djibouti	3.20
7	Luxembourg	1.95	88	Mongolia	3.20
7	Taiwan	1.95	90	Algeria	3.25
7	United Kingdom	1.95	90	Brazil	3.25
11	Bahamas	2.00	90	Lebanon	3.25
12	Czech Republic	2.05	90	Senegal	3.25
12	Japan	2.05	90	Tanzania	3.25
14	Australia	2.10	95	Nigeria	3.30
14	Belgium	2.10	95	Romania	3.30
14	Canada	2.10	97	Cambodia	3.35
14	United Arab Emirates	2.10	97	Dominican Republic	3.35
18	Austria	2.15	97	Egypt	3.35
18	Chile	2.15	97	Guinea	3.35
18	Estonia	2.15	97	Ivory Coast	3.35
18	Netherlands	2.15	97	Moldova	3.35
22	Denmark	2.25	97	Pakistan	3.35
22	El Salvador	2.25	104	Nepal	3.40
22	Finland	2.25	104	Venezuela	3.40
25	Germany	2.30	106	Armenia	3.45
25	Iceland	2.30	106	Bulgaria	3.45
27	Norway	2.35	106	Lesotho	3.45
28	Korea, South	2.40	106	Madagascar	3.45
28	Kuwait	2.40	106	Russia	3.45
28	Malaysia	2.40	111	Burkina Faso	3.50
28	Panama	2.40	111	Cameroon	3.50
28	Thailand	2.40	111	Guyana	3.50
33	Sweden	2.45	111	Nicaragua	3.50
34	Argentina	2.50	115	Gambia	3.60
34	France	2.50	116	Croatia	3.65
34	Italy	2.50	116	Georgia	3.65
34	Spain	2.50	116	Malawi	3.65
38	Portugal	2.55	119	Cape Verde	3.67
38	Sri Lanka	2.55	120	Ethiopia	3.70
38	Trinidad and Tobago	2.55	120	India	3.70
41	Barbados	2.60	120	Niger	3.70
41	Peru	2.60	123	Congo	3.75
43	Bolivia	2.65	124	Chad	3.80
43	Mauritius	2.65	124	China	3.80
45	Cyprus	2.70	124	Mauritania	3.80
45	Jamaica	2.70	124	Ukraine	3.80
45	Uruguay	2.70	124	Zimbabwe	3.80
48	Botswana	2.75	129	Albania	3.85
48	Guatemala	2.75	129	Bangladesh	3.85
48	Jordan	2.75	129	Mozambique	3.85
48	Namibia	2.75	129	Suriname	3.85
48	Oman	2.75	133	Burundi	3.90
48	Philippines	2.75	134	Togo	3.95
54	Belize	2.80	135	Haiti	4.00
54	Costa Rica	2.80	135	Kyrgyz Rep.	4.00
54	Israel	2.80	137	Kazakhstan	4.05
54	Swaziland	2.80	137	Sierra Leone	4.05
54	Turkey	2.80	139	Yemen	4.10
54	Uganda	2.80	140	Belarus	4.15
54	Samoa	2.80	141	Sudan	4.20
61	Latvia	2.85	141	Syria	4.20
62	Greece	2.90	143	Azerbaijan	4.30
62	Hungary	2.90	143	Equatorial Guinea	4.30
62	So. Africa	2.90	143	Myanmar	4.30
65	Ecuador	2.95	143	Rwanda	4.30
65	Gabon	2.95	147	Tajikistan	4.40
65	Indonesia	2.95	147	Uzbekistan	4.40
65	Malta	2.95	149	Angola	4.45
65	Morocco	2.95	149	Turkmenistan	4.45
65	Poland	2.95	151	Guinea-Bissau	4.55
65	Tunisia	2.95	152	Vietnam	4.60
72	Ghana	3.00	153	Congo (Zaire)	4.70
72	Lithuania	3.00	153	Iran	4.70
72	Saudi Arabia	3.00	155	Bosnia	4.80
75	Benin	3.05	155	Somalia	4.80
75	Kenya	3.05	157	Iraq	4.90
75	Paraguay	3.05	157	Laos	4.90
75	Qatar	3.05	157	Libya	4.90
75	Slovak Republic	3.05	160	Cuba	5.00
75	Zambia	3.05	160	Korea, North	5.00
81	Colombia	3.10			

Mostly Unfree

MONETARY POLICY
Score: 4–Stable (high level of inflation)

Paraguay's average annual rate of inflation from 1986 to 1996 was 23.45 percent. Inflation data for 1997 are not available.

CAPITAL FLOWS AND FOREIGN INVESTMENT
Score: 1–Stable (very low barriers)

There are few restrictions on foreign investment. Foreign and domestic companies are treated equally, and full repatriation of capital and profits is guaranteed by law. Some exceptions include bans on investment in the cement industry and in such public utilities as electricity, telephones, and water. According to the U.S. Department of Commerce, "There are no formal restrictions to foreign investment in Paraguay. National treatment of foreign investors is guaranteed, as is full repatriation of capital and profits. Paraguay's tax burden is the lowest in South America, with no personal income tax, a 30% earnings tax for businesses, and a 10% value added tax."[5]

BANKING
Score: 2–Stable (low level of restrictions)

Banks may engage in most financial activities, including the sale of stocks, bonds, and other securities. According to the U.S. Department of Commerce, "The financial system includes over 60 finance companies dedicated to smaller consumer operations off-limits to banks. Four banks are state-owned, 13 are foreign and the remainder are owned by nationals. The banking system operates mostly on short to medium term credit (12 months is the usual maximum for commercial transactions, although private finance of vehicles and homes is available on longer terms) in both local and foreign currency."[6]

WAGE AND PRICE CONTROLS
Score: 3–Stable (moderate level)

The government controls the prices of utilities, petroleum products, pharmaceuticals, and bus fares. It also maintains a minimum wage.

PROPERTY RIGHTS
Score: 4–Stable (low level of protection)

Expropriation of property is still possible; in fact, recent reports indicate a decrease in the level of protection of private property. As the U.S. Department of Commerce explains, "Increasing pressure for land has led to invasions of rural properties and expropriations by the government. Over the past two years, the Congress has approved several expropriations, but the President has vetoed them. In many cases invasions are politically motivated, with parcels of land being awarded as political bounty by local politicians. The 1992 law calls for adequate compensation, but the financial straits of the Government make this difficult."[7] There also is increasing evidence that the judicial system has failed to protect private property rights adequately: "A complicated and sometimes non-transparent legal system makes upholding property rights difficult," reports the U.S. Department of Commerce.[8]

REGULATION
Score: 4– (high level)

The government owns and operates several industries, including public utilities and companies involved in manufacturing cement and steel. These industries are tightly regulated by government officials who oversee production levels and pricing. Environmental, consumer, labor, financial, and other regulations also are burdensome. Another problem is bureaucratic corruption; according to the U.S. Department of Commerce, "One of the most serious problems facing Paraguay is the legacy of institutional corruption after decades of dictatorship. There have been mechanisms created to combat corruption, such as the Congressional Bicameral Investigative Unit or the Comptroller's Office, but investigations often become political and are seldom completed. The slow pace of judicial reform, and the continued lack of transparency of the system, continue to serve as a barrier to development. The law protecting government employees, which makes it impossible to fire public servants even if caught in the act, complicates things further. While more people were jailed in the past two years than ever before for corrupt practices, none of them remains in jail."[9] The lack of success in combating corruption and its apparent continued burden on business cause Paraguay's regulation score to be 1 point worse this year.

BLACK MARKET
Score: 5–Stable (very high level of activity)

Although the government has removed most restrictions on imports, the smuggling of illegal agricultural goods and products still can be lucrative. According to the U.S. Department of Commerce, the black market in Paraguay is immense: "The government has made little headway in formalizing the economy. Some claim that informal activity could match the formal $10 billion economy."[10] Black market activity in pirated intellectual property alone, especially pirated audio and video products, costs U.S.-based businesses alone over $100 million in losses each year.[11]

NOTES
[1] U.S. Department of Commerce, *Country Commercial Guide*, 1998.
[2] World Bank, *World Development Indicators 1997*, 1998.
[3] Paraguay levies a 30 percent tax on individuals engaged in sole proprietorship. This tax, if applied across the entire population, would be negligible, however.
[4] U.S. Department of Commerce, *Country Commercial Guide*, 1998.
[5] *Ibid.*
[6] *Ibid.*
[7] *Ibid.*
[8] *Ibid.*
[9] *Ibid.*
[10] *Ibid.*
[11] U.S. Department of State, *Country Reports on Economic Policy and Trade Practices*, 1997.

Peru   2.60

1998 Score: **2.80**   1997 Score: **2.90**   1996 Score: **3.00**

Trade	2	Banking	2
Taxation	3	Wages and Prices	2
Government Intervention	1	Property Rights	2
Monetary Policy	5	Regulation	3
Foreign Investment	2	Black Market	4

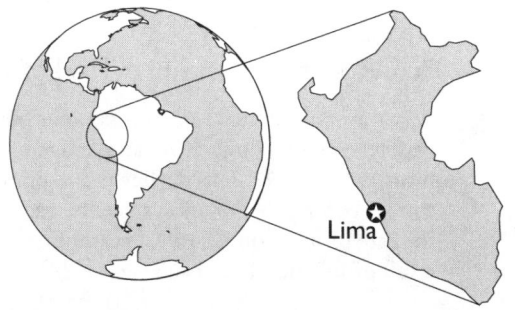

Lima

During the 1980s, Peru was among the world's most socialist and inefficient economies. Under the leadership of Alberto Fujimori, who was elected to the presidency in 1990 and re-elected in 1995, many important economic and trade reforms have been implemented, and subversive guerrilla activity has been virtually eliminated. Although far from achieving full liberalization, Peru has made great strides toward the free market. Peru has reduced corruption in its judicial system and has reduced its regulatory burden on businesses; as a result, its overall score is 0.2 point better than last year.

TRADE POLICY
Score: 2–Stable (low level of protectionism)

Peru has an average tariff rate of 9.46 percent,[1] down from the 13.2 percent reported last year in the *Index*. It maintains few, if any, substantial non-tariff barriers. "Almost all barriers to U.S. exports and direct investment have been eliminated over the past seven years," reports the U.S. Department of State. "Import licenses have been abolished for all products except firearms, munitions, and explosives; chemical precursors (used in cocaine production); and ammonium nitrate fertilizer, which has been used as a blast enhancer for terrorist car bombs."[2]

TAXATION
Score–Income taxation: 2–Stable (low tax rates)
Score–Corporate taxation: 3–Stable (moderate tax rates)
Total Taxation Score: 3–Stable (moderate tax rates)

Peru's top income tax rate is 30 percent, and the average income is taxed at 0 percent. The corporate tax rate is a flat 30 percent. Peru also has a 30 percent capital gains tax and a sales tax.

GOVERNMENT INTERVENTION IN THE ECONOMY
Score: 1–Stable (very low level)

Government consumes only 8.3 percent of GDP. President Fujimori has succeeded in expanding the private sector while privatizing the public sector; the only areas in which the state has the primary role are education, mining, defense, and telecommunications. Many utilities are being privatized or at least opened to private investment. According to the U.S. Department of State, "In the short span of six years, Peru has been converted from an economy dominated by a protectionist and interventionist state to a liberal economy dominated by the private sector and market forces. Several major state-owned businesses have been privatized in the past four years. Although the timetable for the privatization program has slipped over the past couple of years, the government has said it plans to sell the remaining state-owned enterprises by the end of 1998."[3]

1	Hong Kong	1.25	81	Fiji	3.10
2	Singapore	1.30	81	Mali	3.10
3	Bahrain	1.70	81	Slovenia	3.10
4	New Zealand	1.75	85	Honduras	3.15
5	Switzerland	1.85	85	Mexico	3.15
6	United States	1.90	85	Papua New Guinea	3.15
7	Ireland	1.95	88	Djibouti	3.20
7	Luxembourg	1.95	88	Mongolia	3.20
7	Taiwan	1.95	90	Algeria	3.25
7	United Kingdom	1.95	90	Brazil	3.25
11	Bahamas	2.00	90	Lebanon	3.25
12	Czech Republic	2.05	90	Senegal	3.25
12	Japan	2.05	90	Tanzania	3.25
14	Australia	2.10	95	Nigeria	3.30
14	Belgium	2.10	95	Romania	3.30
14	Canada	2.10	97	Cambodia	3.35
14	United Arab Emirates	2.10	97	Dominican Republic	3.35
18	Austria	2.15	97	Egypt	3.35
18	Chile	2.15	97	Guinea	3.35
18	Estonia	2.15	97	Ivory Coast	3.35
18	Netherlands	2.15	97	Moldova	3.35
22	Denmark	2.25	97	Pakistan	3.35
22	El Salvador	2.25	104	Nepal	3.40
22	Finland	2.25	104	Venezuela	3.40
25	Germany	2.30	106	Armenia	3.45
25	Iceland	2.30	106	Bulgaria	3.45
27	Norway	2.35	106	Lesotho	3.45
28	Korea, South	2.40	106	Madagascar	3.45
28	Kuwait	2.40	106	Russia	3.45
28	Malaysia	2.40	111	Burkina Faso	3.50
28	Panama	2.40	111	Cameroon	3.50
28	Thailand	2.40	111	Guyana	3.50
33	Sweden	2.45	111	Nicaragua	3.50
34	Argentina	2.50	115	Gambia	3.60
34	France	2.50	116	Croatia	3.65
34	Italy	2.50	116	Georgia	3.65
34	Spain	2.50	116	Malawi	3.65
38	Portugal	2.55	119	Cape Verde	3.67
38	Sri Lanka	2.55	120	Ethiopia	3.70
38	Trinidad and Tobago	2.55	120	India	3.70
41	Barbados	2.60	120	Niger	3.70
41	Peru	2.60	123	Congo	3.75
43	Bolivia	2.65	124	Chad	3.80
43	Mauritius	2.65	124	China	3.80
45	Cyprus	2.70	124	Mauritania	3.80
45	Jamaica	2.70	124	Ukraine	3.80
45	Uruguay	2.70	124	Zimbabwe	3.80
48	Botswana	2.75	129	Albania	3.85
48	Guatemala	2.75	129	Bangladesh	3.85
48	Jordan	2.75	129	Mozambique	3.85
48	Namibia	2.75	129	Suriname	3.85
48	Oman	2.75	133	Burundi	3.90
48	Philippines	2.75	134	Togo	3.95
54	Belize	2.80	135	Haiti	4.00
54	Costa Rica	2.80	135	Kyrgyz Rep.	4.00
54	Israel	2.80	137	Kazakhstan	4.05
54	Swaziland	2.80	137	Sierra Leone	4.05
54	Turkey	2.80	139	Yemen	4.10
54	Uganda	2.80	140	Belarus	4.15
54	Samoa	2.80	141	Sudan	4.20
61	Latvia	2.85	141	Syria	4.20
62	Greece	2.90	143	Azerbaijan	4.30
62	Hungary	2.90	143	Equatorial Guinea	4.30
62	So. Africa	2.90	143	Myanmar	4.30
65	Ecuador	2.95	143	Rwanda	4.30
65	Gabon	2.95	147	Tajikistan	4.40
65	Indonesia	2.95	147	Uzbekistan	4.40
65	Malta	2.95	149	Angola	4.45
65	Morocco	2.95	149	Turkmenistan	4.45
65	Poland	2.95	151	Guinea-Bissau	4.55
65	Tunisia	2.95	152	Vietnam	4.60
72	Ghana	3.00	153	Congo (Zaire)	4.70
72	Lithuania	3.00	153	Iran	4.70
72	Saudi Arabia	3.00	155	Bosnia	4.80
75	Benin	3.05	155	Somalia	4.80
75	Kenya	3.05	157	Iraq	4.90
75	Paraguay	3.05	157	Laos	4.90
75	Qatar	3.05	157	Libya	4.90
75	Slovak Republic	3.05	160	Cuba	5.00
75	Zambia	3.05	160	Korea, North	5.00
81	Colombia	3.10			

Mostly Free

MONETARY POLICY
Score: 5–Stable (very high level of inflation)

Peru's average annual rate of inflation from 1986 to 1996 was 447 percent, down from an average of 615.6 percent from 1985 to 1993. This decline is due primarily to progress toward controlling inflation since the early 1990s. In 1997, the rate of inflation fell to 8.2 percent. Historically, however, levels of inflation have been very high.

CAPITAL FLOWS AND FOREIGN INVESTMENT
Score: 2–Stable (low barriers)

The few restrictions imposed on foreign investment in Peru apply mainly to industries defined as vital to the national defense. According to the U.S. Department of State, "There are virtually no barriers to investing in Peru, and national treatment for investors is guaranteed in the 1993 constitution."[4]

BANKING
Score: 2–Stable (low level of restrictions)

There are few restrictions on foreign banks. All banks may sell securities, real estate, and insurance policies, and all may make some investments, although they are restricted in their ability to invest in industrial firms. According to the U.S. Department of Commerce, "Peruvian law allows banks to freely take deposits and to make loans in both foreign and domestic currency. The Peruvian banking system is highly 'dollarized' and at present about 63 percent of liquidity in the banking system is denominated in dollars."[5]

WAGE AND PRICE CONTROLS
Score: 2–Stable (low level)

The market sets most wages and prices. The U.S. Department of State reports that "Price controls, direct subsidies, and restrictions on foreign investment have been eliminated."[6] Peru maintains a minimum wage.

PROPERTY RIGHTS
Score: 2+ (low level of protection)

By global standards, private property is moderately protected in Peru; but the court system is inefficient. According to the U.S. Department of Commerce, "Enforcement of property and contractual rights has generally been effective, although the Peruvian legal system remains slow and inefficient. Improving the efficiency of the judicial system is a high priority of the Fujimori government. Government interference in the court system in commercial cases has rarely been a problem in recent years."[7] Moreover, there is little evidence that corruption still plagues the court system, and the Fujimori government seems to have been successful in eradicating corruption in the judicial system. As a result, Peru's property rights score is 1 point better this year.

REGULATION
Score: 3+ (moderate level)

Even though the government has made significant progress toward stamping out corruption, Peru remains plagued by an inefficient bureaucracy; even so, its regulatory environment has become more streamlined. For example, according to the U.S. Department of Commerce, the government "has adopted a transparent policy and effective laws to promote competition, backed by the establishment of INDECOPI [Peru's consumer watchdog agency]. Bureaucratic procedures (e.g., the registration of security licensing) are sufficiently streamlined and transparent, although difficulties have been encountered in obtaining licenses for casino operations."[8] Thus, this progress leaves Peru with only moderately burdensome regulations by global standards. As a result, Peru's regulation score is 1 point better this year.

BLACK MARKET
Score: 4–Stable (high level of activity)

Despite Peru's tremendous progress toward reducing many black market operations (for example, in transportation), much of its labor force still operates in the informal sector. According to the U.S. Department of State, "More than half the workforce is employed in the informal sector, beyond government regulation and supervision."[9] Black market activity in the sale of pirated items from the United States and Europe is rampant.

NOTES

[1]   Based on taxes on international trade as a percentage of total imports.
[2]   U.S. Department of State, *Country Reports on Economic Policy and Trade Practices*, 1998.
[3]   *Ibid.*
[4]   *Ibid.*
[5]   U.S. Department of Commerce, *Country Commercial Guide*, 1998.
[6]   U.S. Department of State, *Country Reports on Economic Policy and Trade Practices*, 1998.
[7]   U.S. Department of Commerce, *Country Commercial Guide*, 1998.
[8]   *Ibid.*
[9]   U.S. Department of State, *Country Reports on Economic Policy and Trade Practices*, 1998.

The Philippines 2.75

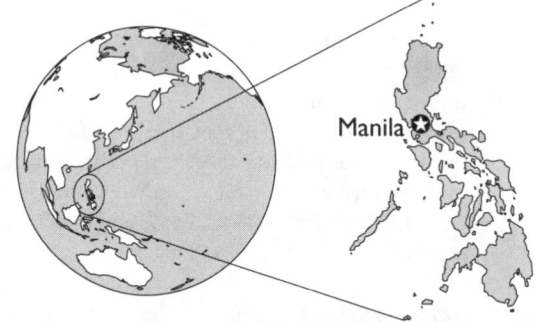
Manila

1998 Score: **2.65**   1997 Score: **2.80**   1996 Score: **2.90**

Trade	3	Banking	3
Taxation	3.5	Wages and Prices	2
Government Intervention	1	Property Rights	2
Monetary Policy	2	Regulation	4
Foreign Investment	3	Black Market	4

The Philippines was a U.S. colony from 1900 to 1948. Much of the country's infrastructure was destroyed during World War II, and the United States played a major role in reconstruction after the war. Nationalist economic policies pursued during the late 1950s and early 1960s laid the groundwork for protectionism and government interventionism, and successive administrations were plagued by ineffectiveness and corruption. Under the 1992–1998 administration of President Fidel Ramos, the Philippines established a solid record of economic reform. In addition to dismantling some monopolies, opening banking to greater foreign competition, and reducing the level of regulation, the government recently managed to cut tariffs, reduce its consumption of economic output, and achieve lower levels of inflation. The new president, Joseph Estrada, elected in May 1998, has promised to continue most of his predecessor's economic policies and reforms. There is recent evidence, however, that the burden of regulation and corruption are increasing in some branches of government; as a result, the Philippines' overall score is 0.1 point worse than last year.

TRADE POLICY
Score: 3–Stable (moderate level of protectionism)

A recent law passed to reduce the tariff rate to 5 percent over the next several years has led to an average tariff rate of 13.34 percent.[1] Republic Act 8179, passed in March 1996, eliminates all quantitative import restrictions on agricultural products (except rice) and replaces them with tariffs. According to the U.S. Department of State, however, "To assess import duty, the Bureau of Customs has shifted from 'home consumption value' to 'export value' as an interim step towards a shift to 'transaction value' before the year 2000. Many U.S. exporters assert that the use by the Bureau of Customs of the 'export value' method of valuation has resulted in unwarranted 'uplifts' in valuation (and in the assessed dutiable value)."[2]

TAXATION
Score–Income taxation: 3–Stable (moderate tax rates)
Score–Corporate taxation: 3–Stable (moderate tax rates)
Final Taxation Score: 3.5–Stable (high tax rates)

The top income tax rate in the Philippines is 35 percent, and the rate for the average income level is 11 percent. The top corporate tax is 34 percent. There also is a 20 percent capital gains tax and a 10 percent value-added tax.

GOVERNMENT INTERVENTION IN THE ECONOMY
Score: 1–Stable (very low level)

Government consumes 11.4 percent of GDP. Most state-owned companies are confined to utilities, and the government has made significant progress toward privatizing other state-owned industries. According to the U.S. Department of Commerce, "The Ramos administration continues to 'reprivatize' a once large portfolio of public sector-controlled firms. The original scope of privatization has, furthermore, been expanded from mere divestment to broadening private

1	Hong Kong	1.25	
2	Singapore	1.30	
3	Bahrain	1.70	
4	New Zealand	1.75	
5	Switzerland	1.85	
6	United States	1.90	
7	Ireland	1.95	
7	Luxembourg	1.95	
7	Taiwan	1.95	
7	United Kingdom	1.95	
11	Bahamas	2.00	
12	Czech Republic	2.05	
12	Japan	2.05	
14	Australia	2.10	
14	Belgium	2.10	
14	Canada	2.10	
14	United Arab Emirates	2.10	
18	Austria	2.15	
18	Chile	2.15	
18	Estonia	2.15	
18	Netherlands	2.15	
22	Denmark	2.25	
22	El Salvador	2.25	
22	Finland	2.25	
25	Germany	2.30	
25	Iceland	2.30	
27	Norway	2.35	
28	Korea, South	2.40	
28	Kuwait	2.40	
28	Malaysia	2.40	
28	Panama	2.40	
28	Thailand	2.40	
33	Sweden	2.45	
34	Argentina	2.50	
34	France	2.50	
34	Italy	2.50	
34	Spain	2.50	
38	Portugal	2.55	
38	Sri Lanka	2.55	
38	Trinidad and Tobago	2.55	
41	Barbados	2.60	
41	Peru	2.60	
43	Bolivia	2.65	
43	Mauritius	2.65	
45	Cyprus	2.70	
45	Jamaica	2.70	
45	Uruguay	2.70	
48	Botswana	2.75	
48	Guatemala	2.75	
48	Jordan	2.75	
48	Namibia	2.75	
48	Oman	2.75	
48	Philippines	2.75	
54	Belize	2.80	
54	Costa Rica	2.80	
54	Israel	2.80	
54	Swaziland	2.80	
54	Turkey	2.80	
54	Uganda	2.80	
54	Samoa	2.80	
61	Latvia	2.85	
62	Greece	2.90	
62	Hungary	2.90	
62	So. Africa	2.90	
65	Ecuador	2.95	
65	Gabon	2.95	
65	Indonesia	2.95	
65	Malta	2.95	
65	Morocco	2.95	
65	Poland	2.95	
65	Tunisia	2.95	
72	Ghana	3.00	
72	Lithuania	3.00	
72	Saudi Arabia	3.00	
75	Benin	3.05	
75	Kenya	3.05	
75	Paraguay	3.05	
75	Qatar	3.05	
75	Slovak Republic	3.05	
75	Zambia	3.05	
81	Colombia	3.10	
81	Fiji	3.10	
81	Mali	3.10	
81	Slovenia	3.10	
85	Honduras	3.15	
85	Mexico	3.15	
85	Papua New Guinea	3.15	
88	Djibouti	3.20	
88	Mongolia	3.20	
90	Algeria	3.25	
90	Brazil	3.25	
90	Lebanon	3.25	
90	Senegal	3.25	
90	Tanzania	3.25	
95	Nigeria	3.30	
95	Romania	3.30	
97	Cambodia	3.35	
97	Dominican Republic	3.35	
97	Egypt	3.35	
97	Guinea	3.35	
97	Ivory Coast	3.35	
97	Moldova	3.35	
97	Pakistan	3.35	
104	Nepal	3.40	
104	Venezuela	3.40	
106	Armenia	3.45	
106	Bulgaria	3.45	
106	Lesotho	3.45	
106	Madagascar	3.45	
106	Russia	3.45	
111	Burkina Faso	3.50	
111	Cameroon	3.50	
111	Guyana	3.50	
111	Nicaragua	3.50	
115	Gambia	3.60	
116	Croatia	3.65	
116	Georgia	3.65	
116	Malawi	3.65	
119	Cape Verde	3.67	
120	Ethiopia	3.70	
120	India	3.70	
120	Niger	3.70	
123	Congo	3.75	
124	Chad	3.80	
124	China	3.80	
124	Mauritania	3.80	
124	Ukraine	3.80	
124	Zimbabwe	3.80	
129	Albania	3.85	
129	Bangladesh	3.85	
129	Mozambique	3.85	
129	Suriname	3.85	
133	Burundi	3.90	
134	Togo	3.95	
135	Haiti	4.00	
135	Kyrgyz Rep.	4.00	
137	Kazakhstan	4.05	
137	Sierra Leone	4.05	
139	Yemen	4.10	
140	Belarus	4.15	
141	Sudan	4.20	
141	Syria	4.20	
143	Azerbaijan	4.30	
143	Equatorial Guinea	4.30	
143	Myanmar	4.30	
143	Rwanda	4.30	
147	Tajikistan	4.40	
147	Uzbekistan	4.40	
149	Angola	4.45	
149	Turkmenistan	4.45	
151	Guinea-Bissau	4.55	
152	Vietnam	4.60	
153	Congo (Zaire)	4.70	
153	Iran	4.70	
155	Bosnia	4.80	
155	Somalia	4.80	
157	Iraq	4.90	
157	Laos	4.90	
157	Libya	4.90	
160	Cuba	5.00	
160	Korea, North	5.00	

Mostly Free

sector participation in activities which were once the government's sole domain, such as the provision of public utilities and infrastructure. Because of limited financial resources, the Government is relying increasingly on the private sector to undertake vital infrastructure construction, maintenance and rehabilitation work under its Build-Operate-Transfer (BOT) scheme and similar arrangements."[3]

MONETARY POLICY
Score: 2–Stable (low level of inflation)

The average annual rate of inflation from 1986 to 1996 was 8.13 percent. In 1997, the rate was 6 percent.

CAPITAL FLOWS AND FOREIGN INVESTMENT
Score: 3–Stable (moderate barriers)

The Philippines maintains some barriers to foreign investment. Foreigners may not invest in advertising, the mass media, or public utilities, among other areas.

BANKING
Score: 3–Stable (moderate level of restrictions)

Although the government recently privatized the Philippines National Bank, the country's largest state-owned financial institution, it also continues to own shares in it. According to the U.S. Department of State, "May 1994 banking legislation permitted 10 foreign banks to open branches in the Philippines. Presently, foreign entry is limited to 60% ownership of either a new local subsidiary or an existing domestic bank. Foreign branch banks are limited to putting up six branches each. Four foreign banks that had been operating in the Philippines since before 1948 are allowed to add six branches each to their respective networks. Current regulations provide that majority Filipino-owned domestic banks should, at all times, control at least 70% of total banking system assets."[4]

WAGE AND PRICE CONTROLS
Score: 2–Stable (low level)

Although the Philippine government controls the prices of basic public utilities, such as electricity, water, and related utilities, the market sets most wages and prices. The Philippines also has a minimum wage.

PROPERTY RIGHTS
Score: 2–Stable (high level of protection)

Expropriation of private property is unlikely. According to the U.S. Department of Commerce, however, "Although the Government of the Philippines has established procedures and systems for registering claims on property...delays and uncertainty associated with a cumbersome court system continues to be a concern to investors."[5] Still, by global standards, the Philippines offers a high level of property rights protection.

REGULATION
Score: 4– (high level)

The Philippine government has eliminated some significantly burdensome regulations, but its regulatory regime is inconsistent, and regulations are applied haphazardly. "The Philippines has taken several significant steps to reduce bureaucratic regulations and to foster competition," reports the U.S. Department of Commerce. "Still, the perception remains that, to do business in the Philippines, one must overcome substantial bureaucratic red tape.... The Philippines has tax, labor, health, safety, environmental and other laws and policies with the aim of efficiently regulating industry and investment. The impact of these laws is sometimes skewed, however, by difficulties to effectively and uniformly enforce them. Selective enforcement reduces the intended benefits of policies to the country and sometimes adds to the risk of doing business."[6] Moreover, there is increasing evidence that corruption remains a problem. For example, the U.S. Department of Commerce also reports, "Although there are government mechanisms directed at combating corruption, a large body of anecdotal evidence suggests that corruption remains a problem at almost all levels in all branches of the Philippine government. Stories and rumors abound about corrupt officials managing government procurement, or bureaucrats demanding 'facilitation money' to expedite paper work, issue permits or other documents, or to skirt or reduce taxes or fees owed, even for basic traffic penalties." Thus, as a result of the increased evidence that regulations are becoming a greater burden and that corruption also is a problem, the Philippines' regulation score is 1 point worse than last year.

BLACK MARKET
Score: 4–Stable (high level of activity)

Even with an increase in the number of duty-free shops and a decline in smuggling, a substantial black market in pirated items exists in the Philippines. According to the U.S. Department of Commerce, "Video and other forms of piracy is a problem in the Philippines, but private-sector representatives report continuing vigorous cooperation with government authorities in identifying and taking action against pirates. Most computer software is pirated, but this past year strong action has been taken against some blatant transgressors. More such action is planned for the future. An agreement between software producers and the government has virtually eliminated software piracy in government offices."[7] Furthermore, the U.S. Department of State reports, "Software and video piracy remains widespread; according to the Business Software Alliance, the piracy rate for software is estimated at between 90–95%, while that for motion pictures is around 70%. Enforcement actions have not effectively reduced these figures. The illegal retransmission of copyrighted works by cable television stations, i.e. without authorization from or payment to the copyright owners, is also a significant problem, especially outside Manila. The U.S. IP [intellectual property] industry estimates potential trade losses in 1996 due to piracy of software at $82 million; for motion pictures, $22 million; and for sound recordings, $3 million."[8]

NOTES

[1]   U.S. Department of Commerce, *Country Commercial Guide,* 1998.
[2]   U.S. Department of State, *Country Reports on Economic Policy and Trade Practices,* 1998.
[3]   U.S. Department of Commerce, *Country Commercial Guide,* 1998.
[4]   U.S. Department of State, *Country Reports on Economic Policy and Trade Practices,* 1998.
[5]   U.S. Department of Commerce, *Country Commercial Guide,* 1998.
[6]   *Ibid.*
[7]   *Ibid.*
[8]   U.S. Department of State, *Country Reports on Economic Policy and Trade Practices,* 1998.

Poland   2.95

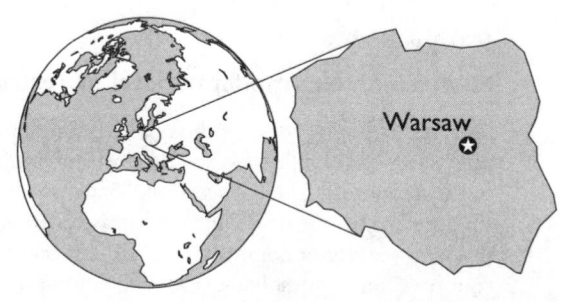

1998 Score: **2.95**		1997 Score: **3.15**		1996 Score: **3.05**

Trade	2	Banking	3
Taxation	3.5	Wages and Prices	3
Government Intervention	3	Property Rights	2
Monetary Policy	5	Regulation	3
Foreign Investment	2	Black Market	3

Poland, a former member of the Soviet-dominated Warsaw Pact, has progressed economically since the fall of the Iron Curtain. A six-party coalition led by Prime Minister Hanna Suchocka collapsed in September 1993 and was replaced by a two-party alliance of the former Communist Party and the Agrarian Party, which came to power in 1994 and was reaffirmed in 1995. The current government of Prime Minister Jerzy Buzek, formed after the Solidarity Electoral Action party won elections in 1997, is committed to continuing economic reform.

TRADE POLICY
Score: 2–Stable (low level of protectionism)

Poland had an average tariff rate of 6 percent in 1997. Non-tariff barriers (which, in Poland's case, in practice rarely hinder imports) include strict product standards and labeling requirements.

TAXATION
Score–Income taxation: 2–Stable (low tax rates)
Score–Corporate taxation: 4–Stable (high tax rates)
Final Taxation Score: 3.5–Stable (high tax rates)

Poland's top income tax rate is 45 percent; the average income level is taxed at a rate of 0 percent. The top corporate tax rate is 36 percent. Poland also has a 36 percent capital gains tax and a 22 percent value-added tax.

GOVERNMENT INTERVENTION IN THE ECONOMY
Score: 3–Stable (moderate level)

Government consumes 17.8 percent of GDP. The public sector still produces about 30 percent of GDP.[1]

MONETARY POLICY
Score: 5–Stable (very high level of inflation)

Poland's average annual rate of inflation between 1990 and 1994 was 147.9 percent. In 1994, the rate of inflation fell to 22 percent; in 1995, it was 23 percent; in 1996, it was 19.1 percent; and in 1997, it was 13 percent. Despite this obvious progress, however, it remains very high by global standards.

CAPITAL FLOWS AND FOREIGN INVESTMENT
Score: 2–Stable (low barriers)

Domestic and foreign firms receive equal treatment under Poland's investment laws, and recent economic reforms are attracting increased foreign investment. According to the U.S. Department of State, "Poland has steadfastly pursued a policy of liberalizing trade, investment, and capital flows measures; it stands out as one of the most successful and open transition economies."[2]

1	Hong Kong	1.25
2	Singapore	1.30
3	Bahrain	1.70
4	New Zealand	1.75
5	Switzerland	1.85
6	United States	1.90
7	Ireland	1.95
7	Luxembourg	1.95
7	Taiwan	1.95
7	United Kingdom	1.95
11	Bahamas	2.00
12	Czech Republic	2.05
12	Japan	2.05
14	Australia	2.10
14	Belgium	2.10
14	Canada	2.10
14	United Arab Emirates	2.10
18	Austria	2.15
18	Chile	2.15
18	Estonia	2.15
18	Netherlands	2.15
22	Denmark	2.25
22	El Salvador	2.25
22	Finland	2.25
25	Germany	2.30
25	Iceland	2.30
27	Norway	2.35
28	Korea, South	2.40
28	Kuwait	2.40
28	Malaysia	2.40
28	Panama	2.40
28	Thailand	2.40
33	Sweden	2.45
34	Argentina	2.50
34	France	2.50
34	Italy	2.50
34	Spain	2.50
38	Portugal	2.55
38	Sri Lanka	2.55
38	Trinidad and Tobago	2.55
41	Barbados	2.60
41	Peru	2.60
43	Bolivia	2.65
43	Mauritius	2.65
45	Cyprus	2.70
45	Jamaica	2.70
45	Uruguay	2.70
48	Botswana	2.75
48	Guatemala	2.75
48	Jordan	2.75
48	Namibia	2.75
48	Oman	2.75
48	Philippines	2.75
54	Belize	2.80
54	Costa Rica	2.80
54	Israel	2.80
54	Swaziland	2.80
54	Turkey	2.80
54	Uganda	2.80
54	Samoa	2.80
61	Latvia	2.85
62	Greece	2.90
62	Hungary	2.90
62	So. Africa	2.90
65	Ecuador	2.95
65	Gabon	2.95
65	Indonesia	2.95
65	Malta	2.95
65	Morocco	2.95
65	Poland	2.95
65	Tunisia	2.95
72	Ghana	3.00
72	Lithuania	3.00
72	Saudi Arabia	3.00
75	Benin	3.05
75	Kenya	3.05
75	Paraguay	3.05
75	Qatar	3.05
75	Slovak Republic	3.05
75	Zambia	3.05
81	Colombia	3.10

81	Fiji	3.10
81	Mali	3.10
81	Slovenia	3.10
85	Honduras	3.15
85	Mexico	3.15
85	Papua New Guinea	3.15
88	Djibouti	3.20
88	Mongolia	3.20
90	Algeria	3.25
90	Brazil	3.25
90	Lebanon	3.25
90	Senegal	3.25
90	Tanzania	3.25
95	Nigeria	3.30
95	Romania	3.30
97	Cambodia	3.35
97	Dominican Republic	3.35
97	Egypt	3.35
97	Guinea	3.35
97	Ivory Coast	3.35
97	Moldova	3.35
97	Pakistan	3.35
104	Nepal	3.40
104	Venezuela	3.40
106	Armenia	3.45
106	Bulgaria	3.45
106	Lesotho	3.45
106	Madagascar	3.45
106	Russia	3.45
111	Burkina Faso	3.50
111	Cameroon	3.50
111	Guyana	3.50
111	Nicaragua	3.50
115	Gambia	3.60
116	Croatia	3.65
116	Georgia	3.65
116	Malawi	3.65
119	Cape Verde	3.67
120	Ethiopia	3.70
120	India	3.70
120	Niger	3.70
123	Congo	3.75
124	Chad	3.80
124	China	3.80
124	Mauritania	3.80
124	Ukraine	3.80
124	Zimbabwe	3.80
129	Albania	3.85
129	Bangladesh	3.85
129	Mozambique	3.85
129	Suriname	3.85
133	Burundi	3.90
134	Togo	3.95
135	Haiti	4.00
135	Kyrgyz Rep.	4.00
137	Kazakhstan	4.05
137	Sierra Leone	4.05
139	Yemen	4.10
140	Belarus	4.15
141	Sudan	4.20
141	Syria	4.20
143	Azerbaijan	4.30
143	Equatorial Guinea	4.30
143	Myanmar	4.30
143	Rwanda	4.30
147	Tajikistan	4.40
147	Uzbekistan	4.40
149	Angola	4.45
149	Turkmenistan	4.45
151	Guinea-Bissau	4.55
152	Vietnam	4.60
153	Congo (Zaire)	4.70
155	Iran	4.70
155	Bosnia	4.80
155	Somalia	4.80
157	Iraq	4.90
157	Laos	4.90
157	Libya	4.90
160	Cuba	5.00
160	Korea, North	5.00

Mostly Free

BANKING
Score: 3–Stable (moderate level of restrictions)

Poland's banking system, although becoming increasingly privatized, is still influenced by the government. According to the Economist Intelligence Unit, "Bank privatization was supposed to be one of Poland's showcase economic reforms. But nine years after communism's fall, just one of the country's four biggest banks has been put in private hands.[3]" Interest rates are not always set by market standards and may be driven by government budgetary concerns. This makes it more difficult for Poland's banks to provide affordable credit to needy businesses. According to the U.S. Department of Commerce, "Poland's banking system continues in the process of adaptation and modernization. With the gradual installation of new telecommunications and in the advent of increased competition amongst domestic and foreign banks, services are becoming increasingly more user friendly and efficient."[4]

WAGE AND PRICE CONTROLS
Score: 3–Stable (moderate level)

Firms must gain permission from the government to raise prices on certain products (for example, fuel and electricity). Obtaining permission to do so may take as long as three months. Poland has a minimum wage law.

PROPERTY RIGHTS
Score: 2–Stable (high level of protection)

Private property is a constitutional right. Therefore, even though property does not receive adequate protection from the courts and the legal system, expropriation is unlikely. According to the U.S. Department of Commerce, "There is a functioning non-discriminatory legal system accessible to foreign investors that protects and facilitates acquisition and disposition of all property rights, such as land, buildings and mortgages."[5]

REGULATION
Score: 3–Stable (moderate level)

Despite some efforts at liberalization, Poland's regulatory regime remains an obstacle to the creation of new businesses. Some corruption persists, and labor, health, and safety regulations are applied randomly, creating uncertainty on the part of business owners and investors. According to the U.S. Department of Commerce, "Foreign investors often complain about difficulties in completing bureaucratic requirements and subsequent delays when investing in Poland."[6]

BLACK MARKET
Score: 3–Stable (moderate level of activity)

By global standards, Poland's black market is moderate. It also is shrinking. Although some labor, transportation, construction, and other services once were supplied routinely on the black market, an increasingly free market is reducing black market activity. Poland also has made significant progress toward protecting intellectual property, although the black market trade in computer software is growing. The U.S. Department of Commerce has reported that as much as 80 percent of all computer software in Poland is pirated.[7]

NOTES

[1] U.S. Department of Commerce, *Country Commercial Guide,* 1998.
[2] U.S. Department of State, *Country Reports on Economic Policy and Trade Practices,* 1997, p. 152.
[3] Economist Intelligence Unit, "Poland Finance: A Banking Champion?" EIU ViewsWire, June 25, 1998.
[4] U.S. Department of Commerce, *Country Commercial Guide,* 1998.
[5] *Ibid.*
[6] *Ibid.*
[7] U.S. Department of Commerce, *Country Commercial Guide,* 1997.

Portugal   2.55

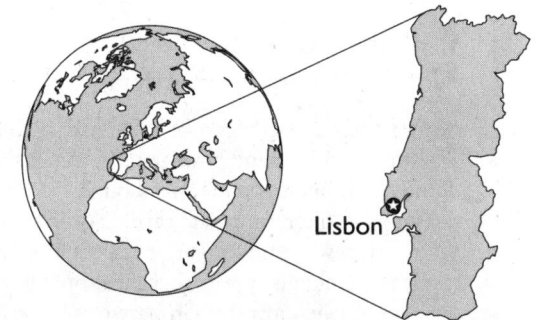

1998 Score: **2.60**   1997 Score: **2.60**   1996 Score: **2.60**

Trade	2	Banking	3
Taxation	4.5	Wages and Prices	2
Government Intervention	3	Property Rights	2
Monetary Policy	2	Regulation	3
Foreign Investment	2	Black Market	2

During the 1970s, Portugal overthrew a dictatorship, entered a period of political chaos, and finally emerged as a constitutional republic. During the first few years following this political revolution, Portugal's government adopted socialist economic policies that were enshrined in the 1982 constitution. Economic growth sputtered during most of the 1980s. Portugal acceded to the European Union (EU) in 1986. Because of this change in policy, subsequent governments gradually liberalized the economy. In January 1996, the voters elected a Socialist Party government led by Prime Minister Antonio Guterres. The Guterres government is privatizing state-owned industries and cutting non–social service spending to meet the budget deficit criteria of the Maastricht Treaty. Portugal recently reduced corporate taxes; as a result, its overall score is 0.05 point better than last year.

TRADE POLICY
Score: 2–Stable (low level of protectionism)

As a member of the EU, Portugal has an average tariff rate of 3.6 percent. As is common among EU members, however, it also requires import certificates for some agricultural products, and these may act as a barrier to foreign agricultural imports.

TAXATION
Score–Income taxation: 5–Stable (very high tax rates)
Score–Corporate taxation: 3+ (moderate tax rates)
Final Taxation Score: 4.5+ (very high tax rates)

Portugal's top income tax rate is 40 percent, and the average income level is taxed at 25 percent. The top corporate tax rate is 34 percent, down from 36 percent last year; as a result, the country's corporate tax rate is 1 point lower than it was last year. This makes Portugal's overall tax score 0.5 point better this year. Portugal also has a 36 percent capital gains tax, a 4 percent to 17 percent value-added tax, a 10 percent real estate tax, and a 50 percent inheritance tax.

GOVERNMENT INTERVENTION IN THE ECONOMY
Score: 3–Stable (moderate level)

Government consumes 19.1 percent of GDP and continues to maintain major stakes in banking, chemicals, food, glass, electricity, pulp and paper, railways, steel, transport, television, tobacco, and telecommunications. To meet the Maastricht budget deficit criteria, however, the Socialist Party government has initiated a major privatization program.

MONETARY POLICY
Score: 2–Stable (low level of inflation)

Portugal's average annual rate of inflation from 1986 to 1996 was 10.1 percent. In 1997, the rate was 2.2 percent.

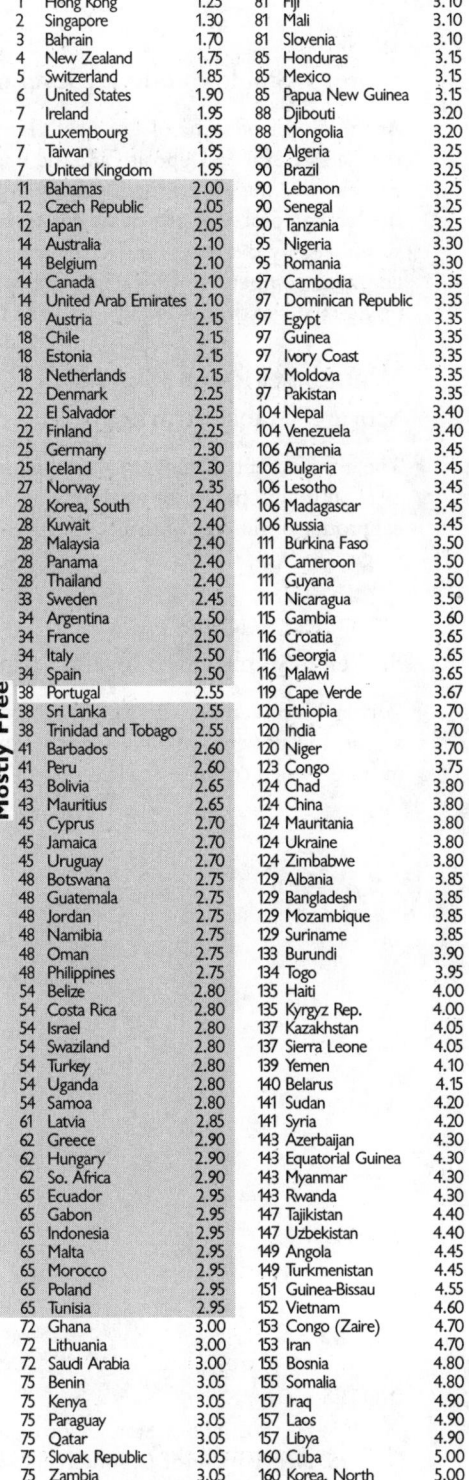

1	Hong Kong	1.25
2	Singapore	1.30
3	Bahrain	1.70
4	New Zealand	1.75
5	Switzerland	1.85
6	United States	1.90
7	Ireland	1.95
7	Luxembourg	1.95
7	Taiwan	1.95
7	United Kingdom	1.95
11	Bahamas	2.00
12	Czech Republic	2.05
12	Japan	2.05
14	Australia	2.10
14	Belgium	2.10
14	Canada	2.10
14	United Arab Emirates	2.10
18	Austria	2.15
18	Chile	2.15
18	Estonia	2.15
18	Netherlands	2.15
22	Denmark	2.25
22	El Salvador	2.25
22	Finland	2.25
25	Germany	2.30
25	Iceland	2.30
27	Norway	2.35
28	Korea, South	2.40
28	Kuwait	2.40
28	Malaysia	2.40
28	Panama	2.40
28	Thailand	2.40
33	Sweden	2.45
34	Argentina	2.50
34	France	2.50
34	Italy	2.50
34	Spain	2.50
38	Portugal	2.55
38	Sri Lanka	2.55
38	Trinidad and Tobago	2.55
41	Barbados	2.60
41	Peru	2.60
43	Bolivia	2.65
43	Mauritius	2.65
45	Cyprus	2.70
45	Jamaica	2.70
45	Uruguay	2.70
48	Botswana	2.75
48	Guatemala	2.75
48	Jordan	2.75
48	Namibia	2.75
48	Oman	2.75
48	Philippines	2.75
54	Belize	2.80
54	Costa Rica	2.80
54	Israel	2.80
54	Swaziland	2.80
54	Turkey	2.80
54	Uganda	2.80
54	Samoa	2.80
61	Latvia	2.85
62	Greece	2.90
62	Hungary	2.90
62	So. Africa	2.90
65	Ecuador	2.95
65	Gabon	2.95
65	Indonesia	2.95
65	Malta	2.95
65	Morocco	2.95
65	Poland	2.95
65	Tunisia	2.95
72	Ghana	3.00
72	Lithuania	3.00
72	Saudi Arabia	3.00
75	Benin	3.05
75	Kenya	3.05
75	Paraguay	3.05
75	Qatar	3.05
75	Slovak Republic	3.05
75	Zambia	3.05
81	Colombia	3.10

81	Fiji	3.10
81	Mali	3.10
81	Slovenia	3.10
85	Honduras	3.15
85	Mexico	3.15
85	Papua New Guinea	3.15
88	Djibouti	3.20
88	Mongolia	3.20
90	Algeria	3.25
90	Brazil	3.25
90	Lebanon	3.25
90	Senegal	3.25
90	Tanzania	3.25
95	Nigeria	3.30
95	Romania	3.30
97	Cambodia	3.35
97	Dominican Republic	3.35
97	Egypt	3.35
97	Guinea	3.35
97	Ivory Coast	3.35
97	Moldova	3.35
97	Pakistan	3.35
104	Nepal	3.40
104	Venezuela	3.40
106	Armenia	3.45
106	Bulgaria	3.45
106	Lesotho	3.45
106	Madagascar	3.45
106	Russia	3.45
111	Burkina Faso	3.50
111	Cameroon	3.50
111	Guyana	3.50
111	Nicaragua	3.50
115	Gambia	3.60
116	Croatia	3.65
116	Georgia	3.65
116	Malawi	3.65
119	Cape Verde	3.67
120	Ethiopia	3.70
120	India	3.70
120	Niger	3.70
123	Congo	3.75
124	Chad	3.80
124	China	3.80
124	Mauritania	3.80
124	Ukraine	3.80
124	Zimbabwe	3.80
129	Albania	3.85
129	Bangladesh	3.85
129	Mozambique	3.85
129	Suriname	3.85
133	Burundi	3.90
134	Togo	3.95
135	Haiti	4.00
135	Kyrgyz Rep.	4.00
137	Kazakhstan	4.05
137	Sierra Leone	4.05
139	Yemen	4.10
140	Belarus	4.15
141	Sudan	4.20
141	Syria	4.20
143	Azerbaijan	4.30
143	Equatorial Guinea	4.30
143	Myanmar	4.30
143	Rwanda	4.30
147	Tajikistan	4.40
147	Uzbekistan	4.40
149	Angola	4.45
149	Turkmenistan	4.45
151	Guinea-Bissau	4.55
152	Vietnam	4.60
153	Congo (Zaire)	4.70
153	Iran	4.70
155	Bosnia	4.80
155	Somalia	4.80
157	Iraq	4.90
157	Laos	4.90
157	Libya	4.90
160	Cuba	5.00
160	Korea, North	5.00

CAPITAL FLOWS AND FOREIGN INVESTMENT
Score: 2–Stable (low barriers)

Portugal has opened most of its industries to foreign investment. As a member of the EU, it treats foreign and domestic companies equally, although it does not permit foreign investment in postal carriers or in such public utilities as sewage treatment, transportation, and water services. Foreign investors may face some government opposition when investing in state-owned businesses undergoing privatization.

BANKING
Score: 3–Stable (moderate level of restrictions)

As full owner of some of Portugal's large banks, including the Caixa Geral de Deposito and the Banco Fomento Exterior SA, the government plays a large role in controlling the lending practices of private banks. Because they are subsidized by the government, the state-owned banks enjoy an unfair competitive advantage against unsubsidized private banks, some of which have had to close as a result.

WAGE AND PRICE CONTROLS
Score: 2–Stable (low level)

The government eliminated almost all price controls in 1993, although prices for electricity, water, and pharmaceutical products still are controlled. Portugal has a minimum wage.

PROPERTY RIGHTS
Score: 2–Stable (high level of protection)

Portugal is privatizing parts of its bloated state-owned sector, and citizens are increasing their purchases of shares in state-owned companies. This provides an expanding base of private property. Portugal has a relatively efficient legal system that protects property adequately in most cases. According to the U.S. Department of State, "The judicial system provides citizens with a fair legal process. It has been much criticized, however, for a large backlog of pending trials resulting from inefficient functioning of the courts."[1]

REGULATION
Score: 3–Stable (moderate level)

Despite some liberalization, the government still maintains significant regulation. As a result of Portugal's 1987 environmental protection law (the most stringent in the EU), for example, both new businesses and proposed business expansion projects must undergo cumbersome environmental impact reviews by various government bureaucracies—a hurdle that often proves too high for some businesses. For example, according to the U.S. Department of Commerce, "Standard operating procedures in Portugal are often inconsistent with efficient investment and business operations. Decision-making tends to be overly centralized and obtaining government approvals or permits can be time-consuming and costly, particularly for small- and medium-sized foreign investors and entrepreneurs. Some U.S. firms report substantial delays and red tape in accomplishing such basic tasks as registering companies, filing taxes, receiving value-added tax refunds, and importing vehicles."[2]

BLACK MARKET
Score: 2–Stable (low level of activity)

Portugal's black market is confined to such scarce goods as auto parts and pharmaceutical products. These scarcities are created by government-imposed price controls and trade quotas. Despite strong protection of intellectual property with stiff fines, there is black market activity in such pirated items as prerecorded music and video tapes.

NOTES

[1]   U.S. Department of State, "Portugal Country Report on Human Rights Practices for 1997," 1998.
[2]   U.S. Department of Commerce, *Country Commercial Guide,* 1998.

1999 Index of Economic Freedom

Qatar

3.05

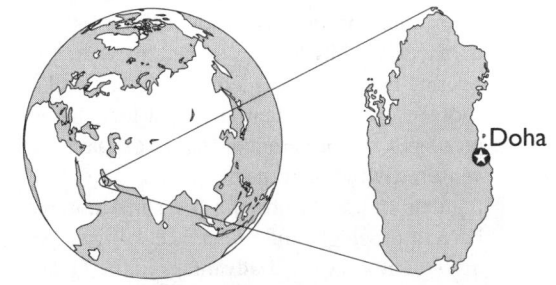
Doha

1998 Score: **n/a**   1997 Score: **n/a**   1996 Score: **n/a**

Trade	3	Banking	4
Taxation	2.5	Wages and Prices	4
Government Intervention	5	Property Rights	3
Monetary Policy	1	Regulation	4
Foreign Investment	3	Black Market	1

The Persian Gulf emirate of Qatar received its independence from the United Kingdom in 1971 and, after independence, became a constitutional monarchy. The state dominates the economy: The government either owns or has controlling ownership of the country's mineral resources, the largest manufacturers, and much of the financial services industry. Although Qatar has been trying to diversify its economy by encouraging the creation of many industrial and commercial sectors, its economy remains dominated by oil and gas resources. Still, Qatar has developed some industrial capacity in fertilizers, petrochemicals, and steel.

TRADE POLICY
Score: 3–Stable (moderate level of protectionism)

Qatar's average tariff rate is about 5 percent. Non-tariff barriers include strict licensing requirements, import bans, and quotas.

TAXATION
Score–Income taxation: 1–Stable (very low tax rates)
Score–Corporate taxation: 3–Stable (moderate tax rates)
Total Taxation Score: 2.5–Stable (moderate tax rates)

The government does not impose income taxes on individuals, but the top corporate tax rate is 35 percent. Qatar also has a 35 percent capital gains tax and a 35 percent branch tax.

GOVERNMENT INTERVENTION IN THE ECONOMY
Score: 5–Stable (very high level)

Government consumes 45.2 percent of GDP. The government owns nearly all of the country's oil production. According to the U.S. Department of State, "The State owns most basic industries and services."[1] Government-owned companies produce most of the country's GDP.

MONETARY POLICY
Score: 1–Stable (very low level of inflation)

Qatar's average annual rate of inflation from 1986 to 1996 was about 5 percent. Inflation data for 1997 are unavailable.

CAPITAL FLOWS AND FOREIGN INVESTMENT
Score: 3–Stable (moderate barriers)

With few exceptions, companies must be owned fully by Qataris. Foreign investment is allowed only through joint ventures and joint-stock companies. There are some tax incentives for investment, but there also are increasing indications that the country is undertaking a program aimed at encouraging businesses to hire only, or primarily, Qatari citizens. According to the U.S. Department of Commerce, "The Government of Qatar encourages foreign

1	Hong Kong	1.25	81	Fiji	3.10
2	Singapore	1.30	81	Mali	3.10
3	Bahrain	1.70	81	Slovenia	3.10
4	New Zealand	1.75	85	Honduras	3.15
5	Switzerland	1.85	85	Mexico	3.15
6	United States	1.90	85	Papua New Guinea	3.15
7	Ireland	1.95	88	Djibouti	3.20
7	Luxembourg	1.95	88	Mongolia	3.20
7	Taiwan	1.95	90	Algeria	3.25
7	United Kingdom	1.95	90	Brazil	3.25
11	Bahamas	2.00	90	Lebanon	3.25
12	Czech Republic	2.05	90	Senegal	3.25
12	Japan	2.05	90	Tanzania	3.25
14	Australia	2.10	95	Nigeria	3.30
14	Belgium	2.10	95	Romania	3.30
14	Canada	2.10	97	Cambodia	3.35
14	United Arab Emirates	2.10	97	Dominican Republic	3.35
18	Austria	2.15	97	Egypt	3.35
18	Chile	2.15	97	Guinea	3.35
18	Estonia	2.15	97	Ivory Coast	3.35
18	Netherlands	2.15	97	Moldova	3.35
22	Denmark	2.25	97	Pakistan	3.35
22	El Salvador	2.25	104	Nepal	3.40
22	Finland	2.25	104	Venezuela	3.40
25	Germany	2.30	106	Armenia	3.45
25	Iceland	2.30	106	Bulgaria	3.45
27	Norway	2.35	106	Lesotho	3.45
28	Korea, South	2.40	106	Madagascar	3.45
28	Kuwait	2.40	106	Russia	3.45
28	Malaysia	2.40	111	Burkina Faso	3.50
28	Panama	2.40	111	Cameroon	3.50
28	Thailand	2.40	111	Guyana	3.50
33	Sweden	2.45	111	Nicaragua	3.50
34	Argentina	2.50	115	Gambia	3.60
34	France	2.50	116	Croatia	3.65
34	Italy	2.50	116	Georgia	3.65
34	Spain	2.50	116	Malawi	3.65
38	Portugal	2.55	119	Cape Verde	3.67
38	Sri Lanka	2.55	120	Ethiopia	3.70
38	Trinidad and Tobago	2.55	120	India	3.70
41	Barbados	2.60	120	Niger	3.70
41	Peru	2.60	123	Congo	3.75
43	Bolivia	2.65	124	Chad	3.80
43	Mauritius	2.65	124	China	3.80
45	Cyprus	2.70	124	Mauritania	3.80
45	Jamaica	2.70	124	Ukraine	3.80
45	Uruguay	2.70	124	Zimbabwe	3.80
48	Botswana	2.75	129	Albania	3.85
48	Guatemala	2.75	129	Bangladesh	3.85
48	Jordan	2.75	129	Mozambique	3.85
48	Namibia	2.75	129	Suriname	3.85
48	Oman	2.75	133	Burundi	3.90
48	Philippines	2.75	134	Togo	3.95
54	Belize	2.80	135	Haiti	4.00
54	Costa Rica	2.80	135	Kyrgyz Rep.	4.00
54	Israel	2.80	137	Kazakhstan	4.05
54	Swaziland	2.80	137	Sierra Leone	4.05
54	Turkey	2.80	139	Yemen	4.10
54	Uganda	2.80	140	Belarus	4.15
54	Samoa	2.80	141	Sudan	4.20
61	Latvia	2.85	141	Syria	4.20
62	Greece	2.90	143	Azerbaijan	4.30
62	Hungary	2.90	143	Equatorial Guinea	4.30
62	So. Africa	2.90	143	Myanmar	4.30
65	Ecuador	2.95	143	Rwanda	4.30
65	Gabon	2.95	147	Tajikistan	4.40
65	Indonesia	2.95	147	Uzbekistan	4.40
65	Malta	2.95	149	Angola	4.45
65	Morocco	2.95	149	Turkmenistan	4.45
65	Poland	2.95	151	Guinea-Bissau	4.55
65	Tunisia	2.95	152	Vietnam	4.60
72	Ghana	3.00	153	Congo (Zaire)	4.70
72	Lithuania	3.00	153	Iran	4.70
72	Saudi Arabia	3.00	155	Bosnia	4.80
75	Benin	3.05	155	Somalia	4.80
75	Kenya	3.05	157	Iraq	4.90
75	Paraguay	3.05	157	Laos	4.90
75	Qatar	3.05	157	Libya	4.90
75	Slovak Republic	3.05	160	Cuba	5.00
75	Zambia	3.05	160	Korea, North	5.00
81	Colombia	3.10			

Mostly Unfree

investment, particularly in joint ventures with Qatari partners. Wholly foreign owned firms are permitted to operate in Qatar, provided they have a local agent or a sponsor. However, there is a clear local hierarchy of privileges and preferences that favor Qatari firms and joint ventures with Qatari participation.... Despite some laws and regulations adopted by the government in recent years, the current privileges and preferences can still put a foreign investor at a severe disadvantage in the Qatari market"[2] Because there is no evidence of corruption in the investment approval process, however, and because Qatar does conform to an established foreign investment code, its restrictions on foreign investment are moderate by global standards.

BANKING
Score: 4–Stable (very high level of restrictions)

Qatar's government owns most of the financial services industry. Competition, both foreign and domestic, is severely curtailed.

WAGE AND PRICE CONTROLS
Score: 4–Stable (very high level)

There are few official price controls, but the government is the main consumer of goods and services and its purchases therefore affect prices. Qatar has a minimum wage law. Moreover, the high level of government ownership of business greatly affects prices, too.

PROPERTY RIGHTS
Score: 3–Stable (moderate level of protection)

Property expropriation is not likely; however, the court system often is inefficient. According to the U.S. Department of Commerce, judicial proceedings in Qatar frequently are long and bureaucratic.[3] Moreover, according to the U.S. Department of State, "The judiciary is nominally independent, but most judges are foreign nations who hold residence permits granted by the civil authorities and thus hold their positions at the Government's pleasure."[4]

REGULATION
Score: 4–Stable (high level)

Qatar's regulations are not applied consistently in all cases. The government enforces some regulations more rigorously on foreign companies and those engaged in joint ventures. Moreover, because the government owns so many businesses, they often are exempt from some regulations while private companies bear a greater regulatory burden. Thus, the overall regulatory burden is significant.

BLACK MARKET
Score: 1–Stable (very low level of activity)

Qatar has a negligible black market. There is some traffic in pirated intellectual property (primarily sound and video recordings), but the laws are strictly enforced, and black market activity in this area is minimal.

NOTES

1. U.S. Department of State, "Qatar Country Report on Human Rights Practices for 1997," 1998.
2. U.S. Department of Commerce, *Country Commercial Guide,* 1998.
3. *Ibid.*
4. U.S. Department of State, "Qatar Country Report on Human Rights Practices for 1997," 1998.

Romania   3.30

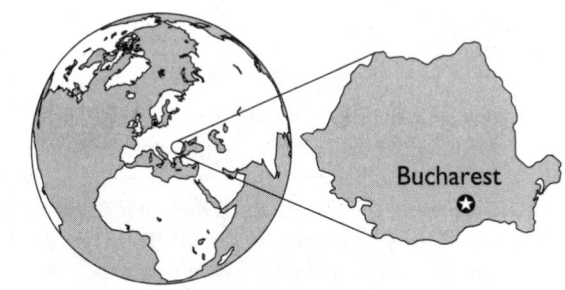

Bucharest ✪

1998 Score: **3.30**	1997 Score: **3.40**	1996 Score: **3.70**

Trade	2	Banking	3
Taxation	5	Wages and Prices	2
Government Intervention	3	Property Rights	4
Monetary Policy	5	Regulation	4
Foreign Investment	2	Black Market	3

Romania's transition to democracy and free markets has been troubled and at times even violent. After the execution of former communist strongman Nicolae Ceausescu in 1989, Romania was ruled by a party controlled by former communists who were corrupt and lukewarm about free markets. Since the early 1990s, Romania has passed laws on taxation, foreign investment, and small business privatization. It also has reduced some barriers to trade. At the same time, however, the large state-owned sector continues to resist further reform. As a result of national elections held in November 1996, a coalition led by center-right President Emil Constantinescu of the Democratic Convention party came to power. Constantinescu has promised economic liberalization and reform, and developed a comprehensive program of privatization, currency stabilization, and deregulation. The efforts of Prime Minister Victor Ciorbea to implement this program, however, were stalled by disagreements within the government coalition. New hopes for reform grew with the appointment of Radu Vasile as prime minister in April 1998. Although Vasile set forth strict deadlines for the implementation of Romania's most ambitious post–Cold War reform plans so far, some of these deadlines already have passed.

TRADE POLICY
Score: 2–Stable (low level of protectionism)

Romania's average tariff rate is 5.52 percent.[1] According to the U.S. Department of State, "There are no known laws that directly prejudice foreign trade or business operations [in Romania]."[2]

TAXATION
Score–Income taxation: 5–Stable (very high tax rates)
Score–Corporate taxation: 4–Stable (high tax rates)
Final Taxation Score: 5–Stable (very high tax rates)

Romania's top income tax rate is 60 percent, and the average income is taxed at 34 percent. The top corporate income tax rate is 38 percent. Romania also has a 38 percent capital gains tax and an 18 percent value-added tax.

GOVERNMENT INTERVENTION IN THE ECONOMY
Score: 3–Stable (moderately high level)

Government consumes 10.8 percent of GDP, most of which is produced by the public sector.

MONETARY POLICY
Score: 5–Stable (very high level of inflation)

Romania's rate of inflation was 295 percent in 1993, 61 percent in 1994, 29 percent in 1995, 38.8 percent in 1996, and 151.4 percent in 1997. Thus, the average annual rate of inflation since the collapse of the Soviet empire remains very high.

1	Hong Kong	1.25	81	Fiji	3.10
2	Singapore	1.30	81	Mali	3.10
3	Bahrain	1.70	81	Slovenia	3.10
4	New Zealand	1.75	85	Honduras	3.15
5	Switzerland	1.85	85	Mexico	3.15
6	United States	1.90	85	Papua New Guinea	3.15
7	Ireland	1.95	88	Djibouti	3.20
7	Luxembourg	1.95	88	Mongolia	3.20
7	Taiwan	1.95	90	Algeria	3.25
7	United Kingdom	1.95	90	Brazil	3.25
11	Bahamas	2.00	90	Lebanon	3.25
12	Czech Republic	2.05	90	Senegal	3.25
12	Japan	2.05	90	Tanzania	3.25
14	Australia	2.10	95	Nigeria	3.30
14	Belgium	2.10	95	Romania	3.30
14	Canada	2.10	97	Cambodia	3.35
14	United Arab Emirates	2.10	97	Dominican Republic	3.35
18	Austria	2.15	97	Egypt	3.35
18	Chile	2.15	97	Guinea	3.35
18	Estonia	2.15	97	Ivory Coast	3.35
18	Netherlands	2.15	97	Moldova	3.35
22	Denmark	2.25	97	Pakistan	3.35
22	El Salvador	2.25	104	Nepal	3.40
22	Finland	2.25	104	Venezuela	3.40
25	Germany	2.30	106	Armenia	3.45
25	Iceland	2.30	106	Bulgaria	3.45
27	Norway	2.35	106	Lesotho	3.45
28	Korea, South	2.40	106	Madagascar	3.45
28	Kuwait	2.40	106	Russia	3.45
28	Malaysia	2.40	111	Burkina Faso	3.50
28	Panama	2.40	111	Cameroon	3.50
28	Thailand	2.40	111	Guyana	3.50
33	Sweden	2.45	111	Nicaragua	3.50
34	Argentina	2.50	115	Gambia	3.60
34	France	2.50	116	Croatia	3.65
34	Italy	2.50	116	Georgia	3.65
34	Spain	2.50	116	Malawi	3.65
38	Portugal	2.55	119	Cape Verde	3.67
38	Sri Lanka	2.55	120	Ethiopia	3.70
38	Trinidad and Tobago	2.55	120	India	3.70
41	Barbados	2.60	120	Niger	3.70
41	Peru	2.60	123	Congo	3.75
43	Bolivia	2.65	124	Chad	3.80
43	Mauritius	2.65	124	China	3.80
45	Cyprus	2.70	124	Mauritania	3.80
45	Jamaica	2.70	124	Ukraine	3.80
45	Uruguay	2.70	124	Zimbabwe	3.80
48	Botswana	2.75	129	Albania	3.85
48	Guatemala	2.75	129	Bangladesh	3.85
48	Jordan	2.75	129	Mozambique	3.85
48	Namibia	2.75	129	Suriname	3.85
48	Oman	2.75	133	Burundi	3.90
48	Philippines	2.75	134	Togo	3.95
54	Belize	2.80	135	Haiti	4.00
54	Costa Rica	2.80	135	Kyrgyz Rep.	4.00
54	Israel	2.80	137	Kazakhstan	4.05
54	Swaziland	2.80	137	Sierra Leone	4.05
54	Turkey	2.80	139	Yemen	4.10
54	Uganda	2.80	140	Belarus	4.15
54	Samoa	2.80	141	Sudan	4.20
61	Latvia	2.85	141	Syria	4.20
62	Greece	2.90	143	Azerbaijan	4.30
62	Hungary	2.90	143	Equatorial Guinea	4.30
62	So. Africa	2.90	143	Myanmar	4.30
65	Ecuador	2.95	143	Rwanda	4.30
65	Gabon	2.95	147	Tajikistan	4.40
65	Indonesia	2.95	147	Uzbekistan	4.40
65	Malta	2.95	149	Angola	4.45
65	Morocco	2.95	149	Turkmenistan	4.45
65	Poland	2.95	151	Guinea-Bissau	4.55
65	Tunisia	2.95	152	Vietnam	4.60
72	Ghana	3.00	153	Congo (Zaire)	4.70
72	Lithuania	3.00	153	Iran	4.70
72	Saudi Arabia	3.00	155	Bosnia	4.80
75	Benin	3.05	155	Somalia	4.80
75	Kenya	3.05	157	Iraq	4.90
75	Paraguay	3.05	157	Laos	4.90
75	Qatar	3.05	157	Libya	4.90
75	Slovak Republic	3.05	160	Cuba	5.00
75	Zambia	3.05	160	Korea, North	5.00
81	Colombia	3.10			

Mostly Unfree

CAPITAL FLOWS AND FOREIGN INVESTMENT
Score: 2–Stable (low barriers)

Romania maintains a fairly free market in foreign investment, and most barriers are the result of bureaucratic red tape and inefficiency. The Constantinescu administration announced the attraction of foreign investment would be a top priority. According to the U.S. Department of State, "Investment barriers are few in Romania."[3]

BANKING
Score: 3–Stable (moderate level of restrictions)

Although more private banks are opening in Romania, the banking environment has yet to mature. Banks are subject to strict government control. According to the U.S. Department of Commerce, "The system remains concentrated, with a relatively small number of wholly or predominately state-owned banks accounting for a substantial majority of loans and deposits."[4] Over the past seven years, however, the number of banks has grown more than fourfold, thereby increasing competition. Bank liberalization is expected to continue under the reformist government of Prime Minister Vasile.

WAGE AND PRICE CONTROLS
Score: 2–Stable (low level)

The market sets most prices, although exceptions include residential heat and energy supply. Romania has minimum wage laws.

PROPERTY RIGHTS
Score: 4–Stable (low level of protection)

Romania is beginning to establish a system of property protection, but the legal system remains unable to arbitrate property rights disputes. "The judicial system," reports the U.S. Department of State, "has been subject to executive branch influence, although it is increasingly independent."[5] According to the U.S. Department of Commerce, "Property and contractual rights are recognized, but enforcement is not always effective."[6]

REGULATION
Score: 4–Stable (high level)

Regulations remain subject to haphazard application. Romania has made progress toward streamlining its bureaucracy, which makes it easier for businesses to obtain licenses, but the bureaucracy continues to be both cumbersome and inefficient. According to the U.S. Department of Commerce, "The Romanian government does not yet have a transparent policy to foster competition. The presence of state-owned government-subsidized enterprises in the economy is a major impediment to the efficient mobilization of capital. Cumbersome and non-transparent bureaucratic procedures are a major problem. Foreign investors point to the excessive time it takes to secure the necessary zoning permits, property titles, licenses, and utility hookups."[7] In addition, corruption remains endemic: "U.S. businesses have complained of corruption in all levels of government in Romania.... In some cases, demands for payoffs by mid- to low-level officials can reach the point of harassment. Corruption in Romania can constitute an actual business risk."[8]

BLACK MARKET
Score: 3–Stable (moderate level of activity)

Almost half of Romania's economic activity is performed in the black market. Laws protecting intellectual property rights have reduced piracy in these items, however.

NOTES

[1] Based on total taxes on international trade as a percentage of total imports.
[2] U.S. Department of State, *Country Reports on Economic Policy and Trade Practices*, 1998.
[3] *Ibid.*
[4] U.S. Department of Commerce, *Country Commercial Guide*, 1998.
[5] U.S. Department of State, "Romania Country Report on Human Rights Practices for 1997," 1998.
[6] U.S. Department of Commerce, *Country Commercial Guide*, 1998.
[7] *Ibid.*
[8] *Ibid.*

Russia   3.45

1998 Score: **3.45**   1997 Score: **3.65**   1996 Score: **3.50**

Trade	4	Banking	2
Taxation	3.5	Wages and Prices	3
Government Intervention	3	Property Rights	3
Monetary Policy	5	Regulation	4
Foreign Investment	3	Black Market	4

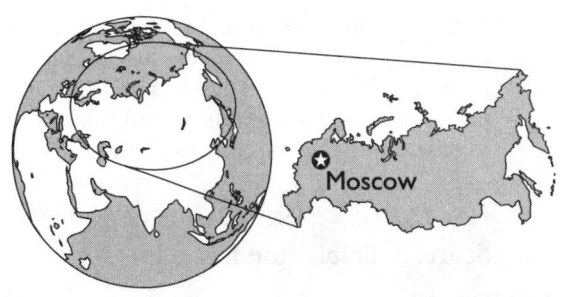

Moscow

Russia, the largest of the former Soviet republics, has struggled for several years to establish democratic political institutions and a free-market economy. Significant progress has been achieved, although much needs to be done. Privatization has been disorderly, and corruption rampant. The banking and investment systems were in disarray and millions of investors were defrauded in 1994 and 1995. The flight of capital to the West has slowed considerably, although accurate estimates are not available. The result has been economic stagnation, civil unrest, coup attempts, and political polarization. At the same time, however, the orderly 1995 parliamentary and 1996 presidential elections indicate that reforms have begun to take root. Having rejected both the communists and the ultranationalists, Russia's voters generally continue to support economic reform. This reform has been slow in coming, however, and Russia's economy went into a tailspin in May 1998. The ruble was under pressure and had to be supported by the currency reserves of the Central Bank; the government was forced to increase interest rates on domestic ruble-denominated bonds to 150 percent. The government also ran out of funds to pay soldiers, bureaucrats, teachers, and medical care providers in the public sector. In July 1998, Russia secured a $15.1 billion loan from the International Monetary Fund (IMF) and an additional $7.5 billion in loans from other sources. In August 1998 and afterward, the government imposed a host of new regulations and laws that restrict economic freedom. Not only is Russia's banking system in a state of collapse; the government also is raising taxes and import duties as well as imposing currency regulations on the ruble. This represents a significant barrier to foreign investment. These events occurred after the cutoff date for consideration in this edition of the *Index of Economic Freedom;* however, had this information been included in this edition, Russia surely would have received a worse score. If these events remain unchanged—or worsen—they will be reflected in next year's score.

TRADE POLICY
Score: 4–Stable (high level of protectionism)

Russia's tariff rates range from 5 percent to 30 percent, with an average rate of 13.4.[1] One result of the recent agreement with the IMF, however, was an increase in taxes on imports. This may frustrate further Russia's accession into the World Trade Organization. Corruption is a problem in the customs service, and bribes often are necessary to bring goods into the country and to obtain access to oil- and gas-exporting pipelines. According to the U.S. Department of State, "[C]ustoms regulations change frequently (often without sufficient notice), are subject to arbitrary application, and can be quite burdensome."[2]

TAXATION
Score–Income taxation: 3–Stable (moderate tax rates)
Score–Corporate taxation: 3–Stable (moderate tax rates)
Final Taxation Score: 3.5–Stable (high tax rates)

Russia's top income tax rate is 35 percent, and the average income level is taxed at 12 percent. The top corporate income tax rate (including both federal and regional taxes) is 35 percent. Russia also has a 35 percent capital gains tax, a 20

1	Hong Kong	1.25		81	Fiji	3.10
2	Singapore	1.30		81	Mali	3.10
3	Bahrain	1.70		81	Slovenia	3.10
4	New Zealand	1.75		85	Honduras	3.15
5	Switzerland	1.85		85	Mexico	3.15
6	United States	1.90		85	Papua New Guinea	3.15
7	Ireland	1.95		88	Djibouti	3.20
7	Luxembourg	1.95		88	Mongolia	3.20
7	Taiwan	1.95		90	Algeria	3.25
7	United Kingdom	1.95		90	Brazil	3.25
11	Bahamas	2.00		90	Lebanon	3.25
12	Czech Republic	2.05		90	Senegal	3.25
12	Japan	2.05		90	Tanzania	3.25
14	Australia	2.10		95	Nigeria	3.30
14	Belgium	2.10		95	Romania	3.30
14	Canada	2.10		97	Cambodia	3.35
14	United Arab Emirates	2.10		97	Dominican Republic	3.35
18	Austria	2.15		97	Egypt	3.35
18	Chile	2.15		97	Guinea	3.35
18	Estonia	2.15		97	Ivory Coast	3.35
18	Netherlands	2.15		97	Moldova	3.35
22	Denmark	2.25		97	Pakistan	3.35
22	El Salvador	2.25		104	Nepal	3.40
22	Finland	2.25		104	Venezuela	3.40
25	Germany	2.30		106	Armenia	3.45
25	Iceland	2.30		106	Bulgaria	3.45
27	Norway	2.35		106	Lesotho	3.45
28	Korea, South	2.40		106	Madagascar	3.45
28	Kuwait	2.40		106	Russia	3.45
28	Malaysia	2.40		111	Burkina Faso	3.50
28	Panama	2.40		111	Cameroon	3.50
28	Thailand	2.40		111	Guyana	3.50
33	Sweden	2.45		111	Nicaragua	3.50
34	Argentina	2.50		115	Gambia	3.60
34	France	2.50		116	Croatia	3.65
34	Italy	2.50		116	Georgia	3.65
34	Spain	2.50		116	Malawi	3.65
38	Portugal	2.55		119	Cape Verde	3.67
38	Sri Lanka	2.55		120	Ethiopia	3.70
38	Trinidad and Tobago	2.55		120	India	3.70
41	Barbados	2.60		120	Niger	3.70
41	Peru	2.60		123	Congo	3.75
43	Bolivia	2.65		124	Chad	3.80
43	Mauritius	2.65		124	China	3.80
45	Cyprus	2.70		124	Mauritania	3.80
45	Jamaica	2.70		124	Ukraine	3.80
45	Uruguay	2.70		124	Zimbabwe	3.80
48	Botswana	2.75		129	Albania	3.85
48	Guatemala	2.75		129	Bangladesh	3.85
48	Jordan	2.75		129	Mozambique	3.85
48	Namibia	2.75		129	Suriname	3.85
48	Oman	2.75		133	Burundi	3.90
48	Philippines	2.75		134	Togo	3.95
54	Belize	2.80		135	Haiti	4.00
54	Costa Rica	2.80		135	Kyrgyz Rep.	4.00
54	Israel	2.80		137	Kazakhstan	4.05
54	Swaziland	2.80		137	Sierra Leone	4.05
54	Turkey	2.80		139	Yemen	4.10
54	Uganda	2.80		140	Belarus	4.15
54	Samoa	2.80		141	Sudan	4.20
61	Latvia	2.85		141	Syria	4.20
62	Greece	2.90		143	Azerbaijan	4.30
62	Hungary	2.90		143	Equatorial Guinea	4.30
62	So. Africa	2.90		143	Myanmar	4.30
65	Ecuador	2.95		143	Rwanda	4.30
65	Gabon	2.95		147	Tajikistan	4.40
65	Indonesia	2.95		147	Uzbekistan	4.40
65	Malta	2.95		149	Angola	4.45
65	Morocco	2.95		149	Turkmenistan	4.45
65	Poland	2.95		151	Guinea-Bissau	4.55
65	Tunisia	2.95		152	Vietnam	4.60
72	Ghana	3.00		153	Congo (Zaire)	4.70
72	Lithuania	3.00		153	Iran	4.70
72	Saudi Arabia	3.00		155	Bosnia	4.80
75	Benin	3.05		155	Somalia	4.80
75	Kenya	3.05		157	Iraq	4.90
75	Paraguay	3.05		157	Laos	4.90
75	Qatar	3.05		157	Libya	4.90
75	Slovak Republic	3.05		160	Cuba	5.00
75	Zambia	3.05		160	Korea, North	5.00
81	Colombia	3.10				

Mostly Unfree

percent value-added tax, and a social payments tax.[3] In compliance with IMF conditions for obtaining a new loan package in July 1998, President Boris Yeltsin signed presidential decrees (over the objections of the State Duma) that aim to raise the amount of tax revenue.[4]

GOVERNMENT INTERVENTION IN THE ECONOMY
Score: 3–Stable (moderate level)

Officially, government consumes 11 percent of GDP. State-owned enterprises, however, still account for a large part of industrial production. The government also subsidizes heavily such money-losing industries as coal mining, ferrous and nonferrous metals, and agriculture.

MONETARY POLICY
Score: 5–Stable (very high level of inflation)

The government has achieved significant progress toward bringing inflation under control. In 1992, the rate of inflation exceeded 1,300 percent. In 1993, it fell to 843 percent; in 1994, 203 percent; and in 1995, 133 percent. In 1996, the rate fell to 26 percent and then to 15 percent in 1997.[5] Historically, however, and despite significant progress toward reducing inflation from its extremely high level in 1992, Russia has had very high rates of inflation by global standards.

CAPITAL FLOWS AND FOREIGN INVESTMENT
Score: 3–Stable (moderate barriers)

A 1991 law permits foreigners to acquire newly privatized firms and to establish wholly owned companies. By global standards, there are few legal restrictions on foreign investment; exceptions include investments in banking, securities, and insurance firms. The most significant barriers to foreign investment are legal uncertainty, crime and corruption, poor infrastructure, and political instability. "While the policy of the Russian government is to encourage foreign investment," reports the U.S. Department of Commerce, "it has had difficulties in creating a stable and attractive investment climate. Economic and political uncertainties are disincentives to companies looking for investment opportunities. Although there are no significant legal barriers to doing business in Russia, the absence of sufficiently developed civil, commercial and criminal codes is a major constraint. In addition, high and unstable taxation, a rise in violent crime, capital flight and a lag in development of local long-term capital are problems for business. Bureaucratic requirements can be confusing and burdensome to investors and bureaucratic discretion may be capricious in awarding tenders or development rights to companies."[6] Foreign investment in 1998 began to decline from 1997 levels.

BANKING
Score: 2–Stable (low level of restrictions)

Many of Russia's state-owned banks have been privatized, and there is fierce competition in the commercial banking market. Foreign banks now operate in Russia, although they are allowed to offer only a limited range of services; most maintain only representative offices. The environment is becoming more competitive, with only limited government influence. According to the U.S. Department of Commerce, "The commercial banking system has been developing rapidly and the largest banks offer a full range of modern banking services."[7]

WAGE AND PRICE CONTROLS
Score: 3–Stable (moderate level)

Free enterprise sets some 90 percent of all prices. The government fixes another 5 percent; and government limits on the amount of profitability determine the remaining 5 percent. Price controls still are in place for fuel and energy, grain, public transportation, medicine, and municipally owned housing rent.[8] Because the government controls a part of the economy through its ownership of the public sector, however, it also exercises a high level of indirect control over wages and prices. Russia also has a minimum wage.

PROPERTY RIGHTS
Score: 3–Stable (moderate level of protection)

Although private property is guaranteed in the constitution adopted in 1993, protection remains significantly lax. The court system works poorly, and no clear and concise method for the settlement of property disputes has been developed. Moreover, protection of private property receives different levels of police attention in different localities, and both corruption and organized crime remain significant threats. In the assessment of the U.S. Department of Commerce, "Russia has a body of conflicting, overlapping and rapidly changing laws, decrees and regulations which has resulted in an ad hoc and unpredictable approach to doing business. Independent dispute resolution in Russia is difficult to obtain; the judicial system is poorly developed. Regional and local courts are not accustomed to adjudicating either commercial or international matters, and they (as well as courts in Moscow) are often subject to political pressure."[9] Courts often lack even minimal funding, and judges and support personnel frequently go unpaid.

REGULATION
Score: 4–Stable (high level)

Some regulations are arbitrary and unevenly enforced, and corruption in the bureaucracy remains a serious problem. According to the U.S. Department of Commerce, "The legal system in Russia is in a state of flux, with various parts of government struggling to create new laws on a broad array of topics. In this environment negotiations and contracts for commercial transactions are complex and protracted. Russia has implemented only part of its new commercial code (contained within the civil code) and investors must carefully research all aspects of Russian law to ensure that each contract conforms with Russian law and embodies the basic provisions of the new, and where still valid, old codes. Contracts must likewise seek to protect the foreign partner against contingencies which often arise. Keeping up with legislative changes and presidential decrees is a daunting task. Uneven implementation of laws creates further complications; various officials, branches of government and jurisdictions interpret and apply regulations with little consistency and the decisions of one may be overruled or contested by another. In addition, while a foreign investor may win a favorable decision from a Russian court, enforcement of judgments is problematic."[10] In addition, the U.S. Department of Commerce also reports, "U.S. firms have identified corruption as a pervasive and growing problem, both in number of instances and in the size of bribes sought. Russia has laws and regulations against bribery and other forms of corruption, but penalties are often insufficient to act as a deterrent."[11]

BLACK MARKET
Score: 4–Stable (high level of activity)

Despite recent moves to establish a free market, Russia's informal sector is massive even though it has shrunk considerably since 1991. The government has not enforced its intellectual property laws, and piracy is rampant. According to the U.S. Department of Commerce, "Until the legislative and judicial measures have been taken to provide for effective IPR enforcement,... there is widespread marketing of pirated U.S. (and other) video-cassettes, recordings, books, computer software, clothes and toys. Losses to manufacturers, authors and others are estimated to be in the hundreds of millions of dollars."[12] Russian organized crime has moved from such traditional activities as prostitution, drug trafficking, and illegal arms sales to money laundering, commodity smuggling, and bank fraud.

NOTES

1. World Bank, *World Development Indicators*, 1998.
2. U.S. Department of State, *Country Reports on Economic Policy and Trade Practices*, 1998.
3. Russia has many overlapping, contradictory, and arbitrarily applied taxes. It also has varying and sometimes rapidly changing municipal and local taxes that could raise overall rates to more than 100 percent of profit. For purposes of methodological consistency, however, the author uses only those taxes that are reported in Ernst & Young's *Worldwide Executive Tax Guide* and *Worldwide Corporate Tax Guide*. The arbitrary application of many taxes is taken into account in the regulation factor.
4. The tax rates reported here, however, are the rates that apply to taxable year 1998. See Ernst & Young, *Worldwide Executive Tax Guide 1998* and *Worldwide Corporate Tax Guide 1998*.
5. Based on the consumer price index; from U.S. Department of State, *Country Reports on Economic Policy and Trade Practices*, 1998.
6. U.S. Department of Commerce, *Country Commercial Guide*, 1998.
7. *Ibid.*
8. Economist Intelligence Unit, *ILT Reports*, November 1997.
9. U.S. Department of Commerce, *Country Commercial Guide*, 1998.
10. *Ibid.*
11. *Ibid.*
12. *Ibid.*

Rwanda   4.30

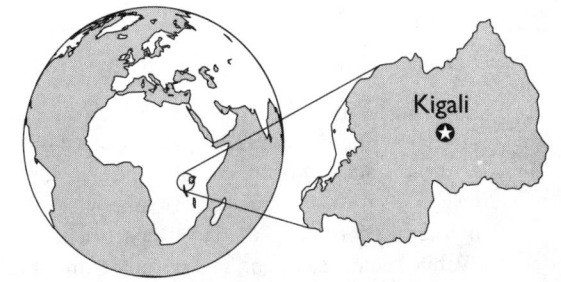

1998 Score: **4.30**	1997 Score: **4.20**	1996 Score: **n/a**

Trade	5	Banking	5
Taxation	5	Wages and Prices	3
Government Intervention	4	Property Rights	5
Monetary Policy	2	Regulation	5
Foreign Investment	4	Black Market	5

After winning its independence from a Belgian-administered United Nations (UN) trusteeship in 1962, Rwanda almost immediately became a major recipient of foreign aid. It received its first foreign aid dollars from the United States in the mid-1960s and has been a major recipient ever since. Despite this and other assistance, however, Rwanda remains one of the most economically repressed countries in the world. The UN ranks Rwanda as the second-least developed country in world: GDP contracted an average of 20.7 percent from 1992 to 1994, although it improved dramatically to grow an average of nearly 18 percent in 1995 and 1996. GDP per capita, however, was only $221 in 1996. In fiscal years 1997–1998, the United States sent some $78 million in aid to Rwanda, which continues to be a source of ethnic unrest and political instability in Central Africa. Not only did Rwanda support Laurent Kabila's successful 1997 coup in the Democratic Republic of Congo, it also is alleged to have supported a 1998 coup attempt against Kabila.

TRADE POLICY
Score: 5–Stable (very high level of protectionism)

Import duties range from 10 percent to 60 percent, and the average tariff rate is about 23 percent.[1] The borders are virtually closed to commerce, however, mainly because of civil unrest. According to the U.S. Department of State, "The country continues to suffer from insurgent attacks, particularly in the northwest quadrant of the country. Poor communication, transportation and health services continue to make travel in Rwanda difficult and potentially hazardous."[2] Thus, commerce across the border is significantly curtailed. In addition, the government has turned to import substitution. For example, according to the U.S. Department of Commerce, "While industry has recovered to at least 70 percent of pre-war levels, it is characterized by inefficient import substitution, with the brewery and soft drink plants topping the list of producers.... The import licensing system is simple and fast, but customs clearance on imports is fraught with bureaucratic hurdles."[3]

TAXATION
Score–Income taxation: 5–Stable (very high tax rates)
Score–Corporate taxation: 5–Stable (very high tax rates)
Final Taxation Score: 5–Stable (very high tax rates)

Rwanda's central government has begun to establish official taxation guidelines and collection services. Corruption in tax collection remains rampant, however, and tax evasion is massive. According to the U.S. Commerce Department, "A revenue authority will increase collections and decrease corruption.... Tax codes are being revised, with a drop in the tax on business profits but an increase in a value added tax from 10 to 15 percent."[4]

1	Hong Kong	1.25	81	Fiji	3.10
2	Singapore	1.30	81	Mali	3.10
3	Bahrain	1.70	81	Slovenia	3.10
4	New Zealand	1.75	85	Honduras	3.15
5	Switzerland	1.85	85	Mexico	3.15
6	United States	1.90	85	Papua New Guinea	3.15
7	Ireland	1.95	88	Djibouti	3.20
7	Luxembourg	1.95	88	Mongolia	3.20
7	Taiwan	1.95	90	Algeria	3.25
7	United Kingdom	1.95	90	Brazil	3.25
11	Bahamas	2.00	90	Lebanon	3.25
12	Czech Republic	2.05	90	Senegal	3.25
12	Japan	2.05	90	Tanzania	3.25
14	Australia	2.10	95	Nigeria	3.30
14	Belgium	2.10	95	Romania	3.30
14	Canada	2.10	97	Cambodia	3.35
14	United Arab Emirates	2.10	97	Dominican Republic	3.35
18	Austria	2.15	97	Egypt	3.35
18	Chile	2.15	97	Guinea	3.35
18	Estonia	2.15	97	Ivory Coast	3.35
18	Netherlands	2.15	97	Moldova	3.35
22	Denmark	2.25	97	Pakistan	3.35
22	El Salvador	2.25	104	Nepal	3.40
22	Finland	2.25	104	Venezuela	3.40
25	Germany	2.30	106	Armenia	3.45
25	Iceland	2.30	106	Bulgaria	3.45
27	Norway	2.35	106	Lesotho	3.45
28	Korea, South	2.40	106	Madagascar	3.45
28	Kuwait	2.40	106	Russia	3.45
28	Malaysia	2.40	111	Burkina Faso	3.50
28	Panama	2.40	111	Cameroon	3.50
28	Thailand	2.40	111	Guyana	3.50
33	Sweden	2.45	111	Nicaragua	3.50
34	Argentina	2.50	115	Gambia	3.60
34	France	2.50	116	Croatia	3.65
34	Italy	2.50	116	Georgia	3.65
34	Spain	2.50	116	Malawi	3.65
38	Portugal	2.55	119	Cape Verde	3.67
38	Sri Lanka	2.55	120	Ethiopia	3.70
38	Trinidad and Tobago	2.55	120	India	3.70
41	Barbados	2.60	120	Niger	3.70
41	Peru	2.60	123	Congo	3.75
43	Bolivia	2.65	124	Chad	3.80
43	Mauritius	2.65	124	China	3.80
45	Cyprus	2.70	124	Mauritania	3.80
45	Jamaica	2.70	124	Ukraine	3.80
45	Uruguay	2.70	124	Zimbabwe	3.80
48	Botswana	2.75	129	Albania	3.85
48	Guatemala	2.75	129	Bangladesh	3.85
48	Jordan	2.75	129	Mozambique	3.85
48	Namibia	2.75	129	Suriname	3.85
48	Oman	2.75	133	Burundi	3.90
48	Philippines	2.75	134	Togo	3.95
54	Belize	2.80	135	Haiti	4.00
54	Costa Rica	2.80	135	Kyrgyz Rep.	4.00
54	Israel	2.80	137	Kazakhstan	4.05
54	Swaziland	2.80	137	Sierra Leone	4.05
54	Turkey	2.80	139	Yemen	4.10
54	Uganda	2.80	140	Belarus	4.15
54	Samoa	2.80	141	Sudan	4.20
61	Latvia	2.85	141	Syria	4.20
62	Greece	2.90	143	Azerbaijan	4.30
62	Hungary	2.90	143	Equatorial Guinea	4.30
62	So. Africa	2.90	143	Myanmar	4.30
65	Ecuador	2.95	143	Rwanda	4.30
65	Gabon	2.95	147	Tajikistan	4.40
65	Indonesia	2.95	147	Uzbekistan	4.40
65	Malta	2.95	149	Angola	4.45
65	Morocco	2.95	149	Turkmenistan	4.45
65	Poland	2.95	151	Guinea-Bissau	4.55
65	Tunisia	2.95	152	Vietnam	4.60
72	Ghana	3.00	153	Congo (Zaire)	4.70
72	Lithuania	3.00	153	Iran	4.70
72	Saudi Arabia	3.00	155	Bosnia	4.80
75	Benin	3.05	155	Somalia	4.80
75	Kenya	3.05	157	Iraq	4.90
75	Paraguay	3.05	157	Laos	4.90
75	Qatar	3.05	157	Libya	4.90
75	Slovak Republic	3.05	160	Cuba	5.00
75	Zambia	3.05	160	Korea, North	5.00
81	Colombia	3.10			

Repressed

GOVERNMENT INTERVENTION IN THE ECONOMY
Score: 4–Stable (very high level)

In 1993 (the most recent year for which a figure is available), government consumed 22.6 percent of GDP.[5] Today, little economic activity occurs outside the public sector, and most private-sector economic activity takes place in the black market. According to the U.S. Department of Commerce, "While the government has a strong commitment to creating an enabling environment for the private sector and investors, measures have not yet coalesced into a consistent policy."[6]

MONETARY POLICY
Score: 2–Stable (low level of inflation)

The average annual rate of inflation from 1986 to 1996 was 10 percent. The inflation rate for 1997 is unavailable.

CAPITAL FLOWS AND FOREIGN INVESTMENT
Score: 4–Stable (high barriers)

Rwanda remains in economic ruin, with no clear protection of foreign investment. The most significant threats to investment continue to be armed bandits, rampant street crime, and the lack of individual freedom of movement. The government is attempting, however, to limit criminal activity, establish an up-to-date investment code, and reform its legal institutions to protect contracts.

BANKING
Score: 5–Stable (very high level of restrictions)

Rwanda's banking system has collapsed, forcing banks to operate in primitive conditions. Although it is beginning to recover, the financial system remains in disarray. The U.S. Department of State reports that "The Rwandan franc is exchangeable for hard currencies in Bureaux de Change and Banks. Several Kigali Banks can handle wire transfers from U.S. banks; banks outside Kigali are slowly re-opening. Credit cards are accepted at only a few hotels in Kigali and only to settle hotel bills. Travelers should expect to handle most expenses, including air tickets, in cash."[7]

WAGE AND PRICE CONTROLS
Score: 3–Stable (moderate level)

For the most part, the market sets wages and prices, albeit through barter. The government does not have the strength to enforce the laws that set prices, although there are official price controls on coffee and tea. Rwanda maintains a minimum wage.

PROPERTY RIGHTS
Score: 5–Stable (very low level of protection)

Private property is virtually nonexistent in Rwanda, and property is subject to frequent confiscation by warring clans and corrupt government officials. According to the U.S. Department of Commerce, "Many properties were occupied by squatters after the genocide, and while the law states that such properties should be returned to the owners on their return to Rwanda, the execution of the law is proving difficult given the shortage of housing and commercial properties."[8]

REGULATION
Score: 5–Stable (very high level)

Rwanda's government has yet to establish a regulatory regime for the country. Most business regulations are chaotic and subject to change, depending on which ministry is in charge of implementing them, and the jurisdictions of the various ministries often overlap.

BLACK MARKET
Score: 5–Stable (very high level of activity)

Most economic activity occurs in the black market.

NOTES

[1]   World Bank, *World Development Report,* 1998.
[2]   U.S. Department of State Travel Advisory, 1998.
[3]   U.S. Department of Commerce, "Rwanda—Investment Climate," *Market Research Reports,* 1998.
[4]   *Ibid.*
[5]   Economist Intelligence Unit, "EIU Country Report," 3rd Quarter 1997.
[6]   U.S. Department of Commerce, "Rwanda—Investment Climate," *Market Research Reports,* 1998.
[7]   U.S. Department of State Travel Advisory, 1997.
[8]   U.S. Department of Commerce, "Rwanda—Economic Overview," *Market Research Reports,* 1997.

Samoa   2.80

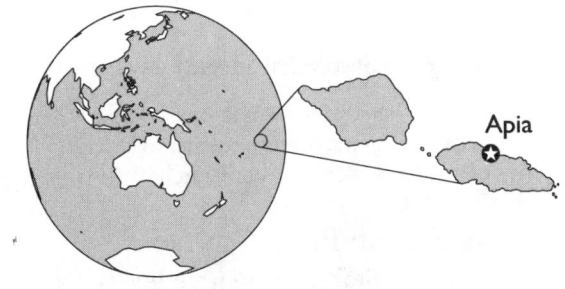

Apia

1998 Score: **2.80**	1997 Score: **2.80**	1996 Score: **2.80**

Trade	3	Banking	3
Taxation	4	Wages and Prices	3
Government Intervention	2	Property Rights	3
Monetary Policy	2	Regulation	3
Foreign Investment	3	Black Market	2

Samoa—known prior to July 1997 as Western Samoa—gained its independence from a New Zealand–administered United Nations trusteeship in 1962. Its primarily agricultural economy is engaged chiefly in the production of coconuts, cocoa, bananas, and taro. Most consumer goods and raw materials must be imported, which creates a chronic trade deficit.

TRADE POLICY
Score: 3–Stable (moderate level of protectionism)

Samoa has a 7.5 percent tariff rate for most so-called essential items and a varying tariff rate of between 5 percent and 75 percent on many consumer goods. The average rate is about 9 percent. The principal non-tariff barrier is a stringent inspection process that can delay entry of some imports. Samoa began a schedule to reduce tariffs in July 1998 that will remove all tariffs by the year 2010. A value-added goods and services tax will remain, however.

TAXATION
Score–Income taxation: 3–Stable (moderate tax rates)
Score–Corporate taxation: 4–Stable (high tax rates)
Final Taxation Score: 4–Stable (high tax rates)

Samoa's top income tax rate is 45 percent, with the average taxpayer in the 10 percent bracket. The top marginal corporate tax rate is 39 percent.[1] Samoa also has a 10 percent goods and services tax and a 10 percent to 15 percent tax on interest, royalties, and dividends.

GOVERNMENT INTERVENTION IN THE ECONOMY
Score: 2–Stable (low level)

Government consumes 17.9 percent of GDP.

MONETARY POLICY
Score: 2–Stable (low level of inflation)

Samoa's average annual rate of inflation from 1986 to 1996 was 6.85 percent. Inflation data for 1997 are not available.

CAPITAL FLOWS AND FOREIGN INVESTMENT
Score: 3–Stable (moderate barriers)

Foreigners may lease land in Samoa but are not permitted to own it. Permission must be granted for most investments, although registering foreign investments is becoming easier. In this respect, the government favors export industries.

1	Hong Kong	1.25	81	Fiji	3.10
2	Singapore	1.30	81	Mali	3.10
3	Bahrain	1.70	81	Slovenia	3.10
4	New Zealand	1.75	85	Honduras	3.15
5	Switzerland	1.85	85	Mexico	3.15
6	United States	1.90	85	Papua New Guinea	3.15
7	Ireland	1.95	88	Djibouti	3.20
7	Luxembourg	1.95	88	Mongolia	3.20
7	Taiwan	1.95	90	Algeria	3.25
7	United Kingdom	1.95	90	Brazil	3.25
11	Bahamas	2.00	90	Lebanon	3.25
12	Czech Republic	2.05	90	Senegal	3.25
12	Japan	2.05	90	Tanzania	3.25
14	Australia	2.10	95	Nigeria	3.30
14	Belgium	2.10	95	Romania	3.30
14	Canada	2.10	97	Cambodia	3.35
14	United Arab Emirates	2.10	97	Dominican Republic	3.35
18	Austria	2.15	97	Egypt	3.35
18	Chile	2.15	97	Guinea	3.35
18	Estonia	2.15	97	Ivory Coast	3.35
18	Netherlands	2.15	97	Moldova	3.35
22	Denmark	2.25	97	Pakistan	3.35
22	El Salvador	2.25	104	Nepal	3.40
22	Finland	2.25	104	Venezuela	3.40
25	Germany	2.30	106	Armenia	3.45
25	Iceland	2.30	106	Bulgaria	3.45
27	Norway	2.35	106	Lesotho	3.45
28	Korea, South	2.40	106	Madagascar	3.45
28	Kuwait	2.40	106	Russia	3.45
28	Malaysia	2.40	111	Burkina Faso	3.50
28	Panama	2.40	111	Cameroon	3.50
28	Thailand	2.40	111	Guyana	3.50
33	Sweden	2.45	111	Nicaragua	3.50
34	Argentina	2.50	115	Gambia	3.60
34	France	2.50	116	Croatia	3.65
34	Italy	2.50	116	Georgia	3.65
34	Spain	2.50	116	Malawi	3.65
38	Portugal	2.55	119	Cape Verde	3.67
38	Sri Lanka	2.55	120	Ethiopia	3.70
38	Trinidad and Tobago	2.55	120	India	3.70
41	Barbados	2.60	120	Niger	3.70
41	Peru	2.60	123	Congo	3.75
43	Bolivia	2.65	124	Chad	3.80
43	Mauritius	2.65	124	China	3.80
45	Cyprus	2.70	124	Mauritania	3.80
45	Jamaica	2.70	124	Ukraine	3.80
45	Uruguay	2.70	124	Zimbabwe	3.80
48	Botswana	2.75	129	Albania	3.85
48	Guatemala	2.75	129	Bangladesh	3.85
48	Jordan	2.75	129	Mozambique	3.85
48	Namibia	2.75	129	Suriname	3.85
48	Oman	2.75	133	Burundi	3.90
48	Philippines	2.75	134	Togo	3.95
54	Belize	2.80	135	Haiti	4.00
54	Costa Rica	2.80	135	Kyrgyz Rep.	4.00
54	Israel	2.80	137	Kazakhstan	4.05
54	Swaziland	2.80	137	Sierra Leone	4.05
54	Turkey	2.80	139	Yemen	4.10
54	Uganda	2.80	140	Belarus	4.15
54	Samoa	2.80	141	Sudan	4.20
61	Latvia	2.85	141	Syria	4.20
62	Greece	2.90	143	Azerbaijan	4.30
62	Hungary	2.90	143	Equatorial Guinea	4.30
62	So. Africa	2.90	143	Myanmar	4.30
65	Ecuador	2.95	143	Rwanda	4.30
65	Gabon	2.95	147	Tajikistan	4.40
65	Indonesia	2.95	147	Uzbekistan	4.40
65	Malta	2.95	149	Angola	4.45
65	Morocco	2.95	149	Turkmenistan	4.45
65	Poland	2.95	151	Guinea-Bissau	4.55
65	Tunisia	2.95	152	Vietnam	4.60
72	Ghana	3.00	153	Congo (Zaire)	4.70
72	Lithuania	3.00	153	Iran	4.70
72	Saudi Arabia	3.00	155	Bosnia	4.80
75	Benin	3.05	155	Somalia	4.80
75	Kenya	3.05	157	Iraq	4.90
75	Paraguay	3.05	157	Laos	4.90
75	Qatar	3.05	157	Libya	4.90
75	Slovak Republic	3.05	160	Cuba	5.00
75	Zambia	3.05	160	Korea, North	5.00
81	Colombia	3.10			

Mostly Free

BANKING
Score: 3–Stable (moderate level of restrictions)

Samoa's banking system is small. The government continues to be a joint venture partner in at least one commercial bank, the Bank of Western Samoa.

WAGE AND PRICE CONTROLS
Score: 3–Stable (moderate level)

The market sets most wages and prices, although there is a government-mandated minimum wage. The government controls some prices, mainly in the utilities sector, and also influences prices through its direct ownership of companies (for example, in the agricultural sector).

PROPERTY RIGHTS
Score: 3–Stable (moderate level of protection)

Samoa's government owns large tracts of public land that are closed to business development. Most private land already has been developed.

REGULATION
Score: 3–Stable (moderate level)

Establishing a business in Samoa is relatively easy, and regulations are applied evenly in most cases, although some regulations make it difficult for businesses to operate. The government, for example, requires all businesses to contribute 5 percent of gross earnings for each Samoan employee to a retirement fund, the Samoan National Provident Fund; it also requires that employees contribute 5 percent of their earnings to this fund. Businesses are not free to hire foreigners if there is a Samoan who can perform the same job.

BLACK MARKET
Score: 2–Stable (low level of activity)

The size of Samoa's black market is negligible.

NOTE

[1]   This rate applies to resident-owned companies; foreign-owned companies pay a top rate of 48 percent.

Saudi Arabia   3.00

1998 Score: **2.80**	1997 Score: **2.80**	1996 Score: **2.90**

Trade	4	Banking	3
Taxation	4	Wages and Prices	3
Government Intervention	4	Property Rights	2
Monetary Policy	1	Regulation	3
Foreign Investment	4	Black Market	2

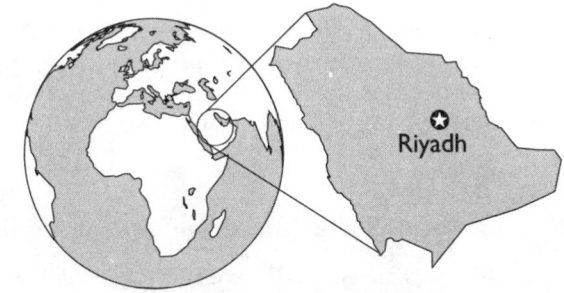

Riyadh

Saudi Arabia takes its name from the Saud family, which rose to prominence in central Arabia around 1750. The modern Saudi state was formed in 1902 under King Abdul Aziz Ibn Saud, who enlarged his holdings until uniting them as the Kingdom of Saudi Arabia in 1932. Oil was discovered in the 1930s, and large-scale production began after World War II. Saudi Arabia today has the world's largest oil reserves and, as the world's largest oil exporter, holds a dominant role within the Organization of Petroleum Exporting Countries. It also has a developing economy with a large government sector. Regulations favor Saudi businesses and often discriminate against foreigners. Recently there has been an increase in regulations and corruption and a decrease in protection for private property; as a result, Saudi Arabia's overall score is 0.2 point worse than last year.

TRADE POLICY
Score: 4–Stable (high level of protectionism)

Saudi Arabia's average tariff rate is about 13 percent. Non-tariff barriers include strict labeling and certification requirements, import licenses, and import bans.

TAXATION
Score–Income taxation: 3–Stable (moderate tax rates)
Score–Corporate taxation: 4–Stable (high tax rates)
Final Taxation Score: 4–Stable (high tax rates)

Saudi Arabia's top income tax rate is 30 percent, and the average taxpayer is in the 10 percent bracket. The top marginal corporate tax rate is 45 percent. The government imposes several other taxes, including a 45 percent capital gains tax.

GOVERNMENT INTERVENTION IN THE ECONOMY
Score: 4–Stable (high level)

Government consumes 26.1 percent of GDP; it also generates most of the country's GDP. According to the Economist Intelligence Unit, "Although the government emphasises its basic commitment to free enterprise, it maintains a monopoly role in the oil sector and a virtual monopoly in infrastructure development and the provision of most utilities and communications services."[1]

MONETARY POLICY
Score: 1–Stable (very low level of inflation)

Saudi Arabia's average annual rate of inflation from 1986 to 1996 was less than 2 percent. In 1997, the rate was about 1 percent.

CAPITAL FLOWS AND FOREIGN INVESTMENT
Score: 4–Stable (high barriers)

Although Saudi Arabia imposes few restrictions on foreign investment and allows 100 percent foreign ownership, complete foreign ownership is uncommon in practice. The government must review and accept all investments. "It is

1	Hong Kong	1.25
2	Singapore	1.30
3	Bahrain	1.70
4	New Zealand	1.75
5	Switzerland	1.85
6	United States	1.90
7	Ireland	1.95
7	Luxembourg	1.95
7	Taiwan	1.95
7	United Kingdom	1.95
11	Bahamas	2.00
12	Czech Republic	2.05
12	Japan	2.05
14	Australia	2.10
14	Belgium	2.10
14	Canada	2.10
14	United Arab Emirates	2.10
18	Austria	2.15
18	Chile	2.15
18	Estonia	2.15
18	Netherlands	2.15
22	Denmark	2.25
22	El Salvador	2.25
22	Finland	2.25
25	Germany	2.30
25	Iceland	2.30
27	Norway	2.35
28	Korea, South	2.40
28	Kuwait	2.40
28	Malaysia	2.40
28	Panama	2.40
28	Thailand	2.40
33	Sweden	2.45
34	Argentina	2.50
34	France	2.50
34	Italy	2.50
34	Spain	2.50
38	Portugal	2.55
38	Sri Lanka	2.55
38	Trinidad and Tobago	2.55
41	Barbados	2.60
41	Peru	2.60
43	Bolivia	2.65
43	Mauritius	2.65
45	Cyprus	2.70
45	Jamaica	2.70
45	Uruguay	2.70
48	Botswana	2.75
48	Guatemala	2.75
48	Jordan	2.75
48	Namibia	2.75
48	Oman	2.75
48	Philippines	2.75
54	Belize	2.80
54	Costa Rica	2.80
54	Israel	2.80
54	Swaziland	2.80
54	Turkey	2.80
54	Uganda	2.80
54	Samoa	2.80
61	Latvia	2.85
62	Greece	2.90
62	Hungary	2.90
62	So. Africa	2.90
65	Ecuador	2.95
65	Gabon	2.95
65	Indonesia	2.95
65	Malta	2.95
65	Morocco	2.95
65	Poland	2.95
65	Tunisia	2.95
72	Ghana	3.00
72	Lithuania	3.00
72	Saudi Arabia	3.00
75	Benin	3.05
75	Kenya	3.05
75	Paraguay	3.05
75	Qatar	3.05
75	Slovak Republic	3.05
75	Zambia	3.05
81	Colombia	3.10

81	Fiji	3.10
81	Mali	3.10
81	Slovenia	3.10
85	Honduras	3.15
85	Mexico	3.15
85	Papua New Guinea	3.15
88	Djibouti	3.20
88	Mongolia	3.20
90	Algeria	3.25
90	Brazil	3.25
90	Lebanon	3.25
90	Senegal	3.25
90	Tanzania	3.25
95	Nigeria	3.30
95	Romania	3.30
97	Cambodia	3.35
97	Dominican Republic	3.35
97	Egypt	3.35
97	Guinea	3.35
97	Ivory Coast	3.35
97	Moldova	3.35
97	Pakistan	3.35
104	Nepal	3.40
104	Venezuela	3.40
106	Armenia	3.45
106	Bulgaria	3.45
106	Lesotho	3.45
106	Madagascar	3.45
106	Russia	3.45
111	Burkina Faso	3.50
111	Cameroon	3.50
111	Guyana	3.50
111	Nicaragua	3.50
115	Gambia	3.60
116	Croatia	3.65
116	Georgia	3.65
116	Malawi	3.65
119	Cape Verde	3.67
120	Ethiopia	3.70
120	India	3.70
120	Niger	3.70
123	Congo	3.75
124	Chad	3.80
124	China	3.80
124	Mauritania	3.80
124	Ukraine	3.80
124	Zimbabwe	3.80
129	Albania	3.85
129	Bangladesh	3.85
129	Mozambique	3.85
129	Suriname	3.85
133	Burundi	3.90
134	Togo	3.95
135	Haiti	4.00
135	Kyrgyz Rep.	4.00
137	Kazakhstan	4.05
137	Sierra Leone	4.05
139	Yemen	4.10
140	Belarus	4.15
141	Sudan	4.20
141	Syria	4.20
143	Azerbaijan	4.30
143	Equatorial Guinea	4.30
143	Myanmar	4.30
143	Rwanda	4.30
147	Tajikistan	4.40
147	Uzbekistan	4.40
149	Angola	4.45
149	Turkmenistan	4.45
151	Guinea-Bissau	4.55
152	Vietnam	4.60
153	Congo (Zaire)	4.70
153	Iran	4.70
155	Bosnia	4.80
155	Somalia	4.80
157	Iraq	4.90
157	Laos	4.90
157	Libya	4.90
160	Cuba	5.00
160	Korea, North	5.00

Mostly Unfree

extremely rare for the government to award a license to any 100 percent-foreign-owned operation," reports the Economist Intelligence Unit.[2] Restrictions still apply to many services, such as insurance and real estate.

BANKING
Score: 3–Stable (moderate level of restrictions)

The banking system is competitive, and there are more than 24 commercial banks. A budgetary crisis, however, forced the government to finance its debt through Saudi banks; the government has resisted seeking financing from foreign banks because that would require it to release data on Saudi Arabia's financial status. The increased government pressure on commercial banks for more loans to meet this crisis has hindered the free operation of these banks. Foreign participation is limited to 40 percent ownership.

WAGE AND PRICE CONTROLS
Score: 3–Stable (moderate level)

The market sets most wages and prices, although the government determines some prices on basic utilities. The government also subsidizes agriculture and some other enterprises. There is no minimum wage.

PROPERTY RIGHTS
Score: 2– (high level of protection)

Private property is safe from expropriation in Saudi Arabia. As the U.S. Department of State reports, "The independence of the judiciary is prescribed by law and is usually respected in practice. However, judges occasionally accede to the influence of the executive branch, particularly members of the royal family and their associates. Moreover, the Ministry of Justice exercises judicial, financial, and administrative control of the courts."[3] Moreover, there is increasing evidence the court system in Saudi Arabia is becoming more inefficient. For example, the U.S. Department of Commerce notes, "Dispute settlement in Saudi Arabia continues to be time-consuming and uncertain. Even after a decision is reached in a dispute, effective enforcement of the judgment can still take years."[4] As a result, Saudi Arabia's score in the property rights factor is 1 point worse this year.

REGULATION
Score: 3– (low level)

Establishing a business in Saudi Arabia is a simple process. There are, however, increasing indications that both the regulatory burden and corruption are in the rise. For example, according to the U.S. Department of Commerce, "There are few aspects of the Saudi Government which are transparent.... Bureaucratic procedures are cumbersome, but Saudi red tape can generally be overcome with persistence.... U.S. firms have identified corruption as an obstacle to investment in Saudi Arabia. Government procurement is an area often cited, as is de facto protection of businesses in which senior officials or elite individuals have a stake. Bribes, often disguised as 'commissions' are commonplace. Giving or accepting a bribe is not a criminal act." As a result, Saudi Arabia's regulation score is 1 point worse than last year.

BLACK MARKET
Score: 2–Stable (low level of activity)

The size of Saudi Arabia's black market is relatively small. The government has been very successful in stamping out pirated videotapes and related copyrighted material.

NOTES

[1] Economist Intelligence Unit, "Saudi Arabia," *ILT Reports,* March 1998, p. 9.
[2] *Ibid.,* p. 8.
[3] U.S. Department of State, "Saudi Arabia Country Report on Human Rights Practices for 1997," 1998
[4] U.S. Department of Commerce, *Country Commercial Guide,* 1998.

Senegal   3.25

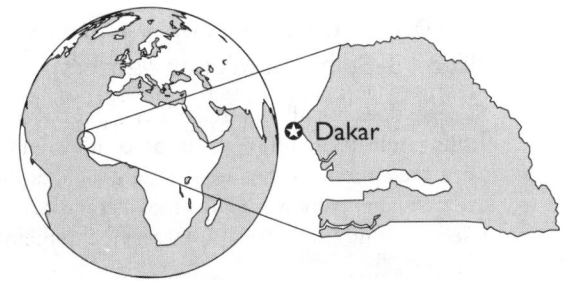
Dakar

1998 Score: **3.25**	1997 Score: **3.25**	1996 Score: **3.40**

Trade	4	Banking	3
Taxation	4.5	Wages and Prices	4
Government Intervention	3	Property Rights	3
Monetary Policy	1	Regulation	4
Foreign Investment	3	Black Market	3

Senegal, a small, semi-arid country with limited natural resources, gained its independence from France in 1960. Its economy is primarily agricultural, although the fishing, mining, and chemical industries are well established. From 1989 to 1994, economic growth was poor; growth in GDP averaged only 0.85 percent annually. The government has sought to reduce spending and reform the economy. In 1995, it began to implement an economic liberalization program aimed at stimulating economic growth. This program included the liberalization of prices, the elimination of state-granted monopolies, the privatization of some state industries, and the limited liberalization of trade. With economic growth averaging 5.1 percent from 1995 to 1997, the signs are positive that these policies are working, but the future of the program may be in question after the resignation of its chief architect, Minister of the Economy Papa Ousmane Sakho.

TRADE POLICY
Score: 4–Stable (high level of protectionism)

Senegal has adopted a flat external tariff rate of 10 percent, down from an average tariff rate of 27 percent in 1994 and over 30 percent for the 1990–1993 period. Other trade restrictions include some import bans, import licenses, and strict documentation requirements. There are some complaints of limited corruption within the customs bureau. According to the U.S. Department of Commerce, "Corruption can range from large scale customs fraud, including invoice under-valuation, to bribe-taking by inspectors and public safety officials."[1]

TAXATION
Score–Income taxation: 5–Stable (very high tax rates)
Score–Corporate taxation: 3–Stable (moderate tax rates)
Final Taxation Score: 4.5–Stable (very high tax rates)

Senegal's top income tax rate is 78 percent.[2] The tax on the average income level is 18 percent. The top marginal corporate tax rate is 35 percent. The country also has a 35 percent capital gains tax and a 10 percent to 20 percent turnover tax.

GOVERNMENT INTERVENTION IN THE ECONOMY
Score: 3–Stable (moderate level)

Government consumes about 10.6 percent of GDP. The government also remains heavily involved in agriculture (although the number of private firms is increasing) and continues to control railroads, electrical production, telecommunications, and postal services.

MONETARY POLICY
Score: 1–Stable (very low level of inflation)

Senegal's average annual rate of inflation from 1986 to 1996 was 5.7 percent. In 1997, the rate was 1.8 percent.

1	Hong Kong	1.25		81	Fiji	3.10
2	Singapore	1.30		81	Mali	3.10
3	Bahrain	1.70		81	Slovenia	3.10
4	New Zealand	1.75		85	Honduras	3.15
5	Switzerland	1.85		85	Mexico	3.15
6	United States	1.90		85	Papua New Guinea	3.15
7	Ireland	1.95		88	Djibouti	3.20
7	Luxembourg	1.95		88	Mongolia	3.20
7	Taiwan	1.95		90	Algeria	3.25
7	United Kingdom	1.95		90	Brazil	3.25
11	Bahamas	2.00		90	Lebanon	3.25
12	Czech Republic	2.05		90	Senegal	3.25
12	Japan	2.05		90	Tanzania	3.25
14	Australia	2.10		95	Nigeria	3.30
14	Belgium	2.10		95	Romania	3.30
14	Canada	2.10		97	Cambodia	3.35
14	United Arab Emirates	2.10		97	Dominican Republic	3.35
18	Austria	2.15		97	Egypt	3.35
18	Chile	2.15		97	Guinea	3.35
18	Estonia	2.15		97	Ivory Coast	3.35
18	Netherlands	2.15		97	Moldova	3.35
22	Denmark	2.25		97	Pakistan	3.35
22	El Salvador	2.25		104	Nepal	3.40
22	Finland	2.25		104	Venezuela	3.40
25	Germany	2.30		106	Armenia	3.45
25	Iceland	2.30		106	Bulgaria	3.45
27	Norway	2.35		106	Lesotho	3.45
28	Korea, South	2.40		106	Madagascar	3.45
28	Kuwait	2.40		106	Russia	3.45
28	Malaysia	2.40		111	Burkina Faso	3.50
28	Panama	2.40		111	Cameroon	3.50
28	Thailand	2.40		111	Guyana	3.50
33	Sweden	2.45		111	Nicaragua	3.50
34	Argentina	2.50		115	Gambia	3.60
34	France	2.50		116	Croatia	3.65
34	Italy	2.50		116	Georgia	3.65
34	Spain	2.50		116	Malawi	3.65
38	Portugal	2.55		119	Cape Verde	3.67
38	Sri Lanka	2.55		120	Ethiopia	3.70
38	Trinidad and Tobago	2.55		120	India	3.70
41	Barbados	2.60		120	Niger	3.70
41	Peru	2.60		123	Congo	3.75
43	Bolivia	2.65		124	Chad	3.80
43	Mauritius	2.65		124	China	3.80
45	Cyprus	2.70		124	Mauritania	3.80
45	Jamaica	2.70		124	Ukraine	3.80
45	Uruguay	2.70		124	Zimbabwe	3.80
48	Botswana	2.75		129	Albania	3.85
48	Guatemala	2.75		129	Bangladesh	3.85
48	Jordan	2.75		129	Mozambique	3.85
48	Namibia	2.75		129	Suriname	3.85
48	Oman	2.75		133	Burundi	3.90
48	Philippines	2.75		134	Togo	3.95
54	Belize	2.80		135	Haiti	4.00
54	Costa Rica	2.80		135	Kyrgyz Rep.	4.00
54	Israel	2.80		137	Kazakhstan	4.05
54	Swaziland	2.80		137	Sierra Leone	4.05
54	Turkey	2.80		139	Yemen	4.10
54	Uganda	2.80		140	Belarus	4.15
54	Samoa	2.80		141	Sudan	4.20
61	Latvia	2.85		141	Syria	4.20
62	Greece	2.90		143	Azerbaijan	4.30
62	Hungary	2.90		143	Equatorial Guinea	4.30
62	So. Africa	2.90		143	Myanmar	4.30
65	Ecuador	2.95		143	Rwanda	4.30
65	Gabon	2.95		147	Tajikistan	4.40
65	Indonesia	2.95		147	Uzbekistan	4.40
65	Malta	2.95		149	Angola	4.45
65	Morocco	2.95		149	Turkmenistan	4.45
65	Poland	2.95		151	Guinea-Bissau	4.55
65	Tunisia	2.95		152	Vietnam	4.60
72	Ghana	3.00		153	Congo (Zaire)	4.70
72	Lithuania	3.00		153	Iran	4.70
72	Saudi Arabia	3.00		155	Bosnia	4.80
75	Benin	3.05		155	Somalia	4.80
75	Kenya	3.05		157	Iraq	4.90
75	Paraguay	3.05		157	Laos	4.90
75	Qatar	3.05		157	Libya	4.90
75	Slovak Republic	3.05		160	Cuba	5.00
75	Zambia	3.05		160	Korea, North	5.00
81	Colombia	3.10				

Mostly Unfree

CAPITAL FLOWS AND FOREIGN INVESTMENT
Score: 3–Stable (moderate barriers)

Senegal does not allow foreign investment in the food and fishing industries, although 100 percent ownership is permitted in most other areas. Foreign and domestic firms are treated equally. Such industries as railroads, electricity, telecommunications, and postal services remain under state control.

BANKING
Score: 3–Stable (moderate level of restrictions)

French banks dominate Senegal's banking system. There is a moderate level of competition, and borrowing capital can be expensive. There is no stock market.

WAGE AND PRICE CONTROLS
Score: 4–Stable (high level)

Both the market and the large state-owned sector set wages and prices in Senegal. The government continues to set prices on some goods and services, including some agricultural products and electricity.

PROPERTY RIGHTS
Score: 3–Stable (moderate level of protection)

Private property in Senegal is protected by an efficient legal system, and expropriation is unlikely. Although the judiciary is independent, reports the U.S. Department of State, it also is "subject to governmental influence and pressure."[3]

REGULATION
Score: 4–Stable (high level)

Establishing a business can be onerous if the business is to compete with a state-owned enterprise. Government-sanctioned monopolies often bribe government officials to keep out new entrants. According to the U.S. Department of Commerce, "The potential for corruption is a significant factor obstructing economic development and competitiveness in Senegal.... Credible allegations of corruption have been made concerning government procurement, dispute settlement, and regulatory and enforcement agencies. Corruption can range from large-scale customs fraud, including invoice under-valuation, to bribe taking by inspectors and public safety officials."[4]

BLACK MARKET
Score: 3–Stable (moderate level of activity)

Black market activity in Senegal is limited principally to labor, construction, and transportation.

NOTES
[1] U.S. Department of Commerce, *Country Commercial Guide,* 1998.
[2] The top income tax rate includes a top rate of 50 percent and a mandatory proportional tax of 28 percent.
[3] U.S. Department of State, "Senegal Country Report on Human Rights Practices for 1997," 1998.
[4] U.S. Department of Commerce, *Country Commercial Guide,* 1998.

Sierra Leone   4.05

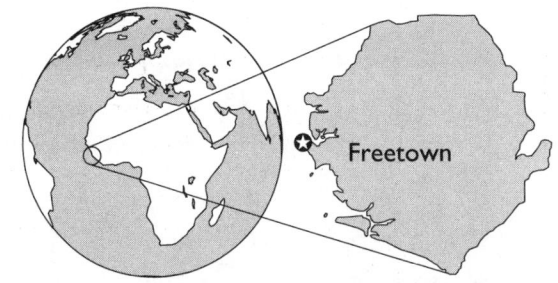

Freetown

Trade	4	Banking	4
Taxation	4.5	Wages and Prices	4
Government Intervention	3	Property Rights	4
Monetary Policy	5	Regulation	4
Foreign Investment	3	Black Market	5

Sierra Leone gained its independence from the United Kingdom in 1961. Over the next 10 years, its economy grew by 4 percent a year. Regular growth ended in the 1970s, however, when the oil crisis devastated the economy. For the past 15 years, the government has made some halfhearted efforts to reform the economy, but recovery has remained elusive, with the economy shrinking by an average of 5.7 percent from 1992 to 1996. In May 1997, a coup led by army officers toppled the government of President Ahmad Tejan Kabbah. In 1998, the military junta was forced from power by troops from the Economic Community of West African States, and Kabbah was reinstated as president. Junta rebels are still active, however, especially in the diamond-rich Kono region. Rationing has become more prevalent in the distribution of goods and services over the past year. Moreover, there has been a significant increase in corruption. As a result, Sierra Leone's overall score is 0.2 point worse than last year.

TRADE POLICY
Score: 4–Stable (high level of protectionism)

The average tariff rate is about 18 percent.[1] Non-tariff barriers include excessive government red tape and chaos resulting from the recent political crisis.

TAXATION
Score–Income taxation: 3–Stable (moderate tax rates)
Score–Corporate taxation: 5–Stable (very high tax rates)
Final Taxation Score: 4.5–Stable (very high tax rates)

Sierra Leone's top income tax rate is 50 percent, with the average income taxed at 5 percent. The corporate income tax rate is a flat 47.2 percent. The government also levies property taxes and a goods and services tax.

GOVERNMENT INTERVENTION IN THE ECONOMY
Score: 3–Stable (moderate level)

Government consumes 11 percent of GDP. The country's large state-owned sector produces more than 30 percent of GDP.

MONETARY POLICY
Score: 5–Stable (very high level of inflation)

Sierra Leone's average annual rate of inflation from 1986 to 1996 was 60.35 percent. Inflation data for 1997 are unavailable.

CAPITAL FLOWS AND FOREIGN INVESTMENT
Score: 3–Stable (moderate barriers)

The government must approve all investments; it also established an investment code. Foreigners are not permitted to invest either in "local industries," such as cement-block manufacturing or granite and sandstone excavation, or in the manufacture of certain durable consumer goods.

1	Hong Kong	1.25	81	Fiji	3.10
2	Singapore	1.30	81	Mali	3.10
3	Bahrain	1.70	81	Slovenia	3.10
4	New Zealand	1.75	85	Honduras	3.15
5	Switzerland	1.85	85	Mexico	3.15
6	United States	1.90	85	Papua New Guinea	3.15
7	Ireland	1.95	88	Djibouti	3.20
7	Luxembourg	1.95	88	Mongolia	3.20
7	Taiwan	1.95	90	Algeria	3.25
7	United Kingdom	1.95	90	Brazil	3.25
11	Bahamas	2.00	90	Lebanon	3.25
12	Czech Republic	2.05	90	Senegal	3.25
12	Japan	2.05	90	Tanzania	3.25
14	Australia	2.10	95	Nigeria	3.30
14	Belgium	2.10	95	Romania	3.30
14	Canada	2.10	97	Cambodia	3.35
14	United Arab Emirates	2.10	97	Dominican Republic	3.35
18	Austria	2.15	97	Egypt	3.35
18	Chile	2.15	97	Guinea	3.35
18	Estonia	2.15	97	Ivory Coast	3.35
18	Netherlands	2.15	97	Moldova	3.35
22	Denmark	2.25	97	Pakistan	3.35
22	El Salvador	2.25	104	Nepal	3.40
22	Finland	2.25	104	Venezuela	3.40
25	Germany	2.30	106	Armenia	3.45
25	Iceland	2.30	106	Bulgaria	3.45
27	Norway	2.35	106	Lesotho	3.45
28	Korea, South	2.40	106	Madagascar	3.45
28	Kuwait	2.40	106	Russia	3.45
28	Malaysia	2.40	111	Burkina Faso	3.50
28	Panama	2.40	111	Cameroon	3.50
28	Thailand	2.40	111	Guyana	3.50
33	Sweden	2.45	111	Nicaragua	3.50
34	Argentina	2.50	115	Gambia	3.60
34	France	2.50	116	Croatia	3.65
34	Italy	2.50	116	Georgia	3.65
34	Spain	2.50	116	Malawi	3.65
38	Portugal	2.55	119	Cape Verde	3.67
38	Sri Lanka	2.55	120	Ethiopia	3.70
38	Trinidad and Tobago	2.55	120	India	3.70
41	Barbados	2.60	120	Niger	3.70
41	Peru	2.60	123	Congo	3.75
43	Bolivia	2.65	124	Chad	3.80
43	Mauritius	2.65	124	China	3.80
45	Cyprus	2.70	124	Mauritania	3.80
45	Jamaica	2.70	124	Ukraine	3.80
45	Uruguay	2.70	124	Zimbabwe	3.80
48	Botswana	2.75	129	Albania	3.85
48	Guatemala	2.75	129	Bangladesh	3.85
48	Jordan	2.75	129	Mozambique	3.85
48	Namibia	2.75	129	Suriname	3.85
48	Oman	2.75	133	Burundi	3.90
48	Philippines	2.75	134	Togo	3.95
54	Belize	2.80	135	Haiti	4.00
54	Costa Rica	2.80	135	Kyrgyz Rep.	4.00
54	Israel	2.80	137	Kazakhstan	4.05
54	Swaziland	2.80	137	Sierra Leone	4.05
54	Turkey	2.80	139	Yemen	4.10
54	Uganda	2.80	140	Belarus	4.15
54	Samoa	2.80	141	Sudan	4.20
61	Latvia	2.85	141	Syria	4.20
62	Greece	2.90	143	Azerbaijan	4.30
62	Hungary	2.90	143	Equatorial Guinea	4.30
62	So. Africa	2.90	143	Myanmar	4.30
65	Ecuador	2.95	143	Rwanda	4.30
65	Gabon	2.95	147	Tajikistan	4.40
65	Indonesia	2.95	147	Uzbekistan	4.40
65	Malta	2.95	149	Angola	4.45
65	Morocco	2.95	149	Turkmenistan	4.45
65	Poland	2.95	151	Guinea-Bissau	4.55
65	Tunisia	2.95	152	Vietnam	4.60
72	Ghana	3.00	153	Congo (Zaire)	4.70
72	Lithuania	3.00	153	Iran	4.70
72	Saudi Arabia	3.00	155	Bosnia	4.80
75	Benin	3.05	155	Somalia	4.80
75	Kenya	3.05	157	Iraq	4.90
75	Paraguay	3.05	157	Laos	4.90
75	Qatar	3.05	157	Libya	4.90
75	Slovak Republic	3.05	160	Cuba	5.00
75	Zambia	3.05	160	Korea, North	5.00
81	Colombia	3.10			

Repressed

BANKING
Score: 4–Stable (high level of restrictions)

Sierra Leone's banking system is in disarray. Banks are heavily regulated, and the government sets interest rates for commercial banks.

WAGE AND PRICE CONTROLS
Score: 4– (high level)

The government imposes price controls on certain foods. Prices also are influenced by the state-owned industries, which the government subsidizes. Sierra Leone has no minimum wage. The recent political crisis has damaged the operation of the economy, however; many formal pricing regimes have been dismantled, and rationing and barter have replaced many economic transactions. As a result, Sierra Leone's score in this factor is 1 point worse than last year.

PROPERTY RIGHTS
Score: 4–Stable (low level of protection)

Although private property is permitted, it also can be expropriated. An inefficient legal and law enforcement environment provides little protection. In 1996, the U.S. Department of State issued a warning on travel to Sierra Leone, mainly because of crime and corruption: "Petty crime and theft of wallets and passports are common. Requests for payments at military roadblocks are common. Robberies and burglaries of residences also occur."[2]

REGULATION
Score: 4– (high level)

Regulations are applied haphazardly, making compliance difficult. The less-than-uniform enforcement of health and safety standards creates uncertainty among businesses. Moreover, during the time Sierra Leone was controlled by a military junta, corruption quickly became commonplace. Since the restoration of the government, however, little progress has been made in reducing corruption. As a result, the country's regulation score is 1 point worse than last year.

BLACK MARKET
Score: 5–Stable (very high level of activity)

The level of black market activity is nearly as high as that of legal activity. High tariffs encourage smugglers to sell many products on the black market, and some products like coffee and rice are sold at much lower prices on the black market than in state-owned stores.

NOTES

[1] World Bank, *World Development Indicators,* 1998.
[2] U.S. Department of State, "Sierra Leone—Travel Conditions," *Market Research Reports* No. IMI960208, 1996.

Singapore   1.30

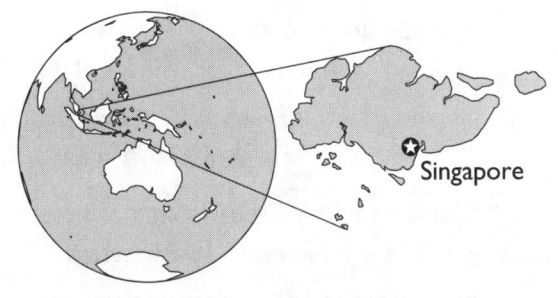
Singapore

Trade	1	Banking	2
Taxation	3	Wages and Prices	1
Government Intervention	1	Property Rights	1
Monetary Policy	1	Regulation	1
Foreign Investment	1	Black Market	1

Singapore became independent of Malaysia in August 1965. Since that time, thanks to economic liberalization, it has been transformed into a developed country. From 1965 to 1995, Singapore enjoyed average annual growth rates of almost 9 percent; it is one of the wealthiest countries in Asia today. Singapore has made this remarkable progress by maintaining an economic environment open to trade and investment; a corruption-free, pro-business regulatory system; political stability; an efficient, strike-free labor force; and tax incentives for foreign investors. Indeed, Singapore is one of the world's freest economies. In fact, this year, Singapore officially ranks as the second most economically free country. While many Asian countries are reacting to the international financial crisis by decreasing economic freedom, Singapore is moving in the opposite direction. Although its score remains the same as last year, there are signs that Singapore may curtail the requirement on businesses to contribute to its central provident fund. If these changes indeed are made, they may be reflected in an improvement in next year's score.

TRADE POLICY
Score: 1–Stable (very low level of protectionism)

Singapore has an exceptionally low average tariff rate: from 0.3 percent to 0.5 percent. Nearly 99 percent of all imports enter duty-free. The government maintains straightforward labeling requirements, no import quotas, and no non-tariff barriers to foreign trade. Import licenses are not required, and customs procedures are minimal. The code regulating product standards is not an impediment to trade.

TAXATION
Score–Income taxation: 2–Stable (low tax rates)
Score–Corporate taxation: 3–Stable (moderate tax rates)
Final Taxation Score: 3–Stable (moderate tax rates)

Singapore's top income tax rate is 28 percent, down from 30 percent in 1996. The average income is taxed at 8 percent. There are no taxes on capital gains. The corporate tax rate is a flat 26 percent, down from 27 percent in 1996. Singapore also has a 3 percent value-added tax as well as a mandatory retirement fund.

GOVERNMENT INTERVENTION IN THE ECONOMY
Score: 1–Stable (very low level)

Government consumed 9.4 percent of GDP in 1997. Although some critics of Singapore's economic reforms claim the government is involved heavily in the private sector, most businesses are privately owned, and direct government control of corporations is negligible.[1]

Rank	Country	Score
1	Hong Kong	1.25
2	Singapore	1.30
3	Bahrain	1.70
4	New Zealand	1.75
5	Switzerland	1.85
6	United States	1.90
7	Ireland	1.95
7	Luxembourg	1.95
7	Taiwan	1.95
7	United Kingdom	1.95
11	Bahamas	2.00
12	Czech Republic	2.05
12	Japan	2.05
14	Australia	2.10
14	Belgium	2.10
14	Canada	2.10
14	United Arab Emirates	2.10
18	Austria	2.15
18	Chile	2.15
18	Estonia	2.15
18	Netherlands	2.15
22	Denmark	2.25
22	El Salvador	2.25
22	Finland	2.25
25	Germany	2.30
25	Iceland	2.30
27	Norway	2.35
28	Korea, South	2.40
28	Kuwait	2.40
28	Malaysia	2.40
28	Panama	2.40
28	Thailand	2.40
33	Sweden	2.45
34	Argentina	2.50
34	France	2.50
34	Italy	2.50
34	Spain	2.50
38	Portugal	2.55
38	Sri Lanka	2.55
38	Trinidad and Tobago	2.55
41	Barbados	2.60
41	Peru	2.60
43	Bolivia	2.65
43	Mauritius	2.65
45	Cyprus	2.70
45	Jamaica	2.70
45	Uruguay	2.70
48	Botswana	2.75
48	Guatemala	2.75
48	Jordan	2.75
48	Namibia	2.75
48	Oman	2.75
48	Philippines	2.75
54	Belize	2.80
54	Costa Rica	2.80
54	Israel	2.80
54	Swaziland	2.80
54	Turkey	2.80
54	Uganda	2.80
54	Samoa	2.80
61	Latvia	2.85
62	Greece	2.90
62	Hungary	2.90
62	So. Africa	2.90
65	Ecuador	2.95
65	Gabon	2.95
65	Indonesia	2.95
65	Malta	2.95
65	Morocco	2.95
65	Poland	2.95
65	Tunisia	2.95
72	Ghana	3.00
72	Lithuania	3.00
72	Saudi Arabia	3.00
75	Benin	3.05
75	Kenya	3.05
75	Paraguay	3.05
75	Qatar	3.05
75	Slovak Republic	3.05
75	Zambia	3.05
81	Colombia	3.10
81	Fiji	3.10
81	Mali	3.10
81	Slovenia	3.10
85	Honduras	3.15
85	Mexico	3.15
85	Papua New Guinea	3.15
88	Djibouti	3.20
88	Mongolia	3.20
90	Algeria	3.25
90	Brazil	3.25
90	Lebanon	3.25
90	Senegal	3.25
90	Tanzania	3.25
95	Nigeria	3.30
95	Romania	3.30
97	Cambodia	3.35
97	Dominican Republic	3.35
97	Egypt	3.35
97	Guinea	3.35
97	Ivory Coast	3.35
97	Moldova	3.35
97	Pakistan	3.35
104	Nepal	3.40
104	Venezuela	3.40
106	Armenia	3.45
106	Bulgaria	3.45
106	Lesotho	3.45
106	Madagascar	3.45
106	Russia	3.45
111	Burkina Faso	3.50
111	Cameroon	3.50
111	Guyana	3.50
111	Nicaragua	3.50
115	Gambia	3.60
116	Croatia	3.65
116	Georgia	3.65
116	Malawi	3.65
119	Cape Verde	3.67
120	Ethiopia	3.70
120	India	3.70
120	Niger	3.70
123	Congo	3.75
124	Chad	3.80
124	China	3.80
124	Mauritania	3.80
124	Ukraine	3.80
124	Zimbabwe	3.80
129	Albania	3.85
129	Bangladesh	3.85
129	Mozambique	3.85
129	Suriname	3.85
133	Burundi	3.90
134	Togo	3.95
135	Haiti	4.00
135	Kyrgyz Rep.	4.00
137	Kazakhstan	4.05
137	Sierra Leone	4.05
139	Yemen	4.10
140	Belarus	4.15
141	Sudan	4.20
141	Syria	4.20
143	Azerbaijan	4.30
143	Equatorial Guinea	4.30
143	Myanmar	4.30
143	Rwanda	4.30
147	Tajikistan	4.40
147	Uzbekistan	4.40
149	Angola	4.45
149	Turkmenistan	4.45
151	Guinea-Bissau	4.55
152	Vietnam	4.60
153	Congo (Zaire)	4.70
153	Iran	4.70
155	Bosnia	4.80
155	Somalia	4.80
157	Iraq	4.90
157	Laos	4.90
157	Libya	4.90
160	Cuba	5.00
160	Korea, North	5.00

MONETARY POLICY
Score: 1–Stable (very low level of inflation)

Singapore's average annual rate of inflation from 1986 to 1996 was 2.8 percent. The rate was 2 percent in 1997.

CAPITAL FLOWS AND FOREIGN INVESTMENT
Score: 1–Stable (very low barriers)

Investment laws in Singapore are clear and fair, and pose few problems for business. Foreign and domestic businesses are treated equally under the investment laws, and there are no production or local content requirements. According to the Economist Intelligence Unit, "Restrictions on equity, licensing and joint ventures are negligible."[2]

BANKING
Score: 2–Stable (low level of restrictions)

Foreign banks are restricted as to the number of branches and automated teller machines they may operate, mainly because of bank overcrowding. Even though it has just under 3.6 million people, Singapore has over 150 foreign banks—more than the number of domestic banks (there are six local banking groups). All banks may participate in securities exchanges, sell insurance policies, engage in some real estate ventures, and invest in industrial firms. It is easy to form new banks.

WAGE AND PRICE CONTROLS
Score: 1–Stable (very low level)

The market sets almost all wages and prices. There is no minimum wage.

PROPERTY RIGHTS
Score: 1–Stable (very high level of protection)

Singapore has a solid history of protecting private property, and there is no threat of expropriation. The court system is highly efficient and strongly protects private property.

REGULATION
Score: 1–Stable (very low level)

Obtaining a business license can be easy. Government regulations are straightforward, and corruption is nonexistent. Occupational safety and health regulations are not burdensome, and there are no antitrust regulations. The government does not tolerate price gouging, however, and will act to eliminate such practices whenever it finds them.

BLACK MARKET
Score: 1–Stable (very low level of activity)

The size of Singapore's black market is very small. The levels of smuggling and black market activity in pirated intellectual property are negligible.

NOTES

[1] Some economists suggest that the existence of government-linked companies (GLCs) in Singapore constitutes a significant intervention of the government in the economy. As the consumption of GDP figures for Singapore show, however, these companies consume very little of the country's economic output. In fact, most of the GLCs are either joint ventures with private companies or a mixture of private companies and government holding companies. Because government consumption of GDP figures are so low, it would appear that the GLCs are not a drain on Singapore's budget and thus do not constitute a significant intervention in the output of the economy. The explanation for this apparent anomaly could be either that the GLCs are profitable, in which case they are not a drain on the government's budget, or that their earnings are not being reflected accurately in the government's budget figures. In either case, neither the level of government ownership nor its level of expenditures for the GLCs is known exactly; therefore, until the extent of the government's involvement in the GLCs is known with greater accuracy, Singapore is graded solely on the level of government consumption as a percentage of GDP, which remains very low by global standards.

[2] Economist Intelligence Unit, *ILT Reports, Singapore,* May 1997, p. 8.

Slovak Republic 3.05

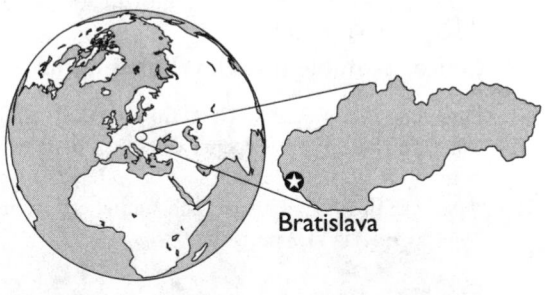

Bratislava

1998 Score: **3.05**	1997 Score: **3.05**	1996 Score: **2.95**

Trade	3	Banking	3
Taxation	4.5	Wages and Prices	3
Government Intervention	3	Property Rights	3
Monetary Policy	2	Regulation	3
Foreign Investment	3	Black Market	3

The Slovak Republic's split from the Czech Republic in 1993 left much of its banking, experienced personnel, data analysis capability, and competitive industry across the border. In addition to its struggle to transform its centrally controlled economy into a market-based economy, the Slovak Republic has had to create a democratic government. Reform has been slower in the Slovak Republic than in the Czech Republic. Although the Slovak Republic experienced a few years of economic growth following its split from the Czech Republic, the domestic policies of Prime Minister Vladimir Meciar prevented the country from being included in the first wave of former Warsaw Pact countries to join the North Atlantic Treaty Organization and the European Union. These policies included restrictions on the freedom of speech and infringement on the rights of the country's large Hungarian minority. Meciar announced his retirement from politics after his party won only a narrow majority in September 1998 elections. As of this writing, a coalition government had not yet been formed.

TRADE POLICY
Score: 3–Stable (moderate level of protectionism)

The Slovak Republic's average tariff rate is about 6 percent.[1] Import licensing requirements, according to the U.S. Department of State, are not burdensome: "For most of the approximately 100 groups of items in the 'general' category, obtaining a license is a formality."[2] In an attempt to curb its mounting trade deficit, however, the government established a requirement that importers place 20 percent of an import's value in an interest-bearing account for 180 days. it recently replaced this requirement with a 7 percent surcharge on the value of all imported items.

TAXATION
Score–Income taxation: 4–Stable (high tax rates)
Score–Corporate taxation: 4–Stable (high tax rates)
Final Taxation Score: 4.5–Stable (high tax rates)

The Slovak Republic's top marginal income tax rate is 42 percent, with the average taxpayer subject to a rate of about 20 percent. The top corporate income tax rate is 40 percent. The government also levies a 40 percent capital gains tax, a 23 percent value-added tax, and a 38 percent social contributions tax.

GOVERNMENT INTERVENTION IN THE ECONOMY
Score: 3–Stable (moderate level)

Government consumes 24 percent of GDP. The Slovak Republic has undergone significant privatization: The government has sold most smaller state-owned enterprises, and it is trying to privatize many of the larger ones. Although the private sector is the largest part of the economy, the state still produces some 35 percent of GDP.

1	Hong Kong	1.25	81	Fiji	3.10
2	Singapore	1.30	81	Mali	3.10
3	Bahrain	1.70	81	Slovenia	3.10
4	New Zealand	1.75	85	Honduras	3.15
5	Switzerland	1.85	85	Mexico	3.15
6	United States	1.90	85	Papua New Guinea	3.15
7	Ireland	1.95	88	Djibouti	3.20
7	Luxembourg	1.95	88	Mongolia	3.20
7	Taiwan	1.95	90	Brazil	3.25
7	United Kingdom	1.95	90	Algeria	3.25
11	Bahamas	2.00	90	Lebanon	3.25
12	Czech Republic	2.05	90	Senegal	3.25
12	Japan	2.05	90	Tanzania	3.25
14	Australia	2.10	95	Nigeria	3.30
14	Belgium	2.10	95	Romania	3.30
14	Canada	2.10	97	Cambodia	3.35
14	United Arab Emirates	2.10	97	Dominican Republic	3.35
18	Austria	2.15	97	Egypt	3.35
18	Chile	2.15	97	Guinea	3.35
18	Estonia	2.15	97	Ivory Coast	3.35
18	Netherlands	2.15	97	Moldova	3.35
22	Denmark	2.25	97	Pakistan	3.35
22	El Salvador	2.25	104	Nepal	3.40
22	Finland	2.25	104	Venezuela	3.40
25	Germany	2.30	106	Armenia	3.45
25	Iceland	2.30	106	Bulgaria	3.45
27	Norway	2.35	106	Lesotho	3.45
28	Korea, South	2.40	106	Madagascar	3.45
28	Kuwait	2.40	106	Russia	3.45
28	Malaysia	2.40	111	Burkina Faso	3.50
28	Panama	2.40	111	Cameroon	3.50
28	Thailand	2.40	111	Guyana	3.50
33	Sweden	2.45	111	Nicaragua	3.50
34	Argentina	2.50	115	Gambia	3.60
34	France	2.50	116	Croatia	3.65
34	Italy	2.50	116	Georgia	3.65
34	Spain	2.50	116	Malawi	3.65
38	Portugal	2.55	119	Cape Verde	3.67
38	Sri Lanka	2.55	120	Ethiopia	3.70
38	Trinidad and Tobago	2.55	120	India	3.70
41	Barbados	2.60	120	Niger	3.70
41	Peru	2.60	123	Congo	3.75
43	Bolivia	2.65	124	Chad	3.80
43	Mauritius	2.65	124	China	3.80
45	Cyprus	2.70	124	Mauritania	3.80
45	Jamaica	2.70	124	Ukraine	3.80
45	Uruguay	2.70	124	Zimbabwe	3.80
48	Botswana	2.75	129	Albania	3.85
48	Guatemala	2.75	129	Bangladesh	3.85
48	Jordan	2.75	129	Mozambique	3.85
48	Namibia	2.75	129	Suriname	3.85
48	Oman	2.75	133	Burundi	3.90
48	Philippines	2.75	134	Togo	3.95
54	Belize	2.80	135	Haiti	4.00
54	Costa Rica	2.80	135	Kyrgyz Rep.	4.00
54	Israel	2.80	137	Kazakhstan	4.05
54	Swaziland	2.80	137	Sierra Leone	4.05
54	Turkey	2.80	139	Yemen	4.10
54	Uganda	2.80	140	Belarus	4.15
54	Samoa	2.80	141	Sudan	4.20
61	Latvia	2.85	141	Syria	4.20
62	Greece	2.90	143	Azerbaijan	4.30
62	Hungary	2.90	143	Equatorial Guinea	4.30
62	So. Africa	2.90	143	Myanmar	4.30
65	Ecuador	2.95	143	Rwanda	4.30
65	Gabon	2.95	147	Tajikistan	4.40
65	Indonesia	2.95	147	Uzbekistan	4.40
65	Malta	2.95	149	Angola	4.45
65	Morocco	2.95	149	Turkmenistan	4.45
65	Poland	2.95	151	Guinea-Bissau	4.55
65	Tunisia	2.95	152	Vietnam	4.60
72	Ghana	3.00	153	Congo (Zaire)	4.70
72	Lithuania	3.00	153	Iran	4.70
72	Saudi Arabia	3.00	155	Bosnia	4.80
75	Benin	3.05	155	Somalia	4.80
75	Kenya	3.05	157	Iraq	4.90
75	Paraguay	3.05	157	Laos	4.90
75	Qatar	3.05	157	Libya	4.90
75	Slovak Republic	3.05	160	Cuba	5.00
75	Zambia	3.05	160	Korea, North	5.00
81	Colombia	3.10			

Mostly Unfree

MONETARY POLICY
Score: 2–Stable (low level of inflation)

Since becoming independent, the Slovak Republic has had inflation rates of 10 percent in 1992, 23 percent in 1993, 13 percent in 1994, 10 percent in 1995, 5.8 percent in 1996, and 6 percent in 1997.[3] The average annual rate of inflation from 1992 to 1997 is 11.3 percent.

CAPITAL FLOWS AND FOREIGN INVESTMENT
Score: 3–Stable (moderate barriers)

Foreign citizens may not own land in the Slovak Republic, but there are few other restrictions on foreign direct investment. Foreign and domestic firms are treated equally, and there is a well-established foreign investment code. Political instability caused by the populist Meciar government, however, has made the Slovak Republic less attractive to investors than the neighboring Czech Republic, Hungary, and Poland.

BANKING
Score: 3–Stable (moderate level of restrictions)

Permission from the Central Bank is required to open new banks, although this requirement has become a simple formality. Of the 29 banks operating in the Slovak Republic at the end of 1994, 10 were branches of foreign banks. The banking system has yet to become completely independent of government coercion and control.

WAGE AND PRICE CONTROLS
Score: 3–Stable (moderate level)

Almost 96 percent of the Slovak Republic's price controls have been removed, but controls on the prices of some products (for example, food, fuel, electricity, and heat) remain in effect. In 1994, the government imposed some restrictions on wages in certain money-losing state-owned industries. The Slovak Republic has a minimum wage.

PROPERTY RIGHTS
Score: 3–Stable (moderate level of protection)

Expropriation is unlikely in the Slovak Republic, which has a moderately efficient legal system. According to the U.S. Department of State, "The Constitution provides for courts that are independent, impartial, and separate from the other branches of government. Some critics allege, however, that the dependence of judges upon the Ministry of Justice for logistical support and other services undermines their independent status."[4]

REGULATION
Score: 3–Stable (moderate level)

The government has reduced its level of regulation, and most businesses do not need a license. But because political allies of the government control the remaining state-owned sector, private firms may find themselves subject to regulations that state-run firms are able to avoid.

BLACK MARKET
Score: 3–Stable (moderate level of activity)

The size of the black market remains fairly large. About 15 percent of the working public is employed in the informal sector.[5]

NOTES

[1]   U.S. Department of State, *Country Reports on Economic Policy and Trade Practices,* 1996, p. 270.
[2]   *Ibid.,* p. 269.
[3]   Based on consumer price inflation.
[4]   U.S. Department of State, "Slovak Republic Country Report on Human Rights Practices for 1997," 1998.
[5]   Economist Intelligence Unit, *EIU Country Profile, 1995–97.*

Slovenia   3.10

1998 Score: **3.10**	1997 Score: **3.10**		1996 Score: **3.35**

Trade	4	Banking	2
Taxation	4	Wages and Prices	3
Government Intervention	3	Property Rights	2
Monetary Policy	5	Regulation	3
Foreign Investment	2	Black Market	3

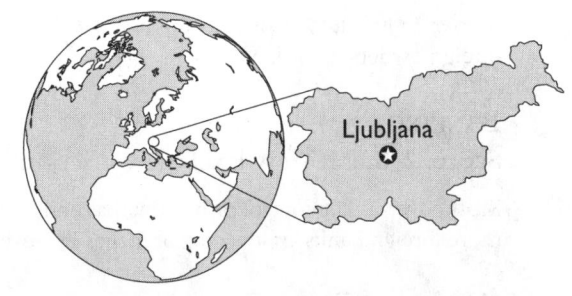

Since the breakup of the former Yugoslavia, Slovenia has pursued an economic liberalization policy aimed at promoting international trade, attracting private investment, and privatizing the state-owned sector. The government also has made substantial progress toward curbing inflation. Despite these advances, overall progress has been relatively slow, and many hurdles still exist. Slovenia recently opened its borders to foreign investment and improved its protection of private property. At the same time, however, the government increased its control of some industries. The political climate has been stable: President Milan Kucan has been president since1990 and Janez Drnovsek had been prime minister since 1992. The current government consists of a coalition of conservative, liberal, and pensioners parties.

TRADE POLICY
Score: 4–Stable (high level of protectionism)

Slovenia's average tariff rate is 13 percent. Non-tariff barriers take the form of quotas in textiles.

TAXATION
Score–Income taxation: 5–Stable (very high tax rates)
Score–Corporate taxation: 2–Stable (low tax rates)
Final Taxation Score: 4–Stable (high tax rates)

Slovenia's top income tax rate is 50 percent; the average taxpayer is in the 35 percent bracket. The top marginal corporate tax rate is 25 percent. Slovenia also has a 20 percent sales tax, among other additional taxes.

GOVERNMENT INTERVENTION IN THE ECONOMY
Score: 3–Stable (moderate level)

Government consumes about 20.8 percent of GDP, and the state sector generates a significant portion of GDP overall. The government remains heavily involved in the banking, transportation, and utility sectors.

MONETARY POLICY
Score: 5–Stable (very high level of inflation)

Slovenia has made substantial progress toward bringing down inflation. The rate of inflation was 201.3 percent in 1992, 32.3 percent in 1993, 19.8 percent in 1994, 12.6 percent in 1995, 9.7 percent in 1996, and 9 percent in 1997. Thus, from 1992 to 1997, the average annual rate of inflation was about 47 percent.

CAPITAL FLOWS AND FOREIGN INVESTMENT
Score: 2–Stable (low barriers)

The government allows foreign investment in most industries, although it requires that the managing director of a business be a Slovenian national. With foreign investment continuing to increase, this does not appear to be a significant

1	Hong Kong	1.25	81	Fiji	3.10
2	Singapore	1.30	81	Mali	3.10
3	Bahrain	1.70	81	Slovenia	3.10
4	New Zealand	1.75	85	Honduras	3.15
5	Switzerland	1.85	85	Mexico	3.15
6	United States	1.90	85	Papua New Guinea	3.15
7	Ireland	1.95	88	Djibouti	3.20
7	Luxembourg	1.95	88	Mongolia	3.20
7	Taiwan	1.95	90	Algeria	3.25
7	United Kingdom	1.95	90	Brazil	3.25
11	Bahamas	2.00	90	Lebanon	3.25
12	Czech Republic	2.05	90	Senegal	3.25
12	Japan	2.05	90	Tanzania	3.25
14	Australia	2.10	95	Nigeria	3.30
14	Belgium	2.10	95	Romania	3.30
14	Canada	2.10	97	Cambodia	3.35
14	United Arab Emirates	2.10	97	Dominican Republic	3.35
18	Austria	2.15	97	Egypt	3.35
18	Chile	2.15	97	Guinea	3.35
18	Estonia	2.15	97	Ivory Coast	3.35
18	Netherlands	2.15	97	Moldova	3.35
22	Denmark	2.25	97	Pakistan	3.35
22	El Salvador	2.25	104	Nepal	3.40
22	Finland	2.25	104	Venezuela	3.40
25	Germany	2.30	106	Armenia	3.45
25	Iceland	2.30	106	Bulgaria	3.45
27	Norway	2.35	106	Lesotho	3.45
28	Korea, South	2.40	106	Madagascar	3.45
28	Kuwait	2.40	106	Russia	3.45
28	Malaysia	2.40	111	Burkina Faso	3.50
28	Panama	2.40	111	Cameroon	3.50
28	Thailand	2.40	111	Guyana	3.50
33	Sweden	2.45	111	Nicaragua	3.50
34	Argentina	2.50	115	Gambia	3.60
34	France	2.50	116	Croatia	3.65
34	Italy	2.50	116	Georgia	3.65
34	Spain	2.50	116	Malawi	3.65
38	Portugal	2.55	119	Cape Verde	3.67
38	Sri Lanka	2.55	120	Ethiopia	3.70
38	Trinidad and Tobago	2.55	120	India	3.70
41	Barbados	2.60	120	Niger	3.70
41	Peru	2.60	123	Congo	3.75
43	Bolivia	2.65	124	Chad	3.80
43	Mauritius	2.65	124	China	3.80
45	Cyprus	2.70	124	Mauritania	3.80
45	Jamaica	2.70	124	Ukraine	3.80
45	Uruguay	2.70	124	Zimbabwe	3.80
48	Botswana	2.75	129	Albania	3.85
48	Guatemala	2.75	129	Bangladesh	3.85
48	Jordan	2.75	129	Mozambique	3.85
48	Namibia	2.75	129	Suriname	3.85
48	Oman	2.75	133	Burundi	3.90
48	Philippines	2.75	134	Togo	3.95
54	Belize	2.80	135	Haiti	4.00
54	Costa Rica	2.80	135	Kyrgyz Rep.	4.00
54	Israel	2.80	137	Kazakhstan	4.05
54	Swaziland	2.80	137	Sierra Leone	4.05
54	Turkey	2.80	139	Yemen	4.10
54	Uganda	2.80	140	Belarus	4.15
54	Samoa	2.80	141	Sudan	4.20
61	Latvia	2.85	141	Syria	4.20
62	Greece	2.90	143	Azerbaijan	4.30
62	Hungary	2.90	143	Equatorial Guinea	4.30
62	So. Africa	2.90	143	Myanmar	4.30
65	Ecuador	2.95	143	Rwanda	4.30
65	Gabon	2.95	147	Tajikistan	4.40
65	Indonesia	2.95	147	Uzbekistan	4.40
65	Malta	2.95	149	Angola	4.45
65	Morocco	2.95	149	Turkmenistan	4.45
65	Poland	2.95	151	Guinea-Bissau	4.55
65	Tunisia	2.95	152	Vietnam	4.60
72	Ghana	3.00	153	Congo (Zaire)	4.70
72	Lithuania	3.00	153	Iran	4.70
72	Saudi Arabia	3.00	155	Bosnia	4.80
75	Benin	3.05	155	Somalia	4.80
75	Kenya	3.05	157	Iraq	4.90
75	Paraguay	3.05	157	Laos	4.90
75	Qatar	3.05	157	Libya	4.90
75	Slovak Republic	3.05	160	Cuba	5.00
75	Zambia	3.05	160	Korea, North	5.00
81	Colombia	3.10			

Mostly Unfree

barrier. In July 1997, Slovenia eliminated its law barring foreign ownership of land.

BANKING
Score: 2–Stable (low level of restrictions)

Most government control of banking has ended. As a result, more foreign banks are opening branches in Slovenia.

WAGE AND PRICE CONTROLS
Score: 3–Stable (moderate level of wage and price controls)

The market drives wages and prices, but price controls continue on such items as electricity, gas, and tele-communications. Slovenia has a minimum wage.

PROPERTY RIGHTS
Score: 2–Stable (high level of protection)

Private property is guaranteed by Slovenia's constitution. The country has made significant progress toward reforming its judicial system by making it more independent and more efficient. According to the U.S. Department of State,

"The Constitution provides for an independent judiciary, and the Government respects this provision in practice.... The Constitution provides great detail for the right to a fair trial, including provisions for: Equality before the law, presumption of innocence, due process, open court proceedings, guarantees of appeal, and a prohibition against double jeopardy. These rights are respected in practice."[1]

REGULATION
Score: 3–Stable (moderate level)

Establishing a business is becoming easier, and the number of private businesses is growing. An entrenched and sometimes inefficient bureaucracy continues to hinder the rapid growth of a free market.

BLACK MARKET
Score: 3–Stable (moderate level of activity)

Slovenia has a large black market, primarily because of high tariffs. Black market activity also results from government control of the transportation industry. Slovenia has made significant progress toward protecting intellectual property, however, and piracy has been curtailed significantly.

NOTE
[1]   U.S. Department of State, "Slovenia Country Report on Human Rights Practices for 1997," 1998.

Somalia   4.80

1998 Score: 4.70	**1997 Score: 4.70**	**1996 Score: 4.70**	

Trade	5	Banking	5
Taxation	5	Wages and Prices	4
Government Intervention	5	Property Rights	5
Monetary Policy	5	Regulation	5
Foreign Investment	4	Black Market	5

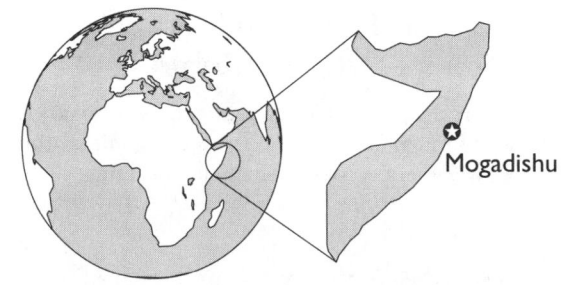

Mogadishu

Modern-day Somalia was established in 1960 when British Somaliland gained its independence from the United Kingdom and joined Italian Somaliland, an Italian-administered United Nations trusteeship that also gained independence that year. Somalia's primarily agricultural economy has been devastated by civil war. There has been no central authority since the fall of Major General Muhammed Siad Barre's dictatorship in 1991. Local authority lies with regional militias, and no international recognition has been given either to the various self-proclaimed governments or to the breakaway northwest province claiming independence as the Republic of Somaliland. Over two dozen militia groups formed the National Salvation Council in 1997 to formalize a lasting peace agreement and establish a national government. So far, it has made little progress. Somalia remains one of the world's poorest countries, with an estimated per capita GNP of $150 in 1996. The pricing system has collapsed; as a result, the country's overall score is 0.1 point worse than last year.

TRADE POLICY
Score: 5–Stable (very high level of protectionism)

Tariff rates play a minor role in restricting imports and exports. The average tariff rate is over 30 percent, but the most significant impediment is the tendency of corrupt customs officials to confiscate goods for personal gain. Clan militias have destroyed what was left of a centralized customs service, although the government is trying to restore order.

TAXATION
Score–Income taxation: 5–Stable (very high tax rates)
Score–Corporate taxation: 5–Stable (very high tax rates)
Final Taxation Score: 5–Stable (very high tax rates)

Little is left of Somalia's centralized government. The country is run primarily by warlords who operate a primitive feudal system. Taxation often takes the form of confiscation of crops and private property, and it is not uncommon for citizens to be taxed by more than one group.

GOVERNMENT INTERVENTION IN THE ECONOMY
Score: 5–Stable (very high level)

Somalia has no official government and very little economic output. The entire economic system is in ruins. The level of crime, banditry, and looting—much of it carried out by warring clans and militias—makes it nearly impossible to conduct business activity.

MONETARY POLICY
Score: 5–Stable (very high level of inflation)

Somalia's average annual rate of inflation from 1985 to 1995 was over 70 percent. No data for 1996 or 1997 are available.

1	Hong Kong	1.25	
2	Singapore	1.30	
3	Bahrain	1.70	
4	New Zealand	1.75	
5	Switzerland	1.85	
6	United States	1.90	
7	Ireland	1.95	
7	Luxembourg	1.95	
7	Taiwan	1.95	
7	United Kingdom	1.95	
11	Bahamas	2.00	
12	Czech Republic	2.05	
12	Japan	2.05	
14	Australia	2.10	
14	Belgium	2.10	
14	Canada	2.10	
14	United Arab Emirates	2.10	
18	Austria	2.15	
18	Chile	2.15	
18	Estonia	2.15	
18	Netherlands	2.15	
22	Denmark	2.25	
22	El Salvador	2.25	
22	Finland	2.25	
25	Germany	2.30	
25	Iceland	2.30	
27	Norway	2.35	
28	Korea, South	2.40	
28	Kuwait	2.40	
28	Malaysia	2.40	
28	Panama	2.40	
28	Thailand	2.40	
33	Sweden	2.45	
34	Argentina	2.50	
34	France	2.50	
34	Italy	2.50	
34	Spain	2.50	
38	Portugal	2.55	
38	Sri Lanka	2.55	
38	Trinidad and Tobago	2.55	
41	Barbados	2.60	
41	Peru	2.60	
43	Bolivia	2.65	
43	Mauritius	2.65	
45	Cyprus	2.70	
45	Jamaica	2.70	
45	Uruguay	2.70	
48	Botswana	2.75	
48	Guatemala	2.75	
48	Jordan	2.75	
48	Namibia	2.75	
48	Oman	2.75	
48	Philippines	2.75	
54	Belize	2.80	
54	Costa Rica	2.80	
54	Israel	2.80	
54	Swaziland	2.80	
54	Turkey	2.80	
54	Uganda	2.80	
54	Samoa	2.80	
61	Latvia	2.85	
62	Greece	2.90	
62	Hungary	2.90	
62	So. Africa	2.90	
65	Ecuador	2.95	
65	Gabon	2.95	
65	Indonesia	2.95	
65	Malta	2.95	
65	Morocco	2.95	
65	Poland	2.95	
65	Tunisia	2.95	
72	Ghana	3.00	
72	Lithuania	3.00	
72	Saudi Arabia	3.00	
75	Benin	3.05	
75	Kenya	3.05	
75	Paraguay	3.05	
75	Qatar	3.05	
75	Slovak Republic	3.05	
75	Zambia	3.05	
81	Colombia	3.10	
81	Fiji	3.10	
81	Mali	3.10	
81	Slovenia	3.10	
85	Honduras	3.15	
85	Mexico	3.15	
85	Papua New Guinea	3.15	
88	Djibouti	3.20	
88	Mongolia	3.20	
90	Algeria	3.25	
90	Brazil	3.25	
90	Lebanon	3.25	
90	Senegal	3.25	
90	Tanzania	3.25	
95	Nigeria	3.30	
95	Romania	3.30	
97	Cambodia	3.35	
97	Dominican Republic	3.35	
97	Egypt	3.35	
97	Guinea	3.35	
97	Ivory Coast	3.35	
97	Moldova	3.35	
97	Pakistan	3.35	
104	Nepal	3.40	
104	Venezuela	3.40	
106	Armenia	3.45	
106	Bulgaria	3.45	
106	Lesotho	3.45	
106	Madagascar	3.45	
106	Russia	3.45	
111	Burkina Faso	3.50	
111	Cameroon	3.50	
111	Guyana	3.50	
111	Nicaragua	3.50	
115	Gambia	3.60	
116	Croatia	3.65	
116	Georgia	3.65	
116	Malawi	3.65	
119	Cape Verde	3.67	
120	Ethiopia	3.70	
120	India	3.70	
120	Niger	3.70	
123	Congo	3.75	
124	Chad	3.80	
124	China	3.80	
124	Mauritania	3.80	
124	Ukraine	3.80	
124	Zimbabwe	3.80	
129	Albania	3.85	
129	Bangladesh	3.85	
129	Mozambique	3.85	
129	Suriname	3.85	
133	Burundi	3.90	
134	Togo	3.95	
135	Haiti	4.00	
135	Kyrgyz Rep.	4.00	
137	Kazakhstan	4.05	
137	Sierra Leone	4.05	
139	Yemen	4.10	
140	Belarus	4.15	
141	Sudan	4.20	
141	Syria	4.20	
143	Azerbaijan	4.30	
143	Equatorial Guinea	4.30	
143	Myanmar	4.30	
143	Rwanda	4.30	
147	Tajikistan	4.40	
147	Uzbekistan	4.40	
149	Angola	4.45	
149	Turkmenistan	4.45	
151	Guinea-Bissau	4.55	
152	Vietnam	4.60	
153	Congo (Zaire)	4.70	
153	Iran	4.70	
155	Bosnia	4.80	
155	Somalia	4.80	
157	Iraq	4.90	
157	Laos	4.90	
157	Libya	4.90	
160	Cuba	5.00	
160	Korea, North	5.00	

Repressed

CAPITAL FLOWS AND FOREIGN INVESTMENT
Score: 4–Stable (high barriers)

Somalia remains in economic ruins, with no clear protection of foreign investment. The most significant threat to foreign investment is continued military fighting.

BANKING
Score: 5–Stable (very high level of restrictions)

Somalia's banking system has collapsed, and banks operate in primitive conditions. Most lending is performed unofficially among family members and friends, some of whom reside in other countries.

WAGE AND PRICE CONTROLS
Score: 4– (high level)

The pricing system has collapsed; most economic trading occurs through barter. Moreover, large sums of international aid have distorted market pricing to the extent that it rarely exists at all. The few wages and prices that do exist are usually determined by the local warlords. As a result, Somalia's score for this factor is 1 point worse than last year.

PROPERTY RIGHTS
Score: 5–Stable (very low level of protection)

Private property is virtually nonexistent in Somalia, and clans and corrupt government officials often confiscate property. The U.S. Department of State reports, "There is no national judicial system."[1]

REGULATION
Score: 5–Stable (very high level)

Although the lack of a national government means that there are few formal government regulations left, informal regulations exist nonetheless. Corruption is rampant and local warlords often pillage what little economic activity still manages to occur.

BLACK MARKET
Score: 5–Stable (very high level of activity)

Most economic activity occurs in the black market.

NOTE
[1]   U.S. Department of State, "Somalia Country Report on Human Rights Practices for 1997," 1998.

South Africa 2.90

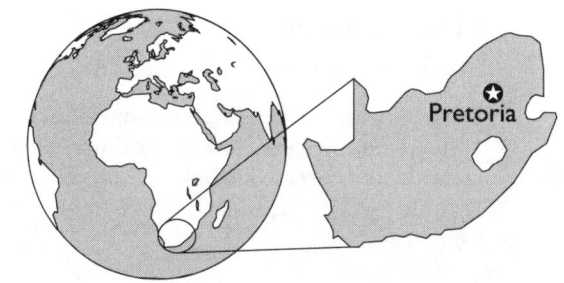

1998 Score: **2.90**	1997 Score: **3.00**	1996 Score: **3.00**

Trade	4	Banking	3
Taxation	4	Wages and Prices	2
Government Intervention	3	Property Rights	3
Monetary Policy	2	Regulation	2
Foreign Investment	2	Black Market	4

South Africa's transition from apartheid to democracy has gone well, but racial issues remain a significant political concern. South Africa enjoys many economic assets, including a modern infrastructure, plentiful natural resources, and the most developed communications, energy, financial, and legal structures in Africa. Emigration of educated and skilled workers is a concern, however. The African National Congress, which is expected to retain the presidency and control of the National Assembly after the 1999 elections, has wavered in its commitment to economic liberalization, fiscal austerity, and privatization after criticism from allied parties and trade unions. Actions to curb unemployment have been unsuccessful, and nearly 30 percent of the economically active population remains unemployed. As a result, economic growth, which has averaged over 2.7 percent since 1994, is expected to slow. South Africa's rate of inflation is shrinking, but the size of its black market is growing. Because these two score changes cancel each other out, South Africa's overall score remains unchanged from last year.

TRADE POLICY
Score: 4–Stable (high level of protectionism)

South Africa's average tariff rate now is 12 percent,[1] down from an average of 21 percent in 1993.[2] According to the U.S. Department of State, "Under terms of the Import and Export Control Act of 1963, South Africa's Minister of Trade and Industry may act in the national interest to prohibit, ration, or otherwise regulate imports. In recent years, the list of restricted goods requiring import permits has been reduced, but still includes such goods as foodstuffs, clothing, fabrics, wood and paper products, refined petroleum products and chemicals."[3]

TAXATION
Score–Income taxation: 4–Stable (high tax rates)
Score–Corporate taxation: 3–Stable (moderate tax rates)
Final Taxation Score: 4–Stable (high tax rates)

South Africa has a progressive tax system, with the highest income level taxed at a rate of 45 percent and the average income level taxed at a rate of 19 percent. The corporate tax is 35 percent. South Africa also has a 14 percent value-added tax, a financial services tax, and regional taxes.

GOVERNMENT INTERVENTION IN THE ECONOMY
Score: 3–Stable (moderate level)

Government consumes 20.8 percent of GDP, and 6 state-owned companies rank among the country's 25 largest firms. State assets include the national airline and electric utilities. The government is studying the possible "reconstruction" of state-owned enterprises.

1	Hong Kong	1.25	81	Fiji	3.10
2	Singapore	1.30	81	Mali	3.10
3	Bahrain	1.70	81	Slovenia	3.10
4	New Zealand	1.75	85	Honduras	3.15
5	Switzerland	1.85	85	Mexico	3.15
6	United States	1.90	85	Papua New Guinea	3.15
7	Ireland	1.95	88	Djibouti	3.20
7	Luxembourg	1.95	88	Mongolia	3.20
7	Taiwan	1.95	90	Algeria	3.25
7	United Kingdom	1.95	90	Brazil	3.25
11	Bahamas	2.00	90	Lebanon	3.25
12	Czech Republic	2.05	90	Senegal	3.25
12	Japan	2.05	90	Tanzania	3.25
14	Australia	2.10	95	Nigeria	3.30
14	Belgium	2.10	95	Romania	3.30
14	Canada	2.10	97	Cambodia	3.35
14	United Arab Emirates	2.10	97	Dominican Republic	3.35
18	Austria	2.15	97	Egypt	3.35
18	Chile	2.15	97	Guinea	3.35
18	Estonia	2.15	97	Ivory Coast	3.35
18	Netherlands	2.15	97	Moldova	3.35
22	Denmark	2.25	97	Pakistan	3.35
22	El Salvador	2.25	104	Nepal	3.40
22	Finland	2.25	104	Venezuela	3.40
25	Germany	2.30	106	Armenia	3.45
25	Iceland	2.30	106	Bulgaria	3.45
27	Norway	2.35	106	Lesotho	3.45
28	Korea, South	2.40	106	Madagascar	3.45
28	Kuwait	2.40	106	Russia	3.45
28	Malaysia	2.40	111	Burkina Faso	3.50
28	Panama	2.40	111	Cameroon	3.50
28	Thailand	2.40	111	Guyana	3.50
33	Sweden	2.45	111	Nicaragua	3.50
34	Argentina	2.50	115	Gambia	3.60
34	France	2.50	116	Croatia	3.65
34	Italy	2.50	116	Georgia	3.65
34	Spain	2.50	116	Malawi	3.65
38	Portugal	2.55	119	Cape Verde	3.67
38	Sri Lanka	2.55	120	Ethiopia	3.70
38	Trinidad and Tobago	2.55	120	India	3.70
41	Barbados	2.60	120	Niger	3.70
41	Peru	2.60	123	Congo	3.75
43	Bolivia	2.65	124	Chad	3.80
43	Mauritius	2.65	124	China	3.80
45	Cyprus	2.70	124	Mauritania	3.80
45	Jamaica	2.70	124	Ukraine	3.80
45	Uruguay	2.70	124	Zimbabwe	3.80
48	Botswana	2.75	129	Albania	3.85
48	Guatemala	2.75	129	Bangladesh	3.85
48	Jordan	2.75	129	Mozambique	3.85
48	Namibia	2.75	129	Suriname	3.85
48	Oman	2.75	133	Burundi	3.90
48	Philippines	2.75	134	Togo	3.95
54	Belize	2.80	135	Haiti	4.00
54	Costa Rica	2.80	135	Kyrgyz Rep.	4.00
54	Israel	2.80	137	Kazakhstan	4.05
54	Swaziland	2.80	137	Sierra Leone	4.05
54	Turkey	2.80	139	Yemen	4.10
54	Uganda	2.80	140	Belarus	4.15
54	Samoa	2.80	141	Sudan	4.20
61	Latvia	2.85	141	Syria	4.20
62	Greece	2.90	143	Azerbaijan	4.30
62	Hungary	2.90	143	Equatorial Guinea	4.30
62	So. Africa	2.90	143	Myanmar	4.30
65	Ecuador	2.95	143	Rwanda	4.30
65	Gabon	2.95	147	Tajikistan	4.40
65	Indonesia	2.95	147	Uzbekistan	4.40
65	Malta	2.95	149	Angola	4.45
65	Morocco	2.95	149	Turkmenistan	4.45
65	Poland	2.95	151	Guinea-Bissau	4.55
65	Tunisia	2.95	152	Vietnam	4.60
72	Ghana	3.00	153	Congo (Zaire)	4.70
72	Lithuania	3.00	153	Iran	4.70
72	Saudi Arabia	3.00	155	Bosnia	4.80
75	Benin	3.05	155	Somalia	4.80
75	Kenya	3.05	157	Iraq	4.90
75	Paraguay	3.05	157	Laos	4.90
75	Qatar	3.05	157	Libya	4.90
75	Slovak Republic	3.05	160	Cuba	5.00
75	Zambia	3.05	160	Korea, North	5.00
81	Colombia	3.10			

Mostly Free

MONETARY POLICY
Score: 2+ (low level of inflation)

South Africa's average annual rate of inflation from 1986 to 1996 was 13.1 percent, down from almost 14 percent annually from 1985 to 1995. As a result, its score in this factor is 1 point better than last year. In 1997, the rate was 8.6 percent.

CAPITAL FLOWS AND FOREIGN INVESTMENT
Score: 2–Stable (low barriers)

No government approval is required for foreign investment, and foreign investors are subject to the same laws as domestic investors. In addition, there are no requirements for South African participation in management; only a few areas of the economy are reserved for South Africans, and foreign investors are free to acquire land. Foreign-controlled firms, however, are subject to domestic borrowing restrictions.

BANKING
Score: 3–Stable (moderate level of restrictions)

The government eliminated legal restrictions that discriminate against foreign-owned financial institutions, and over 30 foreign banks now operate in South Africa. The banking and insurance industries, however, are tightly controlled by the Reserve Bank, with which interest-free reserve balances must be deposited. Exchange controls preclude international investment by South African financial institutions. Licenses for new banks and insurance companies are not granted readily. The new government also may pressure banks into investing in its Reconstruction and Development Program, which is designed to promote the economic advancement of black South Africans.

WAGE AND PRICE CONTROLS
Score: 2–Stable (low level)

Price controls, once pervasive, now exist only on coal, gasoline, and some utilities. There is no national minimum wage, but labor legislation currently under consideration could lead to the de facto imposition of wage controls.

PROPERTY RIGHTS
Score: 3–Stable (moderate level of protection)

No private-sector company, whether South African or foreign-controlled, has been nationalized since the 1920s. The judiciary is both professional and effective. There is the danger, however, that redistributionist policies, including the land reform program, may weaken private property rights. Squatters and crime are problems, and the state may assume control of communal land controlled by tribes.

REGULATION
Score: 2–Stable (low level)

Regulation of economic activity is minimal. It takes only 4 to 10 days to incorporate a business, and most businesses can be started with a minimum of formalities. Licenses, required for certain activities, can be obtained with relative ease. There has been a proliferation of once-banned street vendors. The establishment of an affirmative action directorate within the Ministry of Labour is a sign that increased political pressure to practice more affirmative action in the hiring and firing of personnel can be expected.

BLACK MARKET
Score: 4– (high level of activity)

In 1991, the government lifted legal restrictions that prevented black South Africans from owning businesses, obtaining skilled jobs, or living in major urban centers. There still is significant informal activity, however, in retail textiles and pirated intellectual property. Piracy accounts for as much as 58 percent of the trade in computer software. Moreover, new estimates show that the size of the black market is quite large;[4] as a result, South Africa's black market score is 1 point worse this year.

NOTES

[1] South Africa is a member of the Southern African Customs Union, which has a common external tariff of 12 percent. Other members include Botswana, Lesotho, Namibia, and Swaziland.

[2] Economist Intelligence Unit, *ILT Reports, South Africa,* February 1996, p. 27.

[3] U.S. Department of State, *Country Reports on Economic Policy and Trade Practices,* 1997, p. 14.

[4] See "30% of Companies Still Not Registered to Pay Tax," FT Asia Intelligence Wire, *International Market Insight Reports,* May 13, 1998.

Spain   2.50

1998 Score: **2.50**	1997 Score: **2.60**	1996 Score: **2.70**

Trade	2	Banking	2
Taxation	5	Wages and Prices	3
Government Intervention	2	Property Rights	2
Monetary Policy	2	Regulation	3
Foreign Investment	2	Black Market	2

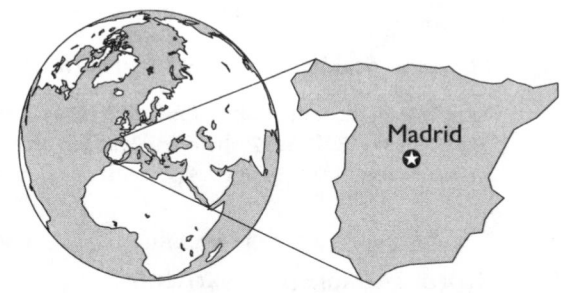

From the end of the Spanish Civil War until 1975, Spain was ruled by Francisco Franco. Following the accession of King Juan Carlos, it became a constitutional monarchy with a parliamentary government. Because of its years under dictatorship, Spain's economy lags behind those of many of its European neighbors. Since joining the European Union (EU) in 1986, the government has opened the economy, removed oppressive, government-run bureaucracies from many economic decisions, and expanded the free market. In March 1996, dissatisfied with a multiyear recession and official corruption under the Socialist Party, Spain elected a new, conservative government headed by Prime Minister José Maria Aznar of the Popular Party. The Aznar government is accelerating economic reform. As Spain scrambles to meet its EU directives and liberalize large sections of its economy, it is enjoying lower unemployment and stronger economic growth. The government has liberalized the banking sector, making it more accessible to foreign investment. Aznar also has begun to liberalize Spain's highly regulated labor market to lower unemployment, and the government has pledged additional privatizations.

TRADE POLICY
Score: 2–Stable (low level of protectionism)

Spain has an average tariff rate of about 3.6 percent. It also maintains restrictive customs procedures, strict labeling and testing requirements, and many other non-tariff barriers.

TAXATION
Score–Income taxation: 5–Stable (very high tax rates)
Score–Corporate taxation: 3–Stable (moderate tax rates)
Final Taxation Score: 5–Stable (very high tax rates)

Spain's top income tax rate is 56 percent, and the average income level is taxed at 23 percent. The top corporate rate is 35 percent. Spain also has a 35 percent capital gains tax and a 4 percent to 16 percent value-added tax.

GOVERNMENT INTERVENTION IN THE ECONOMY
Score: 2–Stable (Low level)

Government consumes 16.2 percent of GDP, and state ownership of industry remains extensive. According to the Economist Intelligence Unit, "State ownership remains extensive in Spanish industry, utilities, public services, and transport facilities, although it has been reduced significantly by a privatization program pursued since the mid-1980s."[1] The Aznar government is accelerating the privatization of state-owned industries. By global standards, Spain's overall level of government intervention in the economy is low.

1	Hong Kong	1.25	81	Fiji	3.10
2	Singapore	1.30	81	Mali	3.10
3	Bahrain	1.70	81	Slovenia	3.10
4	New Zealand	1.75	85	Honduras	3.15
5	Switzerland	1.85	85	Mexico	3.15
6	United States	1.90	85	Papua New Guinea	3.15
7	Ireland	1.95	88	Djibouti	3.20
7	Luxembourg	1.95	88	Mongolia	3.20
7	Taiwan	1.95	90	Algeria	3.25
7	United Kingdom	1.95	90	Brazil	3.25
11	Bahamas	2.00	90	Lebanon	3.25
12	Czech Republic	2.05	90	Senegal	3.25
12	Japan	2.05	90	Tanzania	3.25
14	Australia	2.10	95	Nigeria	3.30
14	Belgium	2.10	95	Romania	3.30
14	Canada	2.10	97	Cambodia	3.35
14	United Arab Emirates	2.10	97	Dominican Republic	3.35
18	Austria	2.15	97	Egypt	3.35
18	Chile	2.15	97	Guinea	3.35
18	Estonia	2.15	97	Ivory Coast	3.35
18	Netherlands	2.15	97	Moldova	3.35
22	Denmark	2.25	97	Pakistan	3.35
22	El Salvador	2.25	104	Nepal	3.40
22	Finland	2.25	104	Venezuela	3.40
25	Germany	2.30	106	Armenia	3.45
25	Iceland	2.30	106	Bulgaria	3.45
27	Norway	2.35	106	Lesotho	3.45
28	Korea, South	2.40	106	Madagascar	3.45
28	Kuwait	2.40	106	Russia	3.45
28	Malaysia	2.40	111	Burkina Faso	3.50
28	Panama	2.40	111	Cameroon	3.50
28	Thailand	2.40	111	Guyana	3.50
33	Sweden	2.45	111	Nicaragua	3.50
34	Argentina	2.50	115	Gambia	3.60
34	France	2.50	116	Croatia	3.65
34	Italy	2.50	116	Georgia	3.65
34	Spain	2.50	116	Malawi	3.65
38	Portugal	2.55	119	Cape Verde	3.67
38	Sri Lanka	2.55	120	Ethiopia	3.70
38	Trinidad and Tobago	2.55	120	India	3.70
41	Barbados	2.60	120	Niger	3.70
41	Peru	2.60	123	Congo	3.75
43	Bolivia	2.65	124	Chad	3.80
43	Mauritius	2.65	124	China	3.80
45	Cyprus	2.70	124	Mauritania	3.80
45	Jamaica	2.70	124	Ukraine	3.80
45	Uruguay	2.70	124	Zimbabwe	3.80
48	Botswana	2.75	129	Albania	3.85
48	Guatemala	2.75	129	Bangladesh	3.85
48	Jordan	2.75	129	Mozambique	3.85
48	Namibia	2.75	129	Suriname	3.85
48	Oman	2.75	133	Burundi	3.90
48	Philippines	2.75	134	Togo	3.95
54	Belize	2.80	135	Haiti	4.00
54	Costa Rica	2.80	135	Kyrgyz Rep.	4.00
54	Israel	2.80	137	Kazakhstan	4.05
54	Swaziland	2.80	137	Sierra Leone	4.05
54	Turkey	2.80	139	Yemen	4.10
54	Uganda	2.80	140	Belarus	4.15
54	Samoa	2.80	141	Sudan	4.20
61	Latvia	2.85	141	Syria	4.20
62	Greece	2.90	143	Azerbaijan	4.30
62	Hungary	2.90	143	Equatorial Guinea	4.30
62	So. Africa	2.90	143	Myanmar	4.30
65	Ecuador	2.95	143	Rwanda	4.30
65	Gabon	2.95	147	Tajikistan	4.40
65	Indonesia	2.95	147	Uzbekistan	4.40
65	Malta	2.95	149	Angola	4.45
65	Morocco	2.95	149	Turkmenistan	4.45
65	Poland	2.95	151	Guinea-Bissau	4.55
65	Tunisia	2.95	152	Vietnam	4.60
72	Ghana	3.00	153	Congo (Zaire)	4.70
72	Lithuania	3.00	153	Iran	4.70
72	Saudi Arabia	3.00	155	Bosnia	4.80
75	Benin	3.05	155	Somalia	4.80
75	Kenya	3.05	157	Iraq	4.90
75	Paraguay	3.05	157	Laos	4.90
75	Qatar	3.05	157	Libya	4.90
75	Slovak Republic	3.05	160	Cuba	5.00
75	Zambia	3.05	160	Korea, North	5.00
81	Colombia	3.10			

Mostly Free

MONETARY POLICY
Score: 2–Stable (low level of inflation)

Spain's average annual rate of inflation from 1986 to 1996 was 6.3 percent. In 1997, the rate fell to 2.2 percent. For most of 1998, it was about 2.4 percent.

CAPITAL FLOWS AND FOREIGN INVESTMENT
Score: 2–Stable (low barriers)

Membership in the EU has forced the government to remove most restrictions on foreign investment. Some restrictions remain, however, in such areas as telecommunications. According to the U.S. Department of Commerce, "The Spanish government is interested in attracting new foreign investment to modernize the economy. It has created new regulations for investment and foreign exchange to make the country more attractive to investors. Spanish law permits foreign investment of up to 100 percent of equity, except in a few strategic sectors. Capital movements have been completely liberalized."[2]

BANKING
Score: 2–Stable (low level of restrictions)

Integration into the EU has forced Spain's banking system to accept banks from other EU members. Spain has made some progress toward opening its banking system to foreign competition by removing restrictions on investments from non-EU investors. This has made the Spanish banking system very competitive. The U.S. Department of Commerce reports, "Private and savings banks are important because of their volume of business and because their activities cover all segments of the economy. There are more than 165 registered private banks in Spain with about 17,500 branch offices. Many of them also have an international presence."[3]

WAGE AND PRICE CONTROLS
Score: 3–Stable (moderate level)

Spain's government imposes price controls on farm insurance, electricity, telephone services, rail transport, gasoline, postal service, and some pharmaceutical products. Spain maintains a minimum wage.

PROPERTY RIGHTS
Score: 2–Stable (high level of protection)

Property is safe from government expropriation. As the U.S. Department of Commerce reports, "Spanish law protects property rights. Enforcement is carried out at the administrative and judicial level. Any decision pertaining to a property right by the Administration can be appealed first at the administrative level, and then at the judicial level, which has three levels of court appeals. Property protection is effective in Spain, although the system is slow."[4]

REGULATION
Score: 3–Stable (moderate level)

The government has streamlined its regulations, but still maintains some regulations on businesses, including labor and environmental laws and regulations dealing with fringe benefits. All are moderately burdensome. According to the U.S. Department of Commerce, "Spain has modernized its commercial laws and regulations following its 1986 entry into the E.U. Local regulatory framework compares favorably with other major European countries. Bureaucratic procedures have been streamlined and most red tape has been eliminated. Labor laws and regulations have been the exception, although the 1994 Labor Reform Laws and the recently signed pact between labor and business in April 1997 may signal a change."[5]

BLACK MARKET
Score: 2–Stable (low level of activity)

Spain's black market is confined mainly to pirated computer software, prerecorded music and video tapes, and illegal local cable transmissions of copyrighted movies. "Despite overall improvement," reports the U.S. Department of Commerce, "software piracy remains a serious problem in Spain; the Business Software Alliance (BSA) estimates that 73 percent of PC software in use has been copied illegally. An amendment to the law in December 1993 allows unannounced civil search procedures. If a software developer has reasonable suspicion of an infringement of his copyright, he or she may ask a judge to permit a search of the alleged wrongdoers' premises without warning. This measure has already produced some searches and prosecution of software pirates."[6] Still, these activities are minuscule compared with the overall size of Spain's economy.

NOTES
1 Economist Intelligence Unit, *ILT Reports, Spain,* 1998.
2 U.S. Department of Commerce, *Country Commercial Guide,* 1998.
3 *Ibid.*
4 *Ibid.*
5 *Ibid.*
6 *Ibid.*

Sri Lanka　　2.55

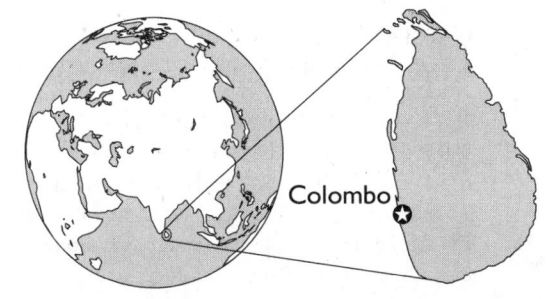

1998 Score: **2.45**	1997 Score: **2.45**	1996 Score: **2.65**

Trade	3	Banking	2
Taxation	3.5	Wages and Prices	1
Government Intervention	2	Property Rights	3
Monetary Policy	2	Regulation	3
Foreign Investment	3	Black Market	3

Sri Lanka declared its independence from the United Kingdom in 1948. It adopted a new constitution in 1972, creating a republic, and began a series of economic reforms in 1977. Since 1983, civil unrest and (more recently) civil war have been serious drains on the economy. Despite domestic turmoil, however, an economic restructuring plan started in 1995 has helped to fuel substantial economic growth. The government has focused on reducing trade barriers, privatizing businesses, and expanding the role of the private sector. Regulation is on the rise, however; as a result, Sri Lanka's overall score is 0.1 point worse this year.

TRADE POLICY
Score: 3–Stable (Moderate level of protectionism)

Sri Lanka has a three-tiered system of 10 percent, 25 percent, and 30 percent tariffs on various imports. For some items, such as automobiles, rates range from 50 percent to 100 percent. The government also imposes a 4.5 percent defense levy, an excise tax on selected consumer and nonessential goods, and a 10 percent export-development access surcharge on a few items subject to an import duty of 45 percent or more, bringing the average tariff rate to 8.5 percent.[1] This is down from 12 percent last year. Although there are no significant formal non-tariff barriers, there are other informal barriers that restrict imports. The U.S. Department of Commerce reports, for example, that corruption can be a problem in customs clearance.[2]

TAXATION
Score–Income taxation: 3–Stable (moderate tax rates)
Score–Corporate taxation: 3–Stable (high tax rates)
Final Taxation Score: 3.5–Stable (high tax rates)

The top marginal income tax rate is 35 percent, with the average income level taxed at 15 percent. The top corporate income tax rate is 35 percent. Sri Lanka also has a 1 percent to 20 percent turnover tax and a social contributions tax.

GOVERNMENT INTERVENTION IN THE ECONOMY
Score: 2–Stable (low level)

Government consumes 10.5 percent of GDP, up from 8.5 percent in 1980. It also owns some sectors of the economy. According to the U.S. Department of Commerce, "The state retains control of all infrastructure (ports, roads, phones, rail and electricity). It owns the two largest commercial banks, two insurance companies, the national airline, a national shipping line, and many other companies."[3]

MONETARY POLICY
Score: 2–Stable (low level of inflation)

Sri Lanka's average annual rate of inflation from 1986 to 1996 was 9.8 percent. The rate was 10 percent in 1997.

1	Hong Kong	1.25	81	Fiji	3.10
2	Singapore	1.30	81	Mali	3.10
3	Bahrain	1.70	81	Slovenia	3.10
4	New Zealand	1.75	85	Honduras	3.15
5	Switzerland	1.85	85	Mexico	3.15
6	United States	1.90	85	Papua New Guinea	3.15
7	Ireland	1.95	88	Djibouti	3.20
7	Luxembourg	1.95	88	Mongolia	3.20
7	Taiwan	1.95	90	Algeria	3.25
7	United Kingdom	1.95	90	Brazil	3.25
11	Bahamas	2.00	90	Lebanon	3.25
12	Czech Republic	2.05	90	Senegal	3.25
12	Japan	2.05	90	Tanzania	3.25
14	Australia	2.10	95	Nigeria	3.30
14	Belgium	2.10	95	Romania	3.30
14	Canada	2.10	97	Cambodia	3.35
14	United Arab Emirates	2.10	97	Dominican Republic	3.35
18	Austria	2.15	97	Egypt	3.35
18	Chile	2.15	97	Guinea	3.35
18	Estonia	2.15	97	Ivory Coast	3.35
18	Netherlands	2.15	97	Moldova	3.35
22	Denmark	2.25	97	Pakistan	3.35
22	El Salvador	2.25	104	Nepal	3.40
22	Finland	2.25	104	Venezuela	3.40
25	Germany	2.30	106	Armenia	3.45
25	Iceland	2.30	106	Bulgaria	3.45
27	Norway	2.35	106	Lesotho	3.45
28	Korea, South	2.40	106	Madagascar	3.45
28	Kuwait	2.40	106	Russia	3.45
28	Malaysia	2.40	111	Burkina Faso	3.50
28	Panama	2.40	111	Cameroon	3.50
28	Thailand	2.40	111	Guyana	3.50
33	Sweden	2.45	111	Nicaragua	3.50
34	Argentina	2.50	115	Gambia	3.60
34	France	2.50	116	Croatia	3.65
34	Italy	2.50	116	Georgia	3.65
34	Spain	2.50	116	Malawi	3.65
38	Portugal	2.55	119	Cape Verde	3.67
38	Sri Lanka	2.55	120	Ethiopia	3.70
38	Trinidad and Tobago	2.55	120	India	3.70
41	Barbados	2.60	120	Niger	3.70
41	Peru	2.60	123	Congo	3.75
43	Bolivia	2.65	124	Chad	3.80
43	Mauritius	2.65	124	China	3.80
45	Cyprus	2.70	124	Mauritania	3.80
45	Jamaica	2.70	124	Ukraine	3.80
45	Uruguay	2.70	124	Zimbabwe	3.80
48	Botswana	2.75	129	Albania	3.85
48	Guatemala	2.75	129	Bangladesh	3.85
48	Jordan	2.75	129	Mozambique	3.85
48	Namibia	2.75	129	Suriname	3.85
48	Oman	2.75	133	Burundi	3.90
48	Philippines	2.75	134	Togo	3.95
54	Belize	2.80	135	Haiti	4.00
54	Costa Rica	2.80	135	Kyrgyz Rep.	4.00
54	Israel	2.80	137	Kazakhstan	4.05
54	Swaziland	2.80	137	Sierra Leone	4.05
54	Turkey	2.80	139	Yemen	4.10
54	Uganda	2.80	140	Belarus	4.15
54	Samoa	2.80	141	Sudan	4.20
61	Latvia	2.85	141	Syria	4.20
62	Greece	2.90	143	Azerbaijan	4.30
62	Hungary	2.90	143	Equatorial Guinea	4.30
62	So. Africa	2.90	143	Myanmar	4.30
65	Ecuador	2.95	143	Rwanda	4.30
65	Gabon	2.95	147	Tajikistan	4.40
65	Indonesia	2.95	147	Uzbekistan	4.40
65	Malta	2.95	149	Angola	4.45
65	Morocco	2.95	149	Turkmenistan	4.45
65	Poland	2.95	151	Guinea-Bissau	4.55
65	Tunisia	2.95	152	Vietnam	4.60
72	Ghana	3.00	153	Congo (Zaire)	4.70
72	Lithuania	3.00	153	Iran	4.70
72	Saudi Arabia	3.00	155	Bosnia	4.80
75	Benin	3.05	155	Somalia	4.80
75	Kenya	3.05	157	Iraq	4.90
75	Paraguay	3.05	157	Laos	4.90
75	Qatar	3.05	157	Libya	4.90
75	Slovak Republic	3.05	160	Cuba	5.00
75	Zambia	3.05	160	Korea, North	5.00
81	Colombia	3.10			

Mostly Free

CAPITAL FLOWS AND FOREIGN INVESTMENT
Score: 3–Stable (moderate barriers)

Sri Lanka generally welcomes foreign investment. Its well-defined and accessible foreign investment code treats foreign and domestic firms equally. Equity restrictions of up to 40 percent apply to some businesses, however, and foreign investment is prohibited in non-bank money lending, pawn shops, retail trade outlets with capital investments of less than $1 million, some personal services, and coastal fishing. According to the U.S. Department of Commerce, "Investment in certain restricted sectors is subject to screening and approval on a case-by-case basis where foreign equity exceeds 40 percent. The restricted sectors include: shipping and travel agencies; freight forwarding; professional services; education; mass transportation; telecommunications; supply of water; mining; deep sea fishing; timber-based industries; growing and primary processing of tea, rubber, coconut, rice, cocoa, sugar and spices; and, finally, the production for export of goods subject to international quota."[4] Still, by global standards, Sri Lanka maintains only moderate barriers to foreign investment.

BANKING
Score: 2–Stable (low level of restrictions)

Sri Lanka has over 20 commercial banks, most of them foreign-owned. The banking sector includes both private and state-owned banks, and competition has caused the industry to become increasingly efficient.

WAGE AND PRICE CONTROLS
Score: 1–Stable (very low level)

The market determines most wages and prices, although the government imposes some controls on the prices of such items as foodstuffs and some energy products. A minimum wage is established by wage boards for specific sectors, but the market determines wages in other areas.

PROPERTY RIGHTS
Score: 3–Stable (moderate level of protection)

Sri Lanka's court system is efficient and free of government influence. According to the U.S. Department of State, "The Constitution provides for an independent judiciary, and the Government respects these provision in practice."[5] Court delays are not uncommon, however. For example, according to the U.S. Department of Commerce, "Although the legal system is well-established and non-discriminatory, it is fraught with long delays."[6]

REGULATION
Score: 3– (moderate level)

Sri Lanka's regulations generally have been straightforward and direct. There is increasing evidence, however, that regulations sometimes are applied haphazardly, creating a burden on some business activity. For example, according to the U.S. Department of Commerce, "Laws pertaining to tax, labor and labor standards, exchange controls, customs, environmental norms, building and construction standards are in place. Some laws and regulations are not freely available, however, and are difficult to access. Foreign and domestic investors at times complain that the regulatory system allows far too much leeway for bureaucratic discretion. Effective enforcement mechanisms are sometimes lacking and coordination problems between the BOI [Bank of India] and relevant line agencies periodically emerge. Lethargy and indifference on the part of mid- and lower-level public servants compound transparency problems."[7] As a result, Sri Lanka's regulation score is 1 point worse this year.

BLACK MARKET
Score: 3–Stable (moderate level of activity)

In general, Sri Lanka has strong and efficient intellectual property rights laws, but there is a growing black market in pirated computer software, prerecorded music and video tapes, and compact discs. According to the U.S. Department of Commerce, "Necessary amendments to Sri Lankan IPR [intellectual property rights] law have not yet been enacted and it will likely take years before new laws, procedures, and court precedents are established."[8]

NOTES

[1] Based on total taxes on international trade as a percentage of imports.
[2] U.S. Department of Commerce, *Country Commercial Guide*, 1998.
[3] *Ibid.*
[4] *Ibid.*
[5] U.S. Department of State, "Sri Lanka Country Report on Human Rights Practices for 1997," 1998.
[6] U.S. Department of Commerce, *Country Commercial Guide*, 1998.
[7] *Ibid.*
[8] *Ibid.*

Sudan

4.20

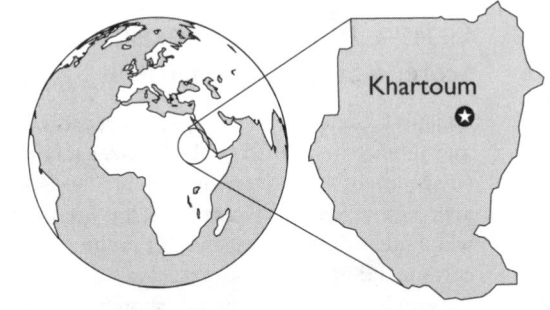

Khartoum ✪

1998 Score: **4.20**	1997 Score: **4.20**	1996 Score: **4.10**

Trade	5	Banking	4
Taxation	5	Wages and Prices	4
Government Intervention	3	Property Rights	4
Monetary Policy	5	Regulation	4
Foreign Investment	4	Black Market	4

Africa's largest country, Sudan, gained its independence from the United Kingdom in 1956. In 1989, President Omar Hassan al-Bashir's Islamic fundamentalist authoritarian regime seized power and suspended the 1985 constitution, rescinded freedom of the press, and outlawed political parties. A new constitution was signed into law on July 1, 1998, but its implementation, along with the rights of opposition political parties, remains unclear. The ruling National Islamic Front is engaged in the 16th year of an expensive and brutal civil war. Sudan has poor relations and border disputes with most of its neighbors, and has become increasingly isolated internationally, even among Arab countries. The United States continues to list Sudan as a state sponsor of terrorism. The United States imposed sweeping economic sanctions on Sudan in late 1997 for its sponsorship of terrorism and launched air strikes against a suspected terrorist site in Khartoum in August 1998. On the other hand, however, the United States has continued to supply humanitarian aid to Sudan: some $16 million in 1998. Although the government has implemented modest economic liberalization, the economy is hindered by internal strife and international sanctions. According to the U.S. Department of Commerce, "Sudan is buffeted by civil war, chronic political instability, adverse weather, high inflation, a drop in remittances from abroad, and counterproductive economic policies."[1]

TRADE POLICY
Score: 5–Stable (very high level of protectionism)

Sudan's average tariff rate is 24 percent,[2] although some estimates put it as high as 56 percent.[3] The government has eliminated import and export licenses, but it continues to ban the importation of some 30 items. Corruption within the customs service is rampant.

TAXATION
Score–Income taxation: 5–Stable (very high tax rates)
Score–Corporate taxation: 5–Stable (very high tax rates)
Final Taxation Score: 5–Stable (very high tax rates)

Sudan has top income and corporate tax rates of 60 percent.[4] Moreover, it levies a special agricultural tax of 15 percent to 20 percent on production.

GOVERNMENT INTERVENTION IN THE ECONOMY
Score: 3–Stable (moderate level)

Government consumes about 24 percent of GDP, a large portion of which is generated by the state-owned sector.

MONETARY POLICY
Score: 5–Stable (very high level of inflation)

Sudan's average annual rate of inflation from 1986 to 1996 was 64.5 percent. In 1997, the rate was 85 percent.

1	Hong Kong	1.25	81	Fiji	3.10
2	Singapore	1.30	81	Mali	3.10
3	Bahrain	1.70	81	Slovenia	3.10
4	New Zealand	1.75	85	Honduras	3.15
5	Switzerland	1.85	85	Mexico	3.15
6	United States	1.90	85	Papua New Guinea	3.15
7	Ireland	1.95	88	Djibouti	3.20
7	Luxembourg	1.95	88	Mongolia	3.20
7	Taiwan	1.95	90	Algeria	3.25
7	United Kingdom	1.95	90	Brazil	3.25
11	Bahamas	2.00	90	Lebanon	3.25
12	Czech Republic	2.05	90	Senegal	3.25
12	Japan	2.05	90	Tanzania	3.25
14	Australia	2.10	95	Nigeria	3.30
14	Belgium	2.10	95	Romania	3.30
14	Canada	2.10	97	Cambodia	3.35
14	United Arab Emirates	2.10	97	Dominican Republic	3.35
18	Austria	2.15	97	Egypt	3.35
18	Chile	2.15	97	Guinea	3.35
18	Estonia	2.15	97	Ivory Coast	3.35
18	Netherlands	2.15	97	Moldova	3.35
22	Denmark	2.25	97	Pakistan	3.35
22	El Salvador	2.25	104	Nepal	3.40
22	Finland	2.25	104	Venezuela	3.40
25	Germany	2.30	106	Armenia	3.45
25	Iceland	2.30	106	Bulgaria	3.45
27	Norway	2.35	106	Lesotho	3.45
28	Korea, South	2.40	106	Madagascar	3.45
28	Kuwait	2.40	106	Russia	3.45
28	Malaysia	2.40	111	Burkina Faso	3.50
28	Panama	2.40	111	Cameroon	3.50
28	Thailand	2.40	111	Guyana	3.50
33	Sweden	2.45	111	Nicaragua	3.50
34	Argentina	2.50	115	Gambia	3.60
34	France	2.50	116	Croatia	3.65
34	Italy	2.50	116	Georgia	3.65
34	Spain	2.50	116	Malawi	3.65
38	Portugal	2.55	119	Cape Verde	3.67
38	Sri Lanka	2.55	120	Ethiopia	3.70
38	Trinidad and Tobago	2.55	120	India	3.70
41	Barbados	2.60	120	Niger	3.70
41	Peru	2.60	123	Congo	3.75
43	Bolivia	2.65	124	Chad	3.80
43	Mauritius	2.65	124	China	3.80
45	Cyprus	2.70	124	Mauritania	3.80
45	Jamaica	2.70	124	Ukraine	3.80
45	Uruguay	2.70	124	Zimbabwe	3.80
48	Botswana	2.75	129	Albania	3.85
48	Guatemala	2.75	129	Bangladesh	3.85
48	Jordan	2.75	129	Mozambique	3.85
48	Namibia	2.75	129	Suriname	3.85
48	Oman	2.75	133	Burundi	3.90
48	Philippines	2.75	134	Togo	3.95
54	Belize	2.80	135	Haiti	4.00
54	Costa Rica	2.80	135	Kyrgyz Rep.	4.00
54	Israel	2.80	137	Kazakhstan	4.05
54	Swaziland	2.80	137	Sierra Leone	4.05
54	Turkey	2.80	139	Yemen	4.10
54	Uganda	2.80	140	Belarus	4.15
54	Samoa	2.80	141	Sudan	4.20
61	Latvia	2.85	141	Syria	4.20
62	Greece	2.90	143	Azerbaijan	4.30
62	Hungary	2.90	143	Equatorial Guinea	4.30
62	So. Africa	2.90	143	Myanmar	4.30
65	Ecuador	2.95	143	Rwanda	4.30
65	Gabon	2.95	147	Tajikistan	4.40
65	Indonesia	2.95	147	Uzbekistan	4.40
65	Malta	2.95	149	Angola	4.45
65	Morocco	2.95	149	Turkmenistan	4.45
65	Poland	2.95	151	Guinea-Bissau	4.55
65	Tunisia	2.95	152	Vietnam	4.60
72	Ghana	3.00	153	Congo (Zaire)	4.70
72	Lithuania	3.00	153	Iran	4.70
72	Saudi Arabia	3.00	155	Bosnia	4.80
75	Benin	3.05	155	Somalia	4.80
75	Kenya	3.05	157	Iraq	4.90
75	Paraguay	3.05	157	Laos	4.90
75	Qatar	3.05	157	Libya	4.90
75	Slovak Republic	3.05	160	Cuba	5.00
75	Zambia	3.05	160	Korea, North	5.00
81	Colombia	3.10			

Repressed

CAPITAL FLOWS AND FOREIGN INVESTMENT
Score: 4–Stable (high barriers)

Sudan's Islamic government is very sensitive to outside interference in its affairs, which makes for an inhospitable environment for foreign investment. Foreign investment is approved on a case-by-case basis; it is not permitted in wholesale or retail companies or in the production of cotton; and bureaucratic procedures designed to encourage the employment of domestic laborers are cumbersome. There is no tax discrimination against foreign investment, but foreigners often find it nearly impossible to move about the country.

BANKING
Score: 4–Stable (high level of restrictions)

The regime has moved to "Islamicize" Sudan's state-controlled banking system, increasing its control of economic enterprise. There is little freedom to exchange currency.

WAGE AND PRICE CONTROLS
Score: 4–Stable (high level)

Although Sudan has liberalized some prices, price controls on foodstuffs remain in effect, and many goods are subsidized. The government regulates public and private salaries. Sudan has a minimum wage.

PROPERTY RIGHTS
Score: 4–Stable (low level of protection)

There is little respect for private property in Sudan. According to the U.S. Department of State, "The judiciary is not independent and is largely subservient to the Government."[5] The wanton destruction of private property by government troops is widespread in southern parts of the country, and petty crime and thievery are common.

REGULATION
Score: 4–Stable (high level)

Bureaucratic inefficiency makes business activity difficult. As is true in many developing countries, Sudan's regulatory burden is heavy and inefficient. Businesses often find it difficult to obtain licenses to operate, and business owners may be harassed by corrupt bureaucrats. Despite a government crackdown, corruption remains a problem.

BLACK MARKET
Score: 4–Stable (high level of activity)

Rationing has led to a black market in several items, including petroleum and sugar, and the ban on some imports encourages smuggling. In the war zone, the illicit economy dominates.

NOTES

[1] U.S. Department of Commerce, *Stat–USA* Internet site (*http://www.stat-usa.gov*).
[2] This figure is for 1992 to 1993 and includes a defense tax. From U.S. Department of State, Bureau of African Affairs, Office of Economic Policy.
[3] World Bank, "Open Economies Work Better!" *Policy Research Working Paper* No. 1636, 1996.
[4] The most recent reliable information is based on 1989 tax data from World Bank sources. There is not enough information to determine the tax rate on the average income level; thus, Sudan was graded on its top tax rate.
[5] U.S. Department of State, "Sudan Country Report on Human Rights Practices for 1996," 1997.

Suriname   3.85

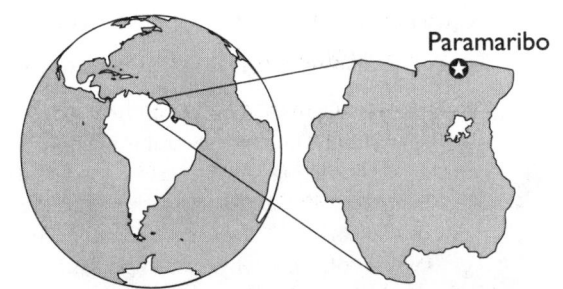

Paramaribo

| 1998 Score: **3.90** | 1997 Score: **4.00** | 1996 Score: **3.90** |

Trade	5	Banking	4
Taxation	3.5	Wages and Prices	3
Government Intervention	3	Property Rights	3
Monetary Policy	5	Regulation	4
Foreign Investment	3	Black Market	5

Suriname gained its independence from the Netherlands in 1975. Throughout the 1980s, Suriname experienced political strife, and relations with its former colonial power deteriorated. In 1982, the Netherlands suspended cash development grants to Suriname because of political violence, but reinstated this aid in 1988. Most aid to Suriname has been squandered and has served as the primary obstacle to economic reform. Suriname recently has reduced some taxes; as a result, its overall score is 0.05 point better than last year.

TRADE POLICY
Score: 5–Stable (very high level of protectionism)

"According to Ministry of Trade and Industry Officials," reports the U.S. Department of Commerce, "average import duties are between 30 and 40 percent."[1] Trade restrictions include strict import licensing and import bans.

TAXATION
Score–Income taxation: 2+ (low tax rates)
Score–Corporate taxation: 4–Stable (high tax rates)
Final Taxation Score: 3.5+ (high tax rates)

Suriname's top income tax rate is 40 percent, down from 50 percent in 1997; as a result, its income taxation score is 1 point better this year. The average taxpayer is in the 10 percent bracket. The top marginal corporate tax rate is 38 percent. Suriname also has a 38 percent capital gains tax. Averaged together with the income taxation score, Suriname's final taxation score is 0.5 point better than last year.

GOVERNMENT INTERVENTION IN THE ECONOMY
Score: 3–Stable (moderately high level)

Government consumes about 12 percent of GDP, and the state sector generates a substantial amount of GDP overall.

MONETARY POLICY
Score: 5–Stable (very high level of inflation)

Suriname's average annual rate of inflation from 1986 to 1996 was 73.5 percent. In 1997, the rate was 7.1 percent.

CAPITAL FLOWS AND FOREIGN INVESTMENT
Score: 3–Stable (moderate barriers)

Suriname is developing a sound foreign investment climate rapidly. Because the foreign investment climate is still evolving, the appropriate ministry deals with investors on an ad hoc basis. "Surinamese investment legislation, formulated in 1960, is now outdated," according to the U.S. Department of Commerce. "As a result, companies negotiate directly with the Surinamese government on concessions, licenses and hiring."[2]

1	Hong Kong	1.25	
2	Singapore	1.30	
3	Bahrain	1.70	
4	New Zealand	1.75	
5	Switzerland	1.85	
6	United States	1.90	
7	Ireland	1.95	
7	Luxembourg	1.95	
7	Taiwan	1.95	
7	United Kingdom	1.95	
11	Bahamas	2.00	
12	Czech Republic	2.05	
12	Japan	2.05	
14	Australia	2.10	
14	Belgium	2.10	
14	Canada	2.10	
14	United Arab Emirates	2.10	
18	Austria	2.15	
18	Chile	2.15	
18	Estonia	2.15	
18	Netherlands	2.15	
22	Denmark	2.25	
22	El Salvador	2.25	
22	Finland	2.25	
25	Germany	2.30	
25	Iceland	2.30	
27	Norway	2.35	
28	Korea, South	2.40	
28	Kuwait	2.40	
28	Malaysia	2.40	
28	Panama	2.40	
28	Thailand	2.40	
33	Sweden	2.45	
34	Argentina	2.50	
34	France	2.50	
34	Italy	2.50	
34	Spain	2.50	
38	Portugal	2.55	
38	Sri Lanka	2.55	
38	Trinidad and Tobago	2.55	
41	Barbados	2.60	
41	Peru	2.60	
43	Bolivia	2.65	
43	Mauritius	2.65	
45	Cyprus	2.70	
45	Jamaica	2.70	
45	Uruguay	2.70	
48	Botswana	2.75	
48	Guatemala	2.75	
48	Jordan	2.75	
48	Namibia	2.75	
48	Oman	2.75	
48	Philippines	2.75	
54	Belize	2.80	
54	Costa Rica	2.80	
54	Israel	2.80	
54	Swaziland	2.80	
54	Turkey	2.80	
54	Uganda	2.80	
54	Samoa	2.80	
61	Latvia	2.85	
62	Greece	2.90	
62	Hungary	2.90	
62	So. Africa	2.90	
65	Ecuador	2.95	
65	Gabon	2.95	
65	Indonesia	2.95	
65	Malta	2.95	
65	Morocco	2.95	
65	Poland	2.95	
65	Tunisia	2.95	
72	Ghana	3.00	
72	Lithuania	3.00	
72	Saudi Arabia	3.00	
75	Benin	3.05	
75	Kenya	3.05	
75	Paraguay	3.05	
75	Qatar	3.05	
75	Slovak Republic	3.05	
75	Zambia	3.05	
81	Colombia	3.10	
81	Fiji	3.10	
81	Mali	3.10	
81	Slovenia	3.10	
85	Honduras	3.15	
85	Mexico	3.15	
85	Papua New Guinea	3.15	
88	Djibouti	3.20	
88	Mongolia	3.20	
90	Algeria	3.25	
90	Brazil	3.25	
90	Lebanon	3.25	
90	Senegal	3.25	
90	Tanzania	3.25	
95	Nigeria	3.30	
95	Romania	3.30	
97	Cambodia	3.35	
97	Dominican Republic	3.35	
97	Egypt	3.35	
97	Guinea	3.35	
97	Ivory Coast	3.35	
97	Moldova	3.35	
97	Pakistan	3.35	
104	Nepal	3.40	
104	Venezuela	3.40	
106	Armenia	3.45	
106	Bulgaria	3.45	
106	Lesotho	3.45	
106	Madagascar	3.45	
106	Russia	3.45	
111	Burkina Faso	3.50	
111	Cameroon	3.50	
111	Guyana	3.50	
111	Nicaragua	3.50	
115	Gambia	3.60	
116	Croatia	3.65	
116	Georgia	3.65	
116	Malawi	3.65	
119	Cape Verde	3.67	
120	Ethiopia	3.70	
120	India	3.70	
120	Niger	3.70	
123	Congo	3.75	
124	Chad	3.80	
124	China	3.80	
124	Mauritania	3.80	
124	Ukraine	3.80	
124	Zimbabwe	3.80	
129	Albania	3.85	
129	Bangladesh	3.85	
129	Mozambique	3.85	
129	Suriname	3.85	
133	Burundi	3.90	
134	Togo	3.95	
135	Haiti	4.00	
135	Kyrgyz Rep.	4.00	
137	Kazakhstan	4.05	
137	Sierra Leone	4.05	
139	Yemen	4.10	
140	Belarus	4.15	
141	Sudan	4.20	
141	Syria	4.20	
143	Azerbaijan	4.30	
143	Equatorial Guinea	4.30	
143	Myanmar	4.30	
143	Rwanda	4.30	
147	Tajikistan	4.40	
147	Uzbekistan	4.40	
149	Angola	4.45	
149	Turkmenistan	4.45	
151	Guinea-Bissau	4.55	
152	Vietnam	4.60	
153	Congo (Zaire)	4.70	
153	Iran	4.70	
155	Bosnia	4.80	
155	Somalia	4.80	
157	Iraq	4.90	
157	Laos	4.90	
157	Libya	4.90	
160	Cuba	5.00	
160	Korea, North	5.00	

Mostly Unfree

BANKING
Score: 4–Stable (high level of restrictions)

The government has significant influence over Suriname's banking system. There are several government-owned banks, and the Central Bank exerts a good deal of control over the system. For example, according to the U.S. Department of Commerce, "The Central Bank of Suriname is the legal supplier of the foreign exchange market. Therefore, the market remains vulnerable to shortages or delays in securing foreign exchange based on the Central Bank's ability to meet demand."[3]

WAGE AND PRICE CONTROLS
Score: 3–Stable (moderate level)

Both the market and the government set wages and prices. The large state-owned sector continues to influence the setting of prices.

PROPERTY RIGHTS
Score: 3–Stable (moderate level of protection)

Private property is guaranteed by Suriname's constitution and protected by law. The time involved in getting a dispute resolved in the court system can be considerable, however. According to the U.S. Department of Commerce, "Settlement of ownership disputes or damage to property, buildings or equipment can be an extremely long process in an undermanned, overworked, legal system."[4]

REGULATION
Score: 4–Stable (high level)

Establishing a business is generally easy, although the bureaucracy is both substantial and corrupt. The U.S. Department of State reports that there is a "high degree of state involvement and regulation."[5]

BLACK MARKET
Score: 5–Stable (very high level of activity)

Suriname has an extensive black market, primarily in pirated video and audio cassettes, computer software, and consumer goods. There is much smuggling along the borders. According to the U.S. Department of Commerce, "With the exception of reexport of goods to eastern Guyana, and illegal smuggling to French Guyana, Suriname is not a distribution point for shipping or air cargo."[6]

NOTES

[1]   U.S. Department of Commerce, *Country Commercial Guide*, 1998.
[2]   *Ibid.*
[3]   *Ibid.*
[4]   *Ibid.*
[5]   U.S. Department of State, "Suriname Country Report on Human Rights Practices for 1996," 1997.
[6]   U.S. Department of Commerce, *Country Commercial Guide*, 1998.

Swaziland 2.80

1998 Score: **2.70**	1997 Score: **2.80**	1996 Score: **2.90**

Trade	3	Banking	3
Taxation	3	Wages and Prices	3
Government Intervention	2	Property Rights	2
Monetary Policy	3	Regulation	3
Foreign Investment	2	Black Market	4

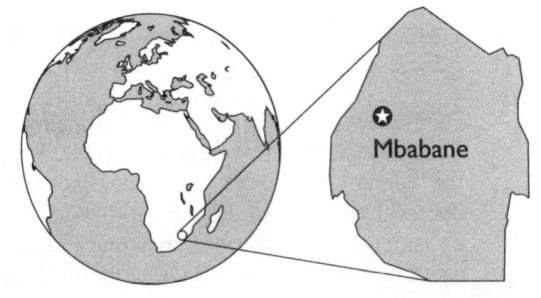

Mbabane

Swaziland gained its independence from the United Kingdom in 1968 and established a monarchy, with all executive and some judicial and legislative powers resting with the king. This system of government remains in effect today. Although Swaziland traditionally has had a largely agrarian society, industry produced 43 percent of GDP in 1995 and is becoming the dominant sector of the economy. Economic growth has been low but positive, averaging 2.7 percent annually from 1992 to 1996. Swaziland's average annual rate of inflation has increased recently, so its overall score is 0.1 point worse this year.

TRADE POLICY
Score: 3–Stable (moderate level of protectionism)

Swaziland is a member of the Southern African Customs Union,[1] which has an average external tariff rate of less than 12 percent. There is no evidence of significant non-tariff barriers.

TAXATION
Score–Income taxation: 2–Stable (low tax rates)
Score–Corporate taxation: 4–Stable (moderate tax rates)
Final Taxation Score: 3–Stable (moderate tax rates)

Swaziland's top income tax rate is 39 percent; there are no taxes on the average level of income. The top corporate tax rate is 37.5 percent. These are the only significant taxes.

GOVERNMENT INTERVENTION IN THE ECONOMY
Score: 2–Stable (low level)

Government consumes 22.9 percent of GDP. It also owns the larger public utilities, such as some transportation and telecommunications enterprises. The rest of the economy is privately owned, and the government is developing plans to privatize most remaining state-owned enterprises. The U.S. Department of Commerce describes Swaziland as a "free-market economy with relatively little government intervention. The government actively encourages foreign investment and is generally committed to an open market policy."[2]

MONETARY POLICY
Score: 3– (moderate level of inflation)

Swaziland's average annual rate of inflation from 1986 to 1996 was 14 percent, up from 11 percent from 1985 to 1995; as a result, its score for this factor is 1 point worse than last year. Inflation data for 1997 are unavailable.

1	Hong Kong	1.25	81	Fiji	3.10
2	Singapore	1.30	81	Mali	3.10
3	Bahrain	1.70	81	Slovenia	3.10
4	New Zealand	1.75	85	Honduras	3.15
5	Switzerland	1.85	85	Mexico	3.15
6	United States	1.90	85	Papua New Guinea	3.15
7	Ireland	1.95	88	Djibouti	3.20
7	Luxembourg	1.95	88	Mongolia	3.20
7	Taiwan	1.95	90	Algeria	3.25
7	United Kingdom	1.95	90	Brazil	3.25
11	Bahamas	2.00	90	Lebanon	3.25
12	Czech Republic	2.05	90	Senegal	3.25
12	Japan	2.05	90	Tanzania	3.25
14	Australia	2.10	95	Nigeria	3.30
14	Belgium	2.10	95	Romania	3.30
14	Canada	2.10	97	Cambodia	3.35
14	United Arab Emirates	2.10	97	Dominican Republic	3.35
18	Austria	2.15	97	Egypt	3.35
18	Chile	2.15	97	Guinea	3.35
18	Estonia	2.15	97	Ivory Coast	3.35
18	Netherlands	2.15	97	Moldova	3.35
22	Denmark	2.25	97	Pakistan	3.35
22	El Salvador	2.25	104	Nepal	3.40
22	Finland	2.25	104	Venezuela	3.40
25	Germany	2.30	106	Armenia	3.45
25	Iceland	2.30	106	Bulgaria	3.45
27	Norway	2.35	106	Lesotho	3.45
28	Korea, South	2.40	106	Madagascar	3.45
28	Kuwait	2.40	106	Russia	3.45
28	Malaysia	2.40	111	Burkina Faso	3.50
28	Panama	2.40	111	Cameroon	3.50
28	Thailand	2.40	111	Guyana	3.50
33	Sweden	2.45	111	Nicaragua	3.50
34	Argentina	2.50	115	Gambia	3.60
34	France	2.50	116	Croatia	3.65
34	Italy	2.50	116	Georgia	3.65
34	Spain	2.50	116	Malawi	3.65
38	Portugal	2.55	119	Cape Verde	3.67
38	Sri Lanka	2.55	120	Ethiopia	3.70
38	Trinidad and Tobago	2.55	120	India	3.70
41	Barbados	2.60	120	Niger	3.70
41	Peru	2.60	123	Congo	3.75
43	Bolivia	2.65	124	Chad	3.80
43	Mauritius	2.65	124	China	3.80
45	Cyprus	2.70	124	Mauritania	3.80
45	Jamaica	2.70	124	Ukraine	3.80
45	Uruguay	2.70	124	Zimbabwe	3.80
48	Botswana	2.75	129	Albania	3.85
48	Guatemala	2.75	129	Bangladesh	3.85
48	Jordan	2.75	129	Mozambique	3.85
48	Namibia	2.75	129	Suriname	3.85
48	Oman	2.75	133	Burundi	3.90
48	Philippines	2.75	134	Togo	3.95
54	Belize	2.80	135	Haiti	4.00
54	Costa Rica	2.80	135	Kyrgyz Rep.	4.00
54	Israel	2.80	137	Kazakhstan	4.05
54	Swaziland	2.80	137	Sierra Leone	4.05
54	Turkey	2.80	139	Yemen	4.10
54	Uganda	2.80	140	Belarus	4.15
54	Samoa	2.80	141	Sudan	4.20
61	Latvia	2.85	141	Syria	4.20
62	Greece	2.90	143	Azerbaijan	4.30
62	Hungary	2.90	143	Equatorial Guinea	4.30
62	So. Africa	2.90	143	Myanmar	4.30
65	Ecuador	2.95	143	Rwanda	4.30
65	Gabon	2.95	147	Tajikistan	4.40
65	Indonesia	2.95	147	Uzbekistan	4.40
65	Malta	2.95	149	Angola	4.45
65	Morocco	2.95	149	Turkmenistan	4.45
65	Poland	2.95	151	Guinea-Bissau	4.55
65	Tunisia	2.95	152	Vietnam	4.60
72	Ghana	3.00	153	Congo (Zaire)	4.70
72	Lithuania	3.00	153	Iran	4.70
72	Saudi Arabia	3.00	155	Bosnia	4.80
75	Benin	3.05	155	Somalia	4.80
75	Kenya	3.05	157	Iraq	4.90
75	Paraguay	3.05	157	Laos	4.90
75	Qatar	3.05	157	Libya	4.90
75	Slovak Republic	3.05	160	Cuba	5.00
75	Zambia	3.05	160	Korea, North	5.00
81	Colombia	3.10			

Mostly Free

CAPITAL FLOWS AND FOREIGN INVESTMENT
Score: 2–Stable (low barriers)

Foreign investment generally is encouraged, and the nationalization of foreign-owned property is prohibited by law. Foreign firms receive the same legal treatment as domestic firms. According to the U.S. Department of Commerce, "Far from discriminating against foreign participation in the country's development, Swaziland's government has been accused of favoring expatriate business over local entrepreneurs. The Swazi government has advanced a policy welcoming foreign investment for over a decade. Nevertheless, government has not been very effective in implementing that policy. Government has largely left events to take their own course, following the trends, interests and opportunities that the country's location and resources offer. The emphasis on foreign investment is more a matter of policy statements by the government and individual ministers than a matter of laws and institutions to support such policy."[3] Thus, the economy is largely open to foreign investment and has few formal barriers. The government is working to develop a consistent and cohesive foreign investment code.

BANKING
Score: 3–Stable (moderate level of restrictions)

By African standards, banks in Swaziland are relatively free of government control. But the government still controls the lending policies of some banks, including the Swaziland Development and Savings Bank, which went bankrupt in 1995 and now is being restructured. The government also maintains strict control of credit.

WAGE AND PRICE CONTROLS
Score: 3–Stable (moderate level)

Cotton, corn, milk, petroleum, energy, and tobacco products all remain subject to price controls. Swaziland has a minimum wage.

PROPERTY RIGHTS
Score: 2–Stable (high level of protection)

Property is legally protected against government expropriation, but enforcement of property rights in the court system can be weak. According to the U.S. Department of Commerce, "Swaziland has a dual legal system comprised of Roman-Dutch law and customary law. This parallel system can be confusing and has, at times, presented problems for foreign-owned business."[4] By global standards, however, the level of private property protection is high.

REGULATION
Score: 3–Stable (moderate level)

Swaziland has streamlined its regulatory system. The government encourages private companies to establish their own safety and health standards. Some government regulations (especially those dealing with safety conditions) are applied erratically, however; this can lead to uncertainty and confusion.

BLACK MARKET
Score: 4–Stable (high level of activity)

Swaziland has an active black market, primarily in the supply of labor, transportation services, the construction industry, and pirated computer software. The illegal software trade is mainly the result of poor protection for intellectual property. "Protection for patents, trademarks and copyrights is currently inadequate under Swazi law," according to the U.S. Department of Commerce.[5]

NOTES
1. The Southern African Customs Union consists of Botswana, Lesotho, Namibia, Swaziland, and South Africa.
2. U.S. Department of Commerce, *Country Commercial Guide*, 1998.
3. *Ibid.*
4. *Ibid.*
5. *Ibid.*

Sweden   2.45

1998 Score: **2.45**   1997 Score: **2.45**   1996 Score: **2.55**

Trade	2	Banking	2
Taxation	4.5	Wages and Prices	2
Government Intervention	5	Property Rights	2
Monetary Policy	1	Regulation	3
Foreign Investment	2	Black Market	1

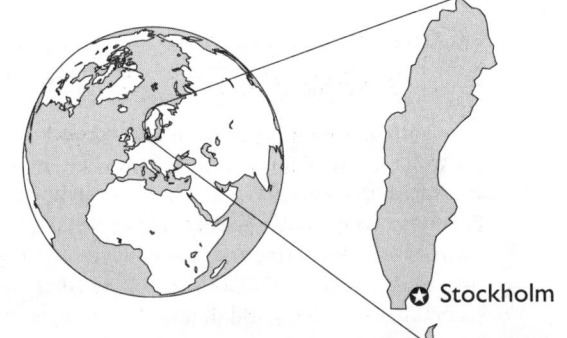

⊛ Stockholm

Sweden's economy has changed dramatically over the past several years. By the end of the 1980s, it was clear that high levels of government spending on social welfare, worker retraining, and unemployment compensation—to say nothing of tax rates as high as 98 percent—could not be sustained. Because of the government's economic policies, GDP shrank by 4 percent from 1991 to 1993, and unemployment rose to around 8 percent in 1994. The government has been forced to abandon most of its highly interventionist economic policies and follow a more market-oriented path. Sweden joined the European Union in 1995 and has managed to reduce its rate of inflation and some of its banking regulations.

TRADE POLICY
Score: 2–Stable (low level of protectionism)

Sweden's tariff rates average about 2.8 percent.[1] The government maintains significant import licensing procedures, however, for such items as agricultural goods, ferroalloys, and semi-finished iron and steel.

TAXATION
Score—Income taxation: 5–Stable (very high tax rates)
Score—Corporate taxation: 3–Stable (moderate tax rates)
Final Taxation Score: 4.5–Stable (very high tax rates)

The tax burden in Sweden is one of the heaviest among the world's industrialized economies: a 56 percent top income tax rate,[2] a 31 percent average income tax rate, a 28 percent top corporate tax rate, a 30 percent capital gains tax, and a 6 percent to 25 percent value-added tax.

GOVERNMENT INTERVENTION IN THE ECONOMY
Score: 5–Stable (very high level)

The level of government spending in Sweden has fallen from around 75 percent of GDP to about 50 percent.[3] The government is privatizing some companies; of those that employ more than 50 workers, 90 percent now are privately owned.

MONETARY POLICY
Score: 1–Stable (very low level of inflation)

Sweden's average annual rate of inflation from 1986 to 1996 was 4.8 percent. In 1997, the rate was less than 1 percent.

CAPITAL FLOWS AND FOREIGN INVESTMENT
Score: 2–Stable (low barriers)

Sweden presents few barriers to foreign investment, but some restrictions remain on foreign ownership of air transportation companies, the maritime industry, and items considered necessary during time of war, such as arms manufacturing. According to the U.S. Department of Commerce, "Up to the mid-1980's,

1	Hong Kong	1.25	81	Fiji	3.10
2	Singapore	1.30	81	Mali	3.10
3	Bahrain	1.70	81	Slovenia	3.10
4	New Zealand	1.75	85	Honduras	3.15
5	Switzerland	1.85	85	Mexico	3.15
6	United States	1.90	85	Papua New Guinea	3.15
7	Ireland	1.95	88	Djibouti	3.20
7	Luxembourg	1.95	88	Mongolia	3.20
7	Taiwan	1.95	90	Algeria	3.25
7	United Kingdom	1.95	90	Brazil	3.25
11	Bahamas	2.00	90	Lebanon	3.25
12	Czech Republic	2.05	90	Senegal	3.25
12	Japan	2.05	90	Tanzania	3.25
14	Australia	2.10	95	Nigeria	3.30
14	Belgium	2.10	95	Romania	3.30
14	Canada	2.10	97	Cambodia	3.35
14	United Arab Emirates	2.10	97	Dominican Republic	3.35
18	Austria	2.15	97	Egypt	3.35
18	Chile	2.15	97	Guinea	3.35
18	Estonia	2.15	97	Ivory Coast	3.35
18	Netherlands	2.15	97	Moldova	3.35
22	Denmark	2.25	97	Pakistan	3.35
22	El Salvador	2.25	104	Nepal	3.40
22	Finland	2.25	104	Venezuela	3.40
25	Germany	2.30	106	Armenia	3.45
25	Iceland	2.30	106	Bulgaria	3.45
27	Norway	2.35	106	Lesotho	3.45
28	Korea, South	2.40	106	Madagascar	3.45
28	Kuwait	2.40	106	Russia	3.45
28	Malaysia	2.40	111	Burkina Faso	3.50
28	Panama	2.40	111	Cameroon	3.50
28	Thailand	2.40	111	Guyana	3.50
33	**Sweden**	**2.45**	111	Nicaragua	3.50
34	Argentina	2.50	115	Gambia	3.60
34	France	2.50	116	Croatia	3.65
34	Italy	2.50	116	Georgia	3.65
34	Spain	2.50	116	Malawi	3.65
38	Portugal	2.55	119	Cape Verde	3.67
38	Sri Lanka	2.55	120	Ethiopia	3.70
38	Trinidad and Tobago	2.55	120	India	3.70
41	Barbados	2.60	120	Niger	3.70
41	Peru	2.60	123	Congo	3.75
43	Bolivia	2.65	124	Chad	3.80
43	Mauritius	2.65	124	China	3.80
45	Cyprus	2.70	124	Mauritania	3.80
45	Jamaica	2.70	124	Ukraine	3.80
45	Uruguay	2.70	124	Zimbabwe	3.80
48	Botswana	2.75	129	Albania	3.85
48	Guatemala	2.75	129	Bangladesh	3.85
48	Jordan	2.75	129	Mozambique	3.85
48	Namibia	2.75	129	Suriname	3.85
48	Oman	2.75	133	Burundi	3.90
48	Philippines	2.75	134	Togo	3.95
54	Belize	2.80	135	Haiti	4.00
54	Costa Rica	2.80	135	Kyrgyz Rep.	4.00
54	Israel	2.80	137	Kazakhstan	4.05
54	Swaziland	2.80	137	Sierra Leone	4.05
54	Turkey	2.80	139	Yemen	4.10
54	Uganda	2.80	140	Belarus	4.15
54	Samoa	2.80	141	Sudan	4.20
61	Latvia	2.85	141	Syria	4.20
62	Greece	2.90	143	Azerbaijan	4.30
62	Hungary	2.90	143	Equatorial Guinea	4.30
62	So. Africa	2.90	143	Myanmar	4.30
65	Ecuador	2.95	143	Rwanda	4.30
65	Gabon	2.95	147	Tajikistan	4.40
65	Indonesia	2.95	147	Uzbekistan	4.40
65	Malta	2.95	149	Angola	4.45
65	Morocco	2.95	149	Turkmenistan	4.45
65	Poland	2.95	151	Guinea-Bissau	4.55
65	Tunisia	2.95	152	Vietnam	4.60
72	Ghana	3.00	153	Congo (Zaire)	4.70
72	Lithuania	3.00	153	Iran	4.70
72	Saudi Arabia	3.00	155	Bosnia	4.80
75	Benin	3.05	155	Somalia	4.80
75	Kenya	3.05	157	Iraq	4.90
75	Paraguay	3.05	157	Laos	4.90
75	Qatar	3.05	157	Libya	4.90
75	Slovak Republic	3.05	160	Cuba	5.00
75	Zambia	3.05	160	Korea, North	5.00
81	Colombia	3.10			

Mostly Free

Sweden's approach to direct investment from abroad was quite restrictive and governed by a complex system of laws and regulations. During the later part of the decade, doubts were raised about the effectiveness and desirability of controlling foreign direct investment (FDI) in Sweden. Such considerations, and Sweden's present membership in the European Union (EU), have drastically changed the investment climate and attracted foreign investors to the country. According to recent OECD statistics Sweden takes the second place in the world in inflow of foreign direct investments as a percentage of GDP."[4]

BANKING
Score: 2–Stable (low level of restrictions)

With one exception, all commercial banks in Sweden are domestically owned and operated; two are owned directly by the government. Foreign banks have been permitted to establish subsidiaries and branches since 1986, but the application process remains a barrier. The government is trying to liberalize the banking system, however, so that opening new banks will become easier and banks will be able to operate more freely.

WAGE AND PRICE CONTROLS
SCORE: 2–STABLE (LOW LEVEL)

The market sets most wages and prices. There is no national minimum wage law, although the government influences wage rates by establishing a minimum wage for employees of state-owned industries. State-owned enterprises often set the prices of the products they produce.

PROPERTY RIGHTS
Score: 2–Stable (high level of protection)

Sweden has a well-developed and efficient legal system. According to the U.S. Department of Commerce, "There have been no major disputes over investment in Sweden in recent years. The country has written and consistently applied commercial and bankruptcy laws, and secured interests in property are recognized and enforced."[5]

REGULATION
Score: 3–Stable (moderate level)

Obtaining a business license in Sweden is relatively easy. Businesses must register with the Patent and Registration Office and the appropriate tax offices. Sweden also maintains, however, a comprehensive and burdensome safety, environmental, and consumer regulatory structure. For example, the Environmental Protection Act of 1969 requires all businesses to obtain permission from the government before releasing any pollutants into the environment. In cases in which the expansion of a business may result in more pollution, a company must undergo a lengthy and sometimes extremely burdensome investigation. Businesses also must comply with many other regulatory strictures, such as a government-imposed five-week vacation.

BLACK MARKET
Score: 1–Stable (very low level of activity)

Sweden once had a large black market in the construction industry, but economic reforms are making it easier to exchange most goods and services legally. Sweden's protection of intellectual property is among the most efficient in the world.

NOTES
[1] Arrowhead International, *World Trade and Customs Directory*, 1998.
[2] *Worldwide Executive Tax Guide and Directory*, 1998 edition (New York, N.Y.: Ernst & Young, 1998).
[3] Based on central government expenditures; from U.S. Department of State, *Country Reports on Economic Policy and Trade Practices*, 1997, p. 178.
[4] U.S. Department of Commerce, *Country Commercial Guide*, 1998.
[5] *Ibid.*

Switzerland (including Liechtenstein)[1]

1.85

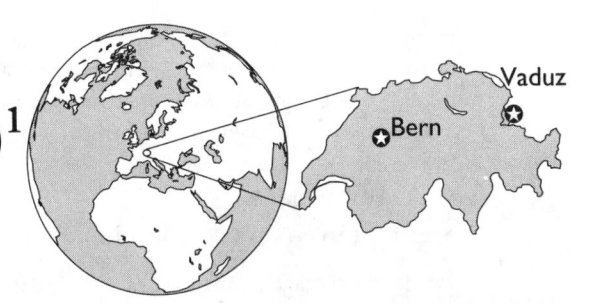

Vaduz

Bern

1998 Score: **1.90**   1997 Score: **1.90**   1996 Score: **1.80**

Trade	2	Banking	1
Taxation	2.5	Wages and Prices	2
Government Intervention	3	Property Rights	1
Monetary Policy	1	Regulation	3
Foreign Investment	2	Black Market	1

Having maintained its neutrality throughout most of the 20th century's major international conflicts, Switzerland has become a favorite site for conventions, peace accords, and international agreements. Today, Geneva is the seat of the World Trade Organization. In 1992, the Swiss electorate voted against joining the European Economic Area (EEA), a free trade area mainly recognized among members of the European Union (EU) and other European countries that have yet to join the EU. As a result of this popular vote, Switzerland is a member of neither the EEA nor the EU. Recently available information indicates that Switzerland's tax rates are lower than previously thought; therefore, its overall score is .05 point better than last year.

TRADE POLICY
Score: 2–Stable (low level of protectionism)

Switzerland's average tariff rate is 1.7 percent, which is lower than those of most other EU members,[2] but other trade restrictions include licensing, subsidies to the agricultural sector, and import quotas. As part of the Uruguay Round of the General Agreement on Tariffs and Trade, Switzerland has pledged to reduce its subsidies to agriculture and transform its quota system on agricultural imports into tariffs while reducing these tariffs by 30 percent by the year 2000. Although Switzerland restricts foreign participation in telecommunications, legislation currently undergoing consideration in parliament would privatize this sector. Thus, by global standards, Switzerland's level of trade protectionism is low.

TAXATION
Score–Income taxation: 1–Stable (very low tax rates)
Score–Corporate taxation: 3+ (moderate tax rates)
Final Taxation Score: 2.5+ (moderate tax rates)

Switzerland's top federal income tax rate is 11.5 percent. According to the international accounting firm Ernst & Young, "Because of the multilayered tax system, there are no average tax rates. Taxes are calculated based on specific figures for specific cantons and municipalities. The maximum overall rate of federal income tax is 11.5 percent."[3] The top marginal corporate tax rate is 32 percent, down from 36 percent last year; as a result, Switzerland's corporate taxation score is 1 point better this year, making its final taxation score 0.5 point better than last year.[4] Switzerland also has a capital gains tax that is levied at the regular business income rate, a 6.5 percent value-added tax, and a 35 percent withholding tax.

GOVERNMENT INTERVENTION IN THE ECONOMY
Score: 3–Stable (moderate level)

Government consumes about 15.2 percent of GDP and, even though it has begun to privatize public corporations, it remains involved in certain parts of the

1	Hong Kong	1.25		81	Fiji	3.10
2	Singapore	1.30		81	Mali	3.10
3	Bahrain	1.70		81	Slovenia	3.10
4	New Zealand	1.75		85	Honduras	3.15
5	Switzerland	1.85		85	Mexico	3.15
6	United States	1.90		85	Papua New Guinea	3.15
7	Ireland	1.95		88	Djibouti	3.20
7	Luxembourg	1.95		88	Mongolia	3.20
7	Taiwan	1.95		90	Algeria	3.25
7	United Kingdom	1.95		90	Brazil	3.25
11	Bahamas	2.00		90	Lebanon	3.25
12	Czech Republic	2.05		90	Senegal	3.25
12	Japan	2.05		90	Tanzania	3.25
14	Australia	2.10		95	Nigeria	3.30
14	Belgium	2.10		95	Romania	3.30
14	Canada	2.10		97	Cambodia	3.35
14	United Arab Emirates	2.10		97	Dominican Republic	3.35
18	Austria	2.15		97	Egypt	3.35
18	Chile	2.15		97	Guinea	3.35
18	Estonia	2.15		97	Ivory Coast	3.35
18	Netherlands	2.15		97	Moldova	3.35
22	Denmark	2.25		97	Pakistan	3.35
22	El Salvador	2.25		104	Nepal	3.40
22	Finland	2.25		104	Venezuela	3.40
25	Germany	2.30		106	Armenia	3.45
25	Iceland	2.30		106	Bulgaria	3.45
27	Norway	2.35		106	Lesotho	3.45
28	Korea, South	2.40		106	Madagascar	3.45
28	Kuwait	2.40		106	Russia	3.45
28	Malaysia	2.40		111	Burkina Faso	3.50
28	Panama	2.40		111	Cameroon	3.50
28	Thailand	2.40		111	Guyana	3.50
33	Sweden	2.45		111	Nicaragua	3.50
34	Argentina	2.50		115	Gambia	3.60
34	France	2.50		116	Croatia	3.65
34	Italy	2.50		116	Georgia	3.65
34	Spain	2.50		116	Malawi	3.65
38	Portugal	2.55		119	Cape Verde	3.67
38	Sri Lanka	2.55		120	Ethiopia	3.70
38	Trinidad and Tobago	2.55		120	India	3.70
41	Barbados	2.60		120	Niger	3.70
41	Peru	2.60		123	Congo	3.75
43	Bolivia	2.65		124	Chad	3.80
43	Mauritius	2.65		124	China	3.80
45	Cyprus	2.70		124	Mauritania	3.80
45	Jamaica	2.70		124	Ukraine	3.80
45	Uruguay	2.70		124	Zimbabwe	3.80
48	Botswana	2.75		129	Albania	3.85
48	Guatemala	2.75		129	Bangladesh	3.85
48	Jordan	2.75		129	Mozambique	3.85
48	Namibia	2.75		129	Suriname	3.85
48	Oman	2.75		133	Burundi	3.90
48	Philippines	2.75		134	Togo	3.95
54	Belize	2.80		135	Haiti	4.00
54	Costa Rica	2.80		135	Kyrgyz Rep.	4.00
54	Israel	2.80		137	Kazakhstan	4.05
54	Swaziland	2.80		137	Sierra Leone	4.05
54	Turkey	2.80		139	Yemen	4.10
54	Uganda	2.80		140	Belarus	4.15
54	Samoa	2.80		141	Sudan	4.20
61	Latvia	2.85		141	Syria	4.20
62	Greece	2.90		143	Azerbaijan	4.30
62	Hungary	2.90		143	Equatorial Guinea	4.30
62	So. Africa	2.90		143	Myanmar	4.30
65	Ecuador	2.95		143	Rwanda	4.30
65	Gabon	2.95		147	Tajikistan	4.40
65	Indonesia	2.95		147	Uzbekistan	4.40
65	Malta	2.95		149	Angola	4.45
65	Morocco	2.95		149	Turkmenistan	4.45
65	Poland	2.95		151	Guinea-Bissau	4.55
65	Tunisia	2.95		152	Vietnam	4.60
72	Ghana	3.00		153	Congo (Zaire)	4.70
72	Lithuania	3.00		153	Iran	4.70
72	Saudi Arabia	3.00		155	Bosnia	4.80
75	Benin	3.05		155	Somalia	4.80
75	Kenya	3.05		157	Iraq	4.90
75	Paraguay	3.05		157	Laos	4.90
75	Qatar	3.05		157	Libya	4.90
75	Slovak Republic	3.05		160	Cuba	5.00
75	Zambia	3.05		160	Korea, North	5.00
81	Colombia	3.10				

Free

economy. The government continues to own shares in the state postal system as well as in Swisscom, the state telecommunications company, although partial privatization has been under way and has increased competition significantly.

MONETARY POLICY
Score: 1–Stable (very low level of inflation)

Switzerland's average annual rate of inflation from 1986 to 1996 was 2.8 percent. In 1997, the rate was about 0.5 percent. Inflation in 1998 was less than 1 percent.

CAPITAL FLOWS AND FOREIGN INVESTMENT
Score: 2–Stable (low barriers)

Switzerland is open to foreign investment, although it restricts investment in hydroelectric and nuclear power plants, oil pipelines, the operation of television and radio broadcasting, and transportation.

BANKING
Score: 1–Stable (very low level of restrictions)

Switzerland's banking system is one of the freest and most competitive in the world. Banks may offer a wide range of financial services with virtually no government interference.

WAGE AND PRICE CONTROLS
Score: 2–Stable (low level)

The market sets most wages and prices. The government heavily regulates and subsidizes the agricultural sector, however, which serves to influence the price of agricultural goods. Switzerland has no minimum wage.

PROPERTY RIGHTS
Score: 1–Stable (very high level of protection)

From the standpoint of private property rights, Switzerland may be one of the world's safest countries. According to the U.S. Department of State, "The Constitution provides for an independent judiciary, and the Government respects this provision in practice. The judiciary provides citizens with a fair and efficient judicial process."[5]

REGULATION
Score: 3–Stable (moderate level)

Establishing a business can be easy. Even though the government heavily regulates such industries as agriculture, television and broadcasting, and utilities, it applies regulations evenly in most cases.

BLACK MARKET
Score: 1–Stable (very low level of activity)

The size of Switzerland's black market is negligible. There is virtually no black market in pirated intellectual property. As the U.S. Department of State reports, "Switzerland has one of the best regimes in the world for the protection of intellectual property, and protection is afforded equally to foreign and domestic rights holders."[6]

NOTES

[1] Liechtenstein's economy is linked closely with Switzerland's.

[2] This rate includes all duty-free trade. From *World Trade and Customs Directory* (Washington, D.C.: Arrowhead International, 1998).

[3] Ernst & Young, *1998 Worldwide Executive Tax Guide,* September 1997.

[4] The score in this factor has changed from a 4 in 1998 to a 3 in 1999. Previously unavailable data provide a more accurate understanding of the country's performance. This information comes from Ernst & Young, which states, "The total effective maximum tax burden, which consists of federal, cantonal, and communal taxes, ranges from 16.5 % to 32%, depending on the canton in which an enterprise is located." See Ernst & Young, *1998 Worldwide Corporate Tax Guide,* January 1998. The methodology for this factor, however, remains the same.

[5] U.S. Department of State, "Switzerland Country Report on Human Rights Practices for 1997," 1998.

[6] U.S. Department of State, *Country Reports on Economic Policy and Trade Practices,* 1997, p. 182.

Syria

4.20

1998 Score: **4.00**   1997 Score: **4.20**   1996 Score: **4.20**

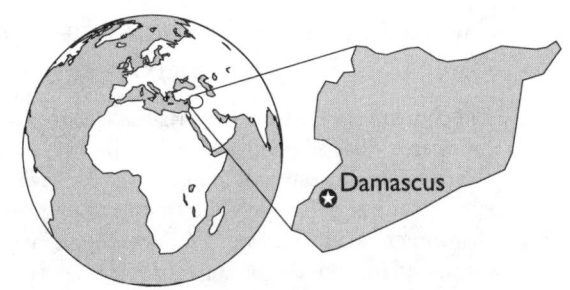

Damascus

Trade	5	Banking	5
Taxation	5	Wages and Prices	4
Government Intervention	3	Property Rights	4
Monetary Policy	3	Regulation	4
Foreign Investment	4	Black Market	5

Syria gained its independence from France in 1946 and has played a leading role in Arab politics and the Arab–Israeli struggle. It was plagued by political instability and a series of military coups until General Hafez al-Assad seized power in 1970; since that time, Syria has developed a state-dominated socialist economy and has depended heavily on foreign aid, first from the Soviet Union and more recently from the oil-rich Persian Gulf states. In 1992, the government sought to spur private and foreign investment by loosening restrictive regulations, but a swollen public sector remains an obstacle to free-market reform. The United States maintains trade sanctions against Syria because of the regime's longstanding support of terrorism. Recent studies demonstrate that corruption within the bureaucracy is having a greater impact on business. Because of an increase in regulation and corruption, Syria's overall score is 0.2 point worse than last year.

TRADE POLICY

Score: 5–Stable (very high level of protectionism)

Syria's average tariff rate is 28.6 percent.[1] The customs service is both onerous and confusing, and all imports require a license. According to the U.S. Department of Commerce, "Customs procedures are cumbersome, tedious, and time-consuming because of complex regulations."[2] Many imports are banned.

TAXATION

Score–Income taxation: 5–Stable (very high tax rates)

Score–Corporate taxation: 5–Stable (very high tax rates)

Final Taxation Score: 5–Stable (very high tax rates)

Syria's top income tax rate is 64 percent.[3] The top marginal corporate tax rate is over 50 percent.[4]

GOVERNMENT INTERVENTION IN THE ECONOMY

Score: 3–Stable (moderate level)

Government consumes about 14.3 percent of GDP, and the public sector accounts for approximately 36 percent of total GDP. According to the U.S. Department of Commerce, the "public sector is still expanding and the government continues to control all 'strategic' sectors such as oil, electricity, banking and chemicals as well as much of the textile and food processing industries."[5] Still, because the government consumption rate is only 14.3 percent, by global standards, Syria's government intervention in the economy is moderate.

MONETARY POLICY

Score: 3–Stable (moderate level of inflation)

Syria's average annual rate of inflation from 1986 to 1996 was 17 percent. In 1997, the rate was about 10 percent.

1	Hong Kong	1.25	81	Fiji	3.10
2	Singapore	1.30	81	Mali	3.10
3	Bahrain	1.70	81	Slovenia	3.10
4	New Zealand	1.75	85	Honduras	3.15
5	Switzerland	1.85	85	Mexico	3.15
6	United States	1.90	85	Papua New Guinea	3.15
7	Ireland	1.95	88	Djibouti	3.20
7	Luxembourg	1.95	88	Mongolia	3.20
7	Taiwan	1.95	90	Algeria	3.25
7	United Kingdom	1.95	90	Brazil	3.25
11	Bahamas	2.00	90	Lebanon	3.25
12	Czech Republic	2.05	90	Senegal	3.25
12	Japan	2.05	90	Tanzania	3.25
14	Australia	2.10	90	Nigeria	3.30
14	Belgium	2.10	95	Romania	3.30
14	Canada	2.10	97	Cambodia	3.35
14	United Arab Emirates	2.10	97	Dominican Republic	3.35
18	Austria	2.15	97	Egypt	3.35
18	Chile	2.15	97	Guinea	3.35
18	Estonia	2.15	97	Ivory Coast	3.35
18	Netherlands	2.15	97	Moldova	3.35
22	Denmark	2.25	97	Pakistan	3.35
22	El Salvador	2.25	104	Nepal	3.40
22	Finland	2.25	104	Venezuela	3.40
25	Germany	2.30	106	Armenia	3.45
25	Iceland	2.30	106	Bulgaria	3.45
27	Norway	2.35	106	Lesotho	3.45
28	Korea, South	2.40	106	Madagascar	3.45
28	Kuwait	2.40	106	Russia	3.45
28	Malaysia	2.40	111	Burkina Faso	3.50
28	Panama	2.40	111	Cameroon	3.50
28	Thailand	2.40	111	Guyana	3.50
33	Sweden	2.45	111	Nicaragua	3.50
34	Argentina	2.50	115	Gambia	3.60
34	France	2.50	116	Croatia	3.65
34	Italy	2.50	116	Georgia	3.65
34	Spain	2.50	116	Malawi	3.65
38	Portugal	2.55	119	Cape Verde	3.67
38	Sri Lanka	2.55	120	Ethiopia	3.70
38	Trinidad and Tobago	2.55	120	India	3.70
41	Barbados	2.60	120	Niger	3.70
41	Peru	2.60	123	Congo	3.75
43	Bolivia	2.65	124	Chad	3.80
43	Mauritius	2.65	124	China	3.80
45	Cyprus	2.70	124	Mauritania	3.80
45	Jamaica	2.70	124	Ukraine	3.80
45	Uruguay	2.70	124	Zimbabwe	3.80
48	Botswana	2.75	129	Albania	3.85
48	Guatemala	2.75	129	Bangladesh	3.85
48	Jordan	2.75	129	Mozambique	3.85
48	Namibia	2.75	129	Suriname	3.85
48	Oman	2.75	133	Burundi	3.90
48	Philippines	2.75	134	Togo	3.95
54	Belize	2.80	135	Haiti	4.00
54	Costa Rica	2.80	135	Kyrgyz Rep.	4.00
54	Israel	2.80	137	Kazakhstan	4.05
54	Swaziland	2.80	137	Sierra Leone	4.05
54	Turkey	2.80	139	Yemen	4.10
54	Uganda	2.80	140	Belarus	4.15
54	Samoa	2.80	141	Sudan	4.20
61	Latvia	2.85	141	Syria	4.20
62	Greece	2.90	143	Azerbaijan	4.30
62	Hungary	2.90	143	Equatorial Guinea	4.30
62	So. Africa	2.90	143	Myanmar	4.30
65	Ecuador	2.95	143	Rwanda	4.30
65	Gabon	2.95	147	Tajikistan	4.40
65	Indonesia	2.95	147	Uzbekistan	4.40
65	Malta	2.95	149	Angola	4.45
65	Morocco	2.95	149	Turkmenistan	4.45
65	Poland	2.95	151	Guinea-Bissau	4.55
65	Tunisia	2.95	152	Vietnam	4.60
72	Ghana	3.00	153	Congo (Zaire)	4.70
72	Lithuania	3.00	153	Iran	4.70
72	Saudi Arabia	3.00	155	Bosnia	4.80
75	Benin	3.05	155	Somalia	4.80
75	Kenya	3.05	157	Iraq	4.90
75	Paraguay	3.05	157	Laos	4.90
75	Qatar	3.05	157	Libya	4.90
75	Slovak Republic	3.05	160	Cuba	5.00
75	Zambia	3.05	160	Korea, North	5.00
81	Colombia	3.10			

Repressed

Capital Flows and Foreign Investment
Score: 4–Stable (high barriers)

"The Syrian government," reports the U.S. Department of Commerce, "has adopted a hesitantly positive attitude toward foreign investment in recent years. However, most representatives of foreign firms find Syria's business environment a difficult one."[6] A new foreign investment law was passed in 1991. According to the U.S. Department of Commerce, "All applications for investment under the law must be screened and vetted through the Higher Council for Investment. The Council meets at least once every two months. Membership includes the Prime Minister, and the Ministers of Economy, Agriculture, Transportation, Supply, Industry, Planning, Finance, and the Director of the Investment Bureau. No definitive criteria for approving investment is [sic] made explicit under the new law."[7]

Banking
Score: 5–Stable (very high level of restrictions)

The banking system is completely controlled by the government, which also owns all of the country's major banks. The U.S. Department of Commerce reports that "Syria's government-controlled banking system consists of five banks: the Commercial Bank of Syria, the Agricultural Cooperative Bank, the Industrial Bank, the Real Estate Bank, and the People's Credit Bank. The Central Bank of Syria oversees banking operations and manages the money supply. According to Syrian bank regulations, only the Central Bank and the Commercial Bank may engage in international transactions and hold foreign exchange deposits outside Syria. Within Syria, only the Commercial Bank may sell Syrian pounds for foreign currencies. Except for a few exceptions, unused Syrian pounds cannot be sold back to the Commercial Bank. Moreover, Law 24 of 1986 criminalizes the private exchange of foreign currencies and Syrian pounds.... Besides monopolizing the exchange of foreign currencies, the Syrian government maintains one of the last remaining fixed, multiple exchange rate systems in the world. At present the government exchanges money at four different rates."[8]

Wage and Price Controls
Score: 4–Stable (high level)

In general, the government sets wages and prices; in addition, according to the U.S. Department of Commerce, the government "continues to control all 'strategic' sectors such as oil, electricity, banking, and chemicals as well as much of the textile and food processing industries."[9]

Property Rights
Score: 4–Stable (low level of protection)

Private property is not safe. Although the legal and judicial system recognizes the free exchange of property and some contractual agreements, private property also is subject to expropriation. "The judiciary," reports the U.S. Department of State, "is constitutionally independent, but this is not the case in the exceptional (state of emergency) security courts, which are subject to political influence."[10] Moreover, the U.S. Department of Commerce reports that there is "considerable government interference in the court system and judgments by foreign courts are generally accepted only if the verdict favors the Syrian government."[11]

Regulation
Score: 4– (high level)

Establishing a business can be easy if the business does not intend to compete directly with the state-owned sector. The private sector is growing rapidly. In the past, regulations often were ignored or not enforced; at the current time, however, evidence is mounting that the regulatory burden and corruption within the bureaucracy both are on the rise. For example, according to the U.S. Department of Commerce, "Bureaucratic procedures for licensing and necessary documentation move slowly and require official approval from many levels within the government. In this regard, under-the-table payments are often required as corruption is endemic at nearly all levels of government."[12] As a result, Syria's regulation score is 2 points worse this year.

BLACK MARKET
Score: 5–Stable (very high level of activity)

The size of Syria's black market is quite large, although the smuggling of many consumer goods has prompted the government to expand its list of permitted legal imports. Moreover, the pirating of books, computer software, and videos is rampant. According to the U.S. Department of Commerce, "instances of copyright infringement especially of Arabic translations of English texts, have occurred. Pirated records, cassettes, and videos are widely available.... Despite government efforts, pirated computer software is also readily available.... The motion picture industry estimates the home video market in Syria is 100 percent pirated, and is also concerned with unauthorized hotel video performances, which are said to be common.... Additionally, 100 percent of both Arab and non-Arab commercial music products are pirated."[13]

NOTES

[1] Based on total taxes on international trade as a percentage of total imports.

[2] U.S. Department of Commerce, *Country Commercial Guide,* 1998.

[3] The tax level for the average income is not available, and tax evasion is rampant. See U.S. Department of State, *Country Reports on Economic Policy and Trade Practices,* 1998.

[4] Because Syria's tax system is complicated and unclear, this figure includes a host of taxes and fees and provides only a rough estimate.

[5] U.S. Department of Commerce, *Country Commercial Guide,* 1998.

[6] *Ibid.*

[7] *Ibid.*

[8] *Ibid.*

[9] *Ibid.*

[10] U.S. Department of State, "Syria Country Report on Human Rights Practices for 1997," 1998.

[11] U.S. Department of Commerce, *Country Commercial Guide,* 1998.

[12] *Ibid.*

[13] *Ibid.*

Tajikistan   4.40

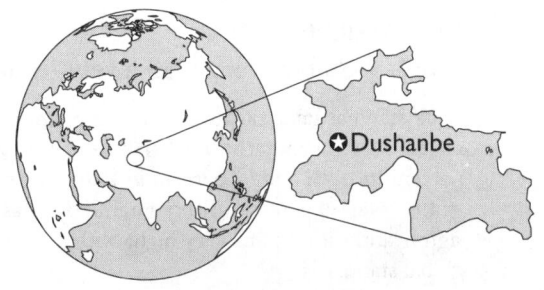

●Dushanbe

1998 Score: **4.40**	1997 Score: **n/a**	1996 Score: **n/a**

Trade	5	Banking	4
Taxation	5	Wages and Prices	4
Government Intervention	4	Property Rights	4
Monetary Policy	5	Regulation	4
Foreign Investment	4	Black Market	5

Subjected to continual conquest throughout much of its early history, Tajikistan became part of Ghengis Khan's Mongol empire in the 13th century. Russia established its control in 1868 by annexing the northern part of the country. In 1916, tsarist Russia attempted to enlist many Tajiks into its army. The ensuing rebellion continued through the revolution in Russia in 1917. The country became part of the Russian Federation in 1921 as the Turkistan Autonomous Soviet Socialist Republic, a region that included portions of present-day Kazakhstan, Turkmenistan, and Uzbekistan. The area that now comprises Tajikistan was made autonomous in 1924 and fully incorporated into the Soviet Union in 1929. After Tajikistan gained its independence in 1991, the Soviet-era government retained control of large portions of the new regime; a civil war between the pro-communists and Islamic and democratic groups ensued in 1992. The pro-communists eventually gained control of the country and began to persecute the Islamic and democratic groups. A ceasefire was reached in 1994, but ethnic and civil unrest continues, leaving little time for economic reform.

TRADE POLICY
Score: 5–Stable (very high level of protectionism)

The average tariff rate is unavailable, primarily because of the lack of a fully functioning customs service. Although most tariffs range between 10 percent and 20 percent, customs rates charged at the border vary constantly. In addition, there is very little private trade. According to the U.S. Department of State, "The government conducts virtually all trade."[1] There also is little economic freedom for individuals in the trade sector.

TAXATION
Score–Income taxation: 5–Stable (very high tax rates)
Score–Corporate taxation: 5–Stable (very high tax rates)
Final Taxation Score: 5–Stable (very high tax rates)

Tajikistan's tax system is in disarray, with redundant and overlapping taxes. According to the U.S. Department of Commerce, the government "abolished the regulation providing for exemptions for major taxes, including the profit tax, excise tax, value added tax, and customs duties."[2] Without these exemptions, businesses and individuals are held responsible for a variety of taxes. Rates vary widely, and the collection system remains arbitrary. The government gets the bulk of its revenue from state ownership of most medium and large businesses, as well as from its ownership share (usually limited to 40 percent) of businesses that have been privatized. It also consumes much of the profit produced by these state-owned and privatized companies—in effect, taxing profits. The government also has a 20 percent value-added tax and a sales tax.

GOVERNMENT INTERVENTION IN THE ECONOMY
Score: 4–Stable (high level)

Tajikistan is privatizing some of its state-owned sector, but the government continues to own shares in many privatized companies. Most GDP is produced by the state-owned sector.

1	Hong Kong	1.25
2	Singapore	1.30
3	Bahrain	1.70
4	New Zealand	1.75
5	Switzerland	1.85
6	United States	1.90
7	Ireland	1.95
7	Luxembourg	1.95
7	Taiwan	1.95
7	United Kingdom	1.95
11	Bahamas	2.00
12	Czech Republic	2.05
12	Japan	2.05
14	Australia	2.10
14	Belgium	2.10
14	Canada	2.10
14	United Arab Emirates	2.10
18	Austria	2.15
18	Chile	2.15
18	Estonia	2.15
18	Netherlands	2.15
22	Denmark	2.25
22	El Salvador	2.25
22	Finland	2.25
25	Germany	2.30
25	Iceland	2.30
27	Norway	2.35
28	Korea, South	2.40
28	Kuwait	2.40
28	Malaysia	2.40
28	Panama	2.40
28	Thailand	2.40
33	Sweden	2.45
34	Argentina	2.50
34	France	2.50
34	Italy	2.50
34	Spain	2.50
38	Portugal	2.55
38	Sri Lanka	2.55
38	Trinidad and Tobago	2.55
41	Barbados	2.60
41	Peru	2.60
43	Bolivia	2.65
43	Mauritius	2.65
45	Cyprus	2.70
45	Jamaica	2.70
45	Uruguay	2.70
48	Botswana	2.75
48	Guatemala	2.75
48	Jordan	2.75
48	Namibia	2.75
48	Oman	2.75
48	Philippines	2.75
54	Belize	2.80
54	Costa Rica	2.80
54	Israel	2.80
54	Swaziland	2.80
54	Turkey	2.80
54	Uganda	2.80
54	Samoa	2.80
61	Latvia	2.85
62	Greece	2.90
62	Hungary	2.90
62	So. Africa	2.90
65	Ecuador	2.95
65	Gabon	2.95
65	Indonesia	2.95
65	Malta	2.95
65	Morocco	2.95
65	Poland	2.95
65	Tunisia	2.95
72	Ghana	3.00
72	Lithuania	3.00
72	Saudi Arabia	3.00
75	Benin	3.05
75	Kenya	3.05
75	Paraguay	3.05
75	Qatar	3.05
75	Slovak Republic	3.05
75	Zambia	3.05
81	Colombia	3.10
81	Fiji	3.10
81	Mali	3.10
81	Slovenia	3.10
85	Honduras	3.15
85	Mexico	3.15
85	Papua New Guinea	3.15
88	Djibouti	3.20
88	Mongolia	3.20
90	Algeria	3.25
90	Brazil	3.25
90	Lebanon	3.25
90	Senegal	3.25
90	Tanzania	3.25
95	Nigeria	3.30
95	Romania	3.30
97	Cambodia	3.35
97	Dominican Republic	3.35
97	Egypt	3.35
97	Guinea	3.35
97	Ivory Coast	3.35
97	Moldova	3.35
97	Pakistan	3.35
104	Nepal	3.40
104	Venezuela	3.40
106	Armenia	3.45
106	Bulgaria	3.45
106	Lesotho	3.45
106	Madagascar	3.45
106	Russia	3.45
111	Burkina Faso	3.50
111	Cameroon	3.50
111	Guyana	3.50
111	Nicaragua	3.50
115	Gambia	3.60
116	Croatia	3.65
116	Georgia	3.65
116	Malawi	3.65
119	Cape Verde	3.67
120	Ethiopia	3.70
120	India	3.70
120	Niger	3.70
123	Congo	3.75
124	Chad	3.80
124	China	3.80
124	Mauritania	3.80
124	Ukraine	3.80
124	Zimbabwe	3.80
129	Albania	3.85
129	Bangladesh	3.85
129	Mozambique	3.85
129	Suriname	3.85
133	Burundi	3.90
134	Togo	3.95
135	Haiti	4.00
135	Kyrgyz Rep.	4.00
137	Kazakhstan	4.05
137	Sierra Leone	4.05
139	Yemen	4.10
140	Belarus	4.15
141	Sudan	4.20
141	Syria	4.20
143	Azerbaijan	4.30
143	Equatorial Guinea	4.30
143	Myanmar	4.30
143	Rwanda	4.30
147	Tajikistan	4.40
147	Uzbekistan	4.40
149	Angola	4.45
149	Turkmenistan	4.45
151	Guinea-Bissau	4.55
152	Vietnam	4.60
153	Congo (Zaire)	4.70
153	Iran	4.70
155	Bosnia	4.80
155	Somalia	4.80
157	Iraq	4.90
157	Laos	4.90
157	Libya	4.90
160	Cuba	5.00
160	Korea, North	5.00

Repressed

MONETARY POLICY
Score: 5–Stable (very high level of inflation)

Tajikistan has been plagued by hyperinflation: 1,157 percent in 1992, 2,195 percent in 1993, 452 percent in 1994, 635 percent in 1995, and 65 percent in 1996. The rate of inflation in 1997 was 40 percent. Although inflation has fallen significantly, it remains very high, both historically and by global standards.

CAPITAL FLOWS AND FOREIGN INVESTMENT
Score: 4–Stable (high barriers)

The government has opened some of the economy to foreign investment and wants to promote increased investment, but the bureaucratic procedure is arbitrary and restricts many investments. According to the U.S. Department of State, "Although legislation encourages foreign investment, contradictory and unclear decrees make doing business in Tajikistan a labyrinthine process."[3]

BANKING
Score: 4–Stable (high level of restrictions)

The banking system is not yet fully functional. As described by the U.S. Department of Commerce, "The Tajik banking sector is dominated by large specialized banks, a heritage from the state banks of the former Soviet Union. These banks—Agroprombank, Orientbank, and Tajikbankbusiness—account for over 96 percent of bank financing."[4] Because the state owns these three major banks, most of the financial system's assets fall under state control. According to the U.S. Department of State, "Tajikistan is a cash-only economy. International banking services are not available. Credit cards and traveler's checks are not accepted. Travel with large amounts of cash can be dangerous. Although some private shops continue to accept Russian rubles, Tajikistan has introduced its own currency, the Tajik ruble."[5]

WAGE AND PRICE CONTROLS
Score: 4–Stable (high level)

The large number of state-owned enterprises controls wages and prices. Price controls continue on such items as agricultural products, transportation, and utilities, and government subsidies to many industries continue to prohibit market pricing.

PROPERTY RIGHTS
Score: 4–Stable (low level of protection)

Private property does not enjoy sufficient protection under the legal system. According to the U.S. Department of State, "Judicial officials at all levels of the court system are heavily influenced by both the political leadership and, in many instances, armed paramilitary groups.... Judges at the local, regional, and republic level are, for the most part, poorly trained and lack understanding of an independent judiciary.... Pressure continues to be exerted on the judicial system by local strongmen, their armed paramilitary groups, and vigilantes who operate outside of government control, sometimes leading to the dismissal of charges and dropping of cases. Bribery of prosecutors and judges is also considered to be widespread."[6]

REGULATION
Score: 4–Stable (high level)

Establishing a business can be a tedious and time-consuming procedure that requires individuals to overcome numerous bureaucratic barriers. According to the U.S. Department of State, "A convoluted and corrupt bureaucracy adds to the difficulty of doing business."[7]

BLACK MARKET
Score: 5–Stable (very high level of activity)

Smuggling is rampant, and despite laws to protect intellectual property rights, significant piracy in computer software continues. According to the U.S. Department of Commerce, "Present laws on intellectual property protection are adhered to in Tajikistan, if the cases ever get to court. However, despite a flourishing video and cassette pirating business, which no one seems to be interested in addressing, only one action, concerning published literature, was brought to court in 1996."[8]

NOTES

[1]   U.S. Department of State, *Country Reports on Economic Policy and Trade Practices, 1996.*
[2]   U.S. Department of Commerce, "Current Status of Economic Reform in Tajikistan," June 1996.
[3]   U.S. Department of State, *Country Reports on Economic Policy and Trade Practices, 1996.*
[4]   U.S. Department of Commerce, "Banking in Tajikistan," May 1997.
[5]   U.S. Department of State, "Travel Conditions," *Market Research Reports,* 1998.
[6]   U.S. Department of State, "Tajikistan Country Report on Human Rights Practices for 1997," 1998.
[7]   U.S. Department of State, *Country Reports on Economic Policy and Trade Practices, 1996.*
[8]   U.S. Department of Commerce, "Intellectual Property Protection in Tajikistan," March 12, 1997.

Tanzania   3.25

Trade	3	Banking	3
Taxation	3.5	Wages and Prices	2
Government Intervention	3	Property Rights	3
Monetary Policy	4	Regulation	4
Foreign Investment	3	Black Market	4

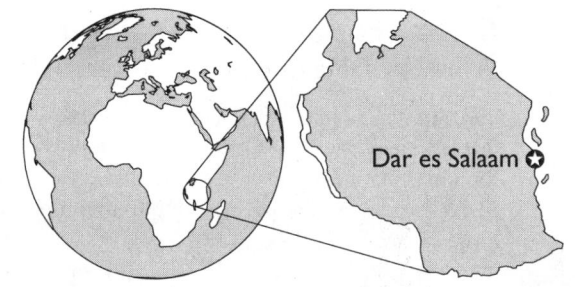

Dar es Salaam ✪

Tanzania was founded in 1964 from the union of Tanganyika and Zanzibar, which had gained their independence from the United Kingdom in 1961 and 1963, respectively. Until the late 1980s, the government controlled most aspects of the economy, with nationalized industry and collectivized agriculture. Tanzania's per capita GNP remains among the world's lowest (estimated by the World Bank at $170 in 1996) despite billions of dollars in foreign aid from developed countries and multilateral aid institutions. Market reforms introduced by the government of President Ali Hassan Mwinyi and continued by President Benjamin Mkapa have made limited progress toward liberalizing the economy and have led to improved growth in GDP, which averaged 3.8 percent from 1993 to 1997. Tanzania still relies heavily on foreign aid, but relations with international donors remain fragile because of political concerns on Zanzibar and widespread graft and corruption.

TRADE POLICY

Score: 3–Stable (moderately high level of protectionism)

Tanzania has an average tariff rate of 8.6 percent.[1] A major non-tariff barrier is the inefficient customs system. "Despite the existence of regulations and laws," reports the U.S. Department of Commerce, "the customs department is the greatest hindrance to importers throughout Tanzania. Clearance delays and extra-legal levies are commonplace when dealing with the Tanzanian Customs Department. These hindrances can cause unpredictable delays when importing goods into the country."[2]

TAXATION

Score–Income taxation: 3–Stable (moderate tax rates)
Score–Corporate taxation: 3–Stable (moderate tax rates)
Final Taxation Score: 3.5–Stable (high tax rates)

Tanzania's highest income tax rate is 35 percent. The average income level is in the 10 percent tax bracket. The corporate tax rate is 30 percent. Tanzania also has a sales tax of up to 30 percent.

GOVERNMENT INTERVENTION IN THE ECONOMY

Score: 3–Stable (moderate level)

Government consumes 13 percent of GDP.[3] Although some industries have undergone privatization, inefficient state-owned enterprises continue to play a major role in the industrial sector, and government monopolies in agriculture still exist.

MONETARY POLICY

Score: 4–Stable (high level of inflation)

Tanzania's average annual rate of inflation from 1986 through 1996 was 34.6 percent. It is estimated that the current rate of inflation is 18 percent.

1	Hong Kong	1.25	81	Fiji	3.10
2	Singapore	1.30	81	Mali	3.10
3	Bahrain	1.70	81	Slovenia	3.10
4	New Zealand	1.75	85	Honduras	3.15
5	Switzerland	1.85	85	Mexico	3.15
6	United States	1.90	85	Papua New Guinea	3.15
7	Ireland	1.95	88	Djibouti	3.20
7	Luxembourg	1.95	88	Mongolia	3.20
7	Taiwan	1.95	90	Algeria	3.25
7	United Kingdom	1.95	90	Brazil	3.25
11	Bahamas	2.00	90	Lebanon	3.25
12	Czech Republic	2.05	90	Senegal	3.25
12	Japan	2.05	90	Tanzania	3.25
14	Australia	2.10	95	Nigeria	3.30
14	Belgium	2.10	95	Romania	3.30
14	Canada	2.10	97	Cambodia	3.35
14	United Arab Emirates	2.10	97	Dominican Republic	3.35
18	Austria	2.15	97	Egypt	3.35
18	Chile	2.15	97	Guinea	3.35
18	Estonia	2.15	97	Ivory Coast	3.35
18	Netherlands	2.15	97	Moldova	3.35
22	Denmark	2.25	97	Pakistan	3.35
22	El Salvador	2.25	104	Nepal	3.40
22	Finland	2.25	104	Venezuela	3.40
25	Germany	2.30	106	Armenia	3.45
25	Iceland	2.30	106	Bulgaria	3.45
27	Norway	2.35	106	Lesotho	3.45
28	Korea, South	2.40	106	Madagascar	3.45
28	Kuwait	2.40	106	Russia	3.45
28	Malaysia	2.40	111	Burkina Faso	3.50
28	Panama	2.40	111	Cameroon	3.50
28	Thailand	2.40	111	Guyana	3.50
33	Sweden	2.45	111	Nicaragua	3.50
34	Argentina	2.50	115	Gambia	3.60
34	France	2.50	116	Croatia	3.65
34	Italy	2.50	116	Georgia	3.65
34	Spain	2.50	116	Malawi	3.65
38	Portugal	2.55	119	Cape Verde	3.67
38	Sri Lanka	2.55	120	Ethiopia	3.70
38	Trinidad and Tobago	2.55	120	India	3.70
41	Barbados	2.60	120	Niger	3.70
41	Peru	2.60	123	Congo	3.75
43	Bolivia	2.65	124	Chad	3.80
43	Mauritius	2.65	124	China	3.80
45	Cyprus	2.70	124	Mauritania	3.80
45	Jamaica	2.70	124	Ukraine	3.80
45	Uruguay	2.70	124	Zimbabwe	3.80
48	Botswana	2.75	129	Albania	3.85
48	Guatemala	2.75	129	Bangladesh	3.85
48	Jordan	2.75	129	Mozambique	3.85
48	Namibia	2.75	129	Suriname	3.85
48	Oman	2.75	133	Burundi	3.90
48	Philippines	2.75	134	Togo	3.95
54	Belize	2.80	135	Haiti	4.00
54	Costa Rica	2.80	135	Kyrgyz Rep.	4.00
54	Israel	2.80	137	Kazakhstan	4.05
54	Swaziland	2.80	137	Sierra Leone	4.05
54	Turkey	2.80	139	Yemen	4.10
54	Uganda	2.80	140	Belarus	4.15
54	Samoa	2.80	141	Sudan	4.20
61	Latvia	2.85	141	Syria	4.20
62	Greece	2.90	143	Azerbaijan	4.30
62	Hungary	2.90	143	Equatorial Guinea	4.30
62	So. Africa	2.90	143	Myanmar	4.30
65	Ecuador	2.95	143	Rwanda	4.30
65	Gabon	2.95	147	Tajikistan	4.40
65	Indonesia	2.95	147	Uzbekistan	4.40
65	Malta	2.95	149	Angola	4.45
65	Morocco	2.95	149	Turkmenistan	4.45
65	Poland	2.95	151	Guinea-Bissau	4.55
65	Tunisia	2.95	152	Vietnam	4.60
72	Ghana	3.00	153	Congo (Zaire)	4.70
72	Lithuania	3.00	153	Iran	4.70
72	Saudi Arabia	3.00	155	Bosnia	4.80
75	Benin	3.05	155	Somalia	4.80
75	Kenya	3.05	157	Iraq	4.90
75	Paraguay	3.05	157	Laos	4.90
75	Qatar	3.05	157	Libya	4.90
75	Slovak Republic	3.05	160	Cuba	5.00
75	Zambia	3.05	160	Korea, North	5.00
81	Colombia	3.10			

Mostly Unfree

CAPITAL FLOWS AND FOREIGN INVESTMENT
Score: 3–Stable (moderate barriers)

Tanzania's new investment code has created a more favorable environment for foreign investment. A single-stop foreign investment approval office has been established, majority government participation in mining projects no longer is required, the government offers investment incentives, and there is a free trade zone on the island of Zanzibar. Bureaucratic impediments, however, include the necessity to acquire business licenses, company registrations, and other documentation from a variety of ministries that frequently are corrupt. For example, according to the U.S. Department of Commerce, "Tanzania is formally open to all foreign investment, although many procedural barriers must be overcome by the successful investor."[4] Foreign ownership of land is prohibited.

BANKING
Score: 3–Stable (moderate level of restrictions)

At least five foreign banks have opened over the past two years, and a Tanzanian-owned bank opened in 1995. These are the first private banks to take advantage of a 1991 law that allows private banking (the banking sector had been nationalized in 1967). The market now determines interest rates. Despite reforms, however, financial services still are provided largely by inefficient and corrupt state banks.

WAGE AND PRICE CONTROLS
Score: 2–Stable (low level)

The government has removed most price controls and liberalized the pricing of agricultural products. Wage controls are imposed indirectly by the government's extensive control of economic enterprise. Tanzania has a minimum wage.

PROPERTY RIGHTS
Score: 3–Stable (moderate level of protection)

No nationalization of private enterprises has taken place since 1973. There is a great deal of resentment, however, against individuals (particularly Asians) who have acquired privatized properties. According to the U.S. Department of State, "The Constitution provides for an independent judiciary; in practice, the higher courts have demonstrated their independence of the Government." At the same time, however, "Independent observers...continue to criticize the judiciary, especially at lower levels, as corrupt and inefficient and question the system's ability to provide a defendant with an expeditious and fair trial."[5] Nevertheless, the judicial system is not in disarray, and Tanzania maintains a moderate level of private property protection by global standards.

REGULATION
Score: 4–Stable (high level)

Excessive regulation is throttling the private sector, and corruption is rampant throughout the bureaucracy. As the U.S. Department of Commerce reports, "Tanzania has in place an extensive set of policies, regulations and procedures that greatly influence trade, commerce, employment, and resource utilization. Many of these provisions are outdated and reflect conditions in the colonial era; many others reflect socialist-era circumstances and have yet to be adjusted to serve the needs of a liberal market based economy."[6]

BLACK MARKET
Score: 4–Stable (high level of activity)

The size of Tanzania's black market is huge. High tariffs on textiles have produced a vibrant market in smuggled textiles, and the free trade zone on Zanzibar has led to the smuggling of goods to the mainland. Protection of intellectual property rights remains lax.

NOTES
1   Based on total taxes on international trade as a percentage of total imports.
2   U.S. Department of Commerce, *Country Commercial Guide,* 1998.
3   The World Bank, *World Development Indicators,* 1998.
4   U.S. Department of Commerce, *Country Commercial Guide,* 1998.
5   U.S. Department of State, "Tanzania Country Report on Human Rights Practices for 1997," 1998.
6   U.S. Department of Commerce, *Country Commercial Guide,* 1998.

Thailand 2.40

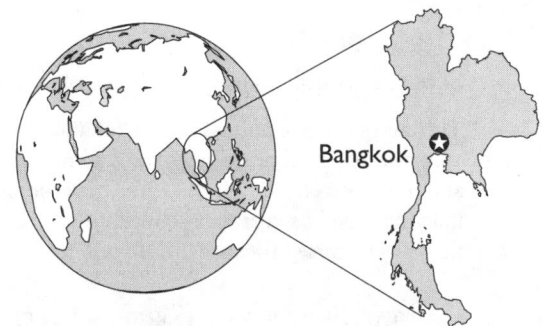

Bangkok

Trade	3	Banking	3
Taxation	3	Wages and Prices	3
Government Intervention	2	Property Rights	2
Monetary Policy	1	Regulation	3
Foreign Investment	2	Black Market	2

Thailand, a constitutional monarchy with a parliamentary government, is suffering from a major economic contraction following the government's decision in July 1997 to devalue the currency in excess of 25 percent against the U.S. dollar. GDP, which grew at an annual rate of about 10 percent from 1987 to 1991, has grown by about 8 percent a year thereafter. This rapid growth has not been without difficulty: roads, bridges, and rail systems have failed to keep up with industrial expansion, and pockets of poverty exist in most cities. The bureaucracy has resisted the government's privatization program, and many companies remain publicly owned. Now under a financial bailout by the International Monetary Fund (IMF), Thailand is struggling to recover from its currency devaluation. The government has closed many failed financial institutions but faces challenges in creating greater transparency in the country's financial sector and in the collection of government statistics. A new bankruptcy law that could improve corporate accountability was expected in 1998.

TRADE POLICY
Score: 3–Stable (moderate level of protectionism)

Thailand has an average tariff rate of 6.9 percent[1] and maintains non-tariff barriers in many areas. For example, import licenses still are required for 42 item categories, 23 of which are agricultural products. According to the Office of the United States Trade Representative, "Many importers, both Thai and foreign, charge that Customs Department procedures are nontransparent, arbitrary, and inconsistently applied."[2]

TAXATION
Score–Income taxation: 2–Stable (low tax rates)
Score–Corporate taxation: 3–Stable (moderate tax rates)
Final Taxation Score: 3–Stable (moderate tax rates)

Thailand's top marginal income tax rate is 37 percent, with the average income level taxed at 5 percent. The top corporate tax rate is 30 percent. Thailand also has a 30 percent capital gains tax and a 10 percent value-added tax, up from 7 percent in 1997.

GOVERNMENT INTERVENTION IN THE ECONOMY
Score: 2–Stable (low level)

Government consumes 9.7 percent of GDP. Although much of Thailand's privatization is moving forward (the government, for example, recently sold off shares in its major oil refinery), recent evidence indicates that part of this program may have stalled. The number of state-owned enterprises has declined in recent years, but 57 still exist.[3]

1	Hong Kong	1.25	81	Fiji	3.10
2	Singapore	1.30	81	Mali	3.10
3	Bahrain	1.70	81	Slovenia	3.10
4	New Zealand	1.75	85	Honduras	3.15
5	Switzerland	1.85	85	Mexico	3.15
6	United States	1.90	85	Papua New Guinea	3.15
7	Ireland	1.95	88	Djibouti	3.20
7	Luxembourg	1.95	88	Mongolia	3.20
7	Taiwan	1.95	90	Algeria	3.25
7	United Kingdom	1.95	90	Brazil	3.25
11	Bahamas	2.00	90	Lebanon	3.25
12	Czech Republic	2.05	90	Senegal	3.25
12	Japan	2.05	90	Tanzania	3.25
14	Australia	2.10	95	Nigeria	3.30
14	Belgium	2.10	95	Romania	3.30
14	Canada	2.10	97	Cambodia	3.35
14	United Arab Emirates	2.10	97	Dominican Republic	3.35
18	Austria	2.15	97	Egypt	3.35
18	Chile	2.15	97	Guinea	3.35
18	Estonia	2.15	97	Ivory Coast	3.35
18	Netherlands	2.15	97	Moldova	3.35
22	Denmark	2.25	97	Pakistan	3.35
22	El Salvador	2.25	104	Nepal	3.40
22	Finland	2.25	104	Venezuela	3.40
25	Germany	2.30	106	Armenia	3.45
25	Iceland	2.30	106	Bulgaria	3.45
27	Norway	2.35	106	Lesotho	3.45
28	Korea, South	2.40	106	Madagascar	3.45
28	Kuwait	2.40	106	Russia	3.45
28	Malaysia	2.40	111	Burkina Faso	3.50
28	Panama	2.40	111	Cameroon	3.50
28	Thailand	2.40	111	Guyana	3.50
33	Sweden	2.45	111	Nicaragua	3.50
34	Argentina	2.50	115	Gambia	3.60
34	France	2.50	116	Croatia	3.65
34	Italy	2.50	116	Georgia	3.65
34	Spain	2.50	116	Malawi	3.65
38	Portugal	2.55	119	Cape Verde	3.67
38	Sri Lanka	2.55	120	Ethiopia	3.70
38	Trinidad and Tobago	2.55	120	India	3.70
41	Barbados	2.60	120	Niger	3.70
41	Peru	2.60	123	Congo	3.75
43	Bolivia	2.65	124	Chad	3.80
43	Mauritius	2.65	124	China	3.80
45	Cyprus	2.70	124	Mauritania	3.80
45	Jamaica	2.70	124	Ukraine	3.80
45	Uruguay	2.70	124	Zimbabwe	3.80
48	Botswana	2.75	129	Albania	3.85
48	Guatemala	2.75	129	Bangladesh	3.85
48	Jordan	2.75	129	Mozambique	3.85
48	Namibia	2.75	129	Suriname	3.85
48	Oman	2.75	133	Burundi	3.90
48	Philippines	2.75	134	Togo	3.95
54	Belize	2.80	135	Haiti	4.00
54	Costa Rica	2.80	135	Kyrgyz Rep.	4.00
54	Israel	2.80	137	Kazakhstan	4.05
54	Swaziland	2.80	137	Sierra Leone	4.05
54	Turkey	2.80	139	Yemen	4.10
54	Uganda	2.80	140	Belarus	4.15
54	Samoa	2.80	141	Sudan	4.20
61	Latvia	2.85	141	Syria	4.20
62	Greece	2.90	143	Azerbaijan	4.30
62	Hungary	2.90	143	Equatorial Guinea	4.30
62	So. Africa	2.90	143	Myanmar	4.30
65	Ecuador	2.95	143	Rwanda	4.30
65	Gabon	2.95	147	Tajikistan	4.40
65	Indonesia	2.95	147	Uzbekistan	4.40
65	Malta	2.95	149	Angola	4.45
65	Morocco	2.95	149	Turkmenistan	4.45
65	Poland	2.95	151	Guinea-Bissau	4.55
65	Tunisia	2.95	152	Vietnam	4.60
72	Ghana	3.00	153	Congo (Zaire)	4.70
72	Lithuania	3.00	153	Iran	4.70
72	Saudi Arabia	3.00	155	Bosnia	4.80
75	Benin	3.05	155	Somalia	4.80
75	Kenya	3.05	157	Iraq	4.90
75	Paraguay	3.05	157	Laos	4.90
75	Qatar	3.05	157	Libya	4.90
75	Slovak Republic	3.05	160	Cuba	5.00
75	Zambia	3.05	160	Korea, North	5.00
81	Colombia	3.10			

Mostly Free

Monetary Policy
Score: 1–Stable (very low level of inflation)

Thailand's average annual rate of inflation from 1986 to 1996 was 4.8 percent. In 1997, the rate of inflation was about 9.5 percent. In July 1997, the government substantially devalued its currency—an action that, among other things, has caused the rate of inflation to increase.

Capital Flows and Foreign Investment
Score: 2–Stable (low barriers)

There are several restrictions on foreign investment. The government restricts foreign entry into such service areas as telecommunications and insurance, although in November 1996 it instituted a new banking law that permits increased foreign investment in this area. Moreover, part of Thailand's agreement with the IMF is to liberalize its investment laws further to allow for greater foreign investment.

Banking
Score: 3–Stable (moderate level of restrictions)

Foreign banks now are permitted to establish offices and engage in local currency transactions, but restrictions on the establishment of branches by foreign banks continue. Domestic banks are prohibited from participating in some financial activities and do not receive full national treatment. As the U.S. Department of Commerce explains, "Foreign banks perform many of the same activities as Thai domestic banks. However, they do not receive national treatment in Thailand. They are prohibited from opening more than three branches and are not permitted to operate off-site automated teller machines (ATMs). Recently, regulations were changed to permit foreign banks to participate in the local ATM network. However, some have not yet been able to negotiate agreements to participate in the ATM network with domestic banks. Foreign banks are required to maintain a ratio of capital fund to risk assets of 7.5 percent as of October 1996. The number of expatriate management personnel is generally limited to six, which tends to restrict their scope of operations. Foreign full-license banks can have two additional expatriate management personnel, and if they operate as Provincial International Banking Facility (PIBF) they can have an additional two expatriates for each branch. Foreign representative offices can have no more than two expatriate management personnel. Still, U.S. bankers have cited the lack of qualified managers as a problem which prevents them from upgrading services. The effect of this restriction is heightened by the difficulty many banks, domestic and foreign, have in hiring and retaining qualified Thai personnel due to Bangkok's booming and highly competitive market for skilled labor."[4]

Wage and Price Controls
Score: 3–Stable (moderate level)

The government imposes price controls on such items as agricultural products, matches, milk, sugar, toiletries, and vegetable oil. It also has a minimum wage.

Property Rights
Score: 2–Stable (high level of protection)

The court system protects property rights adequately, although there are recent indications of corruption. According to the U.S. Department of State, "The Constitution provides for an independent judiciary, and, although generally regarded as independent, the judiciary has a reputation for venality."[5]

Regulation
Score: 3–Stable (moderate level)

Thailand has a large but efficient bureaucracy. Bureaucrats, however, tend to view businesses as exploitable and often apply taxes, fines, and charges arbitrarily. These and other actions prove moderately burdensome.

Black Market
Score: 2–Stable (low level of activity)

Thailand's black market is confined principally to drugs and prostitution. According to the U.S. Department of State, "Piracy remains a serious problem, however. The U.S. pharmaceutical, film, and software industries estimate lost sales at over $200 million annually. Despite new and improved laws, judicial proceedings remain slow and the fines actually imposed are light. To date, no one has served time in jail for copyright infringement. The police have not always been cooperative, let alone proactive, in combating piracy. Partly as a result, arrests and seizures of illicit goods have fallen sharply since 1994. In an October 1997 off-cycle review under Special 301, the USTR [United States Trade Representative] determined that Thailand should remain on the Watch List."[6] The $200 million U.S. industries lose annually to copyright piracy in Thailand is only a small part, however, of the country's $177.5 billion economy. The overall level of the black market activity is low by global standards.

Notes

1. Based on total taxes on international trade as a percentage of total imports.
2. Office of the United States Trade Representative, *1998 National Trade Estimate Report on Foreign Trade Barriers*, p. 379.
3. Economist Intelligence Unit, *ILT Reports*, 1996.
4. U.S. Department of Commerce, *Country Commercial Guide*, 1998.
5. U.S. Department of State, *1997 Human Rights Report: Thailand*, March 1998.
6. U.S. Department of State, *Country Reports on Economic Policy and Trade Practices*, 1998.

Togo   3.95

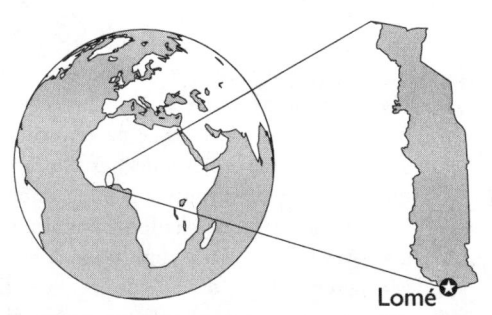

Loné ⊙

1997 Score: **n/a**   1996 Score: **n/a**   1995 Score: **n/a**

Trade	4	Banking	4
Taxation	4.5	Wages and Prices	4
Government Intervention	3	Property Rights	4
Monetary Policy	2	Regulation	5
Foreign Investment	4	Black Market	5

Togo, a small country with a predominantly agricultural economy, gained its independence from France in 1960. Togo's first president, Sylvanus Olympio, was assassinated in 1963, and his successor, Nicolas Grunitzky, was overthrown in a military coup in 1967. Lieutenant Colonel Etienne Eyadéma, who now calls himself Gnassingbé Eyadéma, led a 1967 coup and abrogated the constitution, banned all political parties, and dissolved the legislature. Eyadéma allowed a new constitution, which was ratified in 1992 but has not been implemented in full. Eyadéma won election as president in 1993 and re-election in a controversial contest in 1998. Political unrest, including armed combat, remains common. Togo's political instability has hindered economic reform and foreign investment, but economic growth has been strong, averaging over 9 percent from 1994 to 1996. Togo remains extremely poor, however, with per capita GNP of just $300 in 1996.

TRADE POLICY
Score: 4–Stable (high level of protectionism)

Togo's average tariff rate is about 11 percent. Non-tariff barriers come in the form of an inefficient and corrupt customs service.

TAXATION
Score–Income taxation: 4–Stable (high tax rates)
Score–Corporate taxation: 4–Stable (high tax rates)
Final Taxation Score: 4.5–Stable (very high tax rates)

Togo's tax revenue as a percentage of GDP is about 22 percent.[1] The government imposes a top corporate tax rate of 40 percent in addition to a capital gains tax, an 18 percent value-added tax, and some sales taxes.

GOVERNMENT INTERVENTION IN THE ECONOMY
Score: 3–Stable (moderate level)

Government consumes 13 percent of GDP. The government remains heavily invested in the economy, however. Government-owned businesses produce a large portion of the GDP.

MONETARY POLICY
Score: 2–Stable (low level of inflation)

From 1990 to 1996, Togo's average annual rate of inflation was 9.4 percent.[2] Inflation data for 1997 are not available.

CAPITAL FLOWS AND FOREIGN INVESTMENT
Score: 4–Stable (high barriers)

Although Togo has a transparent investment code, many restrictions still exist, including local content restrictions and requirements on hiring Togo citizens. According to the U.S. Department of Commerce, "The investment code covers

1	Hong Kong	1.25	81	Fiji	3.10
2	Singapore	1.30	81	Mali	3.10
3	Bahrain	1.70	81	Slovenia	3.10
4	New Zealand	1.75	85	Honduras	3.15
5	Switzerland	1.85	85	Mexico	3.15
6	United States	1.90	85	Papua New Guinea	3.15
7	Ireland	1.95	88	Djibouti	3.20
7	Luxembourg	1.95	88	Mongolia	3.20
7	Taiwan	1.95	90	Algeria	3.25
7	United Kingdom	1.95	90	Brazil	3.25
11	Bahamas	2.00	90	Lebanon	3.25
12	Czech Republic	2.05	90	Senegal	3.25
12	Japan	2.05	90	Tanzania	3.25
14	Australia	2.10	95	Nigeria	3.30
14	Belgium	2.10	95	Romania	3.30
14	Canada	2.10	97	Cambodia	3.35
14	United Arab Emirates	2.10	97	Dominican Republic	3.35
18	Austria	2.15	97	Egypt	3.35
18	Chile	2.15	97	Guinea	3.35
18	Estonia	2.15	97	Ivory Coast	3.35
18	Netherlands	2.15	97	Moldova	3.35
22	Denmark	2.25	97	Pakistan	3.35
22	El Salvador	2.25	104	Nepal	3.40
22	Finland	2.25	104	Venezuela	3.40
25	Germany	2.30	106	Armenia	3.45
25	Iceland	2.30	106	Bulgaria	3.45
27	Norway	2.35	106	Lesotho	3.45
28	Korea, South	2.40	106	Madagascar	3.45
28	Kuwait	2.40	106	Russia	3.45
28	Malaysia	2.40	111	Burkina Faso	3.50
28	Panama	2.40	111	Cameroon	3.50
28	Thailand	2.40	111	Guyana	3.50
33	Sweden	2.45	111	Nicaragua	3.50
34	Argentina	2.50	115	Gambia	3.60
34	France	2.50	116	Croatia	3.65
34	Italy	2.50	116	Georgia	3.65
34	Spain	2.50	116	Malawi	3.65
38	Portugal	2.55	119	Cape Verde	3.67
38	Sri Lanka	2.55	120	Ethiopia	3.70
38	Trinidad and Tobago	2.55	120	India	3.70
41	Barbados	2.60	120	Niger	3.70
41	Peru	2.60	123	Congo	3.75
43	Bolivia	2.65	124	Chad	3.80
43	Mauritius	2.65	124	China	3.80
45	Cyprus	2.70	124	Mauritania	3.80
45	Jamaica	2.70	124	Ukraine	3.80
45	Uruguay	2.70	124	Zimbabwe	3.80
48	Botswana	2.75	129	Albania	3.85
48	Guatemala	2.75	129	Bangladesh	3.85
48	Jordan	2.75	129	Mozambique	3.85
48	Namibia	2.75	129	Suriname	3.85
48	Oman	2.75	133	Burundi	3.90
48	Philippines	2.75	134	Togo	3.95
54	Belize	2.80	135	Haiti	4.00
54	Costa Rica	2.80	135	Kyrgyz Rep.	4.00
54	Israel	2.80	137	Kazakhstan	4.05
54	Swaziland	2.80	137	Sierra Leone	4.05
54	Turkey	2.80	139	Yemen	4.10
54	Uganda	2.80	140	Belarus	4.15
54	Samoa	2.80	141	Sudan	4.20
61	Latvia	2.85	141	Syria	4.20
62	Greece	2.90	143	Azerbaijan	4.30
62	Hungary	2.90	143	Equatorial Guinea	4.30
62	So. Africa	2.90	143	Myanmar	4.30
65	Ecuador	2.95	143	Rwanda	4.30
65	Gabon	2.95	147	Tajikistan	4.40
65	Indonesia	2.95	147	Uzbekistan	4.40
65	Malta	2.95	149	Angola	4.45
65	Morocco	2.95	149	Turkmenistan	4.45
65	Poland	2.95	151	Guinea-Bissau	4.55
65	Tunisia	2.95	152	Vietnam	4.60
72	Ghana	3.00	153	Congo (Zaire)	4.70
72	Lithuania	3.00	153	Iran	4.70
72	Saudi Arabia	3.00	155	Bosnia	4.80
75	Benin	3.05	155	Somalia	4.80
75	Kenya	3.05	157	Iraq	4.90
75	Paraguay	3.05	157	Laos	4.90
75	Qatar	3.05	157	Libya	4.90
75	Slovak Republic	3.05	160	Cuba	5.00
75	Zambia	3.05	160	Korea, North	5.00
81	Colombia	3.10			

Mostly Unfree

the expansions of existing enterprises if the cost of the expansion is at least half the value of the existing enterprise. Investors must provide at least 25 percent of the value of a new investment. At least 60 percent of the payroll must go to Togolese citizens. Applications for approval under the law must be submitted to the planning ministry, which, in consultation with the national investment commission, approves or rejects the applications within 30 days, as compared to three to six months under the old law. In practice, approvals take slightly longer than the required 30 days. The government decree granting approval spells out the conditions of the investment."[3]

BANKING
Score: 4–Stable (high level of restrictions)

The banking system is nearly all government-owned and -operated. According to the U.S. Department of Commerce, "The larger banks, wholly or partially state-owned, have over-concentrations of loans to the government and parastatal sector."[4]

WAGE AND PRICE CONTROLS
Score: 4–Stable (high level)

Togo's large government sector affects prices. The government continues to subsidize some industries and controls prices of such essential goods and services as housing, rent, electricity and many other utilities, and some agricultural products.

PROPERTY RIGHTS
Score: 4–Stable (low level of protection)

The judicial system does not protect private property sufficiently. In addition, the judicial system's freedom from government manipulation is in question. According to the U.S. Department of State, "Although the Constitution provides for an independent judiciary, in practice the executive branch continued to influence the judiciary.... Real property rights are frequently contentious in Togo, as inheritance laws are poorly defined and property transmission outcomes are frequently challenged. Only Togolese citizens, or those granted citizenship by court decision, are allowed to possess real property in Togo. Real and chattel property disputes are further complicated by judicial non-transparency, which will often favor national over foreign entities."[5] Corruption is present as well.

REGULATION
Score: 5–Stable (very high level)

The regulatory burden is quite large. Regulations often are not applied evenly; nor are all the enforced regulations transparent. Corruption remains a problem, too. According to the U.S. Department of Commerce, "Lack of judicial and regulatory transparency remain significant obstacles.... [A]lthough Togo has laws on the books that make corruption a crime, it has spread as a business practice in recent years. Togo is still a more straightforward place to do business than many other African countries, but deals, especially in government procurement and dispute settlements, are more likely to go forward with 'greased palms' than in the past."[6]

BLACK MARKET
Score: 5–Stable (very high level of activity)

Togo has a large black market in such pirated intellectual property as computer software and video and cassette recordings. In addition, much labor takes place in the black market as individuals seek to avoid paying taxes by working in the informal sector.

NOTES

[1]   Togo's top income tax is not known; thus, the author uses total tax revenue as a percentage of GDP to categorize the level of taxation. Official taxation figures are misleading, however, in part because the government also imposes random taxation on the population.

[2]   The rate of inflation from 1986 to 1996 is not available.

[3]   U.S. Department of Commerce, *Country Commercial Guide*, 1998.

[4]   *Ibid.*

[5]   U.S. Department of State, "Togo Country Report on Human Rights Practices for 1997," 1998.

[6]   U.S. Department of Commerce, *Country Commercial Guide*, 1998.

Trinidad and Tobago 2.55

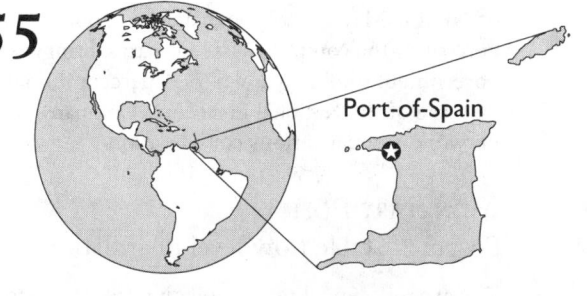

Port-of-Spain

1998 Score: **2.55**	1997 Score: **2.55**	1996 Score: **2.50**

Trade	5	Banking	2
Taxation	4.5	Wages and Prices	2
Government Intervention	2	Property Rights	1
Monetary Policy	2	Regulation	3
Foreign Investment	1	Black Market	3

Christopher Columbus visited Trinidad in 1498 during his third voyage to the New World. Spain established a permanent settlement there in 1592, and the island remained under Spanish control until 1802. In 1888, Trinidad and Tobago were merged to create a single island state. In 1958, the country became a member of the Federation of the West Indies, which was established by the United Kingdom. Trinidad and Tobago declared its independence in 1962 and adopted a new constitution in 1976. Since that time, it has developed a generally free and prosperous economy.

TRADE POLICY
Score: 5–Stable (very high level of protectionism)

Trinidad and Tobago's trade liberalization law was to have reduced tariff rates drastically by 1998. The average tariff rate before that time was 16.7 percent.[1] But because the country is a member of the Caribbean Common Market, the government is working to bring tariffs in line with the market's common external tariff (currently between 5 percent and 20 percent for most goods). Principal non-tariff barriers include strict licensing requirements for such products as poultry parts, live poultry, crab meat, fish, lobster, most coconut products, oilseeds, unrefined animal fats, vegetable fats, left-hand-drive vehicles, used fully assembled right-hand-drive vehicles, cigarette paper, ships and boats under 250 tons, and certain pesticides.

TAXATION
Score–Income taxation: 5–Stable (very high tax rates)
Score–Corporate taxation: 3–Stable (moderate tax rates)
Final Taxation Score: 4.5–Stable (very high tax rates)

Trinidad and Tobago's top income tax rate is 38 percent, and the tax on the average income is 28 percent. The top marginal corporate tax rate is 35 percent. There also is a 35 percent capital gains tax and a 15 percent value-added tax.

GOVERNMENT INTERVENTION IN THE ECONOMY
Score: 2–Stable (low level)

Government consumes about 16 percent of GDP and is involved heavily in various state-owned companies and industries. It owns and operates the telecommunications industry, for example, and manages the sugar industry. It also is working to privatize many state-owned companies, however; for example, according to the U.S. Department of Commerce, "Reductions in subsidies to state enterprises have contributed to fiscal soundness and lent credibility to the government's ongoing divestment program. Companies all or partially divested since 1994 include the National Fisheries Company, BWIA International Airways, National Flour Mills (NFM), the Trinidad and Tobago Electricity Commission (T&TEC), and the Water and Sewerage Authority (WASA). In early 1997 the Government sold its 69 percent interest in the Trinidad and Tobago Methanol Company to a consortium consisting of the local firm CL Financial and Germany s Ferrostaal and Helm companies. There was further divestment

1	Hong Kong	1.25	81	Fiji	3.10
2	Singapore	1.30	81	Mali	3.10
3	Bahrain	1.70	81	Slovenia	3.10
4	New Zealand	1.75	85	Honduras	3.15
5	Switzerland	1.85	85	Mexico	3.15
6	United States	1.90	85	Papua New Guinea	3.15
7	Ireland	1.95	88	Djibouti	3.20
7	Luxembourg	1.95	88	Mongolia	3.20
7	Taiwan	1.95	90	Algeria	3.25
7	United Kingdom	1.95	90	Brazil	3.25
11	Bahamas	2.00	90	Lebanon	3.25
12	Czech Republic	2.05	90	Senegal	3.25
12	Japan	2.05	90	Tanzania	3.25
14	Australia	2.10	95	Nigeria	3.30
14	Belgium	2.10	95	Romania	3.30
14	Canada	2.10	97	Cambodia	3.35
14	United Arab Emirates	2.10	97	Dominican Republic	3.35
18	Austria	2.15	97	Egypt	3.35
18	Chile	2.15	97	Guinea	3.35
18	Estonia	2.15	97	Ivory Coast	3.35
18	Netherlands	2.15	97	Moldova	3.35
22	Denmark	2.25	97	Pakistan	3.35
22	El Salvador	2.25	104	Nepal	3.40
22	Finland	2.25	104	Venezuela	3.40
25	Germany	2.30	106	Armenia	3.45
25	Iceland	2.30	106	Bulgaria	3.45
27	Norway	2.35	106	Lesotho	3.45
28	Korea, South	2.40	106	Madagascar	3.45
28	Kuwait	2.40	106	Russia	3.45
28	Malaysia	2.40	111	Burkina Faso	3.50
28	Panama	2.40	111	Cameroon	3.50
28	Thailand	2.40	111	Guyana	3.50
33	Sweden	2.45	111	Nicaragua	3.50
34	Argentina	2.50	115	Gambia	3.60
34	France	2.50	116	Croatia	3.65
34	Italy	2.50	116	Georgia	3.65
34	Spain	2.50	116	Malawi	3.65
38	Portugal	2.55	119	Cape Verde	3.67
38	Sri Lanka	2.55	120	Ethiopia	3.70
38	Trinidad and Tobago	2.55	120	India	3.70
41	Barbados	2.60	120	Niger	3.70
41	Peru	2.60	123	Congo	3.75
43	Bolivia	2.65	124	Chad	3.80
43	Mauritius	2.65	124	China	3.80
45	Cyprus	2.70	124	Mauritania	3.80
45	Jamaica	2.70	124	Ukraine	3.80
45	Uruguay	2.70	124	Zimbabwe	3.80
48	Botswana	2.75	129	Albania	3.85
48	Guatemala	2.75	129	Bangladesh	3.85
48	Jordan	2.75	129	Mozambique	3.85
48	Namibia	2.75	129	Suriname	3.85
48	Oman	2.75	133	Burundi	3.90
48	Philippines	2.75	134	Togo	3.95
54	Belize	2.80	135	Haiti	4.00
54	Costa Rica	2.80	135	Kyrgyz Rep.	4.00
54	Israel	2.80	137	Kazakhstan	4.05
54	Swaziland	2.80	137	Sierra Leone	4.05
54	Turkey	2.80	139	Yemen	4.10
54	Uganda	2.80	140	Belarus	4.15
54	Samoa	2.80	141	Sudan	4.20
61	Latvia	2.85	141	Syria	4.20
62	Greece	2.90	143	Azerbaijan	4.30
62	Hungary	2.90	143	Equatorial Guinea	4.30
62	So. Africa	2.90	143	Myanmar	4.30
65	Ecuador	2.95	143	Rwanda	4.30
65	Gabon	2.95	147	Tajikistan	4.40
65	Indonesia	2.95	147	Uzbekistan	4.40
65	Malta	2.95	149	Angola	4.45
65	Morocco	2.95	149	Turkmenistan	4.45
65	Poland	2.95	151	Guinea-Bissau	4.55
65	Tunisia	2.95	152	Vietnam	4.60
72	Ghana	3.00	153	Congo (Zaire)	4.70
72	Lithuania	3.00	153	Iran	4.70
72	Saudi Arabia	3.00	155	Bosnia	4.80
75	Benin	3.05	155	Somalia	4.80
75	Kenya	3.05	157	Iraq	4.90
75	Paraguay	3.05	157	Laos	4.90
75	Qatar	3.05	157	Libya	4.90
75	Slovak Republic	3.05	160	Cuba	5.00
75	Zambia	3.05	160	Korea, North	5.00
81	Colombia	3.10			

Mostly Free

of NFM in May 1997 through a market offering of 14 percent of the company's issued shares, bringing the government's holding down to 51 percent. Initial divestment of some of the National Petroleum Company gas station network is under serious consideration."[2]

MONETARY POLICY
Score: 2–Stable (low level of inflation)

The average annual rate of inflation from 1986 to 1996 was 5.1 percent. In 1997, the rate was 3.3 percent.

CAPITAL FLOWS AND FOREIGN INVESTMENT
Score: 1–Stable (very low barriers)

There are few restrictions on foreign investment. The government grants incentives in the form of tax breaks and holidays. According to the U.S. Department of Commerce, "Foreign direct investment is actively encouraged by the Government of Trinidad and Tobago (GOTT) in almost all sectors. Generally speaking, there are no restrictions on investment, and most disincentives to investment have been removed."[3]

BANKING
Score: 2–Stable (low level of restrictions)

The banking system is open and competitive. Foreigners may own banks entirely. "Trinidad and Tobago," according to the U.S. Department of Commerce, "has a well-developed, reliable banking system, which operates under Central Bank oversight. There are no restrictions on borrowing by foreign investors, and there are no foreign exchange controls."[4]

WAGE AND PRICE CONTROLS
Score: 2–Stable (low level)

The market sets most wages and prices, although the government determines prices on some services and such goods as sugar, school books, and pharmaceuticals. There is no national minimum wage.

PROPERTY RIGHTS
Score: 1–Stable (very high level of protection)

Private property is safe on Trinidad and Tobago, which has an efficient legal and judicial system. "The Constitution provides for an independent judiciary, and the Government respects this provision in practice. The judiciary provides citizens with a fair judicial process," reports the U.S. Department of State.[5]

REGULATION
Score: 3–Stable (moderate level)

Establishing a business can be a simple process, and regulations are applied evenly in most cases. Both regulations and bureaucratic red tape, however, are burdensome. Rigid environmental regulations, for example, are enforced by 28 different agencies. The government has announced a plan to create a new agency that would consolidate all environmental regulation.

BLACK MARKET
Score: 3–Stable (moderate level of activity)

Although the government has made significant strides toward cracking down on black market activity, intellectual property laws are not enforced. This has created a black market in pirated videos, computer software, recorded music, and other products. According to the U.S. Department of Commerce, "Although the new legislation provides for intellectual property protection comparable to that in the United States, it is likely that enforcement will remain lax in the near term. The most visible examples of copyright infringement are pirated copies of music and video cassettes. There have also been several cases of trade mark infringement brought before the registrar's office."[6]

NOTES
[1]   Based on a trade weighted average mean tariff. From World Bank, *1998 World Development Indicators*, 1998.
[2]   U.S. Department of Commerce, *Country Commercial Guide*, 1998.
[3]   *Ibid.*
[4]   *Ibid.*
[5]   U.S. Department of State, "Trinidad and Tobago Country Report on Human Rights Practices for 1997," 1998.
[6]   U.S. Department of Commerce, *Country Commercial Guide*, 1998.

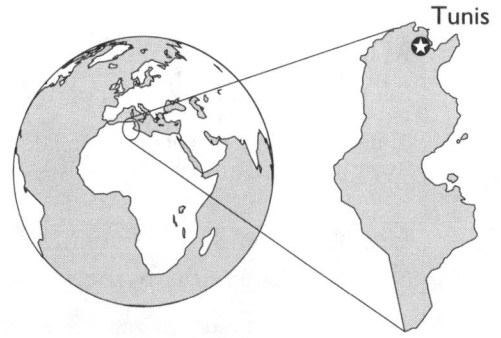

Tunis

Tunisia 2.95

1998 Score: **2.75**	1997 Score: **2.75**	1996 Score: **2.65**

Trade	5	Banking	3
Taxation	3.5	Wages and Prices	2
Government Intervention	3	Property Rights	3
Monetary Policy	2	Regulation	3
Foreign Investment	2	Black Market	3

Tunisia gained its independence from France in 1956. In 1964, the government nationalized all foreign-owned land, causing prolonged tension with France. In the early 1990s, after more than 30 years of unproductive socialist economic policies, Tunisia began to reform its economy. Among the results of this effort are liberalized trade, a large privatization program, and cuts in government subsidies. Tunisia remains one of the most modern, stable, and cosmopolitan countries in the Arab world. The government, however, recently increased regulations in the banking sector in response to the failure of many state-owned banks, and the burden regulation places on businesses is becoming heavier. As a result, Tunisia's overall score is 0.2 point worse than last year.

TRADE POLICY

Score: 5–Stable (very high level of protectionism)

Tunisia has an average tariff rate of 19.22 percent, down from 25 percent last year.[1] Moreover, according to the U.S. Department of Commerce, "Tunisia still has non-tariff barriers such as import licenses or quotas on certain products, particularly consumer goods that compete against locally produced equivalents manufactured by 'developing' industries, such as textiles. Another major category affected by these barriers are motor vehicles, for which there is a strong local demand that could adversely affect the short-term balance of payments. For such products an importer must obtain a license from the Ministry of Commerce specifying the product, quantity and amount of foreign exchange needed. Without this license a bank will not authorize the foreign currency transaction. Certain imported products, including weapons or security-related materials and health-care products, remain strictly controlled."[2]

TAXATION

Score–Income taxation: 3–Stable (moderate tax rates)
Score–Corporate taxation: 3–Stable (moderate tax rates)
Final Taxation Score: 3.5–Stable (high tax rates)

Tunisia's top income tax rate is 35 percent, and the average income level is taxed at 15 percent. The top corporate tax rate is 35 percent. Tunisia also has a 35 percent capital gains tax, a 6 percent to 29 percent value-added tax, and a property tax.

GOVERNMENT INTERVENTION IN THE ECONOMY

Score: 3–Stable (moderate level)

Government consumes 16.3 percent of GDP. The government also has an aggressive privatization program in place and has identified some 20 to 30 companies that are to undergo privatization. Several large state-owned companies continue to receive subsidies, however, and the government retains its controlling interests in cement, tobacco manufacturing, oil refining, and telecommunications.

1	Hong Kong	1.25
2	Singapore	1.30
3	Bahrain	1.70
4	New Zealand	1.75
5	Switzerland	1.85
6	United States	1.90
7	Ireland	1.95
7	Luxembourg	1.95
7	Taiwan	1.95
7	United Kingdom	1.95
11	Bahamas	2.00
12	Czech Republic	2.05
12	Japan	2.05
14	Australia	2.10
14	Belgium	2.10
14	Canada	2.10
14	United Arab Emirates	2.10
18	Austria	2.15
18	Chile	2.15
18	Estonia	2.15
18	Netherlands	2.15
22	Denmark	2.25
22	El Salvador	2.25
22	Finland	2.25
25	Germany	2.30
25	Iceland	2.30
27	Norway	2.35
28	Korea, South	2.40
28	Kuwait	2.40
28	Malaysia	2.40
28	Panama	2.40
28	Thailand	2.40
33	Sweden	2.45
34	Argentina	2.50
34	France	2.50
34	Italy	2.50
34	Spain	2.50
38	Portugal	2.55
38	Sri Lanka	2.55
38	Trinidad and Tobago	2.55
41	Barbados	2.60
41	Peru	2.60
43	Bolivia	2.65
43	Mauritius	2.65
45	Cyprus	2.70
45	Jamaica	2.70
45	Uruguay	2.70
48	Botswana	2.75
48	Guatemala	2.75
48	Jordan	2.75
48	Namibia	2.75
48	Oman	2.75
48	Philippines	2.75
54	Belize	2.80
54	Costa Rica	2.80
54	Israel	2.80
54	Swaziland	2.80
54	Turkey	2.80
54	Uganda	2.80
54	Samoa	2.80
61	Latvia	2.85
62	Greece	2.90
62	Hungary	2.90
62	So. Africa	2.90
65	Ecuador	2.95
65	Gabon	2.95
65	Indonesia	2.95
65	Malta	2.95
65	Morocco	2.95
65	Poland	2.95
65	Tunisia	2.95
72	Ghana	3.00
72	Lithuania	3.00
72	Saudi Arabia	3.00
75	Benin	3.05
75	Kenya	3.05
75	Paraguay	3.05
75	Qatar	3.05
75	Slovak Republic	3.05
75	Zambia	3.05
81	Colombia	3.10
81	Fiji	3.10
81	Mali	3.10
81	Slovenia	3.10
85	Honduras	3.15
85	Mexico	3.15
85	Papua New Guinea	3.15
88	Djibouti	3.20
88	Mongolia	3.20
90	Algeria	3.25
90	Brazil	3.25
90	Lebanon	3.25
90	Senegal	3.25
90	Tanzania	3.25
95	Nigeria	3.30
95	Romania	3.30
97	Cambodia	3.35
97	Dominican Republic	3.35
97	Egypt	3.35
97	Guinea	3.35
97	Ivory Coast	3.35
97	Moldova	3.35
97	Pakistan	3.35
104	Nepal	3.40
104	Venezuela	3.40
106	Armenia	3.45
106	Bulgaria	3.45
106	Lesotho	3.45
106	Madagascar	3.45
106	Russia	3.45
111	Burkina Faso	3.50
111	Cameroon	3.50
111	Guyana	3.50
111	Nicaragua	3.50
115	Gambia	3.60
116	Croatia	3.65
116	Georgia	3.65
116	Malawi	3.65
119	Cape Verde	3.67
120	Ethiopia	3.70
120	India	3.70
120	Niger	3.70
123	Congo	3.75
124	Chad	3.80
124	China	3.80
124	Mauritania	3.80
124	Ukraine	3.80
124	Zimbabwe	3.80
129	Albania	3.85
129	Bangladesh	3.85
129	Mozambique	3.85
129	Suriname	3.85
133	Burundi	3.90
134	Togo	3.95
135	Haiti	4.00
135	Kyrgyz Rep.	4.00
137	Kazakhstan	4.05
137	Sierra Leone	4.05
139	Yemen	4.10
140	Belarus	4.15
141	Sudan	4.20
141	Syria	4.20
143	Azerbaijan	4.30
143	Equatorial Guinea	4.30
143	Myanmar	4.30
143	Rwanda	4.30
147	Tajikistan	4.40
147	Uzbekistan	4.40
149	Angola	4.45
149	Turkmenistan	4.45
151	Guinea-Bissau	4.55
152	Vietnam	4.60
153	Congo (Zaire)	4.70
153	Iran	4.70
155	Bosnia	4.80
155	Somalia	4.80
157	Iraq	4.90
157	Laos	4.90
157	Libya	4.90
160	Cuba	5.00
160	Korea, North	5.00

Mostly Free

MONETARY POLICY
Score: 2–Stable (low level of inflation)

Tunisia's average annual rate of inflation from 1986 to 1996 was 5.6 percent. In 1997, the rate was 3.7 percent.

CAPITAL FLOWS AND FOREIGN INVESTMENT
Score: 2–Stable (low barriers)

Tunisia is open to foreign investment, treating domestic firms the same as foreign firms and offering attractive tax holidays to investors. It prohibits the ownership of land by non-Tunisians, however.

BANKING
Score: 3– (moderate level of restrictions)

Banks are becoming more independent of the government. Recent laws have eased some Central Bank regulations on foreign and domestic banks. According to the U.S. Department of Commerce, "The Tunisian banking system is a mixture of private and state-owned institutions with varying ranges of financial instruments and services.... However, many banks are thought to have substantial amounts (up to 20 percent) of non-performing or delinquent debt in their portfolios, despite the strict new requirements. The government's dominant presence in the banking sector—it is the controlling shareholder in eight of the banks, which account for 70 percent of the credit and 55 percent of the deposits—has retarded liberalization."[3] Thus, government regulation has failed to curtail bad loans by state-owned banks; as a result, these banks are having a negative effect on the competitiveness and soundness of the country's entire banking system. As such, Tunisia's banking score is 1 point worse this year.

WAGE AND PRICE CONTROLS
Score: 2–Stable (low level)

Tunisia maintains a minimum wage as well as some price controls.

PROPERTY RIGHTS
Score: 3–Stable (moderate level of protection)

Property rights are relatively secure, although foreigners are not allowed to own land. Most of the judiciary is part of the country's Department of Justice; therefore, the judicial system is not totally independent of the executive branch. According to the U.S. Department of Commerce, "The Tunisian legal system is based upon the French Napoleonic Code. There are means to enforce property and contractual rights. The judiciary is not independent of the executive branch, however, and local legal experts assert that courts are susceptible to political pressure."[4]

REGULATION
Score: 3– (moderate level)

Regulations are applied fairly in most cases, although sanitary, health, and product quality regulations can be somewhat burdensome. There is increasing evidence that regulations are more burdensome on business. For example according to the U.S. Department of Commerce, "Although the 1994 investment code substantially improved, standardized, and codified incentives for foreign investors, several aspects of existing tax and labor law remain impediments to efficient business operations. Among the latter are greatly increased and complex tariff schedules and unclear requirements concerning the dismissal of employees. Bureaucratic procedures, while slowly improving in some areas, remain cumbersome and time-consuming. Foreign employee work permits, infrastructure-related services (e.g., telecommunications installation, Internet access), and customs clearance for imported goods are usually cited as the lengthiest and most opaque of the necessary procedures in the local business environment."[5] As a result, Tunisia's regulation score is 1 point worse this year. By global standards, however, Tunisia's level of regulation is moderate.

BLACK MARKET
Score: 3–Stable (moderate level of activity)

As Tunisia's market becomes more accessible to foreign goods, the moderately large black market is shrinking. There is some black market activity in pirated trademarks and prerecorded music and video tapes. As the U.S. Department of Commerce reports, "Print, audio, and video media are considered particularly susceptible to copyright infringement, and there is evidence of widespread commercial sales of illegal products in these media."[6]

NOTES

[1]   Based on total taxes on international transactions as a percentage of total imports.
[2]   U.S. Department of Commerce, *Country Commercial Guide*, 1998.
[3]   *Ibid.*
[4]   *Ibid.*
[5]   *Ibid.*
[6]   *Ibid.*

Turkey   2.80

1998 Score: **2.80**   1997 Score: **2.80**   1996 Score: **3.00**

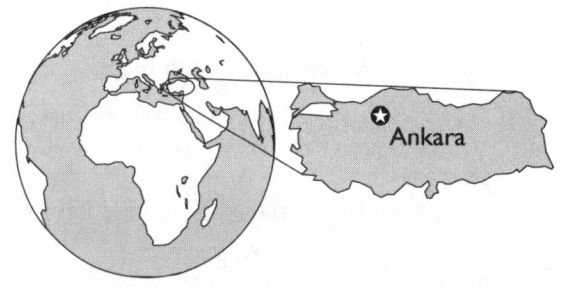

Ankara

Trade	2	Banking	2
Taxation	4	Wages and Prices	3
Government Intervention	2	Property Rights	2
Monetary Policy	5	Regulation	3
Foreign Investment	2	Black Market	3

Turkey became an independent state in 1923 in the wake of the final collapse of the Ottoman Empire. After decades of one-party rule, a multiparty system was adopted in 1950, and in 1951 Turkey joined the North Atlantic Treaty Organization. Turkey enjoyed an economic boom during the 1980s, which some analysts attribute to the broad free-market reforms that were instituted under Prime Minister Turgut Özal,. Since then, the economy has been hurt both by the United Nations economic sanctions imposed on Iraq in 1990 and by an intensifying war against Kurdish separatists in the eastern part of the country. The government of former prime minister Tansu Çiller halfheartedly implemented a privatization program, but the June 1996 formation of a coalition government headed by Prime Minister Necmettin Erbakan, leader of the pro-Islamist Refah Party, was a major setback for economic liberalization. Although Erbakan's resignation and the formation of a secular coalition government in June 1997 have revived the prospects for free-market reform, Turkey remains hampered by a large national debt, skyrocketing inflation, high rates of unemployment, and a growing regulatory burden.

TRADE POLICY
Score: 2–Stable (low level of protectionism)

Turkey has an average tariff rate of 5.3 percent. Although the government has eliminated most import licenses, it still requires that importers obtain a certificate before selling their products in the country. This certificate is relatively easy to get, but the procedure imposes an administrative and financial burden on the importer. Beyond this, there are no significant restrictions on imports.

TAXATION
Score–Income taxation: 5–Stable (very high tax rates)
Score–Corporate taxation: 2–Stable (low tax rates)
Final Taxation Score: 4–Stable (high tax rates)

Turkey's top marginal income tax rate is 55 percent; the average income level is taxed at 45 percent. The top corporate tax rate is 25 percent.[1] Turkey also has a value-added tax that can reach as high as 23 percent, as well as a social contributions tax.

GOVERNMENT INTERVENTION IN THE ECONOMY
Score: 2–Stable (low level)

Government consumes about 11.9 percent of GDP, and the government still owns significant portions of the economy. Although Turkey has a privatization program, the government owns many companies in such areas as ports, railways, iron and steel, airports, mineral mining, airlines, petroleum, and electronics.

1	Hong Kong	1.25	81	Fiji	3.10
2	Singapore	1.30	81	Mali	3.10
3	Bahrain	1.70	81	Slovenia	3.10
4	New Zealand	1.75	85	Honduras	3.15
5	Switzerland	1.85	85	Mexico	3.15
6	United States	1.90	85	Papua New Guinea	3.15
7	Ireland	1.95	88	Djibouti	3.20
7	Luxembourg	1.95	88	Mongolia	3.20
7	Taiwan	1.95	90	Algeria	3.25
7	United Kingdom	1.95	90	Brazil	3.25
11	Bahamas	2.00	90	Lebanon	3.25
12	Czech Republic	2.05	90	Senegal	3.25
12	Japan	2.05	90	Tanzania	3.25
14	Australia	2.10	95	Nigeria	3.30
14	Belgium	2.10	95	Romania	3.30
14	Canada	2.10	97	Cambodia	3.35
14	United Arab Emirates	2.10	97	Dominican Republic	3.35
18	Austria	2.15	97	Egypt	3.35
18	Chile	2.15	97	Guinea	3.35
18	Estonia	2.15	97	Ivory Coast	3.35
18	Netherlands	2.15	97	Moldova	3.35
22	Denmark	2.25	97	Pakistan	3.35
22	El Salvador	2.25	104	Nepal	3.40
22	Finland	2.25	104	Venezuela	3.40
25	Germany	2.30	106	Armenia	3.45
25	Iceland	2.30	106	Bulgaria	3.45
27	Norway	2.35	106	Lesotho	3.45
28	Korea, South	2.40	106	Madagascar	3.45
28	Kuwait	2.40	106	Russia	3.45
28	Malaysia	2.40	111	Burkina Faso	3.50
28	Panama	2.40	111	Cameroon	3.50
28	Thailand	2.40	111	Guyana	3.50
33	Sweden	2.45	111	Nicaragua	3.50
34	Argentina	2.50	115	Gambia	3.60
34	France	2.50	116	Croatia	3.65
34	Italy	2.50	116	Georgia	3.65
34	Spain	2.50	116	Malawi	3.65
38	Portugal	2.55	119	Cape Verde	3.67
38	Sri Lanka	2.55	120	Ethiopia	3.70
38	Trinidad and Tobago	2.55	120	India	3.70
41	Barbados	2.60	120	Niger	3.70
41	Peru	2.60	123	Congo	3.75
43	Bolivia	2.65	124	Chad	3.80
43	Mauritius	2.65	124	China	3.80
45	Cyprus	2.70	124	Mauritania	3.80
45	Jamaica	2.70	124	Ukraine	3.80
45	Uruguay	2.70	124	Zimbabwe	3.80
48	Botswana	2.75	129	Albania	3.85
48	Guatemala	2.75	129	Bangladesh	3.85
48	Jordan	2.75	129	Mozambique	3.85
48	Namibia	2.75	129	Suriname	3.85
48	Oman	2.75	133	Burundi	3.90
48	Philippines	2.75	134	Togo	3.95
54	Belize	2.80	135	Haiti	4.00
54	Costa Rica	2.80	135	Kyrgyz Rep.	4.00
54	Israel	2.80	137	Kazakhstan	4.05
54	Swaziland	2.80	137	Sierra Leone	4.05
54	Turkey	2.80	139	Yemen	4.10
54	Uganda	2.80	140	Belarus	4.15
54	Samoa	2.80	141	Sudan	4.20
61	Latvia	2.85	141	Syria	4.20
62	Greece	2.90	143	Azerbaijan	4.30
62	Hungary	2.90	143	Equatorial Guinea	4.30
62	So. Africa	2.90	143	Myanmar	4.30
65	Ecuador	2.95	143	Rwanda	4.30
65	Gabon	2.95	147	Tajikistan	4.40
65	Indonesia	2.95	147	Uzbekistan	4.40
65	Malta	2.95	149	Angola	4.45
65	Morocco	2.95	149	Turkmenistan	4.45
65	Poland	2.95	151	Guinea-Bissau	4.55
65	Tunisia	2.95	152	Vietnam	4.60
72	Ghana	3.00	153	Congo (Zaire)	4.70
72	Lithuania	3.00	153	Iran	4.70
72	Saudi Arabia	3.00	155	Bosnia	4.80
75	Benin	3.05	155	Somalia	4.80
75	Kenya	3.05	157	Iraq	4.90
75	Paraguay	3.05	157	Laos	4.90
75	Qatar	3.05	157	Libya	4.90
75	Slovak Republic	3.05	160	Cuba	5.00
75	Zambia	3.05	160	Korea, North	5.00
81	Colombia	3.10			

Mostly Free

MONETARY POLICY
Score: 5–Stable (very high level of inflation)

The average annual rate of inflation in Turkey from 1986 to 1996 was 66 percent. In 1997, the rate was 85 percent.

CAPITAL FLOWS AND FOREIGN INVESTMENT
Score: 2–Stable (low barriers)

Turkey is relatively open to foreign investment, but some barriers remain. There are no limits on how much of a Turkish business a foreign investor may own, for example, but local labor groups may pressure the government not to permit full foreign ownership of some newly privatized state-owned enterprises.

BANKING
Score: 2–Stable (low level of restrictions)

Banks are open to foreign ownership, and over 20 foreign banks have been established. Although several banks are state-owned, the domestic banking market is very competitive. According to the U.S. Department of Commerce, "Even though still dominated by a few large state and commercial banks—some 60 percent of all assets are held by the seven largest banks—the Turkish banking system offers the same services found in Western Europe in terms of project finance, letters of credit, and correspondent relationships."[2] By global standards, however, the level of restrictions on banking is relatively low.

WAGE AND PRICE CONTROLS
Score: 3–Stable (moderate level)

There are few official price controls, but prices are controlled indirectly by large state-owned corporations whose wholesale prices are controlled by the government (although the government plans to allow most of these corporations to set their own prices). Turkey has a minimum wage law.

PROPERTY RIGHTS
Score: 2–Stable (high level of protection)

Expropriation is unlikely. Turkey's legal system, although imperfect, protects most private property. "There is a legal system that protects and facilitates acquisition and disposition of all property rights—land, building and mortgages," reports the U.S. Department of Commerce.[3] Court rulings can take several months, however.

REGULATION
Score: 3–Stable (moderate level)

Turkey has reduced the size of its bureaucracy, imposed a performance evaluation test for civil servants, and centralized government economic decision-making under the office of the prime minister. Regulations are aimed at providing more freedom for businesses. Turkey has few environmental laws, but more may be added in the future. There are recent signs, however, of bribery within the bureaucracy. According to the U.S. Department of State, "Corruption appears to be most pervasive in government procurement, although it is present in nearly all sectors."[4]

BLACK MARKET
Score: 3–Stable (moderate level of activity)

Turkey used to have a rather large black market, especially in such foreign goods as pirated recordings and printed materials like books and magazines. The government has enacted and enforced a variety of intellectual property rights laws, however, perhaps to smooth the path to membership in the European Union. As a result, black market activity in pirated intellectual property has fallen dramatically, even though significant black market activity in pirated computer software continues; some estimates place the piracy rate in computer software at 97 percent.[5]

NOTES

[1]   This rate does not include a 10 percent surtax on the corporate income tax rate of 25 percent.
[2]   U.S. Department of Commerce, *Country Commercial Guide,* 1998.
[3]   *Ibid.*
[4]   *Ibid.*
[5]   U.S. Department of Commerce, National Trade Data Bank and Economic Bulletin Board, products of *Stat–USA* (*http://www.stat-usa.gov*), 1997.

Turkmenistan 4.45

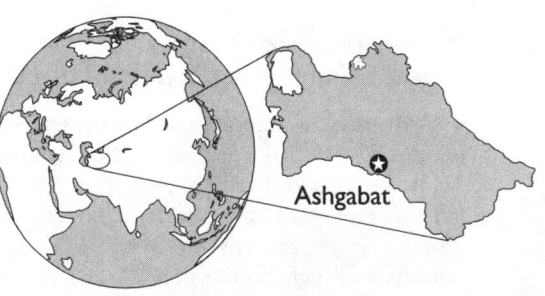

Ashgabat

1998 Score: **4.50**	1997 Score: **n/a**	1996 Score: **n/a**

Trade	5	Banking	5
Taxation	4.5	Wages and Prices	4
Government Intervention	4	Property Rights	4
Monetary Policy	5	Regulation	4
Foreign Investment	4	Black Market	5

The area now known as Turkmenistan has been invaded and conquered by various armies throughout its history. The region was converted to Islam by Arabs during the 7th and 8th centuries, became part of the Mongol empire under Ghengis Khan in the 13th century, and fell to Russia in 1881. After the 1917 Bolshevik Revolution in Russia, the people revolted and enjoyed a brief period of autonomy until 1918, when the region was incorporated into the Turkistan Autonomous Soviet Socialist Republic, which included portions of present-day Kazakhstan, Tajikistan, and Uzbekistan. The region became known as Turkmenistan and was fully incorporated into the Soviet Union in 1924. Turkmenistan today is predominately Sunni Muslim and Turkic-speaking. It is extremely rich in natural gas and other resources. Since becoming independent again in 1991, Turkmenistan has been slow to change to a market-based economy. Much Soviet-era central planning continues, as do government corruption and an inefficient public bureaucracy. Turkmenistan has made some small progress toward lowering taxes; as a result, its overall score is 0.05 point better than last year.

TRADE POLICY
Score: 5–Stable (very high level of protectionism)

Turkmenistan imposes official tariffs on only a few imports like alcohol, tobacco, and some food, including fish (which has tariff rates ranging from 45 percent to over 100 percent). Instead, it uses an agency called the Commodity and Raw Materials Exchange (CRME) to restrict imports. According to the U.S. Department of Commerce, "As the sole conduit for foreign trade, the CRME plays a centralized, regulatory role in Turkmenistan's economy."[1] This bureaucracy makes it difficult to get goods into and out of the country. Some labeling requirements also hinder imports.

TAXATION
Score—Income taxation: 4+ (high tax rates)
Score—Corporate taxation: 4+ (high tax rates)
Final Taxation Score: 4.5+ (very high tax rates)

The government established a formal tax system in July 1997 with lower rates than those that had existed previously, so Turkmenistan's final taxation score is 0.5 point better this year. The country has a top income tax and corporate tax rate of 45 percent.[2] The government also imposes a 20 percent value-added tax, a 15 percent capital gains tax, and a significant payroll tax, among others. Previous rates reached over 65 percent.

GOVERNMENT INTERVENTION IN THE ECONOMY
Score: 4–Stable (high level)

Turkmenistan is privatizing some of its state-owned sector, but the government still produces most GDP and continues to own significant sectors of the economy, including most utilities and cotton operations.

1	Hong Kong	1.25	81	Fiji	3.10
2	Singapore	1.30	81	Mali	3.10
3	Bahrain	1.70	81	Slovenia	3.10
4	New Zealand	1.75	85	Honduras	3.15
5	Switzerland	1.85	85	Mexico	3.15
6	United States	1.90	85	Papua New Guinea	3.15
7	Ireland	1.95	88	Djibouti	3.20
7	Luxembourg	1.95	88	Mongolia	3.20
7	Taiwan	1.95	90	Algeria	3.25
7	United Kingdom	1.95	90	Brazil	3.25
11	Bahamas	2.00	90	Lebanon	3.25
12	Czech Republic	2.05	90	Senegal	3.25
12	Japan	2.05	90	Tanzania	3.25
14	Australia	2.10	95	Nigeria	3.30
14	Belgium	2.10	95	Romania	3.30
14	Canada	2.10	97	Cambodia	3.35
14	United Arab Emirates	2.10	97	Dominican Republic	3.35
18	Austria	2.15	97	Egypt	3.35
18	Chile	2.15	97	Guinea	3.35
18	Estonia	2.15	97	Ivory Coast	3.35
18	Netherlands	2.15	97	Moldova	3.35
22	Denmark	2.25	97	Pakistan	3.35
22	El Salvador	2.25	104	Nepal	3.40
22	Finland	2.25	104	Venezuela	3.40
25	Germany	2.30	106	Armenia	3.45
25	Iceland	2.30	106	Bulgaria	3.45
27	Norway	2.35	106	Lesotho	3.45
28	Korea, South	2.40	106	Madagascar	3.45
28	Kuwait	2.40	106	Russia	3.45
28	Malaysia	2.40	111	Burkina Faso	3.50
28	Panama	2.40	111	Cameroon	3.50
28	Thailand	2.40	111	Guyana	3.50
33	Sweden	2.45	111	Nicaragua	3.50
34	Argentina	2.50	115	Gambia	3.60
34	France	2.50	116	Croatia	3.65
34	Italy	2.50	116	Georgia	3.65
34	Spain	2.50	116	Malawi	3.65
38	Portugal	2.55	119	Cape Verde	3.67
38	Sri Lanka	2.55	120	Ethiopia	3.70
38	Trinidad and Tobago	2.55	120	India	3.70
41	Barbados	2.60	120	Niger	3.70
41	Peru	2.60	123	Congo	3.75
43	Bolivia	2.65	124	Chad	3.80
43	Mauritius	2.65	124	China	3.80
45	Cyprus	2.70	124	Mauritania	3.80
45	Jamaica	2.70	124	Ukraine	3.80
45	Uruguay	2.70	124	Zimbabwe	3.80
48	Botswana	2.75	129	Albania	3.85
48	Guatemala	2.75	129	Bangladesh	3.85
48	Jordan	2.75	129	Mozambique	3.85
48	Namibia	2.75	129	Suriname	3.85
48	Oman	2.75	133	Burundi	3.90
48	Philippines	2.75	134	Togo	3.95
54	Belize	2.80	135	Haiti	4.00
54	Costa Rica	2.80	135	Kyrgyz Rep.	4.00
54	Israel	2.80	137	Kazakhstan	4.05
54	Swaziland	2.80	137	Sierra Leone	4.05
54	Turkey	2.80	139	Yemen	4.10
54	Uganda	2.80	140	Belarus	4.15
54	Samoa	2.80	141	Sudan	4.20
61	Latvia	2.85	141	Syria	4.20
62	Greece	2.90	143	Azerbaijan	4.30
62	Hungary	2.90	143	Equatorial Guinea	4.30
62	So. Africa	2.90	143	Myanmar	4.30
65	Ecuador	2.95	143	Rwanda	4.30
65	Gabon	2.95	147	Tajikistan	4.40
65	Indonesia	2.95	147	Uzbekistan	4.40
65	Malta	2.95	149	Angola	4.45
65	Morocco	2.95	149	Turkmenistan	4.45
65	Poland	2.95	151	Guinea-Bissau	4.55
65	Tunisia	2.95	152	Vietnam	4.60
72	Ghana	3.00	153	Congo (Zaire)	4.70
72	Lithuania	3.00	153	Iran	4.70
72	Saudi Arabia	3.00	155	Bosnia	4.80
75	Benin	3.05	155	Somalia	4.80
75	Kenya	3.05	157	Iraq	4.90
75	Paraguay	3.05	157	Laos	4.90
75	Qatar	3.05	157	Libya	4.90
75	Slovak Republic	3.05	160	Cuba	5.00
75	Zambia	3.05	160	Korea, North	5.00
81	Colombia	3.10			

Repressed

MONETARY POLICY
Score: 5–Stable (very high level of inflation)

Turkmenistan has been plagued by hyperinflation: 493 percent in 1992, 3,102 percent in 1993, 2,400 percent in 1994, 775 percent in 1995, and 600 percent in 1996. In 1997, the inflation rate was 50 percent. Thus, even though inflation dropped so precipitously after 1996, its average annual rate remains very high, both historically and by global standards.

CAPITAL FLOWS AND FOREIGN INVESTMENT
Score: 4–Stable (high barriers)

Although the government wants to promote foreign investment, Turkmenistan does not have a foreign investment code that reduces bureaucratic procedures. According to the U.S. Department of Commerce, "Having no expertise to judge competing bids fairly and accurately and desiring to maintain strict control over all economic transactions, the government sometimes created impediments to investment. Personal relations with government officials often play a decisive role in winning a bid or running a successful business in Turkmenistan."[3]

BANKING
Score: 5–Stable (very high level of restrictions)

Turkmenistan's banking system is not fully functional yet. According to the U.S. Department of Commerce, "The banking system in Turkmenistan consists of the State Central Bank of Turkmenistan; two state banks—the State Bank for Foreign Economic Affairs...and the State Savings Bank...and 17 commercial banks."[4] The state owns most of these banks and controls almost all of the financial system's assets.

WAGE AND PRICE CONTROLS
Score: 4–Stable (high level)

Turkmenistan's large number of state-owned enterprises controls wages and prices. Price controls continue on such items as agricultural products, transportation, and utilities, and government subsidies to many industries continue to prevent market pricing of goods and services. The U.S. Department of State reports that the government "continues to control and subsidize prices for staples, medicines, housing, public transportation services, and some production costs."[5]

PROPERTY RIGHTS
Score: 4–Stable (low level of protection)

The legal system does not protect private property sufficiently. "Currently," reports the U.S. Department of Commerce, "there is no legal system in place to enforce effectively property and contractual rights."[6] According to the U.S. Department of State, "in practice, the judiciary is not independent; the President's power to select and dismiss judges subordinates the judiciary to the Presidency.... The court system has not been reformed since the Soviet era."[7]

REGULATION
Score: 4–Stable (high level)

Establishing a business in Turkmenistan can be a tedious and time-consuming procedure that requires individuals to overcome numerous bureaucratic barriers. In addition, the legal reforms necessary for a market economy to develop are not in place. According to the U.S. Department of Commerce, the "absence of a fully-developed commercial code inhibits foreign trade and investment. The numerous presidential decrees, legislative acts, and administrative rules regulating commercial activity are often contradictory and changes are often applied retroactively."[8] There has been recent movement toward legalizing some private production, but little progress has been made.

BLACK MARKET
Score: 5–Stable (very high level of activity)

Smuggling is rampant and, despite laws protecting intellectual property rights, significant piracy in computer software continues.

NOTES

[1]   U.S. Department of Commerce, "Turkmenistan—Commodity Exchange," *Market Research Reports,* January 1997.
[2]   The tax on the average income level is unknown. Thus, this score is based solely on the top tax bracket.
[3]   U.S. Department of Commerce, *Country Commercial Guide,* 1998.
[4]   *Ibid.*
[5]   U.S. Department of State, *Country Reports on Economic Policy and Trade Practices,* 1997.
[6]   U.S. Department of Commerce, *Country Commercial Guide,* 1998.
[7]   U.S. Department of State, "Turkmenistan Country Report on Human Rights Practices for 1997," 1998.
[8]   U.S. Department of Commerce, "Turkmenistan: Economic and Trade Overview," September 1996.

Uganda   2.80

1998 Score: **2.80**   1997 Score: **2.90**   1996 Score: **2.83**

Trade	5	Banking	3
Taxation	4	Wages and Prices	1
Government Intervention	2	Property Rights	2
Monetary Policy	5	Regulation	2
Foreign Investment	2	Black Market	2

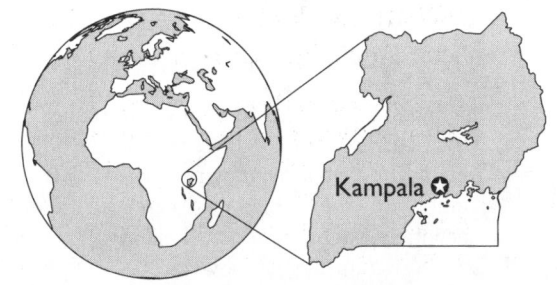

Kampala ✪

Uganda has endured civil strife since gaining its independence from the United Kingdom in 1962. It also is moving toward political liberalization. The 1995 constitution established a democratic system for independent elections of the president and parliament, which were held in May 1996 for the first time in 16 years. Restrictions on political parties continue, however, and rebels are active in north and southwest Uganda. President Yoweri Museveni's economic liberalization agenda has yielded positive results: GDP growth averaged 7.8 percent from 1992 to 1996 and 5 in 1997. Although other sectors of the economy are becoming increasingly important, agriculture continues to dominate, making Uganda's economic performance vulnerable to weather fluctuations.

TRADE POLICY
Score: 5–Stable (very high level of protectionism)

In 1993, Uganda lowered its highest import duty from 80 percent to 20 percent and reduced its lowest import duty from 50 percent to 10 percent. The average tariff rate now stands at approximately 30 percent. The Ministry of Commerce reserves the right to restrict the import of goods that compete with locally produced items. Imports of beer, cigarettes, and a few other items are banned, but plans exist to lift these bans.

TAXATION
Score–Income taxation: 4–Stable (high tax rates)
Score–Corporate taxation: 3–Stable (moderate tax rates)
Final Taxation Score: 4–Stable (high tax rates)

Uganda's top income tax rate is 30 percent, with the average income level taxed at 20 percent. The corporate tax rate is 30 percent. Uganda also has a 17 percent value-added tax.

GOVERNMENT INTERVENTION IN THE ECONOMY
Score: 2-Stable (low level)

Government consumes 9.7 percent of GDP. The government has divested itself of 49 state enterprises and liquidated 14 others, including Uganda Air. Despite preliminary opposition, several other state-owned companies are slated for privatization. The government still owns the postal service, some major banking institutions, hotel chains, and similar companies.

MONETARY POLICY
Score: 5–Stable (very high level of inflation)

The Museveni government has made significant strides toward controlling Uganda's long-standing inflation problem. From 1986 to 1996, the average annual rate of inflation was 88.2 percent.

1	Hong Kong	1.25	
2	Singapore	1.30	
3	Bahrain	1.70	
4	New Zealand	1.75	
5	Switzerland	1.85	
6	United States	1.90	
7	Ireland	1.95	
7	Luxembourg	1.95	
7	Taiwan	1.95	
7	United Kingdom	1.95	
11	Bahamas	2.00	
12	Czech Republic	2.05	
12	Japan	2.05	
14	Australia	2.10	
14	Belgium	2.10	
14	Canada	2.10	
14	United Arab Emirates	2.10	
18	Austria	2.15	
18	Chile	2.15	
18	Estonia	2.15	
18	Netherlands	2.15	
22	Denmark	2.25	
22	El Salvador	2.25	
22	Finland	2.25	
25	Germany	2.30	
25	Iceland	2.30	
27	Norway	2.35	
28	Korea, South	2.40	
28	Kuwait	2.40	
28	Malaysia	2.40	
28	Panama	2.40	
28	Thailand	2.40	
33	Sweden	2.45	
34	Argentina	2.50	
34	France	2.50	
34	Italy	2.50	
34	Spain	2.50	
38	Portugal	2.55	
38	Sri Lanka	2.55	
38	Trinidad and Tobago	2.55	
41	Barbados	2.60	
41	Peru	2.60	
43	Bolivia	2.65	
43	Mauritius	2.65	
45	Cyprus	2.70	
45	Jamaica	2.70	
45	Uruguay	2.70	
48	Botswana	2.75	
48	Guatemala	2.75	
48	Jordan	2.75	
48	Namibia	2.75	
48	Oman	2.75	
48	Philippines	2.75	
54	Belize	2.80	
54	Costa Rica	2.80	
54	Israel	2.80	
54	Swaziland	2.80	
54	Turkey	2.80	
54	Uganda	2.80	
54	Samoa	2.80	
61	Latvia	2.85	
62	Greece	2.90	
62	Hungary	2.90	
62	So. Africa	2.90	
65	Ecuador	2.95	
65	Gabon	2.95	
65	Indonesia	2.95	
65	Malta	2.95	
65	Morocco	2.95	
65	Poland	2.95	
65	Tunisia	2.95	
72	Ghana	3.00	
72	Lithuania	3.00	
72	Saudi Arabia	3.00	
75	Benin	3.05	
75	Kenya	3.05	
75	Paraguay	3.05	
75	Qatar	3.05	
75	Slovak Republic	3.05	
75	Zambia	3.05	
81	Colombia	3.10	
81	Fiji	3.10	
81	Mali	3.10	
81	Slovenia	3.10	
85	Honduras	3.15	
85	Mexico	3.15	
85	Papua New Guinea	3.15	
88	Djibouti	3.20	
88	Mongolia	3.20	
90	Algeria	3.25	
90	Brazil	3.25	
90	Lebanon	3.25	
90	Senegal	3.25	
90	Tanzania	3.25	
95	Nigeria	3.30	
95	Romania	3.30	
97	Cambodia	3.35	
97	Dominican Republic	3.35	
97	Egypt	3.35	
97	Guinea	3.35	
97	Ivory Coast	3.35	
97	Moldova	3.35	
97	Pakistan	3.35	
104	Nepal	3.40	
104	Venezuela	3.40	
106	Armenia	3.45	
106	Bulgaria	3.45	
106	Lesotho	3.45	
106	Madagascar	3.45	
106	Russia	3.45	
111	Burkina Faso	3.50	
111	Cameroon	3.50	
111	Guyana	3.50	
111	Nicaragua	3.50	
115	Gambia	3.60	
116	Croatia	3.65	
116	Georgia	3.65	
116	Malawi	3.65	
119	Cape Verde	3.67	
120	Ethiopia	3.70	
120	India	3.70	
120	Niger	3.70	
123	Congo	3.75	
124	Chad	3.80	
124	China	3.80	
124	Mauritania	3.80	
124	Ukraine	3.80	
124	Zimbabwe	3.80	
129	Albania	3.85	
129	Bangladesh	3.85	
129	Mozambique	3.85	
129	Suriname	3.85	
133	Burundi	3.90	
134	Togo	3.95	
135	Haiti	4.00	
135	Kyrgyz Rep.	4.00	
137	Kazakhstan	4.05	
137	Sierra Leone	4.05	
139	Yemen	4.10	
140	Belarus	4.15	
141	Sudan	4.20	
141	Syria	4.20	
143	Azerbaijan	4.30	
143	Equatorial Guinea	4.30	
143	Myanmar	4.30	
143	Rwanda	4.30	
147	Tajikistan	4.40	
147	Uzbekistan	4.40	
149	Angola	4.45	
149	Turkmenistan	4.45	
151	Guinea-Bissau	4.55	
152	Vietnam	4.60	
153	Congo (Zaire)	4.70	
153	Iran	4.70	
155	Bosnia	4.80	
155	Somalia	4.80	
157	Iraq	4.90	
157	Laos	4.90	
157	Libya	4.90	
160	Cuba	5.00	
160	Korea, North	5.00	

Mostly Free

CAPITAL FLOWS AND FOREIGN INVESTMENT
Score: 2–Stable (low barriers)

Uganda's government has moved to reduce foreign investment barriers. Foreign investors may own Ugandan companies in full, and foreign-owned investments are treated in a nondiscriminatory manner. There also are investment incentives, such as some tax holidays. Foreigners may not own agricultural land, however.

BANKING
Score: 3–Stable (moderate level of restrictions)

Uganda's small financial sector is dominated by several government-owned banks, although the government is trying to establish liberal banking legislation. A small number of foreign banks operate in Uganda, which also has many non-bank financial institutions, including 21 insurance companies. The U.S. Department of Commerce characterizes Uganda's formal financial system as "small and weak."[1]

WAGE AND PRICE CONTROLS
Score: 1–Stable (very low level)

The government dismantled price controls in January 1994, and the abolition of coffee, cotton, and other government monopolies has allowed the market to set wages and prices in these important sectors. There are over 100 private coffee trading companies. Uganda has no minimum wage.

PROPERTY RIGHTS
Score: 2–Stable (high level of protection)

The government is proceeding slowly to privatize state assets and is returning property confiscated by previous regimes. The Departed Asians Property Custodian Board has returned over 4,000 properties in the past few years. According to the U.S. Department of State, "The Constitution provides for an independent judiciary; however, the President has extensive legal and extralegal powers that may influence exercise of this independence."[2]

REGULATION
Score: 2–Stable (low level)

Uganda's government has made significant progress toward reducing bureaucratic red tape. Because many state-owned businesses have undergone privatization, they have been allowed to operate relatively free of burdensome regulations on such things as established work weeks and worker and consumer health and safety standards.

BLACK MARKET
Score: 2–Stable (low level of activity)

The smuggling of cigarettes and oil is widespread, and some electronic goods are smuggled to escape high tariffs. Black market activity has decreased as Uganda's economy has become more liberalized.

NOTES
[1] U.S. Department of Commerce, *Country Commercial Guide,* 1998.
[2] U.S. Department of State, "Uganda Country Report on Human Rights Practices for 1996," 1997.

Ukraine   3.80

Kiev ◉

1998 Score: **3.80**	1997 Score: **3.75**	1996 Score: **4.00**

Trade	4	Banking	4
Taxation	4	Wages and Prices	3
Government Intervention	3	Property Rights	4
Monetary Policy	5	Regulation	4
Foreign Investment	3	Black Market	4

Formerly part of the Soviet Union, Ukraine became an independent republic in 1991 but has been slow to implement economic reform. The government of President Leonid Kravchuk was composed of old Communist Party *apparatchiki* who resisted reform. Some progress has been achieved since the election of President Leonid Kuchma in 1994. Kuchma moved, for example, to reduce subsidies to some state-owned industries, privatize others, and reduce barriers to trade; however, a corrupt, entrenched bureaucracy continues to stifle reform. In July 1997, Prime Minister Pavlo Lazarenko resigned under pressure from critics who claimed that the government's economic reforms harmed most common Ukrainians in favor of the wealthy. The new cabinet of Prime Minister Valery Pustovoitenko and the Supreme Council (Ukraine's legislature) forwarded an economic reform plan that includes streamlining the bureaucracy and deregulating foreign trade and domestic business activities. The government intends to cut taxes and reduce the budget, speed up the privatization of major state-owned enterprises, encourage foreign and domestic investment, and target existing social benefits to the truly needy while trimming the overall welfare burden. The ability of the new cabinet to stick to this plan is not certain in view of the government's past performance. Election of a communist-dominated Supreme Council in spring 1998 has complicated further the movement toward reform.

TRADE POLICY
Score: 4–Stable (high level of protectionism)

According to the Office of the United States Trade Representative, "Most MFN [most favored nation] tariffs in Ukraine range from zero to 30 percent."[1] The U.S. Department of Commerce reports that "Import duties vary, but generally are around 16 percent."[2] According to the U.S. Department of State, Ukraine no longer maintains any significant non-tariff barriers and has eased import licensing requirements, so that now the only requirements relate to technical, safety, and environmental standards, as well as to efficacy standards with regard to pharmaceutical and veterinary products.[3] Moreover, the U.S. State Department also reports that "The daunting menu of a VAT (20 percent), import duties (ranging from 5–200 percent) and excise taxes (10–300 percent) present a major obstacle to trade with Ukraine."[4]

TAXATION
Score–Income taxation: 4–Stable (high tax rates)
Score–Corporate taxation: 3–Stable (moderate tax rates)
Final Taxation Score: 4–Stable (high tax rates)

Ukraine's top income tax rate is 40 percent. The rate for the average income is 20 percent. The top corporate tax rate is 30 percent. Ukraine also maintains a 30 percent capital gains tax and a 20 percent value-added tax.

1	Hong Kong	1.25
2	Singapore	1.30
3	Bahrain	1.70
4	New Zealand	1.75
5	Switzerland	1.85
6	United States	1.90
7	Ireland	1.95
7	Luxembourg	1.95
7	Taiwan	1.95
7	United Kingdom	1.95
11	Bahamas	2.00
12	Czech Republic	2.05
12	Japan	2.05
14	Australia	2.10
14	Belgium	2.10
14	Canada	2.10
14	United Arab Emirates	2.10
18	Austria	2.15
18	Chile	2.15
18	Estonia	2.15
18	Netherlands	2.15
22	Denmark	2.25
22	El Salvador	2.25
22	Finland	2.25
25	Germany	2.30
25	Iceland	2.30
27	Norway	2.35
28	Korea, South	2.40
28	Kuwait	2.40
28	Malaysia	2.40
28	Panama	2.40
28	Thailand	2.40
33	Sweden	2.45
34	Argentina	2.50
34	France	2.50
34	Italy	2.50
34	Spain	2.50
38	Portugal	2.55
38	Sri Lanka	2.55
38	Trinidad and Tobago	2.55
41	Barbados	2.60
41	Peru	2.60
43	Bolivia	2.65
43	Mauritius	2.65
45	Cyprus	2.70
45	Jamaica	2.70
45	Uruguay	2.70
48	Botswana	2.75
48	Guatemala	2.75
48	Jordan	2.75
48	Namibia	2.75
48	Oman	2.75
48	Philippines	2.75
54	Belize	2.80
54	Costa Rica	2.80
54	Israel	2.80
54	Swaziland	2.80
54	Turkey	2.80
54	Uganda	2.80
54	Samoa	2.80
61	Latvia	2.85
62	Greece	2.90
62	Hungary	2.90
62	So. Africa	2.90
65	Ecuador	2.95
65	Gabon	2.95
65	Indonesia	2.95
65	Malta	2.95
65	Morocco	2.95
65	Poland	2.95
65	Tunisia	2.95
72	Ghana	3.00
72	Lithuania	3.00
72	Saudi Arabia	3.00
75	Benin	3.05
75	Kenya	3.05
75	Paraguay	3.05
75	Qatar	3.05
75	Slovak Republic	3.05
75	Zambia	3.05
81	Colombia	3.10

81	Fiji	3.10
81	Mali	3.10
81	Slovenia	3.10
85	Honduras	3.15
85	Mexico	3.15
85	Papua New Guinea	3.15
88	Djibouti	3.20
88	Mongolia	3.20
90	Algeria	3.25
90	Brazil	3.25
90	Lebanon	3.25
90	Senegal	3.25
90	Tanzania	3.25
95	Nigeria	3.30
95	Romania	3.30
97	Cambodia	3.35
97	Dominican Republic	3.35
97	Egypt	3.35
97	Guinea	3.35
97	Ivory Coast	3.35
97	Moldova	3.35
97	Pakistan	3.35
104	Nepal	3.40
104	Venezuela	3.40
106	Armenia	3.45
106	Bulgaria	3.45
106	Lesotho	3.45
106	Madagascar	3.45
106	Russia	3.45
111	Burkina Faso	3.50
111	Cameroon	3.50
111	Guyana	3.50
111	Nicaragua	3.50
115	Gambia	3.60
116	Croatia	3.65
116	Georgia	3.65
116	Malawi	3.65
119	Cape Verde	3.67
120	Ethiopia	3.70
120	India	3.70
120	Niger	3.70
123	Congo	3.75
124	Chad	3.80
124	China	3.80
124	Mauritania	3.80
124	Ukraine	3.80
124	Zimbabwe	3.80
129	Albania	3.85
129	Bangladesh	3.85
129	Mozambique	3.85
129	Suriname	3.85
133	Burundi	3.90
134	Togo	3.95
135	Haiti	4.00
135	Kyrgyz Rep.	4.00
137	Kazakhstan	4.05
137	Sierra Leone	4.05
139	Yemen	4.10
140	Belarus	4.15
141	Sudan	4.20
141	Syria	4.20
143	Azerbaijan	4.30
143	Equatorial Guinea	4.30
143	Myanmar	4.30
143	Rwanda	4.30
147	Tajikistan	4.40
147	Uzbekistan	4.40
149	Angola	4.45
149	Turkmenistan	4.45
151	Guinea-Bissau	4.55
152	Vietnam	4.60
153	Congo (Zaire)	4.70
153	Iran	4.70
155	Bosnia	4.80
155	Somalia	4.80
157	Iraq	4.90
157	Laos	4.90
157	Libya	4.90
160	Cuba	5.00
160	Korea, North	5.00

Mostly Unfree

GOVERNMENT INTERVENTION IN THE ECONOMY
Score: 3–Stable (moderate level)

Government consumes 22 percent of GDP. The public sector, however, still generates most GDP overall.

MONETARY POLICY
Score: 5–Stable (very high level of inflation)

Since becoming an independent state, Ukraine has made tremendous progress toward reducing its rate of inflation: 1,310 percent in 1992, 4,735 percent in 1993, 891 percent in 1994, 377 percent in 1995, and 80 percent in 1996. In 1997, inflation fell to around 12 percent. As important as this progress is, however, Ukraine's average annual rate of inflation is very high by global standards.[5]

CAPITAL FLOWS AND FOREIGN INVESTMENT
Score: 3–Stable (moderate barriers)

Foreign and domestic businesses are treated equally under Ukraine's foreign investment law. There are no regulatory restrictions on repatriation of capital or profits, and few restrictions on foreign ownership of businesses. The government passed a new foreign investment law in 1996 that provides for a more open and stable environment than the one that existed previously. The unpredictable application of the country's laws, widespread corruption among local and central government officials, a lack of understanding of basic economic principles among the bureaucracy, and the slow progress of reform, however, continue to deter foreign investors, who often are forced to pay bribes or kickbacks to facilitate the necessary paperwork, permits, and licenses. According to the U.S. Department of Commerce, "The U.S.–Ukraine Bilateral Investment Treaty, which took effect on November 16, 1996, provides further protection for U.S. investors. Investors have, however, had difficulties in reaching agreements with individual enterprises; this has been in part due to obstructions at the regional or local levels, problems with tax enforcement, the uncertain regulatory climate, and a lack of transparency in the legal system. Individual complaints of corruption within Ukrainian Ministries have also surfaced."[6]

BANKING
Score: 4–Stable (high level of restrictions)

Ukraine's banking environment remains in regulatory chaos, subject to heavy government intervention and the strict control of credit. Even though their number has grown, private banks remain in direct competition with government-controlled and -subsidized institutions. "Generally, Ukrainian banking is unstable and in a painful transitional period," according to the U.S. Department of Commerce. "Foreign investors confront difficulties in transferring funds both domestically and internationally, in converting currency, and in the repatriation of profits in foreign currency."[7]

WAGE AND PRICE CONTROLS
Score: 3–Stable (moderate level)

The government controls wages for jobs in Ukraine's industrial sectors. It also controls some prices, especially in housing, transportation services, and public utilities.

PROPERTY RIGHTS
Score: 4–Stable (low level of protection)

Although its new constitution provides for the protection of private property, Ukraine has yet to establish a legal system that can enforce property rights adequately. Despite an ambitious government program to privatize large sectors of the economy, property remains subject to government expropriation. According to the U.S. Department of State, "Under the new Constitution, the judiciary is funded independently, instead of through the Ministry of Justice. However, the court system remains subject to political interference.... The judiciary is overburdened and lacks sufficient funding and staff. Long delays in trials are a problem."[8]

REGULATION
Score: 4–Stable (high level)

Regulations are applied haphazardly, posing a significant impediment to business activity. Another problem is widespread bureaucratic corruption, which limits the ability of businesses to obtain the necessary permits to conduct operations. According to the U.S. Department of Commerce, "Corruption pervades much of Ukraine's civil service and regulatory system, according to many press articles and foreign business complaints. Conflict of interest is a poorly-developed concept at this point, and many bureaucrats retain their commercial interests while in power. A complicated and non-transparent regulatory system has also encouraged petty corruption at all levels of government.... [T]he current bureaucracy is not transparent and foreign companies have encountered difficulties by not knowing which government and administrative organizations at the national, regional, and local levels need to be consulted."[9]

BLACK MARKET
Score: 4–Stable (high level of activity)

Because the government controls large portions of the economy, the informal sector performs much business activity. According to the U.S. Department of Commerce, "The World Bank estimates that the informal economy accounts for nearly half of estimated total GDP (official plus unofficial economies). Some Ukrainian estimates claim that the informal sector accounts for 60% of Ukraine's economic activity."[10]

NOTES

[1] Office of the United States Trade Representative, *1998 National Trade Estimate Report on Foreign Trade Barriers*, 1998.

[2] U.S. Department of Commerce, "Ukraine: Economic and Trade Overview," March 1997.

[3] U.S. Department of State, *Country Reports on Economic Policy and Trade Practices*, 1998.

[4] *Ibid.*

[5] These figures represent consumer price inflation.

[6] U.S. Department of Commerce, *Country Commercial Guide*, 1998.

[7] *Ibid.*

[8] U.S. Department of State, "Ukraine Country Report on Human Rights Practices for 1997," 1998.

[9] U.S. Department of Commerce, *Country Commercial Guide*, 1998.

[10] *Ibid.*

United Arab Emirates

2.10

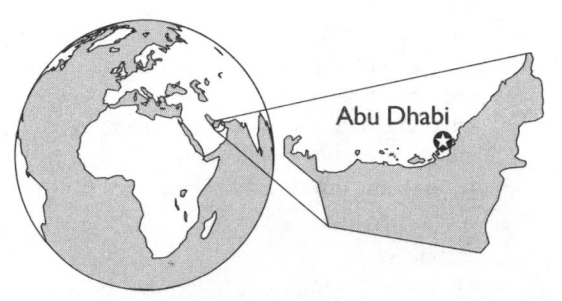

Abu Dhabi

Trade	2	Banking	3
Taxation	1	Wages and Prices	3
Government Intervention	3	Property Rights	1
Monetary Policy	1	Regulation	2
Foreign Investment	4	Black Market	1

The United Arab Emirates (UAE) is a federation of seven emirates: Abu Dhabi, Ajman, Dubai, Fujairah, Ras al-Khaimah, Sharjah, and Umm al-Qaiwain. The individual emirates maintain considerable power over their own legal and economic affairs. Oil revenues—the single largest source of income—allow the government to keep import tariffs and taxation to a minimum. Most oil production remains in the hands of the government.

TRADE POLICY
Score: 2–Stable (low level of protectionism)

The UAE is essentially a huge duty-free port. According to the U.S. Department of Commerce, "In a step toward establishing a common external tariff, the UAE in 1994 took the decision to raise its import duties from one to four percent. However, over 75 percent of imports still enter duty free."[1] One major non-tariff barrier is the government's requirement that UAE nationals own at least 51 percent of some distributing companies not located in free-trade zones.

TAXATION
Score–Income taxation: 1–Stable (very low tax rates)
Score–Corporate taxation: 1–Stable (very low tax rates)
Final Taxation Score: 1–Stable (very low tax rates)

The UAE has no income tax, no corporate tax, and no other significant taxes.

GOVERNMENT INTERVENTION IN THE ECONOMY
Score: 3–Stable (moderate level)

Government consumes about 16 percent of GDP. Much of this GDP is derived from oil, which is owned primarily by the government. The government also heavily subsidizes such services as education, health care, and utilities.

MONETARY POLICY
Score: 1–Stable (very low level of inflation)

The UAE's average rate of inflation from 1990 to 1995 was about 5 percent. In 1996, the rate of inflation was about 5.2 percent, the level at which it remains today.

CAPITAL FLOWS AND FOREIGN INVESTMENT
Score: 4–Stable (high barriers)

The UAE is open to some types of foreign investment, but there are significant restrictions. According to the U.S. Department of Commerce, "The regulatory and legal framework favors local over foreign investors. There is no national treatment for investors in the UAE. Foreign ownership of land and stocks is

#				#		
1	Hong Kong	1.25		81	Fiji	3.10
2	Singapore	1.30		81	Mali	3.10
3	Bahrain	1.70		81	Slovenia	3.10
4	New Zealand	1.75		85	Honduras	3.15
5	Switzerland	1.85		85	Mexico	3.15
6	United States	1.90		85	Papua New Guinea	3.15
7	Ireland	1.95		88	Djibouti	3.20
7	Luxembourg	1.95		88	Mongolia	3.20
7	Taiwan	1.95		90	Algeria	3.25
7	United Kingdom	1.95		90	Brazil	3.25
11	Bahamas	2.00		90	Lebanon	3.25
12	Czech Republic	2.05		90	Senegal	3.25
12	Japan	2.05		90	Tanzania	3.25
14	Australia	2.10		95	Nigeria	3.30
14	Belgium	2.10		95	Romania	3.30
14	Canada	2.10		97	Cambodia	3.35
14	United Arab Emirates	2.10		97	Dominican Republic	3.35
18	Austria	2.15		97	Egypt	3.35
18	Chile	2.15		97	Guinea	3.35
18	Estonia	2.15		97	Ivory Coast	3.35
18	Netherlands	2.15		97	Moldova	3.35
22	Denmark	2.25		97	Pakistan	3.35
22	El Salvador	2.25		104	Nepal	3.40
22	Finland	2.25		104	Venezuela	3.40
25	Germany	2.30		106	Armenia	3.45
25	Iceland	2.30		106	Bulgaria	3.45
27	Norway	2.35		106	Lesotho	3.45
28	Korea, South	2.40		106	Madagascar	3.45
28	Kuwait	2.40		106	Russia	3.45
28	Malaysia	2.40		111	Burkina Faso	3.50
28	Panama	2.40		111	Cameroon	3.50
28	Thailand	2.40		111	Guyana	3.50
33	Sweden	2.45		111	Nicaragua	3.50
34	Argentina	2.50		115	Gambia	3.60
34	France	2.50		116	Croatia	3.65
34	Italy	2.50		116	Georgia	3.65
34	Spain	2.50		116	Malawi	3.65
38	Portugal	2.55		119	Cape Verde	3.67
38	Sri Lanka	2.55		120	Ethiopia	3.70
38	Trinidad and Tobago	2.55		120	India	3.70
41	Barbados	2.60		120	Niger	3.70
41	Peru	2.60		123	Congo	3.75
43	Bolivia	2.65		124	Chad	3.80
43	Mauritius	2.65		124	China	3.80
45	Cyprus	2.70		124	Mauritania	3.80
45	Jamaica	2.70		124	Ukraine	3.80
45	Uruguay	2.70		124	Zimbabwe	3.80
48	Botswana	2.75		129	Albania	3.85
48	Guatemala	2.75		129	Bangladesh	3.85
48	Jordan	2.75		129	Mozambique	3.85
48	Namibia	2.75		129	Suriname	3.85
48	Oman	2.75		133	Burundi	3.90
48	Philippines	2.75		134	Togo	3.95
54	Belize	2.80		135	Haiti	4.00
54	Costa Rica	2.80		135	Kyrgyz Rep.	4.00
54	Israel	2.80		137	Kazakhstan	4.05
54	Swaziland	2.80		137	Sierra Leone	4.05
54	Turkey	2.80		139	Yemen	4.10
54	Uganda	2.80		140	Belarus	4.15
54	Samoa	2.80		141	Sudan	4.20
61	Latvia	2.85		141	Syria	4.20
62	Greece	2.90		143	Azerbaijan	4.30
62	Hungary	2.90		143	Equatorial Guinea	4.30
62	So. Africa	2.90		143	Myanmar	4.30
65	Ecuador	2.95		143	Rwanda	4.30
65	Gabon	2.95		147	Tajikistan	4.40
65	Indonesia	2.95		147	Uzbekistan	4.40
65	Malta	2.95		149	Angola	4.45
65	Morocco	2.95		149	Turkmenistan	4.45
65	Poland	2.95		151	Guinea-Bissau	4.55
65	Tunisia	2.95		152	Vietnam	4.60
72	Ghana	3.00		153	Congo (Zaire)	4.70
72	Lithuania	3.00		153	Iran	4.70
72	Saudi Arabia	3.00		155	Bosnia	4.80
75	Benin	3.05		155	Somalia	4.80
75	Kenya	3.05		157	Iraq	4.90
75	Paraguay	3.05		157	Laos	4.90
75	Qatar	3.05		157	Libya	4.90
75	Slovak Republic	3.05		160	Cuba	5.00
75	Zambia	3.05		160	Korea, North	5.00
81	Colombia	3.10				

Mostly Free

extremely restricted."[2] Moreover, there are restrictions on the shares of certain companies that foreigners can own. Exemptions are given to companies operating in the Jebel Ali Free Zone in Dubai. Some sectors, including oil and gas operations, petrochemicals, electricity, and water desalination, are closed to foreign investment.

BANKING
Score: 3–Stable (moderate level of restrictions)

The UAE's banking system is large and competitive. The government's largely liberal economic policies have led to a proliferation of private banks, although the government still owns some banks. The UAE has no corporate income tax, but there is a 30 percent tax on bank earnings.

WAGE AND PRICE CONTROLS
Score: 3–Stable (moderate level)

The market sets many wages and prices. The government continues to offer subsidies to many businesses, however, and this affects the price of utilities, health care, education, and food. The government also owns many services that affect free-market pricing.

PROPERTY RIGHTS
Score: 1–Stable (very high level of protection)

Private property is protected in the UAE. The emirate has an effective and modern legal and judicial system.

REGULATION
Score: 2–Stable (low level)

Establishing a business in the UAE is easy if the business is not to compete directly with state-owned concerns. Regulations are applied evenly in most cases.

BLACK MARKET
Score: 1–Stable (very low level of activity)

The size of the black market is negligible. There are three laws to protect intellectual property, and the economy is virtually free of pirated material.

NOTES

[1]   U.S. Department of Commerce, *Country Commercial Guide,* 1998.

[2]   *Ibid.*

United Kingdom   1.95

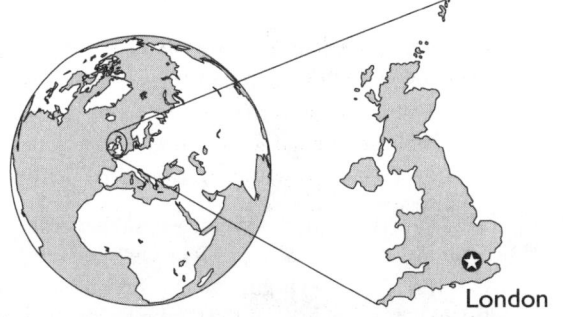

London

1998 Score: **1.95**		1997 Score: **1.95**		1996 Score: **1.95**

Trade	2	Banking	2
Taxation	4.5	Wages and Prices	2
Government Intervention	2	Property Rights	1
Monetary Policy	1	Regulation	2
Foreign Investment	2	Black Market	1

The United Kingdom is a constitutional monarchy with a parliamentary government that has moved from socialism to free-market capitalism. Facing near economic collapse in the 1970s, the United Kingdom turned to free-market reform under the leadership of Prime Minister Margaret Thatcher. The result was extensive market liberalization that made the economy one of the strongest in the European Union (EU). In May 1997 elections, Labour Party candidate Tony Blair ousted the Conservative Party's John Major by a landslide, ending 18 years of Conservative Party rule. Blair ran on a campaign promise to maintain the previous administration's economic liberalization policies; specifically, he promised not to increase income taxes or alter spending plans through 1999, as established by the Conservative Party. Although Labour's first budget maintained Conservative spending caps and cut corporate income taxes from 33 percent to 31 percent, it also levied a one-time windfall tax on privatized utilities and reduced tax benefits for private medical insurance. So far, Blair has demonstrated that he is not likely any time soon to embrace the more socialist policies of the Labour Party; instead, he has shown a willingness to build on the success of the Conservative Party, with no major departures since taking office. According to the Economist Intelligence Unit, "Despite being the architect of its electoral success, Mr. Blair remains an object of suspicion within his own party, particularly among its older members who resent the weakening of the party's links with the trade union movement and apparent abandonment of many of its most cherished ideals."

TRADE POLICY
Score: 2–Stable (low level of protectionism)

The United Kingdom's average tariff rate is 3.6 percent. Some progress has been made toward opening its market to imports, but non-tariff barriers still remain in air services and the energy industry.

TAXATION
Score–Income taxation: 5–Stable (very high tax rates)
Score–Corporate taxation: 3–Stable (moderate tax rates)
Final Taxation Score: 4.5–Stable (very high tax rates)

The top income tax rate is 40 percent, and the average income level is taxed at 23 percent. The top corporate tax rate is 31 percent, down from 33 percent for the 1996–1997 taxable year. The United Kingdom also has a capital gains tax and a 17.5 percent value-added tax.

GOVERNMENT INTERVENTION IN THE ECONOMY
Score: 2–Stable (low level)

Government consumes about 20.8 percent of GDP. The United Kingdom has made progress toward privatization, a sign that the government is becoming less involved in the market. The government has sold its interests in the automotive, steel, coal mining, and aircraft and air transportation sectors. The government also has privatized electric power (except nuclear), rail transportation, and water

1	Hong Kong	1.25	81	Fiji	3.10
2	Singapore	1.30	81	Mali	3.10
3	Bahrain	1.70	81	Slovenia	3.10
4	New Zealand	1.75	85	Honduras	3.15
5	Switzerland	1.85	85	Mexico	3.15
6	United States	1.90	85	Papua New Guinea	3.15
7	Ireland	1.95	88	Djibouti	3.20
7	Luxembourg	1.95	88	Mongolia	3.20
7	Taiwan	1.95	90	Algeria	3.25
7	United Kingdom	1.95	90	Brazil	3.25
11	Bahamas	2.00	90	Lebanon	3.25
12	Czech Republic	2.05	90	Senegal	3.25
12	Japan	2.05	90	Tanzania	3.25
14	Australia	2.10	95	Nigeria	3.30
14	Belgium	2.10	95	Romania	3.30
14	Canada	2.10	97	Cambodia	3.35
14	United Arab Emirates	2.10	97	Dominican Republic	3.35
18	Austria	2.15	97	Egypt	3.35
18	Chile	2.15	97	Guinea	3.35
18	Estonia	2.15	97	Ivory Coast	3.35
18	Netherlands	2.15	97	Moldova	3.35
22	Denmark	2.25	97	Pakistan	3.35
22	El Salvador	2.25	104	Nepal	3.40
22	Finland	2.25	104	Venezuela	3.40
25	Germany	2.30	106	Armenia	3.45
25	Iceland	2.30	106	Bulgaria	3.45
27	Norway	2.35	106	Lesotho	3.45
28	Korea, South	2.40	106	Madagascar	3.45
28	Kuwait	2.40	106	Russia	3.45
28	Malaysia	2.40	111	Burkina Faso	3.50
28	Panama	2.40	111	Cameroon	3.50
28	Thailand	2.40	111	Guyana	3.50
33	Sweden	2.45	111	Nicaragua	3.50
34	Argentina	2.50	115	Gambia	3.60
34	France	2.50	116	Croatia	3.65
34	Italy	2.50	116	Georgia	3.65
34	Spain	2.50	116	Malawi	3.65
38	Portugal	2.55	119	Cape Verde	3.67
38	Sri Lanka	2.55	120	Ethiopia	3.70
38	Trinidad and Tobago	2.55	120	India	3.70
41	Barbados	2.60	120	Niger	3.70
41	Peru	2.60	123	Congo	3.75
43	Bolivia	2.65	124	Chad	3.80
43	Mauritius	2.65	124	China	3.80
45	Cyprus	2.70	124	Mauritania	3.80
45	Jamaica	2.70	124	Ukraine	3.80
45	Uruguay	2.70	124	Zimbabwe	3.80
48	Botswana	2.75	129	Albania	3.85
48	Guatemala	2.75	129	Bangladesh	3.85
48	Jordan	2.75	129	Mozambique	3.85
48	Namibia	2.75	129	Suriname	3.85
48	Oman	2.75	133	Burundi	3.90
48	Philippines	2.75	134	Togo	3.95
54	Belize	2.80	135	Haiti	4.00
54	Costa Rica	2.80	135	Kyrgyz Rep.	4.00
54	Israel	2.80	137	Kazakhstan	4.05
54	Swaziland	2.80	137	Sierra Leone	4.05
54	Turkey	2.80	139	Yemen	4.10
54	Uganda	2.80	140	Belarus	4.15
54	Samoa	2.80	141	Sudan	4.20
61	Latvia	2.85	141	Syria	4.20
62	Greece	2.90	143	Azerbaijan	4.30
62	Hungary	2.90	143	Equatorial Guinea	4.30
62	So. Africa	2.90	143	Myanmar	4.30
65	Ecuador	2.95	143	Rwanda	4.30
65	Gabon	2.95	147	Tajikistan	4.40
65	Indonesia	2.95	147	Uzbekistan	4.40
65	Malta	2.95	149	Angola	4.45
65	Morocco	2.95	149	Turkmenistan	4.45
65	Poland	2.95	151	Guinea-Bissau	4.55
65	Tunisia	2.95	152	Vietnam	4.60
72	Ghana	3.00	153	Congo (Zaire)	4.70
72	Lithuania	3.00	153	Iran	4.70
72	Saudi Arabia	3.00	155	Bosnia	4.80
75	Benin	3.05	155	Somalia	4.80
75	Kenya	3.05	157	Iraq	4.90
75	Paraguay	3.05	157	Laos	4.90
75	Qatar	3.05	157	Libya	4.90
75	Slovak Republic	3.05	160	Cuba	5.00
75	Zambia	3.05	160	Korea, North	5.00
81	Colombia	3.10			

supply utilities. In addition, local bus transportation is in the process of being privatized, too.

MONETARY POLICY
Score: 1–Stable (very low level of inflation)

The United Kingdom's average annual rate of inflation from 1986 to 1996 was 4.3 percent. In 1997, the rate was 2.4 percent. The Labour government's recent grant of "operational independence" to the Bank of England should reduce the government's influence on monetary policy and lead to lower rates of inflation.

CAPITAL FLOWS AND FOREIGN INVESTMENT
Score: 2–Stable (low barriers)

Many non-European companies use the United Kingdom as a base for setting up businesses in Europe. The United Kingdom also is the largest recipient of U.S. and Japanese foreign investment in Europe. Despite a generally hospitable environment, however, the United Kingdom still restricts some foreign investment in the aerospace industry and some media services.

BANKING
Score: 2–Stable (low level of restrictions)

The banking system of the United Kingdom is fairly open to competition. Privately owned banks supply most credit, and they are permitted to sell securities, insurance policies, and real estate as well as invest in industrial firms. The 1987 Banking Act, however, gives the Bank of England the right to prevent the foreign ownership of more than 15 percent of any bank in the United Kingdom.

WAGE AND PRICE CONTROLS
Score: 2–Stable (low level)

The market sets most prices in the United Kingdom, although the government caps maximum prices charged by public utilities. The government also controls the prices of some products and services, such as matches, milk, and some public utilities, and often controls rent prices for housing. Landlords are required to inform renters that they may challenge a rent increase to a "rent assessment committee" that has the power to force a landlord to lower the price if it is determined to be too high. The only area currently subject to minimum wage laws is agriculture; however, the Labour government is committed to implementing a new minimum wage for all workers over 18 years of age.

PROPERTY RIGHTS
Score: 1–Stable (very high level of protection)

The government has accepted the privatization initiatives backed by former prime ministers, especially those of Thatcher. Most of the economy is private, and the court system, in addition to being efficient, provides maximum protection of private property.

REGULATION
Score: 2–Stable (low level)

Opening a business is easy. The regulatory system can be somewhat burdensome, but the United Kingdom also has done more than most other industrialized countries to reduce the level of regulation. For example, companies may self-regulate their industries: Businesses subscribe voluntarily to a code of conduct that, if violated, causes them to be penalized by consumers, who see their products as shoddy. The Labour government is considering a host of regulations, however, that could decrease economic freedom. For example, it has agreed to join the EU's Social Charter, which will force employers to provide a three-month leave for a new parent, allow employees to refuse to work more than 48 hours a week, grant employees three weeks of annual paid leave, and subsidize businesses that hire workers under age 25. The government has pledged, however, not to reverse the Conservative Party's industrial relations reforms, which give the United Kingdom one of Europe's most flexible labor markets. In addition, Prime Minister Blair has criticized other European leaders for not liberalizing their labor markets.

BLACK MARKET
Score: 1–Stable (very low level of activity)

Like those in other developed countries, the black market in the United Kingdom is restricted to the illegal trafficking and possession of drugs and guns. The country's protection of intellectual property rights is among the best in the world.

United States   1.90

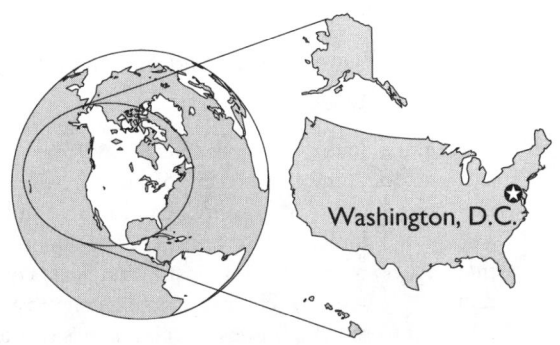

Washington, D.C.

1998 Score: **1.90**	1997 Score: **1.90**	1996 Score: **1.90**

Trade	2	Banking	2
Taxation	4	Wages and Prices	2
Government Intervention	2	Property Rights	1
Monetary Policy	1	Regulation	2
Foreign Investment	2	Black Market	1

The United States remains one of the world's most industrialized countries. It is the biggest exporter and importer of goods, has the largest economy, and enjoys the highest standard of living. It has one of the world's freest economies—but not *the* freest. During its two terms in office, the Reagan Administration made significant progress toward deregulating specific industries, such as railroads, trucking, airlines, and banking. President Bill Clinton signed a major telecommunications deregulation law in 1996. In addition, the United States has enacted some minor tax reform and has worked out a balanced budget for the first time in over 30 years. Still, these changes have been incremental and not sufficient enough to change the country's overall score.

TRADE POLICY
Score: 2–Stable (low level of protectionism)

The average U.S. tariff rate is 3.3 percent. The United States maintains trade restrictions on dairy products, animal feed, chocolate, some beers and wines, cotton, peanuts, syrups, molasses, cheese, wheat, sugar, textiles, and other items. It also is an aggressive user of unilateral trade retaliation. By global standards, however, the level of protectionism is low.

TAXATION
Score–Income taxation: 4–Stable (high tax rates)
Score–Corporate taxation: 3–Stable (moderate tax rates)
Final Taxation Score: 4–Stable (high tax rates)

The top income tax rate is 39.6 percent, and the average taxpayer is in the 15 percent bracket. The top marginal corporate tax rate is 35 percent. The United States also has state and local income taxes, federal estate taxes, a capital gains tax, and local property taxes. The government reduced some taxes as part of a balanced budget agreement; the maximum rate on capital gains, for example, fell from 28 percent to 20 percent. None of these tax changes, however, is sufficient to affect the final taxation score.

GOVERNMENT INTERVENTION IN THE ECONOMY
Score: 2–Stable (low level)

The federal government currently consumes about 16 percent of GDP, but the balanced budget agreement may reduce government consumption significantly while boosting economic activity. Congress has limited government spending in programs for the first time in decades, and this, coupled with increased economic activity, has reduced the overall government consumption rate slightly—but not enough to change the overall government intervention score.

MONETARY POLICY
Score: 1–Stable (very low level of inflation)

From 1986 to 1996, the United States maintained an average rate of inflation of 2.8 percent. In 1997, the rate was 2.4 percent, and it remained less than 3 percent for most of 1998.

1	Hong Kong	1.25	81	Fiji	3.10
2	Singapore	1.30	81	Mali	3.10
3	Bahrain	1.70	81	Slovenia	3.10
4	New Zealand	1.75	85	Honduras	3.15
5	Switzerland	1.85	85	Mexico	3.15
6	United States	1.90	85	Papua New Guinea	3.15
7	Ireland	1.95	88	Djibouti	3.20
7	Luxembourg	1.95	88	Mongolia	3.20
7	Taiwan	1.95	90	Algeria	3.25
7	United Kingdom	1.95	90	Brazil	3.25
11	Bahamas	2.00	90	Lebanon	3.25
12	Czech Republic	2.05	90	Senegal	3.25
12	Japan	2.05	90	Tanzania	3.25
14	Australia	2.10	95	Nigeria	3.30
14	Belgium	2.10	95	Romania	3.30
14	Canada	2.10	97	Cambodia	3.35
14	United Arab Emirates	2.10	97	Dominican Republic	3.35
18	Austria	2.15	97	Egypt	3.35
18	Chile	2.15	97	Guinea	3.35
18	Estonia	2.15	97	Ivory Coast	3.35
18	Netherlands	2.15	97	Moldova	3.35
22	Denmark	2.25	97	Pakistan	3.35
22	El Salvador	2.25	104	Nepal	3.40
22	Finland	2.25	104	Venezuela	3.40
25	Germany	2.30	106	Armenia	3.45
25	Iceland	2.30	106	Bulgaria	3.45
27	Norway	2.35	106	Lesotho	3.45
28	Korea, South	2.40	106	Madagascar	3.45
28	Kuwait	2.40	106	Russia	3.45
28	Malaysia	2.40	111	Burkina Faso	3.50
28	Panama	2.40	111	Cameroon	3.50
28	Thailand	2.40	111	Guyana	3.50
33	Sweden	2.45	111	Nicaragua	3.50
34	Argentina	2.50	115	Gambia	3.60
34	France	2.50	116	Croatia	3.65
34	Italy	2.50	116	Georgia	3.65
34	Spain	2.50	116	Malawi	3.65
38	Portugal	2.55	119	Cape Verde	3.67
38	Sri Lanka	2.55	120	Ethiopia	3.70
38	Trinidad and Tobago	2.55	120	India	3.70
41	Barbados	2.60	120	Niger	3.70
41	Peru	2.60	123	Congo	3.75
43	Bolivia	2.65	124	Chad	3.80
43	Mauritius	2.65	124	China	3.80
45	Cyprus	2.70	124	Mauritania	3.80
45	Jamaica	2.70	124	Ukraine	3.80
45	Uruguay	2.70	124	Zimbabwe	3.80
48	Botswana	2.75	129	Albania	3.85
48	Guatemala	2.75	129	Bangladesh	3.85
48	Jordan	2.75	129	Mozambique	3.85
48	Namibia	2.75	129	Suriname	3.85
48	Oman	2.75	133	Burundi	3.90
48	Philippines	2.75	134	Togo	3.95
54	Belize	2.80	135	Haiti	4.00
54	Costa Rica	2.80	135	Kyrgyz Rep.	4.00
54	Israel	2.80	137	Kazakhstan	4.05
54	Swaziland	2.80	137	Sierra Leone	4.05
54	Turkey	2.80	139	Yemen	4.10
54	Uganda	2.80	140	Belarus	4.15
54	Samoa	2.80	141	Sudan	4.20
61	Latvia	2.85	141	Syria	4.20
62	Greece	2.90	143	Azerbaijan	4.30
62	Hungary	2.90	143	Equatorial Guinea	4.30
62	So. Africa	2.90	143	Myanmar	4.30
65	Ecuador	2.95	143	Rwanda	4.30
65	Gabon	2.95	147	Tajikistan	4.40
65	Indonesia	2.95	147	Uzbekistan	4.40
65	Malta	2.95	149	Angola	4.45
65	Morocco	2.95	149	Turkmenistan	4.45
65	Poland	2.95	151	Guinea-Bissau	4.55
65	Tunisia	2.95	152	Vietnam	4.60
72	Ghana	3.00	153	Congo (Zaire)	4.70
72	Lithuania	3.00	153	Iran	4.70
72	Saudi Arabia	3.00	155	Bosnia	4.80
75	Benin	3.05	155	Somalia	4.80
75	Kenya	3.05	157	Iraq	4.90
75	Paraguay	3.05	157	Laos	4.90
75	Qatar	3.05	157	Libya	4.90
75	Slovak Republic	3.05	160	Cuba	5.00
75	Zambia	3.05	160	Korea, North	5.00
81	Colombia	3.10			

Free

CAPITAL FLOWS AND FOREIGN INVESTMENT
Score: 2–Stable (low barriers)

The United States welcomes foreign investment, which accounts for some 11.5 percent of manufacturing employment and 5.2 percent of overall employment. It treats foreign and domestic enterprises equally under the law; there are no restrictions on repatriation, local content requirements, or ownership restrictions on most industries. Restrictions remain, however, on industries considered vital to national security. For example, the United States continues to restrict foreign investment in commercial and civil aviation, some telecommunications industries, and public utilities.

BANKING
Score: 2–Stable (low level of restrictions)

Federal, state, and local governments minimally regulate the banking system. There are some limits on foreign banks, such as restrictions on the extent to which foreign interests may own U.S. banks. The United States has made some progress toward achieving further deregulation of banking. For example, Congress passed legislation in 1996 to permit domestically owned banks to open branches across state lines—something foreign banks already were allowed to do. Other reforms currently before Congress would allow banks to engage in commercial banking, insurance, and securities underwriting services.

WAGE AND PRICE CONTROLS
Score: 2–Stable (low level)

The market sets wages and prices, although the federal government continues to determine prices on some goods and services (such as peanuts and other agricultural goods) by purchasing excess production, closing borders to imports, and manipulating prices through subsidies to companies like Amtrak. The government controls prices of some dairy products by subsidizing dairy farmers. The federal government also imposes a minimum wage.

PROPERTY RIGHTS
Score: 1–Stable (very high level of protection)

Private property rights are a fundamental principle of the U.S. Constitution. The legal and judicial system is efficient and provides adequate protection of private property. The likelihood of government expropriation without just compensation is low. There have been situations in which governments at various levels have been known to expropriate property without due process (for example, in cases involving suspected drug dealers or those who proposition prostitutes), however, and many environmental policies have resulted in government confiscation of property without due process. The Army Corps of Engineers sometimes has used environmental laws to infringe on the property rights of citizens.

REGULATION
Score: 2–Stable (low level)

Establishing a business can be easy and affordable. Regulations are applied evenly and consistently in most cases, although they also can make it more difficult for businesses to keep their doors open. Despite some progress in recent years toward deregulating the economy, such as the 1996 deregulation of the telecommunications industry, government regulations cost U.S. consumers about $700 billion each year.[1] Many regulations—for example, the Americans with Disabilities Act, various civil rights regulations, environmental laws, health and product safety standards, and food and drug labeling requirements—although well-intentioned, also are onerous in some cases. In addition, many states have adopted such regulations at much higher levels than those imposed by the federal government. For example, California has imposed regulations that require automobile manufacturers to produce and sell electric-powered automobiles; companies failing to do so will not be permitted to sell automobiles in the state. This increase in regulations is occurring at the local level as well. San Francisco, for example, has mandated that any firm doing business with the city must provide the same benefits to domestic partner couples that it provides to legally married couples wherever it does business throughout the world. If evidence continues to grow that the increase in regulations has become a significantly greater burden on business, the U.S. score in this area could change. By global standards, however, the level of regulation remains low.

BLACK MARKET
Score: 1—Stable (very low level of activity)

The black market is confined primarily to goods and services considered harmful to public safety, such as narcotics, prostitution, guns, and stolen goods. The level of intellectual property protection is among the highest in the world.

NOTE

[1]   Thomas Hopkins, "Regulatory Costs in Profile," Center for the Study of American Business *Policy Study* No. 132, August 1996, p. 6.

Uruguay 2.70

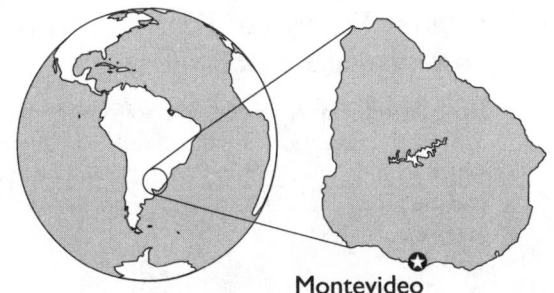

Montevideo

1998 Score: **2.70**   1997 Score: **2.70**   1996 Score: **2.80**

Trade	2	Banking	2
Taxation	3	Wages and Prices	2
Government Intervention	3	Property Rights	2
Monetary Policy	5	Regulation	3
Foreign Investment	2	Black Market	3

Uruguay is wealthy by Latin American standards and has a relatively high level of literacy. Once a major international banking center, it experienced economic stagnation because of statist economic policies introduced in the 1960s. Today, however, Uruguay has a relatively free and open market. The government has been working to liberalize the economy and bring back respectable levels of economic growth. Recent reforms in the banking sector promote greater competition among both foreign and domestic banks, and the government has reduced its barriers to trade. Uruguay is a member of Mercosur, the South American common market that includes Brazil, Argentina, and Paraguay.

TRADE POLICY
Score: 2–Stable (low level of protectionism)

Uruguay's average tariff rate is about 5.98 percent, down from 11 percent in 1992.[1] Few other restrictions on imports remain in effect. Import licenses are easy to obtain and do not serve to restrict imports.

TAXATION
Score–Income taxation: 1–Stable (very low tax rates)
Score–Corporate taxation: 3–Stable (moderate tax rates)
Final Taxation Score: 3–Stable (moderate tax rates)

There is no income tax in Uruguay.[2] The top corporate tax rate is 30 percent. Uruguay also has a value-added tax of 23 percent, up from 22 percent in 1995, and a social security contributions tax of 37 percent to 38 percent.

GOVERNMENT INTERVENTION IN THE ECONOMY
Score: 3–Stable (moderate level)

Government consumes 12.8 percent of GDP, down from 14 percent in 1995. The government has made significant progress toward privatizing state-owned industries. Many port facilities and electricity generation plants were privatized in 1993, and the natural gas company was privatized in 1994. The government continues to play a significant role in the economy, however, and still owns many banks and financial companies, as well as the telephone company. According to the U.S. Department of Commerce, "The Government owns, outright or partially, companies in the sectors of insurance, water supply, electricity, telephone service, petroleum refining, postal service, railways, banking and aviation. These activities generate about 18 percent of the gross domestic product and employ a similar percentage of the total labor force."[3] As of June 1998, however, a new energy law came into effect that will open up electricity generation to private-sector competition.

MONETARY POLICY
Score: 5–Stable (very high level of inflation)

Uruguay's average annual rate of inflation from 1986 to 1996 was 60.4 percent. In 1997, the rate was around 16 percent.

1	Hong Kong	1.25	81	Fiji	3.10
2	Singapore	1.30	81	Mali	3.10
3	Bahrain	1.70	81	Slovenia	3.10
4	New Zealand	1.75	85	Honduras	3.15
5	Switzerland	1.85	85	Mexico	3.15
6	United States	1.90	85	Papua New Guinea	3.15
7	Ireland	1.95	88	Djibouti	3.20
7	Luxembourg	1.95	88	Mongolia	3.20
7	Taiwan	1.95	90	Algeria	3.25
7	United Kingdom	1.95	90	Brazil	3.25
11	Bahamas	2.00	90	Lebanon	3.25
12	Czech Republic	2.05	90	Senegal	3.25
12	Japan	2.05	90	Tanzania	3.25
14	Australia	2.10	95	Nigeria	3.30
14	Belgium	2.10	95	Romania	3.30
14	Canada	2.10	97	Cambodia	3.35
14	United Arab Emirates	2.10	97	Dominican Republic	3.35
18	Austria	2.15	97	Egypt	3.35
18	Chile	2.15	97	Guinea	3.35
18	Estonia	2.15	97	Ivory Coast	3.35
18	Netherlands	2.15	97	Moldova	3.35
22	Denmark	2.25	97	Pakistan	3.35
22	El Salvador	2.25	104	Nepal	3.40
22	Finland	2.25	104	Venezuela	3.40
25	Germany	2.30	106	Armenia	3.45
25	Iceland	2.30	106	Bulgaria	3.45
27	Norway	2.35	106	Lesotho	3.45
28	Korea, South	2.40	106	Madagascar	3.45
28	Kuwait	2.40	106	Russia	3.45
28	Malaysia	2.40	111	Burkina Faso	3.50
28	Panama	2.40	111	Cameroon	3.50
28	Thailand	2.40	111	Guyana	3.50
33	Sweden	2.45	111	Nicaragua	3.50
34	Argentina	2.50	115	Gambia	3.60
34	France	2.50	116	Croatia	3.65
34	Italy	2.50	116	Georgia	3.65
34	Spain	2.50	116	Malawi	3.65
38	Portugal	2.55	119	Cape Verde	3.67
38	Sri Lanka	2.55	120	Ethiopia	3.70
38	Trinidad and Tobago	2.55	120	India	3.70
41	Barbados	2.60	120	Niger	3.70
41	Peru	2.60	123	Congo	3.75
43	Bolivia	2.65	124	Chad	3.80
43	Mauritius	2.65	124	China	3.80
45	Cyprus	2.70	124	Mauritania	3.80
45	Jamaica	2.70	124	Ukraine	3.80
45	Uruguay	2.70	124	Zimbabwe	3.80
48	Botswana	2.75	129	Albania	3.85
48	Guatemala	2.75	129	Bangladesh	3.85
48	Jordan	2.75	129	Mozambique	3.85
48	Namibia	2.75	129	Suriname	3.85
48	Oman	2.75	133	Burundi	3.90
48	Philippines	2.75	134	Togo	3.95
54	Belize	2.80	135	Haiti	4.00
54	Costa Rica	2.80	135	Kyrgyz Rep.	4.00
54	Israel	2.80	137	Kazakhstan	4.05
54	Swaziland	2.80	137	Sierra Leone	4.05
54	Turkey	2.80	139	Yemen	4.10
54	Uganda	2.80	140	Belarus	4.15
54	Samoa	2.80	141	Sudan	4.20
61	Latvia	2.85	141	Syria	4.20
62	Greece	2.90	143	Azerbaijan	4.30
62	Hungary	2.90	143	Equatorial Guinea	4.30
62	So. Africa	2.90	143	Myanmar	4.30
65	Ecuador	2.95	143	Rwanda	4.30
65	Gabon	2.95	147	Tajikistan	4.40
65	Indonesia	2.95	147	Uzbekistan	4.40
65	Malta	2.95	149	Angola	4.45
65	Morocco	2.95	149	Turkmenistan	4.45
65	Poland	2.95	151	Guinea-Bissau	4.55
65	Tunisia	2.95	152	Vietnam	4.60
72	Ghana	3.00	153	Congo (Zaire)	4.70
72	Lithuania	3.00	153	Iran	4.70
72	Saudi Arabia	3.00	155	Bosnia	4.80
75	Benin	3.05	155	Somalia	4.80
75	Kenya	3.05	157	Iraq	4.90
75	Paraguay	3.05	157	Laos	4.90
75	Qatar	3.05	157	Libya	4.90
75	Slovak Republic	3.05	160	Cuba	5.00
75	Zambia	3.05	160	Korea, North	5.00
81	Colombia	3.10			

Mostly Free

CAPITAL FLOWS AND FOREIGN INVESTMENT
Score: 2–Stable (low barriers)

Uruguay remains relatively open to foreign investment. Among the exceptions are the so-called strategic industries, which include telecommunications, transportation, banks, and the press. There are some tax incentives for foreign investment.

BANKING
Score: 2–Stable (low level of restrictions)

Foreign banks are assuming a larger role in the banking industry. Domestic banks are permitted to sell securities, but they also are prohibited from involvement in insurance, real estate, and investment transactions.

WAGE AND PRICE CONTROLS
Score: 2–Stable (low level)

Uruguay maintains a minimum wage. The market determines most prices, although some price controls remain in effect on such items as bread, milk, alcohol, and fuels. The list of products subject to price controls changes frequently.

PROPERTY RIGHTS
Score: 2–Stable (low level of protection)

Uruguay's court and legal system is becoming more efficient. Private property no longer is in danger of expropriation, although bureaucratic corruption often results in weak enforcement of private property laws.

REGULATION
Score: 3–Stable (moderate level)

Establishing a business can be a lengthy process. The bureaucracy is cumbersome and inefficient, and the government has yet to dismantle some of its most burdensome regulations, such as its strict environmental requirements. According to the U.S. Department of Commerce, "[L]egislated labor and social security benefits add significantly to the firm's cost structure. Furthermore, the Government from time to time creates a series of regulations that allow local debtors to refinance debt on extremely favorable terms and conditions. This practice has the effect of sustaining inefficient firms which compete with well-managed firms."[4]

BLACK MARKET
Score: 3–Stable (moderate level of activity)

As in the case of most other Latin American countries, Uruguay has its share of black market activity. Transportation and labor, for example, are found frequently on the black market, and there is considerable black market activity in pirated computer software, video and music recordings, and compact discs. By global standards, however, these activities remain moderate.

NOTES

[1] Based on total tax revenues from taxes on international transactions as a percentage of total imports.

[2] There is, however, a 30 percent income tax rate for workers in the agricultural sector. Because the agricultural sector contributes only about 8 percent of GDP, the author determined the income tax equivalent of the agricultural tax—if applied across the board to the entire population—to be less than 10 percent.

[3] U.S. Department of Commerce, *Country Commercial Guide,* 1998.

[4] *Ibid.*

Uzbekistan   4.40

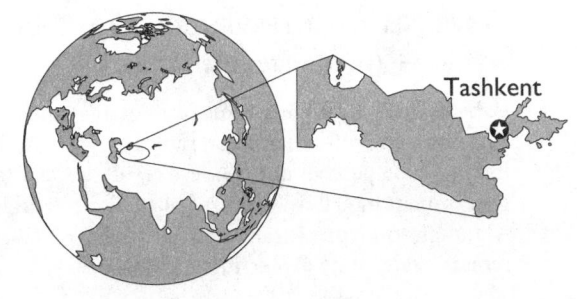

Tashkent

Trade	5	Banking	5
Taxation	4	Wages and Prices	4
Government Intervention	3	Property Rights	4
Monetary Policy	5	Regulation	5
Foreign Investment	4	Black Market	5

The area now known as Uzbekistan was the site of the ancient Persian province of Sogdiana, conquered by Alexander the Great in the 4th century B.C. By the 8th century A.D., it had been conquered by the Arabs. An elaborate Turkic–Muslim civilization flourished in the principalities of Samarkand and Bukhara in the 10th through 12th centuries, and the region became part of the Mongol empire under Ghengis Khan in the 13th century. Between 1865 and 1873, the Khorezm, Khiva, and Bukhara principalities were conquered by Russia but retained a degree of autonomy. Tsarist Russia quickly extended its control over the region, leading to lingering hostilities between the Uzbeks and Russians. After the Bolshevik Revolution of 1917 in Russia, citizens revolted and continued to fight a guerrilla war against Russia into the 1920s. Present-day Uzbekistan became an autonomous region but was incorporated fully into the Soviet Union in 1924. Since becoming independent in 1991, Uzbekistan has seen its economy shrink by over 30 percent. Most economic reforms have been slow in coming, and resistance to free-market reform and democracy remains strong. Uzbekistan is a Turkic-speaking Sunni Muslim country with an ethnic Russian population in urban areas. Uzbekistan recently reduced some taxes and its government consumption rate. As a result, its overall score is 0.15 point better than last year.

TRADE POLICY
Score: 5–Stable (very high level of protectionism)

Uzbekistan has an average tariff rate of about 15 percent, but the most significant barrier to trade is a regulation that requires importers to convert all currency into the Uzbek currency. This increases actual tariff rates because the government, not the market, artificially sets the exchange rates. According to the Office of the United States Trade Representative, "In an attempt to husband its foreign currency reserves, the GOU [government of Uzbekistan] has implemented a system of import contract licensing which severely restrict imports by restricting the availability of foreign exchange.... A recent formal survey of foreign businesses concluded that the GOU's foreign currency restrictions are the greatest single barrier to doing business in Uzbekistan."[1] If these import costs also are taken into account, the effective average tariff rate is higher than 15 percent. The Office of the United States Trade Representative also reports that "Customs clearance is a tedious and capricious bureaucratic process."[2]

TAXATION
Score–Income taxation: 4–Stable (high tax rates)
Score–Corporate taxation: 3+ (moderate tax rates)
Final Taxation Score: 4+ (high tax rates)

Uzbekistan's tax system is in disarray. The top income tax rate is 45 percent.[3] The top corporate tax rate is 35 percent, down from 37 percent last year. As a result, Uzbekistan's corporate taxation score is 1 point better this year. Uzbekistan also levies a 20 percent capital gains tax, a 20 percent value-added tax, a natural resources tax, local taxes, and a 40 percent payroll tax. When averaged with the income tax score, the reduction in the corporate tax rate improves Uzbekistan's final taxation score by 0.5 point.

1	Hong Kong	1.25	81	Fiji	3.10
2	Singapore	1.30	81	Mali	3.10
3	Bahrain	1.70	81	Slovenia	3.10
4	New Zealand	1.75	85	Honduras	3.15
5	Switzerland	1.85	85	Mexico	3.15
6	United States	1.90	85	Papua New Guinea	3.15
7	Ireland	1.95	88	Djibouti	3.20
7	Luxembourg	1.95	88	Mongolia	3.20
7	Taiwan	1.95	90	Algeria	3.25
7	United Kingdom	1.95	90	Brazil	3.25
11	Bahamas	2.00	90	Lebanon	3.25
12	Czech Republic	2.05	90	Senegal	3.25
12	Japan	2.05	90	Tanzania	3.25
14	Australia	2.10	95	Nigeria	3.30
14	Belgium	2.10	95	Romania	3.30
14	Canada	2.10	97	Cambodia	3.35
14	United Arab Emirates	2.10	97	Dominican Republic	3.35
18	Austria	2.15	97	Egypt	3.35
18	Chile	2.15	97	Guinea	3.35
18	Estonia	2.15	97	Ivory Coast	3.35
18	Netherlands	2.15	97	Moldova	3.35
22	Denmark	2.25	97	Pakistan	3.35
22	El Salvador	2.25	104	Nepal	3.40
22	Finland	2.25	104	Venezuela	3.40
25	Germany	2.30	106	Armenia	3.45
25	Iceland	2.30	106	Bulgaria	3.45
27	Norway	2.35	106	Lesotho	3.45
28	Korea, South	2.40	106	Madagascar	3.45
28	Kuwait	2.40	106	Russia	3.45
28	Malaysia	2.40	111	Burkina Faso	3.50
28	Panama	2.40	111	Cameroon	3.50
28	Thailand	2.40	111	Guyana	3.50
33	Sweden	2.45	111	Nicaragua	3.50
34	Argentina	2.50	115	Gambia	3.60
34	France	2.50	116	Croatia	3.65
34	Italy	2.50	116	Georgia	3.65
34	Spain	2.50	116	Malawi	3.65
38	Portugal	2.55	119	Cape Verde	3.67
38	Sri Lanka	2.55	120	Ethiopia	3.70
38	Trinidad and Tobago	2.55	120	India	3.70
41	Barbados	2.60	120	Niger	3.70
41	Peru	2.60	123	Congo	3.75
43	Bolivia	2.65	124	Chad	3.80
43	Mauritius	2.65	124	China	3.80
45	Cyprus	2.70	124	Mauritania	3.80
45	Jamaica	2.70	124	Ukraine	3.80
45	Uruguay	2.70	124	Zimbabwe	3.80
48	Botswana	2.75	129	Albania	3.85
48	Guatemala	2.75	129	Bangladesh	3.85
48	Jordan	2.75	129	Mozambique	3.85
48	Namibia	2.75	129	Suriname	3.85
48	Oman	2.75	133	Burundi	3.90
48	Philippines	2.75	134	Togo	3.95
54	Belize	2.80	135	Haiti	4.00
54	Costa Rica	2.80	135	Kyrgyz Rep.	4.00
54	Israel	2.80	137	Kazakhstan	4.05
54	Swaziland	2.80	137	Sierra Leone	4.05
54	Turkey	2.80	139	Yemen	4.10
54	Uganda	2.80	140	Belarus	4.15
54	Samoa	2.80	141	Sudan	4.20
61	Latvia	2.85	141	Syria	4.20
62	Greece	2.90	143	Azerbaijan	4.30
62	Hungary	2.90	143	Equatorial Guinea	4.30
62	So. Africa	2.90	143	Myanmar	4.30
65	Ecuador	2.95	143	Rwanda	4.30
65	Gabon	2.95	147	Tajikistan	4.40
65	Indonesia	2.95	147	Uzbekistan	4.40
65	Malta	2.95	149	Angola	4.45
65	Morocco	2.95	149	Turkmenistan	4.45
65	Poland	2.95	151	Guinea-Bissau	4.55
65	Tunisia	2.95	152	Vietnam	4.60
72	Ghana	3.00	153	Congo (Zaire)	4.70
72	Lithuania	3.00	153	Iran	4.70
72	Saudi Arabia	3.00	155	Bosnia	4.80
75	Benin	3.05	155	Somalia	4.80
75	Kenya	3.05	157	Iraq	4.90
75	Paraguay	3.05	157	Laos	4.90
75	Qatar	3.05	157	Libya	4.90
75	Slovak Republic	3.05	160	Cuba	5.00
75	Zambia	3.05	160	Korea, North	5.00
81	Colombia	3.10			

Repressed

GOVERNMENT INTERVENTION IN THE ECONOMY
Score: 3+ (moderate level)

Uzbekistan is privatizing some of its state-owned sector. The government consumption rate is 22 percent, down from over 35 percent in 1995. As a result, Uzbekistan's government intervention score is 1 point better this year. Although some privatization has occurred, many companies remain under state ownership.

MONETARY POLICY
Score: 5–Stable (very high level of inflation)

Uzbekistan has been plagued with hyperinflation: 645 percent in 1992, 534 percent in 1993, 1,568 percent in 1994, 305 percent in 1995, 64 percent in 1996, and 58.8 percent in 1997. Thus, even though inflation has fallen, its average annual rate remains very high, both historically and by global standards.

CAPITAL FLOWS AND FOREIGN INVESTMENT
Score: 4–Stable (high barriers)

Although the government wants to promote increased foreign investment, it still maintains some barriers. Uzbekistan has what appears to be a relatively free and open foreign investment code, but the Office of the United States Trade Representative reports that "The GOU's [government of Uzbekistan's] Foreign Investment Act of October 1996 defines enterprises with foreign investment as companies with a $300,000 capital fund which includes at least 30% foreign ownership. At present, there is no legal means for smaller foreign-owned companies to register. The GOU seeks foreign investment and new jobs, but this law essentially excludes small companies which have proven to be engines of growth and job creation in other countries."[4]

BANKING
Score: 5–Stable (very high level of restrictions)

Uzbekistan's banking system is not yet fully functional. According to the U.S. Department of Commerce, "As with so many other economic relationships, the collapse of the Soviet Union destroyed Uzbekistan's banking system, which had relied on central bank accounts in Moscow."[5]

WAGE AND PRICE CONTROLS
Score: 4–Stable (high level)

The large number of state-owned enterprises controls wages and prices. Price controls continue on such items as oil and oil products, natural gas, wheat, cotton, transportation, distribution, and utilities.

PROPERTY RIGHTS
Score: 4–Stable (low level of protection)

Private property does not enjoy sufficient protection under the legal system. According to the U.S. Department of State, "Although the Constitution provides for an independent judicial authority, the judicial branch takes its direction from the executive branch.... Uzbekistan continues to use the Soviet legal system."[6]

REGULATION
Score: 5–Stable (very high level)

Establishing a business can be a tedious and time-consuming process that requires individuals to overcome numerous bureaucratic barriers. According to the U.S. Department of Commerce, "The bureaucratic and often inscrutable process governing the process of registering a foreign firm or joint venture in Uzbekistan is another source of frustration for those wishing to do business there."[7]

BLACK MARKET
Score: 5–Stable (very high level of activity)

Smuggling is rampant. The level of drug production and smuggling is growing. There is a large black market in tobacco. According to the U.S. Department of Commerce, "The bulk of tobacco trade involves cigarettes. Sources estimate that Uzbekistan imports 14 to 15 billion cigarettes annually, most of which are smuggled."[8] Despite laws protecting intellectual property rights, there continues to be significant piracy in computer software.

NOTES

[1] Office of the United States Trade Representative, *National Trade Estimate Report on Foreign Trade Barriers,* 1998.

[2] U.S. Department of State, *Country Reports on Economic Policy and Trade Practices,* 1996, p. 317.

[3] The tax on the average level of income is unavailable. Thus, the income tax score is based solely on the top rate.

[4] Office of the United States Trade Representative, *National Trade Estimate Report on Foreign Trade Barriers,* 1998.

[5] U.S. Department of Commerce, "Uzbekistan: Trade and Investment Overview," March 1997.

[6] U.S. Department of State, "Uzbekistan Country Report on Human Rights Practices for 1997," 1998.

[7] U.S. Department of Commerce, "Uzbekistan: Trade and Investment Overview," March 1997.

[8] U.S. Department of Commerce, "Uzbekistan: Tobacco Update; Voluntary Report," *Agworld Attaché Reports,* 1996.

Venezuela

3.40

1998 Score: **3.50**   1997 Score: **3.60**   1996 Score: **3.50**

Trade	3	
Taxation	3	
Government Intervention	3	
Monetary Policy	5	
Foreign Investment	3	

Banking	3
Wages and Prices	3
Property Rights	3
Regulation	3
Black Market	5

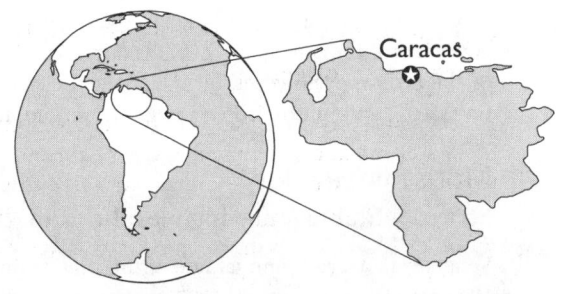

Caracas

Venezuela, a multiparty electoral democracy, is heavily dependent on oil exports to sustain its economy. After decades of statist and interventionist policies that crippled its economy, Venezuela began to adopt free-market policies in 1989. The reform process ended in 1992, however, when then president Carlos Andres Perez was impeached for corruption and forced to resign. When President Rafael Caldera took office in 1994, he immediately froze all economic reform and reinstated economic controls. The economy went into a tailspin, the currency devalued by over 400 percent, and inflation soared. In 1996, the government signed an agreement with the International Monetary Fund (IMF) following pressure from the IMF to reinstitute some degree of fiscal responsibility, but little progress has been made. A new presidential election was scheduled for December 1998: The front-running candidate, Hugo Chávez Frías, has pledged to return to policies of state intervention and reflation of the economy. The tax on the average income level recently was reduced; as a result, Venezuela's overall score is 0.1 point better this year.

TRADE POLICY
Score: 3–Stable (moderate level of protectionism)

The average tariff rate is 9.84 percent.[1] Non-tariff barriers include special taxes designed to protect local producers and health standards designed to minimize imports of grain. Moreover, according to the U.S. Department of State, "Venezuelan customs is plagued by corruption and antiquated procedures which frequently delay clearance of incoming goods."[2]

TAXATION
Score–Income taxation: 2+ (low tax rates)
Score–Corporate taxation: 3–Stable (moderate tax rates)
Final Taxation Score: 3+ (moderate tax rates)

Venezuela's top marginal income tax rate is 34 percent, and the average income is taxed at 6 percent, down from 16 percent last year. As a result, Venezuela's income taxation score is 2 points better this year, and the final taxation score 1 point better. The top corporate tax rate is 34 percent. Venezuela also has a 16.5 percent to 36.5 percent value-added tax and a 34 percent capital gains tax.

GOVERNMENT INTERVENTION IN THE ECONOMY
Score: 3–Stable (moderate level)

Government consumes 10.2 percent of GDP. According to the U.S. Department of Commerce, "Following two years of statist policies, the government is returning to the 1989–1993 trend toward privatizing and deregulating the economy. The government's measures during 1994–95 originated in response to the economic and financial crisis which came to a head in early 1994. Subsequently, a myriad of measures were introduced to eliminate capital flight, soak up excess liquidity, rein in inflation, reduce the Republic's debt burden, stabilize the financial sector, open the petroleum sector to joint ventures with foreign firms, introduce incentives for direct foreign investment in the non-petroleum

1	Hong Kong	1.25	81	Fiji	3.10
2	Singapore	1.30	81	Mali	3.10
3	Bahrain	1.70	81	Slovenia	3.10
4	New Zealand	1.75	85	Honduras	3.15
5	Switzerland	1.85	85	Mexico	3.15
6	United States	1.90	85	Papua New Guinea	3.15
7	Ireland	1.95	88	Djibouti	3.20
7	Luxembourg	1.95	88	Mongolia	3.20
7	Taiwan	1.95	90	Algeria	3.25
7	United Kingdom	1.95	90	Brazil	3.25
11	Bahamas	2.00	90	Lebanon	3.25
12	Czech Republic	2.05	90	Senegal	3.25
12	Japan	2.05	90	Tanzania	3.25
14	Australia	2.10	95	Nigeria	3.30
14	Belgium	2.10	95	Romania	3.30
14	Canada	2.10	97	Cambodia	3.35
14	United Arab Emirates	2.10	97	Dominican Republic	3.35
18	Austria	2.15	97	Egypt	3.35
18	Chile	2.15	97	Guinea	3.35
18	Estonia	2.15	97	Ivory Coast	3.35
18	Netherlands	2.15	97	Moldova	3.35
22	Denmark	2.25	97	Pakistan	3.35
22	El Salvador	2.25	104	Nepal	3.40
22	Finland	2.25	104	Venezuela	3.40
25	Germany	2.30	106	Armenia	3.45
25	Iceland	2.30	106	Bulgaria	3.45
27	Norway	2.35	106	Lesotho	3.45
28	Korea, South	2.40	106	Madagascar	3.45
28	Kuwait	2.40	106	Russia	3.45
28	Malaysia	2.40	111	Burkina Faso	3.50
28	Panama	2.40	111	Cameroon	3.50
28	Thailand	2.40	111	Guyana	3.50
33	Sweden	2.45	111	Nicaragua	3.50
34	Argentina	2.50	115	Gambia	3.60
34	France	2.50	116	Croatia	3.65
34	Italy	2.50	116	Georgia	3.65
34	Spain	2.50	116	Malawi	3.65
38	Portugal	2.55	119	Cape Verde	3.67
38	Sri Lanka	2.55	120	Ethiopia	3.70
38	Trinidad and Tobago	2.55	120	India	3.70
41	Barbados	2.60	120	Niger	3.70
41	Peru	2.60	123	Congo	3.75
43	Bolivia	2.65	124	Chad	3.80
43	Mauritius	2.65	124	China	3.80
45	Cyprus	2.70	124	Mauritania	3.80
45	Jamaica	2.70	124	Ukraine	3.80
45	Uruguay	2.70	124	Zimbabwe	3.80
48	Botswana	2.75	129	Albania	3.85
48	Guatemala	2.75	129	Bangladesh	3.85
48	Jordan	2.75	129	Mozambique	3.85
48	Namibia	2.75	129	Suriname	3.85
48	Oman	2.75	133	Burundi	3.90
48	Philippines	2.75	134	Togo	3.95
54	Belize	2.80	135	Haiti	4.00
54	Costa Rica	2.80	135	Kyrgyz Rep.	4.00
54	Israel	2.80	137	Kazakhstan	4.05
54	Swaziland	2.80	137	Sierra Leone	4.05
54	Turkey	2.80	139	Yemen	4.10
54	Uganda	2.80	140	Belarus	4.15
54	Samoa	2.80	141	Sudan	4.20
61	Latvia	2.85	141	Syria	4.20
62	Greece	2.90	143	Azerbaijan	4.30
62	Hungary	2.90	143	Equatorial Guinea	4.30
62	So. Africa	2.90	143	Myanmar	4.30
65	Ecuador	2.95	143	Rwanda	4.30
65	Gabon	2.95	147	Tajikistan	4.40
65	Indonesia	2.95	147	Uzbekistan	4.40
65	Malta	2.95	149	Angola	4.45
65	Morocco	2.95	149	Turkmenistan	4.45
65	Poland	2.95	151	Guinea-Bissau	4.55
65	Tunisia	2.95	152	Vietnam	4.60
72	Ghana	3.00	153	Congo (Zaire)	4.70
72	Lithuania	3.00	153	Iran	4.70
72	Saudi Arabia	3.00	155	Bosnia	4.80
75	Benin	3.05	155	Somalia	4.80
75	Kenya	3.05	157	Iraq	4.90
75	Paraguay	3.05	157	Laos	4.90
75	Qatar	3.05	157	Libya	4.90
75	Slovak Republic	3.05	160	Cuba	5.00
75	Zambia	3.05	160	Korea, North	5.00
81	Colombia	3.10			

Mostly Unfree

sector, and assist small- and medium-sized industry."[3] The government remains heavily involved in several key sectors of the economy, however, including electricity, oil production, steel, aluminum, iron mining, and development.

MONETARY POLICY
Score: 5–Stable (very high level of inflation)

Venezuela's average annual rate of inflation from 1986 to 1996 was 41.35 percent. In 1997, the rate was 40 percent.

CAPITAL FLOWS AND FOREIGN INVESTMENT
Score: 3–Stable (moderate barriers)

Most industries are open to foreign investment, although some significant restrictions remain in effect. Foreign ownership of a few service industries, including television, radio, the Spanish-language press, and some professional services, is limited to no more than 19.9 percent. Foreign investment is restricted in the petroleum sector and in the mining of iron ore.

BANKING
Score: 3–Stable (moderate level of restrictions)

Even though the government has removed most restrictions on foreign bank branches, it still owns about 50 percent of all banks in the country. Banks based in countries that provide reciprocal treatment now may open 100 percent foreign-owned subsidiaries or purchase 100 percent of existing banks.

WAGE AND PRICE CONTROLS
Score: 3–Stable (moderate level)

Venezuela maintains a minimum wage. The government has broad authority to impose price controls, such as those in effect on some basic foodstuffs, medicines, fuel, and public transportation.

PROPERTY RIGHTS
Score: 3–Stable (moderate level of protection)

Private property is a staple of Venezuela's economy, but the government is prone to expropriation, and the judicial system frequently rules against foreign investors in property rights disputes. According to the U.S. Department of Commerce, "Foreign investors may pursue property claims through Venezuela's legal system, but procedures are lengthy and judgments are uneven."[4]

REGULATION
Score: 3–Stable (moderate level)

Opening a business usually is not difficult. The recent economic downturn has led to increased corruption, however, and some regulations are not applied uniformly. According to the U.S. Department of Commerce, "Foreign direct investment is hindered by corruption, although this varies on a sectoral basis. Government tenders are the most vulnerable to corruption because the tender process frequently lacks transparency."[5]

BLACK MARKET
Score: 5–Stable (very high level of activity)

Venezuela's black market is active in areas in which the government maintains controls (as in the transportation services sector). For example, the black market provides about 40 percent of labor services in Caracas. Although Venezuela has established intellectual property laws, enforcement is lax and piracy in copyrighted material continues.

NOTES
[1] Based on total taxes on international trade as a percentage of total imports.
[2] U.S. Department of State, *Country Reports on Economic and Trade Practices,* 1998.
[3] U.S. Department of Commerce, *Country Commercial Guide,* 1998.
[4] *Ibid.*
[5] U.S. Department of Commerce, "Venezuela Investment Climate," *Market Research Reports,* November 1997.

Vietnam   4.60

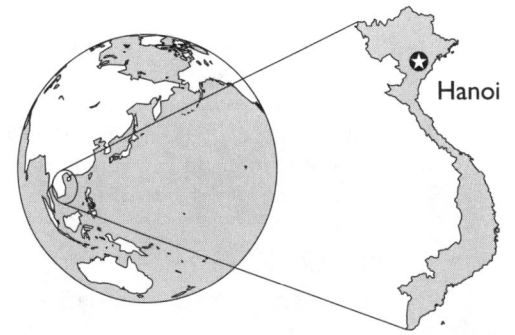
Hanoi

1998 Score: **4.70**   1997 Score: **4.70**   1996 Score: **4.70**

Trade	5	Banking	4
Taxation	5	Wages and Prices	4
Government Intervention	4	Property Rights	5
Monetary Policy	4	Regulation	5
Foreign Investment	4	Black Market	5

Vietnam, divided for most of its early history by warring factions, was occupied by France in the 19th century. In 1954, following its defeat at Dien Bien Phu, France agreed to withdraw from the northern part of Vietnam and moved south below the 17th parallel. The communists in the north established the Democratic Republic of Vietnam, while the non-communists in the south established the Republic of South Vietnam. After the defeat of South Vietnam in 1975, the Hanoi government established a communist system throughout all of Vietnam. In 1995, Vietnam joined the Association of Southeast Asian Nations, and the Clinton Administration extended U.S. diplomatic relations. As a result, U.S. companies now are free to invest in the country. Even though the regime has begun to liberalize some areas of its centrally planned economy, Vietnam remains a communist dictatorship, and the state still owns most means of production. Inflation recently has been reduced; as a result, Vietnam's overall score is 0.1 point better than last year.

TRADE POLICY
Score: 5–Stable (very high level of protectionism)

Vietnam's average tariff rate ranges from 15 percent to 20 percent.[1] A corrupt bureaucracy, however, creates very high barriers to imports. Border officials confiscate many imports. According to the Economist Intelligence Unit, "Outside the bounds of legitimate trading, smuggling remains a problem in Vietnam. Although difficult to quantify, estimates place the value of smuggled goods at one-third to one-quarter of official imports."[2] This demonstrates the high level of protectionism that Vietnam has adopted in an attempt to protect domestic industries from foreign competition.

TAXATION
Score–Income taxation: 5–Stable (very high tax rates)
Score–Corporate taxation: 5–Stable (very high tax rates)
Final Taxation Score: 5–Stable (very high tax rates)

Vietnam's top income tax rate is 60 percent, with the average income level taxed at a rate of 40 percent. The tax on foreign corporate profits is as high as 45 percent.[3] Because the economy is centrally planned and the government owns most businesses, actual tax rates are much higher than these levels suggest.

GOVERNMENT INTERVENTION IN THE ECONOMY
Score: 5–Stable (very high level)

Progress toward privatization has been anemic. The government still owns most means of production and maintains central planning, and it has yet to subject the economy to the basic principles of supply and demand. The government produces almost 60 percent of GDP, up from 33 percent in 1990. According to the U.S. Department of Commerce, "The government plays a significant role in the economy. Vietnam's Constitution calls for state-management of the economy and the Communist Party of Vietnam believes the state sector should continue indefinitely as Vietnam's 'leading' economic sector. State-owned

1	Hong Kong	1.25	81	Fiji	3.10
2	Singapore	1.30	81	Mali	3.10
3	Bahrain	1.70	81	Slovenia	3.10
4	New Zealand	1.75	85	Honduras	3.15
5	Switzerland	1.85	85	Mexico	3.15
6	United States	1.90	85	Papua New Guinea	3.15
7	Ireland	1.95	88	Djibouti	3.20
7	Luxembourg	1.95	88	Mongolia	3.20
7	Taiwan	1.95	90	Algeria	3.25
7	United Kingdom	1.95	90	Brazil	3.25
11	Bahamas	2.00	90	Lebanon	3.25
12	Czech Republic	2.05	90	Senegal	3.25
12	Japan	2.05	90	Tanzania	3.25
14	Australia	2.10	95	Nigeria	3.30
14	Belgium	2.10	95	Romania	3.30
14	Canada	2.10	97	Cambodia	3.35
14	United Arab Emirates	2.10	97	Dominican Republic	3.35
18	Austria	2.15	97	Egypt	3.35
18	Chile	2.15	97	Guinea	3.35
18	Estonia	2.15	97	Ivory Coast	3.35
18	Netherlands	2.15	97	Moldova	3.35
22	Denmark	2.25	97	Pakistan	3.35
22	El Salvador	2.25	104	Nepal	3.40
22	Finland	2.25	104	Venezuela	3.40
25	Germany	2.30	106	Armenia	3.45
25	Iceland	2.30	106	Bulgaria	3.45
27	Norway	2.35	106	Lesotho	3.45
28	Korea, South	2.40	106	Madagascar	3.45
28	Kuwait	2.40	106	Russia	3.45
28	Malaysia	2.40	111	Burkina Faso	3.50
28	Panama	2.40	111	Cameroon	3.50
28	Thailand	2.40	111	Guyana	3.50
33	Sweden	2.45	111	Nicaragua	3.50
34	Argentina	2.50	115	Gambia	3.60
34	France	2.50	116	Croatia	3.65
34	Italy	2.50	116	Georgia	3.65
34	Spain	2.50	116	Malawi	3.65
38	Portugal	2.55	119	Cape Verde	3.67
38	Sri Lanka	2.55	120	Ethiopia	3.70
38	Trinidad and Tobago	2.55	120	India	3.70
41	Barbados	2.60	120	Niger	3.70
41	Peru	2.60	123	Congo	3.75
43	Bolivia	2.65	124	Chad	3.80
43	Mauritius	2.65	124	China	3.80
45	Cyprus	2.70	124	Mauritania	3.80
45	Jamaica	2.70	124	Ukraine	3.80
45	Uruguay	2.70	124	Zimbabwe	3.80
48	Botswana	2.75	129	Albania	3.85
48	Guatemala	2.75	129	Bangladesh	3.85
48	Jordan	2.75	129	Mozambique	3.85
48	Namibia	2.75	129	Suriname	3.85
48	Oman	2.75	133	Burundi	3.90
48	Philippines	2.75	134	Togo	3.95
54	Belize	2.80	135	Haiti	4.00
54	Costa Rica	2.80	135	Kyrgyz Rep.	4.00
54	Israel	2.80	137	Kazakhstan	4.05
54	Swaziland	2.80	137	Sierra Leone	4.05
54	Turkey	2.80	139	Yemen	4.10
54	Uganda	2.80	140	Belarus	4.15
54	Samoa	2.80	141	Sudan	4.20
61	Latvia	2.85	141	Syria	4.20
62	Greece	2.90	143	Azerbaijan	4.30
62	Hungary	2.90	143	Equatorial Guinea	4.30
62	So. Africa	2.90	143	Myanmar	4.30
65	Ecuador	2.95	143	Rwanda	4.30
65	Gabon	2.95	147	Tajikistan	4.40
65	Indonesia	2.95	147	Uzbekistan	4.40
65	Malta	2.95	149	Angola	4.45
65	Morocco	2.95	149	Turkmenistan	4.45
65	Poland	2.95	151	Guinea-Bissau	4.55
65	Tunisia	2.95	152	Vietnam	4.60
72	Ghana	3.00	153	Congo (Zaire)	4.70
72	Lithuania	3.00	153	Iran	4.70
72	Saudi Arabia	3.00	155	Bosnia	4.80
75	Benin	3.05	155	Somalia	4.80
75	Kenya	3.05	157	Iraq	4.90
75	Paraguay	3.05	157	Laos	4.90
75	Qatar	3.05	157	Libya	4.90
75	Slovak Republic	3.05	160	Cuba	5.00
75	Zambia	3.05	160	Korea, North	5.00
81	Colombia	3.10			

Repressed

enterprises (SOEs) probably account for 40–45 percent of industrial output and absorb 60–65 percent of available credit. Vietnam's four state-owned commercial banks account for 80 percent of lending. Almost all joint-venture deals involving foreign firms have been struck with SOEs, to the exclusion of local private firms."[4]

MONETARY POLICY
Score: 4+ (high level of inflation)

From 1990 to 1996, Vietnam's average annual rate of inflation was 22.7 percent, down from 33.2 percent from 1990 to 1994. As a result, Vietnam's monetary policy score is 1 point better this year. In 1997, the rate of inflation was about 10 percent.

CAPITAL FLOWS AND FOREIGN INVESTMENT
Score: 4–Stable (high barriers)

One of the world's few remaining communist states, Vietnam has gone farther to open its economy to foreign investment than either Cuba or North Korea. Even so, much of the economy remains inaccessible to foreigners, investments still need prior government approval, and repatriation of profits remains subject to some restrictions. Even though the government allows 100 percent ownership in principle, in actuality it has approved few investments. The government heavily favors joint ventures (50–50) with foreign firms, and allows investments on a case-by-case basis. According to the U.S. Department of Commerce, "Despite this promising start, Vietnam remains a difficult investment environment. Currently in a period of transition toward a 'state-supervised' market economy 'with socialist characteristics,' away from its previous purely command economy model, Vietnam is trying to implement a vast array of reforms that will enable its fast-growing but developing market to function more efficiently. As the government engages in this complex and challenging process, foreign investors are trying to cope with problems and costs stemming from Vietnam's poorly developed infrastructure (including transportation and power supply); underdeveloped legal and financial systems; its unwieldy bureaucracy; high start-up costs; arcane land-transfer and acquisition rules; and shortage of trained personnel. Gaining licenses for and implementing investment plans is sometimes a lengthy process in Vietnam and foreign investors must also deal with relatively high rents, a shifting tax code, and a number of administrative fees."[5]

BANKING
Score: 4–Stable (high level of restrictions)

Banking services are reserved almost exclusively for the government, although there have been attempts to modernize the financial system. The government heavily influences the few private banks that do exist; they operate at a disadvantage because of the unfair competition from large state-owned banks. The state owns the four largest banks, which control some 85 percent of all banking assets. According to the U.S. Department of Commerce, the banking system "continues to suffer from a lack of consumer confidence, inexperience in capital markets and the slow pace of institutional reform."[6] The government-owned banking system controls over 80 percent of the available credit, too.

WAGE AND PRICE CONTROLS
Score: 4–Stable (high level)

At least 50 percent of the goods produced by Vietnamese companies is subject to some type of central planning. Vietnam has lifted price controls on some products, including steel and printing paper, but controls on the prices of electricity, water, telecommunications, and transportation services remain in place. The government sets many wages.

PROPERTY RIGHTS
Score: 5–Stable (very low level of protection)

The government has become more tolerant of private ownership of property, but property still enjoys almost no legal protection. Moreover, the government does not fully permit foreign companies to seek arbitration in foreign courts; all disputes must be settled within Vietnam. The court system is subject to extensive government influence, especially in cases in which disputes arise among parties with close ties to the government. According to the U.S. Department of State, "While the Constitution provides for the independence of judges and jurors, in practice the VCP [Vietnamese Communist Party] controls the courts closely at all levels, selecting judges primarily for political reliability. Credible reports indicate the party officials, including top leaders, instruct courts on how to rule on politically important cases."[7] In addition, according to the U.S. Department of Commerce, "The Vietnamese legal system is still developing the framework necessary to sustain a market economy. Still in a state of evolution, Vietnam's legal structure is undergoing significant frequent change. Vietnamese officials have limited experience drafting legislation and laws are sometimes unclear or contradictory. In addition, different officials, even within the same ministry, may interpret the same laws differently. There is a shortage of trained lawyers, judges, and law professors. In many instances, procedures for legal process and enforcement either are new, untested or nonexistent."[8]

REGULATION
Score: 5–Stable (very high level)

Vietnam erects many obstacles to private enterprise. According to the U.S. Department of Commerce, "MPI [Ministry of Planning and Investment], local authorities, and other government agencies retain a great deal of discretion in the investment-licensing process. In addition, the experience of U.S. investors suggests that the 'real' problems only begin after the licensing process is completed.... U.S. firms have identified corruption in Vietnam as a growing obstacle in pursuing their business activities. Vietnam's bureaucratic system of licensing investment encourages many forms of corruption, such as bribery and kickbacks."[9]

BLACK MARKET
Score: 5–Stable (very high level of activity)

Vietnam has a large black market in such basic goods and services as foodstuffs and labor. Smuggling and piracy of intellectual property are widespread.

NOTES

[1] U.S. Department of Commerce, *Country Commercial Guide,* 1998.

[2] Economist Intelligence Unit, *ILT Reports, Vietnam,* April 1998.

[3] This is the top rate for companies that have no foreign-owned capital. Vietnam taxes companies that have foreign-owned capital at a top rate of 25 percent.

[4] U.S. Department of Commerce, *Country Commercial Guide,* 1998.

[5] *Ibid.*

[6] *Ibid.*

[7] U.S. Department of State, "Vietnam Report on Human Rights Practices for 1997," 1998.

[8] U.S. Department of Commerce, *Country Commercial Guide,* 1998.

[9] *Ibid.*

Yemen
4.10

1998 Score: **4.10**   1997 Score: **3.90**   1996 Score: **3.75**

Trade	5	Banking	4
Taxation	3	Wages and Prices	3
Government Intervention	4	Property Rights	4
Monetary Policy	5	Regulation	4
Foreign Investment	4	Black Market	5

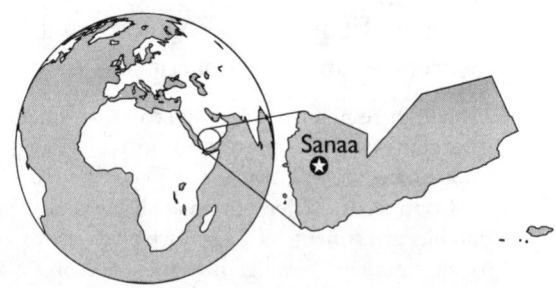

Sanaa

For centuries, Yemen was dominated by various empires, including both the Roman and the Ottoman. The southern part of the country became a British protectorate in 1839; Turkey controlled the northern part until after World War I, but the North became fully independent in 1934. Inspired by this success, southern Yemen fought successfully to gain its independence from the United Kingdom in 1967. Soon afterward, a Marxist government took control but devastated the economy. In 1990, after two decades of political and civil chaos, North and South Yemen united. The outbreak of civil war in 1994 cut short the limited progress the country had made toward economic liberalization. Since that time, there has been little economic growth.

TRADE POLICY
Score: 5–Stable (very high level of protectionism)

Tariffs range from 5 percent to 30 percent; the average tariff is 20 percent. Special duties apply to some so-called luxury items; automobiles, for example, are assessed at 67 percent, and tobacco imports are assessed at a rate of 145 percent. Yemen also maintains non-tariff barriers in several areas; there are import bans, for example, on pork and pork products, coffee, alcohol, and all types of fresh fruits and vegetables. There is evidence of corruption within the government bureaucracy, which also can hinder imports.

TAXATION
Score–Income taxation: 2–Stable (low tax rates)
Score–Corporate taxation: 3–Stable (moderate tax rates)
Final Taxation Score: 3–Stable (moderate tax rates)

Yemen's top income tax rate is 36 percent. The average income level is taxed at 6 percent. The top corporate tax rate is 35 percent. Yemen also has a 35 percent capital gains tax and other taxes.

GOVERNMENT INTERVENTION IN THE ECONOMY
Score: 4–Stable (high level)

Government consumes 21.3 percent of GDP, but this figure fails to provide an accurate picture of the level of government intervention in the economy. According to the U.S. Department of State, "Yemen is a very poor country. Its embryonic market-based economy, despite a major economic reform program, remains impeded by excessive government interference and endemic corruption."

MONETARY POLICY
Score: 5–Stable (very high level of inflation)

Yemen's average annual rate of inflation from 1990 to 1994 was 109 percent. In 1995, the rate was 65 percent; in 1996, 30 percent; and, in 1997, 20.5 percent.

1	Hong Kong	1.25		81	Fiji	3.10
2	Singapore	1.30		81	Mali	3.10
3	Bahrain	1.70		81	Slovenia	3.10
4	New Zealand	1.75		85	Honduras	3.15
5	Switzerland	1.85		85	Mexico	3.15
6	United States	1.90		85	Papua New Guinea	3.15
7	Ireland	1.95		88	Djibouti	3.20
7	Luxembourg	1.95		88	Mongolia	3.20
7	Taiwan	1.95		90	Algeria	3.25
7	United Kingdom	1.95		90	Brazil	3.25
11	Bahamas	2.00		90	Lebanon	3.25
12	Czech Republic	2.05		90	Senegal	3.25
12	Japan	2.05		90	Tanzania	3.25
14	Australia	2.10		95	Nigeria	3.30
14	Belgium	2.10		95	Romania	3.30
14	Canada	2.10		97	Cambodia	3.35
14	United Arab Emirates	2.10		97	Dominican Republic	3.35
18	Austria	2.15		97	Egypt	3.35
18	Chile	2.15		97	Guinea	3.35
18	Estonia	2.15		97	Ivory Coast	3.35
18	Netherlands	2.15		97	Moldova	3.35
22	Denmark	2.25		97	Pakistan	3.35
22	El Salvador	2.25		104	Nepal	3.40
22	Finland	2.25		104	Venezuela	3.40
25	Germany	2.30		106	Armenia	3.45
25	Iceland	2.30		106	Bulgaria	3.45
27	Norway	2.35		106	Lesotho	3.45
28	Korea, South	2.40		106	Madagascar	3.45
28	Kuwait	2.40		106	Russia	3.45
28	Malaysia	2.40		111	Burkina Faso	3.50
28	Panama	2.40		111	Cameroon	3.50
28	Thailand	2.40		111	Guyana	3.50
33	Sweden	2.45		111	Nicaragua	3.50
34	Argentina	2.50		115	Gambia	3.60
34	France	2.50		116	Croatia	3.65
34	Italy	2.50		116	Georgia	3.65
34	Spain	2.50		116	Malawi	3.65
38	Portugal	2.55		119	Cape Verde	3.67
38	Sri Lanka	2.55		120	Ethiopia	3.70
38	Trinidad and Tobago	2.55		120	India	3.70
41	Barbados	2.60		120	Niger	3.70
41	Peru	2.60		123	Congo	3.75
43	Bolivia	2.65		124	Chad	3.80
43	Mauritius	2.65		124	China	3.80
45	Cyprus	2.70		124	Mauritania	3.80
45	Jamaica	2.70		124	Ukraine	3.80
45	Uruguay	2.70		124	Zimbabwe	3.80
48	Botswana	2.75		129	Albania	3.85
48	Guatemala	2.75		129	Bangladesh	3.85
48	Jordan	2.75		129	Mozambique	3.85
48	Namibia	2.75		129	Suriname	3.85
48	Oman	2.75		133	Burundi	3.90
48	Philippines	2.75		134	Togo	3.95
54	Belize	2.80		135	Haiti	4.00
54	Costa Rica	2.80		135	Kyrgyz Rep.	4.00
54	Israel	2.80		137	Kazakhstan	4.05
54	Swaziland	2.80		137	Sierra Leone	4.05
54	Turkey	2.80		139	Yemen	4.10
54	Uganda	2.80		140	Belarus	4.15
54	Samoa	2.80		141	Sudan	4.20
61	Latvia	2.85		141	Syria	4.20
62	Greece	2.90		143	Azerbaijan	4.30
62	Hungary	2.90		143	Equatorial Guinea	4.30
62	So. Africa	2.90		143	Myanmar	4.30
65	Ecuador	2.95		143	Rwanda	4.30
65	Gabon	2.95		147	Tajikistan	4.40
65	Indonesia	2.95		147	Uzbekistan	4.40
65	Malta	2.95		149	Angola	4.45
65	Morocco	2.95		149	Turkmenistan	4.45
65	Poland	2.95		151	Guinea-Bissau	4.55
65	Tunisia	2.95		152	Vietnam	4.60
72	Ghana	3.00		153	Congo (Zaire)	4.70
72	Lithuania	3.00		153	Iran	4.70
72	Saudi Arabia	3.00		155	Bosnia	4.80
75	Benin	3.05		155	Somalia	4.80
75	Kenya	3.05		157	Iraq	4.90
75	Paraguay	3.05		157	Laos	4.90
75	Qatar	3.05		157	Libya	4.90
75	Slovak Republic	3.05		160	Cuba	5.00
75	Zambia	3.05		160	Korea, North	5.00
81	Colombia	3.10				

Repressed

CAPITAL FLOWS AND FOREIGN INVESTMENT
Score: 4–Stable (high barriers)

Although Yemen has streamlined its investment laws and procedures in an attempt to attract more foreign investment, barriers still exist. According to the U.S. Department of Commerce, "[C]orruption at all levels of the government inhibits investment, as does a lack of security in certain parts of the country.... Foreign investors must obtain appropriate visas and work permits for themselves and expatriate staff, an often tedious process."[1]

BANKING
Score: 4–Stable (high level of restrictions)

Although the government plans to allow more foreign banks to operate, not much progress has been made so far. Domestic banks remain heavily regulated, and there are only seven commercial banks.

WAGE AND PRICE CONTROLS
Score: 3–Stable (moderate level)

The government controls some prices (part of southern Yemen's socialist legacy) but imposes no minimum wage.

PROPERTY RIGHTS
Score: 4–Stable (low level of protection)

The government has expropriated no property since 1990, but the threat of expropriation still exists because of uncertain economic conditions. Terrorism is a major threat to private property, as is auto theft. According to the U.S. Department of Commerce, "Inefficiency and corruption characterize Yemen's court system. Cases often take years to be decided and usually go to the highest bidder. Often the government cannot enforce court decisions."[2]

REGULATION
Score: 4–Stable (high level)

Businesses must conduct an environmental impact study before engaging in new investments or expanding their enterprises. The government has turned down almost no investments, but the process still causes delays. Bureaucratic inefficiency and rising corruption also remain problems. According to the U.S. Department of Commerce, "Often described as the 'open drawer' policy, corruption of government officials is pervasive throughout the bureaucracy. U.S. companies trying to invest and/or trade complain often about bribes being solicited by officials ranking from clerk to higher levels. U.S. companies operating businesses in Yemen also note that government officials have offered bribes to their employees for proprietary information or to influence company hiring or contracting decisions. While Yemen may have an anticorruption law on the books, it is not enforced."[3]

BLACK MARKET
Score: 5–Stable (very high level of activity)

Because of high trade barriers, smuggling essentially equals official trade in Yemen. Smuggling of some scarce items, such as certain foodstuffs, is particularly widespread. Protection of intellectual property is weak, and piracy of these products is substantial.

NOTES
1. U.S. Department of Commerce, *Country Commercial Guide,* 1998.
2. *Ibid.*
3. *Ibid.*

Zambia   3.05

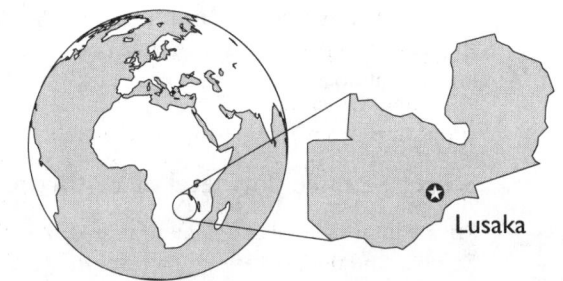

1998 Score: **3.05**	1997 Score: **2.85**	1996 Score: **2.95**

Trade	3	Banking	2
Taxation	3.5	Wages and Prices	2
Government Intervention	3	Property Rights	3
Monetary Policy	5	Regulation	4
Foreign Investment	2	Black Market	3

Lusaka

Zambia gained its independence from the United Kingdom in 1964 and remained a one-party socialist state until 1989, when political opposition was legalized. It currently operates as a unitary republic under its 1996 constitution. President Frederick Chiluba successfully put down a coup attempt in 1997; his heavy-handed actions against opposition parties has attracted domestic and international criticism. Economic liberalization has been sluggish and has fallen considerably short of official targets. Government corruption remains a problem, and privatization has been slow. Economic growth best can be described as erratic: 5.1 percent in 1993, -3.1 percent and -3.9 percent in 1994 and 1995, respectively, and 6.9 percent in 1996 and 2.5 percent in 1997, respectively.

TRADE POLICY
Score: 3–Stable (moderate level of protectionism)

Zambia's average tariff rate is 6 percent. Import restrictions have eased, but resentment against an increase in imports from South Africa has generated protectionist sentiment. Corruption in the Customs Bureau continues.

TAXATION
Score–Income taxation: 3–Stable (moderate tax rates)
Score–Corporate taxation: 3–Stable (moderate tax rates)
Final Taxation Score: 3.5–Stable (high tax rates)

Zambia's top marginal income tax rate is 35 percent, and the average taxpayer finds himself in the 15 percent bracket. In 1993, the corporate tax rate was reduced to 35 percent.[1] The government also imposes a 20 percent value-added tax and property transfer taxes.

GOVERNMENT INTERVENTION IN THE ECONOMY
Score: 3–Stable (moderate level)

Government consumes 18 percent of GDP. During the regime of President Kenneth Kaunda, who ruled from independence until 1991, state-owned enterprises accounted for more than 50 percent of GDP. The state sector still dominates the economy.

MONETARY POLICY
Score: 5–Stable (very high level of inflation)

Zambia's average annual rate of inflation from 1986 to 1996 was 76 percent. Inflation currently is running at approximately 25 percent.

CAPITAL FLOWS AND FOREIGN INVESTMENT
Score: 2–Stable (low barriers)

The government has improved Zambia's foreign investment laws, and there is no legal discrimination between foreign and domestic investors. Few investment opportunities are off-limits, and privatized firms are open to investment, too.

1	Hong Kong	1.25	81	Fiji	3.10
2	Singapore	1.30	81	Mali	3.10
3	Bahrain	1.70	81	Slovenia	3.10
4	New Zealand	1.75	85	Honduras	3.15
5	Switzerland	1.85	85	Mexico	3.15
6	United States	1.90	85	Papua New Guinea	3.15
7	Ireland	1.95	88	Djibouti	3.20
7	Luxembourg	1.95	88	Mongolia	3.20
7	Taiwan	1.95	90	Algeria	3.25
7	United Kingdom	1.95	90	Brazil	3.25
11	Bahamas	2.00	90	Lebanon	3.25
12	Czech Republic	2.05	90	Senegal	3.25
12	Japan	2.05	90	Tanzania	3.25
14	Australia	2.10	95	Nigeria	3.30
14	Belgium	2.10	95	Romania	3.30
14	Canada	2.10	97	Cambodia	3.35
14	United Arab Emirates	2.10	97	Dominican Republic	3.35
18	Austria	2.15	97	Egypt	3.35
18	Chile	2.15	97	Guinea	3.35
18	Estonia	2.15	97	Ivory Coast	3.35
18	Netherlands	2.15	97	Moldova	3.35
22	Denmark	2.25	97	Pakistan	3.35
22	El Salvador	2.25	104	Nepal	3.40
22	Finland	2.25	104	Venezuela	3.40
25	Germany	2.30	106	Armenia	3.45
25	Iceland	2.30	106	Bulgaria	3.45
27	Norway	2.35	106	Lesotho	3.45
28	Korea, South	2.40	106	Madagascar	3.45
28	Kuwait	2.40	106	Russia	3.45
28	Malaysia	2.40	111	Burkina Faso	3.50
28	Panama	2.40	111	Cameroon	3.50
28	Thailand	2.40	111	Guyana	3.50
33	Sweden	2.45	111	Nicaragua	3.50
34	Argentina	2.50	115	Gambia	3.60
34	France	2.50	116	Croatia	3.65
34	Italy	2.50	116	Georgia	3.65
34	Spain	2.50	116	Malawi	3.65
38	Portugal	2.55	119	Cape Verde	3.67
38	Sri Lanka	2.55	120	Ethiopia	3.70
38	Trinidad and Tobago	2.55	120	India	3.70
41	Barbados	2.60	120	Niger	3.70
41	Peru	2.60	123	Congo	3.75
43	Bolivia	2.65	124	Chad	3.80
43	Mauritius	2.65	124	China	3.80
45	Cyprus	2.70	124	Mauritania	3.80
45	Jamaica	2.70	124	Ukraine	3.80
45	Uruguay	2.70	124	Zimbabwe	3.80
48	Botswana	2.75	129	Albania	3.85
48	Guatemala	2.75	129	Bangladesh	3.85
48	Jordan	2.75	129	Mozambique	3.85
48	Namibia	2.75	129	Suriname	3.85
48	Oman	2.75	133	Burundi	3.90
48	Philippines	2.75	134	Togo	3.95
54	Belize	2.80	135	Haiti	4.00
54	Costa Rica	2.80	135	Kyrgyz Rep.	4.00
54	Israel	2.80	137	Kazakhstan	4.05
54	Swaziland	2.80	137	Sierra Leone	4.05
54	Turkey	2.80	139	Yemen	4.10
54	Uganda	2.80	140	Belarus	4.15
54	Samoa	2.80	141	Sudan	4.20
61	Latvia	2.85	141	Syria	4.20
62	Greece	2.90	143	Azerbaijan	4.30
62	Hungary	2.90	143	Equatorial Guinea	4.30
62	So. Africa	2.90	143	Myanmar	4.30
65	Ecuador	2.95	143	Rwanda	4.30
65	Gabon	2.95	147	Tajikistan	4.40
65	Indonesia	2.95	147	Uzbekistan	4.40
65	Malta	2.95	149	Angola	4.45
65	Morocco	2.95	149	Turkmenistan	4.45
65	Poland	2.95	151	Guinea-Bissau	4.55
65	Tunisia	2.95	152	Vietnam	4.60
72	Ghana	3.00	153	Congo (Zaire)	4.70
72	Lithuania	3.00	153	Iran	4.70
72	Saudi Arabia	3.00	155	Bosnia	4.80
75	Benin	3.05	155	Somalia	4.80
75	Kenya	3.05	157	Iraq	4.90
75	Paraguay	3.05	157	Laos	4.90
75	Qatar	3.05	157	Libya	4.90
75	Slovak Republic	3.05	160	Cuba	5.00
75	Zambia	3.05	160	Korea, North	5.00
81	Colombia	3.10			

Mostly Unfree

Zambia attracts commercial farmers from South Africa and Zimbabwe. Foreign investment must be screened by an investment board, which operates quickly and efficiently.

BANKING
Score: 2–Stable (low level of restrictions)

Private international and domestic banks operate in Zambia, and the market sets interest rates for loans and deposits. Merchant banking has been legalized. The country still has two state-owned banks, however, and the government has taken over the management of a failed major commercial bank.

WAGE AND PRICE CONTROLS
Score: 2–Stable (low level)

The government has removed price controls and eliminated most subsidies. State subsidization of government-owned enterprises distorts the pricing system, however. There is a minimum wage.

PROPERTY RIGHTS
Score: 3–Stable (moderate level of protection)

Former president Kenneth Kaunda's socialist regime, voted out of power in 1991, left a legacy of nationalized property. Businesses were expropriated as recently as 1989. Legislation enacted in 1993, however, provides for full compensation for newly nationalized property in convertible currency. According to the U.S. Department of Commerce, "Enforcement of property rights in general is weak.... Planned legal reforms include the strengthening of commercial law and property rights."[2]

REGULATION
Score: 4–Stable (high level)

Acquiring a business license involves complex procedures and delays. An investment board screens domestic investment. Corruption is a growing problem, and labor laws (including the requirement that employers provide housing to employees) are both burdensome and expensive. Residence permits are difficult to acquire. The U.S. Department of Commerce reports that "Current business laws are outdated and some modern business practices are not covered under current law."[3]

BLACK MARKET
Score: 3–Stable (moderate level of activity)

The trade in illegal gemstones thrives because of a government monopoly, and the lack of protection for intellectual property (for example, computer software) has led to increased piracy.

NOTES

[1] Banking profits in excess of 1 billion kwachas are taxed at 45 percent. This one exception to an otherwise flat tax rate was judged not significant enough to earn Zambia a grade of 4, which is reserved for countries with a tax system in which the top marginal rate is between 36 percent and 45 percent.

[2] U.S. Department of Commerce, *Country Commercial Guide,* 1998.

[3] *Ibid.*

Zimbabwe   3.80

1998 Score: **3.90**   1997 Score: **3.70**   1996 Score: **3.70**

Trade	5	Banking	3
Taxation	4	Wages and Prices	3
Government Intervention	3	Property Rights	4
Monetary Policy	4	Regulation	4
Foreign Investment	4	Black Market	4

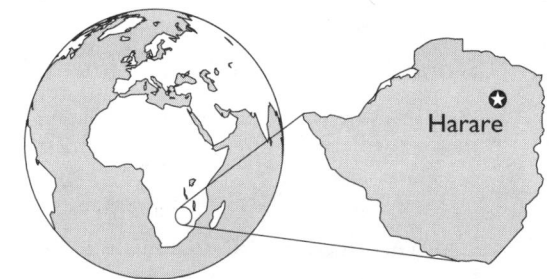

Harare

Zimbabwe gained its independence from the United Kingdom in 1980 on its acceptance of a ceasefire negotiated by the United Kingdom that had ended years of internal conflict between the white minority government and several black nationalist groups. Although it allows opposition parties and periodically holds elections, Zimbabwe is a de facto one-party state under President Robert Mugabe. Zimbabwe has one of Africa's more industrialized economies, but the government exercises considerable control over economic activity. President Mugabe's economic liberalization agenda has been derailed, and little progress has been made toward privatization. The economy has suffered during the latter half of 1997 and so far in 1998 with rapid devaluation of the currency and erosion of investor confidence in the wake of announcements that the government plans to expropriate white-owned farms. Nevertheless, the government recently reduced government spending as a percentage of the economy, resulting in a 0.1 point improvement in Zimbabwe's overall score.

TRADE POLICY
Score: 5–Stable (very high level of protectionism)

The average tariff rate is 23.4 percent.[1] Customs procedures are complex, and concern over cheaper South African imports could lead to additional protectionist measures. Some textile and clothing imports are banned.

TAXATION
Score–Income taxation: 3–Stable (moderate tax rates)
Score–Corporate taxation: 4–Stable (high tax rates)
Final Taxation Score: 4–Stable (high tax rates)

Zimbabwe's top income tax rate is 40 percent, and the average income level is taxed at 0 percent. The top corporate income tax rate is 37.5 percent. Branches of foreign companies are subject to an additional tax of 8.4 percent. Zimbabwe also has a 10 percent to 20 percent capital gains tax and a 10 percent to 25 percent sales tax.

GOVERNMENT INTERVENTION IN THE ECONOMY
Score: 3+ (moderate level)

Government consumes 20 percent of GDP, down from 27 percent last year. As a result, Zimbabwe's score in this factor is 1 point better this year. The government owns many enterprises, some of which require subsidies. These include the postal, telecommunications, and broadcasting services; railroads; and the national air service—all of which are closed to private investment. The government has refused to adopt a program of privatization despite donor encouragement. According to the Office of the United States Trade Representative, "The Government of Zimbabwe has not had a well-defined privatization program, largely due to the absence of a single organizational entity with overall responsibility for the design and implementation of the program."[2]

1	Hong Kong	1.25		81	Fiji	3.10
2	Singapore	1.30		81	Mali	3.10
3	Bahrain	1.70		81	Slovenia	3.10
4	New Zealand	1.75		85	Honduras	3.15
5	Switzerland	1.85		85	Mexico	3.15
6	United States	1.90		85	Papua New Guinea	3.15
7	Ireland	1.95		88	Djibouti	3.20
7	Luxembourg	1.95		88	Mongolia	3.20
7	Taiwan	1.95		90	Algeria	3.25
7	United Kingdom	1.95		90	Brazil	3.25
11	Bahamas	2.00		90	Lebanon	3.25
12	Czech Republic	2.05		90	Senegal	3.25
12	Japan	2.05		90	Tanzania	3.25
14	Australia	2.10		95	Nigeria	3.30
14	Belgium	2.10		95	Romania	3.30
14	Canada	2.10		97	Cambodia	3.35
14	United Arab Emirates	2.10		97	Dominican Republic	3.35
18	Austria	2.15		97	Egypt	3.35
18	Chile	2.15		97	Guinea	3.35
18	Estonia	2.15		97	Ivory Coast	3.35
18	Netherlands	2.15		97	Moldova	3.35
22	Denmark	2.25		97	Pakistan	3.35
22	El Salvador	2.25		104	Nepal	3.40
22	Finland	2.25		104	Venezuela	3.40
25	Germany	2.30		106	Armenia	3.45
25	Iceland	2.30		106	Bulgaria	3.45
27	Norway	2.35		106	Lesotho	3.45
28	Korea, South	2.40		106	Madagascar	3.45
28	Kuwait	2.40		106	Russia	3.45
28	Malaysia	2.40		111	Burkina Faso	3.50
28	Panama	2.40		111	Cameroon	3.50
28	Thailand	2.40		111	Guyana	3.50
33	Sweden	2.45		111	Nicaragua	3.50
34	Argentina	2.50		115	Gambia	3.60
34	France	2.50		116	Croatia	3.65
34	Italy	2.50		116	Georgia	3.65
34	Spain	2.50		116	Malawi	3.65
38	Portugal	2.55		119	Cape Verde	3.67
38	Sri Lanka	2.55		120	Ethiopia	3.70
38	Trinidad and Tobago	2.55		120	India	3.70
41	Barbados	2.60		120	Niger	3.70
41	Peru	2.60		123	Congo	3.75
43	Bolivia	2.65		124	Chad	3.80
43	Mauritius	2.65		124	China	3.80
45	Cyprus	2.70		124	Mauritania	3.80
45	Jamaica	2.70		124	Ukraine	3.80
45	Uruguay	2.70		124	Zimbabwe	3.80
48	Botswana	2.75		129	Albania	3.85
48	Guatemala	2.75		129	Bangladesh	3.85
48	Jordan	2.75		129	Mozambique	3.85
48	Namibia	2.75		129	Suriname	3.85
48	Oman	2.75		133	Burundi	3.90
48	Philippines	2.75		134	Togo	3.95
54	Belize	2.80		135	Haiti	4.00
54	Costa Rica	2.80		135	Kyrgyz Rep.	4.00
54	Israel	2.80		137	Kazakhstan	4.05
54	Swaziland	2.80		137	Sierra Leone	4.05
54	Turkey	2.80		139	Yemen	4.10
54	Uganda	2.80		140	Belarus	4.15
54	Samoa	2.80		141	Sudan	4.20
61	Latvia	2.85		141	Syria	4.20
62	Greece	2.90		143	Azerbaijan	4.30
62	Hungary	2.90		143	Equatorial Guinea	4.30
62	So. Africa	2.90		143	Myanmar	4.30
65	Ecuador	2.95		143	Rwanda	4.30
65	Gabon	2.95		147	Tajikistan	4.40
65	Indonesia	2.95		147	Uzbekistan	4.40
65	Malta	2.95		149	Angola	4.45
65	Morocco	2.95		149	Turkmenistan	4.45
65	Poland	2.95		151	Guinea-Bissau	4.55
65	Tunisia	2.95		152	Vietnam	4.60
72	Ghana	3.00		153	Congo (Zaire)	4.70
72	Lithuania	3.00		153	Iran	4.70
72	Saudi Arabia	3.00		155	Bosnia	4.80
75	Benin	3.05		155	Somalia	4.80
75	Kenya	3.05		157	Iraq	4.90
75	Paraguay	3.05		157	Laos	4.90
75	Qatar	3.05		157	Libya	4.90
75	Slovak Republic	3.05		160	Cuba	5.00
75	Zambia	3.05		160	Korea, North	5.00
81	Colombia	3.10				

Mostly Unfree

MONETARY POLICY
Score: 4–Stable (high level of inflation)

Zimbabwe's average annual rate of inflation from 1986 to 1996 was 19.8 percent. The estimated rate for 1997 was 18.9 percent.

CAPITAL FLOWS AND FOREIGN INVESTMENT
Score: 4–Stable (high barriers)

A 1992 investment code liberalized foreign investment regulations substantially. The government introduced investor incentives, including duty-free imports in some cases, and the Zimbabwe Stock Exchange is open to foreign investment. Prior government approval, however, still is required for all foreign direct investment. In 1994, the government banned foreign participation in several sectors, including much of agriculture, forestry, and transportation. As noted by the Office of the United States Trade Representative, "Notwithstanding such commitments to investment liberalization, Zimbabwe has yet to embrace the concept of national treatment or discontinue its sizable 'reserve list' of sectors that are closed to all but domestic investors and foreign investors in joint ventures with local partners."[3] President Mugabe's administration notified some 1,772 landowners (mostly white) that it plans to seize their farms without compensation. According to the Office of the United States Trade Representative, "Such extensive expropriation of land would have a crippling effect on local and foreign investor confidence."[4] There are indications, however, that the government is backing away from this plan and is considering a policy in which landowners would receive some compensation.

BANKING
Score: 3–Stable (moderate level of restrictions)

Only a few commercial banks are foreign-owned. The government allows foreign commercial and merchant banks to have majority shareholder status, but it discourages this. Recent attempts by foreign banks to obtain operating licenses have failed. The government owns some financial institutions. Some banks, however, are becoming more independent. According to the U.S. Department of Commerce, the Central Bank "is becoming increasingly independent of government in its exercising of monetary controls and advising government on fighting inflation, including on occasion criticizing, for example, the GOZ's [Government of Zimbabwe's] lack of fiscal discipline."[5]

WAGE AND PRICE CONTROLS
Score: 3–Stable (moderate level)

The government has succeeded in removing all but a few price controls, although some subsidies of food goods remain in effect. The government sets minimum wages by employment sector, and government marketing boards continue to control exports of traditional crops.

PROPERTY RIGHTS
Score: 4–Stable (low level of protection)

Expropriation of property remains a possibility, and there is no official requirement that the government compensate the property owner for expropriations. According to the U.S. Department of State, "The judiciary is independent, but the Government occasionally refuses to abide by court decisions."[6]

REGULATION
Score: 4–Stable (high level)

Wages and employment are heavily regulated. Government permission is required not only to terminate an employee, but also to commence virtually any commercial activity. The private sector is under increasing pressure to hire and train more Zimbabweans, and the use of foreign nationals is severely restricted. The bureaucracy lacks transparency and is highly arbitrary. According to the U.S. Department of Commerce, "Presently, many bureaucratic functions in this still heavily controlled economy are less than fully transparent and can by no means be considered streamlined.... Although not rampant, corruption is increasing."[7]

BLACK MARKET
Score: 4–Stable (high level of activity)

About 20 percent of GDP is produced in the black market, primarily because of government monopolies in such areas as transportation services.

NOTES

[1] World Bank, *World Development Indicators,* 1998.
[2] Office of the United States Trade Representative, *1998 National Trade Estimate Report on Foreign Trade Barriers,* 1998.
[3] Ibid.
[4] Ibid.
[5] U.S. Department of Commerce, *Country Commercial Guide,* 1998.
[6] U.S. Department of State, "Zimbabwe Country Report on Human Rights Practices for 1997," 1998.
[7] U.S. Department of Commerce, *Country Commercial Guide,* 1998.

Statistical Appendix

by Denise H. Froning

This appendix provides statistical data for each of the 161 countries graded in the 1999 *Index of Economic Freedom*. I have made every effort to use the same source in each factor for each country to ensure reliability of data; I utilize secondary sources when data are unavailable from the primary source; I indicate such instances whenever necessary. Information reflects the most recent data available at publication deadline. In most cases, and unless otherwise indicated, data are as of 1996 and are expressed in millions of current international dollars. An international dollar has the same purchasing power over gross domestic product as the U.S. dollar does inside the United States.

Guide to Statistics

- **Population:** July 1997 estimate. From Central Intelligence Agency (CIA), *World Factbook 1997*, using U.S. Bureau of the Census statistics from population censuses, vital statistics registration systems, or recent sample surveys and assumptions about future trends.
- **Land area:** Total area in square kilometers. From CIA, *World Factbook 1997*.
- **GDP:** Gross domestic product—the country's total production of goods and services based on purchasing power parity (PPP). GDP PPP is converted to international dollars using PPP rates. The PPP method employs standardized international dollar price weights, which are applied to the quantities of final goods and services produced in a given economy. The division of a GDP estimate in domestic currency by the corresponding PPP estimate in dollars provides the PPP conversion rate. When converted at PPP rates, $1,000 will buy the same market basket of goods in any country. From World Bank, *World Development Indicators on CD–ROM 1998*. Secondary source: CIA, *World Factbook 1997*.
- **GDP growth rate:** Annual percentage growth rate of GDP at market prices based on constant 1987 local currency. Aggregates are based on constant 1987 U.S. dollars. From World

Bank, *World Development Indicators on CD–ROM 1998*. Secondary source: CIA, *World Factbook 1997*.

- **Per capita GDP:** GDP per capita based on PPP. Data are in current international dollars. From World Bank, *World Development Indicators on CD–ROM 1998*. Secondary source: CIA, *World Factbook 1997*.
- **Average annual rate of inflation:** Average from 1986 to 1996. Extrapolated from World Bank, *World Development Indicators on CD–ROM 1998* annual inflation rate data as measured by the annual growth rate of the GDP implicit deflator. The GDP implicit deflator measures the average annual rate of price change in the economy as a whole for the periods shown.
- **Exports of goods and services:** Exports of goods and services represent the value of all goods and other market services. Included is the value of merchandise, freight, insurance, travel, and other non-factor services. Factor and property income, such as investment income, interest, and labor income, is excluded. Data are in current U.S. dollars. From World Bank, *World Development Indicators on CD–ROM 1998*. Secondary source: CIA, *World Factbook 1997*.
- **Major export trading partners:** Main destination of exports from each country and percentage of overall exports. From Economist Intelligence Unit, *Country Reports, 1997–1998*. Secondary source: CIA, *World Factbook 1997*.
- **Imports of goods and services:** Imports of goods and services represent the value of all goods and other market services. Included is the value of merchandise, freight, insurance, travel, and other non-factor services. Factor and property income, such as investment income, interest, and labor income, is excluded. Data are in current U.S. dollars. From World Bank, *World Development Indicators on CD–ROM 1998*. Secondary source: CIA, *World Factbook 1997*.
- **Major import trading partners:** Main countries from which imports originate and percentage of overall imports. From Economist Intelligence Unit, *Country Reports, 1997–1998*. Secondary source: CIA, *World Factbook 1997*.
- **Foreign direct investment:** Foreign direct investment is net inflows of investment to acquire a lasting management interest (10 percent or more of voting stock) in an enterprise operating in an economy other than that of the investor. It is the sum of equity capital, reinvestment of earnings, other long-term capital, and short-term capital as shown in the balance of payments. Data are in current U.S. dollars. From World Bank, *World Development Indicators on CD–ROM 1998*.
- **Aid from the United States, 1946–1999:** Total amount of U.S. aid, both military and economic, from 1946 to1999. Data for 1999 from U.S. Agency for International Development's request for funds for U.S. economic and military assistance; data for all other years reflect actual appropriations. From *Foreign Operations, Export Financing, and Related Programs Appropriations Bill, 1994*, U.S. Senate Report No. 103–142, and *USAID Congressional Presentation Summary Tables, Fiscal Years 1991–1999*.

Terms Used in Import/Export Statistics

- **AFTA:** Association of Southeast Asian Nations Free Trade Area
- **Andean Group:** Trade bloc consisting of Bolivia, Colombia, Ecuador, Peru, and Venezuela
- **APEC:** Asia–Pacific Economic Cooperation forum, consisting of Australia, Brunei, Canada, Chile, China, Hong Kong, Indonesia, Japan, South Korea, Malaysia, Mexico, New Zealand, Papua New Guinea, the Philippines, Singapore, Taiwan, Thailand, and the United States
- **ASEAN:** Association of Southeast Asian Nations, consisting of Singapore, Indonesia, Thailand, the Philippines, Malaysia, Brunei, Laos, Myanmar, and Vietnam
- **BLEU:** Belgium–Luxembourg Economic Union
- **Caricom:** Caribbean Community and Common Market, consisting of the Bahamas, Barbados, Belize, Guyana, Haiti, Jamaica, Suriname, Trinidad, and the Windward and Leeward Islands in the eastern Caribbean
- **CEFTA:** Central European Free Trade Agreement, consisting of Poland, Hungary, the Czech Republic, Slovenia, and the Slovak Republic

- **CIS:** Commonwealth of Independent States
- **EFTA:** Europe Free Trade Association, consisting of Iceland, Liechtenstein, Norway, and Switzerland
- **EU–15:** European Union, consisting of Austria, Belgium, Denmark, Finland, France, Germany, Greece, Ireland, Italy, Luxembourg, the Netherlands, Portugal, Spain, Sweden, and the United Kingdom
- **FSU:** Former Soviet Union
- **NICs:** Newly industrialized countries
- **OPEC:** Organization of Petroleum Exporting Countries, consisting of Algeria, Indonesia, Iran, Iraq, Kuwait, Libya, Nigeria, Qatar, Saudi Arabia, the United Arab Emirates, and Venezuela
- **SACU:** Southern African Customs Union, consisting of Namibia, Botswana, Lesotho, Swaziland, and South Africa

Sources

Central Intelligence Agency, *The World Factbook 1997*.

Economist Intelligence Unit Limited, *EIU Country Reports*, London, 1997–1998.

World Bank, *World Development Indicators on CD–ROM 1998*, Washington, D.C., 1998.

Foreign Operations, Export Financing, and Related Programs Appropriations Bill, 1994, U.S. Senate Report No. 103–142, September 14, 1993.

U.S. Agency for International Development, *USAID Congressional Presentation Summary Tables, Fiscal Years 1991–1999*, Washington, D.C., 1991–1998.

Individual Country Statistics

Albania

Population: 3,286,000

Land area: 28,750 sq. km

Major industries: food processing, textiles and clothing, lumber, oil, cement, chemicals, mining, basic metals, hydropower

Major agricultural products: wide range of temperate-zone crops and livestock

GDP: $4,400 million (1996 est.)

GDP growth rate: 9%

Per capita GDP: $1,339

Average annual rate of inflation: 33.7%

Exports of goods and services: $338 million

Major export trading partners: Italy 51.5%, Greece 9.9%, Turkey 6.2%, Germany 6.1% (1995)

Imports of goods and services: $1,073 million

Major import trading partners: Italy 37.9%, Greece 26.8%, Bulgaria 8.0%, Germany 4.6% (1995)

Foreign direct investment: $90 million

Aid from the United States, 1946–1999: $228.9 million

Algeria

Population: 28,733,550

Land area: 2,381,740 sq. km

Major industries: petroleum, light industries, natural gas, mining, electrical, petrochemical, food processing

Major agricultural products: wheat, barley, oats, grapes, olives, citrus, fruits, sheep, cattle

GDP: $139,945 million

GDP growth rate: 4%

Per capita GDP: $4,870

Average annual rate of inflation: 17.1%

Exports of goods and services: $14,450 million

Major export trading partners: Italy 20.2%, U.S. 16.8%, France 13.0%, Spain 8.7%, Germany 7.5%, Netherlands 5.7%

Imports of goods and services: $11,226 million

Major import trading partners: France 31.9%, Italy 9.5%, Spain 9.1%, U.S. 8.2%, Germany 5.3%, Canada 3.7%

Foreign direct investment: $4 million

Aid from the United States, 1946–1999: $208.5 million

Angola

Population: 11,099,770

Land area: 1,246,700 sq. km

Major industries: petroleum, diamonds, iron ore, phosphates, feldspar, bauxite, uranium, gold, cement, basic metal products, fish processing, food processing, brewing, tobacco products, sugar, textiles

Major agricultural products: bananas, sugarcane, coffee, sisal, corn, cotton, manioc (tapioca), tobacco, vegetables, plantains, livestock, forest products, fish

GDP: $22,244 million

GDP growth rate: 7%

Per capita GDP: $2,004

Average annual rate of inflation: 553.7%

Exports of goods and services: $5,201 million

Major export trading partners:[1] U.S. 70%, Taiwan 6.2%, China 5.0%, BLEU 5.0%

Imports of goods and services: $2,702 million

Major import trading partners: Portugal 23.8%, U.S. 16.0%, South Africa 9.5%, France 9.3%

Foreign direct investment: $300 million

Aid from the United States, 1946–1999: $334.9 million

Argentina

Population: 35,220,000

Land area: 2,766,890 sq. km

Major industries: food processing, motor vehicles, consumer durables, textiles, chemicals and petrochemicals, printing, metallurgy, steel

Major agricultural products: wheat, corn, sorghum, soybeans, sugar beets, livestock

GDP: $339,943 million

GDP growth rate: 4%

Per capita GDP: $9,652

Average annual rate of inflation: 458.4%

Exports of goods and services: $27,082 million

Major export trading partners: Brazil 27.8%, U.S. 8.2%, Chile 7.4%, Netherlands 5.1%, Italy 3.3%

Imports of goods and services: $27,908 million

Major import trading partners: Brazil 22.4%, U.S. 19.9%, Italy 6.3%, Germany 6.0%, France 5.0%

Foreign direct investment: $4,285 million

Aid from the United States, 1946–1999: $509.3 million

Armenia

Population: 3,774,000

Land area: 29,800 sq. km

Major industries: metal-cutting machine tools, forging-pressing machines, electric motors, tires, knitted wear, hosiery, shoes, silk fabric, washing machines, chemicals, trucks, watches, instruments, microelectronics; much of industry is shut down

Major agricultural products: fruit (especially grapes), vegetables, vineyards near Yerevan famous for brandy and other liqueurs, minor livestock sector

GDP: $7,540 million (1995)

GDP growth rate: 7% (1995)

Per capita GDP: $2,005 (1995)

Average annual rate of inflation: 449.1%

Exports of goods and services: $345 million (1995)

Major export trading partners: Russia 33.1%, Belgium 15.4%, South Africa 12.5%

Imports of goods and services: $901 million (1995)

Major import trading partners: Iran 17.4%, Russia 14.6%, U.S. 12.0%

Foreign direct investment: $18 million

Aid from the United States, 1946–1999:[2] $396.2 million

Australia

Population: 18,312,000

Land area: 7,686,850 sq. km

Major industries: mining, industrial and transportation equipment, food processing, chemicals, steel

Major agricultural products: wheat, barley, sugarcane, fruits, cattle, sheep, poultry

GDP: $377,154 million

GDP growth rate: 4%

Per capita GDP: $20,596

Average annual rate of inflation: 4.2%

Exports of goods and services: $72,845 million (1995)

Major export trading partners: developing countries 45.7%, Japan 21.6%, ASEAN 15.5%, EU–15 11.1%, U.S. 6.1%

Imports of goods and services: $73,258 million (1995)

Major import trading partners: developing countries 29.2%, EU–15 24.9%, U.S. 22.6%, Japan 13.9%, ASEAN 9.4%

Foreign direct investment: $6,321 million

Aid from the United States, 1946–1999: $123.6 million

Austria

Population: 8,059,000

Land area: 83,850 sq. km

Major industries: food, iron and steel, machines, textiles, chemicals, electrical, paper and pulp, tourism, mining, motor vehicles

Major agricultural products: grains, fruit, potatoes, sugar beets, cattle, pigs, poultry, sawed wood

GDP: $174,888 million

GDP growth rate: 1%

Per capita GDP: $21,701

Average annual rate of inflation: 2.9%

Exports of goods and services: $89,362 million (1995)

Major export trading partners: Germany 37.4%, Italy 8.3%, Switzerland 5.4%, France 4.3%, Hungary 3.6%, UK 3.5%, U.S. 3.2%, EU–15 64.1%, Eastern Europe 15.4%

Imports of goods and services: $91,124 million (1995)

Major import trading partners: Germany 42.9%, Italy 8.8%, France 4.8%, U.S. 4.5%, Switzerland 3.6%, Netherlands 3.2%, UK 3.0%, EU–15 70.8%, Eastern Europe 10.0%

Foreign direct investment: $3,826 million

Aid from the United States, 1946–1999: $1,258.0 million

Azerbaijan

Population: 7,581,000

Land area: 86,600 sq. km

Major industries: petroleum and natural gas, petroleum products, oil field equipment, steel, iron ore, cement, chemicals and petrochemicals, textiles

Major agricultural products: cotton, grain, rice, grapes, fruit, vegetables, tea, tobacco, cattle, pigs, sheep, goats

GDP: $11,486 million

GDP growth rate: 1%

Per capita GDP: $1,515

Average annual rate of inflation: 298.0%

Exports of goods and services: $758 million

Major export trading partners: Iran 35.8%, Russia 18.9%, Georgia 14.5%, Turkey 6.2%, Sweden 2.8%

Imports of goods and services: $1,517 million

Major import trading partners: Turkey 22.5%, Russia 16.5%, UAE[3] 11.3%, Germany 8.0%, Iran 6.9%

Foreign direct investment: $601 million

Aid from the United States, 1946–1999:[4] $86.5 million

The Bahamas

Population: 284,000

Land area: 13,940 sq. km

Major industries: tourism, banking, cement, oil refining and transshipment, salt production, rum, aragonite, pharmaceuticals, spiral-welded steel pipe

Major agricultural products: citrus, vegetables, poultry

GDP: $3,030 million (1995)

GDP growth rate: 0% (1995)

Per capita GDP: $10,091 (1995)

Average annual rate of inflation: 3.5%

Exports of goods and services:[5] $267.5 million (1995)

Major export trading partners: U.S. 24%, Spain 14%, UK 7%, Norway 7%, France 6%, Italy 5% (1995 est.)

Imports of goods and services:[6] $1,170 million (1995)

Major import trading partners: U.S. 29%, Finland 10%, Iran 10%, Denmark 8% (1995)

Foreign direct investment: $87 million

Aid from the United States, 1946–1999: $13.7 million

Bahrain

Population: 599,000

Land area: 620 sq. km

Major industries: petroleum processing and refining, aluminum smelting, offshore banking, ship repair, tourism

Major agricultural products: fruit, vegetables, poultry, dairy products, shrimp, fish

GDP: $8,921 million (1995)

GDP growth rate: 3% (1995)

Per capita GDP: $15,462 (1995)

Average annual rate of inflation: -2.8%

Exports of goods and services:[7] $4,200 million (1996 est.)

Major export trading partners: India 22%, Japan 12%, Saudi Arabia 6%, U.S. 6%, UAE[8] 5% (1995)

Imports of goods and services:[9] $3,500 million (1996 est.)

Major import trading partners: Saudi Arabia 40%, U.S. 13%, UK 7%, Japan 5%, Switzerland 5% (1995)

Foreign direct investment: n/a

Aid from the United States, 1946–1999: $6.0 million

Bangladesh

Population: 121,671,130

Land area: 144,000 sq. km

Major industries: jute manufacturing, cotton textiles, food processing, steel, fertilizer

Major agricultural products: rice, jute, tea, wheat, sugarcane, potatoes, beef, milk, poultry

GDP: $122,911 million

GDP growth rate: 5%

Per capita GDP: $1,010

Average annual rate of inflation: 7.0%

Exports of goods and services: $4,508 million

Major export trading partners:[10] U.S. 32.1%, UK 11.4%, Germany 10.2%, France 6.9%, Netherlands 4.9%, Italy 4.8%, Hong Kong 2.8%

Imports of goods and services: $7,614 million

Major import trading partners: India 16.2%, China 10.3%, Japan 8.6%, Singapore 5.9%, South Korea 5.8%, U.S. 3.3%, UK 2.3%

Foreign direct investment: $15 million

Aid from the United States, 1946–1999: $3,565.1 million

Barbados

Population: 264,300

Land area: 430 sq. km

Major industries: tourism, sugar, light manufacturing, component assembly for export

Major agricultural products: sugarcane, vegetables, cotton

GDP: $2,797 million

GDP growth rate: 0% (1995)

Per capita GDP: $10,586 (1995)

Average annual rate of inflation: 3.0%

Exports of goods and services: $850 million (1994)

Major export trading partners: UK 16.4%, U.S. 13.2%, Venezuela 8.7%, Jamaica 7.4%

Imports of goods and services: $804 million (1994)

Major import trading partners: U.S. 37.7%, Trinidad and Tobago 10.8%, UK 8.3%, Canada 5.1%

Foreign direct investment: $13 million

Aid from the United States, 1946–1999: $4.6 million

Belarus

Population: 10,298,000

Land area: 207,600 sq. km

Major industries: tractors, metal-cutting machine tools, off-highway dump trucks with load capacity of up to 110 metric tons, wheel-type earth movers for construction and mining, eight-wheel-drive high-flotation trucks with cargo capacity of 25 metric tons for use in tundra and roadless areas, equipment for animal husbandry and livestock feeding, motorcycles, television sets, chemical fibers, fertilizer, linen fabric, wool fabric, radios, refrigerators, other consumer goods

Major agricultural products: grain, potatoes, vegetables, meat, milk

GDP: $45,238 million

GDP growth rate: 3%

Per capita GDP: $4,393

Average annual rate of inflation: 357.7%

Exports of goods and services: $8,604 million

Major export trading partners: Russia, Ukraine, Poland, Germany (percentages not available)

Imports of goods and services: $9,993 million

Major import trading partners: Russia, Ukraine, Poland, Germany (percentages not available)

Foreign direct investment: $18 million

Aid from U.S., 1946–1999:[11] $35.8 million

Belgium

Population: 10,159,000

Land area: 30,510 sq. km

Major industries: engineering and metal products, motor vehicle assembly, processed food and beverages, chemicals, basic metals, textiles, glass, petroleum, coal

Major agricultural products: sugar beets, fresh vegetables, fruits, grain, tobacco, beef, veal, pork, milk

GDP: $225,428 million

GDP growth rate: 1%

Per capita GDP: $22,190

Average annual rate of inflation: 3.0%

Exports of goods and services: $195,522 million (1995)

Major export trading partners:[12] Germany 20.6%, France 17.8%, Netherlands 13.3%, UK 9.0%, U.S. 4.4%

Imports of goods and services: $182,398 million (1995)

Major import trading partners: Germany 19.9%, Netherlands 18.5%, France 15.3%, UK 9.2%, U.S. 6.1%

Foreign direct investment: $14,688 million

Aid from the United States, 1946–1999:[13] $1,864.4 million

Belize

Population: 222,400

Land area: 22,960 sq. km

Major industries: garment production, food processing, tourism, construction

Major agricultural products: bananas, coca, citrus, sugarcane, lumber, fish, cultured shrimp

GDP: $968,497 million

GDP growth rate: 2%

Per capita GDP: $4,355

Average annual rate of inflation: 3.9%

Exports of goods and services: $290 million

Major export trading partners: UK 42.0%, U.S. 36.4%, Canada 4.3%, EU–15 (excluding UK) 8.6%, Caricom 3.1% (1995)

Imports of goods and services: $313 million

Major import trading partners: U.S. 54.1%, Mexico 11.2%, UK 6.2%, Caricom 5.0%, EU–15 (excluding UK) 4.6% (1995)

Foreign direct investment: $15 million

Aid from the United States, 1946–1999: $173.5 million

Benin

Population: 5,631,620

Land area: 112,620 sq. km

Major industries: textiles, cigarettes, beverages, food, construction materials, petroleum

Major agricultural products: corn, sorghum, cassava (tapioca), yams, beans, rice, cotton, palm oil, peanuts, poultry, livestock

GDP: $7,062 million

GDP growth rate: 6%

Per capita GDP: $1,254

Average annual rate of inflation: 5.3%

Exports of goods and services: $544 million

Major export trading partners: Brazil 18%, Portugal 14%, Morocco 10%, Libya 7.5% (1995)

Imports of goods and services: $723 million

Major import trading partners: France 27%, Thailand 9%, China 9%, Hong Kong 9% (1995)

Foreign direct investment: $2 million

Aid from the United States, 1946–1999: $285.1 million

Bolivia

Population: 7,588,000

Land area: 1,098,580 sq. km

Major industries: mining, smelting, petroleum, food and beverages, tobacco, handicrafts, clothing

Major agricultural products: coffee, coca, cotton, corn, sugarcane, rice, potatoes, timber

GDP: $21,596 million (1995)

GDP growth rate: 4% (1995)

Per capita GDP: $2,913 (1995)

Average annual rate of inflation: 40.1%

Exports of goods and services: $1,113 million

Major export trading partners: U.S. 26%, Argentina 17%, UK 15%, Peru 14% (1995)

Imports of goods and services: $1,500 million (1994)

Major import trading partners: U.S. 18%, Brazil 15%, Japan 13%, Argentina 8% (1995)

Foreign direct investment: $527 million

Aid from the United States, 1946–1999: $2,725.7 million

Bosnia and Herzegovina

Population:[14] 3,222,584 (July 1997 est.)

Land area: 51,233 sq. km

Major industries: steel, coal, iron ore, lead, zinc, manganese, bauxite, vehicle assembly, textiles, tobacco products, wooden furniture, tank and aircraft assembly, domestic appliances, oil refining; much of capacity damaged or shut down (1995)

Major agricultural products: wheat, corn, fruits, vegetables, livestock

GDP: $1.9 billion (1995 est.)

GDP growth rate: n/a

Per capita GDP: $600 (1995 est.)

Average annual rate of inflation: n/a

Exports of goods and services: $152 million (1995 est.)

Major export trading partners: n/a

Imports of goods and services: $1,100 million (1995 est.)

Major import trading partners: n/a

Foreign direct investment: n/a

Aid from the United States, 1946–1999:[15] $1,028.0 million

Botswana

Population: 1,480,000

Land area: 600,370 sq. km

Major industries: diamonds, copper, nickel, coal, salt, soda ash, potash, livestock processing

Major agricultural products: sorghum, maize, millet, pulses, groundnuts (peanuts), beans, cowpeas, sunflower seed, livestock

GDP: $11,341 million

GDP growth rate: 6%

Per capita GDP: $7,663

Average annual rate of inflation: 14.2%

Exports of goods and services: $2,526 million

Major export trading partners:[16] Europe 74%, SACU 21%, Zimbabwe 3%

Imports of goods and services: $1,609 million

Major import trading partners: SACU 78%, Europe 8%, Zimbabwe 6%

Foreign direct investment: $75 million

Aid from the United States, 1946–1999: $428.3 million

Brazil

Population: 161,364,880

Land area: 8,511,965 sq. km

Major industries: textiles, shoes, chemicals, cement, lumber, iron ore, tin, steel, aircraft, motor vehicles and parts, other machinery and equipment

Major agricultural products: coffee, soybeans, wheat, rice, corn, sugarcane, cocoa, citrus, beef

GDP: $1,047,391 million

GDP growth rate: 3%

Per capita GDP: $6,491

Average annual rate of inflation: 628.2%

Exports of goods and services: $49,558 million

Major export trading partners: U.S. 19.5%, Argentina 10.8%, Japan 6.4%, Germany 4.4%

Imports of goods and services: $59,355 million

Major import trading partners: U.S. 22.2%, Germany 12.7%, Argentina 9.0%, Japan 5.2%

Foreign direct investment: $9,889 million

Aid from the United States, 1946–1999: $3,132.2 million

Bulgaria

Population: 8,356,000

Land area: 110,910 sq. km

Major industries: machine building and metalworking, food processing, chemicals, textiles, construction materials, ferrous and nonferrous metals

Major agricultural products: grain, oilseed, vegetables, fruits, tobacco, livestock

GDP: $37,229 million

GDP growth rate: -9%

Per capita GDP: $4,455

Average annual rate of inflation: 40.4%

Exports of goods and services: $6,125 million

Major export trading partners: EU–15 36.5%, CIS, Central and Eastern Europe 31.7% (of which Russia 9.8%)

Imports of goods and services: $5,874 million

Major import trading partners: CIS, Central and Eastern Europe 37.7% (of which Russia 28.4%)

Foreign direct investment: $115 million

Aid from the United States, 1946–1999: $165.2 million

Burkina Faso

Population: 10,668,590

Land area: 274,200 sq. km

Major industries: cotton lint, beverages, agricultural processing, soap, cigarettes, textiles, gold

Major agricultural products: peanuts, shea nuts, sesame, cotton, sorghum, millet, corn, rice, livestock

GDP: $10,177 million

GDP growth rate: 6%

Per capita GDP: $954

Average annual rate of inflation: 3.8%

Exports of goods and services: $294 million

Major export trading partners:[17] France 13.2%, Ivory Coast 10.8%, Italy 10.2%, Thailand 7.8%

Imports of goods and services: $748 million

Major import trading partners: Ivory Coast 24.9%, France 18.8%, Togo 3.4%, Nigeria 2.6%

Foreign direct investment: $0

Aid from the United States, 1946–1999: $465.0 million

Burundi

Population: 6,422,680

Land area: 27,830 sq. km

Major industries: light consumer goods (such as blankets, shoes, soap), assembly of imported components, public works construction, food processing

Major agricultural products: coffee, cotton, tea, corn, sorghum, sweet potatoes, bananas, manioc (tapioca), meat, milk, hides

GDP: $3,837 million

GDP growth rate: -9%

Per capita GDP: $597

Average annual rate of inflation: 8.7%

Exports of goods and services: $50 million

Major export trading partners:[18] BLEU 25.2%, Germany 21.5%, U.S. 7.9%, Rwanda 4.1% (1995)

Imports of goods and services: $160 million

Major import trading partners: BLEU 15.4%, Saudi Arabia 13.1%, Germany 8.8%, France 8.6% (1995)

Foreign direct investment: $1 million

Aid from the United States, 1946–1999: $221.6 million

Cambodia

Population: 10,275,320

Land area: 181,040 sq. km

Major industries: rice milling, fishing, wood and wood products, rubber, cement, gem mining, textiles

Major agricultural products: rice, rubber, corn, vegetables

GDP: $7.7 billion (1996 est.)

GDP growth rate: 7%

Per capita GDP: $710 (1996 est.)

Average annual rate of inflation: 46.4%

Exports of goods and services: $831 million

Major export trading partners: Singapore, Japan, Thailand, Hong Kong, Indonesia, Malaysia (percentages not available)

Imports of goods and services: $1,332 million

Major import trading partners: Singapore, Vietnam, Japan, Australia, Hong Kong, Indonesia (percentages not available)

Foreign direct investment: $294 million

Aid from the United States, 1946–1999: $2,413.4 million

Cameroon

Population: 13,676,200

Land area: 475,440 sq. km

Major industries: petroleum production and refining, food processing, light consumer goods, textiles, lumber

Major agricultural products: coffee, cocoa, cotton, rubber, bananas, oilseed, grains, root starches, livestock, timber

GDP: $26,394 million

GDP growth rate: 5%

Per capita GDP: $1,930

Average annual rate of inflation: 3.0%

Exports of goods and services: $1,721 million

Major export trading partners:[19] Italy 17.7%, France 15.8%, Spain 16.5%, Netherlands 6.7%, Germany 5.5%

Imports of goods and services: $1,200 million

Major import trading partners: France 36.7%, Italy 7.5%, BLEU 7.1%, U.S. 6.5%, UK 4.8%

Foreign direct investment: $35 million

Aid from the United States, 1946–1999: $445.1 million

Canada

Population: 29,964,000

Land area: 9,976,140 sq. km

Major industries: processed and unprocessed minerals, food products, wood and paper products, transportation equipment, chemicals, fish products, petroleum and natural gas

Major agricultural products: wheat, barley, oilseed, tobacco, fruits, vegetables, dairy products, forest products; commercial fisheries provide annual catch of 1.5 million metric tons, of which 75% is exported

GDP: $662,312 million

GDP growth rate: 1%

Per capita GDP: $22,104

Average annual rate of inflation: 2.8%

Exports of goods and services: $211,539 million (1995)

Major export trading partners: U.S. 79.1%, Japan 4.5%, UK 1.7%, other EU–15 4.5%

Imports of goods and services: $197,670 million (1995)

Major import trading partners: U.S. 75.9%, Japan 3.0%, UK 2.3%, other EU–15 6.3%

Foreign direct investment: $6,398 million

Aid from the United States, 1946–1999: $30.5 million

Cape Verde

Population: 389,300

Land area: 4,030 sq. km

Major industries: fish processing, salt mining, garments, ship repair, food and beverages

Major agricultural products: bananas, corn, beans, sweet potatoes, sugarcane, coffee, peanuts, fish

GDP: $776 million

GDP growth rate: 5%

Per capita GDP: $1,994

Average annual rate of inflation: 3.6%

Exports of goods and services: $101 million

Major export trading partners:[20] Portugal 50.0%, Singapore 14.3%, UK 7.1%, Germany 7.1%

Imports of goods and services: $273 million

Major import trading partners: Portugal 45.0%, Netherlands 7.3%, Ivory Coast 5.9%, France 3.8%

Foreign direct investment: $12 million

Aid from the United States, 1946–1999: $155.8 million

Chad

Population: 6,610,870

Land area: 1.284 million sq. km

Major industries: cotton textiles, meat packing, beer brewing, natron (sodium carbonate), soap, cigarettes, construction materials

Major agricultural products: cotton, sorghum, millet, peanuts, rice, potatoes, manioc (tapioca), cattle, sheep, goats, camels

GDP: $6,015 million

GDP growth rate: 3%

Per capita GDP: $910

Average annual rate of inflation: 2.8%

Exports of goods and services: $325 million

Major export trading partners:[21] Portugal 34.7%, Germany 11.3%, U.S. 5.6%, France 5.67%

Imports of goods and services: $521 million

Major import trading partners: France 34.7%, Cameroon 24.1%, BLEU 7.4%, Nigeria 6.5%

Foreign direct investment: $18 million

Aid from the United States, 1946–1999: $370.7 million

Chile

Population: 14,418,800

Land area: 756,950 sq. km

Major industries: copper, other minerals, foodstuffs, fish processing, iron and steel, wood and wood products, transport equipment, cement, textiles

Major agricultural products: wheat, corn, grapes, beans, sugar beets, potatoes, fruit, beef, poultry, wool, timber; fish catch of 6.6 million metric tons in 1991

GDP: $173,211 million

GDP growth rate: 7%

Per capita GDP: $12,013

Average annual rate of inflation: 17.3%

Exports of goods and services: $19,761 million

Major export trading partners: U.S. 16.6%, Japan 16.2%, Brazil 6.1%, UK 5.8%, South Korea 5.6%, Germany 4.8%, Argentina 4.6%

Imports of goods and services: $21,223 million

Major import trading partners: U.S. 23.7%, Argentina 9.4%, Brazil 6.1%, Japan 5.5%, Mexico 5.3%, Germany 4.2%, France 3.4%

Foreign direct investment: $4,091 million

Aid from the United States, 1946–1999: $1,504.0 million

China, People's Republic of

Population: 1,215,414,240

Land area: 9,596,960 sq. km

Major industries: iron and steel, coal, machine building, armaments, textiles and apparel, petroleum, cement, chemical fertilizers, consumer durables, food processing, autos, consumer electronics, telecommunications

Major agricultural products: rice, wheat, potatoes, sorghum, peanuts, tea, millet, barley, cotton, other fibers, oilseed, pork and other livestock products, fish

GDP: $4,088,458 million

GDP growth rate: 10%

Per capita GDP: $3,364

Average annual rate of inflation: 9.8%

Exports of goods and services: $146,174 million (1995)

Major export trading partners: Hong Kong 21.8%, Japan 20.4%, U.S. 17.7%, South Korea 5.0%, Germany 3.9%, Singapore 2.5%, Netherlands 2.3%, Taiwan 1.9%

Imports of goods and services: $135,349 million (1995)

Major import trading partners: Japan 21.0%, Taiwan 11.7%, U.S. 11.6%, South Korea 9.0%, Hong Kong 5.6%, Germany 5.3%, Russia 3.7%, Singapore 2.6%

Foreign direct investment: $40,180 million

Aid from the United States, 1946–1999: $7.9 million

China, Republic of (Taiwan)

Population: 21,699,776 (July 1997 est.)

Land area: 35,980 sq. km

Major industries: electronics, textiles, chemicals, clothing, food processing, plywood, sugar milling, cement, shipbuilding, petroleum refining

Major agricultural products: rice, wheat, corn, soybeans, vegetables, fruit, tea, pigs, poultry, beef, milk, fish

GDP: $315,000 million (1996 est.)

GDP growth rate: 5.7%

Per capita GDP: $14,700 (1996 est.)

Average annual rate of inflation: n/a

Exports of goods and services:[22] $116,000 million

Major export trading partners: U.S. 27.6%, Hong Kong 21.7%, EU–15 countries 15.2%, Japan 10.5% (1994 est.)

Imports of goods and services: $102,400 million (CIF[23])

Major import trading partners: Japan 30.1%, U.S. 21.7%, EU–15 countries 17.6% (1993 est.)

Foreign direct investment: n/a

Aid from the United States, 1946–1999: $6,579.5 million

Colombia

Population: 37,450,510

Land area: 1,138,910 sq. km

Major industries: textiles, food processing, oil, clothing and footwear, beverages, chemicals, cement, gold, coal, emeralds

Major agricultural products: coffee, cut flowers, bananas, rice, tobacco, corn, sugarcane, cocoa beans, oilseed, vegetables, forest products, shrimp farming

GDP: $262,156 million

GDP growth rate: 2%

Per capita GDP: $7,000

Average annual rate of inflation: 24.6%

Exports of goods and services: $14,084 million

Major export trading partners: U.S. 33.7%, Andean Group 27.9%, EU–15 24.2.%, Japan 3.7% (1995)

Imports of goods and services: $17,035 million

Major import trading partners: U.S. 39.1%, EU–15 16.4%, Andean Group 13.2%, Japan 7.6% (1995)

Foreign direct investment: $3,322 million

Aid from the United States, 1946–1999: $2,584.6 million

Congo, Democratic Republic of (formerly Zaire)

Population: 45,233,680

Land area: 2,345,410 sq. km

Major industries: mining, mineral processing, consumer products (including textiles, footwear, cigarettes, processed foods and beverages), cement, diamonds

Major agricultural products: coffee, sugar, palm oil, rubber, tea, quinine, cassava (tapioca), palm oil, bananas, root crops, corn, fruits, wood products

GDP: $40,780 million

GDP growth rate: 1%

Per capita GDP: $902

Average annual rate of inflation: 1,410.6%

Exports of goods and services: $2,425 million

Major export trading partners:[24] BLEU 43%, U.S. 16%, South Africa 5%, Italy 5%

Imports of goods and services: $2,300 million

Major import trading partners: South Africa 19%, BLEU 17%, Hong Kong 6%, U.S. 6%

Foreign direct investment: $2 million

Aid from the United States, 1946–1999: $1,745.3 million

Congo, Republic of

Population: 2,705,290

Land area: 342,000 sq. km

Major industries: petroleum extraction, cement kilning, lumbering, brewing, sugar milling, palm oil, soap, cigarette making

Major agricultural products: cassava (tapioca, accounting for 90% of food output), sugar, rice, corn, peanuts, vegetables, coffee, cocoa, forest products

GDP: $4,850 million

GDP growth rate: 5%

Per capita GDP: $1,793

Average annual rate of inflation: 2.3%

Exports of goods and services: $1,599 million

Major export trading partners:[25] BLEU 24.3%, Taiwan 20.2%, U.S. 14.9%, Italy 14.8% (1995)

Imports of goods and services: $2,325 million

Major import trading partners: France 31.2%, Netherlands 24.6%, Italy 11.4%, U.S. 6.9% (1995)

Foreign direct investment: $8 million

Aid from the United States, 1946–1999: $55.5 million

Costa Rica

Population: 3,442,030

Land area: 51,100 sq. km

Major industries: food processing, textiles and clothing, construction materials, fertilizer, plastic products

Major agricultural products: coffee, bananas, sugar, corn, rice, beans, potatoes, beef, timber; depletion of forest resources has resulted in declining timber output

GDP: $22,300 million

GDP growth rate: -1%

Per capita GDP: $6,479

Average annual rate of inflation: 17.0%

Exports of goods and services: $4,079 million

Major export trading partners:[26] U.S. 44.6%, Benelux[27] 7.2%, Germany 5.7%, Guatemala 4.5%, Italy 4.0% (1997)

Imports of goods and services: $4,132 million

Major import trading partners: U.S. 42.1%, Mexico 7.1%, Venezuela 6.8%, Japan 5.7%, Guatemala 3.2% (1997)

Foreign direct investment: $410 million

Aid from the United States, 1946–1999: $1,833.5 million

Croatia

Population: 4,770,910

Land area: 56,538 sq. km

Major industries: chemicals and plastics, machine tools, fabricated metal, electronics, pig iron and rolled steel products, aluminum, paper, wood products, construction materials, textiles, shipbuilding, petroleum and petroleum refining, food and beverages, tourism

Major agricultural products: wheat, corn, sugar beets, sunflower seed, alfalfa, clover, olives, citrus, grapes, vegetables, livestock breeding, dairy farming

GDP: $20,516 million

GDP growth rate: 4% (1996 est.)

Per capita GDP: $4,300

Average annual rate of inflation: n/a

Exports of goods and services: $8,014 million

Major export trading partners: Italy 23.7%, Germany 21.5%, Slovenia 13.1%, Bosnia and Herzegovina 8.3%, Austria 4.3%, France 3.4% (1995)

Imports of goods and services: $10,200 million

Major import trading partners: Germany 20.1%, Italy 18.2%, Slovenia 10.7%, Austria 7.7%, UK 6.1%, U.S. 2.7% (1995)

Foreign direct investment: $349 million

Aid from the United States, 1946–1999:[28] $67.4 million

Cuba

Population: 11,019,000

Land area: 110,860 sq. km

Major industries: sugar, petroleum, food, tobacco, textiles, chemicals, paper and wood products, metals (particularly nickel), cement, fertilizers, consumer goods, agricultural machinery

Major agricultural products: sugarcane, tobacco, citrus, coffee, rice, potatoes and other tubers, beans, livestock

GDP: $16,200 million (1996 est.)

GDP growth rate: 7.8% (1996 est.)

Per capita GDP: $1,480 (1996 est.)

Average annual rate of inflation: n/a

Exports of goods and services:[29] $1,850 million

Major export trading partners: Russia 20%, Canada 16%, Netherlands 11%, China 7%, Spain 6%

Imports of goods and services: $3,610 million

Major import trading partners: Spain 17%, Russia 17%, Mexico 12%, France 7%, Canada 6%

Foreign direct investment: n/a

Aid from the United States, 1946–1999: $20.1 million

Cyprus

Population: 740,000

Land area: 9,250 sq. km (includes 3,355 sq. km under Turkish control)

Major industries: food, beverages, textiles, chemicals, metal products, tourism, wood products

Major agricultural products: potatoes, citrus, vegetables, barley, grapes, olives, vegetables

GDP: $13,310 million (1994)

GDP growth rate: 5% (1994)

Per capita GDP: $18,334 (1994)

Average annual rate of inflation: 4.0%

Exports of goods and services: $3,547 million (1994)

Major export trading partners: Russia 15.7%, UK 14.5%, Bulgaria 9.9%, Greece 6.6%, Germany 5.8% (1995)

Imports of goods and services: $3,593 million (1994)

Major import trading partners: U.S. 13.4%, UK 12.2%, Italy 10.1%, Germany 8.4%, Greece 7.4% (1995)

Foreign direct investment: $119 million

Aid from the United States, 1946–1999: $452.2 million

Czech Republic

Population: 10,315,000

Land area: 78,703 sq. km

Major industries: fuels, ferrous metallurgy, machinery and equipment, coal, motor vehicles, glass, armaments

Major agricultural products: grains, potatoes, sugar beets, hops, fruit, pigs, cattle, poultry, forest products

GDP: $113,531 million

GDP growth rate: 4%

Per capita GDP: $11,006

Average annual rate of inflation: 9.1%

Exports of goods and services: $29,994 million

Major export trading partners: EU–15 60.9%, CEFTA 21.4%, EFTA 1.7%

Imports of goods and services: $34,176 million

Major import trading partners: EU–15 61.1%, CEFTA 16.3%, EFTA 2.2%

Foreign direct investment: $1,435 million

Aid from the United States, 1946–1999:[30] $26.5 million

Denmark

Population: 5,262,000

Land area: 43,094 sq. km (excluding Faeroe Islands and Greenland)

Major industries: food processing, machinery and equipment, textiles and clothing, chemical products, electronics, construction, furniture and other wood products, shipbuilding

Major agricultural products: grain, potatoes, rape, sugar beets, meat, dairy products, fish

GDP: $119,422 million

GDP growth rate: 2%

Per capita GDP: $22,695

Average annual rate of inflation: 2.9%

Exports of goods and services: $58,904 million

Major export trading partners: Germany 22.5%, Sweden 9.7%, UK 7.9%, Norway 5.9%, France 5.4%, Netherlands 4.4%, U.S. 4.0% (1995)

Imports of goods and services: $51,462 million

Major import trading partners: Germany 21.7%, Sweden 11.7%, Netherlands 7.0%, UK 6.6%, France 5.2%, Norway 4.9%, U.S. 4.7%, Japan 3.5%, FSU 1.7% (1995)

Foreign direct investment: $773 million

Aid from the United States, 1946–1999: $916.6 million

Djibouti, Republic of

Population: 618,680

Land area: 22,000 sq. km

Major industries: limited to a few small-scale enterprises, such as dairy products and mineral-water bottling

Major agricultural products: fruits, vegetables, goats, sheep, camels

GDP: $500 million (1995 est.)

GDP growth rate: -3.1% (1995 est.)

Per capita GDP: $1,200 (1995 est.)

Average annual rate of inflation: n/a

Exports of goods and services: $200 million

Major export trading partners:[31] Somalia 42%, Ethiopia 35%, Yemen 7% (1995)

Imports of goods and services: $282 million

Major import trading partners: Thailand 15%, France 13%, Ethiopia 8%, Saudi Arabia 6% (1995)

Foreign direct investment: $5 million

Aid from the United States, 1946–1999: $76.2 million

Dominican Republic

Population: 7,963,580

Land area: 48,730 sq. km

Major industries: tourism, sugar processing, ferronickel and gold mining, textiles, cement, tobacco

Major agricultural products: sugarcane, coffee, cotton, cocoa, tobacco, rice, beans, potatoes, corn, bananas, cattle, pigs, dairy products, meat, eggs

GDP: $36,053 million

GDP growth rate: 7%

Per capita GDP: $4,527

Average annual rate of inflation: 18.9%

Exports of goods and services: $3,832 million

Major export trading partners: U.S. 45.1%, Canada 5.7%, Japan 3.6%, EU–15 34.2% (1995)

Imports of goods and services: $4,525 million

Major import trading partners: U.S. 44.1%, Venezuela 10.7%, Netherlands Antilles 5.7%, Mexico 5.0%, Japan 3.7%, EU–15 15.6% (1995)

Foreign direct investment: $394 million

Aid from the United States, 1946–1999: $1,678.6 million

Ecuador

Population: 11,698,000

Land area: 283,560 sq. km

Major industries: petroleum, food processing, textiles, metal work, paper products, wood products, chemicals, plastics, fishing, lumber

Major agricultural products: bananas, coffee, cocoa, rice, potatoes, manioc, plantains, sugarcane, cattle, sheep, pigs, beef, pork, dairy products, balsa wood, fish, shrimp

GDP: $59,650 million

GDP growth rate: 2%

Per capita GDP: $5,099

Average annual rate of inflation: 40.3%

Exports of goods and services: $5,813 million

Major export trading partners: U.S. 37.9%, Colombia 6.1%, Chile 4.5%, Italy 4.0%, Germany 3.6%

Imports of goods and services: $5,033 million

Major import trading partners: U.S. 31.5%, Colombia 10.2%, Japan 5.6%, Mexico 5.3%, Venezuela 4.6%

Foreign direct investment: $447 million

Aid from the United States, 1946–1999: $1,153.2 million

Egypt

Population: 59,272,000

Land area: 1,001,450 sq. km

Major industries: textiles, food processing, tourism, chemicals, petroleum, construction, cement, metals

Major agricultural products: cotton, rice, corn, wheat, beans, fruits, vegetables, cattle, water buffalo, sheep, goats; annual fish catch about 140,000 metric tons

GDP: $169,121 million

GDP growth rate: 5%

Per capita GDP: $2,853

Average annual rate of inflation: 13.3%

Exports of goods and services: $13,912 million

Major export trading partners: Italy 20.1%, U.S. 12.4%, UK 7.7%, Germany 5.0%, France 4.0%, Turkey 3.7%

Imports of goods and services: $16,982 million

Major import trading partners: U.S. 17.7%, Germany 9.6%, Italy 8.1%, France 8.0%, Japan 4.5%, UK 3.8%

Foreign direct investment: $636 million

Aid from the United States, 1946–1999: $60,388.8 million

El Salvador

Population: 5,809,730

Land area: 21,040 sq. km

Major industries: food processing, beverages, petroleum, chemicals, fertilizer, textiles, furniture, light metals

Major agricultural products: coffee, sugarcane, corn, rice, beans, oilseed, cotton, sorghum, beef, dairy products, shrimp

GDP: $16,359 million

GDP growth rate: 2%

Per capita GDP: $2,816

Average annual rate of inflation: 15.2%

Exports of goods and services: $2,194 million

Major export trading partners: U.S. 53.4%, Guatemala 11.2%, Germany 8.9%, Costa Rica 4.8%, Honduras 4.8%

Imports of goods and services: $3,496 million

Major import trading partners: U.S. 49.9%, Guatemala 8.7%, Panama 5.5%, Mexico 5.3%, Japan 3.5%

Foreign direct investment: $25 million

Aid from the United States, 1946–1999: $5,920.8 million

Equatorial Guinea

Population: 410,350

Land area: 28,050 sq. km

Major industries: fishing, sawmills

Major agricultural products: coffee, cocoa, rice, yams, cassava (tapioca), bananas, palm oil nuts, manioc, livestock, timber

GDP: $1,299 million

GDP growth rate: 31%

Per capita GDP: $3,165

Average annual rate of inflation: -1.0%

Exports of goods and services: $189 million

Major export trading partners: U.S. 34%, Japan 16%, Spain 15%, China 12% (1995)

Imports of goods and services: $396 million

Major import trading partners: Spain 51%, Cameroon 21%, France 6%, U.S. 4% (1995)

Foreign direct investment: $376 million

Aid from the United States, 1946–1999: $22.2 million

Estonia

Population: 1,466,000

Land area: 45,226 sq. km

Major industries: oil shale, shipbuilding, phosphates, electric motors, excavators, cement, furniture, clothing, textiles, paper, shoes, apparel

Major agricultural products: potatoes, fruits, vegetables, livestock and dairy products, fish

GDP: $6,829 million

GDP growth rate: 4%

Per capita GDP: $4,658

Average annual rate of inflation: 60.4%

Exports of goods and services: $3,176 million

Major export trading partners: Finland 19.8%, Russia 15.7%, Sweden 11.6%, Latvia 7.7%, Germany 6.9%

Imports of goods and services: $3,724 million

Major import trading partners: Finland 36.7%, Russia 10.9%, Germany 9.0%, Sweden 8.7%, Denmark 3.6%

Foreign direct investment: $150 million

Aid from the United States, 1946–1999:[32] $4.4 million

Ethiopia

Population: 58,233,770

Land area: 1,127,127 sq. km

Major industries: food processing, beverages, textiles, chemicals, metals processing, cement

Major agricultural products: cereals, pulses, coffee, oilseed, sugarcane, potatoes, other vegetables, hides, cattle, sheep, goats

GDP: $29,330 million

GDP growth rate: 10%

Per capita GDP: $504

Average annual rate of inflation: 4.6%

Exports of goods and services: $783 million

Major export trading partners:[33] Germany 31.7%, Japan 14.5%, Italy 8.1%, Djibouti 7.4% (1994)

Imports of goods and services: $1,647 million

Major import trading partners: Saudi Arabia 15.0%, U.S. 12.3%, Italy 11.1%, Germany 8.0% (1994)

Foreign direct investment: $5 million

Aid from the United States, 1946–1999: $2,153.0 million

Fiji

Population: 803,000

Land area: 18,270 sq. km

Major industries: sugar, tourism, copra, gold, silver, clothing, lumber, small cottage industries

Major agricultural products: sugarcane, coconuts, cassava (tapioca), rice, sweet potatoes, bananas, cattle, pigs, horses, goats; fish catch 13,796 tons in 1991

GDP: $3,412 million

GDP growth rate: 3%

Per capita GDP: $4,249

Average annual rate of inflation: 5.5%

Exports of goods and services: $1,161 million

Major export trading partners: EU–15 26%, Australia 15%, other Pacific island countries 11%, Japan 6% (1995)

Imports of goods and services: $1,212 million

Major import trading partners: Australia 30%, New Zealand 17%, Japan 13%, EU–15 6%, U.S. 6% (1995)

Foreign direct investment: $9.8 million

Aid from the United States, 1946–1999: $13.7 million

Finland

Population: 5,125,000

Land area: 337,030 sq. km

Major industries: metal products, shipbuilding, pulp and paper, copper refining, foodstuffs, chemicals, textiles, clothing

Major agricultural products: cereals, sugar beets, potatoes, dairy cattle; annual fish catch about 160,000 metric tons

GDP: $96,540 million

GDP growth rate: 3%

Per capita GDP: $18,837

Average annual rate of inflation: 3.8%

Exports of goods and services: $47,896 million (1995)

Major export trading partners: Germany 12.1%, Sweden 10.7%, UK 10.2%, U.S. 7.9%, Russia 6.1%, France 4.2%, EU–15 54.5%

Imports of goods and services: $37,341 million (1995)

Major import trading partners: Germany 15.1%, Sweden 11.9%, UK 8.8%, U.S. 7.3%, Russia 7.3%, Japan 5.1%, EU–15 60.3%

Foreign direct investment: $1,118 million

Aid from the United States, 1946–1999: $52.1 million

France

Population: 58,375,000

Land area: 547,030 sq. km

Major industries: steel, machinery, chemicals, automobiles, metallurgy, aircraft, electronics, mining, textiles, food processing, tourism

Major agricultural products: wheat, cereals, sugar beets, potatoes, wine grapes, beef, dairy products; fish catch of 850,000 metric tons, all of which is used domestically, ranks among world's top 20

GDP: $1,260,031 million

GDP growth rate: 1%

Per capita GDP: $21,585

Average annual rate of inflation: 2.8%

Exports of goods and services: $360,979 million (1995)

Major export trading partners: Germany 17.1%, UK 9.3%, Italy 9.2%, BLEU 8.4%, Spain 7.8%, U.S. 6.1%, Netherlands 4.5%, EU–15 62.9%

Imports of goods and services: $324,354 million (1995)

Major import trading partners: Germany 17.4%, Italy 10.1%, BLEU 8.4%, UK 8.4%, U.S. 7.9%, Spain 7.0%, Netherlands 5.2%, EU–15 63.0%

Foreign direct investment: $21,972 million

Aid from the United States, 1946–1999: $8,465.6 million

Gabon

Population: 1,125,000

Land area: 267,670 sq. km

Major industries: food and beverages, textiles, lumbering and plywood, cement, petroleum extraction and refining, mining (manganese, uranium, gold), chemicals, ship repair

Major agricultural products: cocoa, coffee, sugar, palm oil, rubber, okoume (a tropical softwood), cattle; small fishing operations provide a catch of about 30,000 metric tons

GDP: $8,382 million

GDP growth rate: 3%

Per capita GDP: $7,451

Average annual rate of inflation: 3.3%

Exports of goods and services: $3,398 million

Major export trading partners:[34] U.S. 66.0%, France 8.0%, China 5.0%, Japan 5.0%

Imports of goods and services: $2,089 million

Major import trading partners: France 42.0%, U.S. 6.0%, Netherlands 5.0%, Japan 4.0%

Foreign direct investment: -$65 million

Aid from the United States, 1946–1999: $87.8 million

The Gambia

Population: 1,146,880

Land area: 11,300 sq. km

Major industries: processing of peanuts, fish, hides; tourism, beverages, agricultural machinery assembly, woodworking, metalworking, clothing

Major agricultural products: peanuts, millet, sorghum, rice, corn, cassava (tapioca), palm kernels, cattle, sheep, goats; forest and fishing resources not fully exploited

GDP: $1,416 million (1995)

GDP growth rate: -6% (1995)

Per capita GDP: $1,273 (1995)

Average annual rate of inflation: 11.5%

Exports of goods and services: $210 million (1995)

Major export trading partners:[35] Japan 29.2%, Senegal 10.8%, Hong Kong 9.2%, France 7.7%

Imports of goods and services: $268 million (1995)

Major import trading partners: China 20.3%, Ivory Coast 13.9%, Hong Kong 9.8%, UK 7.6%

Foreign direct investment: $11 million

Aid from the United States, 1946–1999: $207.7 million

Georgia

Population: 5,411,000

Land area: 69,700 sq. km

Major industries: steel, aircraft, machine tools, foundry equipment, electric locomotives, tower cranes, electric welding equipment, machinery for food preparation and meat packing, electric motors, process control equipment, trucks, tractors, textiles, shoes, chemicals, wood products, wine

Major agricultural products: citrus, grapes, tea, vegetables, potatoes; small livestock sector

GDP: $8,871 million (1995)

GDP growth rate: 2% (1995)

Per capita GDP: $1,639

Average annual rate of inflation: 1,141.1%

Exports of goods and services: $715 million (1995)

Major export trading partners: Russia 27%, Azerbaijan 14%, Armenia 12%, Turkey 12%, Bulgaria 6%

Imports of goods and services: $1,191 million (1995)

Major import trading partners: Russia 21%, Turkey 11%, Azerbaijan 10%, Ukraine 5%, U.S. 5%

Foreign direct investment: $40 million

Aid from the United States, 1946–1999:[36] $247.6 million

Germany

Population: 81,912,000

Land area: 356,910 sq. km

Major industries: Western: among world's largest and most technologically advanced producers of iron, steel, coal, cement, chemicals, machinery, vehicles, machine tools, electronics, food and beverages; Eastern: metal fabrication, chemicals, brown coal, shipbuilding, machine building, food and beverages, textiles, petroleum refining

Major agricultural products: Western: potatoes, wheat, barley, sugar beets, fruit, cabbage, cattle, pigs, poultry; Eastern: wheat, rye, barley, potatoes, sugar beets, fruit, pork, beef, chicken, milk, hides

GDP: $1,737,521 million

GDP growth rate:[37] 4%

Per capita GDP: $21,212

Average annual rate of inflation: n/a

Exports of goods and services: $570,191 million (1995)

Major export trading partners: France 10.9%, UK 8.0%, U.S. 7.8%, Italy 7.4%, Netherlands 7.4%, BLEU 6.2%, Japan 2.7%, EU–15 56.7%

Imports of goods and services: $549,956 million (1995)

Major import trading partners: France 10.6%, Netherlands 8.6%, Italy 8.2%, U.S. 7.3%, UK 6.8%, BLEU 6.3%, Japan 5.1%, EU–15 55.1%

Foreign direct investment: -$3,183 million

Aid from the United States, 1946–1999:[38] $4,783.6 million

Ghana

Population: 17,521,800

Land area: 238,540 sq. km

Major industries: mining, lumbering, light manufacturing, aluminum, food processing

Major agricultural products: cocoa, rice, coffee, cassava (tapioca), peanuts, corn, shea nuts, bananas, timber

GDP: $32,077 million

GDP growth rate: 5%

Per capita GDP: $1,831

Average annual rate of inflation: 31.5%

Exports of goods and services: $1,728 million

Major export trading partners:[39] UK 16%, Germany 9%, U.S. 10%, Togo 11%

Imports of goods and services: $2,395 million

Major import trading partners: UK 16%, Nigeria 13%, Germany 5%, U.S. 10%

Foreign direct investment: $120 million

Aid from the United States, 1946–1999: $1,079.1 million

Greece

Population: 10,475,000

Land area: 131,940 sq. km

Major industries: tourism, food and tobacco processing, textiles, chemicals, metal products, mining, petroleum

Major agricultural products: wheat, corn, barley, sugar beets, olives, tomatoes, wine, tobacco, potatoes, meat, dairy products

GDP: $130,691 million

GDP growth rate: 3%

Per capita GDP: $12,476

Average annual rate of inflation: 13.6%

Exports of goods and services:[40] $18,825 million (1995)

Major export trading partners: Germany 27.7%, U.S. 17.7%, Italy 8.9%, France 6.6%, UK 6.6%, Netherlands 2.2%, EU–15 56.5% (1995)

Imports of goods and services: $30,747 million (1995)

Major import trading partners: Germany 17.9%, Italy 15.7%, U.S. 9.0%, France 8.2%, UK 6.9%, Netherlands 6.9%, EU–15 64.5% (1995)

Foreign direct investment: $900 million

Aid from the United States, 1946–1999: $12,127.4 million

Guatemala

Population: 10,928,000

Land area: 108,890 sq. km

Major industries: sugar, textiles and clothing, furniture, chemicals, petroleum, metals, rubber, tourism

Major agricultural products: sugarcane, corn, bananas, coffee, beans, cardamom, cattle, sheep, pigs, chickens

GDP: $42,365 million

GDP growth rate: 3%

Per capita GDP: $3,877

Average annual rate of inflation: 15.5%

Exports of goods and services: $2,815 million

Major export trading partners: U.S. 36.6%, El Salvador 12.7%, Honduras 6.9%, Germany 5.1%, Costa Rica 4.9%

Imports of goods and services: $3,564 million

Major import trading partners: U.S. 43.9%, Mexico 10.3%, Venezuela 4.6%, El Salvador 4.1%, Curacao 3.8%

Foreign direct investment: $76.9 million

Aid from the United States, 1946–1999: $2,027.2 million

Guinea

Population: 6,759,210

Land area: 245,860 sq. km

Major industries: bauxite, gold, diamonds, alumina refining, light manufacturing and agricultural processing

Major agricultural products: rice, coffee, pineapples, palm kernels, cassava (tapioca), bananas, sweet potatoes, cattle, sheep, goats, timber

GDP: $12,084 million

GDP growth rate: 4%

Per capita GDP: $1,788

Average annual rate of inflation: 16.4%

Exports of goods and services: $749 million

Major export trading partners:[41] U.S. 16.5%, Ireland 11.7%, Spain 11.3%, BLEU 9.6%

Imports of goods and services: $870 million

Major import trading partners: France 22.0%, U.S. 11.6%, Ivory Coast 10.6%, BLEU 7.5%

Foreign direct investment: $24 million

Aid from the United States, 1946–1999: $654.6 million

Guinea–Bissau

Population: 1,093,810

Land area: 36,120 sq. km

Major industries: agricultural product processing, beer, soft drinks

Major agricultural products: rice, corn, beans, cassava (tapioca), cashew nuts, peanuts, palm kernels, cotton; fishing and forest potential not fully exploited

GDP: $1,148 million

GDP growth rate: 5%

Per capita GDP: $1,049

Average annual rate of inflation: 67.3%

Exports of goods and services: $28 million

Major export trading partners: Spain 35%, India 30%, Thailand 10%, Italy 10% (1995)

Imports of goods and services: $85 million

Major import trading partners: Thailand 27%, Portugal 23%, Japan 6%, Ivory Coast 7% (1995)

Foreign direct investment: $1 million

Aid from the United States, 1946–1999: $114.4 million

Guyana

Population: 838,500

Land area: 214,970 sq. km

Major industries: bauxite, sugar, rice milling, timber, fishing (shrimp), textiles, gold mining

Major agricultural products: sugar, rice, wheat, vegetable oils, beef, pork, poultry, dairy products; potential exists for fishing and forestry development

GDP: $2,067 million

GDP growth rate:[42] -6%

Per capita GDP: $2,465

Average annual rate of inflation: 64.3%

Exports of goods and services: $723 million

Major export trading partners: Canada 26.2%, U.S. 22.9%, UK 20.6%, Netherlands Antilles 8.6%

Imports of goods and services: $759 million

Major import trading partners: Italy 36.8%, U.S. 21.8%, Netherlands Antilles 9.5%, UK 8.4%

Foreign direct investment: $81 million

Aid from the United States, 1946–1999: $149.6 million

Haiti

Population: 7,336,000

Land area: 27,750 sq. km

Major industries: sugar refining, flour milling, textiles, cement, tourism, light assembly industries based on imported parts

Major agricultural products: coffee, mangoes, sugarcane, rice, corn, sorghum, wood

GDP: $8,325 million

GDP growth rate: 2%

Per capita GDP: $1,135

Average annual rate of inflation: 15.3%

Exports of goods and services: $176 million

Major export trading partners: U.S. 73.5%, EU–15 19.4% (1995)

Imports of goods and services: $732 million

Major import trading partners: U.S. 65.0%, EU–15 13.9% (1995)

Foreign direct investment: $4.1 million

Aid from the United States, 1946–1999: $1,909.8 million

Honduras

Population: 6,101,110

Land area: 112,090 sq. km

Major industries: sugar, coffee, textiles, clothing, wood products

Major agricultural products: bananas, coffee, citrus, beef, timber, shrimp

GDP: $13,017 million

GDP growth rate: 3%

Per capita GDP: $2,133

Average annual rate of inflation: 12.6%

Exports of goods and services: $1,907 million

Major export trading partners: U.S. 68.5%, Germany 7.1%, Japan 5.8%, Spain 3.3%, Benelux[43] 2.1% (1995)

Imports of goods and services: $2,093 million

Major import trading partners: U.S. 55.5%, Guatemala 4.0%, Netherlands Antilles 3.8%, Japan 3.4%, Mexico 3.0% (1995)

Foreign direct investment: $75 million

Aid from the United States, 1946–1999: $2,600.8 million

Hong Kong

Population: 6,311,000

Land area: 1,092 sq. km

Major industries: textiles, clothing, tourism, electronics, plastics, toys, watches, clocks

Major agricultural products: fresh vegetables, poultry

GDP: $153,105 million

GDP growth rate: 5%

Per capita GDP: $24,620

Average annual rate of inflation: 7.9%

Exports of goods and services: $219,822 million

Major export trading partners: China 34.3%, U.S. 21.2%, Japan 6.5%, Germany 4.2%, UK 3.3%, Singapore 2.7%

Imports of goods and services: $221,443 million

Major import trading partners: China 37.1%, Japan 13.6%, Taiwan 8.0%, U.S. 7.9%, Singapore 5.3%, South Korea 4.8%

Foreign direct investment: n/a

Aid from the United States, 1946–1999: $43.8 million

Hungary

Population: 10,193,000

Land area: 93,030 sq. km

Major industries: mining, metallurgy, construction materials, processed foods, textiles, chemicals (especially pharmaceuticals), motor vehicles

Major agricultural products: wheat, corn, sunflower seed, potatoes, sugar beets, pigs, cattle, poultry, dairy products

GDP: $70,864 million

GDP growth rate: 1%

Per capita GDP: $6,952

Average annual rate of inflation: 17.3%

Exports of goods and services: $17,548 million

Major export trading partners: EU–15 62.8%, FSU 8.6%

Imports of goods and services: $18,039 million

Major import trading partners: EU–15 59.8%, FSU 14.9%

Foreign direct investment: $1,982 million

Aid from the United States, 1946–1999: $128.1 million

Iceland

Population: 270,000

Land area: 103,000 sq. km

Major industries: fish processing, aluminum smelting, ferrosilicon production, geothermal power, tourism

Major agricultural products: potatoes, turnips, cattle, sheep; fish catch of about 1.1 million metric tons in 1992

GDP: $5,995 million

GDP growth rate: 6%

Per capita GDP: $22,205

Average annual rate of inflation: 21.2%

Exports of goods and services: $2,474 million

Major export trading partners: UK 19%, Germany 14%, U.S. 12%, Japan 11%, Denmark 8%, France 7% (1995)

Imports of goods and services: $2,612 million

Major import trading partners: Germany 11%, Norway 10%, UK 10%, Denmark 9%, U.S. 8%, Sweden 7% (1995)

Foreign direct investment: $4 million (1995)

Aid from the United States, 1946–1999: $77.2 million

India

Population: 945,120,560

Land area: 3,287,590 sq. km

Major industries: textiles, chemicals, food processing, steel, transportation equipment, cement, mining, petroleum, machinery

Major agricultural products: rice, wheat, oilseed, cotton, jute, tea, sugarcane, potatoes, cattle, water buffalo, sheep, goats, poultry; among world's top 10 fishing nations, with catch of about 3 million metric tons

GDP: $1,517,601 million

GDP growth rate: 7%

Per capita GDP: $1,606

Average annual rate of inflation: 8.6%

Exports of goods and services: $43,871 million

Major export trading partners: U.S., Japan, Germany, UK, Hong Kong (percentages not available)

Imports of goods and services: $53,107 million

Major import trading partners: U.S., Germany, Saudi Arabia, UK, Belgium, Japan (percentages not available)

Foreign direct investment: $2,587 million

Aid from the United States, 1946–1999: $13,282.2 million

Indonesia

Population: 197,054,540

Land area: 1,919,440 sq. km

Major industries: petroleum and natural gas, textiles, mining, cement, chemical fertilizers, plywood, food, rubber, tourism

Major agricultural products: rice, cassava (tapioca), peanuts, rubber, cocoa, coffee, palm oil, copra, other tropical products, poultry, beef, pork, eggs

GDP: $681,037 million

GDP growth rate: 8%

Per capita GDP: $3,456

Average annual rate of inflation: 8.8%

Exports of goods and services: $59,205 million

Major export trading partners: Japan 25.9%, U.S. 13.6%, Singapore 7.8%, South Korea 6.6%, China 4.1%, Netherlands 3.3%

Imports of goods and services: $56,210 million

Major import trading partners: Japan 19.8%, U.S. 11.7%, Germany 7.0%, Singapore 6.7%, Australia 5.9%, South Korea 5.6%

Foreign direct investment: $7,960 million

Aid from the United States, 1946–1999: $4,991.0 million

Iran

Population: 62,509,330

Land area: 1.648 million sq. km

Major industries: petroleum, petrochemicals, textiles, cement and other construction materials, food processing (particularly sugar refining and vegetable oil production), metal fabricating, armaments

Major agricultural products: wheat, rice, other grains, sugar beets, fruits, nuts, cotton, dairy products, wool, caviar

GDP: $327,367 million (1995)

GDP growth rate: 3% (1995)

Per capita GDP: $5,351 (1995)

Average annual rate of inflation: 25.8%

Exports of goods and services:[44] $21,300 million (1996 est.)

Major export trading partners: Japan 13.5%, Italy 8.1%, South Korea 6.8%, South Africa 6.1%, France 5.3%, Spain 4.0%, Netherlands 3.1%, Germany 3.0%

Imports of goods and services:[45] $13,300 million (1996 est.)

Major import trading partners: Germany 14.9%, UAE[46] 8.3%, Japan 6.0%, Argentina 5.8%, France 5.1%, UK 4.8%, Italy 4.7%, Netherlands 2.6%

Foreign direct investment: $10 million

Aid from the United States, 1946–1999: $2,172.6 million

Iraq

Population: 21,366,430

Land area: 437,072 sq. km

Major industries: petroleum, chemicals, textiles, construction materials, food processing

Major agricultural products: wheat, rice, other grains, sugar beets, fruits, nuts, cotton, dairy products, wool, caviar

GDP: $42 billion (1996 est.)

GDP growth rate: 0% (1996 est.)

Per capita GDP: $2,000 (1996 est.)

Average annual rate of inflation: 9.25%

Exports of goods and services: n/a

Major export trading partners: Jordan 83.9%, Greece 5.1%, EU–15 7.6% (1995)

Imports of goods and services: n/a

Major import trading partners: Jordan 48.7%, Hungary 14.6%, Switzerland 7.6%, Germany 2.1%, EU–15 13.4% (1995)

Foreign direct investment: n/a

Aid from the United States, 1946–1999: $126.3 million

Ireland

Population: 3,626,000

Land area: 70,280 sq. km

Major industries: food products, brewing, textiles, clothing, chemicals, pharmaceuticals, machinery, transportation equipment, glass and crystal

Major agricultural products: turnips, barley, potatoes, sugar beets, wheat, meat and dairy products

GDP: $67,747 million

GDP growth rate: 7%

Per capita GDP: $18,684

Average annual rate of inflation: 3.1%

Exports of goods and services: $48,009 million (1995)

Major export trading partners: UK 24.8%, Germany 12.8%, U.S. 9.4%, France 8.3%, Netherlands 6.8%, Italy 3.6%, EU–15 68.6%

Imports of goods and services: $38,271 million (1995)

Major import trading partners: UK 34.8%, U.S. 15.5%, Germany 6.9%, Japan 5.4%, France 3.9%, Netherlands 2.9%, EU–15 56.8%

Foreign direct investment: $2,456 million

Aid from the United States, 1946–1999: $464.5 million

Israel

Population: 5,692,000

Land area: 20,770 sq. km

Major industries: food processing, diamond cutting and polishing, textiles and apparel, chemicals, metal products, military equipment, transport equipment, electrical equipment, potash mining, high-technology electronics, tourism

Major agricultural products: citrus and other fruits, vegetables, cotton, beef, poultry, dairy products

GDP: $105,415 million

GDP growth rate:[47] 5%

Per capita GDP: $18,520

Average annual rate of inflation: 19.6%

Exports of goods and services: $27,068 million (1995)

Major export trading partners: EU–15 32.2%, U.S. 30.1%, Japan 6.9% (1995)

Imports of goods and services: $36,510 million (1995)

Major import trading partners: EU–15 52.3%, U.S. 18.6% (1995)

Foreign direct investment: $2,110 million

Aid from the United States, 1946–1999: $84,748.2 million

Italy

Population: 57,380,000

Land area: 301,230 sq. km

Major industries: tourism, machinery, iron and steel, chemicals, food processing, textiles, motor vehicles, clothing, footwear, ceramics

Major agricultural products: fruits, vegetables, grapes, potatoes, sugar beets, soybeans, grain, olives, meat and dairy products; fish catch of 525,000 metric tons in 1990

GDP: $1,155,551 million

GDP growth rate: 1%

Per capita GDP: $20,139

Average annual rate of inflation: 5.7%

Exports of goods and services: $299,783 million (1995)

Major export trading partners: Germany 17.4%, France 12.5%, U.S. 7.3%, UK 6.5%, Spain 4.9%, Switzerland 3.7%

Imports of goods and services: $254,044 million (1995)

Major import trading partners: Germany 18.5%, France 13.5%, UK 6.6%, Netherlands 6.0%, U.S. 4.9%, BLEU 4.8%

Foreign direct investment: $3,523 million

Aid from the United States, 1946–1999: $5,966.1 million

Ivory Coast

Population: 14,347,060

Land area: 322,460 sq. km

Major industries: foodstuffs, beverages, wood products, oil refining, automobile assembly, textiles, fertilizer, construction materials, electricity

Major agricultural products: coffee, cocoa beans, bananas, palm kernels, corn, rice, manioc (tapioca), sweet potatoes, sugar, cotton, rubber, timber

GDP: $24,735 million

GDP growth rate: 6%

Per capita GDP: $1,724

Average annual rate of inflation: 5.3%

Exports of goods and services: $4,763 million

Major export trading partners: France 18%, Germany 8%, Netherlands 8%, Italy 8%, Mali 6% (1995)

Imports of goods and services: $4,090 million

Major import trading partners: France 32%, Nigeria 20%, U.S. 6%, Ghana 4%, Germany 4% (1995)

Foreign direct investment: $21 million

Aid from the United States, 1946–1999: $203.7 million

Jamaica

Population: 2,546,620

Land area: 10,990 sq. km

Major industries: bauxite, tourism, textiles, food processing, light manufacturing

Major agricultural products: sugarcane, bananas, coffee, citrus, potatoes, vegetables, poultry, goats, milk

GDP: $9,076 million

GDP growth rate: -2%

Per capita GDP: $3,564

Average annual rate of inflation: 25.6%

Exports of goods and services: $2,443 million

Major export trading partners: U.S. 36.8%, UK 13.2%, other EU–15 countries 17.5%, Canada 11.8%, Norway 6.5%, Caricom 4.0%

Imports of goods and services: $3,013 million

Major import trading partners: U.S. 52.1%, Caricom 9.9%, UK 7.2%, other EU–15 countries 3.9%, Canada 3.0%

Foreign direct investment: $175 million

Aid from the United States, 1946–1999: $2,004.6 million

Japan

Population: 125,761,000

Land area: 377,835 sq. km

Major industries: among world's largest and most technologically advanced producers of steel and nonferrous metallurgy, heavy electrical equipment, construction and mining equipment, motor vehicles and parts, electronic and telecommunication equipment, machine tools, automated production systems, locomotives and railroad rolling stock, ships, chemicals, textiles, processed foods

Major agricultural products: rice, sugar beets, vegetables, fruit, pork, poultry, dairy products, eggs; world's largest fish catch of 10 million metric tons in 1991

GDP: $2,912,408 million

GDP growth rate: 4%

Per capita GDP: $23,158

Average annual rate of inflation: 1.0%

Exports of goods and services: $482,597 million (1995)

Major export trading partners: U.S. 27.2%, South Korea 7.1%, Taiwan 6.3%, Hong Kong 6.2%, China 5.3%, Singapore 5.1%

Imports of goods and services: $406,890 million (1995)

Major import trading partners: U.S. 22.7%, China 11.6%, South Korea 4.6%, Indonesia 4.4%, Taiwan 4.3%, Australia 4.1%

Foreign direct investment: $200 million

Aid from the United States, 1946–1999: $3,925.5 million

Jordan

Population: 4,311,720

Land area: 89,213 sq. km

Major industries: phosphate mining, petroleum refining, cement, potash, light manufacturing

Major agricultural products: wheat, barley, citrus, tomatoes, melons, olives, sheep, goats, poultry

GDP: $15,734 million

GDP growth rate: 5%

Per capita GDP: $3,649

Average annual rate of inflation: 7.3%

Exports of goods and services: $3,705 million

Major export trading partners:[48] India 13.1%, Saudi Arabia 7.4%, UAE[49] 4.6%, Iraq 4.4%, EU–15 11.2%

Imports of goods and services: $5,478 million

Major import trading partners: EU–15 40.0%, Germany 8.6%, Italy 8.4%, France 7.7%, U.S. 9.4%

Foreign direct investment: $15.5 million

Aid from the United States, 1946–1999: $4,605.5 million

Kazakhstan

Population: 16,471,000

Land area: 2,717,300 sq. km

Major industries: oil, coal, iron ore, manganese, chromite, lead, zinc, copper, titanium, bauxite, gold, silver, phosphates, sulfur, iron and steel, nonferrous metal, tractors and other agricultural machinery, electric motors, construction materials; much industrial capacity shut down and/or in need of repair

Major agricultural products: grain (mostly spring wheat), cotton, wool, meat

GDP: $53,429 million

GDP growth rate: 1%

Per capita GDP: $3,244

Average annual rate of inflation: 305.2%

Exports of goods and services: $6,436 million

Major export trading partners: Russia 44.5%, China 7.4%, Netherlands 5.2%, former Soviet republics 55.7%, EU–15 17.9%

Imports of goods and services: $7,133 million

Major import trading partners: Russia 55.0%, Germany 4.6%, Turkey 3.6%, former Soviet republics 69.6%, EU–15 13.0%

Foreign direct investment: $310 million

Aid from the United States, 1946–1999: $203.8 million

Kenya

Population: 27,363,550

Land area: 582,650 sq. km

Major industries: small-scale consumer goods (plastic, furniture, batteries, textiles, soap, cigarettes, flour), agricultural product processing, oil refining, cement, tourism

Major agricultural products: coffee, tea, corn, wheat, sugarcane, fruit, vegetables, dairy products, beef, pork, poultry, eggs

GDP: $31,803 million

GDP growth rate: 4%

Per capita GDP: $1,162

Average annual rate of inflation: 12.2%

Exports of goods and services: $3,043 million

Major export trading partners: Uganda 16.1%, Tanzania 12.8%, UK 10.4%, Germany 7.5%

Imports of goods and services: $3,400 million

Major import trading partners: UK 13.2%, UAE[50] 8.2%, South Africa 7.6%, Germany 7.4%

Foreign direct investment: $13 million

Aid from the United States, 1946–1999: $1,468.1 million

Korea, Democratic Republic of (North Korea)

Population: 22,450,520

Land area: 120,540 sq. km

Major industries: military products, machine building, electric power, chemicals, mining (coal, iron ore, magnesite, graphite, copper, zinc, lead, precious metals), metallurgy, textiles, food processing

Major agricultural products: rice, corn, potatoes, soybeans, pulses, cattle, pigs, pork, eggs

GDP: $20.9 billion (1996 est.)

GDP growth rate: -5% (1996 est.)

Per capita GDP: $900 (1996 est.)

Average annual rate of inflation: n/a

Exports of goods and services:[51] $805 million (1995 est.)

Major export trading partners: Japan 27.9%, South Korea 20.8%, China 5.2%, Germany 4.0%, Russia 1.2% (1995)

Imports of goods and services: $1,240 million (CIF,[52] 1995 est.)

Major import trading partners: China 32.6%, Japan 17.2%, Russia 4.7%, South Korea 4.3%, Germany 2.9% (1995)

Foreign direct investment: n/a

Aid from the United States, 1946–1999: $0

Korea, Republic of (South Korea)

Population: 45,545,000

Land area: 98,480 sq. km

Major industries: electronics, automobile production, chemicals, shipbuilding, steel, textiles, clothing, footwear, food processing

Major agricultural products: rice, root crops, barley, vegetables, fruit, cattle, pigs, chickens, milk, eggs; fish catch of 2.9 million metric tons, world's 7th largest

GDP: $600,873 million

GDP growth rate: 7%

Per capita GDP: $13,193

Average annual rate of inflation: 5.5%

Exports of goods and services: $156,865 million

Major export trading partners: U.S. 16.7%, Japan 12.2%, Hong Kong 8.6%, Singapore 5.0%, Germany 3.6%

Imports of goods and services: $176,427 million

Major import trading partners: U.S. 22.2%, Japan 20.9%, Germany 4.8%, Saudi Arabia 4.4%, Australia 4.2%

Foreign direct investment: $2,325 million

Aid from the United States, 1946–1999: $14,883.1 million

Kuwait

Population: 1,589,520

Land area: 17,820 sq. km

Major industries: petroleum, petrochemicals, desalination, food processing, construction materials, salt, construction

Major agricultural products: practically no crops; extensive fishing in territorial waters

GDP: $32.5 billion (1996 est.)

GDP growth rate: 3% (1995)

Per capita GDP: $16,700 (1996 est.)

Average annual rate of inflation: -2.3%

Exports of goods and services: $14,588 million (1995)

Major export trading partners: Japan 23.5%, U.S. 18.2%, Netherlands 17.2%, India 11.1%, South Korea 9.6%, Singapore 8.8%, Pakistan 6.0%, Philippines 4.3% (1995)

Imports of goods and services: $13,076 million (1995)

Major import trading partners: U.S. 16.3%, Japan 12.0%, Germany 7.0%, Italy 7.0%, Saudi Arabia 6.6%, UK 6.2%, France 4.1%, India 3.3%

Foreign direct investment: n/a

Aid from the United States, 1946–1999: $0

Kyrgyz Republic

Population: 4,576,000

Land area: 198,500 sq. km

Major industries: small machinery, textiles, food processing, cement, shoes, sawed logs, refrigerators, furniture, electric motors, gold, rare earth metals

Major agricultural products: wool, tobacco, cotton, potatoes, vegetables, grapes, fruits and berries, sheep, goats

GDP: $9,449 million

GDP growth rate: 6%

Per capita GDP: $2,065

Average annual rate of inflation: 129.4%

Exports of goods and services: $552 million

Major export trading partners:[53] Russia 25.6%, Uzbekistan 17.1%, China 16.8%, Kazakhstan 16.3%, UK 6.7%, Ukraine 2.0% (1995)

Imports of goods and services: $958 million

Major import trading partners: Russia 21.9%, Kazakhstan 21.5%, Uzbekistan 17.0%, Turkey 7.3%, Cuba 4.3%, U.S. 3.7% (1995)

Foreign direct investment: $46.3 million

Aid from the United States, 1946–1999: $118.1 million

Laos

Population: 4,725,580

Land area: 236,800 sq. km

Major industries: tin and gypsum mining, timber, electric power, agricultural processing, construction

Major agricultural products: sweet potatoes, vegetables, corn, coffee, sugarcane, cotton, water buffalo, pigs, cattle, poultry

GDP: $5,907 million

GDP growth rate: 7%

Per capita GDP: $1,250

Average annual rate of inflation: 24.4%

Exports of goods and services: $429 million

Major export trading partners: Thailand 25.7%, Japan 10.0%, France 9.8%, Turkey 8.9%, Germany 7.5% (1995)

Imports of goods and services: $773 million

Major import trading partners: Thailand 60.0%, Turkey 8.2%, Singapore 5.5%, Japan 5.0%, Vietnam 4.3% (1995)

Foreign direct investment: $104 million

Aid from the United States, 1946–1999: $2,545.5 million

Latvia

Population: 2,490,000

Land area: 64,100 sq. km

Major industries: buses, vans, street and railroad cars, synthetic fibers, agricultural machinery, fertilizers, washing machines, radios, electronics, pharmaceuticals, processed foods, textiles; dependent on imports for energy, raw materials, and intermediate products

Major agricultural products: grain, sugar beets, potatoes, vegetables, meat, milk, eggs, fish

GDP: $9,087 million

GDP growth rate: 2%

Per capita GDP: $3,649

Average annual rate of inflation: 55.6%

Exports of goods and services: $2,335 million

Major export trading partners: Russia 22.8%, Germany 13.8%, UK 11.1%, Sweden 6.6%, EU–15 44.7%

Imports of goods and services: $2,781 million

Major import trading partners: Russia 20.2%, Germany 13.8%, Finland 9.2%, Sweden 7.9%, EU–15 49.3%

Foreign direct investment: $328 million

Aid from the United States, 1946–1999: $18.9 million

Lebanon

Population: 4,078,510

Land area: 10,400 sq. km

Major industries: banking, food processing, textiles, jewelry, cement, oil refining, chemicals, metal fabricating, wood

Major agricultural products: citrus, vegetables, potatoes, olives, tobacco, hemp (hashish), sheep, goats

GDP: $24,176 million

GDP growth rate: 4%

Per capita GDP: $5,928

Average annual rate of inflation: 17.2%

Exports of goods and services: $1,413 million

Major export trading partners: UAE[54] 28.7%, Saudi Arabia 11.1%, Syria 8.4%, France 6.0%, Kuwait 3.9%, U.S. 3.7%, Jordan 3.6% (1995)

Imports of goods and services: $7,596 million

Major import trading partners: Italy 13.0%, U.S. 10.6%, Germany 8.4%, France 7.6%, Switzerland 4.6%, UK 3.8%, Syria 3.2% (1995)

Foreign direct investment: $80 million

Aid from the United States, 1946–1999: $799.4 million

Lesotho

Population: 2,022,890

Land area: 30,350 sq. km

Major industries: food, beverages, textiles, handicrafts, construction, tourism

Major agricultural products: corn, wheat, pulses, sorghum, barley, livestock

GDP: $3,466 million

GDP growth rate: 12%

Per capita GDP: $1,713

Average annual rate of inflation: 11.9%

Exports of goods and services: $195 million

Major export trading partners: SACU 53.0%, North America 40.9%, EU–15 5.0% (1995)

Imports of goods and services: $1,017 million

Major import trading partners: SACU 81.8%, Asia 13.1%, EU–15 2.7% (1994)

Foreign direct investment: $28 million

Aid from the United States, 1946–1999: $376.4 million

Libya

Population: 5,166,640

Land area: 1,759,540 sq. km

Major industries: petroleum, food processing, textiles, handicrafts, cement

Major agricultural products: corn, wheat, pulses, sorghum, barley, livestock

GDP: $34.5 billion (1995 est.)

GDP growth rate: 2.2% (1995 est.)

Per capita GDP: $6,570 (1995 est.)

Average annual rate of inflation: -2.0%

Exports of goods and services: $8,400 million (1995 est.)

Major export trading partners:[55] Italy 41.6%, Germany 18.0%, Spain 10.0%, Turkey 4.1%, France 4.0%, Switzerland 2.9%, UK 2.1%, Austria 1.8%

Imports of goods and services:[56] $7,300 million (1995 est.)

Major import trading partners: Italy 21.7%, Germany 13.8%, UK 8.3%, France 6.7%, Turkey 5.5%, Spain 3.7%, Japan 2.9%, BLEU 2.8%

Foreign direct investment: n/a

Aid from the United States, 1946–1999: $230.1 million

Lithuania

Population: 3,709,000

Land area: 65,200 sq. km

Major industries: metal-cutting machine tools, electric motors, television sets, refrigerators and freezers, petroleum refining, shipbuilding (small ships), furniture making, textiles, food processing, fertilizers, agricultural machinery, optical equipment, electronic components, computers, amber

Major agricultural products: grain, potatoes, sugar beets, vegetables, meat, milk, eggs, fish, flax fiber

GDP: $16,475 million

GDP growth rate: 4%

Per capita GDP: $4,442

Average annual rate of inflation: n/a

Exports of goods and services: $4,079 million

Major export trading partners: Russia 23.8%, Germany 13.0%, Belarus 10.1%, Latvia 9.3%, Ukraine 7.7%

Imports of goods and services: $4,834 million

Major import trading partners: Russia 29.1%, Germany 15.7%, Poland 4.4%, Italy 3.9%, Denmark 3.6%

Foreign direct investment: $152 million

Aid from the United States, 1946–1999: $36.7 million

Luxembourg

Population: 415,550

Land area: 2,586 sq. km

Major industries: banking, iron and steel, food processing, chemicals, metal products, engineering, tires, glass, aluminum

Major agricultural products: barley, oats, potatoes, wheat, fruits, wine grapes, livestock products

GDP: $13,385 million

GDP growth rate: 4%

Per capita GDP: $32,211

Average annual rate of inflation: 4.5%

Exports of goods and services: $15,915 million (1995)

Major export trading partners:[57] Germany 20.6%, France 17.8%, Netherlands 13.3%, UK 9.0%, U.S. 4.4%

Imports of goods and services: $13,969 million (1995)

Major import trading partners: Germany 19.9%, Netherlands 18.5%, France 15.3%, UK 9.2%, U.S. 6.1%

Foreign direct investment: n/a

Aid from the United States, 1946–1999:[58] $1,864.4 million

Madagascar

Population: 13,704,620

Land area: 587,040 sq. km

Major industries: meat processing, soap, breweries, tanneries, sugar, textiles, glassware, cement, automobile assembly plant, paper, petroleum, tourism

Major agricultural products: coffee, vanilla, sugarcane, cloves, cocoa, rice, cassava (tapioca), beans, bananas, peanuts, livestock products

GDP: $12,839 million

GDP growth rate: 2%

Per capita GDP: $937

Average annual rate of inflation: 21.7%

Exports of goods and services: $753 million

Major export trading partners: France 41%, U.S., Japan, Italy (1995; percentages for U.S., France, and Italy not available)

Imports of goods and services: $1,004 million

Major import trading partners: France 40%, Japan, Hong Kong, Singapore, U.S. (1995; percentages for Japan, Hong Kong, Singapore, and U.S. not available)

Foreign direct investment: $10 million

Aid from the United States, 1946–1999: $524.3 million

Malawi

Population: 10,016,000

Land area: 118,480 sq. km

Major industries: tea, tobacco, sugar, sawmill products, cement, consumer goods

Major agricultural products: tobacco, sugarcane, cotton, tea, corn, potatoes, cassava (tapioca), sorghum, pulses, cattle, goats

GDP: $7,062 million

GDP growth rate: 14%

Per capita GDP: $705

Average annual rate of inflation: 26.6%

Exports of goods and services: $470 million

Major export trading partners:[59] U.S. 14.3%, South Africa 13.3%, Germany 10.3%, Japan 4.9%

Imports of goods and services: $604 million

Major import trading partners: South Africa 35.7%, Zimbabwe 17.8%, UK 5.0%, Germany 2.4%

Foreign direct investment: $1 million

Aid from the United States, 1946–1999: $758.5 million

Malaysia

Population: 20,565,000

Land area: 329,750 sq. km

Major industries: Peninsular Malaysia: rubber and oil palm processing and manufacturing, light manufacturing, electronics, tin mining and smelting, logging and timber processing; Sabah: logging, petroleum production; Sarawak: agriculture processing, petroleum production and refining, logging

Major agricultural products: Peninsular Malaysia: natural rubber, palm oil, rice; Sabah: subsistence crops, rubber, timber, coconut, rice; Sarawak: rubber, pepper, timber

GDP: $224,264 million

GDP growth rate: 8%

Per capita GDP: $10,905

Average annual rate of inflation: 3.0%

Exports of goods and services: $91,245 million

Major export trading partners: Singapore 20.5%, U.S. 18.2%, Japan 13.4%, Hong Kong 5.9%, Taiwan 4.1%, Thailand 4.1%, UK 3.4%

Imports of goods and services: $90,587 million

Major import trading partners: Japan 24.5%, U.S. 15.5%, Singapore 13.3%, South Korea 5.2%, Taiwan 5.0%, Germany 4.3%, Thailand 3.3%

Foreign direct investment: $4,500 million

Aid from the United States, 1946–1999: $291.7 million

Mali

Population: 9,998,680

Land area: 1.24 million sq. km

Major industries: minor local consumer goods production and food processing; construction, phosphate and gold mining

Major agricultural products: cotton, millet, rice, corn, vegetables, peanuts, cattle, sheep, goats

GDP: $7,270 million

GDP growth rate: 4%

Per capita GDP: $727

Average annual rate of inflation: 5.7%

Exports of goods and services: $553 million

Major export trading partners:[60] Thailand 23.2%, Taiwan 14.3%, Italy 13.6%, Portugal 8.9%

Imports of goods and services: $945 million

Major import trading partners: France 19.2%, Ivory Coast 17.8%, Senegal 5.1%, UK 3.7%

Foreign direct investment: $23 million

Aid from the United States, 1946–1999: $847.5 million

Malta

Population: 373,000

Land area: 320 sq. km

Major industries: tourism, electronics, shipbuilding and repair, construction, food and beverages, textiles, footwear, clothing, tobacco

Major agricultural products: potatoes, cauliflower, grapes, wheat, barley, tomatoes, citrus, cut flowers, green peppers, pork, milk, poultry, eggs

GDP: $4,962 million (1995)

GDP growth rate: 9% (1995)

Per capita GDP: $13,373 (1995)

Average annual rate of inflation: 2.8%

Exports of goods and services: $1,900 million (1995)

Major export trading partners: Italy 38.5%, Germany 17.8%, France 9.0%, UK 7.3%, U.S. 4.2%, Singapore 2.8% (1995)

Imports of goods and services: $3,000 million (CIF,[61] 1995)

Major import trading partners: Italy 27.3%, UK 15.5%, Germany 12.1%, France 8.8%, U.S. 6.0%, Singapore 5.6%

Foreign direct investment: $300 million

Aid from the United States, 1946–1999: $85.5 million

Mauritania

Population: 2,332,480

Land area: 1,030,700 sq. km

Major industries: fish processing, iron ore and gypsum mining

Major agricultural products: dates, millet, sorghum, root crops, cattle, sheep, fish products

GDP: $4,450 million

GDP growth rate: 4%

Per capita GDP: $1,908

Average annual rate of inflation: 7.0%

Exports of goods and services: $587 million

Major export trading partners: Japan 21.8%, Italy 16.1%, France 13.9%, Spain 9.1%

Imports of goods and services: $676 million

Major import trading partners: France 29.2%, Algeria 9.9%, Spain 6.9%, China 6.5%

Foreign direct investment: $5 million

Aid from the United States, 1946–1999: $212.2 million

Mauritius

Population: 1,134,000

Land area: 1,860 sq. km

Major industries: food processing (largely sugar milling), textiles, wearing apparel, chemicals, metal products, transport equipment, non-electrical machinery, tourism

Major agricultural products: sugarcane, tea, corn, potatoes, bananas, pulses, cattle, goats, fish

GDP: $10,330 million

GDP growth rate: 6%

Per capita GDP: $9,109

Average annual rate of inflation: 8.6%

Exports of goods and services: $2,622 million

Major export trading partners: UK 35%, France 20%, U.S. 13%, Germany 6%

Imports of goods and services: $2,787 million

Major import trading partners: South Africa 12%, France 11%, India 9%, UK 6%, Germany 5%, Japan 4%, Hong Kong 4%, Taiwan 3%

Foreign direct investment: $36.7 million

Aid from the United States, 1946–1999: $85.8 million

Mexico

Population: 93,182,000

Land area: 1,972,550 sq. km

Major industries: food and beverages, tobacco, chemicals, iron and steel, petroleum, mining, textiles, clothing, motor vehicles, consumer durables, tourism

Major agricultural products: corn, wheat, soybeans, rice, beans, cotton, coffee, fruit, tomatoes, beef, poultry, dairy products, wood products

GDP: $743,840 million

GDP growth rate: 6%

Per capita GDP: $7,983

Average annual rate of inflation: 52.0%

Exports of goods and services: $75,002 million

Major export trading partners: U.S. 83.9%, Canada 2.3%, Japan 1.4%, Spain 1.0%

Imports of goods and services: $66,764 million

Major import trading partners: U.S. 75.5%, Japan 4.6%, Germany 3.5%, France 1.1%

Foreign direct investment: $7,619 million

Aid from the United States, 1946–1999: $822.6 million

Moldova

Population: 4,327,000

Land area: 33,700 sq. km

Major industries: food processing, agricultural machinery, foundry equipment, refrigerators and freezers, washing machines, hosiery, sugar, vegetable oil, shoes, textiles

Major agricultural products: vegetables, fruits, wine, grain, sugar beets, sunflower seed, tobacco, meat, milk

GDP: $6,342 million

GDP growth rate:[62] -9%

Per capita GDP: $1,466

Average annual rate of inflation: n/a

Exports of goods and services: $937 million

Major export trading partners: Russia, Kazakhstan, Ukraine, Romania, Germany (percentages not available)

Imports of goods and services: $1,193 million

Major import trading partners: Russia, Ukraine, Uzbekistan, Romania, Germany (percentages not available)

Foreign direct investment: $41 million

Aid from the United States, 1946–1999:[63] $134.8 million

Mongolia

Population: 2,516,240

Land area: 1.565 million sq. km

Major industries: copper, construction materials, mining (particularly coal), food and beverages, animal product processing

Major agricultural products: wheat, barley, potatoes, forage crops, sheep, goats, cattle, camels, horses

GDP: $4,667 million

GDP growth rate: 3%

Per capita GDP: $1,855

Average annual rate of inflation: 52.2%

Exports of goods and services: $423 million

Major export trading partners: Russia 20.6%, China 17.7%, Kazakhstan 12.8%, South Korea 8.0%

Imports of goods and services: $444 million

Major import trading partners: Russia 34.2%, Japan 17.5%, China 14.6%, Germany 4.7%

Foreign direct investment: $5 million

Aid from the United States, 1946–1999: $120.2 million

Morocco

Population: 27,020,350

Land area: 446,550 sq. km

Major industries: phosphate rock mining and processing, food processing, leather goods, textiles, construction, tourism

Major agricultural products: barley, wheat, citrus, wine, vegetables, olives, livestock

GDP: $92,759 million

GDP growth rate: 12%

Per capita GDP: $3,433

Average annual rate of inflation: 5.0%

Exports of goods and services: $9,259 million

Major export trading partners: France 28.3%, Spain 9.9%, Japan 6.9%, India 6.3%, Italy 6.3%

Imports of goods and services: $11,010 million

Major import trading partners: France 20.9%, Spain 8.8%, U.S. 7.4%, Italy 7.2%, Germany 6.1%

Foreign direct investment: $311 million

Aid from the United States, 1946–1999: $3,735.7 million

Mozambique

Population: 18,028,000

Land area: 801,590 sq. km

Major industries: food, beverages, chemicals (fertilizer, soap, paints), petroleum products, textiles, cement, glass, asbestos, tobacco

Major agricultural products: cotton, cashew nuts, sugarcane, tea, cassava (tapioca), corn, rice, tropical fruits, beef, poultry

GDP: $10,016 million

GDP growth rate: 6%

Per capita GDP: $556

Average annual rate of inflation: 59.7%

Exports of goods and services: $473 million

Major export trading partners:[64] Spain 17.1%, South Africa 15.8%, Portugal 11.7%, U.S. 10.4%

Imports of goods and services: $959 million

Major import trading partners: South Africa 54.6%, Zimbabwe 6.6%, Saudi Arabia 5.4%, Portugal 3.8%

Foreign direct investment: $29 million

Aid from the United States, 1946–1999: $1,275.5 million

Myanmar (formerly Burma)

Population: 45,882,990

Land area: 678,500 sq. km

Major industries: agricultural processing, textiles and footwear, wood and wood products, copper, tin, tungsten, iron, construction materials, pharmaceuticals, fertilizer

Major agricultural products: paddy rice, corn, oilseed, sugarcane, pulses, hardwood

GDP: $51.5 billion (1996 est.)

GDP growth rate: 6%

Per capita GDP: $1,120 (1996 est.)

Average annual rate of inflation: 24.7%

Exports of goods and services: $1,100 million (1996 est.)

Major export trading partners: Singapore, China, Thailand, Hong Kong, Indonesia, Malaysia, Japan (percentages not available)

Imports of goods and services: $2,000 million (1996 est.)

Major import trading partners: Singapore, Hong Kong, Japan, China, Malaysia, Thailand (percentages not available)

Foreign direct investment: $100 million

Aid from the United States, 1946–1999: $328.0 million

Namibia

Population: 1,584,380

Land area: 825,418 sq. km

Major industries: meat packing, fish processing, dairy products, mining (diamond, lead, zinc, tin, silver, tungsten, uranium, copper)

Major agricultural products: millet, sorghum, peanuts, livestock; fish catch potential of over 1 million metric tons not being fulfilled

GDP: $8,290 million

GDP growth rate: 3%

Per capita GDP: $5,232

Average annual rate of inflation: 11.9%

Exports of goods and services: $1,591 million

Major export trading partners: UK 37%, South Africa 25%, Spain 10%, Japan 8% (1994)

Imports of goods and services: $1,868 million

Major import trading partners: South Africa 85%, Ivory Coast 3%, Japan 3%, Germany 2% (1994)

Foreign direct investment: n/a

Aid from the United States, 1946–1999: $135.0 million

Nepal

Population: 22,037,160

Land area: 140,800 sq. km

Major industries: tourism, carpets, textiles, small mills (rice, jute, sugar, oilseed), cigarettes, cement and brick production

Major agricultural products: rice, corn, wheat, sugarcane, root crops, milk, water buffalo meat

GDP: $23,677 million

GDP growth rate: 5%

Per capita GDP: $1,074

Average annual rate of inflation: 11.3%

Exports of goods and services: $1,003 million

Major export trading partners: India, U.S., Germany, UK (percentages not available)

Imports of goods and services: $1,653 million

Major import trading partners: India, Singapore, Japan, Germany (percentages not available)

Foreign direct investment: $19 million

Aid from the United States, 1946–1999: $722.9 million

The Netherlands

Population: 15,517,000

Land area: 37,330 sq. km

Major industries: agroindustries, metal and engineering products, electrical machinery and equipment, chemicals, petroleum, fishing, construction, microelectronics

Major agricultural products: grains, potatoes, sugar beets, fruits, vegetables, livestock

GDP: $318,140 million

GDP growth rate: 3%

Per capita GDP: $20,503

Average annual rate of inflation: 1.1%

Exports of goods and services: $210,665 million (1995)

Major export trading partners: Germany 28.7%, BLEU 13.2%, France 11.1%, UK 9.6%, Italy 5.9%, EU–15 80.2%

Imports of goods and services: $185,461 million (1995)

Major import trading partners: Germany 22.4%, BLEU 11.2%, UK 10.0%, U.S. 8.1%, France 7.4%, EU–15 64.2%

Foreign direct investment: $7,824 million

Aid from the United States, 1946–1999: $2,312.3 million

New Zealand

Population: 3,635,000

Land area: 268,680 sq. km

Major industries: food processing, wood and paper products, textiles, machinery, transportation equipment, banking and insurance, tourism, mining

Major agricultural products: wheat, barley, potatoes, pulses, fruits, vegetables, wool, meat, dairy products, fish

GDP: $64,551 million

GDP growth rate: 2%

Per capita GDP: $17,758

Average annual rate of inflation: 6.2%

Exports of goods and services: $17,834 million (1995)

Major export trading partners: Australia 20.3%, Japan 15.3%, U.S. 9.1%, UK 6.4%

Imports of goods and services: $17,239 million (1995)

Major import trading partners: Australia 23.5%, U.S. 15.9%, Japan 13.5%, UK 5.1%

Foreign direct investment: $280 million

Aid from the United States, 1946–1999: $8.6 million

Nicaragua

Population: 4,503,120

Land area: 129,494 sq. km

Major industries: food processing, chemicals, metal products, textiles, clothing, petroleum refining and distribution, beverages, footwear

Major agricultural products: coffee, bananas, sugarcane, cotton, rice, corn, cassava (tapioca), citrus, beans, beef, veal, pork, poultry, dairy products

GDP: $9,343 million

GDP growth rate: 5%

Per capita GDP: $2,075

Average annual rate of inflation: 2,408.8%

Exports of goods and services: $803 million

Major export trading partners: U.S. 46.7%, Germany 11.0%, El Salvador 7.1%, France 4.5%, Spain 3.5% (1995)

Imports of goods and services: $1,294 million

Major import trading partners: U.S. 26.3%, Costa Rica 14.9%, Venezuela 9.8%, Guatemala 8.0%, El Salvador 4.7% (1995)

Foreign direct investment: $45 million

Aid from the United States, 1946–1999: $1,379.3 million

Niger

Population: 9,335,410

Land area: 1.267 million sq. km

Major industries: cement, brick, textiles, food processing, chemicals, slaughterhouses, a few other small light industries, uranium mining

Major agricultural products: cowpeas, cotton, peanuts, millet, sorghum, cassava (tapioca), rice, cattle, sheep, goats

GDP: $8,715 million

GDP growth rate: 3%

Per capita GDP: $934

Average annual rate of inflation: 4.0%

Exports of goods and services: $314 million

Major export trading partners:[65] France 73.9%, Burkina Faso 8.1%, Canada 3.7%, Nigeria 3.1% (1994)

Imports of goods and services: $430 million

Major import trading partners: France 19.2%, Ivory Coast 12.0%, China 8.1%, BLEU 3.7% (1994)

Foreign direct investment: $0

Aid from the United States, 1946–1999: $690.7 million

Nigeria

Population: 114,568,100

Land area: 923,770 sq. km

Major industries: crude oil, coal, tin, columbite, palm oil, peanuts, cotton, rubber, wood, hides and skins, textiles, cement and other construction materials, food products, footwear, chemicals, fertilizer, printing, ceramics, steel

Major agricultural products: cocoa, peanuts, palm oil, corn, rice, sorghum, millet, cassava (tapioca), yams, rubber, cattle, sheep, goats, pigs; fishing and forest resources extensively exploited

GDP: $102,460 million

GDP growth rate: 4%

Per capita GDP: $894

Average annual rate of inflation: 33.3%

Exports of goods and services: $5,409 million

Major export trading partners: U.S. 39.4%, Spain 8.9%, France 6.3%, India 4.9%, Germany 4.9% (1995)

Imports of goods and services: $3,605 million

Major import trading partners: UK 13.4%, U.S. 11.8%, Germany 10.9%, France 8.2%, Netherlands 5.7% (1995)

Foreign direct investment: $1,391 million

Aid from the United States, 1946–1999: $553.1 million

Norway

Population: 4,381,000

Land area: 324,220 sq. km

Major industries: petroleum and gas, food processing, shipbuilding, pulp and paper products, metals, chemicals, timber, mining, textiles, fishing

Major agricultural products: oats, other grains, beef, milk; livestock output exceeds value of crops; among world's top 10 fishing nations, with catch of 2.33 million metric tons in 1994

GDP: $102,795 million

GDP growth rate: 5%

Per capita GDP: $23,464

Average annual rate of inflation: 2.9%

Exports of goods and services: $63,983 million

Major export trading partners: UK 19.8%, Germany 12.7%, Sweden 9.8%, Netherlands 9.1%, France 7.8%, EU–15 77.2%, U.S. 6.0% (1995)

Imports of goods and services: $49,612 million

Major import trading partners: Sweden 15.4%, Germany 13.8%, UK 9.7%, Denmark 7.5%, Netherlands 4.4%, EU–15 71.0%, U.S. 6.6% (1995)

Foreign direct investment: $3,960 million

Aid from the United States, 1946–1999: $1,243.7 million

Oman

Population: 2,173,000

Land area: 212,460 sq. km

Major industries: crude oil production and refining, natural gas production, construction, cement, copper

Major agricultural products: dates, limes, bananas, alfalfa, vegetables, camels, cattle; annual fish catch averages 100,000 metric tons

GDP: $20,953 million (1995)

GDP growth rate: 3% (1995)

Per capita GDP: $9,814 (1995)

Average annual rate of inflation: -2.6%

Exports of goods and services: $5,594 million (1994)

Major export trading partners: Japan 27.7%, South Korea 17.2%, Thailand 15.0%, China 11.8%, U.S. 6.4%

Imports of goods and services: $4,494 million (1994)

Major import trading partners: UAE[66] 22.4%, Japan 15.4%, UK 15.1%, France 5.9%, Germany 5.3%

Foreign direct investment: $67 million

Aid from the United States, 1946–1999: $372.3 million

Pakistan

Population: 133,510,380

Land area: 803,940 sq. km

Major industries: textiles, food processing, beverages, construction materials, clothing, paper products, shrimp

Major agricultural products: cotton, wheat, rice, sugarcane, fruits, vegetables, milk, beef, mutton, eggs

GDP: $214,318 million

GDP growth rate: 5%

Per capita GDP: $1,605

Average annual rate of inflation: 8.9%

Exports of goods and services: $10,703 million

Major export trading partners: U.S. 17.8%, Hong Kong 9.3%, Germany 7.5%, UK 7.2%, Japan 5.8%, Dubai 4.6%

Imports of goods and services: $13,567 million

Major import trading partners: U.S. 12.0%, Japan 8.7%, Kuwait 6.9%, Saudi Arabia 5.9%, Germany 5.6%, Malaysia 4.7%

Foreign direct investment: $690 million

Aid from the United States, 1946–1999: $10,924.3 million

Panama

Population: 2,674,000

Land area: 78,200 sq. km

Major industries: construction, petroleum refining, brewing, cement and other construction materials, sugar milling

Major agricultural products: bananas, rice, corn, coffee, sugarcane, vegetables, livestock, fish (shrimp)

GDP: $19,276 million

GDP growth rate: 3%

Per capita GDP: $7,209

Average annual rate of inflation: 2.0%

Exports of goods and services: $7,759 million

Major export trading partners: U.S. 47.6%, Switzerland 10.2%, Costa Rica 6.6%, Germany 4.4%, BLEU 4.2%

Imports of goods and services: $7,520 million

Major import trading partners: U.S. 37.3%, Colón Free Zone 13.6%, Venezuela 7.1%, Japan 6.0%, Ecuador 3.8%

Foreign direct investment: $238 million

Aid from the United States, 1946–1999: $1,204.8 million

Papua New Guinea

Population: 4,401,280

Land area: 462,840 sq. km

Major industries: copra crushing, palm oil processing, plywood production, wood chip production, mining (gold, silver, copper), crude oil production, construction, tourism

Major agricultural products: coffee, cocoa, coconuts, palm kernels, tea, rubber, sweet potatoes, fruit, vegetables, poultry, pork

GDP: $13,402 million

GDP growth rate: 2%

Per capita GDP: $3,045

Average annual rate of inflation: 5.2%

Exports of goods and services: $2,957 million

Major export trading partners: Australia, Japan, U.S., Singapore, New Zealand (percentages not available)

Imports of goods and services: $2,278 million

Major import trading partners: Australia, Japan, UK, New Zealand, Netherlands (percentages not available)

Foreign direct investment: $225 million

Aid from the United States, 1946–1999: $33.8 million

Paraguay

Population: 4,955,000

Land area: 406,750 sq. km

Major industries: meat packing, oilseed crushing, milling, brewing, textiles, other light consumer goods, cement, construction

Major agricultural products: cotton, sugarcane, soybeans, corn, wheat, tobacco, cassava (tapioca), fruits, vegetables, beef, pork, eggs, milk, timber

GDP: $17,440 million

GDP growth rate: 1%

Per capita GDP: $3,520

Average annual rate of inflation: 23.4%

Exports of goods and services: $1,998 million

Major export trading partners: Brazil 49.9%, Argentina 9.2%, Uruguay 4.2%

Imports of goods and services: $2,499 million

Major import trading partners: Brazil 32.7%, Argentina 19.5%, Uruguay 2.0%

Foreign direct investment: $220 million

Aid from the United States, 1946–1999: $309.3 million

Peru

Population: 24,287,500

Land area: 1,285,220 sq. km

Major industries: metals mining, petroleum, fishing, textiles, clothing, food processing, cement, auto assembly, steel, shipbuilding, metal fabrication

Major agricultural products: coffee, cotton, sugarcane, rice, wheat, potatoes, plantains, coca, poultry, red meats, dairy products, wool, fish

GDP: $109,849 million

GDP growth rate: 3%

Per capita GDP: $4,523

Average annual rate of inflation: 447.1%

Exports of goods and services: $7,367 million

Major export trading partners: U.S. 19.9%, Japan 7.3%, UK 7.3%, China 7.2%, Germany 5.2%, Brazil 4.1%, Italy 3.4%

Imports of goods and services: $10,040 million

Major import trading partners: U.S. 30.7%, Colombia 7.3%, Chile 5.7%, Spain 5.7%, Brazil 4.2%, Germany 3.9%, Japan 3.7%

Foreign direct investment: $3,581 million

Aid from the United States, 1946–1999: $3,489.3 million

The Philippines

Population: 71,899,000

Land area: 300,000 sq. km

Major industries: textiles, pharmaceuticals, chemicals, wood products, food processing, electronics assembly, petroleum refining, fishing

Major agricultural products: rice, coconuts, corn, sugarcane, bananas, pineapples, mangoes, pork, eggs, beef; fish catch of 2 million metric tons annually

GDP: $245,586 million

GDP growth rate: 6%

Per capita GDP: $3,416

Average annual rate of inflation: 8.1%

Exports of goods and services: $35,177 million

Major export trading partners: U.S. 35.3%, Japan 15.7%, Singapore 5.7%, UK 5.3%, Hong Kong 4.7%, Netherlands 4.6%, Thailand 4.6% (1995)

Imports of goods and services: $43,386 million

Major import trading partners: Japan 22.4%, U.S. 18.9%, Singapore 5.9%, Saudi Arabia 6.2%, Taiwan 5.4%, South Korea 5.1%, Hong Kong 4.8% (1995)

Foreign direct investment: $1,408 million

Aid from the United States, 1946–1999: $8,864.1 million

Poland

Population: 38,618,000

Land area: 312,683 sq. km

Major industries: machine building, iron and steel, coal mining, chemicals, shipbuilding, food processing, glass, beverages, textiles

Major agricultural products: potatoes, milk, fruits, vegetables, wheat, poultry and eggs, pork, beef

GDP: $232,340 million

GDP growth rate: 6%

Per capita GDP: $6,016

Average annual rate of inflation: 68.0%

Exports of goods and services: $31,113 million

Major export trading partners: Germany 34.5%, Russia 6.8%, France 5.9%, Italy 5.6%, U.S. 4.8%, Netherlands 4.1%, UK 3.9%

Imports of goods and services: $34,872 million

Major import trading partners: Germany 26.5%, Italy 10.4%, Russia 7.3%, UK 6.3%, Netherlands 4.8%, France 4.4%, U.S. 2.3%

Foreign direct investment: $4,498 million

Aid from the United States, 1946–1999: $1,211.3 million

Portugal

Population: 9,930,000

Land area: 92,391 sq. km

Major industries: textiles and footwear, wood pulp, paper, cork, metalworking, oil refining, chemicals, fish canning, wine, tourism

Major agricultural products: grain, potatoes, olives, grapes, sheep, cattle, goats, poultry, meat, dairy products

GDP: $134,399 million

GDP growth rate: 3%

Per capita GDP: $13,535

Average annual rate of inflation: 10.1%

Exports of goods and services: $33,253 million (1995)

Major export trading partners: Germany 21.2%, Spain 14.2%, France 14.1%, UK 10.8%, Netherlands 4.9%, U.S. 4.6%, EU–15 80.0%

Imports of goods and services: $40,428 million (1995)

Major import trading partners: Spain 22.4%, Germany 15.5%, France 11.1%, Italy 8.3%, UK 6.7%, Netherlands 4.4%, EU–15 75.6%

Foreign direct investment: $618 million

Aid from the United States, 1946–1999: $3,655.9 million

Qatar

Population: 658,000

Land area: 11,437 sq. km

Major industries: crude oil production and refining, fertilizers, petrochemicals, steel reinforcing bars, cement

Major agricultural products: fruits, vegetables, poultry, dairy products, beef, fish (all on a small scale)

GDP: $11,119 million (1995)

GDP growth rate:[67] 7% (1995)

Per capita GDP: $17,319 (1995)

Average annual rate of inflation: n/a

Exports of goods and services: $4 billion (1996 est.)

Major export trading partners: Japan 54.3%, Singapore 7.3%, South Korea 5.8%, Australia 3.5%, UAE[68] 3.4% (1995)

Imports of goods and services:[69] $4.4 billion (1996 est.)

Major import trading partners: Italy 15.5%, Germany 11.2%, Japan 10.2%, France 8.7%, UK 8.7% (1995)

Foreign direct investment: n/a

Aid from the United States, 1946–1999: $0

Romania

Population: 22,608,000

Land area: 237,500 sq. km

Major industries: mining, timber, construction materials, metallurgy, chemicals, machine building, food processing, petroleum production and refining

Major agricultural products: wheat, corn, sugar beets, sunflower seed, potatoes, grapes, milk, eggs, meat

GDP: $104,727 million

GDP growth rate: 4%

Per capita GDP: $4,632

Average annual rate of inflation: 67.2%

Exports of goods and services: $9,553 million

Major export trading partners: Germany 17.9%, Italy 16.6%, France 5.5%, Turkey 5.0%, Netherlands 4.2%, China 3.0%

Imports of goods and services: $11,867 million

Major import trading partners: Germany 17.1%, Italy 15.6%, Russia 12.6%, France 5.0%, U.S. 3.8%, Egypt 3.8%

Foreign direct investment: $263 million

Aid from the United States, 1946–1999: $308.0 million

Russia

Population: 147,739,000

Land area: 17,075,200 sq. km

Major industries: complete range of mining and extractive industries producing coal, oil, gas, chemicals, metals; all forms of machine building from rolling mills to high-performance aircraft and space vehicles; shipbuilding, road and rail transportation equipment, communications equipment, agricultural machinery, tractors, construction equipment, electric power generating and transmitting equipment, medical and scientific instruments, consumer durables, textiles, foodstuffs, handicrafts

Major agricultural products: grain, sugar beets, sunflower seed, vegetables, fruits, meat, milk

GDP: $630,735 million

GDP growth rate: -5%

Per capita GDP: $4,269

Average annual rate of inflation: 197.9%

Exports of goods and services: $99,201 million

Major export trading partners: CIS 20.5%, Ukraine 9.0%, Germany 8.0%, U.S. 6.0%, China 6.0%

Imports of goods and services: $84,804 million

Major import trading partners: CIS 29.9%, Ukraine 14.0%, Germany 11.0%, Kazakhstan 7.0%, U.S. 6.0%

Foreign direct investment: $2,479 million

Aid from the United States, 1946–1999:[70] $969.3 million

Rwanda

Population: 6,727,000

Land area: 26,340 sq. km

Major industries: cassiterite (tin ore) and wolframite (tungsten ore) mining, tin, cement, agricultural product processing, small-scale beverage production, soap, furniture, shoes, plastic goods, textiles, cigarettes

Major agricultural products: coffee, tea, pyrethrum (insecticide made from chrysanthemums), bananas, beans, sorghum, potatoes, livestock

GDP: $4,280 million

GDP growth rate: 11%

Per capita GDP: $636

Average annual rate of inflation: 10.0%

Exports of goods and services: $81,319 million

Major export trading partners:[71] Brazil 45.5%, BLEU 14.3%, Germany 7.8%, Netherlands 7.8%, UK 1.9% (1995)

Imports of goods and services: $296 million

Major import trading partners: Kenya 19.3%, BLEU 17.5%, Uganda 7.3%, UAE[72] 6.3%, Tanzania 4.4% (1996)

Foreign direct investment: $1 million

Aid from the United States, 1946–1999: $541.1 million

Samoa (formerly Western Samoa)

Population: 171,700

Land area: 2,860 sq. km

Major industries: timber, tourism, food processing, fishing

Major agricultural products: coconuts, bananas, taro, yams

GDP: $415 million (1995 est.)

GDP growth rate: 6%

Per capita GDP: $2,417

Average annual rate of inflation: 11.5%

Exports of goods and services: $8.7 million (1995)

Major export trading partners: New Zealand 44%, Australia 22%, American Samoa, Germany (percentages for American Samoa and Germany not available)

Imports of goods and services: $91 million (CIF,[73] 1995)

Major import trading partners: New Zealand 37%, Australia 21%, U.S./American Samoa 13%

Foreign direct investment: $4 million

Aid from the United States, 1946–1999: $31.0 million

Saudi Arabia

Population: 19,409,000

Land area: 1,960,582 sq. km

Major industries: crude oil production, petroleum refining, basic petrochemicals, cement, two small steel-rolling mills, construction, fertilizer, plastics

Major agricultural products: wheat, barley, tomatoes, melons, dates, citrus, mutton, chickens, eggs, milk

GDP: $188,049 million (1995)

GDP growth rate: 2%

Per capita GDP: $9,908 (1995)

Average annual rate of inflation: -0.7%

Exports of goods and services: $52,676 million (1995)

Major export trading partners: Japan 16.9%, U.S. 15.0%, South Korea 10.6%, Singapore 7.9%, France 4.5%, Netherlands 3.2%

Imports of goods and services: $37,621 million (1995)

Major import trading partners: U.S. 22.0%, UK 11.9%, Japan 9.1%, Germany 7.7%, Italy 5.6%, South Korea 3.3%

Foreign direct investment: n/a

Aid from the United States, 1946–1999: $324.1 million

Senegal

Population: 8,534,180

Land area: 196,190 sq. km

Major industries: agricultural and fish processing, phosphate mining, petroleum refining, construction materials

Major agricultural products: peanuts, millet, corn, sorghum, rice, cotton, tomatoes, green vegetables, cattle, poultry, pigs, fish

GDP: $14,446 million

GDP growth rate: 6%

Per capita GDP: $1,693

Average annual rate of inflation: 5.7%

Exports of goods and services: $1,587 million

Major export trading partners:[74] France 20.3%, India 18.5%, Italy 8.5%, Mali 6.5%

Imports of goods and services: $1,851 million

Major import trading partners: France 35.5%, Germany 4.7%, U.S. 3.6%, India 3.2% (1995)

Foreign direct investment: $45 million

Aid from the United States, 1946–1999: $1,005.8 million

Sierra Leone

Population: 4,630,000

Land area: 71,740 sq. km

Major industries: mining (diamonds, bauxite, rutile), small-scale manufacturing (beverages, textiles, cigarettes, footwear), petroleum refining

Major agricultural products: rice, coffee, cocoa, palm kernels, palm oil, peanuts, poultry, cattle, sheep, pigs, fish

GDP: $2,409 million

GDP growth rate: 5%

Per capita GDP: $520

Average annual rate of inflation: 60.4%

Exports of goods and services: $111 million

Major export trading partners:[75] BLEU 38.7%, U.S. 10.3%, UK 3.9%, Germany 1.0%

Imports of goods and services: $290 million

Major import trading partners: UK 16.0%, U.S. 8.9%, Ivory Coast 7.7%, BLEU 3.4%

Foreign direct investment: $5 million

Aid from the United States, 1946–1999: $297.0 million

Singapore

Population: 3,044,000

Land area: 647.5 sq. km

Major industries: petroleum refining, electronics, oil drilling equipment, rubber processing and rubber products, processed food and beverages, ship repair, entrepot trade, financial services, biotechnology

Major agricultural products: rubber, copra, fruit, vegetables, poultry

GDP: $81,214 million

GDP growth rate: 7%

Per capita GDP: $26,680

Average annual rate of inflation: 2.8%

Exports of goods and services: $159,434 million (1995)

Major export trading partners: U.S. 18.4%, Malaysia 18.0%, Hong Kong 8.9%, Japan 8.2%, Thailand 5.7%, Germany 3.1%, UK 2.8%

Imports of goods and services: $144,329 million (1995)

Major import trading partners: Japan 18.2%, U.S. 16.3%, Malaysia 15.0%, Thailand 5.5%, Taiwan 4.1%, Saudi Arabia 3.8%, Germany 3.6%

Foreign direct investment: $9,440 million

Aid from the United States, 1946–1999: $22.5 million

Slovak Republic

Population: 5,343,000

Land area: 48,845 sq. km

Major industries: metal and metal products, food and beverages, electricity, gas, coke, oil, nuclear fuel, chemicals and manmade fibers, machinery, paper and printing, earthenware and ceramics, transport vehicles, textiles, electrical and optical apparatus, rubber products

Major agricultural products: grains, potatoes, sugar beets, hops, fruit, hogs, cattle, poultry, forest products

GDP: $39,953 million

GDP growth rate: 7%

Per capita GDP: $7,478

Average annual rate of inflation: 7.7%

Exports of goods and services: $10,896 million

Major export trading partners: EU–15 37.4%, CEFTA 44.3% (Czech Republic 35.2%), FSU 7.1% (1995)

Imports of goods and services: $12,994 million

Major import trading partners: EU–15 34.7%, CEFTA 32.9% (Czech Republic 27.5%), FSU 19.5% (1995)

Foreign direct investment: $281 million

Aid from the United States, 1946–1999:[76] $78.3 million

Slovenia

Population: 1,991,000

Land area: 20,256 sq. km

Major industries: ferrous metallurgy and rolling mill products, aluminum reduction and rolled products, lead and zinc smelting, electronics (including military electronics), trucks, electric power equipment, wood products, textiles, chemicals, machine tools

Major agricultural products: potatoes, hops, wheat, sugar beets, corn, grapes, cattle, sheep, poultry

GDP: $23,911 million

GDP growth rate:[77] 6%

Per capita GDP: $12,010

Average annual rate of inflation: n/a

Exports of goods and services: $10,220 million

Major export trading partners: Germany 30.1%, Italy 14.6%, Croatia 10.5%, France 8.2%, Austria 6.4%, FSU 4.5%, U.S. 3.1%, EU–15 67.0% (1995)

Imports of goods and services: $10,367 million

Major import trading partners: Germany 23.0%, Italy 16.9%, Austria 9.6%, France 8.4%, Croatia 6.1%, U.S. 3.0%, FSU 2.8%, EU–15 68.5% (1995)

Foreign direct investment: $186 million

Aid from the United States, 1946–1999:[78] $12.8 million

Somalia

Population: 9,805,460

Land area: 637,660 sq. km

Major industries: a few small industries, including sugar refining, textiles, petroleum refining (mostly shut down)

Major agricultural products: bananas, sorghum, corn, mangoes, sugarcane, cattle, sheep, goats; fishing potential largely unexploited

GDP: $3.6 billion (1995 est.)

GDP growth rate: 2% (1995 est.)

Per capita GDP: $367

Average annual rate of inflation: 58.5%

Exports of goods and services: $130 million (1994 est.)

Major export trading partners:[79] Saudi Arabia 57%, Yemen 14%, Italy 13% (1995)

Imports of goods and services: $269 million (1994 est.)

Major import trading partners: Kenya 24%, Djibouti 18%, Pakistan 6% (1995)

Foreign direct investment: $0

Aid from the United States, 1946–1999: $1,146.6 million

South Africa

Population: 37,643,000

Land area: 1,219,912 sq. km

Major industries: mining (world's largest producer of platinum, gold, chromium), automobile assembly, metalworking, machinery, textiles, iron and steel, chemicals, fertilizer, foodstuffs

Major agricultural products: corn, wheat, sugarcane, fruits, vegetables, beef, poultry, mutton, wool, dairy products

GDP: $286,961 million

GDP growth rate: 3%

Per capita GDP: $7,623

Average annual rate of inflation: 13.1%

Exports of goods and services: $33,419 million

Major export trading partners: Japan 6.8%, U.S. 5.9%, Italy 5.8%, Germany 4.9%, UK 4.6%

Imports of goods and services: $32,481 million

Major import trading partners: Germany 12.9%, U.S. 11.0%, UK 10.4%, Japan 7.3%, Italy 4.2%

Foreign direct investment: $136 million

Aid from the United States, 1946–1999: $996.2 million

Spain

Population: 39,259,930

Land area: 504,750 sq. km

Major industries: textiles and apparel (including footwear), food and beverages, metals and metal manufacturing, chemicals, shipbuilding, automobiles, machine tools, tourism

Major agricultural products: grain, vegetables, olives, wine grapes, sugar beets, citrus, beef, pork, poultry, dairy products; fish catch of 866,831 metric tons in 1993

GDP: $608,498 million

GDP growth rate: 2%

Per capita GDP: $15,499

Average annual rate of inflation: 6.3%

Exports of goods and services: $132,405 million (1995)

Major export trading partners: EU–15 71.4%, U.S. 4.2%, Japan 1.2%, NICs 2.0%, OPEC 2.7%, Latin America 5.3%

Imports of goods and services: $130,290 million (1995)

Major import trading partners: EU–15 66.3%, U.S. 6.3%, Japan 2.8%, NICs 1.8%, OPEC 6.2%, Latin America 3.1%

Foreign direct investment: $6,396 million

Aid from the United States, 1946–1999: $4,531.9 million

Sri Lanka

Population: 18,300,000

Land area: 65,610 sq. km

Major industries: agricultural commodity (rubber, tea, coconuts, other) processing, clothing, cement, petroleum refining, textiles, tobacco

Major agricultural products: rice, sugarcane, grains, pulses, oilseed, roots, spices, tea, rubber, coconuts, milk, eggs, hides, meat

GDP: $42,526 million

GDP growth rate: 4%

Per capita GDP: $2,324

Average annual rate of inflation: 9.8%

Exports of goods and services: $4,881 million

Major export trading partners: U.S. 34.1%, UK 9.5%, Japan 6.2%, Germany 5.8%, BLEU 5.3%, Russia 2.8%

Imports of goods and services: $6,093 million

Major import trading partners: India 11.2%, Japan 9.9%, Hong Kong 7.0%, South Korea 7.0%, Singapore 7.0%, Taiwan 5.7%

Foreign direct investment: $120 million

Aid from the United States, 1946–1999: $1,595.7 million

Sudan

Population: 27,272,130

Land area: 2,505,810 sq. km

Major industries: cotton ginning, textiles, cement, edible oils, sugar, soap distilling, shoes, petroleum refining

Major agricultural products: cotton, groundnuts, sorghum, millet, wheat, gum arabic, sesame, sheep

GDP: $26.6 billion (1996 est.)

GDP growth rate: 5% (1994)

Per capita GDP: $975

Average annual rate of inflation: 64.5%

Exports of goods and services: $500 million (1996 est.)

Major export trading partners: Saudi Arabia 19.6%, Thailand 10.1%, Italy 8.4%, China 7.4%, Japan 5.7%, Germany 4.4%, France 4.0%

Imports of goods and services: $1,000 million (1996 est.)

Major import trading partners: Libya 18.3%, Saudi Arabia 9.1%, UK 7.0%, France 5.4%, Germany 4.9%, Iran 4.1%, U.S. 3.9%

Foreign direct investment: $0

Aid from the United States, 1946–1999: $2,082.5 million

Suriname

Population: 432,100

Land area: 163,270 sq. km

Major industries: bauxite and gold mining, alumina and aluminum production, lumbering, food processing, fishing

Major agricultural products: paddy rice, bananas, palm kernels, coconuts, plantains, peanuts, beef, chicken; forest products and shrimp of increasing importance

GDP: $1.4 billion (1996 est.)

GDP growth rate: 3% (1996 est.)

Per capita GDP: $3,240

Average annual rate of inflation: 8.5%

Exports of goods and services: $432 million (1995 est.)

Major export trading partners: Norway 24.1%, U.S. 18.8%, Netherlands 13.1%, Netherlands Antilles 8.9%

Imports of goods and services:[80] $418 million (1995 est.)

Major import trading partners: U.S. 42.6%, Netherlands 13.2%, Trinidad and Tobago 12.2%, Japan 4.8%

Foreign direct investment: n/a

Aid from the United States, 1946–1999: $17.5 million

Swaziland

Population: 926,100

Land area: 17,360 sq. km

Major industries: coal and asbestos mining, wood pulp, sugar, soft drink concentrates

Major agricultural products: sugarcane, cotton, maize, tobacco, rice, citrus, pineapples, corn, sorghum, peanuts, cattle, goats, sheep

GDP: $3,089 million

GDP growth rate: 3%

Per capita GDP: $3,335

Average annual rate of inflation: 17.5%

Exports of goods and services: $901 million

Major export trading partners: South Africa 58.3%, North Korea 3.4%, Mozambique 3.1%, EU–15 16.8% (1995)

Imports of goods and services: $996 million

Major import trading partners: South Africa 96.7%, Japan 0.7%, UK 0.7%, Singapore 0.7% (1995/1996)

Foreign direct investment: $13 million

Aid from the United States, 1946–1999: $219.7 million

Sweden

Population: 8,843,000

Land area: 449,964 sq. km

Major industries: iron and steel, precision equipment (bearings, radio and telephone parts, armaments), wood pulp and paper products, processed foods, motor vehicles

Major agricultural products: grains, sugar beets, potatoes, meat, milk

GDP: $173,219 million

GDP growth rate: 1%

Per capita GDP: $19,588

Average annual rate of inflation: 4.8%

Exports of goods and services: $99,971 million

Major export trading partners: Germany 11.7%, UK 9.5%, Norway 8.4%, U.S. 8.3%, Denmark 6.1%, Finland 5.1%, EU–15 54.9%

Imports of goods and services: $83,239 million

Major import trading partners: Germany 18.7%, UK 10.0%, Norway 7.8%, Denmark 7.5%, U.S. 5.8%, Finland 5.6%, EU–15 66.2%

Foreign direct investment: $5,492 million

Aid from the United States, 1946–1999: $109.0 million

Switzerland (including Liechtenstein)

Population: 7,074,000

Land area: 41,290 sq. km

Major industries: machinery, chemicals, watches, textiles, precision instruments

Major agricultural products: grains, fruits, vegetables, meat, eggs

GDP: $175,510 million

GDP growth rate: -1%

Per capita GDP: $24,811

Average annual rate of inflation: 2.8%

Exports of goods and services: $105,671 million

Major export trading partners: Germany 23.3%, France 9.4%, U.S. 9.0%, Italy 7.7%, UK 5.7%, Japan 4.1%, EU–15 61.4%

Imports of goods and services: $94,247 million

Major import trading partners: Germany 32.8%, France 12.0%, Italy 11.3%, U.S. 6.6%, Netherlands 5.0%, Japan

2.8%, EU–15 80.2%

Foreign direct investment: $3,512 million

Aid from the United States, 1946–1999: $0

Syria

Population: 14,501,690

Land area: 185,180 sq. km

Major industries: petroleum, textiles, food processing, beverages, tobacco, phosphate rock mining

Major agricultural products: wheat, barley, cotton, lentils, chickpeas, beef, lamb, eggs, poultry, milk

GDP: $44,291 million (1995)

GDP growth rate: 6% (1995)

Per capita GDP: $3,139 (1995)

Average annual rate of inflation: 17.4%

Exports of goods and services: $4,400 million (1996 est.)

Major export trading partners: Italy 17.5%, Germany 14.0%, France 9.6%, Turkey 9.3%, Lebanon 6.9%, Spain 6.0%, Saudi Arabia 5.3%

Imports of goods and services: $5,200 million (CIF,[81] 1996 est.)

Major import trading partners: Italy 8.1%, Germany 6.2%, South Korea 4.9%, France 4.5%, Japan 4.5%, U.S. 3.8%, UK 2.6%

Foreign direct investment: $89 million

Aid from the United States, 1946–1999: $353.1 million

Tajikistan

Population: 5,927,000

Land area: 143,100 sq. km

Major industries: aluminum, zinc, lead, chemicals and fertilizers, cement, vegetable oil, metal-cutting machine tools, refrigerators and freezers

Major agricultural products: cotton, grain, fruits, grapes, vegetables, cattle, sheep, goats

GDP: $5,342 million

GDP growth rate: -4%

Per capita GDP: $901

Average annual rate of inflation: 198.7%

Exports of goods and services: $2,090 million (1995)

Major export trading partners: CIS 33.6%, Netherlands 34.1%, Uzbekistan 17.6%, Russia 12.7%, Switzerland 5.0% (1995)

Imports of goods and services: $2,077 million (1995)

Major import trading partners: CIS 59.8%, Uzbekistan 31.5%, UK 19.3%, Russia 17.0%, Turkmenistan 7.2%

Foreign direct investment: $16 million

Aid from the United States, 1946–1999:[82] $50.7 million

Tanzania

Population: 30,493,860

Land area: 945,090 sq. km

Major industries: primarily agricultural processing (sugar, beer, cigarettes, sisal twine), diamond and gold mining, oil refining, shoes, cement, textiles, wood products, fertilizer

476

Major agricultural products: coffee, sisal, tea, cotton, pyrethrum (insecticide made from chrysanthemums), cashews, tobacco, cloves (Zanzibar), corn, wheat, cassava (tapioca), bananas, fruits, vegetables, cattle, sheep, goats

GDP: $18,900 million (1995 est.)

GDP growth rate: 3.5% (1995 est.)

Per capita GDP: $650 (1995 est.)

Average annual rate of inflation: 43.25%

Exports of goods and services: $1,225 million

Major export trading partners:[83] India 9.1%, Germany 8.1%, Japan 7.3%, Malaysia 6.0%, Rwanda 5.3%, Netherlands 4.7%

Imports of goods and services: $2,113 million

Major import trading partners: South Africa 12.6%, Kenya 9.9%, UK 8.0%, Saudi Arabia 6.4%, Japan 4.8%, China 4.0%

Foreign direct investment: $150 million

Aid from the United States, 1946–1999: $752.7 million

Thailand

Population: 60,003,000

Land area: 514,000 sq. km

Major industries: tourism, textiles and garments, agricultural processing, beverages, tobacco, cement, light manufacturing (such as jewelry), electric appliances and components, integrated circuits, furniture, plastics, tungsten (world's 2nd largest producer), tin (world's 3rd largest producer)

Major agricultural products: rice, cassava (tapioca), rubber, corn, sugarcane, coconuts, soybeans

GDP: $412,388 million

GDP growth rate: 6%

Per capita GDP: $6,873

Average annual rate of inflation: 4.8%

Exports of goods and services: $71,370 million

Major export trading partners: U.S. 18.0%, Japan 16.8%, Singapore 12.9%, Hong Kong 5.8%, China 3.6%

Imports of goods and services: $81,917 million

Major import trading partners: Japan 28.3%, U.S. 12.5%, Singapore 5.5%, Germany 5.1%, Taiwan 5.0%

Foreign direct investment: $2,336 million

Aid from the United States, 1946–1999: $3,465.6 million

Togo

Population: 4,230,000

Land area: 56,790 sq. km

Major industries: phosphate mining, agricultural processing, cement, handicrafts, textiles, beverages

Major agricultural products: coffee, cocoa, cotton, yams, cassava (tapioca), corn, beans, rice, millet, sorghum, meat; annual fish catch of 10,000–14,000 tons

GDP: $7,137 million

GDP growth rate: 6%

Per capita GDP: $1,687

Average annual rate of inflation: 6.2%

Exports of goods and services: $439 million

Major export trading partners: Canada 9.2%, U.S. 8.1%, Taiwan 7.5%, Nigeria 6.7% (1995 est.)

Imports of goods and services: $543 million

Major import trading partners: Ghana 17.1%, China 13.3%, France 12.5%, Cameroon 6.0% (1995 est.)

Foreign direct investment: $0

Aid from the United States, 1946–1999: $239.1 million

Trinidad and Tobago

Population: 1,297,000

Land area: 5,130 sq. km

Major industries: petroleum, chemicals, tourism, food processing, cement, beverages, cotton textiles

Major agricultural products: cocoa, sugarcane, rice, citrus, coffee, vegetables, poultry

GDP: $8,661 million

GDP growth rate: 3%

Per capita GDP: $6,678

Average annual rate of inflation: 5.1%

Exports of goods and services: $2,883 million

Major export trading partners: U.S. 44.3%, Caricom 24.8%, Latin America 7.6%

Imports of goods and services: $2,309 million

Major import trading partners: U.S. 37.5%, Venezuela 12.2%, EU–15 10.0%

Foreign direct investment: $320 million

Aid from the United States, 1946–1999: $48.1 million

Tunisia

Population: 9,131,820

Land area: 163,610 sq. km

Major industries: petroleum, mining (particularly phosphate and iron ore), tourism, textiles, footwear, food, beverages

Major agricultural products: olives, dates, oranges, almonds, grain, sugar beets, grapes, poultry, beef, dairy products

GDP: $43,929 million

GDP growth rate: 7%

Per capita GDP: $4,811

Average annual rate of inflation: 5.675%

Exports of goods and services: $8,252 million

Major export trading partners: France 25.4%, Italy 19.7%, Germany 15.6%, Belgium 7.1%, Spain 3.6%

Imports of goods and services: $8,540 million

Major import trading partners: France 24.3%, Italy 18.7%, Germany 12.9%, U.S. 4.5%, BLEU 4.4%

Foreign direct investment: $320 million

Aid from the United States, 1946–1999: $2,106.3 million

Turkey

Population: 62,697,000

Land area: 780,580 sq. km

Major industries: textiles, food processing, mining (coal, chromite, copper, boron), steel, petroleum, construction, lumber, paper

Major agricultural products: tobacco, cotton, grain, olives, sugar beets, pulses, citrus, livestock

GDP: $374,719 million

GDP growth rate: 7%

Per capita GDP: $5,977

Average annual rate of inflation: 66.0%

Exports of goods and services: $39,050 million

Major export trading partners: Germany 23.6%, U.S. 7.9%, Italy 6.5%, Russia 4.3%, UK 6.0%, France 5.0%, EU–15 51.5%

Imports of goods and services: $49,842 million

Major import trading partners: Germany 18.9%, U.S. 7.8%, Italy 10.6%, France 6.8%, UK 6.3%, Saudi Arabia 3.7%, EU–15 54.6%

Foreign direct investment: $722 million

Aid from the United States, 1946–1999: $21,327.9 million

Turkmenistan

Population: 4,598,000

Land area: 488,100 sq. km

Major industries: natural gas, oil, petroleum products, textiles, food processing

Major agricultural products: cotton, grain, livestock

GDP: $9,165 million

GDP growth rate: -2%

Per capita GDP: $1,993

Average annual rate of inflation: 538.4%

Exports of goods and services: $1,800 million to states outside the FSU (1996 est.)

Major export trading partners: Germany 11.4%, other EU–15 11.4%, Bulgaria 9.3%, Czech Republic 7.1%, other Eastern Europe 17.1% (1995)

Imports of goods and services: $1,300 million from states outside the FSU (1996 est.)

Major import trading partners: Germany 25.4%, other EU–15 4.2%, Poland 9.0%, Czech Republic 8.1%, other Eastern Europe 18.7% (1995)

Foreign direct investment: $108 million

Aid from the United States, 1946–1999:[84] $40.5 million

Uganda

Population: 19,740,830

Land area: 236,040 sq. km

Major industries: sugar, brewing, tobacco, cotton textiles, cement

Major agricultural products: coffee, tea, cotton, tobacco, cassava (tapioca), potatoes, corn, millet, pulses, beef, goat meat, milk, poultry

GDP: $20,486 million

GDP growth rate: 9%

Per capita GDP: $1,038

Average annual rate of inflation: 88.2%

Exports of goods and services: $725 million

Major export trading partners:[85] Spain 22.8%, France 14.1%, Germany 13.9%, Italy 9.5%, Netherlands 8.3% (1995)

Imports of goods and services: $1,347 million

Major import trading partners: Kenya 26.2%, UK 12.1%, Germany 8.0%, Japan 8.0%, India 5.5% (1995)

Foreign direct investment: $121 million

Aid from the United States, 1946–1999: $654.0 million

Ukraine

Population: 50,718,000

Land area: 603,700 sq. km

Major industries: coal, electric power, ferrous and nonferrous metals, machinery and transport equipment, chemicals, food processing (especially sugar)

Major agricultural products: grain, sugar beets, vegetables, meat, milk

GDP: $114,588 million

GDP growth rate: -10%

Per capita GDP: $2,259

Average annual rate of inflation: 401.8%

Exports of goods and services: $20,023 million

Major export trading partners: Russia, Belarus, U.S., Germany, China (1995; percentages not available)

Imports of goods and services: $21,079 million

Major import trading partners: Russia, Turkmenistan, Belarus, Germany, Switzerland (percentages not available)

Foreign direct investment: $350 million

Aid from the United States, 1946–1999:[86] $1,081.1 million

United Arab Emirates

Population: 2,532,260

Land area: 82,880 sq. km

Major industries: petroleum, fishing, petrochemicals, construction materials, some boat building, handicrafts, pearling

Major agricultural products: dates, vegetables, watermelons, poultry, eggs, dairy products, fish

GDP: $38,720 million (1995)

GDP growth rate:[87] 4% (1995)

Per capita GDP: $15,740 (1995)

Average annual rate of inflation: 1.5%

Exports of goods and services: $25,225 million (1994)

Major export trading partners: Japan 37.2%, South Korea 7.3%, Singapore 6.6%, India 5.8%, Oman 3.4%, Iran 3.3%

Imports of goods and services: $25,034 million (1994)

Major import trading partners: U.S. 9.6%, Japan 8.7%, UK 8.3%, Italy 6.0%, Germany 5.5%, India 5.5%

Foreign direct investment: n/a

Aid from the United States, 1946–1999: $0

United Kingdom

Population: 58,782,000

Land area: 244,820 sq. km

Major industries: production machinery including machine tools, electric power equipment, automation equipment, railroad equipment, shipbuilding, aircraft, motor vehicles and parts, electronics and communications equipment, metals, chemicals, coal, petroleum, paper and paper products, food processing, textiles, clothing, other consumer goods

Major agricultural products: cereals, oilseed, potatoes, vegetables, cattle, sheep, poultry, fish

GDP: $1,170,754 million

GDP growth rate: 2%

Per capita GDP: $19,917

Average annual rate of inflation: 4.3%

Exports of goods and services: $313,462 million (1995)

Major export trading partners: Germany 12.0%, U.S. 10.6%, France 9.8%, Netherlands 7.7%, BLEU 4.9%, EU–15 56.9%

Imports of goods and services: $322,118 million (1995)

Major import trading partners: Germany 14.1%, U.S. 12.5%, France 9.2%, Netherlands 6.5%, Japan 4.9%, EU–15 54.0%

Foreign direct investment: $32,347 million

Aid from the United States, 1946–1999: $8,779.5 million

United States

Population: 265,284,000

Land area: 9,629,091 sq. km

Major industries: petroleum, steel, motor vehicles, aerospace, telecommunications, chemicals, electronics, food processing, consumer goods, lumber, mining; world's leading industrial power, highly diversified and technologically advanced

Major agricultural products: wheat, other grains, corn, fruits, vegetables, cotton, beef, pork, poultry, dairy products, forest products, fish

GDP: $7,434,169 million

GDP growth rate: 2%

Per capita GDP: $28,023

Average annual rate of inflation: 2.9%

Exports of goods and services: $793,600 million (1995)

Major export trading partners: Canada 22.3%, Mexico 10.5%, Japan 9.7%, UK 5.4%, South Korea 3.7%, Germany 3.6%, Taiwan 3.0%, EU–15 20.8% (1997)

Imports of goods and services: $902,000 million (1995)

Major import trading partners: Canada 19.2%, Japan 13.8%, Mexico 9.8%, China 7.1%, Germany 4.9%, UK 3.7%, Taiwan 3.7%, EU–15 18.0% (1997)

Foreign direct investment: $76,955 million

Aid from the United States, 1946–1999: n/a

Uruguay

Population: 3,203,000

Land area: 176,220 sq. km

Major industries: meat processing, wool and hides, sugar, textiles, footwear, leather apparel, tires, cement, petroleum refining, wine

Major agricultural products: wheat, rice, corn, sorghum, livestock, fish

GDP: $25,113 million

GDP growth rate: 5%

Per capita GDP: $7,841

Average annual rate of inflation: 60.4%

Exports of goods and services: $3,350 million

Major export trading partners: Brazil 34.6%, Argentina 11.5%, U.S. 7.0%, EU–15 21.6%, Asia 8.4%

Imports of goods and services: $3,636 million

Major import trading partners: Brazil 26.1%, Argentina 24.1%, U.S. 13.7%, EU–15 24.8%, Asia 7.9%

Foreign direct investment: $169 million

Aid from the United States, 1946–1999: $277.2 million

Uzbekistan

Population: 23,228,000

Land area: 447,400 sq. km

Major industries: textiles, food processing, machine building, metallurgy, natural gas

Major agricultural products: cotton, vegetables, fruits, grain, livestock

GDP: $59,980 million

GDP growth rate: 2%

Per capita GDP: $2,582

Average annual rate of inflation: 273.3%

Exports of goods and services: $7,693 million

Major export trading partners: CIS 22.9%, UK 8.0%, Switzerland 7.2%, South Korea 5.9%, U.S. 4.7%, Netherlands 2.9%

Imports of goods and services: $9,568 million

Major import trading partners: CIS 32.1%, Germany 12.3%, U.S. 9.2%, Turkey 7.6%, South Korea 6.9%, Switzerland 3.9%

Foreign direct investment: $55 million

Aid from the United States, 1946–1999:[88] $111.1 million

Venezuela

Population: 22,311,000

Land area: 912,050 sq. km

Major industries: petroleum, iron ore mining, construction materials, food processing, textiles, steel, aluminum, motor vehicle assembly

Major agricultural products: corn, sorghum, sugarcane, rice, bananas, vegetables, coffee, beef, pork, milk, eggs, fish

GDP: $185,641 million

GDP growth rate: -2%

Per capita GDP: $8,321

Average annual rate of inflation: 41.4%

Exports of goods and services: $24,701 million

Major export trading partners: U.S. 53.9%, Colombia 5.2%, Brazil 4.2%, Germany 1.7%, Japan 1.1%

Imports of goods and services: $16,037 million

Major import trading partners: U.S. 43.8%, Colombia 7.2%, Germany 4.7%, Italy 4.6%, Japan 3.3%

Foreign direct investment: $1,833 million

Aid from the United States, 1946–1999: $371.7 million

Vietnam

Population: 75,355,000

Land area: 329,560 sq. km

Major industries: food processing, garments, shoes, machine building, mining, cement, chemical fertilizer, glass, tires, oil

Major agricultural products: paddy rice, corn, potatoes, rubber, soybeans, coffee, tea, bananas, poultry, pigs, fish

GDP: $118,307 million

GDP growth rate: 9%

Per capita GDP: $1,570

Average annual rate of inflation: 153.5%

Exports of goods and services: $9,695 million

Major export trading partners: Japan 28.5%, Germany 9.4%, Singapore 7.5%, China 5.2%, France 5.1%, Taiwan 4.5% (1995)

Imports of goods and services: $12,870 million

Major import trading partners: Singapore 17.0%, South Korea 12.9%, Taiwan 9.6%, Japan 8.8%, China 6.2%, Hong Kong 6.1% (1994)

Foreign direct investment: $1,500 million

Aid from the United States, 1946–1999:[89] $23,366.6 million

Yemen

Population: 15,778,060

Land area: 527,970 sq. km

Major industries: crude oil production and petroleum refining, small-scale production of cotton textiles and leather goods, food processing, handicrafts, small aluminum products factory, cement

Major agricultural products: grain, fruits, vegetables, qat (mildly narcotic shrub), coffee, cotton, dairy products, poultry, meat, fish

GDP: $14,181 million

GDP growth rate:[90] 16%

Per capita GDP: $899

Average annual rate of inflation: n/a

Exports of goods and services: $2,430 million

Major export trading partners: China 22.8%, South Korea 18.6%, Thailand 14.4%, Brazil 12.6%, Japan 12.5%

Imports of goods and services: $3,023 million

Major import trading partners: UAE[91] 8.5%, Saudi Arabia 7.6%, U.S. 7.6%, France 6.7%, Japan 5.7%

Foreign direct investment: $100 million

Aid from the United States, 1946–1999: $557.5 million

Zambia

Population: 9,214,890

Land area: 752,610 sq. km

Major industries: copper mining and processing, construction, foodstuffs, beverages, chemicals, textiles, fertilizer

Major agricultural products: corn, sorghum, rice, peanuts, sunflower seed, tobacco, cotton, sugarcane, cassava (tapioca), cattle, goats, pigs, poultry, beef, pork, poultry meat, milk, eggs, hides

GDP: $8,150 million

GDP growth rate: 5%

Per capita GDP: $884

Average annual rate of inflation: 76.0%

Exports of goods and services: $1,301 million

Major export trading partners:[92] Japan 18%, Thailand 12%, Saudi Arabia 9%, India 7%

Imports of goods and services: $1,530 million

Major import trading partners: South Africa 34%, Saudi Arabia 12%, UK 9%, Zimbabwe 8%

Foreign direct investment: $58 million

Aid from the United States, 1946–1999: $739.4 million

Zimbabwe

Population: 11,247,950

Land area: 390,580 sq. km

Major industries: mining (coal, clay, numerous metallic and non-metallic ores), copper, steel, nickel, tin, wood products, cement, chemicals, fertilizer, clothing and footwear, foodstuffs, beverages

Major agricultural products: corn, cotton, tobacco, wheat, coffee, sugarcane, peanuts, cattle, sheep, goats, pigs

GDP: $25,851 million

GDP growth rate: 7%

Per capita GDP: $2,298

Average annual rate of inflation: 19.8%

Exports of goods and services: $3,110 million

Major export trading partners: UK 10.1%, South Africa 9.6%, Germany 7.9%, U.S. 6.7%, Japan 5.1%

Imports of goods and services: $3,100 million

Major import trading partners: South Africa 38.3%, UK 7.9%, Japan 5.1%, U.S. 5.0%, Germany 4.9%

Foreign direct investment: $63 million

Aid from the United States, 1946–1999: $706.7 million

Notes

[1] Data on export and import trading partners based on trading partners' returns; subject to a wide margin of error.

[2] Does not include aid given to the former Soviet Union, which totaled $191.4 million, or collectively to the New Independent States, which amounted to $319.2 million.

[3] United Arab Emirates, consisting of Abu Dhabi, Ajman, Dubai, Fujairah, Ras al-Khaimah, Sharjah, and Umm al-Qaiwain.

[4] Does not include aid given to the former Soviet Union, which totaled $191.4 million, or collectively to the New Independent States, which amounted to $319.2 million.

[5] From Central Intelligence Agency, *World Factbook 1997*. Import and export data represent the FOB (free on board) value of goods and services unless otherwise indicated.

[6] From Central Intelligence Agency, *World Factbook 1997*. Import and export data represent the FOB value of goods and services unless otherwise indicated.

[7] From Central Intelligence Agency, *World Factbook 1997*. Import and export data represent the FOB value of goods and services unless otherwise indicated.

[8] United Arab Emirates, consisting of Abu Dhabi, Ajman, Dubai, Fujairah, Ras al-Khaimah, Sharjah, and Umm al-Qaiwain.

[9] From Central Intelligence Agency, *World Factbook 1997*. Import and export data represent the FOB value of goods and services unless otherwise indicated.

[10] Data on export and import trading partners from Economist Intelligence Unit estimates.

[11] Does not include aid given to the former Soviet Union or collectively to the New Independent States.

[12] Data on import/export trading partners for BLEU.

[13] Includes aid to Luxembourg.

[14] Data dealing with population are subject to considerable error because of the dislocations caused by military action and "ethnic cleansing."

[15] Denotes only aid given to Bosnia–Herzegovina as a separate entity. An additional $144.1 million was given to Bosnia–Herzegovina, Croatia, and Kosovo together, as well as $2,459.3 million to Yugoslavia.

[16] Data on export and import trading partners from January–June 1996.

[17] Data on export and import trading partners based on trading partners' returns; subject to a wide margin of error.

[18] Data on export and import trading partners based on trading partners' returns; subject to a wide margin of error.

[19] Data on export and import trading partners based on trading partners' returns; subject to a wide margin of error.

[20] Data on export and import trading partners based on trading partners' returns; subject to a wide margin of error.

[21] Data on export and import trading partners based on trading partners' returns; subject to a wide margin of error.

[22] From Central Intelligence Agency, *World Factbook 1997*. Import and export data represent the FOB value of goods and services unless otherwise indicated.

[23] Cost, insurance, and freight.

[24] Data on export and import trading partners based on trading partners' returns; subject to a wide margin of error.

[25] Data on export and import trading partners based on trading partners' returns; subject to a wide margin of error.

[26] Data on export and import trading partners based on preliminary official estimates.

[27] Belgium–Netherlands–Luxembourg.

[28] Denotes only aid given to Croatia as a separate entity. An additional $144.1 million was given to Bosnia–Herzegovina, Croatia, and Kosovo together, as well as $2,459.3 million to Yugoslavia.

[29] Import and export data, including major trading partners, from *Economist Intelligence Unit Country Report*, Fourth Quarter 1997, based on government figures.

[30] Denotes only aid given to the Czech Republic as a separate entity. An additional $203.4 million was given to Czechoslovakia from 1946–1993.

[31] Data on export and import trading partners based on trading partners' returns; subject to a wide margin of error.

[32] Does not include aid given to the former Soviet Union, which totaled $191.4 million, or collectively to the New Independent States, which amounted to $319.2 million; additionally, $16.5 million altogether was given to the Baltic States.

[33] Data on export and import trading partners based on fiscal years starting July 8. Fiscal years are used widely by national statistical sources; calendar years are favored by international publications.

[34] Data on export and import trading partners based on trading partners' returns; subject to a wide margin of error.

[35] Data on export and import trading partners based on trading partners' returns; subject to a wide margin of error.

[36] Does not include aid given to the former Soviet Union, which totaled $191.4 million, or collectively to the New Independent States, which amounted to $319.2 million.

[37] Calculated using GDP data from World Bank, *1998 World Development Indicators on CD–ROM*.

[38] Includes aid given to the former East Germany.

[39] Data on export and import trading partners based on trading partners' returns; subject to a wide margin of error.

[40] Data on export and import trading partners based on latest available full-year Bank of Greece figures.

[41] Data on export and import trading partners exclude trade with the former Soviet Union; based on trading partners' returns; subject to a wide margin of error.

[42] Calculated using GDP data from World Bank, *1998 World Development Indicators on CD–ROM*.

[43] Belgium–Netherlands–Luxembourg.

[44] From Central Intelligence Agency, *World Factbook 1997*. Import and export data represent the FOB value of goods and services unless otherwise indicated.

[45] From Central Intelligence Agency, *World Factbook 1997*. Import and export data represent the FOB value of goods and services unless otherwise indicated.

[46] United Arab Emirates, consisting of Abu Dhabi, Ajman, Dubai, Fujairah, Ras al-Khaimah, Sharjah, and Umm al-Qaiwain.

[47] Calculated using GDP data from World Bank, *1998 World Development Indicators on CD–ROM*.

[48] Data on export and import trading partners based on IMF estimate.

[49] United Arab Emirates, consisting of Abu Dhabi, Ajman, Dubai, Fujairah, Ras al-Khaimah, Sharjah, and Umm al-Qaiwain.

[50] United Arab Emirates, consisting of Abu Dhabi, Ajman, Dubai, Fujairah, Ras al-Khaimah, Sharjah, and Umm al-Qaiwain.

[51] From Central Intelligence Agency, *World Factbook 1997*. Import and export data represent the FOB value of goods and services unless otherwise indicated.

[52] Cost, insurance, and freight.

[53] Data on export and import trading partners based on World Bank estimates.

[54] United Arab Emirates, consisting of Abu Dhabi, Ajman, Dubai, Fujairah, Ras al-Khaimah, Sharjah, and Umm al-Qaiwain.

[55] Data on export and import trading partners based on IMF *Direction of Trade Statistics* estimate.

[56] From Central Intelligence Agency, *World Factbook 1997*. Import and export data represent the FOB value of goods and services unless otherwise indicated.

[57] Data on import/export trading partners for BLEU.

[58] Includes aid to Belgium.

[59] Data on export and import trading partners excludes trade with the former Soviet Union; based on trading partners' returns; subject to a wide margin of error.

[60] Data on export and import trading partners based on trading partners' returns; subject to a wide margin of error.

[61] Cost, insurance, and freight.

[62] Calculated from GDP data from World Bank, *1998 World Development Indicators on CD–ROM*.

[63] Does not include aid given to the former Soviet Union, which totaled $191.4 million, or collectively to the New Independent States, which amounted to $319.2 million.

[64] Data on export and import trading partners based on trading partners' returns; subject to a wide margin of error.

[65] Data on export and import trading partners based on trading partners' returns; subject to a wide margin of error.

[66] United Arab Emirates, consisting of Abu Dhabi, Ajman, Dubai, Fujairah, Ras al-Khaimah, Sharjah, and Umm al-Qaiwain.

[67] Calculated from GDP data from World Bank, *1998 World Development Indicators on CD–ROM*.

[68] United Arab Emirates, consisting of Abu Dhabi, Ajman, Dubai, Fujairah, Ras al-Khaimah, Sharjah, and Umm al-Qaiwain.

[69] From Central Intelligence Agency, *World Factbook 1997*. Import and export data represent the

FOB value of goods and services unless otherwise indicated.

70 Does not include aid given to the former Soviet Union, which totaled $191.4 million.

71 Data on export and import trading partners based on trading partners' returns; subject to a wide margin of error.

72 United Arab Emirates, consisting of Abu Dhabi, Ajman, Dubai, Fujairah, Ras al-Khaimah, Sharjah, and Umm al-Qaiwain.

73 Cost, insurance, and freight.

74 Data on export and import trading partners based on trading partners' returns; subject to a wide margin of error.

75 Data on export and import trading partners based on trading partners' returns; subject to a wide margin of error.

76 Denotes only aid given to the Slovak Republic as a separate entity. An additional $203.4 million went to Czechoslovakia from 1946 to1993.

77 Calculated from GDP data from World Bank *1998 World Development Indicators on CD–ROM.*

78 Denotes only aid given to Slovenia as a separate entity. An additional $2,459.3 million was given to Yugoslavia.

79 Data on export and import trading partners based on trading partners' returns; subject to a wide margin of error.

80 From Central Intelligence Agency, *World Factbook 1997.* Import and export data represent the FOB value of goods and services unless otherwise indicated.

81 Cost, insurance, and freight.

82 Does not include aid given to the former Soviet Union, which totaled $191.4 million, or collectively to the New Independent States, which amounted to $319.2 million.

83 Data on export and import trading partners based on trading partners' returns; subject to a wide margin of error.

84 Does not include aid given to the former Soviet Union, which totaled $191.4 million, or collectively to the New Independent States, which amounted to $319.2 million.

85 Data on export and import trading partners based on trading partners' returns; subject to a wide margin of error.

86 Does not include aid given to the former Soviet Union, which totaled $191.4 million, or collectively to the New Independent States, which amounted to $319.2 million.

87 Calculated from GDP data from World Bank, *1998 World Development Indicators on CD–ROM.*

88 Does not include aid given to the former Soviet Union, which totaled $191.4 million, or collectively to the New Independent States, which amounted to $319.2 million.

89 Aid to South Vietnam.

90 Calculated from GDP data from World Bank, *1998 World Development Indicators on CD–ROM.*

91 United Arab Emirates, consisting of Abu Dhabi, Ajman, Dubai, Fujairah, Ras al-Khaimah, Sharjah, and Umm al-Qaiwain.

92 Data on export and import trading partners based on trading partners' returns; subject to a wide margin of error.

Major Works Cited

The following sources provided the basis for the country factor analyses in the 1999 *Index of Economic Freedom*. In addition, the authors and analysts of the various elements of the *Index* relied on supporting documentation and information from various government agencies and sites on the Internet, numerous news reports and journal articles, and official responses to inquiries. These sources are cited in each chapter where appropriate. All data and information received from government sources were verified with independent, internationally recognized nongovernmental sources as well.

Arrowhead International, *World Trade and Customs Directory*, Washington, D.C., Winter 1998.

Barro, Robert J., presentation to The Heritage Foundation Roundtable on Economic Growth, June 26, 1996; copies available on request from The Heritage Foundation.

Bruno, Michael, and William Easterly, "Inflation Crises and Long-Run Growth," *Journal of Monetary Economics;* data available through the World Bank Growth Project Web site: *http://www.worldbank.org/html/prdmg/grthweb/datasets.htm*.

Dori, John T., and Richard D. Fisher, Jr., eds., *U.S. and Asia Statistical Handbook, 1998–1999 Edition* (Washington, D.C.: The Heritage Foundation, 1998).

Economist Intelligence Unit Limited, *EIU Country Reports*, London, U.K., 1998.

——, *Investing, Licensing and Trading Conditions Abroad (ILT Reports)*, London, U.K., 1998.

International Monetary Fund, "Adjusting to New Realities: MENA, The Uruguay Round, and the EU–Mediterranean Initiative," Working Paper WP/97/5, Washington, D.C., January 1997.

——, *Direction of Trade Statistics Yearbook*, Washington, D.C., 1997.

——, *Government Finance Statistics Yearbook*, Washington, D.C., 1997.

——, *International Financial Statistics Yearbook*, Washington, D.C., 1997.

Johnson, Bryan T., Kim R. Holmes, and Melanie Kirkpatrick, eds., 1998 *Index of Economic Freedom*, (Washington, D.C.: The Heritage Foundation and Dow Jones & Company, Inc., 1998).

Karatnycky, Adrian, Alexander Motyl, and Boris Shor, eds., *Nations in Transit 1997* (New York, N.Y., Freedom House, Inc., 1997).

Michalopoulos, Constantine, and David G. Tarr, *Trade Performance and Policy in the New Independent States* (Washington, D.C.: The World Bank, 1996).

Ng, Francis, and Alexander Yeats, *Open Economies Work Better!* Washington, D.C.: The World Bank, International Trade Division, August 1996.

Ricardo, David, *On the Principles of Political Economy and Taxation*, Third Edition, Piero Sraffa, ed. (Cambridge, U.K.: Cambridge University Press, 1951); published originally in 1821.

Smith, Adam, *An Inquiry into the Nature and Causes of the Wealth of Nations*, R. H. Campbell and A. S. Skinner, eds., Glasgow Edition (Oxford, U.K.: Oxford University Press, 1976); published originally in 1776.

Taxation in Central and South America (New York, N.Y.: Deloitte Touche Tohmatsu International, 1998).

United Nations Development Programme, *Human Development Report 1998*, New York, N.Y., 1998.

U.S. Department of Commerce, *Country Commercial Guides*, Washington, D.C., 1998.

——, *National Trade Data Bank and International Bulletin Board, Stat–USA* Internet site (*http://www.stat-usa.gov*), Washington, D.C., 1998.

U.S. Department of State, *Country Reports on Economic Policy and Trade Practices*, Report Submitted to the Committee on International Relations and Committee on Ways and Means, U.S. House of Representatives, and the Committee on Foreign Relations and Committee on Finance, U.S. Senate, 105th Cong., 2nd Sess., January 1998.

——, *Country Reports on Human Rights Practices for 1997*, released by the Bureau of Democracy, Human Rights, and Labor, January 30, 1998; available at the U.S. Department of State Web site: *http://www.state.gov/www/ind.html*.

United States Trade Representative, Office of, *1998 National Trade Estimate Report on Foreign Trade Barriers* (Washington, D.C.: U.S. Government Printing Office, 1998).

World Bank, *Statistical Handbook 1996: States of the Former USSR*, Washington, D.C., 1996.

——, *World Bank World Atlas 1998*, Washington, D.C., 1998.

——, *World Bank World Development Indicators on CD–ROM 1998*, Washington, D.C., 1997.

——, *World Bank World Development Report 1998*, (Oxford, U.K.: Oxford University Press for the International Bank for Reconstruction and Development/World Bank, 1998).

Worldwide Corporate Tax Guide and Directory, Ernst & Young International, Ltd., New York, N.Y., 1998.

Worldwide Executive Tax Guide and Directory, Ernst & Young International, Ltd., New York, N.Y., 1998.